INTERNATIONAL LAW AND THE ENVIRONMENT

This boo' ⸱fore
the d⸱

⸱

BPP

INTERNATIONAL LAW AND THE ENVIRONMENT

Third Edition

PATRICIA BIRNIE

ALAN BOYLE

CATHERINE REDGWELL

OXFORD
UNIVERSITY PRESS

OXFORD
UNIVERSITY PRESS

Great Clarendon Street, Oxford OX2 6DP

Oxford University Press is a department of the University of Oxford.
It furthers the University's objective of excellence in research, scholarship,
and education by publishing worldwide in

Oxford New York

Auckland Cape Town Dar es Salaam Hong Kong Karachi
Kuala Lumpur Madrid Melbourne Mexico City Nairobi
New Delhi Shanghai Taipei Toronto

With offices in

Argentina Austria Brazil Chile Czech Republic France Greece
Guatemala Hungary Italy Japan Poland Portugal Singapore
South Korea Switzerland Thailand Turkey Ukraine Vietnam

Oxford is a registered trade mark of Oxford University Press
in the UK and in certain other countries

Published in the United States
by Oxford University Press Inc., New York

First published 2009

British Library Cataloguing in Publication Data

Data available

Library of Congress Cataloging in Publication Data

Birnie, Patricia W.
International law and the environment / Patricia Birnie, Alan Boyle,
Catherine Redgwell.—3rd ed.
p. cm.
Includes index.
ISBN 978–0–19–876422–9
1. Environmental law, International. I. Boyle, Alan E. II. Redgwell,
Catherine. III. Title.
K3585.B57 2009
344.04'6—dc22   2008048609

Typeset by Newgen Imaging Systems (P) Ltd., Chennai, India
Printed in Great Britain
on acid-free paper by
Ashford Colour Press Ltd, Gosport, Hampshire

ISBN 978–0–19–876422–9

3 5 7 9 10 8 6 4

PREFACE

The development of modern international environmental law, starting essentially in the 1960s, has been one of the most remarkable exercises in international lawmaking, comparable to the law of human rights and international trade law in the scale and form it has taken. Since the Rio Conference in 1992, the subject as a whole has come of age. Its gestation may have been slow, but international environmental law has proved a very vigorous plant. If the 1980s and 1990s are best remembered for 'treaty congestion' because of the large number of multilateral environmental agreements under negotiation, the first decade of the new millennium has seen an unparalleled growth in the environmental jurisprudence of international tribunals. No longer is it necessary to squeeze every drop of life out of the immortal trio of arbitrations—*Bering Sea Fur Seals*, *Trail Smelter* and *Lac Lanoux*—which have sustained international environmental law throughout most of its existence.

In this third edition we have concentrated on revising and updating the text rather than adding significant amounts of new material. A small number of treaties are covered for the first time, but the principal additions are from the case law of the ICJ, the ITLOS, the WTO, international arbitral awards, and decisions of human-rights courts and commissions. The treatment of climate change and the Kyoto Protocol has been expanded, as has the introductory chapter. We have also taken the opportunity to reorganize some chapters and relocate material to places where it now seems more appropriate, including the waste bin, but the basic structure of the book remains the same. Our intention has been to cover significant developments up to mid-2008, but in such a large and ever-expanding topic it is impossible to be comprehensive, and there is much more that could be said on everything. The book remains primarily an introduction to the general corpus of international environmental law, including the lawmaking and regulatory processes, approached from the perspective of generalist international lawyers rather than specialist environmental lawyers. Experience of international litigation suggests that this is the right way to approach the subject, at least in that context.

The most significant change has been the retirement from active participation by Patricia Birnie, co-author of the first and second editions. Her inspiration and unrivalled understanding of the law and context of international protection of the environment have been indispensable from the very beginning of what has proved a far larger project than was ever imagined. In her place, Catherine Redgwell has taken over responsibility for revising Chapters 11 and 12, as well as Chapter 14, originally drafted by Tom Schoenbaum. In order to keep abreast of the vitally important and fast developing subject of climate change we were very pleased when Navraj Ghaleigh of the University of Edinburgh agreed to deploy his expertise on a substantial revision of what is now Chapter 6.

We are indebted to several colleagues and friends for sharing their knowledge on various topics, but especial thanks are due to Lorand Bartels, Bradnee Chambers, Louise de La Fayette, Bill Edeson, Sebastian Lopez Escarcena, David Freestone, James Harrison, Na Li, and Richard Tarasofsky.

As always we have been well served by a series of research assistants who have greatly eased the task of keeping on top of new material. Safiya Ali, Daniela Diz, Pierre Harcourt, Bonnie Holligan, Sam McIntosh, Frida Petersson, Danielle Rached, Meerim Razbaeva, Christian Schall, Felicity Stewart, Emmanuel Ugirashebuja, and Andreas Woitecki, all of Edinburgh University, and Silvia Borelli of University College London, have been a great help. We are very grateful to them all, and to our many PhD, LLM and LLB students for asking the questions that keep any author alert and conscious. Eleanor Williams of OUP has provided timely and above all patient support for authors who may at times have seemed unlikely ever to deliver, and our thanks go to all those working for OUP who have made this edition happen.

Alan Boyle and Catherine Redgwell
31 July 2008

CONTENTS

ABBREVIATIONS: JOURNALS AND REPORTS

ACHPR	African Convention/Commission on Human and Peoples' Rights
AC	Appeal Cases (House of Lords) (UK)
ACOPS	Advisory Committee on Pollution of the Sea
All ER	All England Reports
AFDI	Annuaire Français de Droit International
AIR	All India Reports
AJIL	American Journal of International Law
ALJ	Australian Law Journal
ALJR	Australian Law Journal Reports
ALR	Australian Law Reports
Ann Droit Mar & Océanique	Annuaire de Droit Maritime et Océanique
Ann Rev Ecol Syst	Annual Review of Ecological Systems
Ann Rev Energy & Env	Annual Review of Energy and Environment
Ann Inst DDI	Annuaire de l'Institut de Droit International
Ann Suisse DDI	Annuaire Suisse de Droit International
Am UJILP	American University Journal of International Law and Politics
ASIL	American Society of International Law Proceedings
AULR	American University Law Review
AYIL	Australian Yearbook of International Law
BAT	Best Available Techniques
BEP	Best Environmental Practice
BFSP	British and Foreign State Papers
Boston CICLJ	Boston College International and Comparative Law Journal
BISD	Basic Instruments and Selected Decisions of the GATT
Boston Coll Env Aff LR	Boston College Environmental Affairs Law Review
BTA	Border Tax Adjustment
Brooklyn JIL	Brooklyn Journal of International Law

Burhenne	*International Environmental Law: Multilateral Treaties, ed. W. Burhenne (Berlin, 1974)*
BYIL	*British Yearbook of International Law*
Colorado JIELP	*Colorado Journal of International Environmental Law and Policy*
Columbia JTL	*Columbia Journal of Transnational Law*
Columbia JEL	*Columbia Journal of Environmental Law*
CLB	*Commonwealth Law Bulletin*
CLP	*Current Legal Problems*
CLR	*Commonwealth Law Reports*
CMLR	*Common Market Law Review*
Columbia HRLR	*Columbia Human Rights Law Review*
Cornell ILJ	*Cornell International Law Journal*
CWILJ	*California Western International Law Journal*
CWRJIL	*Case Western Reserve Journal of International Law*
CYIL	*Canadian Yearbook of International Law*
CBD	*Convention on Biological Diversity*
CCAMLR	*Convention for the Conservation of Antarctic Marine Living Resources*
CDM	*Clean Development Mechanism*
CEC	*Commission for Environmental Co-operation*
CITES	*Convention on International Trade in Endangered Species*
CDM	*Clean development mechanism*
CEC	*Commission for Environmental Co-operation*
CITES	*Convention on International Trade in Endangered Species*
COLREGS	*Collision Regulations*
COP	*Conference of the Parties*
CSCE	*Conference on Security and Cooperation in Europe*
CTE	*Committee on Trade and Environment*
Dal LJ	*Dalhousie Law Journal*
Den JILP	*Denver Journal of International Law and Politics*
DLR (AD)	*Dominion Law Reporter (Appellate Division) (Bangladesh)*
Duke LJ	*Duke Law Journal*
ECHR	*European Court of Human Rights Reports*
ECJ	*European Court of Justice*
ECR	*European Court Reports*

EHRR	*European Human Rights Reports*
EJIL	*European Journal of International Law*
ELQ	*Environmental Law Quarterly*
ELR	*European Law Review*
DSB	*Dispute Settlement Body*
Emory Int LR	*Emory International Law Review*
Envtl L	*Environmental Lawyer*
Ency of Pub Int L	*Encyclopaedia of Public International Law*
EPL	*Environmental Policy and Law*
ETS	*Council of Europe Treaty Series*
Eur Env LR	*European Environmental Law Review*
Eur J of Crime, Crim L & Crim Just	*European Journal of Crime, Criminal Law & Criminal Justice*
EC	*European Community*
ECHR	*European Convention/Court of Human Rights*
ECOSOC	*Economic and Social Committee*
EEZ	*Exclusive Economic Zone*
EFZ	*Exclusive Fishery Zone*
EIA	*Environmental Impact Assessment*
EMEP	*Programme for Monitoring and Evaluation of Long-range Transmission of Air Pollutants in Europe*
EPA	*Environmental Protection Agency*
EU	*European Union*
FAO	*Food and Agriculture Organization*
FC	*Federal Courts (Canada)*
FNI	*Fishing News International*
Fordham ELJ	*Fordham Environmental Law Journal*
GATT	*General Agreement on Tariffs and Trade, 1947*
Georgia LR	*Georgia Law Review*
Georgetown IELR	*Georgetown International Environmental Law Review*
GYIL	*German Yearbook of International Law*
Hague YIL	*Hague Yearbook of International Law*
Harv ELR	*Harvard Environmental Law Review*
Harv HRYB	*Harvard Human Rights Yearbook*
FSIC	*Flag State Implementation Committee*

GEF	Global Environmental Facility
GESAMP	Group of Experts on Scientific Aspects of Marine Pollution
Harv ILJ	Harvard International Law Journal
Harv LR	Harvard Law Review
HRLJ	Human Rights Law Journal
HRR	Human Rights Reports
Hum & Ecol Risk Assessment	Human and Ecological Risk Assessment
HMS	Highly migratory species
ICJ	International Court of Justice
ICLQ	International and Comparative Law Quarterly
Idaho LR	Idaho Law Review
IJECL	International Journal of Estuarine and Coastal Law
IJMCL	International Journal of Marine and Coastal Law
ILA	International Law Association
ILC	International Law Commission
ILM	International Legal Materials
ILR	International Law Reports
Indian JIL	Indian Journal of International Law
Int Affairs	International Affairs
Inter-American YB on Hum Rts	Inter-American Yearbook on Human Rights
Int Env L Reps	International Environmental Law Reports
Int Org	International Organisation
Int Orgs LR	International Organisations Law Review
Ital YIL	Italian Yearbook of International Law
ITLOS	International Tribunal for the Law of the Sea
IUCN Bull	International Union for the Conservation of Nature Bulletin
IACHR	Inter-American Court of Human Rights
IAEA	International Atomic Energy Agency
ICCPR	International Covenant on Civil and Political Rights
ICES	International Council on Exploration of the Seas
ICESCR	International Covenant on Economic, Social and Cultural Rights
ICRW	International Convention for the Regulation of Whaling
IFC	International Finance Corporation

INC	*Intergovernmental Negotiating Committee*
INSC	*International North Sea Conference*
IOPC	*International Oil Pollution Compensation Fund*
IPCC	*Intergovernmental Panel on Climate Change*
ISBA	*International Seabed Authority*
ITTA	*International Tropical Timber Agreement*
ITTO	*International Tropical Timber Organization*
Jap Ann IL	*Japanese Annual of International Law*
JEL	*Journal of Environmental Law*
J Env & Dev'mnt	*Journal of Environment and Development*
J Eur Env & Plng L	*Journal of European Environmental and Planning Law*
JIEL	*Journal of International Economic Law*
JIWLP	*Journal of International Wildlife Law and Policy*
JIELP	*Journal of International Environmental Law and Policy*
JLS	*Journal of Law and Society*
JMLC	*Journal of Maritime Law and Commerce*
Jnl of Bus Admin	*Journal of Business Administration*
JPEL	*Journal of Planning and Environmental Law*
JPL	*Journal of Planning Law*
J Transnatl L & Pol	*Journal of Transnational Law and Policy*
JWT	*Journal of World Trade Law*
LGERA	*Local Government and Environment Reports of Australia*
LJIL	*Leiden Journal of International Law*
LNTS	*League of Nations Treaty Series*
Loyola ICLJ	*Loyola University International and Comparative Law Journal*
LOSB	*Law of the Sea Bulletin*
Mar Poll Bull	*Marine Pollution Bulletin*
Max Planck YbUNL	*Max Planck Yearbook of United Nations Law*
McGill LR	*McGill Law Review*
Melb ULR	*Melbourne University Law Review*
Mich JIL	*Michigan Journal of International Law*
Minn J Global Trade	*Minnesota Journal of Global Trade*

MLJ	*Malaysia Law Journal*
MLR	*Modern Law Review*
ND	*New Directions in the Law of the Sea (Dobbs, Ferry, 1974-)*
NILR	*Netherlands International Law Review*
NLB	*Nuclear Law Bulletin*
Nordic JIL	*Nordic Journal of International Law*
NRJ	*Natural Resources Journal*
NYIL	*Netherlands Yearbook of International Law*
NYJILP	*New York Journal of International Law and Policy*
NY Law School LR	*New York Law School Law Review*
NYUEnvLJ	*New York University Environmental Law Journal*
NZLR	*New Zealand Law Reports*
O&C Man	*Ocean and Coastal Management*
Ocean YB	*Ocean Yearbook*
ODIL	*Ocean Development and International Law*
OGTLR	*Oil and Gas Taxation Law Review*
OJ	*Official Journal (of the European Community)*
Oregon LR	*Oregon Law Review*
OPN	*Ocean Policy News*
OsHLJ	*Osgoode Hall Law Journal*
PACE ELR	*Pace Environmental Law Review*
Otago LJ	*University of Otago Law Journal*
PCIJ	*Permanent Court of International Justice Reports*
Proc ASIL	*Proceedings of the American Society of International Law*
Pub.Admin	*Public Administration*
RBDI	*Revue Belge de Droit International*
RECIEL	*Review of European Community and International Environmental Law*
Rev Int de Droit Pénal	*Revue International de Droit Pénal*
Rev jurid de l'env	*Revue juridique de l'environnement*
Rev Espanola DI	*Revista Espanola Derecho Internacional*
Rev Eur Droit de l'Env	*Revue Européen du Droit de l'Environnement*
RGDIP	*Revue Général de Droit International Public*
RIAA	*Reports of International Arbitration Awards*

Ruster and Simma	*International Protection of the Environment, ed. B. Ruster and B. Simma, (Dobbs Ferry, 1975-)*
SALJ	*South African Law Journal*
Scal LR	*Southern California Law Review*
SCC	*Supreme Court Cases (India)*
S Ct	*Supreme Court (US)*
San Diego LR	*San Diego Law Review*
Stanford JIL	*Stanford Journal of International Law*
Stan ELJ	*Stanford Environmental Law Journal*
Sydney LR	*Sydney Law Review*
Texas ILJ	*Texas International Law Journal*
Tulane ELJ	*Tulane Environmental Journal*
Tulane JICL	*Tulane Journal of International and Comparative Law*
UBCLR	*University of British Columbia Law Review*
UCLA J Envtl L & Pol'y	*University of California at Los Angeles Journal of Environmental Law and Policy*
UCLALR	*University of California at Los Angeles Law Review*
UKTS	*United Kingdom Treaty Series*
UNCLOS	*United Nations Convention on the Law of the Sea, 1982*
UN Doc	*United Nations Document*
UNGA	*United Nations General Assembly*
UNGAOR	*United Nations General Assembly Official Records*
UNHRC	*United Nations Human Rights Commission*
UN Jurid YB	*United Nations Juridical Yearbook*
UN Leg Ser	*United Nations Legislative Series*
UNTS	*United Nations Treaty Series*
U Penn LR	*University of Pennsylvania Law Review*
US	*United States Reports*
USPQ	*United States Patents Quarterly*
UST	*United States Treaties*
UTLJ	*University of Toronto Law Journal*
Vand JTL	*Vanderbilt Journal of Transnational Law*
Va Envtl LJ	*Virginia Environmental Law Journal*
VJIL	*Virginia Journal of International Law*
VUWLR	*Victoria University of Wellington Law Review*
Wash & Lee LR	*Washington and Lee Law Review*

Wis ILJ	*Wisconsin International Law Journal*
WLR	*Weekly Law Reports (England)*
Wm & Mary Envtl L & Pol Rev	*William and Mary Environmental Law & Policy Review*
Yale LJ	*Yale Law Journal*
Ybk of the AAA	*Yearbook of the Hague Academy of International Law*
YEL	*Yearbook of European Law*
YbIEL	*Yearbook of International Environmental Law*
YBILC	*Yearbook of the International Law Commission*
ZAÖRV	*Zeitschrift für Ausländisches und Öffentliches Recht und Völkerrecht*

TABLE OF CASES

TABLE OF MAJOR TREATIES
AND INSTRUMENTS

Only those treaties and other instruments which are cited frequently in the text or are of particular significance are listed here. References to other treaties will be found in the footnotes. 'Not in force' indicates that the treaty had not come into force by 31 December 2007. Most of the major agreements can be found in Birnie and Boyle, *Basic Documents on International Law and the Environment* (Oxford, 1995)[hereafter '*B&B Docs*']. Almost all of these treaties and other instruments are readily accessible on the internet via a Google search.

1

INTERNATIONAL LAW AND THE ENVIRONMENT

The Court also recognizes that the environment is not an abstraction but represents the living space, the quality of life and the very health of human beings, including generations unborn. The existence of the general obligation of States to ensure that activities within their jurisdiction and control respect the environment of other States or of areas beyond national control is now part of the corpus of international law relating to the environment.[1]

1 INTRODUCTION

The development of modern international environmental law, starting essentially in the 1960s, has been one of the most remarkable exercises in international lawmaking, comparable only to the law of human rights and international trade law in the scale and form it has taken. Authors rightly draw attention to 'la grande fertilité de cette branche du droit international'.[2] The law which has emerged from this process is neither primitive nor unsystematic, though unsurprisingly it has weaknesses, as we will see. It is of course possible to argue that other approaches to global environmental management might be more desirable, or more efficacious. But to say that economic or political models have as much or more to contribute than international law is merely to observe that protecting the environment is not exclusively a problem for lawyers. Moreover, given the shallowness of some of their theorizing about the environment, it is far from clear that economists or international relations theorists can save the planet. Similarly, it would be naïve to expect international law to remedy problems of the complexity the world's environment now faces without an underlying political, scientific, and technical commitment on the part of states, and a corresponding response in national legal and political systems. Whether that commitment is more than superficial or symbolic

---

[1] *Nuclear Weapons Advisory Opinion*, ICJ Reports (1996) 241–2, para 29.

[2] Dupuy, 101 *RGDIP* (1997) 873, 900.

remains an open question.[3] It is not the purpose of this book to explore the place of international environmental law within this broader context, but we do attempt to show how it has provided the framework for cooperation between developed and developing states, for measures aimed at equitable and sustainable use of natural resources, for the resolution of international environmental disputes, for the promotion of greater transparency and public participation in national decision-making, and for the adoption and harmonization of a great deal of national environmental law. These developments have created the system of international environmental law and regulation that we examine in the following chapters.

1(1) WHAT IS INTERNATIONAL ENVIRONMENTAL LAW?

A number of preliminary problems arise in any attempt to identify 'international environmental law'. Although international courts make use of the term,[4] some scholars have avoided doing so,[5] arguing that there is no distinct body of 'international environmental law' with its own sources and methods of lawmaking deriving from principles peculiar or exclusive to environmental concerns. Rather, they stress the application of rules and principles of general international law and its sources.

It is unquestionably correct that international environmental law is part of international law as a whole, not some separate, self-contained discipline, and no serious lawyer would suggest otherwise. The problem with over-emphasising the role of general international law, however, is that 'the traditional legal order of the environment is essentially a *laissez-faire* system oriented toward the unfettered freedom of states. Such limitations on freedom of action as do exist have emerged in an *ad hoc* fashion and have been formulated from perspectives other than the specifically environmental.'[6] As environmental problems have risen in importance it has been necessary to develop a body of law more specifically aimed at protection of the environment. Moreover, international environmental law also includes relevant aspects of private international law, and in some instances has borrowed heavily from national law. A study of contemporary international environmental law thus requires us to consider this evolving body of specifically environmental law, as well as the application of general international law to environmental problems.

In this work the expression 'international environmental law' is thus used simply as a convenient way to encompass the entire corpus of international law, public and private, relevant to environmental problems, in the same way that the terms 'Law of the Sea', 'International Criminal Law', or 'International Economic Law' are widely

---

[3] See in particular the section on climate change in Ch 6.

[4] See e.g *Gabčíkovo-Nagymaros Case,* ICJ Reports (1997) 7, paras 92, 104, 141; *Iron Rhine Arbitration,* PCA (2005) paras 58, 222–3.

[5] E.g. Brownlie, *Principles of Public International Law* (6th edn, Oxford, 2005) Ch XII.

[6] Schneider, *World Public Order of the Environment: Towards an Ecological Law and Organization* (Toronto, 1979) 30. See also Fitzmaurice, 25 *NYIL* (1994) 181; Chinkin, in Jewell and Steele (eds), *Law in Environmental Decision-making* (Oxford, 1998) Ch 8; Bodansky, Brunnée, and Hey (eds), *The Oxford Handbook of International Environmental Law* (Oxford, 2007) Ch 1.

accepted. It is not intended thereby to indicate the existence of some new discipline based exclusively on environmental perspectives and principles, though these have played an increasingly important role in stimulating legal developments in this field, as we shall observe. It has become common practice to refer to international environmental law in this way.[7]

Used in the above sense, 'international environmental law' is of course different from international human-rights law, the law of the sea, natural resources law, or international economic law, inter alia, but there are significant overlaps and interactions with these categories, and the categorization is in some cases a matter only of choice and perspective. Our chapters on the protection of the marine environment, or the conservation of marine living resources, would not be out of place in books on law of the sea.[8] Our discussion of environmental rights in Chapter 5 draws heavily on international human-rights law, but books on that subject more rarely address its environmental implications. The interplay of international trade law and international environmental law is considered in Chapter 14 but many of the issues covered in other chapters could equally well be addressed from the perspective of international economic law, including climate change and sustainable use of natural resources. Much of contemporary international environmental law deals with sustainable use of fresh water, fisheries, forests, biological diversity or endangered species. This is simply natural-resources law—or perhaps elements of the law of sustainable development—from another perspective. Moreover, even within otherwise discrete bodies of law, specifically environmental norms or applications can also be found. Part XII of the 1982 UN Convention on the Law of the Sea ('UNCLOS') deals with 'Protection and Preservation of the Marine Environment', and is one of the most important environmental agreements currently in existence. The Preamble to the 1994 WTO Agreement refers to 'sustainable development', and to that extent encompasses environmental concerns, as do the exceptions listed in Article XX of the GATT. Human-rights law has an increasingly important environmental dimension, as we observe in Chapter 5. There is no magic in any of these categorizations.

What matters, as Chapter 3 and later chapters try to make clear, is that the resolution of international environmental problems, however categorized, entails the application of international law as a whole, in an integrated manner. In the real world, it is simply not possible to address many of the legal issues posed by international environmental problems without also considering the law of treaties, state responsibility, jurisdiction, the law of the sea, natural resources law, dispute settlement, private international law, human rights law, international criminal law, and international trade law, to name only the most obvious. All of these topics have environmental dimensions or affect the

---

[7] See e.g. Teclaff and Utton (eds), *International Environmental Law* (New York, 1974); Sands, *Principles of International Environmental Law* (2nd edn, Cambridge, 2005); Kiss and Shelton, *International Environmental Law* (3rd edn, New York, 2004); Louka, *International Environmental Law* (Cambridge, 2006).

[8] See e.g. O'Connell, *The International Law of the Sea* (Oxford, 1984) vol II, Chs 14, 25; Churchill and Lowe, *The Law of the Sea* (3rd edn, Manchester, 1999) Chs 14, 15; Brown, *The International Law of the Sea* (Aldershot, 1994) I, Chs 12, 15.

resolution of environmental problems and disputes. Bearing that in mind, it is worth re-emphasising that 'international environmental law' is nothing more, or less, than the application of public and private international law to environmental problems.[9]

A more difficult issue is the distinction, if there is one, between international law relating to the environment, and international law relating to sustainable development. The 1992 Rio Declaration of the UN Conference on Environment and Development refers to the 'further development of international law in the field of sustainable development',[10] and it is sometimes suggested that this has subsumed international environmental law. A more nuanced approach was endorsed by the UN Environment Programme, whose 1997 Nairobi Declaration refers to 'international environmental law aiming at sustainable development'.[11] In subsequent chapters of this book a great deal of attention will be paid to the concept of sustainable development, whose importance for the resolution of environmental problems is undisputed. Yet, although much of international environmental law could be regarded as law 'in the field of' or 'aiming at' sustainable development,[12] there remain important differences. International environmental law encompasses both more and less than the law of sustainable development. There is a major overlap in rules, principles, techniques and institutions, but the goals are by no means identical. Most obviously, sustainable development is as much about economic development as about environmental protection; while these two goals have to be integrated, they remain distinct. Moreover, not all environmental questions necessarily involve sustainable development, or vice versa. We may wish to preserve Antarctica, or endangered species such as the great whales or the giant panda, for reasons that have little or nothing to do with sustainable development; or put another way, we may wish to preserve them *from* sustainable development. In this sense, international law may in some cases reflect environmental concerns that override or trump development, however sustainable. At the same time, developmental priorities may in other cases override environmental concerns without thereby ceasing to be 'sustainable development'. Of course, much depends on what is meant by sustainable development, a notoriously uncertain term.[13] Once again the question is not whether there is law in the field of sustainable development, but the perspective from which one looks at the existing law. Our principal concern in this book is to address the question of how international law deals with problems which can plausibly be seen as environmental, while accepting that many of these are also problems of sustainable development. To that extent, this is indeed also a book about international environmental law 'aiming at sustainable development'.

1(2) WHAT IS MEANT BY 'THE ENVIRONMENT'?

Defining the term 'environment' presents further difficulties. None of the major treaties, declarations, codes of conduct, guidelines, etc referred to throughout this work

---

[9] Dupuy, 101 *RGDIP* (1997) 873, 899.   [10] Principle 27. See *infra*, Ch 3.
[11] Adopted by UNEP Governing Council decision 19/1 (1997). See *infra*, Ch 2, section 3(3).
[12] See Sands, 65 *BYIL* (1994) 303.   [13] See *infra*, Ch 2.

attempts directly to do so. No doubt this is because it is difficult both to identify and to restrict the scope of such an amorphous term, which could be used to encompass anything from the whole biosphere to the habitat of the smallest creature or organism. Dictionary definitions range from 'something that environs' to 'the whole complex of climatic, edaphic and biotic factors that act upon an organism or an ecological community and ultimately determine its form or survival; the aggregate of social or cultural conditions that influence the life of an individual or a community'[14] or, more simply, 'the surroundings or conditions in which a person, animal, or plant lives or operates'.[15] The Declaration of the 1972 Stockholm Conference on the Human Environment (UNCHE) merely referred obliquely to man's environment, adding that 'both aspects of man's environment, the natural and the man-made, are essential for his well-being and enjoyment of basic human rights'.[16] The World Commission on Environment and Development (WCED) relied on an even more succinct approach; it remarked that 'the environment is where we all live'.[17] The 1992 Rio Declaration on Environment and Development refers at many points to environmental needs, environmental protection, environmental degradation and so on, but nowhere identifies what these include. Interestingly it eschews the term entirely in Principle 1, declaring instead that human beings 'are entitled to a healthy and productive life *in harmony with nature*'(emphasis added). One of the few bodies to proffer a definition is the European Commission. In developing an 'Action Programme on the Environment', it defined 'environment' as 'the combination of elements whose complex inter-relationships make up the settings, the surroundings and the conditions of life of the individual and of society as they are and as they are felt'.[18] Many conventions avoid the problem, however, no doubt because, as Caldwell remarks 'it is a term that everyone understands and no one is able to define'.[19]

Some understanding of what 'the environment' may encompass can be discerned from other treaty provisions, however. Those agreements which define 'environmental effects', 'environmental impacts' or 'environmental damage' typically include harm to flora, fauna, soil, water, air, landscape, cultural heritage, and any interaction between these factors.[20] Others take an approach that additionally introduces the equally problematic concept of ecosystem protection, albeit defined differently for the purposes of

[14] Webster's *New World Dictionary* (3rd edn, Cleveland, 1988) 454.

[15] *Concise Oxford Dictionary* (11th edn, Oxford, 2006) 406.

[16] Stockholm Declaration, Preamble, para 1, in UN, *Rept of UN Conference on the Human Environment*, A/CONF 48/14/Rev 1 (New York, 1972) 3, and see *infra*, Ch 2.

[17] WCED, *Our Common Future* (Oxford, 1987) xi. The WCED's Legal Expert Group on Environmental Law did not define the terms; see Munro and Lammers, *Environmental Protection and Sustainable Development* (Dordrecht, 1986).

[18] Council Regulation (EEC) No 1872/84 on Action by the Community Relating to the Environment, OJL 176 (1984) 1.

[19] Caldwell, *International Environmental Policy and Law* (1st edn, Durham, NC, 1980) 170.

[20] 1992 Convention on the Transboundary Effects of Industrial Accidents, Article 1 (c); 1992 Convention on the Protection of Transboundary Watercourses and Lakes, Article 1 (2); 1993 Convention on Civil Liability for Damage Resulting from Activities Dangerous to the Environment, Article 2 (7) and (10). See *infra*, Ch 3, section 4(6).

each treaty. Although conventions limited to the 'marine environment' avoid defining that term,[21] it seems to have been generally understood at the 3rd UN Conference
on the Law of the Sea that it included the atmosphere and marine life, as well as 'rare
and fragile ecosystems'.[22] Likewise, none of the agreements forming the Antarctic
Treaty System defines the Antarctic environment, but all the relevant ones include
'dependent and associated ecosystems' within that term. Thus the 1980 Convention
on Conservation of Antarctic Marine Living Resources applies to the Antarctic marine ecosystem, defined for this purpose as 'the complex of relationships of marine
living resources with each other and with their physical environment',[23] while the
1988 Convention on the Regulation of Antarctic Mineral Resource Activities defined
damage to the Antarctic environment or dependent or associated ecosystems as 'any
impact on the living or non-living components of that environment or those ecosystems, including harm to atmospheric, marine or terrestrial life…'.[24] The 1991 Protocol
on Environmental Protection also adds 'the intrinsic value of Antarctica, including its
wilderness and aesthetic values'.[25]

Probably the broadest approach is found in the 1992 Framework Convention on
Climate Change, which defines adverse effects on the environment to include 'changes
in the physical environment or biota, resulting from climate change, which have significant deleterious effects on the composition, resilience and productivity of natural
and managed ecosystems, or on the operation of natural and managed ecosystems or
on the operation of socio-economic systems or human health and welfare'.[26]

While there are obvious patterns discernible from these treaty provisions, there is a
danger of reading too much into what are intended only as definitions for the different
purposes of each treaty.[27] Another indication of what the environment encompasses
at an international level is given by the broad range of issues now addressed by international environmental law, including conservation and sustainable use of natural
resources and biodiversity; conservation of endangered and migratory species; prevention of deforestation and desertification; preservation of Antarctica and areas of
outstanding natural heritage; protection of oceans, international watercourses, the
atmosphere, climate and ozone layer from the effects of pollution; safeguarding human
health and the quality of life.[28] Inevitably, however, any definition of 'the environment'
will have the Alice-in-Wonderland quality of meaning what we want it to mean. This
should be borne in mind in later chapters.

---

[21] As in the 1982 United Nations Convention on the Law of the Sea (UNCLOS) although Malta had proposed that the term 'comprises the surface of the sea, the air space above, the water column and the sea-bed
beyond the high-tide mark including the bio-systems therein or dependent thereon'. See Nordquist (ed), *The
United Nations Convention on the Law of the Sea: A Commentary* (Dordrecht, 1991) iv, 42–3.

[22] Ibid, and see Article 194 (5) and *infra*, Ch 7.

[23] Article 1. See Redgwell, in Boyle and Freestone (eds), *International Law and Sustainable Development*
(Oxford, 1999) Ch 9. On the evolution of ecosystem management see Scheiber, 24 *ELQ* (1997) 631, and
infra, Ch 11.

[24] This convention is unlikely to enter into force.   [25] Article 3(1).

[26] Article 1(1) See *infra*, Ch 6. This is an expanded version of a very similar definition used in Article 1(2)
of the 1985 Convention for the Protection of the Ozone Layer.

[27] See *infra*, Ch 3, section 4(6).   [28] See *Iron Rhine Arbitration*, PCA (2005) para 58.

1(3) WHY PROTECT THE ENVIRONMENT?

Quite apart from the obvious difficulty posed by the previous section, this is too large a question to be answered simply. Much depends on the context. The ethical, aesthetic, or symbolic reasons for saving the great whales or Antarctica from further exploitation are quite different from the economic and health related objectives behind pollution regulation. However, almost all justifications for international environmental protection are predominantly and in some sense anthropocentric.[29] This is true especially of the 1972 Stockholm Declaration, which focused explicitly on protecting 'the human environment', and proclaimed:

Man is both creature and moulder of his environment, which gives him physical sustenance and affords him the opportunity for intellectual, spiritual, moral and social growth...[30]

Likewise, the 1992 Rio Declaration on Environment and Development asserts that 'Human beings are at the centre of concerns for sustainable development'.[31]

As we shall see in Chapter 5, the emergence of an environmental dimension in human-rights law has a strongly anthropocentric motivation, most notable in attempts to develop a new human right to a decent environment. Some advocates assert that such a right is indispensable for the enjoyment of other human rights and freedoms,[32] but they usually fail to explain how competing environmental, economic, and social priorities can be accommodated in what necessarily becomes a judgement about what we value most. A more explicit relativism characterizes most environmental measures aimed at protecting human health or safety, including those in which responsibility for the welfare of future generations is a prominent feature, such as the conventions on nuclear radiation risks or climate change.[33] In this context the principal question is the level of socially acceptable risk, but the underlying objective is nevertheless anthropocentric. Economic justifications are also strongly anthropocentric, focusing partly on efficiency considerations and the sustainable use of resources, partly on the perceived desirability of 'internalizing' the true economic costs of pollution damage and control, and partly on the need to minimize the competitive disadvantages of failure to harmonise national environmental policy and law.[34]

Nature, ecosystems, natural resources, wildlife, and so on, are thus of concern to international lawmakers primarily for their value to humanity. This need not be limited to economic value, although most of the early wildlife treaties were so limited, but can include aesthetic, amenity or cultural value, or be motivated by religious or moral concerns.[35] The preamble to the 1992 Convention on Biological Diversity evinces

---

[29] See generally Gillespie, *International Environmental Law, Policy and Ethics* (Oxford, 1997); Eckersley, *Environmentalism and Political Theory* (London, 1992); Redgwell, in Boyle and Anderson (eds), *Human Rights Approaches to Environmental Protection* (Oxford, 1996) Ch 4.

[30] Declaration, Preamble, para 1.   [31] See *infra*, Ch 2.

[32] E.g. Pathak, in Brown Weiss (ed), *Environmental Change and International Law* (Tokyo, 1993) Ch 8.

[33] See *infra*, Chs 6, 9.

[34] See e.g. Jacobs, *The Green Economy* (London, 1991); Gillespie, *International Environmental Law, Policy and Ethics*, Ch 3.

[35] Gillespie, op cit, Chs 4, 5.

the complex mixture of objectives which characterises much of contemporary international environmental law:

Conscious of the intrinsic value of biological diversity and of the ecological, social, economic, scientific, educational, cultural, recreational and aesthetic value of biological diversity and its components,

   Conscious also of the importance of biological diversity for evolution and for maintaining life-sustaining systems of the biosphere...

The last part of this extract illustrates what can be referred to as a 'holistic' approach to environmental protection, a recognition of the interdependence of humanity and the entire natural world, expressed most characteristically in the notion of the world as a 'biosphere', and implicit in both the 1992 Conventions on Biological Diversity and Climate Change.

   But other, potentially non-anthropocentric, justifications are apparent here, in references to the 'intrinsic value' of biodiversity, or of Antarctica and other wilderness areas. Intrinsic value and the 'moral considerability' of animals also provide arguments for international attempts to regulate cruelty and protect endangered species.[36] Such ecological or ecocentric perspectives can lead to a rather different vision of respect for the natural world than those which typify most of international environmental law. Apart from their potential for incoherence, claims based on the intrinsic value of nature, at their most extreme, pose the question 'how does humanity fit within such an ethical view of the world?'[37] It is clear from the opening paragraph of the Rio Declaration quoted above that the international community has not truly embraced this alternative vision of the purposes of environmental protection, but has at most sought to ensure that ecological concerns are accommodated and given weight within a broader process of balancing which remains essentially anthropocentric.[38]

1(4) THE ENVIRONMENT AS A PROBLEM OF INTERNATIONAL CONCERN

International law addresses environmental issues at several levels. Transboundary problems, such as air or water pollution, or conservation of migratory animals, provide examples of the earliest and most developed use of international law to regulate environmental concerns. In many cases these problems are regional in extent, and are regulated by regional organizations and regional agreements, particularly in Europe and North America, or in regional seas such as the Mediterranean or Caribbean.[39] Some environmental problems, for example climate change or depletion of the stratospheric ozone layer, are inherently global in character and affect all states, not necessarily equally but at least to the extent that impacts are global and global solutions are required. The Climate Change Convention, the Ozone Convention, the Biological Diversity Convention, and their respective protocols, typify the emergence of such

---

[36] Id, Ch 7.   [37] Id, 173.   [38] See infra, Ch 2.   [39] Infra, Chs 6, 8, 10.

global regulatory regimes.[40] Increasingly, international law addresses national or domestic environmental problems, whether through international human rights law, conservation of biological diversity, protection of natural heritage areas, or promotion of sustainable development. There is thus no single sense in which an environmental issue can be described as 'international': it could be global, regional, transboundary, domestic, or a combination of all or any of these.

What must be appreciated, however, is that the law governing these rather different contexts is likely itself to differ, both in the content of any applicable rules, and in the form they take. Some of the law relating to transboundary problems takes the form of customary or general international law, while very little customary law applies to global environmental concerns, where regulatory treaties instead provide most of the substantive content. Such differences also affect the processes by which disputes are settled or compliance enforced. Transboundary disputes are rather more likely to be suitable for adjudication or arbitration than global or regional environmental problems. These differences are more fully explored in Chapters 3 and 4.

1(5) THE ROLE OF LAW IN INTERNATIONAL ENVIRONMENTAL PROTECTION

The role played by international law in protecting the environment is not fundamentally different from, or any less varied than, domestic environmental law. Nor, in many cases, is it necessarily any less sophisticated; indeed rather the reverse is true in the case of some countries.

First, in its constitutional role international law provides mechanisms and procedures for negotiating the necessary rules and standards, settling disputes, and supervising implementation and compliance with treaties and customary rules. In this context it facilitates and promotes cooperation between states, international organizations, and non-governmental organizations; and constitutes the processes of international environmental governance, international lawmaking and regulation and, in a few cases, of international trusteeship.[41] Although international environmental law has historically been focused mainly on interstate relations and the rights and duties of states, the human-rights dimensions have become increasingly prominent.[42] NGO participation has also given non-state actors significant influence in environmental treaty negotiations and the environmental agenda of international bodies. In a very real sense modern international environmental law is no longer made by states alone.

Second, like national environmental law, much of international environmental law is concerned with regulating environmental problems, providing common standards and practices for prevention or mitigation of pollution, or promoting conservation and sustainable use of natural resources and biodiversity. A flexible rule-making process allows for easy and regular amendment in the light of technological developments and advances in scientific and other knowledge. Most of this regulatory system is based on

---

[40] *Infra*, Chs 6, 11.   [41] See *infra*, Ch 2.   [42] See *infra*, Ch 5.

multilateral treaties, but soft-law instruments, including codes of conduct, guidelines and recommendations, are also employed. So-called framework agreements allow for successive negotiation of additional protocols, annexes and decisions of the parties to create an increasingly more detailed regulatory regime.[43]

Third, an additional purpose, or at least effect, of some international environmental agreements is to harmonize national laws, either globally or regionally. Treaties on civil liability for nuclear accidents or oil-pollution damage at sea afford good examples of such harmonization: in effect national law will largely have to replicate the provisions of these treaties and will essentially be the same in each state party. Here the objective is to facilitate access to justice for litigants who have suffered loss in large-scale international accidents. Regulatory treaties have different objectives in mind when seeking to harmonize national law: the economic impact of implementing environmental protection measures may be such that states are willing to participate in such treaties once they can be assured that the same regulatory standards will prevail in competitor states. This will not always be possible, and as we shall see, developing states often insist on differential standards.

But the mere fact that certain states have become parties to a treaty committing them to take measures to deal with some environmental problem does not per se ensure, or even necessarily promote, harmonization of national law. First, states will often have considerable discretion in the methods of implementation they use, and possibly also in the standards and timetables they set. It is in this respect that regulatory conflicts can arise, since the result will often be a lack of uniformity in what individual governments actually do. They may all be working to the same goal, but doing so in very different ways. The possibility of the parties adopting the same standards does exist if they are able to reach further agreement, but in practice there may be little to stop each government pursuing its own particular priorities. Not surprisingly some treaties have for these reasons proved very difficult to implement in a coordinated, consistent way. Second, the degree and form of national implementation will largely determine how successful the treaty is as an instrument of change, assuming its objectives and techniques are themselves realistic, and that the parties intend to make more than symbolic gestures, which is not always the case. This is why so much attention has been paid both at UNCED and elsewhere to the methods and institutions which can be used to supervise compliance with environmental treaties, and ensure, through international inspection and reporting procedures, that they are adequately implemented.[44]

Should international environmental agreements therefore aim to lay down more detailed and precise rules and try to ensure greater harmonization of national law and practice? The problem is that this is unlikely to be either possible or desirable in some cases. It may not be possible because a degree of flexibility is often the price that has to be paid to secure international agreement. Much will then depend on how far the parties are prepared subsequently to adopt more specific rules. This has been

---

[43] See *infra*, section 2.   [44] See *infra*, Ch 4.

true of agreements regarding land-based sources of marine pollution and dumping at sea. But greater harmonization may also be undesirable. Because environmental problems tend to require flexible solutions to allow for changing scientific evidence, new control technologies, new political priorities, and the differing circumstances of various states, a treaty which casts precise rules in stone may be hard to renegotiate and thus too inflexible to respond to changing conditions. Most environmental treaties therefore tend to lay down only general principles, relegating the detailed standards to annexes which can be easily amended by decisions of the parties, or easily supplemented by new annexes or soft law provided the parties can agree. This is essentially the core of the problem: whereas the European Community now has the competence to legislate on environmental matters by qualified majority for all its member states, more orthodox treaty-based institutions are merely coalitions of the willing. Harmonization of national law is possible, based on rules agreed within such a treaty, but since the rules may themselves be controversial, as in the case of the Kyoto Protocol to the Climate Change Convention,[45] it is no easy task to bring this about. Inevitably therefore, a lot of discretion is often left to governments as the only way to achieve agreement on something. This is one reason why harmonization of national law can be a much more prominent objective of EC environmental policy than of international environmental policy.

Finally, reinstatement of or compensation for environmental damage is a more limited but still important function of the international legal system. It is more limited because only those who suffer damage can secure such redress, whether they are states relying on the international law of state responsibility,[46] or individuals relying in various ways on their right to bring transboundary actions in national law,[47] and because not all environmental damage is necessarily capable of reinstatement or has an economically assessable value. We explore these questions in Chapter 5.

1(6) DOES EXISTING INTERNATIONAL LAW ADEQUATELY PROTECT THE ENVIRONMENT?

This is an important question to which there is no easy or single answer. International environmental law has evolved at a time when the heterogeneity of the international community has rapidly intensified and when, simultaneously, the economic problems and development needs and aspirations of the less-developed states have become more prominent. Given these problems, the progress made in developing a body of international law with an environmental focus is a remarkable achievement, given the strains imposed on the international legislative process.[48] It has been pointed out, however, that the Rio Conference's endorsement of sustainable development evinces a strictly utilitarian, anthropocentric, non-preservationist, view of environmental protection,[49] which, because it entails negotiating balanced solutions taking account

---

[45] See *infra*, Ch 6.   [46] See *infra*, Ch 4.   [47] See *infra*, Ch 5.
[48] See also Handl, 1 *YbIEL* (1991) 3.   [49] Id, 24.

of environmental and developmental concerns, is likely to inhibit the scope for further development of a more truly 'environmental' perspective to the international legal system.[50] Ultimately, whether the protection offered to the environment by international law is 'adequate' in scope and stringency is of course a value judgement, which will depend on the weight given to the whole range of competing social, economic, and political considerations. All that this book can do is try help the reader to understand what the existing international legal system does provide.

As far as measuring the effectiveness of international environmental law is concerned, much depends on the criteria used. Effectiveness has multiple meanings: it may mean solving the problem for which the regime was established (for example, avoiding further depletion of the ozone layer); or achieving goals set out in the constitutive instrument (for example, attaining a set percentage reduction of sulphur emissions); or altering behaviour patterns (for example, moving from use of fossil fuels to solar or wind energy production); or enhancing national compliance with rules in international agreements, such as those restricting trade in endangered species.[51] As we shall see in subsequent chapters, the effectiveness of different regulatory and enforcement techniques is largely determined by the nature of the problem. What works in one case may not work in others. In this respect considerable advantage has been taken of the flexibility of international lawmaking processes, and their ability to incorporate new concepts and techniques.[52]

2 LAWMAKING PROCESSES AND SOURCES OF LAW

2(1) INTERNATIONAL LAWMAKING PROCESSES

Crucial to any assessment of the current state of international environmental law is an understanding of the sources and the lawmaking processes from which it derives. Although there is no international legislature as such, there are generally accepted sources from which international law derives, and a variety of processes through which new law is made or existing law changed. Much of international environmental law is the product of an essentially legislative process involving international organizations, conference diplomacy, codification and progressive development, international courts, and a relatively subtle interplay of treaties, non-binding declarations

---

[50] For fuller consideration of sustainable development see *infra*, Chs 2, 3.

[51] See Victor, Raustiala, and Skolnikoff (eds), *The Implementation and Effectiveness of International Environmental Commitments* (Cambridge, Mass, 1998) and *infra*, Ch 4, section 3.

[52] For examples of innovatory techniques used in standard setting and implementation, see Sand, *Lessons Learned in Global Environmental Governance* (Washington DC, 1990) 5–20.

or resolutions, and customary international law.[53] Three features have helped to make this lawmaking process both inclusive and relatively rapid.

First, international institutions, including the UN and its specialized and regional agencies and programmes, have played a leading role in setting lawmaking agendas and providing negotiating forums and expertise. The indispensable involvement of these bodies, and of the intergovernmental conferences they have convened, is considered more fully in Chapter 2.

Second, following the model of the 3rd UN Conference on the Law of the Sea, the use of consensus negotiating procedures and 'package deal' diplomacy[54] has created a real potential for securing general acceptance of negotiated texts. In a world of nearly two hundred states with disparate interests, and particularly sharp differences on environmental issues between developed and developing states, such techniques have been essential when dealing with global environmental problems. The 1992 Rio Conference on Environment and Development and the negotiation of the Conventions on Climate Change and Ozone Depletion illustrate particularly well the importance of a process capable of securing universal, or near universal, participation and support.[55]

Third, the use of 'framework treaties', setting out broad principles, while providing for detailed rules to be elaborated through regular meetings of the parties, has given the process, at least in its treaty form, a dynamic character, allowing successive protocols, annexes, and related agreements to be negotiated, adding to or revising the initial treaty. These treaties, together with the institutions they create, have become regulatory regimes.[56] They provide a basis for progressive action to be taken as scientific knowledge expands, and as regulatory priorities evolve or change. As a result, what may begin as a very bare outline agreement, such as the Ozone Convention, can become a complex system of detailed law with its own machinery for ensuring compliance and implementation.[57]

Above all these processes are political, involving lawmaking primarily by diplomatic means rather than codification and progressive development by legal experts, although the International Law Commission and judicial decisions do play a part in affirming the status of customary rules and general principles, leading in some cases to modest evolution in international law.[58] But it is the political processes referred to above which represent a real vehicle for lawmaking, with evidently wide appeal to the international community. Moreover, even where, as in the Stockholm and Rio

---

[53] For a much fuller account see Boyle and Chinkin, *The Making of International Law* (Oxford, 2007).

[54] See UNGA Res 2750 XXV (1970) and 3067 XXVIII (1973); UN, *Official Text of the 1982 UNCLOS* (New York, 1983) Introduction, xix-xxvii, and Final Act; Buzan, 75 *AJIL* (1981) 529; Caminos and Molitor, 79 *AJIL* (1985) 871.

[55] On the Rio Conference see *Rept of the UNCED*, UN Doc A/CONF151/26/Rev 1, vol 1; Sand, 3 *YbIEL* (1992) 3; Freestone, 6 *JEL* (1994) 193, and *infra*, Ch 2, section 2(4). On the Climate Change Convention see Mintzer and Leonard, *Negotiating Climate Change* (Cambridge, 1994) and *infra*, Ch 6. On the Ozone Convention see Benedick, *Ozone Diplomacy* (Cambridge, Mass, 1991) and *infra*, Ch 6. See generally Susskind, *Environmental Diplomacy* (Oxford, 1994).

[56] Gehring, 1 *YbIEL* (1990) 35. On international regimes see *infra*, Ch 2, section 5.

[57] See *infra*, Ch 6.

[58] See *Gabčíkovo-Nagymaros Case,* ICJ Reports (1997) 7, on which see Boyle, 8 *YbIEL* (1997) 13.

Declarations, the instruments adopted are not formally binding on states, they have in many cases contributed to the development of consistent state practice, or provided evidence of existing law, or of the lawmaking intention which is necessary for the evolution of new customary international law, or have lead to the negotiation of binding treaty commitments. While it is not yet the case that states can simply 'declare' new law, it is clear from the development of international environmental law, and from other branches of international law, that a relatively dynamic and creative approach to international lawmaking is possible.[59]

2(2) SOURCES OF INTERNATIONAL LAW IN AN ENVIRONMENTAL PERSPECTIVE

The sources of international environmental law are, of course, the same as those from which all international law emanates, since international environmental law is, as we have seen, simply a branch of general international law. But it can be observed, as this chapter will illustrate, that international environmental law is also particularly rich in illustrations of the problems posed by taking too narrow a view of the traditional sources of international law in a divided[60] or multicultural world.[61] Indeed, given the vast increase in the number of states, from fifty to over 190 since the establishment of the United Nations in 1945, and the diversity of political, racial, and religious systems, as well as of relative size and economic weight, it has been asked whether it is even possible to maintain the proposition that any universal international law can exist in modern international society, and if so how, and by what techniques, we identify it.[62] It is well established and widely accepted that newly independent states have to take international law as they find it but that they can then seek to change and influence its development. This they have done, successfully ensuring that international environmental law has taken account of their development interests from the time of the 1972 United Nations Conference on the Human Environment (UNCHE) onwards.[63] Their influence remains apparent in the development of strategies and approaches to international environmental lawmaking today.

Recognition of the need to protect the global environment as a whole, and to lay down new law on certain priority issues, has required that international law be developed more quickly and in a more flexible manner than in the past, entailing the adoption of new concepts and principles, and taking into account the imperatives of sustainable development. The corpus of environmental treaties that has developed in

---

[59] See especially Charney, 87 *AJIL* (1993) 529; Szasz, in Brown-Weiss (ed), *Environmental Change and International Law* (Tokyo, 1992) 61; Brölmann, 74 *Nordic JIL* (2005) 383; and Boyle and Chinkin, *The Making of International Law* (Oxford, 2007) Chs 3–5.

[60] Cassese, *International Law in a Divided World* (Oxford, 1986) esp 171–99.

[61] Dupuy (ed), *The Future of International Law in a Multicultural World* (The Hague, 1984); Mosler, in TMC Asser Institute (ed), *International Law and the Grotian Heritage* (The Hague, 1985) 173–85; Dinstein, *NYJILP* (1986–7) 1–32; Friedman, *The Changing Structure of International Law* (London, 1964) 121–3.

[62] Jennings, 37 *Ann Suisse DDI* (1981) 59–88; Charney, 87 *AJIL* (1993) 529.   [63] See *infra*, Ch 2.

the last twenty-five years reflects these imperatives, but there has also been resort to a so-called soft-law approach, through the use of non-binding declarations, codes, guidelines, or recommended principles.[64]

2(3) TRADITIONAL SOURCES OF INTERNATIONAL LAW[65]

Treaties and custom have historically been the main sources of binding international law, augmented since the adoption of Article 38(1) of the Statute of the Permanent Court of International Justice in 1920 by general principles of law and, as secondary sources, judicial decisions and the teachings of the most highly qualified publicists.[66] Though drafted before the growth in the number and diversity of states or the emergence of environmental consciousness, Article 38(1) remains the only generally accepted statement of the sources of international law to be applied by the ICJ. It is open to question whether it represents an exhaustive listing. Other possible candidates include General Assembly Resolutions, Declarations of Principles adopted by the UN or by ad hoc conferences, treaty provisions agreed by general consensus among the majority of states but not yet in force, and the proposals of the International Law Commission. Some commentators consider that norms drawn from these sources have to be embodied in treaties or state practice before they can become binding on states. Others are content to regard such sources as good evidence of existing customary law, or at least of the *opinio juris* necessary to turn state practice into custom.[67]

(a) Treaties[68]

Treaties are now the most frequently used instruments for creating generally applicable multilateral rules relating to the environment. The 1992 Conventions on Climate Change and Biological Diversity, or the 1982 UNCLOS, are, in this sense, lawmaking treaties.[69] They create regimes to which almost all states are party and from which no reservations or derogations are possible unless expressly authorized. Treaties of this kind are the most important basis for international environmental law.

Essentially, a treaty is a written or oral agreement between states, or between states and international organizations, governed by international law. The terminology is immaterial: the variety of alternatives includes treaty, convention, protocol, covenant,

---

[64] See generally Fitzmaurice, 25 *NYIL* (1994) 181, and *infra*, section 2(6).

[65] For succinct accounts of sources, a discussion of the term itself, and analysis of Article 38 of the ICJ Statute, see Brownlie, *Principles of Public International Law* (6th edn, Oxford, 2005) Ch 1, and Higgins, *International Law and How we Use it* (Oxford, 1994) Ch 2. See also Danilenko, in Butler (ed), *Perestroika and International Law* (Dordrecht, 1990) 61; Cassese, *International Law in a Divided World* (Oxford, 1986); Macdonald and Johnston (eds), *The Structure and Process of International Law* (Dordrecht, 1983) and van Hoof, *Rethinking the Sources of International Law* (Deventer, 1983).

[66] See now Statute of the International Court of Justice, Article 38(1).

[67] See generally Boyle and Chinkin, *The Making of International Law*, Chs 4, 5.

[68] See Brownlie, *Principles of Public International Law*, Ch 27; Aust, *Modern Treaty Law and Practice* (2nd edn, Cambridge, 2007); Sinclair, *The Vienna Convention on Treaties* (2nd edn, Manchester, 1984); Reuter, *Introduction to the Law of Treaties* (2nd edn, London, 1995).

[69] On lawmaking treaties see Brölmann, 74 *Nordic JIL* (2005) 383.

pact, act, etc. There are no rules prescribing their form but the 1969 Vienna Convention on the Law of Treaties codifies rules applicable to written treaties concluded after its entry into force in 1980. Whilst not all provisions of this convention have necessarily attained the status of customary law, in practice it has been applied without question in many international and national judicial decisions.[70] It deals with such matters as entry into force, reservations, interpretation, termination, and invalidity. Some agreements are executed in a simplified form, by exchange of notes or letters, and become binding on signature without need for reference to parliaments. Others, concluded at the administrative level in the form of Memoranda of Understanding (MOU), are not necessarily binding but they may still be taken into account or create good faith expectations.[71]

A brief summary of the provisions of the Vienna Convention concerning the process of concluding a treaty will assist the uninitiated reader. The underlying principle of customary law is that *pacta sunt servanda* (treaties are made to be kept). Treaties are normally signed following their adoption, but unless there is specific agreement to be bound by signature, it is not until instruments of ratification or accession have subsequently been deposited (which generally requires approval by national parliamentary or other internal processes) and any other requirements for entry into force have been fulfilled (for example a specified number of ratifications) that the treaty enters into force and becomes binding on its parties. Delays frequently occur at this stage. This is not always the case, however—the rapid entry into force of the 1985 Vienna Convention for Protection of the Ozone Layer and its Montreal Protocol indicates that multilateral treaties can provide an efficient means of urgent global or regional law-making when necessary.

Treaties do not *ipso facto* bind non-parties, unless the intention to do so is clearly expressed and the state concerned expressly accepts the benefits or obligations in question; in the latter case this must be done in writing. This is relatively unusual. Much more commonly treaty provisions bind non-parties through their evolution into customary international law, an argument considered in the next section. To be capable of so doing the ICJ has ruled in the *North Sea Continental Shelf Case* that 'It would in the first place be necessary that the provision concerned should, at all events potentially, be of a fundamentally norm-creating character such as could be regarded as forming the basis of a general rule of law'.[72] As we shall see in Chapter 3, this first requirement is one reason for doubting the status of sustainable development or the precautionary principle as 'rules' of customary international law. The second requirement laid down by the ICJ is that the provision in question should have been adopted in the practice of a sufficiently widespread and representative number of states, including those that are *not* parties to the treaty. Moreover, the requirement of *opinio juris*, which establishes the legally binding character of state practice in customary law, must also be satisfied.

---

[70] See in particular *Gabčíkovo-Nagymaros Case*, ICJ Reports (1997) 7.
[71] *Iron Rhine Arbitration*, PCA (2005) paras 142, 157. See generally Aust, 35 *ICLQ* (1986) 787–812.
[72] ICJ Reports (1969) 3, para 72.

These two constitutive elements of custom—state practice and *opinio juris*—are considered further below.

However, many environmental treaties do not necessarily contain clear, detailed, or specific rules. Sometimes they lay down only a framework of general principles or requirements for states 'to take measures' or 'all practicable measures', as in the case of the 1992 Framework Convention on Climate Change, the 1985 Convention for the Protection of the Ozone Layer or the 1979 Convention on Long-range Transboundary Air Pollution.[73] Insofar as these require further action by states to prescribe the precise measures to be taken, they may necessitate the conclusion of more specific agreements, adding protocols or annexes to existing conventions, or adopting non-binding guidelines or recommendations. Another example of this 'framework treaty' approach is the 1979 Bonn Convention on Conservation of Migratory Species of Wild Animals whose implementation requires conclusion of agreements between 'range states' and the listing of species on its appendices for its effective operation.[74] In effect such treaties become regulatory regimes through which an increasingly complex pattern of detailed rules and standards evolves.[75] Regulatory treaties can also be concluded in the form of an 'umbrella' instrument consisting of a general convention linked to one or more treaties on specific issues. The 1982 UNCLOS is an example. Although lacking any formal provision for the adoption of further protocols or annexes, it makes frequent reference to 'generally accepted international rules and standards',[76] it envisages the adoption of regional agreements on various matters, and it must be read together with subsequently adopted 'implementation agreements', including the 1994 Agreement Relating to Part XI,[77] and the 1995 UN Fish Stocks Agreement.[78] Rather like protocols to a framework convention, these agreements interpret, amplify and develop the existing provisions of UNCLOS. They also provide alternative models for what is in effect, although not in form, *inter se* amendment of the Convention.[79] Unlike protocols to environmental framework treaties, however, implementing agreements can be free-standing treaties, independent of participation in UNCLOS itself.

Framework or umbrella treaties can still influence the development of customary law insofar as they establish support for certain basic rules or principles, but this may not apply to the more detailed standards laid down in regulatory protocols or annexes,

---

[73] See *infra*, Ch 6, and on the principle of due diligence, Ch 3, section 4.   [74] See *infra*, Ch 12.

[75] See e.g. the 1973/8 MARPOL Convention, *infra*,Ch 7, the 1985 Ozone Convention, and the 1979 Convention on Long-range Transboundary Air Pollution, *infra*, Ch 6.

[76] See *infra*, Ch 7.   [77] See Anderson, 43 *ICLQ* (1994) 886; Charney, 35 *VJIL* (1995) 381.

[78] See FAO, *Structure and Process of the 1993–1995 UN Conference on Straddling Fish Stocks and Highly Migratory Fish Stocks* (Rome, 1995) and *infra*, Ch 13.

[79] The use of an 'implementing agreement' was deliberately intended to avoid 'amendment' of the Convention. Nevertheless, the 1994 Agreement on Part XI disapplies certain provisions of Part XI and revises others. It also prevails over inconsistent provisions of the Convention. Non-parties are assumed to have acquiesced in the changes made to the Convention. This looks very like amendment in practice. The 1995 Fish Stocks Agreement neither specifically amends UNCLOS nor does it prevail over it, but it does make significant changes in the applicable law.

which are in any case less likely to be followed in practice by non-parties. It is common, moreover, to separate such technical standards from the basic provisions of the treaty in order to allow for ease of amendment in the light of technical or scientific experience. This is why they will usually be found in protocols or annexes, as in most marine pollution conventions, or in schedules, as in the 1946 International Convention for the Regulation of Whaling (ICRW).[80] The provisions of protocols, annexes or schedules of this kind are not always binding on all the parties to a treaty; in many cases states are free to opt out by objecting within an appropriate time after adoption or subsequently.[81] Thus it should not be assumed that every treaty provision has been transformed into customary law, even if widely followed, or that every part of a treaty is binding on all parties.

The 1969 Vienna Convention on the Law of Treaties liberalized treaty-making in a number of ways. In particular, it allowed states to participate à la carte—i.e. with reservations excluding provisions to which they objected, subject only to consistency with the treaty's object and purpose.[82] However, most global environmental treaties prohibit all reservations in order to preserve the integrity of what is usually a 'package deal' compromise text,[83] or they permit only certain kinds of reservations.[84] The possibility of making reservations normally encourages wider participation in treaties; it is partly their impermissibility under the 1982 UNCLOS that delayed this treaty achieving the sixty ratifications required for entry into force and that has kept the US out of several environmental agreements. On the other hand, reservations also undermine the effectiveness of treaties by enabling states to protect their own economic and other interests. In practice, most multilateral environmental treaties are very widely ratified despite the ban on reservations. But most also allow any party to opt of detailed regulatory annexes, amendments, or additional protocols, either by withholding their consent or through 'objection procedures'.[85] This weakness is especially pertinent to adoption of stronger control measures or the listing of additional polluting substances or endangered species.[86] These details matter; participation only in an empty framework treaty amounts to little more than symbolic commitment to a process without the substance.

So far as interpretation of treaties is concerned, the Vienna Convention's provisions[87] include all three major schools of thought on the subject—the literal, the

---

[80] See *infra*, Chs 7, 8, 12, 13.   [81] See *infra*, Ch 2.

[82] Articles 19–23. See *Reservations to the Genocide Convention Case*, ICJ Reports (1951) 15; Brownlie, *Principles of Public International Law*, Ch 27; Redgwell, 64 *BYIL* (1993) 245.

[83] E.g. 1982 UNCLOS, Articles 309–10; 1985 Ozone Layer Convention, Article 18; 1989 Convention on Transboundary Movements of Hazardous Wastes, Article 26; 1992 Climate Change Convention, Article 24; 1992 Biological Diversity Convention, Article 37; 1994 Desertification Convention, Article 37.

[84] E.g. 1946 International Convention for the Regulation of Whaling.   [85] *Infra*, Ch 2, section 5.

[86] E.g. the 1997 Kyoto Protocol, *infra*, Ch 6; 1998 PIC Convention, *infra*, Ch 8; 1973 CITES, *infra*, Ch 12; 1946 Whaling Convention, *infra*, Ch 13.

[87] Articles 31–3.

'effective', and the teleological approaches.[88] Thus, the ordinary meaning of the words to be interpreted must first be sought but in their broad context in the convention. The interpretation must be made in good faith and be compatible with the objects and purposes of the convention, which means that an interpretation must be adopted, so far as is possible, which makes the convention effective, a particularly valuable rule in the case of treaties with environmental objectives.[89] Lastly, if the wording is ambiguous, recourse may be had to the *travaux préparatoires* (preparatory documents) to verify the interpretation derived from the above processes. Although the Convention formally applies only to treaties concluded by parties after its entry into force, its provisions on interpretation have been treated by all international courts as customary law, and on that basis they have been used to interpret earlier treaties or treaties between states not party to the Vienna Convention.[90]

The Vienna Convention's articles on interpretation provide one of the most important techniques for integrating different treaties or bodies of law. The subsequent practice of the parties, or any agreement regarding interpretation of a treaty, must obviously be taken into account.[91] The task of giving guidance on or amplifying the terms of environmental treaties is performed most frequently by resolutions, recommendations, and decisions of other international organizations, and by the conferences of parties to treaties. Environmental soft law is quite often important for this reason, setting detailed rules or more general standards of best practice or due diligence to be achieved by the parties in implementing their obligations. These 'ecostandards' are essential in giving hard content to the open-textured terms of framework environmental treaties.[92] Thus UNEP's Cairo Guidelines on the Transport of Hazardous Wastes[93] can be regarded as an amplification of the obligation of 'environmentally sound management' provided for in Article 4 of the 1989 Basel Convention on the Control of Transboundary Movements of Hazardous Wastes. The advantages of regulating environmental risks in this way are that the detailed rules and standards can easily be changed or strengthened as scientific understanding develops or as political priorities change. They could of course be adopted in treaty form, using easily amended annexes to provide flexibility, but the parties may prefer a more cautious option.

Article 31(3)(c) of the Vienna Convention additionally provides that in interpreting a treaty, account shall also be taken of any other 'relevant rules of international law applicable in the relations between the parties'.[94] Doing so may help to avoid

---

[88] Sinclair, *The Vienna Convention on Treaties*, 114–58.

[89] See e.g. the *Iron Rhine Arbitration*, PCA (2005) paras 45–8, 85–91.

[90] *Territorial Dispute (Libyan Arab Jamahiriya/Chad)*, ICJ Reports (1994) 6, para 41; *Kasikili/Sedudu Island (Botswana/Namibia)*, ICJ Reports (1999) 1045, para 18; *Sovereignty over Pulau Ligitan and Pulau Sipadan (Indonesia/Malaysia)*, ICJ Reports (2002) 625, paras 37–8; *Iron Rhine Arbitration (Belgium/Netherlands)*, PCA (2005) para 45.

[91] Article 31(3)(a)–(b).

[92] See Contini and Sand, 66 *AJIL* (1972) 37; Bodansky, 98 *Proc ASIL* (2004) 275.

[93] UNEP/WG 122/3 (1985), *infra*, Ch 8.

[94] See McLachlan, 54 *ICLQ* (2005) 279; French, 55 *ICLQ* (2006) 281.

conflicts between agreed norms, or save negotiated agreements from premature obsolescence, or the need for constant amendment.[95] Changes in international law and changing social values expressed in international policy can be taken into account and reflected in the jurisprudence, a point particularly well observed in international human-rights law.[96]

How far, if at all, might re-interpretation of a lawmaking treaty be possible under this provision? The terms within which 'evolutionary interpretation' is permissible under Article 31(3)(c) have been narrowly circumscribed in the jurisprudence, and over-ambitious attempts to reinterpret or 'cross-fertilize' treaties by reference to later treaties or other rules of international law have had only limited success.[97] Nevertheless, while accepting 'the primary necessity of interpreting an instrument in accordance with the intentions of the parties *at the time of its conclusion*', the ICJ has acknowledged that treaties are to be 'interpreted and applied within the framework of the entire legal system prevailing at the time of the interpretation'.[98] Thus, its approach in cases such as the *Namibia Advisory Opinion* and *Aegean Sea* is based on the view that the concepts and terms in question 'were by definition evolutionary',[99] not on some broader conception applicable to all treaties. The WTO Appellate Body has given a similarly evolutionary interpretation to certain terms in the 1947 GATT Agreement. In the *Shrimp-Turtle* decision, for example, it referred inter alia to the 1992 Rio Declaration on Environment and Development, the 1982 UNCLOS, the 1973 CITES Convention, the 1979 Convention on Conservation of Migratory Species, and the 1992 Convention on Biological Diversity in order to determine the present meaning of 'exhaustible natural resources'.[100]

In all of these cases the question at issue was not general revision or re-interpretation of the treaty. Rather, each case was concerned with the interpretation of particular provisions or phrases, such as 'natural resources', or 'jurisdiction', which necessarily import—or at least suggest—a reference to current general international law. Ambulatory incorporation of the existing law, whatever it may be, enables treaty provisions to change and develop as the general law itself changes, without the need for

---

[95] For a particularly good example see the *Iron Rhine Arbitration*, PCA (2005) paras 58–9.

[96] See *infra*, Ch 5.

[97] Eg Ireland's unsuccessful attempt to rewrite UNCLOS in the *Mox Plant Arbitration* (PCA, 2002). For a contrary view see Sands, in Boyle and Freestone (eds), *International Law and Sustainable Development*, 39.

[98] *Namibia Advisory Opinion*, ICJ Reports (1971) 16, 31; *Aegean Sea Continental Shelf Case*, ICJ Reports (1978) 3, 32–3. The ICJ's approach, combining both an evolutionary and an inter-temporal element, reflects the ILC's commentary to what became Article 31(3)(c). See ILC, 'The law of treaties', commentary to draft Article 27, para (16), in Watts (ed), *The International Law Commission 1949–1998* (Oxford, 1999), vol II, 690.

[99] See also *Oil Platforms Case*, ICJ Reports (2003) paras 40–1; *La Bretagne Arbitration* (Canada/France) (1986) 82 ILR 591, paras 37–51.

[100] *Import Prohibition of Certain Shrimp and Shrimp Products*, WTO Appellate Body (1998) WT/DS58/AB/R, paras 130–1.

any amendment. As the ICJ points out in the *Oil Platforms Case*, such treaty provisions are not intended to operate independently of general international law.[101]

Evolutionary interpretation is thus a relatively limited task, usually justified by reference to the intention of the parties and the object and purpose of the treaty. It does not entitle a court or tribunal to engage in a process of constant revision or updating every time a newer treaty is concluded that relates to similar matters.[102] On this view, interpretation is interpretation, not amendment or rewriting of treaties. The result must remain faithful to the ordinary meaning and context of the treaty, 'in the light of its object and purpose'.[103]

Whether another treaty is regarded as an agreement on interpretation, or as a guide to the interpretation of inherently evolutionary provisions, or simply as evidence of a common understanding of comparable provisions, the level of participation cannot be ignored. Some authors read Article 31(3)(c) as referring only to rules applicable between all the parties to a treaty *dispute*, rather than all the parties to a treaty. Apart from being inconsistent with the ILC commentary to Article 31(3), this interpretation leaves unanswered the question how the article should be applied in other contexts, e.g. by treaty COPs, the UN, or foreign ministries, and risks a serious Balkanization of global treaties implemented by regional agreements. It is true that under many treaties individual states are free to agree alternative interpretations *inter se*, within the terms of VCLT Article 41.[104] However, where there is a clear need for uniform interpretation, given the express terms of Article 31(3) and the ILC commentary thereto, the stronger argument is that a treaty cannot realistically be regarded as an agreement on interpretation or as a 'relevant rule applicable in relations between the parties' unless it has the consensus support of all the parties, or there is no objection.[105] This does not mean that all the parties to one treaty would have to be party to the other treaty. The 1994 Agreement on the Implementation of UNCLOS is assumed to be effective on the basis that non-parties have tacitly consented to or acquiesced in the revision of UNCLOS.[106] Alternatively, a treaty rule may also be binding in customary international law, and become applicable on that basis. Thus in *Shrimp-Turtle* the WTO Appellate Body noted that although not a party to UNCLOS, the US did accept the relevant provisions as customary law. These are significant qualifications to the ILC's general principle regarding universality of participation.

---

[101] ICJ Reports (2003) paras 40–1. See also *Gabčíkovo-Nagymaros Case*, ICJ Reports (1997) 7, paras 140–1.

[102] Bedjaoui, *Gabčíkovo-Nagymaros Case*, sep op, para 12. See also *SW Africa Case*, ICJ Reports (1966) 3, 48.

[103] VCLT, Article 31(1). See *OSPAR Arbitration*, PCA (2003) paras 101–5; *Iron Rhine Arbitration*, PCA (2005) paras 47, 81, 221.

[104] See e.g. Bartels, 36 *JWT* (2002) 353, 361, and see the next section.

[105] ILC commentary in Watts (ed), *The ILC*, vol II, 688–9. The arguments are reviewed extensively by Pauwelyn, 95 *AJIL* (2001) 535, 575–6; McLachlan, 54 *ICLQ* (2005) 279, 315, para 16, (but note his qualifications para 17); French, 55 *ICLQ* (2006) 300–7.

[106] Boyle, 54 *ICLQ* (2005) 563–84.

An agreement lacking such general support will no longer fall strictly within the obligatory terms of Article 31(3)(a) or (c), and its persuasive force as a basis for evolutionary interpretation will necessarily be weaker the fewer parties there are. In the *OSPAR Arbitration* the arbitrators declined even to take into account a convention which was not in force, and which Ireland had not ratified, although the better view is probably that such an agreement may nevertheless provide some guidance.[107] In practice much will depend on whether other non-parties acquiesce or not, and on the issue in dispute. In *Shrimp-Turtle* the United States did not object to the Appellate Body taking the Biological Diversity Convention into account. It is difficult to see how any tribunal could do otherwise, given the almost universal participation by other states in this treaty and the specific reasons for US non-participation.

(b) Custom[108]

Although treaties are the most frequently used form of international environmental lawmaking, customary international law remains important. The burdensome procedures of treaty ratification are absent, and customary rules may more easily acquire universal application, since acquiescence will often be enough to ensure that 'the inactive are carried along by the active',[109] a particular advantage in environmental matters. On the other hand, many states, including the United States and those which accord particular priority to developmental policies, tend to emphasize the importance of persistent objection in preventing the crystallization and application of particular customary rules to the objecting state.[110] Although most writers consider that it is not necessary for a state to have expressly or impliedly consented to a rule of customary law that *has* crystallized as such in order to be bound by it, the creation of new customary rules does in the end depend on some form of consent, whether express or implied, and this remains a limitation of some importance.

Article 38(1) of the ICJ Statute instructs the Court to apply 'international custom, as evidence of a general practice accepted as law'. This formulation is often criticized on the ground that it inverts the actual process whereby state practice supported by *opinio juris* (the conviction that conduct is motivated by a sense of legal obligation) provides the evidence necessary to establish a customary rule. Both conduct and conviction on the part of the state are usually thought to be essential before it can be said that a custom has become law, whether universally, regionally, or as between particular states involved in its formation. Thus it is 'axiomatic that the material of customary international law is to be looked for primarily in the actual practice and *opinio juris* of states'.[111] However, it has been pertinently remarked that deciding which norms have crystallized into customary law is in many areas not just a matter of inquiry but

---

[107] Griffith, sep op, *OSPAR Arbitration*, PCA (2003) paras 101–5.

[108] Brownlie, *Principles of Public International Law*, Ch 1; Akehurst, 43 *BYIL* (1974–5) 1–53.

[109] Meijers, 9 *NYIL* (1978) 4.

[110] See Brownlie, *Principles of Public International Law*, Ch 1; Charney, 56 *BYIL* (1985) 1–24.

[111] *Libya-Malta Continental Shelf Case*, ICJ Reports (1985) 29–30. See also *North Sea Continental Shelf Case*, ICJ Reports (1969) 3, 32–3, 47, 53.

of policy choice, a consideration of great importance in the development of environmental law.[112] Thus the identification of customary law always has been, and remains, a task requiring research and the exercise of judgement. This is where codification or judicial decisions can be particularly helpful.

In a world of over 190 states of diverse cultures, policies, interests, and legal systems, the task of identifying consistent, general state practice is not necessarily easy. Without some means of bringing about agreement or coordination, the practice of individual states would be difficult to reconcile even on questions of general principle, let alone on specific details of policy, and changes in customary law would emerge only slowly, if at all. Deciding what has become customary law involves at least an examination of official statements, unilateral and multilateral declarations, agreements, legislation, law enforcement actions, and judicial decisions. Most international lawyers would also agree that we should not take too narrow a view of what constitutes state practice for the purpose of identifying customary law.[113] The PCIJ took account of omissions to act,[114] and the ICJ has relied on the practice of organs of international organizations, and of the UN Secretariat itself.[115] The acts of non-state bodies are more difficult to categorize in the custom-creating process. Here it is more a question of states' reaction to acts of their nationals—whether they approve or authorize them or reject or prosecute them—that is significant. Thus, although individuals may form non-governmental pressure groups, such as Greenpeace, the Sierra Club, Friends of the Earth, or the World Wide Fund for Nature, that actively campaign for development of or change in the law to protect the environment, it is the adoption of their proposals by states or the significance attributed to them by international courts that is determinative.[116]

Jennings pointed out many years ago that the old tests of customary law are increasingly irrelevant since much new law is not custom in the orthodox sense: 'it is recent, it is innovatory, it involves topical policy decisions, and it is the focus of contention'.[117] In practice, new international law—and especially new law relating to the environment—is largely negotiated by states through the medium of multilateral treaties, UN General Assembly resolutions, or various forms of non-binding soft law. Two of the most important examples relied on very often in this work are the 1982 UN Convention on the Law of the Sea and the 1992 Rio Declaration on Environment and Development. Both were negotiated by consensus and reflect a series of interlocking compromises and concessions involving all participants with a variety of sometimes very different interests and priorities. The lawmaking effect of such instruments can be very powerful.

[112] Jennings, 37 *Ann Suisse DDI* (1981) 67.

[113] See the résumé of views in Akehurst, 43 *BYIL* (1974–5) 1–11.

[114] *Lotus Case*, PCIJ Ser A, No 10 (1927) 28.

[115] *Nottebohm Case*, ICJ Reports (1955) 4; *Paramilitary Activities in Nicaragua Case*, ICJ Reports (1986) 14, 98.

[116] On the role of NGOs in international lawmaking see Boyle and Chinkin, *The Making of International Law*, Ch 2.

[117] Jennings, 37 *Ann Suisse DDI* (1981) 59, 67. For a more sceptical view see Bodansky, 3 *Indiana Jo Global Legal Studies* (1995) 105.

A treaty does not 'make' customary law as such, but like GA resolutions and other soft-law instruments it may both codify existing law and contribute to the process by which new customary law is created and develops. This process has been fully explored by the ICJ in two cases, the *North Sea Continental Shelf Case* and the *Nicaragua Case*. The approach taken by the court is subtly different in both cases. In the *North Sea Case* the court accepted that a normatively worded provision of a multilateral treaty could contribute to the formation of a new rule of customary law if the subsequent practice of a sufficiently widespread and representative selection of non-parties conformed to the treaty and there was additionally evidence of *opinio iuris*.[118] In the *Nicaragua Case*, the ICJ reiterated that 'the shared view of the parties as to the content of what they regard as the rule is not enough. The court must satisfy itself that the existence of the rule in the *opinio juris* of states is confirmed by practice'.[119] However, that practice need not be perfectly consistent or conform rigorously in order to establish its customary status, provided inconsistent conduct is treated by the states concerned as a breach of the rule, not as an indication of a new rule. Attempts to justify inconsistent conduct serve, on this view, merely to confirm the rule in question. In this context only conduct amounting to an outright rejection of the alleged rule will constitute genuinely inconsistent practice. The *Nicaragua Case* also recognized that the embodiment of a rule in a treaty provision (in this case the UN Charter) does not displace an existing rule of customary international law or prevent its continued development.[120]

The court's findings of law in *Nicaragua* do not rest only on the normative impact of the UN Charter. As this case shows, the *opinio juris* of states may also evidenced by consensus adoption of comparable resolutions in the UN General Assembly. Although the court is careful to avoid any suggestion that custom can be established simply by states declaring the law in treaties and soft-law resolutions, it comes close to doing so. The only significant caveat is that there must be no *inconsistent* state practice. This reverses the approach taken in the *North Sea Case*, where the court emphasized the need for *consistent* state practice. The circumstances of the two cases are different, however. In *North Sea*, the supposed equidistance rule was not acceptable to a number of states, and certainly not to Germany, nor was the practice of non-parties to the treaty consistent. By contrast, both parties in the *Nicaragua Case* consistently expressed support for the same rule on the use of force, even in the face of flagrant violations. Moreover, it should not be forgotten that the United States is a party to the UN Charter, even if in the circumstances of the *Nicaragua Case* the Court was precluded from applying the Charter to the dispute. Finally, the use of force in violation of international law contravenes a norm of *ius cogens*. By definition, such rules are recognized by the international community as a whole. The delimitation of seabed boundaries on the basis of equidistance is not in the same category.

What conclusions about the normative force of lawmaking treaties can we draw from the ICJ case law? First, the Court has no difficulty accepting that treaties 'may

---

[118] ICJ Reports (1969) 3.　　[119] *Nicaragua Case*, ICJ Reports (1986) 14, para 184.
[120] Ibid, paras 174–9.

have an important role in recording and defining rules deriving from custom, or indeed in developing them'.[121] Second, the cases accept that there is a lawmaking intention behind the negotiation of certain multilateral treaties. This can constitute evidence of *opinio juris* in favour of new general rules of international law, especially if the treaty was negotiated by consensus or has the consistent support of a large majority of states. Third, we can see that support for a treaty rule, however universal, cannot by itself create 'instant' law. Such treaties will only create new law if supported by consistent and representative state practice over a period of time. That practice can in appropriate cases consist mainly of acquiescence, or the absence of inconsistent practice. How long a time is required will depend on the circumstances. It may be very short indeed if the subsequent practice is widespread and consistent, as in the case of the exclusive economic zone,[122] or if the treaty is a codification treaty, as we will see below when considering the *Gabčíkovo Case*.[123] Fourth, it evidently matters little whether the treaty is in force, or widely ratified. What is most important is simply that the more widely supported the treaty text is shown to be, the easier it will be to establish its lawmaking effect. The longer it takes to establish consistent *opinio juris* or consistent state practice the harder it will be to establish a new rule of customary law.

While it is clear that multilateral treaties—even those that are not yet in force—can initiate the development of new customary international law, and in that sense some of them can be described as 'lawmaking', it does not follow that law which develops in this fashion will necessarily bind all states. Apart from the obvious proviso that customary law may be regional or local rather than global, certain states may also object to attempts to change the law. They may do so in the form of reservations, or they may remain non-parties and oppose the treaty, even if they participated in its consensus negotiation—a position in which the United States frequently finds itself. Either way, if they maintain their persistent objection to new rules that emerge from a treaty, these rules will not be opposable against those states.[124] Charney argues that persistent objectors can at best maintain this position only while the status of a new rule is in doubt; they will be bound once the rule is firmly established.[125] As a matter of diplomatic reality this will be true in many cases, including those on which Charney relies, but much depends on the circumstances and the states involved. Moreover, if customary law may be local or regional in scope, there can be no inherent reason why persistent objectors cannot successfully remain bound by different rules, unless one accepts the possibility that majorities make law for minorities.[126] There is no support for such a position in the present case law of the ICJ.

---

[121] *Tunisia/Libya Continental Shelf Case*, ICJ Reports (1982) para 27.

[122] Ibid. See also *Libya-Malta Continental Shelf Case*, ICJ Reports (1985) 29–30.

[123] *Infra*, section 2(4).   [124] See *Fisheries Jurisdiction Case*, ICJ Reports (1974) 3, 6–7, 22–35.

[125] Charney, 58 *BYIL* (1987) 1.   [126] See Charney's discussion of the literature.

(c) General principles of international law[127]

General principles of law are important in the current development of international environmental law because there now exist an increasing number of instruments expressed as 'Declarations of Principles', ranging from the Stockholm and Rio Declarations, the World Charter for Nature, to UNEP's various sets of Principles on, for example, the use of shared natural resources.[128] We have to ask whether these are the kind of principles referred to in Article 38(1)(c) of the ICJ Statute or whether a narrower view limiting the role of general principles to common legal maxims is all this that was intended.

Article 38(1)(c) allows the International Court to apply 'the general principles of law recognised by civilized nations'. Not only is the reference to 'civilized nations' outdated in the context of modern international society, but it is unclear whether the principles referred to are merely those commonly applied in all municipal legal systems, such as the maxims relied on to ensure a fair and equitable legal process—*audi alteram partem, res judicata,* etc—or whether they also include 'principles' recognized by international law itself—for example, the prohibition on the non-use of force; basic principles of human rights; the freedom of the seas; the need for good faith evidenced in the maxim *pacta sunt servanda,* and so on. The ambiguity arises from the need to compromise, which arose in the early 1920s when the Statute of the PCIJ was being drafted. One group on the relevant preparatory committee thought that the traditional sources of custom and treaty should be expanded to enable the Court to apply 'the rules of international law as recognised by the *legal conscience* of civilised nations',[129] based on the concept that certain principles existed in so-called 'natural law', principles of 'objective justice' that could be identified by all rational human beings. The purpose of this group has been described as revolutionary, namely to place as a 'wedge between the crevices of existing law principles derived from Western civilization',[130] since the principles would not rest on the free will of states. The rival group adopted the traditional 'positivist' approach, namely that the Court should apply only rules and principles derived from the will of states. This view has been supported in more recent times by lawyers from developing countries and formerly by the Soviet bloc. The compromise adopted in Article 38(1)(c) was regarded by this group as referring only to general principles accepted by all nations in *foro domestico.*

Other writers, however, conclude that Article 38 does not codify an existing unwritten rule on general principles, but endeavours to establish a new secondary source,

---

[127] See Brownlie, *Principles of Public International Law,* 15–19; Cheng, *General Principles of International Law* (London, 1953). See also Bos and Brownlie (eds), *Liber Amicorum for Lord Wilberforce* (Oxford, 1987) 259–85; Lammers, in Kalshoven, Kuypers, and Lammers, *Essays on the Development of the International Legal Order* (Alphen den Rijn, 1980) 53–75; Mosler, in TMC Asser Institute (ed), *International Law and the Grotian Heritage,* 173–85.

[128] Draft Principles of Conduct in the Field of the Environment for the Conduct of States on the Conservation and Harmonious Utilization of Natural Resources Shared by Two or More States, UNEP/I G 12/2 (1978), and see *infra,* Ch 3, section 5.

[129] Cassese, *International Law in a Divided World,* 170, citing Lord Phillimore; emphasis added.

[130] Ibid, 171.

leaving it to the Court, not states, to enunciate the relevant principles by induction.[131] This would give the Court a more creative role within certain limits and is thought by some to avoid any possibility of a *non liquet* where they may be gaps in the law. Such an approach could be helpful in developing international environmental law, allowing some scope for constructing new principles by means of analogy with national systems in order to fill gaps in fields in which legal development is at an embryonic stage. At the same time such a power should be viewed and used with caution, especially where general principles of national law are not reflected in state practice at the international level, as, for example, in the case of strict liability for environmental damage.[132]

In the few cases where it has relied on general principles of national law, the International Court has not considered in detail the practice of domestic courts but has drawn on its own jurisprudential perceptions, mainly to support conclusions on other bases rather than as the sole basis of decision.[133] Tribunals have not mechanically borrowed from domestic law 'lock, stock, and barrel', but have invoked elements of legal reasoning and private law analogies 'as an indication of policy and principles rather than as directly importing these rules and institutions'.[134] As early as 1937, in the *Diversion of Water from the Meuse Case*,[135] the PCIJ considered that equitable principles might be derived from 'general principles of law recognised by civilized nations'. In the *Chorzow Factory Case*[136] the same court enunciated the general principles of state responsibility and reparation, including the principle of *restitutio in integrum*, while in the *Free Zones Cases*[137] it made reference to the doctrines of abuse of rights and good faith. In the *South West Africa Case*[138] one judge considered that elements of natural law were inherent in general principles and could provide a foundation for human rights. Most importantly, general principles of national law were relied on in the *Trail Smelter Arbitration* to support a finding that 'no state has the right to use or permit the use of its territory in such a manner as to cause injury by fumes in or to the territory of another'.[139] Nonetheless, it has to be recognized that general principles derived by analogy from domestic law are only marginally useful in an environmental context.

Of far greater significance are general principles found in the 1992 Rio Declaration, other soft law instruments and certain treaties, including the 1992 Framework Convention on Climate Change. The precautionary principle, the polluter-pays principle, and the principle of common but differentiated responsibility have all been endorsed by states in this form. Such general principles do not have to create rules of customary law to have legal effect, nor do they need to be incorporated in treaties or

---

[131] Ibid, 171–2.   [132] See *infra*, Ch 4.

[133] Cassese, *International Law in a Divided World,* 174. Relevant cases include the *Chorzow Factory Case (Indemnity) (Jurisdiction)* PCIJ Ser A, No 8/9 (1927) 31; *Corfu Channel Case,* ICJ Reports (1949) 18; *South West Africa Case (Second Phase)* ICJ Reports (1966) 294–9.

[134] Lord McNair, *South West Africa Case,* ICJ Reports (1950) 128, 148.

[135] PCIJ Ser A/B No 70 (1937) 4, 73, 76.   [136] See *infra,* Ch 4, section 2.

[137] *Free Zones Case (Second Phase)* Final Order, PCIJ Ser A, No 24 (1932) 12, and *Free Zones Case* (Merits) Ser A/B, No 46 (1932) 167.

[138] ICJ Reports (1966) 294–9, on which see *infra*, Ch 4.   [139] 35 *AJIL* (1941) 716. See *infra*, Ch 3.

reflect national law. They cannot override or amend the express terms of a treaty,[140] so their importance derives principally from the influence they may exert on the interpretation, application, and development of treaties in accordance with Article 31(3) of the 1969 Vienna Convention on the Law of Treaties. General principles of this kind may also influence the interpretation and application of customary law. Thus the precautionary principle, considered further in Chapter 3, has influenced state practice, the negotiation of treaties, and the judgments of international courts. What gives these general principles their authority and legitimacy is simply the endorsement of states—*opinio juris* in other words.[141] Such principles have legal significance in much the same way that Dworkin uses the idea of constitutional principles.[142] They lay down parameters which affect the way courts decide cases or how an international institution exercises its discretionary powers. They can set limits, or provide guidance, or determine how conflicts between other rules or principles will be resolved. They may lack the supposedly harder edge of a 'rule' or 'obligation', but they should not be confused with 'non-binding' or emerging law. The ICJ's references to sustainable development in the *Gabčíkovo-Nagymaros Case* remain perhaps the best illustration of the role of internationally endorsed principles in international environmental law.[143] What these examples show is that subtle changes in the existing law and in existing treaties may come about through the application of such general principles.

(d) Judicial decisions

The reference in the ICJ Statute to judicial decisions as a 'subsidiary means' for determining rules of law[144] is apt to mislead. In reality the ICJ and other international tribunals have an important and often innovatory role in pronouncing on matters of international law. Though judicial decisions cannot be said to be a formal source as such, since the court does not ostensibly make the law but merely identifies and applies it, they clearly provide authoritative evidence of what the law is. In doing so, courts can exercise a formative influence on the law, giving substance to new norms and principles such as self-determination or sustainable development. While there is no doctrine of precedent in the ICJ or in other international courts, including arbitral tribunals,[145] these courts will not lightly disregard their own pronouncements, though they may find ways of distancing themselves from earlier decisions. Thus a body of jurisprudence accumulates, particularly in the ICJ, and contributes to the progressive

---

[140] *Beef Hormones Case* (1998) WTO Appellate Body, paras 124–5.

[141] Lowe, in Boyle and Freestone (eds), *International Law and Sustainable Development* (Oxford, 1999) 33, dispenses even with *opinio juris*, but unless such norms emerge from thin air at the whim of judges the endorsement of states must be a necessary element. All the norms Lowe relies on do in fact have such endorsement.

[142] Dworkin, *Taking Rights Seriously* (London, 1977). This argument is developed by Sands, in Lang (ed), *Sustainable Development and International Law* (London, 1995) Ch 5.

[143] ICJ Reports (1997) 7, para 140. See *infra*, Ch 3

[144] ICJ Statute, Article 38(1)(d). See Fitzmaurice, *Symbolae Verzijl* (1958) 174.

[145] For an analysis of the significance and interrelationship of the different kinds of tribunal and their decisions, see Brownlie, *Principles of Public International Law*, 19–24, and Jennings, 45 *ICLQ* (1996) 1.

development of international law. As we will see in Chapter 3, a growing number of ICJ and arbitral decisions are directly relevant to environmental issues. Other courts whose decisions will be considered in later chapters include the European Court of Human Rights, the International Tribunal for the Law of the Sea, and national courts. Though decisions of these bodies are not all of equal weight and significance they may be persuasive precedents and provide evidence of customary law.

(g) Writings of publicists

The ICJ Statute also cites 'the teachings of the most highly qualified publicists of the various nations' as a 'subsidiary means for the determination of rules of law'. The works and views of some writers have been referred to in the ICJ and other tribunals and are especially cited by law officers and counsel preparing opinions, or pleadings for court cases; arbitrators and, especially, municipal courts less familiar with the concepts and practice of international law are perhaps more inclined to give weight to writers than is the ICJ.[146] As we have seen, reports of international codification bodies are also much quoted and relied on for this purpose. These include the reports and articles drafted by the International Law Commission, and the reports and resolutions of the Institute of International Law, the International Law Association, the World Commission on Environment and Development, and IUCN.[147]

2(4) CODIFICATION AND PROGRESSIVE DEVELOPMENT

The International Law Commission's work on the codification of international law is generally regarded as providing good evidence of the existing law. The Commission was established in 1947 with the object of promoting 'the progressive development of international law and its codification'.[148] Since then it has worked on nearly thirty topics and produced conventions on a wide range of issues including the law of treaties, law of the sea, state responsibility, international watercourses, diplomatic immunity and the statute of an international criminal court.[149] Many of its codifications have become widely regarded as authoritative statements of the law and are relied on by international courts, international organizations and governments. Some, including those on international watercourses, state responsibility, and transboundary risk are directly relevant to this study, and are considered in detail in later chapters.

Because the Commission has never drawn a sharp distinction between codification ('the more precise formulation and systematisation of rules of international law in fields where there already has been extensive state practice, precedent, and doctrine') and progressive development ('the preparation of draft conventions on subjects which have not yet been regulated by international law or in regard to which the law has

---

[146] See Brownlie, *Principles*, 24–5.   [147] See *infra*, Ch 3, and on IUCN, see *infra*, Ch 2, section 7(2).
[148] ILC Statute, Article 1.
[149] See Anderson et al (eds), *The International Law Commission and the Future of International Law* (London, 1998); Ago, 92 *RGDIP* (1988) 532f; Sinclair, *The International Law Commission* (Cambridge, 1987); Boyle and Chinkin, *The Making of International Law*, Ch 4.

not yet been sufficiently developed in the practice of states'),[150] it has been possible for it to engage in a certain amount of creative lawmaking or law reform. This has also enabled the ICJ and other tribunals to rely on ILC conventions without overtly enquiring whether particular articles represent existing law or a new development of the law. Moreover, the deliberative and sometimes slow pace of its work allows states to influence, appreciate, and in some cases apply the law as articulated and shaped by the Commission. Use by foreign ministries of the Vienna Convention on the Law of Treaties and the draft articles on state responsibility are the most obvious examples, but by no means the only ones. Although the ILC does not 'make' international law it has become a significant part of the subtle process by which international law both changes and comes into being.

The best example is the *Gabčíkovo-Nagymaros Case*,[151] decided by the ICJ in 1997. Here the Court showed remarkably little inclination to search for evidence of widespread, consistent, and prolonged state practice as it did for example in its judgment in the *North Sea Continental Shelf Cases*.[152] Instead, on questions of treaty law, the law relating to international watercourses, state responsibility, and state succession, it relied more heavily than in any previous case on the work of the ILC as representing customary law. The Commission's work on state responsibility was then incomplete, its articles on watercourses had only just been adopted as a treaty, and its convention on state succession had not been widely ratified. Here we can see very clearly the interplay of codification by the ILC, re-negotiation and revision of the text by states in a diplomatic forum, and application of that revised text by an international court, even though it was not in force or binding on the parties. Moreover, the fortuitous conjunction of litigation so soon after the UN's adoption of the 1997 UN Watercourses Convention resulted in a rapid endorsement of its efforts at redrafting the law in a more integrated and systematic way. It also helped that although the Watercourses Convention was not adopted by consensus, very few states opposed the text as a whole and only a handful voted against individual articles.[153] Thus the Commission's work has a potential double impact: on the one hand it provides good evidence of the existing law, on the other it helps constitute new law, sometimes quite quickly. There are few better examples of the process of international lawmaking.

At the same time, as one study of the Commission shows, the very subtlety of its approach may have precluded the Commission from contributing in a more overtly creative way to the development of those new and important areas of international law which have emerged since 1945.[154] In advancing the process of codification it may have diminished the scope for progressive development in its work and thereby limited its own role in the contemporary lawmaking process. The resulting displacement of the Commission by other lawmaking bodies can be observed very clearly in the development of international environmental law. The ILC has played no part in creating

---

[150] Statute, Article 15.   [151] ICJ Reports (1997) 7.   [152] ICJ Reports (1969) 3.

[153] McCaffrey, *The Law of International Watercourses* (2nd edn, Oxford, 2007) 360–75.

[154] Anderson et al (eds), *The International Law Commission and the Future of International Law*.

what might be called the architecture of this subject: sustainable development, global environmental responsibility, transboundary risk management, and environmental rights. It has instead confined itself to the more modest role of refining those parts of the law which have become established law during the twenty-year period of its work on this topic—in practice the law relating to transboundary risk.[155] Even then, its efforts have in earlier years been deeply troubled and confused, and inevitably raise the question whether the Commission should have any role in the development of new areas of law, including the law relating to sustainable development.[156]

2(5) STATUS OF UN GENERAL ASSEMBLY RESOLUTIONS AND DECLARATIONS

Resolutions of international organizations and multilateral declarations by states may also have effects on customary international law.[157] Whether they provide evidence of existing law, or of the *opinio juris* necessary for new law, or of the practice of states, will depend on various factors which must be assessed in each case. A lawmaking resolution or declaration need not necessarily proclaim rights or principles as law, but as with treaties, the wording must be 'of a fundamentally norm-creating character such as could be regarded as forming the basis of a general rule of law'.[158] It is also obvious that declarations or resolutions setting out agreed norms or general principles 'will usually have greater influence than recommendations'.[159] The context within which resolutions are negotiated and the accompanying statements of delegations will also be relevant if assessing the *opinio juris* of states. Lastly, the degree of support is significant. A resolution adopted by consensus or by unanimous vote will necessarily carry more weight than one supported only by a two-thirds majority of states. Resolutions opposed by even a small number of states may have little effect if those states are among the ones most immediately affected.[160] The attempt by the General Assembly in the 1970s to change the law on expropriation of foreign investments is a well-known example of the inability of majorities of states to legislate for minorities in this fashion.[161] The General Assembly's ban on deep seabed mining outside the framework of UNCLOS is another. In this case, the minority of objecting states maintained their own parallel regime, until eventually an agreement was reached.[162] In an international

---

[155] See *infra*, Ch 3.

[156] Responsibility for the development of international environmental law relating to sustainable development has been given specifically to UNEP: see *infra*, Ch 2.

[157] See e.g. Abi-Saab, 207 *Recueil des Cours* (1987) 33, 160–1.

[158] *North Sea Continental Shelf Cases,* ICJ Reports (1969) 3, para 72.

[159] Schermers and Blokker, *International Institutional Law* (The Hague, 1995) 777.

[160] See the cautionary dissent of Schwebel in the *Nuclear Weapons Advisory Opinion,* ICJ Reports (1996) 226, 318–9.

[161] See Charter of Economic Rights and Duties of States, UNGA Res 3281 XXX (1974) and *Texaco v Libya* (1977) 53 ILR 422, paras 80–91. One hundred and twenty states voted for the resolution, six voted against, ten abstained.

[162] The Declaration of Principles Governing the Seabed and Ocean Floor etc, UNGA Res 2749 XXX (1970) was adopted by 108 votes in favour with fourteen abstentions.

system where the consent or acquiescence of states is still an essential precondition for the development of new law or changes to existing law, these examples show that opposing votes matter. Even if such resolutions can change the law for states which vote in favour, it is clear that they do not do so for the dissenting minority.[163] Moreover, even consensus adoption will not be as significant as it may at first appear if accompanied by statements which seriously qualify what has been agreed, or if it simply papers over an agreement to disagree without pressing matters to a vote. For all these reasons, the adoption of resolutions by international organizations or of declarations by states should not be confused with lawmaking per se.

Three problems arise in according binding force to such resolutions. First, except for a few special issues, Article 10 of the UN Charter gives the General Assembly power only to make recommendations—it has no prima facie legislative power. Secondly, resolutions can be adopted by simple or weighted (three-quarters) majority vote according to whether they relate to procedural or substantive matters respectively—unanimity is not required. Dissenting minorities may undermine the authority and lawmaking significance of a resolution, particularly if they comprise states most affected. Thirdly, an alternative practice has grown up of continuing negotiations until a resolution can be adopted by consensus, without resort to any voting. States are not expected to raise any objections unless they are vital to their interests (there is pressure on them not to do so if the vast majority support the resolution). Some states may nevertheless retain serious reservations regarding such resolutions, which may be expressed before or after formal adoption. Care thus has to be taken, in evaluating the legal status of resolutions, to ascertain the views of states, even in relation to resolutions that have achieved apparent consensus.

Despite these reservations, however, it has to be acknowledged that though resolutions are not per se binding, they may help make new law. It is a matter of controversy whether the resolution itself provides the *opinio juris* which, taken together with the practice of states, constitutes customary law, or whether the opinions expressed in the debate and the support expressed by voting for or abstaining on the resolution are themselves evidence of state practice. Although many lawyers continue to maintain that resolutions per se, without supporting state practice, can never be regarded as part of customary law,[164] others hold the opposite view.[165] At the very least, consensus resolutions may create strong expectations of conforming conduct and by these means the votes and views of states in international organizations come to have some lawmaking significance, especially when resolutions are repeated or acquiesced in with sufficient frequency.[166]

---

[163] *Texaco v Libya*, 53 ILR (1977) 422. But for a different view compare Charney, (1987) *BYIL* 1.

[164] See MacGibbon, in Cheng (ed), *International Law: Teaching and Practice* (London, 1982) 10–25, who maintains that 'however many times nothing was multiplied by nothing the result was still nothing' (p 17).

[165] There is a large literature on this subject, but see esp Cheng, 5 *Indian JIL* (1965) 23–48, reprinted in Cheng (ed), *International Law Teaching and Practice*, 237, and Roberts, 95 *AJIL* (2001) 757 who makes a similar argument.

[166] Higgins goes no further than to say that if adopted unanimously or without the negative vote of the states most concerned, they raise strong expectations of compliance: Higgins, *The Development*

Nonetheless, in the *Nicaragua Case*, the ICJ concluded, in the context of the obligation not to use force, that *opinio juris* may, 'though with all due caution', be deduced from, inter alia, the attitude of the parties and states towards certain General Assembly resolutions and, in particular, from a resolution adopted without a vote and expressed in the form of a Declaration of Principles interpreting the UN Charter.[167] Consent to such a resolution expressed, in the Court's view, not merely reiteration of the treaty commitment laid down in the Charter but acceptance of the rules concerned, separately from the relevant Charter provisions, albeit not subject to all the constraints concerning their application that are prescribed in the Charter. On this view the attitudes of states expressed in the debates of the UN or other international bodies and their voting on resolutions (including their abstention) may be regarded as constituting the *opinio juris* required to confirm a customary rule as set out in the Resolution or Declaration. The status in customary international law of the rule concerned in the *Nicaragua Case* was further confirmed by the fact that states had frequently referred to it as a fundamental or cardinal principle of international law, and that the International Law Commission had expressed the view during its work on the codification of treaties that it was a 'conspicuous example of a rule in international law having the character of *jus cogens*'.[168] The Court also relied on the 1975 Helsinki Final Act[169] to the same effect, as evidencing *opinio juris*, since the states concerned therein iterated their *undertaking* to refrain from the use of threat of force 'in their international relations in general'. The *Nicaragua Case* is not without its critics; it has been contended that the court completely reversed the normal process for formation of custom based on actual state practice accompanied by a psychological element of legal conviction, that is, that it took account of state practice only after first using the UN resolutions as evidence of the *opinio juris*.[170]

As we shall see, lawmaking in the environmental field now includes a large number of UN resolutions and declarations, starting with the 1972 Stockholm Declaration on the Human Environment, and more recently the 1992 Rio Declaration on Environment and Development,[171] the significance of which will become fully apparent in subsequent chapters. The importance of such instruments or enunciations of principles is that they authorize, even if they do not oblige, states to act upon the basis of the principles concerned; they are, to put it another way, 'directly enforceable in interstate relations', and potentially of significant lawmaking effect, even though they will often require further elaboration through treaties or state practice.[172]

---

of International Law through the Political Organs of the United Nations (Oxford, 1963); id, in Cheng, *International Law: Teaching and Practice*, 27–44.

[167] UNGA Res 2625 (XXV) (1970) Declaration of Principles of International Law concerning Friendly Relations and Cooperation among States.

[168] *Nicaragua Case*, ICJ Reports (1986) para 190.

[169] Declaration of the Conference on Security and Cooperation in Europe, Helsinki, 1975.

[170] See in particular D'Amato, 81 *AJIL* (1987) 101.   [171] See *infra*, Ch 3.

[172] See generally Brownlie, *Principles*, 14; Van der Mensbrugghe, 5 *IJECL* (1990) 15–22.

2(6) 'SOFT LAW'

In the absence of any international body with lawmaking powers, and given the diversity of contemporary international society, the point has already been made that it is not always easy to secure widespread consent to new rules, whether by treaty or custom. Securing agreement even on issues of urgent importance is often fraught with difficulty, results in compromises and ambiguities, and is seldom global in scope. These constraints on the lawmaking process present particular problems in relation to development of the universal standards for environmental protection. As we have seen, it is difficult, especially in the short term, to create the precise constraints required through customary law. Treaties may be a more useful medium for codifying the law, or for concerted lawmaking, but many either do not enter into force, or more frequently, do so for only a limited number of parties which do not necessarily include the states whose involvement is most vital. This is especially true of environmental issues, whose regulation may require modification of economic policies and be perceived as inhibiting development and growth. Treaties thus present problems as vehicles for changing or developing the law.

For this reason increasing use has been made of half-way stages in the lawmaking process, especially on environmental and economic matters, in the form of codes of practice, recommendations, guidelines, resolutions, declarations of principles, often within the context of so-called 'framework' or 'umbrella' treaties, in a way that does not fit neatly into the categories of sources referred to in Article 38(1) of the ICJ Statute. These instruments are clearly not law in the sense used by that article but nonetheless they do not lack all authority. It is characteristic that they are carefully negotiated and drafted statements, intended in many cases to have some normative significance despite their non-binding, non-treaty form. There is at least an element of good faith commitment, an expectation that they will be adhered to if possible, and in many cases, a desire to influence the development of state practice. Thus they may provide good evidence of *opinio juris*, or constitute authoritative guidance on the interpretation or application of a treaty, or serve as agreed standards for the implementation of more general treaty provisions or rules of customary law.[173] Like lawmaking treaties, such instruments can be vehicles for focusing consensus on rules and principles, and for mobilizing a consistent, general response on the part of states. Typical examples include the joint Ministerial Declarations adopted at the end of the series of conferences held on the protection of the North Sea. After remarking on their controversial status, Van der Mensbrugghe[174] concludes that these North Sea Declarations are not legally binding instruments: non-compliance does not entail international responsibility or resort to judicial tribunals. But the policies adopted therein may later be cast in legal form at the appropriate national, regional, or international level. They can also give rise to estoppel and negate the argument that the issues are of purely domestic concern. Their adoption has a legitimizing effect on policy and practice and may lead eventually to the emergence of new customary law or the negotiation of new treaties.

[173] Boyle, 48 *ICLQ* (1999) 901.   [174] Van der Mensbrugghe, 5 *IJECL* (1990) 15–22.

It is these instruments that have attracted the description 'soft law'.[175] 'Soft law' has a range of possible meanings.[176] From a lawmaking perspective the term is simply a convenient description for a variety of non-binding instruments used in contemporary international relations. It encompasses, inter alia, interstate conference declarations such as the 1992 Rio Declaration on Environment and Development; UN General Assembly instruments such as the 1948 Universal Declaration of Human Rights, the 1970 Declaration on the Principles of Friendly Relations Among States, and resolutions dealing with disarmament, outer space, the deep seabed, decolonization, or natural resources; interpretative guidance adopted by human rights treaty bodies and other autonomous intergovernmental institutions; codes of conduct, guidelines and recommendations of international organizations, such as UNEP's 1987 Guidelines on Environmental Impact Assessment, FAO's Code of Conduct on Responsible Fisheries or many others adopted by IMO, IAEA, FAO and so on. Also potentially included are the common international standards adopted by transnational networks of national regulatory bodies, NGOs, and professional and industry associations.[177] Finally, the term 'soft law' can also be applied to non-treaty agreements between states or between states and other entities that lack capacity to conclude treaties.[178] Soft law is perhaps an unfortunate description insofar as it suggests something that is not law at all, but merely a 'second best' approach.[179] Others welcome it on the ground that it enables cautious states more readily to reach agreement on common aims and standards.[180] Even if we ignore its potential impact on customary law, the fact that a great deal of environmental soft law is subsequently transformed into binding treaty commitments, or is otherwise incorporated by reference into binding treaties, demonstrates that this is not a pointless process.

Soft law is by its nature the articulation of a 'norm' in a non-binding written form. The norms which have been agreed by states or in international organizations are thus *recorded*, and this is its essential characteristic; another is that a considerable degree of discretion on how and when to conform to the requirements is left open. Its great advantage over 'hard law' is that, as occasion demands, it can enable states to take on commitments that otherwise they would not, because they are non-binding, or to formulate them in a more precise and restrictive form that could not at that point be agreed in treaty form. The soft-law approach thus allows states to tackle a problem collectively at a time when they do not want too strictly to shackle their freedom of action. On environmental matters this might be either because scientific evidence is

---

[175] See especially Baxter, 29 *ICLQ* (1980) 549–66; Sztucki, in Ramberg et al (eds), *Festskrift till Lars Hjerner: Studies in International Law* (Stockholm, 1990) 549; Dupuy, 12 *Michigan JIL* (1991) 420; Chinkin, 38 *ICLQ* (1989) 850; Bothe, 11 *NYIL* (1980) 65; Tammes, in *Essays on International and Comparative Law in Honour of Judge Erades* (The Hague, 1983) 187–95; Seidl-Hohenveldern, 163 *Recueil des cours* (1980) 164; Sonio, 28 *Jap Ann IL* (1985) 47; Riphagen, 17 *VUWLR* (1987) 81; Elias and Lim, 28 *NYIL* (1997) 3; Shelton (ed), *Commitment and Compliance: The Role of Non-binding Norms in the International Legal System* (Oxford, 2000). For more sceptical views see Weil, 77 *AJIL* (1983) 413; Klabbers, 67 *Nordic JIL* (1998) 381–91.

[176] Other uses are noted by Boyle in 48 *ICLQ* (1999) 901.

[177] See e.g. Roht-Arriaza, 6 *YbIEL* (1995) 107.   [178] Hillgenberg, 10 *EJIL* (1999) 499–515.

[179] Gruchalla-Wesierski, 30 *McGill LJ* (1984) 58, 62.   [180] Boyle, 48 *ICLQ* (1999) 901.

not conclusive or complete, but nonetheless a precautionary approach is required,[181] or because the economic costs are uncertain or over-burdensome. Despite the fact that states retain control over the degree of commitment, the very existence of such an instrument encourages the trend towards hardening the international legal order; not all 'soft' instruments necessarily themselves become 'hard' law nor is that an inherent aim of each one, but several have done so. Examples are numerous, but they include the IAEA Guidelines on Early Notification of a Nuclear Accident which formed the basis for the rapid adoption of the 1986 Convention on Early Notification of a Nuclear Accident following the Chernobyl accident; UNEP Guidelines on Environmental Impact Assessment which were subsequently substantially incorporated in the 1991 ECE Convention on Environmental Impact Assessment in a Transboundary Context; and UNEP's Guidelines on Land-based Sources of Marine Pollution, which provided a model for regional treaties such as the Kuwait Protocol for the Protection of the Marine Environment against Marine Pollution from Land-based Sources.[182] Nor does it follow that all soft-law instruments are unenforceable; those which have been adopted within a treaty framework have to be taken into account in interpreting and applying the treaty,[183] while others may have acquired customary status. Moreover, even soft-law texts can be made the subject of international supervisory and reporting processes.[184]

It is not surprising, therefore, that international environmental law provides numerous examples of the soft-law approach; these are illustrated in almost all of our chapters. Several international bodies have made special use of soft law, most notably the UN Environmental Programme (UNEP), many of whose non-binding principles and codes have served as a starting point for the evolution of new regulatory treaties.[185] Soft-law instruments adopted by the International Atomic Energy Agency (IAEA) provide the detailed rules and technical standards required for implementation of the Nuclear Safety Convention. Its nuclear safety codes and principles generally represent an authoritative technical and political consensus, approved by the Board of Governors or General Conference of the Agency. Despite their soft-law status it is relatively easy to see them as minimum internationally endorsed standards of conduct, and to regard failure to comply as presumptively a failure to fulfil relevant treaty commitments or the customary obligation of due diligence in the regulation and control of nuclear activities.[186] Nuclear soft law thus sets standards of best practice or due diligence to be achieved by the parties in implementing their obligations. Such 'eco-standards' are essential in giving hard content to the overly general and open-textured terms of framework environmental treaties.[187]

---

[181] See e.g. the Declaration adopted by the 1990 Third North Sea Ministerial Conference, which incorporated the 'precautionary principle', accepting that states may need to take measures before clear scientific proof of harmful effects is obtainable, on which see *infra*, Ch 8.

[182] See *infra*, Chs 3, 8, 9.   [183] Vienna Convention on the Law of Treaties, Article 31(3)(a).

[184] Shelton (ed), *Commitment and Compliance: The Role of Non-binding Norms in the International Legal System* (Oxford, 2000) and see *infra*, Ch 4.

[185] On UNEP soft law see *infra*, Ch 2, section 3(3).   [186] See *infra*, Ch 9.

[187] Contini and Sand, 66 *AJIL* (1972) 37.

Although soft law has been described by one writer as no more than 'a convenient shorthand to include vague legal norms',[188] this is a serious misreading of the concept and is belied by many of the examples referred to in this book. Soft law can make an important contribution to establishing a new legal order in a fast-growing and unsettled field. Soft-law guidelines and norms manifest general consent to certain basic principles and detailed standards that are acceptable and practicable for both developed and developing countries. To this extent it contributes to the evolution of new international and national law and to the harmonization of environmental law and standards at the global level.

3 OVERVIEW

Many writers and environmentalists have sometimes been critical of international law's ability to provide adequate protection for the environment and to respond quickly to the changes required as scientific knowledge advances. Much of this criticism is misconceived. It is true that international environmental law has developed on a sectoral basis, often in response to disasters, and that it does not always reflect the interdependence of the various issues and their solutions, but this failing does not derive from the inherent nature and structure of international law—municipal legal systems have also not developed on a holistic basis so far as environmental protection is concerned. International law offers many vehicles for the necessary developments—custom, treaty, soft law, general principles, framework agreements and so on—which can be used in a variety of ways to develop and revise the law to meet new environmental perspectives. This development does not have to be slow; progress depends on the willingness of states to resort to these processes. The speed with which they do so depends not only on the social, economic, and political implications which it is the responsibility of governments to weigh against environmental demands, but also on the availability and reliability of scientific information. Soft-law solutions may sometimes enable agreement to be reached more quickly but, as the following chapters show, there has since the Stockholm Conference been a remarkable growth not only in legally binding measures of environmental protection, but also in new legal concepts and principles which increasingly call into question traditional boundaries between 'public' and 'private' international law, and between national and international law.

Since the Rio Conference in 1992, the subject as a whole has come of age. Its gestation may have been slow, but international environmental law has proved a very vigorous plant. If the 1980s and 1990s are best remembered for 'treaty congestion' because of the large number of multilateral environmental agreements under negotiation, the first decade of the new millennium has seen an unparalleled growth in the environmental jurisprudence of international tribunals. No longer is it necessary to squeeze

---

[188] Gruchalla-Wesierski, 30 *McGill LJ* (1984) 44.

every drop of life out of the immortal trio of arbitrations—*Bering Sea Fur Seals*, *Trail Smelter* and *Lac Lanoux*—which have sustained international environmental law throughout most of its existence. A modern account now has nearly twenty cases decided between 1996 and 2007 on which to draw. By any measure this is a substantial jurisprudence. Equally remarkable is the number of courts and tribunals which have contributed to the jurisprudence. They include the ICJ, the PCA, and the ITLOS, but also the WTO and the European, African and Inter-American human-rights commissions and courts.

The recognition that human-rights law has an environmental dimension—both internally and in a transboundary context—is shown by the developments taking place in this context since the previous edition of this book.[189] Civil and political rights have been the focus of the strongest environmental claims. Economic and social rights provide a less well-established basis for environmental rights, but even they have become significant in African and Latin American litigation. Moreover, the emergence of specifically environmental rights is evidenced by the Aarhus Convention and the ILC's support for principles of non-discriminatory access to effective remedies for transboundary environmental nuisances. International environmental law has thus moved well beyond its original focus on interstate problems, while placing humans 'at the centre of concerns for sustainable development' and giving some substance to Principle 1 of the Rio Declaration.

The growing case law affords little comfort for those who have sometimes doubted the very existence of international law dealing with the environment, or who tend to see it all as soft law or comprised only of specific treaty regimes. Judicial decisions have applied rules of customary law to the control of transboundary environmental risks and the conservation and sustainable use of shared or common resources.[190] In this respect they have drawn heavily on the work of the ILC and the provisions of the 1992 Rio Declaration. The Rio Declaration has also stimulated the development of new general principles with direct relevance to the global environment—the precautionary principle, the polluter-pays principle, common but differentiated responsibility, and sustainable development.[191] While the status of all of these principles in customary law is doubtful or disputed, they have nevertheless become important modifiers of existing rules and treaties, or influenced the negotiation and elaboration of treaty regimes. They are too important for courts, governments, or international organizations and treaty bodies to ignore.

Nevertheless, it must be accepted that the main part of international environmental law comprises the major multilateral treaty regimes which are the subject of the second half of the present study. Participation in many of these MEAs is sufficiently widespread that they represent applicable law for most states. Quite apart from the obvious impact this has had on customary international law, their growing sophistication testifies to their character as evolutionary regimes. At the same time the explosion of treaty-making has visibly diminished. Many of the newer treaties deal

---

[189] *Infra*, Ch 5.   [190] *Infra*, Ch 3.   [191] Ibid.

with matters of detail rather that broader issues of principle, suggesting that the era of environmental lawmaking has reached a plateau. The focus of international attention has shifted instead towards a stronger emphasis on treaty coordination, effectiveness, and compliance. Contrary to a frequently asserted claim, there is little evidence of systematic non-compliance by states parties with MEAs. As we will see in Chapter 4, a more pertinent critique is that some international regulatory regimes are inadequate, ineffective, and constrained, understandably, by the competing demands of economic development.[192] Some, such as the Ozone Convention, have clearly been a success. Others, such as the Climate Change Convention, have yet to prove their value. A few, including the fisheries provisions of the 1982 Law of the Sea Convention, have made matters worse. This mixed record should not be surprising. A focus on sustainable development, as we note in Chapter 2, does not inevitably mean giving greater weight to environmental protection, or nature conservation, or environmental rights. It simply highlights the great difficulty that integrating the needs of environmental protection and economic development poses, not merely for lawyers, but above all for politicians and lawmakers.

What these developments have done, as argued in Chapters 3 and 5, is to change the basis and perspective of international environmental law.[193] Having started as a system of rules limited largely to state responsibility for transboundary harm, resource allocation, and the resolution of conflicting uses of common spaces, international law now accommodates a preventive and precautionary approach to the management of environmental risk and the protection of the environment on a global level. This is a necessary and inevitable development if international environmental law is to address major global and regional environmental issues. It involves greater emphasis on environmental regulation, and gives less prominence to liability for damage as the law's main response to environmentally harmful activities. To this extent, the development of international environmental law reflects the comparable transformation in national environmental law throughout much of the developed, industrialized world. As a consequence, the most convincing characterization is no longer that of neighbourly relations, but of environmental trusteeship, with certain institutional similarities to the protection of social and economic rights, and a comparable concern for community interests at a global level, not merely those of states *inter se*. At the same time the system still displays a largely anthropocentric perspective—the environment as such does not have rights and there is little support for giving it 'intrinsic value' beyond the protection of 'charismatic megafauna' or the wilderness value of Antarctica.[194]

We explain in Chapters 2 and 4 how multilateral supervisory institutions constitute the predominant model of environmental regulation and compliance control. The role of courts is inevitably secondary in this context, limited to the settling of bilateral problems, or to providing judicial review of the operation of treaty regimes and

---

[192] Pallemaerts, *Toxics and Transnational Law* (Oxford, 2003) Ch 2.

[193] See also Bodansky, Brunnée, Hey (eds), *The Oxford Handbook of International Environmental Law* (Oxford, 2007) Ch 1.

[194] *Supra*, section 1(3).

international institutions. While international courts could be given greater power to act in the public interest in environmental matters, for example in the protection of common spaces, such proceedings should preferably be initiated by international organizations such as the UN General Assembly, UNEP, ECOSOC, or regional groupings of states rather than by NGOs. But even if their role is widened in this way it is still difficult to envisage courts doing more than supplementing the work of other international institutions. Thus the primary concern of future development should properly be to address the deficiencies of existing institutions, not to introduce radical innovations in the judicial machinery and process.

From this perspective, the problems of environmental lawmaking, implementation and compliance are essentially political and institutional in character. They are best seen as a reflection of the difficulties of securing international cooperation on global environmental management within a complex and diffuse structure of political authority, and of the deeply conflicting priorities among developed and developing states. As Hurrell and Kingsbury perceptively argue:

> Collective environmental management poses a severe and therefore politically sensitive challenge because it involves the creation of rules and institutions that embody notions of shared responsibilities and shared duties that impinge very heavily on the domestic structures and organization of states, that invest individuals and groups within states with rights and duties and that seek to embody some notion of a common good for the planet as a whole.[195]

Some environmentalists have argued for the radical restructuring of international authority, abandoning the present model of cooperation between sovereign states in favour of some form of majoritarian decision-making. Perhaps the most far-reaching proposal in this respect is to invest the UN Security Council, or some other UN organ, with power to act in the interests of 'ecological security', taking universally binding decisions in the interests of all mankind and the environment. Other proposals, so far unfulfilled, would turn UNEP into an international environmental organization modelled on the WTO.

Yet the major virtue of the present international political system is precisely that in matters of global interdependence, such as protection of the environment, it compels negotiation of a balance of interests and requires consensus if a framework of rules is to attain global acceptance. No group of states, including developing nations, are deprived of influence in this system, as they might well be under a majoritarian model of decision-making; competing priorities, including those of economic development, must be fully accommodated. In this sense the attempt to negotiate the 1982 UNCLOS on a consensus basis represents the kind of bargaining process arguably essential if global environmental needs are to command a global response.[196] Moreover, as the experience of the European Community illustrates, it is by no means clear that a

---

[195] Hurrell and Kingsbury, *The International Politics of the Environment* (Oxford 1992) 6.
[196] See Boyle and Chinkin, *The Making of International Law*, 141–51.

supranational model of interstate regulation necessarily leads to better environmental management in the face of equally pressing claims to higher priority for other issues, or that it generates environmental law more quickly than the present decentralized international system. It took the EC longer to decide how to implement the 1989 Basel Convention than it took for the convention itself to be drafted, negotiated and enter into force, and similar problems have been encountered in attempts to negotiate directives on ocean dumping or liability for environmental harm.

If states have generally preferred to avoid resort to supranational lawmaking institutions, or supranational enforcement, it does not follow that their sovereignty has remained unaffected by the growth of international environmental law and the emergence of the environment as an issue of global concern. Not only are states subject to obligations of restraint and control over the extraterritorial effects of activities within their jurisdiction or control, as well as in the exploitation of shared natural resources and common spaces but, more significantly, notions of common heritage, common interest, common concern, and inter-generational equity have extended the scope of international law and the legitimate interest of other states into the management of every state's domestic environment, at least in respect of certain issues such as global climate change and conservation of biodiversity.[197] Moreover, the characterization of environmental quality as a human-rights issue, potentially affording individuals a claim to protection in national and international law against their own government and those of other states, has effected another radical transformation in the nature of sovereignty or sovereign rights over natural resources and the environment in general.[198] These developments indicate that while sovereignty may remain a focus of conflict and resistance to further encroachments on national autonomy, it is not a decisive objection.[199]

International law empowers, constrains, and compels governments in various ways and at various levels. Its impact on environmental protection policies and laws is complex. For example, a country that enters into free-trade agreements gains economic advantages it would not otherwise enjoy, but at the same time its freedom to pursue other policies will be affected. Parts of its economy may develop more rapidly, putting pressure on land, natural resources, water supply, and air quality leading to unsustainable development, environmental degradation, and poorer conditions of health. It may thus be harder to meet commitments undertaken in the International Covenant on Economic, Social and Cultural Rights, or at the UN Conference on Environment and Development. Equally, those same commitments may restrict certain forms of economic development and limit the ability to benefit from free trade in natural resources. Ultimately, governments make policy choices about how to balance competing objectives of this kind on political, social, economic, or ethical grounds. These choices will be reflected in the agreements they sign or in the state practice that contributes to general international law. The relationship between environmental concerns, international-trade policy and human-rights law is best negotiated by states

---

[197] *Supra* Ch 3.   [198] *Supra* Ch 5.   [199] Handl, 1 *YBIEL* (1990) 3.

acting through the UN, the WTO, and other international organizations. However, few governments can foresee in detail all the consequences of the commitments they make; even when they do foresee them, it is not always possible to secure the agreement of other governments on how to address whatever tensions may arise out of the interaction of commitments into which they have entered.

Neither conflict nor fragmentation are necessary consequences of the inter-action of international environmental law with other branches of international law. In practice, international tribunals have usually found various ways of applying international law as an integrated whole, except where the parties themselves have made this difficult through the Balkanization of dispute settlement and the selective choice of applicable law. Rules of interpretation, priority of treaties, or a balancing of competing interests have generally provided an ample range of techniques for promoting coherence in the application of international law.[200]

This does not mean there are no problems. On the contrary, there will always be uncertainty about how different legal regimes or different bodies of law interact. Our examination of the interrelationship of trade, environment, and human-rights law shows that difficult judgements have to be made, and that there remains much for lawyers to argue over.[201] Do these regimes interact at all? Has the right balance between environmental regulation and individual rights been maintained? Are the terms of a treaty inherently evolutionary? Are environmental measures a *lex specialis* or a *lex generalis*, or do they form part of an integral, non-derogable regime that will prevail over subsequent agreements? What law is applicable in any dispute? The answers to such questions will rarely be obvious and the outcomes are unlikely to be predictable with certainty. For those reasons, these are in practice some of the most challenging questions any international lawyer will have to deal with.

---

[200] See Boyle, in Bodansky, Brunnée, Hey (eds), *Handbook of IEL*, Ch 7.
[201] See Francioni (ed), *Environment, Human Rights and International Trade* (Oxford, 2001).

2

INTERNATIONAL GOVERNANCE AND THE FORMULATION OF ENVIRONMENTAL LAW AND POLICY

1 INTRODUCTION

In this chapter we consider the institutions of global governance responsible for formulating and implementing international environmental policy and law. Global governance has been defined as 'a continuing process through which conflicting or diverse interests may be accommodated and cooperative action may be taken. It includes formal institutions and regimes empowered to enforce compliance, as well as informal arrangements... There is no single model or form of global governance, nor is there a single structure or set of structures. It is a broad, dynamic, complex, process of interactive decision-making'.[1] Although their powers vary widely, a growing number of UN specialized agencies and other international bodies with some measure of competence over environmental matters have become important institutions of global and regional environmental governance.

Used in this sense, the term 'governance' when applied to the UN and its agencies implies rather less than global government, a task for which no international organization is equipped,[2] but more than the power to determine policy or initiate the process

---

[1] Commission on Global Governance, *Our Global Neighbourhood* (Oxford, 1995) 2–4. For a succinct account of 'governance' literature in international relations see Toope, in Byers (ed), *The Role of Law in International Politics* (Oxford, 2000) 94–9.

[2] *Our Global Neighbourhood*, 4; Roberts and Kingsbury (eds), *United Nations, Divided World* (2nd edn, Oxford, 1993) 14–17.

of international lawmaking. At the very least it captures the idea of a community of states with responsibility for addressing common problems through a variety of political processes which are inclusive in character, and which to some degree 'embody a limited sense of a collective interest, distinct in specific cases from the particular interests of individual states'.[3] Such bodies may potentially be universal in membership, like the UN or the World Trade Organization, or regional, like the Council of Europe or the Organization of American States, or have limited membership based on common interests, as in the Organization for Economic Cooperation and Development. They may operate on the basis of one-member-one-vote, as in the UN General Assembly or the World Trade Organization, or votes may be weighted on some other basis, as in the World Bank, controlled by major donor states, or the UN Security Council, dominated by the five permanent members, or the Council of the International Maritime Organization, where the major flag states enjoy a privileged position.

There is nothing new in international organizations exercising powers of international governance: they have done so for over a century. The Congress of Vienna in 1815 and the series of conferences that followed it were the precursors of the political cooperation that takes place today in the UN. The creation of international bodies for functional, administrative purposes began with the innovative nineteenth-century public unions, including the Universal Postal Union, the International Telegraphic Union, and the International Railway Union. The first major lawmaking conferences, the Hague Peace Conferences of 1899 and 1907, represent another development in the institutionalization of international cooperation.[4] These nineteenth-century developments have contributed to and are reflected in modern intergovernmental organizations—their political role deriving from the Congress approach, their lawmaking role from the Hague Conferences, and their constitutional powers synthesized from experience with the public unions. All three strands were embodied first in the League of Nations and then further elaborated in the UN Charter, which established the United Nations in 1945.

The UN and other organizations considered in this chapter are only part of this process of international governance. Equally important is the extensive network of supervisory bodies, conferences of the parties and commissions established by environmental treaties. These autonomous treaty bodies have been likened to a species of international organization, whose main role is to promote implementation and compliance with specific regulatory regimes.[5] They have also contributed to the evolution of what has been termed 'global administrative law'.[6] In contrast, the most valuable contribution made by the UN and related international organizations considered in this chapter has been their ability to influence the international policymaking agenda,

---

[3] Roberts and Kingsbury, *United Nations, Divided World*, 16–17, and see generally, *Our Global Neighbourhood*, 2–6 and Hey, in Bodansky, Brunnée, and Hey (eds), *Oxford Handbook of International Environmental Law* (Oxford, 2007) 750–69.

[4] See Aldrich and Chinkin, 94 *AJIL* (2000) 1–98.

[5] Churchill and Ulfstein, 94 *AJIL* (2000) 623, 658–9.

[6] Kingsbury, Krisch, and Stewart, 68 *Law & Cont Problems* (2005) 15.

and to initiate or facilitate many of the most important lawmaking developments. Nevertheless, there is, as we shall see, a considerable overlap between conventional international organizations and autonomous treaty institutions, and too sharp a distinction between their respective lawmaking and implementation roles would be misleading. In reality, both types of institution perform both functions, and the difference between them is largely one of degree. Thus, some intergovernmental organizations, such as IMO, also offer a means of supervising, monitoring, revising and promoting compliance with regulatory treaties and other international standards.[7] The range and diversity of organizations and institutions involved in some aspect of global environmental governance points to one obvious problem: the immense difficulty of ensuring coordination and consistency within such a diffuse and multilayered system.[8] This is an issue to which we return later.

Intergovernmental organizations such as the United Nations, the International Maritime Organization, the Food and Agriculture Organization, and the International Atomic Energy Agency, among others, have provided the principal forums in which much of the interstate cooperation necessary for developing international environmental policy and regulatory regimes has been realized. UN conferences, and especially the 1972 Stockholm Conference on the Human Environment and the 1992 Rio Conference on Environment and Development, have set agendas for the environment-related work of these bodies. Non-governmental organizations have been especially influential in certain areas of environmental policy and lawmaking, most notably the International Union for the Conservation of Nature.[9] International organizations and NGOs also provide a reservoir of legal and technical expertise and diplomatic machinery not always possessed by individual governments. For many developing states, these organizations thus offer an important source of 'capacity-building' and personnel training, a role which the 1992 Rio Conference on Environment and Development especially attributed to the UN Development Programme, the World Bank, and regional development banks.[10]

International organizations have become an important part of the lawmaking process, even if they are not in themselves *the* process.[11] In this context their most obvious and indispensable role is to provide a permanent forum where states and other participants can engage in dialogue and negotiations, facilitating the compromises necessary for lawmaking by states at very different stages of economic and social development and representing an array of legal, cultural, and religious systems and values. Brunnée and Toope argue that periodic meetings of the parties to multilateral treaties—and by extension the argument must also apply to intergovernmental organizations and lawmaking conferences such as the 3rd UN Conference on the Law of the Sea—constitute

---

[7] See *infra*, section 4(3).

[8] See generally Dunoff, in Bodansky, Brunnée and Hey, *Handbook of IEL*, 85–106.

[9] Membership of IUCN is open both to governments and non-governmental bodies: see *infra*, section 6.

[10] UNCED Agenda 21, Ch 37, para 9. See *infra*, section 4.

[11] See generally Boyle and Chinkin, *The Making of International Law* (Oxford, 2007) Ch 3.

'ongoing, interactional processes', and that 'It is this broader process and not the formal act of consent that infuses the legal norms generated within [a multilateral agreement] with the ability to influence state conduct'.[12] Their central point is that a lawmaking process perceived as legitimate by states and other relevant actors is more likely to be an effective process. An illegitimate process will either fail to make law at all or will undermine the likelihood of compliance with adopted rules or standards.

It is important to recall, however, that although many intergovernmental organizations will have a legal personality separate from their members,[13] they have few, if any, powers of independent action, and progress in the development of policy and law depends entirely on the willingness of member states to propose, to adopt and to implement whatever is agreed. What emerges from any international organization will inevitably reflect the interests and concerns of its members, as well as the voting structure within each organization, and may not always coincide with the priorities of the international community of states as a whole, still less with those of environmental NGOs. The International Maritime Organization and the International Atomic Energy Agency both illustrate the influence wielded by states representing powerful and important industries.[14] International organizations are not immune from the phenomenon of 'agency capture' well documented by administrative lawyers.[15]

The significance of viewing any of these bodies as processes of international governance is twofold. Firstly, it suggests an understanding of international society as 'something more than a crucible for the resolution of competitive state interests, with law the mere handmaiden of power'.[16] Whether this is true of international environmental relations will have to be judged on the evidence of subsequent chapters, but it is certainly true that major environmental treaties, like the 1992 Climate Change and Biological Diversity Conventions, or the 1982 UN Convention on the Law of the Sea, cannot easily be explained by conventional realist conceptions of an international society dominated by power relations. In this respect the role played by international organizations in institutionalizing cooperation on the basis of a community of interest has been crucial. Secondly, governance implies a more cosmopolitan notion of international society than one composed solely of states. Most notions of governance thus envisage participation by other entities, including non-governmental organizations, industry and business, and civil society in general.[17] Here too, international

---

[12] Brunnée, 15 *LJIL* (2002) 1, 6. For a fuller account see also Brunnée and Toope, 39 *Columbia JTL* (2000) 19.

[13] *Reparations for Injuries Case*, ICJ Reports (1949) 174.   [14] See *infra*, Chs 7, 9, respectively.

[15] For a succinct account see Baldwin and McCrudden (eds), *Regulation and Public Law* (London, 1987) 9–12, and literature at 333–4.

[16] Toope, in Byers (ed), *The Role of Law in International Politics*, 96.

[17] Commission on Global Governance, *Our Global Neighbourhood*, 253–60; Boyle and Chinkin, *The Making of International Law*, Ch 2. On NGO participation in the work of international organizations see *infra*, section 6. Higgins, *Problems and Process: International Law and How We Use it* (OUP, 1994) Ch 3, argues strongly that discussion of the 'subjects' of international law is outmoded and should be replaced by 'participants'. On participation by individuals see 1998 Aarhus Convention on Access to Information, Public Participation in Decision-making and Access to Justice in Environmental Matters, *infra*, Ch 5 and 1989 ILO Convention No 169 Concerning Indigenous and Tribal Peoples.

organizations have been notably progressive, especially in environmental affairs. One of the most striking features of modern international lawmaking is the interaction of states, intergovernmental organizations (IGOs), and non-governmental organizations (NGOs) in what have been variously described as 'epistemic communities' or 'transnational networks' of officials, experts, and interest groups whose quasi-autonomous character allows them to constitute a broader international community than the states that nominally make the decisions.[18] This perspective helps explain why some states—or their representatives—appear to have more (or less) influence on outcomes than the relative size or importance of that state might suggest. But studying the list of observers at meetings of environmental treaty parties is also instructive. To take one example, the 6th COP of the Basel Convention on the Transboundary Movement of Hazardous Waste was attended by observers from the Association of Plastics Manufacturers, the International Council on Mining and Metals, and no fewer than nine electronics or mobile phone companies, including Nokia, Sony, LG Electronics and Motorola.[19] What was on the agenda? Negotiation of an end-of-life management agreement with the manufacturers of mobile phones. There were also two environmental NGOs present—WWF and the Basel Action Network. Knowing who participates in such meetings is essential to an understanding of the politics of international lawmaking. In some treaty bodies, environmental NGOs and industry observers are more active and influential than many of the states that participate as full members.[20]

Two objections are commonly made to the involvement of intergovernmental bodies in international governance. First, they may be seen as fundamentally undemocratic in taking power away from elected governments and national legislatures, locating it instead in unaccountable institutions where decisions are taken by national representatives insulated from open public scrutiny, and promoting forms of globalization remote from the concerns of ordinary people.[21] Such a 'democratic deficit' is only partially mitigated by greater transparency and the growing involvement of NGOs and business in the work of some intergovernmental bodies. From this perspective conceptions of a more cosmopolitan international order may appear essentially false. Secondly, without real lawmaking authority or, in most cases, the ability to take binding decisions by majority vote, they lack the necessary power to take effective action for the common good and to impose their collective will on individual states. From this perspective the problems international organizations encounter in addressing environmental issues may be seen as evidence of the continuing power of national sovereignty and of a need to transcend the outdated structures of an international society dominated by states. Although both characterizations are widely prevalent,

---

[18] Haas, in Bodansky, Brunnée and Hey (eds), *Handbook of IEL*, 791; Szasz, in Joyner (ed), *The UN and International Law*, 34–5; Slaughter, 76 *Foreign Affairs* (1997) 183.

[19] 1989 Basel Convention, *Rept of 6th COP*, UNEP/CHW 6/40 (2003), para 21.

[20] For examples see *infra*, section 7.

[21] The arguments reviewed in Bodansky, 93 *AJIL* (1999) 596, have general relevance.

they are also mutually incompatible, and in any case considerably over-simplified.[22] Nevertheless, they do capture the dilemma of how to address the evident need for more effective means of promoting international cooperation to tackle global problems within a politically legitimate and publicly accountable process.[23] Despite these concerns, in an environmental context it will be seen in later chapters that the role and form of cooperation through international organizations has evolved well beyond its rudimentary origins and has at least to some extent been responsive to the needs of contemporary international society.

2 THE DEVELOPMENT OF INTERNATIONAL ENVIRONMENTAL POLICY

2(1) THE 1972 UNITED NATIONS CONFERENCE ON THE HUMAN ENVIRONMENT

It was pressure from NGOs, especially in the United States, that led to the convening of the first intergovernmental conference devoted to environmental issues, the 1972 Stockholm Conference on the Human Environment (UNCHE).[24] A preliminary meeting of experts drew particular attention to the developmental aspects of the problem.[25] This report encouraged many developing countries to participate in the Conference on the understanding that any environmentally protective measures resulting from it would not be used as the medium for inhibiting their economic development.

The Conference resulted in four major initiatives at the normative, institutional, programmatic, and financial levels, which together provided the driving force for developments in the UN during the next decade and beyond.[26] The first was the adoption of the Stockholm Declaration on the Human Environment, intended to 'inspire and guide the peoples of the world in the preservation and enhancement of the human

---

[22] Koskenniemi, *From Apology to Utopia: The Structure of International Legal Argument* (Helsinki, 1989) and Allott, *Eunomia* (Oxford, 1990) exemplify the opposing arguments in a much more sophisticated form. See also Toope, in Byers (ed), *The Role of Law in International Politics*, 99–104, and Roberts and Kingsbury, *United Nations, Divided World*, Ch 1.

[23] The literature is too extensive to cite but see in particular Brunnée and Toope, 39 *Columbia JTL* (2000) 19; Franck, *Fairness in International Law and Institutions* (Oxford, 1995).

[24] A number of seminal books had stimulated awareness, including Carson, *Silent Spring* (New York, 1962); Commoner, *The Closing Circle* (New York, 1971); Falk, *This Endangered Planet* (Toronto, 1971); Meadows et al, *The Limits to Growth* (London, 1972).

[25] *Development and Environment: Report and Working Papers of Experts Convened by the Secretary General of the United National Conference on the Human Environment*, Founex, Switzerland, 4–12 June 1971.

[26] The *Report of the Conference on the Human Environment*, together with the Action Plan, is found in UN Doc A/CONF 48/14/Rev 1 (1972). For a full account see Caldwell, *International Environmental Policy* (3rd edn, Durham NC, 1996) Chs 2, 3.

environment'.[27] The second was the establishment of a new institution within the UN, the UN Environment Programme (UNEP). The third was the adoption of an Action Plan for the development of environmental policy, to be administered by UNEP, and the fourth was the institution, by voluntary contributions, of an Environment Fund.

The human-rights perspective with which the Stockholm Declaration opens was innovative at the time, and has had some influence on the development of national environmental law, but it was not repeated in the same terms twenty years later in the Rio Declaration.[28] However, the responsibility for future generations also articulated in Principle 1 was not entirely novel, and has subsequently become an important element of the Rio Declaration and the concept of sustainable development.[29] The key normative provision in the Stockholm Declaration, Principle 21, is purportedly drawn from existing treaty and customary law. While recognizing both sovereignty and developmental concerns, it is clear that transboundary environmental harm must be controlled.[30]

Other provisions of the Stockholm Declaration are more policy-oriented than normative in character. The need to take account of nature conservation and wildlife protection in economic development planning was identified, but not in terms which would rule out exploitation of natural resources. Principles 2–5 proclaim that the earth's natural resources 'must be safeguarded for the benefit of present and future generations', 'that its capacity to produce vital renewable resources must be maintained and, if practical, restored or improved', and that humans have a responsibility to 'safeguard and wisely manage the heritage of wildlife and its habitat'. Principles 6 and 7 relate to pollution control, calling for cessation of the discharge of toxic and other substances into the environment in quantities that exceed the capacity to render them harmless, to ensure that no irreversible damage is inflicted on ecosystems, and to prevent pollution of the sea. The reference to preservation of ecosystems was considered a significant step, long advocated by NGOs, but still controversial today. In deference to the economic concerns of developing countries, Principles 8–11 recognize, inter alia, that economic and social development is essential, and that environmental policies should 'enhance and not adversely affect the present or future development potential of developing countries'. Principles 12–17 set out policies on environmental and resource management that are in many respects repeated twenty years later in the Rio Declaration. These include the need for capacity-building and financial assistance for developing states (Principle 12); integration of development planning and environmental protection (Principles 13 and 14); adoption of policies on urbanisation and population planning (Principles 15 and 16),[31] and the creation of national institutions with responsibility for 'enhancing environmental quality'. Finally, Principle 22 requires states to further develop international law on liability and compensation for

---

[27] *Reports of the Preparatory Committee* relevant to the Declaration are in UN Doc A/CONF 48/PC 9, 13, 17. The *Final Report of the Working Group on the Declaration* is in UN Doc A/CONF 48/14/Rev 1/Annex II. See Sohn, 14 *Harv ILJ* (1973) 423.

[28] See *infra*, Ch 5.   [29] See *infra*, Ch 3, section 2(2).   [30] See *infra*, Ch 3, section 4.

[31] No comparable provisions were included in the Rio Declaration: see *infra*.

pollution and other forms of environmental damage to areas beyond their jurisdiction; subsequent progress in this regard has been very slow.[32]

2(2) THE 1992 UN CONFERENCE ON ENVIRONMENT AND DEVELOPMENT

(a) The negotiations

Following Stockholm, the International Union for Conservation of Nature began to promote *sustainable* use of resources,[33] but it was not until the World Commission on Environment and Development (WCED) published the 'Brundtland Report' calling for a new approach, articulated as 'sustainable development', that a turning point in UN policy was reached.[34] The Brundtland Report recommended that the UN transform its conclusions into a Programme of Action on Sustainable Development, hold a conference to review implementation of this programme, and institute follow-up arrangements to 'set benchmarks and maintain human progress within the guidance of human needs and natural law'. The General Assembly decided to convene the UN Conference on Environment and Development (UNCED) for 1992, and it established a Preparatory Commission (Prepcom) in which most of the negotiations took place.[35] Political objections from developing countries ensured that intergovernmental negotiating committees established by the General Assembly were given responsibility for drafting conventions on climate change and biological diversity, rather than UNEP, the World Meteorological Organization (WMO) or the Food and Agriculture Organization (FAO).[36] Developing states also worked hard to coordinate their negotiating position,[37] although in the intergovernmental negotiating committee on climate

---

[32] See *infra*, Chs 4, 5, 7, 8, 9.

[33] *World Conservation Strategy: Living Resource Conservation for Sustainable Development* (1980) prepared by the International Union for Conservation of Nature (IUCN) in collaboration with UNEP, the World Wildlife Fund for Nature, FAO and UNESCO; see also the updated version prepared for the UNCED, *Caring for the Earth: A Strategy for Sustainable Living* (1991).

[34] World Commission on Environment and Development, *Our Common Future* (Oxford, 1987); see also report of the WCED's Legal Expert Group on Environmental Law, in Munro and Lammers (eds), *Environmental Protection and Sustainable Development* (London, 1986). See generally Ginther, Denters and De Waart (eds), *Sustainable Development and Good Governance* (Dordrecht, 1995) esp Ch by Matsui; Schrijver, *Sovereignty over Natural Resources* (Cambridge, 1997) esp Ch 4; Bugge and Voigt (eds), *Sustainable Development in International and National Law* (Groningen, 2008) esp Chs 1, 2, and see *infra*, Chs 3, 11.

[35] UNGA Res 44/228 (1989). On the negotiations and the conference see Campiglio et al (eds), *The Environment after Rio* (London, 1994); Spector, Sjöstedt, and Zartman (eds), *Negotiating International Regimes: Lessons Learned from the UNCED* (London, 1994); Johnson (ed), *The Earth Summit* (London, 1993); Sand, 3 *YbIEL* (1992) 3; Freestone, 6 *JEL* (1994) 193; 'Symposium: UNCED', 4 *Colorado JIELP* (1993) 1ff; and report in 22 *EPL* (1992) 204–25.

[36] See Bodansky, *Yale JIL* (1993) 451, 471–92.

[37] See Beijing Ministerial Declaration on Environment and Development, UN Doc A/CONF151/PC/85 (1991); South Centre, *Environment and Development: Towards a Common Strategy of the South in the UNCED Negotiations and Beyond* (Geneva, 1991); Mensah, in Campiglio et al, *The Environment after Rio* (London, 1994) 33–54.

change they could not agree on a common position and separated into different groups.[38]

Two unusual features of UNCED were: first, its sponsorship not only by donor governments but also by major companies (e.g. ICI) and foundations (e.g. the MacArthur and Rockefeller Foundations) and, secondly, the fact that NGOs were allowed to play a major role in the preparatory committees. The negotiating climate in these meetings was often hostile, as major differences emerged on such basic questions as the weight to be accorded to development, as opposed to environment; whether the two could be separated; and the content of 'sustainable development'. As in earlier negotiations, developing states characterized the environmental crisis as a long-term developmental one, while developed states saw it as a more immediate technical problem. The former thus endeavoured to direct discussion, as in the 1974 debates on the 'New International Economic Order', towards reform of the international economic system as a prerequisite for effective environmental action. Major differences thus again arose along a North–South divide on issues relating to sovereignty over natural resources, economic costs, equitable burden-sharing, funding, the role of multilateral institutions, transfer of technology, climate change, biological diversity, and deforestation. The North's proposals on the last two issues, in particular, were regarded as a threat to the sovereign rights of developing states over their own natural resources, while pressure for global action on climate change was seen as an inequitable attempt to force developing states to share the costs and burdens of a problem created almost entirely by the industrialized states.

Many governments and NGOs expressed regret that the Rio Conference was not asked to adopt the more ambitious proposals for an Earth Charter, that the Climate Change Convention was weakened, that many crucial issues were removed from or diluted in Agenda 21, and that the USA initially refused to sign the treaty on biological diversity in order to protect its pharmaceutical industry.[39] Malaysia also blocked consideration of a treaty on tropical forests, and only vague commitments were made by developed states on provision of financial resources and debt reduction. Despite these deficiencies, some spirit of solidarity (referred to as the 'Spirit of Rio') did prevail, enabling these new instruments and an agenda for future action to emerge from the negotiations. A contributing factor was the unprecedented level of NGO participation in the negotiations leading up to UNCED, the vast number of NGO observers who were present in Rio to lobby government delegates, and the presence of so many heads of state and government.

(b) The UNCED Conference instruments

The Rio Conference adopted a range of instruments whose legal status and implications we explore in greater depth in later chapters.

(i) The Rio Declaration on Environment and Development   This set of twenty-seven principles, finely balanced between the priorities of developed and developing states,

---

[38] Bodansky, *Yale JIL* (1993) 451.   [39] See *infra*, Ch 11.

sets out the principal contours of sustainable development as now endorsed by the UN, but it also has much greater legal significance than its 1972 predecessor. It is examined in detail in the next section and in Chapter 3.

(ii) Agenda 21[40]   This is a programme of action covering many issues, including climate change, deforestation, desertification and protection of the oceans. Although not legally binding it is potentially relevant to interpretation of treaties and other instruments adopted in accordance with its provisions. It recognizes more explicitly than the Stockholm Action Plan the interconnections between economic, environmental, social, and development issues, and endeavours to integrate these objectives. Agenda 21 is directed primarily at states, but it also gives international agencies, including the UN and the World Bank, a role in supporting and complementing action by states, including the promotion of enhanced international cooperation and capacity building.

(iii) The Framework Convention on Climate Change and the Convention on Biological Diversity   These important agreements create new regulatory regimes for two of the most significant problems facing contemporary society: the consequences of energy use, and large-scale natural resource depletion. Both treaties were and remain controversial, despite their adoption by consensus, and both exemplify the difficult policy choices facing governments trying to integrate economic and environmental considerations. The continuing inability of the United States to reconcile itself to either agreement illustrates the gulf between commitment in principle to sustainable development and implementation in practice in national law and economic policy. Both agreements are considered in more detail in Chapters 6 and 11 respectively.

(iv) The Non-legally Binding Authoritative Statement of Principles for a Global Consensus on the Management, Conservation and Sustainable Development of all Types of Forests   As the full title suggests, the Statement of Forest Principles is not a treaty, and represents the most that could be agreed at UNCED after strong opposition from countries in Latin America, Africa and South-east Asia to the negotiation of a convention on tropical forests alone.[41] Its adoption did lead to revision of the International Tropical Timber Agreement in 1994, and continuing negotiations on forests within the UN thereafter.

2(3) THE 2002 WORLD SUMMIT ON SUSTAINABLE DEVELOPMENT

The third, and quite possibly the last, UN conference on environment and development convened at Johannesburg in 2002. Like the others the World Summit on Sustainable Development (WSSD) adopted a declaration and an action plan, known respectively

---

[40] UNCED, *Report,* I (1992). It is so called because implementation of the plan would extend well into the 21st century.

[41] See Schally, 4 *YbIEL* (1993) 30; Tarasofsky (ed), *Assessing the International Forests Regime* (IUCN, 1999) and *infra,* Ch 12.

as the Declaration on Sustainable Development and the Plan of Implementation.[42] Unlike the earlier conferences neither document articulates new principles or policies, nor do they specifically set an agenda for further lawmaking. Their value lies mainly in the reaffirmation and refinement of existing policies and principles, and in giving a little more substance to the contours of sustainable development as a concept. They are best seen as a modest programme of incremental progress towards strengthening implementation of goals and commitments previously endorsed. Of particular environmental significance are the paragraphs on protection and management of natural resources, trade and environment, energy efficiency, and strengthening the Commission on Sustainable Development (CSD). Otherwise, for lawyers, their only real importance is that they reiterate the main legal principles endorsed by the Rio Declaration, including the precautionary principle, the polluter-pays principle, and public participation.

However, if the 2002 WSSD has generally been seen as a disappointment for environmental policy, the 2005 UN Summit showed that other priorities now dominate international policymaking and the attention of the UN.[43] But it is doubtful whether the world needs more grand statements of environmental policy or even reiteration of existing policy: what is needed is implementation of the Rio instruments and more progress towards the goals already agreed. From this perspective it is the continued failure of states to grapple seriously with the implications of climate change and loss of biodiversity which adds most to the perception that environmental issues have once again become peripheral concerns of global governance.[44]

2(4) THE CONCEPT OF SUSTAINABLE DEVELOPMENT

With the adoption of the Rio instruments, sustainable development became and has so far remained the leading concept of international environmental policy. The Brundtland Report characterized sustainable development as a process that 'meets the needs of the present without compromising the ability of future generations to meet their own needs'.[45] UNEP's Governing Council helpfully added that this artful formulation 'does not imply in any way encroachment upon national sovereignty'.[46] Although 'sustainable development' is used throughout the Rio Declaration, it was not until the 2002 World Summit on Sustainable Development that anything approaching

---

[42] UN, *Report of the WSSD*, UN Doc A/Conf 199/20 (2002), Resolution 1 and Annex. See Beyerlin and Reichard, 63 *ZAÖRV* (2003) 213–38. For background see Dodds (ed), *Earth Summit 2002* (London, 2001).

[43] See Galizzi, 29 *Fordham ILJ* (2006) 952–1008.   [44] See *infra*, Chs 6, 11.

[45] WCED, *Our Common Future*, 43. Compare the definition of sustainable development developed by the FAO Committee on Fisheries in 1991: 'the management and conservation of the natural resource base, and the orientation of technological and institutional change in such a manner as to ensure the attainment and continued satisfaction of human needs for present and future generations. Such development conserves land, water, plant genetic resources, is environmentally non-degrading, technologically appropriate, economically viable and socially acceptable.'

[46] Annex II to UNEP GC decision 15/2, May 1989; Thacher, in Hurrell and Kingsbury (eds), *The International Politics of the Environment: Actors, Interests and Institutions* (Oxford, 1992) 183–211, 190.

a definition of the concept could be attempted by the UN. Three 'interdependent and mutually reinforcing pillars of sustainable development' were identified in the Johannesburg Declaration—economic development, social development, and environmental protection.[47]

However defined, the notion of sustainable development is inherently complex and its implementation obliges governments to think in somewhat different terms from those to which they have been accustomed. Social, political, and economic choices abound: what weight should be given to natural-resource exploitation over nature protection, to industrial development over the air and water quality, to land-use development over conservation of forests and wetlands, to energy consumption over the risks of climate change, and so on. These choices may result in wide diversities of policy and interpretation, as different governments and international organizations pursue their own priorities and make their own value judgements, moderated only to some extent by international agreements on such matters as climate change and conservation of biological diversity. Twenty years on from the Brundtland Report we are still little nearer to an internationally agreed understanding of what constitutes sustainable development in any detail, and the concept itself has proved almost infinitely malleable.

Agenda 21 refers in its preamble to the need for a 'global partnership for sustainable development', and most of its provisions, together with the principles laid down in the Rio Declaration on Environment and Development, are intended to promote implementation of the concept. But, as one author has pertinently asked, 'Can a term which commands such support actually mean anything?'[48] Does this crucial concept have a solid core of meaning, or does the content of sustainable development lie mainly in the eye of the beholder? Certain interpretations can be discarded immediately. Firstly, sustainable development is not to be confused with zero growth. Economists readily accept that in some cases even zero growth may be unsustainable: zero growth in the output of CFCs will not save the ozone layer, for example. Conversely, growth, if defined in terms of GNP, is not inevitably unsustainable, since GNP is not per se a measure of natural resource consumption or of pollution. One economist has put this point succinctly: 'As a mere monetary aggregate, GNP does not distinguish between different types of economic activity: it simply records the overall total. It is quite possible for GNP to go up with fewer resources being used, and less pollution being generated, if the *content* of growth tends away from environmentally—degrading activities'.[49] The switch from coal or oil to gas-fired or nuclear power stations is one example of environmentally friendly growth of this kind, and in general more environmentally

---

[47] UN, *Report of the WSSD*, UN Doc A/CONF 199/20 (2002), Resolution 1, para 5.

[48] Jacobs, *The Green Economy* (London, 1991) 59. See generally Redclift, *Sustainable Development: Exploring the Contradictions* (London, 1987); Reid, *Sustainable Development* (London, 1995); Moffat, *Sustainable Development: Principles, Analysis and Policies* (London, 1995) esp Ch 3; Goldin and Winters (eds), *The Economics of Sustainable Development* (OECD, Cambridge, 1995); Dresner, *The Principles of Sustainability* (London, 2002); Neumayer, *Weak Versus Strong Sustainability* (2nd edn, 2003).

[49] Jacobs, op cit, 54.

efficient use of natural resources or energy is more likely to promote economic growth rather than retard it.

Whatever else it means therefore, sustainable development need not imply a policy of zero growth. Nor does the Rio Declaration envisage such an outcome. It firmly reiterates the sovereign right of states to exploit their own resources in accordance with their own environmental and development policies, although subject, as at Stockholm, to a responsibility for transboundary environmental protection; it asserts a right to development,[50] albeit so as to meet equitably the needs of present and future generations, and it calls for an 'open international economic system that would lead to economic growth and sustainable development in all countries'.

A more plausible interpretation is that sustainable development entails a compromise between environmental protection and economic growth. The integration of environmental protection and economic development was for that reason an important objective of the UNCED Conference, expressed in Principle 4 of the Rio Declaration. Much of Agenda 21, and of international environmental law, has been concerned with attaining this integration. Clearly, a policy of economic growth which disregards environmental considerations, or vice versa, will not meet the criterion of sustainable development. But to view sustainable development as amounting to a compromise between equally desirable ends fails to explain either the nature of sustainability or of development, and gives us no criteria for determining the parameters and the ultimate objective of this integration of development and environment. Nor does it tell us what the needs of future generations will be.

On one view, sustainable development implies not merely limits on economic activity in the interests of preserving or protecting the environment, but an approach to development which emphasizes the fundamental importance of equity within the economic system. This equity is both intra-generational, in that it seeks to redress the imbalance in wealth and economic development between the developed and developing worlds by giving priority to the needs of the poor,[51] and inter-generational, in seeking a fair allocation of costs and benefits across succeeding generations.[52] Put simply, development will only be 'sustainable' if it benefits the disadvantaged, without disadvantaging the needs of the future. These points are well observed in Principles 3–9 of the Rio Declaration, and in the Conventions on Climate Change and Biodiversity. What is characteristic of all these instruments is their commitment to protecting the interests of future generations (an inherently problematic notion),[53] and of developing countries. The latter benefit more immediately from access to funding and capacity-building through the Global Environment Facility and other sources,[54] from access to the benefits derived from exploitation of their own genetic resources and transfer

---

[50] See *infra*, Ch 3, section 2.   [51] WCED, *Our Common Future*, 44–5; Rio Declaration, Principle 5.

[52] Rio Declaration, Principle 3, and see Brown-Weiss, *In Fairness to Future Generations* (Dobbs Ferry, NY, 1989).

[53] See *infra*, Ch 3, section 2(2).   [54] See *infra*, section 4(4).

of technology,[55] and from a recognition that in a system of 'common but differentiated responsibilities' developed countries bear a larger responsibility for ensuring sustainable development 'in view of the pressures their societies place on the global environment and of the technologies and financial resources they command'.[56] Thus 'sustainable development' is intended to serve not simply the needs of the environment, but entails a reorientation of the world's economic system in which the burdens of environmental protection will fall more heavily on the developed Northern states and the economic benefits will accrue more significantly to the underdeveloped South, for the common benefit of all.

A further element of sustainable development, however, is 'a notion of economic welfare which acknowledges non-financial components',[57] in particular the quality of the environment, health, and the preservation of culture and community. At some level these concerns require preservation of natural capital, not simply a substitution of man-made capital of equivalent value. Some economists have used the term 'strong sustainability' in this context.[58] We can see some of these concerns in Principle 1 of the Rio Declaration, which places human beings 'at the centre of concerns for sustainable development', and proclaims their entitlement to 'a healthy and productive life in harmony with nature', but more especially in such international agreements as the 1972 Convention for the Protection of World Cultural and National Heritage,[59] which protects areas like Stonehenge and the Great Barrier Reef. Similarly, the 1991 Protocol to the Antarctic Treaty on Environmental Protection[60] designates Antarctica a Special Conservation Area, and acknowledges its 'intrinsic value', including its 'wilderness and aesthetic values'. However, the Rio Declaration is somewhat less 'ecocentric' than its 1972 predecessor, and it lacks any express reference to such values, or to conservation of wildlife and habitat.

Defined in these terms, sustainable development has not been an objective of industrialized or developing countries until now, and its implementation requires a considerable departure from earlier global economic policy. This is most obviously true of the United States, where less than 5 per cent of the world's population consume annually over 30 per cent of global energy output, and each American generates as much CO_2 as four Chinese. Developing countries not only have problems securing a more equitable balance of resource consumption, but control over their own natural resources and environmental policies may be significantly limited by external indebtedness and resulting dependence on short-term resource exploitation, influenced by patterns of international trade within the WTO system. It is in this context that the failure of the present WTO system to take greater account of environmental concerns

---

[55] 1992 Convention on Biological Diversity, Articles 12, 15, 16, 19, *infra*, Ch 11; 1992 Convention on Climate Change, Articles 4(2)–(3), *infra*, Ch 6.

[56] Rio Declaration, Principle 7, and see *infra*, Ch 3, section 3(3).

[57] Jacobs, *The Green Economy*, 60.

[58] See Neumayer, *Weak Versus Strong Sustainability* (2nd edn, Cheltenham, 2003).

[59] See *infra*, Ch 12.   [60] Ibid.

or of the development interests of developing states has become a structural inhibition on implementation of the policies adopted at Rio in 1992.[61]

Other structural impediments are technological and scientific. Governments and economists tend to assume that scientists can identify all the adverse environmental consequences of economic and industrial activity, whether now or in the future, and that appropriate technical solutions can then be found. Given the real state of environmental deterioration identified by UN reports, this optimism may well be naïve. A somewhat more prudent concept of sustainability would take account of the limitations of scientific knowledge and prediction in evaluating and addressing environmental risks.[62]

Sustainable development requires political action if it is to be implemented, and it may be easier to deliver in certain systems than in others. While on the one hand a measure of authoritarian dirigisme may appear superficially attractive if strong environmental controls are required, in reality totalitarian societies such as the former Soviet Union, China, or the former communist regimes in Eastern Europe have proved far less successful in managing their environment and in avoiding environmental disasters than participatory democracies. It is no coincidence that both the Soviet and Hungarian democratic revolutions of the period 1989–91 can be related directly to the environmental consequences of the Chernobyl accident and the Gabčíkovo-Nagymaros dam controversy, nor is it surprising that the Bhopal disaster has greatly strengthened the emphasis which Indian courts now place on human rights and public-interest litigation in environmental matters.[63] Environmental impact assessment, access to information, and public participation in national policy formation and domestic environmental governance are for this reason among the more important elements of the Rio Declaration.[64] As we shall see in the next chapter, sustainable development is as much about processes as about outcomes, and for lawyers this may be the key point to grasp.

While it is one of the roles of international environmental law to give the concept of sustainable development more concrete content, chiefly through multilateral environmental treaties, this process is still very far from complete. Only a few governments, such as New Zealand's, have legislated specifically for sustainable development.[65] Despite the demands of the Rio Declaration for integration, many other governments will approach the matter piecemeal, with inevitable incoherence.[66] In any event the nature of sustainable development is such that it cannot usefully be defined.[67] At best, international law can only facilitate its implementation in specific situations, such as conservation of high-seas fisheries, or trade in elephant ivory, or allocation of shared watercourses, and so forth. This will be evident in the following chapters. Sustainable development offers us a unifying concept for the exploitation of natural resources and

[61] See infra, Ch 14.   [62] See Principle 15, the 'precautionary approach', and infra, Ch 3, section 4.
[63] See infra, Ch 5.   [64] See Principles 10 and 17, and infra, Ch 5.
[65] Resources Management Act of 1991.
[66] E.g. the United Kingdom. See Jenkins, 22 Legal Studies (2002) 578.
[67] See infra, Ch 3, section 2.

the integration of environment and development. However, it does not encompass the totality of international environmental law. In Chapter 3 we will explore further the contours and legal implications of the concept, as well as the Rio Declaration's codification and development of certain principles of international law relating to sustainable development and environmental protection.

3 THE UN AND ENVIRONMENTAL GOVERNANCE

3(1) THE UN'S ENVIRONMENTAL COMPETENCE

The United Nations has become the most significant political embodiment of the international community, 'a central institution in the conduct of international relations'.[68] Nevertheless, although the UN Charter expressed the UN's aims and purposes in far wider terms than those of the League of Nations, nowhere is there any explicit reference to the aim of protecting, preserving, or conserving the natural environment or promoting sustainable development. This is hardly surprising. There was little awareness in 1945 of any need to protect the environment, except on a limited and ad hoc basis, and it was not anticipated that UN action would be needed. Thus, the subsequent evolution of the UN's power to adopt policies or take measures directed at environmental objectives has to be derived from a broad interpretation of the Charter and of the implied powers of the organization. Article 1 includes among the purposes of the UN the furtherance of 'international cooperation in solving international problems of an economic, social, cultural, or humanitarian character, and in promoting and encouraging respect for human rights...'. Article 55 also requires the UN to promote conditions of economic and social progress and development, solutions to international economic, social, health and related problems, and observance of human rights and fundamental freedoms.

In the *Reparations for Injuries Case* the ICJ held that 'the rights and duties of an entity such as the Organization must depend upon its purpose and functions as specified or implied in its constituent documents and developed in practice'.[69] It can readily be assumed that environmental protection is an essential element in the promotion of social progress and in solving economic and social problems as referred to in Articles 1 and 55.[70] On that basis the UN Environment Programme was established in 1972 following the Stockholm Conference, and the Commission on Sustainable Development in 1992 following the Rio Conference. Both bodies report to the UN through the Economic and Social Council (ECOSOC). The same articles of the UN Charter also support the environmental programmes of UN regional agencies: the

---

[68] See Roberts and Kingsbury, *United Nations, Divided World*, 1.   [69] ICJ Reports (1949) 174, 180.
[70] On the interpretation of these articles see Simma (ed), *The Charter of the United Nations: A Commentary* (2nd edn, Oxford, 2002).

UN Economic Commissions for Africa, Asia and the Pacific, Europe, Latin America, and Western Asia.[71]

A particularly important feature of the UN system has been the linking of the UN to various specialized agencies, established autonomously by intergovernmental agreement. Like the UN, most of the specialized agencies were not endowed with explicit power over environmental matters, but have had to develop such a competence through interpretation and practice.[72] Those whose responsibilities for environmental protection or sustainable use of natural resources have evolved in this way include the International Maritime Organization (IMO), the Food and Agriculture Organization (FAO), the World Bank, and the UN Educational, Scientific and Cultural Organization (UNESCO).[73] The International Atomic Energy Agency (IAEA) is not formally a UN specialized agency, but it too has acquired an environmental dimension through interpretation of its constituent instrument.[74]

The powers of all of these bodies are necessarily more limited than those of the UN. In its *Advisory Opinions on the Legality of the Threat or Use of Nuclear Weapons*,[75] the ICJ distinguished the general power of the UN General Assembly from the exclusively health-related powers of the WHO, and denied the latter body the competence to seek an advisory opinion on the legality of nuclear weapons, notwithstanding their obvious potential for harming human health and the natural environment. This decision illustrates how closely the express and implied powers of specialized agencies must be related to their specific objects and purposes. Thus IMO has confined its regulatory competence to marine pollution from ships, FAO deals with the environment as an aspect of sustainable use of natural resources, and so on.

3(2) THE UN PRINCIPAL ORGANS AND PROTECTION OF THE ENVIRONMENT

(a) The General Assembly

The General Assembly and the Security Council, along with the Economic and Social Council, are 'principal organs' of the UN.[76] Every member state has one vote in the General Assembly, giving developing states an overwhelming majority, while certain non-member states and international NGOs have observer status. The General Assembly has limited power, but may discuss any matter within the scope of the Charter, and make recommendations to member states or to the Security Council.[77] In particular, Article 13 provides that it 'shall initiate studies and make recommendations' for the purpose of promoting political cooperation, encouraging the progressive

---

[71] See *infra*, section 4(2).

[72] See Werksman (ed), *Greening International Institutions* (London, 1996); White, *The Law of International Organizations*, Ch 10; Desai, *Institutionalizing International Environmental Law* (Ardsley, 2004) Ch 5.

[73] *Infra*, section 4.   [74] Ibid.   [75] ICJ Reports (1996) 66 (WHO) and 226 (UNGA).

[76] UN Charter, Article 7. The others are the Trusteeship Council, the ICJ and the secretariat.

[77] Article 10. See generally Peterson, *The General Assembly in World Politics* (London, 1986); id, in Weiss and Daws (eds), *The Oxford Handbook on the UN* (Oxford, 2007) Ch 5.

development and codification of international law, and furthering the social and economic objectives of Article 55. The General Assembly is thus the UN's most important political body.

While the General Assembly has no lawmaking power as such, its ability to adopt resolutions, convene lawmaking conferences and initiate codification projects has given it a central role in the development of international policy and law relating to many aspects of the environment.[78] As we shall see in later chapters, UNGA resolutions on the legal status of the deep seabed, natural resources, and the global climate have influenced the evolution of treaties and customary law on these matters, as has UN endorsement of the Stockholm and Rio Declarations. Decisions to convene UN Conferences on, inter alia, the Human Environment (Stockholm, 1972), the Law of the Sea (Caracas, 1973), and Environment and Development (Rio, 1992) were taken by the General Assembly. With regard to the codification of international law the General Assembly usually acts through one of its subsidiary bodies, mainly the International Law Commission (ILC), or in some cases through ad hoc committees. Two ILC projects have particular relevance to environmental issues: codification of the law relating to international watercourses and the prevention of transboundary harm.[79]

Even when it does not itself promote the negotiation of new treaties or other instruments, the General Assembly's power to coordinate the legal and policy agendas of specialized agencies and other UN bodies gives it a continuing role at the heart of the lawmaking process. With so many different bodies potentially involved in international lawmaking, the task of allocating responsibilities and coordinating policy is an increasingly important feature of the General Assembly's role. Where, for example, should responsibility for developing international law relating to forests be located? FAO's mandate covers forestry, while promoting trade in timber is the main objective of the International Tropical Timber Organization. The World Heritage Convention adopted by UNESCO protects some forest areas, while forests generally are also covered by the Convention on Biological Diversity. Sustainable use of natural resources falls within the mandate of UNEP, while afforestation and deforestation are potentially significant issues for parties to the Kyoto Protocol and the Convention on Climate Change. Where such cross-cutting areas of policy are involved, no single forum is self-evidently the right one to undertake the development of new law.[80] Yet the choice of forum may affect not only the perspective from which the issues are approached but also the constituencies most likely to become involved and whose interests are most strongly favoured by the governmental representatives concerned. To give responsibility for a convention on forests to FAO, for example, would tend to

---

[78] On the UN's general contribution to international law see Joyner (ed), *The United Nations and International Law* (Cambridge, 1997) and on the environment see Birnie, in Roberts and Kingsbury, *United Nations, Divided World*, Ch 10.

[79] See *infra*, Chs 10, 3 respectively.

[80] The UN first established an Intergovernmental Panel on Forests, then an Intergovernmental Forum on Forests, then finally the UN Forum on Forests to co-ordinate policy and to recommend a programme of action. For the outcome see the Non-Legally Binding Instrument on All Types of Forests adopted by UNGA Res 62/98 (2008).

favour the perspectives of agriculture and forestry ministries and the relevant industries. To give it to UNEP would be more likely to favour environmental ministries
and organizations. In either case, the influence of developing countries may not be as
strong as it is in the General Assembly, and forests are a matter of strong interest to a
number of important developing states. In such circumstances there is a tendency for
the UNGA to take upon itself responsibility for coordinating action.[81]

Moreover, even a specialized agency with undisputed competence may not be the
best forum to take the relevant measures. Specialized agencies, both national and
international, tend to be strongly influenced by special interests and particular ministries. For instance, IMO, dominated by shipping states, has been notably reluctant to
strengthen international law relating to flag of convenience vessels.[82] FAO, in which
fishing states have a powerful voice, may be slow to react to unsustainable practices
such as drift-netting or flag of convenience trawling. In all of these cases it may become
necessary for the General Assembly with its universal membership and broader view
to take action, as it did when adopting a ban on driftnet fishing,[83] or establishing an
inter-agency task force on flags of convenience in response to lobbying by Greenpeace,
the International Union for the Conservation of Nature (IUCN), and the International
Transport Workers' Federation.[84]

Coordination of the policies of so many different international organizations necessarily falls to the UN, specifically the General Assembly, the Secretary General, or
ECOSOC. Thus, when the General Assembly endorsed the 1992 Rio Declaration
on Environment and Development, referring to its 'fundamental principles for
the achievement of sustainable development', it also called on the Commission on
Sustainable Development and the UN Secretary General to promote incorporation
of the principles of the declaration in the implementation of Agenda 21 *and in UN
programmes and processes*, and urged governments to promote their widespread dissemination.[85] The Rio Agenda has gradually affected the application and the development of law and policy by most of the relevant international organizations, including
FAO, IMO, The World Bank, and the WTO, as well as by treaty bodies such as the
International Tropical Timber Organization and the European Energy Charter.[86]
International lawmaking by all of these organizations on issues such as the precautionary approach, sustainable use of natural resources, and environmental impact
assessment reflects the changes brought about through the mechanism of UN soft law
since 1992.

The point is not that the General Assembly has usurped the powers of other bodies,
merely that it can perform a necessary role in bringing some measure of consistency to

---

[81] For another example see UNGA Res 59/25 (2004), which gives directions on fisheries policy to FAO,
IMO, and UNEP.

[82] See *infra*, section 4.

[83] UNGA Res 44/225 (1989); 45/197 (1990); 46/215 (1991); 59/25 (2004). See Rothwell, in Shelton (ed),
Commitment and Compliance (Oxford, 2000) 121–45.

[84] Consisting of the UN, FAO, IMO, UNEP, UNCTAD, ILO, and OECD. See UN Doc A/59/63 (2004) *Rept
of the Consultative Group on Flag State Implementation*.

[85] UNGA Res 47/190 (1992) and 48/191 (1993).   [86] See *infra*, Ch 3.

the policies and lawmaking activities of an otherwise diverse range of organizations. However, there is also good reason for scepticism concerning the UN's performance in coordinating the complex array of institutions of global environmental governance. ECOSOC is notoriously 'unable to rise to this task'.[87] Frequent complaints are that it does not use the resources at its disposal adequately, and that the relationship between the internal divisions and activities of the UN vis-à-vis the rest of the UN 'family' is incoherent and unnecessarily complex.[88] As a Director General of IUCN pointed out: 'Despite all the emphasis on co-ordination...the programmes of UN agencies, and other organizations, including my own, are still conceived too independently, operated too separately and involve too many overlaps and inefficiencies'.[89] Nor does UNGA have the constitutional power to direct the policies of bodies such as the WTO, The World Bank, or ad hoc treaty COPs and commissions: at most it can only request or urge them to act.

(b) The Security Council

The Security Council has more power, but a narrower role, than the General Assembly. Composed of fifteen states, and dominated by the five permanent members, its decisions on measures to restore international peace and security under Chapter VII of the Charter are binding on all UN member states unless vetoed by one of the permanent members.[90] Its post-cold war practice shows how broad an interpretation can be given to the phrase 'international peace and security'.[91] Some authors have used the concept of 'environmental security' to envisage a greater role for the Security Council in dealing with environmental threats and emergencies.[92] Measures to promote environmental protection may in some circumstances be necessary for the maintenance of international peace and security, thus giving the Security Council power to take mandatory action under Chapter VII, but 'the language of the Charter, not to speak of the clear record of the original meaning, does not easily lend itself to such an interpretation'.[93] The Council has acted cautiously in this respect, using its Chapter VII powers only once, to hold Iraq responsible in international law for environmental damage inflicted on Kuwait during the 1991 Gulf war.[94] In 2007 it also held its first ever debate on climate change. Moreover, although the Security Council is not formally a lawmaking body, since 9/11 it has started to use its mandatory powers to adopt a small

---

[87] Chambers (ed), *Reforming International Environmental Governance* (Tokyo, 2005) 35.

[88] For a succinct analysis see Chambers, loc cit, 13–39.

[89] Holdgate, 19 *EPL* (1989) 86, 92. See also Szasz, in Brown Weiss, *Environmental Change and International Law* (Tokyo, 1992) 340–84.

[90] UN Charter, Articles 23–5, 27, 41–2.

[91] For differing views of the limits to Security Council powers see chapters by Gowlland-Debbas and Nolte in Byers (ed), *The Role of Law in International Politics* (Oxford, 2000).

[92] Timoshenko, in Weiss (ed), *Environmental Change and International Law* (Tokyo, 1992) Ch 13; Elliott, in Chambers (ed), *Reforming International Environmental Governance* but for contrary views see Szasz, ibid, 359–61; Tinker, 59 *Tennessee LR* (1992) 787.

[93] Szasz, in Brown Weiss, *Environmental Change and International Law*, 359.

[94] UNSC Res 687. See *infra*, Ch 4, section 2.

number of binding resolutions on anti-terrorism measures laying down general rules for all states.[95] There is no inherent reason why the Council should not also legislate in the same way on environmental matters in sufficiently serious circumstances.

(c) ECOSCOC and the Commission on Sustainable Development

In the UN Charter the Economic and Social Council (ECOSOC) is the principal UN organ responsible for the promotion of international cooperation on economic and social matters.[96] In respect to the implementation of Rio Agenda 21, the 2002 World Summit on Sustainable Development (WSSD) reaffirmed ECOSOC as 'the central mechanism for the co-ordination of the United Nations system and its specialized agencies and supervision of subsidiary bodies, in particular its functional commissions…'.[97] It is also the body to which UN specialized agencies, commissions and programmes report, and with which NGOs may have consultative status.[98]

If the perceived weakness of the UN has been the duplication of effort in the sectorally organized, unsystematic array of UN in-house bodies, specialized agencies, and other entities concerned with sustainable development and the environment, then ECOSOC is part of the problem.[99] UNCED rejected proposals for re-instituting UNEP's coordinating role, or establishing an Intergovernmental Standing Committee in a supervisory role, or adapting the role of the Security Council or Trusteeship Council to take on environmental responsibilities.[100] Instead, proposals for the establishment of a further subsidiary body of ECOSOC were regarded as the most attractive and politically feasible idea, and were adopted in the form of a Commission on Sustainable Development (CSD).[101] The CSD consists of representatives of 53 states elected by ECOSOC for three-year terms. It meets annually and had its first substantive session in June 1993.

The principal responsibility of the CSD is to 'Keep under review the implementation of Agenda 21, recognizing that it is a dynamic programme that could evolve over time…'[102] Specifically, the General Assembly gave it the following tasks: to promote incorporation of the Rio Declaration and the Forest Principles in the implementation of Agenda 21; to monitor progress in the implementation of Agenda 21, the Rio Declaration and the Forest Principles by governments and the UN system; to review the adequacy of the financial and technology transfer provisions, inter alia; to enhance

---

[95] Two striking and unprecedented examples are SC resolutions 1373 (2001) and 1540 (2005) both Chapter VII resolutions passed in the aftermath of the 11 September 2001 attacks in New York and Washington and later atrocities.

[96] UN Charter, Articles 55, 62. See Rosenthal, in Weiss and Daws, *Oxford Handbook on the UN*, Ch 7.

[97] UN, *Report of the WSSD*, UN Doc A/CONF 199/20 (2002), 'Plan of Implementation', para 144.

[98] UN Charter, Articles 64, 71.

[99] See Sand, *Issues Learned in Global Environmental Governance* (Washington, 1990); Ayling, 9 *JEL* (1997) 243.

[100] See Birnie in Roberts and Kingsbury (eds), *United Nations, Divided World*, 373–9.

[101] The CSD was created by UNGA Res47/191 (1992). See Mensah, in Werksman (ed), *Greening International Institutions*, Ch 2; Desai, *Institutionalizing International Environmental Law*, 189–94.

[102] UNGA Res 47/191, para 4 (c).

the dialogue between the UN, NGOs and other outside bodies; to consider information on implementation of environmental conventions, and to make recommendations to ECOSOC and the General Assembly on all these matters.

These responsibilities are potentially wide-ranging and significant, but also over-
broad and vague.[103] In effect the CSD is a permanent diplomatic forum for continued
negotiation on all matters concerned with sustainable development policy, but one
with no powers, few resources, and limited influence. Although Agenda 21 is not a
legally binding document and is not written in normative language, review by the
CSD of its implementation and of the problems faced by governments could give it
somewhat greater significance. Some comparison can be drawn in this respect with
the UN Human Rights Commission, which for many years has monitored and promoted implementation of the non-legally binding Universal Declaration on Human
Rights. It took over twenty years before the UNHRC decided to establish its present
system of review and complaint investigation by independent experts, but in doing so
it clearly demonstrated the possibility that significant new powers can emerge from
unpromising beginnings.[104]

It remains difficult to point to any comparable progress resulting from the CSD's
deliberations. Although it receives voluntary reports from states and other UN institutions, with limited time and little continuity of membership, none of it independent, the Commission has not chosen to review either the performance of individual
countries or the implementation and effectiveness of environmental treaties. Its deliberations have remained entirely within the confines of policy recommendations, such
as the 'Programme for the Further Implementation of Agenda 21' prepared by the
Commission, adopted by the General Assembly in 1997 and reaffirmed by the WSSD
in 2002.[105] Significantly, in its report to the WSSD , the Commission felt it necessary to
stress that this should not be seen as an opportunity to renegotiate Agenda 21, indicating the obvious fragility of whatever commitments that document may represent.[106]
Another unresolved problem is that UNCED and the WSSD left unchanged the separate and independent status of the UN Environment Programme (UNEP), the UN
Development Programme (UNDP), the UN Conference on Trade and Development
(UNCTAD), and the specialized agencies. The report of the 2002 World Summit
acknowledged some of these problems, and called for the CSD to be strengthened,
but that body can do little about the competing institutional agendas beyond pointing
them out and attempting to instil some policy coherence.

---

[103] Beyerlin, 56 *ZAÖRV* (1996) 602, 622. UNGA Res S/19-2 (1997) calls for a more focused approach
[104] See the Resolution 1235 and 1503 procedures as described in Alston (ed), *The UN and Human Rights*
(Oxford, 1992) 144–81, and Farer and Gaer, in Roberts and Kingsbury (eds), *UN, Divided World*, 260–3.
[105] See UN, *Report of the WSSD*, UN Doc A/Conf 199/20 (2002), 'Plan of Implementation', paras 145–50.
[106] ECOSOC, *Off Recs* (2000) Supp 9, UN Doc E/CN 17/2000.

3(3) THE UN ENVIRONMENT PROGRAMME

(a) UNEP's mandate

UNEP is the only UN body with a mandate to focus specifically on environmental issues. Although only a 'programme' it has been the most active UN body in the development of multilateral environmental agreements, as well as promoting treaty implementation and coordinating some of the growing number of treaty secretariats and meetings of parties.[107] It was established as a subsidiary body by the General Assembly in 1972, following the Stockholm Conference.[108] Fifty-eight member states are elected triennially to its General Council by the General Assembly on the basis of equitable geographic distribution. UNEP's original terms of reference envisaged a limited role:

To promote international cooperation in the field of the environment and to recommend, as appropriate, policies to this end; [and] to provide general policy guidance for the direction and co-ordination of environmental programmes within a United Nations System.[109]

UNEP was thus expected to act as a catalyst in developing and coordinating an environmental focus in the programmes of other UN bodies rather than initiate action itself. Its first director said its role was 'to complexify', that is, to 'remind others of, and help them to take into account all the systems, interactions and ramifications implied in their work'. He observed that it was the lack of this cross-sectoral, cross-disciplinary view that had led to many environmental problems.[110]

The status and future role of UNEP were the subject of debate before, during, and after the Rio Conference in 1992.[111] Although its activities had to some extent helped in 'greening' specialized agencies, including The World Bank, and resulted in some important lawmaking innovations, it had not succeeded in coordinating the environmental work of UN and other bodies. Moreover, the creation of the CSD, the Global Environment Facility (GEF), and an Inter-agency Committee on Sustainable Development, added yet more competing institutions with overlapping responsibilities, and potentially diluted UNEP's influence within the UN system still further. Thus it did not have a clear role in the 1992 Rio Conference. Proposals for transforming it into a specialized agency, or creating a new environmental agency, attracted little support in the UNCED preparatory meetings. Developed states rejected both

---

[107] UNCED Agenda 21, Ch 38, para H (1)(h); UNGA Res S/19-2, 19 September 1997; UNGA Res 53/242, 28 July 1999; 1997 Nairobi Declaration on the Role and Mandate of UNEP, adopted by UNEP Governing Council decision 19/1 (1997).

[108] UNGA Res 2997 (XXVII) (1972). See generally, Birnie, 20 *Melb ULR* (1995) 80–93.   [109] Ibid.

[110] UNEP Governing Council, *Introductory Statement by the Executive Director* (11 February 1975) UNEP/GC/31, UNEP/GC/31/Add 1, UNEP/GC/31/Add 2, UNEP/GC/31/Add 3.

[111] See Tarasofsky in Chambers (ed), *Reforming International Environmental Governance*, 66; Desai, *Institutionalizing International Environmental Law*, 166–88; Kimball, *Forging International Agreements: Strengthening Intergovernmental Institutions for Environment and Development* (Washington, 1992); Szasz, in Brown Weiss (ed), *Environmental Change and International Law* (Tokyo, 1992) 340; Thacher, in Hurrell and Kingsbury (eds), *The International Politics of the Environment*, 183; Sand, *Lessons Learned in Global Environmental Governance* (Washington DC, 1990).

the extra costs and political implications of such a change, and there was no enthusiasm for more bureaucratization of the UN. There was more support for strengthening
UNEP in its existing role and location. Agenda 21 called on UNEP to promote cooperation on policymaking, monitoring, and assessment, and mandated it specifically to
give priority, inter alia, to development of international environmental law, environmental impact assessment and auditing, dissemination of information, and promotion of regional and subregional cooperation.[112] Yet another 'priority' was accorded to
coordinating ('clustering') the growing number of environmental treaties, and their
secretariats.[113]

A further attempt to enhance UNEP's role flowed from a special session of the
General Assembly held in 1997 to review progress since Rio. The decision was taken
to try to revitalize UNEP, establishing a Global Ministerial Forum to give it a more
authoritative sense of direction and greater prominence within the UN system.[114] The
UN Environmental Programme was described as 'the leading global environmental
authority that sets the global environmental agenda, promotes the coherent implementation of the environmental dimension of sustainable development within the United
Nations system, and serves as an authoritative advocate for the global environment'.
The extended mandate envisaged in Agenda 21 was confirmed. In particular, UNEP
would assume responsibility for coordination of UN environmental treaties and their
implementation, as well as the further development of international environmental
law. It would also provide scientific, technical and policy advice to the Commission on
Sustainable Development.

Subsequent decisions have sought to improve UNEP's funding to enable it to carry
out its responsibilities, have called for stronger linkages between UNEP and the GEF,
and initiated a broader review of the UN's whole range of environment-related bodies.[115] These are potentially significant developments, which are consistent with the
2002 WSSD's emphasis on greater coherence and collaboration between international
institutions.[116] It remains the case, however, that the WSSD specifically affirmed the
coordinating role of ECOSOC, not that of UNEP, and did nothing to re-arrange the
present architecture of international environmental governance. It is hard to see how
this can redress the 'sense of policy incoherence among the different international
bodies dealing with environmental issues'.[117]

(b) UNEP's role in developing international environmental law

It is notable that UNEP was not initially given a specific mandate to develop international environmental law. Not until the adoption of Agenda 21 was such a task

---

[112] UNCED Agenda 21, Ch 29.

[113] Ibid, Ch 38, and UNGA Res 55/198 (2001). See *infra*, section 3(3).

[114] UNGA Res S/19-2, Programme for the Further Implementation of Agenda 21, endorsing the Nairobi
Declaration adopted at the 19th Governing session of UNEP in 1997. See Desai, 40 *Ind JIL* (2000) 455.

[115] UNGA Res 53/242 (1999); 1997 Nairobi Declaration on the Role and Mandate of UNEP, adopted by
UNEP Governing Council decision 19/1 (1997).

[116] UN, *Report of the WSSD*, UN Doc A/CONF 199/20 (2002), 'Plan of Implementation', paras 139–40.

[117] Tarasofsky in Chambers (ed), *Reforming International Environmental Governance*, 70.

explicitly envisaged. Nonetheless the necessity for promotion of both binding and non-binding instruments to achieve its purposes was appreciated from the outset. An ambitious Environment Programme initiated in 1975 had only been partially achieved by the end of UNEP's first decade.[118] In order to give greater focus to its subsequent lawmaking efforts, a 'Programme for the Development and Periodic Review of Environmental Law' (referred to as the 'Montevideo Programme')[119] was adopted in 1982. This established priorities for the following decade, and included the adoption of conventions on the ozone layer and transboundary transport of hazardous wastes. The Montevideo Programme would be implemented both by UNEP itself and jointly with other UN bodies, regional organizations, and NGOs including IUCN. It was revised in 1993 and again in 2001 to respond to the recommendations and decisions of UNCED and subsequent reviews.[120]

Agenda 21, together with subsequent resolutions and decisions, for the first time expressly mandated UNEP to undertake further development of international environmental law, as well as promoting its implementation and coordinating the growing number of treaty secretariats and meetings of parties.[121] The task of coordination was intended 'to achieve coherence and compatibility, and to avoid overlapping or conflicting regulation', between existing environmental regulatory regimes and new ones,[122] but in performing this role, UNEP 'should strive to promote the effective implementation of those conventions in a manner consistent with the provisions of the conventions and the decisions of the parties'.[123]

Principle 27 of the Rio Declaration and Chapter 39 of Agenda 21 also called for development of international law on sustainable development and set out certain objectives. Particular emphasis was placed on participation by developing countries, on taking account of their different capabilities, on the need for international standards to be based on consensus and non-discrimination, and for improvements in the implementation and administration of international agreements. At the request of the Commission on Sustainable Development, UNEP initiated a study of 'the concept, requirements and implications of sustainable development and international law'.[124]

---

[118] See generally UNEP, *Environmental Law in the UNEP* (Nairobi, 1990); Petsonk, 5 *Am UJILP* (1990) 351; Desai, 40 *Ind JIL* (2000) 455.

[119] *Report of the Ad Hoc Meeting of Senior Government Officials Expert in Environmental Law*, UNEP/GC 10/5/Add 2, Annex, Ch 11 (1981).

[120] UNEP/Env Law/2/3 (1991), UNEP/Env Law/4/4 (2001).

[121] Agenda 21, Ch 38, para H (1)(h); UNGA Res S/19-2 (1997); UNGA Res 53/242 (1999); Desai, 40 *Ind JIL* (2000) 455. See also the 1997 Nairobi Declaration on the Role and Mandate of UNEP, adopted by UNEP Governing Council decision 19/1 (1997) which refers to 'international environmental law aiming at sustainable development.' Timoshenko and Berman, in Werksman (ed), *Greening International Institutions*, 43, conclude that: 'Apparently, this mandate is wider than just the co-ordination of the environmental conventions' secretariats, and includes the co-ordination of the whole process of international lawmaking in the field of sustainable development.'

[122] Timoshenko and Berman, loc cit, 43.

[123] UNGA Res S/19-2 (1997) para 123. On the pros and cons of clustering MEAs see Oberthur in Chambers (ed), *Reforming International Environmental Governance*, 40–65.

[124] *Infra*, Ch 3, section 3.

UNEP's achievements are considerable, if measured purely by the number and importance of the legal instruments for which it has been responsible, but its catalytic role in the legal field was clearly strongest during its first two decades. Its contribution to international lawmaking can be grouped loosely into three categories: (i) conclusion of international agreements;[125] (ii) development of soft-law principles, guidelines, and standards;[126] (iii) provision of assistance for drafting of national environmental legislation and administration in developing countries.[127] It pioneered both the use of so-called 'framework treaties' and 'soft law' instruments.[128] It has also sought to codify the law on shared natural resources.[129] The Regional Seas Programme introduced some innovatory concepts, such as protected areas and especially sensitive areas, and now covers some fourteen regions.[130] UNEP guidelines provided the basis for negotiation of the 1989 Basel Convention for the Control of Transboundary Movement of Hazardous Waste, and resulted in the adoption of further regional agreements, and more recently (with FAO) a Convention on the Prior Informed Consent Procedure for Certain Hazardous Chemicals and Pesticides in International Trade.[131] Guidelines on environmental impact assessment have resulted in refinement and adoption of these practices on a wider basis and their inclusion in the 1991 Espoo Convention on Environmental Impact Assessment in a Transboundary Context.[132]

We will examine in later chapters the results of UNEP's lawmaking efforts. Their approach has been based on first formulating the scientific positions, then developing legal strategies, and in the process building political support. In the support-building process many compromises have to be arrived at, especially in the interests of maintaining a 'sustainable development' policy. Thus the conventions are replete with constructive ambiguities and the more controversial issues are often left, at least initially, to soft law, the procedures and status of which are often made deliberately obscure.

---

[125] These include the so-called 'Regional Seas Conventions', on which see *infra*, Ch 7; 1979 Convention on the Conservation of Migratory Species of Wild Animals 1979, *infra*, Ch 12; 1985 Vienna Convention for the Protection of the Ozone Layer, *infra*, Ch 6; 1989 Basel Convention on the Control of Transboundary Movements of Hazardous Wastes and their Disposal, *infra*, Ch 8; 1992 Convention on Biological Diversity, *infra*, Ch 11; 1998 Convention on the Prior Informed Consent for Certain Hazardous Chemicals and Pesticides in International Trade (in collaboration with FAO), *infra*, Ch 8; 2001 Convention on Persistent Organic Pollutants, *infra*, Ch 8.

[126] These include the 1978 Principles of Conduct in the Field of the Environment for the Guidance of states in the Conservation and Harmonious Utilisation of Natural Resources Shared by Two or More States; 1985 Montreal Guidelines for the Protection of the Marine Environment against Pollution from Land-based Sources; 1987 Conclusions on Legal Aspects Concerning the Environment related to Offshore Mining and Drilling Carried Out Within the Limits of National Jurisdiction; 1987 Cairo Guidelines and Principles for the Environmentally Sound Management of Hazardous Waste; 1987 Goals and Principles of Environmental Impact Assessment; 1989 London Guidelines for the Exchange of Information on Chemicals in International Trade; 1995 Global Programme of Action for the Protection of the Marine Environment from Land-based Activities; 2002 Guidelines on Compliance with and Enforcement of MEAs.

[127] See UNEP, *New Directions in Environmental Legislation and Administration Particularly in Developing Countries* (Nairobi, 1989) and *Environmental Law in the UNEP*, 36–40.

[128] *Supra*, Ch 1.

[129] 1978 Principles of Conduct etc in the Conservation and Harmonious Utilisation of Natural Resources Shared by Two or More States, *infra*, Chs 6, 11.

[130] *Infra*, Ch 7.   [131] *Infra*, Ch 8.   [132] *Infra*, Ch 3, section 4(3).

The General Assembly only asked states to 'use' the UNEP Principles on Shared National Resources as 'guidelines and recommendations in formulating conventions'; the Weather Modification Provisions were for 'consideration in the formulation and implementation of programmes and activities' relating to that field;[133] the Offshore Mining Conclusions were to be considered 'when formulating national legislation or undertaking negotiations for the conclusion of international agreements'.[134] In promulgating the World Charter for Nature the General Assembly was more peremptory: it stated that 'the principles set forth in the present Charter *shall* be reflected in the law and practice of each State, as well as at the international level', though this phraseology alone does not render this Charter binding.[135] The Montreal Guidelines on Land-based Pollution were addressed to 'states and international organizations', which were asked to 'take them into account' in the process of developing appropriate agreements and national legislation.[136] The Cairo Guidelines on Waste Management were merely addressed to states 'with a view to assisting them in the process of developing *policies*' for this purpose[137] and the London Guidelines on Information Exchange on Traded Chemicals were presented to them to '*help* them in the process of increasing chemical safety in all countries'.[138] Nonetheless, the distinction between 'hard' and 'soft' law becomes blurred as states begin to act on these recommendations or incorporate them in treaties.

3(4) A GLOBAL ENVIRONMENTAL ORGANIZATION?

UNEP remains a programme of the UN; in that sense it may have been revitalized, but it has not yet been reformed. Should it be turned into a fully-fledged UN specialized agency, comparable, perhaps, to the World Trade Organization?[139] The main arguments in favour are that its standing, funding, and political influence would be enhanced, especially if it were more closely linked or integrated with the GEF, and perhaps the CSD, as well as hosting and coordinating the secretariats of the major environmental treaties. This, it is said, would reduce overlaps and duplication, while improving effectiveness. Protagonists rightly point to fragmentation of existing structures, the relative weakness of UNEP as the principal UN body with general environmental competence, and the powerful focus the IMF, the World Bank, and the WTO bring to economic development. Several models are canvassed by those in favour. The most radical would merge existing bodies into a powerful new intergovernmental environmental organization with decision-making and enforcement powers. A less

---

[133] UNEP G/C Decision 8/74 (1980).   [134] UNGA Res 37/217 (1982).

[135] UNGA Res 37/7 (1982). See *infra*, Ch 3.   [136] UNEP GC Decision 13/18 (II) (1985).

[137] UNEP GC Decision 14/30 (1987) emphasis added

[138] UNEP GC Decision 14/27 (1987) emphasis added

[139] On proposals for a new UN specialized agency see Palmer, 86 *AJIL* (1992) 259; Esty, *Greening the GATT: Trade, Environment and the Future* (Washington, 1994); Dunoff, 19 *Harv.ELR* (1995) 241, 257–70; Ayling, 9 *JEL* (1997) 243; Desai, 40 *Ind JIL* (2000) 455; Charnovitz in Chambers (ed), *Reforming International Environmental Governance*, 93–123; Desai, *Institutionalizing International Environmental Law*, Ch 6; Biermann and Bauer, *A World Environment Organization* (Aldershot, 2005).

radical vision would merge existing environmental institutions and treaties into a new organization similar to the WTO. The least radical choice would simply upgrade UNEP into a UN specialized agency rather like IMO. Sceptics remain unconvinced by some of these arguments. To them a new environmental organization is politically unrealistic and would not be any better at securing the necessary decisions. Insofar as reform is necessary to enhance the efficiency of the present eclectic system, they favour a simple clustering of MEAs within UNEP and greater efforts to coordinate international action.[140]

There is room for some scepticism. A UN environment agency could not monopolize the field. It could not take over the environmental responsibilities of other specialized agencies, such as FAO or IMO: the work of these bodies has an important environmental dimension which cannot be separated from their general responsibilities. Nor is it evident how coordination of environmental treaty regimes would be any easier if UNEP were a specialized agency instead of a programme. The diversity of decision-making requirements and non-compliance procedures is the most obvious element of MEAs that could benefit from greater coherence and the stronger institutional framework provided by WTO, but there are strong political reasons why it is easier to list endangered species under the Convention on International Trade in Endangered Species (CITES) than to list dangerous chemicals under the PIC Convention,[141] and why MEA non-compliance procedures differ radically.[142] States are no more likely to negotiate or revise such agreements under a new agency than they are at present. Nor has UNEP's existing status stopped it performing a considerable lawmaking role. It already provides a forum for negotiation, if desired. States would be no more or less likely than before to comply with their treaty commitments. Unlike the WTO, which faces a barrage of disputes concerning compliance with trade treaties, there is no evidence of any need for new institutional arrangements to handle the far smaller number of disputes that arise under environmental treaties, and which have been quite satisfactorily resolved through existing non-compliance procedures or negotiation.[143] Moreover, the reluctance or inability of IMO and IAEA to monitor compliance with treaty commitments[144] does not suggest that having the status of an international organization necessarily contributes anything to the effectiveness of environmental treaties; in many cases the non-compliance procedures of autonomous treaty supervisory bodies considered in Chapter 4 are significantly more impressive in this role. There may well be efficiencies to be gained from a 'clustering' of secretariat services and non-compliance procedures within UNEP. Certainly, there is a need for a system that can ensure the integration of environmental and development objectives in a more balanced and efficient manner,[145] but a more centralized, bureaucratic,

---

[140] All of these are arguments are comprehensively addressed in Biermann and Bauer, op cit. On clustering see Von Moltke, in Winter (ed), *Multilevel Governance of Global Environmental Change* (Cambridge, 2006) 409–29.

[141] See *infra*, Chs 8, 12.   [142] See *infra*, Ch 4, section 3.

[143] See *infra*, Ch 4, section 3.   [144] See *infra*, Chs 7, 9.

[145] Ayling, 9 *JEL* (1997) 243, 268; Chambers (ed), *Reforming International Environmental Governance*, 13–39.

and entrenched institution may be less likely to influence the system as a whole, or to facilitate the cross-sectoral integration that Agenda 21 seeks to promote. As the UN's principal environmental body, UNEP needs to be more effective; what remains to be demonstrated is that changing its status will have that result.

4 OTHER INTERNATIONAL ORGANIZATIONS

4(1) UN SPECIALIZED AGENCIES AND RELATED BODIES

Space does not permit a detailed explanation of the environment-related work of all the agencies which, through agreements with ECOSOC, have entered into a special relationship with the UN. Some have a clearly defined mandate to protect the environment and promote sustainable development, others only a tangential involvement in these tasks.[146] For our purposes the most directly relevant are the Food and Agricultural Organization (FAO), the International Maritime Organization (IMO), the World Bank, and other related organizations, including the International Atomic Energy Agency (IAEA) and the World Trade Organization (WTO). There are also a number of UN regional bodies with environmental responsibilities. Within the UN system specialized agencies and regional commissions are the principal repositories and disseminators of technical expertise, and it is this attribute which arguably constitutes their most significant contribution to the lawmaking process. Moreover, NGOs and national experts often work closely with specialized agencies, sometimes to a greater extent than is possible in the UN itself.

The range of lawmaking activities undertaken by the specialized agencies and related bodies is very varied. Their most important role is best understood as international standard setting.[147] The adoption of soft-law codes and guidelines on nuclear installations by the IAEA, the Codex Alimentarius of the WHO and FAO, the radiological protection standards established by the International Commission on Radiation Protection, or the annexes to IMO treaties on ship safety and pollution typify this aspect of their work.[148] Essentially technical in character, these instruments seek to establish internationally agreed minimum standards for the regulation of internationally important industries. Their precise legal status will depend on the organization involved, the basis on which the standards are adopted and the form of the instrument.

Specialized agencies and regional commissions also negotiate and adopt multilateral treaties. In many cases, these treaties provide the legal framework for international

---

[146] E.g. the World Health Organization (WHO), the World Meteorological Organization (WMO), and the International Labour Organization (ILO). The work of these bodies is referred to when appropriate in later chapters.

[147] The seminal study is Contini and Sand, 66 *AJIL* (1972) 37.

[148] See Kirgis in Joyner (ed), *The UN and International Law*, 82–8.

regulatory regimes which provide the basis for standard-setting, monitoring processes, and compliance mechanisms. The regulation of maritime and nuclear safety, security, and liability by IMO and IAEA respectively are among the most important examples of this genre. Both organizations are responsible for adopting new treaties and treaty amendments, revising or adding annexes, and setting additional soft-law standards on related matters. In effect they each constitute a standing diplomatic forum, whose ongoing oversight enables lawmaking to evolve relatively quickly in response to new problems, priorities, or opportunities. Less convincingly, they also enable member states to exercise some degree of oversight over implementation and compliance by member states.

Lastly, major UN agreements such as the 1982 UNCLOS and the Convention on Biological Diversity, or policy statements such as Agenda 21 of the Rio Conference, often require further implementation by specialized agencies.

4(2) UN REGIONAL COMMISSIONS

There are five UN regional economic commissions but only the UN Economic Commission for Europe (UNECE) has made a significant contribution to the development of regional environmental law. This organization has fifty-five member states, including all of the former Soviet states in the Caucasus and Central Asia, as well as the United States and Canada. A Committee on Environmental Protection, established in 1994, provides policy direction on environment and sustainable development, but much of the political impetus has come from the Organization for Security and Cooperation in Europe (OSCE). It is this organization which has been the principal catalyst for environmental lawmaking by the UN body.

UNECE's most important environmental achievement has been to establish a framework for environmental cooperation and the harmonization of environmental law in Eastern Europe and the former Soviet Union, thus ensuring greater compatibility with standards in Western Europe. This development began in 1975, when the Helsinki Final Act recognized the existence of a duty in international law to ensure that activities carried out within the territory of member states do not cause environmental degradation in other states and designated UNECE to coordinate cooperation on matters of air and water pollution control, protection of the marine environment, land use, nature conservation, and human settlements.[149] The first substantive achievement of these commitments was the negotiation under UNECE auspices of the 1979 Convention on Long-range Transboundary Air Pollution.[150]

The 1989 Sofia Declaration on Protection of the Environment recommended the elaboration of conventions on pollution of watercourses and transboundary accidents, and the 1990 Paris Charter committed the organization to intensification of efforts to protect and improve the environment 'in order to restore and maintain a

---

[149] See Chossudovsky, *East-West Diplomacy for Environment in the United Nations* (New York, 1989).
[150] *Infra*, Ch 6.

sound ecological balance in air, water and soil'. It emphasized the 'significant' role of a well-informed society in enabling the public and individuals to take environmental initiatives, as well as the need to encourage clean and low-waste technology and the importance of effective implementation of environmental agreements and systematic evaluation of compliance. The 1995 Sofia Declaration and the 1998 Aarhus Declaration by the Ministers of Environment of the UNECE also set out further objectives for the development of environmental policy and law in the region, stressing in particular the need for energy efficiency, nuclear safety, minimization of transboundary water pollution, elimination of persistent organic pollutants, and protection of biodiversity and landscapes.

These objectives have once again been pursued through UNECE. The results include the 1991 Espoo Convention on Environmental Impact Assessment in a Transboundary Context, the 1992 Helsinki Convention on Transboundary Effects of Industrial Accidents, the 1992 Helsinki Convention on Protection and Use of Transboundary Watercourses and Lakes, and the 1998 Aarhus Convention on Access to Information, Public Participation in Decision-making and Access to Justice in Environmental Matters,[151] in addition to the adoption of further protocols to the 1979 Convention on Transboundary Air Pollution. The impact of some of these agreements has been significant, notably in harmonizing legislation and practice on EIA,[152] and in the negotiation of further agreements covering environmental protection of the Rhine, Meuse, Scheldt and Danube.[153]

4(3) THE FOOD AND AGRICULTURE ORGANIZATION

FAO was created for the purpose, inter alia, of improving efficiency in the production of food and agricultural produce.[154] Broadly defined, its mandate also covers forestry, plant genetic resources, fisheries, and freshwater resources. It is empowered to collect information, promote research, furnish assistance to governments, and make recommendations on conservation of natural resources and other matters. All member states belong to a Conference of the Parties. A smaller Council, assisted by various committees, exercises powers delegated by the Conference.

Within its specialized sphere, FAO has promoted international environmental law-making in various ways.[155] Article XIV of its constitution empowers the Organization to 'approve' conventions and agreements negotiated, drafted and submitted by a technical commission or conference composed of member states. While the majority of Article XIV treaties mainly establish regional fisheries commissions rather than adding to the corpus of international law, a few have laid down rules of more general significance, most notably the 1993 Agreement to Promote Compliance with International Conservation and Management Measures by Fishing Vessels on the

---

[151] *Infra*, Ch 5.   [152] *Infra*, Ch 3, section 4(3).   [153] *Infra*, Ch 10.
[154] 1945 Constitution of the FAO.
[155] See Dobbert in Schachter and Joyner (eds), *United Nations Legal Order* (ASIL, 1995) 902.

High Seas ('Compliance Agreement') and the 2001 International Treaty on Plant Genetic Resources for Food and Agriculture. FAO technical consultations have provided expert and influential advice in the negotiation of several UN treaties, including the 1958 Convention on Fishing and Conservation of the Living Resources of the High Seas, the 1982 UNCLOS and the 1995 Agreement on Straddling and Highly Migratory Fish Stocks. The Organization collaborated with UNEP in securing the negotiation and adoption of the 1998 Convention on the Prior Informed Consent Procedure for Certain Hazardous Chemicals and Pesticides in International Trade. Finally, when the adoption of binding agreements is not possible, FAO has made some use of non-binding agreements, including the 1983 International Undertaking on Plant Genetic Resources, now superseded by the 2001 treaty considered below.

FAO has also been the principal body responsible for developing international fisheries law and promoting implementation of the fisheries provisions of the 1982 UNCLOS, the 1995 UN Fish Stocks Agreement and Agenda 21 of the 1992 UN Conference on Environment and Development.[156] It has employed a mixture of hard and soft law for this purpose, including the 1993 Agreement to Promote Compliance with Conservation Measures on the High Seas,[157] the 1995 Code of Conduct on Responsible Fishing,[158] the 2001 Reykjavik Declaration on Sustainable Fisheries, and various voluntary undertakings.[159] As required by Article XIV of the FAO Constitution, all of these fisheries instruments were considered initially by a 'technical consultation' of industry and government experts; they were then negotiated by consensus in the Committee on Fisheries before adoption by the FAO Council. Here we can see how, in the framework of a UN lawmaking treaty—the 1982 UNCLOS—a specialized agency can further develop the law within its own special field in response to emerging needs and priorities. At the same time, we can also see that a variety of lawmaking instruments allows added flexibility and increases the likelihood of reaching agreement.

FAO played only a limited role in the negotiation of the Convention on Biological Diversity (CBD), but it has subsequently been involved in implementation of the Convention and related elements of Agenda 21. To this end, the International Treaty on Plant Genetic Resources for Food and Agriculture adopted in 2001 replaces the earlier non-binding 1983 Undertaking and creates a multilateral scheme for access to certain agricultural crops, an issue not specifically dealt with in the CBD.[160] Negotiations were initiated by the FAO Council and conducted mainly in the Commission on Genetic Resources for Food and Agriculture, in which a large number of states participated,

---

[156] See Edeson, in Boyle and Freestone (eds), *International Law and Sustainable Development* (Oxford, 1999) Ch 8, and *infra*, Ch 13.

[157] Moore, in Hey (ed), *Developments in International Fisheries Law* (The Hague, 1999) 91–2.

[158] See Edeson, 11 *IJMCL* (1996) 97.

[159] E.g. the International Plans of Action on Longline Fisheries, Conservation and Management of Sharks, Management of Fishing Capacity, adopted by FAO in 1999, and the International Plan of Action on Illegal, Unreported and Unregulated Fishing, adopted in 2001. Some states expressed significant reservations when adopting the 2001 Plan of Action: see FAO, *Rept of the Committee on Fisheries*, 24th Session (2001).

[160] See Dobbert, in Schachter and Joyner (eds), *United Nations Legal Order* 930–8; Raustiala and Victor, 58 *Int Org* (2004) 277.

together with observers from WIPO, the CBD Secretariat, the International Union for the Protection of New Varieties of Plants, and a variety of NGOs and agricultural research institutes. However, the negotiations straddled issues of concern to several other international bodies, including UNEP, WTO, UNCTAD, WIPO, and the Conference of the Parties to the CBD and could have been allocated accordingly.[161] Three factors helped ensure the choice of FAO. First, that is where the issue had previously been dealt with, mainly at the insistence of developing countries, which did not have the same influence or level of participation in WTO. Secondly, the CBD recognized that further negotiations on agricultural biodiversity would be required, and should take place within FAO.[162] FAO's promotion of a new treaty whose objectives included 'harmony with the Convention on Biological Diversity'[163] was not inherently problematic. At Brazil's insistence it became a 'treaty', rather than a 'convention', a meaningless gesture supposed to minimize confusion with the CBD. Thirdly, the United States and other developed countries had already largely secured their objectives in intellectual property negotiations at the WTO, and to that extent whatever happened in FAO would matter less.[164]

4(4) THE INTERNATIONAL MARITIME ORGANIZATION

IMO is the principal body responsible for the international regulation of shipping and thus for the prevention of pollution of sea by ships. Its role as 'the competent organization' in this respect is referred to implicitly in several articles of the 1982 UN Convention on the Law of the Sea.[165] It is empowered to promote 'the general adoption of the highest practicable standards in matters concerning the maritime safety, efficiency of navigation and prevention and control of marine pollution from ships'.[166] Responsibility for regulatory developments is divided between a Maritime Safety Committee (MSC), a Marine Environment Protection Committee (MEPC) established following a recommendation of the 1972 Stockholm Conference,[167] and a Legal Committee.[168] The IMO Council, whose thirty-two members are drawn on an equitable geographical basis from the largest maritime states and other states with a 'special interest in maritime transport and navigation', supervises the work of these

---

[161] See Petit et al, *Why Governments Can't Make Policy: The Case of Plant Genetic Resources* (Lima, 2001) 6; Chambers, 6 *J World Intellectual Property* (2003) 311.

[162] Resolution 3, Nairobi Final Act, 1992 CBD. The parties to the CBD subsequently adopted the Bonn Guidelines on Access to Genetic Resources, but like the CBD itself these are broader than the 2001 Treaty. Moreover they are non-binding. See Chambers, previous note.

[163] Article 1.

[164] See TRIPS Agreement, Article 27(3)(b); Raustiala and Victor, 58 *Int Org* (2004) 277.

[165] Notably Articles 211, 217, 218. See IMO, *Implications of the Entry into Force of the UNCLOS for the IMO*, LEG/MISC/2 (1997).

[166] Article 1, 1948 Convention Establishing the International Maritime Consultative Organization (changed to IMO in 1982).

[167] IMO Res A297 (VIII) (1973). See de La Fayette, 16 *IJMCL* (2001) 155.

[168] See Gaskell, 18 *IJMCL* (2003) 155.

bodies. As a result, the Council is dominated by shipping states,[169] but all member states are represented in the Assembly, the governing body of the organization, and in the various committees referred to above. Coastal states and those with limited maritime interests can thus participate fully in the Organization's main rule-making bodies; however, it does not follow that they will necessarily be influential.

Agenda 21 reiterated the need for IMO to adopt further regulatory measures to address 'degradation of the marine environment', and this is reflected in its subsequent work, which addresses a broader range of environmental concerns than hitherto, including protection of sensitive sea areas and regulation of air and ballast-water pollution from ships.[170] The main criticism of IMO, however, has been the failure of its member states to give enough attention to non-implementation and non-compliance with existing conventions and standards, especially by flag states, many of which are members of the IMO Council. In 1993 IMO established a sub-committee on Flag State Implementation, whose task is 'to identify measures necessary to ensure effective and consistent global implementation of IMO instruments, paying particular attention to the special difficulties faced by developing countries', but the committee has made little progress, and the problem highlights IMO's limited powers as a supervisory body.[171]

IMO has negotiated almost forty conventions, as well as adopting non-binding codes, recommendations and guidelines on related matters. For environmental purposes the most important regulatory treaties are the 1973/78 Convention for the Prevention of Marine Pollution from Ships (MARPOL), the 1974 Convention on the Safety of Life at Sea (SOLAS), and the 2004 Convention for the Control and Management of Ships' Ballast Water.[172] These agreements establish internationally recognized standards for the construction and operation of ships and the prevention of pollution at sea. The principal regulations are found not in the text of the conventions themselves but in annexes which are easily and regularly supplemented or amended by decision of the MEPC or MSC.[173] Apart from their character as treaty law, many of the relevant provisions of these annexes have become 'generally accepted international rules and standards' for the purposes of the 1982 UNCLOS.[174] Another important role for IMO lawmaking is the development of treaty regimes whose principal purpose is to harmonize and progressively develop national law on liability for marine pollution. Some states have begun to question whether these agreements are too favourable to

---

[169] See M'Gonigle and Zacher, *Pollution, Politics and International Law* (London, 1979); Tan, *Vessel-Source Marine Pollution* (Cambridge, 2006) 29–102.

[170] Agenda 21, Ch 17.30. See *Report of the IMO to the Commission on Sustainable Development*, IMO Doc MEPC 37/Inf (1995) and *Report on Follow-Up Action to UNCED*, MEPC 37/10/1, 23 March 1995. On subsequent IMO regulatory developments see Nordquist and Moore (eds), *Current Maritime Issues and the International Maritime Organization* (The Hague, 1999) and *infra*, Ch 7.

[171] Roach, in Nordquist and Moore (eds), *Current Maritime Issues and the IMO*, 151; de La Fayette, 16 *IJMCL* (2001) 215–26, and see *infra*, Ch 7.

[172] See *infra*, Ch 7.

[173] But only the states parties have a vote: see MARPOL Convention, Article 16; Ballast Water Convention, Article 19.

[174] See *infra*, Ch 7.

the interests of the shipping and oil industries.[175] This criticism points to one of the main problems with bodies like IMO.

IMO exhibits many of the strengths and weaknesses of international regulatory agencies. In its favour it enables the lawmaking process to draw upon appropriate technical expertise and it is rather more than a forum within which interested states negotiate and revise global standards. Industry associations, mainly representing shipping companies, seafarers, and insurers, participate actively and they are often influential, as are some environmental NGOs.[176] Bodies typically involved include the International Chamber of Shipping, the International Confederation of Trade Unions, P&I Clubs, Friends of the Earth International, and IUCN. Among its weaknesses, IMO inevitably finds it difficult to act against the opposition of flag of convenience states, many of which coordinate their positions in advance and are influential members of the IMO Council. This has been a significant factor in its inability to deliver stronger regulation and better compliance mechanisms. Like some other regulatory agencies IMO is thus open to the criticism that it too often serves the interests of the industry it is meant to regulate.[177] Pressure for action on flags of convenience has thus come from the UNGA rather than from IMO. Lastly, the whole process of negotiating and renegotiating maritime conventions can be very slow. The 1989 Salvage Convention took eleven years to negotiate, the 1996 HNS Liability Convention almost twenty, and ten years later it was still not in force. In this respect IMO compares unfavourably with the work of the CMI in the years prior to IMO's involvement in maritime law-making.[178] IMO can act quickly, as its response to disasters such as the sinking of the *Torrey Canyon*, the *Erika* or the *Prestige* shows.[179] Nevertheless, it is unsurprising if some states opt for unilateral measures rather than waiting for IMO.

4(5) THE INTERNATIONAL ATOMIC ENERGY AGENCY

The IAEA was established principally to facilitate dissemination of nuclear technology for peaceful purposes and to prevent the proliferation of nuclear weapons.[180] It has over one hundred member states, meeting annually in a General Conference, and a Board of Governors of thirty-five members, which must include the ten members most advanced in the technology of atomic energy or production of its source materials, and representatives of the eight major UN regions, if not already included. Although this agency is associated with the UN, it is an independent intergovernmental organization without specialized agency status. It is responsible, inter alia, for setting international standards on nuclear safety, a task which became more important

---

[175] See e.g. the discussion of the 2004 Ballast Water Convention in Tsimplis, 19 *IJMCL* (2004) 444–5.

[176] Gaskell, 18 *IJMCL* (2003) 172–4; de La Fayette, 16 *IJMCL* (2001) 213–6; Tan, *Vessel-Source Marine Pollution*, 34–46.

[177] See Hayashi, 16 *IJMCL* (2001) 501; de La Fayette, 16 *IJMCL* (2001) 215–20.

[178] Gaskell, 18 *IJMCL* (2003) 212–4.

[179] See de La Fayette, 16 *IJMCL* (2001) 195–6; Frank, 20 *IJMCL* (2005) 1, 62–4.

[180] 1956 IAEA Statute. See further Ch 9, *infra*.

following the Chernobyl disaster in 1986. Conventions on nuclear safety, radioactive waste, liability for nuclear accidents, and notification and cooperation in emergencies have subsequently been negotiated through IAEA. It is thus the principal international regulatory agency for civil nuclear activities. Its role is considered in more detail in Chapter 9.

4(6) THE WORLD TRADE ORGANIZATION

The WTO is not part of the UN system. It was created by an intergovernmental conference in 1994 for the purpose of furthering free trade and facilitating implementation and operation of the General Agreement on Tariffs and Trade and other related agreements.[181] Like IMO and various other international organizations, it is in effect a regulatory agency. All WTO members must sign up to all the main agreements adopted in 1994. While many of these agreements are detailed and comprehensive, some are little more than an outline or framework requiring further negotiations, while the whole package of WTO law assumes the need for continued evolution. In this respect the WTO is the forum for agenda-setting and policy review, as well as the negotiation, adoption, amendment, and authoritative interpretation of WTO agreements.[182] For these purposes all members are represented on the General Council and the Ministerial Conference, the two main political organs of the organization. The 1947 GATT allowed decisions to be taken by majority vote,[183] but the parties have normally operated on the basis that consensus is desirable (defined for this purpose to mean the absence of objections by any member present when a decision is taken) and that practice is retained expressly in the WTO Agreement.[184] Voting is thus allowed only if the objections of a member government cannot otherwise be overcome.

What can the WTO legitimately regulate? The Agreement Establishing the WTO envisages that it will provide a 'common institutional framework for the conduct of trade relations among its Members…'.[185] At the same time, in the preamble to the Marrakesh agreement the members recognized the need to do so in accordance with sustainable development and protection and preservation of the environment. Despite this explicit reference, the Organization has shown great reluctance to reflect environmental concerns in its lawmaking agenda, and it is largely through decisions of its quasi-judicial Dispute Settlement Body that serious conflict between trade law and international environmental law has so far been avoided.[186] Moreover, trade regulation is not the exclusive preserve of the WTO, and there is nothing in the WTO Agreement which gives WTO treaties priority over other treaties.[187] A small number of non-WTO multilateral treaties thus regulate environmentally harmful forms of international trade. These include the 1988 UN Convention against Illicit Traffic in

---

[181] 1994 Marrakesh Agreement Establishing the World Trade Organization.
[182] 1994 Agreement, Articles 3, 9–10.   [183] Article 25(4).
[184] Article 9(1).   [185] Article 2(1).
[186] See generally Boyle, in Bodansky, Brunnée and Hey, *Handbook of IEL*, 125–46 and *infra*, Ch 14.
[187] Boyle, ibid, and see *infra*, Ch 14.

Narcotic Drugs, the Conventions on International Trade in Endangered Species and on Transboundary Movements of Hazardous Wastes negotiated by UNEP in 1973 and 1989 respectively, and a protocol on trade in genetically modified organizms adopted by the parties to the Convention on Biological Diversity.[188] Provided any trade restraints they adopt are non-discriminatory and not a 'disguised restriction on international trade',[189] there is no obligation for states to choose the WTO as the forum in which to conduct negotiations on such matters. At the same time, since trade regulation is the central purpose of all of these agreements there is no reason in principle why the WTO should not address similar concerns. Because the WTO is not a UN specialized agency, its lawmaking activities cannot easily be coordinated or dictated by the UN General Assembly. Member governments are largely free therefore to decide for themselves what the scope of WTO lawmaking should be.

A more difficult question is whether the WTO can also regulate issues that do not themselves involve trade but which have a direct impact on conditions of trade. Obvious examples would include the establishment of health, safety, or environmental standards for goods or agricultural produce traded internationally. In all these examples other international bodies with primary responsibility for international regulation already exist, including FAO, WHO and the various treaty COPs. There are no hard and fast jurisdictional boundaries between these organizations and the WTO, and it is possible to advance policy arguments for and against the WTO taking on a more expansive role in regard to the regulation of these matters and many others.[190] It might well make sense, for example, to link negotiations on trade issues with setting standards for reducing CO_2 emissions and promoting energy efficiency, since it is far from obvious why a country that subsidizes pollution by failing to take action on climate change should reap the benefits of free trade. We should not assume therefore that such trade-related issues could not be dealt with by the WTO.

Ultimately it is for the contracting parties to decide on the forum in which they wish to negotiate, and if, for example, they choose to conclude the TRIPS Agreement in a WTO context rather than at the World Intellectual property Organization (WIPO) they are free to do so. This is no different from the similar choices made when preferring to negotiate a plant genetic resources agreement at FAO rather than the CBD, or a tobacco convention at WHO rather than FAO or WTO. In all these cases states have treated the question as essentially a pragmatic one: which forum is more appropriate and why? The answer in many instances is best understood in political rather than jurisdictional or constitutional terms.[191] But, while the boundaries between different organizations cannot be laid down in a systematic way, the need for a supportive relationship between WTO and other international bodies is obvious.[192]

---

[188] 2000 Protocol on Biosafety.

[189] See especially 1992 Rio Declaration on Environment and Development, Principle 12.

[190] See Alvarez and others, 96 *AJIL* (2002) 1–158.

[191] See generally Boyle and Chinkin, *The Making of International Law* (Oxford, 2007) Ch 3.

[192] See in particular Cass, *The Constitutionalization of the WTO* (Oxford, 2005) who argues against expansion of the role of the WTO.

The substantive law of the WTO and its relationship to environmental concerns are dealt with more fully in Chapter 14.

4(7) THE WORLD BANK AND THE GLOBAL ENVIRONMENT FACILITY

(a) The Bank

The World Bank and its private finance arm the International Finance Corporation (IFC) fund long-term capital loans to promote structural reforms that will lead to economic growth in developing countries or that support reconstruction and development projects. The states contributing most to the Bank's capital appoint five of its twenty-two executive directors, and it is predominantly controlled by the developed industrialized economies. Some of its more grandiose projects, such as the funding of power stations, dams, pipelines, or the building of roads through forests, have caused serious environmental harm and dislocated the lives of many local people. Largely through strong NGO and US Congressional pressure the Bank has become increasingly responsive to these environmental side-effects.[193] Its mandate, like that of most of the regional development banks, requires it to be guided exclusively by economic considerations.[194] Only the European Bank for Reconstruction and Development has an explicit obligation to promote 'environmentally sound and sustainable development'.[195] Nevertheless, like other agencies within the UN system, the Bank's programmes are expected to promote sustainable development in accordance with Agenda 21 and to incorporate the principles of the Rio Declaration.[196] In practice, it has proved politically essential to take account of the needs of sustainable development, environmental protection, and human-rights concerns in its lending decisions.

Current World Bank policy is to structure and condition loans in such a way that development which it funds is ecologically sound. Environmental Action Plans outline the borrower countries' environmental problems and strategies for addressing them. Environmental assessments are aimed at ensuring that development proposals take account of environmental factors. Of particular note is the policy of the IFC which forbids the financing of new business activity that cannot meet the IFC's environmental

---

[193] See Fox and Brown (eds), *The Struggle for Accountability: the World Bank, NGOs and Grassroots Movements* (Cambridge, Mass, 1998).

[194] World Bank, Articles of Agreement, Article V(10); Inter-American Development Bank Agreement, Article VIII(5); Asian Development Bank Agreement, Article 36(2); African Development Bank Agreement, Article 38(2). See generally Handl, *Multilateral Development Banking* (The Hague, 2001).

[195] Agreement Establishing the EBRD, Article 2(1).

[196] UNGA Res 47/190 and 47/191 (1992) paras 21–3; See World Bank, *The World Bank and the Global Environment* (Washington DC, 2000). Handl, *Multilateral Development Banking*, 25, argues that the incorporation of environmental and sustainable development considerations represents subsequent practice which interprets or modifies the Bank's mandate. See also id, 92 *AJIL* (1998) 642 and Muldoon, 22 *Texas ILJ* (1987) 1.

and social performance standards.[197] These standards require inter alia compatibility with the following MEAs:

1971 Convention on Wetlands of International Importance

1972 Convention Concerning the Protection of World Cultural and Natural Heritage

1973 Convention on International Trade in Endangered Species

1973 Convention on Conservation of Migratory Species

1979 Convention on Long-range Transboundary Air Pollution

1989 Basel Convention on the Control of Transboundary Movements of Hazardous Wastes

1991 Espoo Convention on Environmental Impact Assessment in a Transboundary Context

1992 Convention on Biological Diversity

1998 Rotterdam Convention on Prior Informed Consent for Certain Hazardous Chemicals and Pesticides in International Trade

2001 Stockholm Convention on Persistent Organic Pollutants.

It is open to the Bank and its agencies to set the conditions applicants must meet. In doing so it is not limited to ensuring compatibility with applicable national or international law. Some of the above treaties are European regional agreements and not all World Bank members are parties to all of the global treaties. Nevertheless, when Finnish developers sought IFC funding for a new pulp mill on the River Uruguay, Uruguay's ability to meet the requirements of all of the above treaties was assessed, even those not applicable in Latin America (e.g. the EIA Convention). The IFC's decision to fund the project was made only after it concluded that all the requirements set out in those standards were satisfied.

An Inspection Panel has been created with the object of providing affected groups or communities with some means of challenging any failure by the Bank to observe its own operational policies and procedures.[198] This is an innovative and so far unique method for introducing a measure of public accountability to the operations of an international organization. The IFC's equivalent body was involved in assessing complaints during the *Pulp Mills* dispute between Uruguay and Argentina.[199] It has also been argued that all the development banks have an obligation in international law to avoid causing harm to other states and to refrain from funding activities that

---

[197] International Finance Corporation, *Policy on Social and Environmental Sustainability* (2006) para 17. See Morgera, 18 *Colorado JIELP* (2007) 151.

[198] Res No 93/10 (1993) in 4 *YbIEL* (1993) 883. See Schlemmer-Schulte, 58 *ZAÖRV* (1998) 353; Orakhelashvili, 2 *Int Orgs LR* (2005) 57; Nurmukhametova, 10 *Max Planck YbUNL* (2006) 397.

[199] The Compliance Advisor/Ombudsman (CAO) who is independent of IFC management and reports directly to the President of the World Bank Group.

undermine international environmental agreements.[200] The Bank's policies require that possible harmful impacts on neighbouring states must be assessed,[201] and it is most unlikely to fund projects which would be likely to cause significant transboundary harm. However, despite all these changes and constraints, one study concluded that the Bank's approach to incorporating environmental concerns remains inadequate, and 'has demonstrated that environmental sustainability cannot be added on [to] the business-as-usual approach to development'.[202]

(b) The Global Environment Facility

The World Bank acts as trustee for the Global Environment Facility (GEF), which provides additional funding to developing states and has become an important environmental institution in its own right. The GEF was established in 1991 by the World Bank, UNEP, and UNDP. Following decisions taken at UNCED to restructure the GEF in accordance with principles of 'universality, transparency and democracy', a new instrument was adopted by the three implementing agencies and further revised in 2002.[203] The GEF's general function is to provide funds to enable developing countries to meet 'agreed incremental costs' of measures taken pursuant to UNCED Agenda 21 and intended to achieve 'agreed global environmental benefits' with regard to climate change, biological diversity, international waters, ozone-layer depletion, deforestation, desertification, and persistent organic pollutants. It has also been designated to act as the financial mechanism established by the Climate Change Convention, the Biological Diversity Convention, and the Persistent Organic Pollutants (POPS) Convention. It works closely with other international bodies and regional development banks and also funds related NGO activities, including those of IUCN.

Although formally an inter-agency body, the GEF is a separate and distinct entity from the World Bank and its partners,[204] with a voting structure that was redesigned in 1994 to avoid the World Bank's pattern of dominance by major Western donors. It has its own Council, responsible for developing, adopting, and evaluating operational policies and programmes for GEF-financed activities. Composed of thirty-two members with an equal balance of developed and developing states (or 'recipient' and 'non-recipient' states), decisions require a double majority of 60 per cent of all members plus a majority of 60 per cent (by contribution) of donors. An Assembly, in which all member states have one vote, reviews the general policies of the Facility and reports received from the Council. Although the GEF Instrument specifies that 'use of the GEF resources for purposes of [the relevant MEAs] shall be in conformity with the policies, program priorities and eligibility criteria decided by the Conference of

---

[200] Handl, *Multilateral Development Banking*, 26–31.   [201] See *infra*, Ch 3, section 4(4).

[202] Fox and Brown (eds), *The Struggle for Accountability: the World Bank, NGOs and Grassroots Movements*, 9, citing a WWF assessment.

[203] 1994 Instrument for the Establishment of the Restructured Global Environment Facility, revised 2002. See generally Freestone, in Ndiaye and Wolfrum (eds), *Law of the Sea, Environmental Law and Settlement of Disputes* (Leiden, 2007) 1077–107.

[204] Werksman, 6 *YbIEL* (1995) 55–8 reviews the legal status of the GEF.

the Parties of each of those conventions',[205] as one commentator has noted, the GEF's voting structure 'does not preclude the possibility of conflict between the objectives of the Conventions, the implementing agencies, and the GEF in the context of particular decisions'.[206]

The GEF is thus an important instrument for promoting participation by developing countries in policies and conventions intended to protect the global environment, and for assisting their implementation through capacity-building, as envisaged in Agenda 21. As such, it funds measures that do not necessarily benefit the country concerned, but which do benefit the international community as a whole. Its creation and remit reflect notions of 'common but differentiated responsibility' and 'additionality' in funding allocations which are core elements of the equitable treatment of developing countries in the Rio Declaration and the two Rio Conventions.[207] The scale and impact of GEF funding have been substantial. Inter alia, it has become the principal instrument for funding biodiversity conservation in developing countries; it has supported negotiation and implementation of MEAs, including the elimination of ozone depleting substances; and it has helped to promote the objectives of the 1982 UNCLOS, Agenda 21 and the Rio Conventions.[208]

4(8) THE ORGANIZATION FOR ECONOMIC COOPERATION AND DEVELOPMENT

The OECD is an economic grouping of industrialized states, not a UN agency. It has twenty-four members, mainly European, but also Canada, Japan, Mexico, South Korea and the United States. Recognizing the economic interdependence of its members, its objectives are to promote growth, help less-developed states, and encourage world trade. On this basis, and because its members undertake to 'promote the efficient use of their economic resources' and in scientific and technological fields to encourage research, the OECD has been able to develop an environmental programme.[209] Its Nuclear Energy Agency has played a significant role in the development of national and international nuclear law in Europe.[210]

The OECD acts through a Council, an Executive Committee of fourteen member states, and various committees, covering, inter alia, the environment, energy, fisheries, and scientific and technological policy. The Council can make recommendations, or take decisions that bind members if they so agree, and in this role it has provided a forum for crystallization of some important principles that have subsequently been adopted into national and international law. The Environment Committee analyses the national environment policies of its members and their economic implications

---

[205] Ch V, para 26.   [206] Werksman, 6 *YbIEL* (1995) 60.   [207] See *infra*, Ch 3, section 3(3).

[208] For a detailed assessment see GEF, *3rd Overall Performance Study* (2005) and Freestone, in Ndiaye and Wolfrum (eds), *Law of the Sea, Environmental Law and Settlement of Disputes*, 1105–7; id, in Freestone, Barnes and Ong (eds), *The Law of the Sea* (Oxford, 2006) Ch 16.

[209] Article 2, OECD Constitution.   [210] *Infra*, Ch 9.

and makes recommendations on guiding principles.[211] It did much early work on finding solutions to transboundary pollution problems for which, as early as 1972, it developed the influential polluter-pays principle, as well as the principle of 'equal access' for transboundary claimants to national remedies, procedures and information.[212] Following the stranding of the *Amoco Cadiz* oil tanker, an OECD evaluation of the nature of oil-pollution impacts provided better methods of assessing the economic value of environmental loss (see Chapter 7). An OECD recommendation on environmental information is aimed at improving the reporting, collection, and dissemination of environmental information held by public bodies.[213] This recommendation applies the principles of the 1998 Arhus Convention to all OECD member states. More recently the Fisheries Committee has reviewed policies on sustainable fisheries and illegal and unreported fishing, but no lawmaking initiatives or recommended principles have emerged.

5 INTERNATIONAL REGULATORY REGIMES

5(1) INTRODUCTION

Often referred to as 'international regimes', multilateral environmental agreements (MEAs) with their related protocols and soft law have been employed by states and international institutions to provide a regulatory system capable of dynamic evolution.[214] The strength of the regime model of governance is the opportunity it offers for multilateral solutions to environmental problems and the negotiated application and development of international legal standards. It enables states to exercise a fiduciary or trusteeship role in the protection of the environment, other species, and future generations. No other model of governance offers adequate solutions to the problem of controlling phenomena of global character, such as global warming or ozone depletion, where no single state's acts are responsible and where the interests of all are at stake. While some theorists see international regimes creating 'epistemic communities' of experts and interest groups,[215] others argue that they offer a new basis for integrating international law and international relations.[216]

---

[211] See OECD, *Environmental Performance Review of OECD Countries* (Paris, 1998). Most of OECD's environment-related recommendations will be found in *OECD and the Environment* (Paris, 1986).

[212] See *infra*, Ch 5, section 3.   [213] Council Rec C(98) 67 (1998).

[214] See Gehring, 1 *YbIEL* (1990) 35; Kimball, 3 *YbIEL* (1992) 18; Thacher, 1 *ColJIELP* (1989) 101; Sand, *Lessons Learned in Global Environmental Governance* (New York, 1990); Young, Demko and Ramakrishna, *Global Environmental Change and International Governance* (Dartmouth, 1991); Haas, Keohane and Levy (eds), *Institutions for the Earth: Sources of Effective Environmental Protection* (Cambridge, Mass, 1993); Yoshida, *The International Legal Regime for the Protection of the Stratospheric Ozone Layer* (The Hague, 2001) Ch 1.

[215] *Supra* n 18.

[216] See Rittberger (ed), *Regime Theory and International Relations* (Oxford, 1993); Slaughter, 87 *AJIL* (1993) 205; Byers, *Custom, Power and the Power of Rules* (Cambridge, 1999) Ch 2.

The application of regime theory to environmental relations can be observed in numerous treaties considered in later chapters, including the 1946 International Convention for the Regulation of Whaling, the 1972 London Dumping Convention (replaced in 1996 by a new protocol), the 1973 Convention on International Trade in Endangered Species, the 1985 Ozone Convention and 1987 Montreal Protocol, and the 1992 Framework Convention on Climate Change and 1997 Kyoto Protocol, as well as many regional agreements. Both the Ozone Convention and the Climate Change Convention have evolved into complex regulatory regimes following regular meetings of the parties, with additional protocols, amendments, adjustments and decisions.[217] In order to facilitate this further development most MEAs establish regulatory institutions, usually intergovernmental and autonomous in character,[218] but in a few cases this role is performed by existing international organizations such as IMO or the IAEA. The autonomous treaty bodies created by these agreements have become the international community's primary institutional model for the regulation and control of environmental risks. Even when the problems are regional, such as the conservation of fish stocks, the allocation of water resources, or transboundary air pollution, some form of international management and cooperation will usually offer a necessary means for the equitable allocation and conservation of such resources. In the following sections we consider the role and operation of these international regulatory bodies.

Whether they are autonomous bodies or part of an international organization, the essential elements of intergovernmental treaty institutions are threefold. First, and most importantly, the parties must meet regularly. Conferences or meetings of the parties (COPs/MOPs) may be provided for in the treaty itself, or may be convened by the UN or one of its specialized agencies, or by a commission established to manage the treaty. It is this ongoing role which institutionalizes these gatherings. Second, it will usually be the responsibility of the parties to keep the relevant treaty under review and take whatever measures they are empowered to adopt to further its object and purpose. Some treaties, usually described as 'framework' or 'umbrella' treaties, are specifically designed to facilitate further development through the addition of protocols, annexes, additional agreements, amendments, decisions, or recommendations which give detailed content to the outline legal regime created by the treaty.[219] COPs are usually the forum in which these measures are negotiated and adopted, and it is in this sense that they are lawmaking bodies. They must therefore have power to adopt the necessary measures. Third, they will usually be assisted by expert bodies providing scientific, technical and legal advice where appropriate. These bodies may be the

---

[217] See *infra*, Ch 6.

[218] Churchill and Ulfstein, 94 *AJIL* (2000) 623; Brunnée, 15 *LJIL* (2002) 1; Ulfstein, in Bodansky, Brunnée and Hey, *Handbook of IEL*, 878.

[219] For example the 1973/78 MARPOL Convention, the 1985 Ozone Convention and the 1992 Climate Change Convention all provide for the adoption of annexes and protocols containing more detailed rules. The 1982 UNCLOS is not a framework agreement in this sense, but it does envisage further elaboration in other ways: see Boyle, 54 *ICLQ* (2005) 563–84.

source of recommendations for further regulation, or they may be concerned with treaty implementation, or they may have other functions. Additionally, some treaty bodies also have a responsibility for supervising compliance with the treaty regime, but this is not a necessary feature of a lawmaking agreement.[220]

In general, effective treaty institutions are those which combine political direction and inclusive, transparent, informed decision-making processes with the availability of technical, financial, and capacity-building support for developing state parties from UN specialized agencies, the Global Environment Facility, or developed states.[221] In all these respects environmental treaties have been notably innovative. Not all such bodies have been a success, however. Some lack a wide-enough remit, or sufficient resources. In other cases a weakness has been the inability to ensure the full participation of all the states most closely concerned. Rather than any failure to ensure compliance with agreed standards of environmental protection, where MEA institutions are most likely to fail is in reaching consensus on the more stringent measures that may be needed to tackle environmental problems effectively, such as climate change. Such bodies are often open to the criticism that their decisions represent only the lowest common denominator of agreement: the conventions on toxic chemicals considered in Chapter 8 are good examples. Those failings are the product of political choice, or the lack of adequate political commitment, rather than of inherent institutional weakness. In that respect they are no different from the United Nations, or from any of the other political institutions considered earlier in this chapter. Thus a commitment to a multi-lateral approach may in some cases prove an obstacle to stronger action at international level. The International Maritime Organization, whose record was considered above, is perhaps the best current example of this phenomenon. The true role of such bodies may in some cases be closer to legitimation of policies acceptable to the relevant industry than to acting as a trustee for the interests of the environment. For the same reasons, it does not follow that replacing the present fragmented structure of treaty supervision with a single global environmental organization would necessarily improve the effectiveness of international environmental regimes. As one experienced participant observes, 'each IEA [international environmental agreement], regardless of how superficially similar, develops its own unique sense of what is politically possible'.[222]

5(2) AUTONOMOUS REGULATORY BODIES

Two principal forms of autonomous regulatory body are found in the majority of MEAs. One consists of regular meetings of the parties, with institutional continuity usually provided by a permanent secretariat.[223] This model is adopted by the London

---

[220] See *infra*, Ch 4, section 3.

[221] See Sand, 56 ZAÖRV (1996) 754; Gündling, ibid, 796; Victor, Raustiala and Skolnikoff (eds), *Implementation and Effectiveness of International Environmental Commitments*, Ch 16; Wettestad, *Designing Effective Environmental Regimes* (Cheltenham, 1999).

[222] Werksman, 6 *YbIEL* (1995) 62.

[223] See Werksman (ed), *Greening International Institutions* (London, 1996) Ch 4.

Dumping Convention (see Chapter 8), the UNEP Regional Seas Conventions (see Chapter 8), the Antarctic Treaty,[224] the Convention on International Trade in Endangered Species (see Chapter 12) and the Conventions on Ozone Depletion and Climate Change (see Chapter 6). The alternative approach is to establish a commission in which member states are represented. This model is employed by the 1974 and 1992 Paris Conventions, the 1976 and 1999 Rhine Conventions, the Helsinki Convention on the Protection of the Baltic Sea and, as we shall observe in Chapter 13, it is common in the case of multilateral fisheries or marine living resources treaties, including the 1980 Convention for the Conservation of Antarctic Marine Living Resources and the 1946 International Convention for the Regulation of Whaling. The International Joint Commission (IJC), established by the United States and Canada in the 1909 Boundary Waters Treaty represents a third model, unique among environmental bodies in exercising quasi-judicial functions and having a composition independent of its member governments.[225] It is noteworthy, however, that these states have been reluctant to allow the IJC to perform a truly regulatory role, probably because of its independent structure. In all other cases considered in this work the regulatory body, whether a meeting of the parties or a commission, is in substance no more than a diplomatic conference, and the existence in some cases of a separate legal personality does not alter the reality that these institutions are in no sense independent of their member states. This is not necessarily a weakness, however. Because the development of regulatory standards and further measures is essentially a political task, entailing adoption and implementation by governments, in practice it can only be performed by an intergovernmental body with appropriate negotiating authority. The idea of an 'independent' regulatory agency in this context is thus an unhelpful analogy.

This does not mean that questions of structure and due process are irrelevant.[226] Several general considerations apply. First, community interests will only be protected if the right community of interest is defined. Institutions whose membership is too narrowly drawn are more likely to legitimize pollution or the over-exploitation of resources than to tackle them. Second, transparency is an essential ingredient if these institutions are to be made responsive to a wider public. That may entail a greater willingness to facilitate NGO participation, and to publish reports and findings. Third, scientific recommendations, verification, and review of national reports and environmental data, compliance procedures and inspection regimes will not be successful if the subsidiary bodies which carry them out do not have a measure of independence from the political organs. These functions must be carried out with objectivity and detachment and the institution must therefore be structured in such a way as to facilitate this goal.[227]

---

[224] See Gautier, in Francioni and Scovazzi, *International Law for Antarctica* (2nd edn, The Hague, 1996) Ch 2.

[225] See *infra*, Ch 10.

[226] See generally Kingsbury, Krisch and Stewart, 68 *Law & Cont Problems* (2005) 34ff.

[227] On the role of scientific bodies in MEAs see e.g. *infra*, Chs 6, 13.

(a) Membership

The potential effectiveness of regulatory or management institutions is significantly affected by their composition. A crucial question is whether membership is limited to those who benefit from the activity or resource in question, as in the consultative meetings of the Antarctic Treaty system, or whether membership is drawn from a wider category including those who may be adversely affected. Examples of the latter are the London Dumping Convention Consultative Meeting, and the International Whaling Commission.[228] Both of these bodies now contain a preponderance of members opposed respectively to dumping and whaling and this has greatly facilitated gradual progress towards the decision to phase out dumping and impose a moratorium on whaling, despite inconclusive scientific evidence in both cases. These are institutions in which community pressure is arguably at its strongest because of their broadly drawn membership and because they have allowed significant NGO involvement at meetings of the parties: they have substantially answered the question who may speak for the global commons in their respective areas of competence, and can be regarded as bodies which have successfully fulfilled a fiduciary role on behalf to the environment. Much the same could be said of the Ozone and Climate Change Conventions and their associated protocols.[229]

Other institutions are less favourably composed, especially at regional level. One of the reasons for the ineffectiveness of fisheries commissions has been that their membership has usually been dawn exclusively from those states participating in the exploitation of a particular area or stock. As Koers has observed, 'such restrictions on membership may also result in the organization becoming an instrument to further the interests of its members rather than as an instrument to regulate marine fisheries rationally'.[230] Despite other radical changes made by the 1995 Fish Stocks Agreement, the right to participate in a regional fisheries agreement remains limited to 'states having a real interest in the fisheries concerned'.[231] The same problem affects other regional-seas bodies, including commissions on land-based sources of marine pollution. In the latter case a regional approach is dictated both by geopolitical considerations and the special ecological needs of enclosed or semi-enclosed seas,[232] but it has the effect of leaving environmental protection in the hands of those whose economic and industrial activities would be most affected by high standards or strict enforcement of pollution controls. What is lacking in these cases is a constituency of outside states able to speak for the environmental interests of a wider community.

A second problem arises where membership and functions are too narrowly defined: the wrong states may address the issues from the wrong perspective. Chapter 10 indicates how this problem affects international watercourse commissions. These bodies

---

[228] See *infra*, Chs 8, 13.   [229] See *infra*, Ch 6.
[230] Koers, *International Regulation of Marine Fisheries*, 126.
[231] Article 8(3). See Molenaar, 15 *IJMCL* (2000) 475. See also Article 12, which gives NGOs a right to participate.
[232] See *infra*, Ch 8.

are invariably composed of riparian states,[233] yet they are expected to take account of the needs of the marine environment, and thus of coastal states who may be affected by river-borne pollution. A more appropriate solution would be to broaden membership to include coastal states, or at least ensure coordination of related treaties by combining the institutional machinery. The former Oslo and Paris Commissions applied the latter approach to the control of land-based pollution and dumping off north-west Europe. Both commissions have now been replaced by a single body administering a new treaty applicable both to land-based pollution of the sea and dumping.[234] A similar need for coordination affects living-resource management where the needs of interdependent or associated stocks must be accommodated, and where problems of pollution control may also be relevant.[235] Here the preferable solution, at least in theory, is the ecosystem approach adopted by the Convention on the Conservation of Antarctic Marine Living Resources, although it is not clear that this body has in fact operated as intended.[236] Some regional-seas treaties also combine responsibility for pollution control and ecosystem protection, as envisaged by Article 194(5) of the 1982 UNCLOS.[237] In spite of difficulties in their practical operation, there are advantages in a regional approach to some environmental issues. Such arrangements facilitate policies and rules appropriate to the needs of particular areas. Political consensus may be obtainable at a regional level which could not be achieved globally. Cooperation in enforcement, monitoring, and information exchange may be easier to arrange. These advantages are recognized in a number of treaties, including the 1982 UNCLOS, whose environmental provisions assume the need for appropriate regional and global action. But it is important not to overlook the weaknesses of many regional regimes, or the benefits to be derived from ensuring that such regimes are structured within a framework of minimum global standards with some oversight and supervision at global level. Chapter 8 shows clearly the benefits of coordinating regional action within a global framework such as the London Dumping Convention, and the limitations of leaving the problem to regional solutions alone, as in the case of land-based sources of marine pollution.

(b) Transparency and NGO participation

The importance of transparency in the work of international regulatory bodies is recognized in at least two important treaties which lay down general principles. Article 12 of the 1995 Fish Stocks Agreement requires that states 'shall provide for transparency in the decision-making process and other activities of . . . fisheries

---

[233] A position maintained in Article 4 of the 1997 UN Watercourses Convention.

[234] 1992 Paris Convention for the Protection of the Marine Environment of the NE Atlantic, on which see *infra*, Ch 8.

[235] See 1995 Fish Stocks Agreement, Articles 3, 5–7.

[236] Howard, 38 *ICLQ* (1989) 135; Redgwell, in, Boyle and Freestone (eds), *International Law and Sustainable Development* (Oxford, 1999) Ch 9, but compare Miller, Sabourenkov and Ramm, 19 *IJMCL* (2004) 317, and see *infra*, Ch 13.

[237] See *infra*, Ch 7, section 3.

management organizations'. The 1998 Aarhus Convention commits UNECE member states to 'promote the application of the principles of this Convention in international environmental decision-making processes and within the framework of international organizations in matters relating to the environment'.[238] Some treaties provide for reports to be made public, while a few insist on the maintenance of confidentiality.[239]

There is now widespread provision for national and international NGOs qualified in relevant fields to be accorded observer status at meetings of treaty parties.[240] While there is no general right to observer status, and some treaties continue to exclude NGOs,[241] the usual empowering formulation presumes admission unless at least one-third of member states object.[242] Unusually, relevant NGOs have a right to take part in the meetings of regional fisheries bodies by virtue of Article 12 of the 1995 Straddling and Highly Migratory Fish Stocks Agreement, but there is no comparable provision in the 1997 UN Watercourses Convention. Non-governmental organizations play an increasingly important role as 'guardians of the environment' in the processes of international regulation and supervision.[243] This is evident in the presence of many NGOs at the UNCED in 1992, and in the references to NGOs in Agenda 21.[244] In some cases they have provided an effective voice because of their freedom from governmental control and ability to influence public opinion and supranational bodies such as the European Parliament and the Council of Europe. NGOs can turn the fear of adverse publicity into a weapon for putting pressure on states to agree stricter standards or ensure better compliance. Transparency and NGO participation can thus be seen as

---

[238] Article 3(7). See Ebbesson, 8 *YbIEL* (1997) 51, 57, and *infra*, Ch 5.

[239] Compare 1973 CITES Convention, Article 8(8) [reports of parties to be made public]; 1991 Protocol to the Antarctic Treaty, Article 11(5) [reports of the Committee on Environmental Protection to be made public], with 1994 Convention on Nuclear Safety, Article 27 [reports and meetings to be confidential].

[240] See e.g. 1972 World Heritage Convention, Article 8(3); 1973 CITES Convention, Article 11(7); 1979 Migratory Animals Convention, Article 7(9); 1979 European Wildlife Convention, Article 13(3); 1985 Ozone Convention, Article 6(5); 1987 Montreal Protocol, Article 11(5); 1989 Basel Convention on Transboundary Transport of Hazardous Waste, Article 15(6); 1991 Antarctic Environment Protocol, Articles 11–12; 1991 Convention on the Protection of the Alps, Article 5; 1992 Climate Change Convention, Article 7(6); 1992 Biological Diversity Convention, Article 23(5); 1992 Paris Convention for the Protection of the Marine Environment of the North-East Atlantic, Article 11; 1994 Desertification Convention, Article 22(7); 1994 International Tropical Timber Agreement, Article 15; 1995 Agreement on the Conservation of African-Eurasian Migratory Water Birds, Article 7; 1996 Agreement on the Conservation of Cetaceans, Article 3(4). NGO observers have also been admitted to meetings of the parties to the 1946 Convention for the Regulation of Whaling and the 1972/1996 London Dumping Convention even though there is no specific treaty provision: see Victor et al (eds), *Implementation and Effectiveness etc*, Chs 10, 11.

[241] See e.g. the 1994 Nuclear Safety Convention.

[242] See Article 11(7) of the 1973 CITES Convention and Article 6(5) of the Montreal Protocol, which are the two principal provisions repeated in many later treaties.

[243] See Morgenstern, *Legal Problems of International Organizations* (Cambridge, 1986) 86ff; Kimball, in Soons (ed), *Implementation of the Law of the Sea Convention through International Institutions* (Honolulu, 1989) 139; Sands, 30 *Harv ILJ* (1989) 393; Tolbert, in Churchill and Freestone, *International Law and Global Climate Change* (London, 1991) Ch 6; Cameron and Mackenzie, in Boyle and Anderson (eds), *Human Rights Approaches to Environmental Protection* (Oxford, 1996) Ch 7; Victor, Raustiala and Skolnikoff (eds), *Implementation and Effectiveness of International Environmental Commitments*, 664–8; Charnovitz, 18 *Mich JIL* (1997) 183.

[244] UN, *Report of the UNCED* (New York, 1993) paras 27.9, 27.13, 38.42–3.

enhancing both the effectiveness of MEAs and the claim of international regulatory institutions to legitimacy in the exercise of their responsibility for global environmental governance.

NGOs serve four main functions as participants in MEA institutions. First, although they cannot vote as full members, their observer status allows them in many cases to make proposals, to influence other parties, and to join actively in the negotiating process. Their influence on policy in the development of treaty regimes such as the CITES Convention and the Climate Change Convention has been substantial, often more so than the contribution of many of the states parties. Second, NGOs can to some extent further the interests of public participation and transparency in decision-making by treaty bodies. The 1998 Aarhus Convention on Access to Information, Public Participation and Access to Justice recognizes the importance of NGOs in this respect.[245] Third, NGOs may be a source of technical and scientific expertise, and for that reason are sometimes given observer status or even full membership in advisory committees established by several treaties.[246] Fourth, NGOs such as Greenpeace have on some occasions helped monitor implementation and compliance with treaty commitments by exposing, for example, illegal nuclear waste dumping in the Barents Sea.[247] However, the only systematic study concludes that NGOs perform this function only rarely. They are often less concerned with ensuring compliance than with high-profile action aimed at changing the rules.[248]

(c) Regulatory decision-making

The form in which international environmental rules and standards are adopted varies widely. In some cases new treaties may be required. As we have seen, the Antarctic Treaty System has extended its regulatory scope mainly in this way. The 1982 UNCLOS indirectly incorporates by reference regulations drawn from treaties on dumping and pollution from ships among the category of internationally agreed rules and standards of pollution control to which it refers.[249] Other treaties provide for the negotiation of protocols to lay down detailed standards. The 1979 Geneva Convention on Long-range Transboundary Air Pollution and the 1985 Vienna Convention on the Protection of the Ozone Layer are two instruments which have relied on this method.[250] Some treaties also contain technical annexes in which specific standards are set: the 1973 MARPOL Convention regulates various aspects of pollution from ships in this way. These annexes can be amended by a vote of the parties in IMO. More informal methods of rule-making, such as recommendations, resolutions, codes of practice, and guidelines

---

[245] Article 3(7).

[246] See e.g. 1991 Antarctic Environment Protocol, Articles 11–12. The Antarctic Treaty system generally makes use of SCAR, an independent scientific NGO, to provide advice. IUCN is specifically given observer status by several treaties, including the 1972 World Heritage Convention. The 1995 Agreement on African and Eurasian Migratory Water Birds, Article 7, makes it a full member of that agreement's Technical Committee.

[247] See Stokke, in Victor et al (eds), *Implementation and Effectiveness etc*, 475.

[248] Victor et al (eds), *Implementation and Effectiveness etc*, 667–8.

[249] See *infra*, Chs 7, 8.   [250] See *infra*, Ch 6.

all fall into the category of soft law, but they are nevertheless an important means by which states undertake further measures of treaty implementation. The legal status of these instruments was considered in Chapter 1.

Whether formally binding or not, all of these various methods of rule-making have in common that no obligation may be imposed on any state without its consent. Differences exist in the manner in which this is achieved, but it is one of the more serious problems of international regulation that a two-thirds or three-quarters majority vote is typically required for adoption of new measures in whatever form, and states usually remain free to opt out of any measures so adopted. Where consensus is required, as in the listing of additional chemicals in the 1998 Rotterdam Convention on Prior Informed Consent, one state can block any decision, but this is exceptional.[251] Moreover, new treaties, protocols, or amendments thereto will normally require positive ratification to enter into force. This often slow 'opt-in' process can be a serious impediment to necessary lawmaking, since, as we saw in Chapter 1, states which fail to ratify will not be bound. An alternative approach relies on tacit consent or non-objection to bring amendments to technical annexes into force within a set time-limit. This opt-out method of amendment reverses the normal procedure and is now widely used for annexes to treaties such as the MARPOL Convention, the Basel Convention, CITES, the POPS Convention and most fisheries conventions, since it enables schedules of protected species, prohibited substances, or conservation regulations to be changed speedily as circumstances require. Although states still remain free to opt out of these measures if they object within the prescribed time limit, the onus is on them to do.

The 1987 Montreal Protocol shows that a more radical approach to the problem of regulatory opt-outs is possible. Combined majorities of industrialized and developing states are empowered to amend standards set by the protocol for production and consumption of controlled ozone-depleting substances.[252] Once adopted, these adjustments are automatically binding on all parties to the protocol. Withdrawal from the protocol is then the only option left for those states which find such an amendment unacceptable. Clearly the result is to make isolated opposition to majority decisions as difficult and costly as possible. In practice such opposition is pointless and it has never been necessary to adopt amendments using this procedure. However the Montreal Protocol precedent is unique among environmental agreements.

In contrast, the more usual freedom to opt out of regulations adopted by majority vote has seriously limited the ability of a number of commissions to function effectively as regulatory bodies. Fisheries commissions in particular have had difficulty setting appropriate catch quotas.[253] The so-called 'Turbot war' in 1994 between Canada and Spain resulted from the abuse by the European Community of its power to object to quotas set under the 1978 Northwest Atlantic Fisheries Convention.[254] In an attempt to overcome this problem the 1995 Fish Stocks Agreement now requires parties to regional fisheries agreements to 'agree on decision-making procedures

---

[251] See *infra*, Ch 8, section 2(2).   [252] Article 2(9) as amended 1990. See *infra*, Ch 6, section 2.
[253] See *infra*, Ch 13.   [254] See Davies, 44 *ICLQ* (1995) 927.

which facilitate the adoption of conservation and management measures in a timely and effective manner'.[255] Any failure to do so in respect of fishing for straddling or highly migratory fish stocks on the high seas could be dealt with by the FAO or UNGA recommending international minimum standards which become binding under Article 10.[256] The International Whaling Commission has also had difficulty persuading Japan and Norway to accept moratoria on commercial whale catches approved by substantial majorities of non-whaling states. Resort to the objections procedure has enabled whaling states to delay or evade some conservationist proposals. But, due to the relative ease of amending regulations, this convention 'has proved a most useful and flexible instrument for reflecting changes in attitude and practice, and thus in resolving issues'.[257] So too has the CITES Convention, enabling the parties to list and de-list protected species easily and regularly.[258] The success of the parties to the London Dumping Convention and the Basel Convention in progressively adopting stricter standards leading to the elimination of hazardous waste exports for dumping at sea or disposal in developing countries shows how in the right conditions substantial changes can come about within the terms of an existing treaty.[259]

(d) Non-participants

Various techniques have been employed in MEAs to minimize non-participation or objection. Diplomatic and economic pressure applied by other states may help to make persistent objectors comply with majority decisions; such pressure was successfully used by the United States to persuade Japan to accept the whaling moratorium adopted in 1982. Through the Marine Mammal Protection Act, the High Seas Driftnet Fisheries Enforcement Act, the Packwood-Magnuson and Pelly amendments to its fisheries laws, and the Sea Turtle Conservation amendments to the Endangered Species Act, the United States has made extensive use of trade restrictions to enforce compliance with international conservation standards, or with its own national conservation objectives.[260] Unilateral measures of this kind will not always be consistent with international trade agreements, however, nor are they endorsed by Principle 12 of the Rio Declaration. But the *Shrimp-Turtle Case* shows that where Article XX of the GATT can be invoked, and the other party refuses to negotiate, trade sanctions aimed at encouraging treaty participation remain permissible in accordance with GATT rules.[261]

Treaty regulations cannot of course bind states which refuse to participate at all in the treaty.[262] In order to tackle this potential challenge to the universality of major

---

[255] Article 10(j). See *infra*, Ch 13. For an analysis of what this might mean see McDorman, 20 *IJMCL* (2005) 423.

[256] See *infra*, Ch 13, section 5(3).

[257] Birnie, 29 *NRJ* (1989) 913; id, 12 *IJMCL* (1997) 488, and see *infra*, Ch 13.

[258] Sand, 8 *EJIL* (1997) 29, and see *infra*, Ch 12.　　[259] *Infra*, Ch 8.

[260] Zoller, *Enforcing International Law Through US Legislation* (Dobbs Ferry, 1985); Wolfrum, 272 *Recueil des Cours* (1998) 62–5.

[261] See *United States—Import Prohibition of Certain Shrimp and Shrimp Products* ['Shrimp/Turtle Case'] WTO Appellate Body (1998) WT/DS58/AB/R, *infra*, Ch 14.

[262] 1969 Vienna Convention on the Law of Treaties, Article 34.

global environmental agreements, other forms of pressure or persuasion have also been built into some treaty regimes: in effect a mixture of carrots and sticks.[263] The Ozone, Climate Change and Biological Diversity Conventions and their protocols employ trust funds, technology transfer provisions, and other capacity-building measures in order to encourage participation by developing states. As we saw above, the Global Environment Facility (GEF) has played an important role in funding developing-state programmes to implement these and other global environmental agreements. All of these agreements use 'common but differentiated responsibility' to place fewer burdens on developing states. The Biological Diversity Convention goes further than most such agreements in encouraging participation. It seeks to provide resource-rich developing countries with additional economic incentives through participation 'in a fair and equitable way' in the benefits of biotechnology.[264] In much the same way the 1982 UNCLOS was widely ratified by developing states partly because of the benefits from deep-seabed mining and the exclusive economic zone which at one time it appeared to offer them. Non-participants thus deprive themselves of whatever potential benefits any of these treaties may provide.

Some treaties also impose constraints on non-parties. Trade with non-parties is restricted under the Ozone Protocol, the Basel Convention, the CITES Convention, and the Whaling Convention. Article 10 of the 1980 Convention for the Conservation of Antarctic Marine Living resources does not resort to these tactics, but it does allow the Commission for the Conservation of Antarctic Marine Living Resources (CCAMLR) to put pressure on non-parties whose activities affect implementation of the Convention. This attempt to involve non-parties is a distinctive feature of the Antarctic treaty system, but it is probably too limited in scope and insufficiently supported by acquiescence to constitute an assertion of jurisdiction or to create an objective regime binding on all states.[265] However, parties to the 1995 Fish Stocks Agreement must now participate in regional fisheries agreements such as CCAMLR if they wish to continue high-seas fishing,[266] and even non-parties to such regional agreements must comply with their rules and may be subject to compulsory dispute settlement under Part XV of the 1982 UNCLOS if they refuse to cooperate.[267]

5(3) INTERNATIONAL RESOURCE-MANAGEMENT BODIES

Exceptionally, a small number of international institutions perform functions more appropriately described as international resource management. Their responsibilities include protection of the environment but they differ from other control and

---

[263] See generally Wolfrum, 272 *Recueil des Cours* (1998) 110–45.

[264] See Articles 1, 15(7) 16(1) 16(3) 19(1)–(2) and *infra*, Ch 11.

[265] See also 1978 Convention for Future Cooperation in Northwest Atlantic Fisheries, Article 19; 1982 North Atlantic Salmon Convention, Article 2(3); 1995 Fish Stocks Agreement, Article 33. On the status of the Antarctic Treaty system against third states see Charney and Brunner, in Francioni and Scovazzi (eds), *International Law for Antarctica* (2nd edn, The Hague, 1996) Chs 3, 4.

[266] See 1995 Fish Stocks Agreement, Article 8.   [267] *Infra*, Ch 13.

supervisory bodies in that the right of individual states to exploit the resource is subordinated to the authority of collective decision-making. These institutions thus possess considerably stronger powers than is normally the case, since exploitation may take place only with their prior consent and subject to rules some of which are established by qualified majorities which bind all participants. The most prominent example is the International Seabed Authority (ISBA), the institutional manifestation of the concept of common heritage, which came into existence following entry into force of the 1982 UNCLOS.

The ISBA is concerned only with the exploration for and exploitation of deep seabed mineral resources;[268] earlier proposals to extend its authority to include management of high-seas fisheries and protection of the whole marine environment were not pursued.[269] More recently it has been suggested that it might take on the role of regulating access to and conservation of deep-seabed biological resources and bio-prospecting, although that would probably require an amendment of the convention or an implementing protocol.[270] Article 157 of the 1982 UNCLOS provides that 'The Authority is the organization through which states Parties shall...organize and control activities in the [deep seabed] Area, particularly with a view to administering the resources of the Area'. No exploitation of these resources may take place outside the control and administration of this body, which is given the duty to adopt appropriate rules, regulations, and procedures for ensuring effective protection of the marine environment, both in relation to pollution and the protection and conservation of natural resources and flora and fauna.[271]

The ISBA comprises several elements, including the Assembly, a political organ consisting of all member states, to which other organs of the authority are responsible. Its approval is necessary for the adoption of regulations governing exploitation and exploration of the deep seabed, including environmental protection measures, and it also approves arrangements for the equitable sharing of benefits derived from seabed activities. The second component is the Council, a small executive body reflecting a balance of geographical, political, and economic groupings, whose functions are, inter alia, to establish specific policies, to supervise and coordinate the implementation of the convention's provisions on the deep seabed, to approve proposed plans for exploration and exploitation, and to make recommendations to the Assembly.[272] For these purposes the Council may rely on an Economic Planning Commission and Legal and Technical Commission. Thirdly, the authority also controls a body described as

---

[268] 1982 UNCLOS, Articles 156–70, and Annexes III–IV These provisions must now be read together with the 1994 Agreement Relating to Implementation of Part XI, 33 *ILM* (1994) 1309. See Nandan, in Freestone, Barnes and Ong (eds), *The Law of the Sea* (Oxford, 2006) Ch 5.

[269] For earlier proposals, see Carroz, 21 *San Diego LR* (1984) 516–17; Kenya, Draft Articles for the preservation and protection of the marine environment, UN Doc A/CONF 62/C3/L/ 2 (1974).

[270] See Scovazzi, 19 *IJMCL* (2004) 383.

[271] Article 143; Annex II, Article 17; 1994 Agreement on Implementation, Annex, Section 1.5. See also 'Regulations on Prospecting and Exploration for Polymetallic Nodules in the Area', Doc ISBA/6/A/18, approved by the ISBA Assembly on 13 July 2000.

[272] Article 161, as revised by 1994 Implementation Agreement, Annex, section 3.15.

'the Enterprise'. The latter's task is to carry out some seabed mining activities on its behalf.[273] The structure, both complex and controversial, was designed as the means of implementing the concept of the common heritage of mankind, which the 1982 UNCLOS applies to deep seabed mineral resources.[274] Similar institutional support is also envisaged in the 1979 Moon Treaty as an essential condition for the application of the same concept to the exploitation of mineral resources on the celestial bodies, but the treaty leaves the creation of such a body to later negotiation.[275]

For reasons partly of political, economic, and ideological opposition, internationalized management of natural resources has had a troubled history. Establishment of the International Seabed Authority was only possible following reforms agreed in the 1994 Implementation Agreement and intended to reduce its bureaucratic complexity and possible expense. The very similar Antarctic Mineral Resources Commission (AMRC) was stillborn, following French and Australian opposition to the Convention for the Regulation of Antarctic Mineral Resource Activities (CRAMRA),[276] which never entered into force. CRAMRA was replaced in 1991 by a Protocol to the Antarctic Treaty on Environmental Protection, which bans all Antarctic mineral resource activities for fifty years, designates Antarctica as a natural reserve, and lays down new rules for the protection of the Antarctic environment and the management of activities in Antarctica.[277] However, the Protocol creates no management institutions with distinctive powers comparable to those of the AMRC or the ISBA. A Committee on Environmental Protection is established, within the framework of the Antarctic Treaty Consultative Meetings, but it performs only the usual supervisory and regulatory functions associated with other environmental treaty institutions. Although a case can still be made for regarding Antarctica as part of the 'common heritage' of mankind,[278] managed by the Consultative Parties to the 1957 Antarctic Treaty under a form of international trusteeship, regulatory 'measures' under the 1991 Protocol can only be adopted, or the Protocol amended, by unanimous agreement.[279] Thus, although the 1991 Protocol otherwise establishes a strong environmental regime,

---

[273] Article 170 as modified by 1994 Implementation Agreement.

[274] Baslar, *The Concept of the Common Heritage of Mankind in International Law* (The Hague, 1998) Ch 6, and see *infra*, Ch 3.

[275] Cheng, *CLP* (1980) 213; Baslar, op cit.

[276] 1988 CRAMRA, Articles 18–33. See Watts, 39 *ICLQ* (1990) 169; Stokke and Vidas (eds), *Governing the Antarctic* (Cambridge, 1996); Wolfrum, *The Convention on the Regulation of Antarctic Mineral Resource Activities* (Berlin, 1993).

[277] Redgwell, 43 *ICLQ* (1994) 599; Pineschi, in Francioni and Scovazzi (eds), *International Law for Antarctica* (2nd edn, The Hague, 1996) Ch 9; Francioni (ed), *International Environmental Law for Antarctica* (Milan, 1992) Ch 1; Vidas (ed), *Implementing the Environmental Protection Regime for the Antarctic* (The Hague, 2000); Triggs and Riddell (eds), *Antarctica: Legal and Environmental Challenges for the Future* (London, 2007).

[278] Francioni, in Francioni and Scovazzi (eds), *International Law for Antarctica* (2nd edn) 9–10, but compare Charney, ibid, 75–80, and Baslar, *The Concept of the Common Heritage of Mankind*, Ch 7.

[279] 1991 Protocol, Articles 9 and 10, applying Articles 9(4) and 12(1) of the 1959 Antarctic Treaty. Even the annexes can only be amended unanimously, unless the annex itself provides otherwise. On the question whether 'measures' are legally binding see Gautier, in Francioni and Scovazzi (eds), *International Law for Antarctica* (2nd edn) Ch 2.

application of the Treaty's unanimity requirement to decision-making by the parties leaves Antarctica in quite a different category from the newer type of international management exemplified by the ISBA.

The significance of international management for environmental protection and resource conservation is that it represents a model of international trusteeship which, by taking away from states control over resource allocation and regulation of the environment, overcomes the two central problems confronting the more limited regulatory and supervisory institutions established under other treaties. Crucially, it substitutes an obligation to comply with majority or consensus decisions for an obligation merely to cooperate in reaching such decisions through good faith negotiation. As Wijkman points out, the latter type of voluntary agreement under which international fisheries commissions have typically operated quickly breaks down and has proved economically inefficient in utilizing common-property resources or arresting the 'tragedy of the commons'. He concludes that: 'When many governments share a resource, the management authority must be given power to determine harvesting limitations unilaterally and to enforce the observance of national quotas allocated within this general limit'.[280] If this cannot be achieved, it may be preferable to remove the resource from a common-property regime entirely, as has now happened for fish stocks falling within the exclusive economic zone.[281] A similar inability to make international control of the high-seas environment fully effective has also resulted in the transfer to coastal states of pollution jurisdiction in this zone.[282] However, as we shall see in Chapters 7 and 13, it is not clear that this transfer has been successful.

Apart from the ambiguous precedents of Antarctica and the deep seabed, the need for more effective international management institutions for the global commons has not so far been realized. Although the Hague Declaration of 1989 endorsed the creation of a strong institution to combat global warming, the institutional provisions of the Climate Change Convention are a disappointment.[283] They lack even the modest advance in decision-making rules made under the Ozone Protocol. Proposals to give the UN Trusteeship Council responsibility for management of the global commons were not adopted at UNCED and have made no further progress. Instead the Global Environment Facility was reformed, and the Commission on Sustainable Development created. Both bodies have influence, but neither has regulatory power, or a mandate to manage common resources or common interests on behalf of the international community.[284]

---

[280] Wijkman, 36 *Int. Org.* (1982) 511; Koers, *International Regulation of Marine Fisheries: A Study of Regional Fisheries Organizations* (London, 1973).

[281] 1982 UNCLOS, Articles 61–70; see *infra*, Ch 13.

[282] 1982 UNCLOS, Articles 56, 207–12; see *infra*, Ch 7.

[283] See Sands, 30 *Harv ILJ* (1989) 417. On the Climate Change Convention see *infra*, Ch 6.

[284] See *supra*, section 2, and generally Werksman, 6 *YbIEL* (1995) 27; Szasz, in Brown Weiss (ed), *Environmental Change and International Law* (1992) 362.

5(4) CONCLUSIONS

Measures of the type considered above may increase the costs of isolated opposition to majority decisions, but they cannot guarantee either participation or adherence to treaty regimes by all states. Resort to soft-law techniques only partially resolves this dilemma, since there is no obligation to comply. The more radical alternative of allowing majorities of states to impose regulations on dissenting minorities is at variance with the philosophy of consent on which the international legal order is based, and for some governments it would accentuate the problem of democratic legitimacy referred to earlier. Nevertheless, the problem of dissentient minorities must in the end be addressed if environmental protection regimes are to establish common rules and implement collective policies followed by all states.[285] It is for this reason that the tentative steps taken in the 1987 Montreal Protocol to the Ozone Convention towards majority decision-making are of particular significance, since they increase the likelihood of more stringent standards being adopted and enforced. It is notable, however, that no subsequent MEA has followed this precedent. Failing such agreed changes, or action by the UN Security Council, linking MEA participation and compliance to World Bank funding and access to the benefits of free trade under WTO rules represent the only realistic alternatives.

There is plainly room for improvements in existing treaty structures, which themselves represent a pragmatic attempt to find workable answers to difficult problems affecting many states with diverse and competing interests. The essential modesty of what has been achieved falls well short of international management of the global environment, and remains heavily dependent on progress by consensus. Improving and measuring the performance of existing treaty bodies has for this reason been an item on the UN agenda since the UNCED Conference in 1992. Included among the matters considered have been the facilitation and encouragement of wider participation, especially by developing countries, the provision of better financing arrangements, and improvements in the rule-making and amendment procedures of existing treaty institutions.[286] We have also seen earlier in this chapter that many of those issues remain under discussion in the context of proposals to 'cluster' MEAs under the general umbrella of UNEP or create a World Environment Organization. Perhaps the most important development to affect MEAs, however, has been the creation of a growing number of non-compliance procedures. These are considered further in Chapter 4.

---

[285] See Mc Dorman, 20 *IJMCL* (2005) 423 who looks at the problem from the perspective of fisheries commissions.

[286] See e.g. Sand, *Lessons Learned in Global Environmental Governance* (New York, 1990) 6–20; UNCED, *The Effectiveness of International Agreements* (Cambridge, 1992).

6 SCIENTIFIC ORGANIZATIONS

While many IGOs and treaty bodies have established their own scientific advisory committees, a number of international organizations exist specifically to provide independent scientific advice and research on matters of environmental importance.[287] The value of most of these bodies is that they represent 'a diversity of knowledge and expertise',[288] and provide an independent or neutral source of publicly accessible data. Scientists cannot be expected to take policy decisions that are ultimately the responsibility of politicians; rather their role as experts is 'to refine problem definition and to identify and expend the range of response options', setting out uncertainties, assumptions, and the probable consequences of action or inaction.[289]

One of the most active is the International Council for Exploration of the Seas (ICES).[290] ICES was founded informally by scientists in 1902 but put on a treaty basis in 1964. It is open to any state approved by its members, though its scope is limited to the Atlantic Ocean and adjacent seas. Its aim is to promote, encourage, and organize research and investigation for the study of the sea, especially its living resources, and to disseminate the results. It has a coordinating, not a managerial or lawmaking, role but contributes to the latter by supplying advice on request or by formal agreement to such bodies as the FAO, IMO, UNESCO, WHO, UNEP, the EC, the North-East Atlantic Fisheries Commission and the Helsinki and Paris Commissions. It has interpreted its mandate broadly to cover not only fisheries but also pollution from various sources. Though it has no regulatory role, it can come to conclusions and make recommendations, drawing attention to management and legislative needs, indicating whether species or pollutants should be added to regulatory annexes.

ICES has a very small secretariat (Bureau) and a Council that meets annually taking by vote decisions that are executed by the Bureau. Its meetings are attended by delegates, experts, observers from non-member states and international organizations, and scientists invited personally. It has achieved an excellent reputation for offering fair and impartial advice and has published a large number of influential reports. Its use of a grid system for the purposes of collecting information has enabled a detailed picture of fisheries and environmental factors to be built up for the relevant commissions. Similar expert bodies cover other seas, but have been less active bodies than ICES, although there is renewed interest in their role.[291]

---

[287] See generally Andresen et al (eds), *Science and Politics in International Environmental Regimes* (Manchester, 2000).

[288] Kimball, *Treaty Implementation: Scientific and Technical Advice Enters a New Stage* (Washington, 1996) 7. See also Andresen and Skjaerseth, in Bodansky et al, *Handbook of IEL*, 183ff.

[289] Ibid.

[290] 1964 Convention for the International Council for the Exploration of the Seas. See Kimball, *Treaty Implementation*, 187–8.

[291] In 1919 the International Commission for the Scientific Exploration of the Mediterranean Sea was instituted, followed in 1949 by the General Fisheries Council for the Mediterranean (GFCM) and in 1990 the North Pacific Marine Science Organization (PICES).

UNESCO's Intergovernmental Oceanographic Commission (IOC) is also active at the international level in structuring and coordinating marine scientific research projects and has increasingly involved developing countries in joint research programmes.[292] It is notable that the United States and United Kingdom, even when they withdrew from UNESCO, continued to participate in and support the work of the IOC. Scientific research is conducted at the regional level through intergovernmental commissions, such as those dealing with land-based pollution, pollution from dumping, and fisheries discussed in later chapters. The IOC works closely with an inter-agency Group of Experts on the Scientific Aspects of Marine Pollution (GESAMP), whose reports have provided invaluable information on the state of the marine environment.[293]

Other non-governmental groups providing independent, authoritative advice include the International Council for Science (ICSU), which has various environmental programmes and has cooperated, inter alia, with WMO, UNEP and UNESCO in scientific studies relating to climate change and in organizing scientific conferences calling for policy decisions from governments.[294] The ICSU is also prominent in the provision of scientific advice to the Antarctic treaty system, through its Scientific Committee on Antarctic Research (SCAR). The Intergovernmental Panel on Climate Change, established by UNEP and WMO, has assumed the principal responsibility for independent scientific assessment of climate change science and policy.[295] Finally, the UN Scientific Committee on the Effects of Radiation is the principle international body providing independent scientific advice on radiological protection.

7 NON-GOVERNMENTAL ORGANIZATIONS

7(1) ROLE OF NGOS IN GENERAL

Modern non-governmental organizations have existed for over one hundred years, since their creation by Victorian naturalists and philanthropists.[296] NGOs have proliferated in modern times, and they play an important part in contemporary concepts of international governance.[297] More than 8,000 attended the NGO forum during the 1992 Rio Conference. Over one hundred regularly attend meetings of the International

---

[292] See Bernal, in Nordquist et al (eds), *Law, Science and Ocean Management* (Leiden, 2007) 21–63.

[293] See Kimball, *Treaty Implementation*, 194–5, and *infra*, Ch 7.

[294] Kimball, *Treaty Implementation*, 188–9.   [295] Kimball, ibid, 195–6, and see *infra*, Ch 6.

[296] McCormick, *The Global Environmental Movement* (London, 1989) esp 1–24. Some of the earliest NGOs were formed to protect birds, the first in 1867. The movement to save whales began at the 8th International Zoological Congress in 1910.

[297] See generally Tolbert, in Churchill and Freestone (eds), *International Law and Global Climate Change: International Legal Issues and Implications* (London, 1991) 95; Charnovitz, 18 *Mich JIL* (1997) 183; id, 100 *AJIL* (2006) 348; Boyle and Chinkin, *The Making of International Law* (Oxford, 2007) Ch 2; Spiro, in Bodansky, Brunnée and Hey, *Handbook of IEL*, 771–90; Gupta, 63 *ZAÖRV* (2003) 459.

Whaling Commission (IWC).[298] The development of international environmental law has been influenced by the activities and pressure of many industrial and business organizations, as well as those established purely for purposes of environmental protection. Japanese fishermen's unions attend IWC meetings alongside conservationist NGOs. On climate change, organizations representing oil companies and the motor industry are as active in UN bodies as environmentalist NGOs.

NGOs' aims and activities are diverse and often entwined. Some are international professional bodies, usually in the scientific field, such as the International Council of Scientific Unions (ICSU); some have exclusively educational or research purposes, such as the World Resources Institute (WRI), or the International Institute for Environment and Development (IIED); others are campaigning organizations advocating particular courses of action, such as Friends of the Earth International (FOEI), Greenpeace International, the Sierra Club, the National Audubon Society, the International Fund for Animal Welfare (IFAW), and the World Wide Fund for Nature (WWF). Some are purely national, others regional, yet others fully international. Most of the major international environmental NGOs are based in northern-hemisphere developed states, but national NGOs are also beginning to play an important part in some developing countries.

The extent to which NGOs can participate in and influence the work of international organizations depends on the constitution and practice of each organization, and varies considerably. Article 71 of the UN Charter provides only for NGOs to enter into consultation agreements with ECOSOC,[299] but UN resolutions also allow the Secretary General to invite them to attend public sessions of the General Assembly and Security Council as observers when economic and social matters are under discussion. The practice of most UN specialized agencies, such as IMO and FAO, is similar. NGOs are allowed to participate in meetings as observers only if they are concerned with matters within the competence of the relevant organ or organization. NGO participation remains controversial in some international organizations, notably the IAEA and WTO, due to opposition from some member states.[300]

The effectiveness of NGOs varies greatly according to their seriousness of purpose, funding, depth of research, skills in political advocacy, means of exercising pressure, and narrowness of focus. Some have become effective at achieving consultative status at international and regional organizations where their representation and personal lobbying may, if to the point and well researched, influence the negotiating process for conventions and resolutions. Increasingly they have 'networked' their activities, for example at the Rio Conference, where NGOs met to coordinate their policies and actions.

---

[298] In contrast, fewer than 40 states are parties to the convention.

[299] Compare Article 70, which gives observer status to intergovernmental organizations. On Article 71 and UN practice see Simma (ed), *The Charter of the UN: A Commentary* (2nd edn, Oxford, 2002).

[300] On WTO see Marceau and Pedersen, 33 *JWT* (1999) 5–20; Esty, 1 *JIEL* (1998) 123.

7(2) INTERNATIONAL UNION FOR THE CONSERVATION OF NATURE (IUCN)

One of the most important organizations operating at the international level, which merits special mention, is the International Union for the Conservation of Nature (IUCN), also known as the World Conservation Union.[301] Founded in 1948, this is a federative membership organization, consisting primarily of governments or their agencies but also including scientific, professional, and conservation bodies such as the World Wide Fund for Nature (WWF), with which the IUCN has a close association. The diversity of its membership is unique among environmental bodies, comprising 83 states, 110 government agencies, over 800 national and international NGOs, and some 10,000 scientists, lawyers, and experts from 181 countries. As such it is something of a hybrid organization, neither exclusively intergovernmental nor wholly non-governmental in character.

The IUCN has a small secretariat located in Gland, Switzerland, and an Environmental Law Centre in Bonn, which, inter alia, provides a repository of legal information available to members. Many leading legal experts serve on its International Council of Environmental Law. A General Assembly of all members deliberates every three years. Resolutions which members adopt are presented to governments and relevant bodies, but it operates mainly through numerous standing commissions and committees. The former include Ecology, National Parks, and Protected Areas; Environmental Policy, Law and Administration; Species Survival and Environmental Planning. The IUCN lacks real powers; however, its resolutions do not bind and it has no enforcement mechanisms.

Despite these limitations, IUCN's hybrid character has helped it to play a catalytic role in initiating or supporting new legal developments. It early perceived the need to link environment and development and prepared the IUCN/WWF/UNEP World Conservation Strategy, published in 1980, in which FAO and UNESCO also collaborated. This laid down principles for conservation of living resources and for legal developments to ensure their sustainable utilization.[302] The IUCN was also instrumental in drafting the World Charter for Nature, adopted by the UN General Assembly in 1982.[303] Although the IUCN's mission is primarily to provide advice and expertise, it helps governments develop international declarations and conventions. It did preparatory work on the Convention on Biological Diversity and the proposed Earth Charter for UNCED, and contributed to the negotiation of 1972 World Heritage Convention, the 1973 Convention on Trade in Endangered Species, the 1971 Convention on Wetlands of International Importance, and the 1979 Convention on Conservation of Migratory Species of Wild Animals.[304] It seeks, as far as possible, to fill gaps in legal developments, or to cooperate with other organizations in preparing drafts, or in commenting on them, and to provide expert advice and support to developing countries in the drafting of national laws and regional conventions.

---

[301] See *IUCN Bulletin* (1988, Special Issue).   [302] See *infra*, Ch 11.
[303] Ibid.   [304] On all these agreements see *infra*, Ch 12.

The IUCN's most ambitious, but little noticed, undertaking is the drafting of a proposed Covenant on Environment and Development in 1995.[305] With seventy-two articles this represents the most detailed and comprehensive attempt to codify and develop international environmental law yet seen. It is at the same time conservative insofar as it follows closely the previous development of the subject. The draft reiterates and builds on the Rio principles; it seeks to provide a framework for further integration of environment and development and to restate fundamental norms and principles. Unlike all prior attempts, it also sets out to codify the law relating to specific sectoral problems, dividing these into four categories: natural systems (ozone, climate, soil, water, forests, wetlands, marine ecosystems, biological diversity and cultural and natural heritage); processes and activities producing pollution and waste; global issues (such as population, poverty, trade, military activities, and those of foreign firms); and transboundary issues. Further articles deal with implementation, liability, and compliance. There is little here that is novel per se; in essence the draft extrapolates principles from existing treaties or other instruments and elevates them to a higher plane of generality. Not every article is necessarily *lex lata*, but overall this remains perhaps the most accurate portrayal of the present corpus of existing and developing international environmental law.

8 CONCLUSIONS

As this chapter has sought to demonstrate, the historical background and original goals of the UN and its agencies have not generated a system that is well suited to synthesizing environmental and developmental goals, a fusion that UNCED identified as the key issue in the achievement of sustainable development. The UN's original security-oriented purposes, the politicization of its organs along East–West and North–South divides, the sectoralism of the specialized agencies, the proliferation of programmes and autonomous units with different objectives, and the large number of concerned bodies that exist outside the UN, have made coordination difficult. Neither coordinating committees such as the ACC nor UNEP have been given sufficient authority to have a radical impact on this fragmented system so far.

Debates prior to UNCED made clear that there was no political support for creation of a new supranational UN environment and development agency, nor even for endowing any one existing agency with a lead role. It was always unlikely that a conference on the scale of UNCED, divided by such a variety of interests, would adopt strong measures or establish powerful new machinery. Though the UNCED Prepcom undertook the most wide-ranging and thorough review ever conducted of the UN's environmental and developmental activities and the whole range of environmental and developmental agreements and institutions worldwide, UNCED failed to

---

[305] Robinson, 13 Pace ELR (1995) 133; Boyle and Freestone, International Law and Sustainable Development, Ch 4. For the current text see IUCN, Draft International Covenant on Environment and Development (3rd edn, Gland, 2004).

reach agreement on any one radical solution for reforming the UN system. Its review revealed the wide range of available machinery, and concluded that, beyond the creation of the Commission on Sustainable Development, there was little need for new additions. Fifteen years later nothing has significantly changed.

The criteria agreed in 1972 by governments for the institutional aspects of the UNCHE Action Plan remain pertinent to an understanding of UNCED: instituting a mechanism for agreeing on the action required; use of existing organizations; developing institutional networks with linkages and 'switchboard mechanisms' rather than a new supranational agency; providing for flexibility and evolution in the context of incomplete knowledge; avoiding overlap by coordination and rationalization; ensuring that any policy-centres established to influence and coordinate activities do not have operational functions that compete with cooperating organizations; strengthening regional capability; retaining the UN as the main centre for international cooperation but strengthening and reinforcing the whole UN system whilst taking account of the wide variations in environmental conditions among states.[306]

Have the institutional reforms initiated by UNCED been sufficient to set in motion the rethinking, redirection and review necessary to enable Agenda 21 targets to be met?[307] What UNCED produced was a set of tools for achieving these goals in the long term. Much depends, as always, on the will of states to use these tools effectively. Agenda 21 has influenced environmental and developmental cooperation and could provide the basis for further initiatives. This is the most important outcome of UNCED. As Dr Brundtland said in commenting on UNCED's achievements: 'Progress in many fields, too little progress in most fields, and no progress at all in some fields...But the direction of where we are heading has been set'.[308] No doubt it is still possible to mitigate environmental problems to a considerable extent without changing the underlying political and economic factors responsible for environmental degradation: 'discrete, reformist, institutionalised measures have been effective'.[309] International institutions have not been systematically integrated, but their environmental efforts can nevertheless complement each other better than might have been expected; their achievements stem not from large bureaucratic operations or enforcement powers, but from their catalytic role in 'increasing governmental concern, enhancing the contractual environment and increasing national political and administrative capacity'.[310]

---

[306] Thacher, *Global Security and Risk Management: Background to Institutional Options for Management of the Global Environment and Commons* (Geneva, World Federation of United National Associations, 1991).

[307] See French, *After the Earth Summit: The Future of Global Environmental Governance* (Washington DC, 1992); Kimball, *Forging International Agreements* (Washington DC, 1991); Thacher, in Hurrell and Kingsbury (eds), *The International Politics of the Environment* (Oxford, 1992); Sand, *Lessons Learned in Global Environmental Governance* (Washington DC, 1990); Tinker, *Making UNCED Work: Building the Legal and Institutional Framework for Sustainable Development at the Earth Summit and Beyond* (Washington, UNA-USA Occasional Paper No 4, 1992). For a critique of UNCED institutional arrangements see Kimball and Boyd, 1 *RECIEL* (1992) 295 and *ASIL Proc* (1992) 414, on the conclusions of which this section is largely based

[308] As quoted by El-Ashry, *Rio Review* (Centre for Our Common Future, 1992) 11.

[309] Ibid.   [310] Ibid.

While the objectives of all the elements of the UN system are intended to be compatible and complementary, they remain different.[311] Each organization has its own mandate, its own constituency of member states, and its own objectives. Although this functional differentiation makes planning and implementation of programmes across the UN system a more complex process, it may also be a potential strength, because it forces interactions, debate, and diversity; a convergence of planning procedures is required, rather than blank uniformity. UNCED Agenda 21 sets out ways of achieving this in broad and flexible terms while encouraging the embodiment of environmental concerns in the activities of the development agencies and programmes generally and indicating the action required.

The UN system has also not been notably effective in assessing, reviewing, and monitoring either the effects of its programmes or compliance with prescribed measures. Scrutiny has been left mainly to autonomous treaty bodies and NGOs, which have performed the task efficiently in several areas, but their activities are necessarily issue-oriented: they cannot themselves carry out the required reforms to remedy the whole range of weaknesses in the system, especially the coordinative failures. It is governments that have to legislate and to ensure that their national programmes conform to the UN goals for sustainable development. It is here that NGOs can provide a necessary stimulus, as could a more focused Commission on Sustainable Development or UNEP.

Hurrell and Kingsbury have pointed out that: 'It would be wrong to assume...that the universal rhetoric of ecological interdependence translates readily into effective international action'.[312] On the other hand, we can also observe the impact that the Stockholm Conference, Declaration, Action Plan, and institutions have had on the international system as a whole, both inside and outside the UN, despite contemporaneous criticisms of their weakness and of UNCHE's 'failure'. Although 'sovereignty remains the legal cornerstone of the environmental order',[313] and governments thus stress the need for action at the national rather than international level, it is quite clear, as subsequent chapters will show, that new life has also been breathed into the UN system by UNCED and the post-UNCED reforms.

Fundamental questions still remain. One is whether the post-UNCED process has been sufficiently energizing to generate sustainable development—or to overcome fundamental differences on what must be done. Another is whether the balancing of environment and development required by the Rio Declaration will in fact result in the subordination of environmental to developmental goals.[314] A final question, well beyond the scope of this work, is whether the global system of international environmental lawmaking and governance has the legitimacy necessary to ensure comprehensive participation, implementation, and compliance by all the relevant actors.[315]

---

[311] UNEP, *UN System-Wide Medium Term Environment Programme 1990–1995* (Nairobi, 1988) 101.

[312] Hurrell and Kingsbury (eds), *The International Politics of the Environment*, 47.

[313] Levy, Haas, and Keohane, 34/4 *Environment* (1992) 12–17, 29–36.

[314] See Pallemaerts, in Sands (ed), *Greening International Law* (London, 1993) 1.

[315] See in particular Hey, 34 *NYIL* (2003) 3; Bodansky, 93 *AJIL* (1999) 596.

3

RIGHTS AND OBLIGATIONS OF STATES CONCERNING PROTECTION OF THE ENVIRONMENT

1 INTRODUCTION

1(1) CODIFICATION AND DEVELOPMENT OF INTERNATIONAL ENVIRONMENTAL LAW

The main argument in this and the following two chapters is that rules and principles of international law concerning protection of the environment exist and can be identified.[1] In many cases the evidence for this assertion is strong and is considered in more detail in later chapters; in others the need for further clarification is apparent. It must be remembered, as we saw in Chapter 1, that international environmental law is not a separate or self-contained field of law. In some respects it is simply the application of well-established rules, principles and processes of general international law to the resolution of international environmental problems and disputes. Thus the subject

---

[1] See generally Bodansky, Brunnée, Hey (eds), *Oxford Handbook of International Environmental Law* (Oxford, 2007); Louka, *International Environmental Law* (Cambridge, 2006); Atapattu, *Emerging Principles of International Environmental Law* (Ardsley, 2006); Kiss and Shelton, *International Environmental Law* (3rd edn, New York, 2005); Sands, *Principles of International Environmental Law* (2nd edn, Cambridge, 2003); de Sadeleer, *Environmental Principles* (OUP, 2002); Dupuy, 101 *RGDIP* (1997) 873; Dunoff, 19 *Harv ELR* (1995) 241; Freestone, 6 *JEL* (1994) 193; Fitzmaurice, 25 *NYIL* (1994) 181; Brown Weiss, *Environmental Change and International Law* (Tokyo, 1992); Handl, 1 *YbIEL* (1990) 3.

cannot be understood without a good understanding of international law as a whole. Many otherwise novel environmental questions can be answered without the need for creating new law, or even for developing old law. A good example is the defence of necessity in the law of state responsibility. Once it is appreciated that states also have environmental as well as other interests to protect within the terms of the existing rule, the application of this defence in such cases is neither problematic nor innovative.[2] Similarly, it is possible to rely on violation of territorial sovereignty to encompass transboundary pollution,[3] but this immediately begs obvious questions about when such pollution becomes unlawful. Is all transboundary pollution an interference with sovereignty? Or only when it can be attributed to the actions or inactions of a state? Any discussion of these questions tends to become indistinguishable from the rule on transboundary harm codified in Principle 21 of the Stockholm Declaration and considered later.[4]

Modern environmental problems have also prompted the creation of new law, or development and clarification of existing law. Much of this new law has emerged gradually, through a process of incremental development in the fields of pollution control and conservation of the natural environment, or more recently in regard to problems of global environmental concern. The evolution in our understanding of how international law relates to the environment has been too recent to allow for universally acceptable codification.[5] In some cases the rules themselves, their present legal status, or their precise implications, remain controversial or need further consolidation. The most widely ratified treaties, such as the Conventions and related protocols on Climate Change or Ozone Depletion, constitute international regulatory regimes which have become the most important sources of law on these subjects for almost all states.[6] There is also much soft law, whose legal status varies, but which is not necessarily non-binding in all circumstances. A more difficult question is how far the rules and principles found in these treaties and soft-law instruments have been translated into customary international law. Some evidence of existing or developing customary law is found in the 1982 UN Convention on the Law of the Sea (1982 UNCLOS),[7] in the work of UN specialized agencies and programmes,[8] and of bodies such as the International Law Commission (ILC),[9] the International Law Association

---

[2] See *Gabčíkovo-Nagymaros Case,* ICJ Reports (1997) 7, paras 49–58.

[3] See *Nuclear Tests Cases*, ICJ Reports (1974) 175, 253.

[4] See *infra*, section 4, and discussion of the *Trail Smelter Arbitration.*

[5] But see WCED, Legal Experts Group, Draft Convention on Environmental Protection and Sustainable Development, in Munro and Lammers, *Environmental Protection and Sustainable Development: Legal Principles and Recommendations* (London, 1986) and IUCN, *Draft International Covenant on Environment and Development* (3rd edn, Gland, 2004); Robinson, 13 *Pace ELR* (1995) 133; Boyle and Freestone (eds), *International Law and Sustainable Development* (Oxford, 1999) Ch 4.

[6] See *infra*, Ch 6. On regulatory regimes see *supra* Ch 2.   [7] See *infra*, Chs 7, 8, and 13.

[8] The most important of these is UNEP, on which see *supra* Ch 2.

[9] See 2001 Articles on the Prevention of Transboundary Harm from Hazardous Activities, and commentary, *infra*, section 4; on environmental crimes see *infra*, Ch 5, section 6; on international watercourses, see *infra*, Ch 10, and on allocation of loss *infra*, Ch 5, section 4.

(ILA),[10] and the Institut de Droit International (IDI).[11] There is, however, no single treaty or declaration comparable to the 1982 UNCLOS, the 1947 GATT or the 1948 Universal Declaration of Human Rights in systematically setting out the basic rules and principles of the subject.

Since 1992, environmental disputes have formed a significant proportion of the caseload of the International Court of Justice (ICJ),[12] the Dispute Settlement Body of the World Trade Organisation (WTO),[13] the International Tribunal on the Law of the Sea (ITLOS),[14] and arbitration tribunals.[15] Some of these decisions provide evidence for the evolution of customary international law concerning the environment, but they remain at present too few in number and too limited in scope to offer a comprehensive statement of the law. It has been aptly noted by one arbitral tribunal that 'There is considerable debate as to what, within the field of environmental law, constitutes 'rules' or 'principles'; what is 'soft law'; and which environmental treaty law or principles have contributed to the development of customary international law'.[16] What is clear, however, and what needs to be remembered when reading this chapter, is that international law dealing with the environment is still in a state of dynamic development. Propositions about what is or is not customary law are liable to change, in some cases quite quickly, and it cannot be assumed without further enquiry either that recent developments are not law, or that older judicial precedents continue to state existing law. As we saw in Chapter 1, views differ on the relative importance of state practice and declaratory principles adopted by consensus in crystallizing the formation of new law. In some disputes the parties have been happy to rely on unratified treaties, the work of the International Law Commission, or soft-law instruments as evidence of

[10] For the ILA's early work see *Rept of 55th Conference* (1972) 468–500; *57th Conference* (1976) 564–87; *58th Conference* (1978) 383–422. For the Montreal Rules on Transfrontier Pollution see *60th Conference* (1982) 1; transboundary air pollution: *65th Conference* (1992); water pollution: *67th Conference* (1996) 401–15; marine pollution: *69th Conference* (2000) 443–512; sustainable development: *69th Conference* (2000) 655–710; water resources: *71st Conference* (2004) 334–65; transnational enforcement: *72nd Conference* (2006) 655–91. See generally Boyle and Freestone, *International Law and Sustainable Development*, Ch 4.

[11] IDI, *Rept of the Athens Session* (1979) I, 193–380 and II, 197 (pollution of rivers and lakes); id, *Rept of the Cairo Session* (1987) I, 159–294 and II, 296 (transboundary air pollution); IDI, 1997 Resolutions on (i) Environment, (ii) Procedure for the Adoption and Implementation of Rules in the Field of Environment, and (iii) Responsibility and Liability for Environmental Damage, on which see Sands, 30 *RBDI* (1997) 512. He rightly condemns the Institute's 1997 resolutions as 'rubble rather than architecture'.

[12] See *infra*, section 4(1).

[13] WTO cases include *United State—Import Prohibition of Certain Shrimp and Shrimp Products* ['Shrimp-Turtle Case'] WTO Appellate Body (1998) WT/DS58/AB/R and *Art 21.5 Report* (2001) WT/DS58/AB/RW; *EC-Measures Concerning Meat And Meat Products* ['Beef Hormones Case'] WTO Appellate Body (1997) WT/DS26/AB/R; *EC-Measures Affecting Asbestos, etc* ['Asbestos Case'] WTO Appellate Body (2001) WT/DS135/AB/R. See *infra*, Ch 14.

[14] At least three can be regarded as environmental: *Southern Bluefin Tuna Cases (Provisional Measures)* ITLOS Nos 3 & 4 (1999); *MOX Plant Case (Provisional Measures)* ITLOS No 10 (2001); *Case Concerning Land Reclamation by Singapore in and around the Straits of Johor (Provisional Measures)* ITLOS No 12 (2003) ['*Land Reclamation Case*'].

[15] *MOX Plant Arbitration*, PCA (2003); *OSPAR Convention Arbitration*, PCA (2003); *Land Reclamation Arbitration*, PCA (2005); *Iron Rhine Arbitration*, PCA (2005).

[16] *Iron Rhine Arbitration*, para 58.

international law. In others they have taken a more sceptical stance and pointed to the absence of state practice or *opinio juris*. There are also disputes where the parties have not pressed their strict legal rights to the full but have preferred to negotiate equitable solutions,[17] while in others they have been content to interpret older treaties in an evolutionary manner, so that contemporary standards of environmental law can be incorporated.[18] How far what follows can be regarded as *lex lata* thus depends partly on the methodology used to identify international law.

Moreover, even when applicable treaties or customary law are identified, how different rules affecting the same issue interact is not always clear. Conflicts between treaties are in theory resolved in accordance with Articles 30 and 41 of the Vienna Convention on Treaties, and depend to a large extent on the intention of the parties and the *lex specialis* rule.[19] As the *Gabčíkovo-Nagymaros* and *Shrimp-Turtle* cases show, a treaty also has to be interpreted and applied in the light of other rules of international law, including new norms of environmental law.[20] An understanding of customary international law and general principles is thus essential even when the applicable law is treaty-based. The application of norms of international law dealing specifically with environmental problems may also have to take into account other bodies of law dealing inter alia with sustainable development, human rights, international watercourses, law of the sea, armed conflict or free trade. How courts resolve the potential for conflict between simultaneously applicable norms in these situations is essentially a matter of judicial technique, but the case law of the International Court and of other international tribunals suggests that where possible they prefer an integrated conception of international law to a fragmented one.[21] Apart from highlighting the formative role of international courts in determining the applicable law, this conclusion points again to the danger of viewing any part of international law in isolation from the whole. Not only are the rules dynamic, but potentially so is their interaction. What cannot be supposed is that environmental rules have any inherent priority over others save in the exceptional case of *ius cogens* norms. The principle characteristic of a *ius cogens* rule is that 'it may not be trumped by another rule that is not itself *ius cogens*'.[22] No such

---

[17] See *infra*, section 4(5). [18] See e.g. the *Iron Rhine Arbitration*, para 60.

[19] The precedents are reviewed in Boyle and Chinkin, *The Making of International Law* (Oxford, 2007) 250–3.

[20] 1969 Vienna Convention on the Law of Treaties, Article 31(3). See *Gabčíkovo-Nagymaros Case*, ICJ Reports (1997) 7, paras 112 and 140; *Shrimp-Turtle Case*, supra n 13. See also *Nuclear Weapons Advisory Opinion (UNGA)* ICJ Reports (1996) 226, where the Court took into account the law on use of force when interpreting environmental treaties, and *Beef Hormones Case*, WT/DS26/AB/R (1997) paras 120–25. See McLachlan, 54 *ICLQ* (2005) 279; Boyle and Chinkin, *The Making of International Law* (Oxford, 2007) Ch 5.

[21] A conclusion confirmed by Stephens, 25 *AYIL* (2004) 226, 270. See *Gabčíkovo-Nagymaros Case*, ICJ Reports (1997) 7, paras 112, 140; *Nuclear Weapons AO*, ICJ Reports (1996) 226; *Oil Platforms Case*, ICJ Reports (2003) 161, paras 31–45; *Shrimp-Turtle Case* (1998) WT/DS58/AB/R, paras 131–3; *Iron Rhine Arbitration*, PCA (2005), and the discussion of human rights and sustainable development in Ch 5.

[22] Seiderman, *Hierarchy in International Law* (Antwerp, 2001) 35–6.

norms of international environmental law have yet been convincingly identified,[23] nor is there an obvious case for treating them in this way.[24]

To say that rules and principles of international environmental law must be integrated with the rest of international law does not mean that the law is always the same for all states regardless of their capabilities or differing circumstances. In the development of international environmental law the different priorities of mainly southern hemisphere less-developed countries have been given 'special consideration'. For many of these countries poverty and the need for economic development are perceived as the main 'environmental' problem. Their concerns have been a central feature of environmental diplomacy since the Stockholm Conference. Various ways of reconciling the competing priorities of north and south have been employed. The concept of sustainable development,[25] economic assistance and capacity-building through the Global Environment Facility and other trust funds,[26] alterations in the lending policies of the World Bank and other capital providers,[27] and the negotiation of different[28]—usually lower—standards of environmental regulation and resource conservation are all part of a strategy for engaging developing states in the process of regulating the international environment. With regard to global environmental problems the concept of 'common but differentiated responsibility' has helped to mediate North–South disagreements by recognizing their different contribution to generating environmental problems and their different capacities for resolving them.[29] The UN General Assembly has also been careful to formulate the 'right to development' in terms requiring respect for international law on friendly relations and cooperation, as well as sustainable development.[30] Moreover, the emphasis placed on sovereignty over natural resources and freedom to pursue policies of economic growth must be seen in its proper context. UN resolutions, the Stockholm and Rio Declarations, and other international instruments have consistently recognized that although states have permanent sovereignty over their natural resources and the right to determine their own environmental and developmental policies, they are not free to disregard protection of the environment of common spaces or of other states.[31] Nevertheless, developmental priorities remain a major obstacle to stronger environmental regulation for developing and developed economies alike.

Some of the precedents on which this chapter is based are regional or bilateral in scope or reflect environmental concerns appropriate mainly to northern hemisphere industrialized states. There are obvious dangers in assuming that such precedents

---

[23] In *Gabčíkovo-Nagymaros*, para 97, the Court impliedly accepted Slovakia's argument that none of the norms of environmental law on which Hungary relied was *ius cogens*.

[24] Orkhelashvili, *Peremptory Norms in International Law* (Oxford, 2006) 65, suggests otherwise, but while certain norms considered in this chapter may apply *erga omnes*, it does not follow that they are therefore also *ius cogens*. On the contrary, there is no necessary connection between these two categories. See generally Seiderman, op cit, 123–9.

[25] *Supra* Ch 2, section 2(5) and *infra*, section 2.   [26] *Supra* Ch 2, section 4(4).   [27] Ibid.

[28] 1992 Rio Declaration on Environment and Development, Principles 7 and 11; 1972 Stockholm Declaration on the Human Environment, Principles 8–12, and 23, and *infra*, section 3(3).

[29] See *infra*, section 3(3).   [30] See *infra*, section 2(3).   [31] See *infra*, section 4.

necessarily have global force. This does not mean that international environmental law represents only a regional system, or systems, of law, nor does it imply that its rules have no relevance to the problems of the Third World, but it does imply that we need evidence of Third World practice to complement the richer material available from the developed world. Securing Third World participation in treaty regimes of global significance, such as the 1985 Ozone Convention, the 1982 UNCLOS, the 1992 Conventions on Climate Change and Biological Diversity, or the 2001 POPS Convention, is even more important. The particular significance of UNCED Agenda 21 and the Rio Declaration is that they are not simply expressions of the views of developed northern-hemisphere countries, but also reflect the concerns of a broad coalition of developing states.[32] This is clear if we look at the evidence of international litigation or regional treaties.[33]

In contrast to developing states, the reluctance of the United States to be bound by more recent environmental agreements casts some doubt on the extent to which it is subject to contemporary international environmental law.[34] The United States will normally participate in environmental negotiations and advance its own position strongly, but the rarity with which it then ratifies or supports the outcome is noticeable. Its most consistent objective is to protect free trade and its own autonomy. In deference to its industrialists, the United States is not a party to the Biodiversity Convention, the Kyoto Protocol, the POPS Convention, the Basel Convention, the PIC Convention, or the UN Convention on the Law of the Sea, although in practice it treats the latter agreement as largely customary law and it has been an active promoter of the UN Fish Stocks Agreement and of marine conservation in general. The only UNECE treaty to which it is a party is the Convention on Long-range Transboundary Air Pollution, but only two of its protocols.[35] It does not participate in any environmental liability treaties, although it has ratified the Vienna Convention on Supplementary Compensation for Nuclear Damage. Its failure to ratify the Caribbean Protocol on Land-based Sources of Marine Pollutuion has prevented that instrument from coming force. The United States supported the Rio Declaration with extensive reservations, and it remains particularly doubtful how far it accepts the precautionary approach. It is not subject to the compulsory jurisdiction of the ICJ or the International Criminal Court, and is not a party to the Inter-American Convention on Human Rights. The only forums in which it can usefully be sued in environmental disputes are the WTO and NAFTA arbitral tribunals.[36] The *Trail Smelter Arbitration*, the 1972 Stockholm Conference and the Ozone Convention remain as testimony to American dynamism in an earlier era of progressive environmentalism, but they are only faintly echoed in contemporary US policy.

[32] See *supra* Ch 2.

[33] See e.g. the *Pulp Mills Case*, ICJ Reports (2006), human rights cases (Ch 5) and regional agreements on the marine environment (Ch 7), international watercourses (Ch 10) and fisheries (Ch 13).

[34] See Brunnée, 15 *EJIL* (2004) 617–649.   [35] Heavy metals and NOx.

[36] See e.g. *Shrimp/Turtle Case*, WTO Appellate Body (1998) WT/DS58/AB/R; *Methanex Corporation v United States of America*, UNCITRAL Final Award (2005).

1(2) THE 1992 RIO DECLARATION ON ENVIRONMENT AND DEVELOPMENT

The Rio Declaration on Environment and Development,[37] adopted by consensus at the UN Conference on Environment and Development in 1992, constitutes at present the most significant universally endorsed statement of general rights and obligations of states affecting the environment. The Declaration is in part a restatement of existing customary law on transboundary matters, partly an endorsement of new or developing principles of law concerned with protection of the global environment, and partly a statement of policies and ideals set out more fully in Agenda 21, the programme of action for tackling environmental problems also adopted by the Conference, and whose implementation may lead to further lawmaking. This does not mean that the Declaration itself is binding law. Its value, like certain other soft-law declarations, is evidential: it tells us what states believe the law to be in certain cases, or in others what they would like it to become or how they want it to develop. The Declaration's legal significance can therefore only be properly appreciated in conjunction with an examination of the pre-existing customary law, and the development of state practice, further treaties, protocols, regulations, and judicial decisions, in the period since Rio. As we shall see in the following sections, the Declaration has had significant impact in all of these areas of lawmaking; several of the principles have been referred to by the ILC in support of its codification of the law relating to transboundary harm,[38] and it appears to be one of the 'great number of instruments' setting out norms of international environmental law to which the International Court of Justice referred in the *Gabčíkovo-Nagymaros Case*, and on which the Court also relied explicitly in its *Nuclear Weapons Advisory Opinion*.[39]

Three factors give the Rio Declaration significant authority and influence in the articulation and development of contemporary international law relating to the environment. First, unlike the earlier Stockholm Declaration of 1972, it is expressed mainly in obligatory terms. Although some principles use the words 'States should...', most start with the injunction that 'States shall...'.[40] There is little doubt

---

[37] For *Reports of the Preparatory Committee*, see UN Doc A/CONF 151/PC/L 31, Annex (1991); A/CONF 151/PC/78 (1991); A/CONF 151/PC/WG 111.2 (1991); A/CONF 151/PC/WG 111/L5, L6, L8/Rev 1, L 20–8 (1991–2) in Robinson, *Agenda 21 and the UNCED Proceedings* (6 vols, New York, 1992–3). On the Rio Declaration see Sand, 3 *Colorado JIELP* (1992) 1; id, 3 *YbIEL* (1992) 3; Mann, *Proc ASIL* (1992) 405; Sands (ed), *Greening International Law*, 1–34; Kiss, in Campiglio et al, *The Environment after Rio* (London, 1994) 55–64; various authors 4 *Colorado JIELP* (1993) 1–215; Wirth, 29 *Georgia LR* (1995) 599; Malanczuk, in Ginther, Denters, and de Waart (eds), *Sustainable Development and Good Governance* (Dordrecht, 1995) Ch 2.

[38] The commentaries to the 2001 Articles on Transboundary Harm and the 2006 Principles on the Allocation of Loss draw upon Principles 2, 7, 10, 11, 13, 15, 16, 17, 18, and 19. See *ILC Report* (2001) GAOR A/56/10; id (2006) GAOR A/61/10, paras 51–67.

[39] ICJ Reports (1996) 226, paras 29–30, and dissenting opinions of Judges Weeramantry and Palmer in the *Request for an Examination of the Situation*, ICJ Reports (1995) 288. See also *Iron Rhine Arbitration*, PCA (2005) para 59.

[40] On the difference between 'should' and 'shall' see Nordquist (ed), *UNCLOS 1982: A Commentary* (Dordrecht, 1993) II, xlv–xlvi.

that many of its carefully drafted terms are capable of being and were intended potentially to be norm creating or to lay down the parameters for further development of the law. The UN General Assembly endorsed the Declaration, referring to it as containing 'fundamental principles for the achievement of sustainable development, based on a new and equitable global partnership'; it also called on the Commission on Sustainable Development and the UN Secretary General to promote incorporation of the principles of the declaration in the implementation of Agenda 21 and in UN programmes and processes, and urged governments to promote their widespread dissemination.[41]

Second, its twenty-seven principles represent something of a 'package deal', negotiated by consensus, rather like the 1982 UNCLOS,[42] and must be read as a whole. The Rio Declaration has thus been called:

a text of uneasy compromises, delicately balanced interests, and dimly discernible contradictions, held together by the interpretative vagueness of classic UN-ese.[43]

Some of its provisions reflect the interests of developed states, such as Principles 4 (integration of environmental protection and development), 10 (public participation), 15 (the precautionary approach) and 17 (environmental impact assessment). Others were more strongly supported by developing states, including Principle 3 (right to development), Principles 6 and 7 (special needs of developing states and common but differentiated responsibility), and Principles 5 and 9 (poverty alleviation and capacity building). One illustration of the Declaration's package-deal character is the conjunction of Principles 3 and 4, which together form the core of the principle of sustainable development. Throughout, the principal concern of the Declaration, and of those who negotiated it, was to integrate the needs of economic development and environmental protection in a single, if not wholly coherent, ensemble. The implications of this inter-dependence are also apparent in the concept of 'common but differentiated responsibility' referred to in Principle 7 and in the Climate Change Convention, and considered further below.

Third, as we have seen, the Declaration reflects a real consensus of developed and developing states on the need to identify agreed norms of international environmental protection. Despite certain reservations on the part of the United States,[44] the principles and rules it contains have a universal significance and cannot be dismissed as the work of one segment of international society. Indeed, 'insofar as there is evidence of a shift away from the practice of developed country dominance of the process of

---

[41] UNGA Res 47/190 and 191 (1992) and 48/190 (1993). GAOR, 19th Special Session, Supp No 2 (A/S-19/33) para 14 notes progress but concludes that much remains to be done.

[42] On the package deal consensus character of the 3rd UN Conference on the Law of the Sea see *supra* Ch 1, section 2(1). On the Rio negotiations see *supra* Ch 2, section 2(4).

[43] Porras, in Sands (ed), *Greening International Law*, 20.

[44] The United States joined in the consensus but subject to reservations with regard to Principles 3, 7, 12 and 23. See *UNCED*, UN Doc A/CONF 151/26/Rev 1 (Vol II) (1993) para 16.

dictating international norms and priorities',[45] Rio marks the emergence of developing countries as a real and substantial influence on the making of international environmental law in a way that was not so evident during the 1972 Stockholm Conference. For the first time it is now possible to point to a truly international consensus on some core principles of law and policy concerning environmental protection, sustainable development, and their interrelationship. Most of the legally important elements are more fully discussed in the following sections of this chapter.

Also worth noting are those matters which the Rio Declaration does not address, mainly at the insistence of developing countries. The human right to a decent environment articulated in Principle 1 of the Stockholm Declaration is not repeated.[46] Unlike the Stockholm Declaration, the Rio Declaration is explicitly anthropocentric in character (Principle 1) and makes no reference to animal rights, or the conservation of flora, fauna, habitats, and ecosystems.[47] It does not deal with environmental crimes.[48] On liability for environmental damage it merely reiterates the need to develop the law (Principle 13). Lastly, it calls for the further development not of international law relating to the environment but of international law 'in the field of sustainable development' (Principle 27).[49] Moreover, Principle 12 on trade policy and Principle 16 on the polluter-pays principle are, unusually, expressed in aspirational rather than obligatory terms, suggesting a rather weaker commitment on these economic issues than developed states would have liked to see.[50] Despite these qualifications, it is right to view the Rio Declaration in generally positive terms. It is much too pessimistic to characterize it as a backward step in the development of international environmental law.[51] On the contrary the Declaration has articulated the shared expectations of developed and developing states and brought together an important body of new and existing law.

The Rio Declaration should not be underestimated by lawyers. Freestone has argued that at the Rio Conference 'a system of international environmental law has emerged, rather than simply more international law rules about the environment'.[52] The authors of this book claim only that the Declaration's contribution to the codification and progressive development of international law relating to the environment has been and is likely to remain considerable and significant.

---

[45]   Porras, in Sands (ed),*Greening International Law*, 20. But contrast Hey, 34 *NYIL* (2003) 3, although her comments relate mainly to international financial institutions.

[46]   See *infra*, Ch 5.

[47]   See Schrijver, *Sovereignty over Natural Resources* (Cambridge, 1997) 139–40.

[48]   See *infra*, Ch 5.

[49]   On the difference between international environmental law and the law of sustainable development, see *supra* Ch 1.

[50]   On trade and environment see *infra*, Ch 14.

[51]   For pessimistic assessments see Pallemaerts, in Sands (ed),*Greening International Law*, 1–19 and Wirth, 29 *Georgia LR* (1995) 599.

[52]   6 *JEL* (1994) 193. See also Porras, in Sands (ed), *Greening International Law*, 20.

2 SUSTAINABLE DEVELOPMENT: LEGAL IMPLICATIONS

2(1) A RIGHT TO SUSTAINABLE DEVELOPMENT?

There is no explicit reference to a 'right to sustainable development' in the Rio Declaration—nor is there a right to its mirror image, a decent environment.[53] Principle 3 endorses the 'right to development', but emphasises that it 'should be fulfilled so as to meet equitably the developmental and environmental needs of present and future generations'.[54] Principle 2 affirms both the sovereign right of states to exploit their own resources 'pursuant to their own environmental and developmental policies' and their responsibility 'to ensure that activities within their jurisdiction or control do not cause damage to the environment of other states or of areas beyond the limits of national jurisdiction'. As we will see later in this chapter, Principle 2 is neither an absolute prohibition on global or transboundary environmental damage, nor does it confer on states absolute freedom to exploit natural resources.[55] The case law shows that it requires integration or accommodation of economic development and environmental protection, and Principle 4 reiterates that point expressly. Similarly, Article 1 of the 1966 UN Covenants on Civil and Political Rights and Economic, Social and Cultural Rights proclaims the right of all peoples to pursue economic development, and to dispose freely of their natural wealth and resources, but at the same time regional human-rights treaties in Africa and Latin America also recognize a right to some degree of environmental protection and so does the case law of the ECHR.[56]

The essential point of each of these examples is that, while recognizing that the right to pursue economic development is an attribute of a state's sovereignty over its own natural resources and territory, it cannot lawfully be exercised without regard for the detrimental impact on human rights or the environment. Equally, as we will see later in this chapter and again in Chapter 5, neither environmental protection nor human rights necessarily trump the right to economic development. Such potential conflicts have not led international courts to employ the concept of *ius cogens* or to give human rights, environmental protection or economic development automatic priority. Instead, the case law has concentrated on questions of balance, necessity, and the degree of interference. It shows that few rights are ever absolute or unqualified. It is in this sense that we can talk about a 'right to sustainable development' and that the International Court has used the concept. In the *Gabčíkovo-Nagymaros Case* the Court referred for the first time to 'this need to reconcile economic development with protection of the environment [which] is aptly expressed in the concept of sustainable

---

[53] See *infra*, Ch 5.   [54] See *infra*, section 2(3).
[55] See *infra*, section 4.   [56] See *infra*, Ch 5.

development'.[57] Its order in the first *Pulp Mills Case* illustrates the essentially relative character of these competing interests:

Whereas the present case highlights the importance of the need to ensure environmental protection of shared natural resources while allowing for sustainable economic development; whereas it is in particular necessary to bear in mind the reliance of the Parties on the quality of the water of the River Uruguay for their livelihood and economic development; whereas from this point of view account must be taken of the need to safeguard the continued conservation of the river environment and the rights of economic development of the riparian States...[58]

From this perspective, one of the main attractions of sustainable development as a concept is that both sides in any legal argument will be able to rely on it.

2(2) THE ELEMENTS OF SUSTAINABLE DEVELOPMENT

Sustainable development contains both substantive and procedural elements.[59] The substantive elements are set out mainly in Principles 3–8 of the Rio Declaration. They include the integration of environmental protection and economic development; the right to development; the sustainable utilization of natural resources; the equitable allocation of resources both within the present generation and between present and future generations (intra- and inter-generational equity). None of these concepts is new, but the Rio Declaration brings them together in a more systematic form than hitherto. The principal procedural elements are found in Principles 10 and 17 dealing with public participation in decision-making and environmental impact assessment. Again, none of these is new, but never before have they secured such widespread support across the international community.

(a) Integration of environmental protection and economic development

Principle 4 of the Rio Declaration provides that 'environmental protection shall constitute an integral part of the development process and cannot be considered in isolation from it'. Sands rightly argues that Principle 4 'creates the possibility of moving environmental considerations and objectives from the periphery of international relations to the economic core, probably the most important long-term contribution which UNCED will make to international affairs'.[60] Integration permeates the Rio

---

[57] ICJ Reports (1997) 7, para 140. See also *Iron Rhine Arbitration*, PCA (2005) para 59; Lowe and Higgins, in Boyle and Freestone (eds), *International Law and Sustainable Development* (Oxford, 1999) Chs 2 and 5.

[58] *Pulp Mills Case (Provisional Measures) (Argentina v Uruguay)* ICJ Reports (2006) para 80.

[59] Compare Sands, 65 *BYIL* (1994) 303 and ILA, 2002 Conference Report, 'Declaration of Principles of International Law Relating to Sustainable Development', 22–9. See generally Atapattu, *Emerging Principles of International Environmental Law*, Ch 2, and *infra*, section 2(4).

[60] 65 *BYIL* (1994) 324.

instruments,[61] as well as Agenda 21,[62] and it is reflected in subsequent agreements and declarations including the 1994 Convention to Combat Desertification[63] and the 1995 Washington Declaration on Protection of the Marine Environment from Land-based Activities.[64] Integration had also been endorsed, although not in obligatory terms, in the 1972 Stockholm Declaration (Principle 13), and it has since been incorporated in certain regional agreements.[65] As we have seen, the need to integrate environmental protection and economic development was regarded by the ICJ as one of the decisive elements of the *Gabčíkovo-Nagymaros Case*, even for activities 'begun in the past'.[66] In the *Iron Rhine Arbitration,* Principle 4 was regarded as 'a principle of general international law' which 'applies not only in autonomous activities but also in activities undertaken in implementation of specific treaties between the Parties'.[67] The relevant treaty in this case dated from 1839, so the intertemporal implications of Principle 4 for treaty interpretation are plainly significant.

The purpose of Principle 4 is to ensure that development decisions do not disregard environmental considerations. Integration of these competing values is fundamental to the concept of sustainable development and has implications across a broad range of national and international policy, as can be seen from Agenda 21, which refers to the 'more systematic consideration of the environment when decisions are made on economic, social, fiscal, energy, agricultural, transportation, trade and other policies'.[68] Since 1989 the World Bank and other multilateral development banks have sought to integrate environmental assessment into their lending policies.[69] The integration of environmental considerations is also an issue affecting international trade, although here there remains significant scope for improvement. While Principle 12 of the Rio Declaration reflects the concerns of free trade advocates that environmental restrictions should not constitute disguised or arbitrary interference with free trade, the WTO has been slower to take full account of the needs of environmental protection.[70] The relationship between environmental protection and GATT is considered further in Chapter 14.

As later chapters will also show, most of the main global and regional treaties which deal with environmental protection already evidence integration of the concerns of business, industry, and government with regard to economic development.[71] In some cases, such as the regulation of nuclear energy, it may be thought that too little

---

[61] 1992 Convention on Climate Change, Article 3(4); 4(1)(f); 1992 Convention on Biological Diversity, Article 6.

[62] See Agenda 21, Ch 8. [63] Article 4(2). See *infra*, Ch 11.

[64] UNEP/OCA/LBA/IG 2/L 4 (1995). See *infra*, Ch 8.

[65] On integrated water resource management see *infra*, Ch 10; on integrated coastal zone management see *infra*, Ch 8. See also 1978 Treaty for Amazonian Cooperation, Preamble; 1978 Kuwait Regional Convention for Cooperation on the Protection of the Marine Environment from Pollution, Preamble; 1985 ASEAN Agreement on the Conservation of Nature and Natural Resources, Article 2(1).

[66] ICJ Reports (1997) 7, para 140. [67] PCA (2005) para 59.

[68] Agenda 21, Chapter 8.2. [69] See *infra*, section 4(4).

[70] But see the Appellate Body's decision in the *Shrimp-Turtle Case*, *infra*, Ch 14.

[71] See e.g. regional agreements on land-based sources of marine pollution, *infra*, Ch 8, and nuclear energy, *infra*, Ch 9.

attention has been paid to environmental concerns. One criticism of Principle 4 is that it 'ambiguously stands as much for the subordination of environmental policies to economic imperatives in the eyes of some, as for the converse to others'.[72] But this is to view integration in isolation from the broader context of the Rio Declaration as a whole; nonetheless the criticism should remind us that the pursuit of purely 'environmental' values is not what the concept of sustainable development is intended to serve. Yet, if integration may not be a panacea, it remains the most likely means to secure a balanced view of environmental needs within competing priorities.

Qualifications of this kind apart, integration is a well-established and intrinsic feature of international environmental regulation, and of most developed economies. To this extent the real implications of Principle 4 are more to be found in its impact on developing countries, where environmental considerations have historically not been prominent in development planning, and in the World Bank and other development agencies. The establishment of environmental standards by the Bank and its agencies is thus an important contribution to the promotion of sustainable development.[73] The *Pulp Mills Case* provides clear evidence of the impact this 'greening' of the Bank can have in compelling governments to take environmental protection seriously when promoting foreign investment in natural resource exploitation.

(b) The right to development

Principle 3 of the Rio Declaration is the first example of the international community fully endorsing the previously controversial concept of a 'right to development'.[74] Critics have argued that this is not a right at all and point to its uncertain character in the 'Declaration on the Right to Development' adopted by the General Assembly in 1986, and reiterated in the 1993 Vienna Declaration on Human Rights.[75] This amorphous concept embraces not just the promotion of economic development by states but also the social and cultural aspects of human development found in the 1966 UN Covenant on Economic, Social and Cultural Rights. Often referred to by its proponents as a 'third generation' human right, others see it as unnecessary and unhelpful to the promotion either of development or of human rights.[76] Although partly drawn from existing UN General Assembly resolutions and conventions on economic and social rights, the legal status of the right to development has been and remains doubtful.

---

[72] Pallemaerts, in Sands (ed), *Greening International Law*, 17.   [73] See *infra*, Ch 5, section 5.

[74] See Dupuy (ed), *Le Droit au Développement au Plan International* (Dordrecht, 1980); Alston, 1 *Harv HRYb* (1988) 21; Rich, in Crawford (ed), *The Right of Peoples* (Oxford, 1988) Ch 3; Chowdury, Denters and de Waart (eds), *The Right to Development in International Law* (Dordrecht, 1992); Rosas, in Eide, Krause and Rosas (eds), *Economic, Social and Cultural Rights: A Textbook* (Dordrecht, 1995) Ch 16, and references cited there; Schrijver, in Bugge and Voigt (eds), *Sustainable Development in International and National Law* (Groningen, 2008) Ch 2.3.

[75] UNGA Res 41/128 (1986) adopted by 146 votes to 1 (USA) with 8 abstentions (Denmark, FRG, Finland, Iceland, Israel, Japan, Sweden, UK); 1993 World Conference on Human Rights: Vienna Declaration and Programme of Action, 32 *ILM* (1993) 1661, adopted by consensus. For an account of the subsequent work of the Working Group on the Right to Development see Rosas, *supra* n 93.

[76] Alston, 1 *Harv HRYb* (1988) 21. But for a spirited defence see Mansell and Scott, 21 *JLS* (1994) 171. See generally Andreassen and Marks (eds), *Development as a Human Right* (Cambridge, Mass, 2006).

Inclusion in the Rio Declaration represents a success for developing country advocates, and reflects concerns that environmental protection should not outweigh their need for economic development. It was thus intended as a counterweight to Principle 4. At the same time, Principle 3 introduces the further important limitation that the right to development must be fulfilled 'equitably' so as to meet both developmental and environmental needs of present and future generations. The point has already been made that it is not an absolute right but one whose scope is defined only in relation to other competing factors. This may help explain why the United States continues to assert that development is not a right at all but only a 'goal'.[77] Moreover, as we saw earlier, the right to develop requires 'full respect for the principles of international law concerning friendly relations and co-operation among states in accordance with the Charter of the United Nations'.[78] To that extent it cannot override, but must be integrated with, existing international law concerning protection of the environment and human rights.[79] From that perspective, 'Environmental law and the law on development stand not as alternatives but as mutually reinforcing, integral concepts, which require that where development may cause significant harm to the environment there is a duty to prevent, or at least mitigate, such harm'.[80]

(c) Sustainable utilization and conservation of natural resources

Although an important element of sustainable development, sustainable utilization is an autonomous concept best understood in the context of international law concerning the conservation of natural resources and it is considered in section 5 below.

(d) Inter-generational equity

The theory of inter-generational equity has been advanced to explain the optimum basis for the relationship between one generation and the next. The theory requires each generation to use and develop its natural and cultural heritage in such a manner that it can be passed on to future generations in no worse condition than it was received.[81] Central to this idea is the need to conserve options for the future use of resources, including their quality, and that of the natural environment.

The Brundtland Commission's definition of sustainable development as 'development that meets the needs of the present without compromising the ability of future

---

[77] *Supra* n 44.
[78] Declaration on the Right to Development, UNGA Res 41/128 (1986) Article 3(2).
[79] See discussion of *Pulp Mills Case, supra* section 2(1). On human rights aspects see *infra*, Ch 5.
[80] *Iron Rhine Arbitration*, PCA (2005) para 59, and see *infra*, section 4. See generally Schrijver, in Bugge and Voigt (eds), *Sustainable Development in International and National Law*, Ch 2.3.
[81] Brown Weiss, *In Fairness to Future Generations* (Dobbs Ferry, 1989); 1988 Goa Guidelines on Inter-generational Equity, ibid, Appendix A. Lowe provides a critique of the theory as expounded by Brown Weiss in Boyle and Freestone, *International Law and Sustainable Development*, Ch 2. See also Redgwell, *Intergenerational Trusts and Environmental Protection* (Manchester, 1999); id, in Churchill and Freestone (eds), *International Law and Global Climate Change* (London, 1991) Ch 3; D'Amato, 84 *AJIL* (1990) 190; Gundling, ibid, 207; Supanich, 3 *YbIEL* (1992) 94; Agius et al, *Future Generations and International Law* (London, 1998).

generations to meet their own needs' begs elaboration, but it does emphasize the centrality of inter-generational equity.[82] As early as 1946, the International Convention
for the Regulation of Whaling recognized the interest of the nations of the world in
safeguarding whale stocks for 'future generations'. The same generational perspective
underlies references in the 1972 Stockholm Declaration to man's responsibility to protect the environment and the earth's natural resources.[83] Inter-generational equity is
explicitly referred to in Principle 3 of the 1992 Rio Declaration, which provides for the
right to development to be fulfilled 'so as to equitably meet developmental and environmental needs of present and future generations', and is reiterated in the same terms
in the 1993 Vienna Declaration on Human Rights. Article 3(1) of the 1992 Convention
on Climate Change calls for inter-generational equity to be taken into account in decisions of the parties to that convention. These international declarations indicate the
importance now attached in international policy to the protection of the environment
for the benefit of future generations. However, although the idea of moral responsibility to future generations is well established in the writings of Rawls and other philosophers, it is less easy to translate into law, or, more specifically, into rights for future
indeterminate generations.[84]

Weiss argues that inter-generational equity is already part of the fabric of international law.[85] It is true that the policy which underlies a number of global environmental treaties is the avoidance of irreversible harm, as in the Ozone Convention, the
Convention on Biological Diversity and the Convention on Climate Change.[86] It is also
possible to point to new fisheries conservation treaties which require cooperation in
the management of stocks and ecosystems for the purpose of maintaining sustainable
utilization.[87] The phasing out of dumping at sea, particularly of radioactive waste, the
elaboration of a comprehensive regime of ecosystem protection for Antarctica, including the prohibition on mineral extraction and the designation of the continent as a
world park, and the adoption of further controls on whaling through the International
Whaling Commission and regional conventions, also demonstrate a real concern for
the interests of future generations.[88] Future generations will benefit to the extent that
these regimes are successful, and the record of actual practice will doubtless demonstrate the level of commitment to any theory of inter-generational equity. What they
do not demonstrate is endorsement of the generational rights perspective promoted

[82] WCED, *Our Common Future* (Oxford, 1987) 43. See *supra* Ch 2.

[83] Principles 1 and 2. See also 1968 African Convention on the Conservation of Nature and Natural
Resources.

[84] Rawls, *A Theory of Justice* (Oxford, 1972); Gillespie, *International Environmental Law, Policy and
Ethics* (Oxford, 1997) Ch 6; D'Amato, 84 *AJIL* (1990) 190. On the different meanings of 'rights' in this context see *infra*, Ch 5.

[85] *Supra* n 81. See also Judge Weeramantry in *Advisory Opinion on Nuclear Weapons,* ICJ Reports
(1996) 266.

[86] See *infra,* Chs 6, 11.

[87] See 1995 Agreement on the Conservation of Straddling and Highly Migratory Fish Stocks, *infra,* Ch 13.

[88] *Infra,* Chs 8, 11, 13.

by Brown Weiss or the conclusion that future generations have been endowed with justiciable rights in international law.[89]

But the essential point of the theory, that mankind has a responsibility for the future, and that this is an inherent component of sustainable development, is incontrovertible, however expressed. The question then becomes one of implementation.[90] The examples of the London Dumping Convention, the Climate Change Convention, and the International Whaling Convention show that some international institutions already accommodate the interests of future generations in a balancing of interests. Wider adoption of the precautionary principle, and of policies of sustainable development, will entail more institutions following this lead. The Commission on Sustainable Development and the restructured Global Environment Facility also reflect the evolution of a more fiduciary or trusteeship model of man's relationship with the environment, which may enhance inter-generational perspectives.[91]

Representation of future generations in legal proceedings before international courts is a less well-developed possibility. What is lacking is a theory of representation before international tribunals capable of according standing to future generations independently of the states and international institutions which are at present the only competent parties in international litigation. Although some interstate or advisory proceedings before the ICJ can be interpreted as involving generational responsibilities, as can a few international human-rights decisions, these cases all involve the present generation suing in respect of the misdeeds of the past, rather than a future generation challenging those of the present.[92] Moreover, in none of these cases has an international court expressly recognized the rights of future generations.[93] There is, however, no inherent reason why national courts should not permit representative proceedings on behalf of the unborn, as is not uncommon in English trust law, but much will turn on the procedural rules and the context in each legal system and no generalizations with regard to generational rights in national law are possible. In the Philippines Supreme Court plaintiffs seeking to challenge the grant of timber licences

[89] Supanich, 3 *YbIEL* (1992) 94, but compare Agius et al, *Future Generations and International Law* (London, 1998) and Pathak, in Brown Weiss (ed), *Environmental Change and International Law* (Tokyo, 1992) 226ff. On the failure of the Rio Declaration to give prominence to human rights approaches see *infra,* Ch 5.

[90] Gundling, 84 *AJIL* (1990) 207.

[91] On the GEF and CSD see *supra* Ch 2. A proposal to establish the CSD with stronger powers of guardianship on behalf of future generations was not adopted: see UN Doc A/CONF 151/PC/WG III/L 8/Rev 1/Add 2 (1992). See also the earlier institutional proposals of the WCED in Munro and Lammers, *Environmental Protection and Sustainable Development,* and Redgwell, *Intergenerational Trusts and Environmental Protection,* Ch 6.

[92] See *Certain Phosphate Lands in Nauru,* ICJ Reports (1993) 322; *Advisory Opinion on Nuclear Weapons,* ICJ Reports (1996) 266; and *LCB v United Kingdom,* 27 EHRR (1999) 212, in which the respondent government was held to owe a duty to protect the offspring of servicemen engaged in nuclear tests. On the possible international legal capacity of future generations see Agius et al, *Future Generations and International Law,* Chs 5–7.

[93] Brown Weiss, in de Chazournes and Sands (eds), *International Law, the ICJ and Nuclear Weapons* (Cambridge, 1999) 338. See also Lowe, in Boyle and Freestone (eds), *International Law and Sustainable Development,* Ch 2.

were held to have standing on behalf of themselves and future generations, but this precedent was not followed in comparable proceedings before the Supreme Court of Bangladesh.[94]

Despite its conceptual elegance, the apparent simplicity of the theory of inter-generational equity is deceptive. It provides an essential reference point within which future impacts and concerns must be considered and taken into account by present generations, as well as a process by which these and other concerns can be addressed. Nevertheless, viewing inter-generational equity as an element of sustainable development does not resolve the argument for stronger generational rights or international guardianship, nor does it determine the optimal balance between this generation and its successors. Moreover, while accepting the right of present generations to use resources for economic development, it fails to answer the question how we should value the environment for the purpose of determining whether future generations will be worse off.[95] Nor does concentration on relations between one generation and the next convincingly answer the equally pressing question of how benefits and burdens should be shared within each generation.[96] Thus, although the content of the theory is well defined, it rests on some questionable assumptions concerning the nature of economic equity.

(e) Intra-generational equity

If the theory of inter-generational equity can be criticized for neglecting intra-generational considerations, the same cannot be said of the concept of sustainable development. Both in the Brundtland Report, and in Agenda 21, there is no doubt that redressing the imbalance in wealth between the developed and developing worlds and giving priority to the needs of the poor are important policy components of sustainability. Unlike inter-generational equity, intra-generational equity addresses inequity within the existing economic system.

The Rio Declaration does not refer by name to any concept of intra-generational equity, but several of its substantive provisions, and of the Climate Change and Biological Diversity Conventions, imply that intra-generational concerns are now an element in the contemporary development of international environmental law. Apart from Principle 5, which calls for cooperation to eradicate poverty, intra-generational equity is served mainly by a recognition of the special needs of developing countries. In global environmental conventions such as the Ozone and Climate Change Conventions this takes the form of financial assistance, capacity-building and the principle of common but differentiated responsibility. These elements are considered below. The Biological Diversity Convention, unusually, goes further by establishing

---

[94] *Minors Oposa v Secretary of the Department of Environment and Natural Resources*, 33 *ILM* (1994) 173; *Farooque v Government of Bangladesh* (1997) 49 *DLR (AD)* 1.

[95] Redgwell, in Churchill and Freestone (eds), *International Law and Global Climate Change*, Ch 3; Christenson, 1 *YbIEL* (1990) 392. For an economist's analysis of how to value the environment on a sustainable basis, see Pearce, *Blueprint for a Green Economy* (London, 1989).

[96] Gundling, 84 *AJIL* (1990) 211.

a framework under which developing countries are entitled to a 'fair and equitable' sharing of the benefits arising from the use of genetic resources found in their territory.[97] In effect, a trade-off between conservation and economic equity is at the core of this convention, although troubled by unsettled questions concerning intellectual property rights and the feasibility of controlling the activities of multinational drug companies.[98]

Equity, and equitable utilization, are well-established general principles of international law;[99] their use in an intra-generational context is more novel however. At present it cannot easily be argued that equity in this form has any applicability outside the limited context of the Rio instruments in which it has so far been employed.

(f) Procedural elements of sustainable development

No discussion of sustainable development should overlook the procedural elements which facilitate implementation at national level. Cooperation between states, environmental impact assessment, public participation in environmental decision-making, and access to information perform the function of legitimizing decisions and, if properly employed, may also improve their quality. Their role is not limited to the pursuit of sustainability, however, but has equal relevance to global and transboundary environmental law and they are further discussed below.[100]

2(3) THE INFLUENCE OF SUSTAINABLE DEVELOPMENT ON THE LAW

As we saw in the previous chapter, the concept of 'sustainable development' had already begun to emerge prior to the UN Conference on Environment and Development in 1992,[101] but its defining role in the evolution of international law and policy on protection of the environment secured near universal endorsement at Rio.[102] Sustainable development informs much of the Rio Declaration, as well as the Conventions on Climate Change and Biological Diversity, and it is central to the elaboration of global environmental responsibility by these and other instruments.[103] Agenda 21, the non-binding programme of action adopted by the Rio Conference, also refers in its preamble to the need for a 'global partnership for sustainable development', and most

---

[97] Article 15(7). See also Agenda 21, Ch 15.4(d); 1992 Forest Principles; Shelton, 5 *YbIEL* (1994) 83–4.

[98] See generally Bowman and Redgwell (eds), *International Law and the Conservation of Biological Diversity* (London, 1996) and *infra*, Ch 14.

[99] See *infra*, section 5(3).

[100] On cooperation and EIA see *infra*, sections 4(3)–(4). On public access to information and participation in decision-making see *infra*, Ch 5.

[101] See *Development and Environment: Report and Working Papers of a Panel of Experts Convened by the UNCHE* (Founex, 1971); WCED, *Our Common Future* (Oxford, 1987) Ch 2 and 3, endorsed by UNGA Res 42/186 and 187 (1987); 1982 World Charter for Nature, endorsed by UNGA Res 37/7; UNEP GC Res 14/4 (1982).

[102] *Supra* Ch 2, section 2.

[103] See 1992 Convention on Climate Change, Article 3; 1992 Convention on Biological Diversity, Articles 8 and 10; 1994 Convention to Combat Desertification, Articles 4, 5.

of its provisions are intended to promote the concept, whose implementation is monitored by the Commission on Sustainable Development.[104] Since Rio, sustainable development has been adopted as a policy by numerous governments, both at national and regional level. It has influenced the application and the development of law and policy by various international organizations, including FAO, IMO, The World Bank, the WTO, and UNDP, as well as treaty bodies such as the International Tropical Timber Organization and the European Energy Charter.[105] Various studies have assessed the relevance of the concept to international law.[106]

As we also saw earlier, Principle 27 of the Rio Declaration and Chapter 39 of Agenda 21 call specifically for further development of international law 'in the field of sustainable development'.[107] The impact of sustainable development on the evolution of existing international law can be observed in the *Gabčíkovo-Nagymaros Case*. The Court's judgment goes some way towards modernizing international watercourses law along the lines indicated by the International Law Commission and the 1997 UN Convention on the Non-Navigational Uses of International Watercourses.[108] The latter convention was amended in its final drafting stages to take explicit account of the principle of sustainable utilization,[109] which is also one of the new principles applied to high seas fisheries by the 1995 Agreement Relating to the Conservation and Management of Straddling and Highly Migratory Fish Stocks.[110] Together these treaties have the effect of redefining existing legal concepts of equitable utilization of shared resources and freedom of fishing on the high seas, and for the first time they introduce important environmental constraints into this part of international law relating to natural resources.

The most potentially far-reaching aspect of sustainable development is that for the first time it makes a state's management of its own domestic environment a matter of international concern in a systematic way.[111] This is most apparent in the Convention

---

[104] UNGA Res 47/191 (1992). See Osborn and Bigg, *Earth Summit II: Outcomes and Analysis* (London, 1998) 60–8.

[105] *Supra* Ch 2.

[106] See Sands, 65 *BYIL* (1994) 303; Lang (ed), *Sustainable Development and International Law* (London, 1995); Ginther, Denters and de Waart (eds), *Sustainable Development and Global Governance* (London, 1995); McGoldrick, 45 *ICLQ* (1996) 796; Boyle and Freestone (eds), *International Law and Sustainable Development* (Oxford, 1999); Cordonnier Segger (ed), *Sustainable Development Law: Principles, Practices and Prospects* (Oxford, 2004); Schrijver and Weiss (eds), *International Law and Sustainable Development: Principles and Practice* (Leiden, 2004); French, *International Law and Policy of Sustainable Development* (Manchester, 2005); Bugge and Voigt (eds), *Sustainable Development in International and National Law* (Groningen, 2008).

[107] UNEP GC Decision 18/9 (1995); Working Papers UNEP/IEL WS/1/2 (1995), UNEP/IEL WS/2/1 (1995) and *Final Report of the Expert Group on International Law Aiming at Sustainable Development* UNEP/IEL/WS/3/2 (1996). See also UN, Dept for Policy Co-ordination and Sustainable Development, *Report of the Expert Group Meeting on Identification of Principles of International Law for Sustainable Development* (Geneva, 1995) prepared for 4th Meeting of the CSD.

[108] *Infra*, Ch 10.

[109] Compare Article 5 of the ILC Draft Convention, UN Doc A/CN 4/L492 and Add 1 (1994) with Article 5 of the 1997 Convention as finally adopted

[110] Articles 5 and 6. See Freestone and Makuch, 7 *YbIEL* (1996) 3 and *infra*, Ch 13.

[111] See *infra*, section 3(1)(b).

on Biological Diversity, but the point is evident throughout Agenda 21. It also has potential implications for the future development of national and international human rights law, as we shall see in Chapter 5.

However, as we noted in Chapter 2, there remain fundamental uncertainties about the nature of sustainable development which the Rio Declaration does not resolve, but which have a direct bearing on the question whether sustainable development can in any sense be considered a legal principle.[112] If it is to be interpreted, applied, and achieved primarily at national level by individual governments, there may be only a limited need for international definition and oversight. If, however, it is intended that states should be held internationally accountable for achieving sustainability, whether globally or nationally, then the criteria for measuring this standard must be made clear, as must the evidential burden for assessing the performance of individual states. Although the Commission on Sustainable Development has a role in assessing national reports on implementation of Agenda 21, and in determining future policy,[113] at present it is not the job of the Commission to answer the question whether any particular development is or is not sustainable, or to hold governments to account, although such a role may in time evolve. It may then become clearer what are the parameters of sustainability and the criteria for measuring it. Moreover, although it is possible to identify the main elements of the concept of sustainable development, it is far from certain what their specific normative implications are, or indeed, how they relate to each other, or to human-rights law and international economic law.[114] As we saw at the beginning of this chapter, international law cannot be applied in a fragmented way, and sustainable development has no more claim to priority than any other element.

2(4) THE LEGAL STATUS OF SUSTAINABLE DEVELOPMENT

No easy answer can be given to the question whether international law now requires that all development should be sustainable, or if so, what that would mean in specific terms.[115] It is clear, given the breadth of international endorsement for the concept, that few states would quarrel with the proposition that development should in principle be sustainable and that all natural resources should be managed in this way. What is lacking is any comparable consensus on the meaning of sustainable development, or on how to give it concrete effect in individual cases. As Handl observes, 'without authoritative third-party decision-making, conflicting claims about the concept's specific normative implications will abound and disputes over application will

---

[112] See Handl, in Lang (ed), *Sustainable Development and International Law*, 35–43. Judge Kooijmans, 56 *ICLQ* (2007) 751 has drawn attention to the Court's deliberate characterisation of sustainable development as a 'concept' rather than a 'principle'.

[113] See UNGA Res 47/191 (1992) and *supra* Ch 2.

[114] Handl, 1 *YbIEL* (1990) 24–8, and see infra, Chs 11–13. But compare McGoldrick, 45 *ICLQ* (1996) 796.

[115] See in particular, Lowe, in Boyle and Freestone, *International Law and Sustainable Development*, Ch 2; French, *International Law and Policy of Sustainable Development*, Ch 3; Sands, 65 *BYIL* (1994) 303.

be exceedingly difficult to resolve'.[116] In these circumstances, states retain substantial discretion in interpreting and giving effect to the alleged principle, unless specific international action has been agreed. Given the social, political and economic value judgements involved in deciding on what is sustainable, and the necessity of weighing conflicting factors, of which environmental protection is only one, it is difficult to see an international court reviewing national action and concluding that it falls short of a standard of 'sustainable development', save possibly in an extreme case. The International Court of Justice did not do so in the *Gabčíkovo-Nagymaros Case*,[117] preferring instead to address more readily justiciable questions such as the equitable allocation of water flow or the applicability of international environmental standards in the operation of the hydroelectric system. It is possible that other international bodies, such as the Commission on Sustainable Development, or a Watercourse Commission, might be better able to identify criteria for deciding whether a particular development is sustainable, but this too is unlikely to be easy except in an extreme case. As we saw earlier, such a task is not at present within the mandate of the CSD.[118] Normative uncertainty, coupled with the absence of justiciable standards for review, strongly suggest that decisions on what constitutes sustainability rest primarily with individual governments.

This is not the end of the matter, however, for two reasons. First, courts could readily review the sustainability of economic development by reference to detriment to human rights, including the right to life, private life or property, or economic, social, and cultural rights such as health and the right to water.[119] Thus, in the *Ogoniland Case*, after noting '[t]he destructive and selfish role-played by oil development in Ogoniland, closely tied with repressive tactics of the Nigerian Government, and the lack of material benefits accruing to the local population', the African Commission on Human and Peoples' Rights found, inter alia, that the right of peoples to dispose freely of their own natural resources had been violated as well as their right to 'ecologically sustainable development'.[120] Here, in contrast to the *Gabčíkovo-Nagymaros Case*, we can see an international tribunal taking a critical view of the merits of economic development, albeit in an admittedly extreme case. Any challenge to the sustainability of economic development on this basis will be most effective if focused on the long-term impact on the environment on which those most affected depend for their livelihood. Other cases in the Inter-American and European Courts of Human Rights exemplify the same argument,[121] which we explore more fully in Chapter 5.

Second, although international law may not require development to be sustainable, it does require development decisions to be the outcome of a process which promotes

---

[116] Handl, 1 *YbIEL* (1990) 25. For the same reasons Handl also rejects the possibility that sustainable development is a peremptory norm of international law.

[117] ICJ Reports (1997) 7.   [118] *Supra* section 2(3).

[119] On the right to water see *infra*, Ch 10, section 2(5).

[120] *The Social and Economic Rights Action Center and the Center for Economic and Social Rights v Nigeria*, ACHPR Communication 155/96 (2002) paras 52–5.

[121] Compare *Maya indigenous community of the Toledo District v Belize*, Inter-Am CHR, OEA/Ser L/V/II 122 Doc 5 rev 1, 727 (2004) and *Hatton v UK* [2003] ECHR (Grand Chamber), *infra*, Ch 5.

sustainable development. Specifically, if states do not carry out environmental impact assessments (EIAs), or they refuse to cooperate in the management of global and transboundary risks or the conservation of natural resources, or they fail to integrate development and environmental considerations in their decision-making, or do not take account of the needs of intra- and inter-generational equity, they will have failed to implement the main tools employed by the Rio Declaration and other international instruments for the purpose of facilitating sustainable development. There is, as we shall see below, ample state practice to support the normative significance of most of these elements. Moreover, an interpretation which makes the process of decision-making the key legal test of sustainable development, rather than the nature of the development, is implicitly supported by the *Gabčíkovo-Nagymaros Case*. In that decision, while not questioning whether a project conceived in 1977 was sustainable, the ICJ required the parties in the interests of sustainable development to 'look afresh' at the environmental consequences and to carry out monitoring and abatement measures to contemporary standards set by international law.[122] Such an approach enables international courts to further the objective of sustainable development in accordance with the Rio Declaration while relieving them of the impossible task of deciding what is and what is not sustainable.

An argument of this kind would thus focus on the components of sustainable development, rather than on the concept itself. Even if there is no legal obligation to develop sustainably, there may nevertheless be law 'in the field of sustainable development'.[123] Moreover, a court or international institution can also ensure that elements such as inter-generational equity or integration of environment and development are taken account of in decision-making, even if it cannot review judgements made in the light of them. Principles of this kind may be 'soft', but as Lowe convincingly demonstrates, sustainable development and its components are very relevant when courts or international bodies have to interpret, apply, or develop, treaties or general international law.[124] That is perhaps the most important lesson to be drawn from the ICJ's references to the concept of sustainable development in the *Pulp Mills* and *Gabčíkovo-Nagymaros Cases* and from the WTO Appellate Body's decision in the *Shrimp-Turtle Case*.[125] Whether or not sustainable development is a legal obligation, and as we have seen this seems unlikely, it does represent a policy which can influence the outcome of cases, the interpretation of treaties, and the practice of states and international organizations, and may lead to significant changes and developments in the existing law. In that very important sense, international law does appear to require states and international bodies to take account of the objective of sustainable development, and to employ appropriate processes for doing so.

[122] ICJ Reports (1997) 7, para 140.   [123] Sands, 65 *BYIL* (1994) 303.

[124] Lowe, in, Boyle and Freestone, *International Law and Sustainable Development*, Ch 2; Handl, 1 *YbIEL* (1990) 24–8; Sands, in Lang (ed), *Sustainable Development and International Law*, 53–66, but for more cautious views see Handl, in Lang (ed), op cit, 35–43 and Mann, ibid, 67–72.

[125] *Pulp Mills Case*, ICJ Reports (2006) paras 68–84; *Gabčíkovo-Nagymaros Case*, ICJ Reports (1997) 7, para 140; *Shrimp/Turtle Case*, WTO Appellate Body (1998) WT/DS58/AB/R, paras 126–30, and see Preamble to 1994 WTO Agreement, *infra*, Ch 14. See also *Iron Rhine Arbitration*, PCA (2005) paras 81, 221–3.

3 PRINCIPLES OF GLOBAL ENVIRONMENTAL RESPONSIBILITY

3(1) THE ENVIRONMENT AS A 'COMMON CONCERN'

As we saw earlier, the 1992 Rio Conference on Environment and Development marked a distinctive evolution in the scope of international environmental law. For the first time, the Rio instruments set out a framework of global environmental responsibilities, as distinct from those responsibilities which are merely regional or transboundary in character, such as air or river pollution, or which relate to common spaces, such as Part XII of the 1982 UNCLOS. Whereas the 1972 Stockholm Declaration on the Human Environment had simply distinguished between responsibility for areas within and beyond national jurisdiction,[126] the Rio treaties use the concept of 'common concern' to designate those issues which involve global responsibilities.[127] Thus climate change and biological diversity are each expressly denominated as the 'common concern of mankind' and have become the subject of global regulatory treaties.[128]

(a) The global environment

The features which appear important in defining climate change and biological diversity as global concerns are their universal character and the need for common action by all states if measures of protection are to work.[129] Global environmental responsibility is not necessarily confined to these two phenomena, however. Although the ozone layer is nowhere referred to as a 'common concern', it is in substance treated by the Ozone Convention and the Montreal Protocol in essentially the same way.[130] Many of the elements of global responsibility can also be identified in provisions of the 1982 UNCLOS dealing with protection of the marine environment, in the 1995 Agreement on Straddling and Highly Migratory Fish Stocks, and in Chapter 17 of Agenda 21, which refers to the oceans, seas and adjacent coastal areas as an 'integrated whole that is an essential component of the global life-support system'.[131]

(b) The domestic environment of states

In certain contexts it might also be arguable that the management of a state's own domestic environment is a matter of international concern independently of any transboundary effects. Even before the Rio Conference, multilateral treaties dealing

---

[126] Principle 21.

[127] See also UN General Assembly Resolution 43/53 on Global Climate Change; Noordwijk Declaration of the Conference on Atmospheric Pollution and Climate Change, 19 *EPL* (1989) 229; UNEP GC Resolution 15/36 (1989). Note, however, that the Rio Declaration does not itself use the term.

[128] Convention on Climate Change, Preamble; Convention on Biological Diversity, Preamble.

[129] See the preambles to both Conventions.   [130] *Infra*, Ch 6.

[131] See also preamble to the 1982 UNCLOS: '*Conscious* that the problems of ocean space are closely interrelated and need to be considered as a whole'. See *infra*, Chs 7, 8, 13.

with wildlife conservation,[132] world heritage areas,[133] disposal of hazardous wastes,[134] and human rights[135] had already touched on the international regulation of matters internal to the states concerned. The Rio Declaration significantly extends the domestic reach of international environmental law by requiring states to enact effective environmental legislation,[136] to facilitate access for individuals to information, decision-making processes and judicial and administrative proceedings at national level,[137] to apply the precautionary approach 'widely',[138] and to undertake environmental impact assessment 'as a national instrument'.[139] Some authors see the precautionary principle as the basis for comprehensive environmental protection both nationally and internationally.[140] It has also been suggested that the so-called 'preventive principle' applies to domestic environmental harm, requiring states to regulate and control pollution regardless of possible global or transboundary effects.[141] The POPS Convention and protocols on various forms of air pollution exemplify this approach.[142] Moreover, to the extent that sustainable development can be regarded as a legal principle involving some degree of international supervision—and as we saw earlier this is not certain—it might be said that this aspect of domestic environmental protection may by implication also be a matter of 'common concern', although the Declaration itself does not say so.

(c) Implications of 'common concern'

Although in some cases the developments just referred to are tentative and of uncertain legal status and scope, they do point to a 'globalization' of international environmental law, in the sense of addressing contemporary needs for global cooperation to deal with global environmental problems.[143] What is clear after Rio is that for this reason it is no longer possible to characterize international environmental law as simply a system governing transboundary relations among neighbouring states. It is in this context that the concept of common concern becomes important.

'Common concern' is not a concept previously employed in international law and its present legal implications remain unsettled. The choice of language was itself the outcome of political compromise, agreed after initial proposals using the term 'common heritage of mankind' for the global climate and biological diversity encountered predictable opposition.[144] Nonetheless, 'common concern' indicates a legal status both for climate change and biological resources which is distinctively different from the

---

[132] *Infra*, Ch 12.   [133] 1972 World Heritage Convention.   [134] *Infra*, Ch 8.
[135] *Infra*, Ch 5.   [136] Principle 11.   [137] Principle 10.
[138] Principle 15.   [139] Principle 17.
[140] E.g. Trouwborst, *Evolution and Status of the Precautionary Principle in International Law*, 284.
[141] De Sadeleer, *Environmental Principles*, Ch 2, 64ff.   [142] See *infra*, Chs 6, 8.
[143] Kiss, 32 *GYIL* (1989) 241; Handl, 1 *YbIEL* (1990) 3.
[144] The original Maltese draft of UNGA Resolution 43/53 on Climate Change used the term 'common heritage'; early drafts of the Biological Diversity Convention also referred to the 'common heritage of all peoples': see UNEP, Ad hoc Working Group of Experts on Biological Diversity, 2nd session, Geneva, February 1990, para 11. The draft convention was amended following Brazilian opposition to the possibility that this might be seen as conferring rights on indigenous peoples.

concepts of permanent sovereignty, common property, shared resources, or common heritage which generally determine the international legal status of natural resources.[145] In relation to climate change, UNGA Resolution 43/53 and the Climate Change Convention do not make the global atmosphere common property beyond the sovereignty of individual states, but like the ozone layer, they do treat it as a global unity insofar as injury in the form of global warming or climate change may affect the community of states as a whole. It is thus immaterial whether the global atmosphere comprises airspace under the sovereignty of a subjacent state or not: it is a 'common resource' of vital interest to mankind.[146] By approaching the matter from a global perspective, the UN has acknowledged not only the artificiality of spatial boundaries in this context but also the inappropriateness of treating the phenomena of global warming and climate change in the same way as transboundary air pollution, which is regional or bilateral in character.[147] Similarly the Convention on Biological Diversity does not internationalize biological resources in the same way that the 1982 UNCLOS treats mineral resources of the deep seabed; still less does it turn them into common property accessible for exploitation by all states.[148]

If 'common concern' is neither common property nor common heritage, and if it entails a reaffirmation of the existing sovereignty of states over their own resources, what legal content, if any, does this concept have? Its main impact appears to be that it gives the international community of states both a legitimate interest in resources of global significance and a common responsibility to assist in their sustainable development.[149] Moreover, insofar as states continue to enjoy sovereignty over their own natural resources and the freedom to determine how they will be used, this sovereignty is not unlimited or absolute, but must now be exercised within the confines of the global responsibilities set out principally in the Climate Change and Biological Diversity Conventions, and also in the Rio Declaration and other relevant instruments.

Global responsibility differs from existing transboundary environmental law in three respects. First, like human rights law, the global responsibilities in question may have an *erga omnes* character, owed to the international community as a whole, and not merely to other states inter se. Second, although held in common by all states, global environmental responsibilities are differentiated in various ways between developed and developing states, and contain strong elements of equitable balancing not found in the law relating to transboundary harm. Third, although the commitment to a precautionary approach is now relevant to many aspects of environmental law, it is particularly evident in matters of global concern.

---

[145] *Infra*, section 5.

[146] See recommendations of the International Meeting of Legal and Policy Experts, Ottawa, Canada, 19 *EPL* (1989) 78. On the status of the ozone layer, see *infra*, Ch 6.

[147] See Boyle, in Churchill and Freestone, *International Law and Global Climate Change*, Ch 1.

[148] *Infra*, section 5.

[149] UNEP, *Report of the Group of Legal Experts to Examine the Concept of the Common Concern of Mankind in Relation to Global Environmental Issues* (1990); Boyle, in Churchill and Freestone, *International Law and Global Climate Change*; Kirgis, 84 *AJIL* (1990) 525; but for a more sceptical view see Brunnée, 49 *ZAÖRV* (1989) 791.

3(2) *ERGA OMNES* STATUS OF GLOBAL ENVIRONMENTAL RESPONSIBILITY

International lawyers have traditionally distinguished between legal obligations owed to another state, which can be enforced only by that state, and legal obligations owed to the whole international community of states, which can be enforced by or on behalf of that community. The latter are sometimes referred to as *erga omnes* obligations. It was this distinction which the ICJ had in mind in the *Barcelona Traction Case*[150] when it contrasted interstate claims for the taking of property, which could only be brought by the state of nationality of the claimant, and claims based on a violation of international human-rights law, which could be brought by any state. The same distinction is reflected in the International Law Commission's articles on the law of state responsibility, which recognize explicitly that any state may bring an international claim in respect of the breach of an obligation owed to the international community of states as a whole.[151]

Outside the human-rights context, the International Court has made little use of the concept of *erga omnes* obligations. The issue arose in an environmental context in the 1974 *Nuclear Tests Cases* when New Zealand and Australia complained of interference with the high-seas freedoms of all states.[152] It is also referred to in the dissenting judgment of Judge Weeramantry in the *Gabčíkovo-Nagymaros Case*, where sustainable development is seen as an *erga omnes* obligation.[153] For various reasons considered more fully in Chapter 4, it may be right to take a cautious view of the *erga omnes* character of environmental obligations when the question to be determined is one of standing to bring proceedings before an international court, but if the ILC is correct, those customary obligations which concern protection of the global environment will have an *erga omnes* character.[154]

The idea that some legal obligations are owed to the international community as a whole can be viewed from a broader perspective, however. Characterization of issues such as climate change and biological diversity as the 'common concern of humankind' is important in this context because it places them on the international agenda and declares them to be a legitimate object of international regulation and supervision, thereby overriding the reserved domain of domestic jurisdiction or the possible contention that they relate to economic activities and resources which fall mainly within the exclusive territorial sovereignty of individual states.[155] The concept is more than a rhetorical gesture, moreover. What gives such obligations a real *erga omnes* character is not that all states have standing before the ICJ in the event of breach, but that the international community can hold individual states accountable for compliance

---

[150] ICJ Reports (1970) 3. See also *East Timor Case*, ICJ Reports (1995) 2, para 29, where the Court holds that self-determination has an *erga omnes* character.

[151] *ILC Report* (2001) GAOR A/56/10, Article 48. See *infra*, Ch 4, section 2(5).

[152] ICJ Reports (1974) 253 and 457. See *infra*, Ch 4, section 2(5).

[153] ICJ Reports (1997) 7. However, as we saw earlier, the assumption that sustainable development is a legal obligation seems incorrect.

[154] See *infra*, Ch 4, section 2(5).   [155] *Supra* section 3(1)(c).

with their obligations through institutions such as the Conference of the Parties to the Climate Change Convention,[156] or other comparable bodies endowed, whether by treaty or General Assembly resolution, with supervisory powers.[157] The Ozone Convention and Protocol provide perhaps the best-developed examples of the exercise of *erga omnes partes* rights by the states through the institutions set up by those agreements.[158] The concept of the common heritage of mankind represents another parallel development in the international management of mineral resources of the deep seabed, outer space, and possibly, Antarctica.[159] Multilateral accountability of this kind is considered more fully in Chapter 4, but it is clearly central to the notion of *erga omnes* global environmental responsibilities considered here.

3(3) COMMON BUT DIFFERENTIATED RESPONSIBILITY

It should not be assumed that international law always applies equally to all states. In practice, distinctions have been drawn most often between developed and developing states. Usually this entails acknowledging contextual differences, most notably the differing capabilities of states; more rarely the normative treatment of developed and developing states is expressly differentiated. In international environmental law the evolution of 'common but differentiated responsibility' can best be observed in the Ozone, Climate Change and Biological Diversity Conventions.[160] The commitments undertaken in these treaties are dependent on further elaboration and agreement in protocols such as those concluded at Montreal in 1987 and Kyoto in 1997. The very widespread ratification of all three treaties, and the terms on which subsequent negotiations have been conducted, including the Kyoto Protocol, point to near universal acceptance of the principle of common but differentiated responsibility for global environmental change, even if differences remain on its implications. The broad terms of that responsibility differ significantly from the older customary law regarding transboundary harm found in Principle 2. Principle 7 elaborates 'common but differentiated' responsibility in the following terms:

States shall co-operate in a spirit of global partnership to conserve, protect and restore the health and integrity of the Earth's ecosystem. In view of the different contributions to global environmental degradation States have common but differentiated responsibilities. The developed countries acknowledge the responsibility that they bear in the international pursuit of sustainable development in view of the pressures their societies place on the global environment and of the technologies and financial resources they command.[161]

---

[156] See 1992 Convention on Climate Change, Article 7(2)(e) and Article 10; *infra*, Ch 6.

[157] See generally *infra*, Ch 4. It is also possible that the Commission on Sustainable Development may in future acquire such a role: see *supra* section 2(3).

[158] *Infra*, Ch 4, section 3(3).   [159] See *infra*, section 5 and Kiss, 175 *Recueil des Cours* (1985) 99.

[160] The most comprehensive treatment is Rajamani, *Differential Treatment in International Environmental Law* (Oxford, 2006). See also Cullet, 10 *EJIL* (1999) 549; French, 49 *ICLQ* (2000) 35; various authors, 96 *Proc ASIL* (2002) 358–68; Atapattu, *Emerging Principles of IEL*, Ch 5.

[161] See also Convention on Climate Change, Article 3(1) and 1987 Protocol on Substances that Deplete the Ozone Layer, Article 5.

This is principally an obligation to cooperate in developing the law, but it has signifi-cant normative value in setting parameters within which responsibilities are to be allocated between developed and developing states in the subsequent negotiation of further implementing agreements or in the interpretation of existing agreements.[162] Common but differentiated responsibility can thus be seen to define an explicit equit-able balance between developed and developing states in at least two senses: it allows for different standards for developing states and it makes their performance depend-ent on the provision of solidarity assistance by developed states.

(a) Differentiated responsibility

Although responsibility is common to all states, developed and developing alike, higher standards of conduct are explicitly set for developed states on the grounds that they have both contributed most to causing problems such as ozone depletion and cli-mate change and that they also possess greater capacity to respond than is generally available to developing states. The differentiation of standards of conduct between developed and developing states is most apparent in Article 4 of the Climate Change Convention and Article 5 of the Ozone Protocol (see Chapter 6). Under the former all parties are required to undertake certain measures, mainly concerned with cooper-ation and information exchange, while only developed countries and others listed in an annex are bound by any commitments to takes measures to deal with greenhouse gases. The same broad distinction is maintained in the Kyoto Protocol. Under Article 5 of the Ozone Protocol all parties are bound by the same commitments, but develop-ing country parties are given a longer timescale within which to phase out production and consumption of ozone depleting substances. In some cases these states may even increase production and consumption within that period.

Although the phraseology of Principle 7 is not repeated in the Biological Diversity Convention or in the 1982 UNCLOS, nor is there any explicit differentiation in these treaties between the responsibilities of developed and developing states, in practice the latter do not bear the same burdens and contextual differences are recognized. Thus there are frequent references to what is 'possible and appropriate' throughout the Biological Diversity Convention, and Article 6 allows account to be taken of the 'par-ticular conditions and capabilities' of each party.[163] Article 194(2) of the 1982 UNCLOS uses similar terminology, whose practical effect is to require less from developing states in protecting the marine environment than from developed states.[164] The equitable differentiation of responsibilities is evidently less strong in these two treaties than in those dealing with climate change and ozone depletion, but it is still apparent, and all four agreements share, in a unique way, the element of solidarity and conditionality.

---

[162] On the role of principles in structuring the negotiation of further agreements see *supra* Ch 1. On the influence of the Principle 7 in negotiation of the Kyoto Protocol see *infra*, Ch 6.

[163] *Infra*, Ch 11 and see Boyle, in Bowman and Redgwell, *International Law and the Conservation of Biological Diversity*, 44–7.

[164] *Infra*, Chs 7, 8.

(b) Solidarity and conditionality

In addition to setting higher standards for developed states, Principle 7 of the Rio Declaration also entails obligations of solidarity assistance to developing states in the form of access to new and additional funds and the transfer of environmentally sound technologies or substitutes. Provisions on all of these matters are found in the Climate Change, Biological Diversity and Ozone Conventions and Protocol, and to a more limited extent in the 1982 UNCLOS.[165] Their purpose is to help developing countries implement their commitments by meeting the incremental costs and building up their capacity to do so. Trust funds and the Global Environment Facility[166] provide access to funding for these purposes and for projects likely to result in global benefits, including protection of the marine environment.

The extent of this commitment to solidarity should not be exaggerated. Not surprisingly, the developed states which would have to provide the necessary resources under these treaties have been carefully ambiguous about the terms of any commitments they have made. For example, under the Biological Diversity Convention the undertaking to provide or facilitate access to technology is in most cases dependent on mutual agreement of terms and conditions,[167] making it uncertain how far any real obligations or rights are created. Nor is the provision of financial resources open-ended. The incremental costs to be covered under Article 21 must also be agreed between the developing states in question and the financial mechanism created by the convention. The view of many developed states is that contributions to this fund are in effect voluntary and determined by each party.[168] Similar comments can be made about technology transfer and funding provisions of the Montreal Protocol and Climate Change Convention.[169] It is doubtful whether at best these represent more than very weak commitments on the part of developed states.

Developing states have, however, found a much better solution to the problem of financial assistance and technology-transfer which obviates the need to express their expectations in terms of strong obligations or solidarity rights. A common feature of the Montreal Protocol, the Biological Diversity Convention and the Climate Change Convention is that the obligations of developing states to comply with these conventions 'will depend upon' the effective implementation of their provisions on financial assistance and transfer of technology by developed states.[170] While this might simply

---

[165] Convention on Climate Change, Articles 4(1)(c), 4(3), 4(5), 11; Convention on Biological Diversity, Articles 16, 20, 21; 1987 Protocol on Substances that Deplete the Ozone Layer, Articles 10 and 10A; 1982 UNCLOS, Articles 202–3. See Rajamani, *Differential Treatment*, 108–18. On the role of funding in treaty compliance see Cameron, Werksman and Roderick (eds), *Improving Compliance with International Environmental Law* (London, 1996) Ch 12; Burhenne-Guilmin and Casey-Lefkowitz, 3 *YbIEL* (1992) 55–6.

[166] *Supra* Ch 2, section 4(4).   [167] Article 16.

[168] The United Kingdom and nineteen other states made declarations on signature asserting that the amount, nature, frequency and size of contributions under Articles 20 and 21 are to be determined by individual states, not by the Conference of the Parties. See Boyle in Bowman and Redgwell, *International Law and the Conservation of Biological Diversity*, 46–7.

[169] See *infra*, Ch 6.

[170] Convention on Biological Diversity, Article 20(4); Convention on Climate Change, Article 4(7); Protocol on Substances that Deplete the Ozone Layer, Article 10.

be a statement of the obvious, it could also be read as making implementation of these conventions by developing countries conditional on receipt of assistance from developed states. Agenda 21 makes the same point with regard to the marine environment. It provides that implementation of its provisions by developing countries:

shall be commensurate with their technological and financial capacities and priorities in allocating resources for development needs and ultimately depends on technology transfer and financial resources required and made available to them.[171]

The effect of making obligations conditional in this way is to give developing states the means to put pressure on developed states. From this perspective it becomes irrelevant whether developed states have a legal duty to provide assistance: if they want developing states to participate actively in securing the goals of each agreement they must honour the expectation that the necessary resources will be provided.[172] It is in this sense that solidarity is a key element of the common but differentiated responsibility of the parties.

(c) An assessment of Principle 7

Principle 7 of the Rio Declaration has to be viewed in the context of negotiated global regulatory regimes, rather than as a principle of customary international law, but it is nonetheless legally significant. It may not provide a basis for interstate claims for global environmental damage,[173] but it does provide an equitable basis for cooperation between developed and developing states on which the latter are entitled to rely in the negotiation of new law to address global environmental concerns. In this sense it is far from being merely soft law, but can be regarded as a 'framework principle', as we saw in Chapter 1.

Acceptance of the principle of common but differentiated responsibility was one of the conditions for ensuring the widest possible participation by developing countries in the Rio instruments. It is this consideration which provides the main justification for differentiation. Consensus on common higher standards would have been impossible to achieve; consensus based on common lower standards would, at least in the case of climate change, have meant failure to achieve any notable advance on the status quo. Principle 7 is undoubtedly preferable to either of these outcomes. At the same time there is a loss of legal uniformity, which may entail higher costs and ultimately weaken the legitimacy and credibility of global environmental regimes.[174] Some of these considerations underlay the US insistence at Kyoto, and subsequently, that

---

[171] Agenda 21, Ch 17.2.

[172] In 1995 the G77 developing countries expressed concern that 'effective implementation of Agenda 21 on developing countries is severely jeopardized by the insufficient transfer of financial and technological resources from developed to developing countries', 26 *EPL* (1996) 59.

[173] A point stressed by the United States at Rio and Johannesburg: see UN Doc A/Conf 151/26, vol iv (1992) 20 and UN Doc A/Conf 199/20 (2002) 146.

[174] Handl, 1 *YbIEL* (1990) 8–10, but cf Sand, *Lessons Learned in Global Environmental Governance*, (Washington, 1990) who points out that asymmetrical standard-setting may be the best way of avoiding consensus on the lowest acceptable standards.

developing states should accept greater responsibility for averting climate change in future negotiations.

The idea of differentiated responsibility is not entirely new in international environmental law. The obligation to use due diligence in mitigating and controlling transboundary environmental risks already takes account of the differing capabilities of individual states,[175] although to a more limited extent and without the elements of conditionality and solidarity found in Principle 7 and the Climate and Ozone Conventions. But it should not be assumed that differentiated responsibility applies universally to all environmental risks. On the contrary, it finds no place in regulatory treaties dealing with ultrahazardous activities, such as nuclear safety[176] and pollution from ships,[177] or in the regulation of dumping at sea[178] and trade in endangered species,[179] or in the conduct of activities in Antarctica, outer space, or on the deep seabed.[180] In all these cases observance of common international standards is essential for effective international regulation. It is also evident that in the Convention on Biological Diversity the element of common but differentiated responsibility is more attenuated than in other global conventions. Moreover it would clearly be wrong to suggest that the obligations of developing states in cases of transboundary risk are in any sense conditional on the provision of technical and financial assistance by their neighbours. Any such view would not only be subversive of existing law on transboundary risks[181] but would be detrimental to the interests of developing states themselves. Common but differentiated responsibility is based on the perception that global environmental risks, such as climate change, have mainly been caused by and should therefore be tackled primarily by developed states. It was never intended to be a justification for allowing developing states to dump pollution on each other.

3(4) THE PRECAUTIONARY APPROACH AND GLOBAL ENVIRONMENTAL RESPONSIBILITY

The precautionary approach is a common feature of all the Rio and post-Rio global environmental agreements. Its purpose is to make greater allowance for uncertainty in the regulation of environmental risks and the sustainable use of natural resources. Principle 15 of the Rio Declaration requires that a precautionary approach 'shall be widely applied by states according to their capabilities'. Like sustainable development, the precautionary approach is not limited to global environmental concerns, but encompasses in addition transboundary and domestic environmental harm, and for this reason the principle and its legal status is considered in the next section below. For

---

[175] *Infra*, section 4(2)(g).   [176] 1994 Convention on Nuclear Safety, *infra*, Ch 9.

[177] 1973/78 Convention on the Prevention of Marine Pollution from Ships, *infra*, Ch 7.

[178] 1996 Protocol to the London Dumping Convention, *infra*, Ch 8.

[179] 1973 Convention on International Trade in Endangered Species, *infra*, Ch 12.

[180] 1991 Protocol to the Antarctic Treaty on Environmental Protection; 1972 Moon Treaty; 1982 UNCLOS, Part XI.

[181] See *infra*, section 4.

present purposes it is necessary only to note that a precautionary approach is of particular importance in cases of global environmental concern, such as ozone depletion, climate change, or protection of the marine environment, because of the seriousness and possible irreversibility of the risks involved. Its adoption in this context confirms the status of the precautionary approach as an important principle of global environmental regulation.

4 PREVENTION OF POLLUTION AND ENVIRONMENTAL HARM

4(1) INTRODUCTION

International law does not allow states to conduct or permit activities within their territories, or in common spaces, without regard for the rights of other states or for the protection of the global environment. This point is sometimes expressed by reference to the maxim *sic utere tuo, ut alienum non laedas* or 'principles of good neighbourliness', but the contribution of customary law in environmental matters is neither as modest nor as vacuous as these phrases might suggest. Two rules enjoy significant support in state practice, judicial decisions, multilateral environmental agreements, and the work of the International Law Commission. They can be regarded as customary international law, or in certain aspects as general principles of law:

1. States have a duty to prevent, reduce, and control transboundary pollution and environmental harm resulting from activities within their jurisdiction or control.

2. States also have a duty to cooperate in mitigating transboundary environmental risks and emergencies, though notification, consultation, negotiation, and in appropriate cases, environmental impact assessment.

Both propositions are reflected in the 1992 Rio Declaration on Environment and Development. It should be noted immediately that neither rule prohibits transboundary harm, and it is erroneous to refer to a 'no harm' rule in this context. The precedents reviewed below confirm this observation.

(a) The Rio Declaration and transboundary environmental harm

Although the Rio Declaration is primarily concerned with sustainable development and the global environment,[182] three principles apply specifically to transboundary harm and environmental risks. Principle 2 requires states to ensure that activities within their jurisdiction do not cause harm to the environment of other states or of

---

[182] *Supra* section 1(2).

common spaces; Principle 18 requires them to notify emergencies likely to affect the environment of other states, and Principle 19 requires them to give prior notification and consult in good faith before undertaking activities that may have significant adverse transboundary environmental effects. On these matters the more convincing view is that the Rio Declaration is merely restating existing law;[183] it is neither soft law nor mere aspiration. A number of other Rio Principles, although not limited to transboundary risks, are also important in that context: Principle 10 on public participation, Principle 15 on the application of the precautionary approach, and Principle 17 on environmental impact assessment. These principles all reflect more recent developments in international law and state practice, but the evidence of consensus support provided by the Rio Declaration, subsequent codification by the ILC, and the case law of international tribunals, are an important indication of their present status as general international law.[184] Taken as a whole, the Rio Declaration is a much more significant statement of the law on transboundary environmental harm than the Stockholm Declaration, and it has provided a strong starting point for the further elaboration of this part of international environmental law by the International Court of Justice and the International Law Commission.

(b) Jurisprudence of the ICJ relating to the environment

Until 1995, the ICJ had contributed very little to the evolution of international environmental law.[185] Since then, four cases have added significantly to the jurisprudence, and have either explicitly or implicitly relied on Rio Principles 2, 4, 24, 26, 27, and probably also Principle 17, as evidence of existing international law. In the *Request for an Examination of the Situation Case*[186] New Zealand reactivated its earlier 1974 *Nuclear Tests Case* application, asking the Court inter alia to order that France carry out an environmental impact assessment in accordance with international law before resuming underground nuclear tests in the Pacific. It further argued that such tests would be illegal unless the EIA showed that no pollution of the marine environment would result, in accordance with its view of the precautionary principle. Having found itself without jurisdiction over the dispute, the Court gave no judgment on these issues, but the dissenting opinions of three judges do address them. Judge ad hoc Palmer noted that the trend of developments from Stockholm to Rio 'has been to establish a comprehensive set of norms to protect the global environment'. Judge Weeramantry gave the most comprehensive judgment, finding that there was prima facie an obligation to conduct an EIA and to show that no harm would result to the marine environment; he

---

[183] See *infra*, sections 4(2)–(3).

[184] On Principle 10 see *infra*, Ch 5. On Principles 15 and 17 see *infra*.

[185] See *Nuclear Tests Cases (Australia and New Zealand v France)* ICJ Reports (1974) 253 and 457, and *infra*, Ch 9; *Fisheries Jurisdiction Cases (UK and Germany v Iceland)* ICJ Reports (1974) 3 and 175, and *infra*, Ch 13. Two other cases with potential importance for the development of international environmental law were settled: *Certain Phosphate Lands in Nauru*, ICJ Reports (1993) 322; *Case Concerning Passage Through the Great Belt*, ICJ Reports (1991) 12 and ibid, (1992) 348.

[186] *Request for an Examination of the Situation in Accordance with the Court's Judgment in the Nuclear Tests Case*, ICJ Reports (1995) 288. ['*Request for an Examination Case*']

also referred to international support for the precautionary principle and the concept of inter-generational equity. Both he and, more cautiously, Judge Koroma, accepted that international law requires states not to cause or permit serious damage in accordance with Principle 21 of the Stockholm Declaration of 1972.

In its *Advisory Opinion on the Legality of the Threat or Use of Nuclear Weapons* the Court took the opportunity to affirm for the first time that:

The existence of the general obligation of states to ensure that activities within their jurisdiction and control respect the environment of other states or of areas beyond national control is now part of the corpus of international law relating to the environment.[187]

It held that states had an obligation to protect the natural environment against widespread, long-term and severe environmental damage in times of armed conflict and to refrain from methods of warfare or reprisals intended to cause such damage. Although treaties on protection of the environment did not take away or restrict a state's right of self-defence if attacked, states must nevertheless take environmental considerations into account when assessing what is necessary and proportionate in the pursuit of legitimate military objectives.[188]

The Court's most important judgment on environmental law remains the *Case Concerning the Gabčíkovo-Nagymaros Dam*.[189] In this dispute Hungary argued that a treaty to build a series of hydroelectric dams on the Danube had been terminated on a number of grounds, including ecological necessity. It also alleged that in unilaterally implementing the project Slovakia had failed to take account of the ecological problems or to do an adequate EIA. The Court accepted that grave and imminent danger to the environment could constitute a state of necessity, but it found no such danger to exist in this case. The contention that the treaty between the parties had terminated was also rejected, but the Court held that in operating the works which had been constructed the parties were obliged to apply new norms of international environmental law, not only when undertaking new activities but also when continuing activities begun in the past. The Court referred, as we saw earlier, to the concept of sustainable development and concluded that the parties must negotiate in good faith, 'look afresh' at the effects on the environment, and find an agreed solution consistent with the objectives of the treaty and the principles of international environmental law and the law of international watercourses. The effect of the judgment is to require the parties to cooperate in the joint management of the project, and to institute a continuing process of environmental protection and monitoring, although only Judge Weeramantry draws this conclusion explicitly. Slovakia's abstraction of over 80 per cent of the flow of water was found to be inequitable and required adjustment.[190]

As we saw earlier, the *Pulp Mills on the River Uruguay Case*[191] provided another opportunity to affirm the importance of integrating sustainable development and

---

[187] ICJ Reports (1996) 226, para 29 ['*Nuclear Weapons AO*'].   [188] See *infra*, section 6.
[189] ICJ Reports (1997) 7 ['*Gabčíkovo-Nagymaros Case*']. See 'Symposium' in 8 *YbIEL* (1997) 3–50.
[190] See *infra*, Ch 10.   [191] ICJ Reports (2006) para 80 ['*Pulp Mills Case*']. See *supra* section 2.

environmental protection. The ICJ's order illustrates the essentially relative character of these competing interests and the need for balance. Argentina argued that the development should not proceed unless shown to be harmless, in accordance with the strongest version of the precautionary principle, and unless prior consent had been given by the River Uruguay Commission. Uruguay rejected these arguments as unsupported by international law or the terms of the 1975 River Uruguay Statute, and relied on the right to sustainable development in support of its own position. At the same time, Uruguay accepted that it must regulate and control a potentially harmful activity to the highest international standards, after conducting a thorough EIA, with public consultation. In the absence of any evidence of imminent harm to the environment, however, the Court refused Argentina's application for a provisional measures order halting construction of the mills, while calling on the parties to renew cooperation in accordance with the terms of the 1975 Statute.

Judgments of international courts provide the most authoritative guidance on the state of the law at the time they are decided. While the environmental jurisprudence is not extensive, it nevertheless affirms the existence of a legal obligation to prevent, reduce and control transboundary environmental harm, to cooperate in the management of environmental risks, to utilize shared natural resources equitably and sustainably, and albeit less certainly, to carry out environmental impact assessment and monitoring. Equally importantly, states parties to litigation before international tribunals, including the ICJ and the International Tribunal on the Law of the Sea (ITLOS), have not sought to argue that general international law does not require them to control transboundary pollution, or to carry out EIAs, or to cooperate in the management of environmental risks. They have not challenged the standard textbook accounts of the subject or the ILC's codification of the law relating to transboundary harm.[192] Rather, the focus of most of the litigation has been on the adequacy or inadequacy of the measures states have taken, or failed to take—on whether, for example, an appropriate EIA has been carried out, or diligent pollution control laws exist, not on whether they are necessary at all. Moreover, as we saw in Chapter 1, the International Court has not been unsympathetic to the needs of international lawmaking on environmental matters using soft law and other declaratory processes. Nor has it been unresponsive to the claims of sustainable development, as we saw earlier in this chapter.[193] Only in one area has judicial activity been noticeably absent: liability for damage to the environment. Not surprisingly, however, the jurisprudence leaves a number of other questions unanswered, including the legal status of the precautionary principle and the extent to which an EIA is judicially reviewable.[194]

---

[192] See *MOX Plant Case (Provisional Measures)* (2001) ITLOS No 10; *MOX Plant Arbitration (Jurisdiction and Provisional Measures)* (2003) PCA; *Land Reclamation Case (Provisional Measures)* (2003) ITLOS No 12; *Pulp Mills Case*, ICJ Reports (2006).

[193] *Supra* section 2(1).

[194] See *infra*, section 4(3). At the time of writing the precautionary principle and environmental impact assessment were among the matters awaiting argument on the merits in the *Pulp Mills Case*.

(c) The International Law Commission

Transboundary environmental harm has been on the agenda of the ILC since 1978, under the improbable title of 'Liability for Injurious Consequences of Acts Not Prohibited by International Law'.[195] The Commission's early work on this topic was fundamentally misconceived, and is of no real value to an understanding of the subject,[196] but draft articles and commentary proposed in 1996 were a significant advance,[197] and for the first time afforded a more realistic view of the law. There were three elements in that draft—prevention, cooperation, and strict liability for damage. In the absence of any consensus on the latter topic, the Commission decided to postpone further work on liability. Amended Articles on the Prevention of Transboundary Harm from Hazardous Activities were finally adopted in 2001, and recommended to the UN General Assembly.[198]

The 2001 Articles on Transboundary Harm essentially codify existing obligations of environmental impact assessment, notification, consultation, monitoring, prevention, and diligent control of activities likely to cause transboundary harm. These articles are securely based in existing precedents. They draw on case law, treaties, the Rio Declaration, the quite elaborate regime established for the marine environment by the 1982 UNCLOS, the 1991 UNECE Convention on Environmental Impact Assessment in a Transboundary Context, and the ILC's own articles on protection of international watercourses. The articles on non-discriminatory access to justice and other procedures in transboundary cases and on provision of information to the public also reflect developments in state practice, treaties, and in other codifications.[199] On all of these matters the 2001 Articles offer an authoritative exposition of the existing law. Not surprisingly, they have been heavily cited by parties to international environmental litigation.[200]

The 2001 articles apply to all activities within the jurisdiction or control of states which involve a risk of causing significant transboundary harm, including environmental harm. Risk is broadly defined to include both the possibility of unlikely but disastrous accidents, such as exploding nuclear power plants (e.g. Chernobyl), and

---

[195] See II *YbILC* (1980) Pt1, 160, paras 138–9; I *YbILC* (1981) 224, para 10; the special rapporteur's first schematic outline in II *YbILC* (1982) Pt 1, 62 and II *YbILC* (1983) Pt 1, 204, para 10; the special rapporteur's 4th and 5th reports in (1983) II *YbILC* 201; II *YbILC* (1984) Pt 1, 155 and the *Survey of State Practice Relevant to International Liability for Injurious Consequences (etc)* (1984) UN Doc ST/LEG/15.

[196] For critical analysis see Akehurst, 16 *NYIL* (1985) 8; Boyle, 39 *ICLQ* (1990) 1; Fitzmaurice, 25 *NYIL* (1994) 181; for more favourable views see Magraw, 80 *AJIL* (1986) 305; Lefeber, *Transboundary Interference and the Origin of State Liability*, Ch 6; Handl, 16 *NYIL* (1985) 49.

[197] *Report of the Working Group on International Liability*, in *ILC Report* (1996) GAOR A/51/10, Annex 1, 235.

[198] See *ILC Report* (2001) GAOR A/56/10, 366. [Hereafter referred to as '2001 Articles on Transboundary Harm']. For drafting history see Special Rapporteur's *1st Report* (1998) UN Doc A/CN 4/487/Add 1; *2nd Report* (1999) UN Doc A/CN 4/501; *3rd Report* (2000) UN Doc A/CN 4/510 and Boyle and Freestone (eds), *Sustainable Development and International Law* (Oxford, 1999) Ch 4.

[199] On all these issues see *infra*, Ch 5.

[200] See e.g. the pleadings in the *MOX Plant Arbitration* (2003) PCA and the *Pulp Mills Case* (2006) ICJ Reports.

probable but smaller scale harm, such as industrial air pollution (e.g. *Trail Smelter*).[201]
Whether there is such a risk has to be determined objectively: 'as denoting an appreciation of possible harm resulting from an activity which a properly informed observer
had or ought to have had'.[202] The articles would not therefore apply to an activity not
reasonably foreseeable as potentially harmful. Hypothetical risks do not fall within
this standard.[203] Harm is 'significant' if it is 'more than detectable', but it need not
be 'serious' or 'substantial'; what is significant depends on the circumstances of each
case, and may vary over time.[204] Trivial or speculative harm will not be covered: '[t]
he harm must lead to a real detrimental effect on matters such as, for example, human
health, industry, property, environment or agriculture in other states. Such detrimental effects must be susceptible of being measured by factual and objective standards.'[205]
The articles do not cover prohibited activities, although there is no reason why a more
comprehensive codification should not do so. Ocean dumping of waste, or the export
of waste to developing countries, both of which international law now prohibits,[206]
would thus not be included. However, the Commission no longer took the erroneous
view that activities which cause harm are for that reason prohibited, a fallacy which
underlay its earlier efforts.[207] Most industrial activities which cause environmental
harm are not prohibited; what is needed is a legal regime to regulate the risks and consequences of those activities. This the 2001 Articles now provide.

The second element of the ILC's codification of the law on transboundary harm
takes the form of Principles on Allocation of Loss, adopted in 2006. These complete its
previous work on liability, and are examined in more detail in Chapter 5. Additionally,
Article 5 also reiterates the requirement that states notify and consult their neighbours
and take appropriate response measures when accidents involving hazardous activities occur. This article builds on state practice and the development of specific environmental response regimes for Antarctica, industrial accidents, accidents at sea, and
nuclear incidents.[208]

The ILC's work thus reflects the relevant provisions of the Rio Declaration, notably
Principles 2, 10, 11, 17, 18, and 19, but formulates them in greater detail. Inter alia, all
appropriate measures must be taken to prevent or minimize the risk of transboundary
harm or to minimize its effects (Article 3); states must cooperate to this end (Article 4);
no such activity may be undertaken without prior impact assessment and authorization by the state in which it is to be conducted (Articles 6 and 7); states likely to be
affected must be notified and consulted with a view to agreeing measures to minimize
or prevent the risk of harm (Articles 8 and 9); relevant information on the risks must

---

[201] Article 2, and commentary, *ILC Report* (2001) GAOR A/56/10, 387 paras (3) & (4).
[202] *ILC Report* (2001) GAOR A/56/10, 385 para (15).
[203] See *Japan—Measures Affecting the Import of Apples*, WT/DS245/AB/R (2003) para 202.
[204] *ILC Report* (2001) GAOR A/56/10, 389 para (7).
[205] Id, para (4).   [206] See *infra*, Ch 8.
[207] Boyle, 39 *ICLQ* (1990) 1. In his *3rd Report* the special rapporteur noted that 'none of the authorities he
had surveyed had indicated that non-compliance with the obligation of due diligence made the activity itself
prohibited': *ILC Report* (2000) GAOR A/55/10, para 678.
[208] See *infra*, section 4(5).

be given to the public likely to be affected (Article 14); and measures must be taken to deal with and notify other states of any emergency (Articles 16 and 17). The 2001 Articles do not prohibit the conduct of activities which create a transboundary risk, however serious, and the preamble recognizes the freedom of states to carry on or permit activities under their jurisdiction subject to the above obligations.[209]

4(2) THE DUTY TO PREVENT, REDUCE AND CONTROL ENVIRONMENTAL HARM

It is beyond serious argument that states are required by international law to regulate and control activities within their territory or subject to their jurisdiction or control that pose a significant risk of global or transboundary pollution or environmental harm.[210] This is an obligation to take appropriate measures to prevent or minimize as far as possible the risk of significant harm, not merely a basis for reparation after the event.[211] It follows that states must also take measures to identify such risks, for example by environmental impact assessment or monitoring.[212] The obligation is a continuing one: 'It implies the need for States to review their obligations of prevention in a continuous manner to keep abreast with the advances in scientific knowledge.'[213] Although some writers and treaties use the term 'preventive principle',[214] the obligation referred to here is more than a principle—in regard to transboundary environmental risks it is an obligatory rule of customary international law. It has been identified as such in arbitral and judicial decisions, in a wide range of global and regional treaties, and in the Stockholm and Rio Declarations.

(a) Customary law and Principle 2 of the Rio Declaration

In the *Nuclear Weapons Advisory Opinion* the ICJ held, as we saw earlier, that the terms of Principle 2 of the Rio Declaration are 'now part of the corpus of international law relating to the environment'.[215] The origins of a rule on transboundary harm can be traced to the well-known *Trail Smelter Arbitration*,[216] in which a tribunal awarded

---

[209] But see Articles 9 and 10, and the discussion of equitable balancing, *infra*, section 4(5).

[210] On the meaning of 'jurisdiction or control' see ILC Report (2001) GAOR A/56/10, 383–5. It includes ships, aircraft, spacecraft, and occupied territory.

[211] Article 3, ILC 2001 Articles on Transboundary Harm. See generally Handl in Bodansky, Brunnée, and Hey, *Oxford Handbook of IEL*, 532. On the origins of this rule see Dupuy in OECD, *Legal Aspects of Transfrontier Pollution* (Paris, 1977) 345; Smith, *State Responsibility and the Marine Environment* (Oxford, 1988) 36ff, 72ff; Handl, 26 *NRJ* (1986) 405, 427ff; Kirgis, 66 *AJIL* (1972) 290, 315; Quentin-Baxter, II *YbILC* (1980) Pt 1, 246–62; Lefeber, *Transboundary Environmental Interference and the Origin of State Liability*, Ch 2.

[212] *ILC Report* (2001) GAOR A/56/10, 391, para (5). On EIA see *infra*, next section.

[213] *ILC Report* (2001) GAOR A/56/10, 415, para (7). See *Gabčíkovo-Nagymaros Case*, ICJ Reports (1997) 7, para 140.

[214] See e.g. de Sadeleer, *Environmental Principles*, Ch 2, and 1999 Rhine Convention, Article 4. The 'preventive principle' is derived from EC law where it is not limited to global or transboundary harm.

[215] ICJ Reports (1996) 226, para 29. See also *Iron Rhine Arbitration*, PCA (2005) paras 222–3.

[216] 33 *AJIL* (1939) 182 and 35 *AJIL* (1941) 684. See Read, 1 *CYIL* (1963) 213; Rubin, 50 *Oregon LR* (1971) 259; Kirgis, 66 *AJIL* (1972); Smith, *State Responsibility*, 72ff; Quentin-Baxter, II *YbILC* (1981) Pt 1, 108ff.

damages to the United States and prescribed a regime for controlling future emissions from a Canadian smelter which had caused air pollution damage. It concluded that 'no state has the right to use or permit the use of its territory in such a manner as to cause injury by fumes in or to the territory of another or the properties or persons therein, when the case is of serious consequence and the injury is established by clear and convincing evidence', and prescribed control measures to avert future transboundary pollution.[217] The judgment of the ICJ in the *Corfu Channel Case* supports a similar conclusion, although the context is rather different and its application to the environment more doubtful. Here the court held Albania responsible for damage to British warships caused by a failure to warn them of mines in territorial waters, and it indicated that it was 'every state's obligation not to allow knowingly its territory to be used for acts contrary to the rights of other states'.[218] This judgment does not suggest what the environmental rights of other states might be, and its true significance may be confined to a narrower point about warning other states of known dangers, considered below.

While the significance of these older judicial or arbitral precedents should not be overrated, there is ample evidence of continued international support for the broad proposition that states must control sources of harm to others or to the global environment arising within their territory or subject to their jurisdiction and control.[219] In particular, Principle 21 of the 1972 Stockholm Declaration on the Human Environment is important, because it affirms both the sovereign right of states to exploit their own resources 'pursuant to their own environmental policies' and their responsibility 'to ensure that activities within their jurisdiction or control do not cause damage to the environment of other states or to areas beyond the limits of national jurisdiction'. Although, as Professor Sohn has observed, the first part of this principle comes 'quite close' to asserting that a state has unlimited sovereignty over its environment, the totality of the provision, including its emphatic reference to responsibility for environmental damage, was regarded by many states present at the Stockholm Conference,

---

[217] 35 *AJIL* (1941) 716. This finding relied on the *Alabama Claims Arbitration* (1872) Moore, 1 *International Arbitrations*, 485, and Eagleton, *Responsibility of States in International Law* (1928) 80, for the general proposition that 'A state owes at all times a duty to protect other states against injurious acts by individuals from within its jurisdiction', and on the evidence of US Federal case law dealing with interstate air and water pollution, which it held 'may legitimately be taken as a guide in this field of international law...where no contrary rule prevails', 35 *AJIL* (1941) 714. Reliance on domestic case law by analogy was *not* required by the *compromis*, which called for application of US law and practice only in respect of issues of proof of damage, indemnity, and the regime of future operations of the smelter, ibid, 698. The use of domestic law analogies is better treated as an invocation of 'general principles of law' referred to in Article 38(1) of the Statute of the ICJ. For criticism of the tribunal's approach, see Rubin, 50 *Oregon LR* (1971) 267; Goldie, 14 *ICLQ* (1965) 1229, and for explanation, see Read, 1 *CYIL* (1963) 213.

[218] ICJ Reports (1949) 22. See also *Nuclear Tests Case (Australia v France)* ICJ Reports (1974) 388, per de Castro; *Lac Lanoux Arbitration*, 24 ILR (1957) 101, 123; and Brownlie, *State Responsibility* (Oxford, 1983) 182.

[219] See e.g. 1979 Convention on Long-range Transboundary Air Pollution; 1982 UNCLOS, Articles 192–212; 1989 Convention on the Control of Transboundary Movements of Hazardous Wastes; 1991 Convention on EIA, Article 2; 1985 Convention for the Protection of the Ozone Layer; 1992 Framework Convention on Climate Change.

and subsequently by the UN General Assembly, as reflecting customary international law.[220]

Moreover, whereas older formulations of the preventive obligation, in cases such as *Trail Smelter*, had dealt only with transboundary harm to other states, Stockholm Principle 21 and later conventions point to international acceptance of the proposition that states are also required to protect global common areas, including Antarctica and those areas beyond the limits of national jurisdiction, such as the high seas, deep sea-bed, and outer space.[221] Article 194(2) of the 1982 UNCLOS makes the same point in relation to the prevention of pollution spreading beyond areas where a state exercises sovereign rights. At the 1972 Stockholm Conference, the United States stated that Principle 21 did not in any way diminish existing international responsibility for damage to areas beyond national jurisdiction; in its view it 'affirmed existing rules'.[222] The UN General Assembly also resolved that in the exploration, exploitation, and development of their natural resources, 'states must not produce significant harmful effects in zones situated outside their national jurisdiction'.[223] An important consequence of this changed perspective is that the obligation to prevent, reduce and control environmental harm is no longer solely bilateral in character but in relation to the high seas or the global atmosphere it benefits the international community as a whole and to that extent operates *erga omnes*.[224]

The Rio instruments confirm the status of Stockholm Principle 21 as a statement of contemporary international law. It is repeated verbatim in Article 3 of the Convention on Biological Diversity, reiterated with one minor change in Principle 2 of the Rio Declaration, and extended to the global atmosphere by the preamble to the Convention on Climate Change.[225] In its revised form Principle 2 now provides that:

States have, in accordance with the Charter of the United Nations and the principles of international law, the sovereign right to exploit their own resources pursuant to their own

---

[220] Sohn, 14 *Harv ILJ* (1973) 491ff. Several states declared that Principle 21 accorded with existing international law: see Canadian and US Comments in UN Doc A/CONF 48/14/Rev 1, 64–6. UNGA Res 2996 (XXVII) (1972) asserts that Principles 21 and 22 of the Stockholm Declaration 'lay down the basic rules governing the matter'. See also UNGA Res 2995 XXVII (1972); 2996 XXVII (1972); 3281 XXIX (1974); 34/186 (1979); UNEP Principles of Conduct in the Field of the Environment Concerning Resources Shared by Two or More States, Principle 3, UNEP/IG/12/2 (1978).

[221] 1967 Outer Space Treaty; 1979 Moon Treaty; 1972 London Dumping Convention; 1982 UNCLOS, Articles 145, 209; 1991 Protocol to the Antarctic Treaty on Environmental Protection. See Sohn, 14 *Harv ILJ* (1973) 423; Smith, *State Responsibility and the Marine Environment* (Oxford, 1988) 76ff; Fleischer, in Bothe, *Trends in Environmental Policy and Law*, 321; Charney, in Francioni and Scovazzi (eds), *International Responsibility for Environmental Harm* (Dordrecht, 1991) 149; Pineschi, in Francioni and Scovazzi (eds), *International Law for Antarctica* (2nd edn, The Hague, 1996) 261.

[222] *Report of the UN Conference on the Human Environment*, UN Doc A/CONF/48/14/Rev 1, (1972) para 327.

[223] UNGA Res 2995 XXVII (1972).

[224] Charney, in Francioni and Scovazzi, *International Responsibility for Environmental Harm*, and see *supra* section 3(2) on *erga omnes* obligations.

[225] See also preambles to 1994 Convention to Combat Desertification; 2001 Convention on Persistent Organic Pollutants; 2006 International Tropical Timber Agreement; 2008 Non-Legally Binding Instrument on all Types of Forests, UNGA Res 62/98.

environmental and developmental policies, and the responsibility to ensure that activities within their jurisdiction or control do not cause damage to the environment of other states or of areas beyond the limits of national jurisdiction.

Although the reference to a state's own developmental policies constitutes an additional qualification of its environmental responsibilities, it is doubtful whether this does more than confirm an existing and necessary reconciliation with the principle of sustainable development and the sovereignty of states over their own natural resources. It is an exaggeration to see this textual change as eviscerating or significantly amending the existing responsibility of states in international law for the control and prevention of environmental harm.[226] As Sands observes:

a careful reading suggests that the additional words merely affirm that states are entitled to pursue their own developmental policies. The introduction of these words may even expand the scope of the responsibility not to cause environmental damage to apply to national developmental policies as well as national environmental policies.[227]

As we noted earlier, Principle 2 is neither an absolute prohibition on environmental damage, nor does it confer on states absolute freedom to exploit natural resources. Like sustainable development, it requires integration or accommodation of both economic development and environmental protection.[228] This feature of Principle 2 must be taken into account when interpreting both parts of the rule which it articulates. In practice, the relationship between the sovereign use of resources and the responsibility for environmental protection has usually been negotiated in the context of specific sectoral treaty regimes, and it may differ in different contexts. Treaties dealing with climate change or land-based sources of marine pollution thus allow rather more latitude for resource use which causes environmental damage than do those concerned with pollution from ships or nuclear accidents.[229] In its work on international watercourses the ILC found it a challenge to determine the right balance between the freedom to make equitable use of an international watercourse and the duty not to cause harm to other riparian states.[230] Both the need for balance and its context-specific nature in individual situations make it more difficult, but certainly not impossible, to apply Principle 2 in legal disputes between states. Despite its age, the *Trail Smelter Arbitration* illustrates very well how even a judicial or arbitral tribunal can find ways of reconciling the prevention of transboundary harm with economic development. In the following sections we consider how this can be achieved, and how Principle 2 should be interpreted.

---

[226] *Contra*, Pallemaerts, in Sands, *Greening International Law*, 5–7.
[227] Sands, *Principles of International Environmental Law*, 54–5.   [228] *Supra* section 2(1).
[229] See *infra*, Ch 6, 7, 8, 9.
[230] Compare Articles 5 and 7 of the 1997 UN Watercourses Convention with the same articles in the ILC's 1994 Draft Convention, UN Doc A/CN 4/L492 and Add 1 and compare the ILA's 1966 Helsinki Rules, Article 10(1) and see *infra*, Ch 10.

(b) The normative contours of Principle 2

Whatever the significance of *Trail Smelter* and older judicial precedents may have been, the main importance of Principle 2 is that it recognizes the need to take measures to prevent or minimize harm to the environment of other states or the global commons. Even in *Trail Smelter*, Canada was ordered by the tribunal to take measures to prevent or reduce future injury, and this is the primary purpose of most modern environmental treaties, including the Ozone Convention, the MARPOL Convention, the London Dumping Convention, the POPS Convention and others dealing with land-based pollution, desertification, or climate change. That the rule is now primarily one of regulation and control is indicated most clearly by its formulation in Article 194 of the 1982 UNCLOS:

(1) States shall take, individually or jointly as appropriate, all measures consistent with this Convention that are necessary to prevent, reduce and control pollution of the marine environment from any source, using for this purpose the best practicable means at their disposal and in accordance with their capabilities, and they shall endeavour to harmonise their policies in this connection.

(2) States shall take all measures necessary to ensure that activities under their jurisdiction or control are so conducted as not to cause damage by pollution to other states and their environment...[231]

The same approach is found in Article 2(1) of the 1991 Convention on Transboundary Environmental Impact Assessment, and in Article 3 of the 2001 Articles on Prevention of Transboundary Harm. The former provides that: 'The parties shall, either individually or jointly, take all appropriate and effective measures to prevent, reduce and control significant adverse transboundary environmental impact from proposed activities.' The latter requires parties to take 'all appropriate measures to prevent or minimise the risk of significant transboundary harm'. What these formulations imply is an obligation to act with due diligence.[232]

In general terms, 'due diligence' addresses two issues. First, it requires the introduction of policies, legislation, and administrative controls applicable to public and private conduct which are capable of preventing or minimizing the risk of transboundary harm to other states or the global environment, and it can be expressed as the conduct to be expected of a good government.[233] Following the Sandoz disaster, Switzerland thus accepted that it had failed to regulate spills from pharmaceutical plants to the standard required by the 1976 Rhine Chemicals Convention.[234] This is not an obligation of result: 'The duty of due diligence... is not intended to guarantee that significant

---

[231] See *infra*, Chs 7, 8.

[232] *ILC Report* (2000) GAOR A/55/10, para 718: 'the special rapporteur was of the opinion that "all appropriate measures" and "due diligence" were synonymous'.

[233] ILC 2001 Articles, Article 3 and commentary, *ILC Report* (2001) GAOR A/56/10, 393–5, paras (10)–(17); OECD, *Legal Aspects of Transfrontier Pollution*, 385f; Dupuy, ibid, 369ff; Smith, *State Responsibility and the Marine Environment*, 36–42; Pisillo-Mazeschi, 35 *GYIL* (1992) 9.

[234] *ILC Report* (2001) GAOR A/56/10, 392. See Kiss, 33 *AFDI* (1987) 719–27.

harm be totally prevented, if it is not possible to do so.'[235] To that extent it remains lawful to conduct inherently harmful or risky activities such as nuclear power plants. Moreover, states are responsible only for their own failure to act diligently, not for any failure by the operator to do so.[236] In the *Pulp Mills Case*, much of the argument thus focused on the adequacy of Uruguay's regulatory system, its provision for EIA, and the choice of technology. Considerations of the effectiveness of territorial control, the resources available to the state, the degree of risk, and the nature of specific activities may also be taken into account and justify differing degrees of diligence.[237] The ILC commentary has summarized the key points:

> The standard of due diligence against which the conduct of State of origin should be examined is that which is generally considered to be appropriate and proportional to the degree of risk of transboundary harm in the particular instance. For example, activities which may be considered ultra-hazardous require a much higher standard of care in designing policies and a much higher degree of vigour on the part of the State to enforce them. Issues such as the size of the operation; its location, special climate conditions, materials used in the activity, and whether the conclusions drawn from the application of these factors in a specific case are reasonable, are among the factors to be considered in determining the due diligence requirement in each instance. What would be considered a reasonable standard of care or due diligence may change with time; what might be considered an appropriate and reasonable procedure, standard or rule at one point in time may not be considered as such at some point in the future. Hence, due diligence in ensuring safety requires a State to keep abreast of technological changes and scientific developments.[238]

Secondly, due diligence entails an evolving standard of technology and regulation. This is commonly expressed by reference to the use of 'best available techniques', 'best practicable means', or 'best environmental practices'.[239] Comparison with standards followed by other states will often be a good guide in this context. This approach allows for the standard of diligence to change as technology and operating techniques develop and for new industrial plants to operate to higher standards than existing

---

[235] *ILC Report* (2001) GAOR A/56/10, 391–2, para (7), and to the same effect but in a rather different context, *Bosnian Genocide Case*, ICJ Reports (2007) para 430: 'A State does not incur responsibility simply because the desired result is not achieved; responsibility is however incurred if the State manifestly failed to take all measures to prevent the genocide which were within its power and which might have contributed to preventing the genocide.' See generally Handl in Bodansky, Brunnée, and Hey, *Oxford Handbook of IEL*, 538–40, and Dupuy, 10 *EJIL* (1999) 371–85.

[236] *ILC Report* (2001) GAOR A/56/10, 399, para (3); OECD, *Legal Aspects of Transfrontier Pollution*, 380; Dupuy, ibid. See, for a good example, 1982 UNCLOS, Annex III, Article 4(4).

[237] See generally *Alabama Claims Arbitration*, *supra* n 217, 485; *Corfu Channel Case*, ICJ Reports (1949) 89, Judge ad hoc Ecer; *Case Concerning Diplomatic and Consular Staff in Tehran*, ICJ Reports (1980) 29–33; *Bosnian Genocide Case*, ICJ Reports (2007) para 430; Dupuy, in OECD, *Legal Aspects of Transfrontier Pollution*, 375f; Smith, *State Responsibility and the Marine Environment*, 38–41.

[238] *ILC Report* (2001) GAOR A/55/10, 394, para (11).

[239] For a comprehensive definition of the terms 'best available techniques' and 'best environmental practices' see Article 5(f) and Annex C of the 2001 POPS Convention. See also 1992 OSPAR Convention for the Protection of the Marine Environment of the Northeast Atlantic, Article 2(3) and BAT standards adopted by the OSPAR Commission, *infra*, Ch 8.

plants. Thus, in the *Pulp Mills Case*, Uruguay's newly built mills would have to operate to the highest international standards, whereas Argentina's older mills could not be expected to do so.[240]

By requiring states to use the 'best practicable means at their disposal and in accordance with their capabilities' Article 194(1) of the 1982 UNCLOS illustrates how the concerns of less developed states about older technology and lack of regulatory capacity can also be accommodated within a flexible model of due diligence. Similarly, Article 2 of the 1972 London Dumping Convention required parties to take effective measures 'according to their scientific, technical and economic capabilities'. The view that special allowance is to be made for developing countries in determining the content of their legal obligations is also reflected in Principle 23 of the Stockholm Declaration, in Principles 6, 7, and 11 of the Rio Declaration, and in the Ozone Protocol and the Conventions on Climate Change and Biological Diversity. Due diligence can be compared to 'common but differentiated responsibility' insofar as it allows for differentiated standards of conduct for different states, but it lacks the elements of conditionality and solidarity which characterize the latter concept.[241] However, there are dangers in pressing this point too far if the result is that developing states remain free to pollute other developing states. In the *Pulp Mills Case*, Uruguay—a developing state—made no attempt to dispute Argentina's claim that the applicable standard was anything less than state-of-the-art technology that would meet the most demanding regulatory requirements anywhere else. The standard of comparison was the European Union, Canada and the United States, not other developing countries.[242] The argument that developing countries should be free to operate substandard oil tankers or nuclear power plants is even less attractive, and it finds no support in IMO or IAEA regulations, the MARPOL Convention, or the Nuclear Safety Convention.[243]

If the main advantage of due diligence is its flexibility and responsiveness to circumstances, the main disadvantage of a generalized formulation is that it offers limited guidance on what legislation or technology are required in specific cases. Something more may be needed to give it concrete content and predictability. For this purpose a useful approach is to look to internationally agreed minimum standards set out in treaties or in the resolutions and decisions of international bodies such as IMO or IAEA. In the *MOX Plant Case* the core of the United Kingdom's response to Ireland's claims was that it had fully complied with the relevant international standards established by these bodies. For its part Ireland pointed instead to applicable regional standards, including European Community law. These examples show that internationally

---

[240] *Pulp Mills Case* (2006) ICJ Reports. See also 1994 Nuclear Safety Convention, Article 6, *infra*, Ch 9.

[241] See *supra* section 3(3).

[242] Similarly, the United States has consistently sought to ensure that industrial plants in Mexico operate to the same standards as in the United States: see 1993 North American Agreement on Environmental Cooperation. The 1982 UNCLOS recognizes the same point by allowing parties less flexibility under Article 194(2) where the harm is to other states than in cases of pollution affecting common spaces. But for examples of a 'double standard' in practice, see *infra*, Chs 6, 8.

[243] See *infra*, Chs 7, 9.

agreed 'ecostandards' can be very detailed and precise, as in the annexes to the 1973/78 MARPOL Convention or the Ozone Protocol.[244] They can usually be easily updated, often using soft-law instruments or decisions of the parties.[245] The technique of resorting to international standards for the purpose of defining obligations of conduct is employed by several multilateral treaties. The 1982 UNCLOS in effect incorporates the annexes to the MARPOL Convention and the London Dumping Convention by requiring states to give effect to 'generally accepted international rules and standards', whether or not they are independently binding on parties.[246] Other examples include the Basel Convention on Transboundary Movement of Hazardous Wastes and the Nuclear Safety Convention.[247] In some treaties states are given more latitude and need only 'take account of' international standards, but even this formulation gives some guidance as to the content of their general obligation of diligence.[248]

It follows that, quite apart from their incorporation by treaty, such international standards may acquire customary force by virtue of the obligation of due diligence if international support is sufficiently widespread and representative. The annexes to the MARPOL Convention may be one example of this transformation process.[249] IAEA safety standards for the management of nuclear installations are arguably another, an argument reinforced by the Nuclear Safety Convention's requirement to 'take the appropriate steps'.[250] Thus whether or not they are found in legally binding instruments, it will sometimes be possible to point to specific standards of diligent conduct which can be monitored by international supervisory institutions or employed by international tribunals to settle disputes. At the same time, reliance on internationally agreed standards has drawbacks. The most obvious is that states may have agreed standards which represent the lowest common denominator rather than the best available techniques. This is a significant problem with IMO's regulation of shipping standards, as we will see in Chapter 7. The more subtle objection is that overly prescriptive regulation of technology can become an impediment to further technological advance, in some cases resulting in fossilization rather than evolution.

(c) Absolute obligations of prevention and prohibited activities

An alternative interpretation of Rio Principle 2, which itself is ambiguous on the matter, stresses the fact of harm, rather than the conduct of the state in bringing it about or failing to prevent it.[251] Another way of making the same point is to postulate a duty of diligence so demanding that it amounts to an absolute obligation of prevention or an obligation of 'result' rather than of conduct: in effect a prohibition.[252] Since it is

---

[244] See *infra*, Chs 6, 7, 10.   [245] See *supra*, Ch 2, section 3.
[246] Articles 210–11. See *infra*, Chs 7, 8.   [247] See *infra*, Chs 8, 9.
[248] E.g. 1982 UNCLOS, Articles 207–8, *infra*, Ch 8. The question whether national standards must be 'based on' or 'conform to' international standards is considered at length in the *Beef Hormones Case* WT/DS26/AB/R (1997) paras157–77.
[249] See *infra*, Ch 7.   [250] See *infra*, Ch 9.
[251] *Infra,* Ch 4, section 2. See Scovazzi, 12 *YbIEL* (2001) 43.
[252] Smith, *State Responsibility*, 41; II *YbILC* (1977) Pt 2, 11–30.

not plausible to interpret the typical treaty formulation requiring states to 'prevent, reduce and control' pollution in this absolute sense, the more onerous interpretation of Principle 2 is mainly significant in determining the incidence of liability in customary law for unavoidable environmental damage, which by definition could not have been prevented or controlled. The precedents and possible arguments for this view of the law are reviewed in Chapter 4.

One problem with these more onerous interpretations, however, is that they may place unacceptable burdens on the freedom of states to pursue their own environmental and developmental policies, and to exercise their sovereign rights over their own natural resources. Such an interpretation thus risks giving excessive weight to the second part of Rio Principle 2. For this reason some commentators limit the application of this absolute version to ultra-hazardous activities, of which nuclear reactors are an obvious example.[253]

An extreme view, that activities likely to cause significant transboundary harm are unlawful and therefore prohibited, was used by ILC rapporteurs during the early stages of work on 'Injurious Consequences' to justify proposals for a novel legal regime requiring compensation for harm as part of an equitable balance of interests which would allow polluting activities lawfully to continue in operation.[254] The conclusion that obligations of harm prevention however defined can make the activity itself unlawful is widely regarded as misconceived; as Brownlie observes, 'it is the content of the relevant rules which is critical, and a global distinction between lawful and unlawful activities is useless' and unsupported by state practice or international jurisprudence.[255] It is true that some environmentally risky activities *are* prohibited by international law, such as dumping at sea of hazardous waste (see Chapter 8), or atmospheric nuclear tests (see Chapter 9). States must not authorize or conduct such activities themselves and to this end they will have to adopt appropriate laws and exercise the necessary administrative controls. But even this obligation seems more one of conduct than of result: it remains a duty of diligence rather than an absolute obligation.

A further objection to absolute obligations of prevention is that they concentrate more on shifting the burden of proof and liability for loss than on the diligent control of dangerous activities, since standards of conduct will be irrelevant to their performance. Thus even if arguments for prohibition of transboundary harm are accepted as a basis for state responsibility for environmental injury, in practice the elaboration of standards of diligent conduct remains an essential complementary principle,[256] and a better basis for international regulation of the environment and interpretation of Principle 2.

---

[253] E.g. Jenks, 117 *Recueil des Cours* (1966) 105, and see *infra*, Ch 4.

[254] See Quentin-Baxter, II *YbILC* (1981) Pt 1, 112–22; ibid, (1982) Pt 1, 60, para 39; ibid, (1983) Pt 1, 206, paras 19–22; and Barboza, UN Doc A/CN 4/428 (1990) para 10.

[255] Brownlie, *State Responsibility*, 50; see also Akehurst, 16 *NYIL* (1985) 8; Boyle, 39 *ICLQ* (1990) 12–14, but cf Magraw, 80 *AJIL* (1986) 305.

[256] See Barboza, *2nd Report on International Liability*, II *YbILC* (1986) Pt 1, 159, paras 63–9; *4th Report*, UN Doc A/CN 4/413 (1988) 34, paras 103–11.

(d) Non-discrimination and transboundary harm

Non-discrimination is not referred to in the Rio Declaration, but it is listed in the preamble of the 1992 Convention on the Transboundary Effects of Industrial accidents among 'principles of international law and custom'. In a more limited form it is codified in Article 15 of the ILC's 2001 Articles on Transboundary Harm.[257] At least one writer argues that, in an environmental context, it is an emerging general principle, widely accepted in Europe and North America, and, albeit with reservations, in relations with developing states.[258] As defined by OECD, where the environmental application of the concept originated, it entails giving equivalent treatment to the domestic and transboundary effects of polluting or environmentally harmful activities.[259] This is not a restatement of the obligation of due diligence, but neither does it represent a lower standard: in effect it requires states with higher domestic standards to apply the same legal standards to activities with external effects.

One example of such a requirement is found in Article 2 of the 1974 Nordic Convention on Protection of the Environment, which obliges parties to equate domestic and transboundary nuisances when considering the permissibility of environmentally harmful activities. The principle need not be limited to transboundary pollution, however; in OECD recommendations and decisions it has also been applied to export of hazardous wastes and products, export of dangerous installations, and development aid.[260] Potentially it could have implications for such problems as trade in alien or endangered species, export of genetically modified organisms, or sustainable use of natural resources.

The strongest evidence for a principle of non-discrimination in international environmental law will be found in Chapter 5. Outside that context of transboundary access to information, decision-making, and justice, however, the evidence for a broader application of the principle is sparse. There are some parallels with the principle of national treatment in international trade law, and non-discrimination is also a principle of the law of the sea[261] and international human-rights law.[262] The obvious limitation of non-discrimination as a principle of environmental law is that it provides no basis for restraining transboundary effects of harmful activities in states with weak environmental controls.

4(3) THE PRECAUTIONARY PRINCIPLE AND FORESEEABILITY OF HARM

As we have seen, the rule that states must not cause or permit serious or significant harm to other states or to common spaces is not simply one of responsibility for injury

---

[257] *ILC Report* (2001) GAOR A/56/10, 427–9.

[258] Smets, *Rev Eur Droit de l'Env* (2000) 1. See also Knox, 96 *AJIL* (2002) 291.

[259] OECD Council Recommendations C (74) 224 (1974); C (77) 28 (1977); C (78) 77 (1978); C (79) 116 (1979), collected in *OECD and the Environment* (Paris, 1986).

[260] Smets, *Rev Eur Droit de l'Env* (2000) 1, 20–7.

[261] 1982 UNCLOS, Articles 24, 227.   [262] *Infra*, Ch 5.

ex post facto. It is primarily an obligation of diligent prevention and control of fore-seeable risks, and in this sense it can be said that international law already adopts a 'precautionary approach'. The question then arises: at what point does this obligation of diligent control and regulation arise?

This is a question which can only be answered by reference to the foreseeability or likelihood of harm and of its potential gravity. The *Trail Smelter Arbitration*[263] suggests that the obligation arises if there is actual and serious harm which is likely to recur; the *Corfu Channel Case*[264] suggests that it also arises when there is a known risk to other states. In general, however, foreseeability of harm, in the sense of an objectively deter-mined risk, will usually be sufficient to engage the state's duty of regulation and con-trol. This is the position adopted by the ILC, whose 2001 Articles on Transboundary Harm define risk to encompass both 'a low probability of causing disastrous harm', and 'a high probability of causing significant harm'.[265] Thus, both the magnitude and probability of harm are relevant factors; what is objectively foreseeable may vary over time, and will depend on the state of knowledge regarding the risk posed by the activ-ity in question at the time when it has to be appreciated.[266] Moreover, the existence of a risk is not exclusively a scientific question:

It is essential to bear in mind that the risk that is to be evaluated in a risk assessment under Article 5.1 is not only risk ascertainable in a science laboratory operating under strictly con-trolled conditions, but also risk in human societies as they actually exist, in other words, the actual potential for adverse effects on human health in the real world where people live and work and die.[267]

These precedents show that a state cannot be required to regulate activities of which it is not and could not reasonably have been aware; equally clearly the same must be true of activities which the state did not know, and could not reasonably have known, to be potentially harmful. Thus, if no state could have foreseen the ozone-depleting poten-tial of CFCs when first introduced, no duty of diligent regulation and control would arise at that time regardless of their eventual impact. So much is common sense, sub-ject to what is said below concerning a duty to enquire further by conducting environ-mental impact assessments. Risk is a complex concept, however, entailing judgements not only about the probability and scale of harm, but about the causes of harm, the effects of the activities, substances or processes in question, and their interaction over time. These are not easy questions to answer with certainty, even for scientists. Very

---

263 *Supra* n 216.

264 ICJ Reports (1949) 18–22. See also *Bosnian Genocide Case*, ICJ Reports (2007) para 432.

265 Article 2 and commentary in *ILC Report* (2001) GAOR A/56/10, 387 paras (2)–(3). For the ILC's earlier approach, which lists categories of 'activities involving risk' see Barboza, *6th Report*, draft Article 2, UN Doc A/CN 4/428 (1990). Compare the approach to risk assessment adopted by the WTO Appellate Body in *EC Measures Concerning Meat and Meat Products*, WT/DS26/AB/R (1998) para 184: 'Although the utility of a two-step analysis may be debated, it does not appear to us to be substantially wrong.'

266 *ILC Report* (2001) GAOR A/56/10, 385, paras (14)–(15), 387, paras (1)–(3).

267 *EC Measures Concerning Meat and Meat Products*, WT/DS26/AB/R (1998) paras 179–86, referring to Article 5 of the SPS Agreement.

often, they can be understood, if at all, only after prolonged enquiry and monitoring, as in the *Trail Smelter* case.

Some states have asserted that they are not bound to take action to control possible global or transboundary risks until there is 'clear and convincing' scientific proof of actual or threatened harm. As we shall see in Chapter 6, this argument has been used at various times to delay the negotiation of measures to tackle the risk of global climate change, ozone depletion and acid rain. It reflects the formulation of international law in the *Trail Smelter Case*, but makes no allowance for the reality of scientific uncertainty in matters of causation and prediction of long-term effects, or for the different context of a case concerned principally with liability for actual damage. If the high standard of proof applied in *Trail Smelter* were required in contemporary international law, irreversible or very serious harm might occur before the causes could be fully understood or preventive action initiated. At the same time some states may understandably be reluctant to undertake expensive and possibly futile measures to deal with problems whose origin and character remained uncertain. Others may object to measures intended to protect the environment if there is no adequate scientific basis—trade bans on GMOs for example.

(a) Principle 15 of the Rio Declaration

Determining what the standard of proof should be in the above situations, or who bears the burden of proof of risk, are questions of immense practical importance. It is in this context that the so-called precautionary principle or approach has acquired special significance.[268] Inspired by its use in Swedish and German environmental law and policy,[269] the precautionary principle was first employed internationally in the North Sea Conference in 1984 and later affirmed by EC governments in the 1990 Bergen Ministerial Declaration on Sustainable Development. Based on these precedents, a text proposed by the European Union[270] secured global endorsement in the 1992 Rio Declaration on Environment and Development in the following terms:

Principle 15: In order to protect the environment, the precautionary approach shall be widely applied by states according to their capabilities. Where there are threats of serious or irreversible damage, lack of full scientific certainty shall not be used as a reason for postponing cost-effective measures to prevent environmental degradation.

---

[268] See de Chazournes, in Ndiaye and Wolfrum (eds), *Law of the Sea, Environmental Law and Settlement of Disputes* (Leiden, 2007) 21; Wiener, in Bodansky, Brunnée, and Hey (eds), *Handbook of International Environmental Law*, Ch 25; Atapattu, *Emerging Principles of IEL*, Ch 3; Böckenförde, 63 *ZAÖRV* (2003) 313; de Sadeleer, *Environmental Principles* (Oxford, 2002) Ch 3; Bechmann and Mansuy, *Le Principe de Précaution* (Paris, 2002); Trouwborst, *Evolution and Status of the Precautionary Principle in International Law* (The Hague, 2002); Martin-Bidou, 103 *RGDIP* (1999) 631; Freestone and Hey, *The Precautionary Principle and International Law* (The Hague, 1996); O'Riordan and Cameron (eds), *Interpreting the Precautionary Principle* (London, 1994).

[269] Sand, 6 *Hum & Ecol Risk Assessment* (2000) 445, 448; Boehmer-Christiansen, in O'Riordan and Cameron, op cit, 31; Von Moltke, in Royal Commission on Environmental Pollution, *12th Report* (1988) Annex 3, 57.

[270] For the EC's initial draft see UN Doc A/Conf 151/PC/WG 111/L 8/Rev 1 (1991).

At US insistence this formulation favours the term 'precautionary approach' rather than 'precautionary principle'. During negotiation of the 1995 Agreement on Straddling and Highly Migratory Fish Stocks the term 'precautionary approach' was again preferred, in the belief that the 'approach' offers greater flexibility and will be less potentially restrictive than the 'principle'.[271] Few commentators regard the difference in terminology as significant,[272] although one view is that the precautionary *principle* applies in situations of high uncertainty with a risk of irreversible harm entailing high costs, whereas the precautionary *approach* is more appropriate, it is argued, where the level of uncertainty and potential costs are merely significant, and the harm is less likely to be irreversible.[273] However, actual use of the terms in treaties contradicts any such distinction and reveals instead that European treaties and EC law generally refer to the precautionary principle,[274] whereas global agreements more often refer to the precautionary approach or precautionary measures.[275]

Nevertheless, the attempt to distinguish the 'approach' from the 'principle' points to the reality that the concept of precaution appears to mean different things in different contexts. This is not a subject on which consensus is identifiable.[276] Much of the confusion surrounding it stems from a failure to distinguish the identification of risk from the entirely separate question of how to respond to that risk. Thus to suggest that states shall 'apply a precautionary approach (or principle)' may mean that when faced with scientific uncertainty they must be more cautious about identifying risks, or it may mean that they must act more cautiously by taking measures to deal with those risks. Used in the former sense, the precautionary principle is a sensible development in international environmental law. Used in the latter sense, however, it is not clear whether 'precautionary action' or 'precautionary measures' represent a radically new approach to prioritizing environmental protection, or differ only rhetorically from the customary obligation of due diligence codified in Principle 2 of the Rio Declaration and considered earlier.

Whether viewed as a principle or as an approach, the essence of precaution is aptly explained by Freestone:

The precautionary approach then is innovative in that it changes the role of scientific data. It requires that once environmental damage is threatened action should be taken to control

---

[271] See FAO, *The Precautionary Approach to Fisheries with Reference to Straddling Fish Stocks and Highly Migratory Stocks* (1994) UN Doc A/Conf 164/INF/8.

[272] See e.g. Freestone, 6 *JEL* (1994) 212; Hey, 4 *Georgetown IELR* (1992) 303.

[273] See Garcia, in FAO, *Precautionary Approach to Fisheries*, Technical Paper 350/2 (Rome, 1996) 53–5 for the most detailed elaboration of the distinction.

[274] See e.g. 1992 Paris Convention for the Protection of the Marine Environment of the Northeast Atlantic, Article 2; 1992 UNECE Convention for the Protection of Transboundary Watercourses and Lakes, Article 2(5); 1992 Maastricht Treaty on European Union, Article 174; 1994 Danube Convention, Article 2(4); 1999 Rhine Convention, Article 4.

[275] See e.g. 1992 Convention on Climate Change, Article 3; 1992 Convention on Biological Diversity, Preamble and 2000 Protocol on Biosafety; 1994 Sulphur Protocol, 1998 Heavy Metals Protocol, and 1998 Persistent Organic Pollutants Protocol to the 1979 Convention on Long-Range Transboundary Air Pollution; 1996 Protocol to the London Dumping Convention, Article 3; 2001 POPS Convention, Article 1.

[276] See Bodansky, in Caron and Scheiber (eds), *Bringing New Law to Ocean Waters* (Leiden, 2004) 381.

or abate possible environmental interference even though there may still be scientific uncertainty as to the effects of the activities.[277]

This does not mean that science ceases to be relevant in judging the existence of risk, or that states are required or permitted to act on the basis of mere hypothesis or purely theoretical assessments of risk. On the contrary:

Recourse to the precautionary principle presupposes that potentially dangerous effects deriving from a phenomenon, product or process have been identified, and that scientific evaluation does not allow the risk to be determined with sufficient certainty.[278]

Thus there still has to be *some* scientific basis for predicting the possibility of harmful effects, some 'reason to believe' or 'reasonable grounds for concern'.[279] As the European Court put it in the *Pfizer Case*, 'a preventive measure cannot properly be based on a purely hypothetical approach to risk, founded on mere conjecture which has not been scientifically verified'.[280] At the same time, the evidence of risk need not necessarily be based on the majority of expert opinion: 'the very existence of divergent views presented by qualified scientists who have investigated the particular issue at hand may indicate a state of scientific uncertainty'.[281]

To summarize the position: if the evidence is sufficiently conclusive to leave little or no room for uncertainty in the calculation of risk, then there is no justification for the precautionary principle to be applied at all.[282] Rio Principle 15 requires only that *uncertainties* regarding, for example, the capacity of the environment to assimilate pollution, or of living resources to sustain exploitation, or the impact of proposed activities, or any other relevant factor, should be acknowledged and taken into account when determining what the risks of harm may be and what controls are needed. If assumptions about harmful effects are to be made they should, in other words, be more cautious, allowing for the possibility of error or ignorance, and in that sense reflecting a better understanding of science, not less science.[283] Another way of

---

[277] Freestone, 6 *JEL* (1994) 211.

[278] EC, *Communication on the Precautionary Principle*, COM (2000)1, 4.

[279] See *EC Measures Concerning Meat and Meat Products* (1998) WTO Appellate Body, paras 120–5; 1996 Protocol to the London Dumping Convention, Article 3(1) ('reason to believe'); 1992 Paris Convention for the Protection of the NE Atlantic, Article 2 ('reasonable grounds for concern'); 1992 Helsinki Convention on the Protection of the Baltic Sea Area, Article 3(2) ('reason to assume') and see Gray and Bewers, 32 *Mar Poll Bull* (1996) 768–71 who criticize some uses of the precautionary principle for relying on unsustainable suspicion rather than scientific evidence.

[280] *Pfizer Animal Health v Council of the EU* (2002) II ECR 3305, para 143.

[281] *EC Measures Concerning Meat and Meat Products* (1998) WTO Appellate Body, para 194. But dissent is not necessarily evidence of risk: it is usually possible to find a scientist to oppose any conclusion of a body of experts.

[282] *MOX Plant Case (Provisional Measures)* ITLOS No 10 (2001) paras 71–81. See also Uruguay's argument in the *Pulp Mills Case*.

[283] Gray and Bewers, 32 *Mar Poll Bull* (1996), 768–71. On the role of science and the precautionary principle see Calman and Smith, 79 *Pub Admin* (2001) 185; O'Riordan and Cameron, *Integrating the Precautionary Principle*, 69; Freestone and Hey, *The Precautionary Principle and International Law*, 97–146; FAO, *Precautionary Approach to Fisheries*, Technical Papers 350/1&2 (Rome, 1996).

explaining the point is to say that the environment should be given the benefit of the doubt.[284] The main effect of Principle 15 in international law therefore is to lower the standard of proof of risk. Where there is *some* evidence of a risk of serious or irreversible harm, even if uncertainty exists, appropriate action may be called for and 'Lack of full scientific certainty shall not prevent the proposal from proceeding'.[285]

Principle 15 stresses that the precautionary approach must be 'widely applied by states according to their capabilities'. This includes application to problems of global environmental risk, such as climate change and biological diversity, as well as to transboundary and national environmental risks, in furtherance of the objective of sustainable development. The 1985 Ozone Convention and its 1987 Montreal Protocol are perhaps the best examples of the application of the precautionary principle or approach in the form found in Principle 15 of the Rio Declaration because they required action on the part of states before the causal link between ozone depletion and CFCs had been conclusively demonstrated.[286] Since 1990 the precautionary principle or approach has also been adopted by a growing number of treaty institutions, or incorporated in the text of treaties, dealing with marine pollution,[287] international watercourses,[288] persistent organic pollutants,[289] air pollution and climate change,[290] transboundary trade in hazardous waste[291] and endangered species,[292] biosafety,[293] and the conservation of biological diversity and marine living resources.[294] In each of these cases uncertainty in the prediction of causes and long-term effects has induced the parties to adopt precautionary policies, including the phasing out of industrial waste-dumping at sea, the adoption of clean or low-waste technology, the elimination

---

[284] *Landelijke Vereniging tot Behoud van de Waddenzee, Nederlandse Vereniging tot Bescherming van Vogels v Staatssecretaris van Landbouw, Natuurbeheer en Visserij*, I ECR (2004) 7405, para 10 ('*Waddenzee Case*').

[285] See 2001 POPS Convention, Article 8(7)(a) dealing with listing of harmful chemicals. See also 2000 Biosafety Protocol, Article 11(8).

[286] *Infra*, Ch 6.

[287] 1992 Helsinki Convention on the Protection of Baltic Sea Area, Article 3(2); 1992 Paris Convention for the Protection of the NE Atlantic, Article 2; 1996 Protocol to the London Dumping Convention, Article 3; 1996 Syracuse Protocol for the Protection of the Mediterranean Against Pollution form Land-based Activities, preamble. See MacDonald, 26 *ODIL* (1995) 255 and *infra*, Ch 8.

[288] 1992 UNECE Convention on Transboundary Watercourses and Lakes, Article 2(5); 1994 Danube Convention, Article 2(4); 1999 Rhine Convention, Article 4. The principle is *not* included in the 1997 UN Convention on International Watercourses.

[289] 2001 POPS Convention, Article 1; 2001 Convention on the Control of Harmful Anti-fouling Systems on Ships.

[290] 1994 Sulphur Protocol, Preamble; 1998 Heavy Metals Protocol, Preamble; 1998 Persistent Organic Pollutants Protocol, Preamble; 1992 Convention on Climate Change, Article 3. See also 1991 European Energy Charter, Article 19.

[291] 1991 Bamako Convention, Article 4(3)(f); *infra*, Ch 8. The 1989 Basel Convention does not refer to the precautionary principle, but the ban on waste trade between developed and developing states adopted in 1994 may be seen as precautionary: see Ch 8.

[292] See *infra*, Ch 12.   [293] 2000 Biosafety Protocol, Articles 1, 10(6), 11(8).

[294] 1992 Convention on Biological Diversity, Preamble; 1995 FAO International Code of Conduct for Responsible Fisheries, General Principles and Article 6(5); 1995 UN Agreement Relating to the Conservation and Management of Straddling Fish Stocks and Highly Migratory Fish Stocks, Articles 5, 6, and *infra*, Ch 13.

of persistent organic pollutants, and a revised formulation of sustainable yields in international fisheries. Without a precautionary approach, regulatory action might have been delayed pending more compelling evidence of a risk of harm.

(b) Burden of proof of risk

It is sometimes asserted that the precautionary principle requires the promoter of a potentially harmful activity to prove that there is no risk of harm.[295] It is true that, for example, pharmaceutical companies or aeroplane manufacturers must normally show that their products meet acceptable safety standards before they can be licensed for public use. But this has been true for many years; it is not a consequence of any application of Rio Principle 15 and long predates the invention of the precautionary principle. No one would fly or use medicines unless they had been tested and shown to be within acceptable safety standards. In international law, who bears the burden of proving that a risk exists cannot be answered dogmatically, but will depend on the context in which the question arises. International courts have generally required the party alleging a risk of serious environmental harm to adduce enough evidence to establish at least a prima facie case.[296] They have not taken the view that the precautionary principle necessarily shifts the burden of proof to the party proposing to undertake potentially harmful activities. Provisional measures were thus refused in the *MOX Plant Case* and the *Pulp Mills Case* because the applicants failed to establish a serious risk, despite their reliance on the precautionary principle, but granted in *Land Reclamation* and *Southern Bluefin Tuna* because they could do so.[297] But these cases also show that where an environmental impact assessment has not been carried out the promoter of a potentially harmful activity will find it more difficult to rebut evidence of risk, however slender. Similarly, the Biosafety Protocol is significant mainly because it requires the exporting state to carry out a risk assessment: it does not leave the burden of doing so to the importing state. None of these precedents suggests that international law requires a state to prove that activities within its jurisdiction or control are environmentally 'safe'—that is not the purpose of an EIA or risk assessment and if it were the operation of oil tankers and nuclear power plants would be illegal—but there is ample evidence that international law does require environmental risks to be assessed and controlled, as we will see in the next section.

Nevertheless, there are some circumstances where states have agreed that an activity will be impermissible unless it can be shown that it will *not* cause harm to the

---

[295] Argentina made this argument in the *Pulp Mills Case*. Compare the EC *Communication on the Precautionary Principle* (2000) 5, which notes that there is no general rule to this effect, but that requirements of prior approval for products deemed dangerous 'a priori reverse the burden of proving injury, by treating them as dangerous unless and until businesses do the scientific work necessary to demonstrate that they are safe'.

[296] The European Court has taken the same view: see *Pfizer Animal Health v Council of the EU*, II ECR (2002) 3305, paras 136–48, 164–73. So has the WTO: see *EC Measures Concerning Meat and Meat Products* WT/DS26/AB/R (1998) paras 97–109.

[297] *MOX Plant Arbitration (Jurisdiction and Provisional Measures)* paras 53–5; *Pulp Mills Case (Provisional Measures)* (2006) paras 73–7; *Southern Bluefin Tuna Cases (Provisional Measures)* para 79; *Land Reclamation Case (Provisional Measures)* para 96.

environment. Examples include the ban on industrial waste dumping at sea,[298] and the moratorium on whaling, which can be recommenced only with the approval of the parties to the Whaling Convention.[299] The main effect of the precautionary principle in these situations is to require states to submit proposed activities affecting the global commons to international scrutiny and demonstrate that they will not cause harm. This reversal of the burden of proof is exceptional, however. It was quite deliberately not adopted when a precautionary approach to fisheries conservation was elaborated in some detail by Article 6 of the 1995 UN Fish Stocks Agreement,[300] nor does the 2001 Convention on Persistent Organic Pollutants reverse the burden of proof,[301] notwithstanding that both treaties are expressly based on the precautionary approach set out in Principle 15 of the Río Declaration.

(c) Legal status and implications of the precautionary principle

How far the precautionary principle as found in Principle 15 of the Rio Declaration must now be applied by all states as a matter of international law is an open question. On the one hand, it is formulated in obligatory terms in the Rio Declaration; it is very widely endorsed by states, most notably in Agenda 21; it has been applied or adopted by a growing number of international organizations and treaty bodies both as a matter of policy and in legally binding treaty articles and subsidiary rules. At the domestic level it informs environmental policy and law in Australia, France, Germany, the UK, the European Union and certain other states, although the position in US law is less certain.[302] It has also been described as a principle of international law or applied as such by the Supreme Courts of India and Pakistan.[303] How the precautionary principle is used in each of these countries will differ according to the context and legal culture, however.[304] It should not be assumed that national law and international law on the subject are necessarily the same.

On the other hand, although the precautionary principle was relied on by Hungary in *Gabčíkovo-Nagymaros*, and was referred to with approval by Judge Weeramantry in his dissent, the ICJ made no reference to it, despite a willingness to apply new norms of international environmental law.[305] It is not clear whether the court felt that the

---

[298] 1996 Protocol to the London Dumping Convention; 1992 OSPAR Convention, Article 4. See *infra*, Ch 8.

[299] See *infra*, Ch 13.   [300] See *infra*, section 5.   [301] See *infra*, Ch 8.

[302] On the application of the principle in national law see de Sadeleer, *Environmental Principles*, 124–49; Freestone and Hey, *The Precautionary Principle and International Law*, 38–40, 187–230; O'Riordan and Cameron, *Interpreting the Precautionary Principle*, 203–61; Sand, 6 *Hum & Ecol Risk Assessment* (2000) 445; Barton, 22 *Harv ELR* (1998) 509. For the EC's policy on the application of the precautionary principle, see EC, *Communication on the Precautionary Principle*, COM (2000)1, and Fisher, in Vos, Everson, and Scott (eds), *Uncertain Risks Regulated: National, EU and International Regulatory Models Compared* (London, 2007).

[303] India: *A P Pollution Control Board v Nayudu* (2001) 2 SCC 62; *A P Pollution Control Board (I) v Naidu* (1999) 2 SCC 710; *Jagannath v Union of India* (1997) 2 SCC 87; *M C Mehta v Union of India* (1997) 2 SCC 353; *Vellore Citizens Welfare Forum v Union of India* (1996) 7 SCC 375; Pakistan: *Sheila Zia v WAPDA* (1994) SC 693.

[304] Fisher, *supra* n 302.

[305] Nor did it do so in the *Pulp Mills Case*, ICJ Reports (2006) but see the dissent of ad hoc Judge Vinuesa.

environmental risks were sufficiently certain to require no reliance on the precautionary principle or whether it did not regard the principle as having any legal status. Both
views are plausible. And although in the *Beef Hormones Case*[306] the WTO Appellate
Body concluded that the applicable agreement incorporated precautionary elements,
it found the legal status of the precautionary principle in general international law
uncertain. The European Community had argued that it was a principle of customary law, or alternatively a general principle of law; Canada accepted that it was an
emerging principle of international law, but the United States denied that it had any
legal status at all. In the *Southern Bluefin Tuna (Provisional Measures) Cases*,[307] the
International Tribunal for the Law of the Sea relied on scientific uncertainty surrounding the conservation of tuna stocks to justify the grant of provisional measures
to protect the stock from further depletion pending resolution of the dispute. This
can be regarded as an application of the precautionary approach, but it can also be
explained on the basis that the 1982 UN Convention on the Law of the Sea in effect
requires a precautionary approach to fisheries conservation, or alternatively that a precautionary approach is inherent in the award of provisional measures.[308] The Tribunal
took no view on the precautionary principle or approach in general international law,
although its references to scientific uncertainty do focus directly on the core element
of the precautionary approach as set out in Principle 15 of the Rio Declaration.

There are good reasons for this judicial hesitation. The precautionary approach is
not universally applied: states have been selective, adopting it in the Climate Change
and Biological Diversity Conventions, but not in the 1994 Nuclear Safety Convention,
the 1995 Washington Declaration on the Protection of the Marine Environment from
Land-based Activities, or the 1998 Rotterdam PIC Convention. There are also different thresholds of harm: Rio Principle 15 and the Climate Change Convention require
a risk of 'serious or irreversible harm' before the principle becomes applicable, but
treaties on the marine environment do not. In some cases, as we have seen, there is a
reversal of the burden of proof, while in others it merely lowers the standard of proof,
but to what level remains uncertain. A precautionary approach can also be characterized in different ways.[309] Does it require states to act? Does it empower them to act?
Does it merely encourage them to be more cautious?

Some writers and governments have nevertheless argued that the precautionary
principle or approach is a rule of customary international law.[310] This is quite a widely
held view. Nevertheless, the uncertainties in the meaning, application, and implications of the precautionary principle or approach outlined above suggest that the
proposition that it is, or that it is not, customary international law is too simplistic.

---

[306] *Measures Concerning Meat and Meat Products* (1998) WTO Appellate Body, paras 120–5. See Cheyne,
19 *JEL* (2007) 155.

[307] *Southern Bluefin Tuna Cases (Provisional Measures)* ITLOS Nos 3 & 4 (1999) paras 77–9.

[308] See Judges Shearer, Laing, paras 16–19, Treves, para 9.

[309] See Wiener in Bodansky, Brunnée, and Hey, *Handbook of International Environmental Law*, 604–7.

[310] E.g. the EU's argument in the WTO *Asbestos* case. See McIntyre and Mosedale, 9 *JEL* (1997) 221, and
Trouwborst, *Evolution and Status of the Precautionary Principle in International Law*, 284. Trouwborst sees
the principle as the basis for comprehensive environmental protection both nationally and internationally.

It is far from evident that the precautionary approach as articulated in Principle 15 of the Rio Declaration has or could have the normative character of a rule of law. It is phrased in very general terms and says only that scientific uncertainty is not to be used as a reason for postponing cost-effective measures; it does not say anything about what those measures should be. Of course, a pattern of treaty provisions elaborating 'precautionary measures' might enable a new and more specific customary rule to emerge.[311] A number of treaties dealing with the marine environment do have such provisions, including the OSPAR Convention[312] and the POPS Convention,[313] but in essence these agreements strengthen the existing obligation to take preventive measures or eliminate certain pollutants. They are best understood as an elaboration of the obligation of due diligence, not as some separate species of rule.

More fundamentally, the consequences of applying a precautionary approach also differ widely. This should not be surprising. As formulated in Principle 15 of the Rio Declaration, the precautionary approach helps us identify whether a legally significant risk exists by addressing the role of scientific uncertainty, but it says nothing about how to control that risk, or about what level of risk is socially acceptable.[314] Those are policy questions which in most societies are best answered by politicians and by society as a whole, rather than by courts or scientists.[315] This is implicit in the European Community's assertion that, in applying a precautionary approach to trade, each WTO member state has the right to establish whatever level of health and environmental protection it deems appropriate within its own borders.[316] The same point is also reflected in treaty formulations such as the 1992 Helsinki Convention on the Protection of the Baltic, which requires the parties to be 'guided by' the precautionary principle, but leaves them free to decide what action to take. In some cases states have been more specific. Agenda 21, for example, sets out a list of precautionary measures intended to strengthen protection of the marine environment:

A precautionary and anticipatory rather than a reactive approach is necessary to prevent the degradation of the marine environment. This requires, inter alia, the adoption of precautionary measures, environmental impact assessments, clean production techniques,

---

[311] But compare Daillier and Pellet, *Droit International Public* (7th edn, Paris, 2002) 1308, who draw attention to 'leur fréquente imprécision'.

[312] 1992 Convention for the Protection of the Marine Environment of the North-East Atlantic, Article 2(2)(a). See also the 1995 Revised Convention for the Protection of the Mediterranean Sea Against Pollution, Article 4(3)(a); 1996 Protocol for the Protection of the Mediterranean Sea against Pollution from Land-based Sources and Activities, Preamble.

[313] 2001 Stockholm Convention on Persistent Organic Pollutants, Article 1.

[314] See especially EC Court of 1st Instance in *Pfizer Animal Health v Council of the EU*, II ECR (2002) 3305, paras 135–73; Douma, 15 *JEL* (2003) 394.

[315] A point well expressed by the French Prime Minister, M Jospin: 'Appliquer le principe de précaution, enfin, implique que la décision soit prise par le politique. Si le politique doit se fonder pour préparer sa décison sur l'analyse du scientifique, il est le seul à devoir décider. Seuls ceux qui sont responsables devant le peuple sont en situation de faire les choix dont dépend la sécurité sanitaire des citoyens...', *Le Figaro*, 16 March 2001.

[316] EC, *Communication on the Precautionary Principle*, (COM (2000)1, 3. The proposition was accepted by the CFI in *Pfizer Animal Health v Council of the EU*, II ECR (2002) 3305, para 151. See also 2000 Cartagena Protocol on Biosafety, Articles 10 and 11.

recycling, waste audits and minimization, construction and/or improvement of sewage treatment facilities, quality management criteria for the proper handling of hazardous substances, and a comprehensive approach to damaging impacts from air, land and water.[317]

Commitments of this kind do show that governments may be expected to negotiate 'precautionary measures' in response to perceived risks, but there is no general principle for determining what measures to adopt. Although taking a precautionary approach has led to a ban or moratorium on ocean dumping, high-seas whaling, and driftnet fishing, it has resulted only in more cautious criteria for exploitation of straddling and highly migratory fish stocks, but fishing has continued.[318] The precautionary measures required by the POPS Convention involve stricter controls and reductions in the use of chemicals such as dioxin with the aim of ultimate elimination, but the Convention does not ban them outright or require states to show that they are harmless.[319] The Biosafety Protocol subjects international trade in living modified organisms to a precautionary regime of risk assessment and prior consent from the importing state, but this is no different from the Basel Convention on Transboundary Movement of Hazardous Wastes, which makes no reference to a precautionary approach.[320] Despite a commitment to take precautionary measures in Article 3 of the Climate Change Convention there remains great difficulty in persuading states to agree on how to implement this article.[321] Invoking the precautionary principle or approach cannot of itself determine what those measures should be, or how strong they should be. There are similar differences in national law. Whereas Indian and Pakistani courts are prepared to apply the precautionary principle as law imposing duties on governments, and to spell out precise consequences, most national legal systems view it only as a principle which governments and legislatures may lawfully take into account or be guided by. It has thus been relied on by national courts when considering the legality of laws or decisions or when interpreting and applying them, but not normally as a legal obligation which can be used to direct or require stronger action by governments.[322]

If the precautionary principle is viewed not as a rule of customary law but simply as a general principle of law then its use by national and international courts and by

---

[317] UNCED, *Agenda 21*, Ch 17, para 21.   [318] See *infra*, Ch 13, section 5.

[319] 2001 Convention on Persistent Organic Pollutants, Article 5 and Annex C.

[320] *Infra*, Ch 8.   [321] *Infra*, Ch 6.

[322] Australia: *Leatch v National Parks and Wildlife Service*, 81 Local Govt & Env Reps of Australia (1993) 270; *Nicholls v DG of National Parks and Wildlife*, 84 *LGERA* (1994) 397; England: *Gateshead Metropolitan Council v Secretary of State for the Environment* (1995) *JPL* 432; *R v Secretary of State for Trade and Industry ex parte Duddridge*, 2 *CMLR* (1996) 361; European Community: *United Kingdom v EC Commission*, I ECR (1998) 2265; *Pfizer Animal Health v Council of the EU*, II ECR(2002) 3305, paras 139–44; *Waddenzee Case*, I ECR (2004) 7405; France: *World Wildlife Fund Geneva v France* ['*Superphenix Case*'] (1997) *Cahiers Juridique de l'Electricité et Gaz* 217; Germany: *Kalkar Case* 49 *Entscheidungen des Bundesverfassungsgerichts* (1979) 89; *Augsburg v Federal Republic of Germany* ['*Waldsterben Case*'] 103 *Deutsches Verwaltungsblatt* (1988) 232. Failure to take account of the principle may be a ground for judicial review, however: see *Association Greenpeace France v France, Novartis and Monsanto* ['*Transgenic maize Case*'] 2/IR Recueil Dalloz (1998) 240.

international organizations is easier to explain.[323] In this context the precautionary principle does have a legally important core on which there is international consensus—that in performing their obligations of environmental protection and sustainable use of natural resources states cannot rely on scientific uncertainty to justify inaction when there is enough evidence to establish the possibility of a risk of serious harm, even if there is as yet no proof of harm. In this sense the precautionary principle may be relied upon by decision-makers and courts in much the same way that they may be influenced by the principle of sustainable development.[324]

It follows that, as in the *Southern Bluefin Tuna Cases* or the *Gabčíkovo-Nagymaros Case*, the interpretation and application of treaties, or of rules of customary law, may be affected by the precautionary principle. Moreover, in the law of state responsibility, an international tribunal might well take account of scientific uncertainty in determining whether harmful consequences are foreseeable or not. As Brownlie observes, 'The point which stands out is that some applications of the principle, which is based on the concept of foreseeable risk to other states, are encompassed within existing concepts of state responsibility'.[325] For the same reason, the ILC special rapporteur was right to suggest that the precautionary principle is already included in the principles of prevention and prior authorization, and in environmental impact assessment, 'and could not be divorced therefrom'.[326] From this perspective, the real importance of the precautionary principle is that it redefines existing rules of international law on control of environmental risks and conservation of natural resources and brings them into play at an earlier stage than before. No longer is it necessary to prove that serious or irreversible harm is certain or likely before requiring that appropriate preventive measures be taken. Evidence that such harm is possible will be enough to trigger an obligation or to empower states to act.[327]

But in determining whether and how to apply 'precautionary measures', states have evidently taken account of their own capabilities, their economic and social priorities, the cost-effectiveness of proposed measures, and the nature and degree of the environmental risk when deciding what preventive measures to adopt. They have in other words made value judgments about how to respond to environmental risk, and have been more willing to be more precautionary about ozone depletion, dumping at sea or whaling, than about fishing or industrial activities which cause air, river, or marine pollution. This does not imply that Principle 15 is not a principle of international law, only that its implications should not be exaggerated by attempting to turn it into an obligation of precautionary conduct with specific normative implications quite

---

[323] Nollkaemper, in Freestone and Hey (eds), *The Precautionary Principle and International Law: The Challenge of Implementation* (The Hague 1996) 80.

[324] See *Gabčíkovo-Nagymaros Case*, ICJ Reports (1997) 7; Lowe, in Boyle and Freestone, *International Law and Sustainable Development*, Ch 2, and *supra* section 2(3). For an example, see the ECJ Preliminary Ruling in the *Waddenzee Case*, I ECR (2004) 7405.

[325] *Principles of Public International Law* (6th edn, Oxford, 2003) 276. On state responsibility see *infra*, Ch 4, section 2.

[326] *ILC Report* (2000) GAOR A/55/10, para 716.

[327] See *Pfizer Animal Health v Council of the EU* (2002) II ECR 3305, paras 135–73.

separate from those already required by Principle 2 of the Rio Declaration. Thus, to reiterate, while the precautionary principle helps determine whether a risk is sufficiently foreseeable and serious to require a response, regardless of conclusive proof, it cannot determine what that response should be.[328]

(d) Conclusions

There can be little doubt that the need for a more precautionary approach to international risk management now underpins an increasing number of multilateral environmental agreements. In that sense the precautionary principle has become one of the central concepts for organizing, influencing, and explaining contemporary international environmental law and policy.[329] States, acting in their role as international regulators, have to some extent taken it seriously. They have become more cautious about environmental risks, and the use or misuse of scientific evidence. But unlike national regulators who are subject to judicial review, and who must demonstrate both an evidential basis and proportionality in the measures they adopt,[330] the community of states can neither be challenged when they decide to adopt a precautionary approach in an MEA, nor when they fail to do so. In this context the role of the precautionary principle is essentially rhetorical rather than normative. Uniformity of application is not a necessary outcome, and may not be a desirable one given the many different contexts.

The precautionary principle has also had an impact on the way treaties and other rules of law are interpreted and applied. Here, it is a principle with a genuine place in international legal discourse, whether in interstate relations or in international litigation. Lawyers can, and do, make use of it. Beyond that, the evidence does not support some of the more radical characterizations. In particular, the common but essentially incoherent belief that the principle always shifts the burden of proof and requires states to prove that development projects pose no risk of harm misunderstands both the nature of the precautionary principle and its relationship to other rules of international law on risk management. Environmental impact assessment (interpreted in accordance with the precautionary principle), transparency, and public participation all play a much more important role in identifying risk and the measures necessary to manage it in a socially acceptable manner. These have proved more effective weapons in interstate environmental disputes or in the hands of NGOs than the precautionary principle.

4(4) ENVIRONMENTAL IMPACT ASSESSMENT AND MONITORING

Environmental impact assessment (EIA) is 'a procedure for evaluating the likely impact of a proposed activity on the environment'.[331] The object of an EIA is to provide

---

[328] Ibid.   [329] See in particular de Sadeleer, *Environmental Principles*, esp Ch 4.

[330] Compare *Pfizer Animal Health v Council of the EU* (2002) II ECR 3305.

[331] 1991 Convention on Environmental Impact Assessment in a Transboundary Context, Article 1(vi). See generally Wathern (ed), *EIA: Theory and Practice* (London, 1988); Glasson, Therivel, and Chadwick,

national decision-makers with information about possible environmental effects when deciding whether to authorize the activity to proceed. An EIA is fundamental to any regulatory system which seeks to identify environmental risk, integrate environmental concerns into development projects and promote sustainable development. It is a tool which aids informed decision-making, but it does not determine whether a project should proceed or how it should be regulated. Those decisions are for the relevant public authority, balancing the information provided by the EIA against whatever other considerations are considered decisive, including economic development. Seen from this angle, it is clear that a 'satisfactory' EIA need not show that there will be no environmental harm. It will be sufficient if it provides the necessary information about the project's likely impact and follows the proper process. Monitoring is another aid to decision-making whereby states 'observe, measure, evaluate and analyze, by recognized scientific methods, the risks or effects' of pollution or environmental harm.[332] Unlike prior EIA, monitoring is generally undertaken after the project has begun; its purpose is to check initial EIA predictions and provide information to enable national regulatory agencies to determine whether further measures are needed in order to abate or avoid pollution or environmental harm. It is necessarily on ongoing process, which will have to continue over the life of a project and in some cases beyond.

Since its adoption in the US National Environmental Policy Act of 1969, EIA has become an important tool of environmental management in national law. The value of an effective EIA is that it provides an opportunity for public scrutiny and participation in decision-making,[333] it should introduce elements of independence and impartiality to the process,[334] and, ideally, it will facilitate better-informed judgments when balancing environmental and developmental needs. At an international level it alerts governments and international organizations to the likelihood of transboundary harm. Without the benefit of an EIA the duty to notify and consult other states in cases of transboundary risk will in many cases be meaningless. EIA also contributes to the implementation of national policies on sustainable development and precautionary action. Although US experience shows that the process can be cumbersome, expensive and cause delay, when done properly EIA should, inter alia, help governments to foresee and avoid international environmental disputes or harmful consequences for which they might otherwise be held legally responsible.

Introduction to EIA (2nd ed, London, 2005); Wood, *EIA: A Comparative Review* (2nd ed, Harlow, 2003) Ch 1; Holder, *Environmental Assessment* (Oxford, 2004); Holder and McGillivray (eds), *Taking Stock of Environmental Assessment* (London, 2007).

[332] 1982 UNCLOS, Article 204. See Wathern, *EIA: Theory and Practice*, Ch 7; Wood, *EIA: A Comparative Review*, Ch 14.

[333] 1991 Convention on EIA, Articles 2(6), 3(8); 1987 UNEP Goals and Principles of EIA, Principle 7; Glasson, Therivel and Chadwick, *Introduction to EIA*, Ch 6. World Bank practice also requires public consultation as part of an EIA: see World Bank, OP 4.01: Environmental Assessment (1999). On public participation see *infra*, Ch 5.

[334] 1987 UNEP Goals and Principles of EIA, Principle 6: 'The information provided as part of the EIA should be examined impartially prior to the decision'.

A very large number of states now make some provision for EIA.[335] The most sophisticated legislation is found in the USA,[336] Canada,[337] and the European Union.[338] Through the efforts of UNECE the practice is increasingly common in Eastern Europe,[339] while UNEP and the World Bank have promoted its adoption in developing states, particularly in Asia and Latin America.[340] China adopted a law on EIA in 2002.[341] Although there are differences in the frequency and sophistication with which EIA is used across this range of jurisdictions, there has been a worldwide sharing of methodology and the basic features of most schemes are very similar.[342]

(a) Rio Principle 17

International law requires states to conduct environmental impact assessments in certain circumstances.[343] Rio Principle 17 affords the strongest evidence of international support for EIA. It is formulated in the broadest of terms:

Environmental impact assessment, as a national instrument, shall be undertaken for proposed activities that are likely to have a significant impact on the environment and are subject to a decision of a competent national authority.

This would appear to entail a process focused on impacts on the domestic and transboundary environment,[344] on sustainable development,[345] and probably also on global environmental impacts such as climate change and loss of biological diversity, albeit in highly qualified terms.[346] The practice of a number of international lending agencies

---

[335] See UN, *Current Policies, Strategies and Aspects of Environmental Impact Assessment in a Transboundary Context* (New York, 1997).

[336] See Karkkainen, in Holder and McGillivray (eds), *Taking Stock of Environmental Assessment*, Ch 3. NEPA applies only to 'major Federal actions significantly affecting the quality of the human environment'. Projects not regulated by Federal agencies are thus not covered, but may be subject to state law.

[337] Canadian Environmental Assessment Act, SC 1992, c 37; Wood, *EIA: A Comparative Review*, Ch 5.

[338] EC Directive 85/337, OJ 1985 L175, 40 as amended by EC Directive 97/11, OJ 1997 L73, 5. See Kramer in Holder and McGillivray (eds), *Taking Stock of Environmental Assessment*, Ch 5.

[339] A number of East European states are parties to the 1991 Convention on EIA in a Transboundary Context. See generally Winter (ed), *European Environmental Law: A Comparative Perspective* (Aldershot, 1996) Ch 5.

[340] See Wathern, *EIA: Theory and Practice*, Ch 13; Lin and Kurukulasuriya (eds), *UNEP's New Way Forward: Environmental Law and Sustainable Development* (UNEP, 1995) 259.

[341] 2002 Law of the People's Republic of China on the Environmental Impact Assessment, with implementing regulation of 2006 on public participation.

[342] Robinson, 19 *Boston Coll Env Aff LR* (1992) 594. For a review of differences between EIA practice in developed and developing countries see Wood, *EIA: A Comparative Review*, 301–8.

[343] See Craik, *The International Law of Environmental Impact Assessment* (Cambridge, 2008), especially Ch 4; Atapattu, *Emerging Principles of IEL*, Ch 4.

[344] See *infra*.

[345] See 1987 UNEP Goals and Principles of EIA and the numerous references to EIA in Agenda 21, *Report of the UN Conference on Environment and Development* (1992) UN Doc A/CONF 151/26/Rev 1, but especially Chapter 8.4(d) which calls for regular monitoring and evaluation of the development process, including the state of the environment and natural resources. See also Weeramantry in *Gabčíkovo-Nagymaros Case*, ICJ Reports (1997) 7, 111–13.

[346] 1992 Climate Change Convention, Article 4(1)(f); 1992 Convention on Biological Diversity, Article 14. On the very qualified nature of the latter article see Boyle, in Bowman and Redgwell, *International Law and the Conservation of Biological Diversity*, 41–2. EIA is also obligatory in a number of regional conventions

supports this broad interpretation of Principle 17. The World Bank's Environmental Assessment Directive was first issued in 1989,[347] since when Bank-funded projects have routinely been screened for their potential domestic, transboundary, and global environmental impacts. These assessments are meant to ensure that 'development options are environmentally sound and sustainable' and that 'any environmental consequences are recognized early in the project cycle and taken account of in project design'. There is also an obligatory and detailed scheme of EIA in the 1991 Antarctic Protocol, focused on 'the Antarctic environment or on dependent or associated ecosystems', which could include both the marine environment and global climatic impacts.[348]

It might be said that the practice of states or international banks when dealing with impacts that are solely of domestic concern is not evidence of an international legal obligation to conduct an EIA. Evidence of *opinio iuris* for domestic EIA is confined to Principle 17 of the Rio Declaration, UNEP's soft-law Goals and Principles of EIA,[349] and the rather lukewarm reference to EIA in Article 14 of the Convention on Biological Diversity. Moreover, the assessment of global impacts is referred to in such qualified terms by the Climate Change and Biological Diversity Conventions that it too may be difficult to translate into customary law, and there is little evidence of supporting state practice at present. Subject to what is said below about transboundary EIA, and excluding specific treaty commitments such as the Antarctic Protocol or the 1982 UNCLOS, it seems necessary to conclude that at present general international law neither requires states to assess possible global effects nor effects wholly within their own borders.

(b) Transboundary EIA and monitoring

An article on transboundary EIA formed part of the long-standing work of the International Law Commission. Article 7 of the 2001 Articles on Transboundary Harm provides:

Any decision in respect of the authorization of an activity within the scope of the present articles shall, in particular, be based on an assessment of the possible transboundary harm caused by that activity, including any environmental impact assessment.[350]

establishing specially protected areas for flora and fauna: see 1985 ASEAN Agreement on the Conservation of Nature and Natural Resources, Article 14; 1990 Kingston Protocol Concerning Specially Protected Areas and Wildlife, Article 13; 1989 Protocol for the Conservation and Management of Protected Marine and Coastal Areas of the SE Pacific, Article 8.

[347] For current practice see OP 4.01: Environmental Assessment (1999); World Bank, *The World Bank and the Environment* (Washington, DC, 1995) Ch 4. EIAs are also required for development projects funded by the Asian Development Bank, the European Bank for Reconstruction and Development, the European Investment Bank, and the Inter-American Development Bank. See (1993) 4 *YbIEL* 528–49 and Klein-Chesivoir, 30 *VJIL* (1989–1990) 517. On the use of EIA by in bilateral development aid, see Wathern, *EIA: Theory and Practice*, Chs 15–17.

[348] Article 8 and Annex I. See Francioni (ed), *International Law for Antarctica* (Milan, 1992) 149–73.

[349] Bonine, 17 *EPL* (1987) 5.

[350] For commentary see *ILC Report* (2001) GAOR A/56/10, 402–7. For earlier drafts see Barboza, *5th Report on International Liability*, UN Doc A/CN 4/423 (1989) 26–33; Draft Articles on International Liability, Article 11, UN Doc A/CN 4/428 (1990); id, Article 10, UN Doc A/CN 4/L 5333 (1996).

International support for transboundary EIA originated in a series of OECD recommendations which relied on the principle of non-discrimination.[351] UNEP also included provisions on the subject in its soft-law recommendations.[352] It acquired global support in an extensive network of regional and global treaties based on Article 206 of the 1982 UNCLOS which requires states to assess activities likely to affect the marine environment and to report their findings to the relevant international organization.[353] However, the 1991 UNECE Convention on EIA in a Transboundary Context remains the most comprehensive agreement on the subject. At the time of writing it had forty-one mainly European parties, including the European Community, but also Canada, Russia, and Kazakhstan.[354] It has provided a model for amendment of the EC directive on EIA,[355] and for some harmonization of European law and practice.

In much of North America and Europe national legislation, case law, and bilateral agreements or EU directives apply national EIA requirements to transboundary impacts. Although NEPA does not expressly deal with extra-territorial impacts, US courts have allowed standing for Canadian plaintiffs affected by oil development in Alaska to challenge the adequacy of an EIA under the act.[356] They have also held that the legislation applies to Federal actions abroad, including waste disposal in Antarctica, highway construction in Central America, and the spraying of herbicides on marijuana and poppy crops in Mexico.[357] In Canada a federal court granted mandamus requiring extraterritorial impacts of a dam to be assessed.[358] Both states are

---

[351] OECD Council Recommendations C (74) 224 (1974) para 6; C (77) 28 (1977) paras 8–10; C(78) 77 (1978); C (79) 116 (1979) collected in *OECD and the Environment* (Paris, 1986). Reliance on non-discrimination as a basis for transboundary EIA in North America is reviewed by Knox, 96 *AJIL* (2002) 291. However, this article's view of the relationship between EIA and Stockholm Principle 21 should be treated with caution.

[352] See 1987 Goals and Principles of EIA, Principle 12; 1978 Principles of Cooperation in the Utilization of Natural Resources Shared by Two or More States, *infra*, section 5.

[353] This article was the subject of litigation in the *MOX Plant Case* and the *Land Reclamation Case*, *infra*. See also 1983 Convention for the Protection and Development of the Marine Environment of the Wider Caribbean Region, Article 12; 1986 Convention for the Protection of the Natural Resources and Environment of the South Pacific Region, Article 16; 1985 Convention for the Protection, Management and Development of the Marine and Coastal Environment of the Eastern African Region, Article 13; 1990 Kuwait Protocol for the Protection of the Marine Environment against Pollution from Land-based Sources, Article 8; 1992 Convention on the Protection of the Marine Environment of the Baltic Sea Area, Article 7; 1992 Convention on the Protection of the Black Sea Against Pollution, Article 15(5). In effect Annex II of the 1996 Protocol to the London Dumping Convention requires prior EIA before a permit to dump may be granted: see *infra*, Ch 8.

[354] It has been amended to permit non-UNECE states to accede. See generally Woodliffe, in Bowman and Boyle, *Environmental Damage etc*, Ch 8; Knox, 96 *AJIL* (2002) 301–5.

[355] Council Directive 97/11/EC 1997 OJ L 73/5.

[356] *Wilderness Society v Morton* 463 F 2d 1261 (1972).

[357] *Environmental Defense Fund Inc v Massey* 986 F 2d 528 (1993); *Sierra Club v Adams* 578 F 2d 389 (1978); *National Organization for the Reform of Marijuana Laws v US Dept of State* 452 F Supp 1226 (1978). But other cases take different views: see *Natural Resources Defense Council Inc v Nuclear Regulatory Commissions* 647 F 2d 1345 (1981); *NEPA Coalition of Japan v Aspin* 837 F Supp 466 (1993); *Greenpeace v Stone* 748 F Supp 749 (1990); *People of Saipan v US Dept of Interior* 356 F Supp 645 (1973) and Knox, 96 *AJIL* (2002) 298–9 who reviews the literature.

[358] *Canadian Wildlife Federation v Minister of Environment and Saskatchewan Water Comp* (1989) 3 FC 309 (TD). The 1992 Environmental Assessment Act (s 47) now applies to extraterritorial effects.

party to an Air Quality Agreement of 1991 which requires them to assess any activity likely to cause transboundary air pollution,[359] while the 1993 North American Agreement on Environmental Cooperation commits Canada, the United States, and Mexico to assess transboundary environmental effects when 'appropriate'.[360] UK regulations now require assessment of extraterritorial impacts, but in practice these had previously been considered where relevant. When a public hearing was held into the licensing of a proposed nuclear waste dump at Sellafield, bordering the Irish Sea, Ireland made representations.[361] The evidence of possible transboundary effects was one factor in the British government's decision to refuse the plant a licence. There are also some countries whose EIA legislation explicitly covers extraterritorial effects.[362] The EU directive was amended in 1997 partly in order to bring it into line with the 1991 ECE Convention and strengthen its provisions on transboundary EIA.[363] Some European bilateral agreements require assessment of transboundary impacts,[364] as does World Bank practice.[365]

Moreover, even without this evidence of state practice, legal prudence may compel states and international banks to conduct an EIA before authorizing or funding projects likely to result in significant transboundary harm. If they do not do so, and harm subsequently occurs, they may find it very difficult to argue that they acted with due diligence in controlling or preventing harm that should and could have been foreseen.[366] It might also be argued that transboundary EIA is a necessary part of the obligation of transboundary cooperation considered in the next section. Without prior assessment there can be no meaningful notification and consultation in most cases of environmental risk. The duty, in other words, is not merely to notify what is known but to know what needs to be notified. Both arguments were developed by New Zealand in the 1995 *Nuclear Tests Case*.[367]

However, given the independent status of Rio Principle 17 and the evidence of state practice, the better view is simply that customary international law requires states to ensure that a transboundary EIA is carried out in appropriate circumstances. At least five ICJ or ITLOS cases have involved alleged failures to undertake a transboundary

---

[359] *Infra*, Ch 6.

[360] Article 2(1)(e). However no agreement has yet been reached on how to implement this commitment. On a draft North American EIA agreement see Knox, 96 *AJIL* (2002) 305–8.

[361] See Statements by and on behalf of the Minister of State of the Department of Transport, Energy and Communications, Ireland, to the Public Inquiry Concerning an Appeal by UK Nirex Ltd, 12 January 1996. See now UK, 1999 Town and Country Planning (EIA) Regulations, SI 1999/293.

[362] Austria, Federal Act Concerning Environmental Impact Assessment and Public Participation, s 10; Germany, 1990 Act Concerning EIA (amended 2006); Canada, 1992 Environmental Assessment Act; Finland, 1994 Act on EIA Procedure and Decree on EIA Procedure.

[363] EC Directive 97/11, OJ 1997 L 73.

[364] 1994 German–Polish Agreement on Cooperation in Environmental Protection; 1994 Polish–Ukrainian Treaty on Environmental Cooperation.

[365] E.g. in the *Pulp Mills* dispute between Argentina and Uruguay.

[366] Okowa, 72 *BYIL* (1996) 280; Handl, 1 *YbIEL* (1990) 21.

[367] *Request for an Examination of the Situation*, ICJ Reports (1995) 288. New Zealand also relied on Article 16 of the 1987 Convention for the Protection of Natural Resources and Environment of the South Pacific.

EIA.[368] In some of these cases there are explicit treaty articles, while in others customary law or 'evolutionary interpretation' are relied upon. Although none of the judgments says anything very useful on the subject,[369] they provide important evidence of state practice which points consistently in the direction of recognizing that where proposed activities are likely to harm the environment, an EIA directed at transboundary impacts is a necessary preliminary to consultation and cooperation with other potentially affected states. Typically, as in *Gabčíkovo-Nagymaros, MOX Plant, Land Reclamation* or *Pulp Mills*, states argue about whether an EIA took place and what it should cover, not about whether it is obligatory, even in the absence of applicable treaty provisions.[370] In these circumstances it should not be surprising that there has been no need to affirm judicially what states say they already practice, although some of the literature appears to think that EIA can be customary law only if a court spells this out in black and white.

Gabčíkovo-Nagymaros remains the most significant case. Here it was alleged that an EIA had not been carried out before construction of a hydroelectric project.[371] The judgment stresses that new environmental norms and standards have to be taken into account 'not only when States contemplate new activities but also when continuing activities begun in the past'.[372] The court's approach treats prior EIA and subsequent monitoring of the ongoing environmental risks and impacts (or 'post project analysis') as a continuum which will operate throughout the life of a project. This view of the relationship between EIA and monitoring reflects the practice of EIA in many national systems and in the provisions of modern treaties,[373] including the 1991 Convention on Transboundary EIA.[374] A failure to institute proper monitoring, like a failure to undertake an EIA, may well constitute a failure to act with due diligence. That obligation is a continuing one, to which the court's observations on the need to apply contemporary standards are equally applicable.

---

[368] *Request for an Examination of the Situation Case*, ICJ Reports (1995) 288; *Gabčíkovo-Nagymaros Case*, ICJ Reports (1997) 7; *MOX Plant Case*, ITLOS No 10 (2001); *Land Reclamation Case*, ITLOS No 12 (2003); *Pulp Mills Case*, ICJ Reports (2006).

[369] But see the dissenting judgment of Judge Weeramantry in the 1995 *Nuclear Tests Case*, 344.

[370] Craik, *The International Law of EIA*, 119.

[371] ICJ Reports (1997) 7. See also Hungary's declaration terminating the 1977 Treaty with Czechoslovakia at 32 *ILM* (1993) 1260.

[372] At para 140.

[373] See e.g. 1982 UNCLOS, Article 204; 1992 Convention on the Protection and Use of Transboundary Watercourses and Lakes, Articles 4, 11; 1991 Antarctic Protocol, Article 3(2)(d) and (e); 1992 Convention for the Protection of the NE Atlantic, Article 6; 1980 Protocol for the Protection of the Mediterranean Sea Against Pollution from Land-based Sources, Article 8; 1992 Convention on the Protection of the Baltic Sea Area, Article 3(5); 1992 Convention on the Protection of the Black Sea Against Pollution, Article 15; 1983 Protocol for the Protection of the SE Pacific Against Pollution from Land-based Sources, Article 8; 1990 Kuwait Protocol for the Protection of the Marine Environment Against Pollution from Land-based Sources, Article 7; 1983 Convention for the Protection and Development of the Marine Environment of the Caribbean, Article 13.

[374] Article 7. On the relationship between EIA and monitoring see Wathern, *EIA: Theory and Practice*, Ch 7 and Wood, *EIA: A Comparative Review*, Ch 14.

(c) When is an EIA required?

Principle 17 of the Rio Declaration calls for EIA to be undertaken for 'proposed activities that are likely to have a significant adverse impact on the environment'. The majority of precedents follow this formulation and limit the scope of the obligation in two ways.[375] First, it does not apply to minor or transitory impacts—the potential harm must be significant, the threshold adopted by the ILC in its 2001 Articles on Transboundary Harm.[376] Second, a threshold of foreseeability must be met *before* the obligation to do an EIA arises. Herein lies a potential weakness of EIA as a tool of international environmental management and transboundary cooperation. The reason for doing an EIA is to find out whether harm is likely; yet, under most treaties the obligation to do one and to notify other states only arises once it is known that it is likely, or even that it will occur.[377] This is both circular and potentially self-defeating if taken literally. Moreover, although the proponent of the activity in question must exercise good faith in making this determination, the potentially affected state, lacking the necessary information, may find it hard to challenge that determination or justify a request for an EIA.

In practice, the evidential standard in this context is unlikely to be onerous. One possibility is to rely on the precautionary approach as defined in Rio Principle 15 when interpreting references to the likelihood of harm in Principle 17 or in treaty formulations. This would have the virtue of setting a low threshold of risk when deciding whether an EIA is necessary.[378] Article 206 of the 1982 UNCLOS expressly lowers the threshold of foreseeability by requiring only 'reasonable grounds for believing that planned activities…*may* cause substantial pollution of or significant harmful changes to'. The practice of the parties in *MOX Plant* and *Pulp Mills* suggests that where large-scale industrial activities with a known risk of potentially significant pollution are involved, the necessity of an EIA can be presumed, even if the likely risk is a small one.

Another option is to follow the example of the Antarctic Protocol: except in *de minimis* cases, an 'initial environmental examination' is required for all activities covered by the protocol. Only if the likely impact is found to be more than minor is a comprehensive environmental examination then required.[379] UNEP's EIA Principles

---

[375] ILC, 2001 Articles on Transboundary Harm, Articles 1, 2(a) 7; 1987 UNEP Goals and Principles of EIA, Principle 1; 1982 UNCLOS, Article 206; 1991 Convention on Transboundary EIA, Article 2(3); 1992 Convention on Biological Diversity, Article 14; 1992 Convention on the Protection of the Baltic Sea Area, Article 7; 1989 Protocol for the Conservation and Management of Protected Marine and Coastal Areas of the South East Pacific, Article 89. See Craik, *The International Law of EIA*, Ch 5.

[376] *Supra* section 4(1).

[377] See e.g. 1990 Kingston Protocol on Specially Protected Areas and Wildlife, Article 13: 'activities that *would* have a negative environmental impact *and* significantly affect areas or species that have been afforded special protection'.

[378] See also 1990 Kuwait Protocol for the Protection of the Marine Environment from Land-based Sources, Article 8: 'projects…which *may* cause significant risks of pollution'. On the precautionary approach see *supra* section 4(3).

[379] 1991 Protocol to the Antarctic Treaty on Protection of the Environment, Article 8 and Annex I.

similarly distinguish between an initial and a comprehensive assessment but also call for criteria and procedures to be defined clearly by legislation so that 'subject activities can quickly and surely be identified'.[380] In particular, the UNEP Principles suggest that activities likely to cause harm should be listed, as they are in the 1991 Convention on Transboundary EIA. However, an EIA is only necessary under this convention when listed activities are 'likely' to cause significant adverse transboundary impact.[381] While there is thus no presumption that a transboundary EIA is required for all listed activities, in case of dispute other states may invoke an inquiry procedure to determine the question.[382] This procedure has been employed by Romania and Ukraine—the inquiry report in effect constituted an EIA of the proposed project and made various recommendations.[383] The 1991 Convention also provides for activities which are not listed to be the subject of prior assessment if the parties agree, and it sets out criteria to assist in making this judgement, based on the size, location, and effects of the proposed project.

What we can observe from *Southern Bluefin Tuna* and *Land Reclamation* is that, in the absence of any inquiry process comparable to the Espoo Convention, provisional-measures applications to international courts may be the best remedy available to a potentially affected state seeking to enforce the obligation to carry out a transboundary EIA. In both cases the ITLOS found that the risk of harm to the marine environment could not be excluded.[384] In *Land Reclamation* it expressly ordered the parties to assess the risks and effects of the works, while in *Southern Bluefin Tuna* the effect of its order was that catch quotas could only be increased by agreement after further studies of the state of the stock. The outcome in these cases suggests that if an EIA has not been undertaken and there is some evidence of a risk of significant harm to the environment—even if the risk is uncertain and the potential harm not necessarily irreparable—an order requiring the parties to cooperate in prior assessment is likely to result even at the provisional measures stage.

(d) The content of an EIA

Unlike most EIA provisions, the 1991 Convention on Transboundary EIA and UNEP's EIA Goals and Principles specify in some detail the type of information which an EIA should contain. This includes a description of the activity and its likely impact, mitigation measures and practical alternatives, and any uncertainties in the available knowledge.[385] The ILC's 2001 Articles require only that an assessment should include an evaluation of the possible impact on persons, property and the environment of other states, but otherwise they leave the detailed content for individual

---

[380] Principles 1, and 2.   [381] Article 2(2).   [382] Appendix IV.

[383] Espoo Inquiry Commission Report on the Danube–Black Sea Navigation Route (2006).

[384] *Southern Bluefin Tuna (Provisional Measures)*, para 79; *Land Reclamation (Provisional Measures)*, para 96.

[385] UNEP EIA Principles, Principle 4; 1991 Convention on Transboundary EIA, Article 4(1) and Appendix II.

states to determine.[386] Given the wealth of national practice and literature on what an EIA requires,[387] the ILC's caution is arguably misplaced. The evidence suggests that UNEP's definition of the minimum content of an EIA more closely and convincingly reflects national practice. Moreover, the consistent elaboration of the term 'EIA' at the international level may have given it a specialized meaning in international law, based on the UNEP Principles.[388] If the costs and benefits of a project are to be assessed then information of this kind is a necessary aid to decision-makers.

Treaties usually require an EIA only for planned 'activities' or 'projects'. These terms embrace the licensing or approval of industrial, energy and transport undertakings, inter alia,[389] but would not cover government plans or policies of a more general kind—whether to use nuclear energy, for example. However, at the domestic level strategic environmental assessment of this broader kind is being developed in some of the more advanced jurisdictions.[390] Canada and the United States have, for example, subjected free-trade agreements to an EIA.[391] Article 2(7) of the 1991 Convention on Transboundary EIA provides for parties to 'endeavour' to apply EIA to 'policies, plans and programmes', but more importantly a 2003 Protocol on Strategic Environmental Assessment (SEA) has significantly broadened the obligations of states parties in this respect. Unlike the Convention, the protocol is not limited to transboundary effects, and it also requires parties to promote SEA in international organizations and 'decision-making processes' (presumably treaty conferences).[392] It applies in full only to 'plans and programmes', but 'policies and legislation' are covered to a more limited extent.[393] The protocol's strong provision for public participation will represent a considerable expansion of environmental democracy in many states and international organizations if fully implemented.[394]

(e) Judicial review

The question whether an international court can review the adequacy of an EIA was posed by the *MOX Plant* and *Pulp Mills* disputes. In both cases the complainants favoured a prescriptive approach, drawing on detailed standards from European Community law or the 1991 Convention on Transboundary EIA to fill out the applicable treaty provisions. Like the Statute of the River Uruguay, Article 206 of UNCLOS

---

[386] Article 7 and commentary in ILC Report (2001) 405, paras (7), (8).

[387] Wood, *EIA: A Comparative Review*, 143; Wathern, *EIA: Theory and Practice*, 6–7.

[388] Craik, *The International Law of EIA*, 126–7, relying on Article 31(4) of the Vienna Convention on Treaties.

[389] See the activities listed in the 1991 Convention on Transboundary EIA, Annex 1.

[390] In *R (ex parte Greenpeace Ltd) v Secretary of State for Trade and Industry* [2007] EWHC 311 the UK's plans for nuclear power were successfully challenged. See generally Sadler and Veerheem, *Strategic Environmental Assessment: Status, Challenges and Future Directions* (Netherlands Ministry of Housing and Environment, 1996); Therivel and Partidario, *The Practice of Strategic Environmental Assessment* (London, 1996); Therivel, Wilson et al, *Strategic Environmental Assessment* (London, 1992).

[391] US Executive Order 13141 (1999) 39 *ILM* (2000) 766. Canada also conducted an EIA of the North American Free Trade Agreement.

[392] Articles 3(5), 4.   [393] Article 13.

[394] See Article 8. On public participation see *infra*, Ch 5.

is silent about what is required in an EIA, and in contrast to Articles 207–11 it makes no reference to internationally agreed rules and standards. The respondent states argued that their EIAs already met the highest international standards and they relied on scientific evidence and the judgement of independent bodies—the European Commission and the World Bank respectively—to justify the conclusion that other states were not at risk. Using litigation to challenge the adequacy and conclusions of an EIA is not unknown in national law. The national case law tends to emphasize that an EIA need not address every aspect of a project in depth, and that its purpose is to assist the decision-maker and alert the public, not to test every possible hypothesis or provide detailed solutions to problems that have been identified.[395] UNEP's Goals and Principles say only that '[t]he environmental effects in an EIA should be assessed with a degree of detail commensurate with their likely environmental significance' (Principle 5). Plainly this involves an exercise of judgement. In *Pulp Mills*, Uruguay argued that an EIA is not required to assess risks that are unlikely to result in significant harm because they are too remote, or are merely speculative. It remains to be seen how far an international court may be prepared to set aside an EIA carried out in good faith on the basis of substantial scientific and technical evidence.[396]

(e) The process

The process employed for carrying out an EIA is not set out in any international instrument. An EIA will normally take place before authorization is granted, but it may occur in several stages, for example in schemes which require an 'initial environmental examination' followed by a full EIA only if a likelihood of significant harm is then identified.[397] In cases involving complex projects, where the time between initial authorization and eventual operation is prolonged, it may be necessary to conduct several EIAs—or at least to review and revise the initial EIA—before a plant is authorized to commence operations. Some states rely on the operator or developer to carry out the EIA, subject to approval by an environmental agency or ministry. In others, a more formal process is conducted by independent inspectors. However, national EIA procedures typically provide for some element of public participation. The 1991 Convention on Transboundary EIA expressly applies this requirement on a non-discriminatory basis to the public in other states likely to be affected, but other

---

[395] See *Prineas v Forestry Commission of New South Wales*, 49 LGERA (1983) 402; *Belize Alliance of Conservation Non-Governmental Organizations v Dept of Environment*, UKPC (2003) No 63; *Marsh v Oregon Natural Resources Council*, 490 US 360 (1989); *Robertson v Methow Valley Citizens Council*, 490 US 332 (1989).

[396] However, the WTO DSB has reviewed the adequacy of risk assessments. See *Japan— Measures Affecting the Import of Apples*, WTO Appellate Body, WT/DS245/AB/R (2003) para 202: 'Under the SPS Agreement, the obligation to conduct an assessment of "risk" is not satisfied merely by a general discussion of the disease sought to be avoided by the imposition of a phytosanitary measure. The Appellate Body found the risk assessment at issue in *EC—Hormones* not to be "sufficiently specific" even though the scientific articles cited by the importing Member had evaluated the "carcinogenic potential of entire categories of hormones, or of the hormones at issue in general".'

[397] See e.g. 1991 Protocol on Environmental Protection to the Antarctic Treaty, Article 8 and Annex I; UNEP EIA Goals and Principles, Principle 1.

formulations are narrower.[398] Moreover, compliance with international human-rights law also necessitates notification to the public and participation in an 'informed process' wherever environmental impacts may seriously affect life, health, private life, or property.[399]

An EIA is 'a national procedure for evaluating the likely impact of a proposed activity on the environment'.[400] The protection which an EIA affords other states is essentially procedural: it enables them to be better informed, to be consulted, and to try to influence the outcome. It is not a process of prior joint approval. The Convention on Transboundary EIA thus gives a potentially affected state the right to participate in a national EIA only to the extent of providing information and making representations.[401] However, this Convention also envisages the possibility that joint or multilateral assessment and monitoring may be appropriate where data and information might otherwise be incompatible.[402] The scientific enquiries instituted by agreement of the parties in the *Trail Smelter Arbitration* or the *Land Reclamation Case* exemplify such a joint process.[403] An affected state has the right to receive EIA documentation and to be informed of the final decision, including the reasons and considerations on which it is based; thereafter, it is entitled to be consulted regarding measures to reduce or eliminate any transboundary impact.[404] Neighbouring states should therefore be fully aware of the risks, the benefits, and the possible alternatives revealed by the EIA. As we will see in the next section, international law gives affected states no veto on proposed activities, nor does the existence of an adverse EIA place any duty on the proposing state to refrain from proceeding with a project, although in the final decision 'due account' must be taken of the findings, and failure to act in accordance with an EIA may make it more difficult for a state to show that it has acted with due diligence.[405]

4(5) TRANSBOUNDARY COOPERATION IN CASES OF ENVIRONMENTAL RISK

If due diligence is the first rule of transboundary environmental risk management, cooperation is the second. Cooperation provides the essential basis on which

---

[398] Articles 2(6), 3(8). See also 2003 Protocol on Strategic EA, Article 10(4). Compare UNEP EIA Goals and Principles, Principle 5 ['appropriate opportunity to comment on the EIA'] and ILC, 2001 Articles on Transboundary Harm, Article 13 ['provide…relevant information'], and commentary, *ILC Report* (2001) 422–5.

[399] *Taskin v Turkey* [2006] 42 EHRR 50, para 119. See *infra*, Ch 5.

[400] 1991 Convention on Transboundary EIA, Article 1(vi). See to the same effect Rio Principle 17; *ILC Report* (2001) 402, emphasising that the state of origin carries out the EIA.

[401] Articles 3(5)–(6). Contrast Principle 12 of the UNEP Goals and Principles, which provides only for transmission of information.

[402] Article 3 and Appendix VI. See also 1997 Korea–China Agreement on Environmental Cooperation, Article 2(4); 1994 Israel–Jordan Peace Treaty, Annex IV.

[403] See also the *Gabčíkovo-Nagymaros Case* in which the parties were ordered to cooperate in monitoring.

[404] 1991 Convention on Transboundary EIA, Articles 4–7.   [405] Ibid, Article 6.

multilateral environmental agreements are built. It is the foundation for equitable utilisation, management, and conservation of shared natural resources.[406] The obligation of states to cooperate through notification, consultation, and negotiation permeates the ILC's 2001 Articles on transboundary harm and the 1992 Rio Declaration on Environment and Development.[407] It is also very clearly articulated in the *Lac Lanoux Arbitration*,[408] and in various regional treaties, including the 1991 Convention on Transboundary EIA and the 1975 Statute of the River Uruguay at issue in the *Pulp Mills Case*. An obligation to cooperate is rather less clearly set out in the 1982 UNCLOS. Article 123 somewhat weakly says that states bordering enclosed or semi-enclosed seas 'should' cooperate with each other, while Part XII requires states to cooperate, but mainly in the task of adopting global and regional rules and standards. However, in what may become the best-known passage from an ITLOS judgment, the Tribunal has twice said that 'the duty to co-operate is a fundamental principle in the prevention of pollution of the marine environment under Part XII of the Convention and general international law and that rights arise therefrom which the Tribunal may consider appropriate to preserve under Article 290 of the Convention'.[409] In *MOX Plant* and *Land Reclamation* the parties were thus ordered to improve their cooperation, and to consult, exchange information, and monitor or assess the risks and effects of their activities. Similarly, in *Southern Bluefin Tuna* the Tribunal emphasized the need for greater cooperation to ensure conservation and optimum utilization, and it ordered the parties to resume negotiations for that purpose 'without delay'.[410] In *MOX Plant* and *Land Reclamation* these cooperation orders were made notwithstanding findings that irreparable harm was neither imminent nor likely.

The Stockholm Conference recognized in 1972 that cooperation through multilateral or bilateral arrangements or other appropriate means is essential to control, prevent, reduce, and eliminate adverse environmental effects resulting from activities conducted in all spheres, in such a way that due account is taken of the sovereignty and interests of all states.[411] In endorsing this resolution, the UN General Assembly noted that it should not be construed as enabling other states to delay or impede programmes and projects of exploration, exploitation, and development of natural resources within the territory of states, but that it did require the exchange of information 'in a spirit of good neighbourliness'.[412] At that time, agreement could not be reached on more detailed rules and these formulations fall short of explicitly requiring consultation and negotiation with other states, but the broad contours of 'good neighbourliness' can be identified in subsequent legal developments.

---

[406] See UNEP, 1978 Principles of Conduct, etc in the Conservation and Harmonious Utilization of Natural Resources Shared by Two or More States, and *infra*, section 5.

[407] See Principles 7, 9, 12, 13, 14, 18, 19, 27.

[408] *Lac Lanoux Arbitration*, 24 ILR (1957) 101. See also *Gabčíkovo-Nagymaros Case*, paras 140–7.

[409] *MOX Plant Case (Provisional Measures)* para 82; *Land Reclamation (Provisional Measures)* para 92.

[410] *Southern Bluefin Tuna (Provisional Measures)* para 78 and operative para (e).

[411] 1972 Stockholm Declaration, Principle 24.   [412] UNGA Res 2995 XXVII (1972).

(a) Notification and consultation in respect of transboundary risk

Although some writers have doubted whether it is possible to generalize customary procedural rules for transboundary environmental risk from the treaties, case law, and limited state practice,[413] a strong provision was included in the Rio Declaration. Principle 19 provides:

States shall provide prior and timely notification and relevant information to potentially affected states on activities that may have a significant adverse transboundary environmental effect and shall consult with those states at an early stage and in good faith.

This provision fully reflects the precedents referred to below. Moreover, even if notification and consultation in cases of transboundary risk are not independent customary rules, non-compliance with them is likely to be strong evidence of a failure to act diligently in protecting other states from harm under Rio Principle 2.[414] Once notified, a state which raises no objection may find itself estopped from future protest; there are thus significant legal benefits to be gained from following the requirements of Principle 19.

The ILC's 2001 Articles on Transboundary Harm also address procedural issues.[415] A particular feature of these articles is the continuing character of the obligation to notify and consult even after a project has come into operation.[416] Moreover the ILC requires that information be given to the public likely to be affected in other states, not simply to other governments.[417] Subject to one qualification considered later, the ILC articles otherwise follow closely the main principles of the *Lac Lanoux Arbitration* (see below) and are comparable to the relevant articles of the 1997 UN Convention on International Watercourses, which in the ILC's view reflect well-established international practice.[418] As the *Lac Lanoux Arbitration* and the *Nuclear Tests Cases* indicate, Principle 19 and the ILC Articles enjoy some support in state practice.[419] Although the *Pulp Mills* and *MOX Plant Cases* both arose out of allegations of failure to cooperate fully under applicable treaty provisions, all of the parties sought to interpret those provisions by reference to customary international law and the precedents referred to here.

A requirement of prior consultation based on adequate information has a substantial pedigree of international support and is a natural counterpart of the concept of equitable utilization of a shared resource. The *Lac Lanoux* arbitration[420] shows how

---

[413] Okowa, 67 *BYIL* (1996) 275, 317–22. But for a more positive view see Kirgis, *Prior Consultation in International Law* (Charlottesville, Va, 1983).

[414] Okowa, 67 *BYIL* (1996), 332–4.

[415] Articles 9–13, and see commentary in *ILC Report* (2001) GAOR A/55/10.

[416] See especially Articles 11 and 12, and commentary, *ILC Report* (2001) 418–21.

[417] Article 13. On public participation see *infra*, Ch 5.   [418] See *infra*, Ch 10.

[419] On the *Nuclear Tests Cases*, see the French note of 19 Feb 1973, in NZ Ministry of Foreign Affairs, *French Nuclear Testing in the Pacific* (Wellington, 1973) 42. On state practice, see generally Kirgis, *Prior Consultation in International Law*; but for a more sceptical view see Okowa, 67 *BYIL* (1996) 275.

[420] 24 ILR (1957) 101. On the question whether this award is based solely on the 1866 Treaty of Bayonne, or also on customary law, see *infra*, Ch 10.

the rule has been applied in the law of international watercourses. The tribunal held that France had complied with its obligations under a treaty and customary law to consult and negotiate in good faith before diverting a watercourse shared with Spain. It noted that conflicting interests must be reconciled by negotiation and mutual concession.[421] France must inform Spain of its proposals, allow consultations, and give reasonable weight to Spain's interests, but that did not mean that it could act only with Spain's consent: 'the risk of an evil use has so far not led to subjecting the possession of these means of action to the authorization of states which may possibly be threatened'.[422] Spain's rights were thus of a procedural character only; it enjoyed no veto and no claim to insist on specific precautions. In the absence of agreement it was for France to determine whether to proceed with the project and how to safeguard Spain's interests, provided it gave a reasonable place to those interests in the solution finally adopted.[423]

Treaties and state practice apply the basic principles of the *Lac Lanoux* case to the management of transboundary risks posed by hazardous or potentially harmful activities, including nuclear installations near borders,[424] continental-shelf operations and other sources of marine pollution, including dumping and land-based activities,[425] long-range transboundary air pollution,[426] and industrial accidents.[427] In each of these situations some measure of prior notification and consultation has been called for in bilateral, regional, or global treaties, but neighbouring states are not given a veto over potentially harmful developments. Where common areas are affected, negotiation with any one state may be inappropriate, however, and the basic principle is modified to provide for notification and consultation to take place through institutions acting for the international community. Chapter 8 provides the best examples of this development: as we will see, states are no longer free to put common areas or shared natural resources at risk without taking account of the interests of others.[428]

The 1991 Convention on Transboundary EIA is the first regional agreement to make detailed provision for transboundary procedural obligations in cases of environmental risk. As we saw in the previous section, it applies to a range of proposed activities, including oil refineries, power stations, nuclear installations, smelters, and waste disposal installations 'that are likely to cause significant adverse transboundary impact'. Other states likely to be affected must be notified and given the opportunity to enter into consultations and make representations on the environmental impact assessment.[429]

---

[421] 24 ILR (1957) 119.   [422] Ibid, 126.

[423] Ibid, 128–30, 140–1.   [424] See *infra*, Ch 9.

[425] On continental-shelf operations see 1983 Canada–Denmark Agreement for Cooperation Relating to the Marine Environment, 23 *ILM* (1984) 269; 1988 Kuwait Protocol Concerning Marine Pollution Resulting from Exploration and Exploitation of the Continental Shelf, 19 *EPL* (1989) 32; 1981 UNEP Principles Concerning the Environment Related to Offshore Drilling and Mining Within the Limits of National Jurisdiction, 7 *EPL* (1981) 50. On dumping and land-based sources of marine pollution see *infra*, Ch 8.

[426] 1979 Geneva Convention on Long-range Transboundary Air Pollution, Articles 5, 8, *infra*, Ch 6.

[427] 1992 Convention on Transboundary Effects of Industrial Accidents, especially Article 4.

[428] See *infra*, Ch 8, sections 2, 3.   [429] Articles 3, 5, 6.

It does not follow, however, that identical procedural obligations will apply to every case of environmental risk. First, the risk must be significant. This, as we have seen, implies both a degree of probability and a threshold of seriousness of harm, although the risk does not have to be ultra-hazardous in character.[430] Second, as with the obligation of diligent control, much will depend on the circumstances of each case. Procedural obligations in regard to nuclear power, for example, have been narrowly construed, and applied only to border installations, despite the continental implications of accidents at reactors such as Chernobyl.[431] The practice of consultation and notification in respect of activities which affect only common spaces is also more limited in scope.[432] Lastly, it must be recalled that these procedural rules usually lead only to an obligation to negotiate in good faith. Negotiations must be 'meaningful' and each side must be willing to listen and take account of the other's interests.[433] Subject to what is said below about equitable balancing, however, they will not necessarily result in substantive limitations on the activities which states propose to undertake, nor are states required to refrain from acting if negotiations prove unsuccessful, since that would enable others to obstruct or veto any proposed development.[434] At most, the object of negotiation is to provide the opportunity for accommodating any conflict of rights and interests which may exist, not to stifle initiative.[435] In particular, states are not debarred from creating sources of risk to others, even where, as in the case of nuclear installations, these involve the possibility of serious harm.

The most obvious flaw in this approach is that in disputes concerning the acceptability and mitigation of transboundary environmental risks, finding a solution may depend on the ability to negotiate one. The potential difficulties are illustrated by the continuing frustration of the parties to the *Gabčíkovo-Nagymaros Case*. The ICJ judgment required them to cooperate in the joint management of the project, and to institute a process of environmental protection and monitoring. Ten years later, no such agreement had been concluded. This outcome may be exceptional, however. The *Land Reclamation Case* shows how obligations of transboundary cooperation can be enforced using court-ordered provisional measures. In addition to requiring the parties to cooperate in establishing an independent study, exchanging information and assessing the risks, the Tribunal also noted that in the course of the hearing Singapore had given assurances that it would notify, consult, and negotiate with Malaysia before

---

[430] ILC, 2001 Articles on Transboundary Harm, Articles 2, 3; 1982 UNCLOS Articles 206, 210(5); 1991 Convention on Transboundary EIA, Article 2; 1997 Convention on International Watercourses, Article 12.

[431] See *infra*, Ch 9. However, Appendix III of the 1991 Convention on Transboundary EIA requires the parties also to consider 'more remote proposed activities which could give rise to significant transboundary effects far removed from the site of the development'.

[432] See *infra*, Ch 8, sections 2(4), 3(7).

[433] *North Sea Continental Shelf Cases*, ICJ Reports (1969) 46–7, paras 83–5; *Icelandic Fisheries Cases*, ICJ Reports (1974) 32ff; *Gabčíkovo-Nagymaros Case*, ICJ Reports (1997) 7, para 141.

[434] 2001 Articles on Transboundary Harm, Article 9(3) and commentary, paras (2), (10), *ILC Report* (2001) 409–11, and see earlier discussion of *Lac Lanoux Arbitration*. See also the arguments of the parties on this point in the *Pulp Mills* litigation.

[435] See *infra*, Chs 6, 8, 9, 10; UNGA Res 2995 XXVII (1972); and 1991 Convention on Transboundary EIA, Article 6.

proceeding with further works, while giving it the opportunity to comment and produce new evidence. Without any decision on the merits, Malaysia thus secured commitments that in substance addressed all of its rights to cooperation under UNCLOS and general international law. Precedents also exist for successful court-imposed regulatory regimes in similar circumstances, as in the *Behring Sea Fur Seals* and *Trail Smelter* arbitrations.[436] In both cases the parties had jointly requested the arbitrators to indicate an equitable solution. Aided by appropriate scientific investigations, the arbitrators were thus empowered to substitute their own judgment for that of the parties in order to resolve the disputes.

(b) Equitable balancing and impermissible transboundary risks

An important question not addressed directly by the ILC is whether there is ever a point at which activities are so risky to other states that they must not be carried out at all if they cannot be rendered harmless or moved elsewhere. To their codification of existing law the ILC's 2001 Articles on Transboundary Harm add the important modification that states have a duty to negotiate an equitable balance of interests in accordance with factors set out in Article 10.[437] These factors include the degree of risk of transboundary or environmental harm; the possibility of prevention, minimization, or repair; the importance of the activity in relation to the potential harm; the economic viability of the project if preventive measures or alternatives are undertaken; the willingness of states likely to be affected to contribute to the cost of preventive measures; and the standards of prevention applied by those states and in regional or international practice. This is not an exhaustive list and it assigns no particular priority or weight to any of these factors. The parties remain free to take into account whatever they deem relevant, subject only to their over-riding duty to negotiate in good faith. This approach is more than procedural, however. While not prohibiting all risk creation, it requires the parties to establish an equitable balance of interests as the price for undertaking risky activities.[438] The rapporteur noted that the Commission's work was 'guided by the need to evolve procedures enabling States to act in a concerted manner...' and he accepted that in this respect the draft convention was progressive development of the topic.[439] If the parties cannot agree an equitable solution, however, it would remain open to the proposing state to proceed, even if harm is unavoidable.[440]

---

[436] *Behring Sea Fur Seals Arbitration*, Moore, 1 *Int Arb Awards* (1898) 755, repr in 1 *IELR* (1999) 43; *Trail Smelter Arbitration*, *supra* n 216.

[437] Article 9(2).

[438] See *ILC Report* (2001) 413ff. See also id, (1996) *Rept of the Working Group*, 306–16; Quentin-Baxter's 'Schematic Outline', II *YbILC* (1983) Pt 1, 223, section 6, and compare 1991 Convention on Transboundary EIA, and ILA, Montreal Rules on Transfrontier Pollution, *supra* n 10. The ILA's approach is criticized by Quentin-Baxter, II *YbILC* (1983) Pt 1, 209. Compare human rights cases which require states to maintain a fair balance between the interests of affected individuals and the community: see *Hatton v UK, infra,* Ch 5.

[439] *ILC Report* (2000) GAOR A/55/10, para 675.

[440] Article 9(3). Compare Draft Article 20, UN Doc A/CN 4/428 (1990) which had provided that 'If an assessment of the activity shows that transboundary harm cannot be avoided or cannot be adequately compensated, the state of origin shall refuse authorization for the activity unless the operator proposes less harmful alternatives.'

This does not look like a prohibition on risk creation, but it is possible that certain risks can never be rendered equitable if the costs to other states seriously outweigh the benefits to the state undertaking the project. The argument has been made, unsuccessfully on the facts, in both *MOX Plant* and *Pulp Mills*.[441]

The Commission's commentary is unable to cite any significant international practice in support of a requirement of equitable balancing of transboundary risk other than the *Donauversinkung Case*,[442] and some equally old US domestic cases.[443] There is some evidence that states have, even in more modern times, negotiated what might be seen as equitable solutions to transboundary disputes: agreements concerning French potassium emissions into the Rhine,[444] pollution of US–Mexican boundary waters,[445] and North American and European acid rain[446] all display elements of this kind. There is also no doubt that the *Behring Sea Fur Seals* and *Trail Smelter* arbitrations resulted in equitable solutions because that is what the parties asked the arbitrators to indicate in their awards.

On the other hand it is far from clear that the parties to any of these precedents were acting out of any sense of legal obligation to reach an 'equitable' solution. They may be more convincingly explained as cases in which the parties decided that their interests were better served by negotiating compromise outcomes than by insisting on their strict legal rights. Support for a legal obligation to negotiate an equitable solution can also be found in the law of international watercourses, the law of high-seas fisheries, and the law relating to maritime boundary delimitation.[447] Whether it is permissible to generalize from these precedents a broader rule applicable to transboundary risk depends ultimately on whether transboundary environmental relations are more appropriately based on equitable balancing than on legal rules in which a balance between environmental protection and economic development is already inherent, but which afford states a more predictable basis on which to protect their own interests.

There are arguments for and against the Commission's proposed solution. The main argument in favour is that it places some degree of restraint on the permissibility of any activity which poses an inequitably large risk for other states with little or no compensating benefit for the host state. Such activities might even be characterized as unsustainable development. We return to this question in our discussion of nuclear power in Chapter 9. If in these situations equity functions as an element additional to

---

[441] See *MOX Plant Case (Provisional Measures)* ITLOS No 10 (2001); *Pulp Mills Case (Argentina v Uruguay)* ICJ Reports (2006).

[442] In 1 *Int Env LR* (1999) 444.   [443] *ILC Report* (2001) 413–4.

[444] 1976 Convention for the Protection of the Rhine from Pollution by Chlorides, with 1991 Protocol; *infra*, Ch 10.

[445] 1973 Agreement on the Permanent and Definitive Solution of the International Problem of the Salinity of the Colorado River; *infra*, Ch 10.

[446] 1979 Convention on Long-range Transboundary Air Pollution; 1991 Agreement between the United States and Canada on Air Quality; *infra*, Ch 6.

[447] *Gabčíkovo-Nagymaros Case*, ICJ Reports (1997) 7; *Icelandic Fisheries Cases*, ICJ Reports (1974) 3 and 175; *North Sea Continental Shelf Case*, ICJ Reports (1969) 3. The Commission's analogy is Article 6 of the 1997 UN Watercourses Convention, on which see *infra*, Ch 10.

the protection offered by other rules of law, then it can only be beneficial to potentially affected states. If, however, it subsumes and weakens existing rules of law then it may not be so benign, and will tend to favour the more powerful states, even the polluting ones.[448] From this perspective it is worth noting the rapporteur's view that equitable balancing is not intended to dilute the obligation of due diligence.[449] Moreover, as in other contexts, equitable balancing may be hard to achieve without compulsory third-party dispute settlement. Many states, especially in the developing world, may feel that they are not well served by a regime which offers little certainty and only the limited assurance of compulsory fact-finding in the event of a dispute.[450]

(c) Emergency notification, response, and assistance

The customary obligation of cooperation in the management of environmental risks extends to accidents and emergencies likely to cause transboundary harm. Article 17 of the 2001 ILC Articles on Prevention of Transboundary Harm provides that 'The State of origin shall, without delay and by the most expeditious means, at its disposal, notify the State likely to be affected of an emergency concerning an activity within the scope of the present articles and provide it with all relevant and available information.' As we saw earlier, the *Corfu Channel Case* provides an early example of judicial application of this duty to warn. In that case British warships were damaged by mines in Albanian territorial waters. Giving judgment on this point for the United Kingdom, the Court noted: 'The obligations incumbent upon the Albanian authorities consisted in notifying for the benefit of shipping in general, the existence of a minefield in Albanian territorial waters and in warning the approaching British warships of imminent danger to which the minefield exposed them'.[451] Although the context of this case involved interference with freedom of maritime communication, the Court expressly based its conclusion on additional grounds of more general application namely, elementary considerations of humanity and the obligation referred to earlier, that a state should not knowingly allow its territory to be used for acts contrary to the rights of other states. As we have seen, these include the right to protection from environmental harm. For this reason, it is legitimate to view the *Corfu Channel Case* as authority for a customary obligation to give warning of known environmental hazards.

Treaties and state practice support this conclusion. It is unequivocally applied to marine pollution by the 1982 UNCLOS and other treaties now widely ratified.[452] A Convention on Early Notification of Nuclear Accidents, and a network of bilateral

---

[448] For critical assessments see Okowa, 67 *BYIL* (1996) 311–14; Boyle and Freestone (eds), *International Law and Sustainable Development*, 79–84.

[449] *ILC Report* (2000) GAOR A/55/10, para 676. See also the rapporteur's *3rd Report*, UN Doc A/CN 4/510 (2000). Article 18 also provides that 'The present articles are without prejudice to any obligation incurred by states under relevant treaties or rules of customary law.'

[450] Article 19. Disputes may also be referred to the ICJ, arbitration, or any other means of settlement if the parties can agree. For a good illustration of how compulsory dispute settlement can work in these situations see the *Pulp Mills Case*, ICJ Reports (2006).

[451] ICJ Reports (1949) 4, 22.

[452] 1982 UNCLOS, Articles 198, 211(7) and others cited *infra*, Ch 7. See also 1989 Basel Convention on the Control of Transboundary Movements of Hazardous Wastes, Article 13.

agreements apply the same rule to transboundary releases of radioactivity,[453] and it is found in treaties dealing with pollution of international watercourses,[454] in the ILA Montreal Rules on Transfrontier Pollution,[455] and in OECD principles.[456] In all of these instruments the object of notification is the same: states should be given sufficient information promptly enough to enable them to minimize the damage and take whatever measures of self-protection are permitted by international law. Principle 18 of the Rio Declaration codifies this duty to warn other states in situations where 'natural disasters or other emergencies' are likely to produce 'sudden harmful effects' on their environment.

Modern treaties tend also to require states to make contingency plans for pollution emergencies and to cooperate in their response.[457] The ILC has adopted comparable provisions in its articles on transboundary harm.[458] A typical example is Article 199 of the 1982 UNCLOS which requires states to make joint plans. Practice in this respect is well developed in the maritime field.[459] A multilateral convention and a network of bilateral agreements also facilitate emergency cooperation in cases of nuclear accidents.[460] Only in the law of the sea, however, have states assumed a power to intervene unilaterally to forestall accidental harm emanating from outside their territory,[461] although in other cases the defence of necessity may provide some basis for emergency measures of ecological protection taken in violation of the sovereignty of other states.[462] Such measures must be the only means of protecting an essential interest of the state from a grave and imminent peril and must not seriously impair the essential interests of the other state affected.[463]

Where accidents do pose an environmental risk for other states or the global commons, the obligation of due diligence, considered earlier, will additionally require the source state to take whatever measures are necessary to forestall or mitigate their effects. Thus states do not discharge their duty merely by seeking to prevent accidents, or by giving notification of an emergency.[464] It is in this context that treaty obligations

---

[453] See *infra,* Ch 9.

[454] E.g. 1976 Convention on the Protection of the Rhine Against Chemical Pollution, Article 11; 1997 Convention on International Watercourses, Article 28, *infra,* Ch 10; 2003 UNECE Protocol on Civil Liability and Compensation for Damage Caused by Accidents on Transboundary Waters.

[455] *Supra* n 10, Article 5.   [456] Council Recommendation C (74) 224 (1974) Annex, Part F.

[457] 1990 Convention on Oil Pollution Preparedness and Response; 1992 UNECE Convention on the Transboundary Effects of Industrial Accidents; 2005 Annex VI to the Antarctic Environmental Protocol.

[458] 2001 Articles, Article 16; 2006 Principles on Allocation of Loss, Principle 5.

[459] See *infra,* Ch 7.   [460] See *infra,* Ch 9.

[461] 1969 Brussels Convention Relating to Intervention on the High Seas in Cases of Oil Pollution Casualties; 1982 UNCLOS, Article 221; see *infra,* Ch 7.

[462] ILC, 2001 State Responsibility Articles, Article 25. Bilder, 14 *Vand JTL* (1981) 63ff, suggests a broader principle of unilateral action to protect a state from environmental damage caused by another's breach of duty not to cause serious harm to other states.

[463] *Gabčíkovo-Nagymaros Case*, ICJ Reports (1997) 7, paras 49–59. See Jagota, 16 *NYIL* (1985) 269, and Brown, 21 *CLP* (1968) 113.

[464] 1997 Convention on International Watercourses, Article 28(3). The *Corfu Channel Case* refers only to notification of the danger, but this must be read in the context of that case: notification would of itself have been sufficient to avert the disaster.

to maintain contingency plans and respond to pollution emergencies must be seen: they are part of a state's duty of diligence in controlling sources of known environmental harm.

4(6) DEFINING 'ENVIRONMENTAL DAMAGE' AND 'POLLUTION'

(a) Environmental harm or damage

There is no doubt that injury to persons or property falls within the scope of the obligation to prevent or control transboundary harm.[465] In this context harm can also be defined in human rights terms—i.e. adverse impacts on the right to life, private life, and property, including indigenous peoples' lifestyles.[466] The more difficult question is the extent to which protection of the environment or the prevention of environmental harm also do so. Both *Trail Smelter* and the early civil liability conventions took a narrow view, compensating for injury to persons or property but appearing to exclude wider environmental interests such as wildlife, aesthetic considerations, or the unity and diversity of ecosystems.[467] Modern civil-liability conventions and protocols now recognize environmental damage as a distinct interest covered by international tort law.[468] UN Security Council resolution 687, imposing international liability on Iraq for environmental damage in Kuwait, is another important if so far unique precedent pointing in the same direction.[469]

Moreover, when viewed from the perspective of international regulatory conventions, rather than liability for environmental damage, it can be seen that the older approach is outdated and inappropriate. In contrast, Principle 21 of the Stockholm Declaration and Principle 2 of the Rio Declaration refer explicitly to responsibility for controlling 'damage to the environment' of other states or of areas beyond national jurisdiction. So does the ICJ in its *Advisory Opinion on the Threat or Use of Nuclear*

---

[465] *ILC Report* (2001) GAOR A/56/10, 388 para (4); *Trail Smelter Arbitration, supra* section 4(2).

[466] See the ICJ claim Ecuador filed against Colombia in 2008. On human rights impacts see *infra*, Ch 5, section 2, and Handl, in Bowman and Boyle (eds), *Environmental Damage in International and Comparative Law* (OUP, 2002) 85–110.

[467] Rubin, 50 *Oregon LR* (1971) 272–4. On this issue the *Trail Smelter* tribunal was required to follow US law. US tort law is now more generous in allowing for restoration of ecological loss: see *Commonwealth of Puerto Rico v SS Zoe Colocotroni*, 628 F 2d 652 (1980); Schoenbaum, in Wetterstein (ed), *Harm to the Environment* (Oxford, 1997) Ch 9, and Brans, *Liability for Damage to Public Natural Resources* (The Hague, 2001) Ch 4.

[468] 1992 Convention on Civil Liability for Oil Pollution Damage, *infra,* Ch 7; 1993 ECE Convention on Civil Liability for Damage Resulting from Activities Dangerous to the Environment, *infra,* Ch 5; 1997 Vienna Protocol on Civil Liability for Nuclear Damage and 1997 Vienna Convention on Supplementary Compensation for Nuclear Damage, *infra,* Ch 9. See generally de La Fayette, in Boyle and Bowman (eds), *Environmental Damage in International and Comparative Law* (Oxford, 1999) Ch 9; Brans, *Liability for Damage to Public Natural Resources*, Ch 7.

[469] See *infra*, Ch 4, and Decision 7, UN Compensation Commission Governing Council, 31 *ILM* (1992) 1045, para 35; UNEP, *Report of the Working Group of Experts on Liability and Compensation for Environmental Damage arising from Military Activities*, 1996 ['*UNEP Rept of Working Group on Liability*']. See also *Gabčíkovo-Nagymaros Case*, ICJ Reports (1997) 7, in which the ICJ accepted that prospective environmental damage could in an appropriate case justify a plea of necessity.

Weapons, while the ILC specifically includes 'the environment' within the scope of its 2001 Articles on Transboundary Harm. Articles 145 and 194 of the 1982 UNCLOS articulate the obligation to protect the marine environment in particularly broad terms. It includes measures to protect and preserve the 'ecological balance', marine flora and fauna, and 'rare and fragile ecosystems as well as the habitat of depleted, threatened or endangered species and other forms of marine life'.[470] Moreover the convention's definition of pollution in Article 1(4) includes the introduction of substances which may cause 'harm to living resources and marine life'. Similarly, the 1995 Washington Declaration on Protection of the Marine Environment from Land-based Activities refers to 'Setting as their common goal sustained and effective action to deal with all land-based *impacts* upon the marine environment', including 'physical alteration and destruction of habitat'. Instead of 'land-based sources of marine pollution' it refers to 'land-based activities that degrade the marine environment'.

Taken together, these provisions indicate that the scope of the obligation to protect the marine environment is not dependent on actual or intended human usage of the sea and its contents but focuses instead on the interdependence of human activity and nature. Other treaties adopt an even broader perspective. Thus the Antarctic Environment Protocol protects not only the Antarctic environment, 'dependent and associated ecosystems and the intrinsic value of Antarctica, including its wilderness and aesthetic values', but it also covers a very broad range of 'adverse effects' which must be avoided by activities planned to take place there. These include effects on climate and weather, air and water quality, marine and terrestrial environments, fauna and flora, as well as endangered species, and biological diversity.[471] Both the Ozone Convention and the Climate Change Convention likewise apply, inter alia, to controlling adverse effects on 'the composition, resilience or productivity of natural and managed ecosystems'.[472]

As these examples indicate, what is meant by 'the environment', and therefore by 'environmental harm', may differ in individual treaties, and will depend on what each treaty is intended to regulate and protect. It is thus not possible to give a generic definition. What does seem tenable, however, is that while prospective material injury of some kind is a necessary element of the customary obligation to prevent transboundary harm,[473] this is not limited to the loss of resources or amenities of economic value to man, but can extend to the intrinsic worth of natural ecosystems, including biological diversity and areas of wilderness or aesthetic significance. Studies conducted for UNEP and the ILC both concluded that the 'environment' covers at least air, water, soil, flora, fauna, ecosystems, and their interaction and noted that some agreements also include

---

[470] 1982 UNCLOS, Articles 145, 194(5); see *infra*, Ch 7.

[471] 1991 Protocol to the Antarctic Treaty on the Environment, Article 3.

[472] 1985 Convention on the Ozone Layer, Article 1(2); 1992 Framework convention on Climate Change, Article 1(1).

[473] Handl, 69 *AJIL* (1975) 50. In this respect the obligation is an exception to the proposition advanced by some writers and adopted by the ILC that harm is not a necessary element of state responsibility. See Boyle, 39 *ICLQ* (1990) 16.

cultural heritage, landscape, and amenity values.[474] The most radical view, supported by a number of treaties,[475] points to the need to move beyond a focus on the territory of other states in favour of an ecosystem approach, emphasizing 'consideration of whole systems rather than individual components'.[476] The Antarctic Environment Protocol is to date the largest, most comprehensive, and significant example in which an entire continent and the surrounding marine environment have been protected on such an ecosystem basis.[477] The ILC has advanced the view that international law requires states to protect and preserve ecosystems on a comprehensive basis, but for reasons explored in later chapters, this appears to go beyond present state practice.[478] However, whether put in holistic terms, or merely in terms of its component elements, there is now substantial consensus behind the proposition that international law protects the environment of other states and common spaces from harm.[479]

(b) Thresholds of serious or significant harm

Determining the threshold at which harm to the environment becomes a breach of obligation is a question on which there are several possible views. While the *Trail Smelter Case* referred to 'serious' injury,[480] suggesting a relatively high threshold, the ILC initially preferred the term 'appreciable' to qualify the degree of harm.[481] The Commission changed its mind in 1994, however, after analysis of 'more than sixty international instruments' had shown a clear preference for the term 'significant' or equivalents,[482] and this is the term now used in the 1997 Convention on International Watercourses and the 2001 Articles on Prevention of Transboundary Harm. The commentary to both texts notes that significant harm need not be substantial but must be 'more than trivial'.[483] Both the Ozone and Climate Change Conventions also use 'significant' to qualify references to deleterious effects but the latter treaty then sets a higher threshold of threats of 'serious or irreversible damage' when introducing the precautionary principle.[484]

---

[474] UNEP, *Rept of Working Group on Liability*, 1996; ILC, *11th Report on International Liability for Injurious Consequences*, UN Doc A/CN 4/468 (1995). Cultural heritage and landscape are included in the 1992 ECE Convention on the Transboundary Effects of Industrial Accidents and the 1993 ECE Convention on Civil Liability for Damage Resulting from Accidents Dangerous to the Environment.

[475] E.g. 1997 Convention on International Watercourses, Article 20, and see *infra*, Ch 10.

[476] Brunnée and Toope, 5 *YbIEL* (1994) 55.

[477] See Vidas (ed), *Protecting the Polar Marine Environment* (Cambridge, 2000) Chs 1, 4; Redgwell, in, Boyle and Freestone, *International Law and Sustainable Development*, Ch 9.

[478] See *infra*, Ch 7, section 2(4).

[479] See ILC 2001 Articles on Transboundary Harm, Article 2(b).

[480] 35 *AJIL* (1941) 716. See also 1992 ECE Convention on the Transboundary Effects of Industrial Accidents, Article 1.

[481] ILC, Draft Articles on International Liability, UN Doc A/CN 4/428 (1990) and on International Watercourses, II *YbILC* (1984) Pt 1, 112.

[482] II *YbILC* (1993) Pt 2, 93, para 410; II *YbILC* (1994) Pt 2, 102–3. See generally Sachariew, 37 *NILR* (1990) 193.

[483] UNGA, *Report of the 6th Committee*, UN Doc A/51/869 (1997) 5; ILC Report (2001) 388, paras (4)–(7).

[484] Article 1 of both conventions and Article 3(3) 1992 Framework Convention on Climate Change.

Apart from obvious difficulties of definition and assessment of the threshold in individual cases, other formulations, such as Principle 21 of the Stockholm Declaration and Principle 2 of the Rio Declaration, omit any qualifying reference to the level of harm or damage, and cast some doubt on the general assumption.[485] It should also be noted that none of the relevant civil-liability conventions requires environmental harm to be serious or significant, while the 1994 Nuclear Safety Convention merely refers to protection from the 'harmful effects' of radiation without any further explicit threshold. More problematic is the view that any threshold of harm is essentially relative and conditional on equitable considerations or a balance of interests between the states concerned.[486] This could allow the utility of the activity to outweigh the seriousness of the harm and have the effect of converting an obligation to prevent harm into an obligation to use territory equitably and reasonably or into a constraint on abuse of rights. Thus Lefeber argues that the threshold requirement represents a 'balance of interests between the sovereign right of states to develop . . . and the duty to prevent transboundary interference'.[487] There is some support for equitable balancing as a test of the permissibility of pollution of shared resources, such as international watercourses, and some writers would apply the same approach, or a test of reasonableness, to the obligation to prevent transboundary harm.[488]

While states may choose to regulate transboundary harm in this way,[489] neither the international case law nor treaty definitions of harm referred to above support thresholds determined by equitable balancing. The only balancing of interests in *Trail Smelter* related not to the question whether Canada was in breach of its obligations but to the determination of a regime for the future operation of the smelter.[490] Moreover, although the relationship between harm prevention and equitable utilization was the subject of prolonged controversy in the ILC's work on international watercourses,[491] Article 7 of the 1997 Convention on International Watercourses as finally adopted requires watercourse states to 'take all appropriate measures to prevent the causing of significant harm to other watercourse states', without subordinating this obligation to any threshold of equitable balancing.

---

[485] See also 1974 Charter of Economic Rights and Duties of States, Article 30; 1978 UNEP Principles of Conduct Concerning Resources Shared by Two or More States, Principle 3; 1982 UNCLOS, Article 194. Compare however UNGA Res 2995 XXVII (1972) which refers to 'significant harmful effects'. Views differ on whether omission of an explicit threshold is intended to change earlier practice: cf Handl, 26 *NRJ* (1986) 412ff, and Pallemaerts, *Hague YIL* (1988) 206.

[486] Handl, 13 *CYIL* (1975) 156; *id*, 26 *NRJ* (1986) 405; Quentin-Baxter, II *YbILC* (1981) Pt 1, 112–119; McCaffrey, II *YbILC* (1986) Pt 1, 133–4; Lefeber, *Transboundary Environmental Interference and the Origin of State Liability*, 86–9; Wolfrum, 33 *GYIL* (1990) 308.

[487] *Transboundary Environmental Interference*, 86–7.

[488] Quentin-Baxter, 2nd Report on International Liability, II *YbILC*, (1981) Pt 1, 108ff; McDougall and Schlei, 64 *Yale LJ* (1955) 690ff.

[489] Possible examples include the 1979 Convention on Long Range Transboundary Air Pollution and its protocols, dealing with European acid rain, on which see *infra*, Ch 6, and the 1976 Convention for the Protection of the Rhine from Chlorides, on which see *infra*, Ch 10. See also the *Trail Smelter Arbitration* in which the parties requested an equitable solution.

[490] Read, 1 *CYIL* (1963) 213.   [491] *Infra*, Ch 10.

This is almost certainly the correct conclusion, since the case for making the customary threshold of harm dependent on an equitable balance of interests is not a strong one.[492] The notion that states must act with due diligence to prevent significant harm is a formula which already allows for flexibility in individual cases, including taking account of the more limited technical and economic capacity of developing states, while excluding *de minimis* pollution. To add yet more variables would be subversive of efforts to establish minimum standards of environmental protection and prove much too favourable to the polluter. Only if the obligation to prevent harm is an absolute one, rather than an obligation of diligence, might it be justifiable to resort to equitable manipulation of the threshold of harm to mitigate the rigours of what would then be an extreme rule.

(c) Pollution

'Pollution' is a narrower concept than environmental harm, as can be seen clearly when Articles 1 and 2 of the Ozone and Climate Change Conventions are compared with Article 1 of the 1979 Convention on Long-range Transboundary Air Pollution. As a concept it has increasingly been displaced in favour of the broader 'impacts' or 'adverse effects' referred to in the previous section. Nevertheless, pollution represents an important form of environmental harm and many agreements are concerned solely or mainly with its prevention, reduction, and control.[493]

Although several formulations are used, treaty definitions of pollution adopted following the 1972 Stockholm Conference are considerably wider than the *Trail Smelter* approach. The unifying feature of these definitions is their focus on a detrimental alteration in quality, but this can be expressed narrowly, in terms of impact on resources or amenities useful to man, or more broadly, in terms of environmental conservation or amelioration.[494] The former approach is represented by the definition of marine pollution initially adopted by the Group of Experts on Scientific Aspects of Marine Pollution (GESAMP), which referred only to 'harm to living resources, hazard to human health, hindrance to marine activities including fishing, impairment of quality for use of sea water and reduction of amenities'.[495] The latter is found in most subsequent definitions of marine pollution, including the 1982 UNCLOS. The important point is that these definitions, although similar to the GESAMP definition, also include harm or the risk of harm to marine ecosystems, endangered species, and other forms of marine life.[496] As Tomczak observes, this makes the definition independent

---

[492] Handl, 26 *NRJ* (1986) 416–21.   [493] See in particular Chs 7, 8, 10.

[494] See Springer, 26 *ICLQ* (1977) 531; Tomczak, 8 *Marine Policy* (1984) 311; Springer, *International Law of Pollution* (Westport, Conn, 1983).

[495] See e.g. 1974 Paris Convention on Prevention of Marine Pollution from Land-based Sources, Article 1; 1976 Barcelona Convention for the Protection of the Mediterranean Sea Against Pollution, Article 2(a); 1977 OECD Recommendation C (77) 28 (Final) on Implementing a Regime of Equal Access and Non-Discrimination.

[496] See e.g. 1979 Geneva Convention on Long-range Transboundary Air Pollution, Article 1; 1982 UNCLOS, Article 1(4); 1992 OSPAR Convention, Article 1(d); 1995 Barcelona Convention for the Protection of the Mediterranean Sea Against Pollution, Article 2(a) and Tomczak, 8 *Marine Policy* (1984) 317.

of actual or intended human usage of the sea and its contents and focuses instead on the interdependence of human activity and nature. This broader formulation presents a much more clearly environmental perspective,[497] which now predominates in definitions favoured by OECD and the ILA.

Pollution cannot be defined simply in terms of its effects, however. All definitions confine the term to the introduction by man of substances or energy, whether directly or indirectly, into the environment. It is the relationship between these substances and their effects which together constitute pollution. This has several implications. First, it means that over-use of resources, or the impact of urban development on ecosystems, however harmful, is not 'pollution'. Some other concept, such as 'unsustainable utilization' or 'adverse effects', must be found for these problems. Secondly, despite the apparent breadth of conventional definitions, what constitutes pollution will often be limited in practice by reference to the substances whose discharge states have specifically agreed to control. Thus the annexes of prohibited or controlled substances found in treaties concerned with air pollution or land-based sources of pollution are crucial in determining what it is states are meant to regulate.[498] The annexes can be amended, however, so the general concept of pollution serves mainly as a residual category which can be invoked when necessary to deal with additional substances, and which allows the application of a precautionary approach to the listing of potential new pollutants.

In older treaties it is often only when discharges reach a certain level of seriousness, either in volume or in the context of their location, that they will constitute pollution. Treaties on land-based sources of marine pollution show considerable diversity in the range and volume of toxic emissions treated as pollution in different seas.[499] An extreme case is Principle 6 of the Stockholm Declaration, which refers to the discharge of toxic substances 'in such quantities or concentrations as to exceed the capacity of the environment to render them harmless'. Here the damage must be irreversible. Few treaties dealing with toxic substances have found this approach acceptable, however. A more recent development adopts the opposite approach by banning all discharges except those identified as harmless and listed accordingly. This form of 'reverse listing' is found in the 1996 revision of the London Dumping Convention. In effect it treats all waste dumping as 'pollution' unless it can be proved harmless, thus reversing the burden of proof.[500] In some cases any level of discharge will be presumed harmful and banned outright. A good example of this category is the treaty prohibition of any disposal of high-level radioactive material into the global commons.[501]

Thus, we can see that what 'pollution' means is, like the 'environment', significantly dependent on context and objective. While it is possible to talk of an obligation to prevent 'pollution', or to protect 'the environment', there is little point attempting a global definition of what are essentially terms with a variable content. The meaning which these terms have acquired will become more apparent in later chapters.

---

[497] Tomczak, ibid, 319–21.   [498] See *infra*, Chs 6, 8.   [499] *Infra*, Ch 8.
[500] Ibid.   [501] *Infra*, Ch 9.

5 CONSERVATION AND SUSTAINABLE USE
OF NATURAL RESOURCES

International law protecting the environment from pollution and others forms of damage is complemented by other rules, principles, and regulatory regimes which affect the conservation and sustainable utilization of natural resources. In particular, it is now possible to point to treaties which impose on states obligations to cooperate in conservation, sustainable utilization, and ecological protection intended to avoid over-exploitation and permanent loss of some categories of internationally significant resources. Marine fisheries and certain other shared living resources are included, but regional air masses, international watercourses, and common spaces are other examples. We also note below the emerging concept of sustainable utilization with respect to shared water resources and high-seas fisheries. These are potentially important developments in the law relation to natural resources, which we explore in Chapters 10–13. However, other, older, rules and general principles concerning the legal status and utilization of natural resources remain relevant to understanding the limitations of international law in this context.

5(1) LEGAL STATUS OF NATURAL RESOURCES

International law has traditionally regulated the use of natural resources indirectly by determining the basis on which rights are allocated among states. The legal status of natural resources varies according to whether the resource is under the sovereignty of one state, shared by several states, or held in common for the benefit of all. These categorizations have different impacts on the freedom of states to exploit a resource, and they have continuing relevance to an understanding of several important treaties or groups of treaties considered later. Questions of legal status are most significant in the conservation and use of high-seas fisheries, biological diversity, and freshwater resources.

(a) Permanent sovereignty over natural resources

In general, it was assumed in the early development of international law that control of natural resources depended on the acquisition of sovereignty over land territory and territorial seas.[502] Resolution of disputes concerning resources thus often took the form of boundary delimitations, as in the *Norwegian Fisheries Case*,[503] or alternatively centred on the status of a resource as shared or common property falling outside the exclusive control of any one state, as in the *Behring Sea Fur Seals* arbitration,[504] or the

---

[502] Brownlie, 162 *Recueil des Cours* (1979) 272–86.
[503] ICJ Reports (1951) 116. See also *Jan Mayen Case*, ICJ Reports (1991) 38.
[504] Moore, 1 *Int Arb Awards* (1898) 755, repr in 1 *Int Env L Reps* (1999) 43, and see *infra*, Ch 13.

Icelandic Fisheries Cases.[505] No distinction existed in this respect between sovereignty over living resources, or non-renewable resources such as minerals.[506] Once a resource fell within the category of exclusive sovereignty, such as forests, international law placed few limitations on its use.

The principle of permanent sovereignty over natural resources which developed after 1945 was mainly a response by newly independent developing states to the problem of foreign ownership of their mineral resources, notably oil. Their efforts resulted in the adoption in 1962 by the UN General Assembly of resolution 1803 XVII.[507] It proclaimed 'The right of peoples and nations to permanent sovereignty over their natural wealth and resources', and the preamble recommended that 'the sovereign right of every state to dispose of its natural wealth and resources should be respected...in accordance with their national interests'. This resolution draws no distinction between living and non-living resources and makes no reference to any duty of conservation, although it does recognize the desirability of promoting international cooperation for the economic development of developing countries and the benefits 'derivable' from the exchanges of technical and scientific information in the development and use of resources. Whilst not per se binding, resolution 1803 was regarded by some states as declaratory of existing law; it has also been referred to as such by international arbitral tribunals.[508]

In 1974, two years after the Stockholm Conference, the General Assembly adopted two further resolutions. The 'Declaration on the Establishment of a New International Economic Order' (NIEO)[509] reaffirmed permanent sovereignty over natural resources and the right to nationalize them. The Charter of Economic Rights and Duties of States asserted that 'Every state has and shall freely exercise full permanent sovereignty including possession, use and disposal, over all its natural resources'.[510] By emphasizing the apparently untrammelled sovereignty of states over natural resources, these resolutions might be thought to imply that any restrictions would for the most part require agreement between the states concerned. In reality, however, these resolutions, and the strong support given by developing states to the concept of permanent sovereignty, were primarily directed at asserting the right to nationalize or control foreign-owned resources and industries, free from some of the older rules which protected foreign investments. Despite their categorical pronouncements, they have not

---

[505] ICJ Reports (1974) 3, 175. See *infra*, Ch 13.

[506] See e.g. 1958 Continental Shelf Convention, which defines 'natural resources' as consisting of 'the mineral and other non-living resources of the sea-bed and subsoil, together with living organisms belonging to a sedentary species'.

[507] For drafting history see Schrijver, *Sovereignty over Natural Resources*, Ch 2.

[508] *Texaco v Libya*, 53 ILR (1977) 389; *BP v Libya*, 53 ILR (1977) 297. See generally Brownlie, 162 *Recueil des cours* (1979); Schachter, *Sharing the World's Resources* (New York, 1977) 124, and Schrijver, *Sovereignty over Natural Resources*.

[509] UNGA Res 3201 (S-VI) (1974). See Schrijver, *Sovereignty over Natural Resources*, Ch 3.

[510] Article 2, UNGA Res 3281 XXIX (1974). The United States and a number of other Western states voted against this resolution or abstained. See Brownlie, 162 *Recueil des Cours* (1979) 267–9; White, 24 *ICLQ* (1975) 542; Chatterjee, 40 *ICLQ* (1991) 669; Schrijver, *Sovereignty over Natural Resources*, Ch 3; *Texaco v Libya*, 53 ILR (1977) 389.

constrained the development of treaties and rules of customary international law concerning conservation of natural resources and environment protection that qualify
this sovereignty. This will be observed below in the rules applicable to shared natural
resources, and the resources of common spaces, notably the high seas. Nor, as we shall
see, has the concept of permanent sovereignty prevented resource conservation within
a state's territory from being treated as a question of common concern for all states.
Treaties such as the 1968 African Convention on the Conservation of Nature, the 1972
World Heritage Convention, CITES 1973, and the 1992 Convention on Biological
Diversity exemplify this point.[511]

That is not to say that sovereignty does not remain the cornerstone of the rights and
duties of states over natural resources within their own territory.[512] It is reiterated, as
we saw earlier, in Stockholm Principle 21 and Rio Principle 2, and in the Biological
Diversity Convention and other agreements, albeit qualified by responsibilities for the
protection of other states and common spaces. But as Schrijver observes, 'It is clear that
sovereignty has become pervaded with environmental concerns'.[513] Contemporary
sovereignty is in no sense absolute or unfettered. As many writers have argued, new
concepts of resource utilization based on notions of economic security, ecological
protection, and common interest involve a redefinition of sovereignty itself, so that
it is no longer a basis for exclusion of others, but entails instead 'a commitment to
co-operate for the good of the international community at large'.[514] It must be exercised responsibly.

(b) Shared natural resources

'Shared natural resources' represent an intermediate category.[515] These resources
do not fall wholly within the exclusive control of one state, but neither are they the
common property of all states. The essence of this concept is a limited form of community interest, usually involving a small group of states in geographical contiguity,
which exercise shared rights over the resources in question. Examples considered in
later chapters include international watercourses, regional air masses, and migratory
species.

A succession of UN General Assembly resolutions has recognized the general principle that states do not have unlimited sovereignty with regard to shared resources.
In 1973, Resolution 3129 XXVIII called for adequate international standards for the
conservation and utilization of natural resources common to two or more states to
be established and affirmed that there should be cooperation between states on the
basis of information exchange and prior consultation. Article 3 of the 1974 Charter
of Economic Rights and Duties of States set out the same principle more fully: 'In the

---

[511] See *infra*, Chs 11–12.   [512] Schrijver, *Sovereignty over Natural Resources*, 250.
[513] Ibid, 168. See in particular his Chs 4, 8.
[514] Handl, 1 *YbIEL* (1990) 32. See also Schrijver, *Sovereignty over Natural Resources*, Ch 1; Fawcett, 123
Recueil des Cours (1968) 237, 239; Brownlie, 162 *Recueil des cours* (1979) 282; Kiss, 175 *Recueil des cours*
(1982) 229ff; Schachter, *Sharing the World's Resources*, and see *infra*, Chs 12, 13.
[515] See generally Brownlie, 162 *Recueil des Cours* (1979) 289ff.

exploitation of natural resources shared by two or more countries each state must co-operate on the basis of a system of information and prior consultation in order to achieve optimum use of such resources without causing damage to the legitimate interests of others'. Although the stress of this Charter as a whole still lay with the use of resources for the economic benefit of developing states, Article 3 clearly qualified the sovereignty states enjoy with regard to shared resources. However, the terms 'optimum use' and 'legitimate interests' are not defined and we have to look elsewhere in treaties and customary law for their content. These resolutions formed the basis for the adoption by the Governing Council of UNEP in 1978 of the 'Principles of Conduct, etc in the Conservation and Harmonious Utilization of Natural Resources Shared by Two or More States'.[516] The General Assembly took note of these 'Principles', including the statement that they are 'without prejudice to the binding nature of those rules already recognized as such in international law', and it called on states to use them as 'guidelines and recommendations' in the formulation of bilateral or multilateral conventions, in such a way as to enhance the development and interests of all states, in particular developing countries.[517]

The Assembly's reluctance to give its full endorsement to the 'Principles', and the use of language which avoids the implication of existing legal obligation, stems from the controversy and opposition earlier resolutions on the subject had aroused.[518] This indicates that the rules contained in the 1978 Principles were not necessarily regarded as settled law, nor as enjoying the support of all states, although as we shall see in later chapters they do in many respects reflect contemporary international law and the practice of a significant number of countries. Nevertheless, they have not subsequently lost their controversial character. At the time of their adoption several countries declared that the 'Principles' confirmed the sovereign right to exploit their own resources in accordance with national laws and policy, subject only to an obligation not to cause injury to others; continued opposition to the concept of 'shared natural resources' led to the removal of all reference to it in the ILC's codification of the law relating to international watercourses.[519] Moreover, the most notable omission from the 'Principles' and from UN resolutions concerns their failure to define what resources should be treated as shared. The Executive Director of UNEP indicated his belief that at least the following are 'shared natural resources': river systems, enclosed and semi-enclosed seas, air sheds, mountain chains, forests, conservation areas, and migratory species.[520] Another proposed definition refers to 'an element of the natural environment used by man which constitutes a bio-geophysical unity, and is located in the territory of two or

---

[516] 17 *ILM* (1978) 1091. See Schrijver, *Sovereignty over Natural Resources*, 129–33; Sand, in R-J Dupuy, *The Future of International Law of the Environment* (Hague Academy, Dordrecht, 1984) 51–72; Adede, 5 *EPL* (1979) 6; Lammers, *Pollution of International Watercourses* (Dordrecht, 1984) 335–8.

[517] UNGA Res 34/186 (1979).

[518] Five states voted against UNGA Res 3129; 43 abstained, and 77 voted for. See also II *YbILC* (1983) Pt 1, 195, and Adede, 5 *EPL* (1979) 6. The WCED Experts Group preferred the term 'transboundary natural resources'.

[519] UNEP IG/12/2 (1978) para 15, and see *infra*, Ch 10.   [520] UNEP/GC/44 (1975) para 86.

more states'.[521] The working group drafting the 'Principles' did not discuss the issue or reach any conclusions, however.

The UNEP Principles themselves endorse the view that shared resources are subject to obligations of transboundary cooperation and equitable utilization (Principle 1). The requirements of cooperation are comparable to those considered earlier in section 4 of this chapter and follow closely the rules applied to shared watercourses in the *Lac Lanoux* arbitration and state practice, which are considered further in Chapter 6. Principle 4 further calls for states to make environmental impact assessments before engaging in any activity with respect to resources which may significantly affect the environment of another state sharing the resource. In common with the obligation to prevent transboundary harm also outlined in section 4, Principle 3 affirms responsibility for ensuring that adverse environmental effects on other states or on areas beyond national jurisdiction are avoided or reduced to the maximum extent possible, particularly where the utilization or conservation of the resource may be affected, or public health in other states endangered. The Principles call for states to consider establishing joint commissions for consultations on environmental problems relating to the protection and use of shared resources, and they recognize a duty to cooperate in informing other states likely to be affected in cases of emergency or by 'sudden grave natural events' related to shared resources. Principles 13 and 14 adopt the principles of non-discrimination and equal access, considered further in Chapter 5. In many respects therefore, the legal rules and principles applicable to transboundary pollution are also relevant to the broader context of natural resources shared by a number of states.

The main purpose for regulating the use and conservation of a shared resource is to ensure a balance of interests between the parties concerned. The concept of equitable utilization has been employed in arbitral awards, ICJ decisions, treaties, and the work of the ILC and other codification bodies in resolving conflicts of interest affecting shared resources.[522] UNEP's Principles have thus adopted a well-established concept of international law when they rely on equitable utilization as the basis of cooperation, although to regard all fifteen principles as a definition of this concept is to give it an unusually wide interpretation. No attempt is made to determine what constitutes an equitable allocation of a shared resource among the parties concerned, however, or to settle questions of priority and geographical inequity which have proved in practice to be the most contentious questions affecting such resources. Equitable utilization is best understood in the context in which it is employed; reference should be made to chapters on international watercourses, protection of the atmosphere, and marine living resources for examples of its application.

(c) Common property

Common property, in international law, refers primarily to areas beyond national jurisdiction, of which the high seas and superjacent airspace are the most important

---

[521] UNEP/IG/12/2 (1978) para 16.   [522] See *infra*, section 5(2).

examples. These common spaces are open for legitimate and reasonable use by all states, and may not be appropriated to the exclusive sovereignty of any one state.[523]As we have already seen, the principles of international law which require states to prevent and control pollution and environmental damage have been extended to protect these common spaces, which are now regulated by a series of multilateral treaties for this purpose.[524]

The common-property doctrine extends to most of the living resources of these areas, including fish and mammals found in the high seas, a view confirmed in the *Behring Sea Fur Seals Arbitration*[525] and subsequently codified by treaty. Birds and other species of wildlife that inhabit common spaces or migrate through them are similarly regarded. Once living resources are held in common in this way, no single user can have exclusive rights over them, nor the right to prevent others from joining in their exploitation.[526] Such living resources do, however, become exclusive property once reduced into possession by capture or taking. The common-property doctrine is not to be confused with the more recent 'common heritage' concept, a specialized regime applied to certain mineral resources, nor with 'shared natural resources', where, as indicated above, rights are shared by a limited number of states.

An important factor contributing to the classification of living resources as common property is that they have generally been so plentiful that the cost of asserting and defending exclusive rights exceeds the advantages to be gained. A regime of open access has generally been to everyone's advantage. However, as Hardin has observed,[527] the 'inherent logic of the commons remorselessly generates tragedy', as the availability of a free resource leads to over-exploitation and minimizes the interest of any individual state in conservation and restraint. Common-property resources cannot effectively be protected without the cooperation of all states taking the resource; this has generally been difficult to obtain once resource exploitation has become established. As resources become less plentiful, and particular stocks or species accordingly become more valuable, perceptions of the costs and benefits of exclusivity change. This occurred in relation to high-seas fisheries from the 1950s onwards, resulting in increasing pressure for states to extend their jurisdiction over the resources of the sea and of the seabed.[528]

Extension of the limits of coastal states' exclusive jurisdiction over fisheries led to numerous conflicts with those distant water states asserting high-seas freedoms. In the *Icelandic Fisheries Cases* in 1974, the ICJ made significant observations on the character of high-seas fishing resources as common property. While affirming that established fishing states continued to have high-seas rights beyond the twelve-mile

---

[523] 1958 Geneva Convention on the High Seas, Articles 1–2; 1982 UNCLOS, Articles 87, 89. See also 1967 Outer Space Treaty, Article 2.

[524] See *infra*, Chs 6, 7, 8.   [525] *Supra* n 436, and *infra*, Ch 13.

[526] Christy and Scott, *The Commonwealth in Ocean Fisheries* (2nd edn, Baltimore, 1972) Ch 2, and see *infra*, Ch 13.

[527] 162 *Science* (1968) 1243–8. See also Wijkman, 36 *Int Org* (1982) 511, and *infra*, Ch 13.

[528] See *infra*, Ch 13.

limit of coastal state fisheries jurisdiction, the Court found that all the states concerned had an obligation of reasonable use which required them to take account of the needs of conservation and to allow coastal states preferential rights in the allocation of high-seas stocks. There was, in the Court's view, an obligation on all parties to negotiate in good faith with a view to reaching an equitable solution.[529]

This decision is important for two reasons. First, it opened the way for a much more radical transfer to coastal-state jurisdiction of much of the world's fishing resources, effected by the 3rd UN Conference on the Law of the Sea and quickly adopted by coastal states in the form of 200-mile exclusive fisheries or economic zones.[530] Thus marine living resources are now for the most part no longer common property, although significant exceptions to this are found in the form of highly migratory species, other stocks which straddle both coastal zones and the high seas, and surplus stocks located within national maritime zones but available for exploitation by other states.[531] Moreover, transferring resources from common property has in many cases meant not that they fall under the exclusive jurisdiction of any one state, but constitute shared stocks straddling a number of national maritime jurisdictions, as in the North Sea or Mediterranean, and to which the principle of equitable utilization will still apply. Thus there remains a substantial international interest in the conservation of these resources even within national maritime boundaries.

Second, the *Icelandic Fisheries Cases* indicated for the first time that states had a duty in customary law not merely to allocate common resources equitably, but also to conserve them for future benefit in the interests of sustainable utilization. Conservation in this sense has become the basis of a number of multilateral fisheries agreements, starting with the 1958 Geneva Convention on Fishing and Conservation of the Living Resources of the High Seas, and more recently the 1995 Agreement on Straddling and Highly Migratory Fish Stocks, which amplifies the relevant articles of the 1982 UNCLOS. It is also recognized in a number of wildlife agreements, and accords with the emphasis on sustainable utilization favoured by the World Conservation Strategy and the Brundtland Commission.[532]

There remain problems, however, in implementing conservation measures to restrain over-exploitation and ensure sustainable utilization, whether these are based on common property or exclusive jurisdiction solutions. The concept of 'conservation' remains closely related to supplying human needs, albeit on a sustainable basis.[533] Moreover, whether expressed as an obligation of reasonable use, equitable utilization, conservation, or sustainable use, the customary rules, though a useful guide, are often too vague and general to be of practical use. It is, in such circumstances, of vital importance that the activities of all states with regard to common spaces and com-

---

[529] ICJ Reports (1974) 3; Churchill, 24 *ICLQ* (1975) 82, and *infra*, Ch 13. On the principle of 'reasonable use', see *infra*, section 5(2).

[530] See *infra*, Ch 13.

[531] 1982 UNCLOS, Articles 62(2) 63, 64, 66. See also Articles 69, 70, which confer rights on landlocked and geographically disadvantaged states and see *infra*, Ch 13.

[532] See *infra*, Ch 11.   [533] Ibid.

mon property resources be subjected to internationally agreed and prescribed regimes of conservation and environmental control. These are generally best constituted and implemented through treaties, supervised by intergovernmental commissions or similar bodies which can regularly promulgate the necessary rules in a flexible and sustained manner, easily adaptable to changing scientific knowledge and advice and changing economic, social, and political circumstances.[534] The protection of common spaces, and conservation and sustainable use of their living resources is thus a complex issue in which scientific, moral, ethical, political, economic, social, and technological issues are inextricably intertwined and which do not always coincide.

(d) Common heritage

Although the term 'common heritage' is frequently used loosely by environmentalists to refer either to all the living and non-living resources of nature or to the global environment as an ecological entity, for legal purposes the term is currently confined to the narrow meaning attributed to it in two conventions, namely, the 1979 Moon Treaty and the 1982 UNCLOS.[535] Though both apply the concept to areas beyond national jurisdiction, they relate in this respect only to their non-living resources, to which in the latter treaty a precise and narrow definition is given. The concept was put forward by Malta to the United National General Assembly as the basis on which a new regime for exploiting the resources of the sea-bed in the interest of all mankind could be built.[536] It was included both in a 'Declaration of Principles Governing the Sea-bed and Ocean Floor'[537] and in Articles 136 and 137 of the 1982 UNCLOS, which pronounce the resources of the deep sea-bed beyond national jurisdiction (the Area) to be 'the common heritage of mankind', vested in mankind as a whole, on whose behalf an International Sea-bed Authority (ISBA) established under the UNCLOS shall act. All activities in the Area must be conducted under this Authority.

As employed in the Moon Treaty and the 1982 UNCLOS, the concept of common heritage implies that the resources of these areas cannot be appropriated to the exclusive sovereignty of states but must be conserved and exploited for the benefit of all, without discrimination. The concept thus differs from common property in allowing all states to share in the rewards, even if unable to participate in the actual process of extraction. The ISBA represents an elaborate form of international management and regulation in order to control the allocation of exploitation rights and the equitable sharing of benefits.[538] The establishment of some form of international management

---

[534] See *supra*, Ch 2, section 5.

[535] See generally Baslar, *The Concept of the Common Heritage of Mankind in International Law* (The Hague, 1998); Cheng, *Studies in International Space Law* (Oxford, 1997) 365–80; Ogley, *Internationalising the Sea-bed* (Aldershot, 1984); Pardo and Christol, in Macdonald and Johnston (eds), *Structure and Process of International Law* (The Hague, 1983) 643; Kiss, 175 *Recueil des Cours* (1982) 99; Brownlie, 162 *Recueil des Cours* 1979) 289–300.

[536] Permanent Mission of Malta to the UN Sec Gen, *Note verbale*, 17 Aug 1967, UN Doc A/6095. See Ogley, *Whose Common Heritage? Creating a Law for the Sea-bed* (Guildford, 1975) 17–25.

[537] UNGA Res 2749 XXV (1970) adopted 108 to none, with 14 abstentions.   [538] See *supra* Ch 2.

is also envisaged by the Moon Treaty.[539] Both schemes require the states concerned to take measures of environmental protection. Article 145 of the 1982 UNCLOS gives the ISBA authority to adopt 'appropriate rules regulations and procedures' to prevent, reduce, and control pollution or 'interference with the ecological balance of the marine environment', and to protect natural resources, flora and fauna.[540] Article 209 requires states to adopt laws and regulations 'no less effective' than the rules approved by the ISBA. Common heritage resources, unlike common property, are thus subject to regulation by a strong international authority, which, as we saw in Chapter 2, is in this respect unique among international institutions with environmental responsibilities.

Although, in convening the 3rd UNCLOS, the General Assembly stated that it was 'conscious that the problems of ocean space are closely related and need to be considered as a whole',[541] the 1982 UNCLOS neither applied the common heritage regime to the waters above the deep sea-bed, nor to the living resources found anywhere in the oceans. Nor has the concept yet found any further explicit applications and there remains the objection that common heritage is still of doubtful legal status. It was not employed in the Ozone Convention.[542] The General Assembly declined to adopt a Maltese proposal to designate the global climate as the common heritage of mankind, preferring instead to describe it as a matter of 'common concern'. Similarly, the parties to the Antarctic Treaty system have adopted a comprehensive regime for the protection of that area and its dependent and associated ecosystems 'in the interest of mankind as a whole',[543] but they have avoided direct analogy with the moon or deep sea-bed. A case can be made for the proposition that Antarctica nevertheless has many of the features of a common heritage regime, but such a view remains controversial and does not take full account of the complex legal and political status of that continent, nor of the absence of any scheme for sharing resources.[544]

Some conventions do use the term or others such as the 'world heritage of mankind' in their preambles in a hortatory sense.[545] But these are better viewed, like the term 'common concern' as expressions of the common interest of all states in certain forms of ecological protection, and not as attempts to internationalise ownership of resources. Common heritage is important, however, in providing one of the most developed applications of trusteeship or fiduciary relationship in an environmental context,[546] and in that sense it represents a significant precedent whose implications are further explored in the following chapter.

---

[539] Article 11(5).

[540] See Regulations on Prospecting and Exploration for Polymetallic Nodules in the Area, Doc ISBA/6/A/18, approved by the ISBA Assembly on 13 July 2000.

[541] UNGA Res 2750 XXV (1970) adopted by 108 to 7, with 6 abstentions.   [542] See *infra*, Ch 6.

[543] 1991 Protocol to the Antarctic Treaty on Environmental Protection, Preamble, on which see *supra* Ch 2, section 5.

[544] See Kiss, 175 *Recueil des Cours* (1982).

[545] E.g. 1972 World Heritage Convention, and see *infra*, Ch 12 for other examples.

[546] Kiss, 175 *Recueil des Cours* (1982) and see *supra* Ch 2.

5(2) RULES AND PRINCIPLES OF NATURAL RESOURCES LAW

(a) Conservation and sustainable use of natural resources

In 1982 the World Charter for Nature called for 'All areas of the earth, both land and sea' to be subject to principles of conservation.[547] It required 'Special protection' to be given to unique areas, representative ecosystems, and habitats of rare or endangered species; ecosystems and land, atmospheric and marine resources had to be managed to achieve 'optimum sustainable productivity' without endangering other ecosystems or species. Living resources were not be used in excess of their capacity for regeneration, and irreversible damage to 'nature' was to be avoided.

The 1992 Rio Declaration contains nothing as specific in regard to natural resources. Principle 8 of the Rio Declaration talks only of the need to 'reduce and eliminate unsustainable patterns of production and consumption'. Nevertheless, the idea that sustainable development involves limits on the utilization of land, water and other natural resources can be observed in the Biological Diversity and Climate Change Conventions and the terms 'sustainable utilization' or 'sustainable use' are expressly employed in Rio and post-Rio agreements.[548] Article 2 of the Biodiversity Convention defines sustainable use as 'use . . . in a way and at a rate that does not lead to long-term decline of biological diversity.' The UN Fish Stocks Agreement also refers to 'long-term sustainability'. Older agreements refer to 'conservation' of natural resources, 'maximum (or optimum) sustainable yield', or 'optimum sustainable productivity'.[549] While the precise meaning of these terms may not be the same, the idea of sustainable use is common to all of them. The precautionary principle, endorsed by Principle 15 of the Rio Declaration is also an important element of sustainable utilization, because it addresses the key question of uncertainty in the prediction of environmental effects.[550] Underlying all of these agreements is a concern for the more rational use and conservation of natural resources and a desire to strengthen existing conservation law.

How far it can be assumed that international law now imposes on states a general obligation of conservation and sustainable use of natural resources and the natural environment remains an open question. These concepts, and the extent to which they govern the exploitation of natural resources, are considered more fully

---

[547] 23 *ILM* (1983) 455. See *infra*, Ch 11.

[548] 1992 Biological Diversity Convention, Articles 2, 6, 8 and 10, *infra*, Ch 11; 1994 Desertification Convention, Articles 2 and 3; 1995 Agreement for the Conservation of Straddling and Highly Migratory Fish Stocks, Articles 2 and 5, *infra*, Ch 13; 1997 Convention on the Non-Navigational Uses of International Watercourses, Article 5(1), *infra*, Ch 10; 2006 International Tropical Timber Agreement, Article 1. See Wälde, in Schrijver and Weiss, *International Law and Sustainable Development*, Ch 6; Rayfuse, ibid, Ch 19; Beyerlin, 63 *ZAÖRV* (2003) 417; Epiney, ibid, 377; Bekhechi, 101 *RGDIP* (1997) 101.

[549] The World Charter for Nature refers to 'optimum sustainable productivity' (para I 4); the 1958 Geneva Convention on Fishing and the Conservation of the Living Resources of the High Seas uses the term 'optimum sustainable yield' (Article 2); the 1982 UN Convention on the Law of the Sea refers to 'maximum sustainable yield' (Article 61); see *infra*, Ch 11, and for a scientific perspective Hilborn, Walters and Ludwig, 26 *Ann Rev Ecol Syst* (1995) 45–67.

[550] See e.g. 1995 Agreement on Straddling and Highly Migratory Fish Stocks, Article 6; *Southern Bluefin Tuna Case (Provisional Measures)* (1999) ITLOS Nos 3&4, and *supra* section 4(2).

in Chapters 10–13. The *Icelandic Fisheries Cases*[551] and various fisheries treaties do support the existence of a customary obligation to co-operate in the conservation and sustainable use of the common property resources of the high seas. To these precedents must be added the explicit references to 'sustainable utilisation' of water in the 1997 Convention on International Watercourses.[552] The provisions of a growing body of global and regional treaties concerned with biological diversity, wildlife conservation, habitat protection, endangered species, specially protected marine areas, and cultural and natural heritage also suggest that conservation and sustainable use of natural resources and ecosystems have acquired a wider legal significance beyond that implied in the *Icelandic Fisheries Cases*.[553]

Some of these agreements, such as the 1972 World Heritage Convention,[554] and the 1992 Biological Diversity Convention,[555] impose little by way of concrete obligations, however, or deal only with particular aspects of the conservation problem, as in the 1973 Convention on International Trade in Endangered Species, or the 1994 Desertification Convention. It may thus be said that it is difficult to treat these regimes, or the limited indications of customary rules derived from case law, as adding up to the systematic endorsement of an obligation of conservation and sustainable use of all natural resources in international law. A reasonably comprehensive pattern of international co-operation now exists for the protection of common areas, such as the high seas or deep sea-bed, and for Antarctica, based respectively on the 1982 UNCLOS and related agreements,[556] and on treaties forming the Antarctic Treaty System, including the 1991 Protocol to the Antarctic Treaty on Environmental Protection.[557] However, it cannot necessarily be assumed that comparable obligations apply to areas which fall wholly within the boundaries of national sovereignty, such as forests, where the adoption of binding commitments has been more difficult.[558]

The evidence of treaty commitments, coupled with indications of supporting state practice, might be sufficient to crystallize conservation and sustainable use of natural resources into an independent normative standard of international law.[559] However, it is clear that states retain substantial discretion in giving effect to the alleged principle, unless specific international action has been agreed. Thus, to return to the example of tropical forests, little of value can be inferred from a broad principle of sustainable use without reference to state practice and the practice of international

---

[551] ICJ Reports (1974) 3 and 175.   [552] *Infra*, Ch 10.

[553] See Ch 7, 11, and 12, and also New Zealand Resources Management Act, 1991, based explicitly on the WCED'S concept of sustainable development.

[554] Lyster, *International Wildlife Law* (Cambridge, 1985) Ch 11, and see *Commonwealth of Australia v State of Tasmania* (1983) 46 ALR 625, 697 ff, per Mason J, and cf Gibbs CJ, 658–66. See *infra*, Ch 12.

[555] *Infra*, Ch 11.   [556] *Infra*, Ch 7.   [557] *Infra*, Ch 4, section 3(5).

[558] See 1992 Rio Non-Legally Binding Authoritative Statement of Principles for a Global Consensus on the Management, Conservation and Sustainable Development of all Types of Forests, 3 *YbIEL* (1992) 830; UN, Non-Legally Binding Instrument on all Types of Forests, UNGA Res 62/98 (2008).

[559] See Handl, 1 *YbIEL* (1990) 25; Munro and Lammers, *Environmental Protection and Sustainable Development*, 44.

organizations and lending agencies such as the World Bank.[560] Only where specific international regimes have been developed, as in the management of fisheries and water resources, can it be said that the concept of sustainable use has acquired some normative content or could potentially be used to judge the permissibility of natural resource exploitation.[561]

(b) Reasonable use

The principle that common spaces are open for use by all nationals entails an obligation not to abuse this right or to interfere unreasonably with the freedoms of others. Article 2 of the 1958 High Seas Convention requires states to act with reasonable regard for the interests of others, and the same principle is reiterated in the 1982 UNCLOS, Article 87(2). Article 2 of the 1958 Convention formed the basis for the International Court's judgment in favour of the United Kingdom in the *Icelandic Fisheries Case*.[562] The court referred to the parties' obligations to undertake negotiations in good faith to reach an equitable solution of their differences, and to pay due regard to the interests of other states in the conservation and equitable exploitation of high seas fishing resources. Similarly, in the *Nuclear Tests Cases*,[563] Judge De Castro referred to Article 2(2) in the context of alleged high seas pollution emanating from atmospheric nuclear tests. State practice discussed in Chapter 9 has afforded some support for the view that such tests are permissible in so far as they are reasonable, although more recent declarations by nuclear states and the trend of global and regional treaties now favours a complete prohibition.

There is no judicial authority for the application of a reasonableness tests in judging the permissibility of other forms of pollution. But the inference that pollution from any source may be illegal if it unreasonably interferes with fishing or other uses of the oceans is supported by Article 11 of the 1983 Quito Protocol to UNEP's Lima Convention for the Protection of the Marine Environment of the South East Pacific, and by Article 4(6) of the 1986 Noumea Convention for the Protection of the Natural Resources and Environment of the South Pacific Region.[564]

Reasonableness is essentially a basis for resolving competing claims where otherwise lawful activities conflict. It is not as such a principle of substantive environmental protection. While as a last resort it may enable states to argue that pollution or the exploitation of natural resources are illegal if so excessive that the interests of other states are disproportionately affected, it is not a substitute for other, more concrete rules limiting the right of states to pollute or requiring sustainable use of resources.

---

[560] See e.g. World Bank/FAO/UNEP/WRI 1985 Tropical Forest Action Plan, the International Tropical Timber Organization's 1990 Guidelines for the Sustainable Management of Natural Tropical Forests, and its 1992 Criteria for and Measurement of Sustainable Forest Management and generally, Handl, *Multilateral Development Banking: Environmental Principles and Concepts etc.* (The Hague, 2001).

[561] See *infra*, Ch 10 and 13.   [562] ICJ Reports (1974) 3 and 175.

[563] ICJ Reports (1974) 253 and 457.   [564] See *infra*, Ch 8.

(c) Equity and equitable utilization

The role of equity in international environmental law, as in general international law, is controversial. Some writers see most environmental problems as requiring 'equitable solutions', in which more concrete rules of law are displaced or interpreted in favour of an *ad hoc* balancing of interests. Used in this general sense equity is little different from concepts of reasonableness or abuse of rights and suffers the same objections of encouraging instability and relativity in the legal system. There is of course nothing to stop states agreeing to settle disputes on an 'equitable' basis, and in some cases of air and water pollution they have indeed found it in their interests to do so,[565] but political accommodation should not be confused with determinations of international law.

In some situations, however, rules of law may require resort to equity to resolve disputes. 'Equitable utilization' is generally regarded as the primary rule of customary law governing the use and allocation of international water resources,[566] and, as we have seen, UNEP's 'principles' concerning other shared natural resources follow the same view. In the *Icelandic Fisheries Cases* the ICJ also referred to the need for an equitable allocation of common property fishing stocks,[567] while the ILC's proposals for equitable limitations on the entitlement of states to conduct risky activities within their territory suggests the possibility of more novel applications of the principle.[568]

The 'equitable' utilization of shared or common property natural resources entails a balancing of interests and consideration of all relevant factors. What these factors are, and how they should be balanced depends entirely on the context of each case. No useful purpose can be served by attempting generalized definitions of what is essentially an exercise of discretion, whether by judges or other decision-makers. This discretion can be structured, however, and rendered more predictable, by careful analysis of international practice or by explicit recognition of relevant criteria in treaties or other instruments.[569] Moreover, as later chapters will show, the negotiation of equitable entitlements to the exploitation of natural resources can be facilitated by cooperation through intergovernmental institutions.[570]

Apart from its generality, and limited capacity for prescribing predictable outcomes, equitable utilization is sometimes also deficient in addressing environmental problems only from the perspective of those states sharing sovereignty over the resource or engaged in its actual exploitation. It is thus less well suited to accommodating common interests, or the protection of common areas, since these require a wider representation in any process for determining a balance of interests.

---

[565] See *infra*, Chs 6 and 10.   [566] See 1997 UN Watercourses Convention, Article 6, *infra*, Ch 10.
[567] See *infra*, Ch 13.   [568] 2001 Articles on Transboundary Harm, Articles 9–10, *supra* section 4.
[569] See e.g. the 1997 UN Watercourses Convention, *infra*, Ch 10, but cf Brownlie, 162 *Recueil des Cours* (1979) 287. Brownlie is too dismissive of equity as a major source of principles for resource allocation. Cf Schachter, *Sharing the World's Resources*, 64–83.
[570] Schachter, *Sharing the World's Resources*, 70, and see *infra*, Ch 10 and 13.

(d) The precautionary principle and natural resources

The precautionary principle or approach is considered fully in section 4 above, but it is no less relevant to sustainable use of living natural resources, including fisheries, endangered species, biological diversity and forests. The moratorium on commercial whaling is one of the earliest examples of a precautionary approach.[571] Similarly, the 'Berne Criteria' for the listing and de-listing of endangered species under the 1973 Convention on International Trade in Endangered Species require de-listing to be 'approached with caution' and on the basis of 'positive scientific evidence that the plant or animal can withstand the exploitation resulting from the removal of protection'.[572] The 9th Conference of the Parties in 1994 resolved to apply the precautionary principle 'so that scientific uncertainty should not be used as a reason for failing to act in the best interests of conservation of the species'. Both examples show how Rio Principle 15 has come to influence the interpretation and application of multilateral conservation treaties concluded many years earlier.

What action states should take when they decide to adopt precautionary conservation measures varies just as much in this context as in any other, however. For example, application of a precautionary approach to high seas fisheries is justified not only by the level of uncertainty surrounding fisheries data, but also by the lack of EIA procedures for exploitation of fish stocks, the political misuse of scientific input, and the historically weak compliance and enforcement regime for high seas fishing. Article 6 of the 1995 UN Agreement on Straddling and Highly Migratory Fish Stocks seeks to remedy these deficiencies by improving data collection and techniques for dealing with risk and uncertainty. The precautionary approach and other provisions of the Agreement have for the first time given international fisheries law an environmental and inter-generational aspect consistent with the pursuit of sustainable development.[573] At the same time, the parties resisted any suggestion that new or exploratory high seas fishing could not take place in the absence of adequate scientific knowledge. Such fisheries would be subject to 'cautious conservation and management measures' until the impact on long-term sustainability could be assessed properly. Moreover, it would in practice be left to the parties to regional fisheries agreements to decide whether threatened stocks should be subject to a moratorium on fishing. Even if fully implemented, the principal impact of applying a precautionary approach as defined in Article 6 will only be to 'improve decision-making for fishery resource conservation and management'. Any wider implications for the level of fisheries protection, or the stringency of conservation measures, will flow from changes in the attitude and policies of fishing states, or from other provisions of the Agreement, not from any commitment they may have made to 'apply the precautionary approach'.

---

[571] *Infra*, Ch 13.   [572] *Infra*, Ch 12.

[573] Garcia, in, FAO, *Precautionary Approach to Fisheries*, Technical Paper 350/2 (Rome, 1996) 3; Boyle and Freestone, *International Law and Sustainable Development*, Ch 7; Hewison, 11 *IJMCL* (1996) 301, and *infra*, Ch 13, section 6.

Thus, while it is clear that the precautionary principle or approach is now part of international law on sustainable use of natural resources, its precise implications can only be understood in the particular context of specific treaties.

(e) Abuse of rights

It has been said that it is not unreasonable to regard 'abuse of rights' as a general principle of international law, but that it is a doctrine which must be used with 'studied restraint'.[574] Some versions of the principle are more relevant to environmental questions than others. The concept can be treated as one which limits the exercise of rights in bad faith, maliciously or arbitrarily.[575] In this form it is found in the law of the sea,[576] and in some of the rules examined earlier, including the duty to negotiate and consult in good faith referred to in the *Lac Lanoux* arbitration and the *Icelandic Fisheries Cases*. This tells us nothing about the content of legal rights and duties but is essentially a method of interpreting them.[577]

An alternative view treats abuse of rights as simply another way of formulating a doctrine of reasonableness or a balancing of interests. Some authors regard the *Trail Smelter* arbitration and other formulations of the *sic utere tuo* principle as indicative of an implicit abuse of rights doctrine in this form. Once again, the question is not whether it is correct to do so, although some writers deny that it is, but whether this interpretation adds anything useful to the elaboration of substantive rights and obligations concerning transboundary relations, the prevention of pollution, or the conservation and use of resources. Lauterpacht observed that in the relative absence of concrete rules and prohibitions of international law, abuse of rights offered a general principle from which judicial organs might construct an international tort law in accordance with the needs of interdependent states.[578] But this is to observe the generality of nascent rules of law which have subsequently acquired much greater particularity through codification and elaboration, primarily in treaty form. To the extent that present rules of international environmental law require a balancing of interests, or incorporate limitations of reasonableness, it may remain appropriate to describe this as a limitation on abuse of rights, but it does not affect the force of Ago's conclusion that international illegality is constituted by a failure to fulfil an international obligation, and that 'abuse of rights would be nothing else but failure to comply with a positive rule of international law thus enunciated'.[579] On this view, abuse of rights is not an independent principle, but simply an expression of the limits inherent in the

---

[574] Brownlie, *Principles of Public International Law* (6th edn, Oxford, 2003) 430; Lauterpacht, *The Development of International Law by the International Court* (London, 1958) 164.

[575] Cheng, General Principles of Law (London, 1953) 121–36; Kiss, 7 Ency of Pub Int L 1; Byers, 47 McGill LJ (2002) 389.

[576] 1982 UNCLOS, Article 300. Claims based on Article 300 were advanced in the *Southern Bluefin Tuna Case (Australia and New Zealand v Japan)* (1999) ITLOS Nos 3 & 4; *Swordfish Case (Chile v EC)* (2001) ITLOS No 7; *MOX Plant Case* (2001) ITLOS No 10.

[577] Friedman, 57 *AJIL* (1963) 288; Elkind, 9 *Vand JTL* (1976) 57.

[578] *The Function of Law in the International Community* (London, 1933) 295–306.

[579] I *YbILC* (1970) 178, paras 25–31.

formulation of certain rights and obligations which now form part of international law. Any wider use of the doctrine is likely, as Brownlie observes, to encourage instability and relativity.

6 MILITARY ACTIVITIES AND THE ENVIRONMENT[580]

A number of multilateral conventions have sought to place limitations on the deliberate infliction of environmental damage for military purposes or during armed conflict. Some protection is afforded by restraints on methods of warfare and the infliction of unnecessary suffering found in the 1949 Geneva Conventions and in the earlier Hague Conventions,[581] whose provisions were held declaratory of customary law by the Nuremberg Tribunal. More recent agreements make explicit reference to the environment, however. The 1977 Environmental Modification Convention prohibits the hostile use of environmental modification techniques having 'widespread, long-lasting or severe effects'. This Convention is in force and has been ratified by major military powers, although not by Iraq, whose actions in setting fire to Kuwaiti oil wells in 1991 might arguably have been a violation, depending on the uncertain question whether it actually applies to actions of this kind. Violations of the UN Charter will, however, entail responsibility under international law to make reparation, and Security Council Resolution 687 (1991) holds Iraq liable on this ground for 'direct loss, damage, including environmental damage and depletion of natural resources' arising out of its conflict with Kuwait.[582]

Also adopted in 1977, Additional Protocol I to the 1949 Geneva Conventions similarly prohibits methods of warfare intended or expected to cause 'widespread, long-term and severe damage to the natural environment', or to prejudice the health or survival of the civilian population. This terminology was understood to be directed at high-level policy-makers authorizing the use of unconventional weapons such as chemical agents or herbicides, and not at incidental or collateral environmental damage caused by those conducting conventional warfare.[583] The protocol requires parties to take care to protect the natural environment, and places limits on the circumstances in which 'works or installations containing dangerous forces', including dams and

---

[580] See generally Austin and Bruch, *The Environmental Consequences of War* (Cambridge, 2000); Low and Hodgkinson, 35 *VJIL* (1995) 405; Greenwood in Grunawalt, King and McClain (eds), *Protection of the Environment During Armed Conflict* (US Naval War College, 1996) 397; Tarasofsky, 24 *NYIL* (1993) 17; Bothe, 34 GYIL (1992) 54; Kalshoven, *Constraints on the Waging of War* (Dordrecht, 1987); Aldrich, 85 *AJIL* (1991) 1; id, 26 *VJIL* (1986).

[581] See 1899 Hague Convention II with respect to the Laws and Customs of War on Land; 1907 Hague Convention IV respecting the Laws and Customs of War on Land; 1949 Geneva Conventions relating to the Protection of Victims or Armed Conflicts. See also 1972 World Heritage Convention, Article 6.

[582] See *infra*, Ch 4, section 2.

[583] See Articles 35, 54(2) 55(1); Aldrich, 26 *VJIL* (1986) 711; Tarasofsky, 24 *NYIL* (1993) 48–54.

nuclear power plants, can be made the object of attack.[584] The latter limitations are also found in Protocol II dealing with non-international armed conflict. These protocols are widely ratified, but not by major Western military powers. During the 1991 conflict with Iraq, a number of nuclear installations, power plants, and water supply systems were attacked by Western airforces, causing serious damage, and casting doubts on the usefulness or general acceptability of the 1977 protocols. Unsuccessful proposals were subsequently made for the adoption of a fifth Geneva Convention, intended to cover protection of the environment in times of armed conflict.[585] The ILC's Code of Offences Against the Peace and Security of Mankind and the 1998 Statute of the International Criminal Court also treat certain acts of serious and intentional harm to the environment as war crimes and allow for individual responsibility.[586]

It should not be assumed, however, that rules of customary international law do not protect the environment in times of armed conflict, or that further international agreement is necessary to regulate environmentally harmful attacks. Principle 24 of the 1992 Rio Declaration asserts that 'States shall…respect international law providing protection for the environment in times of armed conflict and cooperate in its further development, as necessary'. UN General Assembly Resolution 47/37 (1992) also states that 'destruction of the environment not justified by military necessity and carried out wantonly, is clearly contrary to existing international law'. In the *Nuclear Weapons Advisory Opinion*, the ICJ referred to both these instruments and held that as a matter of general international law:

States must take environmental considerations into account when assessing what is necessary and proportionate in the pursuit of legitimate military objectives. Respect for the environment is one of the elements that go to assessing whether an action is in conformity with the principles of necessity and proportionality.[587]

It seems highly probable that Iraq's attacks on oil wells could not meet the tests of necessity or proportionality which govern military actions in general international law.[588] Similarly, in the *Corfu Channel Case*,[589] the ICJ referred to 'elementary considerations of humanity' in finding Albania bound to notify approaching warships of a known danger from mines, while, in the *Nicaragua Case*,[590] the Court treated restrictions on the threat of use of force as peremptory norms of international law. Moreover, as against states not parties to an international armed conflict, belligerents enjoy no special privileges and remain bound by general rules of international law.

---

[584] Articles 55(1), 56(1).

[585] The International Committee of the Red Cross held three meetings in 1992–3, but decided that no convention was needed: see Gasser, in Grunawalt et al, *Protection of the Environment During Armed Conflict*, 521. For the opposite view see Plant (ed), *Environmental Protection and the Law of War* (London, 1992) and IUCN/ICEL, 1991 Munich Consultation Recommendations, 22 *EPL* (1992) 63. See also UN, *Rept of the SG on the Protection of the Environment in Times of Armed Conflict*, UN Doc A/48/269 (1993).

[586] See *infra*, Ch 5, section 6(3).

[587] ICJ Reports (1996) 266, paras 30–2. See Gardam and Momtaz in de Chazournes and Sands (eds), *International Law, the ICJ and Nuclear Weapons* (Cambridge, 1999) 275 and 355.

[588] See Tarasofsky, 24 *NYIL* (1993) 23–26, 29–30, 38–9. On the environmental aspects of the Gulf war, see Roberts, in, Grunawalt et al, *Protection of the Environment During Armed Conflict*, 222.

[589] ICJ Reports (1949) 4.   [590] ICJ Reports (1986) 14.

Multilateral treaties for the protection of the environment may be affected in times of armed conflict by the doctrine of *rebus sic stantibus*,[591] and must be interpreted according to the intention of the parties, but their continued validity as regards relations between belligerent and non-belligerent states is not otherwise affected.[592] Even between belligerent states, such treaties will not necessarily be suspended; *a fortiori*, if the conflict is not international, treaty rules will in general continue to apply. Few environmental treaties make explicit provision for derogation or suspension in time of war; in the view of one group of writers this supports their conclusion that the general rule is one of non-suspension of such treaties in time of armed conflict,[593] although as the ICJ pointed out in the *Nuclear Weapons Advisory Opinion*, environmental treaty obligations cannot have been intended to deprive a state of its right of self defence under international law.

Most environmental treaties, however, contain clauses which preclude their application to ships or aircraft entitled to sovereign immunity. Thus, neither the 1969 Intervention Convention nor the 1989 Salvage Convention apply to such vessels, nor do the London or Oslo Dumping Conventions. Some treaties, while denying jurisdiction over foreign vessels entitled to immunity, require their parties to ensure as far as possible that their sovereign vessels act in a manner consistent with the treaty's requirements. Both the 1973 MARPOL Convention, and the marine pollution provisions of the 1982 UNCLOS are in this category.[594] Moreover, although both the 1969 Intervention Convention and the 1969/92 Conventions on Civil Liability for Oil Pollution Damage do not apply to military vessels, several parties to the 1986 Convention on Early Notification of Nuclear Accidents have given notice when nuclear powered military submarines encountered difficulties at sea, although the latter convention is not explicitly applicable to military facilities.[595] Conventions dealing with nuclear safety and liability for nuclear accidents do not apply to military facilities, but, like the 1969 Oil Pollution Convention, the operator or owner is relieved of all liability for incidents due to armed conflict, hostilities, civil war, or insurrection.[596]

The law of armed conflict is one of the least sophisticated parts of contemporary international law.[597] It lacks an institutional structure for supervision of compliance, and relies mainly on the good faith of the parties to a conflict for implementation and application. The possibility of resort to criminal sanctions *ex post facto* is not a reliable means of ensuring its satisfactory operation. Moreover, although it is clear that international law does not relieve states of their obligations of environmental protection during conflicts, and, as in the case of Iraq, responsibility may be imposed for

---

[591] 1969 Vienna Convention on the Law of treaties, Article 62, on which see *Gabčíkovo-Nagymaros Case*, ICJ Reports (1997) 7.

[592] On this and subsequent points, see generally Bothe, Cassese, Kalshoven, Kiss, Salmon, and Simmonds, *Protection of the Environment in Times of Armed Conflict*, European Parliament (1985) section 3.

[593] Ibid, citing Article 19 of the 1954 International Convention for the Prevention of Pollution of the Sea by Oil as one of the few which do provide for suspension. See also Tarasofsky, 24 *NYIL* (1993) 62–67.

[594] 1973 MARPOL Convention, Article 3(3); 1982 UNCLOS, Article 236.

[595] *Infra*, Ch 9.   [596] Ibid.

[597] Greenwood, in Butler (ed), *Control over Compliance with International Law* (Dordrecht, 1991) 195; Cassese, *International Law in a Divided World* (Oxford, 1986) Ch 10.

environmental injury, this does not of itself afford adequate assurance of military restraint. Obligations of prior environmental impact assessment, consultation, and co-operation are inherently difficult to apply in time of war. Certain measures can be taken, however, to ensure that the more precautionary or preventive approach which now characterizes environmental lawmaking is also applied to the military sphere.[598] Chemical and biological weapons, and other forms of warfare can be assessed in advance to determine their likely impact on the environment. A number of treaties place limitations on chemical and biological weapons,[599] and the Environmental Modification Convention was partly inspired by the use of toxic defoliation agents in Vietnam. Sites of special cultural or ecological significance can be protected from attack or military use, and for this purpose the 1972 World Heritage Convention remains relevant. The control of environmental risks posed by the military use of nuclear power and nuclear weapons remains unsatisfactory, partly because it falls largely outside the existing regulation of civil uses of nuclear energy.[600] More fundamentally, the *Nuclear Weapons Advisory Opinion* demonstrates that although international law constrains the use of environmentally destructive weaponry, it does not prohibit the use of nuclear weapons, or of other weapons not specifically banned by international agreements.[601]

What does need to be emphasized is the importance of making environmental consequences a serious concern in military decisions. In this respect it is unfortunate that the 1977 Protocols remain controversial. The active role of the UN Security Council during the 1991 Gulf conflict, and its appreciation of the environmental implications, does offer some means of ensuring that pressure for compliance with the rules governing armed conflict is applied to the parties involved. Moreover, the Gulf conflict also involved UNEP and IMO in co-ordinating international action to mitigate some of the more serious environmental effects. This is a role for appropriate international institutions which could also usefully be developed. In short, the continued relevance of international law governing protection of the environment, and of environmental institutions, in situations of armed conflict needs to be stressed.

7 CONCLUSIONS

This chapter has attempted to draw from the relevant cases, general principles of law and the growing body of treaties, 'soft law' instruments, and state practice indications of the main thrust of international law governing the protection of the environment. The extent to which international courts, the International Law Commission, and

---

[598] See commentary in Plant, *Environmental Protection and the Law of War*, Ch 9.

[599] See 1972 Convention on Biological Weapons; 1993 Convention on the Prohibition of Chemical Weapons. See generally Tarasofsky, 24 *NYIL* (1993) 54–61.

[600] On nuclear weapons, see de Chazournes and Sands (eds), *International Law, the International Court of Justice and Nuclear Weapons*.

[601] ICJ Reports (1996) 266, para 33.

states themselves, have identified customary international law relating to the environment is noteworthy. Nevertheless, the precedents accumulated here do not necessarily reflect the actual practice of all states in all circumstances. There is a risk of appearing to attribute too much weight to what remain in some respects developing trends whose legal status is insecure and not universally established. In particular, it should not be assumed that rules and principles derived mainly from treaties or soft law have acquired the force of customary law binding on all states. Many of the treaties considered here and in later chapters reflect the continued operation of a process of codification and lawmaking which will be complete only when supported by the evidence of widespread, representative, and consistent state practice normally required for creation of customary international law. Some, such as the 1982 UNCLOS, largely meet these conditions, but even here, some of the more novel articles have not yet been acted upon by states, and cannot necessarily be regarded as customary law.[602]

Caution is also needed before drawing general conclusions from the limited context of certain precedents, such as fisheries treaties and the *Icelandic Fisheries Case*. While the law may be well established in areas such as the conservation of marine living resources, it is still necessary to ask what evidence there is for the application of some of these rules to more novel situations, such as the conservation of tropical forests. Thus it remains important to consider in subsequent chapters how far the general norms identified here codify existing law or have influenced the practice of states. This observation applies with equal force to 'soft law' instruments, such as UNEP's Principles of Conduct Concerning Natural Resources Shared by Two or More States, or its Montreal Guidelines for the Prevention of Pollution from Land-based Sources. Such instruments, although lacking legal force, have nevertheless had an impact on the development of state practice, or have led to the conclusion of further regional or global treaties. They should not be dismissed as being of no legal significance, and to this extent their use by UNEP for lawmaking purposes has been in some cases of help to the process of progressive development.

Some of these considerations help explain why customary international law remains of relatively limited utility in providing normative standards for the resolution of evolving environmental problems. As Handl has observed, the pace of change in the scientific, economic, and social aspects of global environmental problems has placed enormous strain on the capability of the international legal system to keep up.[603] Although customary international law and general principles have given legal force to important basic rules, and the importance of this framework in interpreting and applying environmental treaties should not be under-estimated, they lack the capacity to set standards which are precise, flexible, or sufficiently capable of rapid articulation. For this purpose customary law has to be supplemented and implemented through bilateral or multilateral environmental agreements, as we saw in Chapter 2. Much of the more important work of developing precise rules and standards has fallen in practice to the institutions and autonomous intergovernmental bodies which

---

[602] See *infra*, Ch 7.   [603] 1 *YbIEL* (1990) 4.

these environmental treaties have created, and whose operation is examined in later chapters.

It would be misleading in the extreme to view orthodox, customary lawmaking as an apt description of the process just described. Rather, what has occurred is an accretion of negotiating experience and regulatory techniques during almost forty years since the Stockholm Conference. The most notable feature of environmental treaties over this period has been their increasing sophistication, characterized by the greater attention now paid to questions of effective supervision and compliance, the position of non-parties, and the problems of amendment and flexibility. The 1989 Basel Convention on the Control of Transboundary Movements of Hazardous Waste, the 1987 Montreal Protocol for Protection of the Ozone Layer, the 1992 Convention on Climate Change, and the 2001 Convention on Persistent Organic Pollutants represent some of the most developed examples of this sort of international regulatory regime.[604] Within their own sphere, these treaties are far more important than customary law, and the key question is less their contribution to precedent, although that too is important, than their effectiveness in practice in securing their objectives. For this reason subsequent chapters will attempt in appropriate cases not merely to review the content of these treaties, but to assess their operation. In those areas where no such formal structure of regulation and supervision exists, the role of international law is necessarily weaker. Even where the problem of identifying the rules can be resolved, the remedies and processes then available for securing compliance or settling disputes present their own difficulties, which we will explore in Chapters 4 and 5.

---

[604] See *infra*, Chs 6 and 8.

4

INTERSTATE ENFORCEMENT: STATE RESPONSIBILITY, TREATY COMPLIANCE, AND DISPUTE SETTLEMENT

1 INTRODUCTION

The development of rules of international law concerning protection of the environment is of little significance unless accompanied by effective means for ensuring enforcement, compliance, and the settlement of disputes. The more traditional approach to this subject is the familiar one of interstate claims based on the principle of state responsibility, and employing the variety of forms of dispute settlement machinery contemplated in Article 33 of the UN Charter. There are various disadvantages to enforcing international environmental law in this way, particularly if it involves compulsory resort to judicial institutions.[1] These disadvantages include the adverse effect on relations between the states concerned; the complexity, length, and expense of international litigation; the technical character of environmental problems and the difficulties of proof which legal proceedings may entail, and the unsettled character of some of the law. Perhaps the most significant objection is that the traditional model exemplified by the *Trail Smelter Case* is concerned largely with affording reparation as a response to violations of international law rather than preventing environmental harm before it happens. Such a system is inherently bilateral and confrontational in

---

[1] See generally UNEP, *Study on Dispute Avoidance and Dispute Settlement in International Environmental Law*, UNEP/GC 20/INF/16 (1999); Bilder, 144 *Recueil des Cours* (1975) 141; Cooper, 24 *CYIL* (1986) 247; Okowa, in Evans (ed), *Remedies in International Law* (Oxford, 1998) 157; Koskenniemi, 60 *Nordic JIL* (1991) 73; Sand, *Lessons Learned in Global Environmental Governance* (Washington, 1990); de Chazournes, 99 *RGDIP* (1995) 37.

character: it assumes that 'injured states' whose rights are affected are the primary actors in seeking compliance with legal standards of environmental protection. Its closest analogy in national legal systems is tort law, and adjudication is the method of dispute settlement to which it is most suited.

Claims for transboundary pollution damage are thus the most obvious application for this approach, yet in practice even here the obstacles are such that states have preferred to avoid the law of state responsibility and to rely on other methods of establishing liability using national law, considered in the next chapter. No modern pollution disaster, including Chernobyl, Sandoz, or *Amoco Cadiz*, has resulted in the adjudication of an international claim against the state concerned. The only precedent which holds a state unequivocally responsible for environmental damage in international law is UN Security Council Resolution 687, adopted following Iraq's invasion and occupation of Kuwait in 1991.[2] Because of the sparseness, age or doubtful relevance of most of the other precedents and case law, the legal basis on which states may be held liable for such damage remains to some degree uncertain. The main reason for discussing state responsibility at all in this book is thus not its immediate practical utility but because an understanding of what it can and cannot offer is essential to an explanation of other developments in the international legal system that have largely taken its place. However, the possibility that states might have recourse to international claims against their neighbours may itself exercise an influence on the negotiation of environmental agreements and the settlement of disputes. It is thus not to be entirely discounted.

As we have seen in Chapter 3, modern international environmental law focuses principally on the control and prevention of environmental harm and the conservation and sustainable use of natural resources and ecosystems. A preventive, or regulatory, regime of this comprehensive character requires a more sophisticated approach to enforcement than one based primarily on interstate claims for environmental damage. It must be capable, first, of ensuring compliance with the obligations of pollution control, resource conservation, transboundary risk management and cooperation considered in the previous chapter. Second, the emergence of problems of a global character, affecting the atmosphere, oceans, and natural resources necessitates an appropriate community response to matters of enforcement and compliance. A perspective which accords rights only to 'injured states' after the event will be inappropriate to the polycentric character of global environmental problems involving a range of actors and a multiplicity of complex interrelated issues,[3] or for the protection of common interests, common property, or future generations. Third, many environmental problems involve harm which is subtle, cumulative, and manifest only after a long period of time; in these circumstances 'only equitable and preventative remedies may be capable of providing an effective solution'.[4]

Judicial tribunals are in some cases ill-equipped to provide these solutions. Their limitations can be observed in two important decisions of the ICJ concerned with

---

[2] 30 *ILM* (1991) 846.   [3] Fuller, 92 *Harv LR* (1978) 353. See *infra*, Chs 6, 10, 12, 13 for examples.
[4] Bilder, 144 *Recueil des Cours* (1975) 225.

control of environmental risks. In the *Advisory Opinion Concerning the Threat or Use of Nuclear Weapons* the International Court of Justice showed that it is possible to accommodate public-interest multi-party litigation within the procedure for giving advisory opinions,[5] but its authoritative exposition of the law did not alter the need for negotiations to bring about further progress on nuclear disarmament. The *Case Concerning the Gabčíkovo-Nagymaros Dam*[6] is notable as the first contentious case tried by the ICJ in which environmental monitoring and risk management were central to the court's decision, and as the first in which non-governmental organizations sought to file an *amicus* brief.[7] However, it too ended in a judgment requiring the parties to negotiate a solution. Not surprisingly, in cases where the dispute is multi-lateral, or involves fundamental issues of social, economic, and political choice, states will usually prefer to resolve such problems by negotiations, allowing room for flexible regulation or equitable solutions not necessarily dictated by international law, but accommodating as far as possible the interests of all parties.

In Chapter 2 we noted how states increasingly rely on intergovernmental commissions and meetings of treaty parties as a means of coordinating policy, developing the law, supervising its implementation, putting community pressure on individual states, and resolving conflicts of interest. These bodies also have greater flexibility and may be better at securing compliance than traditional forms of dispute settlement. In place of more confrontational approaches, such regimes facilitate 'dispute avoidance', and promote 'alternative dispute resolution' in the event of non-compliance.[8]

The weakness of this approach, however, is that since in most cases it relies for effectiveness on the operation of community pressure, it may be thought to lack real enforcement power. Moreover, its essentially political character may dilute the force of legal standards,[9] and merely serve to legitimize practices otherwise insupportable from an environmental viewpoint. The first of these criticisms misconceives the nature of the international legal system. The resolution of environmental disputes by interstate claims, as in the *Gabčíkovo Case*, is itself substantially dependent on the consent and good faith of the states concerned. Community pressure remains in practice the only real sanction for enforcing compliance with arbitral awards, or with judgments of the ICJ or other international tribunals, and it is only in that very limited sense that we can talk about courts 'enforcing' international law at all. What institutional supervision offers, whether through international organizations, or autonomous treaty bodies, is the opportunity to organize this pressure on a multilateral basis. The second criticism begs the question whether maintaining normative coherence and strict adherence to law are more important than finding mechanisms that settle disputes and secure compliance with agreed commitments. On this question the international legal system has always been pragmatic rather than principled.[10]

---

[5] ICJ Reports (1996) 226. See *infra*, section 4(1).
[6] ICJ Reports (1997) 7. [*Gabčíkovo-Nagymaros Case*]
[7] On NGO participation in litigation see *infra*, section 4(1).   [8] See *infra*, section 3.
[9] Koskenniemi, 3 *YbIEL* (1992) 123.   [10] See Article 33 of the UN Charter.

2 STATE RESPONSIBILITY FOR ENVIRONMENTAL DAMAGE

2.1 INTRODUCTION

(a) The basis of state responsibility

The law of state responsibility regulates the accountability of states under international law.[11] The foundation of responsibility lies in the breach of obligations undertaken by states or imposed on them by international law.[12] Responsibility in environmental cases will normally arise either because of the breach of one or more of the customary obligations referred to in Chapter 3 or because of a breach of a treaty.[13] The concept is not limited to liability for environmental damage, but has a wider application in the enforcement of international obligations concerning protection of the environment and prevention of transboundary harm. It is thus an important element in the *Gabčíkovo-Nagymaros*, *Pulp Mills* and *MOX Plant Cases*, even without proof of actual or imminent damage.

Only the state's own obligations are in issue here. Private parties or companies are not in general bound by public international law, although as we shall see in Chapter 5, the practice of channelling environmental liability towards private actors in national law is now a widely developed alternative to the international liability of states in cases of environmental damage. But the problem of attributing private conduct to states will seldom impinge on responsibility in international law for non-performance of the state's own environmental obligations. Even where an activity causing environmental harm is conducted by private parties, as in the *Trail Smelter* or *Pulp Mills Cases*, the issue remains one of the state's responsibility for prevention, cooperation, and notification, which cannot be avoided by surrendering the activity itself into private hands.[14] In this chapter, therefore, it is important to remember that we are not concerned with

---

[11] See ILC 2001 Articles on State Responsibility ['ILC Articles'], *ILC Report* (2001) GAOR A/56/10, 43–365, reproduced in Crawford (ed), *The ILC's Articles on State Responsibility* (Cambridge, 2002). This final draft reflects important changes made in 1998 and 2000: see Crawford et al, 94 *AJIL* (2000) 660 and 96 *AJIL* (2002) 874. In Resolution 56/83 (2001) the UN General Assembly 'took note' of the draft articles. See generally Brownlie, *System of the Law of Nations: State Responsibility* (Oxford, 1983); de Arechaga, in Sorensen (ed), *Manual of Public International Law* (London, 1968) 530; *id*, 159 *Recueil des Cours* (1978) 267; Brunnée, 36 *NYIL* (2005) 21–56.

[12] Articles 1–3, ILC Articles; Brownlie, *State Responsibility*, 37ff, 60–2.

[13] See Xue, *Transboundary Damage in International Law* (Cambridge, 2003) Ch 8; Scovazzi, 12 *YbIEL* (2001) 43; Lefeber, *Transboundary Environmental Interference and the Origin of State Liability* (The Hague, 1996) esp Ch 4; Francioni and Scovazzi (eds), *International Responsibility for Environmental Harm* (Dordrecht, 1991) esp chapter by Mazzeschi; Okowa, *State Responsibility for Transboundary Air Pollution in International Law* (Oxford, 2000); Smith, *State Responsibility and the Marine Environment* (Oxford, 1988); Dupuy, *La Responsabilité internationale des états pour les dommages d'origine technologique et industrielle* (Paris, 1976); *id*, in OECD, *Legal Aspects of Transfrontier Pollution* (Paris, 1977).

[14] See *Tehran Hostages Case*, ICJ Reports (1980) 3; *Bosnian Genocide Case*, ICJ Reports (2007) paras 390–415. Cf ILC Articles 4–11 and commentary in Crawford (ed), *The International Law Commission's Articles*

the conduct of individual polluters, fishermen, or multinational enterprises, but with states themselves, and in particular with their obligations of due diligence and cooperation. Only in this sense is the state a guarantor of private conduct, but its responsibility is direct, not vicarious.

(b) Fault and due diligence

To describe the responsibility of states in international law as based on fault is misleading and liable to confuse. Both the *Corfu Channel Case*,[15] and the manner in which writers have subsequently interpreted that judgment, illustrate the dangers of trying to make general propositions on this subject. Two points must be borne in mind regarding 'fault' in international law. The term can be used subjectively, requiring intention, malice, or recklessness on the part of the state or its agents,[16] or it can be used objectively, meaning simply the breach of an international obligation.[17] Used in the subjective sense, 'fault' is almost never the basis of responsibility in environmental disputes, although the reckless or intentional infliction of environmental damage in situations such as the Iraqi attack on Kuwait in 1991 could be said to involve subjective fault.[18] But the point is that fault of this subjective kind is not a necessary condition of responsibility. Jiménez de Arechaga aptly explains this view: 'The decisive consideration is that unless the rule of international law which has been violated specifically envisages malice or culpable negligence, the rules of international law do not contain a general floating requirement of malice or culpable negligence as a condition of responsibility'.[19]

Used in the objective sense of breach of obligation, however, 'fault' is essentially tautologous, unless the particular obligation itself incorporates subjective elements. While it is not erroneous to describe the breach of an objective standard of diligent control of harmful activities as amounting to 'fault' it adds little to our understanding of the concept of responsibility to do so. Far more significant, as we saw in Chapter 3, is the question how due diligence is to be defined.[20] For this purpose what matters is

---

on *State Responsibility*. See also Handl, 74 *AJIL* (1980) 525; de Arechaga, in Sorensen, *Manual of Public International Law*, 560ff; Brownlie, *State Responsibility*, 159ff.

[15] ICJ Reports (1949) 4. See *infra*.

[16] For example genocide, which requires proof of intention to destroy a particular group: *Bosnian Genocide Case*, ICJ Reports (2007) paras 186–7.

[17] de Arechaga, in Sorensen, *Manual of Public International Law*, 534–7, and Handl, 13 *CYIL* (1975) 162–7, prefer this interpretation of *Corfu Channel*. Brownlie, *State Responsibility*, 38–48, observes: 'The approach adopted by the majority of the Court fails to correspond with either the *culpa* doctrine or the test of objective responsibility' (p 47).

[18] *Supra* Ch 3, section 4.

[19] In Sorensen, *Manual of Public International Law*, 535. See *ILC Report* (1998) Ch VIII, para 340: 'There was no general requirement of fault or damage for a State to incur responsibility for an internationally wrongful act.' See also Brownlie, *State Responsibility*, 44 ff; Smith, *State Responsibility and the Marine Environment*, 15–20, but contrast the dissent of Judge Krylov, *Corfu Channel Case*, ICJ Reports (1949) 72, requiring *dolus* or *culpa*, and Oppenheim, *International Law*, (5th edn, London, 1955) vol I, 343: 'An act of state injurious to another is nevertheless not an international delinquency if committed neither wilfully and maliciously nor with culpable negligence.'

[20] *Supra* Ch 3, section 4(2).

that there is no additional requirement of intention, malice, or recklessness on the part of the state. References to 'fault' in this chapter are thus to be understood as meaning simply a failure to act with due care or diligence, or a breach of treaty, or the commission of a prohibited act.

Putting all this in an environmental context, the key point is that we can take it for granted that states are responsible ('liable') in international law to make reparation for transboundary damage, or the risk of damage, resulting from their own failure to regulate and control potentially harmful activities to the standard of due diligence required by international law, or from their failure to cooperate.[21] This follows inevitably from the general law of state responsibility codified by the ILC as applied to breach of the obligations outlined Chapter 3. The more difficult question we have to consider in the next section is whether states are also liable in international law for transboundary damage caused *without* fault in the sense just defined. This form of responsibility is sometimes referred to as strict or absolute liability, by analogy with the same concepts in national law and civil-liability treaties. 'Strict liability' differs from 'absolute liability' only in the greater range of defences which may preclude wrongfulness[22]—but in both cases acting with due diligence will *not* be a defence.

2(2) STATE RESPONSIBILITY AND LIABILITY FOR ENVIRONMENTAL DAMAGE

Liability for loss or damage is an elementary feature of a legal system; it remains an important part of most systems of environmental law even when supplemented or in part superseded by regulatory regimes, risk avoidance procedures, and criminal penalties. In international law, liability for transboundary damage, based on analogies going back to Roman law, is one of the oldest concepts available in interstate disputes. The *Trail Smelter* arbitral award delivered in 1938 and 1941, and involving a transboundary air pollution dispute between the United States and Canada, remains the seminal judicial contribution to the international law on the subject.[23] After awarding compensation for damage already proved, the arbitrators ordered payment of further compensation if harm subsequently occurred notwithstanding Canada's compliance with the regime of control laid down in the award. This order can be read in support of a general principle of liability without fault, but the failure of many writers to identify precisely which principle the case supports indicates the difficulty of drawing firm conclusions from it. Because Canada's responsibility for proven damage was accepted by the parties at the outset, the award was not concerned with establishing a standard of responsibility in international law. It does not provide a strong affirmation of liability without fault as a general principle. Nevertheless, despite the limited range of national and international sources on which the tribunal relied in determining

---

[21] Ibid.

[22] Compare liability for oil pollution damage, *infra*, Ch 7, and nuclear accidents, *infra*, Ch 9.

[23] *Supra* Ch 3, section 4(2).

rules of international law, there is no reason to doubt that states remain responsible in international law for harm caused in breach of obligation by transboundary air pollution.[24] Moreover, modern monitoring and sampling techniques have made it possible to calculate with reasonable accuracy the amounts of transboundary air pollution emanating from individual countries and to identify the areas where it is deposited.[25] Furnishing the necessary proof, even to the 'clear and convincing' standard demanded by the tribunal in the *Trail Smelter Case*, need no longer be a potential obstacle to the attribution of responsibility for long-range transboundary air pollution.[26]

(a) State liability for damage

Since *Trail Smelter* there has been little or no judicial elaboration of liability for transboundary damage at an international level, and the precise character of this elementary concept remains unsettled. Academic literature on the subject remains deeply divided, with some authors emphasizing the prohibition of transboundary harm, while others, including the present authors, stress the failure to regulate and control the source of harm.[27] It seems generally accepted that no responsibility of any kind will attach to harm resulting from risks of which the state concerned was not and could not have been objectively aware. This was an essential condition of Albania's responsibility in the *Corfu Channel Case*.[28] However, the common assumption that international law simply prohibits transboundary environmental harm is not reflected in state practice or in the work of the ILC, as we have already observed in Chapter 3. If it were true that transboundary harm is prohibited, there would then be no need to regulate transboundary or global environmental risks and this book could end at Chapter 5.

On the most widely held view states are liable only if the harm is directly caused by a failure of due diligence, or by some other breach of obligation, such as a violation of the UN Charter prohibition on use of force.[29] As Dupuy points out, whatever the *Trail Smelter Case* decides, it must be read in the light of subsequent state practice, which in his view favours liability in such cases if there is a failure to act with due diligence, but not liability without fault.[30] Reviewing the proceedings of the Preparatory Committee for the Stockholm Conference, Handl concluded that they too provide little or no support in favour of any specific theory.[31] Viewed in isolation, Principle 21 of the 1972

---

[24] See *infra*, Ch 6.

[25] Sand, in Helm (ed), *Energy: Production, Consumption and Consequences* (Washington, DC, 1990) 247.

[26] Handl, 26 *NRJ* (1986) 440–7; Kirgis, 66 *AJIL* (1972) 294.

[27] For example, contrast Scovazzi, 12 *YbIEL* (2001) 43, with the views of the present authors. The disagreements on this subject transcend the divide between civil law and common law.

[28] ICJ Reports (1949) 18–22. See *ILC Report* (2001) GAOR A/56/10, 385, para (14) and *supra* Ch 3, section 4(1).

[29] See Lefeber, *Transboundary Environmental Interference*, 172–6.

[30] Dupuy, in Bothe (ed), *Trends in Environmental Policy and Law* (Gland, 1980) 373. See also Kiss and Shelton, in Ndiaye and Wolfrum (eds), *Law of the Sea, Environmental Law and Settlement of Disputes* (Leiden, 2007) 1131–2.

[31] 74 *AJIL* (1980) 535–40 and see also Jiménez de Arechaga, 159 *Recueil des cours* (1978) 272; Dupuy, *La Responsabilité internationale etc*, 355–8.

Stockholm Declaration and Principle 2 of the 1992 Rio Declaration are thus an incon-clusive guide to the precise contours of liability for environmental damage, and must be interpreted within the framework of customary rules on which both are based. As we saw in Chapter 3, their incorporation in environmental treaties points clearly in the direction of a due diligence obligation—an obligation of conduct (regulation and control) rather than result (no transboundary harm). Only exceptionally do treaties adopt a form of state liability for damage without fault.[32] More often, as in Articles 139 and 235 of the 1982 UNCLOS, they specify expressly that only for the non-fulfilment of international obligations will states parties be responsible.[33]

Some writers have argued, however, that a form of strict or absolute liability for environmental harm arises independently through general principles of law, equity, sovereign equality, or good neighbourliness.[34] Jenks identified ultra-hazardous activ-ities as a distinct category for which strict or absolute liability is justified as a means of shifting the burden of proof and ensuring a more equitable distribution of loss.[35] In defining what constitutes 'ultra-hazardous activity' most attempts focus more on the potential harm than on the likelihood of the risk occurring. One candidate is the risk posed by nuclear power plants.[36] Beyond that, the boundaries are more questionable and views are divided on whether the category should extend to activities whose effects are only cumulatively harmful, as in the *Trail Smelter Case*. An alternative approach to the problem of definition is to require specific agreement, but the only clear example is the 1972 Space Objects Liability Convention, under which states bear direct and abso-lute liability for damage on earth.[37] Significantly, treaties concerned with nuclear acci-dents and oil pollution at sea do not follow this example.[38] They focus instead on the liability of the owner or operator, although states may be involved in the provision of insurance or supplementary compensation. Nor do state claims in general support any particular standard of liability for environmental damage. This can be observed most clearly in respect of nuclear accidents or tests. Only the *Cosmos 954* claim[39] brought by Canada explicitly adopts the view that states are absolutely liable for ultra-hazardous activities as a matter of general principle, but this claim was also based on the 1972 Space Objects Liability Convention, and was settled *ex gratia* by the Soviet Union. Other examples of *ex gratia* payments in respect of oil pollution at sea, nuclear tests,

---

[32] See Lefeber, *Transboundary Environmental Interference*, 159–66.

[33] See also 1961 Treaty Relating to the Cooperative Development of the Water Resources of the Columbia River Basin, Article 18; 1988 Convention for the Regulation of Antarctic Mineral Resource Activities, Article 8; 2005 Antarctic Protocol, Liability Annex VI, Article 10.

[34] Lefeber, *Transboundary Environmental Interference and the Origin of State Liability*, esp Ch 5, reviews the literature comprehensively. See also Scovazzi, 12 *YbIEL* (2001) 43 and Kiss and Shelton, in Ndiaye and Wolfrum (eds), *Law of the Sea, Environmental Law and Settlement of Disputes*, 1131–51.

[35] 117 *Recueil des cours* (1966) 105. See also Hardy, 36 *BYIL* (1960) 223; Smith, *State Responsibility and the Marine Environment*, 112–25; Handl, 13 *CYIL* (1975) 68ff; and Brownlie, *State Responsibility*, 50.

[36] See *infra*, Ch 9.

[37] Article II. See Cheng, *Studies in International Space Law* (Oxford, 1997) Ch 11.

[38] See *infra*, Chs 7, 9.

[39] *Claim for damage caused by Cosmos 954*, 18 *ILM* (1979) 902; Schwartz and Berlin, 27 *McGill LJ* (1982) 676 and see *infra*, Ch 9 for other state claims concerning nuclear accidents.

or explosions at borders do not afford evidence of *opinio iuris* regarding an explicit standard of liability.[40] In cases where damage is caused by pollution of international watercourses, states have preferred to channel claims through national courts, relying on principles of civil liability. The Sandoz accident and other cases of Rhine pollution have been dealt with in this manner, and not by interstate claims.[41] The *Trail Smelter Case* remains the only example of an interstate claim for air-pollution damage. If that dispute were to arise today, it seems more likely that it too would be resolved by trans-boundary civil litigation.[42]

Thus, if states can be held liable for transboundary damage caused by activities within their territory or control even when they are not at fault, the examples remain at best exceptional or questionable. After undertaking the most comprehensive review of the precedents Lefeber reluctantly concludes that 'a positivist approach to international law cannot but lead to the rejection of an absolute obligation to prevent transboundary environmental interference causing significant harm or liability *sine delicto*'.[43]

(b) General principles of law

The argument that a standard of liability for environmental damage can be inferred by analogy from general principles of law rests on the use of strict liability in national legal systems and in civil-liability treaties, particularly those dealing with oil pollution at sea and nuclear accidents.[44] It is true that many legal systems entertain strict liability in certain cases. The common law principle employed in *Rylands v Fletcher*[45] and in certain nuisance cases is also found in many civil-law systems, especially in situations of ultra-hazardous activities.[46] There are, however, significant differences in the scope of strict liability. In French law strict liability is an accepted principle of governmental liability, while in England activities conducted by public bodies under statutory authority are usually excluded from *Rylands v Fletcher*.[47] English common law also excludes from its rules on strict liability damage which could not reasonably have been foreseen, thus significantly limiting the utility of no-fault liability in cases of historic pollution damage.[48] Moreover, although there is a legislative trend to

---

[40] Lefeber, *Transboundary Environmental Interference*, who reviews other examples at 166–77.

[41] See *infra*, Ch 10.   [42] See *infra*, Ch 5.   [43] Op Cit, 187.

[44] Goldie, 14 *ICLQ* (1965) 1189; Kelson, 12 *Harv ILJ* (1972) 197; Gaines, 20 *Harv ILJ* (1989) 311 and see *infra*, Chs 7, 9.

[45] (1868) LR 3 HL 330, and see Waite, 18 *JEL* (2006) 423. Not all common law jurisdictions follow *Rylands v Fletcher*: see the High Court of Australia's decision in *Burnie Port Authority v General Jones Pty Ltd* (1994) 179 CLR 520, rejecting strict liability in favour of 'ordinary negligence'.

[46] Lawson and Markesinis, *Tortious Liability for Unintentional Harm in the Common Law and Civil Law* (Cambridge, 1981) vol I, Ch 4; Reid, 48 *ICLQ* (1999) 731; Van Dam, *European Tort Law* (Oxford, 2006) 255–65.

[47] *Dunne v Northwestern Gas Board* [1964] 2 QB 605 and see Brown and Bell, *French Administrative Law* (5th edn, Oxford, 1997) 193–201; Van Dam, *European Tort Law*, 472–97.

[48] *Cambridge Water Co v Eastern Counties Leather plc* [1994] 1 All ER 53; *The Wagonmound (No 2)* [1967] 1 AC 67, per Lord Reid. See Ogus, 6 *JEL* (1994) 151; Wilkinson, 57 *MLR* (1994) 799; Brearley, 7 *JEL* (1995) 119.

create special rules of strict liability for pollution damage or activities dangerous to the environment,[49] these precedents are 'far from presenting a homogeneous approach to the mechanisms for remedying environmental damage'.[50] National legal systems differ not only in their acceptance of strict liability, but also in the extent to which they allow recovery for environmental damage, that is for losses such as wildlife that are not property or have no accepted economic value.[51] Attempts have been made to harmonize the general law on liability for environmental damage, most comprehensively in the 1993 Lugano Convention on Civil Liability, but this treaty has not been widely adopted and has had no impact on existing national law.[52] Some writers have concluded that the analogy of international liability with municipal law is both inappropriate and 'does not, as yet, seem to support the extension of the standard of no-fault liability to all environmentally hazardous activities'.[53] Similarly, although widespread, the use of strict or absolute liability in civil-liability treaties and in the ILC's 2006 Principles for the Allocation of Loss is normally part of a complex scheme whose principles cannot easily be replicated in public international law.[54] These treaties were in any case intended to channel limited liability to the private party responsible for the activity in question: they tell us little or nothing about state liability in international law. Most are not in force and their impact on national law is negligible.[55]

These observations are not necessarily an obstacle to an international court relying on general principles to found a principle of state liability in international law.[56] Given that the decision is thus one of legal policy, an argument based on strict liability as a general principle of law cannot be dismissed. But international courts have been cautious in making use of this source of law, mainly because it constitutes a form of judicial lawmaking independent of the will of states. References to national law in

---

[49] E.g. China, Environmental Protection Law, Article 41; Brazil, 1980 Constitution, Article 262(3); USA, 1980 Comprehensive Environmental Response, Compensation and Liability Act; Portugal, 1986 Law No 11, Article 41; Sweden, 1986 Environmental Damage Act; Greece, Law No 1650, Article 29; Germany, 1990 Environmental Liability Act, Article 1; Norway, 1989 Pollution Control Act; Russia, 1991 Law on the Protection of the Environment, Articles 89–90; Finland, 1994 Environmental Damage Compensation Act. Not all countries have followed this trend: compare Italy, 1986 Law No 349, Article 18; Chile, 1994 Law on the Environment, Article 52. See Bianchi, 6 *JEL* (1994) 21; Wetterstein, 3 *Env Liability* (1995) 41; Hoffman, 38 *NILR* (1991) 27.

[50] EC, *Green Paper on Remedying Environmental Damage*, COM (93) 47 (1993) para 2.2.1. See also Van Dam, *European Tort Law*, 396–405; Lefeber, *Transboundary Environmental Interference and the Origin of State Liability* (The Hague, 1996) 182–3, 276–9.

[51] For reviews of different national and international approaches to the inclusion of 'environmental damage' within the scope of liability for damage see Wetterstein (ed), *Harm to the Environment* (Oxford, 1997) especially Chs 2, 6–9; Bowman and Boyle (eds), *Environmental Damage in International and Comparative Law* (Oxford, 2002) Chs 11–18.

[52] See *infra*, Ch 5, section 3(2).

[53] Lefeber, *Transboundary Environmental Interference*, 182–3, 276–9.

[54] See *infra*, Ch 5, section 4; Handl, 92 *RGDIP* (1988) 35ff; Lefeber, *Transboundary Environmental Interference*, Ch 7; Doecker and Gehring, 2 *JEL* (1990) 1; Brans, *Liability for Damage to Public Natural Resources* (The Hague, 2001) Ch 7.

[55] Churchill, 12 *YbIEL* (2001) 3. But this comment does not apply to the oil pollution and nuclear liability treaties.

[56] See Judge McNair, *South West Africa Case,* ICJ Reports (1950) 128, 148 and *supra* Ch 1, n 134.

the *Trail Smelter Case* were carefully controlled by the *compromis* and agreed by the parties.[57] Where this is not the case, it seems likely that an international court would hesitate to impose a general principle of strict or absolute liability on states, however widely evidenced in national law, in the face of the contrary evidence of state claims and treaty formulations referred to earlier. For this reason objective responsibility for breach of obligation remains a firmer foundation for a standard of state liability for environmental damage in international law. As we will see below, that also appears to represent the final view of the ILC.

2(3) DEVELOPING THE LAW OF STATE LIABILITY FOR DAMAGE

(a) Who should be liable for transboundary harm: states or private parties?

With the deficiencies of the existing law in mind, the UN Conference on the Human Environment in 1972 called on states 'to develop further the international law regarding liability and compensation for the victims of pollution and other environmental damage caused by activities within the jurisdiction or control of such states...'.[58] Six years later, the International Law Commission embarked on a twenty-nine-year odyssey entitled 'Liability for Injurious Consequences of Acts Not Prohibited by International Law'.[59] In this guise, the Commission slowly and uncertainly grappled with the task identified by the Stockholm Conference and reiterated in 1992 by the Rio Conference on Environment and Development.[60]

Why should the International Law Commission address the question of liability for transboundary damage and is its concluded work on state responsibility and the management of transboundary risk not sufficient for the purpose? As we saw above, transboundary environmental damage resulting from the activities of industry or business will not in normal circumstances be attributable to the source state in international law.[61] State liability for such activities based on a failure to regulate and control will not cover damage that is unforeseeable or unavoidable.[62] In these circumstances the state itself is not at fault and the loss will not be recoverable in international law.[63] The ILC's work thus proceeded from the entirely reasonable assumption that transboundary damage may still happen, however diligent the state has been in regulating and controlling the harmful activity, and that some alternative form of redress is desirable. The Commission had two possible options.

First, even though it may not be at fault in such cases, arguments can be made for shifting the burden of loss back to the source state, particularly where the source is

---

[57] See the tribunal's award at 35 *AJIL* (1939) 698, 714ff.

[58] 1972 Stockholm Declaration on the Human Environment, Principle 22.

[59] See Quentin-Baxter, II *YbILC* (1981) Pt 1, 112–22; Barboza, 6th *Report*, UN Doc A/CN 4/428 (1990) with draft articles 1–33 and, *ILC Report* (1990) GAOR A/45/10, 242; Lefeber, *Transboundary Environmental Interference*, Ch 6.

[60] Principle 13.   [61] *Supra* section 2(1).

[62] See e.g. *Corfu Channel Case* (1949) ICJ Reports 1; 1982 UNCLOS, Article 139.

[63] *ILC Report* (2004) GAOR A/59/10, 166, commentary to Principle 1, para 8.

an ultra-hazardous activity such as a nuclear power plant. In the absence of reciprocal acceptance of risk, or some common benefit, making the victim state suffer in the
event of unforeseeable or unavoidable harm is not an attractive policy.[64] The underlying assumption here is that it is inequitable to leave the burden to lie where it falls
merely because the source state has acted with all due diligence. The injured state can
neither control the activities which cause such harm nor does it necessarily benefit
from them, however socially or economically desirable they may be to the source state.
The problem of inequity can readily be observed in the relationship between states
using nuclear power and those non-nuclear states which cannot avoid the risks posed
by nuclear accidents such as Chernobyl: the latter have no veto over their neighbours
and no guarantee of indemnity for accidental harm beyond the limits of what may be
available under nuclear civil-liability conventions.[65] Nor is due diligence always an
easy standard to administer unless clearly accepted international standards defining
the content of this duty can be identified.[66] If accidents can happen even in the best-
regulated and managed installations their occurrence does not necessarily indicate
any fault by the state. A heavy burden of proof will be placed on whoever has to establish a failure of due diligence. In the case of complex processes, such as nuclear reactors, this will be especially difficult unless liberal inferences of fact are allowed, or the
burden of proof is placed on the source state.[67] These arguments all pointed the ILC
towards affirming that states are and should be liable without fault in such cases.

But why make states liable for damage they have not caused? Even where a state is
potentially responsible in international law, to whatever extent, it is far from clear that
states should be the only or even the principal source of recourse for those injured
by transboundary damage. Claiming compensation from a government for pollution
caused by industry amounts in effect to a state subsidy and undermines the 'polluter
pays' principle.[68] Allowing direct recourse against the enterprise causing the damage
would do more to facilitate a 'polluter pays' approach to the allocation of transboundary costs than making states a guarantor for industry.[69] Moreover, only governments
can bring international claims against another state. Finding a forum with jurisdiction will thus depend on the consent of another state, which may not be easy to obtain.
In practice very few claims for transboundary damage have been handled in this way.
It will usually be simpler, quicker, and economically more efficient to make those who

---

[64] Quentin-Baxter, II *YbILC* (1981) Pt 1, 113–8; Barboza, II *YbILC* (1986) Pt 1, 160; Handl, 92 *RGDIP* (1988) 50.

[65] See *infra*, Ch 9.

[66] For example in the 1994 Convention on Nuclear Safety, *infra*, Ch 9.

[67] Cf *Corfu Channel Case*, ICJ Reports (1949) 1, 18 where the court did allow certain inferences from the fact of Albania's exclusive territorial control. McCaffrey, II *YbILC* (1988) Pt 2, 30, para 167, suggests that due diligence is 'essentially a defence' and thus 'the burden of proving it should lie with the state of origin', but the case law reviewed *supra* Ch 3, section 4, does not bear this out.

[68] See 1992 Rio Declaration, Principle 16, *infra*, Ch 5.

[69] See *Vellore Citizens Welfare Forum v Union of India* (1996) 5 SCC 647, where the Indian Supreme Court relied on the principle to justify imposition of absolute liability on the polluter both for injury to private parties and for environmental reinstatement costs which the government would otherwise have borne.

cause pollution or other forms of damage pay, rather than states. From this perspective, state responsibility and the liability of states are and should be no more than residual sources of redress. These arguments favoured a second option—developing the law of civil liability.

(b) The International Law Commission's articles on liability

In an attempt to move beyond the limitations of the existing law on state responsibility, the ILC initially proposed to make states liable for significant transboundary harm caused by any activity covered by their draft liability articles.[70] The obligation to compensate other states would not cover unforeseeable risks, but would include unavoidable harm which the source state could not prevent by exercising due diligence.[71] At the same time the ILC's proposals did not place the source state in the same position as if it were at fault. Equitable compensation would instead be negotiated as part of a balance of interests between the parties, 'in accordance with the principle that the victim of harm should not be left to bear the entire loss'.[72]

These were relatively novel proposals, however, and they did not rest on any clear foundation in general international law. They proved too controversial for many states. Nevertheless, in 2001, largely at the behest of developing states, the General Assembly requested the ILC to resume work on liability, 'bearing in mind the interrelationship between prevention and liability, and taking into account the developments in international law and comments by Governments'.[73] This suggests a recognition by at least some governments that existing law on liability for transboundary damage remained insufficient and that some additional measures were necessary.

The most fundamental question confronted by the Commission was whether to continue to focus on extending the liability of states in international law along the lines envisaged in 1996. However meritorious the idea may be in theory, few governments, in whatever context, have shown any enthusiasm for accepting that no-fault liability for damage caused by activities within their jurisdiction should fall on states themselves.[74] Marking an important change of direction, the ILC did not return to that model of loss allocation. Thus, for essentially pragmatic rather than principled reasons, the Commission opted to focus on 'loss allocation among different actors involved in the operations of the hazardous activities',[75] rather than making states directly liable in international law. Having eschewed state liability as a solution, the ILC's subsequent work necessarily addressed the civil liability of operators. In most cases corporations or other private operators of a harmful activity would become strictly

---

[70] 1996 ILC draft Liability Article 5. For the full text of the 1996 draft see *Report of the Working Group on International Liability etc, ILC Report* (1996) GAOR A/51/10, Annex 1, 235. For a brief resumé see Boyle and Freestone (eds), *International Law and Sustainable Development* (Oxford, 1999) 73–85; de La Fayette, 6 *RECIEL* (1997) 321–33.

[71] 1996 draft Article 1.   [72] 1996 draft Article 21, on which see *ILC Report* (1996) Annex 1, 320.

[73] UNGA Res 56/82 (2001).

[74] Special Rapporteur's *2nd Report*, UN Doc A/CN 4/540 (2003) para 22.

[75] *ILC Report* (2003) GAOR A/58/10, para 168. See Boyle, 17 *JEL* (2005) 3; Kiss and Shelton, in Ndiaye and Wolfrum, *Law of the Sea, Environmental Law and Settlement of Disputes*, 1138–51.

liable in national law for transboundary damage. In effect, therefore, the polluters would have to pay, not the states within whose territory they operate. To that extent the ILC recognized the reality that many, if not most, transboundary environmental problems are caused by and mainly affect private parties, rather than states as such. States would still remain responsible for their own fault in international law, including their failure to provide for liability in the form envisaged by the Commission. Essentially, however, the Commission's proposals would build directly on the private law civil-liability models already adopted for oil, nuclear, and other environmental risks. There would still be strict liability, but it would not fall on states. The outlines of the Principles for Allocation of Loss finally adopted in 2006 are considered fully in Chapter 5.

(c) Interaction of civil liability and interstate claims: the local remedies rule

In general international law, interstate claims involving responsibility for injury to aliens are normally conditional on the prior exhaustion of local remedies, which usually entails resort to the relevant national legal system as a preferred means of redress. Only if civil justice is effectively denied, or if no redress is available, will an international claim then be admissible.[76] The ILC's 2006 Principles for Allocation of Loss are 'without prejudice to the rules relating to state responsibility and any claim that may lie under those rules'.[77] It seems clear that the Commission envisages civil liability and state responsibility as potentially complementary regimes. The preference of states and the ILC for non-discriminatory access to national remedies, civil liability and compensation schemes as a means of dealing with transboundary environmental nuisances is already well established.[78] The view that local remedies should be exhausted when adequate and available would leave interstate claims as a residual option to be exercised only when other remedies have been exhausted or do not exist.

However, it has been suggested that the local remedies rule is inapplicable to cases of transboundary environmental harm. The underlying idea is that the injured party must have assumed the risk of being subject to the jurisdiction of a foreign state:

> even where effective local remedies exist, it would be unreasonable and unfair to require an injured person to exhaust local remedies where his property has suffered environmental harm caused by pollution, radioactive fallout or a fallen space object emanating from a State in which his property is not situated...[79]

The Draft Articles on Diplomatic Protection thus exclude the local remedies rule where there is no 'relevant connection' between the injured party and the state responsible.[80] On this view, governments would remain free to make an interstate claim on behalf

---

[76] *ELSI Case*, ICJ Reports (1989) 15, paras 50–63; ILC, 2001 State Responsibility Article 44(b). See Amerasinghe, *Local Remedies in International Law* (2nd edn, Cambridge, 2004); Trindade, *The Application of the Rule of Exhaustion of Local Remedies in International Law* (Cambridge, 1983); Okowa, *State Responsibility for Transboundary Air Pollution* (Oxford, 2000) 217–21.

[77] *ILC Report* (2006) GAOR A/61/10, 111, para 7.   [78] See *infra*, Ch 5.

[79] *ILC Report* (2006) GAOR A/61/10, 80–1, para 7.   [80] 2006 Draft Article 15(c).

of anyone affected by transboundary damage without first exhausting local remedies. Particularly in cases where the damage is widespread, and the victims are numerous and poor, governmental action at interstate level may well be the only realistic option and should not be excluded. The UN Compensation Commission's procedures for bringing compensation claims against Iraq are the most recent example of governments espousing claims on behalf of a mass of individual victims.[81] Whether such claimants should be left to their local remedies would in that type of case be a matter for their own government to decide.

But in more typical cases of transboundary nuisances it is not obvious why the absence of a relevant connection with the respondent state should exclude the local remedies rule even where the injured victims would suffer no hardship in pursuing local remedies and it would be feasible to do so. This will especially be true where the victim has the choice of suing in the place where the injury has occurred or would occur, rather than in the respondent state. For reasons elaborated at some length in Chapter 5, states have clearly found it desirable to encourage resort to local remedies as a means of de-escalating such transboundary disputes, and the logic of this policy is implicit in Principles 10 and 16 of the Rio Declaration. The ILC accepts that the authority in support of its relevant connection requirement is limited and contradictory, and its conclusion is tentative.[82] In *Trail Smelter* there were no local remedies that could be exhausted in Canada because of the extraterritorial location of the damage and the narrowly territorial jurisdiction of Canadian courts: interstate arbitration was the only possibility.[83] Given this admittedly shaky foundation and the absence of any compelling justification, the Commission's blanket dismissal of the rule in transboundary pollution cases appears questionable.

2(4) REMEDIES

No attempt has yet been made, either in the ILC's articles on state responsibility, or in those on the prevention of transboundary harm, to develop remedies specifically adapted to environmental damage.[84] The remedies available for breach of environmental obligations are thus determined by general international law. Where the responsibility of a state is established, an obligation arises first to discontinue the wrongful conduct, second to offer guarantees of non-repetition, and third to make

---

[81] See Kazazi, in Bowman and Boyle (eds), *Environmental Damage in International and Comparative Law*, 111.

[82] *ILC Report* (2006) GAOR A/61/10, 82, para 9.

[83] Read, 1 *CYIL* (1963) 222. The ILC commentary appears not to appreciate this point. In the Chernobyl disaster there were also no local remedies because there was no liability under Soviet law. But in the Sandoz pollution disaster on the Rhine, and the *Handelskwekerij Case*, local remedies did exist and were used. See *infra*, Ch 5, section 3(2).

[84] See generally Gray, *Judicial Remedies in International Law* (Oxford, 1987); Mann, *Further Studies in International Law* (Oxford, 1990) Ch 4; Brownlie, *State Responsibility*, Ch 13; *id*, in Lowe and Fitzmaurice (eds), *Fifty Years of the International Court of Justice* (Cambridge, 1996) 557–66; Okowa, *State Responsibility for Transboundary Air Pollution in International Law* (Oxford, 2000) 203–21; Shelton, 96 *AJIL* (2002) 833.

'full reparation' for the injury caused.[85] Article 34 of the ILC 2001 Articles on State Responsibility defines full reparation as 'restitution, compensation and satisfaction, either singly or in combination'.

Reparation is not an inflexible concept, however. As Brownlie observes: 'the inter-action of substantive law and issues of reparation should be stressed'.[86] The appropri-ateness of particular forms of reparation, or of other responses, thus depends on the circumstances of individual cases. Recognizing this, the ILC commentary notes that: 'The most suitable remedy can only be determined in each instance with a view to achieving the most complete satisfaction of the injured state's interest in the 'wiping out' of all the injurious consequences of the wrongful act'.[87] In environmental dis-putes, states will primarily be concerned with preventing further harm or the risk of harm, securing better cooperation, or obtaining compensation for damage to people, property and natural resources, clean-up costs and restoration of the environment. The only consistent feature of much of the jurisprudence relating to environmental disputes is that it has usually reiterated the duty to negotiate;[88] in a few cases tribunals have also indicated measures to be taken by the parties,[89] and in only one have they awarded compensation for environmental damage.[90]

(a) Preventive remedies

International tribunals generally have the power to make interim orders to protect the rights of the parties, or the marine environment, pending settlement of a dispute.[91] Provisional-measures applications are dealt with urgently and expeditiously: where there is a risk of imminent and potentially irreparable transboundary environmental damage, such an application will be the most effective means of securing a remedy pending a negotiated settlement or a hearing on the merits.[92] Moreover, as we saw in Chapter 3, interim orders to cooperate in protecting the marine environment have been granted even where there is no proof of imminent harm.[93] In the *Land Reclamation*

---

[85] ILC 2001 Articles on State Responsibility, Articles 30–1, 35–7 and commentary in Crawford, *The ILC's Articles etc*, 196–206, 211–34.

[86] *State Responsibility*, 234. See also Combacau and Alland, 16 *NYIL* (1985) 108, who argue that 'it is above all the consideration of "content" and the primary obligation in its widest meaning, which explains why a certain consequence is attached specifically and *ab initio* to its breach'.

[87] II *YbILC* (1993) Pt 2, 63. See also *Chorzow Factory Case (Indemnity)*, PCIJ Ser A No 17 (1928) 47–8; *Avena Case*, ICJ Reports (2004) 12, para 119.

[88] *Lac Lanoux Arbitration*, 24 *ILR* (1957) 101; *Icelandic Fisheries Cases*, ICJ Reports (1974) 3 and 175; *Gabčíkovo-Nagymaros Case*, ICJ Reports (1997) 7; *Southern Bluefin Tuna Arbitration* (2000); *MOX Plant Case (Provisional Measures)* ITLOS No 10 (2001) para 82; *Land Reclamation (Provisional Measures)* ITLOS No 12 (2003) para 92; *Pulp Mills Case*, ICJ Reports (2006).

[89] See *Behring Sea Fur Seals Arbitration* (1898) 1 Moore's Int Arb 755; *Trail Smelter Arbitration*, 35 *AJIL* (1941) 684; *Land Reclamation (Provisional Measures)* ITLOS No 12 (2003).

[90] *Trail Smelter Arbitration*, 33 *AJIL* (1939) 182, and 35 *AJIL* (1941) 684.

[91] 1945 ICJ Statute, Article 41; 1982 UNCLOS, Article 290; 1995 Agreement on Straddling and Highly Migratory Fish Stocks, Article 31. See Rosenne, *Provisional Measures in International Law* (Oxford, 2005).

[92] *Pulp Mills Case (Provisional Measures)* ICJ Reports (2006) --, paras 72–5; *Southern Bluefin Tuna Cases (Provisional Measures)* ITLOS Nos 3 and 4 (1999). See *supra* Ch 3, section 4(4).

[93] *MOX Plant (Provisional Measures)* ITLOS No 10 (2001); *Land Reclamation (Provisional Measures)* ITLOS No 12 (2003). See *supra* Ch 3, section 4(5).

Case the parties were also required to carry out a study of possible impacts on the marine environment. The *Pulp Mills Case* shows that even an unsuccessful application for provisional measures can be beneficial. In order to resist the application it was necessary for Uruguay to demonstrate to the court that it had carried out an EIA and that adequate measures to prevent or minimize the risk of harm to the River Uruguay had been taken or were planned. Since interim orders are binding on the parties, they must be taken seriously.

In several environmental disputes the applicant has asked the court to order cessation of a potentially harmful activity. No such order has yet been made. Where there has been a failure to notify or consult the only remedy identified by the ILC,[94] case law,[95] or state practice,[96] is for applicant state to request the necessary information and initiate consultations. The only remedy afforded by any international tribunal for failure to carry out an EIA or monitoring is to order appropriate studies to be carried out.[97] Where the measures taken to protect neighbouring states from environmental damage are inadequate, international tribunals have ordered additional measures to be taken.[98] In most such disputes, the parties are ordered to cooperate.[99] Thus in the *Gabčikovo-Nagymaros Case*, the Court concluded that '[i]n this case, the consequences of the wrongful acts of both Parties will be wiped out "as far as possible" if they resume their cooperation in the utilization of the shared water resources of the Danube' and it ordered them to do so.[100]

The *Trail Smelter Case* remains the best illustration of the power of courts and tribunals to prescribe measures to prevent repetition of environmental damage for which a state has been held responsible.[101] In that case Canada was ordered to implement regulations controlling the future operation of the smelter, and to compensate for any damage which recurred notwithstanding compliance. Although Canada had to take measures to protect the United States from serious injury, its right to continue to operate the smelter was maintained. Thus, a balance of interests between the two parties

---

[94] 2001 Articles on Prevention of Transboundary Harm, Article 11; 1997 UN Watercourses Convention, Article 18.

[95] *Lake Lanoux Arbitration*, 24 *ILR* (1957) 138 ('if a neighbouring State has not taken the initiative, the other State cannot be denied the right to insist on notification of works or concessions which are the object of a scheme'). See *infra*, Ch 10.

[96] See e.g. *Sudanese–Egyptian dispute regarding the Aswan High Dam* and *US–Mexico dispute regarding salinity of the Colorado River*, cited in *ILC Report* (1988) GAOR A/43/10, 131–33; see also Kirgis, *Prior Consultation in International Law: A Study in State Practice* (Charlottesville, 1983) 43, 66.

[97] *Trail Smelter Arbitration*, 33 AJIL 182 (1939) 209; *Gabčikovo-Nagymaros Case*, ICJ Reports (1997) 78, para 140; *Land Reclamation (Provisional Measures)* ITLOS No 12 (2003) para 106

[98] *Trail Smelter Arbitration*, 35 AJIL 684 (1941) 726; *Gabčikovo-Nagymaros*, 82, para 155(2); *Land Reclamation (Arbitral Award)* (2005) operative para 2, Annex.

[99] *Gabčikovo-Nagymaros Case*, 80, para 150; *MOX Plant (Provisional Measures)* para 82; *Land Reclamation (Provisional Measures)* para 92; *Land Reclamation (Arbitral Award)* operative para 2 and Annex; *Southern Bluefin Tuna (Provisional Measures)* para 78 and operative para (e).

[100] *Gabčikovo-Nagymaros Case*, 80, para 150.

[101] 35 *AJIL* (1941) 712ff. Gray, *Judicial Remedies in International Law*, 12 emphasizes that the *compromis* expressly empowered the tribunal to prescribe measures.

was achieved through the tribunal's order, and indeed this formed the main object of the arbitration.[102]

Some of the judges in the 1974 *Nuclear Tests Cases* suggested that an international tribunal cannot grant injunctions or prohibitory orders restraining violations of international law.[103] Nevertheless, the ICJ has in later cases decided that a state 'shall take effective steps' to ensure compliance with its obligations.[104] It has also been willing to order the cancellation of warrants and the review of court judgments found to be inconsistent with a state's international obligations.[105] The latter precedents may be relevant in environmental disputes, where for example an authorisation or permit is unlawfully granted. In most cases, ICJ judgments simply declare that a state has or has not acted in accordance with its obligations, and refer to its duty to make reparation. A strong dissent by four judges favoured this form of remedy in the *Nuclear Tests Cases*, although the majority took a more restrictive view of the Court's power in the particular circumstances of that case.[106]

(b) Restitution and compensation

Where injury to persons or damage to property, natural resources, or the environment are suffered by the claimant state, restitution or compensation are likely to be the normal remedy. Controversy surrounding restitution in international law makes it 'difficult to state the conditions of its application with any certainty'.[107] Restitution is given the narrowest possible meaning by the ILC: 'to re-establish the situation which existed before the wrongful act was committed'.[108] It neither includes establishment of the situation that would have existed but for the wrong, nor does it require a transfer of any profit accruing to the wrongdoer because of the wrong. Legal restitution, that is an order for the repeal or alteration of some legislative, judicial, or administrative act, will usually be most appropriate where a treaty provision or international standard has not been complied with.[109] The *Trail Smelter* award comes close to restitution in this sense in so far as it compels the more diligent regulation of the smelter.

What is clear from the ILC's work, as well from the state practice, is that restitution of the *status quo ante*, in the form of restoration of environmental damage, will not necessarily be either adequate or appropriate in every case. The issue will primarily be one of fact: what has been lost and what needs to be done to restore it? It will of

---

[102] Rubin, 50 *Oregon LR* (1971); Read, 1 *CYIL* (1963) 213; Boyle, 39 *ICLQ* (1990) 18–19.

[103] ICJ Reports (1973) 131, per Ignacio Pinto, but cf ICJ Reports (1974) 389, per de Castro.

[104] *Bosnian Genocide Case*, ICJ Reports (2007) operative para 8; *Tehran Hostages Case*, ICJ Reports (1980) 3, operative para 3.

[105] *Arrest Warrant Case*, ICJ Reports (2002) 3, operative para 3; *Avena Case*, ICJ Reports (2004) 12, operative para 9.

[106] See ICJ Reports (1974) 263. Compare the refusal of the Court to treat Australia's application as a request for a declaration, at 263, para 30, with joint dissenting opinion of Judges Waldock, Onyeama, Dillard, Arechaga at 312–17, and see Gray, *Judicial Remedies in International Law*, 104–6.

[107] Brownlie, *State Responsibility*, 222; Gray, *Judicial Remedies in International Law*, 12.

[108] 2001 Article 35. See Crawford, *The ILC's Articles etc*, 213–7.

[109] *Chorzow Factory Case*, PCIJ Ser A, No 17 (1928); *Avena Case*, ICJ Reports (2004) 12, operative para 9.

course be necessary to determine whether and how far restoration of the damaged environment or its equivalent is possible, or is not otherwise disproportionately burdensome to the wrongdoer within the terms of the ILC's article. Moreover, restitution is 'very frequently inadequate to ensure a complete reparation'.[110] In these circumstances, compensation will in many cases become 'the main and central remedy following an internationally wrongful act'.[111]

What is mainly in issue is whether claims can be made for environmental harm not quantifiable in terms of damage to property or economic loss. This question is significantly dependent on the content of a state's primary obligations of environmental protection. To the extent that these do cover the protection of common areas, ecosystems, wildlife, or protected or wilderness areas, reparation should include clean-up costs, damage limitation, and possible reinstatement. State practice and judicial precedent are too limited in this field to draw confident conclusions, but reparation for environmental damage to a state's territory is covered by a number of modern liability treaties,[112] and is the basis for compensation awards made by the UN Compensation Commission in claims against Iraq.[113]

In principle, compensation should fully restore the injured party's position. Thus, the 1972 Space Objects Liability Convention (Article 12) provides that compensation shall be determined in accordance with 'international law and the principles of justice and equity'[114], but must be sufficient to restore the party on whose behalf the claim is presented 'to the condition which would have existed if the damage had not occurred'. Moreover, the negotiators of this treaty deliberately rejected any limits on liability. There is some evidence, however, that the application of a strict or absolute liability principle may entail limiting the amount of compensation. In the *Cosmos 954* claim Canada did not recover its full costs of $14 million, but claimed $6 million, and settled for $3 million.[115] However, this was an ad hoc, *ex gratia* settlement, of limited value as a precedent.

The ILC recognizes that, in making awards of compensation, international arbitral tribunals and claims commissions have drawn on private law analogies, but it concludes that these precedents do not give us detailed general rules on the matter.[116] Its draft articles indicate two important limits on the right to claim compensation, however. First, compensation can only be appropriate where the damage has been caused by the wrongful act. The Commission dismisses the distinction sometimes drawn between direct and indirect damage as ambiguous and of 'scant utility',[117] although its preferred alternative requirement of a 'clear and unbroken causal link' is scarcely

---

[110] *YbILC* (1993) 1, Pt 2, 62.   [111] Ibid, 63, 76.

[112] Convention on Civil Liability for Oil Pollution Damage, *infra*, Ch 7; 1996 Vienna Convention on Civil liability for Nuclear Damage, *infra*, Ch 9.

[113] See *infra*.

[114] This formulation was deliberately adopted in preference to the *lex loci*. See Cheng, *Studies in International Space Law*, 332–41.

[115] See Schwartz and Berlin, 27 *McGill LJ* (1982) 676.   [116] *YbILC* (1993) II, Pt 2, 68.

[117] Ibid, 68–9. Compare UNSC Resolution 687, *infra*, n 126, which allows claims against Iraq only if the damage is direct.

less problematic. Whatever test is used, the obligation to compensate for damage is not unlimited, and is bounded by some inherent notion of remoteness or proximity. Thus regardless of whether international law in principle compensates for environmental damage, however defined, there will inevitably be some cases where compensation is denied on grounds of non-proximity or remoteness.

Second, only 'financially assessable damage' is compensable.[118] The term 'financially assessable' was adopted in the draft articles because the earlier reference to 'economically assessable' damage was thought inappropriate to cover, for example, the wrongful extinction of endangered wildlife of no 'economic' value,[119] although it did include damage to 'the State's territory in general, to its organization in a broad sense, its property at home and abroad...'.[120] This list begs the question whether all damage to a state's territory is assessable in monetary terms. The problem with environmental damage is precisely that it may not be. Although almost everything can be either restored or given a monetary value in some fashion, what is not clear are the limits, if any, to acceptable methods of valuation. Would the attribution of notional or non-market-based valuations to depleted natural resources be covered under this formulation? Such valuations have been employed in US, Italian, and Russian law,[121] but have been rejected by the International Oil Pollution Compensation Fund. The Fund's view is that it cannot compensate for oil pollution damage assessed 'on the basis of an abstract quantification of damage calculated in accordance with theoretical models'.[122] If the rules of international law on compensation are as general and flexible as the ILC believes, then all of these approaches are probably acceptable in principle, even if in practice they are then narrowed for the purposes of specific treaty-based compensation schemes.

These are questions the Commission does not really address, however. The precedents it relies on deal mainly with valuing injury or death of persons, loss of profits, loss of earnings or livelihood, and interest, but they shed no light on the extent to which environmental damage can be compensated. Moreover, although international claims point in a limited way to the availability of compensation for environmental restoration and clean-up costs, as well as for environmental damage that harms people or private property,[123] they do not take in the whole range of what is potentially included in the phrase 'environmental damage', such as loss of biological diversity,

---

[118] ILC, 2001 State Responsibility Article 36.

[119] *ILC Report* (2000) GAOR A/55/10, Ch IV, para 193. Compare 1998 draft Article 44, and commentary at *YbILC* (1993) II, Pt 2, 71.

[120] *YbILC* (1993) II, Pt 2, 72.

[121] *Commonwealth of Puerto Rico v SS Zoe Colocotroni* 456 F Supp 1327 (1978) and 628 F 2d 652 (1980); *Antonio Gramsci* (No 2) and *Patmos* cases, IOPC Fund, *Annual Report* (1990) 23, 27. See Maffei, in Francioni and Scovazzi, *International Responsibility for Environmental Harm* (London, 1991) 381 and generally, Wetterstein (ed), *Harm to the Environment* (Oxford, 1997); Bowman and Boyle (eds), *Environmental Damage in International and Comparative Law* (Oxford, 2002).

[122] See Brown in Butler (ed), *The Law of the Sea and International Shipping* (New York, 1986) 282ff.

[123] See e.g. *Trail Smelter; COSMOS 954 Claim*; the practice of the IOPC Fund, *supra*, n 121, and UNCC practice, *infra*.

or dead wildlife. It may be that at this point we should simply recognize that there are limits to what can be valued and therefore to what interests are worth compensation. Where neither restoration nor compensation for damage to the environment are appropriate then satisfaction is left as the only means of affording some nominal redress.[124]

At the same time we should remember that the ILC's draft articles are a framework of general principles, not a precise prescription for every eventuality. Even if the availability of compensation is limited to 'financially assessable damage', there remains much scope for interpretation of that phrase in a manner which takes full account of the particular demands of environmental valuation. This suggests that we focus on methods of valuation, on overcoming the objection that something which is not necessarily 'property' and which may have no 'market value' has no economic worth. This is clearly not a task for lawyers alone: it requires at least the input of economists and others skilled in techniques of valuation.

In this respect the UN Compensation Commission's (UNCC) decisions dealing with environmental claims against Iraq provide the most relevant contemporary precedents. They are particularly innovative on questions of valuation, restoration and monitoring.[125] The UN Security Council held Iraq liable for 'any direct loss, [or] damage, including environmental damage and the depletion of natural resources...as a result of Iraq's unlawful invasion and occupation of Kuwait'.[126] As interpreted by the UNCC, Resolution 687 covers, inter alia, reimbursement of clean-up assistance costs, compensation for reasonable measures to assess and monitor damage to the environment and public health, and to clean up and restore the environment.[127] While rejecting many of the environmental claims for lack of evidence linking them with the invasion, the Commission allowed some substantial claims for reinstatement of the *status quo ante*, subject to the qualification that the 'primary emphasis must be placed on restoring the environment to pre-invasion conditions, in terms of its overall ecological functioning, rather than on the removal of specific contaminants or restoration of the environment to a particular physical condition'.[128] Where restoration to a natural state was not possible or reasonable the cost of making equivalent provision was awarded.[129] The UNCC found no legal basis for excluding pure environmental damage that has no commercial value.[130] To that extent its approach is comparable to the IOPC Fund's practice of allowing reasonable reinstatement measures aimed at accelerating natural recovery of environmental damage.

---

[124] ILC, 2001 State Responsibility Article 37. Satisfaction may consist of an apology, expression of regret, or a judicial declaration of a breach of obligation.

[125] See Sand, 35 *EPL* (2005) 244; Gautier, in Ndiaye and Wolfrum (eds), *Law of the Sea, Environmental Law and Settlement of Disputes* (Leiden, 2007) 177; Kazazi, ibid, 1109.

[126] UNSC Res 687 (1991).

[127] UNCC Gov Council, Decision 7, revised 16 March 1992, para 35; UNCC F4 Claims 2nd Decision (2002) paras 29 and 32–5.

[128] UNCC F4 Claims 3rd Decision (2003) paras 47–8.

[129] UNCC F4 Claims 5th Decision (2006) para 82.   [130] Ibid, para 57.

One of the panel of commissioners has summarized five elements of UNCC practice:

1. precautionary monitoring to identify and assess long-term risks to public health and the environment

2. reimbursement of mutual assistance costs in environmental emergencies

3. the obligation for claimants to mitigate and contain damage to the environment

4. valuation methods to ensure the remediation of lost ecological services

5. follow-up tracking to ensure the environmental effectiveness of remediation, making the disbursement of compensation awards conditional upon compliance with agreed environmental objectives and standards ('green conditionality').

In his view the multilateral UNCC process was better able to represent the general environmental concerns of the international community than the traditional bilateral perspective of state responsibility.[131] It could only do so, however, because the UNSC had found Iraq liable and created a mechanism for giving effect to that decision. This was an important procedural innovation. It is unlikely that an international court could have handled matters in the same way.

2(5) STANDING TO BRING CLAIMS

Standing to bring international claims is in principle confined to 'injured states'.[132] What this means can be observed in the second phase of the *South West Africa Case*.[133] Liberia and Ethiopia, although original members of the League of Nations with certain rights under the mandates agreement, were held to have no legal right or interest in South Africa's compliance with its obligations towards the inhabitants of the territory. That was a matter for the League alone and individual members acquired no independent standing to bring violations before the ICJ. This was an unusual case, however, whose unsuccessful outcome is a consequence of a narrow analysis of the legal relationship between the League, its members and the mandatory power. Although the term 'injured state' is used by Article 42 of the ILC Articles on State Responsibility in broadly comparable terms, this will cause little difficulty in most interstate environmental disputes. A denial of high-seas fishing rights, as in the *Icelandic Fisheries Cases*,[134] or high-seas pollution affecting a coastal state, would clearly fall within the ILC's conception of an injured state, for example.

---

[131] Sand, 35 *EPL* (2005) 244. See also Kazazi, in Bowman and Boyle (eds), *Environmental Damage in International and Comparative Law*, 111.

[132] ILC, 2001 Articles on State Responsibility Article 42. See generally, Crawford, *The ILC's Articles on State Responsibility*, 254–60; Gray, *Judicial Remedies in International Law*, 211–15; Charney, 10 *Mich JIL* (1989) 57.

[133] ICJ Reports (1966) esp 20–3; Brownlie, *Principles of Public International Law* (6th edn, Oxford, 2003) 449–52.

[134] ICJ Reports (1974) 3.

More problematic, however, are violations of international law affecting only the global commons, or areas of common concern, such as the ozone layer or global climate. As in the *Nuclear Tests Cases*,[135] such violations may not per se affect the rights of any individual state, but rather those of the community of states as a whole. The problem of standing in this context is thus particularly concerned with how community rights can be enforced, it at all, by unaffected states through interstate claims, or by some other form of public interest representation.

International law recognizes the possibility that in exceptional situations certain obligations may be enforceable on behalf of the international community.[136] In the *Barcelona Traction Case*[137] the ICJ referred to obligations *erga omnes* in respect of which all states would enjoy standing to bring claims, and the normal nationality of claims rules would cease to apply. The protection of common areas such as the high seas, or of common interests such as the ozone layer or global climate, presents a comparable problem to the protection of human rights in that without community standing there might be no 'injured' state capable of holding states responsible for the violation of these obligations. While, as we saw in Chapter 3, obligations of global environmental responsibility may have an *erga omnes partes* character, in the sense that they are owed to all states acting through collective institutions of treaty supervision, in the 1974 *Nuclear Tests Cases* the ICJ was unsympathetic to the notion of an *actio popularis* allowing high-seas freedoms to be enforced by any state, and it did not follow its earlier dicta.[138] Nor has it applied the concept in any other case not concerned with human rights or humanitarian law.

Despite this unpromising background, the ILC has recognized the right of states to enforce collective interests in terms broad enough to encompass the more significant global environmental responsibilities and to permit an *actio popularis* in certain circumstances.[139] The 2001 Articles on State Responsibility envisage five categories of potential claimant:

1. An injured state may claim, i.e. when an obligation owed to that state is breached: Article 42(a).

2. A specially affected state may claim if the obligation breached is owed to that state as part of a group of states, or to the international community as a whole: Article 42(b)(i).

---

[135] ICJ Reports (1974) 253, 457.

[136] See generally Crawford, *1st Rept*, UN Doc A/CN4/490/Add 1 (1998) paras 69–71; Tams, *Enforcing Obligations Erga Omnes in International Law* (Cambridge, 2005); Ragazzi, *The Concept of International Obligations Erga Omnes* (Oxford, 1997); Rosenne, in Anghie and Sturgess (eds), *Legal Visions of the 21st Century* (The Hague, 1998) 509; Simma, 250 *Recueil des Cours* (1994) 293–301.

[137] ICJ Reports (1970) 3.

[138] ICJ Reports (1974) 387, per de Castro, but see *contra* Petren, 303, and Weeramantry in *Gabčíkovo-Nagymaros Case*, ICJ Reports (1997) 7, *supra* Ch 3, section 3(2).

[139] ILC, 2001 State Responsibility Articles 42, 48, on which see ILC commentary in Crawford, *The ILC's Articles on State Responsibility*, 254–60, 276–80.

3. Any state may claim if the breach of obligation is of such a character that it affects the enjoyment of rights and obligations by all states concerned: Article 42(b)(ii).

4. Any state may claim if the obligation breached is established for the protection of the collective interests of a group of states, including the claimant state: Article 48(1)(a).

5. Any state may claim if the obligation breached is owed to the international community as a whole: Article 48(1)(b).

Essentially the first three categories of claimant are all 'injured states', i.e. those covered by Article 42. Here the claimant state will be affected by the breach, and will necessarily be enforcing its own rights. Claims falling within the last two categories, i.e. those covered by Article 48, are genuinely public interest claims, enforcing *erga omnes* obligations. They can be initiated by any state within the terms of that article.

Assuming that the ILC has correctly codified the existing law, its draft articles cast serious doubt on the reasoning of those judges in the 1974 *Nuclear Tests Cases* who questioned the applicants' standing to bring the claim. In contrast to that judgement, Article 48 takes account of the growing number of multilateral treaties and customary law concerned with the protection of the global environment or of areas of common interest or concern, such as the Conventions on World Heritage, Trade in Endangered Species, Ozone Depletion, Climate Change, Biological Diversity, Dumping at Sea, or the Law of the Sea. These agreements cannot be dismissed as mere expressions of a principle of good neighbourliness. That they create obligations whose intended beneficiaries are the international community of states as a whole has been partially acknowledged by the new terminology of 'common concern of mankind' found in the Climate Change and Biological Diversity Conventions.[140] The ILC has in effect now acknowledged that all parties have a collective and individual interest in the enforcement of such treaties.[141] In these cases any state party will have standing to sue for breach or non-compliance. The same will be true of *erga omnes* customary obligations, including the duty to protect the marine environment or the environment of common areas beyond national jurisdiction.

However broadly the right to protect community interests is expressed, it does not follow that the full range of reparation will be available to third states acting for this purpose.[142] What is clear is that third states have the same right as injured states to seek cessation of any breaches of obligations owed to the international community

---

[140] *Supra*, Ch 3, section 3(1). See also Kirgis, 84 *AJIL* (1990) 525; Boyle, in Churchill and Freestone (eds), *International Law and Global Climate Change* (Dordrecht, 1991) Ch1.

[141] Crawford, *1st Report* (1998) UN Doc A/CN 4/460, para 100. Cf *SS Wimbledon, PCIJ* Ser A, No 1 (1923) 20, and Gray, *Judicial Remedies in International Law,* 211ff, but compare Hutchinson, 59 *BYIL* (1988) 151 and Chinkin, *Third Parties in International Law* (Oxford, 1993) 282–3 and *infra,* section 4(3)(d). Note that ICJ Statute, Article 63 gives every party to a treaty a right to intervene in ICJ proceedings when the construction of the treaty is in question. See Chinkin, 178–98 and *infra,* section 4(1).

[142] Charney, 10 *Mich JIL* (1989) 57, and *id*, in Francioni and Scovazzi (eds), *International Responsibility for Environmental Harm*, but compare Abi-Saab, in Weiler et al, *International Crimes of State* (Berlin, 1989) 141.

as a whole.[143] Beyond that, the availability of reparation will depend on the circumstances of the breach, the extent to which the claimant's interests are affected, and the nature of the risk to community interests. It is, for example, unlikely that individual states will be entitled to demand reparation for material damage to the global environment beyond any clean-up or reinstatement costs which they may incur.[144] Any further satisfaction will probably be limited to acknowledging that there has been a breach. Account must also be taken of the risk of multiple claimants rendering settlement of a dispute more difficult or resulting in measures disproportionate to the violation or injury.

In practice the protection of community interests will in many cases involve no more than the right to make diplomatic protests. The possibility of third states taking unilateral action or countermeasures, such as refusal of access to EEZ fish stocks or to ports, or embargoes on trade, in order to induce compliance, is increasingly constrained by WTO treaty obligations.[145] Moreover the ILC Articles on State Responsibility specifically allow countermeasures only if taken by an injured state.[146] This would not preclude one state from taking countermeasures where all states are injured states within the terms of Article 48, but the ILC deliberately left open the question whether collective countermeasures can also be applied by non-injured states.[147]

There is one further way of looking at the protection of community interests under the ILC State Responsibility Articles, however. If the wrongful act is a 'serious breach' of a 'peremptory norm of general international law', other states will be under a duty not to recognize its legality and they must cooperate to bring the violation to an end.[148] The intention behind this provision is to allow for an exceptional response in the event of 'gross or systematic failure' to comply with obligations affecting the international community's most important interests. It has some precedent in international law.[149] In its original form the predecessor draft article was intended to apply to obligations for 'the safeguarding and preservation of the human environment such as those prohibiting massive pollution of the atmosphere or the seas'.[150] It is far from clear, however, whether any environmental obligations have been recognized as non-derogable peremptory norms by the international community as a whole in accordance with Article 53 of the Vienna Convention on the Law of Treaties. The issues are

---

[143] ILC, 2001 State Responsibility Article 48(2).

[144] Boyle, in Wetterstein (ed), *Harm to the Environment* (Oxford, 1997) Ch 7; Charney, in Francioni and Scovazzi (eds), *International Responsibility for Environmental Harm.*

[145] On WTO law, see *infra,* Ch 14. See also 1992 Rio Declaration, Principle 12. See generally Wolfrum, 272 *Recueil des Cours* (1998) 9, 59–77; Murase, 253 *Recueil des Cours* (1995) 283, 324ff.

[146] Article 49.   [147] Article 54. See Koskenniemi, 72 *BYIL* (2001) 337.

[148] Articles 40–1. These replace the concept of criminal responsibility previously found in Article 19 of the earlier text of the ILC's draft articles. See Crawford, *1st Rept,* (1998) UN Doc A/CN 4/490, Add 1–3; *ILC Report* (1998) GAOR A/53/10, Ch VII, paras 241–331; *ILC Report* (2000) GAOR A/55/10, ChIV, paras 358–63, 374–83.

[149] See *Namibia Advisory Opinion,* ICJ Reports (1971) 16.

[150] See text of Article 19 in the ILC's 1996 draft articles.

not susceptible to simplistic assumptions, but international courts have so far applied the concept of peremptory norms only to aggression, torture, and genocide.[151]

As we shall see in the next section, however, collective supervision of global environmental responsibilities by intergovernmental commissions, conferences of treaty parties, or international organizations will often be a more effective and realistic remedy than public interest claims and countermeasures by individual states.

2(6) CONCLUSIONS: THE UTILITY OF STATE RESPONSIBILITY

While potentially relevant to environmental disputes, reliance on state responsibility has serious deficiencies in this context. First, claims may be brought only by states; the provision of diplomatic protection is discretionary and the state entitled to claim is the sole judge of whether it should do so.[152] This decision may be made on grounds unrelated to the environmental issues in the individual case. Especially where the harm is to common spaces, or where states may be reluctant to create precedents affecting their own future conduct, there is less likelihood that a willing plaintiff will appear or press claims to the full. Moreover, the jurisdiction of international tribunals is rarely compulsory;[153] without agreement to resort to litigation or a claims settlement process, claims can only proceed by negotiation. Whatever method is used, the process will often be slow and expensive, and it gives the individual victim no control over the negotiation of any settlement.

Second, insofar as claims may be made only by states with standing, and the remedies available may be limited or inadequate, it is potentially more difficult to use international claims as a means of protecting the environment of common areas. This leads one writer to conclude that:

In so far as the concept of responsibility to the international community as a whole is a reality, this is through the functioning of international organizations rather than any formal judicial procedure. International organizations provide a partial substitute for the lack of any general action on behalf of the world community and also for the lack of compulsory judicial settlement.[154]

Third, although compensation for the costs of transboundary environmental damage may be recovered through international claims, making states liable is an inefficient means of allocating these costs. Uncertainty surrounding liability standards, whether states or private parties should be made liable, the type of environmental damage covered, and the role of equitable balancing, means that the outcome of any

[151] *Nicaragua v United States*, ICJ Reports (1986) 14, paras 172–86; *Prosecutor v Furundzija*, 38 ILM (1999) 317 (ICTY); *Al-Adsani v United Kingdom*, 34 EHRR (2002) 11, paras 52–67.

[152] *Barcelona Traction Case*, ICJ Reports (1970) 4, paras 78–9. Claims in respect of injury to individuals must also satisfy the nationality of claims rule: see *Nottebohm Case*, ICJ Reports (1955) 4. See ILC Draft Articles on Diplomatic Protection, *ILC Report* (2006) GAOR A/61/10, commentary to Articles 2 and 3.

[153] See *infra*, section 4.

[154] Gray, *Judicial Remedies in International Law*, 215, and see *infra*, section 3.

claim remains inherently unpredictable and points to the absence of a fully principled basis for determining who should bear transboundary costs.

The most important objection to state responsibility, however, is that it is an inadequate model for the enforcement of international standards of environmental protection. Like tort law, it complements, but does not displace, the need for a system of regulatory supervision. It is this failing which explains the emphasis states have placed on the development of treaty regimes of environmental protection enforced by multilateral non-compliance procedures or resort to transboundary legal proceedings, and the failure to develop or reform the law relating to state liability for environmental harm. Commentators have rightly discerned a 'corresponding decline in recourse to the law of state responsibility'.[155] Moreover, equal access to civil remedies and other civil-liability schemes offer a better means of allowing the recovery of transboundary environmental costs. For most forms of transboundary or marine pollution damage civil liability and insurance schemes now represent the primary recourse available to individual claimants and states.[156] Such schemes also emphasize the responsibility of individual polluters for the protection of the environment. In this respect state responsibility operates too indirectly and may appear to exempt those corporations or officials whose actions, policies, or decisions have led to harmful consequences. One writer concludes that: 'It is not surprising in such circumstances if states behave badly'.[157]

But it does not follow that state responsibility is of no continuing significance. First, without the more comprehensive codification of environmental standards, and the wider use of supervisory institutions, there may be no other basis for enforcing customary international law. Second, civil-liability schemes, although valuable, have their own drawbacks and deficiencies which make it necessary to retain the option of recourse through international claims. This point is particularly clear with regard to major nuclear accidents, such as the Chernobyl disaster.[158] Lastly, non-compliance procedures, whatever their potential, do not always work as an effective substitute.

3 TREATY COMPLIANCE

3(1) BREACH OF TREATY OR NON-COMPLIANCE?

In Chapter 2 we saw how multilateral environmental agreements have become an especially prominent means of developing international environmental law and regulating environmental risks and sustainable use of natural resources. How do states enforce or ensure compliance with this growing body of treaty law? If violations of a multilateral environmental treaty are revealed, what consequences could then follow?

---

[155] Shelton, 96 *AJIL* (2002) 854.
[157] Allott, 29 *Harv IJL* (1988) 1.
[156] See *infra*, Ch 5.
[158] See *infra*, Ch 9.

Several approaches are possible. Breach of treaty is a wrongful act entailing a duty to afford reparation in accordance with the law of state responsibility discussed above. It may additionally entitle the injured party to retaliate by taking proportionate countermeasures aimed at restoring equality between the parties,[159] or by terminating or suspending the treaty if the breach is 'material'.[160] However, termination of a treaty on any ground is not easy to achieve unless all the parties agree. The terms of Article 60 of the Vienna Convention on the Law of Treaties require there to be either repudiation of the treaty or breach of a provision essential to its object and purpose; in practice uncertainty inherent in this wording has resulted in courts almost never finding such a breach. As one writer concludes: 'Article 60 simply does not work. It does not mean what it says and it does not say what it means.'[161] The *Gabčíkovo-Nagymaros Case* illustrates the point. Hungary relied on repudiation by both parties, as well as necessity, fundamental change of circumstances, and impossibility of performance to justify its claim that the 1977 Treaty had terminated. All of these arguments were rejected on the facts. Although the ICJ accepted that important aspects of the treaty had not been complied with and that the scheme now in operation was not even an approximate application of the treaty, it referred to the possibility that reciprocal non-compliance might justify termination as 'a precedent with disturbing implications'.[162] Nevertheless, given the scale of construction work actually undertaken and the fact that a scheme of power generation had come into operation, even if not the one envisaged by the treaty, the Court's reluctance to contemplate a situation no longer regulated by any treaty is almost certainly correct.

In the case of multilateral regulatory treaties, including those intended to protect the global or regional environment, breach is even more unlikely to justify termination. Not only does Article 60 make agreement of all the other parties a precondition, but termination is an inherently inappropriate response in most cases, however serious the breach. Thus, it would have served no purpose to conclude that Russia's non-compliance with the Montreal Protocol on Substances that Deplete the Ozone Layer terminated its participation in that treaty.[163] What needs to be achieved in such situations is compliance with the terms of the treaty. From this perspective emphasis on the continued integrity of the treaty and the widest possible participation are the most important considerations. Demanding reparation for breach is also likely to be unhelpful in such cases because of the implication of wrongdoing. Breach of treaty retains its theoretically wrongful character, but for multilateral regulatory treaties its implications have more often been avoided than observed. Thus, in the case of environmental treaties, states have generally favoured softer procedures which make use

---

[159] On countermeasures see ILC, 2001 State Responsibility Articles 49–54 and *Air Services Arbitration* 54 *ILR* (1978) 304.

[160] 1969 Vienna Convention on Treaties, Article 60; *Chorzow Factory Case,* PCIJ Ser A, No 8/9 (1927) 21; *Namibia Advisory Opinion,* ICJ Reports (1971) 16; *ICAO Council Case,* ICJ Reports (1972) 67; *Gabčíkovo-Nagymaros Case,* ICJ Reports (1997) 7, paras 105–14, and see generally Rosenne, *Breach of Treaty* (Cambridge, 1985); Reuter, *An Introduction to the Law of Treaties* (London, 1989) 150ff.

[161] Klabbers, 8 *YbIEL* (1997) 36–40.   [162] At para 114. See Fitzmaurice, 11 *Leiden JIL* (1998) 321.

[163] See *infra*, Ch 6.

of international institutions, treaty supervisory bodies or diplomatic methods to deal with non-compliance.

Academic studies have shown that ensuring compliance with environmental treaties is not the principal problem which treaty institutions face, for the simple reason that states typically agree to measures that they believe can be complied with at little or no cost.[164] For the same reason, if the treaty is not strong enough, full compliance will not solve the problems it is intended to address.[165] Nevertheless, where problems do arise, intergovernmental bodies can provide both formal and informal methods for settling disputes and monitoring compliance. Their principal importance lies in facilitating multilateral solutions, usually within the Conference of the Parties, both to resolve questions of treaty interpretation and allegations of breach or non-compliance with the treaty. Some scholars have characterized this approach as 'managerialist'—in the sense that active management of compliance is required rather than enforcement.[166] Others refer to it as 'dispute avoidance' because it seeks to minimize resort to arbitration or judicial settlement.[167] The non-compliance procedures considered below are an example, as is the power given to some treaty bodies to undertake inquiry or conciliation, but dispute avoidance in a wider sense is characteristic of many environmental treaties, even when no formal provision is made.

3(2) TREATY SUPERVISORY BODIES

The treaty supervisory bodies we consider in this section are useful insofar as they exercise a form of collective supervision, enabling individual parties to be held accountable to the other parties for non-compliance.[168] Accountability may thus extend to a wider community than the affected state and involve also the participation of NGO observers, although none of the environmental treaties goes as far as the ILO Convention, under which employers and trade union organizations participate directly in the process of scrutiny.

Reliance on autonomous treaty bodies has been identified as part of a general trend away from the solution of problems by strictly judicial means and towards the resolution of conflicts through an equitable balancing of interests and ad hoc political compromise.[169] Used in this way such mechanisms become a forum for negotiation

---

[164] Victor, Raustiala and Skolnikoff (eds), *Implementation and Effectiveness of International Environmental Commitments* (Cambridge, Mass, 1998) 662.

[165] See Mitchell, in Bodansky, Brunnée, and Hey, *Oxford Handbook of International Environmental Law* (Oxford, 2007) 893–921.

[166] Chayes et al, in Brown Weiss and Jacobson (eds), *Engaging Countries: Strengthening Compliance with International Environmental Accords* (Cambridge, Mass, 2000) 39–62. But for an important critique of this approach see Brunnée, in Winter (ed), *Multilevel Governance of Global Environmental Change* (Cambridge, 2006) 387–408.

[167] UNEP, *Study on Dispute Avoidance and Dispute Settlement in International Environmental Law*, UNEP/GC 20/INF/16 (1999).

[168] On the nature of these bodies see Churchill and Ulfstein, 94 *AJIL* (2000) 623 and *supra* Ch 2.

[169] Simma, in Macdonald and Johnston (eds), *Structure and Process of International Law* (The Hague, 1983) 485; Rosenne, *Breach of Treaty* (Cambridge, 1985) 39–44; Gehring, 1 *YbIEL* (1990) 35.

and mutual assistance, rather than adjudication of legal disputes. The underlying perception is that community pressure and the scrutiny of other states in an inter-governmental forum may be more effective in securing a higher level of compliance than more confrontational methods.[170] Moreover, it is possible for supervisory mech-anisms to give a flexible interpretation to treaties of this kind and to apply to this pro-cess experience and knowledge of the issues concerned. The International Whaling Commission, the Meeting of the Parties to the Montreal Protocol on Substances that Deplete the Ozone Layer, and the consultative meeting of the London Dumping Convention afford particularly good examples of this form of conflict resolution.[171] The absence of any provision for institutional supervision is, by contrast, often a sign that a treaty is ineffective and leads to obsolescence. Older treaties in this category, such as the 1940 Western Hemisphere Convention, have for this reason aptly been described as 'sleeping treaties' and their impact on contemporary environmental pro-tection is likely to be limited. As Lyster observes, 'simply by requiring its Parties to meet regularly to review its implementation, a treaty can ensure that it stays at the forefront of its parties' attention'.[172]

The key tasks which treaty supervisory bodies perform are those of information and data collection, receiving and reviewing reports on implementation by states, overseeing independent monitoring and inspection, and facilitating compliance with agreed standards of conduct. These obligations or standards will usually have a treaty basis, but the technique is also capable of application to rules of customary law or to soft law.[173] It is, for example, one method by which the equitable utilization of shared resources can be implemented,[174] or by which preferential or shared rights to common resources such as high seas fisheries can be allocated, as envisaged in the *Icelandic Fisheries Case* and the 1995 Agreement on the Conservation of Straddling and Highly Migratory Fish Stocks.[175]

Another reason for resorting to treaty supervisory mechanisms is that, as we saw earlier in this chapter, individual states may lack standing to bring international claims relating to the protection of global common areas, such as the high seas or global climate. Compliance with the MARPOL Convention, the London Dumping Convention, or the CITES Convention, to take three examples, cannot readily be secured by suspension or termination of the treaty in cases of material breach, as

---

[170] See generally Brown Weiss and Jacobson (eds), *Engaging Countries: Strengthening Compliance with International Environmental Accords*; Victor, Raustiala, and Skolnikoff (eds), *The Implementation and Effectiveness of International Environmental Commitments*; Handl, 5 *Colorado JIELP* (1994) 305; Beyerlin, 56 *ZAÖRV* (1996) 602; Kingsbury, 19 *Mich JIL* (1998) 345; Cameron, Werksman, and Roderick (eds), *Improving Compliance with International Environmental Law* (London 1996); Wolfrum, 272 *Recueil des Cours* (1998) 9; de Chazournes, 99 *RGDIP* (1995) 37.

[171] On the IWC, see Birnie, 29 *NRJ* (1989) 903, and *infra*, Ch 13; on the LDC, see *infra*, Ch 8 and on the Montreal Protocol, *infra*, Ch 6.

[172] Lyster, *International Wildlife Law* (Cambridge, 1985) 12.

[173] Victor et al, *The Implementation and Effectiveness of International Environmental Law*, Ch 6; Shelton (ed), *Commitment and Compliance* (Oxford, 2000).

[174] See *infra*, Ch 10.   [175] See *infra*, Ch 13.

envisaged by Article 60 of the Vienna Convention on Treaties, since that would primarily harm the international community, not the defaulting state, and would run counter to a policy of ensuring the widest possible participation in such agreements.[176] In such cases accountability through international institutions or treaty bodies may be the only practical remedy available.[177]

(a) Trusteeship

The most sophisticated example of an international supervisory regime is UN trusteeship. United Nations trust territories succeeded the mandated territories established by the League of Nations Covenant. In each case the Covenant and the Charter prescribed basic obligations for the administering state to perform in fulfilling its 'sacred trust' to bring the territories in question to full self-determination.[178] The essence of this trust, like the concept of common heritage later employed by the 1982 UNCLOS, was that its performance was subject to international scrutiny and supervision. Although disputes concerning these territories could come before the Permanent Court or the International Court of Justice in certain circumstances,[179] judicial settlement was not the primary method for ensuring compliance by administering powers with their treaty obligations. Instead, the Mandates Commission of the League, or the Trusteeship Council of the UN, were invested with a reporting and reviewing function. As Judge Lauterpacht observed, explaining the role of the former body:

The absence of purely legal machinery and the reliance upon the moral authority of the findings and reports of the Mandates Commission were in fact the essential features of the supervision of the mandates system. Public opinion—the resulting attitude of the Mandatory Powers—were influenced not so much by the formal resolutions of the Council and the Assembly, as by the reports of the Mandates Commission which was the true organ of supervision.[180]

The Trusteeship Council and the Mandates Commission are important precedents because they represent a model of accountability to the whole international community, made more effective by a structure which facilitates open scrutiny and publicity for states failing to meet their obligations, but reinforced by the ultimate authority of the UN General Assembly, or the League Council before it, to pronounce on the conduct of the mandatory power in case of non-compliance. There are obvious parallels here with oversight of MEAs.[181] Not surprisingly, therefore, it has sometimes been suggested that the Trusteeship Council should assume a supervisory responsibility

---

[176] *Supra* section 3(1), and see Macdonald and Johnston (eds), *Structure and Process of International Law* (The Hague, 1983) 485, and Rosenne, *Breach of Treaty*, 39–44.

[177] Handl, 5 *Tulane JICL* (1997) 35–7, and *supra* section 2(5).

[178] Covenant of the League of Nations, Article 22; UN Charter, Ch 12. See Redgwell, *International Trusts and Environmental Protection* (Manchester, 1999) 146–66.

[179] See *South West Africa Case*, ICJ Reports (1950) 128; *South West Africa Cases*, ICJ Reports (1962) 319 and (1966) 9.

[180] *South West Africa (Voting Procedure) Case*, ICJ Reports (1955) 121.

[181] Redgwell, in Chambers (ed), *Reforming International Environmental Governance* (Tokyo, 2005) 183.

for the global commons, or more generally for the global environment.[182] The idea has made no headway in the face of political resistance to UN reform, but elements of international trusteeship can nevertheless be discerned in the environmental responsibilities of the Global Environment Facility and the World Bank.[183] Apart from funding environmental protection projects, what these institutions have in common with trusteeship is that they monitor compliance with a range of MEAs as a condition of any loans or grants they make.[184]

(b) Autonomous treaty bodies

Autonomous treaty bodies offer a more basic model of institutional supervision.[185] The use of autonomous bodies for supervisory purposes is not new. It dates back to the Rhine Commission, established in 1815, with power to regulate navigation on the river, and to settle disputes.[186] Some of the techniques of political supervision and control employed here have become more widely used since 1945, more especially in the field of human rights.[187] As we saw in Chapter 2, modern MEAs have also created an elaborate network of commissions and conferences or meetings of the parties. These are now the principal mechanisms for evaluating MEA effectiveness and supervising compliance. A provision for the parties 'to keep under continuous review and evaluation the effective implementation' of the treaty,[188] or some similar wording, is found in most modern environmental treaties. A variety of supervisory techniques can be used for this purpose.

3(3) SUPERVISORY TECHNIQUES

Effective supervision of the operation and implementation of treaty regimes depends on the availability of adequate information. This can be obtained in several ways.

(a) Reporting and monitoring[189]

Most treaties require states to make periodic reports on matters affecting the treaty. The extent of this obligation varies, but it will usually cover at least the measures taken by the parties towards implementing their obligations. Information must also usually be provided to enable the parties to assess how effectively the treaty is operating.

---

[182] See Redgwell, ibid, 178–95; Palmer, 86 *AJIL* (1992) 259.   [183] Werksman, 6 *YbIEL* (1995) 27.

[184] *Supra*, Ch 2.   [185] See generally Churchill and Ulfstein, 94 *AJIL* (2000) 623.

[186] Congress of Vienna, Final Act, 9 June 1815, Article 32, Annex 16B. See also the 1856 Treaty of Paris which established the first Danube commission and Skubiszewski, 41 *BYIL* (1965) 168; Vitanyi, *The International Regime of River Navigation* (Alphen aan den Rijn, 1979) Chs 1–2.

[187] See Alston and Crawford (eds), *The Future of Human Rights Treaty Monitoring* (Cambridge, 2000).

[188] 1989 Basel Convention on the Control Hazardous Wastes, Article 15; *infra*, Ch 8. See also 2003 Protocol on Pollutant Release Registers, Article 17(2); 2001 POPS Convention, Article 16; 2000 Biosafety Protocol, Article 35; 1998 Aarhus Convention, Article 10.

[189] See Bodansky in Alston and Crawford (eds), *The Future of UN Human Rights Treaty Monitoring*, Ch 17; Wolfrum, 272 *Recueil des Cours* (1998) 9, 36–43; Sachariew, 2 *YbIEL* (1991) 31; Wettestad, in Bodansky, Brunnée and Hey, *Handbook of IEL*, 975–94.

The 1996 Mediterranean Protocol on Land-based Sources of Marine Pollution, for example, calls on the parties to communicate the results of monitoring of levels of marine pollution, as well as measures they have taken, results achieved, and difficulties encountered.[190] The Basel Convention on the Control of Transboundary Movements of Hazardous Wastes requires an annual report on all aspects of transboundary trade and disposal of such substances, and on 'such other matters as the conference of the Parties shall deem relevant'.[191] Similarly, Article 8 of the 1973 CITES Convention provides for the parties to maintain records of trade in listed species and to report on the number and type of permits granted. This information must be made available to the public. The 2001 POPS Convention also requires the parties to report on production, import, and export of listed chemicals; national inventories are made public and can be compared.[192] In some cases reporting requirements are designed to monitor how well the parties are enforcing a treaty. Thus the 1946 International Convention for the Regulation of Whaling and the 1991 Protocol to the Antarctic Treaty on Environmental Protection oblige the parties to communicate reports submitted by national inspectors concerning infractions, while the 1973 MARPOL Convention calls for reports from national authorities on action taken to deal with reported violations and on incidents involving harmful substances.[193]

This sort of information is meant to enable the parties to review and evaluate the treaty's impact. Where the treaty additionally requires the information to be made public, NGOs and other interested groups are also able to monitor progress. The obvious weakness is that much will depend on the diligence and accuracy of the reporting authorities, and the record of many states in this regard is poor. Despite this, many treaty COPs have found it possible to assess implementation and outcomes and, where necessary, non-compliance procedures can be employed to pressurize defaulting states into submitting the necessary data.[194]

(b) Fact-finding and research

Treaty institutions are not necessarily confined to a passive role as recipients of information. In many cases the power they enjoy to commission fact finding or research provides the essential scientific basis for adopting further measures and formulating policies of conservation and pollution control.[195] Some treaties also create scientific or technical committees as subsidiary bodies to provide expert advice. These committees, or the treaty secretariat, may offer a measure of independent verification or peer review of the information supplied by states, a point explicitly recognized in

---

[190] Article 13. See also 1996 Protocol to the London Dumping Convention, Article 9; 1992 Paris Convention for the Protection of the Marine Environment of the Northwest Atlantic, Article 22 and Annex IV, Article 2.

[191] Article 13.

[192] Article 15. See arguments of the parties in the *Pulp Mills Case*, ICJ Reports (2006).

[193] See *infra*, Chs 7, 12.   [194] On non-compliance see *infra*, section 3(4).

[195] See especially the use of the Intergovernmental Panel on Climate Change by the parties to the Climate Change Convention, *infra*, Ch 6.

the 1978 Great Lakes Water Quality Agreement,[196] and in the Kyoto Protocol to the Climate Change Convention.[197] The value of information obtained independently of governments is obvious in the operation of fisheries conservation bodies and other highly contentious situations such as climate change. Thus it is important that these bodies should not be dependent on government scientists for expertise, but should be able to employ their own experts, or call on international scientific bodies such as the International Council for Exploration of the Seas (ICES), or the Scientific Committee for Antarctic Research (SCAR).[198] The latter possibility is essential if small and modestly resourced institutions are to have access to high quality independent advice. The FAO and a variety of NGOs may also provide useful, though in the latter case not always detached, expertise.

(c) Inspection[199]

The most assertive method of information-gathering and supervision allows international institutions to undertake inspections to verify compliance with international agreements and standards. The strongest examples of inspection by international agencies are found in the arms-control field.[200] Here inspections are usually compulsory and reports are sent to the Security Council. The IAEA's inspection powers with regard to non-proliferation of nuclear weapons conform to this pattern. But the powers of inspection of this agency with regard to the safety of nuclear installations are not compulsory and may be employed only if requested by states.[201] This is the more usual pattern of environmental treaties, where provision for compulsory inspection by international institutions is exceptional. The main examples are concerned with the marine environment. The International Whaling Commission has power to place observers on board whaling vessels to report back to the Commission. But these observers are nominated by member states willing to participate in the scheme on a mutual basis. In practice this means that observers from whaling nations are appointed to inspect each other's operations.[202] This falls well short of independent compulsory inspection. A few fisheries treaties have somewhat similar provision for mutual inspection, again reporting to the relevant Commission.[203] Only in the Antarctic treaty system

---

[196] See infra, Ch 10.

[197] Article 8. See infra, Ch 6, where the operation of this provision is examined in more detail.

[198] See e.g. 1980 Convention for the Conservation of Antarctic Marine Living Resources; 1946 International Convention for Regulation of Whaling; 1978 Convention on Future Multilateral Cooperation in the North-West Atlantic Fisheries; 1980 Convention on Future Multilateral Cooperation in the North-East Atlantic Fisheries, infra, Ch 13.

[199] See generally Oeter, 28 NYIL (1997) 101.

[200] See e.g. 1990 Arms Control and Disarmament Agreement; 1968 Nuclear Non-Proliferation Treaty; UN Security Council Resolution 687 (1991) and Butler (ed), Control Over Compliance with International Law (Dordrecht, 1991) 31; Schoenbaum et al, Trilateral Perspectives on International Legal Issues (New York, 1998) Ch 11.

[201] Infra, Ch 9.   [202] Birnie, 29 NRJ (1989) 903; Lyster, International Wildlife Law, 31f.

[203] 1949 International Convention for North-West Atlantic Fisheries, Protocol on Joint Enforcement; 1978 Convention on Future Multilateral Cooperation in North-West Atlantic Fisheries, Article 18. Compare Article 21 of the 1995 Fish Stocks Agreement, which permits unilateral inspection of fishing vessels for law enforcement purposes.

have states accepted compulsory inspection as a means of informing the Consultative Meetings of possible violations of applicable treaties.[204] Thus there is clearly room for the wider adoption of institutional inspection as a means of ensuring compliance with environmental treaties,[205] although this observation must also take account of the additional provision made by some treaties for national inspection and of the role of NGOs in bringing to light violations.

3(4) NON-COMPLIANCE PROCEDURES

Non-compliance procedures are usually designed to secure compliance with the terms of a treaty or legally binding decision, although they are sometimes also applied to non-binding soft law.[206] A number of environmental treaties have introduced formal non-compliance procedures for this purpose,[207] but as Gehring observes, even without such a formal procedure, non-compliance problems are likely to be handled in a similar way in many environmental regimes.[208] When used in a treaty context it is not entirely clear that 'non-compliance' differs in any material sense from 'breach' or 'non-application'.[209] What is at issue is a failure to meet the required legal standard set by the treaty and at this level the distinction is merely terminological. Some writers have also pointed to the importance of distinguishing between non-compliance and failure to take effective action to meet the objectives of a treaty, a situation which can arise even where the parties are in full compliance with its terms.[210] Non-compliance is thus a narrower concept which focuses only on commitments, rather than on broader questions affecting the further development and effectiveness of a regulatory regime.

As we saw earlier, most non-compliance procedures are best understood as a form of 'dispute avoidance' or 'alternative dispute resolution', in the sense that resort to binding third-party procedures is avoided.[211] They are unlike litigation in several respects.

---

[204] The 1959 Antarctic Treaty, Article VII and the 1991 Protocol to the Antarctic Treaty on Environmental Protection, Article 13 provide for national inspectors, but the latter also makes provision for the meeting of the Consultative Parties to appoint observers to act on its behalf. See also 1997 Kyoto Protocol, Article 8, *infra*, Ch 6, which in effect provides for independent inspection.

[205] See generally Wolfrum, 272 *Recueil des Cours* (1998) 9, 43–8.

[206] See generally Shelton (ed), *Commitment and Compliance* (Oxford, 2000). On the non-binding regime for chemicals in international trade see Victor, Raustiala, and Skolnikoff, *Implementation and Effectiveness*, Ch 6.

[207] In addition to those discussed below, compliance procedures are also envisaged or established by 1989 Basel Convention on the Control of Transboundary Movements of Hazardous Wastes, Article 19; 1992 OSPAR Convention, Article 23; 2000 Protocol on Biosafety, Article 34; 2001 POPS Convention, Article 17; 2003 Protocol on Pollutant Release and Transfer Registers, Article 22. UNEP adopted Guidelines on Compliance with MEAs in 2001. See generally UNEP, *Compliance Mechanisms Under Selected MEAs* (UNEP, 2007).

[208] 1 *YbIEL* (1990) 54. See e.g. the 1973 CITES Convention, on which see Sand, 8 *EJIL* (1997) 29, and *infra*, Ch 12.

[209] See Fitzmaurice and Redgwell, 31 *NYIL* (2000) 35 and *supra*, section 3(1).

[210] Victor, Raustiala, and Skolnikoff (eds), *Implementation and Effectiveness of International Environmental Commitments*, 6–8.

[211] See generally Chinkin, in Evans (ed), *Remedies in International Law*, 128–34; Fitzmaurice and Redgwell, 31 *NYIL* (2000) 35; Brown Weiss and Jacobson (eds), *Engaging Countries: Strengthening Compliance*

They are inherently multilateral in character. The consent of the respondent state need not be obtained before the process can be initiated. Standing is not required to make a complaint:[212] in most cases any party to the treaty or the treaty secretariat may do so. In a few cases NGOs and members of the public may also complain, or provide information to secretariats.[213] The fundamental assumption is that when governments voluntarily undertake commitments they normally intend to comply.[214] Non-compliance procedures thus operate on the understanding that it is better to assist and encourage than to penalize them for failing. The treaty parties will usually seek to shape consensus on the issue in dispute, and the process is intended to reinforce the stability, transparency, and legitimacy of the regime as a whole.[215]

Non-compliance procedures represent a logical extension of information gathering, monitoring, and supervision by meetings of the parties referred to in the previous sections. They may resemble conciliation insofar as negotiation with the defaulting state and cooperation are relied on to secure a satisfactory outcome, rather than binding adversarial resolution of questions of legal responsibility or treaty interpretation. They differ from conciliation in that there is usually no formally independent third party seeking to facilitate agreement.[216] The outcome of the procedure can be the provision of assistance or other inducements to encourage future compliance, but if necessary more compelling responses are also possible, ranging from the withholding of funds by the World Bank or the Global Environment Facility to the suspension of treaty rights and privileges pending full compliance. Sanctions of this kind can be remarkably effective, particularly where they involve loss of the right to trade.[217]

(a) The Montreal Protocol as a model non-compliance procedure

Dispute avoidance is best exemplified by the non-compliance procedure adopted by parties to the 1987 Montreal Protocol to the Ozone Convention.[218] This procedure can be invoked by any party to the protocol, by the protocol secretariat, or by the party itself, wherever there are thought to be problems regarding compliance. The matter

with *International Accords* (Cambridge, Mass, 1998); Mitchell, in Bodansky, Brunnée and Hey, *Oxford Handbook of International Environmental Law*, 893–921; Adede, in Lang (ed), *Sustainable Development and International Law* (London, 1995) Ch 8; Lang, 56 *ZAÖRV* (1996) 685; Handl, 5 *Colorado JIELP* (1994) 327; id, 5 *Tulane JICL* (1997) 29.

[212] Compare treaty disputes, *infra*, section 4(3).

[213] See Epiney, in Beyerlin, Stoll, and Wolfrum (eds), *Ensuring Compliance with Multilateral Environmental Agreements* (Leiden, 2006) 319–352.

[214] Bilder in Shelton (ed), *Commitment and Compliance* (Oxford, 2000) 66.

[215] Chayes, in Brown Weiss and Jacobson (eds), *Engaging Countries etc*, 43; Brunnée, in Winter (ed), *Multilevel Governance of Global Environmental Change* (Cambridge, 2006) 387–408.

[216] But compare the Aarhus Convention compliance procedure and Kyoto Protocol enforcement procedure, *infra*.

[217] E.g. suspension of trade under the 1973 CITES, *infra*, Ch 12, and Sand, 8 *EJIL* (1997) 29. On the relationship with countermeasures and other responses to breach of treaty see Fitzmaurice and Redgwell, 31 *NYIL* (2000) 35.

[218] Article 8, and Annex IV, as adopted at Copenhagen in 1992, and amended 1998. See *infra*, Ch 6, section 2(3); Yoshida, 10 *Colorado JIELP* (1999) 95, and UNEP, *Report of the Implementation Committee for the Montreal Protocol, 20th Meeting*, UNEP/OzL Pro/Imp Com/20/4, paras 24–33.

is then referred for investigation by an Implementation Committee consisting of ten parties elected on the basis of equitable geographical representation. The main task of the committee is to consider the submissions, information, and observations made to it with a view to securing an amicable solution of the matter on the basis of respect for the provisions of the Protocol. This is very similar to the provision for negotiation of a friendly settlement under the European Convention on Human Rights.[219] The Implementation Committee can seek whatever information it needs through the secretariat; for this purpose it may also visit the territory of the party under investigation if invited to do so. A report is made to the full Meeting of the Parties, which decides what steps to call for in order to bring about full compliance. These can include the provision of appropriate financial, technical, or training assistance in order to help the party to comply. If these measures are insufficient, cautions can be issued, or, as a last resort, rights and privileges under the treaty can be suspended in accordance with the law of treaties.[220] The meeting of the parties will also decide on appropriate action when a developing state notifies the secretariat of its inability to implement the protocol through the failure of developed states to provide finance or technology.[221]

A very similar procedure has been adopted under the 1979 Convention on Long-Range Transboundary Air Pollution. An Implementation Committee has responsibility for reviewing compliance by the parties with all the Convention's protocols under a common procedure.[222] As in other non-compliance procedures its task is to consider referrals 'with a view to securing a constructive solution'. The Executive Body may decide on non-discriminatory measures to secure compliance, but the only measure specifically indicated is the provision of assistance. Its decisions require consensus, and can thus be easily blocked. The Climate Change Convention provides an even softer 'multilateral consultative process' to resolve questions regarding implementation.[223] Conducted by a panel of experts, rather than by other member states, it remains non-judicial, non-confrontational, and advisory rather than supervisory. No sanctions of any kind can be imposed, not even suspension of rights and privileges; there is power only to recommend measures to facilitate cooperation and implementation and to clarify issues and promote understanding of the Convention.

Where, as in the case of climate change or ozone depletion, non-compliance affects all parties to the treaty, there is considerable merit in designing a process for securing

---

[219] 1950 European Convention on Human Rights, Article 28 provided that the Commission on Human Rights 'shall place itself at the disposal of the parties concerned with a view to securing a friendly settlement of the matter on the basis of respect for human rights as defined in the Convention'.

[220] Montreal Protocol, annex V, as adopted 1992. On suspension or termination of treaties see 1969 Vienna Convention on the Law of Treaties, especially Articles 58, 60.

[221] Montreal Protocol, Article 5(4)–(7) as revised 1990. The NCP cannot be invoked against a party who has made such a notification.

[222] Executive Body, Decision 1997/2, in UNECE, *Report of the 15th Session of the Executive Body* (1997) Annex III and Szell, in Lang (ed), *Sustainable Development and International Law* (London, 1995) 97. See also Article 11 of the POPS Protocol, Article 9 of the Heavy Metals Protocol, and Article 9 of the Acidification Protocol.

[223] Article 13, and see *infra*, Ch 6, section 4(5).

compliance which is multilateral in character and allows all parties, as well as NGOs, to participate. Although it is possible to accommodate a multiplicity of participants in judicial proceedings, it is not easy to do so, and an adversarial procedure is not well suited to the resolution of the kind of non-compliance problems likely to arise under global environmental treaties.[224] Moreover, soft settlement typically facilitates more readily than judicial processes the necessary input of scientific and technical expertise required to deal with issues of compliance under agreements of this kind. Those are probably the major contributions of the processes of review developed from the Montreal Protocol.

(b) The Aarhus Convention Compliance Committee

Although in many respects similar to the Montreal Protocol NCP, the most innovative features of the 'non-confrontational, non-judicial and consultative' procedure established under Article 15 of the 1998 Aarhus Convention are that members of the public and NGOs may bring complaints before a non-compliance committee whose members are not only independent of the parties but may be nominated by NGOs.[225] In all these respects it is somewhat closer to human rights treaty-monitoring bodies such as the UN Human Rights Committee than to the Montreal Protocol NCP.[226] The process was strongly opposed by the United States during negotiations,[227] but it has nevertheless been accepted throughout Europe and the former Soviet states. The committee hearing complaints has given rulings which interpret and clarify provisions of the convention and a body of case law is emerging.[228] There have been findings of non-compliance against several parties resulting in recommendations that the respondent states should change their law, develop better implementation, or engage in capacity-building and training. However, not all respondent governments have cooperated with the Compliance Committee or implemented its recommendations.[229] In theory it is then open to the Meeting of the Parties to suspend a non-complying party's treaty rights and privileges or take other appropriate measures to secure compliance.[230] Kravchenko concludes that 'independence, transparency, and NGO involvement in the Convention's novel compliance mechanism represent an ambitious effort to bring

---

[224] See *infra*, next section.

[225] Aarhus Convention, Decision 1/7: Review of Compliance, *Report of 1st Mtg of Parties*, UN Doc ECE/MP PP/2/Add 8 (2004). See also Report of the Compliance Committee, UN Doc ECE/MP PP/2005/13 (2005) and generally Kravchenko, 18 *Colorado JIELP* (2007) 1; Koester, 2 *J Eur Env & Plng L* (2005) 31. The compliance procedure adopted in 2007 under the 1999 UNECE Protocol on Water and Health is modelled directly on the Aarhus procedure. Other NCPs with independent members but with no public participation include the Compliance Committees of the Biosafety Protocol and the Kyoto Protocol.

[226] See generally Alston and Crawford (eds), *The Future of UN Human Rights Treaty Monitoring* (Cambridge, 2000).

[227] But compare procedures for individual enforcement under the 1993 North American Agreement on Environmental Cooperation, *infra*, Ch 5, section 2(5).

[228] *Infra*, Ch 5.   [229] Kravchenko, 18 *Colorado JIELP* (2007) 46–7.

[230] Decision 1/7: Review of Compliance, para 37. See Koester, in Ulfstein, Marauhn, and Zimmermann (eds), *Making Treaties Work: Human Rights, Environment and Arms Control* (Cambridge, 2007) Ch 8.

democracy and participation to the very heart of compliance itself'.[231] In all of these respects the Aarhus procedure is significantly stronger than any other currently in operation. Nevertheless, individual complainants would be well advised to appreciate that many of the same rights they enjoy under the Aarhus Convention can also be asserted under the European Convention of Human Rights, in a judicial forum, with an established record of compliance by states.[232]

(c) The Kyoto Protocol Compliance Committee

As we will see in Chapter 6, complying with the Kyoto Protocol is not necessarily easy or cheap. However willing states may have been when they became parties, there are substantial economic and political pressures to delay or compromise on commitments. The implementation mechanisms are complex, involving joint implementation, emissions trading between developed states, and a clean-development mechanism requiring reductions in emissions by developing states. In effect, parties have the right to transfer implementation of their commitments to other states. All these complicated arrangements have to be verified, and all parties have a mutual interest in trust and transparency.

The task of ensuring compliance with the Kyoto Protocol is thus particularly crucial to its success.[233] The procedure adopted under Article 18 reflects these concerns.[234] Its purpose is to 'facilitate, promote and enforce compliance' with commitments under the Protocol. It is the last of these objectives—enforcement—which gives it a distinctive character unique among environmental treaties. 'Questions of implementation' may be submitted by the party concerned, or by any other party. They will be considered by a Compliance Committee, elected by the parties, whose members serve 'in their individual capacities'. There is no NGO participation on the Committee, but competent intergovernmental organizations and NGOs may submit relevant information. In practice, initiation of procedures before the Kyoto Compliance Committee is most likely to result from the work of the expert review teams, whose 'in-depth review' of national inventories of greenhouse-gas emissions will provide the initial evidence of non-compliance. The Committee then has a choice when deciding how to deal with non-compliance. Like other compliance committees, it can give advice and make recommendations on implementing the protocol, offer assistance, or arrange technology transfer and capacity building. These are the responsibility of the 'facilitative branch'.

Alternatively, the matter can be referred to the 'enforcement branch'. Members of this body must be lawyers, the party concerned will be entitled to a public hearing and

---

[231] Kravchenko, 18 *Colorado JIELP* (2007) 49.   [232] See *infra*, Ch 5, section 2(5).

[233] The problems are discussed in Werksman, 9 *YbIEL* (1998) 48; *id*, *Responding to Non-Compliance Under the Climate Change Regime* (OECD, 1998); *id*, in Cameron, Werksman, and Roderick (eds), *Improving Compliance with International Environmental Law*, 85ff.

[234] Kyoto Protocol, Decision 27/CMP 1: Procedures and Mechanisms Relating to Compliance, *1st MoP*, FCCC/KP/CMP/2005/8/Add 3 (2006). See Werksman, 9 *YbIEL* (1998) 48; Lefeber, *Hague YIL* (2001) 25; Fitzmaurice, 8 *Singapore YIL* (2004) 23; Stokke, Hovi, and Ulfstein (eds), *Implementing the Climate Regime: International Compliance* (London, 2005) 39ff.

due process, and decisions must be based on evidence, must be reasoned and made public. There can be an appeal to the Conference of the Parties if due process has been denied. The reason for adopting such a quasi-judicial process is that the enforcement branch has the power to impose real penalties on a non-complying party. Inter alia, emissions reductions may be increased and eligibility to participate in emissions trading or the clean-development mechanism may be suspended. In effect, treaty rights can be suspended if necessary in order to restore compliance with the Protocol. This is also possible under other non-compliance procedures,[235] but given the economic significance of the potential penalties in this case a more formal procedure was thought desirable.

At this point we can see that the idea of compliance procedures as non-confrontational and non-judicial has given way to a process that has more in common with the dispute settlement body of the WTO—an entirely deliberate parallel. It does not follow that in this form it will necessarily be more effective than 'softer' non-compliance procedures. The WTO Dispute Settlement Body has not succeeded in resolving every WTO dispute satisfactorily, if by that we mean ensuring compliance with WTO agreements. Nor is it obvious why a state that finds non-compliance with Kyoto advantageous should change its mind if its emissions reduction targets are further increased or its eligibility to meet them by trading emissions is taken away. There are large theoretical questions here about the reasons for compliance and the right balance between incentives and penalties.[236]

4 SETTLEMENT OF INTERNATIONAL ENVIRONMENTAL DISPUTES

4(1) JUDICIAL SETTLEMENT AND ARBITRATION

(a) A choice of forum

General international law takes an eclectic approach to international dispute settlement.[237] Article 33 of the UN Charter gives pre-eminence to the principle that disputes must be settled peacefully, but leaves the choice of means to the parties. Despite its status as the 'principal judicial organ' of the United Nations, the International Court of Justice enjoys no priority as a forum for dispute settlement. The Court's jurisdiction, in common with all international judicial and arbitral tribunals, is based on the

---

[235] See Montreal Protocol, *supra*.

[236] See Haas in Shelton, *Commitment and Compliance*, Ch 2, and Bilder, ibid, Ch 3.

[237] See generally Merrills, *International Dispute Settlement* (4th edn, Cambridge, 2005); Collier and Lowe, *The Settlement of Disputes in International Law* (OUP, 1999) and specifically on environmental disputes see Lowe and Fitzmaurice (eds), *Fifty Years of the International Court of Justice* (Cambridge, 1996) Ch 15; Romano, in Bodansky, Brunnée and Hey, *Handbook of IEL*, Ch 45.

consent of the states parties to each dispute. It has no general jurisdiction to hear applications submitted unilaterally save to the extent provided for by Article 36 (2) of the Statute of the Court, or in other treaties such as the 1982 UNCLOS. Nor is the ICJ necessarily the preferred forum under those treaties which do provide for compulsory binding settlement. As we shall see, the 1991 Antarctic Protocol refers all disputes to arbitration, unless the parties agree otherwise, while the 1994 Agreement Establishing the World Trade Organization creates its own system of specialized panels, an appeal body, and arbitration, for the purpose of settling trade disputes, a number of which have involved environmental questions. Part XV of UNCLOS brings disputes concerning the marine environment and living resources of the high seas within its extensive provision for compulsory settlement of disputes,[238] but it allows the parties to choose various forums, including conciliation, several forms of arbitration, the ICJ, or a specialized court, the International Tribunal for the Law of the Sea (ITLOS).[239] If the parties cannot agree on a forum, arbitration is obligatory. The creation of ITLOS has significantly widened the choice of forum, not only for UNCLOS disputes, but for any dispute concerning the protection of the marine environment or the conservation of marine living resources.[240] There are possible risks in this, of a fragmentation of the international legal system, and of a diminution of the ICJ's authority and centrality as the principal judicial organ of the UN.[241] But there are also benefits, in the specific expertise of 21 judges with 'recognized competence' in the law of the sea, in a stronger and more responsive jurisprudence, and in the encouragement more states may feel when contemplating judicial settlement.[242]

Although international organizations, NGOs, and companies can all be party to an arbitration based on international law,[243] only states can at present be parties to contentious proceedings before the ICJ, while only competent intergovernmental organizations may seek advisory opinions.[244] As Sir Robert Jennings has observed,[245] the ICJ's narrow jurisdiction *ratione personae* reflects a conception of participation in the international legal system that is now seventy-five years old, increasingly anomalous, and out of step with contemporary international society. Other international tribunals, including those concerned with human rights, commercial and investment disputes, international claims, or the European Community, have adopted broader rules on access. In consensual proceedings brought before the ITLOS (but *not* in compulsory jurisdiction cases) the range of potential parties may include not only international organizations, NGOs, and private parties but also entities of uncertain status,

---

[238] See *infra*, section (c).

[239] 1982 UNCLOS, Articles 280–1, 284, 286–7. See Boyle, 46 *ICLQ* (1997) 37.

[240] See Rothwell, in Ndiaye and Wolfrum, *Law of the Sea, Environmental Law and Settlement of Disputes*, 1007–24.

[241] Oda, 244 *Recueil des Cours* (1993) II, 127–55; *id*, 44 *ICLQ* (1995) 863; Guillaume, 44 *ICLQ* (1995) 848.

[242] Charney, 90 *AJIL* (1996) 69; Boyle, 22 *IJMCL* (2007) 369. See generally Merrills, 54 *NILR* (2007) 361.

[243] As under the Permanent Court of Arbitration Optional Rules for Arbitration of Disputes Relating to Natural Resources and/or the Environment, adopted 2001, *infra*, n 269.

[244] Statute, Articles 34, 65.   [245] Jennings, 89 *AJIL* (1995) 493.

such as Taiwan.[246] This offers the possibility of creating a judicial process capable of accommodating conceptions of participation already apparent when we look at international environmental lawmaking, or at environmental institutions, or even at national environmental law.

(b) The drawbacks of litigation

Litigation has played only a limited role in the development of international environmental law—much less than for the law of the sea. States may be more reluctant to litigate where the rules of customary law are themselves unsettled or an underlying consensus on what they should be is not yet fully established. Even where agreed rules are set out in a treaty, there may be uncertainty about the proper forum or the applicable law if the dispute straddles several treaties or the jurisdiction of the forum is limited.[247] In these circumstances a judicial or arbitral award might establish precedents with unwelcome implications for the claimant state, or for the international community as a whole. These factors have often favoured negotiated solutions to environmental disputes such as the Chernobyl disaster, or acid rain in Europe and North America.[248]

Moreover, judicial proceedings and arbitration tend to be less well adapted to the multilateral character of many environmental problems than supervision by meetings of the parties to treaty regimes, including non-compliance procedures.[249] Contentious litigation can be initiated only by states and only if they have standing.[250] In arbitration it is rare to find any provision for third-party intervention. Before the ICJ and the ITLOS third parties may intervene as of right only if the interpretation or application of a treaty to which they are party is in question.[251] This would entitle any party to a multilateral environmental treaty, such as the Ozone or Climate Change Conventions, to intervene and make representations in any litigation concerning those treaties. However, multilateral interests are not so well protected in disputes concerned with customary law, where there is merely a discretion to allow intervention when the legal rights of a third party may be 'affected' by the decision in a case. States are not permitted to intervene in such cases for the purpose of assisting a court to decide what the law is, nor can they use intervention as a means of initiating what is in effect a

---

[246] Article 20(2) of the Statute of the ITLOS provides that: 'The Tribunal shall be open to entities other than States Parties in any case expressly provided for in Part XI *or in any case submitted pursuant to any other agreement conferring jurisdiction on the Tribunal which is accepted by all the parties to that case.*' There seems no reason why 'fishing entities' to which the 1995 Agreement on Straddling and Migratory Fish Stocks applies, such as Taiwan, should not fall under the terms of Article 20(2). Article 187 of UNCLOS gives the Seabed Disputes Chamber compulsory jurisdiction over states, the ISBA, the Enterprise, and seabed contractors, who may be state enterprises or private companies.

[247] See *OSPAR Arbitration*, PCA (2003); *MOX Plant Arbitration*, PCA (2003); *Southern Bluefin Tuna Arbitration*, ICSID (2000) and generally Romano, in Bodansky, Brunnée, and Hey, *Handbook of IEL*, Ch 45.

[248] See *infra*, Chs 6, 9. Compare also the unsuccessful attempt to secure a judicial settlement in the *Gabčíkovo-Nagymaros Case*, ICJ Reports (1997) 7, and 8 *YbIEL* (1997) 3–116.

[249] See *supra* section 3.   [250] See *infra*, section 4(3).

[251] Statute of the ICJ, Article 63; Statute of the ITLOS, Article 32.

new dispute.[252] This narrow interpretation of Article 62 of the ICJ Statute may deny third parties the opportunity to intervene in cases where the respondent state is violating the rights of all states, or of the international community as whole in the case of obligations *erga omnes*. It may be that the International Court would simply view such interventions as attempts to make representations on the law or to turn a bilateral dispute into a multi-party one.[253] It could plausibly be said that the decision in one case does not 'affect' the rights of non-parties to the dispute, who remain free to bring proceedings of their own. There is also an obvious risk of states using intervention to bring claims over which the court would otherwise have no jurisdiction in original proceedings. Allowing multiple third parties with competing interests to intervene in litigation may also make it harder to settle a dispute, may deter states from going to court, and may thus undermine the UN Charter's concern for the peaceful resolution of interstate disputes by whatever means the parties choose.

(c) Public-interest litigation

As we saw earlier in this chapter, international law does not make general provision for a public interest *actio popularis*.[254] Only those environmental obligations which affect the international community as a whole have an *erga omnes* character potentially enforceable by any state; even then the consent of the respondent state is still essential for jurisdictional purposes in any international litigation.[255] An alternative to interstate litigation, however, is to allow international organizations with responsibility for protection of the global environment to act in the public interest. This does not necessarily entail giving these bodies power to initiate or intervene in contentious judicial proceedings against states. At present the International Seabed Authority is the only international body with power to sue states, and only within its restricted field of competence over exploitation of the deep seabed and protection of the marine environment from seabed activities.[256] A better option may be the use of advisory proceedings for public-interest purposes.

The UN General Assembly and the Security Council have competence to seek advisory opinions from the ICJ on any question of international law, while ECOSOC, IMO, WHO, IAEA, and possibly UNEP may do so in respect of environmental matters falling within their specific competence.[257] An advisory opinion from the ICJ carries just

---

[252] Statute of the ICJ, Article 62; Statute of the ITLOS, Article 31; *Land, Island and Maritime Frontier Case (Nicaragua Intervention)* ICJ Reports (1990) 92, paras 52–105; *Continental Shelf Case (Italian Intervention)* ICJ Reports (1984) 3.

[253] For a detailed review of the case law see Chinkin, *Third Parties in International Law* (Oxford, 1993) Chs 7, 12; Ruda, in Lowe and Fitzmaurice (eds), *Fifty Years of the ICJ*, 487; Merrills, in Evans (ed), *Remedies in International Law*, 58–64. See also Okowa's discussion of the attempt by four states to intervene in the 1995 *Nuclear Tests Case*, ibid, 164–7. All four states were in effect making the same claim as New Zealand.

[254] *Supra*, section 2(5).

[255] *East Timor Case*, ICJ Reports (1995) para 29. On *erga omnes* obligations see *supra* section 2(5).

[256] 1982 UNCLOS, Article 187 (b)(i).

[257] ICJ Statute, Articles 65–8; *Advisory Opinions Concerning the Legality of the Treat or Use of Nuclear Weapons*, ICJ Reports (1996) 66, 226.

as much authority as a judgment in interstate proceedings, and represents a very real means of clarifying and developing the law. The UNGA and WHO requests for an *Advisory Opinion on the Legality of the Threat or Use of Nuclear Weapons* are the first such use of this power to bring public-interest legal proceedings in respect of questions which were at least partly environmental. As these cases demonstrate, it is possible for any state or relevant international organization to make representations in advisory proceedings,[258] and to that extent a genuine multilateralism is possible. Requests for advisory opinions thus represent perhaps the best method for litigating breaches of *erga omnes* rules. The earlier *Western Sahara Advisory Opinion* shows how this power can also be used to pose carefully formulated questions of a general kind in matters concerned with interstate controversy.[259]

It is sometimes argued that NGOs and other non-state actors should also have the power to represent the public interest by initiating or intervening in international legal proceedings.[260] Such bodies and groups are already represented as observers in environmental treaty negotiations; their participation in any legal proceedings could be beneficial for the same reasons: provision of information and expertise, detachment from the interests of specific states, the ability to reflect more accurately the real composition of the international 'community' as it presently exists. There are also serious objections to broadening NGO access to international courts, however. NGOs are not in reality representative of the international community, but at best only of their own members. Their policies and priorities may be driven by factors other than a rational appreciation of true global needs. Many of the wealthiest and most influential NGOs are American or European, and do not necessarily reflect Third World concerns or perspectives. For all these reasons it may be preferable to broaden the rights of other states or intergovernmental organizations to represent the public interest in international legal proceedings rather than extend that right to NGOs. It is always open to states to adopt NGO submissions as part of their own case: such a tactic was held admissible by the WTO Appellate Body in the *Shrimp-Turtle Case*,[261] and there is no reason to believe it would not also be permissible before the ICJ or ITLOS.[262]

---

[258] ICJ Statute, Article 66. In the *Nuclear Weapons Advisory Opinion* some forty states made written or oral submissions: see Rosenne, 27 *Israel YbHR* (1998) 263; Sands and de Chazournes (eds), *International Law, the ICJ and Nuclear Weapons* (Cambridge, 1999). On the power of the ICJ to request or receive information from public international organizations in contentious cases see Statute of the ICJ, Article 34.

[259] ICJ Reports (1975) 12. See also *Privileges and Immunities Advisory Opinion*, ICJ Report (1989) 177, para 27.

[260] See generally Shelton, 88 *AJIL* (1994) 611; Sands, 30 *Harv ILJ* (1989) 393.

[261] *United States—Import Prohibition of Certain Shrimp and Shrimp Products* ['*Shrimp/Turtle Case*'] Report of the WTO Appellate Body (1998) WT/DS58/AB/R, paras 79–91. However, the Appellate Body took account of NGO submissions attached to the US submission only insofar as they reflected or were adopted by the United States Government. In the *Asbestos Case*, the Appellate Body for the first time permitted NGOs to apply for leave to file a written brief, but all such applications were then rejected: see *EC—Measures Affecting Asbestos*, WT/DS135/AB/R (2001) paras 50–7.

[262] In the *Pulp Mills Case*, ICJ Reports (2006), Argentina's advocates included the head of an environmental NGO who claimed to speak for the River Uruguay.

4(2) AN INTERNATIONAL ENVIRONMENTAL COURT?

In 1993 the International Court established a special chamber for environmental cases under Article 26(1) of its Statute, composed of seven judges. Thirteen years later no cases had come before the chamber and it was abolished. It was difficult to see what advantages the environmental chamber afforded over the full court, or over an ad hoc chamber, since the parties could not choose the judges and the judges would not necessarily be experts on international environmental law or on the scientific and technical issues which may be relevant to certain kinds of dispute. The cost, the procedure, and the parties would be the same whether the action proceeded in the full court or the chamber. Moreover, it is not easy to identify what is an environmental case. Cases may raise environmental issues, whether legal or factual, but they rarely do so in isolation. The *Gabčíkovo-Nagymaros Case*, for example, is as much about the law of treaties, international watercourses, state responsibility, and state succession, as it is about environmental law. Much the same could be said about the *Pulp Mills* litigation. In these circumstances the parties need a generalist court, not a specialist one.[263]

Nor is the view that there should be a specialist environmental court, similar to the International Tribunal for the Law of the Sea, borne out by experience.[264] Specialist tribunals are most useful when they have a special body of law to apply, usually a treaty such as the European Convention on Human Rights, the 1982 UNCLOS or the GATT and related agreements. There is a case for such bodies, not only because of their specialist expertise and procedures, but also because they relieve the ICJ of a burden of litigation it could not sustain. But as this book has shown, international environmental law is not a self-contained, codified system of this kind. Settling environmental disputes requires a wide-ranging grasp of international law as a whole; it is not a specialism which can readily be detached for the purposes of litigation. Moreover, even specialized tribunals such as the ECHR, the ITLOS, or the WTO Appellate Body may have to decide environmental issues in the course of their normal work. It is difficult to see how an environmental court could either monopolize the field or avoid the risk of over-specializsation and distorted focus for which the WTO disputes system has been criticized.

This does not mean that there is no role for specialized environmental tribunals. The principal potential weakness of the ICJ and the ITLOS as forums for the settlement of some categories of environmental disputes lies not in their comprehension of international law relating to the environment but in their limited ability to handle scientific evidence and technical expertise. In this respect valuable lessons can be derived from the dispute settlement provisions of the 1982 UNCLOS. During the UNCLOS negotiations it was recognized that no single forum would be appropriate for the whole

---

263 See Okowa, in Evans (ed), *Remedies in International Law,* Ch 10.

264 See Lowe and Fitzmaurice (eds), *Fifty Years of the ICJ,* 302–8; Okowa, loc cit, 168–72; Hey, *Reflections on an International Environmental Court* (The Hague, 2000); but for a more positive view compare Postiglione, 23 *EPL* (1993) 73–8; Pauwelyn in Chambers and Green (eds), *Reforming International Environmental Governance: from Institutional Limits to Innovative Reforms* (Tokyo, 2005).

range of issues likely to arise in disputes under that convention. Provision was there-fore be made for specialist bodies, not necessarily composed of lawyers, to deal with the more technical matters.[265] This accounts for the inclusion of arbitration and spe-cial arbitration among the options available to parties in law of the sea disputes. The composition of these bodies reflects differences in their intended functions. Whereas the ITLOS is composed of persons of 'recognized competence in the field of the Law of the Sea'—and functions as an alternative to the ICJ—arbitrators appointed under Annex VII need not be lawyers but must be 'experienced in maritime affairs'. Special arbitrators appointed under Annex VIII similarly do not have to be lawyers, but are instead selected for their expertise in the four areas for which special arbitration is available: fisheries, protection of the marine environment, scientific research, and navigation. FAO, UNEP, the IOC and IMO will maintain lists of appropriate experts in these fields. Technical experts may also be appointed to sit with the ICJ, ITLOS, or an arbitral tribunal in accordance with Article 289. These experts are 'preferably' to be chosen from the list of special arbitrators.

While special arbitrators possess only a limited and specific jurisdiction, the 1982 UNCLOS does not try to allocate a specific functional jurisdiction to each of the four compulsory forums. Rather, as we have seen above, it leaves the choice of forum to the parties to the dispute, and gives them the freedom to select whichever they deem most suitable to the circumstances of their case. Only in default of agreement are the parties compelled to arbitrate. It is thus possible within the UNCLOS scheme to tailor the choice of tribunal to the characteristics of each dispute, and to bring in tech-nical expertise where necessary. The Convention certainly cannot be characterized as favouring adjudication by lawyers. It shows how fisheries and marine environmen-tal disputes can be handled within the Convention's scheme even where they involve mainly technical, or a mix of legal and technical, issues. In such cases resort to special arbitration, or the appointment of experts to sit with judicial or arbitral tribunals, may be the most appropriate way of ensuring that the right fisheries, scientific, or environ-mental expertise is applied to deciding the dispute.[266]

In practice a similar freedom to draw on technical expertise is available to states in environmental disputes not governed by UNCLOS. The *Trail Smelter Arbitration* blends legal and technical expertise to produce an award that is competent and cre-ative in both fields.[267] More recently the UN Compensation Commission's awards on environmental damage have demonstrated the value of combining specialist legal and valuation expertise when assessing compensation.[268] The Permanent Court of Arbitration has adopted new rules intended to reflect the particular characteristics of environmental disputes by allowing, inter alia, for provisional measures, expe-dited procedures, participation of non-state entities, and assistance from scientific

---

[265] See Adede, *The System for Settlement of Disputes under the UN Convention on the Law of the Sea* (Dordrecht, 1987) 242ff; Sohn, 10 *IJMCL* (1995) 205.

[266] See Anderson in Nordquist et al (eds), *Law, Science and Ocean Management* (Leiden, 2007) 505–18.

[267] 33 *AJIL* (1939) 182, and 35 *AJIL* (1941) 684.   [268] *Supra* section 2(4).

experts.[269] The ICJ also possesses a general power either to sit with expert assessors or to request outside bodies to carry out an inquiry or give expert opinion.[270] The Court has been criticized for not doing so in the *Gabčíkovo-Nagymaros Case*,[271] although given its conclusion that the parties should negotiate, taking into account the environmental consequences, technical expertise was evidently not considered relevant to the outcome of the case. A specialist environmental court would have to make the same kind of judgement, however, and is just as likely to be wrong.

The lack of a specialized international environmental court appears to be no handicap to the settlement of environmental disputes. The wide choice of means available to the parties, and their inherent freedom to choose the most appropriate, provides ample scope for ensuring that disputes are competently handled. Nor would the problems of accommodating multilateral participation in legal proceedings necessarily be solved by creating a specialist tribunal. In practice there seems no good reason why the present approach of locating environment-related cases within the existing system of international courts and tribunals should not continue to work, provided the system is used intelligently and appropriately.

4(3) ADJUDICATION OF TREATY DISPUTES

The inclusion of compulsory, binding, third-party dispute settlement provisions in multilateral-treaty regimes can serve a variety of objectives.[272] The commonest is to provide an authoritative mechanism for determining questions relating to the 'interpretation or application' of the treaty. The phrase 'interpretation and application', or other comparable terms, covers not only questions concerning the meaning of a treaty, but also issues of compliance and responsibility for breach of treaty.[273] It can involve application of other rules of international law if the treaty so provides, or interpretation and application taking other rules into account. An element of evolutionary interpretation may thus be possible.[274] Treaties will inevitably be interpreted and applied differently by different states, even when acting entirely in good faith. Judicial institutions can serve as the main guarantors of a treaty's integrity, undertaking not only the task

---

[269] 2001 Optional Rules for Arbitration of Disputes Relating to Natural Resources or the Environment.

[270] ICJ Statute, Articles 30, 50.

[271] Okowa, in Evans (ed), *Remedies in International Law*, 167. The Court's use of Article 50 is examined by White, in Lowe and Fitzmaurice (eds), *Fifty Years of the ICJ*, Ch 28.

[272] Sohn, 150 *Recueil des Cours* (1976) 195; Bilder, 144 *Recueil des Cours* (1975) 139; Chinkin, in Crawford and Rothwell (eds), *The Law of the Sea in the Asian Pacific Region* (Dordrecht, 1995) 237, and see generally Merrills, *International Dispute Settlement* (4th edn, Cambridge, 2005) Ch 12.

[273] *Chorzow Factory Case (Jurisdiction)* PCIJ Sers A, No 9 (1927) 20–5; see also *German Interests in Polish Upper Silesia Case* (1925) PCIJ Sers A (1926) No 6, 24–5 and No 7, 17ff; *Interpretation of the Peace Treaties Case,* ICJ Reports (1950) 75; *Oil Platforms Case,* ICJ Reports (1996) 803.

[274] 1969 Vienna Convention on the Law of Treaties, Article 31(3); *United States—Import Prohibition of Certain Shrimp and Shrimp Products,* Appellate Body Report, WT/DS58/AB/R (1998) 4–7, 32–57; *Iron Rhine Arbitration* (2005) PCA, paras 46–58. But compare *OSPAR Arbitration,* PCA (2003) paras 101–5; *Gabčíkovo-Nagymaros Case,* ICJ Reports (1997) 7, paras 140–1, and Judge Bedjaoui. See generally McLachlan, 54 *ICLQ* (2005) 279.

of interpretation and the adjudication of alleged breach, but also determining the validity of reservations and derogations. As one writer explains:

What is important—what is indeed crucial—is that there should always be in the background, as a necessary check upon the making of unjustified claims, or upon the denial of justified claims, automatically available procedures for the settlement of disputes.[275]

Despite these attractions, provision for compulsory judicial settlement or arbitration remains relatively rare in environmental treaties. A few Western European treaties allow any party to refer disputes concerning 'interpretation or application' to binding arbitration,[276] as does the 1973/78 MARPOL Convention.[277] The London Dumping Convention provides for such cases to be referred unilaterally to binding arbitration or by agreement to the ICJ.[278] Many other environmental treaties have no dispute settlement clause at all or merely provide for negotiation, followed by arbitration or judicial settlement if all parties to the dispute agree.[279] One common provision is for negotiation followed by compulsory non-binding conciliation if agreement cannot be reached on any other means of settlement.[280] Some treaties also allow a party to make an optional declaration accepting compulsory judicial settlement or arbitration, but this operates only against other states making a similar declaration. Like the optional clause in Article 36(2) of the ICJ Statute, this falls well short of a general system of compulsory binding settlement of disputes. Apart from disputes under the 1982 UNCLOS, the only recent environmental case to be brought under a compulsory adjudication clause in a treaty is the *Pulp Mills Case*, initiated by Argentina under Article 60 of the Statute of the River Uruguay.

This pattern is consistent with the view that international adjudication has too many disadvantages in an environmental context to be widely attractive to states as a primary means of multilateral treaty enforcement. The inclusion of non-compliance procedures in a growing number of environmental treaties emphasizes the importance of collective supervision by the parties in this context,[281] while relatively weak dispute settlement clauses indicate the continuing opposition of many states to compulsory

---

[275] Sinclair, *The Vienna Convention on the Law of Treaties*, (2nd edn, Manchester, 1984) 235.

[276] 1976 Rhine Chemicals Convention, Article 15; 1979 Berne Convention on the Conservation of European Wildlife and Natural Habitats, Article 18; 1992 Paris Convention for the Protection of the Marine Environment of the Northeast Atlantic, Article 32; 1999 Rhine Convention, Article 16.

[277] Article 10.

[278] 1972 Convention, procedure agreed by the parties under Article XI; 1996 Protocol, Article 16.

[279] 1973 CITES Convention, Article 28; 1980 Convention for the Conservation of Antarctic Marine Living Resources, Article 25; 1989 Basel Convention on the Regulation of Transboundary Movements of Hazardous Wastes, Article 20; 1991 Convention on Environmental Impact Assessment, Article 15; 1992 Convention on the Transboundary Effects of Industrial Accidents, Article 21; 1992 Convention on the Protection and Use of Transboundary Watercourses and Lakes, Article 22; 1995 Agreement on the Conservation of African-Eurasian Migratory Water Birds, Article 12; 1998 Aarhus Convention, Article 16.

[280] 1979 Convention on Long-range Transboundary Air Pollution, Article 9; 1985 Ozone Convention, Article 11; 1992 Convention on Climate Change, Article 14; 1992 Convention on Biological Diversity, Article 27; 1994 Convention to Combat Desertification, Article 28; 1994 Protocol on the Further Reduction of Sulphur Emissions, Article 9.

[281] *Supra*, section 3.

adjudication.[282] Even where compulsory adjudication is the primary method of dispute settlement, as with the 1973/78 MARPOL Convention, or the 1972 London Dumping Convention, the parties may in practice choose to seek agreement on matters of interpretation, in this case through IMO, without ever resorting to formal dispute settlement. A few treaties formalize this practice explicitly.[283] Although courts are not unmindful of the need for purposive construction, the parties to a treaty are usually best placed to decide for themselves what is appropriate, and can help the regime evolve by their decisions. This may explain why it has been possible to reinterpret some treaties, such as the Whaling Convention, in quite radical ways.[284]

(a) Dispute settlement under the 1982 UNCLOS

The 1982 UNCLOS is one of the very few treaties under which environmental and natural resources disputes fall potentially within the compulsory jurisdiction of international tribunals,[285] although it remains open to the parties to make alternative arrangements which will then prevail over UNCLOS dispute settlement.[286] Article 288 of the 1982 UNCLOS makes general provision for unilateral reference of disputes concerning interpretation or application of the Convention to the International Tribunal for the Law of the Sea, the ICJ, or an arbitral tribunal. The court or tribunal chosen will also have jurisdiction to interpret or apply international agreements 'related to the purposes of the Convention' if they so provide. Article 288 is broad in scope. It applies inter alia to allegations that 'a coastal State has acted in contravention of specified international rules and standards for the protection and preservation of the marine environment which are applicable to the coastal State', and also includes flag state violations of the Convention's marine pollution articles.[287] High-seas fisheries disputes are in general subject to compulsory jurisdiction, but EEZ fishery disputes involving the determination of a total allowable catch, harvesting capacity, and the allocation of surpluses, are not.[288] Allegations of a failure by coastal states to ensure proper conservation and management of stocks must, however, be submitted to conciliation.[289]

The 1995 Agreement Relating to the Conservation of Straddling and Highly Migratory Fish Stocks extends the UNCLOS dispute settlement articles to disputes arising under this agreement or under any related regional fisheries treaty. It is arguable that the exclusion of disputes concerning EEZ sovereign rights incorporated

---

[282] See *infra*, Ch 6. [283] See *infra*, section 4(4). [284] See Birnie, 12 *IJMCL* (1997) 307, 488.

[285] 1982 UNCLOS, Articles 279–99, and Annexes VI–II. See generally Freestone, Barnes and Ong (eds), *The Law of the Sea* (Oxford, 2006) Chs 20, 21; Klein, *Dispute Settlement in the UNCLOS* (Cambridge, 2005); Merrills, *International Dispute Settlement* (4th edn, Cambridge, 2005) Ch 8; Churchill and Lowe, *The Law of the Sea* (3rd edn, Manchester, 1998) Ch 19; Rayfuse, 36 *VUWLR* (2005) 683; Sohn, 10 *IJMCL* (1995) 205; Charney, 35 *VJIL* (1995) 381.

[286] Articles 281–2. See *Southern Bluefin Tuna Arbitration* (2000); *MOX Plant Arbitration* (2002) PCA.

[287] Article 297(1). See Boyle, in Ringbom (ed), *Competing Norms in the Law of Marine Environmental Protection* (The Hague, 1997) 241 and *MOX Plant Case* (2001) ITLOS No 10.

[288] Article 297(3)(a). See also *Southern Bluefin Tuna Arbitration* (2000) excluding compulsory jurisdiction over high seas fisheries covered by a regional agreement. For a fuller account see Boyle, 14 *IJMCL* (1999) 1.

[289] Article 297(1)(b).

in the 1995 Agreement should be construed narrowly, to cover only the exercise of coastal state discretion on matters that are purely of EEZ concern only, i.e. which do not affect straddling or migratory stocks inside or outside the EEZ.[290] If this is correct, then as between parties to UNCLOS or the 1995 Agreement, all or almost all disputes concerning high-seas fisheries or marine mammals will fall within the compulsory jurisdiction of a court or tribunal.[291] The ITLOS also has power to prescribe binding provisional measures to protect the marine environment or living resources.[292] As we saw in Chapter 3 it has used this power quite liberally to set catch quotas, require environmental studies, and promote cooperation.[293]

These provisions are indicative of the importance of judicial supervision in controlling the exercise of jurisdiction and authority conferred by the 1982 Convention on states, particularly coastal states, and on international institutions. It was intended to be a 'package deal' whose provisions represented a global consensus, from which only limited derogation would be permitted. Compulsory third-party dispute settlement is thus an integral element in a Convention whose integrity and consistent application were among the primary interests of many states involved in its negotiation. Judicial supervision can be seen in this context as an essential means of stabilizing a complex balance of rights and duties, while accommodating inevitable pressure for continued development of the law to fit new circumstances.[294] Few of these considerations apply with the same force to other environmental treaties, which in most cases are less concerned with the allocation and control of power than with facilitating cooperative solutions to common problems. In this context institutional supervision remains in general the more appropriate means of control and development.

(b) The Protocol to the Antarctic Treaty on Environmental Protection[295]

Apart from the 1982 UNCLOS and related treaties, the only other comprehensive scheme for the settlement of environmental disputes is found in the 1991 Protocol to the Antarctic Treaty. No new court is created, but disputes concerning interpretation or application of certain articles of the protocol are subject to compulsory arbitration, once attempts at negotiation and conciliation have been exhausted.[296] Any party to the treaty may also make a declaration accepting as compulsory the jurisdiction of the ICJ and/or arbitration. The arbitral tribunal provided for in the schedule is composed

---

[290] See Boyle, 14 *IJMCL* (1999) 1.

[291] But see *Southern Bluefin Tuna Arbitration* (2000) in which the arbitrators held that the 1993 Convention on the Conservation of Southern Bluefin Tuna had deprived them of jurisdiction under UNCLOS to decide the dispute. See Boyle, 50 *ICLQ* (2001) 447. This decision is inconsistent with the arbitral decision in the *MOX Plant Case*.

[292] 1982 UNCLOS, Article 290; 1995 Fish Stocks Agreement, Article 31. See *Southern Bluefin Tuna Cases* (1999) ITLOS Nos 3, 4; *MOX Plant Case* (2001) ITLOS No 10; *Land Reclamation Case* (2003) ITLOS No 12.

[293] See *supra* Ch 3, section 4.

[294] Oxman, in Soons, *Implementation of the Law of the Sea Convention through International Institutions*, 650.

[295] See Articles 18–20 and Schedule, and see generally, Francioni and Scovazzi (eds), *International Law for Antarctica* (2nd edn, The Hague, 1996) 603–23.

[296] Notably Articles 7, (mining) 8 (EIA), 15 (emergency response) and the Annexes.

of persons 'experienced in Antarctic affairs' with a 'thorough knowledge' of international law. The tribunal has power to 'indicate' provisional measures to preserve the respective rights of the parties to the dispute and to 'prescribe' provisional measures to prevent serious harm to the Antarctic environment or associated ecosystems. Only the latter are binding. Unusually in an arbitration, there is provision for a third party to intervene in the proceedings if it believes it has a legal interest, 'whether general or individual', which may be substantially affected by the award of the tribunal. This wording may be broad enough to allow any party to the protocol to intervene, as would be the case under Article 32 of the Statute of the ITLOS in cases involving interpretation or application of the UNCLOS.[297] The arbitral tribunal is required to apply the Antarctic Protocol, and other applicable rules and principles of international law not incompatible with it, but the parties may alternatively agree to let the tribunal decide *ex aequo et bono*. This is a sophisticated, but so far untested scheme, which draws substantially on Part XV of the 1982 UNCLOS.

(c) The World Trade Organization Dispute Settlement Scheme

The 1994 Understanding on Rules and Procedures Governing the Settlement of Disputes for the first time established a system of compulsory binding adjudication of disputes arising out of the WTO agreements. The operation of this scheme is explained in Chapter 14. It is not possible to refer disputes arising under general international environmental law or under environmental treaties to the WTO dispute settlement system. However, when an environmental dispute raises issues of compliance or compatibility with WTO agreements, then the WTO Dispute Settlement Body will have jurisdiction at least over that issue. It is also possible that both the WTO and other international courts or tribunals may have concurrent compulsory jurisdiction over different aspects of a dispute which straddles various treaties.[298]

The WTO Committee on Trade and Environment has recommended that, where possible, disputes concerning multilateral environmental agreements are settled under these agreements, rather than through the WTO, but of course most environmental agreements make no provision for binding compulsory settlement of disputes. Similarly, if the dispute involves unilateral application of environmental measures in restraint of trade, rather than treaty compliance, then the WTO is likely to be the only available forum for compulsory settlement. Such disputes may require the dispute settlement body of WTO to adjudicate on the scope of environmental exceptions to WTO agreements. Moreover, questions concerning general international environmental law, or the relationship between WTO agreements and environmental

---

[297] Compare the narrower wording of Article 31 of the ITLOS Statute on intervention by interested parties.

[298] See Chile–EC: *Case Concerning the Conservation and Sustainable Exploitation of Swordfish Stocks in the South-Eastern Pacific Ocean*, ITLOS No 7, Order No 2000/3 (2000) and EC–Chile: *Measures Affecting the Transit and Importation of Swordfish* (WTO, 2000)(WT/DS193). The 2006 *Pulp Mills* dispute between Argentina and Uruguay involved concurrent litigation before the ICJ under the statute of the River Uruguay and a MERCOSUR arbitral tribunal under the MERCOSUR Agreement.

agreements, may also have to be decided.[299] Thus, even if the WTO is not a general forum for the settlement of international environmental disputes, important trade and environment issues will inevitably come before it.

(d) Standing to sue under MEAs

The question whether all parties have standing to sue for breach or non-compliance with a multilateral environmental agreement is not straightforward. In principle, as we saw when considering the law of state responsibility, any treaty which creates *erga omnes* rights for all parties can be enforced by any of those states.[300] Any party to the Montreal Protocol, the Kyoto Protocol, or the Aarhus Convention, for example, will therefore be entitled to initiate proceedings under the dispute settlement provisions of those treaties. But it does not follow that all MEAs create *erga omnes* rights or that any party may sue in respect of any breach by any other party. Consistently with the ILC articles on state responsibility, transboundary pollution will normally engage only the rights of the states directly affected.[301] Unaffected states will thus have no standing to sue for violations of the Convention on Long-Range Transboundary Air Pollution, the Basel Convention on Transboundary Movement of Waste, or certain articles of Part XII of the 1982 UNCLOS. Much depends, however, on the treaty in question, and on when the rights of other parties—or of individuals—are implicated. WTO agreements, for example, create a network of essentially bilateral trade relations.[302] Nevertheless, any party may complain of a violation of the GATT if it 'should consider' that its trade benefits have been nullified or impaired.[303] This provision has allowed quite broad access to the dispute-settlement procedure, even for states which do not engage in the trade in question.[304] It is probable that certain provisions of the 1982 UNCLOS would have a similarly broad effect even if they are not *erga omnes partes*.[305]

4(4) DISPUTE SETTLEMENT BY TREATY SUPERVISORY BODIES

Formal settlement of environmental disputes may also fall within the competence of treaty bodies. The US–Canadian International Joint Commission (ICJ) is a leading

---

[299] See *United States—Import Prohibition of Certain Shrimp and Shrimp Products* ['*Shrimp/Turtle Case*'] Appellate Body (1998) WT/DS58/AB/R.

[300] ILC, 2001 Articles on State Responsibility, Article 48, *supra* section 2(5).   [301] Ibid, Article 42.

[302] Pauwelyn, *Conflict of Norms in Public International Law* (Cambridge, 2003) 315–24; id, 14 *EJIL* (2003) 925–41.

[303] 1994 GATT, Article XXIII.

[304] *European Communities—Regime for the Importation, Sale and Distribution of Bananas*, WT/DS27/AB/R (1997) paras 135–6. See also *United States—Sections 301–10 of the Trade Act of 1974*, WT/DS152/R (2000) para 7.81 ('Indirect impact on individuals is, surely, one of the principal reasons. In treaties which concern only the relations between States, State responsibility is incurred only when an actual violation takes place. By contrast, in a treaty the benefits of which depend in part on the activity of individual operators the legislation itself may be construed as a breach, since the mere existence of legislation could have an appreciable 'chilling effect' on the economic activities of individuals.') See Schoenbaum, 47 *ICLQ* (1998) 653, but compare the more cautious explanation of these cases in Pauwelyn, *Conflict of Norms*, 81–5, where the need for some detriment to the rights of a complainant state is stressed.

[305] E.g. the articles on transit passage through international straits or freedom of navigation in the EEZ.

example. Article 10 of the 1909 Boundary Waters Treaty permits it to act as an arbitrator, with the consent of both parties, but for reasons explained in Chapter 10 it has not found favour in this role. More use has been made of its power of conciliation under Article 9 of the Treaty, because this places no obligation on the parties to comply with its recommendations. It was asked to conciliate in the early stages of the *Trail Smelter* dispute, but without ultimate success. In the early 1980s the IJC also acted as mediator between British Columbia and the City of Seattle in the Skagit River dispute.[306]

Some dispute settlement powers have been given to the Commission for Environmental Cooperation (CEC), established under the 1993 North American Agreement on Environmental Cooperation as part of the NAFTA accords. This agreement is principally concerned with ensuring that each party 'effectively' enforces its own environmental laws through appropriate government action. There is limited provision for private access to remedies in each party's legal system, and NGOs or private individuals may also complain about inadequate law enforcement to the secretariat of the CEC, which has power to investigate and report, but no power to compel action.[307] Unresolved disputes concerning law enforcement may be taken up at interstate level, however. In such cases the CEC then has power to investigate, mediate or conciliate between the parties to see whether a mutually satisfactory solution can be agreed. If this proves impossible, and if trade or competition are affected, a dispute may go to arbitration. The arbitrators have power to approve remedial measures, to impose a substantial fine, or to suspend NAFTA benefits. This is a potentially powerful dispute settlement scheme, but it is principally aimed at Mexico; Canadian provinces are bound only if they agree on ratification. Moreover, while the Agreement's focus on disputes about enforcement of national law represents a novel but useful extension of international dispute settlement,[308] it also precludes it from operating as a mechanism for settling disputes about international environmental law.

A few agreements involve the relevant body in settling treaty disputes. Disputes arising out of the 1995 Mekong River Agreement may be referred to the Mekong River Commission,[309] while the 1994 International Tropical Timber Agreement provides that any dispute arising under the agreement shall be referred to the Council of the ITTO for a 'final and binding' decision.[310] This enables the Council to interpret the agreement definitively. The benefit of dealing with such disputes in this way is that it keeps control over interpretation and development of the treaty in the hands of the parties collectively, rather than surrendering it to an independent third party, or to the parties acting unilaterally.

---

[306] Cooper, 24 *CYIL* (1986) 247, 285–90, who also notes the Commission's role as a mediator; Bilder, 70 *Michigan LR* (1972) 513ff.

[307] Fitzmaurice, 52 *ICLQ* (2003) 334, and see *infra*, Ch 5.

[308] Compare the approach to transborder law enforcement adopted in the 1974 Nordic Environmental Protection Convention. This convention allows public bodies as well as individuals to initiate legal action in neighbouring jurisdictions, and it provides for a commission to give 'an opinion' on the permissibility of environmentally harmful activities. See *infra*, Ch 5.

[309] Articles 18(c), 24(f), 34, 35.

[310] Article 31. Producing and consuming states have an equal number of votes in the Council and decisions which cannot be agreed by consensus are taken by majority vote.

4(5) DIPLOMATIC METHODS OF DISPUTE SETTLEMENT

Diplomatic methods of settlement facilitate negotiation of a dispute without resort to bilateral adjudication or multilateral non-compliance procedures. They have two principal advantages. First, and most importantly, the parties remain in control of the outcome. They can walk away at any time and, until agreement is reached in the form of a treaty, there will be no final or binding determination of rights or obligations. Second, there are the added benefits of cheapness, flexibility, privacy, and complete freedom to determine who is involved, what expertise is relevant, and the basis on which any solution will be sought. The solution need not be based on international law. In many of these respects diplomatic settlement has much in common with the concept of alternative dispute resolution in national legal systems,[311] although it differs in the important respect that interstate negotiation will not necessarily take place against a background of resort to compulsory adjudication should the parties fail to reach agreement.

(a) Mediation and good offices[312]

These methods of dispute settlement involve the assistance of a third party in facilitating negotiations. The process is voluntary and works only if the parties want to reach agreement. A number of environmental treaties allow for the possibility of mediation or good offices.[313] The main virtue of both types of settlement process is that the parties are able to avoid taking adversarial roles, while the third party is not involved in a formal adjudication. Global or regional organizations may provide good offices, mediation, or conciliation for states involved in environmental disputes. The World Bank mediated a solution to the Indus River dispute, resulting in negotiation of the 1960 Indus Waters Treaty.[314] UNEP could offer its good offices or act as a mediator or conciliator, since its responsibilities include the power to provide 'at the request of all the parties concerned advisory services for the promotion of cooperation in the field of the environment', and the Executive Director can also bring problems to the attention of the Governing Council for its consideration

(b) Conciliation and inquiry[315]

Conciliation and inquiry involve more than facilitating negotiations. In the former a third party can be empowered to indicate possible solutions, which may include findings on matters of law and of fact. Commissions of inquiry will normally deal

---

[311] Chinkin, in Evans (ed), *Remedies in International Law*, 123–40.

[312] Cooper, 24 *CYIL* (1986) 284; Barnes, in Dupuy (ed), *The Future of International Law of the Environment* (Dordrecht, 1985) 167.

[313] E.g. the 1979 Berne Convention on the Conservation of European Wildlife and Natural Habitats, Article 18(1).

[314] Cooper, 24 *CYIL* (1986) 285.

[315] Merrills, *International Dispute Settlement*, Ch 4; Cooper, 24 *CYIL* (1986) 287, and see Bar-Yaacov, *The Handling of International Disputes By Means of Inquiry* (London, 1974). See UN Rules for the Conciliation of Disputes, UN Doc A/50/33 (1995).

only with fact finding, a particularly important issue in many environmental disputes. The parties are not obliged to accept the findings or proposed solutions, however, nor do these necessarily represent an adjudication of the legal issues. Thus the conciliators appointed to settle a maritime boundary dispute between Norway and Iceland described their task in the following terms:

[T]he Conciliation Commission shall not act as a court of law. Its function is to make recommendations to the two governments which in the unanimous opinion of the Commission will lead to acceptable and equitable solutions of the problems involved.[316]

Nevertheless, conciliation is often used in disputes where the main issues are legal, and conciliators are often lawyers. As the *Jan Mayen Conciliation* illustrates, legal precedents and state practice may be taken into account, but in this case they were only 'possible guidelines' for a solution. In a few cases, however, conciliators have been asked to do more than this, and to make recommendations on what the parties merit, rather than what they will accept.[317] Depending on the mandate in specific cases, conciliation can thus vary from a form of institutionalized negotiation to something akin to non-binding arbitration.

Conciliation is widely employed in dispute-settlement provisions in multilateral environmental treaties, including the 1982 UNCLOS.[318] It is also one of the roles of the US–Canadian International Joint Commission.[319] Comparatively few environmental treaties provide for an inquiry procedure, but the 1991 Convention on Transboundary Environmental Impact Assessment is an important example.[320] The first such inquiry assessed the possible risks posed by river works on the Romania–Ukraine border.[321] There are also several instances of states resorting to scientific inquiry to establish the causes or consequences of environmental pollution or depletion of natural resources.[322]

As alternatives to judicial settlement or arbitration, the attractions of conciliation and inquiry are obvious: whatever the outcome of the proceedings, the parties remain free to negotiate a politically acceptable settlement of their differences without being bound to adhere strictly to treaty provisions or rules of international law. This means that conciliation awards are of limited value as legal precedents, and they may also have an adverse effect on the integrity of a treaty if they sanction what are in effect negotiated violations or departures from the formal rules. Compulsory conciliation in

---

[316] *Jan Mayen Conciliation*, 20 *ILM* (1981) 797, 823. See also 1969 Vienna Convention on the Law of Treaties, Annex, para 6; Article 19, 2001 ILC Articles on Prevention of Transboundary Harm, *ILC Report* (2001) GAOR A/56/10; 1974 Nordic Convention for Protection of the Environment, Articles 11–12.

[317] Merrills, *International Dispute Settlement*, Ch 4.

[318] 1982 UNCLOS, Annex V.   [319] See *infra*, Ch 10.

[320] Article 3. See also Article 19, 2001 ILC Articles on Prevention of Transboundary Harm, *ILC Report* (2001) GAOR A/56/10; 1974 Nordic Convention for Protection of the Environment, Articles 11–12.

[321] See Espoo Inquiry Commission Report on the Danube-Black Sea Navigation Route (2006) *supra* Ch 3, section 4(4).

[322] See e.g. the *Trail Smelter Arbitration*, and the use of the IJC under Article 9 of the US–Canada Boundary Waters Treaty.

the context of a multilateral treaty dispute in effect becomes an extension of supervision by the Conference of the Parties and a reflection of the essentially political nature of this process with its emphasis on consensus and persuasion rather than adjudication or sanctions. We need then to recall the variety of functions dispute-settlement provisions may perform and avoid the temptation to see them always as an exercise in rule-based adjudication and enforcement. While the treaties in question remain binding, the parties are free to decide when, how, and how far to implement them. In this obvious sense they can be described as 'soft' rather than 'hard' law.[323] As Koskenniemi points out, 'Though procedure is far from irrelevant, it cannot be successfully used nor interestingly discussed without regard to the types of outcomes it is intended, or likely, to produce'.[324]

5 CONCLUSIONS

In considering how the international legal system handles environmental disputes, the diversity of issues needs to be emphasized. Where the problem is one of compliance with agreed standards of global or regional environmental protection, treaty COPs and non-compliance committees afford multilateral forums appropriate to the protection of common interests. Such procedures will be stronger and more effective if they facilitate openness, informed scrutiny, and resort where necessary to judicial organs by way of review. They should not be seen as an inferior substitute for adjudication, but potentially as a more effective means of exercising a form of international trusteeship over the environment. They give substance to the ILC's conception of certain multilateral treaty obligations having an *erga omnes partes* character. Moreover, effective multilateral supervision also makes unilateral responses less likely and ensures greater consistency and continuity in the development of state practice.

Resort to international judicial machinery remains an alternative means of resolving environmental claims, but its utility should not be exaggerated, despite the increasing environmental caseload of international courts and tribunals. International proceedings will rarely be the best way of settling claims for environmental injury; in this context greater reliance has rightly been placed on facilitating resort to national legal systems, considered in the next chapter, or on international claims procedures. At the same time, litigation has proved its utility as a means of challenging failure to carry out an EIA or to cooperate with neighbouring states in the management of transboundary environmental risks.[325] Like negotiating a new treaty, it can also have the politically satisfying effect of appearing to do something about the environment. Moreover, international adjudication provides a form of third-party determination of rights over natural resources, or over common spaces; but here too, political supervisory institutions

---

[323] See Boyle, 48 *ICLQ* (1999) 909–12.   [324] 60 *Nordic JIL* (1991) 74.

[325] See *supra* Ch 3, section 4.

will usually prove more attractive because of their various advantages, including flexibility, accessibility, and capacity for resolving matters multilaterally without necessarily following existing rules of international law. Finally, advisory opinions have shown how *erga omnes* environmental rules could be adjudicated in a relatively multilateral process outside the normal framework of bilateral contentious litigation.

The ILC's completed work on 'International Liability' remains a missed opportunity to place state responsibility for environmental damage on a more satisfactory basis. It is thus doubtful whether the concept of state liability will assume greater significance than at present in the resolution of environmental disputes, although states will continue to be responsible for damage caused by a breach of their obligation of due diligence, or in breach of treaty, or by a prohibited act.

In the next chapter we consider some alternative approaches to the implementation and enforcement of international environmental law which have begun to change the emphasis of the whole subject. Relying less on interstate claims, or on mechanisms of international supervision, the development of human-rights approaches to environmental protection and the economic logic of the polluter-pays principle have made claims by individuals an increasingly attractive means of dealing with domestic or transboundary environmental problems. But the diversity of the issues needs emphasis in this context also. National remedies are not necessarily alternatives to the system considered in this chapter, but are more often complementary to it, and only in certain respects more useful. The variety of approaches now available for the resolution of international environmental disputes does indicate the increasing sophistication of the international legal system. It is testimony to the fact that considerable efforts have been made over the past twenty years to develop the law in this field, by states parties to various treaties and by international organizations such as OECD, the Council of Europe, IMO, IAEA, UNECE, UNEP and the Permanent Court of Arbitration.

5

NON-STATE ACTORS: ENVIRONMENTAL RIGHTS, LIABILITY, AND CRIMES

1   INTRODUCTION

The two previous chapters were concerned with the law applicable in interstate relations. In this chapter we consider some of the rights and obligations which attach to individuals, corporations, and NGOs in international environmental law. The emergence of individual environmental rights marks perhaps the most significant shift in the focus of international environmental law. It is potentially more significant than the injection of environmental concerns into WTO law because it reaches directly into the core of national policies on a wide range of issues. We explore first what potential there may be for using international human-rights law to compel governments to address environmental conditions within their own territory. Is there or should there be a 'right' to a decent environment? Can the rights to life, private life, or property be useful in environmental cases? Should international law promote democratization of environmental decision-making or public-interest enforcement by NGOs? Second, we consider the rights and liabilities of non-state actors in a transboundary setting. Can individuals affected by transboundary damage seek redress against polluters in other jurisdictions? Should states harmonize their national law on environmental liability or establish compensation schemes and provide other remedies in such cases? These are essentially questions of private international law. Third, we look briefly at mechanisms for promoting corporate environmental responsibility. Corporations are subject to the normal rules of civil liability for transboundary environmental damage, but are they bound to respect international environmental law in general? Should they be accountable for failing to meet internationally agreed standards and by what means? Last, we look at the limited role of international criminal law in enforcing environmental standards.

1(1) ENVIRONMENTAL RIGHTS

The claim that individuals, peoples, generations, animals, or the environment have or should have environmental rights raises the question what is meant in this context by the notion of a 'right'. Such claims do not necessarily entail conferring rights directly enforceable through legal proceedings. Rather, advocates of environmental rights use this terminology to ascribe value or autonomous status to the interests and claims of particular entities.[1] By doing so, they seek to force lawmakers and institutions to take account of those interests, to accord them a priority which they might not otherwise enjoy and to make them part of the context for interpreting legal rules. The entrenchment of such values within the legal system may extend to the appointment of representatives to speak or act on their behalf but, as an articulation of values, such rights do not cease to be significant merely because no formal means can be found for their expression. Used in this sense, even future generations may have 'rights', as we saw in Chapter 3.

Critics point out that it is simply unnecessary to construct 'rights' of this kind to deal with problems of conflicting social priorities.[2] The attempt to do so may lead to the false assumption that social changes are thereby effected. To argue that value should be ascribed to future generations, peoples, animals, or the environment, does not tell us what the value should be or how it should be weighed against other values or 'rights'. It may assume, moreover, that such common interests are incapable of protection unless represented independently of other interests, and that legal procedures are the best means for doing so. The argument for environmental rights in this form shares the problems of expressing and implementing claims to economic and social rights in legal form, with the added complication that the claimants may not yet exist, may be non-human, or inanimate.

Thus the main danger of the rights argument is its overextension. It is not clear that it leads necessarily to any greater protection for the environment than could be made available simply through better regulation or litigation on other issues. But Stone's argument that creating rights is not the same as introducing more protective rules should be noted. He points out that 'rights' introduce a flexibility and open-endedness that no rule can capture.[3] Above all, they trump other claims or values which do not have the status of rights.[4]

---

[1] Merrills, in Bodansky, Brunnée, and Hey (eds), *Oxford Handbook of International Environmental Law* (Oxford, 2007) 663; Hayward, *Constitutional Environmental Rights* (Oxford, 2005); Giagnocavo and Goldstein, 35 *McGill LJ* (1990) 356–7; D'Amato and Chopra, 85 *AJIL* (1991) 21.

[2] Giagnocavo and Goldstein, ibid, 361; Emond, 22 *OsHLJ* (1985) 325; Elder, ibid, 285.

[3] Stone, 45 *SCal LR* (1972) 488.

[4] Merrills, in Bodansky, Brunnée, and Hey (eds), *Handbook of IEL*, 666.

1(2) THE ROLE OF NATIONAL LAW

The argument for individual rights stands apart as the strongest of these environmental claims. The pragmatic point is that by addressing the rights and responsibilities of individuals and other legally significant entities directly, international law facilitates wider participation in processes of national governance and environmental decision-making, and provides a more effective approach to the enforcement and implementation of environmental law, primarily through the use of national legal systems and the promotion of public interest litigation. The importance of national law can be observed at three levels.

First, national law is the medium through which states will usually implement their international obligations and regulate the conduct of their own nationals and companies both inside their borders and beyond. It both serves as the principal source of legal remedies for individual claimants and enables effect to be given to the notion of individual or corporate responsibility in international environmental law. In this context, the obligation to provide 'effective access' to justice before national courts, referred to in Principle 10 of the 1992 Rio Declaration, has provided the basis for some significant developments in environmental rights and liabilities at regional level and in the International Law Commission. The use of criminal sanctions in environmental cases is largely regulated by national law and confined to activities within a states' own territory. Nevertheless, for the purpose of making international environmental regulation more effective, states in certain instances possess extraterritorial criminal jurisdiction exercisable against non-nationals. Exceptionally, some environmental offences may be treated as crimes against international law over which all states have jurisdiction wherever they are committed.

Second, national law may be used as a means of reallocating the costs of transboundary environmental harm. Here it becomes an alternative to reliance on interstate claims, in contrast to which the main advantages are that individual claimants gain control over the proceedings and liability is placed directly on the polluter or enterprise causing environmental damage. The role of international law in this context is to remove obstacles to transboundary litigation and in certain cases to ensure that liability standards are harmonized and an effective remedy guaranteed. More generally, making national remedies available is consistent with the view that there are significant advantages in avoiding resort to interstate remedies for the resolution of transboundary environmental disputes wherever possible.[5] In this broader sense, individuals and NGOs can be empowered to act as part of the enforcement structure of international environmental law.

Finally, international law is in some jurisdictions and in certain circumstances directly applicable as national law. To that limited extent it may in theory be possible for

---

[5] Levin, *Protecting the Human Environment* (New York, 1977) 31–8; Sand, in OECD, *Legal Aspects of Transfrontier Pollution* (Paris, 1977) 146; Bilder, 144 *Recueil des Cours* (1975) 224; Handl, 1 *YbIEL* (1990) 18ff.

claimants to rely on environmental treaties or customary law before national courts. In practice the leading study of the subject concluded that 'the role of national courts in implementing international environmental law has been rather limited to date'.[6] The only notable exception is that some human-rights treaties have become a significant basis for environmental claims and are usually applicable by national courts. The European Convention on Human Rights is the most important example.

2 HUMAN RIGHTS AND THE ENVIRONMENT

2(1) INTRODUCTION

In 1972 the United Nations Conference on the Human Environment declared that 'Man has the fundamental right to freedom, equality and adequate conditions of life, *in an environment of a quality that permits a life of dignity and well-being,* and he bears a solemn responsibility to protect and improve the environment for present and future generations'.[7] This grand statement might have provided the basis for subsequent elaboration of a human right to environmental quality,[8] but its real-world impact has been noticeably modest. It was not repeated in the 1992 Rio Declaration, which merely makes human beings the 'central concern of sustainable development' and refers only to their being 'entitled to a healthy and productive life in harmony with nature'.[9] As Dinah Shelton noted at the time, the Rio Declaration's failure to give greater emphasis to human rights was indicative of uncertainty and debate about the proper place of human-rights law in the development of international environmental law.[10] There is still room for debate.[11]

Environmental rights do not fit neatly into any single category or 'generation' of human rights. They can be viewed from at least three perspectives. First, existing civil and political rights can provide a basis for giving affected individuals access to environmental information, judicial remedies, and political processes.[12] On this view their role is one of empowerment, facilitating participation in environmental

---

[6] See Anderson and Galizzi (eds), *International Environmental Law in National Courts* (London, 2002) 9.

[7] Principle 1, 1972 Stockholm Declaration on the Human Environment.

[8] See Sohn, 14 *Harv ILJ* (1973) 451–5.

[9] Principle 1, 1992 Rio Declaration on Environment and Development. But see also Principle 10, considered below.

[10] Shelton, 3 *YbIEL* (1992) 75, 82ff.

[11] See generally Boyle and Anderson (eds), *Human Rights Approaches to Environmental Protection* (Oxford, 1996); Shelton, in Alston (ed), *Peoples' Rights* (Oxford, 2001) 185; Merrills, in Bodansky, Brunnée and Hey, *Handbook of IEL*, Ch 28.

[12] See McGoldrick, *The Human Rights Committee: Its Role in the Development of the International Covenant on Civil and Political Rights* (Oxford, 1994); Nowak, *UN Covenant on Civil and Political Rights: a Commentary,* (Kehl, 1993); Joseph, Schultz and Castan, *The International Covenant on Civil and Political*

decision-making and compelling governments to meet minimum standards of protection for life, private life, and property from environmental harm. Human-rights commissions and courts can adjudicate on the rights concerned in response to complaints from individuals. A second possibility is to treat a decent, healthy, or sound environment as an economic or social right, comparable to those whose progressive attainment is promoted by the 1966 UN Covenant on Economic Social and Cultural Rights.[13] The main argument for this approach is that it would privilege environmental quality as a value, giving it comparable status to other economic and social rights such as development, and priority over non rights-based objectives. Like other economic and social rights it would be programmatic and in most cases enforceable only through relatively weak international supervisory mechanisms. The third option would treat environmental quality as a collective or solidarity right, giving communities ('peoples') rather than individuals a right to determine how their environment and natural resources should be protected and managed.

The first approach is essentially anthropocentric insofar as it focuses on the harmful impact on individual humans, rather than on the environment itself: it amounts to a 'greening' of human-rights law, rather than a law of environmental rights.[14] The second comes closer to seeing the environment as a good in its own right, but nevertheless one that will always be vulnerable to trade-offs against other similarly privileged but competing objectives, including the right to economic development. The third approach is the most contested. Not all human-rights lawyers favour the recognition of third generation rights, arguing that they devalue the concept of human rights, and divert attention from the need to implement existing civil, political, economic and social rights fully.[15] The concept hardly featured in the agenda of the 1993 UN World Conference on Human Rights, and in general it adds little to an understanding of the nature of environmental rights, which are not inherently collective in character. However, there are some significant examples of collective rights which in certain contexts can have environmental implications, such as the protection of minority cultures and indigenous peoples,[16] or the right of all peoples freely to dispose of their natural resources, recognized in the 1966 UN International Covenants on Civil and Political

---

Rights (2nd edn, Oxford, 2005). However, treatment of environmental rights is noticeably absent from these works.

[13] See Craven, *The International Covenant on Economic, Social, and Cultural Rights* (Oxford, 1995); Eide, Krause and Rosas (eds), *Economic, Social and Cultural Rights* (Dordrecht, 2001); Dennis and Stewart, 98 *AJIL* (2004) 462.

[14] See *infra*, section 2(3).

[15] Alston, 29 *NILR* (1982) 307; id, 78 *AJIL* (1984) 607; Brownlie, in Crawford (ed), *The Rights of Peoples* (Oxford, 1988) 1.

[16] See 1966 ICCPR, Article 27, under which minorities have the right to enjoy their own culture, including the exploitation of natural resources, and 1989 ILO Convention No 169 Concerning Indigenous and Tribal Peoples, Article 7(4) which provides that 'Governments shall take measures, in cooperation with the peoples concerned, to protect and preserve the environment of the territories they inhabit.'

Rights and Economic, Social and Cultural Rights (ICCPR and ICESCR)[17] and in the 1981 African Charter on Human and Peoples Rights.[18]

(a) The environment in human-rights treaties

Among human-rights treaties only the 1981 African Charter on Human and Peoples' Rights proclaims environmental rights in broadly qualitative terms. It protects both the right of peoples to the 'best attainable standard of health' (Article 16) and their right to 'a general satisfactory environment favourable to their development' (Article 24). In the *Ogoniland Case* the African Commission on Human and Peoples Rights held, inter alia, that Article 24 of the Charter imposes an obligation on the State to take reasonable measures 'to prevent pollution and ecological degradation, to promote conservation, and to secure ecologically sustainable development and use of natural resources'.[19] Specific actions required of States in fulfilment of Articles 16 and 24 include 'ordering or at least permitting independent scientific monitoring of threatened environments, requiring and publicising environmental and social impact studies prior to any major industrial development, undertaking appropriate monitoring and providing information to those communities exposed to hazardous materials and activities and providing meaningful opportunities for individuals to be heard and to participate in the development decisions affecting their communities'.[20] The Commission's final order is also the most far-reaching of any environmental rights case. It calls for a 'comprehensive cleanup of lands and rivers damaged by oil operations', the preparation of environmental and social impact assessments, and provision of information on health and environmental risks and 'meaningful access to regulatory and decision-making bodies'.[21] As Shelton observes, 'The result offers a blueprint for merging environmental protection, economic development, and guarantees of human rights'.[22]

Ogoniland is a remarkable decision which goes further than any previous human-rights case in the substantive environmental obligations it places on states. It is unique in also applying for the first time the right of peoples to dispose freely of their own natural resources (Article 21).[23] When combined with the evidence of severe harm to the lives, health, property, and well-being of the local population, the decision must be

---

[17] Common Article 1(2) and see also ICESCR, Article 25 and ICCPR, Article 47. For drafting history of Article 1(2) see Cassese, in Henkin (ed), *The International Bill of Rights: The Covenant on Civil and Political Rights* (New York, 1981) 32ff, and Rosas, in Eide, Krause, Rosas (eds), *Economic, Social and Cultural Rights*, Ch 6, 117, who notes that Article 1 'establishes minimum rules for the right of the entire population to economic and social rights against its own government.'

[18] Article 21.

[19] *The Social and Economic Rights Action Center and the Center for Economic and Social Rights v Nigeria*, ACHPR, No 155/96 (2002) paras 52–53 ['*SERAC v Nigeria*']. See Shelton, 96 *AJIL* (2002) 937; Coomans, 52 *ICLQ* (2003) 749.

[20] Para 54.   [21] Para 69.

[22] Shelton, Decision Regarding case 155/96 (2002) 96 *AJIL* 937, 942.

[23] Although Article 1(2) of the 1966 ICCPR also recognizes the right of peoples to 'freely dispose of their natural wealth and resources...' this provision is not justiciable by the UN Human Rights Committee under the optional procedure for individual complaints: see *Ominayak and Lubicon Lake Band v Canada* (1990) ICCPR No 167/1984, para 32.1.

seen as a challenge to the sustainability of oil extraction in Ogoniland. The most obvi-ous characteristics of unsustainable development include serious long-term environ-mental harm and a lack of material benefits for those most adversely affected. In that sense it is not surprising that the African Commission does not see this case simply as a failure to maintain a fair balance between public good and private rights. The deci-sion gives some indication of how environmental rights could be used, but its excep-tional basis in Articles 21 and 24 of the African Convention has to be remembered. No other treaty contains anything directly comparable, although several decisions of the Inter-American Commission and Court of Human Rights have interpreted the rights to life, health, and property to afford protection from environmental destruction and unsustainable development and they go some way towards achieving the same out-come as Article 24 of the African Convention.[24]

The only other treaty to make specific provision for environmental rights is the 1998 Aarhus Convention on Access to Information, Public Participation in Decision-making and Access to Justice in Environmental Matters. Its preamble not only recalls Principle 1 of the Stockholm Declaration and recognizes that 'adequate protection of the environment is essential to human well-being and the enjoyment of basic human rights, including the right to life itself' but also asserts that 'every person has the right to live in an environment adequate to his or her health and well-being, and the duty, both individually and in association with others, to protect and improve the envir-onment for the benefit of present and future generations'.[25] The Aarhus Convention represents an important extension of environmental rights, but also of the corpus of human-rights law. However, as we will see below, its focus is strictly procedural in content, limited to public participation in environmental decision-making and access to justice and information.[26] As a conception of environmental rights it owes little to Stockholm Principle 1 and everything to Principle 10 of the 1992 Rio Declaration, which gives explicit support in mandatory language to the same category of proced-ural rights.[27] The Aarhus Convention is widely ratified in Europe and has had signifi-cant influence on the jurisprudence of the European Court of Human Rights, whose decisions are considered below. The Convention is also important because, unlike the European Convention on Human Rights, it gives particular emphasis to public interest activism by NGOs.[28] But as one critic has pointed out, while the Convention endorses the right to live in an adequate environment, it 'stops short, however, of pro-viding the means for citizens directly to invoke this right'.[29]

---

[24] See *Mayagna (Sumo) Awas Tingni Community v Nicaragua* (2001) IACHR Ser C, No 20; *Maya Indigenous Community of the Toledo District v Belize,* Case 12.053, Report No 40/04, Inter-Am CHR, OEA/Ser L/V/II.122 Doc 5 rev 1, 727 (2004); *Yanomani Indians v Brazil,* Decision 7615, Inter-Am CHR, *Inter-American YB on Hum Rts* 264 (1985). See *infra,* section 2(3).

[25] The UK made a declaration on signing the Convention that this provision is 'an aspiration', not a legal right.

[26] Section 2(4).   [27] See also UNCED, Agenda 21, Ch 23, esp 23.2, and see *infra.*

[28] Articles 4(1)(a), 6, 9 are considered below.

[29] Hayward, *Constitutional Environmental Rights,* 180.

Other human-rights treaties either make no explicit reference to the environment at all or do so only in relatively narrow terms, focused on human health, which add little or nothing to case law derived from the right to life.[30] Insofar as most human-rights treaties have relevance to environmental rights it is mainly or exclusively through the growing body of jurisprudence in which the 'greening' of other rights has been pursued with increasing vigour. The European Convention on Human Rights, adopted in 1950, says nothing about the environment. Nevertheless, like other such treaties, it is a 'living instrument', pursuant to which changing social values can be reflected in the jurisprudence. The European Court of Human Rights has consistently held that 'the Convention...must be interpreted in the light of present-day conditions'.[31] With regard to environmental rights this is exactly what the Court has done. So extensive is its growing environmental jurisprudence that proposals for the adoption of an environmental protocol have not been pursued.[32] Instead, a *Manual on Human Rights and the Environment* adopted by the Council of Europe in 2005 recapitulates the Court's decisions on this subject and sets out some general principles.[33]

Nevertheless, as the Council of Europe Manual points out, 'The Convention is not designed to provide a general protection of the environment as such and does not expressly guarantee a right to a sound, quiet and healthy environment'.[34] Despite its evolutionary character, therefore, the European Convention still falls short of guaranteeing a right to a decent or satisfactory environment if that concept is understood in broader, essentially qualitative, terms unrelated to impacts on specific humans.

(b) The environment in national constitutions

If Stockholm did little for the development of international environmental rights, it may have had greater impact on national law. Environmental provisions of some kind have been added to an increasing number of constitutions since 1972.[35] Some

---

[30] See *infra*, section 2(2).

[31] *Soering v UK* (1989) 11 EHRR 439, para 102 and *Öcalan v Turkey* (2003) 37 EHRR 10. The Inter-American Court of Human Rights takes the same approach to interpretation of the Inter-American Convention: see *Advisory Opinion on the Right to Information on Consular Assistance* (1999) IACHR Series A, No 16, paras 114–5; *Advisory Opinion on the Interpretation of the American Declaration on the Rights and Duties of Man* (1989) IACHR Series A, No 10, para 43; *Mayagna (Sumo) Awas Tingni Community v Nicaragua* (2001) IACHR Ser C, No 20, paras 146–8.

[32] See Council of Europe: Committee of Experts for the Development of Human Rights, *Final Activity Report on Human Rights and the Environment*, DH-DEV(2005)006rev, Strasbourg, 10 November 2005, 2–3 [Hereinafter 'Council of Europe Report'].

[33] Council of Europe Report, Appendix II. See section 2(3) below, and Loucaides, 75 *BYIL* (2005) 249–67; Desgagné, (1995) 89 *AJIL* 263. For a review of other international developments see Shelton, 'Human Rights and the Environment: Jurisprudence of Human Rights Bodies', *Joint UNEP-OHCHR Expert Seminar on Human Rights and the Environment: Background Paper No 2* (Geneva, 2002).

[34] Council of Europe Report, 7. See also *Kyrtatos v Greece* [2003] ECHR 242, para 52, *infra*, section 2(7).

[35] Countries which have specific constitutional provisions include: Brazil, Articles 170, 225; Chile, Articles 19, 20; China, Articles 9, 26; Cuba, Article 27; Ecuador, Article 19; Greece, Article 24; Guatemala, Article 93; Guyana, Article 36; Honduras, Article 145; Hungary, Articles 18, 70; India, Article 48A; Iran, Article 50; Mozambique, Article 11; Namibia, Article 95; The Netherlands, Article 21; Nicaragua, Article 60; Papua New Guinea, Article 4; Paraguay, Article 93; Peru, Article 123; Portugal, Article 66; Russian Federation,

clearly create no justiciable rights, but may nevertheless influence the interpretation and application of other constitutional rights or of general law. For example, Article 37 of the European Union's Charter of Fundamental Rights merely provides that 'A high level of environmental protection and the improvement of the quality of the environment must be integrated into the policies of the Union and ensured in accordance with the principle of sustainable development.'[36] Similarly, under the heading 'Directive Principles of State Policy', Article 48A of the Indian Constitution provides only that 'The state shall endeavour to protect and improve the environment and to safeguard the forests and wild life of the country.'[37] This article has nevertheless encouraged Indian courts to give other human rights, including the right to life, a very vigorous environmental interpretation.[38] The result has been a jurisprudence which, more than in any other country, uses human-rights law to address questions of environmental quality.[39] Some constitutions draw inspiration from Article 12 of the 1966 UN Covenant on Economic, Social and Cultural Rights. Thus Article 35 of the Constitution of the Republic of Korea declares that 'All citizens shall have the right to a healthy and pleasant environment', but it then goes on to say that the substance of this right shall be determined by legislation.

Other constitutions give environmental rights a stronger focus, although there is no consistent formulation. Article 45 of the Spanish Constitution declares that everyone has 'the right to enjoy an environment suitable for the development of the person as well as the duty to preserve it'. It then directs public authorities to concern themselves with 'the rational use of all natural resources for the purpose of protecting and improving the quality of life and protecting and restoring the environment…'. Article 225 of the Brazilian Constitution declares that everyone has 'the right to an ecologically balanced environment which is an asset of common use and essential to a healthy quality of life, and both the Government and the community shall have the

---

Article 42; South Africa, Section 24; South Korea, Article 35; Spain, Article 45; Thailand, Article 65; Turkey, Article 56; Yemen, Article 16. See generally Brandl and Bungert, 16 *Harvard ELR* (1992) 1; ECOSOC, *Human Rights and the Environment*, UN Doc E/CN 4/Sub 2/1992/7 and 1993/7. For studies of South Africa, India and Brazil, see Boyle and Anderson (eds), *Human Rights Approaches*, Chs 9, 10, 13.

[36] OJEC 2000/C 364/01. See Eleftheriadis in Alston (ed), *The EU and Human Rights* (Oxford, 1999) Ch 16.

[37] Compare the 1982 Constitution of the People's Republic of China, which provides as follows:

Article 9: 'The state ensures the rational use of natural resources and protects rare animals and plants. Appropriation or damaging of natural resources by any organization or individual by whatever means is prohibited.' Article 26: 'The state protects and improves the environment in which people live and the ecological environment. It prevents and controls pollution and other public hazards. The state organizes and encourages afforestation and the protection of forests.'

[38] On the use of 'directive principles' in Indian case law see Anderson and Galizzi (eds), *International Environmental Law in National Courts*, 150–1.

[39] See *Bandhua Mukti Morcha v Union of India* (1984) 3 SCC 161; *MC Mehta v Union of India* (1997) 2 SCC 353; *Jagganath v Union of India* (1997) 2 SCC 87. For an overview of the Indian case law see Razzaque, 'Human Rights and the Environment: the National Experience in South Asia and Africa', *Joint UNEP-OHCHR Expert Seminar on Human Rights and the Environment: Background Paper No 4* (Geneva, 2002).

duty to defend and preserve it for present and future generations'.[40] It sets out in some detail the principal environmental responsibilities of the state, including, inter alia, the protection and preservation of ecological processes, species, ecosystems, flora and fauna, and genetic diversity, and regulation and control of risks to life, the quality of life, and the environment. Article 56 of the Turkish Constitution is similar: 'Everyone has the right to live in a healthy, balanced environment. It shall be the duty of the State and the citizens to improve and preserve the environment and to prevent environmental pollution'.[41] Article 42 of the 1993 Russian Constitution confers on everyone 'the right to a favourable environment, reliable information about its condition and to compensation for the damage caused to his or her health or property by ecological violations'.[42] The 1996 South African Constitution refers instead to the right 'to an environment that is not harmful to their health or well-being; and to have the environment protected, for the benefit of present and future generations, through reasonable legislative and other measures that prevent pollution and ecological degradation; promote conservation; and secure ecologically sustainable development and use of natural resources while promoting justifiable economic and social development'.[43] This provision reflects Article 24 of the African Convention and the *Ogoniland* decision gives some guidance on how it might be interpreted and applied.[44] The Spanish, Brazilian, Turkish, Russian, and South African constitutional provisions suggest that in those jurisdictions there is some form of right to environmental quality along the lines foreseen at Stockholm, although much will depend on how national courts interpret and use them.

2(2) A RIGHT TO A DECENT, HEALTHY, OR SATISFACTORY ENVIRONMENT?

The most far-reaching case for environmental rights comes in the form of claims to a decent, healthy, or satisfactory environment: to a substantive environmental right involvings the promotion of a certain level of environmental quality. Sohn argues that Principle 1 of the 1972 Stockholm Declaration created an individual human right of this kind,[45] but it is significant that no treaty refers explicitly to the right to a decent environment in these terms. When the concept is employed in a similarly broad and autonomous form, as in Article 24 of the African Charter on Human and Peoples' Rights, it appears as a collective right only: 'All peoples shall have the right to a generally satisfactory environment favourable to their development'. However, as the *Ogoniland*

---

[40] In 1995 the Federal Supreme Tribunal held that Article 225 created a collective right for the whole community rather than for a particular individual. However, it is also possible for an individual to bring an environmental claim: see Constitution, Article 5 LXXIII.

[41] A decision of the Turkish Supreme Court relying on this provision is considered in *Taskin v Turkey* [2006] 42 EHRR 50.

[42] But compare the reality revealed in *Fadeyeva v Russia* [2005] ECHR 376.

[43] Constitution of the Republic of South Africa, Act 108 of 1996, s 24. See Glazewski, *Environmental Law in South Africa* (Durban, 2000).

[44] *SERAC v Nigeria*, ACHPR, Communication 155/96 (2002).   [45] 14 *Harv ILJ* (1973) 455.

Case amply demonstrates, it is no less justiciable in legal proceedings. In a somewhat narrower formulation UNGA Resolution 45/94 (1990) declared that 'all individuals are entitled to live in an environment adequate for their health and well-being', while a link between health and the environment is also found in Article 12 of the 1966 UN Covenant on Economic and Social Rights, which refers to the right to improvement of 'environmental and industrial hygiene', and in a number of other treaties.[46] In most cases these appear to endorse a collective right, guaranteed by government action, but with no provision for individual enforcement. A similar approach is found in many of the national constitutions referred to earlier.[47]

(a) The UN Draft Principles on Human Rights and the Environment

Partly in response to these national developments the UN Sub-Commission on the Prevention of Discrimination and Protection of Minorities in 1994 proposed a Declaration of Principles on Human Rights and the Environment.[48] This draft declaration offered a conception of human rights and the environment much closer to Principle 1 of the 1972 Stockholm Declaration than to Principle 1 of the 1992 Rio Declaration. It proclaimed generally that 'All persons [have the right to] a secure, healthy and ecologically sound environment [and to] an environment adequate to meet equitably the needs of present generations and that does not impair the rights of future generations to meet equitably their needs'. This extensive and sophisticated restatement of environmental rights and obligations at the international level was based on a survey of national and international human-rights law and international environmental law. The special rapporteur's most fundamental conclusion was that there had been 'a shift from environmental law to the right to a healthy and decent environment'.

The main arguments the Sub-Commission advanced for adopting an autonomous right to a healthy and decent environment are the enhanced status it would give environmental quality when balanced against competing objectives, and that it would recognize the vital character of the environment as a basic condition of life, indispensable to the promotion of human dignity and welfare, and to the fulfilment of

---

[46] 1981 African Charter on Human and Peoples' Rights, Article 16; 1988 Additional Protocol to the Inter-American Convention on Human Rights, Article 11; 1989 European Charter on Environment and Health; WCED Legal Principles, Article 1; 1989 Convention on the Rights of the Child, Article 24(2)(c); 1961 European Social Charter, Article 11, on which see Trindade, in Brown Weiss (ed), *Environmental Change and International Law*, 281–4 and references there cited. For fuller discussion of other treaty provisions, see Churchill, in Boyle and Anderson (eds), *Human Approaches to Environmental Protection* (Oxford, 1996) Ch 5. On health as the focus for environmental rights see PM Dupuy in RJ Dupuy (ed), *The Right to Health as a Human Right* (Alphen aan den Rijn, 1979) 340; Toebes, *The Right to Health as a Human Right in International Law* (Oxford, 1999).

[47] *Supra*, section 2(1).

[48] ECOSOC, *Human Rights and the Environment*, Final Report (1994) UN Doc E/CN 4/Sub 2/1994/9, 59. The text of the draft declaration is reproduced in Boyle and Anderson (eds), *Human Rights Approaches*, 67–9. See Popovic, 27 *Columbia HRLR* (1996) 487–603.

other human rights.[49] Their report stressed the close link between the right to a decent environment and the right to development, but it also relied on the indivisibility and interdependence of all human rights.

The response of the UN Human Rights Commission and of states generally was not favourable to this approach, and the proposal made no further progress. US and European opposition was particularly strong. Many scholars have also argued that the elaboration of an international right to a decent environment is undesirable and unnecessary given the extent to which international law has already addressed environmental problems.[50] Some regard it as misconceived to assume that environmental protection is furthered by postulating a generic human right to the environment, in whatever form, stressing the difficulty of definition, the inefficiency of developing environmental standards in response to individual complaints, the inappropriateness of human-rights bodies for the task of supervising obligations of environmental protection, and the fundamentally anthropocentric character of viewing environmental issues though a human-rights focus, entailing a form of 'species chauvinism'.[51]

What constitutes a satisfactory, decent or ecologically sound environment is bound to suffer from uncertainty. It may result in cultural relativism, particularly from a North–South perspective, and lack the universal value normally thought to be inherent in human rights. Indeterminacy is an important reason, it is often argued, for not rushing to embrace new rights without considering their implications.[52] Moreover, there is little international consensus on the correct terminology. Even the UN Sub-Commission could not make up its mind, referring variously to the right to a 'healthy and flourishing environment' or to a 'satisfactory environment' in its report and to the right to a 'secure, healthy and ecologically sound environment' in the draft principles. Other formulations are equally diverse. Principle 1 of the Stockholm Declaration talks of an 'environment of a quality that permits a life of dignity and well-being', while Article 24 of the African Charter refers to a 'general satisfactory environment favourable to their development'. What any of these mean is largely a subjective value judgement. An option preferred by Kiss and Shelton is to accept the impossibility of defining an ideal environment in abstract terms, but to let human-rights supervisory institutions and courts develop their own interpretations, as they have done for many other human rights.[53] But do we want courts deciding such cases? Even if definition of a decent or satisfactory environment is justiciable, does it follow that international

[49] See separate opinion of Judge Weeramantry, *Gabčíkovo-Nagymaros Case*, ICJ Reports (1997) 7, and Pathak, in Brown Weiss, *Environmental Change and International Law*, Ch 8.

[50] E.g. Handl, in Trindade (ed), *Human Rights, Sustainable Development and the Environment* (San José, 1992) 117; PM Dupuy in RJ Dupuy (ed), *The Right to Health as a Human Right* (Alphen aan den Rijn, 1979) 91–2; Alston, 78 *AJIL* (1984) 607.

[51] Handl, ibid, 117, but see *contra*, Shelton, 3 *YbIEL* (1992) 91–2, and Pathak, in Brown Weiss (ed), *Environmental Change and International Law*, 212–4.

[52] Alston, 78 *AJIL* (1984) 607; Handl, in Trindade (ed), *Human Rights, Sustainable Development and the Environment*.

[53] Kiss and Shelton, *International Environmental Law* (2nd edn, New York, 2000) 174–8. See also Shelton, 28 *Stanford JIL* (1991) 103.

courts are the best bodies to perform this task and the balancing of options that such cases would entail?[54]

Anthropocentricity is more of a problem than indeterminacy because it goes to the heart of what protection of the environment is for. Is it for the benefit of humans only, as provisions such as Article 12 of the 1966 ICESCR necessarily assume, or does it also recognize the intrinsic or inherent value of other species and ecosystems? The World Commission on Environment and Development concluded in 1987 that the right to a healthy environment applies only vis-à-vis other humans or states, and thus does not imply an anthropocentric approach.[55] But this explanation misses the point that by looking at the problem in moral isolation from other species such a right may reinforce the assumption that the environment and its natural resources exist only for human benefit, and have no intrinsic worth in themselves. This is precisely the kind of non-ecocentric approach which ecological theorists have opposed because they believe it is insufficiently comprehensive and inconsistent with ecological reality and biological diversity.[56]

Nor is it convincing to argue that international law disregards the intrinsic value of the environment, including natural ecosystems and non-human species. This much is demonstrated by treaties concerned with Antarctica,[57] the 1972 World Heritage Convention, the 1979 Berne Convention on the Conservation of European Wildlife and Natural Habitat, the 1973 Convention on International Trade in Endangered Species, and the 1992 Biological Diversity Convention, as well as the World Charter for Nature. These and other such instruments are of course also for human benefit, but not exclusively so. Redgwell characterizes them as examples of 'weak anthropocentrism'.[58] An alternative way of putting the same point is to say that even if their focus remains human benefit this concept is drawn so broadly as to be indistinguishably ecocentric. As we saw above, this is very much the approach adopted by the 1994 UN Draft Principles on Human Rights and the Environment. Although put in terms of human rights, these rights include protection and preservation of flora and fauna, essential processes and areas necessary to maintain biological diversity and ecosystems, as well as conservation and sustainable use of nature and natural resources. Drawn in such a broad way their substance is far from exclusively anthropocentric.

(b) Expanding the corpus of human-rights law

Should we then go the whole way and create a human right to a satisfactory or decent environment? Such a right would be less anthropocentric than the present law. It would benefit society as a whole, not just individual victims. It could enable litigants and NGOs to challenge environmentally destructive or unsustainable development

---

[54] See *infra*, sections 2(4), 2(7).

[55] Munro and Lammers, *Environmental Protection and Sustainable Development*, 39–42.

[56] See Eckersley, *Environmentalism and Political Theory* (London, 1992); Gillespie, *International Environmental Law, Policy and Ethics* (Oxford, 1997) Ch 1.

[57] 1959 Antarctic Treaty and 1991 Protocol on Environmental Protection; 1980 Convention on the Conservation of Antarctic Living Resources.

[58] Redgwell, in Boyle and Anderson (eds), *Human Rights Approaches*, Ch 4.

on public-interest grounds. Moreover, although the interests of humans and the environment, or of animals and species, are at present protected primarily by the collective processes of multilateral regulation established by international organizations and environmental treaties, the addition to these processes of a specifically human-rights argument could be seen as complementary to this wider protection of the biosphere, reflecting the impossibility of separating the interests of mankind from the environment as a whole, or from the needs of future generations.[59] But such a balancing process will not work effectively if human claims are extracted from these broader environmental concerns and elevated to a separate or prior status as 'rights', outside any process for resolving the conflicts that may result with other rights or claims. The implications of the argument from anthropocentricity are thus essentially structural. They point to a need for integration of human claims within a broader decision-making process, capable also of taking account of the competing economic and environmental interests of future generations, other states and the common interest in common spaces and wildlife preservation; in other words, for a balancing of polycentric interests through international cooperation and supervisory institutions.[60] This is a challenging but not impossible task for the relevant international bodies to perform.

From this perspective, a right to a decent or satisfactory environment is arguably best located within the economic, social, and cultural rights set out in the 1966 ICESCR. These rights are generally concerned with encouraging governments to pursue policies which create conditions of life enabling individuals or peoples to develop to their full potential. They are programmatic, entailing progressive realization in accordance with available resources, but nevertheless requiring states to 'ensure the satisfaction of, at the very least, minimum essential levels of each of the rights'.[61] Compliance is monitored by an independent committee which can only make general recommendations to states parties, rather than by litigating individual complaints through commissions and courts.[62] Critics point to the 'built-in defects' of this monitoring process, including poor reporting and excessive deference to states.[63] However, because they are inherently uncertain and require allocation of scarce resources few states have been willing to allow independent adjudication of economic and social rights.[64]

The major problem at present is the narrowness of Article 12 of the UN Covenant, with its focus on health and 'environmental hygiene'. According to the ICESCR Committee, Article 12 includes 'the requirement to ensure an adequate supply of safe

---

[59] Shelton, 28 *Stanford JIL* (1991) 103.

[60] On problems of competing competence among human rights bodies see Meron, 76 *AJIL* (1982) 754. This problem also arises among environmental institutions and regimes: see Sand, 3 *YbIEL* (1992) 14.

[61] UNCESCR, General Comment No 3: The Nature of States' Parties Obligations (1990) interpreting Article 2 of the Covenant. See Craven, *The International Covenant on Economic, Social and Cultural Rights* (Oxford, 1995) Ch 3.

[62] On proposals to create an individual complaints mechanism for the ICESCR see Dennis and Stewart, 98 *AJIL* (2004) 462. The authors regard the idea as misguided.

[63] Leckie, in Alston and Crawford (eds), *The Future of UN Human Rights Treaty Monitoring* (Cambridge, 2000) 129. See also 1966 ICESCR, Articles 16–21; UNCESCR, General Comment No 1: Reporting by States Parties (1989); Craven, *The International Covenant on Economic, Social and Cultural Rights*, Ch 2.

[64] See Dennis and Stewart, 98 *AJIL* (2004) 462.

and potable water and basic sanitation; the prevention and reduction of the population's exposure to harmful substances such as radiation and harmful chemicals or
other detrimental environmental conditions that directly or indirectly impact upon
human health'.[65] It is difficult to see what this adds over and above the case law on
environmental impacts on the right to life. What is needed here is a broader focus on
environmental quality which could be balanced more directly against the covenant's
economic and developmental priorities.[66] The problems of definition and judgement
would still arise but, as in environmental treaty COPs, they could more readily be
handled within the process of 'constructive dialogue' with other governments which
characterizes the ICESCR. Since political processes of this kind are inherently multilateral and normally allow for more extensive NGO participation than international
courts they also have a stronger claim to greater legitimacy.

It remains to be seen in the following sections how far existing human rights can be
or have been used to promote environmental protection.

2(3) GREENING EXISTING HUMAN RIGHTS

Even if no independent right to a decent environment has yet become part of international law, there remains the alternative possibility that environmental rights can
usefully be derived from other existing treaty rights, in particular the rights to life,
private life, property, and access to justice under the 1966 UN Covenant on Civil and
Political Rights,[67] the 1950 European Convention on Human Rights,[68] and the 1969
Inter-American Convention on Human Rights.[69] The virtue of looking at environmental protection through other human rights, such as life, private life, or property, is that
it focuses attention on what matters most: the detriment to important, internationally
protected values from uncontrolled environmental harm. This is an approach which
avoids the need to define such notions as a satisfactory or decent environment, falls
well within the competence of human-rights courts, and involves little or no potential
for conflict with international environmental institutions or treaty COPs. Both the
right to life and the right to respect for private life and property entail more than a simple prohibition on government interference: governments additionally have a positive
duty to take appropriate action to secure these rights,[70] as we can see in many of the
cases, where the problem lay in a failure of government to legislate about the environment or to enforce existing environmental law.

---

[65] UNCESCR, General Comment No 14: The Right to the Highest Attainable Standard of Health (2000).
See also on the human right to water *infra*, Ch 10, section 2(5).

[66] See Willis, 9 *Georgetown IELR* (1996–7) 195.

[67] Articles 6(1), 14(1), 17. There is no right to property in the 1966 Covenant.

[68] Articles 2, 6(1), 8, and Article 1, Protocol 1.

[69] Articles 4(1), 8(1), 11(2), 21. See also the 1948 American Declaration on the Rights of Man, Articles I,
III, XXIII.

[70] See UNHRC, General Comment No 6 on Article 6 of the ICCPR, 16th Session, 1982; Desgagné, 89 *AJIL*
(1995) 263; Churchill, in Boyle and Anderson, *Human Rights Approaches*, 91; Ramcharan, 30 *NILR* (1983)
297, 306; Trindade in Weiss (ed), *Environmental Change and International Law*, 271–7.

The right to life has been a particularly fruitful source of environmental jurisprudence in several national jurisdictions, especially India. Here the courts have not only closed down industries causing harm to health and safety but have held that 'the right to life includes the right to live with human dignity and all that goes along with it', including the right to live in a 'healthy environment with minimal disturbance of [the] ecological balance', and they have drawn an explicit link with environmental quality.[71] Indian courts have also used the right to life and the environmental provisions of the constitution as a basis for attacking state inaction. Some remarkable decisions have compelled the protection of the Taj Mahal, the creation of an Environmental Protection Agency, the closure of factories, the provision of pollution-free air and water, and the restoration of the 'ecological balance'.[72] Although the interpretation of the right to life adopted by Indian courts is expansive, it does show the potential for existing human rights to take on environmental dimensions.[73] In those countries where the failure of governmental action is a major source of environmental harm, human-rights law, both national and international, has significant potential for remedying deficiencies in regulation and enforcement.

(a) Environmental nuisances

As in India, the starting point for any discussion of international human-rights law and the environment is that a sufficiently serious failure by the state to regulate or control environmental nuisances or to protect the environment may amount to an interference with individual rights.[74] Cases before the European Court of Human Rights, such as *Guerra*, *Lopez Ostra*, *Öneryildiz*, *Taskin* and *Fadeyeva*, show in particular how the right to private life, or the right to life, can be used to compel governments to regulate environmental risks, enforce environmental laws, or disclose environmental information.[75]

All of these cases have common features. First, there is an industrial nuisance—a chemical plant, smelter, tannery, mine, or waste disposal site, for example. Second, there is a failure to take adequate preventive measures to control these known sources of serious risk to life, health, private life, or property. In contrast, where the state

---

[71] *Mullin v Union Territory of Delhi* AIR 1981 SC 746; *Rural Litigation & Entitlement Kendra v State of Uttar Pradesh* AIR 1985 SC 652 and AIR 1987 SC 359; *Charan Lal Sahu v Union of India* (1986) 2 SCC 176; *T. Damodhar Rao v Municipal Corp of Hyderabad*, AIR 1987 AP 171; *Subhash Kumar v State of Bihar* AIR 1991 SC 420; *MC Mehta v Kamal Nath* (2000) 6 SCC 213. These and other decisions are collected in UNEP, *Compendium of Summaries of Judicial Decisions in Environment Related Cases* (Colombo, 1997). See Anderson, in, Boyle and Anderson (eds), *Human Rights Approaches*, Ch 10; Razzaque, 'Human Rights and the Environment: the National Experience in South Asia and Africa', *Joint UNEP-OHCHR Expert Seminar on Human Rights and the Environment: Background Paper No 4*, 14–16 January 2002.

[72] Not all of these decisions are based on the right to life, however. See *MC Mehta v Union of India* (1997) 2 SCC 353; *Jaganath v Union of India* (1997) 2 SCC 87, and cases cited *supra*, n 75.

[73] But even in India the activist role of judges has been challenged: see Dam and Tewary, 17 *JEL* (2005) 383. Compare Desgagné, 89 *AJIL* (1995) 266–70.

[74] Council of Europe Report, Appendix II.

[75] *Lopez Ostra v Spain* (1994) 20 EHRR 277; *Guerra v Italy* (1998) 26 EHRR 357; *Fadeyeva v Russia* [2005] ECHR 376; *Öneryildiz v Turkey* [2004] ECHR 657; *Taskin v Turkey* [2006] 42 EHRR 50.

has done all in could to avoid a risk to individuals, there will be no violation of the Convention.[76] Third, it is irrelevant that the state itself does not own or operate the plant or industry in question. As the Court said in *Fadeyeva*,[77] the state's responsibility in environmental cases 'may arise from a failure to regulate private industry'. The state thus has a duty 'to take reasonable and appropriate measures' to secure rights under the convention. In *Öneryildiz* it emphasized that 'The positive obligation to take all appropriate steps to safeguard life for the purposes of Article 2 entails above all a primary duty on the State to put in place a legislative and administrative framework designed to provide effective deterrence against threats to the right to life'.[78] The Court had no doubt that this obligation covered the licensing, setting up, operation, security, and supervision of dangerous activities, and required all those concerned to take 'practical measures to ensure the effective protection of citizens whose lives might be endangered by the inherent risks'.[79]

These practical measures include law enforcement: it is a characteristic feature of *Guerra*, *Lopez Ostra*, *Taskin*, and *Fadeyeva* that the industrial activities in question were either operating illegally or in violation of environmental laws and emissions standards. In *Lopez Ostra* and *Taskin* the national courts ordered the closure of the facility in question, but their decisions had been ignored or overruled by the political authorities. In effect, there is a right to have the law enforced and the judgments of national courts upheld: 'The Court would emphasize that the administrative authorities form one element of a State subject to the rule of law, and that their interests coincide with the need for the proper administration of justice. Where administrative authorities refuse or fail to comply, or even delay doing so, the guarantees enjoyed by a litigant during the judicial phase of the proceedings are rendered devoid of purpose'.[80] The Inter-American Court of Human Rights has taken the same view pursuant to Article 25 of the Inter-American Convention.[81]

We can draw certain obvious conclusions from these cases. First, states have a positive duty to take appropriate measures to prevent industrial pollution or other forms of environmental nuisance from seriously interfering with health or the enjoyment of private life or property.[82] This is not simply a responsibility which can be left to industry to fulfil. Its extent will of course depend on the harmfulness of the activity and the foreseeability of the risk. Once the risk ought to have been foreseen as a result

---

[76] *LCB v United Kingdom* (1999) 27 EHRR 212, a case concerned with exposure to nuclear tests. See also *Bordes v France*, UNHRC No 645/1995, *Rept of UN Human Rights Cttee* (1996) GAOR A/51/40 vol II.

[77] Para 89.   [78] Para 89.

[79] Ibid, para 90. For a comparable case in which precautionary measures were ordered by the Inter-American Commission see *Community of San Mateo de Huanchor and its members v Peru*, Case 504/03, Report No 69/04, Inter-Am CHR, OEA/Ser L/V/II.122 Doc 5 rev 1, 487 (2004).

[80] *Taskin v Turkey* [2006] 42 EHRR 50, paras 124–5.

[81] See *Mayagna (Sumo) Awas Tingni Community v Nicaragua* (2001) IACHR Ser C, No 201, paras 106–14.

[82] *Lopez Ostra v Spain* (1994) 20 EHRR 277; *Guerra v Italy* (1998) 26 EHRR 357; *Fadeyeva v Russia* [2005] ECHR 376; *Öneryildiz v Turkey* [2004] ECHR 657; *Taskin v Turkey* [2006] 42 EHRR 50. See also the IACHR's decision in *Maya Indigenous Community of the Toledo District v Belize*, para 47, where the Commission found that 'the State failed to put into place adequate safeguards and mechanisms, to supervise, monitor and ensure that it had sufficient staff to oversee that the execution of the logging concessions would not cause further environmental damage to Maya lands and communities'.

of an EIA or in some other way (e.g. an official report) then the state has a duty to take appropriate action: it cannot wait until the interference with health or private life has become a reality.[83] In assessing whether a risk is foreseeable for this purpose it is quite likely that the precautionary principle will be relevant in situations of potentially serious or irreversible harm, although the point has not so far been decided by a court.[84] Second, although the European Court refers to the need to balance the rights of the individual with the needs of the community as a whole, in reality the states' failure to apply or enforce their own environmental laws in each of these cases left no room for such a defence. This breach of domestic law necessarily constitutes a violation of the Convention.[85] States cannot expect to persuade a court that the needs of the community can best be met in such cases by not enforcing the law. A fortiori, if a national supreme court has weighed the rights involved and annulled a permit for a harmful activity on the ground that it does not serve the public interest, the European Court is not going to reverse this judgment in favour of a national government.[86] Third, the beneficiaries of this duty to regulate and control sources of environmental harm are not the community at large, still less the environment per se, but only those individuals whose rights will be affected by any failure to act. The duty is not one of protecting the environment, but of protecting humans from significantly harmful environmental impacts.[87]

Attempts to invoke the rights to life or private life for environmental purposes before other international human-rights bodies have been less successful. In *Port Hope Environmental Group v Canada*[88] the UN Human Rights Committee accepted that dumping of nuclear wastes raised a serious right-to-life issue for local residents and future generations under Article 6 of the 1966 Civil and Political Rights Covenant, but the application was dismissed due to failure to exhaust local remedies. In *Bordes v France*[89] a complaint to the Committee about nuclear tests in the Pacific was dismissed because there was no evidence of serious risk to life. In a report on Ecuador the Inter-American Commission found that 'where environmental contamination and degradation pose a persistent threat to human life, the foregoing rights viz right to life are implicated',[90] while in *Yanomani Indians v Brazil* it concluded that the construction of a road through the applicants' traditional lands had so seriously affected their way of life that it violated both the right to life and the right to health.[91]

---

[83] *Taskin*, para 113; *Öneryildiz*, paras 100–1.

[84] Principle 15 of the 1992 Rio Declaration. See Ch 3.   [85] See e.g. *Fadeyeva*, para 95.

[86] *Taskin v Turkey* [2006] 42 EHRR 50, para 117.

[87] See *Kyrtatos v Greece* [2003] ECHR 242, para 52, and *infra*, section 2(7).

[88] *Port Hope Environmental Group v Canada*, Comm No 67/1980, 2 *Selected Decisions UNHRC* (1990) 20.

[89] *Bordes v France*, UNHRC No 645/1995, *Rept Human Rights Committee* (1996) GAOR A/51/40 vol II.

[90] IACHR, *Report on the Human Rights Situation in Ecuador*, OEA/Ser L/V/II.96, Doc 10 rev 1 (1997) 88.

[91] *Yanomani Indians v Brazil*, Decision 7615, Inter-Am CHR, *Inter-American YB on Hum Rts* 264 (1985). On this and other cases in Latin America see Fabra, in Boyle and Anderson (eds), *Human Rights Approaches*, Ch 12, but cf Fernandes, ibid, Ch 13.

(b) Indigenous culture and the environment

A small number of environmental cases have concerned interference with the rights of indigenous peoples or other minorities to enjoy their own culture under Article 27 of the ICCPR. In *Ilmari Lansman and Ors v Finland* the UNHRC held that 'measures whose impact amount to a denial of the right will not be compatible with the obligations under article 27. However, measures that have a certain limited impact on the way of life of persons belonging to a minority will not necessarily amount to a denial of the right under article 27'.[92] The Committee concluded that Finland had taken adequate measures to minimize the impact of stone quarrying on reindeer herding.

In somewhat similar circumstances, the Inter-American Commission and Court of Human Rights have relied instead on a broad reading of the right to property in order to afford indigenous peoples protection from environmental destruction and unsustainable development and they go some way towards achieving the same outcome as Article 27 of the ICCPR or Article 24 of the African Convention. In the *Maya Indigenous Community of Toledo Case*,[93] the IACHR accepted that logging concessions threatened long-term and irreversible damage to the natural environment on which the petitioners' system of subsistence agriculture depended. Citing *Ogoniland*, the IACHR concluded that there had been violations of the petitioners' right to property in their ancestral lands. Its final order required Belize to repair the environmental damage and to take measures to demarcate and protect their land in consultation with the community. The Commission's decision notes the importance of economic development but reiterates that 'development activities must be accompanied by appropriate and effective measures to ensure that they do not proceed at the expense of the fundamental rights of persons who may be particularly and negatively affected, including indigenous communities and the environment upon which they depend for their physical, cultural and spiritual well-being'.[94] Despite the different rights at issue in these cases, they all show a similar willingness to use whatever treaty provisions are available in order to protect the natural environment—in effect the habitat—of vulnerable indigenous peoples confronted by serious interference with their traditional livelihood and surroundings.

---

[92] (1996) ICCPR Communication No 511/1992, paras 9.4. See also *Ominayak and Lubicon Lake Band v Canada* (1990) ICCPR Communication No 167/1984, para 32.2; *Apirana Mahuika and Ors v New Zealand* (2000) Communication No 547/1993.

[93] *Maya indigenous community of the Toledo District v Belize*, Case 12.053, Report No 40/04, IACHR, OEA/Ser L/V/II.122 Doc 5 rev 1, 727 (2004). See also *Mayagna (Sumo) Awas Tingni Community v Nicaragua* (2001) IACHR Ser C, No 20. Several other claims have been held admissible: *Yakye Axa Indigenous Community of the Enxet-Lengua People v Paraguay*, Case 12.313, Report No 2/02, Inter-Am CHR, Doc 5 rev 1, 387 (2002); *The Kichwa Peoples of the Sarayaku Community and Its Members v Ecuador*, Case 167/03, Report No 62/04, Inter-Am CHR., OEA/Ser L/V/II.122 Doc 5 rev 1, 308 (2004).

[94] Para 150. The decision is based on the 1948 American Declaration of the Rights of Man, not on the 1969 Inter-American Convention.

2(4) ENVIRONMENTAL PROTECTION AS A LEGITIMATE AIM

Inevitably there will be circumstances where environmental objectives and the rights of particular individuals or groups may come into conflict. Establishing wild-life reserves, regulating polluting activities, or controlling resource extraction, for example, may impair the use or value of property, hamper economic development, or restrict the right of indigenous peoples to make traditional use of natural resources. In extreme cases environmental regulation may amount to a taking of property or an interference with private and family life, entitling the owner to compensation.[95] Particularly in cases involving alleged interference by the state with peaceful enjoy-ment of possessions and property, the Strasbourg Court has consistently taken the view that environmental protection is a legitimate objective of public policy.[96] It has refused to give undue pre-eminence to property rights, despite their supposedly pro-tected status under the 1st Protocol.[97] Regulation in the public interest is not inconsist-ent with the terms of the protocol, provided it is authorized by law and proportionate to a legitimate aim.[98]

In other cases before the European Court states have been allowed a wide margin of appreciation to pursue environmental objectives provided they maintain a fair bal-ance between the general interests of the community and the protection of the indi-vidual's fundamental rights. They are also free to give economic development priority over environmental protection provided the rights of individuals to private and family life or protection of possessions and property are sufficiently balanced against eco-nomic benefits for the community as a whole. Environmental protection and human rights do not necessarily trump economic development. In *Hatton v United Kingdom* the applicants challenged the extension of night flights at Heathrow Airport.[99] In the European Court's view the United Kingdom had acted lawfully, had done its best to mitigate the impact on the private life of those affected and had maintained a fair balance between the economic benefit to the community as a whole and the rights of individuals who lived near the airport. The state would be failing in its duty to those affected if it did not regulate or mitigate environmental nuisances or environmen-tal risk caused by airport development projects,[100] but it was required to do so only

---

[95] See *Sporrong and Lonnroth v Sweden* (1982) EHCR Sers A/52.

[96] See e.g. *Matos e Silva Lda v Portugal* (1996) IV ECHR; *Jacobsson v Sweden* No 2 (1998) I ECHR; *Katte Klitsche and de la Grange v Italy* (1994) ECHR Sers A/293B; *Pine Valley Developments Ltd v Ireland* (1991) ECHR, Sers A/222; *Svidranova v Slovak Republic,* (1998) ECHR App No 35268/97; *Chassagnou v France* (1999) ECHR; *Denev v Sweden* (1989) ECHR App No 12570/86.

[97] *Pine Valley Developments Ltd v Ireland* (1991) ECHR Sers A/222, paras 57–9; *Katsoulis and Ors v Greece,* (2004) ECHR. Contrast *Mateos e Silva Ltd v Portugal* [1996] IV ECHR where restrictions on property were found to be unnecessary.

[98] *Fredin v Sweden* (1991) ECHR Sers A/192, paras 41–51. See also *Apirana Mahuika and Ors v New Zealand* (2000) ICCPR Comm No 547/1992, in which the UNHRC upheld the state's right to conserve and manage natural resources in the interests of future generations provided this did not amount to a denial of the applicant's rights.

[99] *Hatton v UK* [2003] ECHR (Grand Chamber).

[100] See also *Öneryildiz,* para 107; *Taskin,* paras 116–7.

to the extent necessary to protect life, health, enjoyment of property, and family life from disproportionate interference. In its judgment the Grand Chamber leaves little room for the Court to substitute its own view of the extent to which the environment should be protected from economic development. On this basis, decisions about where the public interest lies are for politicians, not for the court, save in the most extreme cases.[101]

At the same time the equally important case of *Taskin v Turkey* shows that the balance of interests to be maintained is not only a substantive one, but has important procedural dimensions. In particular, the most important feature of *Taskin* is that it envisages an informed process. The Court put the matter like this: 'Where a State must determine complex issues of environmental and economic policy, the decision-making process must first involve appropriate investigations and studies in order to allow them to predict and evaluate in advance the effects of those activities which might damage the environment and infringe individuals' rights and to enable them to strike a fair balance between the various conflicting interests at stake'.[102] The words 'environmental impact assessment' are not used, but in many cases that is exactly what will be necessary to give effect to the evaluation process envisaged here. The Inter-american Commission of Human Rights[103] and the UN Human Rights Committee[104] have taken a similar approach in cases concerning logging, oil extraction, and mining on land belonging to indigenous peoples.

2(5) PARTICIPATORY RIGHTS

(a) In general

The strongest argument for specifically environmental rights focuses not on environmental quality but on procedural rights, including access to environmental information, access to justice and participation in environmental decision-making.[105] This approach rests on the view that environmental protection and sustainable development cannot be left to governments alone but require and benefit from notions of civic participation in public affairs already reflected in existing civil and political rights.[106] At its broadest, it can be represented as the application to environmental

---

[101] But compare the views of the dissenting judges and of the 1st instance chamber, and see Hart and Wheeler, 16 *JEL* (2004) 132–9.

[102] *Taskin*, para 119.

[103] See *Maya Indigenous Community of the Toledo District v Belize*, Case 12.053, Report No 40/04, Inter-Am CHR, OEA/Ser L/V/II.122 Doc 5 rev 1, 727 (2004) para 150.

[104] See *Ilmari Lansman and Ors v Finland* (1996) ICCPR Communication No 511/1992, para 9.4, and *Lubicon Lake Band v Canada* (1990) ICCPR Communication No 167/1984, para 32.2.

[105] See Zillman, Lucas and Pring (eds), *Human Rights in Natural Resource Development* (Oxford, 2002) especially Ch 1; Ebbesson, in Bodansky, Brunnée and Hey (eds), *The Oxford Handbook of International Environmental Law* (Oxford, 2007) Ch 29; Francioni (ed), *Access to Justice as a Human Right* (Oxford, 2007) Chs 1, 5.

[106] Universal Declaration on Human Rights, Articles 19, 21; 1966 International Covenant on Civil and Political Rights, Articles 19, 25; 1969 Inter-American Convention on Human Rights, Article 23; but

matters of arguments for democratic governance as a human right.[107] At its narrowest it is an argument for improving the quality and transparency of governmental decisions and promoting more effective enforcement.[108] The public-interest role of non-governmental organizations is especially important in this respect. Not only do environmental NGOs use access to information and lobbying to raise awareness of environmental concerns, but research has also shown that they tend to have high success rates in enforcement actions and public-interest litigation.[109]

The argument for participatory rights assumes that governments which operate with openness, accountability, and civic participation are more likely to promote environmental justice, to balance the needs of present and future generations in the protection of the environment, to integrate environmental considerations in governmental decisions, and to implement and enforce existing environmental standards than are closed, totalitarian, or undemocratic societies governed in a heavily centralized fashion. Empirically this is not difficult to demonstrate, especially by reference to countries with a disastrous environmental record such as East European states pre-1991 or contemporary China. In the old Soviet Union, awareness of the environmental costs of totalitarianism appears to have been a significant factor in that country's post-communist revolution and its initial support for policies of environmental openness adopted by CSCE and the UNECE.[110] But cases such as *Ogoniland* or *Maya Indigenous Community* show that the same criticism can sometimes be made of democratic states, insofar as certain groups such as indigenous peoples are ignored or excluded from participation in decision-making relating to exploitation of natural resources. This is an important reason for emphasizing the special claims of these groups to 'meaningful consultation'.[111]

Although the Rio Declaration contains no explicit human right to a decent environment, Principle 10 lends substantial support in mandatory language for participatory rights of a comprehensive kind. It provides:

Environmental issues are best handled with the participation of all concerned citizens, at the relevant level. At the national level, each individual shall have appropriate access to information concerning the environment that is held by public authorities, including information

compare 1950 European Convention on Human Rights, Protocol No 1, Article 3 of which provides only for free elections. See Partsch, in Henkin (ed), *The International Bill of Rights* (New York, 1981) 241–5 and cf *Nicaragua Case*, ICJ Reports (1986) 14, 131–2, and 1990 Charter of Paris (CSCE) 30 *ILM* (1991) 193.

[107] See Mason, *Environmental Democracy* (London, 1999); Franck, 86 *AJIL* (1992) 46; Crawford, 64 *BYIL* (1993) 113; Fox, 17 *Yale JIL* (1992) 539; Steiner, 1 *Harv HRYb* (1988) 77; Ebbesson, 8 *YbIEL* (1997) 51; 1993 UN Conference on Human Rights, Vienna Declaration, para 8.

[108] See preamble to the 1998 Aarhus Convention.

[109] See de Sadeleer/Roller/Dross, *Access to Justice in Environmental Matters*, Final Report, Doc ENVA 3/ETU/2002/0030, Part I, section 3.

[110] See Charter of Paris (OSCE) *supra*, n 106; 1995 Sofia Ministerial Declaration (UNECE) 26 *EPL* 34.

[111] *Maya Indigenous Community Case*, paras 154–5. See 1992 Rio Declaration Principle 22; Agenda 21, Chapter 26 and 1989 ILO Convention No 169 Concerning Indigenous and Tribal Peoples in Independent Countries. See also Agenda 21, Ch 24 on the role of women, and generally Shelton, 3 *YbIEL* (1992) 82–9; Ebbesson, 8 *YbIEL* (1997) 70–73; Triggs, in Zillman, Lucas, and Pring, *Human Rights in Natural Resource Development*, Ch 3.

on hazardous materials and activities in their communities, and the opportunity to participate in decision-making processes. States shall facilitate and encourage public awareness and participation by making information widely available. Effective access to judicial and administrative proceedings, including redress and remedy, shall be provided.

Whether one describes such rights in terms of a generic right to a decent environment is largely a matter of terminology. What is important is the recognition that they would add significantly to the protection of the environment and sustainable development.[112]

What distinguishes Principle 10 from participatory rights in the ICCPR and regional human-rights conventions is its greater specificity and environmental focus, and its emphasis both on participation in environmental decision-making, including access to information, and on effective access to justice. These features justify the proposition that there is a role for human-rights law in promoting procedures for protection of the environment, and a need for further development over and above those more general rights already protected in human-rights treaties.[113] For example, Article 10 of the European Convention only guarantees freedom to receive and impart information. It creates neither a right of access to information nor a duty to communicate information.[114] Access to, or communication of, environmental information may nevertheless be required under general human-rights law but only insofar as necessary in order to give effect to rights to life, private life, or access to justice.[115] In contrast, the 1998 Aarhus Convention recognizes a rather broader duty to inform, which it formulates in terms requiring an imminent threat to human health or the environment,[116] and as we will see in the next section the importance of this convention is that it requires environmental information to be more generally accessible than would be necessary under general human-rights law. Crucially, Aarhus Convention information rights are not dependent on showing that the applicant is a victim of a violation of the right to life, private life, or property.

Similarly, while access to justice articles of human-rights treaties will normally apply to environmental disputes where civil rights and obligations are at stake,[117] they do not facilitate NGO standing, public-interest litigation, or judicial review and appeal in respect of decisions which affect the environment but not the rights of individuals.

---

[112] See also UNGA Res 42/186 (1987); Principle 23, World Charter for Nature; UNCED Agenda 21, Ch 23, especially 23.2. Cf 1992 Climate Change Convention, Article 6, however.

[113] See ECOSOC, *Human Rights and the Environment: Preliminary Report*, UN Doc E/CN 4/Sub 2/1991/8; Kane, 18 *Yale LJ* (1993) 389; Handl, in Trindade (ed), *Human Rights, Sustainable Development and the Environment*, 117; Ebbesson, 8 *YbIEL* (1997) 51.

[114] *Guerra v Italy* (1998) 26 EHRR 357, para 55.

[115] See Gavouneli, 13 *Tulane ELJ* (2000) 303, and see *infra*, section 2(5)(c).

[116] Article 5(1)(c). See also 2001 ILC Draft Articles on the Prevention of Transboundary Harm, Article 13, *ILC Report* (2001) GAOR A/56/10.

[117] 1966 ICCPR, Article 14; 1969 ACHR, Article 8; 1950 ECHR, Article 6(1) on which see *Taskin v Turkey* [2006] 42 EHRR 50. Cf *Athanassoglou v Switzerland* (2001) 31 EHRR 13 and *Balmer-Schafroth v Switzerland* (1998) 25 EHRR 598 where claims based on Article 6 were rejected because the applicants could not show they were exposed to any imminent danger.

Other agreements make broader provision for environmental claims, including the 1998 Aarhus Convention, considered in the next section. The 1993 North American Agreement on Environmental Cooperation is another example. Article 6 gives persons with a 'legally recognized interest' the right to bring proceedings to enforce national environmental laws and to seek remedies for environmental harm; Article 7 provides for these proceedings to be fair, open, and equitable and to conform to standards of due process. One unusual provision of this agreement allows individuals and NGOs to complain to the secretariat that a state party is failing to enforce its environmental legislation. This has already resulted in several complaints against Mexico; these are investigated by the secretariat, which then reports its findings to the Commission.[118]

The public-participation and access-to-information requirements of Rio Principle 10 are to some extent reflected in various treaties and international instruments. One of the most far-reaching is Article 8(1) of the 2003 UNECE Protocol on Strategic Environmental Assessment, under which 'Each party shall ensure early, timely and effective opportunities for public participation, when all options are open, in the strategic environmental assessment of plans and programmes'.[119] The public for this purpose includes relevant NGOs. Other treaties include the 1991 UNECE Convention on EIA in a Transboundary Context,[120] the 1992 Biological Diversity Convention,[121] the 1992 OSPAR Convention,[122] the 1992 UNECE Convention on the Protection and use of Transboundary Watercourses,[123] the 1993 Council of Europe Convention on Civil Liability for Damage Resulting from Activities Dangerous to the Environment,[124] and the 1993 North American Agreement on Environmental Cooperation.[125] In addition, the OAS has adopted a strategy on promotion of public participation.[126]

(b) Participatory rights under the Aarhus Convention

The most comprehensive multilateral scheme for giving effect to Rio Principle 10 remains the 1998 Aarhus Convention on Access to Information, Public Participation in Decision-making and Access to Justice in Environmental Matters.[127] This is a regional convention, whose participants include European Union states and most of

---

[118] See Articles 14, 15, and Raustiala, 36 *VJIL* (1996) 123; McCallum, 8 *Colorado JIELP* (1997) 395–422; Di Mento and Doughman, 10 *Georgetown IELR* (1998) 651–743; Markell, 12 *Georgetown IELR* (2000) 545–74; Knox, 28 *ELQ* (2001) 53ff.

[119] *Supra*, Ch 3, section 4(4).   [120] Articles 2(6), 3(8). See *supra*, Ch 3.

[121] Article 14 provides for public participation in EIA, but only 'where appropriate'.

[122] Article 9 provides only for access to information. See *Dispute Concerning Access to Information under the OSPAR Convention (Ireland v UK)* PCA (2003).

[123] Article 16 provides only for access to information.

[124] Articles 14–16. See *Explanatory Report* in Council of Europe CDCJ (92) 50.

[125] See Fitzmaurice, 52 *ICLQ* (2003) 334.

[126] 2000 Inter-American Strategy for the Promotion of Public Participation in Decision-making for Sustainable Development.

[127] See UNECE, *The Aarhus Convention: An Implementation Guide* (New York, 2000); Koester, in Ulfstein, Marauhn, Zimmermann (eds), *Making Treaties Work: Human Rights, Environment and Arms Control* (Cambridge, 2007) 179; Davies, in Zillman, Lucas, and Pring, *Human Rights in Natural Resource Development* (Oxford, 2002) Ch 4; Lee and Abbott, 66 *MLR* (2003) 80; Ebbesson, 8 *YbIEL* (1997) 51. The convention takes account of the UNECE Guidelines on Access to Environmental Information and Public

the former Soviet states, but it is open to any state to participate. As Kofi Annan, formerly Secretary General of the UN, observed: 'Although regional in scope, the significance of the Aarhus Convention is global... [I]t is the most ambitious venture in the area of "environmental democracy" so far undertaken under the auspices of the United Nations'.[128] In his view the Convention has the 'potential to serve as a global framework for strengthening citizens' environmental rights'.[129] The substantive provisions of the Aarhus Convention focus exclusively on participatory rights, and reflect the opposition of the OECD members to the broader environmental-rights approach of the draft UN declaration. Parties to the convention guarantee rights of access to information, public participation in decision-making, and access to justice in environmental matters. They are required by Article 9 to make those rights enforceable by a national court or independent tribunal. There is also a non-compliance procedure to which NGOs and individuals can take complaints.[130]

Under Article 4 of the Aarhus Convention anyone ('the public') is entitled to environmental information covered by the Convention, including NGOs 'promoting environmental protection' in accordance with national law. Access is not dependent on being personally affected or having some right or interest in the matter. In this respect it simply reflects the many national laws on the subject, including US law and EC directives.[131] Nor is access limited to nationals of the state concerned: Article 3(9), the convention's non-discrimination article, ensures that in transboundary cases foreign nationals and NGOs have the same rights as anyone else.[132] 'Environmental information' is very broadly defined by Article 2(3) and includes information concerning the physical elements of the environment, such as water and biological diversity, as well as information about activities, administrative measures, agreements, policies, legislation, plans, and programmes likely to affect the environment, human health, safety, or conditions of life. Cost benefit and other economic analyses and assumptions used in environmental decision-making are also included. There are also detailed provisions on collection and dissemination of environmental information (Article 5). In all of these respects the Convention goes further than the case law based on general human-rights law referred to earlier. However, Article 4 applies only to information held by public authorities. Very important information held by industry or subject to the convention's commercial and industrial exception is not covered, although a Protocol on Pollutant Release and Transfer Registers adopted in 2003 will require

---

Participation in Decision-making adopted at Sofia in 1995 and is another example of soft law transformed into hard law.

[128] Annan, 'Foreword', UNECE, *The Aarhus Convention: An Implementation Guide*, v

[129] Ibid.   [130] See *supra*, Ch 4, section 3.   [131] See Gavouneli, 13 *Tulane ELJ* (2000) 303.

[132] UNECE, Compliance Committee, *Bystre Deep-water Navigation Canal—Findings and Recommendation with regard to compliance by Ukraine* (Comms ACCC/C/2004/01 and 03) ECE/MP PP/C 1/2005/2/Add 3 (14 March 2005) paras 26–8; UNECE, *The Aarhus Convention: An Implementation Guide*, 41, and see *infra*, section 2(6).

industry to collect and report information about pollution emissions which parties must then make publicly available.[133]

Unlike access to information, participatory rights under Article 6 of the Aarhus Convention are available only to 'the public concerned', but this is broadly defined in Article 2(5) as 'the public affected or likely to be affected by, or having an interest in, the environmental decision-making; for the purposes of this definition, non-governmental organizations promoting environmental protection and meeting any requirements under national law shall be deemed to have an interest'. This would again require that national, foreign, or international NGOs be allowed to participate in decisions on a non-discriminatory basis, subject only to any legal requirements consistent with the convention.[134] Article 6 applies to decisions regarding a wide range of activities, including the oil, chemical, and nuclear industries, smelters, wood pulp mills, and waste-management sites, motorways and airports, and the release of genetically modified organisms.[135] It does not specify what kind of public procedure is required, but Article 6(6) focuses instead on the information to be made available to the public, including:

1. a description of the site and the physical and technical characteristics of the proposed activity, including an estimate of the expected residues and emissions

2. a description of the significant effects of the proposed activity on the environment

3. a description of the measures envisaged to prevent and/or reduce the effects, including emissions

4. an outline of the main alternatives studied by the applicant.

As a comparison with Annex II of the 1991 Espoo Convention on EIA shows, these are all matters normally included in an EIA: in effect implementing Aarhus will thus require some kind of EIA process.[136] The *Taskin* decision of the ECHR, considered earlier, takes a very similar approach and makes explicit reference to Rio Principle 10 and the Aarhus Convention.[137]

Finally, Article 9 also makes general provision for access to justice in order to challenge breaches of national law relating to the environment when either the applicant's

---

[133] Comparable national schemes exist in the United States and European Union. See generally Sand, 63 *ZAÖRV* (2003) 487.

[134] *Supra*, n 132.

[135] See Annex I. Article 6 is amended by Decision II/1 on Release of GMOs. See UNECE, *Rept of 2nd Meeting of Parties to the Aarhus Convention*, ECE/MP PP/2005/2/Add 2 (2005).

[136] See UNECE, *The Aarhus Convention: An Implementation Guide*, 90–2. Annex II of the Espoo Convention additionally includes an indication of predictive methods, underlying assumptions, relevant data, gaps in knowledge and uncertainties, as well as an outline of monitoring plans.

[137] *Taskin*, paras 98–99. The Court also relied upon Council of Europe Parliamentary Assembly Recommendation 1614 (2003) which declares that member states should 'safeguard the individual procedural rights to access to information, public participation in decision-making and access to justice in environmental matters set out in the Aarhus Convention' (Principle 9 iii).

rights are impaired or they have a 'sufficient interest'.[138] In English administrative law whether an interest is sufficient will depend on the strength of the case and the seriousness of the illegality; on this view an appropriate NGO will have standing if it has a suitable case.[139] 'Sufficient interest' is not defined by the Aarhus Convention, it appears to be narrower than the 'public concerned' employed in Article 6, and the parties could not agree on how far it provides for public-interest litigation by NGOs.[140] In its first ruling, the Aarhus Compliance Committee held that 'Although what constitutes a sufficient interest and impairment of a right shall be determined in accordance with national law, it must be decided with "the objective of giving the public concerned wide access to justice" within the scope of the Convention'.[141] While Article 9(2) preserves the stricter requirements of legal systems that confer standing only on those whose rights have been violated,[142] parties must nevertheless ensure that they 'take fully into account the objective of the Convention to guarantee access to justice'.[143] They are not required to establish an *actio popularis*, but they must not use national law 'as an excuse for introducing or maintaining so strict criteria that they effectively bar all or almost all environmental organizations from challenging acts or omissions that contravene national law relating to the environment'.[144] Access to such procedures 'should thus be the presumption, not the exception'.[145] Under Article 9(3) applicants entitled to participate in decision-making will also have the right to seek administrative or judicial review of the legality of the resulting decision. A general failure to enforce environmental law will also violate Article 9(3).[146] Article 9(4) also requires that adequate, fair, and effective remedies are provided.[147] This reflects the decisions in *Lopez Ostra* and *Guerra* referred to earlier.

The Aarhus Convention is an important achievement; strongly supported by participating governments and the European Community, to whose institutions it expressly applies,[148] and it has helped shape national law and practice throughout Europe. Moreover, as we have seen above, the non-discriminatory application of rights of

---

[138] For a fuller account see Redgwell, in Francioni (ed), *Access to Justice as a Human Right* (Oxford, 2007) 153, although, following decisions of the compliance committee, standing under Article 9 may be less restrictive than suggested there.

[139] Cf *R v Secretary of State for Foreign and Commonwealth Affairs, ex parte World Development Movement* [1995] 1 All ER 611 and *R v Secretary of State ex parte Greenpeace* [1994] 4 All ER 352 and see Hilson and Cram, 16 *Legal Studies* (1996) 1.

[140] UNECE, *The Aarhus Convention: An Implementation Guide*, 129.

[141] *Bond Beter Leefmilieu Vlaanderen VZW: Findings and Recommendation with Regard to Compliance by Belgium*, Compliance Committee, UNECE/MP PP/C 1/2006/4/Add 2 (2006) para 33.

[142] E.g. Germany: see Section 42(2) of the Administrative Courts Act and Decision of the Administrative Court of Cologne (25 January 2007) 13 K 2858/06, para 41.

[143] Aarhus Convention, Decision II/2, Para 16; *Bond Beter Leefmilieu Vlaanderen VZW*, para 36.

[144] Ibid, para 35.   [145] Ibid, para 36. See also Article 9(3).

[146] *Gatina, Gatin, Konyushkova: Findings and Recommendation with Regard to Compliance by Kazakhstan*, Compliance Committee, UNECE/MP PP/C 1/2006/4/Add 1 (2006) paras 30–1.

[147] On the right to adequate remedies see section 4 below.

[148] Article 2(2)(d) implemented by Regulation (EC) No 1367/2006 on the application of the Aarhus Convention to Community institutions and bodies (OJ L 264, 25.9.2006, 13).

public participation and access to environmental justice under Article 3(9) will also include transboundary claimants, and may thus facilitate resolution of transboundary environmental disputes.[149] The Aarhus Convention is significantly broader than the 1991 Convention on Transboundary EIA in two important respects, however: it is not limited to a transboundary context, and in accordance with Articles 7 and 8 it also applies, with some important qualifications, to plans, policies and legislation.[150] Ultimately, it is public participation at this level, rather than at the project level to which Article 6 applies, that has the greatest potential to promote—or to retard—environmental protection. Article 7 provides that 'To the extent appropriate, each Party shall endeavour to provide opportunities for public participation in the preparation of policies relating to the environment'. Like Article 8, which deals with legislation, this wording is somewhat weaker than Article 6. Nevertheless, this has not stopped the Compliance Committee from finding at least one state in breach.[151] It has also provided a basis for further development of state practice,[152] and no other human-rights treaty goes this far.

(c) Participatory rights under human-rights treaties

An important question posed by developments in the case law of the ECHR is the extent to which the participatory rights contained in the Aarhus Convention and Principle 10 of the Rio Declaration have become part of general human-rights law.

The most significant case is *Taskin v Turkey*, about the licensing of a mine, in which the European Court held that 'whilst Article 8 [of the European Convention] contains no explicit procedural requirements, the decision-making process leading to measures of interference must be fair and such as to afford due respect to the interests of the individual as safeguarded by Article 8'.[153] This passage and the Court's emphasis on taking into account the views of affected individuals strongly suggests that their participation in the decision-making process will be essential for compliance with Article 8. Similarly, the right to 'meaningful consultation' is upheld by the Inter-American Commission in the *Maya Indigenous Community of Toledo Case*,[154] by the African Commission in the *Ogoniland Case*,[155] and by the UN Human Rights Committee.[156]

---

[149] *Infra*, section 2(6).   [150] See also the 2003 Protocol on Strategic Environmental Assessment.

[151] *Dalma Orchards: Armenia*, Compliance Committee, UNECE/MP PP/C 1/2006/2/Add 1 (2006).

[152] In the Almaty Guidelines adopted in 2005 the parties endorsed public participation in the decision-making of international bodies concerned with environmental protection: UNECE, *Rept of 2nd Meeting of Parties to the Aarhus Convention*, ECE/MP PP/2005/2/Add 5 (2005) paras 28–39.

[153] *Taskin v Turkey* [2006] 42 EHRR 50, para 118.

[154] Paras 154–5. The Commission relies, inter alia, on the right to life and the right to private life, in addition to finding consultation a 'fundamental component of the State's obligations in giving effect to the communal property right of the Maya people in the lands that they have traditionally used and occupied'.

[155] *SERAC v Nigeria* (2002) ACHPR Comm 155/96.

[156] *Ilmari Lansman and Ors v Finland* (1996) ICCPR Comm No 511/1992, para 9.5, which stresses the need 'to ensure the effective participation of members of minority communities in decisions which affect them', and *Apirana Mahuika and Ors v New Zealand* (2000) ICCPR Comm No 547/1993, para 9.8. See also ILO Convention No 169 Concerning Indigenous and Tribal Peoples.

In *Öneryildiz v Turkey* the European Court placed 'particular emphasis' on the public's right to information about dangerous activities which posed a threat to life.[157] Where governments engage in or permit dangerous activities with unknown consequences for health, such as nuclear tests, there is a duty to establish an 'effective and accessible' procedure for allowing those involved to obtain relevant information.[158] In appropriate cases there is a duty to inform, not simply a right of access. In *Guerra*, Italy's failure to provide 'essential information' about the severity and nature of toxic emissions from a chemical plant was held to constitute a breach of the right to private life.[159] The judgment notes that the applicants were 'particularly exposed to danger' in the event of an accident at the factory, and there had been a violation of Italian legislation requiring that information concerning hazardous activities be made public. Finally, the *Taskin* judgment stipulates that 'the individuals concerned must also be able to appeal to the courts against any decision, act or omission where they consider that their interests or their comments have not been given sufficient weight in the decision-making process'.[160]

All of these decisions would also be covered by the terms of the Aarhus Convention but where the threat is to the environment, rather than to individuals, only the Aarhus Convention will apply. Moreover, the ECHR right of participation in decision-making is plainly not available to everyone, nor does it apply to decisions concerning the environment in general. Only those whose convention rights are in some way affected will benefit from this protection. This is significantly narrower than under Article 6 of the Aarhus Convention. If Aarhus can be viewed as promoting public interest participation, the ECHR case law remains firmly grounded in individual rights. It is likely to prove harder to influence the outcome of any balancing of interests from this perspective.

Nevertheless, if *Hatton* shows a reluctance on the part of the European Court to grapple with the merits of a decision interfering with individual rights, *Taskin* convincingly demonstrates an unequivocal willingness to address the proper procedures for taking decisions relating to the environment in human-rights terms. This is a profound extension of the scope of Article 8 of the European Convention. It goes some way towards translating into European human-rights law the procedural requirements set out in Principle 10 of the Rio Declaration and elaborated in European environmental-treaty law, despite the fact that Turkey was not a party to the Aarhus Convention at the time. However, the broader public-interest approach of the Aarhus Convention and the narrower ECHR focus on the convention rights of affected individuals is also very evident in the case law. This distinction has important implications for any debate about the need for an autonomous right to a decent or satisfactory environment, a question to which we return in the final section.

---

[157] Para 90.
[158] *McGinley and Egan v United Kingdom* [1998] III ECHR, paras 97, 101; *LCB v UK* (1999) 27 EHRR 212.
[159] Para 60.   [160] Ibid.

(d) Participatory rights in national law

The real test of Rio Principle 10's significance lies less in international treaties, however, than in national law. It is here that most of the important applications of the principle have taken place. In particular, public interest litigation has become an important feature of access to environmental justice, whether in the form of class actions, or liberal rules of standing, or allowing intervention by NGOs. Decisions of courts in common-law countries such as England, the United States, and New Zealand have generally granted *locus standi* in administrative-review proceedings to environmental groups and NGOs on a liberal basis, although such groups must usually demonstrate some interest in the issue beyond a mere concern for the environment.[161] In some cases influenced by the Aarhus Convention, certain civil-law jurisdictions also allow an *actio popularis* in environmental cases,[162] although standing before the European Court of Justice remains very restrictive.[163] Nor is this trend confined to developed states. India,[164] Pakistan,[165] Bangladesh,[166] the Philippines,[167] Malaysia[168] and several Latin American jurisdictions[169] have also embraced public-interest litigation on environmental issues. Judicial activism can be overdone, however, and some studies have questioned whether government by judges is equitable or environmentally effective.[170]

[161] For the US position see *Sierra Club v Morton* 405 US 727 (1972); *Lujan v Defenders of Wildlife* 504 US 555 (1992); *Friends of the Earth v Laidlaw*, 120 SCt 693 (2000) and Miller, 12 *JEL* (2000) 370. On New Zealand see *Environmental Defence Society v South Pacific Aluminium* (No 3) (1981) 1 NZLR 216. On English law see n 139.

[162] See especially the liberal approach adopted in the Italy: *Comitato Communa Bellis e Sanctuario v Commune di Ostiglia* (2006) Consiglio di Stato No 5760/2006 and in France: Conseil d'Etat, Decision of 26 April 1985 '*Ville de Tarbes*'. NGO standing in Germany is limited to s 61(2) of the 2002 Nature Conservation Act: see Federal Administrative Court (19 March 2003) 22 *Neue Zeitschrift für Verwaltungsrecht* (2003) 1120. In the Netherlands the formerly liberal rules on NGO standing are under review and may be abolished: see de Sadeleer/Roller/Dross, *Access to Justice in Environmental Matters*, Final Report, Doc ENVA 3/ETU/2002/0030, Part II, 76ff. Part I of this study surveys access to environmental justice in Western Europe.

[163] See *Stichting Greenpeace Council v EC Commission* (1998) ECR I-1651; 3 *CMLR* (1998) 1; Gérard, 10 *JEL* (1998) 331; Davies, in Zillman/Lucas/Pring (eds), *Human Rights in Natural Resources Development*, 176.

[164] E.g. *Bandhua Mukti Morcha v Union of India*, AIR 1984 SC 802; *Rural Litigation and Entitlement Kendra v State of Uttar Pradesh*, AIR 1985 SC 652; id, AIR 1987 SC 359; id, AIR 1988 SC 2187; *T Damodhar Rao v Municipal Corporation of Hyderabad*, AIR 1987 AP 171; *MC Mehta v Union of India* (1987) 1 SCC 395; id, (1987) 4 SCC 463; id, (1988) 1 SCC 471; id, (1997) 2 SCC 353.

[165] *Shela Zia v WAPDA*, PLD 1994 SC 416. See Lau, in, Boyle and Anderson (eds), *Human Rights Approaches to Environmental Protection*, Ch 14, who notes the Islamic-law basis for expanded public-interest litigation, expressed by Pakistan's Supreme Court and the four provincial High Courts in the 1991 Quetta Declaration.

[166] *Farooque v Govt of Bangladesh* (1997) 49 DLR (AD) 1.

[167] *Minors Oposa v Secretary of the Department of Environment and Natural Resources*, 33 *ILM* (1994) 173.

[168] See *Ketua Pengarah Jabatan Sekitar and Anor v Kajing Tubek and Ors* [1997] 3 *MLJ* 23, but cf Harding, in Boyle and Anderson (eds), *Human Rights Approaches*, Ch 11.

[169] See Colombian Constitutional Court decisions in *Fundepublico v Mayor of Bugalagrande* (1992) and *Organizión Indigena de Antioquia v Codechoco and Madarien* (1993) noted in ECOSOC, UN Doc E/CN 4/ Sub 2/1993/7, 16; and on Brazil see Fernandes, in Boyle and Anderson, *Human Rights Approaches*, Ch 13.

[170] See Rajamani, 19 *JEL* (2007) 293.

The main advantage of focusing on procedural rights is that it enables individuals and NGOs to enforce domestic environmental law and may help them shape domestic environmental policy. As we saw earlier, public-interest litigation may also diminish problems of anthropocentricity to the extent that rights can be exercised on behalf of the environment or of its non-human components, and not solely for human benefit. They can also be employed in the interests of future generations.[171] A further advantage of such litigation is that it can serve as a means of making public bodies accountable for their actions under international law. It has enabled environmental groups in the United States to seek review of governmental decisions affecting the Conventions on Trade in Endangered Species and Whaling,[172] while in India international environmental law, including treaties and the Rio Declaration, have been relied on in public-interest cases.[173] The extent to which public international law and treaties can be invoked or enforced by national courts varies across jurisdictions, however, and is beyond the scope of this book.[174]

It should not be overlooked, moreover, that governments also have a role as public-interest plaintiffs. Following the Bhopal disaster in India, the government assumed *parens patriae* power to negotiate a mass settlement of claims against Union Carbide.[175] In Australia, the Commonwealth government has relied on its treaty-making power in actions concerning non-compliance by state governments with the World Heritage Convention.[176] The European Commission is similarly empowered to bring proceedings against member states for non-compliance with directives implementing treaties to which the EC is a party.[177] Indeed, where the EC has legislative competence to implement international environmental commitments, it is no longer possible for EC member states to bring international judicial or arbitral proceedings inter se. They must either invite the Commission to use its enforcement powers or must initiate proceedings against the other member state before the ECJ.[178]

---

[171] See Philippines Supreme Court decision in *Minors Oposa v Secretary of the Department of Environment and Natural Resources*, 33 *ILM* (1994) 173; *Rural Litigation and Entitlement Kendra v State of Uttar Pradesh* AIR (1987) SC 359.

[172] *Defenders of Wildlife Inc v Endangered Species Authority*, 659 F 2d 168 (1981); *Japanese Whaling Association v American Cetacean Society*, 478 US 221 (1986); Gibson, 14 *ELQ* (1987) 485.

[173] See *T Damodhar Rao v Municipal Corporation of Hyderabad* AIR 1987 AP 171; *People United for Better Living in Calcutta v West Bengal*, AIR 1993 Cal 215; *Indian Council for Environmental Action v Union of India* (1996) 3 SCC 212; *Vellore Citizens Welfare Forum v Union of India* (1996) 5 SCC 647; *Janannath v Union of India* (1997) 2 SCC 87. See Anderson and Galizzi (eds), *International Environmental Law in National Courts*, Ch 8.

[174] See Anderson and Galizzi (eds), *International Environmental Law in National Courts*.

[175] See Bhopal Gas Leak Disaster (Processing of Claims) Act, 1985, and *Charan Lal Sahu v Union of India*, AIR 1990 SC 1480.

[176] *Commonwealth of Australia v State of Tasmania* (1983) 46 ALR 625; *Richardson v Tasmanian Forestry Commission* (1988) 77 ALR 237; *Queensland v The Commonwealth of Australia* (1989) 167 CLR 232; Tsamenyi and Bedding, 2 *JEL* (1990) 117.

[177] See *EC v France* (1990) ECR I-4337 (violation of CITES); *EC v France* (2004) Case C-239/03 (violation of Athens Protocol for Protection of the Mediterranean). Where treaty provisions have direct effect individuals can also sue: see e.g. *Syndicat Professionel etc v EDF* (2004) Case C-213/03 (Athens Protocol).

[178] *Commission v Ireland* ['*MOX Plant Case*'] ECR [2006] I-4635, and see Churchill and Scott, 22 *IJMCL* (2007) 303.

2(6) EXTRATERRITORIAL APPLICATION OF HUMAN-RIGHTS TREATIES IN ENVIRONMENTAL CASES

International human-rights treaties generally require a state party to secure civil and political rights and freedoms for everyone within its own territory or subject to its jurisdiction.[179] At first sight, this may suggest that a state cannot be held responsible for violating the rights of persons in other countries, but the European Court of Human Rights has in several cases held states responsible for extraterritorial effects.[180] In *Cyprus v Turkey* the Court reaffirmed that 'the responsibility of Contracting States can be involved by acts and omissions of their authorities which produce effects outside their own territory'.[181] In this case the question was whether the respondent state was responsible for the actions of its army of occupation in Northern Cyprus. Although this case turns on the effective control over territory exercised by Turkey, and in that sense it differs from environmental disputes, it may suggest that the Convention could have extraterritorial application if a state's failure to control activities causing environmental harm affects life, private life, or property in neighbouring countries. If states are responsible for their failure to control soldiers and judges abroad, a fortiori they should likewise be held responsible for a failure to control transboundary pollution and environmental harm emanating from industrial activities within their territory. These activities are within their jurisdiction and control in the obvious sense of being subject to their own law and administrative controls. Only the effects are extraterritorial. On this basis an application to the Inter-American Commission on Human Rights was brought against Uruguay in 2006 by a group of Argentine residents concerned about possible transboundary pollution risks from a pulp mill under construction adjacent to the River Uruguay. Uruguay's response to the claim was to emphasize the equal access of Argentine claimants in judicial and administrative procedures, an argument considered in the next section.

Similarly, it would not be unreasonable to expect one state to take into account transboundary impacts in another state when balancing the wider public interest against the possible harm to individual rights.[182] There is no principled basis for suggesting that the outcome of cases such as *Hatton* should depend on whether those affected by the noise are in the same country, or in other countries.[183] From this it also

---

[179] 1950 European Convention on Human Rights, Article 1; 1966 UN Covenant on Civil and Political Rights, Article 2.

[180] See *Loizidou v Turkey (Preliminary Objections)* [1995] ECHR Sers A/310, para 87; *Loizidou v Turkey (Merits)* [1996-VI] ECHR, para 52; *Drozd and Janousek vFrance and Spain* [1992] ECHR Sers A/240, para 91; Merrills and Robertson, *Human Rights in Europe* (4th edn, Manchester, 2001) 23–8. Cf *Bankovic v Belgium and Ors* [2001] ECHR No 52207/99 holding inadmissible a transboundary claim brought against NATO states in respect of the bombing of Serbia.

[181] [2001] ECHR No 25781/94.

[182] 2006 ILA Conference Report, Committee on Transnational Enforcement of Environmental Law, Rule 2, and commentary.

[183] See to the same effect OECD policy on equivalent treatment of domestic and transboundary effects, *infra*, section 3(2)(d).

follows that representations from those affected in other countries should be taken into account and given due weight.[184]

Although the Aarhus Convention does not specifically provide for transboundary application, as we saw earlier its provisions must be applied on a non-discriminatory basis.[185] Moreover, insofar as the principal elements of the Aarhus Convention have now been incorporated into European Convention case law it follows that they too 'must be secured without discrimination on any ground' in accordance with Article 14.

To deny transboundary claimants the protection afforded by human-rights treaties when otherwise appropriate would be hard to reconcile with standards of equality of access to justice and non-discriminatory treatment required by these precedents. Available national procedures would have to be exhausted before any human-rights claims could be brought, but there is little point requiring that national remedies be made available to transboundary claimants if they cannot also resort to human-rights law when necessary to compel the state to enforce its own laws or to take adequate account of extraterritorial effects. Given that transboundary claimants may have to subject themselves to the jurisdiction of the state causing the damage when seeking redress for environmental harm, it seems entirely consistent with the case law and the 'living instrument' conception of human-rights treaties to conclude that a state party must balance the rights of persons in other states against its own economic benefit, and must adopt and enforce environmental protection laws for their benefit, as well as for the protection of its own population. The same proposition applies just as much to other human-rights treaties as to the European Convention.[186]

2(7) THE VALUE OF HUMAN RIGHTS APPROACHES

The case law of the ECHR clearly demonstrates how far environmental protection can be extracted from existing human-rights law without creating specifically environmental rights. In particular, we can see that the European convention fully guarantees everything a right to a *healthy* environment would normally be thought to cover. Through evolutionary interpretation it now also guarantees the main procedural requirements of the Aarhus Convention, including in various ways the rights of access to environmental information and public participation in decision-making. In that sense environmental rights are already entrenched in European human-rights law, as they are also in the African Charter and the Inter-American Convention. The European, African, and Inter-American precedents are clearly relevant to the interpretation of comparable rights in global human-rights conventions, and Principle 10 of the Rio Declaration would also sustain reading into the UN Covenants the procedural requirements found in the Aarhus Convention. Judge Higgins has drawn attention to

---

[184] Ibid. See also Article 13 of the 2001 ILC Draft Articles on Prevention of Transboundary Harm.

[185] Article 3(9). See UNECE, *The Aarhus Convention: An Implementation Guide*, 48; and *supra*, section 2(5)(b).

[186] See 2006 ILA Conference Report, Committee on Transnational Enforcement of Environmental Law, Rule 2, and commentary.

the way human-rights courts 'work consciously to co-ordinate their approaches'.[187] In environmental cases there is certainly evidence of convergence in the case law and a cross-fertilization of ideas between the different human-rights systems.

Despite its evolutionary character, however, human-rights law still falls short of guaranteeing a right to a decent or satisfactory environment if that concept is under-stood in broader, essentially qualitative, terms unrelated to impacts on specific humans. It remains true, as the European Court reiterated in *Kyrtatos*, that 'neither Article 8 nor any of the other articles of the Convention are specifically designed to provide general protection of the environment as such...'.[188] This case involved the illegal draining of a wetland. The European Court could find no violation of their right to private life or enjoyment of property arising out of the destruction of the area in question. Although they lived nearby, the applicants' rights were not affected. They were not entitled to live in any particular environment, or to have the surrounding environment indefinitely preserved. The Court's conclusion in *Kyrtatos* points to a larger issue which goes to the heart of the problem: human-rights protection ben-efits only the victims of a violation of convention rights. If the individual applicant's health, private life, property, or civil rights are not sufficiently affected by environ-mental loss, then he or she has no standing to proceed. There is, as Judge Loucaides has observed, no *actio popularis* under the European convention.[189] The Inter-American Commission on Human Rights has taken a similar view, rejecting as inadmissible a claim on behalf of all the citizens of Panama to protect a nature reserve from devel-opment.[190] In a comparable case, concerning objections to the growing of genetically modified crops, the UN Human Rights Committee likewise held that 'no person may, in theoretical terms and by *actio popularis*, object to a law or practice which he holds to be at variance with the Covenant'.[191]

There is little doubt that the UN Sub-Commission's 1994 report[192] is right to empha-size the potential within existing human-rights law for environmental protection, and this can be fully observed in much of the national and international case law. What is less clear is whether there is any need for a separate, generic right in international law to a decent, viable, or satisfactory environment, or for the re-conceptualizsation of international environmental law into the international law of environmental rights, as proposed by the Sub-Commission. The strongest argument in favour of qualita-tive environmental rights is that other human rights are themselves dependent on adequate environmental quality, and cannot be realized without governmental action

---

[187] Higgins, 55 *ICLQ* (2006) 791, 798. See also the separate opinion of Judge Trindade in *Caesar v Trinidad and Tobago* (2005) IACHR Sers C, No 123, paras 6–12: 'The converging case law to this effect has generated the common understanding, in the regional (European and inter-American) systems of human rights protection...'. (para 7).

[188] *Kyrtatos v Greece* [2003] ECHR 242, para 52.   [189] Loucaides, 75 *BYIL* (2004) 249.

[190] *Metropolitan Nature Reserve v Panama*, Case 11.533, Report No 88/03, Inter-Am CHR, OEA/Ser L/V/II.118 Doc 70 rev 2 (2003) 524, para 34.

[191] *Brun v France* (2006) ICCPR Communication No 1453/2006, para 6.3.   [192] *Supra*, n 48.

to protect the environment.[193] This is doubtless true but it does not demonstrate that such action requires an extension of international human-rights law, rather than better regulation or stronger international cooperation. Climate change and unsustainable use of natural resources represent by far the greatest contemporary challenge to a decent environment, but these are not problems that human-rights law can solve.

Nor does the argument for a right to a decent environment offer convincing solutions to the problems of supervision, definition and anthropocentricity which are its inherent weaknesses. The claims of humanity, both now and in future generations, to live in a decent environment capable of sustaining life of acceptable quality, need little justification. When viewed against the need for biological diversity, unity of ecosystems, and the preservation of options implicit in sustainable development, the claims of animals and nature to international protection appear controversial. The fundamental difficulty lies in reconciling these claims with economic development and other competing objectives and, for the lawyer, in identifying the most appropriate means for doing so. For this purpose the role of international human-rights courts is important but limited to the protection of individual civil and political rights and ill-suited to broader forms of public interest litigation. Larger questions of economic and social welfare have been and should remain within the confines of the more political supervisory processes envisaged by the ICESCR and the European Social Charter. At the substantive level a 'right' to a decent or satisfactory environment can best be envisaged within that context, but at present it remains largely absent from the relevant global and regional treaties. This is an omission which should be addressed if environmental considerations are to receive the weight they deserve in the balance of other economic, social, and cultural rights.

As the internationalization of the domestic environment becomes more extensive, through policies of sustainable development, protection of biodiversity, and mitigation of climate change, the role of human-rights law in democratizing national decision-making processes and making them more rational, open, and legitimate will become more and not less significant. Public participation, as foreseen in UNCED Agenda 21, is thus a central element in sustainable development. The Aarhus Convention and the incorporation of Aarhus-style procedural rights into general human-rights law significantly advance this objective. Adequate protection of the global environment depends on the interplay of international and national measures; the use of national legal systems by individuals and environmental groups not only influences the policy and decisions of government and helps resolve transboundary disputes, it also puts pressure on governments to comply with their international commitments and obligations. It is entirely realistic for international law to encourage these trends. In that sense, the inclusion of Principle 10 in the Rio Declaration, combined with a 'greening' of existing human-rights law, is arguably of greater significance than the omission of an explicit right to an environment of decent, healthy, or viable quality.

---

[193] See Pathak, in Brown Weiss (ed), *Environmental Change and International Law*, Ch 8; Weeramantry, sep op, *Gabčíkovo-Nagymaros Case*, ICJ Reports (1997) 7.

3 TRANSBOUNDARY ENVIRONMENTAL RIGHTS

3(1) INTRODUCTION

The problems of resorting to public international law to deal with transboundary environmental disputes have been explored in previous chapters: the lack of a forum with universal compulsory jurisdiction, the complexity and uncertainty of the law of state responsibility as regards environmental damage, and the absence of clarity concerning the remedies available to states and their scope. These problems have not so far been significantly mitigated by the International Law Commission either in its work on state responsibility or international liability.

It is against this background that we can now examine the somewhat greater progress in opening up national legal systems to transboundary environmental litigation, particularly in Europe and North America, but also through civil liability conventions covering ultra-hazardous activities, such as oil transportation or nuclear power. There are three good reasons for encouraging resort to private-law remedies in transboundary environmental disputes. First, it de-escalates disputes 'to their ordinary neighbourhood level',[194] where they can be resolved using national law, and avoids turning them into interstate controversies based on problematic concepts of state responsibility in international law. Second, by allowing direct recourse against the enterprise causing the damage, it facilitates implementation of a 'polluter pays' approach to the allocation of environmental costs. A policy of internalizing the true economic costs of pollution is endorsed in Principle 16 of the Rio Declaration and by OECD and the EC.[195] Third, it empowers individuals by enabling the private plaintiff to act without the intervention of a government, and to that extent facilitates further development of a rights-based approach to environmental issues. This is consistent in general terms with the policy, considered earlier in this chapter, of promoting environmental rights through '[e]ffective access to judicial and administrative proceedings, including redress and remedy' in accordance with Principle 10 of the Rio Declaration. Moreover, a policy of encouraging resort to transboundary civil litigation and remedies recognizes the reality that many, if not most, transboundary environmental problems are mainly caused by and affect private parties, rather than states as such. In this context transboundary litigation not only provides an effective mechanism for dealing with transboundary harm, but may also offer the possibility of securing redress from multinationals whose operations in developing countries are sometimes difficult to control through local law.

---

[194] Sand, *Lessons learned in Global Environmental Governance* (New York, 1990) 31. For a succinct survey of the problems of transboundary litigation see McCaffrey, in Von Bar (ed), *Internationales Umwelthaftungsrecht I* (Köln, 1995) 81.

[195] OECD, Council Recommendations C (72)128; C (74)223; C (89) 88 and C (90) 177, and European Community Treaty, Article 174. On the polluter pays principle, see *infra*, section 4(4).

Encouraging the solution of transboundary problems through national law also has disadvantages, which must be recognized. There may be no remedy, or no effective remedy, if the applicable legal system is favourable to the activities of polluters. No common legal standards will necessarily govern the availability of remedies in different states unless there is parallel progress in harmonizing environmental standards and liability for damage. Even where adequate laws exist, problems of jurisdiction, the availability of remedies and enforcement in transboundary cases may limit the usefulness of this form of litigation. Public and private international law can have a role in securing access to justice by removing some or all of these disadvantages and by ensuring that adequate national remedies are available to plaintiffs in transboundary cases. These objectives can be achieved in a variety of ways, but will usually involve addressing some or all of the following elements:

1. non-discriminatory treatment of transboundary plaintiffs and equal access to available national procedures and remedies

2. resolving problems of private international law, particularly jurisdiction and choice of law in transboundary cases

3. harmonization of national laws dealing with liability for environmental damage.

3(2) EQUAL ACCESS TO NATIONAL REMEDIES

(a) The principle

Equality of access to transboundary remedies and procedures is based on the principle of non-discrimination: where domestic remedies are already available to deal with internal pollution or environmental problems, international or regional law can be used to ensure that the benefit of these remedies and procedures is extended to transboundary claimants. As defined by OECD,[196] equal access and non-discrimination should ensure that any person who has suffered transboundary environmental damage or who is exposed to a significant risk of such damage obtains at least equivalent treatment to that afforded to individuals in the country of origin. This includes the provision of and access to information concerning transboundary environmental risks; participation in hearings, preliminary enquiries and the opportunity to make objections; and resort to administrative and judicial procedures in order to prevent pollution, secure its abatement, or obtain compensation—in other words, access to justice.[197] These rights of equal access are to be accorded not only to individuals affected by the risk of transboundary injury but also to foreign NGOs and public

---

[196] OECD Council Recommendations C74 (224); C (76) 55; C (77) 28, in OECD, *OECD and the Environment* (Paris, 1986). See generally McCaffrey, 1 *EPL* (1975) 1; Smets, 9 *EPL* (1982) 110; Willheim, 7 *AYIL* (1976) 174.

[197] *Supra*, section 2(5) and see generally Francioni, *Access to Justice as a Human Right*, Ch 1.

authorities, insofar as comparable entities possess such rights in the country of origin of the pollution.

The principle of non-discrimination as defined by OECD also entails giving equivalent treatment to the domestic and transboundary effects of polluting activities, and requires that polluters causing transboundary pollution should be subject to legal standards no less severe than would apply to pollution with domestic effects only. In effect, transboundary pollution should not, under this principle, exceed levels that would be considered acceptable if occurring within the country of origin. To a limited extent Canadian and US legislation accepts OECD's non-discrimination standard. Section 115 of the US Clean Air Act[198] permits the administrator of the US Environmental Protection Agency to direct US state governments to take stronger air-pollution abatement measures where an 'international agency' or the Secretary of State believes that pollution emanating from these states is endangering health and welfare in a foreign country. This provision was invoked by the EPA in 1980 on the basis of a report of the International Joint Commission concerning air pollution of the Great Lakes. However, the discretionary nature of the legislation meant that it was not a reliable mechanism for ensuring that Canadian interests received equal, or any, consideration in the control of US air pollution.[199] The Canadian Clean Air Act is intended to provide reciprocal protection for the United States. Article 2 of the 1974 Nordic Convention also requires parties to equate domestic and transboundary nuisances when considering the permissibility of environmentally harmful activities.[200] As we noted earlier, human-rights law points in the same direction when balancing the interests of the community at large against the impact on the rights of particular individuals.

(b) Non-discrimination and equal access in international law

Although non-discrimination was included in the legal principles on environmental protection proposed by the World Commission on Environment and Development, this body concluded that it was still an 'emerging principle of international law', at least in the context of transboundary environmental claims.[201] International policy declarations, including the Stockholm and Rio Declarations, do not explicitly refer to equal access, nor do they demonstrate clear support for the principle of non-discrimination. However, given the ILC's consistent endorsement of the non-discrimination principle in a transboundary environmental context, and other precedents considered below, it

---

[198] 42 USC 7415. See Schmandt, Clarkson, and Roderick, *Acid Rain and Friendly Neighbors* (Durham, NC, 1988) 226f.

[199] *New York v Thomas*, 802 F 2d 1443, reversing 613 F Suppl 1472 (1985); *HM Queen in Right of Ontario v US*, 912 F 2d 1525 (1990). The United States finally responded to Canadian complaints by amending the federal Clean Air Act in 1990.

[200] *Infra*, n 207. It also makes provision for reciprocal access by administrative agencies to regulatory or licensing procedures.

[201] Munro and Lammers, *Environmental Protection and Sustainable Development* (London, 1986) 88. See *supra*, Ch 3, section 4(2)(d).

can probably be assumed that it already reflects existing international law.[202] Article 15 of the ILC's 2001 Articles on Prevention of Transboundary Harm prohibits discrimination based on nationality, residence, or place of injury in granting access to judicial or other procedures, or compensation, in cases of significant transboundary harm.[203] Article 32 of the 1997 UN Watercourses Convention is comparable.[204] Both allow victims of transboundary pollution or damage to have direct recourse to local remedies in the state where the source of the harm is located. The rule as formulated by the ILC is residual. States are thus free to deal with questions of transboundary justice in some other way if they agree.[205] As we shall see below, an altogether different approach has been adopted in regional and global treaties dealing with liability for damage, including accidents involving oil tankers and nuclear installations.

Discriminatory restrictions on transboundary access to justice may also violate the right to a fair trial under Article 6(1) of the European Human Rights Convention,[206] or under Article 14 of the 1966 UN Covenant on Civil and Political Rights, which specifically states: 'All persons shall be equal before the courts and tribunals'.

Insofar as it is possible to review the state practice on such a disparate topic, it is not easy to point to any clear picture. There are rules in some national legal systems which are difficult to reconcile with equality of access, such as the principle of *forum non conveniens*, the denial of jurisdiction in actions affecting foreign land, or the refusal to allow transboundary access to administrative proceedings on the ground that national legislation does not have extraterritorial application. At the same time there is significant regional support for equality of access to justice, and some undoubted examples of its application.

(c) Regional provision for equal access to remedies

It is mainly at regional level, in Europe and North America, that equal access and non-discrimination have received significant support. OECD and the UNECE are the principal international organizations to have elaborated the content of the principle in detail and to have relied on it as an important element in the development of international environmental policy and law. Although OECD's recommendations and

---

[202] Smets, *Rev Eur Droit de l'Env* (2000) 3. In *Juridical Situation and Rights of Undocumented Migrants* (17 September 2003) I/A Court HR, OC-18/03, para 83, the IACHR held that 'the fundamental principle of equality and non-discrimination constitutes a part of general international law, which is applicable to all states, independent of whether or not they are a party to a particular international treaty. In the present stage of the evolution of international law, the fundamental principle of equality and non-discrimination has entered the realm of jus cogens.'

[203] See also the ILC's 2006 Principles on Allocation of Loss, Principle 8(2) *infra*, section 4(3).

[204] The inclusion of this article was questioned by several states, including India, Russia and Tanzania: see McCaffrey, 92 *AJIL* (1998) 97, 104. See also 1909 US–Canada Boundary Waters Treaty, Article 2, but compare *Soucheray and Ors v US Corps of Engineers*, 483 F Supp 352, denying relief on ground that no action lay in respect of IJC decisions under this treaty; ILA, Montreal Rules on Water Pollution in an International Drainage Basin, 1982, Article 8; id, Helsinki Rules on Private Law Remedies for Transboundary Damage in International Watercourses, 1996, Articles 1–3, and *infra*, Ch 10.

[205] ILC Report (2001) Prevention of Transboundary Harm, commentary to Article 15, para (4).

[206] See *Lubbe v Cape plc* [2000] 1 WLR 1545, *supra*.

decisions in this respect are not binding, they have had some influence on arrangements among certain member states, most notably in the 1974 Nordic Convention for the Protection of the Environment,[207] and in conventions adopted by the UNECE. Its 1991 Convention on Environmental Impact Assessment in a Transboundary Context requires that members of the public in the affected state be given the equivalent opportunity to participate in relevant environmental impact assessment procedures available to the public in the party of origin.[208] The 1992 Convention on the Transboundary Effects of Industrial Accidents 'underlines' the principle of non-discrimination, reiterates the EIA Convention's provision for equivalent access to procedures, and affords reciprocal access to justice.[209] Last, but most importantly, as we saw earlier, Article 3(9) of the 1998 Aarhus Convention requires the parties to afford access to information, justice, and decision-making without discrimination as to citizenship, domicile or place of registration or business. Because of this convention's extensive impact on the provision of domestic remedies and procedures, this article is potentially the most significant legal basis for claims of equal access in transboundary cases in UNECE states. In particular, it may ensure that cases are not dismissed on grounds of *forum non conveniens*, and may also limit denial of jurisdiction on grounds of extraterritoriality.

European Community law does not explicitly provide for equal access, but the Regulation on Jurisdiction and the Recognition and Enforcement of Judgments in Civil and Commercial Matters[210] has the effect of securing access to justice for transboundary litigants, and of precluding reliance on exclusionary doctrines such as *forum non conveniens*. It will be considered further below. In North America the Commission established by the 1993 Agreement on Environmental Cooperation has power to make recommendations on reciprocal access to courts and administrative agencies, but the agreement otherwise contains no non-discrimination clause.[211] Ontario has made use of provisions in the US Clean Air Act allowing citizen suits for violation of Federal environmental standards while the Trans-Alaska Pipeline Act explicitly permits transboundary plaintiffs to do so.[212] A model Uniform Transboundary Pollution

---

[207] Kiss, 20 *AFDI* (1978) 808; Broms, in Flinterman, Kwiatkowska, and Lammers (eds), *Transboundary Air Pollution* (Dordrecht, 1986) 141; Phillips, ibid, 153; Ebbeson, in Hollo and Marttinen (eds), *North European Environmental Law* (Helsinki, 1995) 41. Only one case is recorded: *Saugbruksforeningen Case*, *Norsk Retstidende* (1992) 1618. Public-interest litigants do not have standing in Sweden but do in Norway. See Ebbeson, loc cit.

[208] Article 2(6). See Ch 3 section 4(4).   [209] Preamble and Article 9.

[210] Council Regulation (EC) No 44/2001 (2000) (OJL 12 of 16.01.2001). The regulation replaces the 1968 Brussels Convention on Jurisdiction and Judgments.

[211] 1993 North American Agreement on Environmental Cooperation, Article 10(9). Canada, Mexico, and the United States are parties to the agreement. It is possible that Article 6, which provides for 'interested persons' to have access to legal remedies for violation of environmental laws, may also apply to transboundary litigants.

[212] See *Her Majesty the Queen in Right of Ontario v US Environmental Protection Agency*, 912 F 2d 1525(1990); Ontario's application for review of EPA action was refused: its standing to bring the action was not challenged or considered. See also Clean Air Act, 42 USC § 7415 and 7604; Clean Water Act, 33 USC § 1365(a) and (g); although these acts make no reference to transboundary plaintiffs, in *Pfizer Inc v Govt of India*, 434 US 308 (1978) the Supreme Court held that a foreign state is a 'person' for the purpose of entitlement to sue under anti-trust law. The Trans Alaska Pipeline Authorization Act, 43 USC § 1635(c)(1) allows

Reciprocal Access Act is also intended to remove jurisdictional limits on actions for transboundary damage, but it has been not been adopted in either Washington state or British Columbia, the two jurisdictions involved in the *Trail Smelter* dispute.[213]

The effect of these developments is that in North America and Europe transboundary legal proceedings have become a feasible, though still uncommon, method for recovering damages for air and water pollution injury affecting plaintiffs in other states. A good example is the litigation resulting from the Sandoz chemical spillage in the Rhine, which was successfully handled without any resort to interstate claims or international proceedings.[214] There is less information on the treatment of transboundary plaintiffs in other regions of the world, and especially in developing countries. However, the Pulp Mills dispute has shown that Argentine citizens enjoy equal access to remedies and procedures under Uruguayan law in respect of possible transboundary harm.[215] A protocol to the MERCOSUR Convention also provides for equal access to judicial procedures throughout the member states.[216]

(d) Implementation of a policy of equal access

Impediments to equal access primarily involve procedural and jurisdictional obstacles. One example is a rule found in some legal systems which denies jurisdiction over actions involving foreign land. In some cases it applies only to actions concerning title or trespass to land, but in others it includes extraterritorial effects of activities within the territory of the forum.[217] There is no obvious reason in principle why a forum in which activities causing transboundary damage are situated should refuse jurisdiction merely because the effects are extraterritorial, but it is this rule which explains why the *Trail Smelter Case* was referred not to the Canadian courts but to international arbitration.[218] The US–Canadian Uniform Transboundary Reciprocal Access Act was intended to remove this problem.[219] In *Aguinda v Texaco Inc*,[220] a US case involving oil spills and environmental damage in Ecuador, it was held that the local action rule is inapplicable under US Federal law where the case does not involve

---

'any person or entity, public or private, *including those resident in Canada*' (emphasis added) to invoke the Act's liability provisions. See generally Hsu and Parrish, 48 *VJIL* (2007) 1.

[213] Adopted 1982 and implemented in Colorado, Connecticut, Manitoba, Michigan, Montana, New Jersey, Nova Scotia, Ontario, Oregon, Prince Edward Island, South Dakota, and Wisconsin. Text in *Uniform Laws Annotated*, vol 9B. See Rosencrantz, 15 *EPL* (1985) 105; Bernasconi, *Hague YIL* (1999) 35, 105–6; McCaffrey, in Von Bar (ed), *Internationales Umwelthaftungsrecht I*, 81, 85–6.

[214] See D'Oliviera, in Francioni and Scovazzi (eds), *International Responsibility for Environmental Harm* (Dordrecht, 1991) 429; *Michie v Great Lakes Steel Division* 495 F 2d 213 (1974); Ianni, *CYIL* (1973) 258; this case simply assumed without discussion that Canadian plaintiffs could bring a tort action for transboundary air pollution in the United States.

[215] See 1988 General Code of Procedure.

[216] 1992 Las Leñas Protocol on Jurisdictional Cooperation and Assistance, Ch III, Article 3.

[217] See e.g. *British South Africa Company v Compania de Moçambique* [1893] AC 602; *Hesperides Hotels Ltd v Muftizade* [1979] AC 508; *Albert v Frazer Companies Ltd* [1937] 1 DLR 39; *Dagi v Broken Hill Proprietary Co Ltd* (1997) 1 Victoria Reps 428. UK courts now have jurisdiction over torts affecting immovable property outside the UK under s 30 of the 1982 Civil Jurisdiction and Judgments Act. See generally Bernasconi, *Hague YIL* (1999) 102–6; OECD, *Legal Aspects of Transfrontier Pollution*, 98–102; McCaffrey, 3 *CWILJ* (1973) 191.

[218] Read, 1 *CYIL* (1963) 222.   [219] *Supra*, n 213.   [220] 850 F Supp 282 (1994).

title to land or trespass, but may be relevant if the action relates closely to a specific piece of land. The problem is not significant in transboundary tort cases in Western Europe due in part to the jurisdictional provisions of the EC Regulation on Jurisdiction and the Recognition and Enforcement of Judgments, considered below, but it remains an obstacle in common-law jurisdictions outside Europe.

A more significant obstacle to equal access for the transboundary litigant in Anglo-American law is the discretionary power of courts to dismiss cases on the ground that a foreign forum is a more appropriate venue for trial. Thus, even if it can be established that a national court does have jurisdiction, it does not follow that it will necessarily exercise it. The principle of *forum non conveniens*[221] allows the court to look at all the relevant factors in order to decide which legal system is better placed to decide the case. In the Bhopal litigation,[222] the US courts declined to hear Indian claims against Union Carbide because, in their view, the Indian courts were a more appropriate forum. The plaintiffs were Indian, most of the evidence was in India, the applicable law was likely to be Indian, and India had the stronger interest in setting appropriate standards of care. It was not, the court held, a matter of determining the most favourable forum for the plaintiff, but of balancing the public and private interests. The US courts had no public interest in trying cases of this kind. In effect, the judgment ensured that the plaintiffs' claims would never come before a court in either country, and left Union Carbide free to negotiate a very favourable settlement with the Indian government.

Similarly, in *Aguinda*,[223] a US district court was persuaded that Ecuador was the more appropriate forum, on grounds similar to those relied on in *Union Carbide*. The *forum non conveniens* doctrine as applied in these cases thus discriminates against foreign plaintiffs while at the same time protecting the forum's own companies from liability for their actions abroad.[224] This may not matter as between developed countries, but when the plaintiffs are from developing countries it may in some cases amount to a denial of justice if no effective local redress is available, or if the plaintiffs are prevented by intimidation, corruption, civil war, or cost from resorting to local courts. Moreover, as we saw earlier, because of its inherently discriminatory character, dismissal on grounds of *forum non conveniens* may be incompatible with a number of recent UNECE treaties, most notably the 1998 Aarhus Convention. In some circumstances it is also arguably a breach of the right to a fair hearing of a civil claim guaranteed by a number of human-rights conventions, including Article 6 of the European Convention on Human Rights.[225]

---

[221] *Piper Aircraft Co v Reyno* 454 US 235 (1981); *Spiliada Maritime Corp v Cansulex Ltd* [1987] AC 460; *Connelly v RTZ Corp plc* [1998] AC 854. See Fawcett, *Declining Jurisdiction in Private International Law* (Oxford, 1995); Robertson, 103 *LQR* (1987) 398; id, 29 *Texas ILJ* (1994) 353; Weintraub, 29 *Texas ILJ* (1994) 321; Brand, 37 *Texas ILJ* (2002) 467.

[222] *In re Union Carbide Corporation Gas Plant Disaster at Bhopal* 634 F Supp 842 (1986); 809 F 2d 195 (1987); Muchlinski, 50 *MLR* (1987) 545.

[223] *Aguinda v Texaco Inc* 945 F Supp 625 (1996). The case was reinstated on appeal in 1998.

[224] Prince, 47 *ICLQ* (1998) 573; Robertson, 103 *LQR* (1987) 398.

[225] See also 1966 UN Covenant on Civil and Political Rights, Article 14. The point was argued before but not decided by the UK House of Lords in *Lubbe v Cape plc* [2000] 1 WLR 1545. See *Axen v Federal Republic of*

Not all jurisdictions are as hostile to the human-rights and denial of justice issues as US courts appear to be. When persuaded that justice so requires, United Kingdom courts have declined to dismiss actions on *forum non conveniens* grounds, for example where no legal aid or financial assistance would be available to enable a suit to be brought abroad.[226] Moreover, in some jurisdictions, the test for dismissal is stricter than in the United States. Whereas American courts apply a US public-interest test, Australian courts require an abuse of process and will dismiss an action only if the defendant can show that Australia is clearly an inappropriate forum on this ground. Thus, in circumstances similar to Bhopal, indigenous peoples harmed by Australian mining operations in New Guinea, and denied access to justice there, were able to bring proceedings in Australia.[227] On the other hand Anglo-American case law does provide some limit on excessive jurisdictional claims over extraterritorial events and relieves judges of the burden of hearing sometimes complex cases.[228] *Forum non conveniens* is generally unknown in civil-law systems, which exercise a more restrained jurisdiction than under common law, and it is incompatible with EC law on civil jurisdiction.[229]

(e) The limitations of equal access

The evident advantages of opening up local remedies to foreign parties as a means of settling transboundary disputes must be set against certain weaknesses or disadvantages inherent in what is a relatively limited form of access to justice. These problems need to be appreciated to understand why it is necessary to go beyond equal access if a satisfactory regional or international approach is sought:

1. Equal access guarantees no substantive standard of environmental protection, and no procedural rights of any kind save to the extent that these are already available for domestic claimants.

2. Equal access does not solve the problems of choice of law which arise in transboundary litigation.

3. Equal access to a foreign forum may be disadvantageous on various grounds of inconvenience, language, unfamiliarity, and the plaintiff may be better off suing in his own domestic jurisdiction.

Germany (1983) ECHR Ser A, No 72; *Dombo Beheer v Netherlands* (1993) ECHR Ser A, No 274. See generally Fawcett, (2007) 56 *ICLQ* 1, 39–41.

[226] *Connelly v RTZ Corp plc* [1998] AC 854; *Lubbe v Cape plc* [2000] 1 WLR 1545. See Muchlinski, 50 *ICLQ* (2001) 1; Ward, 12 *YbIEL* (2001) 105.

[227] *Dagi v Broken Hill Proprietary Co Ltd* (1997) 1 Victoria Reps 428; see Prince, 47 *ICLQ* (1998) 573. On the 'clearly inappropriate forum' test see *Voth v Manildra Flour Mills* (1990) 171 CLR 538. In *Lubbe v Cape plc* [2000] 1 WLR 1545, the UK House of Lords rejected the view that public policy questions of the kind considered decisive in the Bhopal litigation had any role to play. See in particular the judgment of Lord Hope, Muchlinski, 50 *ICLQ* (2001) 1 and Ward, 12 *YbIEL* (2001) 105.

[228] *In re Union Carbide Corp*, 634 F Supp 842 (1986) 861. But cf *Lubbe v Cape plc* [2000] 1 WLR 1545, and Muchlinski, 50 *ICLQ* (2001) 1.

[229] *Owusu v Jackson* (2005) ECJ C-281/02.

Why then, should the plaintiff be forced to sue abroad? The answer to this of course is that equal access to the polluting jurisdiction does not preclude access to any other forum: it leaves open the issue of jurisdiction and choice of forum in private international law, just as it does not resolve the question of choice of law. It is to these issues that we can now turn.

3(3) PRIVATE INTERNATIONAL LAW ISSUES IN TRANSBOUNDARY ENVIRONMENTAL LITIGATION

(a) Choice of law

Given that a claim for transboundary environmental damage may involve events, impacts, and persons in several countries, and possibly on the high seas, the question which legal system should determine liability and other issues is a real and important one. One study has shown that as regards choice of law in transboundary environmental claims there is 'no discernible consensus'.[230] There are various possibilities, each of which is adopted in a number of legal systems:

1. The forum applies the law of the place where the harmful activity is located. This allows the legal consequences to be regulated by the jurisdiction within whose territory the activity takes place and gives legal effect to administrative licensing or statutory authorization by that state.

2. The forum applies the law of the place where the injury occurred. This solution is favoured by the 1973 Hague Convention on the Law Applicable to Products Liability, and is consistent with the application of Dutch law by the Dutch Court of Appeal in the *Handelskwekerij* litigation,[231] which arose out of pollution of the Rhine by a French undertaking. Products liability and transboundary environmental torts are not necessarily comparable, however. The former usually involves the deliberate supply of goods, while the latter may entail harm accidentally spread across several countries, including the place in which the activity causing the harm is situated. Moreover, applying the law of the place of injury may make it more difficult to integrate with the administrative or statutory authorization of the activity by the state where the harmful activity is located.[232]

3. The forum applies some other law, such as that of the place in which the defendant company is domiciled or has its principal place of business. Some common-law

---

[230] Kreuzer, 44 *Rev Espanola DI* (1992) 57. See also Hague Conference on Private International Law, *Note on the Law Applicable to Civil Liability for Environmental Damage* (1992); Beaumont, *Juridical Review* (1995) 28; Bernasconi, *Hague YIL* (1999) 74–88; Von Bar, 268 *Recueil des Cours* (1997) 303; ILA, *70th Conference Report* (2004) 896.

[231] *Handelskwekerij GJ Bier and Stichting Reinwater v Mines de Potasse d'Alsace*, reported in 19 *NYIL* (1988) 496.

[232] For an example of the problems see *Pakootas v Teck Cominco Metals Ltd* 452 F 3d 1066 (2006) ['*Trail Smelter II*'].

countries are more likely to apply their own law if the defendant is domiciled or has its business there.

4. The forum applies whichever is the more favourable law for the plaintiff, the so-called 'ubiquity' principle. This approach is adopted in German, Swiss, Czech, and Portuguese law.[233] The Swiss statute allows the plaintiff to nominate the better law.

Each of these choices has advantages and disadvantages, and no attempt will be made here to assess which represents the best approach. But the problem with the present diversity of choice of law rules, and the lack of any consensus, particularly in Europe, is that they add to the unpredictability, complexity, and expense of transboundary litigation, and are in that sense obstacles to better transboundary access to environmental justice. Moreover, it does not follow that a court will apply the same choice of law to all aspects of the case before it. US courts have often applied US law to determine the liability of American defendants but then applied the plaintiff's legal system when it comes to assessing the compensation due. This is what happened in the *Amoco Cadiz Case*,[234] denying US damages to French plaintiffs.

As we have seen, neither the OECD nor the EC scheme of transboundary jurisdiction addresses the question of choice of law, which is thus determined by each national legal system.[235] Other possible approaches include giving the plaintiff a choice of forum, or undertaking measures to harmonize substantive liability in national law.

(b) Jurisdiction and 'forum shopping'

Transboundary environmental damage cases may involve elements in several countries. For that reason, private international law will often afford victims of transboundary harm a choice of forum in which to sue. The general principle most widely accepted is that proceedings may be brought (i) in the courts of the place where damage occurs (i.e. the transboundary victim's own state) or (ii) in the place where harmful activity is located, or (iii) in the place where the defendant is domiciled.[236] There is no consensus on whether jurisdiction is mandatory in these circumstances or may nevertheless be declined, and no agreement has been possible in negotiations on a global jurisdiction convention.

---

[233] Swiss Private International Law Act, 1987, Article 138; Czechoslovakian Conflict of Laws Act, 1963, s 15; and on Germany and Portugal see Kreuzer, 44 *Rev Espanola DI* (1992) 64–5.

[234] *In re Oil Spill by Amoco Cadiz* 954 F 2d 1279 (1992). See generally Lowenfeld, *International Litigation and the Quest for Reasonableness* (Oxford, 1996) 86–90.

[235] The Hague Conference on Private International Law considered whether to negotiate a convention to harmonize choice of law in transboundary environmental suits: see Bernasconi, *Hague YIL* (1999) 35; Beaumont, *Juridical Review* (1995) 28; Von Bar (ed), *Internationales Umwelthaftungsrecht I* (Köln, 1995).

[236] See respectively *Handelskwekerij GJ Bier v Mines de Potasse d'Alsace*, Case 21/76 [1976] II ECJ Reports, 1735; *Re Union Carbide Corporation* 634 F Supp 842 (1986); *In re Oil Spill by Amoco Cadiz* 954 F 2d 1279 (1992). All three jurisdictional bases are recognized by Articles 2 and 5 of the 2000 EC Regulation on Jurisdiction and Judgments, by the 2003 Kiev Protocol on Civil Liability and Compensation, Article 13, and by the 1993 Convention on Civil Liability for Damage to the Environment, Article 19. See generally 2006 ILA Conference Report, Committee on Transnational Enforcement of Environmental Law, 664–5.

Jurisdiction will generally exist in the courts of the defendant's residence, domicile or place of business.[237] There may, however, be exceptions to this general rule. As we saw above when discussing equality of access to justice, in some legal systems extraterritorial environmental damage is excluded from the jurisdiction of courts outside the state where the injury occurs, while in others the principle of *forum non conveniens* is resorted to as a means of declining jurisdiction over actions brought by foreigners.

Jurisdiction will usually also exist in the place where the injury occurs, as for example in *Aguinda v Texaco* and in the Bhopal case, where there was no doubt that Ecuador and India respectively had territorial jurisdiction. Similarly, in the *Trail Smelter II* litigation, US courts held a Canadian company potentially liable under US legislation for transboundary damage caused by water pollution emanating from a smelter in Canada.[238] By virtue of international liability conventions pollution incidents at sea also fall under the jurisdiction of the courts of the states where the damage occurs.[239] The same is true under EC law, which in matters relating to tort or delict gives exceptional jurisdiction to the courts of the place 'where the harmful event occurred'.[240] But it cannot be assumed that this is always the general rule. In US law there is some doubt as to whether it is constitutional to assert jurisdiction when injury in the United States is merely fortuitous, and there are no other significant connecting factors, such as the place of business. If product liability cases are an apt analogy, which is far from certain, it would be necessary to show some 'purposeful direction' of transboundary pollutants, for example by locating a smelter or nuclear plant close to a border.[241]

A plaintiff who litigates where the damage occurs, rather than where the defendant is located, may also have to overcome the defence of sovereign immunity, if the enterprise responsible for the damage is part of a foreign state rather than a separate entity. Some states now deny immunity from suit where the tort is deemed to have taken place within their own territory, or where it is not committed 'in the exercise of sovereign authority'.[242] The latter point could be relied on to exclude immunity for most industrial activities on the ground that they are *iure gestionis*, which is the view taken by German and Austrian courts when the Soviet Union was sued in respect of the Chernobyl disaster.[243] Schreuer notes that a rigid requirement that the act or omission alleged to constitute a non-immune tort take place entirely within the territory of the forum, as required by Article 12 of the 2004 UN Convention on State Immunity,

---

[237] E.g. 2000 EC Regulation Regulation on Jurisdiction and Judgments, Article 2. See generally McLachlan and Nygh (eds), *Transnational Tort Litigation* (Oxford, 1996) esp Chs 1, 4, 12.

[238] *Pakootas v Teck Cominco Metals Ltd* 452 F 3d 1066 (2006). See generally Hsu and Parrish, 48 *VJIL* (2007) 1.

[239] See *infra*, Ch 7. [240] 2000 EC Regulation on Jurisdiction and Judgments, Article 5.

[241] See *Ohio v Wyandotte Chemicals Corp* 401 US 493 (1971); *Asahi Metal Co. Ltd v Superior Court* 480 US 102 (1987); Am Law Inst, *2nd Restatement: Conflict of Laws* (1971) § 37, on which see Juenger, in McLachlan and Nygh, *Transnational Tort Litigation*, 201ff, and McLachlan, ibid, 17.

[242] See for example UK State Immunity Act, 1978, ss 3(3)(c), 5; US Foreign Sovereigns Immunity Act, 28 USCA s 1605; Schreuer, *Sovereign Immunity* (Cambridge, 1988) Ch 3.

[243] ILA Conference Report (1992) *Second Report on State Immunity*, 11; Rest, 24 *EPL* (1994) 173. Note however that the nuclear liability conventions require immunities to be waived: see *infra*, Ch 9.

would continue to allow immunity in cases of transboundary harm. At the same time, for jurisdictional purposes, international judicial decisions and state practice generally give territoriality a more extended definition under which it is sufficient if the effects are present in the forum state.[244]

One important consequence of the variety of jurisdictional rules applicable to transboundary tort cases is that the courts of several countries may have concurrent jurisdiction. In this situation, and subject to the exercise of any discretion to dismiss on *forum non conveniens* grounds, the plaintiff will have a choice of jurisdiction in which to proceed: in effect to go 'forum shopping'. Giving the plaintiff the choice of where to sue recognizes that a transboundary environmental tort will generally if not invariably involve elements located within at least two jurisdictions.

In the European Union and European Economic Area such a choice is provided by Article 5 of the Regulation on Jurisdiction and Judgments, which, as we have seen, allows an action in tort to be brought 'in the courts of the place where the harmful event occurred'. As interpreted by the ECJ in the case of *Handelskwekerij GJ Bier v Mines de Potasse d'Alsace*[245] this means both the place where the harmful effects are felt, and where the harmful activity is located. Article 5 was used in this case to enable Dutch plaintiffs to proceed in the Dutch courts against a French mining company whose polluting activities in France caused loss downstream to crops in Holland. The same article would also have allowed them to opt for suit in France, where the mine was located, or under Article 2 in the defendant's domicile, also France. The German Environmental Liability Act of 1990 also gives the plaintiff a choice of forum in transboundary pollution cases.[246]

At this point it is not proposed to consider how the plaintiff chooses the forum in which to sue, but merely to confine our attention to the advantages and disadvantages of forum shopping as an element in a regional or international system of transboundary environmental justice. Its virtues in an environmental context are fairly obvious: the plaintiff decides which system offers the most advantageous procedural and substantive rules and remedies, and thereby maximizes the chances of recovery. But the problems are also obvious: making this choice is no easy task, it adds to the complexity and expense of the case, and is further complicated if the question of choice of law to be applied in each jurisdiction is also uncertain.

Moreover, there are certain advantages and disadvantages inherent in particular jurisdictional preferences. The forum in which the harmful activity is located is the

---

[244] Schreuer, *Sovereign Immunity*, 61, but cf *Handelskwekerij GJ Bier v Mines de Potasse d'Alsace*, Case 21/76, II ECR (1976) 1735, and *Lotus Case* (1927) PCIJ Ser A, No 10. See generally Fox, *The Law of State Immunity* (Oxford, 2002) 51–64.

[245] Case 21/76, II *ECR* (1976) 1735. See also *Shevill v Presse Alliance SA* [1995] 2 WLR 499 in which the same interpretation of Article 5 was applied to a transboundary defamation case.

[246] Hoffman, 38 *NILR* (1991) 27. So do the 1962 Nuclear Ships Convention, and the 1977 Convention on Civil Liability for Oil Pollution Damage Resulting from Sea-bed Exploration or Exploitation of Submarine Mineral Resources, neither of which is likely ever to enter into force.

one best able to handle multiple suits against a single defendant; courts in this position can more easily obtain evidence of fault and discovery of documents, grant and enforce preventive remedies, and apply limits on liability and insurance requirements. Against this, as observed earlier, are the problems of unfamiliarity, language, etc of proceeding in a foreign forum.

The forum in which the damage is suffered is best placed to assess that harm, and this is why the 1969 Convention on Civil Liability for Oil Pollution Damage opted for this choice.[247] But it is harder then to enforce remedies against a foreign defendant, to obtain evidence, and to handle multiple suits rationally if the damage affects several states. The possibility in Europe of a single transboundary pollution incident giving rise to suits in a variety of jurisdictions points to the impracticability of this kind of forum shopping for any business attempting to order its affairs so as to comply with its legal responsibilities: it will never be able to predict with certainty where it may be sued or by what laws it will be judged. This is not an approach which benefits access to environmental justice. Moreover, a foreign defendant may have no assets within the jurisdiction of the court or, in the case of ships or nuclear installations, the defendant's main or only asset may have been lost in the accident giving rise to the proceedings. Although a judgment or injunction may be recognized and enforced in other countries, this can only be guaranteed where there are appropriate treaty provisions in force.[248]

A much better variant of the *Handelskwekerij* approach is found in the 1993 Council of Europe Convention on Civil Liability for Damage Resulting from Activities Dangerous to the Environment, considered further below. This convention gives the plaintiff a choice of jurisdiction, but avoids problems of choice of law by providing for harmonization of national laws on a basis of strict liability and by defining what forms of damage are actionable. If widely ratified it would achieve what the EC's Regulation on Jurisdiction and Judgments does not do: create a common regime of liability for environmental damage regardless of where the action is brought.[249] Thus consideration of the forms of transboundary justice becomes ultimately inseparable from the substance of the law. This leads us to consider the role of harmonization of national law on liability for environmental damage.

---

[247] *Infra*, Ch 7.

[248] But the treaty provision is now extensive: see 2000 EC Regulation on Jurisdiction and Judgments; 1993 Convention on Civil Liability for Damage Resulting From Activities Dangerous to the Environment, Article 23; 1992 Convention on Civil Liability for Oil Pollution Damage, Article 10; 1997 Vienna Convention on Civil Liability for Nuclear Damage, Article 12. On the position where there is no treaty see Lowenfeld, *International Litigation and the Quest for Reasonableness* (Oxford, 1996) Ch 6, and on Europe see Kennet, *The Enforcement of Judgments in Europe* (Oxford, 2000).

[249] But see Directive 2004/35/EC of 21 April 2004 on environmental liability with regard to the prevention and remedying of environmental damage, OJ 2004 L 143/56 (30/4/2004).

4 HARMONIZATION OF ENVIRONMENTAL LIABILITY

4(1) INTRODUCTION

Harmonization of national law on environmental liability, both at the substantive and procedural levels, serves three principal roles. First, it provides a common minimum standard for all legal systems. To that extent it is another means for ensuring the provision of 'effective access to judicial and administrative proceedings, including redress and remedy' required by Principle 10 of the Rio Declaration and considered in previous sections of this chapter. Second, harmonization has an important role in any scheme for transboundary access to justice. It can mitigate the conflict of laws problems referred to above, and contributes to the creation of shared expectations on a regional basis. If the principal criteria for assessing progress towards environmental justice are the reduction of unpredictability, complexity, and cost, balancing the interests of plaintiffs in the widest possible choice of law and jurisdiction against the interests of defendants in ordering their affairs in an environmentally responsible manner, then greater harmonization, at least at regional level, remains a desirable goal. Third, it can help promote implementation of the polluter-pays principle referred to in Principle 16 of the Rio Declaration and considered below.

Transboundary litigation will only be fully effective in environmental cases if common minimum standards apply regardless of where the proceedings are brought. The issues which need to be addressed in this context include the following:

- Liability: is it based on fault, strict liability or absolute liability?
- Remedies: to what extent are compensation for environmental damage, restoration costs, and injunctive relief available?
- Recognition and enforcement of judgments: can the defendant's assets be reached and his activities controlled outside the territory of the forum?
- Compensation funds: are these necessary to allow adequate recovery in cases of serious loss?

Several examples of harmonization of civil liability already exist, including conventions dealing with pollution damage from ships and nuclear accidents. Although there are differences in detail, their main elements are (in most cases) a common scheme of strict liability for all parties, liability channelled to the owner or operator, limited in amount and supported by compulsory insurance and compensation funds. These conventions are examined in more detail in Chapters 7 and 9, but they have the merits of clarity, predictability, and relative simplicity for the plaintiff. No problems of forum-shopping or choice of law arise, the schemes are operational and they provide an assurance that any compensation awarded will be recovered. They are important precedents for the sort of provision necessary to make such risks internationally acceptable, although they raise questions about the distribution of loss. None of the schemes follows the polluter-pays principle in full. Instead the burden of major losses is borne partly by the operator, partly by the industry or state concerned, and beyond that it falls on the innocent victim, or must be recovered in interstate claims. It is in these circumstances that state responsibility retains an important subsidiary role, as we saw in Chapter 4. Although compensation limits have not always been realistic, civil liability conventions of this kind afford litigants significant benefits when compared with equal access to national remedies.[250]

Principle 13 of the Rio Declaration calls on states to develop national law regarding liability and compensation for pollution victims and other environmental damage, and also requires them to cooperate 'in a more expeditious and determined manner' to develop international law in this respect. Some progress has been made in implementing Principle 13. The conventions on oil pollution damage and nuclear accidents have been strengthened,[251] and new treaties or protocols on liability for hazardous and noxious substances, wastes, and bunker fuel oil have been adopted.[252] There is a liability annex to the Antarctic Protocol,[253] and attempts have been made to reach international agreement on civil liability for other potential hazards, including the adoption of draft principles by the ILC in 2006, considered below.[254] One key issue is the extent to which there can be liability for environmental damage not otherwise included under categories of property loss or personal injury. Here Articles 2(7)–(10) of the 1993 Lugano Convention on Civil Liability provide a useful model, and these provisions build on those already found in a number of other liability conventions.[255]

---

[250] For an overview, see Boyle, 17 *JEL* (2005) 3; Xue, *Transboundary Damage in International Law* (Cmbridge, 2003) Ch 2.

[251] See *infra*, Chs 7, 9.

[252] 1996 Convention on Liability and Compensation for the Carriage of Hazardous and Noxious Substances by Sea, *infra*, Ch 7; 1999 Protocol on Liability and Compensation for Damage Resulting from the Transboundary Movements of Hazardous Wastes, *infra*, Ch 8; 2001 Convention on Civil Liability for Bunker Oil Pollution Damage, *infra*, Ch 7.

[253] Annex VI, adopted in 2005. See Bederman and Keskar, 19 *Emory Int LR* (2005) 1383; de La Fayette, in Triggs and Riddell (eds), *Antarctica: Legal and Environmental Changes* (London, 2007) 109.

[254] On GMOs see 2000 Biosafety Protocol, Article 27.

[255] Other conventions which also cover liability for environmental damage include 1989 Convention on Civil Liability for Damage Caused During Carriage of Dangerous Goods by Road etc, Article 1(10); 1992 Convention on Civil Liability for Oil Pollution Damage, Article 6; 1996 Convention on Liability and Compensation for Damage in Connection with the Carriage of Hazardous and Noxious Substances by Sea; 1997 Protocol to the Vienna Convention on Civil Liability for Nuclear Damage, Article 2(2), (4); 1999 Protocol on Liability and Compensation for Damage Resulting from Transboundary Movements of Hazardous Waste; 2001 Convention on Civil Liability for Bunker Oil Pollution Damage; 2003 Protocol on Civil Liability and Compensation for Damage Caused by the Transboundary Effects of Industrial Accidents on Transboundary Waters; 2005 Annex VI to the Protocol to the Antarctic Treaty on Environmental Protection, Article 6(1). See de La Fayette, in Bowman and Boyle, *Environmental Damage in International and Comparative Law* (Oxford, 2002) Ch 9; and *infra*, Chs 7, 9.

Sceptics rightly question whether liability treaties have had much impact on industry or contribute to improving environmental standards.[256] Lack of participation is a problem with many of the newer liability schemes; at best it casts serious doubt on their acceptability or relevance, and on the wisdom of negotiating any more of them.[257] The prospect of possibly extensive changes to national tort law is one reason for this hesitation; the selective application of strict liability in some areas but not others is another, insofar as it challenges fundamental concepts of national law and is incompatible with a principled approach to tort law as a whole. This is an area in which some serious rethinking is overdue.[258]

4(2) THE 1993 LUGANO CONVENTION

The Council of Europe's Convention on Civil Liability for Damage Resulting from Activities Dangerous to the Environment[259] is the only existing scheme for comprehensive harmonization of environmental liability, in Europe, or elsewhere. It imposes a common scheme of strict liability for dangerous activities or dangerous substances on the operator of the activity in question. Liability is not limited in amount and thus reflects the polluter-pays principle more closely than other treaties under which the loss is spread. 'Damage' is widely defined and covers impairment of the environment, as well as injury to persons and property. For this purpose the 'environment' is also broadly defined and includes natural resources, cultural heritage areas, and 'characteristic aspects of the landscape'. However, apart from loss of profit, recovery of compensation for environmental impairment is limited to the costs of 'reasonable measures of prevention and reinstatement actually undertaken or to be undertaken'. Reinstatement includes the introduction 'where reasonable' of the equivalent of destroyed or damaged elements of the environment, for example where exact restoration is impossible. Possible defences to liability include war, hostilities, exceptional and irresistible natural phenomena, and act of a third party. Administrative authorization is not a defence, but 'tolerable' pollution is not actionable. The liability of the operator is assured by compulsory insurance. Jurisdiction is based on the provisions of the EC Regulation on Jurisdiction and Judgments. This is a sophisticated scheme, but it has attracted few ratifications, and appears likely to have little impact unless the EC decides to participate. The Lugano Convention provided an obvious model for the ILC to draw upon in its attempts to codify principles of liability (considered below) but the main risk, had the Commission tried to follow this approach, was that it would prove over-prescriptive and result in an outcome unwelcome to many states. If such a solution is unappealing even in Europe what chance of success would it have elsewhere?

---

[256] See Brunnée, 53 *ICLQ* (2004) 351; Bergkamp, *Liability and the Environment: Private and Public Law Aspects of Civil Liability for Environmental Harm in an International Context* (The Hague, 2001).

[257] Churchill, 12 *YbIEL* (2001) 3.   [258] See Sachs, 55 *UCLALR* (2008) 837.

[259] See *Explanatory Report*, in Council of Europe CDCJ (92) 50; Bianchi, 6 *JEL* (1994) 21, 26–32.

4(3) ILC PRINCIPLES ON ALLOCATION OF LOSS FOR TRANSBOUNDARY DAMAGE

Draft principles on liability and compensation for environmental damage were finally adopted by the ILC in 2006 after many years of deliberation.[260] Rather than making states directly liable in international law as originally envisaged,[261] the Commission's final text provides for states to make the polluter liable to transboundary victims in national law. The principles apply only to damage occurring on the territory of another state or in some other place under its jurisdiction or control.[262] In contrast to the Lugano Convention they do not as such require or envisage a general harmonization of national law relating to environmental damage, but in practice that will necessarily be the outcome to some extent.

At the heart of its scheme is an international standard of liability which affects not only compensation for damage but also the procedures and remedies through which it is to be obtained. Principle 6(1) sets out the core principle of prompt, adequate and effective compensation:

"States shall provide their domestic judicial and administrative bodies with the necessary jurisdiction and competence and ensure that these bodies have prompt, adequate and effective remedies available in the event of transboundary damage caused by hazardous activities located within their territory or otherwise under their jurisdiction or control."

Underlying this formulation is the understanding that non-discriminatory access to national remedies may not be enough to satisfy an international standard of access to justice.[263] The Commission refers to the *Trail Smelter Arbitration* as authority, noting that 'the basic principle established in that case entailed a duty of a State to ensure payment of prompt and adequate compensation for any transboundary damage'.[264] Moreover, in requiring 'effective redress', 'adequate and effective remedies', or 'prompt and adequate compensation or other relief', Principle 10 of the Rio Declaration, Article 9(4) of the Aarhus Convention, and Article 235(2) of the 1982 Law of the Sea Convention all suggest that there are international standards of compensation and remedy for victims of environmental damage. As we saw earlier, the failure of a state to provide adequate redress to its own citizens for pollution or other forms of damage

---

[260] ILC Report (2006) GAOR A/61/10, paras 51–67. For preparatory work see *ILC Report* (2004) GAOR A/59/10, paras 158–76; *ILC Report* (2003) GAOR A/58/10, paras 154–231; *ILC Report* (2002) GAOR A/57/10, paras 430–57; Special Rapporteur Rao's 1st Report (2003) A/CN 4/531; 2nd Report (2004) A/CN 4/540; 3rd Report (2006) A/CN 4/566.

[261] *Supra,* Ch 4, section 2.

[262] Principle 2. E.g. occupied territory such as present day Iraq or Palestine. See *Namibia Advisory Opinion* (1971) ICJ Reports 16; *Advisory Opinion on Legal Consequences of the Construction of a Wall in the Occupied Palestinian Territory* (2004) ICJ Reports, para 139.

[263] Compare ILA, *67th Conference Report* (1996) 401–15, International Watercourses, Article 2(1): 'States, individually or jointly, shall ensure the availability of *prompt, adequate and effective* administrative and judicial remedies for persons in another State who suffer or may suffer damage…' (emphasis added).

[264] *ILC Report* (2004) GAOR A/59/10, International Liability, commentary to Principle 4, para 11. See also commentary to Principle 6, para 7.

may in sufficiently serious cases also violate the rights to life, health, private life, property, and freedom to dispose of natural resources under international human-rights
agreements.[265] An alternative foundation would draw from precedents on the taking
of property in international law, making an obvious analogy with damage by pollution.[266] These precedents all show that Principle 6(1) builds on existing law. This
element of the ILC scheme could represent its most significant contribution to the
progressive development of the subject. The rest of the scheme then goes on to set
out a model for transboundary liability drawn from existing civil liability conventions. These elements are essentially optional and open to implementation in a variety
of ways.

Three important points about allocation of loss stand out when comparing the ILC
Principles to existing civil liability and compensation schemes. First, strict liability
is the universally accepted standard,[267] albeit with minor variations in the permitted defences. The ILC commentary accepts the argument that hazardous activities
carry inherent risks and that it would be unjust and inappropriate to require proof
of fault when accidents happen. It notes the adoption of strict liability in treaties and
in national law, and on this point refers to its own draft as 'a measure of progressive development of international law'.[268] Second, as the examples of the Bunker Fuel
Convention and the Protocol on Liability for Transboundary Waste show, channelling
liability to a single owner or operator is not always a realistic option, and the choice
of 'owner/operator liability' without more would represent in some cases too simplistic a solution without a broader definition of these terms.[269] Significantly, while the
ILC scheme chooses to focus liability on operators, it also allows for alternatives. The
'operator' of the harmful activity should be primarily liable, not the state, but 'where
appropriate' liability may be imposed on some other person or entity.[270] In practice
the Commission's draft seems to assume that there may be more than one operator
and, by implication, that liability may be joint and several. Third, while most liability
schemes spread the burden of loss through additional compensation funds,[271] each
scheme has its own unique funding arrangements. There is no common pattern. In

---

[265] *SERAC v Nigeria* (2002) ACHPR Comm 155/96 (2002) para 69; *Maya Indigenous Community of the Toledo District v Belize*, Case 12.053, Report No 40/04, IACHR OEA/Ser L/V/II.122 Doc 5 rev 1 (2004); *Fadeyeva v Russia* [2005] ECHR 376; *Taskin v Turkey* [2006] 42 EHRR 50, para 119. See above.

[266] See for example *Sporrong and Lonnroth v Sweden* (1983) 5 EHRR 617, where planning blight was held to constitute a taking of property without compensation, contrary to Article 1, Protocol 1 of the European Convention on Human Rights. The 'prompt, adequate and effective' standard of compensation for expropri-ation is not universally accepted, however. See Amerasinghe, 41 *ICLQ* (1992) 22.

[267] See ILC Principle 4. But the 2003 Kiev Protocol retains additional fault-based liability as provided for by national law. See also 1992 CLC, Articles 3, 5(2); 1993 Lugano Convention, Article 8(b) and 1999 Protocol on Liability for Transboundary Waste.

[268] *ILC Report* (2004) commentary to Principle 4, paras 15–17.

[269] The 2001 Bunker Fuel Convention makes the shipowner, charterer, manager and operator jointly and severally liable. Under the 1999 Transboundary Waste Protocol generators, exporters, importers and disposers are all potentially liable at different stages of the wastes' journey to its eventual destination.

[270] ILC Principle 4.

[271] The 1993 Lugano Convention and the 2003 Kiev Protocol are notable exceptions.

some cases, states carry the ultimate burden of residual compensation funding, as well as a residual liability in the event of operator insolvency; in others the costs are borne wholly by industry. This makes them difficult models from which to derive any general scheme of loss allocation that might secure universal agreement beyond the proposition that some such provision should be made. It may also suggest that different contexts require different solutions. Again, the ILC scheme allows for such diversity. In 'appropriate cases' additional compensation funding should be provided by industry, or if necessary by States.[272]

The Commission's text also replicates the definition of 'environmental damage' in the more modern liability treaties, and is consistent with the practice of the UNCC and developments in national law.[273] Thus draft Principle 2(a) expressly includes damage to cultural property, the costs of reasonable measures of reinstatement of the environment, and reasonable response measures. In one respect the ILC Principles are potentially more progressive, however, because Principle 2(a)(iii) envisages liability for environmental damage per se, unrelated to the cost of response or restoration measures.[274] While some national laws already allow recovery of compensation for pure environmental damage, no previous liability agreement has gone this far.[275] The Commission says nothing on the question of valuation of such damage, although it notes that damages awarded do not have a punitive function. It defines 'victim' as the person or state that suffers damage, but its commentary notes that the term can include groups of local authorities, NGOs, or public trustees.[276]

While the 2006 ILC Principles as a whole cannot be viewed as an exercise in codifying customary international law, they show how the Commission has made use of general principles of law as 'an indication of policy and principle'.[277] The draft successfully reflects the modern development of civil-liability treaties, without in any way compromising or altering those which presently exist, or the right of victims to sue in their own state.[278] This is a notable achievement, but it may also be a double-edged attribute. On the one hand it is prudent to build on what states themselves have already negotiated. On the other, the reluctance of states to ratify those same treaties may indicate a

---

[272] ILC Principle 7.

[273] *ILC Report* (2004) commentary to Principle 2, paras 1–21. For fuller analysis of recent trends see Bowman and Boyle (eds), *Environmental Damage in International and Comparative Law.*

[274] *ILC Report* (2004) commentary to Principle 2, para 12; *ILC Report* (2006) commentary to Principle 2, paras (13)–(15). See also Special Rapporteur's *2nd Report*, para 31.

[275] Compare 2004 Protocol to Amend the Paris Convention on Third Party Liability in the Field of Nuclear Energy, Article IB; 1992 Convention on Civil Liability for Oil Pollution Damage, Article 1(6); de La Fayette, 20 *IJMCL* (2005) 167, 202–5, and see generally Bowman and Boyle, *Environmental Damage in International and Comparative Law*, 213–322.

[276] *ILC Report* (2004) commentary to Principle 3, paras 3–6; *ILC Report* (2006) commentary to Principle 2, paras (11)–(14), (29)–(30). The focus on 'victims' reflects Principle 13 of the 1992 Rio Declaration on Environment and Development. Compare the 2005 Antarctic Liability Annex under which states parties may sue the operator for the cost of environmental response and cleanup measures, but not for environmental damage per se. For comprehensive analysis of valuation of environmental damage and standing to sue see Brans, *Liability for Damage to Public Natural Resources* (The Hague, 2001).

[277] See *South West Africa, Advisory Opinion*, ICJ Reports (1950) 128, sep op Lord McNair, 148.

[278] See Principles 6(3), 7.

less than wholehearted commitment to the idea of shifting the focus away from state responsibility for transboundary harm in favour of civil liability and individual access to justice. Given the unwillingness of states to extend their own liability on a non-fault basis, it is difficult to see what other choice the Commission could have made.

4(4) LIABILITY AND THE POLLUTER PAYS PRINCIPLE

The 'polluter-pays' principle is essentially an economic policy for allocating the costs of pollution or environmental damage borne by public authorities, but it also has implications for the development of international and national law on liability for damage. As defined by OECD in a series of recommendations starting in the 1970s,[279] the principle entailed that the polluter should bear the expense of carrying out measures decided by public authorities to ensure that the environment is in an 'acceptable state' and that 'the cost of these measures should be reflected in the cost of goods and services which cause pollution in production and or in consumption'. The purpose of OECD policy and recommendations on the subject was thus to internalize the economic costs of pollution control, clean-up and protection measures, and to ensure that governments did not distort international trade and investment by subsidizing these environmental costs.

It was not until the UNCED Conference that the polluter-pays principle for the first time secured international support as an environmental policy. Principle 16 of the Rio Declaration provides, in somewhat qualified terms, that:

National authorities should endeavour to promote the internalisation of environmental costs and the use of economic instruments, taking into account the approach that the polluter should, in principle, bear the cost of pollution, with due regard to the public interest and without distorting international trade and investment.[280]

Given this wording, it cannot be said that the polluter-pays principle is intended to be legally binding. Principle 16 simply lacks the normative character of a rule of law.[281]

---

[279] OECD, Recommendations C (72) 128 (1972); C (74) 223 (1974) reprinted in OECD, *OECD and the Environment*, (Paris, 1986) and C (89) 88 (1988) reprinted in 28 *ILM* (1989) 1320. See generally OECD, *The Polluter Pays Principle*, OCDE/GD(92)81 (1992); Smets, 97 *RGDIP* (1993) 339; id, in Campiglio, Pineschi, Siniscalco, and Treves (eds), *The Environment After Rio* (London, 1994) 131; de Sadeleer, *Environmental Principles: From Political Slogans to Legal Rules* (Oxford, 2002) 21–59.

[280] See generally Atapattu, *Emerging Principles of IEL* (Ardsley, 2006) Ch 6. The principle is defined in broadly similar terms in the 1992 Paris Convention, the 1992 Helsinki Convention on Transboundary Watercourses, the 1995 Barcelona Convention, and the 1996 Protocol to the London Dumping Convention. See also 1991 European Energy Charter, Article 19(1). Other treaties simply refer to the polluter pays principle without attempting to define it.

[281] See *North Sea Continental Shelf Case*, ICJ Reports (1969) 3, para 72. Cf *Rhine Chlorides Convention Arbitral Award* (France/Netherlands) PCA (2004) para 103: 'Le Tribunal observe que ce principe figure dans certains instruments internationaux, tant bilatéraux que multilatéraux, et se situe à des niveaux d'effectivité variables. Sans nier son importance en droit conventionnel, le Tribunal ne pense pas que ce principe fasse partie du droit international général.' However, the preambles to the 1990 Oil Pollution Preparedness and Response Convention, the 1992 UNECE Convention on the Transboundary Effects of Industrial Accidents,

Moreover, while some treaties require parties to 'apply the polluter pays principle',[282] others use the softer language of guidance.[283] The principle only appears in a limited range of post-Rio treaties dealing with pollution of international watercourses, marine pollution, transboundary industrial accidents, and energy. Although there are examples where it has been used more broadly in national environmental policy and legislation,[284] it is impossible to point to any general pattern of state practice. Implementation has largely been left to national rather than international action. As a result, both the choice of methods—taxation, charges, liability laws—and the degree of implementation, have been very variable, and few states have been fully consistent in their policy.[285] The most that can be said is that states, intergovernmental regulatory institutions and courts can and should take account of the principle in the development of environmental law and policy, but they are in no sense bound by international law to 'make polluters pay'. Moreover, reference to the public interest in Principle 16 leaves ample room for exceptions and thus for continued governmental subsidy. As adopted at Rio, the polluter-pays principle is neither absolute nor obligatory.

How then could the polluter-pays principle be used and developed in its more limited incarnation as a guiding principle? This is a more difficult question than it might first appear. Taxation is a relatively crude way to recoup the external costs of environmentally harmful activities. Charges to meet the cost of preventing, reducing, or restoring environmental damage can be more accurately targeted, but their impact in deterring environmentally harmful activities will vary. As experience with charging for disposal of oily residues from ships shows, charges can be counter-productive if they make the polluter more likely to evade environmental protection measures in order to cut costs. The US practice of attempting to internalize environmental costs by making the polluter rather than public agencies directly responsible for conducting the clean-up and restoration after accidents such as the *Exxon Valdez* may also be counter-productive if the result is a dilatory and inadequate response. Charges and taxes cannot easily be targeted at accidental damage, nor can they be applied to transboundary polluters. In this sort of case there may be no practical alternative to

and the 2003 Kiev Protocol on Liability for Pollution of Transboundary Waters and Lakes describe the 'polluter pays' principle as a 'general principle of international environmental law'.

[282] 1992 Paris Convention for the Protection of the Marine Environment of the NE Atlantic, Article 2(2)(b); 1992 Helsinki Convention on the Protection of the Marine Environment of the Baltic Sea Area, Article 3(4); 1994 Danube River Protection Convention, Article 2(4); 1995 Barcelona Convention for the Protection of the Marine Environment and the Coastal Region of the Mediterranean, Article 4.

[283] 1990 Convention on Oil Pollution Preparedness, Response and Cooperation, Preamble; 1992 Helsinki Convention on the Protection and Use of Transboundary Watercourses and Lakes, Article 2(5); 1996 Protocol to the London Dumping Convention, Article 3; 1999 Convention on the Protection of the Rhine, Article 4.

[284] See e.g. Article 174 of the EC Treaty, which provides that 'Action by the Community relating to the environment shall be based on the principles that preventive action should be taken, that environmental damage should as a priority be rectified at source and that the polluter should pay'. See Jans, *European Environmental Law* (London, 1995) 23–5.

[285] On environmental taxes and trade see *infra*, Ch 14.

state-organised action, with the taxpayer recovering the costs through liability laws and compensation schemes.

Thus full implementation of a polluter-pays approach may entail consideration of civil liability and compensation, especially if accidental damage to the environment is to be included.[286] The commentary on the ILC's 2006 draft principles on allocation of loss notes that: 'The Commission considers the polluter-pays principle as an essential component in underpinning the present draft principles to ensure that victims that suffer harm as a result of an incident involving a hazardous activity are able to obtain prompt and adequate compensation'.[287] Individual civil-liability actions are limited by the need to identify specific polluters, although this problem can be eased by the willingness of courts to impose joint liability on multiple tortfeasors, for example in cases of air pollution damage.[288] The extent to which civil liability then makes the polluter pay for environmental damage will depend on a variety of factors. If liability is based on negligence, not only does this have to be proved, but harm which is neither reasonably foreseeable nor avoidable will not be compensated and the victim or the taxpayer, not the polluter, will bear the loss. Strict liability is a better approximation of the polluter-pays principle, but not if limited in amount, as in internationally agreed schemes involving oil tankers or nuclear installations.[289] The limit for environmental damage in Antarctica is a mere 3 million SDRs: rather less than the sum paid by the USSR to Canada for clean-up costs after the Cosmos 954 satellite crashed in the Arctic.[290] Moreover, a narrow definition of damage may exclude environmental losses which cannot easily be quantified in monetary terms, such as wildlife, or which affect the quality of the environment without causing actual physical damage. An illustration of this problem is the case of *Merlin v BNFL*[291] where a house was rendered radioactive but the operator of the installation responsible was absolved from liability because there had been no damage to property within the terms of the statute, despite the building's loss of market value. A significant amount of environmental injury is likely to remain uncompensated under civil liability in English law, and the same is true of some other legal systems, though not uniformly.[292] To this extent the polluter remains free to off-load certain environmental costs even under a strict liability regime.

---

[286] See OECD, *The Polluter Pays Principle*, but cf Smets, 97 *RGDIP* (1993) 339.

[287] ILC Report (2006) International Liability, commentary to the preamble, at para (2). See also the commentary to Principle 3 where the ILC's view is set out more fully.

[288] *Michie v Great Lakes Steel Division* 495 F 2d 213 (1974); Ianni, 11 *CYIL* (1973) 258.

[289] See 1992 Conventions on Civil Liability for Oil Pollution Damage and on the Establishment of an International Fund for Compensation for Oil Pollution Damage, *infra*, Ch 7; 1960 Paris Convention on Third Party Liability in the Field of Nuclear Energy and 1997 Vienna Convention on Civil Liability for Nuclear Damage, *infra*, Ch 9.

[290] Annex VI to the Antarctic Environmental Protocol, Article 9. See *supra*, Ch 4.

[291] [1990] 2 QB 557. But compare *Blue Circle Industries Plc v Ministry of Defence* [1998] 3 All ER 385.

[292] See also s 1 of the German Environmental Liability Act, 1990 which confines liability to cases of 'death, personal injury or property damage'. Cf the more generous approach to environmental compensation under the 1990 US Oil Pollution Act, s 1006(d)(1) and under US tort law, on which see *Commonwealth of Puerto Rico v SS Zoe Colocotroni* 628 F 2d 652 (1980). See also 2006 ILC Loss Allocation Principles, *infra*, section 4(3).

A more fundamental problem with broader use of the polluter-pays principle is that it does not indicate who is the polluter, and cannot as such determine liability.[293] OECD and the ILC treat the operator of a hazardous installation as the 'polluter' in cases of accidental damage.[294] On this view the operator of an oil tanker is the polluter and should be responsible if the ship sinks. But it can equally be said that the cargo causes the damage and that the cargo owner is in that sense the polluter. Sensibly, the present internationally agreed scheme of liability and compensation for oil pollution treats both the ship's owner and the cargo owner as sharing responsibility, while excluding the liability of any other potential defendant in order to facilitate recovery by plaintiffs.[295] In this case what matters is *how* the responsibility is shared, and how the compensation is funded: asking who the polluter is will not answer these questions, nor will it do so in other complex transactions such as the carriage of hazardous wastes, a point fully recognized by the ILC draft principles on allocation of loss.[296]

An altogether different problem arises in the case of nuclear accidents. Here it is usually clear who the polluter is—the operator of the nuclear installation—but the adoption of a strict polluter-pays approach to liability is simply not economically feasible, and would not be in the public interest. In the event of a serious accident, the scale of absolute and unlimited liability would be uninsurable and quickly bankrupt even the largest utility company. Unless the losses are to fall mainly on the innocent victims, some other approach to allocating them must be found, almost certainly by involving other states which use nuclear power. Thus in Western Europe the uninsured risks are borne first by the state in which the installation is located and then above a certain level by a compensation fund to which participating governments contribute in proportion to their installed nuclear capacity and GNP.[297] In this case the basic concept is not one of making the polluter pay but of an equitable sharing of the risk, with a large element of state subsidy. An even more extensive departure from the polluter-pays principle has emerged with regard to Eastern European nuclear installations. The costs of remedial measures are so high, and the local economies so weak, that Western European governments, who represent one large group of potential victims of any accident, have funded the work needed to improve safety standards. The same approach has reluctantly been adopted by the Dutch and other riparians on the Rhine in order to persuade the French to reduce pollution from their potassium mines.[298] Here, it is in effect the victim who pays.

---

[293] Smets, 97 *RGDIP* (1993) 339, 357.

[294] See Rec C (89) 88 (1989) and OECD, *The Polluter Pays Principle*.

[295] See *infra*, Ch 7, section 6.

[296] See *infra*, section 4; 1999 Protocol on Liability and Compensation for the Transboundary Movement of Hazardous Wastes, *infra*, Ch 8, section 4, and the 1996 Convention on Liability and Compensation for the Carriage of Hazardous and Noxious Substances by Sea, *infra*, Ch 7, section 6(2).

[297] 1960 Paris Convention on Third Party Liability in the Field of Nuclear Energy and 1963 Brussels Supplementary Agreement, on which see *infra*, Ch 9.

[298] 1976 Convention for the Protection of the Rhine from Pollution by Chlorides, on which see *infra*, Ch 10. For a general survey of this approach to the funding of environmental measures see OECD Environment

Thus the polluter-pays principle and the general policy of internalizing environmental costs cannot be treated as a rigid rule of universal application, nor are the means used to implement it going to be the same in all cases. A great deal of flexibility will be inevitable, taking full account of differences in the nature of the risk and the economic feasibility of full internalization of environmental costs in industries whose capacity to bear them will vary. As one author comments, 'The main difficulty with the full internalisation policy is that it cannot be implemented in practice unless some agreement is reached on the respective rights of the polluters and the victims'.[299] No doubt considerations of this kind account for the heavily qualified nature of Principle 16 of the Rio Declaration. Whatever its legal status, or its relationship to sustainable development, the polluter-pays principle cannot supply guidance on the content of national or international liability without further definition.

5 CORPORATE ENVIRONMENTAL ACCOUNTABILITY

Corporations are entitled to the protection of human-rights treaties and can also sue and be sued in transboundary litigation before national courts in the same way as individuals. As we have seen in the previous section, they may be held liable for transboundary environmental damage in the courts of the state where they are domiciled, the state where they conduct business, and the state where their activities cause environmental damage.[300] In reality, multinational corporations not infrequently escape effective accountability for their activities, especially in those countries where regulation is weak, enforcement lax, the judicial system ineffective, the government corrupt, or simply inadequate. But even where none of these problems exist, in order to encourage and protect foreign investment, developing states may have to conclude bilateral investment treaties (BITs) which restrict their ability to regulate foreign investors, who can if necessary resort to binding arbitration in case of breach. Regulatory measures designed to protect the environment have in some cases been treated by arbitrators as expropriation of property—a 'regulatory taking'.[301] Some of the more recent BITs are intended to avoid such outcomes provided the regulatory measures

Committee, *The Use of International Financial Transfers in Resolving Transfrontier and Global Pollution Problems*, ENV/EC (90) 25 (1990).

[299] Smets, in Campliglio, Pinsechi, Siniscalco, and Treves (eds), *The Environment After Rio* (London, 1994) 131.

[300] See generally Muchlinski, *Multinational Enterprises and the Law* (2nd edn, Oxford, 2007); Sornarajah, *The Interrnational Law of Foreign Investment* (Cambridge, 2004).

[301] See eg *Metalclad Corporation v United Mexican States*, ICSID No ARB(AF)/97/1 (2000); *SD Myers Inc v Canada*, UNCITRAL Partial Award (2000); *Methanex Corporation v United States of America*, UNCITRAL Final Award (2005). See Waelde and Kolo, 50 *ICLQ* (2001) 811. Cf the ECHR cases on environmental restrictions on property cited *supra*, section 2(4).

are non-discriminatory.[302] In other cases changes in national law may amount to a denial of 'fair and equitable treatment' if there has been a failure to respect legitimate expectations, a lack of transparency or disregard for due process.[303] Faced with these constraints some governments may simply shy away from trying too hard to protect the environment. Moreover, as we saw when considering the Bhopal case, attempts to sue multinationals in their home state may also encounter obstacles, such as the *forum non conveniens* defence, which effectively protects US corporations from suit in US courts for their overseas activities.[304]

There are several possible responses to these problems. One is to rely on human-rights litigation. The *Ogoniland Case* is a striking reminder that unregulated foreign investment which contributes little to the welfare of the local population may amount to a denial of human rights for which the host government is responsible. In such cases it seems improbable that a BIT could provide the investor with any protection against changes in local law or policy necessary to give effect to fundamental human-rights obligations. As a straightforward matter of treaty law a BIT would have to be interpreted and applied consistently with any applicable human-rights treaties.[305] While this strategy may protect the population from investment-led environmental damage, it will not protect the environment itself in situations falling short of a human-rights abuse. Attempts to hold corporations liable for breaches of international environmental law in such situations have generally not worked, even in the United States, where the Alien Tort Claims Act has been invoked unsuccessfully in environmental claims.[306] Corporations are not directly bound by environmental treaties or by customary international law,[307] and as we saw earlier, national courts have not been notably receptive to arguments based on international law in environmental cases.[308]

An alternative, softer, strategy focuses on promoting corporate social accountability, in which compliance with agreed environmental standards is monitored through transparent reporting, NGO activism, and shareholder accountability.[309] The earliest and most significant standards adopted for this purpose are the OECD's Guidelines

---

[302] See Baughen, 18 *JEL* (2006) 207, 227.

[303] *Metalclad Corporation v United Mexican States*, ICSID No ARB(AF)/97/1 (2000); *Emilio Agustin Maffezini v The Kingdom of Spain*, ICSID No ARB/97/7 (2000); *CME Czech Republic BV v The Czech Republic*, UNCITRAL Partial Award (2001). The conduct of the investor may also be relevant in assessing what is fair and equitable, however: see Muchlinski, 55 *ICLQ* (2006) 527. See generally Fauchald, 17 *YbIEL* (2006) 3.

[304] *Supra*, section 3(2)(d).   [305] 1969 Vienna Convention on the Law of Treaties, Article 31(3).

[306] Following the US Supreme Court's ruling in *Sosa v Alvarez-Machain* 124 S Ct 2739 (2004) it has become clear that ATCA only constitutes a ground of jurisdiction—not a statutory cause of action—and that it does not include international environmental law as actionable norms in any event. See 2006 ILA Conference Report, Committee on Transnational Environmental Law, 671–3.

[307] For an incisive study of the problems see Nollkaemper, in Winter (ed), *Multilevel Governance of Global Environmental Change* (Cambridge, 2006) 179–99.

[308] Anderson and Galizzi, *International Environmental Law in National Courts*, 9.

[309] The literature is extensive. See generally Zerk, *Multinationals and Corporate Social Responsibility* (Cambridge, 2006); Morgera, *Corporate Accountability in International Environmental Law*, PhD thesis (EUI, 2007); Ong, 12 *EJIL* (2001) 685.

for Multinational Enterprises.[310] These have the support of the main capital exporting states, whose responsibility it is to ensure that companies comply. While not
legally binding on companies, the OECD Guidelines are not without impact. They
represent a standard of public interest which may affect decisions of national courts.[311]
Non-compliance complaints can be investigated by 'National Contact Points' (NCP).
OECD also has a procedure for investigating complaints, although it is generally perceived as ineffective by NGOs and by UNCTAD.[312] In extreme cases, involving illegal
exploitation of natural resources in areas of conflict, the UN Security Council has
used the OECD Guidelines as a basis for monitoring the conduct of multinational
corporations and requiring governments to take action against companies found in
breach.[313] However, governments have not generally been good at doing so. Human
Rights Watch reported that 'The NCP procedure for dealing with these complaints in
all relevant countries has been slow and ineffective. Most government representatives
have chosen to use the most narrow, and sometimes unjustified, interpretations of
the guidelines'.[314] The Security Council could if necessary apply UN sanctions under
Chapter 7 of the UN Charter, but it has not so far chosen to do so.

Another method of promoting environmental accountability is through the work
of the multilateral investment banks. The World Bank's corporate investment arm,
the International Finance Corporation, applies a 'Policy on Social and Environmental
Sustainability',[315] which requires compliance with various environmental standards.
As we saw in Chapter 2, these standards include many of the major MEAs, as well as
applicable national law. The World Bank Inspection Panel and the IFC ombudsman
system have power to investigate complaints from member governments, NGOs or
individuals alleging a failure by the Bank to apply these standards.[316] Moreover, compliance may become an issue in interstate litigation. In the *Pulp Mills Case* compatibility with IFC standards by Botnia, the investor company, was one of the issues in
dispute between Uruguay and Argentina.

Following several unsuccessful attempts by the UN to adopt its own global standards, a 'Global Compact' was promulgated by the Secretary General in 1999 with the
object of securing business support for established UN principles, including the 1992
Rio Declaration on Environment and Development.[317] It is difficult to evaluate the
impact these may have.

Nevertheless, while international environmental law does not apply directly to
corporations, it is not irrelevant to their activities, as the examples discussed above

[310] For the current text see OECD, *The OECD Guidelines for Multinational Enterprises: Text, Commentary and Clarifications* (Paris, 2001). See Tully, 50 *ICLQ* (2001) 394.
[311] Muchlinski, 50 *ICLQ* (2001) 24.   [312] Morgera, *Corporate Accountability*, Ch 12.
[313] UNSC 1457 (2003), 1499 (2003).   [314] HRW, *The Curse of Gold* (New York, 2005) Ch IX.
[315] IFC, *Performance Standards on Social and Environmental Sustainability* (2006). See Morgera, 18 *Colorado JIELP* (2007) 151 and *supra*, Ch 2.
[316] See *supra*, Ch 2.
[317] See *UN Guide to the Global Compact*; Morgera, *Corporate Accountability*, Ch 12.

show.[318] Nor, as we have seen from successful litigation, can governments afford to ignore the environmental impact of multinationals operating within their territory. At the same time, it is clear that international efforts to promote corporate environmental accountability are underdeveloped and frequently ineffective against powerful multinationals. The best method for controlling these companies remains the well-established one habitually deployed by developed states: effective regulation via national law and enforcement agencies. An alternative approach may entail application of international criminal law, considered further in the following section.

6 ENVIRONMENTAL CRIMES

The notion that individuals and corporations bear a responsibility towards the environment is not new. The Stockholm Declaration referred in Principle 1 to man's 'solemn responsibility' to protect and improve the environment. Subsequent formulations have preferred to emphasize the individual character of this obligation. Thus the World Charter for Nature talks of the duty of 'each person' to act in accordance with its terms.[319] The 1994 Draft Principles on Human Rights and the Environment state: 'All persons...have the duty to protect and preserve the environment'.[320] Moreover, a number of constitutions, including Article 51A of the Indian Constitution, refer to the individual's duty to protect and improve the natural environment or some similar concept.[321] None of the international instruments creates legally binding obligations for individuals or corporations as such. But they do provide a justification for using criminal responsibility as a means of enforcing international environmental law. The importance of criminal responsibility is that it provides added incentive to refrain from harmful conduct by emphasizing its culpable character, and, in many cases, by allowing more stringent enforcement measures or penalties to be imposed.[322] Its use can be observed in the requirements of treaty enforcement in national law, in instances of extraterritorial jurisdiction, and in the concept of environmental crimes against international law.

6(1) ENFORCEMENT THROUGH CRIMINAL LAW

The implementation of most environmental treaties will usually require legislative and enforcement measures to be taken by governments. In general these are part of the obligation of due diligence which states are called on to perform. How a state gives

---

[318] See Nollkaemper, in Winter (ed), *Multilevel Governance of Global Environmental Change* (Cambridge, 2006) 179–99.

[319] Principle 24. See *infra*, Ch 11.   [320] Paragraph 21. *Supra*, n 48.

[321] See also Yemen, Article 16; Papua-New Guinea, Article 5; Peru, Article 123; Poland, Article 71; Sri Lanka, Article 28; Vanuatu, Article 7.

[322] See generally Richardson, Ogus, and Burrows, *Policing Pollution* (Oxford, 1982) 15–17.

effect to this obligation will depend on what is required by the particular treaty, but in many cases the choice of means is left to the state's discretion.[323] Whether it relies on the criminal law to regulate individual or corporate conduct will then depend on the legal system in question. Other possible options include civil remedies, administrative or fiscal measures, and voluntary restraints.[324] But there are some situations for which states have agreed that conduct is sufficiently objectionable that criminal penalties are required. This is typically the case in treaties covering trade in hazardous wastes, marine pollution, and trade in or possession of endangered species.[325] Criminal penalties are normally also employed to deal with illegal fishing.[326]

In 1998 the Council of Europe adopted a Convention for the Protection of the Environment through Criminal Law.[327] The purpose of this agreement is to further a 'common criminal policy aimed at protection of the environment'. It is based on the belief that there is an important role for criminal law in this respect, and that serious violations of environmental law should be criminalized and made subject to adequate penalties. In general, Article 2 requires the parties to criminalize polluting discharges, disposal, treatment, storage, export and import of hazardous waste, the operation of dangerous plant, and nuclear hazards, when these are unlawful, intentional, and reach a threshold of substantial injury. Article 3 allows this obligation to be extended to the same acts when committed negligently, and Article 4 applies to a wider range of unlawful activities, including interfering with protected areas and protected species of flora and fauna, without requiring any harm. The convention confers jurisdiction only on the state on whose territory, ships, or aircraft the offence is committed, and it provides for sanctions to take into account the seriousness of the offence. Imprisonment, fines, confiscation of assets, and measures of reinstatement of the environment are envisaged. This agreement is purely European, still not in force, and its very general character suggests that it is unlikely to influence the practice of many states, even in Europe; most of the potential parties already employ criminal sanctions in many of the cases covered by the convention, while it can scarcely be said that it offers a minimum standard for criminal law, or criminal penalties.

---

[323] The distinction between obligations of conduct and obligations of result is relevant here. See in particular II *YbILC* (1977) Pt 2, 11–30.

[324] For a review of differing national approaches to the enforcement of environmental law see Macrory, *Regulatory Justice: Making Sanctions Effective: Final Report* (2006); Mushal, 19 *JEL* (2007) 201.

[325] 1989 Basel Convention for the Control of Transboundary Movements of Hazardous Wastes, Article 4(3)–(4); 1991 Bamako Convention on the Ban of the Import into Africa, etc, of Hazardous Wastes, Article 9(2); 1973 MARPOL Convention, Article 4(2), (4); 1972 London Dumping Convention, Article 6(2); Paris Convention for the Prevention of Marine Pollution from Land-based Sources, Article 12(1); 1987 Protocol for the Prevention of Pollution of the South Pacific by Dumping, Article 12(2); 1982 UNCLOS, Articles 217(8), 230; 1973 CITES Convention, Article 8(1).

[326] Subject to limitations set out in 1982 UNCLOS, Article 73.

[327] Draft Convention and Explanatory Report in CDPC (96) 12, 13, Addendum I. See Ercmann, 65 *Rev Int de Droit Pénal* (1994) 1199. On European practice see Ringelmann, 5 *Eur J of Crime, Crim L & Crim Just* (1997) 393, and for an international survey see reports collected in 65 *Rev Int de Droit Pénal* (1994) 653–921.

6(2) EXTRATERRITORIAL CRIMINAL JURISDICTION

Jurisdiction in this context means the capacity of a state under international law to prescribe and enforce laws. It is primarily an attribute of the sovereignty of states over their own territory, or over their own nationals.[328] Jurisdiction based on nationality is not confined to individuals, but applies also to companies, ships, aircraft, and spacecraft. The state retains jurisdiction over its nationals even when they are abroad or on the high seas; it is on this basis that flag states remain responsible for regulating pollution or fishing from ships on the high seas or in the maritime zones of other states.[329] Nationality is also in practice the only accepted basis for regulating persons and activities in Antarctica.[330] Although in principle there is nothing to stop states regulating their nationals when operating in other states, in practice most states will confine such cases of concurrent jurisdiction to serious criminal offences.[331]

In addition to these general principles of jurisdiction in customary law, international law also recognizes certain forms of extraterritorial jurisdiction based on the so-called protective principle. This is particularly important in the law of the sea. It provides the justification for the extension of coastal state jurisdiction within the exclusive economic zone for the purposes of protecting the marine environment and conserving living resources. The content of this jurisdiction is carefully defined by treaty and customary law, and it is not unlimited. Moreover the power to enforce coastal state laws within the EEZ is more restricted than the power to prescribe. These limitations are more fully considered in later chapters.[332] The important point, however, is that this extended jurisdiction enhances the enforcement machinery in these two areas of environmental law. In both cases the main argument in favour of extraterritorial criminal jurisdiction has been the failure or inability of the flag state to police the high seas effectively. A similar argument underlies the possible extension of the concept of universal jurisdiction to cover certain environmental offences.

6(3) UNIVERSAL JURISDICTION AND CRIMES AGAINST INTERNATIONAL LAW

Universal jurisdiction entitles a state to prosecute an offence even in the absence of any connection based on nationality, territory, or the protective principle.[333] Piracy is the clearest example in customary international of this form of jurisdiction, which rests on the assumption that the crimes in question are contrary to international public

---

[328] See generally Bowett, in McDonald and Johnston, *The Structure and Process of International Law* (Dordrecht, 1983) 555; Brownlie, *Principles of International Law* (6th edn, Oxford, 2005) Ch 15.

[329] See *infra*, Ch 7.

[330] 1959 Antarctic Treaty, Article 8; Triggs (ed), *The Antarctic Treaty Regime* (Cambridge, 1987) 88.

[331] States are not entitled to *enforce* their laws on the territory of another state, however. On the more complex problems of jurisdiction over companies and their subsidiaries, see Muchlinski, *Multinational Enterprises and the Law*, Ch 5.

[332] See *infra*, Chs 7, 13.

[333] Bowett, in McDonald and Johnston, *The Structure and Process of International Law*, 563ff.

order. Thus it is the interest of every state in suppressing such offences which justifies their status as crimes which all states may prosecute.[334] The basis of the ILC's 'Code of Offences Against the Peace and Security of Mankind', and of conventions dealing with torture and hijacking, is to ensure that every state in whose territory the alleged offender is present shall either try or extradite, and in contemporary international law this is in effect what is now meant by 'universal jurisdiction'.[335] Moreover, in 1998 a Statute establishing a permanent International Criminal Court was adopted. This court will have concurrent jurisdiction to try war crimes, crimes against humanity, genocide and aggression, making these offences truly universal crimes under international law.[336]

It is the ILC's version of the universality principle with which the concept of port-state jurisdiction found in Article 218 of the 1982 UNCLOS is broadly comparable. The crucial feature of this article is that it gives the state in whose port a foreign vessel is present the right to prosecute for pollution offences committed on the high seas or in the maritime zones of other states, subject to a right of pre-emption by the flag state. Although this article represented progressive development when first adopted, today it is widely regarded as accepted law.[337]

A limited category of environmental crimes subject to universal jurisdiction are included in the ILC's 1996 Code of Offences, and in the 1998 Statute of the International Criminal Court. The ILC initially took an expansive view: its 1986 formulation referred to 'any serious breach of an international obligation of essential importance for the safeguarding and preservation of the human environment', and treated the offence as a crime against humanity.[338] Thereafter the scope and character of the offence was progressively narrowed. The 1991 draft covered only those who wilfully caused or ordered 'widespread, long-term and severe damage to the natural environment'.[339] The article finally adopted in 1996 retains the same very high threshold of intentional harm, and moves the offence into the narrower category of war crimes which, when committed 'in a systematic manner or on a large scale' amount to crimes against the peace and security of mankind.[340]

The effect of this re-classification and re-drafting is that the offence can be committed only during armed conflict, only when the methods and means of warfare

---

[334] *Lotus Case*, PCIJ Ser A, No 10 (1927) 70. It is of course necessary for states to adopt appropriate national legislation to give effect to their right of prosecution.

[335] See 1996 Code of Offences, Articles 8, 9, and commentary in *ILC Report* (1996) GAOR A/51/10, 42–55. See McCormack and Simpson, 5 *Crim L Forum* (1994) 1.

[336] Statute of the International Criminal Court, Article 5. See generally Graefrath, 1 *EJIL* (1990) 67; Charney, 93 *AJIL* (1999) 452.

[337] See *infra*, Ch 7. No comparable attempt has been made to extend jurisdiction over high seas fishing offences. Cf Articles 21 and 23 of the 1995 Agreement on Straddling Fish Stocks, which allow for boarding and inspection on the high seas and in port, but in either case reserve the right of prosecution to the flag state.

[338] Article 12(4) II *YbILC* (1986), Pt 1, 86.

[339] Article 14(6) *ILC Report* (1989) GAOR A/44/10, 168f; Article 26, *ILC Report* (1991) GAOR A/46/10. See also draft Article 22(2)(d).

[340] Article 20(g) *ILC Report* (1996) GAOR A/51/10, 110–20.

are 'not justified by military necessity', and only when the intended environmental damage 'gravely prejudices the health or survival of the population'. As defined by the Commission, the offence is far removed from its original form and has lost its autonomous character. Moreover, although it reflects some of the contemporary concern arising out of Iraq's environmental warfare against Kuwait in 1991, the final ILC text 'has been emasculated to such an extent that its conditions of applicability will almost never be met'.[341]

The Commission's basic approach is retained in the Statute of the International Criminal Court adopted in 1998, but in a less emasculated form. The requirements that environmental damage must be the *intentional result* of an attack that gravely prejudices the population are dropped. There remain five essential elements of the crime as defined by Article 8 of the Statute. The attack itself must be intentional; it must be known that damage to the environment will be caused; the damage must be widespread, long-term, and severe; it must also be excessive in relation to the overall military advantage; and the crime must have been committed as part of a plan or policy *or* on a large scale.[342] It is unclear that such a rule in whatever form is at present part of international law. Although the 1977 Additional Protocol I to the Geneva Conventions includes provisions on protection of the environment in time of armed conflict, which some writers see as representing customary law, it does not place these articles in the category whose grave breach constitutes a war crime.[343] Similarly, the ILC's commentary on the Code of Offences sought to 'avoid giving the impression that this type of conduct necessarily constitutes a war crime under existing international law'.[344] Article 8 of the 1998 Statute can thus be regarded only as a step towards broadening the category of universal crimes under international law.

Nevertheless the inclusion of environmental offences in the ICC Statute may prove to be a significant development if widely adopted in practice. There is a case for treating very serious and deliberate environmental harm as a universal crime, since the public interest of all states is affected, and more effective enforcement is facilitated if individual states are empowered to take action to protect community concerns. It might be said that the same argument applies equally strongly in peacetime, but the case for a broader offence, within the category of crimes against humanity, has not been accepted by the international community or the ILC. This does not preclude further incremental developments in universal jurisdiction tied to more specific forms of conduct, such as illegal trade in hazardous waste or the dumping of radioactive waste. In this respect Article 218 of the 1982 UNCLOS remains an important precedent.

---

[341] Tomuschat, 26 *EPL* (1996) 242.   [342] Articles 8(1), 8(2)(a)(iv).

[343] Additional Protocol I Relating to the Victims of International Armed Conflicts, Articles 35, 55, 56, 85; see Cassese, *International Law in a Divided World* (Oxford, 1986) 273–5; see *supra*, Ch 3, section 7.

[344] *ILC Report* (1996) 120.

7 CONCLUSIONS

This chapter points first to the increasing importance of environmental rights perspectives in national and international environmental law. At a procedural level, strengthening individual participatory rights in national law has become an instrument for legitimizing national policies aimed at sustainable development, with implications principally for public-interest litigation, standing, and access to justice. At a substantive level, though less well developed internationally and still controversial, environmental quality has become a human-rights issue, offering an approach to environmental protection very different from the regulatory system explored in the previous two chapters. Such developments may not necessarily make the task of reconciling developmental and environmental objectives any easier, since human-rights law can be used to obstruct greater environmental protection as well as to advance it.

Second, as studies for the Hague Conference have shown, unless greater harmonization of substantive environmental law can be achieved, the need for more coherence in the private international-law aspects of transnational environmental litigation becomes more apparent. The increasing international emphasis on free movement of goods, capital, and investment has not yet been matched by a willingness to address the accountability of multinational corporations for environmental and human-rights abuses in developing countries. Nevertheless, cases such as *Lubbe v Cape* show how national conflict-of-laws rules which have hitherto shielded business are beginning to be affected by human-rights and access-to-justice issues in novel and important ways that have implications for future environmental litigation.

The development of environmental liability law called for in so many international agreements and declarations remains largely an aspiration, save in the discrete areas of marine pollution and nuclear accidents. The great caution shown by states on this question, both in Europe and elsewhere, suggests that little is likely to change in this respect. Finally, the evolution of international environmental criminal law appears equally tentative, confined at present largely to war crimes and jurisdiction over offences at sea. Despite these qualifications, we can see from this chapter that the Stockholm and Rio Declarations have promoted individual environmental rights and addressed to some degree the responsibilities of individuals and corporations for environmentally harmful consequences.

6

CLIMATE CHANGE AND ATMOSPHERIC POLLUTION[*]

1 INTRODUCTION

The present chapter looks at how international law has been used or could be used to help tackle the most significant environmental challenge of our time—global climate change. Few topics provide a better illustration of the importance of a globally inclusive regulatory regime focused on preventive and precautionary approaches to environmental harm—or of the problems of negotiating one on such a complex subject. In this context the 'framework treaty'[1] has provided the key regulatory tool. The 1992 Framework Convention on Climate Change is not the first such treaty to address atmospheric pollution, however, and it is best approached with two earlier, models in mind: the 1979 Convention on Long-range Transboundary Air Pollution and the 1985 Convention for the Protection of the Ozone Layer. Although both were initially little more than empty frameworks for further negotiation, they have evolved progressively to the point where they now represent two of the leading examples of international regulation providing a basis for real solutions to pollution problems.[2]

Solutions to global climate change have not been so easily forthcoming. In principle, the same legal tools could be used successfully to regulate greenhouse gas emissions and construct an international regime for tackling climate change but, with its causes and effects more deeply embedded, the intimate connection with economic growth has made international agreement in this area especially hard to achieve. The stance of the United States vis-à-vis the Kyoto Protocol is perhaps the best-known example of this problem. Emerging economies have been similarly reluctant to engage in international agreements which might compromise economic performance, reflecting

---

[*] We are grateful to Navraj Singh Ghaleigh, School of Law, Edinburgh University, for revising the sections on climate change.

[1] *Supra*, Ch 1.   [2] *Infra*, sections 2, 3.

their sense of where historical culpability lies. Tackling climate change is thus as much a political and economic challenge as a legal one. The efforts of the international regulatory regime to address these challenges by recourse to novel 'market based' mechanisms and differentiated treatment are discussed below, as are the prospects for the post-Kyoto scheme of regulating global climate change.

1(1) DEGRADATION OF THE GLOBAL ATMOSPHERE

Climate change and depletion of the ozone layer are the two principal threats to the global atmosphere.[3] They are to some extent interlinked because some ozone-depleting substances also contribute to global warming (the so-called 'greenhouse effect'). During the 1980s evidence emerged linking the release of chlorofluorocarbons (CFCs), halons, and other chlorine-based substances with the gradual destruction of the ozone layer. This layer, located in the stratosphere but still well within the earth's atmosphere, is important because it filters sunlight and protects the earth from ultraviolet radiation. Loss of the atmospheric shield would have serious implications for human health, agriculture, and fisheries productivity over a long period, and could leave future generations a legacy of irreversible harm.[4]

It is 'very likely' that the major risk of global climate change comes from anthropogenic increases in greenhouse gases.[5] The greenhouse effect is the result of certain gases (principally water vapour, carbon dioxide, and, to a lesser extent, methane) which envelop the earth, regulate the in- and out-flow of the sun's energy and make the earth habitable. In its absence, the earth's temperature would be about $-18°C$. Carbon dioxide, the most voluminous of the greenhouse gases, was present in the pre-industrial (1750) atmosphere at a concentration of 280 parts per million (ppm). Its rise to 379 ppm by 2005 is substantially a function of global industrialization, which is in turn driven by fossil fuel combustion. In the same period, methane (which has a global warming potential approximately 70 times greater than CO_2 by mass) has increased in concentration from 715 to 1774 ppm.[6]

Other human activities, such as deforestation, also contribute to global climate change, as to do emissions of methane from agricultural sources and the loss of soil carbon due to excessive ploughing and intensive agriculture. In addition to such 'forcings' (human-induced changes in greenhouse gas (GHG) concentrations), 'feedbacks' are also important—internal climate processes that may amplify the climate's response to certain conditions. For example, warmer atmospheres hold more moisture which in turn operates as a greenhouse gas causing further warming. This is known

---

[3] For a comparison of the ozone depletion and climate change legal regimes, see Sunstein, 31 *Harv ELR* (2007) 1.

[4] WMO, *Atmospheric Ozone 1985* (Geneva 1986); EPA, *An Assessment of the Risks of Stratospheric Modification* (Washington, DC, 1987); Benedick, *Ozone Diplomacy* (2nd edn, London, 1998).

[5] IPCC, 'Summary for Policy Makers' in *Climate Change 2007: The Physical Science Basis: Contribution of Working Group 1 to the Fourth Assessment Report* (Cambridge, 2007).

[6] Ibid.

as a positive feedback.[7] The effects of global climate change are likely to be felt world-wide, but with differential impacts. Some countries might benefit from a change to more temperate climates; others, such as low-lying Pacific islands, might disappear altogether. Predicted rises in global temperatures would potentially have world-wide effects on sea levels, forests, agriculture, natural ecosystems, and population distribution.[8] The ability to adapt to such changes is not unconnected to the economic wealth, technical capabilities and government structures of different societies.

Science has played a decisive role in the formation of the current regime of climate change. Indeed, the Intergovernmental Panel on Climate Change (IPCC) was established in 1988 by UNEP and WMO 'anticipating the critical role that scientific consensus would play in building the political will to respond to climate change'.[9] Established to review the scientific evidence and make recommendations, the IPCC's reports are recognized as the definitive source of information on climate change. Assessment reports are published every six years: on the physical basis of climate change; impacts, adaptation and vulnerability; and mitigation. The most recent Assessment Reports of 2007 give the lie to suggestions that climate change is a natural, not anthropogenic, phenomenon, finding that the rise in global average temperature since the mid twentieth century is 'very likely' (that is, more than 90 per cent certain) to result from the increase in human-induced greenhouse gas emissions. If continued unchecked, such increased emissions are 'likely' (more than 66 per cent certain) to result in an average temperature change of up to 6.4°C by 2099. In addition, the IPCC predicts an average sea-level rise due to thermal expansion and melting of ice of up to 65 cm by the year 2100, with the probability of reduced precipitation in Africa, Southern Europe, Amazonia, and central North America due to temperature increases.

The IPCC's use of the language of certainty is an admission that there are many 'unknowns' in the timing, magnitude, and regional patterns of climate change due to the complexity of the subject and the need for further research. Nonetheless, the Kyoto Protocol does not contain measures as far-reaching as the IPCC's findings might suggest it should.[10] When compared with the Montreal Protocol, this can be explained by the relative absence of controversy surrounding ozone depletion and the Kyoto Protocol's characterization as a regime of high political conflict. What consensus has been achieved is largely a product of the IPCC's work.

1(2) THE LEGAL STATUS OF THE ATMOSPHERE

The atmosphere is not a distinct category in international law. Because it consists of a fluctuating and dynamic air mass, it cannot be equated with airspace which, above land, is simply a spatial dimension subject to the sovereignty of the subjacent states.[11]

---

[7] Hunter et al, *International Environmental Law and Policy* (3rd edn, New York, 2007).

[8] Op cit, n 5.   [9] Op cit, n 5.

[10] See Andressen and Skjaerseth, in Brunée, Bodansky and Hey (eds), *Handbook of International Environmental Law* (Oxford, 2007) 183–200.

[11] 1944 Chicago Convention on International Civil Aviation, 15 *UNTS* 295.

But this overlap with territorial sovereignty also means that the atmosphere cannot be treated as an area of common property beyond the jurisdiction of any state, comparable in this sense to the high seas.[12] The alternative possibility of regarding it as a shared resource is relevant in situations of bilateral or regional transboundary air pollution, affecting other states or adjacent regional seas. UNEP has referred to 'airsheds' as examples of shared natural resources,[13] and this status is consistent with regional approaches to the control and regulation of transboundary air pollution adopted in the 1979 Geneva Convention on Long-range Transboundary Air Pollution, and in regional seas agreements limiting air pollution of the marine environment of the North Sea, the Baltic, and the Mediterranean.[14]

The shared-resources concept is much less useful in relation to global atmospheric problems such as ozone depletion or climate change. What is needed here is a concept which recognizes the unity of the global atmosphere and the common interest of all states in its protection. The traditional category of common property is inadequate for this purpose. The same objection applies to the use of 'common heritage' in this context, with the additional difficulty that this concept has so far been applied only to mineral resources of the deep seabed and outer space and that its legal status remains controversial.[15] The atmosphere is clearly not outer space, despite the difficulty of defining the boundaries of that area. Moreover, Article 135 of the 1982 UNCLOS provides that the status of the seabed does not affect superjacent airspace, and thus offers no support for any wider use of the common heritage concept. Significantly, common heritage was not employed in the 1985 Vienna Convention for the Protection of the Ozone Layer,[16] or in the 1992 Convention on Climate Change (UNFCCC). The 1985 Convention defines the 'ozone layer' as 'the layer of atmospheric ozone above the planetary boundary layer'.[17] This does not mean that the ozone layer is either legally or physically part of outer space. It remains part of the atmosphere, and falls partly into areas of common property, and partly into areas of national sovereignty. One purpose of the convention's definition is to indicate that it is concerned with stratospheric ozone,[18] and not with low-level ozone, an air pollutant regulated by a protocol to the 1979 Convention. More importantly, however, the definition treats the whole stratospheric ozone layer as a global unity, without reference to legal concepts of sovereignty, shared resources, or common property. It points to the emergence of a distinct status for the global atmosphere, which makes it appropriate to view the ozone layer as an area of common interest, regardless of who enjoys sovereignty over the airspace which it occupies.[19]

The same conclusion can also be drawn from UN General Assembly resolution 43/53 which declares that global climate change is 'the common concern of

---

[12] 1958 Geneva Convention on the High Seas, Articles 1–2; 1982 UNCLOS, Articles 87, 89.

[13] *Report of the Executive Director*, UNEP/GC/44 (1975) para 86; *supra*, Ch 3, section 5(1).

[14] Handl, 26 *NRJ* (1986) 405.   [15] See *supra*, Ch 3, section 5(1).

[16] See *infra*, section 3(2).   [17] Article 1(1).

[18] The stratosphere begins between 5 and 10 miles from the earth's surface and reaches a height of approximately 30 miles. Powered aircraft typically operate to heights of 10 miles, and exceptionally to about 20 miles.

[19] International Meeting of Legal and Policy Experts, 1989, Ottawa, Canada, 19 *EPL* (1989) 78.

mankind'.[20] This phraseology was the outcome of a political compromise over Malta's initial proposal to treat the global climate as the common heritage of mankind. It has subsequently been followed in the Noordwijk Declaration of the Conference on Atmospheric Pollution and Climate Change,[21] by UNEP,[22] and in the preamble to the Climate Change Convention. What it suggests is that the global climate has a status comparable to the ozone layer, and that the totality of the global atmosphere can now properly be regarded as the 'common concern of mankind'. By approaching the issues from this global perspective, the UN has recognized both the artificiality of territorial boundaries in this context, and the inadequacy of treating global climate change in the same way as transboundary air pollution, for which regional or bilateral solutions remain more appropriate.

As we have seen in Chapter 4, the status of 'common concern' is primarily significant in indicating the common legal interest of all states in protecting the global atmosphere, whether directly injured or not, and in enforcing rules concerning its protection.[23] While it is not clear that a General Assembly resolution alone is sufficient to confer this status, the 1985 Ozone Convention and the 1992 UNFCCC unquestionably do so.[24]

1(3) CUSTOMARY LAW AND GLOBAL ENVIRONMENTAL RESPONSIBILITY

The argument that the due diligence obligation considered in Chapter 3 applies to the protection of the global atmosphere is not difficult to make. Principle 21 of the Stockholm Declaration on the Human Environment already forms the basis for the 1979 Convention on Long-range Transboundary Air Pollution, the 1985 Convention for the Protection of the Ozone Layer, and the 1992 Framework Convention on Climate Change. Although the global atmosphere is not an area 'beyond the limits of national jurisdiction', and thus does not quite fit the precise terms of Principle 21 or of Rio Principle 2,[25] it should by analogy fall within the protection afforded by international law to common areas such as the high seas. This conclusion is implicit in the Ozone Convention and in UNGA Resolution 43/53, and in the designation of climate change as a matter of 'common concern' in the Climate Change Convention.[26]

Moreover, international claims concerning the conduct of atmospheric nuclear tests provide some precedent for the inference that, like the high seas, the global atmosphere must be used with reasonable regard for the rights of other states, including the protection of their environment and human health. As we will see in Chapter 9, such tests are arguably unreasonable and contrary to customary international law. This

---

[20] Boyle, in Churchill and Freestone (eds), *International Law and Global Climate Change* (London, 1991).

[21] 19 *EPL* (1989) 220.   [22] UNEP/GC 15/36 (1989).

[23] *Supra*, Ch 4, section 2(5); Kirgis, 84 *AJIL* (1990) 585, but cf Brunnée, 49 *ZAÖRV* (1989) 791.

[24] *Supra*, Ch 3, section 3(1).   [25] *Supra*, Ch 3, section 4(2).

[26] See also UNGA Resolution 44/207 (1989) para 4, and UNEP Principles of Cooperation in Weather Modification (1980).

conclusion may be specific to the discharge of radioactivity, however, and it cannot be assumed that discharges of greenhouse gases or ozone-depleting substances are necessarily unlawful or subject to similar limitations of reasonableness. But the 1977 Convention on the Prohibition of Military or Other Hostile Use of Environmental Modification Techniques does indicate that many states regard the hostile modification of the atmosphere as contrary to international law.[27] Moreover, UNEP Principles concerning weather modification for peaceful purposes recommend that states should cooperate in informing, notifying, and consulting international organizations and other states in cases of proposed weather modification activities, and that these should only be carried out after an assessment of their environmental consequences and in a manner 'designed to ensure that they do not cause damage to the environment of other states or of areas beyond the limits of national jurisdiction'.[28]

Customary international law, and the responsibility of states for the performance of their customary obligations, may therefore provide some legal restraint on the production of greenhouse gases or on the conduct of other activities likely to result in global climate change. But it is not easy to extrapolate from this conclusion precise standards for the diligent conduct of states. It does not follow that standards adopted under the 1987 Montreal Protocol to the Ozone Convention and the 1997 Kyoto Protocol to the Climate Change Convention can be generalized into customary law.[29] Although most states are now committed to the elimination of ozone-depleting substances and have put these commitments into effect, it is clear that some significant states—most notably the United States—remain opposed to any commitment to specific action on CO_2 emissions. The extent to which customary law can usefully be employed to compel states to give priority to preventing global climate change or to the adoption and application of international standards thus remains questionable. The precautionary principle might alter this conclusion if it required states to refrain from increasing or continuing with their present emission levels until they had demonstrated that no harm would ensue, but there is no evidence that the principle has this effect.[30] Without dismissing the relevance of customary law as a basis for negotiation, it seems clear that, as in the case of transboundary air pollution and ozone depletion, legally binding standards for the abatement of greenhouse gas emissions can only come through agreement on detailed commitments and international supervisory mechanisms.

1(4) INTERNATIONAL POLICY AND THE REGULATION OF THE ATMOSPHERE

The foregoing considerations indicate something of the legal and scientific complexity surrounding the protection of the atmosphere and its various components. No single approach or legal regime is likely to be appropriate or possible. Moreover, the control of transboundary air pollution, ozone depletion, and climate change have posed difficult choices for many states in matters of economic and industrial policy.

---

[27] *Supra*, Ch 3, section 7.   [28] UNEP Principles of Cooperation in Weather Modification (1980).
[29] See Churchill and Freestone, *Global Climate Change*, Ch 9.   [30] *Supra*, Ch 3, section 4(3).

For these reasons, attempts to negotiate international controls have made relatively slow progress, and for many states the preferable policy, at least initially, has been to delay action pending clearer scientific evidence and proof of harm. This explains the initial emphasis in the recommendations of the 1972 Stockholm Conference on the need for monitoring programmes and more scientific research.[31] The same pattern has been repeated with regard to long-range transboundary air pollution, ozone depletion, and climate change. Only gradually have states been persuaded of the need for a precautionary approach to the risk of irreversible atmospheric harm. Although reinforced by a growing body of scientific evidence, a precautionary approach is apparent in the negotiations for the 1985 Ozone Convention and its later protocol and amendments,[32] but the need for precautionary action to deal with the risk of climate change remains only weakly recognized in the Climate Change Convention and the 1997 Kyoto Protocol.[33]

A second reason for the slow pace of international negotiations has been the need to ensure global participation. Fundamental questions of economic equity between developed and developing states are raised by ozone depletion and climate change, both of which are substantially the result of policies pursued principally by the developed, industrialized states. Yet, without constraints on the pursuit of comparable policies by the developing states no control strategy will work. Thus the Ozone and Climate Change Conventions represent attempts to balance the economic concerns of developing countries with controls sought by developed states.[34] To these equitable considerations must also be added the competing claims of future generations to inter-generational equity.[35]

A third important consideration in evaluating legal developments relevant to the protection of the atmosphere is the realization that transboundary air pollution, ozone depletion, and climate change are problems whose solution goes to the heart of a policy of sustainable development. This is recognized in the declaration of the 1990 Bergen Conference on Sustainable Development,[36] in Agenda 21 of the 1992 Rio Conference, and in the 2002 Johannesburg Declaration on Sustainable Development, all of which support a range of measures to promote energy efficiency, energy conservation, and the use of environmentally sound and renewable energy sources in order to reduce harmful atmospheric emissions.[37] It should not be assumed that the most appropriate or effective means of implementing these policies are necessarily to be afforded by international law or international regulation. Rather, international law is one element

---

[31] Recommendations 70, 71, 73, 77, 79, 81, and 83, UN Doc A/CONF/48/14/Rev. 1 (1972).

[32] Freestone, in Churchill and Freestone (eds), *International Law and Global Climate Change*, Ch 2, and see *infra*, section 3(2).

[33] *Infra*, section 3(3).

[34] On common but differentiated responsibility see *supra*, Ch 3. See also Benedick, *Ozone Diplomacy*; Handl, 1 *EJIL* (1990) 250; Gardiner, 114 *Ethics* (2004) 555.

[35] Redgwell, in Churchill and Freestone (eds), *International Law and Global Climate Change*, Ch 3; Franck, *Fairness in International Law* (Oxford, 1995) Ch 12.

[36] 20 *EPL* (1990) 100. See also 1989 Declaration of the Hague, 19 *EPL* (1989) 78; 1989 Noordwijk Declaration, 19 *EPL* (1989) 220; 1989 Cairo Compact, 20 *EPL* (1990) 59, and UNEP/GC/15/36 (1989).

[37] *Supra*, Ch 2, section 2.

in a broader strategy, whose success may depend at least in part on the willingness of states to commit themselves to and to implement economic and trade policies focused on sustainable use of energy. Their record in this respect has improved since the early 1980s, but it is still very far from convincing.[38]

2 TRANSBOUNDARY AIR POLLUTION

2(1) INTRODUCTION

The main contemporary sources of significant transboundary air pollution are the sulphur dioxide (SO_2) and nitrogen oxides (NO_x) produced by the combustion of fossil fuels for power generation and industrial use, to which must be added the increasing volume of vehicle exhaust emissions since the 1960s. Both SO_2 and NO_x are emitted naturally into the atmosphere, for example from volcanoes, but these represent only a small proportion of the global total.[39] Transboundary air pollution first emerged as a significant problem in North America and Europe, and it is here that regional regulation is the most advanced. Agenda 21 pointed out that much less attention has been paid to transboundary air pollution in developing countries.[40] In Brazil, Southern Africa, India, China, and Korea industrialization and traffic growth are producing air pollution problems similar to or in some cases far worse than those of Europe and North America. Transboundary air pollution has also been caused on a substantial scale by natural or man-made disasters such as the deliberate burning of Kuwaiti oil wells by Iraqi forces in 1991, and the extensive forest fires in Borneo in 1997.[41]

Once in the atmosphere, the distribution and deposition of pollution is a function of prevailing winds and weather patterns. Scientific observations and monitoring have shown that sulphur and nitrogen compounds are dispersed atmospherically over thousands of miles. The work of the Programme for Monitoring and Evaluation of Long-range Transmission of Air Pollutants in Europe (EMEP) has succeeded in quantifying the depositions in each country that can be attributed to emissions in any other, and has shown that the problem is not simply a bilateral one between adjacent states, but a regional one, in which most states contribute their own share of pollution, but some emerge as substantial net importers.[42] Moreover, research conducted by GESAMP and in the North Sea and Great Lakes has shown that land-based air

---

[38] *Infra*, section 4(6).   [39] See generally UNECE, *Air Pollution Studies*, Nos 1–12 (1984–96).

[40] *Report of the UNCED* (1992), Agenda 21, Ch 9. On ASEAN action to deal with transboundary air pollution see 8 *YbIEL* (1997) 404 and 9 *YbIEL* (1998) 469.

[41] There is no reason in principle why states should not incur international responsibility for transboundary harm caused by forest fires, provided there has been some failure to act diligently on the part of the state concerned, for example by not controlling deliberate burning. See Tan, 48 *ICLQ* (1999) 826, and *supra*, Ch 4, section 2.

[42] Sand, in Helm (ed), *Energy: Production, Consumption and Consequences* (Washington, DC, 1990) 247.

pollution of the marine environment is also significant, and in the case of metals and nutrients more so than for inputs from rivers, particularly to the open oceans.[43] Sulphur and nitrogen can be deposited in dry form, or as acid rain, although in both cases the ultimate effect is comparable. Dry deposition is more likely to remain a localized problem, however. Greater transboundary effects are generated by reactions of sulphur, nitrogen, and other substances with water vapour in the atmosphere, where they form acidic compounds, deposited as acid rain, or create other pollutants such as ozone gas (O_3). Sunlight, moisture, temperature and the level of concentration of particles are important factors in this complex chemical process, whose effects are also influenced by climate and location.[44]

Acid deposition has been blamed for increased acidity of soil, lakes, and rivers and for other effects including reduced crop growth, death or degradation of forests, and the disappearance of fish and wildlife. It appears to accelerate the decomposition of buildings, poses health risks, and increases the release of toxic metals, either directly, or through leaching from soil or corrosion of plumbing. These effects have been well documented in UN and nationally sponsored research programmes.[45] Ozone pollution of the lower atmosphere is thought also to harm crops and forests, either alone, or in combination with acid rain.[46]

State practice in bilateral disputes involving the United States, Canada, Norway, Sweden, the United Kingdom, Germany, and France does not suggest that the basic rule of customary international codified by Principle 2 of the Rio Declaration is without impact on transboundary air pollution.[47] On the other hand, it did not provide a solution to regional problems of air pollution or acid rain either in North America or Europe. Although those states which are net importers of pollution, such as the Nordic countries or Canada, have from time to time invoked Principle 21 of the Stockholm Declaration or *Trail Smelter*,[48] the preferred approach of all parties has been to negotiate agreed emissions standards with polluting states on a basis which takes account of the interests of both sides, while leaving aside the question of compensation for long-term damage previously inflicted. In the 1979 Geneva Convention on Long-range Transboundary Air Pollution equitable considerations have thus played an important part in tackling transboundary air pollution, although it remains correct to observe that 'it will be customary international legal principles and rules which will principally

---

[43] GESAMP, *The State of the Marine Environment* (Nairobi, 1990) 36; 2nd International Conference on the Protection of the North Sea, *Quality Status of the North Sea* (1987); International Joint Commission, 6th and 7th *Annual Reports on Great Lakes Water Quality* (Ottawa, 1974–1980); US NRC and Royal Society of Canada, *The Great Lakes Water Quality Agreement: An Evolving Instrument for Ecosystem Management* (1985).

[44] UN/ECE, *supra*, n 39.   [45] Ibid.   [46] UN/ECE, *Air Pollution Study* (No 3).

[47] See generally Wetstone and Rosencranz, *Acid Rain in Europe and North America* (Washington, DC, 1983); Flinterman, Kwiatkowska, and Lammers (eds), *Transboundary Air Pollution* (Dordrecht, 1986) 121ff; Schmandt, Clarkson, and Roderick (eds), *Acid Rain and Friendly Neighbours* (Durham, NC, 1988); Pallemaerts, *Hague YIL* (1988) 189; McCormick, *Acid Earth* (London, 1997); Okowa, *State Responsibility for Transboundary Air Pollution in International Law* (Oxford, 2000).

[48] *Supra,* Ch 3, section 4.

shape the parties' respective starting positions and guide states in their negotiations'.[49] Customary international law is not unimportant in the control of air pollution; effective solutions to the problem can only be provided by cooperative regimes of international regulation, however.

2(2) THE 1979 GENEVA CONVENTION ON LONG-RANGE TRANSBOUNDARY AIR POLLUTION

This Convention remains the only major regional multilateral agreement devoted to the regulation and control of transboundary air pollution.[50] It treats the European air mass as a shared resource and the problem as one requiring coordination of pollution-control measures and common emission standards. In this sense it is comparable to the 1974 Paris Convention on Land-based Sources of Marine Pollution or to some of the more advanced international watercourse agreements.[51] Its purpose is thus to prevent, reduce, and control transboundary air pollution, both from new and existing sources, and it contains no provision on liability for air pollution damage, whether under international law or through civil proceedings.

The treaty came into force in 1983, and now has over fifty Northern Hemisphere parties in Europe, including all the major polluter states. Canada and the Unites States have also ratified, although they have stayed out of the SO_2 protocol.[52] The Convention text was weaker than the net importers of pollutants would have liked, but only through compromise of essential interests on both sides could such widespread adherence by both groups have been achieved.[53] However, as a framework treaty, it has for thirty years provided the basis for further development and the elaboration of further regulatory protocols which have made it one of the most successful and highly developed of the older environmental regimes.

'Long-range transboundary air pollution' is defined as pollution having effects at such a distance that 'it is not generally possible to distinguish the contributions of individual emission sources or groups of sources'.[54] Thus it is not aimed at *Trail Smelter* type cases, but at regional problems of acid rain and other widely dispersed pollutants. Nor is it confined to effects harmful to health or property. A much broader definition of 'pollution' is used, comparable to those found in marine pollution treaties, and which includes harm to living resources and ecosystems, and interference with amenities and legitimate uses of the environment.[55] Amelioration of a wide range of potential environmental harm is thus the treaty's basic objective.

---

[49] Handl, 26 *NRJ* (1986) 423, 467. But cf Gundling, *Proc ASIL* (1989) 72.

[50] Gundling, in Flinterman, Kwiatkowska, and Lammers (eds), *Transboundary Air Pollution*, 19; Rosencranz, 75 *AJIL* (1981) 975; Fraenkel, 30 *Harv ILJ* (1989) 447; Okowa, *State Responsibility for Transboundary Air Pollution in International Law*, 24–59.

[51] *Infra*, Chs 8, 10.

[52] But see the 1991 Agreement Between the Government of the United States and the Government of Canada on Air Quality.

[53] Wetstone and Rosencranz, *Acid Rain in Europe and North America*, 140–4.

[54] Article 1(b).   [55] Article 1(a). See *supra*, Ch 3, section 4(6).

No concrete commitments to specific reductions in air pollution are contained in the treaty itself. Instead, the parties committed themselves to broad principles and objectives for pollution-control policy, in language often so weak that one commentary described the treaty as no more than a 'symbolic victory' intended to reassure both the polluters and the victims.[56] Thus there is only an obligation to 'endeavour to limit' and 'as far as possible, gradually reduce and prevent' air pollution.[57] To achieve this, parties undertake to develop the best policies, strategies, and control measures, but these must be compatible with 'balanced development', and use the 'best available technology' which is 'economically feasible'.[58] A great deal of latitude was thus left to individual states to determine what level of effort they would put into pollution control and what cost they would be willing to pay in overall economic development. For major polluters such as the United Kingdom and West Germany, this elastic obligation was the major condition for their acceptance of the treaty in 1979, and it enabled the United States to continue to cause serious pollution in Canada without violating the Convention.[59]

The Geneva Convention also contains provisions on notification and consultation in cases of significant risk of transboundary pollution. These are only loosely comparable to the customary rule requiring consultation regarding shared resources or environmental risk.[60] Only 'major' changes in policy or industrial development likely to cause 'significant' changes in long-range air pollution must be notified to other states.[61] Otherwise, consultations need only be held at the request of parties 'actually affected by or exposed to a significant risk of long-range transboundary air pollution'.[62] However, the 1991 UNECE Convention on Environmental Impact Assessment in a Transboundary Context has provided a stronger regime of assessment and consultation covering proposals to operate refineries, power stations, smelters, and other large-scale, 'combustion installations' since its entry into force.[63] This convention requires the party initiating a proposed activity to take the initiative in providing notification to those likely to be affected, a position much closer to more recent treaty and ILC formulations than is found in the 1979 Geneva Convention.

Despite its evident weaknesses, the Geneva Convention's real value is that it has provided a successful framework for cooperation and the development of further measures of pollution control. Articles 3, 4, 5, and 8 commit the parties to exchange information, conduct research, and consult on policies, strategies, and measures for combating and reducing air pollution. The convention is thus both a basis for continuing study of the problem, and for taking further coordinated action to deal with it. In this sense the weakness of its obligations is deceptive. Given adequate consensus among the parties,

---

[56] Wetstone and Rosencranz, *Acid Rain in Europe and North America*, 145; Gundlling, in Flinterman, Kwiatkowska, and Lammers (eds), *Transboundary Air Pollution*, 21–3.

[57] Article 2. [58] Article 6. This article is directed 'in particular' at new or rebuilt installations.

[59] But see now the 1991 US–Canada Air Quality Agreement. [60] *Supra*, Ch 3, section 4(5).

[61] Article 8(b). Rosencranz, 75 *AJIL* (1981) 977 argues that 'few if any cases are likely to arise to trigger this article' because the threshold is so high.

[62] Article 5. [63] *Supra*, Ch 3, section 4(4). See also 1991 US–Canada Air Quality Agreement.

stronger and more effective measures are possible within this framework. For this reason the creation of institutions is, as in other treaty regimes, of particular importance.
The Executive Body's main task is to keep under review the implementation of the
convention, for which purpose it has instituted periodic reviews of the effectiveness
of national policies.[64] Its success is best measured by the protocols which have been
negotiated setting specific targets for reduction of emissions.

2(3) PROTOCOLS TO THE 1979 CONVENTION

The first SO_2 protocol required the parties to reduce emissions or their transboundary fluxes by 30 per cent by 1993.[65] By then the parties were comfortable with a more
sophisticated approach to the problem. The second sulphur protocol[66] acknowledges
the need for precautionary measures to prevent transboundary air pollution from
continuing to cause damage to forests, natural resources, and the sensitive Arctic
environment. Based on a 'critical loads' approach, its objective is to reduce sulphur
deposition below the level at which there would be significant damage to the areas
where deposition is likely to occur. To this end Article 2 requires parties to control
and reduce sulphur emissions in order to protect human health and the environment
and to ensure 'as far as possible' and 'without entailing excessive cost' that they do not
exceed the critical loads specified in Annex I. These loads are based on mapping of
actual SO_2 deposition and sources. No date is set for reaching this ambitious objective, but each party is also given minimum emissions targets to meet within timescales
which vary between 2000, 2005, and 2010. Instead of the single flat rate reduction for
all parties used in the earlier protocol, the newer one sets differentiated emissions
targets for each party, which range from an 80% reduction by 2010 for Germany to a
49% increase for Greece. The overall SO_2 emissions reduction for all parties combined
is 50.8%, and the effect of this should be to reduce the amount by which deposition
exceeds the critical loads by at least 60% by 2010.

Unlike the first sulphur protocol, whose 30% figure was essentially arbitrary, the
second sulphur protocol's critical loads approach is the product of a high degree of scientific knowledge. For this reason it does not need to apply a precautionary approach,
despite references to scientific uncertainty in the preamble. Its emissions reductions
figures are not derived solely from scientific advice, however; instead they represent
the outcome of a politically negotiated compromise which recognizes that for some
states, such as Germany and the United Kingdom, the critical-loads approach is too
demanding for full implementation.[67] Moreover certain states are not included in
these commitments, such as the United States, which preferred the different approach

---

[64] Article 10.
[65] 1985 Protocol on the Reduction of Sulphur Emissions. See Fraenkel, 30 *Harv ILJ* (1989) 470.
[66] 1994 Protocol on Further Reduction of Sulphur Emissions. See Churchill, Kütting and Warren, 7 *JEL*
(1995) 169; McCormick, *Acid Earth*, 73f; Jhaveri, Gupta, Ott, *The LRTAP Convention/2nd Sulphur Protocol:
Possible Lessons for the Climate Convention* (FIELD, 1998).
[67] Churchill, Kütting, Warren, 7 *JEL* (1995) 169; Wettestad, 4 *J Env & Dev'mnt* (1995) 165.

it had adopted in the Clean Air Act of 1990. Nevertheless the Protocol's differentiated commitments are fairer to all parties because they are based on calculations of actual sources and effects and require reductions only to the extent that they are needed. Not only does it address the problem from a more realistic scientific perspective, it is also more effective in requiring the parties to reduce their total emissions, not merely their transboundary fluxes of SO_2.

Implementation of the Protocol is mainly left to the discretion of each party, with some qualifications. Specific limits and timetables are laid down for cutting major power station emissions; otherwise the 'most effective measures' appropriate to the circumstances of each party are to be used.[68] These can include energy efficiency, use of renewable energy such as wind power, reducing the sulphur content of fuel, the application of best available technology, or the use of economic instruments such as taxes or tradeable permits, but none of these measures is obligatory. There is also an obligation to facilitate technology transfer, mainly to help countries in Eastern Europe.[69] Two or more parties may be permitted by the Executive Body to implement their obligations jointly, subject to certain conditions.[70] The parties are required by Article 5 to report their SO_2 emissions and what steps they have taken to implement their commitments.

The NO_x protocol concluded after prolonged and difficult negotiations requires parties to stabilize their NO_x emissions or their transboundary fluxes at 1987 levels by 1994.[71] By allowing states to specify an earlier base year for emissions levels, however, some parties, such as the United States, may actually be able to increase their emissions. The protocol covers both major stationary sources, including power plants and vehicle emissions. Its approach to the coordination of national measures requires the use of best available technology for national emissions standards, and the eventual negotiation of internationally accepted 'critical loads' for NO_x pollution to take effect after 1996. This approach is more suited to regional environmental protection than flat-rate emissions reductions.[72]

In 1991 a protocol intended to deal with pollution from low-level ozone was adopted. It came into force in 1997.[73] Parties are required either to reduce emissions of volatile organic compounds by 30 per cent by 1999, or to stabilize emissions at specified levels by the same year. Two further protocols concluded in 1998 deal with airborne deposition of persistent organic pollutants (mainly pesticides and industrial chemicals), and heavy metals.[74] The first of these bans production and use of some substances, severely restricts the use of others, and requires destruction and disposal to be carried out in an environmentally sound manner compatible with the Basel Convention. The second

---

[68] Articles 2(4) and (5). [69] Article 5. [70] Article 2(7).
[71] 1988 Protocol Concerning the Control of Emissions of Nitrogen Oxides or Their Transboundary Fluxes. See Fraenkel, 30 *Harv ILJ* (1989) 472. Twelve countries made commitments to reduce emissions by more than is required under the Protocol.
[72] See *Rept of the 8th Session of the Executive Body*, UN Doc ECE/EB AIR/24 (1990).
[73] For background see UN Doc ECE/EBAIR/WG 4/R 12 (1988).
[74] See Executive Body, *Rept of the Special Session*, ECE/EB AIR/55 and ECE/EB AIR/57 (1998).

phases out leaded petrol, reduces other emissions of lead, cadmium, and mercury from industry, incinerators, and power stations to below 1990 levels, and specifies use of best available technology. Additional substances can be added to either proto-col by amendment of the annexes.[75] Some parties to the 1998 protocols voluntarily entered into additional commitments. Finally, in 1999, the UNECE adopted a proto-col to abate adverse effects of acidification, eutrophication, and ground-level ozone on human health, natural ecosystems, and crops resulting from transboundary air pollution.[76] The need for a precautionary approach is recognized, and emissions must not exceed critical loads stipulated in the annexes.

2(4) IMPLEMENTATION AND ASSESSMENT

Transboundary air pollution in Europe has undoubtedly fallen substantially, and especially SO_2 pollution. By 1994 the 30% target for reducing sulphur emissions had been met by all parties, and exceeded by nineteen of them, reducing total emissions by 52%. Even non-parties such as the UK and Poland had also exceeded the 30% tar-get. NO_x emissions had either stabilized as required, or had reduced, giving a net fall of 9%, although those parties who had promised a 30% fall remained a long way short of this target, and further reductions would be difficult to achieve. One study concluded that 'deposition in excess of critical loads of acidification has been greatly reduced in Europe due to emission reductions' and that 'Recovery from acidification damage is particularly evident in the chemistry of acidified lakes and streams and in the reduction of corrosion for many materials'.[77] However, NO_x emissions remained problematic, 'exceeding the critical loads of eutrophication in large areas in Europe and increase[ing] the risk of harmful effects, for example, the loss of biodiversity'. Ozone levels in European and North American cities continued to affect health and caused widespread damage to buildings and plants. Reports from the Implementation Committee show that there are continuing problems of non-compliance by some par-ties with the NO_x and VOC protocols. Overall, although the picture is one of improve-ment and substantial compliance with the sulphur protocols, further measures would be needed to tackle other problems.

What is less clear is how far this improvement can be attributed directly to imple-mentation of the protocols. Any explanation of the reduction in sulphur emissions which has undoubtedly occurred must take account of evidence that this is signifi-cantly due to industrial changes in some areas, such as Eastern Germany, and to the increased use of gas or nuclear power for power generation in countries such

---

[75] Criteria and procedures for doing so are set out in Executive Body Decisions 1998/1 and 1998/2.

[76] Protocol to Abate Acidification, Eutrophication, and Ground-level Ozone. See UNECE, *17th Rept of the Executive Body*, ECE/EB AIR/68 (1999).

[77] Working Group on Effects, *Convention on Long-range Transboundary Air Pollution: Review and assess-ment of air pollution effects and their recorded trends* (UK Natural Environment Research Council, 2004).

as the UK and France, rather than to implementation of the Convention regime.[78] Nevertheless, in their reports to the Executive Body, the parties have concurred in viewing the Convention's impact on air pollution control and air-quality management as a positive one, which has resulted in national and international action to improve the environment, to reduce pollution, and to develop control technologies. Largely through increased knowledge and the building of mutual confidence, the Long-range Transboundary Air Pollution treaty regime has helped to alter perceptions, to change policies in participating states, and to reverse some of the earlier trends.[79]

3 PROTECTING THE OZONE LAYER

3(1) 1985 OZONE CONVENTION

UNEP initiated negotiation of a treaty to protect the ozone layer in 1981.[80] As with the 1979 Convention on Long-range Transboundary Air Pollution, the interests of several groups had to be reconciled. These included developing countries, such as India, China, and Brazil, which were primarily concerned that restraints on the use of ozone-depleting substances might inhibit their industrial development, or that alternative technologies might not be available to them. The United States, which had earlier acted unilaterally to reduce domestic production and consumption of CFCs, did not wish to remain at a disadvantage while others went on using them, and its position was strongly in favour of an international control regime. The EC represented the largest group of producers and was reluctant to commit itself to measures that might prove costly to implement. Moreover, some EC states resisted controls on the grounds that harmful effects had not been proven, and that the risk remained long-term and speculative. Unlike air pollution, however, no regime would be likely to work unless it was global, since the impact of ozone-depleting substances is the same wherever or however they originate, and would affect all states. Thus, as many parties as possible would have to be persuaded to join and there would have to be strong disincentives to deter relocation of CFC production to non-parties.[81]

---

[78] Sand, in Helm (ed), *Energy: Production, Consumption, and Consequences* (Washington, 1990) 246; Wettestad, 7 *Global Environmental Change* (1997) 235. See also *National Strategies and Policies for Air Pollution Abatement*, UN Doc ECE/EB AIR/65 (1999).

[79] See in particular Wettestad, *Acid Lessons? Assessing and Explaining LRTAP Implementation and Effectiveness* (IIASA Working Paper, 1996); Jhaveri, Gupta, and Ott, *The LRTAP Convention/Second Sulphur Protocol: Possible Lessons for the Climate Convention* (FIELD, 1998).

[80] For text and commentary on successive drafts see Ad Hoc Working Group on the Ozone Convention, UNEP/WG 69/8; UNEP/WG 78/2; UNEP/WG 78/4; UNEP/WG 78/10; UNEP/WG 94/3; UNEP/WG 94/4 and Add 1 and 2; UNEP/WG 94/8; UNEP/WG 94/11.

[81] Ad Hoc Working Group, 2nd Session, 1982, 10 *EPL* (1983) 34; UNEP Working Group on CFCs, 16 *EPL* (1986) 139.

Again following the pattern of the 1979 Geneva Convention on Long-range Transboundary Air Pollution, the 1985 Vienna Convention for the Protection of the Ozone Layer (Ozone Convention) made reference in its preamble to Principle 21 of the 1972 Stockholm Declaration on the Human Environment, but imposes few concrete obligations.[82] The weakness of its provisions indicated compromise between demands for more research and a commitment to firm action. Parties would have to take 'appropriate measures', including the adoption of legislation and administrative controls, to protect human health and the environment 'against adverse effects resulting or likely to result from human activities which modify or are likely to modify the ozone layer'.[83] The nature of these measures was not defined, but the parties had to cooperate in harmonizing policies and in formulating 'agreed measures, procedures and standards for the implementation of this Convention'. Nor did the convention specify any particular substances to which these measures must relate; it merely listed in an annex substances 'thought' to have the potential to modify the ozone layer.

The only measures which the convention required the parties to take concern assessment of the causes and effects of ozone depletion, the transmission of information, and the exchange of information and technology.[84] These provisions laid the basis for ensuring adequate monitoring and research, and for making substitute technologies and substances available to all, including developing countries. But Article 4, which dealt with the acquisition of alternative technology, was most unsatisfactory from the perspective of developing countries, since it merely required states to cooperate, in accordance with their own laws, regulations, and practices, in the development and transfer of technology and knowledge. This was significantly weaker than transfer of technology provisions in the 1982 UNCLOS,[85] and essentially left the matter to each state's discretion. Article 4 proved inadequate to satisfy the concerns of developing states that CFC substitutes might not be available to them, or would be prohibitively expensive, and the issue was reopened in later negotiations.

Institutions created by the Convention comprised a regular Conference of the Parties (COP) and a secretariat. Like the Executive Body of the 1979 Geneva Convention on Long-range Transboundary Air Pollution, the Conference of the Parties reviews implementation of the convention, receiving for that purpose reports from the parties and establishing the necessary programmes and policies. It is responsible for adopting new protocols and annexes, and for amending the convention. There is provision for dispute settlement in Article II.

Thus the 1985 Convention is largely an empty framework, requiring further action by the parties, who proved unable in 1985 to agree on proposals for more specific control measures.[86] Nevertheless, it is an important precedent with wider significance

---

[82] See generally Anderson and Sarma (eds), *Protecting the Ozone Layer* (London, 2002); Yoshida, *The International Legal Regime for the Protection of the Stratospheric Ozone Layer* (The Hague, 2001); Benedick, *Ozone Diplomacy* (2nd edn, London, 1998).

[83] Article 2.   [84] Articles 2(2)(a), 4, 5.

[85] Cf 1982 UNCLOS, Article 144 and Annex III, Article 5.

[86] UNEP, Ad Hoc Working Group on the Ozone Convention, UNEP/WG 94/9.

in environmental law. First, it is explicitly concerned with protection of the global environment, and defines adverse effects to mean 'changes in the physical environment or biota, including changes in climate, which have significant deleterious effects on human health or on the composition, resilience and productivity of natural and managed ecosystems, or on materials useful to mankind'.[87] This definition both recognizes the impact of ozone depletion on climate change, and adopts an ecosystem approach in terms which suggest that the natural environment has a significance independent of its immediate utility to man. Second, the Ozone Convention is one of the first to perceive the need for preventive action in advance of firm proof of actual harm, and in that sense it is indicative of the emergence of a more 'precautionary' approach than had been typical for earlier pollution conventions, including the 1979 Geneva Convention on Long-range Transboundary Air Pollution.[88]

3(2) 1987 MONTREAL PROTOCOL

The 1987 Montreal Protocol on Substances that Deplete the Ozone Layer[89] represents a much more significant agreement than the Ozone Convention. First, it sets firm targets for reducing and eliminating consumption and production of a range of ozone-depleting substances. These were supported particularly strongly by the United States, which referred to the need to err on the side of caution and to recall the well-being of future generations, and by the Executive Director of UNEP, whose efforts ensured that a consensus emerged among the scientific experts on predicting the rate of ozone depletion and the regulatory measures needed to protect human health and the environment. Following scientific evidence that the standards adopted in 1987 would not be effective in reducing ozone depletion, however, additional substances were included by the amendments adopted in 1990 and 1992 and the timetable for complete elimination was revised and brought forward to 1996.[90] These changes were made possible by the development of new technology and alternative substances, although in some cases these substitutes may still have an ozone-depleting potential; others are greenhouse gases. Limited allowance is made for increases in production of ozone-depleting substances to meet domestic needs and to facilitate industrial rationalization. Control of consumption and production was necessary in order to protect the interests of producers and importers by deterring price inflation or over-production in the interim period until the eventual phase-out of these gases.[91]

---

[87] Article 1(2).

[88] Preamble, and see Benedick, *Ozone Diplomacy*, 45, and *supra*, Ch 3, section 4(4).

[89] Ad Hoc Working Group of Legal and Technical Experts, First Session, UNEP/WG 151/L 4 (1986); id, Second Session, UNEP/WG 167/2 (1987); id, Third Session, UNEP/WG 172/2 (1987). See Benedick, *Ozone Diplomacy*.

[90] For amendments and adjustments see UNEP, *Handbook of Substances that Deplete the Ozone Layer* (7th edn, Nairobi, 2006) and subsequent updates. Decisions of the parties will also be found there.

[91] Explanatory Note by the Executive Director of UNEP, Montreal, 1987.

Second, acknowledging the inequity of equal treatment for all, and the very small contribution to ozone depletion made by developing states, the protocol makes special provision for their needs. It was essential to encourage participation by these states, given their potential for increased production of CFCs, and the likelihood that this would simply nullify the actions of developed states. Although the 1987 text of the protocol would have allowed them a possibly substantial increase in production and consumption for domestic needs,[92] this option did not prove sufficiently attractive to prompt India and China to ratify, and would in any case have reduced its effectiveness. The accelerated timetable set for eventual phase-out by the subsequent revisions required a different approach in order to encourage the developing states to ratify. Allowance was still made in the revised Article 5 for a ten-year delay in compliance with the control measures by this group, whose obligation to phase out production and consumption thus began to take effect only in 1999, but the protocol revision adopted new financial and technical incentives to encourage such states to switch as quickly as possible to alternative substances and technologies.[93] Article 10 establishes a multilateral fund financed by those parties to the convention that are not taking advantage of the dispensation allowed for developing countries in Article 5. Its purpose is to facilitate technical cooperation and technology transfer so that developing states do not have to rely on Article 5 to protect their interests but are enabled to comply with the protocol's control measures.[94] The revised protocol also requires each party to take 'every practicable step' to ensure that substitutes and technology would expeditiously be transferred under 'fair and most favourable conditions' to developing states.[95] Although this provision by no means overcame the reluctance of chemical companies in the developed world to transfer technology,[96] and did not compel them to do so, the obligation of developing countries to comply with the protocol's control measures 'will depend upon' the effective implementation of these provisions on financial cooperation and transfer of technology. Moreover, if these provisions did not work effectively, developing states could refer the matter to a meeting of the parties, which would decide on appropriate action. Put shortly, developing states were given the power to put pressure on developed states to ensure that they were given the necessary means to meet the protocol's target for elimination of ozone-depleting substances. This was one of a number of innovative measures adopted in the 1990 revision to ensure compliance and effective implementation.

Third, the protocol attempted to deal with the problem of non-parties by banning trade with these states in controlled substances or products containing such

---

[92] Article 5. See Rosencranz and Scott, 20 *EPL* (1990) 201.

[93] Benedick, *Ozone Diplomacy*, Chs 12, 13, 16.

[94] For an optimistic report of its success, see *10th Meeting of the Parties,* UNEP/OZL.Pro. 10/9 (1998) para 83f. The Multilateral Fund is administered by the World Bank, UNEP and UNDP. See UNEP, *Handbook* (7th edn, 2006); Benedick, *Ozone Diplomacy*, 252–68; Keohane and Levy, *Institutions for Environmental Aid* (MIT, 1996) 89–126. The GEF also provides funding.

[95] Article 10A.

[96] Rosencranz and Scott, 20 *EPL* (1990) 201. Lawrence, 2 *JEL* (1990) concludes that reluctance to transfer CFC substitute technology is based primarily on financial rather than legal considerations.

substances.[97] To take only one example, Korea was thus forced to participate if it wished to continue to export cars and fridges.[98] The parties also had to discourage the export of CFC production technology. During the 1987 negotiations the question of compatibility of this article with the General Agreement on Tariffs and Trade was raised.[99] Since the measures proposed were neither arbitrary nor unjustifiable and did not discriminate against non-parties as such, but could only be applied against those not following the protocol's control measures, it was concluded that Article 4 would be in accordance with Article 20(b) of the GATT concerning protection of human, animal, or plant life, or health, although the final judgement in the event of a bilateral dispute would rest with the WTO. There were already precedents for controls on trade with non-parties in the 1973 CITES Convention, and under resolutions of the parties to the 1972 London Dumping Convention and the 1946 International Convention for the Regulation of Whaling.[100]

3(3) REVISION AND COMPLIANCE

The institutional provisions of the 1987 protocol merit special note, since they are the key to its flexible development and enforcement.[101] The powers enjoyed by the meeting of the parties to this protocol are unusual among environmental treaties. First, provided efforts to reach a consensus have been exhausted, certain decisions taken by a two-thirds majority will bind all parties to the protocol, including those who voted against them.[102] To maintain the equitable balance between developed and developing states these decisions must be supported by separate majorities of both groups. In this way further adjustments and reductions in the production and consumption of controlled substances may be adopted and will enter into force within six months. The same rule applies to decisions concerning the financial mechanism and under Article 5. Objecting states retain the option of withdrawing from the protocol on one year's notice.[103] Other amendments to the protocol, including the addition of new controlled substances, must be made in accordance with Article 9 of the Ozone Convention, and will be effective only in respect of parties who ratify or accept them. The inability to add new substances by majority vote does limit the protocol's capacity for rapid evolution but ensures that, for example, oil or natural gas could only become controlled substances for those parties which ratify such an amendment.

Second, Article 8 of the protocol provides for a formal non-compliance procedure, the first multilateral environmental agreement to do so.[104] This procedure, which is

---

[97] Article 4, as revised 1990 and 1997.   [98] Andersen and Sarma, *Protecting the Ozone Layer*, 353.

[99] Ad Hoc Working Group, 2nd Session, 22; id, 3rd Session, 18. See *infra*, Ch 14.

[100] *Infra*, Ch 13.   [101] See *supra*, Ch 2.

[102] Article 2(9) as revised 1990. See *supra*, Ch 2, section 5.   [103] Article 19, but see 1990 revision.

[104] Protocol Annex IV, as adopted at Copenhagen in 1992. Minor revisions were agreed in 1998: see *Rept of 10th MOP, Annex II*, UNEP/OzL Pro 10/9 (1998) and *Rept of Ad Hoc Group of Legal and Technical Experts*, UNEP/OzL Pro/WG 4/1/3 (1998). See UNEP, *Rept of the Implementation Committee for the Montreal Protocol, 20th Meeting*, UNEP/OzL Pro/ImpCom/20/4, paras 24–33; Yoshida, 10 *Colorado JIELP* (1999) 95; Usuki, 43 *Jap Ann IL* (2000) 19. See also Koskenniemi, 3 *YbIEL* (1992) 123, and *supra*, Ch 4, section 3.

described in Chapter 4, has been invoked on several occasions by parties who are in difficulty, including Russia, Belarus, Ukraine and other states from Eastern Europe and the former Soviet Union. Various measures have been recommended by the meeting of the parties to deal with these problems of non-compliance, including the provision of technical assistance, GEF funding, and the issuing of cautions.[105] Further funding from the GEF and the World Bank has been made conditional on the meeting of the parties certifying that compliance by these states is satisfactory. The same procedure has also offered a useful means to ensure that parties provide the data required by Article 7 of the protocol concerning production, imports, and exports of controlled substances. Two developing states, Mauritania and North Korea, have been threatened with loss of Article 5 status for failure to report data.

Thus, although the non-compliance procedure is an example of 'soft enforcement', it is not without teeth, and it has enabled the parties to give serious and sustained attention to their responsibility for reviewing implementation of the protocol. The absence from the protocol of any other dispute settlement provision emphasises the importance of collective supervision and control, through multilateral negotiation and cooperation with the parties, rather than adjudication or arbitration.

3(4) ASSESSING THE MONTREAL PROTOCOL

One measure of the protocol's success is that it has 191 parties, including the EC, the USA, Russia, China, India, and Brazil, the last three having joined following the adoption of the London amendments in 1990.[106] These amendments, together with the availability of significant financial assistance through the GEF and the multilateral fund, helped to ensure a very high participation from developing states. So did trade restraints: the number of Article 5 parties doubled once these came into force. Thus good progress has been made in securing the level of global adherence necessary for the protocol to work.

A second measure of success is evidenced by the dynamic and flexible way in which the regime has operated. Controls on ozone-depleting substances have been strengthened at successive meetings of the parties;[107] new substances have been

---

[105] See UNEP, *Rept of the 7th Meeting of the Parties to the Montreal Protocol*, Decisions VII/15-19 (Poland, Bulgaria, Belarus, Russia, Ukraine) UNEP/OzL Pro 7/12 (1995); id, *Rept of 8th Meeting*, Decisions VIII/22-25 (Latvia, Lithuania, Czech Rep, Russia) UNEP/OzL Pro 8/12 (1996); id, *Rept of 9th Meeting*, Decisions IX/29-32 (Latvia, Lithuania, Russia, Czech Republic) UNEP/OzL Pro 9/12 (1997); id, *Rept of 10th Meeting*, Decisions X/20-28 (Azerbaijan, Belarus, Estonia, Czech Rep, Latvia, Lithuania, Russia, Ukraine, Uzbekistan) UNEP/OzL Pro 10/9 (1998); id, *Rept of 11th Meeting* (Bulgaria, Turkmenistan) UNEP/OzL Pro 11/10 (1999). See generally, Victor, Raustiala and Skolnikoff (eds), *The Implementation and Effectiveness of International Environmental Commitments* (Cambridge, Mass,1998) Chs 3, 4; Werksman, 36 ZAÖRV (1996) 750; Benedick, *Ozone Diplomacy*, Ch 17.

[106] See generally UNEP, *Rept of the Working Group of the Parties*, 17th Meeting (1998) UNEP/OzL Pro/ WG 1/17/3; id, *Rept of the Implementation Committee* (1998) UNEP/OzL Pro/ImpCom/20/4; id, *Rept of the Working Group on Countries with Economies in Transition* (1995); id, *Rept of 10th Meeting of Parties*, UNEP/ OzL Pro 10/9 (1998).

[107] The most recent are those adopted at Beijing in 1999.

added; the supervisory institutions have evolved. Without the protocol and successive adjustments, ozone depletion would be ten times greater than currently.[108]

Third, the level of compliance in developed states appears to have been high, with most phasing out the major ozone-depleting substances by 1996 as required by the accelerated timetable set by the protocol amendments. Problems submitted to the non-compliance procedure have largely been dealt with successfully, albeit at the price of some delay in implementation by states in Eastern Europe. Continued Russian production and export of controlled substances to other CIS states had been a persistent problem, but by 1998 this had been phased out with assistance from the GEF and the World Bank. The Implementation Committee was also reporting large falls in the total consumption of the main ozone-depleting substances. Once the protocol began to take effect, a black market developed, threatening to undermine the entire regime. By 1998, however, a new export/import licensing system to combat smuggling was in operation[109] and rocketing prices for CFCs suggested that illegal trade was being cut. The obligation of Article 5 parties to phase out production and consumption only began to take effect in 1999, so that by 1996 the world's main CFC producers, apart from Russia, were India and China. Thereafter data showed that consumption in a majority of developing countries had begun to fall significantly, and some parties, including China, had accelerated the phase out.[110] However, there continued to be problems obtaining reports from some states under Article 7: this is significant because the whole regime depends ultimately on the ability to monitor performance accurately.

Finally, whereas scientific assessments showed that in its original 1987 form the Montreal Protocol would not have halted an accelerating level of ozone-depleting substances in the stratosphere, subsequent revisions are now predicted to result in a gradually diminishing level after the year 2000, when increases attributable to past emissions were due to stabilize.[111] Provided the protocol is fully adhered to, global ozone losses and the Antarctic ozone hole should have recovered by around 2050. Other problems may affect the success of the protocol, including new ozone-depleting substances which it does not cover. Moreover, although the protocol has encouraged resort to substitute substances and technologies, some of these are greenhouse gases included in the Kyoto Protocol.[112] There is an evident need for coordination of these two regimes. Nevertheless, faced with the relatively straightforward task of eliminating ozone-depleting substances, the Ozone Convention and the Montreal Protocol appear to be working.

---

[108] Andersen and Sarma, *Protecting the Ozone Layer*, 346.

[109] Adopted as Article 4B of the Protocol by the IXth Meeting of the Parties in Decision IX/8 (1997). On the problem of illegal trade see Benedick, *Ozone Diplomacy*, 273–6; Brack, *International Trade and the Montreal Protocol* (London, 1996) 99–114.

[110] UNEP, *Rept. of 10th Meeting of Parties*, UNEP/OzL.Pro.10/9 (1998) paras 72ff.

[111] WMO, *Scientific Assessment of Ozone Depletion* (Geneva, 1994).

[112] E.g. HFCs, included in Annex A of the Kyoto Protocol.

4 THE CLIMATE CHANGE REGIME

4(1) DEVELOPMENT OF THE FRAMEWORK CONVENTION ON CLIMATE CHANGE

Negotiation of a climate change convention proved to be a much more difficult task than reaching agreement on protection of the ozone layer.[113] The range and complexity of issues involved in containing global warming and uncertainty regarding the nature, severity and timescale of possible climatic effects make the task of phasing out production and consumption of ozone-depleting substances seem relatively simple by comparison. The economic implications of climate change are much greater. Whereas industrial processes that deplete the ozone layer are relatively discrete, greenhouse gas production goes to the heart of energy, transport, agricultural, and industrial policy in all developed states and increasingly in developing ones too. Moreover, the role of carbon sinks means that deforestation, protection of natural habitats and ecosystems, sea-level rise, and sovereignty over natural resources are also important elements of the problem. Thus the sectoral approach, which has traditionally dominated international regulation of the environment, is plainly inappropriate to the interconnected and global character of climate change. Pollution control and the use and conservation of natural resources are both involved, within the broader context of sustainable development.

Following the adoption of numerous declarations at regional conferences calling for various measures to be taken to reduce the generation of CO_2 and other greenhouse gases, the elements of a climate-change convention were first considered by a meeting of experts in Ottawa in 1989, and by the Intergovernmental Panel on Climate Change in 1990.[114] Negotiations were then initiated in 1990 by UN General Assembly resolution 45/212, and concluded in 1992 with the adoption at the Rio Conference of a Framework Convention on Climate Change.[115]

---

[113] See Grubb, 66 *Int Affairs* (1990) 67; Churchill and Freestone (eds), *International Law and Global Climate Change*; Barrett, *Convention on Climate Change: Economic Aspects of the Negotiations* (OECD, 1992); Bodansky, 3 *YbIEL* (1992) 60 and 18 *Yale JIL* (1993) 451; Nilsson and Pitt, *Protecting the Atmosphere: The Climate Change Convention and its Context* (London, 1994); Mintzer and Leonard (eds), *Negotiating Climate Change: The Inside Story of the Rio Convention* (Cambridge, 1994); Bodansky, 20 *Ann Rev Energy & Env* (1995) 425; O'Riordan and Jäger (eds), *Politics of Climate Change: A European Perspective* (London, 1996); Luterbacher and Sprinz (eds), *International Relations and Global Climate Change* (Cambridge, Mass, 2001).

[114] Statement of Legal and Policy Experts on Protection of the Atmosphere, Ottawa, 1989; IPCC Working Group III: Formulation of Response Strategies; Legal and Institutional Mechanisms, 1990. These and the series of conference declarations setting out the negotiating policy of various groups of states are reproduced in Churchill and Freestone (eds), *International Law and Global Climate Change,* 280ff.

[115] For documentation on the negotiating history of the Convention see *Reports of the Intergovernmental Negotiating Committee for a Framework Convention on Climate Change,* UN Doc A/AC 237/6 (1st session); -/9 (2nd session); -/L 9 (3rd session); -/18 (5th session). The mandate of the INC is in UNGA Resolutions 44/207 (1989); 45/212 (1990); 46/169 (1991); and 47/195 (1992). See also UNEP Governing Council decisions 14/20 (1987); 15/36 (1989); SS II/3 (1990).

Negotiated by consensus, and intended to attract universal participation, the Climate Change Convention reflects deep differences of opinion among the participating states as to the measures needed and the allocation of responsibility for addressing the problem. Not only was it necessary to acknowledge the differential needs and responsibilities of developed and developing states, but also within each of these groups there were no common positions. Members of the Association of Small Island States, such as Nauru and Vanuatu, which might disappear in the event of modest sea level rise, were much in favour of a strong convention. Their interests were far removed from those of OPEC oil producers such as Saudi Arabia and Kuwait, whose income and economies could seriously suffer if consumption of fossil fuels by developed states were to be reduced. Neither of these groups had much in common with the larger developing states such as China, Brazil, and India, who were mainly concerned not to limit their own economic growth, but had no objection to developed states taking a strong lead. Nor did the developed OECD economies share the same view on the measures that might be needed to tackle climate change. In particular, the United States was not prepared to commit itself to specific emissions reductions or timetables and its opposition resulted in a convention that was significantly weaker than the commitments already undertaken voluntarily by a number of developed states.[116] These divisions among major groups participating in the negotiations must be recalled when assessing and interpreting the Convention.[117]

The political, scientific, and economic complexity of tackling climate change has thus presented the international community with a considerable challenge. Like the Ozone Convention, the 1992 UNFCCC is neither a comprehensive 'law of the atmosphere', nor a fully formed and detailed regulatory regime, but a framework convention establishing a process for reaching further agreement on policies and specific measures to deal with climate change.[118] Although the commitments undertaken by the parties are similarly weak, the 1992 Convention differs significantly from the Ozone Convention in two important respects. First, it specifies objectives and principles to guide implementation of the Convention and further development of related legal instruments by the parties. Second, for the first time, it makes the concept of 'common but differentiated responsibility' the explicit basis for the very different commitments of developed and developing states parties. The same differentiation underpins the Kyoto Protocol. An important and detrimental effect of this approach is that developed states have outsourced industrial production to developing economies not subject to controls on greenhouse gas emissions. To that extent the liberalization of world trade brought about by the WTO Agreement in 1994 has helped the developed economies to

---

[116] Countries that had previously committed themselves voluntarily to stabilise or reduce CO_2 emissions included Australia, Belgium, Canada, France, Germany, Italy, Japan, the Netherlands, New Zealand, the Nordic states, Switzerland, and the UK.

[117] For a sophisticated appraisal of the impact of various methods of allocating responsibility, see the Netherlands Government's *Framework to Assess International Regimes* (FAIR) for the differentiation of future commitments, available at <http://www.rivm.nl/fair>.

[118] On early proposals for a comprehensive 'law of the atmosphere' see Bodansky, 18 *Yale JIL* (1993) 451.

live within their Kyoto Protocol commitments without significantly reducing overall carbon emissions.

4(2) OBJECTIVES, PRINCIPLES, AND COMMITMENTS IN THE 1992 CONVENTION

The objective of the Convention and of related instruments is not to reverse greenhouse gas emissions but to *stabilize* them 'at a level that would prevent dangerous anthropogenic interference with the climate system'. The Convention does not specify what that level might be, nor does Article 2 envisage that it should be achieved immediately, merely that it should be 'within a time frame sufficient to allow ecosystems to adapt naturally to climate change, to ensure that food production is not threatened and to enable economic development to proceed in a sustainable manner'. The wording of Article 2 suggests that the parties envisage some degree of climate change as inevitable, and that they are prepared to tolerate it provided it happens slowly enough to allow natural adaptation.[119]

Article 3 sets out the principles the parties shall be 'guided by' in their efforts to achieve the objective of Article 2. The principles listed in Article 3 reflect the contours of global environmental responsibility elaborated in the Rio Declaration and Agenda 21.[120] Thus they include reference to inter-generational equity, common but differentiated responsibility, the precautionary principle or approach, and the right of all parties to sustainable development, as well as the need to promote 'a supportive and open international economic system'. Article 3 also tries to flesh out some of the policy factors which should be taken into account by the parties, such as policies and measures to be comprehensive and cover all relevant 'sources, sinks and reservoirs' of greenhouse gases. Further, in conformity with the principle of common but differentiated responsibility, the need for developed country parties to 'take the lead' in combating climate change and its adverse effects is stated, with full consideration to be afforded to the specific needs of those developing states that are particularly vulnerable to adverse effects of climate change, such as low-lying states affected by sea-level rise, as well as to those states which would bear a disproportionate or abnormal burden under the Convention.[121] These policies and measures should be cost-effective in the sense that they will ensure 'global benefits at the lowest possible cost'—a consideration that looms large in the architecture of the Kyoto Protocol itself.

---

[119] See Oppenheimer and Petsonk, 73 *Climatic Change* (2005) 195.   [120] See *supra*, Ch 3, section 3.

[121] Article 3(2). Although this provision is aimed 'especially' at developing countries, it is possible that states such as Saudi Arabia or the USA, which rely heavily on oil production or consumption, may have some claim to special treatment under the terms of the Convention. See also Article 4(8) of the Convention which specifically refers inter alia to the needs and concerns of '[c]ountries whose economies are highly dependent on income generated from the production, processing and export, and /or on consumption of fossil fuels and associated energy-intensive products'. Demands from OPEC countries for special treatment in the form of compensation for loss of oil income were made at the Kyoto negotiations but rejected. However Article 2(3) of the Protocol only recognizes the need to minimize the impact of implementing protocol commitments on countries listed in Article 4(8) of the Convention.

Article 3 takes a novel approach to environmental protection, but in the context of a dynamic and evolutionary regulatory regime such as the Climate Change Convention it has the important merit of providing some predictability regarding the parameters within which the parties are required to work towards the objective of the Convention. In particular, they are not faced with a completely blank sheet of paper when entering subsequent protocol negotiations or when the Conference of the Parties takes decisions under the various articles empowering it to do so. It is a nice question what the legal effect of decisions which disregard the principles contained in Article 3 may be. Given their explicit role as guidance, these 'principles' are not necessarily binding rules which must be complied with; their softer legal status is also indicated by the use of the word 'should' throughout this article.[122] However, Article 3 is not without legal effect. At the very least it is relevant to interpretation and implementation of the Convention as well as creating expectations concerning matters which must be taken into account in good faith in the negotiation of further instruments, such as the non-compliance procedure; it was reiterated in the mandate for negotiation of the Kyoto Protocol and is referred to in the Protocol itself.[123]

Article 4, which deals with the commitments undertaken by parties to the Convention, is based on the principle of common but differentiated responsibility.[124] Thus, although obligations in Article 4(1) are subject to 'specific national and regional development priorities, objectives and circumstances', they are nevertheless common to all parties, whereas the more onerous commitments made in Article 4(2) apply only to developed states and the so-called 'economies in transition' of Eastern Europe (collectively referred to as Annex I parties). Article 4(3)–(10) also makes extensive provision for solidarity assistance to developing states in the form of funding and technology transfer. The explicit assumption is that the developed states that have contributed most of the greenhouse gas emissions should also contribute most to tackling the problem, both by providing resources and by 'taking the lead' in adopting control measures.

Article 4(1) deals principally with making national inventories of greenhouse gas emissions and sinks (such as forests); national and regional programmes to mitigate climate change; promotion of scientific and technical cooperation; sustainable management of forests, oceans, and ecosystems; preparation for adaptation to the impact of climate change; and the integration of climate-change considerations in social, economic, and environmental policies. This article is not without importance in encouraging all parties to think about climate change and have policies on the subject but it does not compel them to adhere to any specific international standards for controlling it.

---

[122] Mann, in Lang (ed), *Sustainable Development and International Law* (London, 1995) 67ff notes that the legal effect of Article 3 was deliberately minimized in the final draft.

[123] See preamble to the 1997 Protocol. Article 31(2) of the 1969 Vienna Convention on the Law of Treaties also suggests that Article 3 of the Convention is part of the context for interpreting the Protocol.

[124] *Supra*, Ch 3, section 3(3). See also Rajamani, *Differential Treatment in International Law* (Oxford, 2006).

The commitments undertaken by developed states in Article 4(2) are only marginally more onerous, consisting principally of an obligation to adopt national policies and measures on the mitigation of climate change by limiting emission of greenhouse gases and protecting and enhancing greenhouse gas sinks and reservoirs. In deciding what these policies and measures should be individual Annex I parties are free to take account inter alia of their different starting points, resources, economies and 'other individual circumstances, as well as the need for equitable and appropriate contributions by each of these Parties to the global effort'. No uniformity of approach is required, and economies in transition are additionally allowed a 'certain degree of flexibility' in implementing their commitments under this article. Information concerning the policies and projected emissions of each Annex I party must be communicated to the Conference of the Parties.

There is reference in Articles 4(2)(a) and (b) to the 'aim' of returning emissions to 1990 levels 'by the end of the present decade' (i.e. by 2000). Although the timescale envisaged here is more precise than in Article 2, the wording of these sub-articles creates neither a strong nor clear commitment, although this shortcoming is balanced somewhat by the provision for early review of their adequacy by the Conference of the Parties at its first meeting, and at regular intervals thereafter.[125] In effect the parties recognized that, as in the case of ozone depletion, it would be necessary to strengthen commitments in the light of new scientific information and further assessments of the problem. Following an IPCC report that, even with stabilization of greenhouse gas emissions at current levels, atmospheric concentrations would continue to rise for the next two centuries, the first Conference of the Parties, held at Berlin in 1995,[126] did accept that these commitments were inadequate, and it provided a strong mandate (commonly known as the 'Berlin Mandate') for negotiating new, more rigorous obligations under what eventually became the 1997 Kyoto Protocol.

4(3) THE KYOTO PROTOCOL

(a) Commitments

The Berlin Mandate specified that the new Protocol would cover commitments beyond 2000, would elaborate stronger policies and measures for developed parties, and would set quantified objectives for emissions limitation and removal by sinks within a specific timescale.[127] It was agreed, however, that no new commitments would be applied to developing states. The Kyoto Protocol adopted in 1997 meets most of these objectives.[128] The key feature of the Kyoto Protocol is its establishment, for the first

---

[125] Article 4(2)(d).

[126] For decisions see *Report of the Conference of the Parties on its First Session* UN Doc FCCC/CP/1995/7/ Add 1, on which see Oberthür and Ott, 25 *EPL* (1995) 144.

[127] Decision 1/CPI (1995).

[128] See Oberthür and Ott, *The Kyoto Protocol* (Berlin, 1999); Yamin, 7 *RECIEL* (1998) 113; Freestone and Streck (eds), *Legal Aspects of Implementing the Kyoto Protocol* (Oxford, 2005). For drafting history see Depledge, *Tracing the Origins of the Kyoto Protocol: An Article by Article History*, UN Doc FCCC/TP/2000/2

time, of quantitative restrictions on emissions from industrialized economies. These states—listed in Annex B of the Protocol[129]—are limited in their emissions of the six greenhouse gases listed in Annex A. As stated in Article 3(1) KP,

The Parties included in Annex I shall, individually or jointly, ensure that their aggregate anthropogenic carbon dioxide equivalent emissions of the greenhouse gases listed in Annex A do not exceed their assigned amounts, calculated pursuant to their quantified emission limitation and reduction commitments inscribed in Annex B and in accordance with the provisions of this Article, with a view to reducing their overall emissions of such gases by at least 5 per cent below 1990 levels in the commitment period 2008 to 2012.

Also established are the three 'flexibility mechanisms'—the Clean Development Mechanism (Article 12), Joint Implementation (Article 6), and Emissions Trading (Article 17) by which parties may achieve their emissions reductions.

The quantified emission limitation and reduction commitments contained in Article 3(1) seek to ensure that overall emissions from Annex B states are reduced to at least 5% below 1990 levels within the period 2008 to 2012 but are of course subject to Article 4(2)(a) of the Convention. Article 3(1) sets out different limits for each party, in deference to their particular circumstances, including ability to reduce emissions, access to clean technology, use of energy and so on. In most cases (including the EU, USA, and Japan) a reduction of between 5% and 8% is specified, but New Zealand, Russia, and Ukraine need only stabilize emissions, while Norway, Australia, and Iceland are permitted to increase by amounts ranging from 1% to 10%. All parties listed in Annex I of the Convention must show 'demonstrable progress' in meeting their Kyoto Protocol commitments by 2005.[130]

Whilst reductions of 5% or so may seem low, they are deceptive. Choice of 1990 as the main base year means that percentage reductions of up to 30% or more of *present* emissions will have to be made by those states whose greenhouse gas emissions have increased since 1990. The United States is in this category: in 2000 a cut of some 36% would have been needed to reduce its emissions to 1990 levels. In certain circumstances economies in transition, including Russia and Ukraine, may opt for a base year earlier than 1990[131] in order to enable them to *increase* emissions because their economies have contracted so sharply since then. Developing states are not included in Annex B so no emissions limits apply to them and they are not required to do more than meet their existing commitments under Article 4(1) of the Convention.[132]

The Protocol commits Annex B developed state parties to taking action on a range of matters additional to those already covered by the Convention, including energy

---

(New York, 2000); *Repts of the Ad Hoc Group on the Berlin Mandate* (1995–7) UN Doc FCCC/AGBM/1995/2–1997/8 (8 sessions); COP, Chairman's Draft UN Doc FCCC/CP/1997/CRP.2 and *Rept of the COP* (3rd session, 1998) UN Doc FCCC/CP/1997/7, part V.

[129] The list of parties in Annex B Kyoto Protocol is substantially similar to that in Annex I of the UNFCCC.

[130] 1997 Protocol, Article 3(2).

[131] Ibid, Article 3(5). Annex I parties may use 1995 as a base year for gases listed in Article 3(8).

[132] Ibid, Article 10.

efficiency, promotion of renewable energy, reduction and phasing out of subsidies that contravene the objectives of the Convention, and control of emissions from ships and aircraft.[133] Land-use changes or forestry activities undertaken since 1990, which result in the removal of greenhouse gases (known as 'carbon sinks'), can be offset against emissions to meet the net figures set by the Protocol.[134] In order to host an afforestation or reforestation project,[135] a party must meet both the general eligibility requirements for all projects and the specific eligibility requirements for afforestation and reforestation projects, including the requirements that the host country is a party to the Kyoto Protocol, is participating voluntarily in the project activity, and has designated a national authority for the Clean Development Mechanism (CDM).[136]

The Kyoto Protocol is then a considerable advance on the Framework Convention, which it strengthens by providing means for remedial and precautionary action to address climate change. It shares its foundational principles and objectives with the Convention, as well as its classification of parties. Also common are the Convention's institutions, such as its subsidiary bodies, secretariat and the Conference of the Parties, which functions as the 'meeting of the Parties' for the purposes of the Protocol. Finally, the IPCC also supports the Protocol on scientific, technical and methodological matters.

(b) Entry into force

Any state may become a party to the Kyoto Protocol, but entry into force depends on participation by the developed states with significant greenhouse gas emissions. Pursuant to Article 25, ' "[t]his Protocol shall enter into force [when] not less than 55 Parties to the Convention, incorporating Parties included in Annex I which accounted in total for at least 55 per cent of the total carbon dioxide emissions for 1990 of the Parties included in Annex I, have deposited their instruments of ratification, acceptance, approval or accession".' Given the refusal of the United States to ratify the Protocol,[137] the prospects of its coming into force rested on one party, even after the EU and Japan had ratified. On 16 February 2005, the Russian ratification satisfied the 'double trigger', enabling the Kyoto Protocol to enter into force, following which, formal intergovernmental discussions on the Kyoto Protocol would be known as Meetings of the Parties (MOPs) and would run in parallel to COPs.

The period between COP 3 (signature of the Kyoto Protocol) and COP 7 was consumed by extensive negotiations between the parties about the detailed rules of the flexibility mechanisms. These discussions culminated in decisions at COP 7 in 2001— known as the 'Marrakesh Accords'[138]—which included, amongst other things, a draft

---

[133] Ibid, Article 2.   [134] Ibid, Article 3(3).

[135] Defined in 16/CMP 1, Annex, paras 1(b) and (c), respectively.

[136] See 3/CMP 1, Annex, paras 28–30. More generally, see Streck and Scholz, 82 *International Affairs* (2006) 861.

[137] See Ghaleigh, in O'Connor (ed), *Anti-Americanism: History, Causes, Themes* (Vol 1, Oxford, 2007) 139.

[138] Decision 2/CP7 to Decision 24/CP7 inclusive. These decisions were adopted by the Conference of the Parties serving as the meeting of the Parties (COP/MOP) at its first meeting in Montreal in November 2005.

set of rules for the operation of the CDM modalities and procedures. Decision 17/CP 7 gave the CDM Executive Board authority to commence provisional operation of the CDM (in recognition of lengthy project lead times), pending the Protocol's entry into force. The CDM modalities and procedures were formally adopted at the first Meeting of the Parties to the Protocol, subject to further refinement by the Executive Board.[139]

4(4) FLEXIBILITY MECHANISMS

The most striking aspect of the Kyoto Protocol is its so-called flexibility mechanisms. Not only were these viewed by the United States and other developed state parties as an essential means of meeting their commitments in a cost effective manner,[140] but some of them also provide a means by which developing states may restrain growth in their own emissions.

The possibility that some developed states might find it economically advantageous to meet their commitments jointly, and that developing states might also benefit from such assistance, was envisaged in Articles 4(2)(a) and 4(5) of the Convention and in a decision of the 1st COP, although the commitments of each party would not thereby be modified.[141] Such ideas were more fully articulated in the Kyoto Protocol and in particular, in its three flexibility mechanisms—Clean Development Mechanism under Article 12, Joint Implementation under Article 6, and International Emissions Trading under Article 17. Before each of these is explored at greater length, it is necessary to consider their conceptual underpinnings.

(a) Economic background

The Kyoto's Protocol's use of market-based instruments to generate emission reductions is commonly described as innovative or radical.[142] Whilst this may be true in the context of international environmental regulation, its pedigree in both theory and practice is venerable. Those familiar with Law and Economics theory will recognize in techniques such as carbon trading the legacy of Pigovian and Coasian economics. The former identified the social benefits of compelling companies to pay for the costs of their own pollution,[143] whilst the latter's *The Problem of Social Cost* demonstrated how allocating property rights and allowing trade yields pareto efficient results.[144] These

---

[139] The general supervisory powers of the CDM Executive Board are established by Article 12(4). Its functions are set out in 3/CMP 1, Annex, para 5.

[140] Although not initially by the EU—see Damro and Mendez, 12 *Environmental Politics* (2003) 2, 71–94.

[141] See Decision 5/CP1 (1995) and generally Missfeldt, 7 *RECIEL* (1998) 128; Barrett, in Cameron, Werksman, Roderick (eds), *Improving Compliance with International Environmental Law* (London, 1996) 229.

[142] See Freestone and Streck (eds), *Legal Aspects of Implementing the Kyoto Protocol*, Ch 1.

[143] See Pigou, *The Economics of Welfare* (London, 1920).

[144] See Coase, 3 *Journal of Law and Economics* (1960) 1. See also Kramer, 'A Coda to Coase', in *In the Realm of Legal and Moral Philosophy: Critical Encounters* (Basingstoke, 1998) and Pearce, 27 *Annual Review of Energy and Environment* (2002) 57.

insights laid the foundations for market mechanisms, such as emissions trading, as an alternative to traditional command-and-control methods, based on its claim to deliver environmental outcomes at the least cost. Each of the three Kyoto 'Flexibility Mechanisms' seeks to draw on the logic of the Coasian privatization of the commons and trading the resultant property rights with a view to achieving emission reductions in the most cost-effective manner, in the optimal global location.

The rationale of mechanisms such as emissions-trading is as follows. A regulator sets a cap on aggregate emissions, distributes the right to emit to regulated facilities (with their emission allowances totalling less than the aggregate emissions), and permits the market to determine the emission price and degree of abatement at individual facilities. If the regulator allows regulated facilities to transfer their emission allowances, the distribution of emission reductions among facilities will be equal to the marginal cost of emission reductions among facilities.[145] If the marginal cost of emission reductions varies among facilities, total costs can be lowered by reallocating greater effort to the facility that can lower emissions at a lower cost. Thus, when marginal cost is equal among facilities, total costs are lowest and the environmental target is reached.

Market mechanisms were first used as environmental tools in the USA in the 1990s in the form of Title IV of the Clean Air (Amendment) Act 1990. A response to SO2 generated acid rain, the Act allocated a fixed number of allowances to the electricity industry, with firms being required to surrender allowances for tons of SO2 emitted, with transfers and banking being permitted.[146] The success of the scheme in terms of costs but also as a driver of abatement innovation exceeded expectations. As a consequence, emissions trading gained favour domestically and most significantly at the multilateral level, where it formed a key negotiating strategy for the Clinton administration in negotiations leading to Kyoto.[147]

(b) Clean Development Mechanism

The Clean Development Mechanism enables Annex I parties to establish project-based activities that reduce anthropogenic emissions in non-Annex I parties.[148] The resultant Certified Emission Reductions (CERs) generated by such projects can be used by the Annex I Party to help meet its emissions targets under the Kyoto Protocol. Parties can authorize legal entities to take part in project activities. The CDM is the only flexibility mechanism available to developing states. Article 12 states it dual purposes to be: 'to assist Parties not included in Annex I in achieving sustainable development and in contributing to the ultimate objective of the Convention, and to assist Parties included in Annex I in achieving compliance with their quantified emission limitation and reduction commitments under Article 3'.

---

[145] 'Marginal cost' is the additional cost to achieve an additional unit of emissions at any facility.

[146] See Streck and Gehring, 35 *Environmental Law Reporter* (2005) 10219.

[147] See MacKenzie, *The Political Economy of Carbon Trading*, 29 *London Review of Books* (2007) 29–31, and Damro and Mendez, 12 *Environmental Politics* (2003) 2.

[148] See Freestone and Streck (eds), *Legal Aspects of Implementing the Kyoto Protocol*, Chs 9–13.

Host parties benefit from projects that contribute to sustainable development, facilitating the transfer of technology and capacity building by Annex I parties. For Annex I parties, the CDM enables the use of CERs generated by registered CDM project activities to meet part of their Kyoto targets, although CERs generated by the CDM must be 'supplemental' to domestic action to reduce emissions, and domestic action by parties must therefore constitute a 'significant element' of actions by Annex I parties to reduce emissions.[149] Typical projects include renewable energy (wind, small scale hydro, renewable biomass), fuel switching, and the capture of the most damaging of GHG such as methane and HFCs.

The CDM project cycle encompasses a number of stages and entities which are commonly divided into two phases—the development phase and the implementation phase. The former commences with the Designated National Authority of the host party providing the letter of approval to project participants, confirming that the project activity contributes to sustainable development in the country.[150] This is followed by the preparation of the Project Design Document,[151] which is necessary to obtain validation[152] from a Designated Operational Entity (DOE)[153] and registration by the CDM Executive Board,[154] and which must itself demonstrate 'additionality'. This is the requirement that the GHG emissions after project implementation are lower than would have occurred in the most plausible alternative scenario to the implementation of the CDM project activity.[155] At this stage a project is accepted as a CDM project and thereby eligible to generate CERs. The latter stage commences with monitoring of the project which involves the measurement and analysis of greenhouse gas emissions from a project so as to determine the volume of emission reductions that are attributable to the project.[156] This is followed by periodic independent review and ex post determination of reductions in greenhouse gas emissions by sources which have been monitored, performed by an independent DOE.[157] If verification is satisfactory, it is followed by certification—the formal confirmation by the designated operational entity that the emission reductions which are set out in the verification report were actually achieved.[158] Having been generated, verified, and certified a number of greenhouse

---

[149] Article 12(3) and 15/CP7. In order to ensure supplementarity, reporting obligations are imposed by Articles 5, 7, 8 of the Kyoto Protocol.

[150] 3/CMP 1, Annex, paras 29; 40(a); EB 25, para 95.   [151] 3/CMP 1, Annex, Appendix B.

[152] 3/CMP 1, Annex, para 35: 'Validation is the process of independent evaluation of a project activity by a designated operational entity against the requirements of the CDM as set out in decision 17/CP7 ... on the basis of the project design document.'

[153] DOEs are independent auditors that assess whether a project meets the eligibility requirements of the CDM (validation) and whether the project has achieved greenhouse gas emission reductions (verification and certification). DOEs are accredited by the CDM Executive Board. Although DOEs ordinarily performs either validation or verification and certification, they can be permitted to perform all three tasks for a single project. 3/CMP 1, Annex, para 27(e).

[154] 3/CMP 1, Annex, para 36: 'Registration is the formal acceptance by the Executive Board of a validated project as a CDM project activity. Registration is the prerequisite for the verification, certification and issuance of CERs relating to that project activity.'

[155] See Kyoto Protocol, Article 12(5) and 3/CMP 1, Annex, para 43.

[156] 3/CMP 1, Annex, para 44.   [157] 3/CMP 1, Annex, para 61.   [158] Id.

gas emission reductions in respect of a CDM project activity, an equivalent quantity of CERs are issued[159] and finally forwarded from the Executive Board to parties involved and project participants, as well as to the accounts in the CDM registry relating to the share of proceeds.[160]

This somewhat simplified account indicates the rather complex nature of the CDM project cycle. Whilst rigorous procedural safeguards are necessary, the attendant transaction costs are high—although small-scale projects do benefit from simplified procedures. Similarly, the centrality of the Designated National Authority to the process can operate as a bureaucratic barrier. The DNA's letter of approval is premised on there being a competent and capable DNA in existence. Of necessity in many non-Annex I parties, such an entity may not exist causing at best commercially unattractive delays, at worst a non-functioning system. The World Bank has reported on the CDM's 'creaking structure', resulting in large numbers of projects awaiting validation, delays of up to six months in engaging DOEs, and of two years in the issuance of CERs.[161] It is notable in this respect that the distribution of registered CDM projects is heavily skewed towards the more developed non-Annex I parties such as India (354), China (239), Brazil (141), and Mexico (105) with the whole of Africa hosting only twenty-five projects from a global total of 1,115.[162] In terms of sectoral, rather than geographical, concentration it is noteworthy that many CDM projects focus on HFC-23—a refrigerant coolant that has a global warming potential of approximately 11,700. It follows therefore that huge quantities of CERs can be generated via the CDM without actually contributing to the long-term effort to reduce carbon dependency and at what might not be the lowest cost. Is the HFC-23 case an example where straightforward command-and-control might be more cost-effective? Nonetheless, it should be recognized that, in 2007, the CDM market accounted for transactions worth US$7.4bn, representing emission reductions of 551 MtCO2e (million tonnes of carbon dioxide equivalent).[163]

(c) Joint implementation

Under joint implementation (JI),[164] one Annex I party may implement an emission-reducing project or a project that enhances removals by sinks in another Annex I party and by doing so generate emission reduction units (ERUs) that will count towards meeting its own Kyoto target, as defined by Article 6. As with the CDM, joint implementation aims to offer Parties a flexible and cost-efficient means of fulfilling a part of their Kyoto commitments, while the host party benefits from foreign investment and technology transfer. A JI project must provide a reduction in emissions by sources, or an enhancement of removals by sinks, that is additional to what would otherwise have

---

[159] 3/CMP 1, Annex, para 66.   [160] Article 12(8).

[161] World Bank, *State and Trends of the Carbon Market 2008* (Washington DC, 2008). See more generally, Wara and Victor, *A Realistic Policy on International Carbon Offsets* PESD Working Paper No 74 (Stanford, 2008).

[162] <http://www.cdm.unfccc.int/>, accessed on July 10, 2008.   [163] See World Bank, *supra*, n 161.

[164] See Freestone and Streck (eds), *Legal Aspects of Implementing the Kyoto Protocol*, Chs 6–8.

occurred and projects must have approval of the host Party and participants have to be authorized to participate by a party involved in the project. In comparison with the CDM, there is only modest activity under this mechanism.[165]

(d) International emission trading

Article 17 provides a framework for Annex I parties to 'participate in emissions trading for the purposes of fulfilling their commitments' provided that such trading is 'supplemental to domestic actions for the purpose of meeting quantified emission limitation and reduction commitments'.[166] Parties that may otherwise not meet their commitments are thereby able to trade units in the form of assigned amount units,[167] certified emission reductions,[168] emission reduction units,[169] and removal units.[170]

It is notable that the trade in AAUs has been a matter of some controversy. The economic collapse of the Soviet Union has left its successor states, especially Russia and the Ukraine with large AAU surpluses (as their emissions in the Kyoto commitment period are likely to be significantly below those in the baseline year of 1990). However, as this surplus has not been generated in a manner that is 'supplemental' to domestic action, major market actors in the EU have refused to purchase such AAUs unless they have been 'greened'.[171] International emissions trading under the Kyoto Protocol ought to be linked to regional or domestic trading schemes, such as the European Union Emissions Trading Scheme (EU ETS). However, one of the most serious limitations of IET has been the delay in the international transaction log[172] becoming operational, principally due to the failure to connect to the transaction log of the European Union's Emission Trading Scheme.

Although not created under the legal authority of the Kyoto Protocol, the EU ETS[173] is the keystone in the EU's complex attempts to comply with its commitments. Perhaps ironically, given its initial resistance to the market-based instrument of emissions trading in favour of more command-and-control regulatory and taxation schemes,

---

[165] Transactions under JI in 2007 totalled US$499m, representing emission reductions of 41 MtCO2e—see World Bank, *supra*, n 161.

[166] Ibid, Chs 22–9; Grubb, 7 *RECIEL* (1998) 140; Oberthür and Ott, *The Kyoto Protocol*, 187–205.

[167] AAUs are units issued by Parties to the Kyoto Protocol into their national registry up to their assigned amount.

[168] CERs are the tradeable units of the CDM. CERs are defined in 3/CMP 1, Annex, paragraph 1(b) as 'a unit representing one tonne of carbon dioxide-equivalent sequestered or abated...CERs are issued to project participants in CDM projects pursuant to Article 12 of the Kyoto Protocol and the CDM modalities and procedures.'

[169] ERUs are units converted from either AAUs or removal unit RMU and issued to project participants in Joint Implementation project activities.

[170] RMUs are issued by Parties to the Kyoto Protocol in respect of net removals by sinks from activities covered by Article 3(3) and Article 3(4) (in the land use, land use change and forestry sector).

[171] Tangen et al, *A Russian Green Investment Scheme*, <http://www.climate-strategies.org>.

[172] The purpose of the log is 'to verify the validity of transactions, including issuance, transfer and acquisition between registries, cancellation and retirement of ERUs, CERs, AAUs and RMUs and the carry-over of ERUs, CERs and AAUs'. 13/CMP 1, Annex, paragraph 38.

[173] Directive 2003/87/EC. See Freestone and Streck (eds), *Legal Aspects of Implementing the Kyoto Protocol*, Ch 23.

the scheme has become the single largest carbon market in the world with a traded volume in 2007 of 1.6 gigatons of CO_2 at a value of €28bn.[174] The scheme drives much of the activity in the CDM market and through the Linking Directive[175] has become the hub of the global carbon market. Whilst the EU ETS has undoubtedly greatly contributed to the EU's ability to influence policy-making at the national and international levels, it should not be judged an unqualified success. In its first phase (2005–2007) EU Member State governments granted emission allowances for free.[176] Combined with overly generous National Allocation Plans, the first phase came badly unstuck in May 2006 when the market crashed, losing over 70 per cent of its value. Whilst measures have been taken to avoid a reoccurrence of this episode, critics of emissions trading remain unconvinced of its merits.[177]

4(5) SUPERVISION AND COMPLIANCE

The supervisory role of the parties under the Convention and Protocol is among the most elaborate in any environmental treaty and includes a number of significant innovations. The Conference of the Parties serves as the principal supervisory institution for both the Convention and the Protocol; it is required to meet regularly and to keep the adequacy, implementation and effectiveness of both instruments under review.[178] For this purpose it receives advice from supplementary bodies for science and technology (SBSTA), and implementation (SBI).[179] The former assesses the state of scientific knowledge relating to climate change and the effects of implementation measures. The latter assists the COP in the 'assessment and review of the effective implementation' of the Convention and the Protocol and considers reports from parties under Article 12 of the Convention and Article 7 of the Protocol concerning implementation and projected emissions. It is this body which has also been responsible for developing detailed guidelines on issues such as transfer of technology, the financial mechanism, and consultation with NGOs and business. Both supplementary bodies are composed of experts acting as governmental representatives. Together, the COP and its supplementary bodies provide the essential political oversight and management of the whole climate change regime.

One of the innovative features of the regime, however, is that before national reports are considered by the subsidiary body and the COP an in-depth review is conducted by

---

[174] Roine et al, *Carbon 2008: Post 2012 Is Now* (Point Carbon, 2008).

[175] Directive 2004/101/EC. See Freestone and Streck (eds), *Legal Aspects of Implementing the Kyoto Protocol*, Ch 29.

[176] Phase 3 of the EU ETS (post-2012) is likely to feature auctioned allowances, the inclusion of the aviation and shipping sectors and support for carbon capture and storage projects.

[177] Baldwin, *Regulation Lite: The Rise of Emissions Trading*, LSE Law, Society and Economy Working Paper 3/2008.

[178] FCCC Article 7; 1997 Protocol Article 13. See Werksman, 9 *YbIEL* (1998) 48.

[179] FCCC Articles 9, 10; 1997 Protocol Article15. However, the IPCC continues in existence and remains the principal source of authoritative and independent scientific and technical advice.

a team of experts.[180] These reviews are coordinated by the secretariat and the experts who conduct them are selected from nominees of governments and international organizations. The purpose of the review is to provide 'a thorough and comprehensive technical assessment' of all aspects of implementation by any party, and to identify and report on any problems or other factors influencing the fulfilment of commitments. The teams generally visit each party to discuss the report. Their findings are circulated to all parties. Review by experts serves two useful functions. First, it helps ensure that reporting by parties is adequate, accurate, and consistent. Second, it introduces an important and desirable element of quasi-independent expertise to the process of scrutiny. In effect, review teams have the ability to report on the performance of individual states in implementing the Convention, and to point out any inadequacy in their reporting. Early in-depth reviews showed that the EC, Japan and the United States would not meet 1990 emissions levels in 2000.[181] The secretariat is required to draw such findings to the attention of the COP. It is then up to the COP to take the necessary decisions. The closest analogy to this process is the use of expert assessment teams by the IAEA when invited to review the safety of nuclear installations, but the process established here is probably stronger than anything so far adopted by that organisation.[182] It represents an attempt to provide for a significant measure of transparency and international verification of national reporting.

What happens, however, if such reviews show that a party is failing to fulfil its commitments? There are several options. The Convention makes provision for a 'multilateral consultative process' to resolve questions regarding implementation.[183] This process can be extended to the 1997 Protocol if the parties so decide. It is intended to be an even softer form of dispute avoidance than non-compliance procedures: conducted by a panel of experts, it is non-judicial in character, non-confrontational, and advisory rather than supervisory. No sanctions can be imposed; there is power only to recommend measures to facilitate cooperation and implementation and to clarify issues and promote understanding of the Convention. Parties may bring questions concerning their own implementation or that of other parties to the Multilateral Consultative Committee; the COP may also do so. This new process represents a further move away from formal binding third-party dispute settlement in favour of procedures that facilitate compliance but cannot compel it. Given the lack of real commitments in the Convention this is not a serious weakness in that context. However, reliance on the deterrent effect of inspection and publicity is unlikely to be a sure guarantee of compliance with commitments on a matter as economically fundamental as greenhouse gas emissions. How, in particular, should joint implementation, the clean development mechanism, and emissions trading be policed? Given the possibilities for evasion and

---

[180] The mechanism was first established by decision 20/CP1 (1995) and subsequently incorporated in Article 8 of the 1997 Protocol. See UN Doc FCCC/CP/13 (1996) and Werksman, 9 *YbIEL* (1998) 48.

[181] Werksman, ibid, 66.   [182] *Infra,* Ch 9.

[183] FCCC Article 13; 1997 Protocol, Article 16. For details of the process approved by the 4th COP see *6th Rept of the Ad Hoc Working Group on Article 13* (1998) UN Doc FCCC/AG13/1998/2, Annex II.

abuse this is an important question. For all these reasons, it has been argued that, unlike ozone depletion, 'purely facilitative approaches to non-compliance may not answer parties' concerns about the need to ensure that all parties pull their weight and that the protocol's market mechanisms provide confidence to investors'.[184]

Another option in cases of non-compliance is to resort to dispute settlement as provided for in Article 14 of the Convention and Article 19 of the Protocol. However, negotiation and non-binding conciliation are the only compulsory procedures envisaged here, unless both parties to the dispute have declared their acceptance of ICJ jurisdiction or arbitration. Moreover, even for parties who do accept adjudication or arbitration, these articles are probably not adequate for dealing with the questions likely to be thrown up by joint implementation or clean development projects and emissions trading, all of which may also involve private parties and private law. Neither procedure is multilateral in character, and would not necessarily involve participation by the parties collectively.

Finally, and most importantly, there is provision in Article 18 of the 1997 Protocol for a non-compliance procedure to be negotiated. The unusually complex process adopted in 2006, and involving facilitative and enforcement procedures, is considered further in Chapter 4. It seems likely that these procedures will become the principal mechanism for disputes concerning compliance with the 1997 Protocol and any subsequent commitments.

4(6) ASSESSMENT OF THE CLIMATE CHANGE REGIME

In the long approach to the expiry of the Kyoto Protocol's commitment period on 31 December 2012, issues of climate change have assumed a prominence in public discourse that is unprecedented in international environmental law. The vast range of actors—state and non-state; governmental and non-governmental; commercial and otherwise; national, sub-national and supra-national—engaged in tackling climate change is commensurate with the scale of the challenge. Similarly extensive are the processes, techniques and positions taken in respect of it. The following assessment seeks to provide a point of departure for investigations into the complexity of the post-Kyoto climate-change regime.

(a) The UNFCCC

At the time of its adoption in 1992 the Climate Change Convention was criticized for containing 'only the vaguest of commitments regarding stabilisation and no commitment at all on reductions'.[185] Understandably, the United States' position was that 'there is nothing in any of the language which constitutes a commitment to any specific level of emissions at any time'. It was noted also that 'Many of the Convention's provisions do not attempt to resolve differences so much as paper them over', and that there was

---

[184] Werksman, 9 YbIEL (1998) 48, 100.   [185] Bodansky, 18 Yale JIL (1993) 451.

no provision for international monitoring or fact finding.[186] Nor does the Convention acknowledge responsibility on the part of industrialized states to compensate other states for the harm caused by greenhouse gas emissions beyond a vague commitment to assist vulnerable developing country parties to meet the costs of adaptation.[187]

Whilst valid criticisms in 1992, much has since changed. Even in 1992 the Climate Change Convention contained more substance than the Ozone Convention or the Transboundary Air Pollution Convention. Like those agreements, the test of success lies not in the commitments made in the Convention itself but in its subsequent evolution. Most importantly the Convention did achieve an equitable balance acceptable to the great majority of developed and developing states,[188] and as of July 2008 it had 192 parties. Moreover, the adoption of the Kyoto Protocol in 1997 demonstrated that agreement on stronger emissions limits and earlier timetables was possible, despite the difficulty of maintaining meaningful consensus.

(b) The Kyoto Protocol in changing circumstances

In the previous edition of this work it was noted that 'the Kyoto Protocol is not the last word'. What was purely speculative in 2001 has become commonplace in 2008, indicating the speed at which this area of law and policy has since moved. This has been driven by the rapidly evolving state of scientific knowledge about climate change—not least the IPCC's Fourth Assessment Report of 2007—which has made the case for significantly more demanding multilateral regulation a necessity. Also influential has been *The Economics of Climate Change: The Stern Review*,[189] commissioned by the United Kingdom Treasury. A comprehensive treatment, the report describes anthropogenic climate change in terms of catastrophic market failure. Its main conclusion is that in order to avoid the worst effects of climate change, prompt investment totalling 1 per cent of global gross domestic product per annum is necessary. Investment would be required for mitigation and adaptation, thereby encompassing, inter alia, low-carbon energy technologies and carbon capture and storage. The failure to do so, argues Stern, could risk annual global GDP being up to 20 per cent lower than it otherwise might be.

In this context, emission reductions required by the Kyoto Protocol seem overwhelmingly inadequate. Similarly, whatever the achievements of the Clean

---

[186] Ibid.

[187] Article 4(4). The governments of Nauru, Tuvalu, Kiribati, Fiji, and Papua-New Guinea made declarations on signature or ratification stating that the Convention did not constitute a renunciation of any rights under international law concerning state responsibility for adverse effects of climate change or a derogation from the principles of general international law. On state responsibility for environmental damage see *supra*, Ch 4.

[188] Bodansky, 18 *Yale JIL* (1993) 451. See generally Redgwell, in Churchill and Freestone (eds), *International Law and Global Climate Change*, 41; Franck, *Fairness and International Law and Institutions*, Ch 12, and *supra*, Ch 3, sections 3(3), 6(3).

[189] (Cambridge, 2007). The lead author is the Head of the UK Government Economic Service, and a former Chief Economist of the World Bank. Whilst influential, the report has also attracted criticism—see Tol and Yohe, 7 *World Economics* (2006) 233–50.

Development Mechanism, it is clear that it has so far failed to drive technological innovation at an appropriate rate, or facilitate technology transfer on a scale that meets the needs of the burgeoning new economies of India and China in particular. Indeed a brief analysis of global energy forecasts brings the scale and dynamics of the relative positions of industrialized and emerging economies into sharp relief.

Global demand for energy is forecast to increase by 66% by 2030, with fossil fuels accounting for 86% of the total. Whilst energy usage by OECD and non-OECD states was roughly equal in 2005, the latter's share is set to increase to 59% in 2030, with India and China's accounting for the majority of that extra demand. Global CO_2 emissions are estimated to increase from 28.1 billion metric tons in 2005 to 42.3 billion tons in 2030 and the share of non-OECD economies rising from 51% in 2005 to 63.3% in 2030.[190] If such figures appear to support the argument for uniform emission reductions, it is of course the case that the *historic* responsibility for global emissions lies mainly with developed, not developing economies, and has facilitated a level of welfare the latter are keen to emulate. Moreover, disparities exist in per capita CO_2 totals. Indian and Chinese emissions stood at 3.7 and 1.0 metrics tons per capita in 2004 as compared with 9.5 and 19.7 metric tons per capita for Japan and the USA. Even after the forecast increases by 2030 to 7.1 and 1.8 metrics tons per capita for India and China (with the United States and Europe remaining substantially the same) the gap persists.[191] Nevertheless, it is clear that a future regime which does not engage the major developing states in greenhouse gas reductions will not be successful.

(c) The negotiating context

Before considering possible amendments to the existing regulatory architecture of climate change, we must ask how future agreements will be negotiated. Whilst the negotiations under the auspices of the Framework Convention are clearly central, it is important to note the existence of parallel processes.

The Kyoto Protocol commitment period expires in 2012. At the time of writing, many of the key issues necessary for a successor agreement were expected to be substantially settled at COP 14 in 2008, if not their details. Adoption of a new protocol was scheduled for COP 15 at Copenhagen in December 2009. Both will build upon the Bali Roadmap—a series of decisions taken at COP 13 in December 2007, which include the Bali Action Plan,[192] purporting to chart the course for a new negotiating process, with the aim of completion by Copenhagen. It also includes the AWG-KP[193] negotiations, the launch of the Adaptation Fund, and the Article 9 review of the Kyoto Protocol, as

---

[190] Energy Information Administration, *International Energy Outlook* (2008). Whilst the previous edition of this work recognized the 'risk that emissions from developing states such as Brazil, China and India will overtake those of OECD states as they industrialise further [as] a real one', that possibility has now become a fact, with China soon to become the world's single largest GHG emitter.

[191] International Energy Agency, *World Energy Outlook* (Vienna, 2006).   [192] Decision 1/CP13.

[193] Ad Hoc Working Group on Further Commitments for Annex I Parties under the Kyoto Protocol. Article 3, para 9 of the Kyoto Protocol mandates the Conference of the Parties to initiate consideration of future commitments for Annex I Parties. It aims to complete its work and have its results adopted by the

well as decisions on technology transfer and reducing emissions from deforestation. This is an ambitious agenda.

Running in parallel with the 'Convention' negotiations are two other processes. The Major Economies Meeting (MEM), initiated by President Bush in 2007, is avowedly ' "a new initiative to develop and contribute to a post-Kyoto framework on energy security and climate change" ' that seeks to 'contribute to existing national, bilateral, regional and international programs' and not undermine them.[194] Not surprisingly it has been viewed with some suspicion, given President Bush's less-than-firm commitment to action on climate change at home and abroad. Moreover, participation is limited to major actors (principally OECD nations, USA, China, India, Brazil, EU) rather than the more broadly based Convention processes. A similarly hand-picked parallel process operates under the auspices of the G8. Commenced in 2005 under the British presidency,[195] the G8 has undertaken various actions to combat climate change, including a 'dialogue' with Brazil, Mexico, South Africa, China and India. As with the MEM, the G8+5 process is intended to complement the UN Framework Convention process and recognizes it as the ' "only forum in which binding agreements on future frameworks can be negotiated" '.

The 2008 G8+8 meetings in Hokkaido[196] reaffirmed that future cooperation would be 'rooted in the objective, provisions, and principles of the Convention' and the Bali Roadmap. 'Serious consideration' would be given to the 'ambitious IPCC scenarios', and the role of technology in addressing climate change.[197] Most significantly, governments agreed on the 'goal of achieving at least a 50 per cent reduction in global emissions by 2050'.[198] Compared with the emission reductions of the Kyoto Protocol, this would represent a significant change in the commitments leading economies are prepared to undertake. Whilst the Summit Leaders' Declaration states that 'this global challenge can only be met by a global response, in particular, by the contributions from all major economies, consistent with the principle of common but differentiated responsibilities and respective capabilities',[199] it is far from clear that emerging economies take the same view. The Declaration emerging from the larger meeting of the MEM states the need to 'ensure the agreed outcome [of negotiations] maximizes the efforts of all nations [with] nationally appropriate mitigation actions, supported and enabled by technology, financing and capacity-building, with a view to achieving a

---

Conference of the Parties at the earliest possible time to ensure that there is no gap between the first and second commitment period of the Kyoto Protocol.

[194] Formally known as the 'Major Economies Process on Energy Security and Climate Change'—see <http://www.state.gov/g/oes/climate/mem/>.

[195] See <http://www.g8.gov.uk/>.

[196] UK, United States, Russia, Germany, Japan, Italy, Canada, France. Expanded to include Australia, Indonesia and South Korea, China, India, Brazil, South Africa, and Mexico.

[197] See *G8 Hokkaido Toyako Summit Leaders Declaration*, 8 July 2008, paras 22–35.

[198] Ibid, para 23. Note the absence of a specified base year or shared medium term reduction targets.

[199] Ibid.

deviation from business as usual emissions'.[200] This differently nuanced emphasis is characteristic of post-Kyoto negotiations.

On the relative negotiating positions of Annex I and non-Annex I parties—and hence the future articulation of the principle of common but differentiated responsibility—the most striking development of recent years has been the vast economic expansion of India and China. As we have seen, most of the commitments under the Convention and the Protocol apply only to developed state parties. Given recent patterns of industrialization and trade liberalization, which have seen large-scale relocation of heavy GHG emitters from Europe and North America to China, India and Brazil, is it appropriate, or sustainable, for these non-Annex I parties to continue to be largely unconstrained by the climate change regime? Whilst the Convention and Protocol provide some incentives for developing states to tackle greenhouse gas emissions, through various provisions on technology transfer, the clean development mechanism, and 'additional' funding from developed states, and the Global Environment Facility, they have trenchantly resisted the application of quantified emission limitation and reduction commitments. The background to this position is twofold. First is the historic fact that industrialized economies have long benefited from massive GHG emissions, are substantially responsible for the current problems, and should not as such deprive newly industrializing economies from similarly raising the standard of living of their own citizens. Second, the rejectionist position taken by the Bush administration vis-à-vis the Kyoto Protocol, and its general appearance as a climate change denier, has not persuaded emerging economies that they are obliged to undertake binding commitments. Moreover, pursuant to Article 4(7) '[t]he extent to which developing country Parties will effectively implement their commitments under the Convention will depend on the effective implementation by developed country parties of their commitments'.[201] Here we can see that the already limited obligations of developing states appear to be conditional on provision of benefits by developed states. Whilst a regime in which one group of states bears most of the burdens and another group reaps most of the benefits accurately reflects a sense of historical responsibility for the causes of climate change it is far from clear that this approach is optimally placed to solve the problem at hand. The question thus arises whether the articulation of the principle of common but differentiated responsibility found in the Kyoto Protocol is sustainable given the scientific urgency indicated by the 2007 IPCC Assessment Reports and the economic realities of Indian, Brazilian, and Chinese industrialization.

---

[200] See *Declaration of Leaders' Meeting of Major Economies on Energy Security and Climate Change*, 9 July 2008, paras 2, 5.

[201] Wording of this kind is found also in the Convention on Biological Diversity, Article 20(4), and see *supra*, Ch 3, section 3(3). On cooperation within the UNFCCC and Kyoto Protocol regime, see Baettig et al, 30 *Environmental Science and Policy* (2008) 478–489.

4(7) POST-KYOTO POSSIBILITIES

(a) Bali Action Plan

The preamble to the Bali Action Plan speaks of the need for 'deep cuts' in global GHG emissions and refers to the 'urgency' of the task, with the work of the IPCC playing an important role.[202] The report indicates that global emissions of greenhouse gases (GHGs) need to peak in the next ten to fifteen years and be reduced to very low levels, well below half of levels in 2000 by the middle of the twenty-first century in order to stabilize their concentrations in the atmosphere at the lowest levels assessed by the IPCC to date in its scenarios. This goes further than either the Kyoto Protocol or the UNFCCC in emphasizing the immediacy of the problem. The majority of countries, with EU leadership, wished to consider cuts of between 25 and 40 per cent for rich countries, by 2020, but agreement was blocked by the USA, Canada, and Russia.[203] The commitment to 'Measurable, reportable and verifiable...mitigation commitments or actions including quantified emissions limitation' for all developed country parties is however important in ensuring that the USA, which is not a party to the Kyoto Protocol, remains involved in mitigation efforts.[204] Although it is moving in a positive direction, the Bali Action Plan frustrates hopes of establishing binding targets, which will be the focus of subsequent negotiations.[205]

The Bali conference made significant progress on putting deforestation and forest degradation firmly on the agenda. Decision 2/CP 13 required the SBSTA to undertake a programme of work in relation to this, with a report to be made at COP 14. This builds on the groundwork done in the Marrakesh Accords on defining and adopting methodologies. The same decision invites developing countries to 'explore a range of actions, identify options and undertake efforts, including demonstration activities, to address the drivers of deforestation relevant to their national circumstances'.[206] Developed country parties are 'invited' to mobilize resources in support of this, although it is left open what incentives might be provided.[207] Decision CMP3/6 established Good Practice Guidance for land use, land use change, and forestry activities.

The inclusion of Carbon Capture and Storage Technology in the CDM continues to be discussed by the SBSTA. Strengthening of the previous regime on technology-sharing

---

[202] Decision 5/CP13.

[203] See *Climate Change Strategic Comments* (2008) vol 14, available from the International Institute for Strategic Studies at <http://www.iiss.org>.

[204] Morgan, *Post-Kyoto: The International Context for Progress on Climate Change*, Memorandum to the House of Commons Environmental Audit Committee, 1.5.

[205] Ibid, 1.1. See also UK House of Commons, Environmental Audit Committee, *6th Report: Reaching an International Agreement on Climate Change* (London, 2008).

[206] Ibid, 3.

[207] In addition, the World Bank has launched a Forest Carbon Partnership Facility to help demonstrate the feasibility of accurately accounting for REDD reductions. The two components are a $100 million 'readiness' fund focusing on capacity building and a $200million carbon finance mechanism for pilot projects. The Bank has already raised roughly half of this money from nine industrialized countries and The Nature Conservancy.

is necessary if the potential for cooperation is to be realized. Here the Experts Group on Technology Transfer (EGTT) established by the Marrakesh Accords has an important role to play. Decision CP13/3 establishes a very comprehensive work programme including assessing the gaps and barriers to technology transfer, developing a set of performance indicators to monitor and evaluate the effectiveness of the technology transfer framework, and bringing forth a strategy paper on how to move forward. The issue of secure funding for the EGTT is also given continued precedence. Decision CP13/4 requests the GEF to develop a plan for scaling up funding for transfer of environmentally sound technologies. Decision CMP3/1 on the clean development mechanism reiterates many of the concerns relating to establishing baselines, approval of methodologies and monitoring that have plagued the CDM from its inception. No promises about the long-term future of the CDM were made. In relation to Joint Implementation, there was again little in the way of radical reform.

Important progress was also made in Bali towards operationalizing an Adaptation Fund to develop policies and guidelines, recommending strategic priorities to the COP/MOP, developing criteria to ensure that governments seeking funding are administratively and financially capable, and approving funds for adaptation projects and programmes proposed by governments. A sixteen-member Board will be composed of two representatives of each of the UN's five regional groups, one representative of small island developing states, one representative of the least developing countries, and two each from developed and developing countries.[208] The Adaptation Fund is based on an 'Adaptation Levy', i.e. 2 per cent of certified emission reductions (CERs) approved under the Clean Development Mechanism (CDM). This does not involve national development assistance funds but is a global tax (or levy) on an international transaction. It is estimated that this 'adaptation levy' on CDM transactions will generate several hundred million pounds by 2012.

Post-Kyoto, the two-track framework of Annex 1/non-Annex 1 countries is likely to include further commitments for developing countries. Article 1(b)(ii) of the Bali Action Plan calls for 'nationally appropriate' mitigation actions to be undertaken 'in a measurable, reportable and verifiable manner'. This may be compared to the commitments in Article 10(b) of Kyoto Protocol to:

Formulate, implement, publish and regularly update national and, where appropriate, regional programmes containing measures to mitigate climate change and measures to facilitate adequate adaptation to climate change.

It is clear that, whilst the Bali Action Plan remains informed by the principle of common but differentiated responsibility, developing countries are increasingly expected to play a full role in mitigation efforts. The language used, although short of binding commitments, indicates that concrete evidence of progress will be required. The strengthening of the *Dialogue on Long Term Cooperative Action on Climate Change* to form an Ad hoc Working Group[209] is another step towards a more inclusive

---

[208] Decision COP/MP3/1.   [209] Decision CP13/1, at 2.

international framework. This is a positive step in relation to the long-term actions necessary by all countries to address climate change.

The work of the Least Developed Countries Expert Group is also to continue.[210] Several issues are important in this area, including increases in funding to the Least Developed Countries Fund and other specialist funds administered by the GEF and coordination with official development assistance. By mid 2007, actual multilateral financing delivered under the broad umbrella of initiatives set up under the UNFCCC had reached a total of US$26 million. This is equivalent to one week's spending on flood defence in the United Kingdom.[211] However, for the first time, finance ministers met at Bali during the climate change negotiations to better understand the scale of the challenge and to explore the potential need for transfers. Decision CP13/6 establishes a review of the current financial mechanism by the SBI with a view to facilitating consistency in financing activities and improving the complementarity of the financial mechanism with other sources of investment and financial flows, in addition to exploring options for increasing resource flows. Decision CP13/7 establishes a structure for assessment of the work of the GEF, but falls short of establishing the increases in resource flow that are arguably needed.

5 CONCLUSIONS

This chapter has illustrated several points of general significance. First, that although customary international law remains important in providing a basis for solutions to problems of atmospheric protection, the negotiation of global treaty regimes is essential if detailed and comprehensive international regulation is required. Second, that progress has been made in refining the operation of international regulatory and supervisory regimes, of which the institutional machinery established by the 1985 Ozone Convention and the Montreal Protocol is now among the most significant examples.[212] Third, that whatever the legal status of the precautionary principle or approach, its influence on the evolution of international regimes is apparent in the examples covered by this chapter. But the significance of this conclusion should not be exaggerated. Endorsing the principle does not answer the question what measures are to be taken, or by whom, and it is clear that substantial problems of global and regional economic equity have to be addressed if the necessary action is to be undertaken by a sufficiently large number of relevant states. This conclusion only serves to emphasize that the use of legal controls and the machinery of international justice cannot of themselves ensure the attainment of environmental goals endorsed by international policymakers, given the substantial changes in energy policy, industrial activity, and technology which are needed, and the economic implications this may have for developed and developing states. It is thus not surprising that the various

---

[210] Decision CP13/8.   [211] Morgan, *supra*, 5.1.6.   [212] *Supra*, Ch 2, section 5.

treaties on protection of the global atmosphere examined here represent perhaps the most significant resort to equity in international environmental law and diplomacy.

No other topic covered by this book presents the problems of inter-generational equity and global governance in such stark contours. Climate change potentially affects all elements of the global environment, including land use and food supply, sustainable water resources, preservation of biodiversity, sea levels and the marine environment, the polar ice caps, the survival of tropical forests, and human health. Unchecked, it may change the world as we know it irreversibly. Tackling it represents probably the greatest challenge the UN system has ever faced.

7

THE LAW OF THE SEA AND PROTECTION OF THE MARINE ENVIRONMENT

1 INTRODUCTION

The high seas are the world's largest expanse of common space. They have been freely used for maritime commerce, exploitation of living resources, extraction of oil and gas, and as a disposal area for the waste products of industry, agriculture, domestic life, and war. The pressure of international competition for living resources led to the conclusion of the first multilateral treaties on seals, fisheries, and whaling in the early twentieth century.[1] The emergence of serious environmental problems was evident as early as 1926, when a draft convention on pollution from ships was drawn up at a conference in Washington, but not opened for signature. Only after the Second World War did problems of over-exploitation of resources and the steady increase in the volume and effects of pollution from land and seaborne sources reach an intensity that required concerted international action. The subsequent history and development of international law relating to fisheries, marine living resources and marine biodiversity is considered in Chapter 13. Regulation of marine pollution was somewhat slower to develop, reflecting the more limited interest of states in this problem and the limitations of scientific understanding of oceanic processes.[2]

---

[1] 1911 Convention for the Preservation and Protection of Fur Seals, 104 *BFSP* 175; 1923 Convention for the Preservation of the Halibut Fishing of the Northern Pacific, 32 *LNTS* 94; 1930 Convention Establishing an International Pacific Salmon Fisheries Commission, 184 *LNTS* 306; 1931 Convention for the Regulation of Whaling, 155 *LNTS* 349. See *infra*, Ch 13.

[2] See generally O'Connell, *The International Law of the Sea* (Oxford, 1984) ii, Ch 25; Churchill and Lowe, *The Law of the Sea* (3rd edn, Manchester, 1999) Ch 15; Johnston (ed), *The Environmental Law of the Sea*

By the late 1960s awareness of the impact of pollution on coastal environments, fisheries, and human populations had become widespread. The *Torrey Canyon* disaster in 1967, involving the contamination of large areas of coastline by oil, exemplified the risk posed by the daily transport of large quantities of toxic and hazardous substances at sea. The discovery that mercury emissions from a factory at Minimata in Japan had poisoned fish and endangered the lives and health of coastal communities showed that the problem was not confined to the operation of ships, but required comprehensive control of all potential pollution sources, including those on land. Scientific studies conducted in the 1970s and 80s by GESAMP,[3] and at regional level, showed significant pollution of the sea by oil, persistent organic compounds, chemicals, nuclear waste, and the effluent of urban, industrial society. By the 1990s real problems of over-fishing, loss of marine biological diversity, and degradation of marine ecosystems had also become more apparent.[4] For all these reasons protection of the marine environment and sustainable use of its resources have been significant issues in the modernization of the law of the sea.

Because of the considerable attention devoted since 1954 to the control of oil pollution from ships and dumping of waste at sea, these are today a relatively minor component of marine pollution. By far the major input into the marine environment comes from land-based sources and airborne depositions. Sewage, industrial waste, and agricultural run-off are the most common types of pollutant which enter the sea from land, mostly through rivers. Some of the substances these sources generate are directly toxic to marine life and humans or spread disease. Others contribute to eutrophication and oxygen depletion, resulting in loss of marine biodiversity and altering sensitive ecosystems. Further harmful impacts on the marine ecosystem are caused by the incidental transport of alien invasive species in ships' ballast water and their discharge many thousands of miles distant from their natural habitat. Thus effective pollution control is important not only for the general health of the marine environment but particularly for its impact on the conservation of fish stocks and coastal ecology. Climate change has also begun to affect marine ecosystems, resulting in loss of coral reefs, alterations in the distribution of marine species, melting ice shelves in the polar seas, and ultimately sea level rise.

In 1990, the second GESAMP report concluded that marine pollution had worsened since 1982.[5] Sewage disposal and agricultural run-off were identified as the most urgent problems requiring international attention. Eutrophication had been occurring

---

(Berlin, 1981); Brown, *The International Law of the Sea* (Aldershot, 1994) i, Ch 15; Vidas and Østreng (eds), *Order for the Oceans at the Turn of the Century* (The Hague, 1999); Boyle and Freestone (ed), *International Law and Sustainable Development* (Oxford, 1999).

[3] Group of Experts on the Scientific Aspects of Marine Pollution (GESAMP), *The State of the Marine Environment* (UNEP, 1990) and see *infra*, Ch 8. GESAMP is a body of independent scientists which conducts studies for IMO, IAEA, and UNEP.

[4] GESAMP, *Reports and Studies No 50: Impact of Oil and Related Chemicals and Wastes on the Marine Environment* (IMO, 1993); id, Statement of 1998 Concerning Marine Pollution Problems, in *Reports and Studies No 66* (IMO, 1998) Annex X; Cormack, 16 *Marine Policy* (1992) 5, and see *infra*, Ch 13.

[5] GESAMP, *The State of the Marine Environment*. There has been no comparable study since 1990.

with increasing severity in enclosed waters in the Baltic, North Sea, Mediterranean, Northern Adriatic, and in parts of Japan and the US east coast. The effects on coastal ecosystems of pollution and development had become a serious threat to wildlife and fish resources. But existing controls on certain persistent toxins such as DDT and chlorinated hydrocarbons had begun to prove effective in European and American waters. In tropical and subtropical areas, however, contamination was thought to be rising. In general, the report's conclusions pointed out the strengths and weaknesses of international regulation of the marine environment. Where there were effective international standards, as in the case of nuclear waste disposal, the problem had diminished. Where particular categories of pollutant, such as sewage, were less well regulated, or where no coordinated action had been agreed, as in many Third World coastal areas, the problems were of increasing severity. Moreover, the report concluded that for the first time there was some evidence that pollution was no longer confined to coastal waters and enclosed seas, although these remain the most seriously affected areas, and it is here in the oceans' most biologically productive region that international action is most urgent. Regional agreements concerned with enclosed or semi-enclosed seas such as the North Sea, the Baltic, or the Mediterranean, have attempted to coordinate environmental measures in these areas. Since 1992, they have been strengthened and extended in response to Agenda 21 of the Rio Conference, with renewed emphasis on sustainable development, a precautionary approach, and integrated coastal-zone management. There is some evidence that this has begun to reverse the deterioration. In the north-east Atlantic, for example, OSPAR has concluded that 'The trends towards worsening pollution have been reversed, and in a substantial number of significant cases the source of the pollution has been stopped.'[6]

While highly regulated operational discharges from oil tankers now provide only 4 per cent of oil entering the sea, discharges from other vessels and accidental spills still account for some 450,000 tonnes of oil pollution from ships every year. This is far greater than the very limited input from offshore oil extraction, but somewhat less than the 600,000 tonnes believed to seep into the oceans naturally.[7] Marine pollution is not the only environmental problem posed by international shipping, however, although it is the only one on which international law has anything significant to say at present. Ships burn relatively low-grade fuel oil that causes significant levels of SO_X and NO_X air pollution, which are predicted by IMO to increase 30–40 per cent by 2020. A start has been made on regulating these emissions, but more radical proposals were under discussion in 2008.[8] Another IMO report concluded that CO_2 emissions from ship's engines amounted to 4.5 per cent of the global total, more than twice that of the airline industry.[9] Given continued expansion in world trade, much of it transported by sea,

---

[6] *Quality Status Report* (London, 2000) 102.

[7] See GESAMP, *Reports and Studies No 75: Estimates of oil entering the marine environment from sea-based activities* (IMO, 2007).

[8] See 1973/78 MARPOL Convention, Annex VI. Draft amendments will be submitted to the Marine Environment Protection Committee (MEPC) 57th session, in 2008.

[9] The report is summarized in MEPC 57/4 (2007) paras 87–106.

these emissions will rise unless shipping is brought within efforts to deal with climate change. This will be one of the biggest environmental challenges currently facing the shipping industry.

1(1) THE 1982 UN CONVENTION ON THE LAW OF THE SEA

The process of developing new law, initially based on ad hoc attempts to regulate specific problems such as pollution from ships or dumping, was given substantial impetus by the 1972 Stockholm Conference on the Human Environment and the 1992 Rio Conference on Environment and Development. Recommendations of the Stockholm Conference led directly to the adoption of the 1972 London and Oslo Dumping Conventions, and the 1973 International Convention for the Prevention of Pollution from Ships (MARPOL). General principles for the assessment and control of marine pollution from all sources, including land-based and airborne, were also endorsed, and these formed the basis for articles later incorporated in UNEP's Regional Seas Agreements and in Part XII of the 1982 UN Convention on the Law of the Sea (UNCLOS).[10] Unlike the earlier Geneva Conventions of 1958, the 1982 Convention was intended to be, as far as possible, comprehensive in scope and universal in participation. In these respects it has been largely successful. Not only does it enjoy very wide participation, but on many issues it has been treated as customary law by courts, international organizations, and non-parties.

Negotiated by consensus as an interlocking package deal,[11] the Convention's provisions form an integral whole, protected from derogation by compulsory third-party settlement of disputes, a prohibition on reservations, and a ban on incompatible *inter se* agreements.[12] Within these limits, it is capable of further evolution through amendment,[13] the incorporation by reference of other generally accepted international agreements and standards,[14] and the adoption of additional global and regional implementing agreements and soft law.[15] Multilateral negotiating processes, both at the UN and in other international organizations and conferences, continue to play a central role in the development of the law of the sea. The International Maritime Organization (IMO) provides the principal forum for further lawmaking with respect to pollution from ships, while the Food and Agriculture Organization (FAO) oversees the further development of fisheries law. Both organizations are considered in more detail in Chapter 2. Regulation of the oceans affects many other interests, however, and has continued to generate proposals for further development from various

---

[10] UN Doc A/CONF 48/14/Rev 1, Action Plan, Recommendations 86–94, and see also Intergovernmental Working Group on Marine Pollution, UN Doc A/CONF 48/8, para 197, repr as Annex III to the Conference Report. See Ch 2, *supra*.

[11] UN, *The Law of the Sea: UN Convention on the Law of the Sea* (New York, 1997) 'Introduction', 1–4. See also Caminos and Molitor, 79 *AJIL* (1985) 871; Buzan, 75 *AJIL* (1981) 324; Allott, 77 *AJIL* (1983) 1.

[12] Articles 279–99, 309, 311(3).   [13] Articles 312–14.

[14] See especially Articles 21(2) 119, 207–12. In most cases these global standards are derived from IMO regulatory conventions. See *infra*, section 4.

[15] See e.g. the 1995 Agreement on Straddling Fish Stocks and Highly Migratory Fish Stocks, *infra*, Ch13.

bodies, including the 1992 UN Conference on Environment and Development,[16] the Commission on Sustainable Development,[17] the Conference of the Parties to the Biodiversity Convention,[18] the UN General Assembly,[19] and the Informal Consultative Process on Law of the Sea.[20]

The 1982 UNCLOS was intended to be a comprehensive restatement of almost all aspects of the Law of the Sea. Its basic objective is to establish:

a legal order for the seas and oceans which will facilitate international communication, and will promote the peaceful uses of the seas and oceans, the equitable and efficient utilization of their resources, the conservation of their living resources, and the study, protection and preservation of the marine environment.[21]

The Convention thus attempts for the first time to provide a global framework for the rational exploitation and conservation of the sea's resources and the protection of the environment, while also recognizing the continued importance of freedom of navigation. In many respects it has been a model for the evolution of international environmental law.[22] Moreover, it gives special recognition in various ways to the interests of developing states, in particular though provision for transfer of science and technology and a partial reallocation of fisheries resources. Other measures intended to benefit developing states are noted later in this chapter and in Chapter 8.

The articles of the 1982 UNCLOS on the marine environment represent the outcome of a process of international lawmaking which has effected a number of fundamental changes in the international law of the sea.[23] Of these perhaps the most important here is that pollution can no longer be regarded as an implicit freedom of the seas; rather, its diligent control from all sources is a matter of comprehensive legal obligation affecting the marine environment as a whole, and not simply the interests of other states. A second alteration is to the balance of power between flag states, more concerned with freedom of navigation and fishing, and coastal states, more concerned with effective regulation and control, although many states fall into both categories and thus faced complex policy choices in negotiating the 1982 UNCLOS. Third, the emphasis is no longer placed on responsibility or liability for environmental damage, but rests primarily on international regulation and cooperation focused on protection of the marine environment. In this legal regime, flag states, coastal states, port states, international organizations, and commissions each have important roles, powers, and responsibilities, which in certain respects combine to produce one of the

---

[16] See infra, section 1(2).   [17] See e.g. CSD Rept of 7th Session, Decision 7/1.

[18] See infra, Ch 13.

[19] E.g. the 1995 Fish Stocks Agreement and the annual UNGA resolutions on fisheries and law of the sea.

[20] See de La Fayette, in Freestone, Barnes, and Ong (eds), The Law of the Sea (Oxford, 2006) Ch 4.

[21] Preamble.

[22] UN, Rept of the UN Sec Gen on the Protection and Preservation of the Marine Environment, UN Doc A/44/461 (1989).

[23] Boyle, 79 AJIL (1985) 347; Schneider, 20 CJTL (1981) 243; Kwiatkowska, The 200-Mile EEZ in the Law of the Sea (Dordrecht, 1989) Ch 5; McConnell and Gold, 23 CWRJIL (1991) 83; Charney, 28 Int. Lawyer (1994) 879.

more successful of international environmental regimes. The law of the sea has not remained static, however, and cannot be understood without reference to later developments, including the recommendations of the Rio Conference, considered below, and the 1992 Convention on Biological Diversity, whose impact on conservation of marine living resources is considered in Chapter 13.

1(2) AGENDA 21 AND THE MARINE ENVIRONMENT

The 1982 UNCLOS is referred to in Agenda 21 of the 1992 Rio Conference Report as providing 'the international basis upon which to pursue the protection and sustainable development of the marine and coastal environment and its resources'. Nevertheless, Chapter 17 of Agenda 21 introduces several new elements not found in UNCLOS, including an emphasis on integrated and precautionary approaches to protection of the marine and coastal environment.[24] The focus is no longer principally on the control of sources of marine pollution, but more broadly on the prevention of environmental 'degradation' and the protection of ecosystems. For the first time protection of the exclusive economic zone is linked with sustainable development of coastal areas and sustainable use of marine living resources. Although Agenda 21 cannot amend the 1982 UNCLOS, and is not binding on states, it can be taken into account when interpreting or implementing the Convention and it has had the effect of legitimizing and encouraging legal developments based on these new perspectives. The impact of Agenda 21 thus illustrates how 'a more conceptually sophisticated' focus on protection of the marine environment has evolved out of Part XII of UNCLOS.[25] As one writer observes: 'It is hard to conceive of the development of modern law of the sea and the emerging international law of the environment in ocean-related matters outside the close association and interplay between UNCLOS and Agenda 21'.[26]

How these developments have further changed the law can be seen in the rewriting of regional-seas agreements on the Mediterranean, the Baltic and the Northeast Atlantic, revision of the London Dumping Convention, extension of treaty schemes on liability for pollution damage, and the adoption at Washington in 1995 of a Declaration and Global Programme of Action on Protection of the Marine Environment from Land-based Activities. A precautionary approach to the protection of marine ecosystems and biological diversity is now addressed in many of these treaties and in various other ways, in particular through the Conventions on Biological Diversity and Climate Change, the 1995 Agreement on Straddling and Highly Migratory Fish Stocks

---

[24] Agenda 21, Ch 17, para 17.1. See generally Treves, in Campiglio et al (eds), *The Environment After Rio* (London, 1993) 161; Nollkaemper, *Marine Policy* (1993) 537; Cicin-Sain and Knecht, 24 *ODIL* (1993) 323; Beyerlin, 55 *ZAÖRV* (1995) 544; Birnie, in Norton et al (eds), *The Changing World of International Law in the 21st Century* (The Hague, 1998) 3; Falk and Elver, in Vidas and Østreng (eds), *Order for the Oceans at the Turn of the Century* (The Hague, 1999) 145; Yankov, in Boyle and Freestone (eds), *International Law and Sustainable Development* (Oxford, 1999) 271; Tanaka, 19 *IJMCL* (2004) 483.

[25] Falk and Elver, in Vidas and Østreng (eds), *Order for the Ocean*, 153.

[26] Yankov, op cit, 272.

(UN Fish Stocks Agreement), the 2004 Ballast Water Convention, and the creation of specially protected areas by IMO and under regional-seas agreements.[27]

Not all of the regional agreements fully reflect post-Rio perspectives, however. Problems of coordination between pollution and fisheries regimes remain. Sustainable management of oceans and coasts is far from common in the practice of states.[28] Moreover, although changes to international law brought about by the 1995 Fish Stocks Agreement are more extensive than in instruments affecting land-based sources of marine pollution, in neither case have economic interests necessarily been outweighed by greater concern for the marine environment: as in other contexts, sustainable development does not entail a preservationist approach but a value judgment which may be development-oriented.[29] As we shall see in the next chapter, although industrial waste dumping at sea is now largely prohibited, international law relating to the most significant source of damage to the marine and coastal environment— urbanization and industrial and domestic pollution from land-based activities— remains very weak.

Nor is the objective of integrating protection of the marine and coastal areas, living resources, and associated ecosystems straightforward. First, what are the landward limits of 'the coastal zone'? It has been described as 'the interface where the land meets the ocean', including reefs, deltas, wetlands, beaches, coastal plains, and so on, but the limits 'are often arbitrarily defined' and differ from state to state.[30] Most regional protocols on land-based sources of marine pollution protect internal waters (i.e. those on the landward side of the territorial sea baseline such as bays, deltas, and estuaries) up to the freshwater limit, which would cover some of the areas just listed; those on specially protected wildlife areas usually extend further to include related land areas, such as wetlands and beaches. The most extensive, the revised 1996 Mediterranean Protocol on Pollution from Land-based Sources and Activities, includes not only the Mediterranean Sea, internal waters, brackish waters, coastal marshes, lagoons, and related ground waters, but also 'the entire watershed area within the territories of the Contracting Parties, draining into the Mediterranean Sea Area'.[31] While this definition acknowledges the theory that the 'coastal zone' should extend to the watersheds of all rivers flowing into the sea, in practice so much land is then included that the concept is likely to be unacceptable to some states for the same reason that the drainage basin has been resisted in the law of international watercourses.

Second, what are the seaward limits? Integrated management of marine ecosystems and coastal areas is not easy to reconcile with the unaltered UNCLOS division of the

---

[27] See UN, *Oceans and Law of the Sea: Report of the Sec Gen* (New York, 1998) esp paras 306–28; Freestone and Makuch, 7 *YbIEL* (1996) 3; Freestone, in Boyle and Freestone (eds), *International Law and Sustainable Development* (Oxford, 1999) 135; Hewison, 11 *IJMCL* (1996) 301; Gjerde and Freestone, *Particularly Sensitive Sea Areas*, 9 *IJMCL* (1994) 431, and see *infra*, Chs 8, 11, 13.

[28] GESAMP, *Reports and Studies No 66* (IMO, 1998).

[29] Beyerlin, 55 *ZAÖRV* (1995) 577–9; Nollkaemper, 27 *ODIL* (1996) 153.

[30] 1993 Noordwijk Guidelines for Integrated Coastal Zone Management (World Bank).

[31] Articles 2, 3; Scovazzi (ed), *Marine Specially Protected Areas*, 85. See also 1990 Kingston Protocol on Specially Protected Areas and Wildlife, Article 1(c) which includes related watersheds and terrestrial areas.

oceans into zones of exclusive national jurisdiction out to 200 miles from the coast and high seas thereafter.[32] In ecosystem terms, such national or jurisdictional boundaries are inherently arbitrary and the exclusive economic zone does not reflect a rational basis for integrated management of marine ecosystems, whatever its economic and jurisdictional benefits to coastal states. The failure of US efforts in the UNCED nego-tiations and in the ICJ to secure recognition of the alternative concept of the 'large marine ecosystem' merely serves to re-emphasise that despite post-Rio evolution, eco-system management is a policy tool, not a legal concept,[33] and that effective inter-state cross-boundary cooperation at global and regional level remains essential to the sus-tainable management of marine ecosystems. Moreover, even where, as in Antarctica, national jurisdictional claims are in abeyance, and the landmass and surrounding ocean are treated for regulatory purposes as a common area, cooperative application of integrated ecosystem management has not been an obvious success.[34]

2 CUSTOMARY LAW AND THE 1982 UNCLOS

2(1) HIGH SEAS FREEDOMS AND REASONABLE USE

Protection of the marine environment was not given special importance in the Geneva Conference on the Law of the Sea in 1958, and the Geneva Conventions have little to say on the subject. Articles 24 and 25 of the 1958 High Seas Convention do require states to prevent oil pollution from ships, pipelines, and seabed operations, and pollu-tion from radioactive substances, but they fall short of acknowledging a more compre-hensive duty to prevent marine pollution or protect the marine environment, and offer no definition of the term 'pollution'. The content of even these limited obligations was uncertainly defined, and states were left with much discretion in the choice of measures to take. The articles did refer to 'taking account' of 'existing treaty provisions', a for-mulation intended to cover the 1954 London Convention for Prevention of Pollution of the Sea by Oil, and to 'any standards and regulations which may be formulated by the competent international organizations', which in this instance meant the IAEA's regulations on the disposal of radioactive waste,[35] but this did not mean that states were obliged either to become parties or to follow the standards set by these inter-national regulations. In practice, the 1958 Conventions seemed to suggest that states enjoyed substantial freedom to pollute the oceans, moderated only by the principle

---

[32] See Tanaka, 19 *IJMCL* (2004) 483.

[33] See Wang, 35 *ODIL* (2004) 41; Juda, 30 *ODIL* (1999) 89; Alexander, *Marine Policy* (1993) 186; Cicin-Sain and Knecht, 24 *ODIL* (1993) 339; Treves, in Campiglio et al, *The Environment After Rio*. The ICJ has con-sistently rejected attempts to redraw maritime boundaries in accordance with environmental or ecosystem considerations: see *Gulf of Maine Case*, ICJ Reports (1984) 246 and *Jan Mayen Case*, ICJ Reports (1993) 38.

[34] See 1991 Protocol to the Antarctic Treaty on the Environment, and Redgwell, in Boyle and Freestone (eds), *International Law and Sustainable Development*, Ch 9.

[35] See *infra*, Ch 8.

that high-seas freedoms must be exercised with reasonable regard for the rights of others. This view was not contradicted by the 1954 London Convention, which did not entirely prohibit discharges of oil from ships at sea, nor by the IAEA's regulations, which permitted the disposal of low-level radioactive waste. The test of reasonableness still remains a useful principle for accommodating lawful but conflicting uses of the sea,[36] but evidence now points firmly towards the emergence of more specific rules of international law governing the protection of the marine environment, such as the prohibition of radioactive pollution of the seas, referred to in Chapter 8, or the authoritative exposition of the due-diligence principle in relation to pollution from ships, considered below.

2(2) A DUTY TO PROTECT THE MARINE ENVIRONMENT

The emergence of a more strongly expressed obligation to protect the marine environment is evidenced by Articles 192–5 of the 1982 UNCLOS, by regional treaties, and by other multilateral agreements negotiated progressively since 1954. These include the 1972/96 London Dumping Convention, the 1973/8 MARPOL Convention, which deals with pollution from ships and supersedes the earlier 1954 Convention, and a variety of regional treaties requiring states to control land-based sources of marine pollution, dumping, and seabed operations.[37] The degree of acceptance of these various treaties and the consensus expressed by states in negotiating the environmental provisions of the 1982 UNCLOS suggest that its articles on the marine environment are supported by a strong measure of *opinio juris* and represent an agreed codification of existing principles which have become part of customary law.[38] There is thus nothing essentially novel in the proposition first articulated in Article 192 of the 1982 Convention that 'states have the obligation to protect and preserve the marine environment', although this may not have been the case when the article was first proposed in 1975. Moreover, this obligation is more strongly expressed than in Principle 21 of the Stockholm Declaration, insofar as Article 193 reaffirms the sovereign right of states to exploit their natural resources but only 'in accordance with their duty to protect and preserve the marine environment'.

The content of this obligation is elaborated in more detail by Article 194 and subsequent provisions. It is evident from the Convention, first, that its protection extends not only to states and their marine environment, but to the marine environment as a whole, including the high seas. This goes beyond the older customary rule based on the *Trail Smelter* arbitration, and reflects its extension to global common areas contemplated by Principle 21 of the Stockholm Declaration.[39] The 'environment' for

---

[36] *Supra*, Ch 3, and *Icelandic Fisheries Case*, ICJ Reports (1974) 4.

[37] On regional treaties see *infra*, section 3.

[38] Ch 17 of Rio Agenda 21 refers to 'International law, *as reflected in the provisions of the United Nations Convention on the Law of the Sea*' (emphasis added). On the drafting history of Articles 192–5 see Nordquist (ed), *United Nations Convention on the Law of the Sea: A Commentary*, iv (Dordrecht, 1991) 36ff.

[39] *Supra*, Ch 3, section 4.

this purpose includes 'rare and fragile ecosystems as well as the habitat of depleted, threatened, or endangered species and other forms of marine life'.[40] The obligation of states is thus not confined to the protection of economic interests, private property, or the human use of the sea implied in the Convention's definition of 'pollution'.[41] This conclusion is consistent with the provisions of modern treaties dealing with the wider environmental impact of marine pollution, including the 1992 protocol to the 1969 Convention on Civil Liability for Oil Pollution Damage, the 1989 Salvage Convention, and a number of regional treaties and protocols concerned with especially sensitive ecological areas.[42]

Second, the 1982 UNCLOS represents an important advance over the earlier Geneva Conventions by formulating the obligation of environmental protection in terms which are comprehensive of all sources of marine pollution.[43] Thus it applies to ships, land-based activities, seabed operations, dumping, and atmospheric pollution, and provides a framework for treaties both global and regional on each of these topics. In this respect the comprehensive scope of the 1982 Convention follows the pattern established by the 1974 Helsinki Convention for the Protection of the Marine Environment of the Baltic Sea, and subsequently adopted in UNEP's regional-seas treaties. Moreover, as we saw in Chapter 3, the International Tribunal for the Law of the Sea has held that 'the duty to cooperate is a fundamental principle in the prevention of pollution of the marine environment under Part XII of the Convention and general international law and that rights arise therefrom which the Tribunal may consider appropriate to preserve under Article 290 of the Convention'.[44] Other provisions of the Convention require states to carry out environmental impact assessment and monitoring, to maintain contingency plans against marine pollution, and to notify other states of imminent damage.[45] In all these respects later developments in general international law have come to reflect the Convention's provisions.[46] The Convention must also be interpreted and applied taking later developments in general international law into account, including the precautionary principle.[47] The definition of pollution in Article 1, the obligation to do an environmental impact assessment in Article 206, the general obligation to take measures to prevent, reduce and control pollution under Article 194, and the responsibility of States for protection and preservation of the

---

[40] Article 194(5).   [41] Article 1(4) *supra*, Ch 3, section 4(6).

[42] 1985 Nairobi Protocol Concerning Protected Areas and Wild Flora and Fauna in Eastern Africa; 1990 Kingston Protocol Concerning Specially Protected Areas and Wildlife of the Wider Caribbean; 1996 Barcelona Protocol Concerning Specially Protected Areas and Biological Diversity in the Mediterranean.

[43] Article 194.

[44] *MOX Plant Case (Provisional Measures)* (2001) ITLOS No 10, para 82; *Land Reclamation Case (Provisional Measures)* (2003) ITLOS No 12 para 92, *supra*, Ch 3, section 4(5). See also Articles 123, 197, 199–202 and *Southern Bluefin Tuna Cases (Provisional Measures)* (1999) ITLOS Nos 3 and 4, para 78.

[45] Articles 198, 199, 204, 206.   [46] *Supra*, Ch 3, sections 4(4), (5).

[47] *Supra*, Ch 3, section 4(3) and see *Southern Bluefin Tuna Cases* (1999) ITLOS Nos. 3 & 4, paras 77–79 and Judges Laing at paras 16–19 and Treves at para 9. See also Nordquist (ed), *UNCLOS Commentary*, vol III, 288, and Freestone, in Boyle and Freestone (eds), *International Law and Sustainable Development* (Oxford 1999) 140.

marine environment under Article 235 are all potentially affected by the more liberal approach to proof of environmental risk envisaged by Rio Principle 15.

But perhaps its most significant feature is the way the Convention handles the concept of due diligence. As with other treaties it makes reference to the need to take 'all measures necessary' to prevent and control pollution damage to other states, but moderates this requirement by allowing use of the 'best practicable means at their disposal and in accordance with their capabilities' where the risk is to the marine environment in general, rather than to other states. This wording implies a somewhat greater flexibility and discretion, particularly for developing countries, whose interests received particular attention in the drafting of this part of the Convention.[48] The significance of this point can be seen more clearly in Articles 207 and 212, dealing with the control of land-based and atmospheric sources of pollution, where reference is made to economic capacity, development needs, and 'characteristic regional features'. State practice in this regard is examined in Chapter 8 and confirms the view that the Convention's treatment of both issues largely defers to the priorities set by individual states.

These unhelpful generalities are absent, however, in the provisions dealing with pollution from ships, dumping, and seabed operations, and it is here that the Convention does establish some important and concrete principles. The essential point in these cases is that states must give effect to or apply rules and standards no less onerous than 'generally recognized international rules and standards'. Although precise phraseology varies in detail, and not all writers are agreed on the correct interpretation, Articles 208, 210, and 211 of the Convention have the effect of incorporating into the primary obligation to prevent pollution the evolving standards set by the London Dumping Convention, the MARPOL Convention annexes, relevant IAEA guidelines, IMO codes, and other soft law instruments agreed and adopted by a preponderance of maritime states. If this view is correct, then states parties to the 1982 UNCLOS will thus be compelled as a matter of UNCLOS treaty law to adopt the basic standards set inter alia by the annexes to the Dumping and MARPOL Conventions, even if they are not parties to them.[49] Arguably, ships flagged in non-parties to UNCLOS would similarly be subject to the same standards due to their widespread adoption and the general compliance of non-parties in coastal state and port enforcement measures.[50]

---

[48] Nordquist and Park (eds), *Report of the US Delegation to the UN Convention 3rd UNCLOS* (Honolulu, 1983) 47–51, 74, 89; Kindt, 20 *VJIL* (1979) 313; Nordquist (ed), *UNCLOS Commentary*, iv, 64.

[49] Boyle, 79 *AJIL* (1985) 347. On the variety of meanings attributed to the phrase 'generally accepted', see Vukas, in Soons (ed), *Implementation of the Law of the Sea Convention Through International Institutions* (Honolulu, 1990) 405; Bernhardt, 20 *VJIL* (1980) 265; Van Reenen, 12 *NYIL* (1981) 3; Vignes, 25 *AFDI* (1979) 712; Molenaar, *Coastal State Jurisdiction over Vessel-Source Pollution* (The Hague, 1998) Ch 5; Birnie, in Ringbom (ed), *Competing Norms in the Law of Marine Environmental Protection* (The Hague, 1997) 31. For the status of other IMO and ILO conventions as 'generally accepted international standards' for the purposes of Article 211 of the 1982 UNCLOS, see Valenzuela, in Soons (ed), *Implementation of the Law of the Sea Convention Through International Institutions* (Honolulu, 1990) 187, and more cautiously, Oxman, 24 *NYUJILP* (1991–2) 109.

[50] By December 2007, 146 states representing 98% of world shipping tonnage were parties to Annexes I and II of MARPOL; 82 states were parties to the 1972 London Dumping Convention, on which see *infra*, Ch 8. On coastal state and port enforcement see *infra*, section 4.

Understood in these terms, the 1982 Convention is important because it delegates to the IMO the task of defining and updating the detailed content of the obligation of due diligence as formulated in Article 194. The generality and uncertainty which limit the usefulness of the due diligence rule in other contexts are thus potentially reduced, although as some writers point out, the lack of clarity in defining precisely which rules must be observed may in practice give states some discretion to pick and choose.

More than any other aspect of the 1982 Convention, Part XII is indicative of an altered sense of priorities in the treatment of marine pollution. It is no longer essentially a matter of high-seas freedom moderated by reasonable use, but one of legal obligation to protect the environment. Whereas previously states were to a large degree free to determine for themselves whether and to what extent to control and regulate marine pollution, they will now in most cases be bound to do so on terms laid down by the 1982 Convention and other international instruments. Because of the widespread acceptance of the treaties on pollution from ships and dumping, this proposition held good even before the entry into force of UNCLOS in 1994; the impact of the Convention's articles on the marine environment thus lies essentially in their expression of principles of customary law, whether those reflected in prior state practice, or subsequently developed.

3 REGIONAL PROTECTION OF THE MARINE ENVIRONMENT[51]

3(1) THE 1982 UNCLOS AND REGIONAL RULES

Although the 1982 Convention, like the law of the sea itself, is primarily concerned with a global system of international law governing all aspects of the use of the oceans, the Convention's reference at various points to regional rules, regional programmes, regional cooperation, and so forth does indicate that we are not necessarily dealing with a single legal regime of universal application but with one which allows for significant regional variations. There is specific provision for regional cooperation in the case of enclosed and semi-enclosed seas;[52] in the case of management of living resources regional cooperation and regulation are required if the provisions of UNCLOS and the 1995 UN Fish Stocks Agreement are to be implemented effectively. Part XII of UNCLOS, dealing with protection of the marine environment, also makes significant

---

[51] Boyle, in Vidas (ed), *Protecting the Polar Marine Environment* (Cambridge, 2000) Ch 1; Crawford, in *International Law on the Eve of the Twenty-First Century: Views from the International Law Commission* (UN, 1997) 99; Vallega, 24 *O&C Man* (1994) 17; Knecht, 24 *O&C Man* (1994) 39; Johnston, *Regionalisation of the Law of the Sea* (Cambridge, 1978); Boczek, 16 *CWRJIL* (1984) 39; Johnston and Enomoto, in Johnston (ed), *The Environmental Law of the Sea* (Gland, 1981) 285.

[52] Articles 122–3. The *MOX Plant Arbitration*, PCA (2003) reveals sharply differing views about the implications of these articles for regional cooperation.

reference to regional rules and standards in various contexts. Article 237 specifically preserves the freedom of states to make further agreements relating to the protection and preservation of the marine environment, provided these are 'concluded in furtherance of the general principles and objectives of this Convention'. The same article also preserves obligations under existing agreements on the marine environment, but requires them to be 'carried out in a manner consistent with the general principles and objectives' of the Convention. UNEP's regional-seas agreements, FAO's regional fisheries agreements, and regional schemes for port-state control are thus an important contribution to implementing UNCLOS and meeting the goals of sustainability and integrated ecosystem management set out in Chapter 17 of Rio Agenda 21 and in the 2002 Johannesburg Declaration and Plan of Implementation.

Nowhere does UNCLOS specify what is meant by 'regional', although the term is clearly something less than 'global'. The best interpretation is that a region is defined by the context in which the issue arises. Article 122 offers one approach in its reference to enclosed or semi-enclosed seas;[53] defined as 'a gulf, basin or sea surrounded by two or more states and connected to another sea or the ocean by a narrow inlet or consisting entirely or primarily of the territorial seas and exclusive economic zones of two or more coastal states'. A number of treaties concerned with protection of the marine environment are regional in this sense, notably those relating to the Mediterranean, the Baltic, the Red Sea and Persian Gulf.[54] What makes these areas special is their relative ecological sensitivity and separation from the marine environment of adjacent oceans. They represent in varying degrees 'problem sheds' or areas within which the levels of pollution are relatively or completely independent of discharges elsewhere, and which require regional coordination if control measures are to be effective.[55] These considerations are of particular significance in the control of land-based sources of pollution, and as we shall see in the next chapter, the 1982 Convention's articles largely assume that this source will be controlled nationally and regionally, rather than by global rules. This partly accounts for the extreme generality of the Convention's provisions on the subject, although some progress has subsequently been made in strengthening regional action.

A 'region' does not have to be composed on this ecological basis, however. Political considerations, common interests, or geographical proximity are other factors influencing the conclusion of regional treaties.[56] Some of the UNEP regional-seas treaties relate to oceanic coastal areas where the only factor connecting participants is their location on a common coastline, rather than any identity of interest or shared

---

[53] See Vukas, in Vidas (ed), *Protecting the Polar marine Environment*, Ch 2; Vallega, 24 *O&C Man* (1994) 17; Alexander, 2 *ODIL* (1974) 151.

[54] 1995 Barcelona Convention for the Protection of the Marine Environment and Coastal Region of the Mediterranean; 1992 Helsinki Convention for the Protection of the Marine Environment of the Baltic Sea Area; 1982 Jeddah Convention for the Conservation of the Red Sea and the Gulf of Aden Environment; 1978 Kuwait Convention for Cooperation on the Protection of the Marine Environment from Pollution.

[55] Okidi, 4 *ODIL* (1971) 1; Schachter and Serwer, 65 *AJIL* (1971) 84.

[56] Alexander, 71 *AJIL* (1977) 84; id, 2 *ODIL* (1974) 151; id, 11 *Ocean YB* (1994) 1; Hayward, 8 *Marine Policy* (1984) 106; Boczek, 16 *CWRJIL* (1984) 39; Vallega, 24 *O&C Man* (1994) 17.

ecological problems. The conventions dealing with the south-east Pacific and north-east Pacific coasts of Latin America and the Atlantic and Indian Ocean coasts of Africa fall into this category.[57] Others, in the south Pacific or the Caribbean, are largely defined by the proximity and shared interests of a number of island states.[58] For UNEP, defining a region thus resolves itself largely into a question of policy: what is the most sensible geographical and political area within which to address the interrelated problems of marine and terrestrial environmental protection? As one author points out, 'development of the basic regional concept has not been stimulated by scientific thought but by the decision-making context and practice of the UN system'.[59] From this perspective it does not matter how a region is defined so long as it works. What does seem to be important is that there should be close correspondence between the 'political' region and the 'geographical' region: that is undoubtedly one of the central lessons of UNEP's regional-seas programme.[60]

Leaving aside their composition, the more important question concerns the role which it is appropriate for regional regulation of the marine environment to play. There are several possible answers to this question. At one level, regional arrangements are simply a means of implementing policies which are necessary in the interests of a specific community of states and which can best be tackled on a regional basis. Cooperation in cases of pollution emergencies, or in the exploitation of fishing stocks are good examples, because the range of states affected is relatively limited. In other cases, such as enclosed or semi-enclosed seas or Arctic waters, physical characteristics may dictate the regional application of more onerous standards of pollution prevention than would suffice for oceanic areas. This factor is the main justification for special regional rules governing the discharge of pollution from ships or the dumping of waste at sea. The need to cater for such special cases is recognized in the 1982 UNCLOS,[61] although it is important to observe that for pollution from ships or dumping the Convention insists that regional rules should be no less effective than more generally accepted international rules, and that regional treaties cannot be taken as an opportunity for falling below those rules. By facilitating some regional flexibility, however, regional arrangements do help accommodate the special needs and varying circumstances of a range of seas with diverse ecological and oceanographic characteristics to a general international law of the sea.

A second reason for resort to regional arrangements is that they may facilitate cooperation in negotiating stronger (or more precautionary) environmental standards

---

[57] 1981 Lima Convention for the Protection of the Marine Environment and Coastal Area of the SE Pacific; 1981 Abidjan Convention for Cooperation in the Protection and Development of the Marine and Coastal Environment of West and Central Africa; 1985 Nairobi Convention for the Protection, Management, and Development of the Marine and Coastal Environment of East Africa; 2002 Convention for Cooperation in the Protection and Sustainable Development of the Marine and Coastal Environment of the Northeast Pacific.

[58] 1983 Cartagena Convention for the Protection and Development of the Marine Environment of the Wider Caribbean; 1986 Noumea Convention for the Protection of the Natural Resources and Environment of the South Pacific Region.

[59] Vallega, 24 O&C Man (1994) 26.   [60] Ibid.

[61] 1982 UNCLOS, Articles 211(6), 234; 1972 Oslo Dumping Convention, and see *infra*, Ch 8.

and supervising compliance. This is particularly true in the North Sea, the Baltic, and the Mediterranean, where intergovernmental supervisory institutions have been established;[62] there are other regions, however, where no effective multilateral commissions exist, or where the role played by institutions remains limited to a symbolic presence.[63] A number of UNEP regional-seas institutions fall into this category, having never in practice functioned. Third, regional treaties can be seen as a means of giving effect to the framework provisions of the 1982 Convention, and as evidence of the implementation and adoption of that Convention's main principles at regional level. Their conformity in most respects with the 1982 UNCLOS is some indication of their legislative function in international law, and of the present legal status of the 1982 Convention's provisions on protection of the marine environment.[64]

Lastly, regional regimes offer a more appropriate basis for the integrated ecosystem and coastal zone management called for by Rio Agenda 21. This approach, which takes account of the need to conserve marine biodiversity and fisheries, is reflected inter alia in the 1992 OSPAR Convention,[65] in the 1995/6 revisions of the Mediterranean Convention regime,[66] and in the 1991 Antarctic Environment Protocol.[67] It is a significant innovation. Not only is it now harder to draw a clear dividing line between the marine environment and the land environment, as we saw above, but a state may also be considered to form part of a marine region even if it has no sea-coast, provided its adjacent land area falls sufficiently within the ambit of the 'coastal zone' to require environmental management as a single entity. Thus although they have no coastline on the Arctic Ocean, Sweden and Finland may nevertheless be 'Arctic states' for the purpose of integrated management.[68] This is scarcely surprising, given that the greatest impact on the marine environment comes not from the uses of the sea considered in this chapter, but from land-based activities considered in the next chapter. As we have seen, however, such an interpretation of what is meant by 'coastal zone' may prove in practice too extensive to be readily acceptable to all states.

3(2) REGIONAL SEAS AGREEMENTS

Some twenty treaties can be identified which are 'regional' in the various senses described above and which relate to the protection of the marine environment. These

---

[62] See esp Hey, 17 *IJMCL* (2002) 325.   [63] See *infra*, Ch 8.

[64] Some regional agreements do pose problems of conformity with UNCLOS, however: see 1981 Lima Convention, Article 1 (area of application).

[65] Hey, 17 *IJMCL* (2002) 325.

[66] Vallega, 29 *O&C Man* (1995) 251; id, 31 *O&C Man* (1996) 192 and *infra*, next section.

[67] 1991 Protocol, Articles 2 and 3(1) of which commit parties to 'the comprehensive protection of the Antarctic environment and dependent and associated ecosystems'. For this purpose the cold-water marine ecosystem surrounding Antarctica, known as the 'convergence', would appear to be included. See Boyle, in Vidas (ed), *Protecting the Polar Marine Environment*, Ch 1; Vidas, ibid, Ch 4; Redgwell, in Boyle and Freestone (eds), *International Law and Sustainable Development* (Oxford, 1999) Ch 9.

[68] On the difficulties of defining 'the Arctic' see Rothwell, 6 *YbIEL* (1995) 65; Boyle, in Vidas, *Protecting the Marine Environment*, 29–30; Vanderzwaag, in Vidas and Østreng (eds), *Order for the Oceans*, 231. Similarly, Switzerland now participates in the International North Sea Conference: see *infra*, Ch 8.

fall into two main groups; first, those concerned with enclosed or semi-enclosed seas in the northern hemisphere where the major problems are those of industrial pollution and land-based activities, and second, a group of UNEP-sponsored treaties which establish a broadly uniform pattern of principles for a majority of developing countries in the southern hemisphere. The number of states now involved in these regional-seas treaties, and in other UNEP regional-seas programmes, is such that they cannot be dismissed as special cases; they represent a substantial body of practice of more general significance for the law of the marine environment as a whole. Most have been supplemented, replaced, amended, or reinterpreted to reflect post-UNCED objectives and principles; in this respect they illustrate both the flexibility of framework treaties as regulatory instruments and the continuing evolutionary character of the law of the sea notwithstanding codification in the 1982 UNCLOS.

(a) The North Sea and north-east Atlantic

The North Sea has a longer history of regional environmental cooperation than any other semi-enclosed sea. Initially regulated by a series of overlapping agreements adopted piecemeal, it remains outside UNEP's Regional Seas Programme, and still lacks an over-arching framework treaty.[69] However, the series of International North Sea Conferences (INSC),[70] which first met in 1984, has provided an important political forum in which to define and coordinate increasingly stringent environmental objectives. The declarations of these Conferences are not legally binding treaties, but the principle of good faith does entail an expectation that implementation will be promoted at national and regional level. Some of the Conference undertakings have been translated into action through relevant regional treaty bodies, in particular the Oslo/Paris Commission. This body supervises implementation of the most important regional agreement, the 1992 Paris Convention for the Protection of the Marine Environment (OSPAR Convention),[71] which extends to the north-east Atlantic, the North Sea and adjacent Arctic waters. The 1992 Convention replaces and updates two earlier treaties regulating pollution of the sea from land-based and offshore sources, and dumping.[72] It also empowers the parties to tackle other issues affecting sustainable protection of the marine environment by adopting new annexes or taking binding decisions. The first such measure, an annex on Protection and Conservation of Ecosystems and Biological Diversity, was adopted following the treaty's entry into force in 1998. This may suggest that the 1992 Convention will evolve in ways that

---

[69] See Saetevik, *Environmental Cooperation Among North Sea States* (London, 1986); IJlstra, 3 *IJECL* (1988) 181; papers collected in 5 *IJECL* (1990); Pallemaerts, 7 *IJECL* (1992) 1; Sadowski, in Ringbom (ed), *Competing Norms in the Law of Marine Environmental Protection*, 109; Skjaerseth, in Victor et al (eds), *The Implementation and Effectiveness of International Commitments* (Cambridge, Mass, 1998) 327; id, *North Sea Cooperation* (Manchester, 2000); Hey, 17 *IJMCL* (2002) 325.

[70] See *infra*, Ch 8.

[71] Hey, IJlstra and Nollkaemper, 8 *IJMCL* (1993) 1; Hilf, 55 *ZAÖRV* (1995) 580; de la Fayette, 14 *IJMCL* (1999) 247, and see *infra*, Ch 8.

[72] 1972 Oslo Dumping Convention, and 1974 Paris Convention for the Prevention of Marine Pollution from Land-based Sources: see *infra*, Ch 8.

reflect more fully the commitments undertaken in Agenda 21.[73] Other European regional agreements or arrangements deal with marine pollution emergencies and port-state control of shipping.[74]

(b) The Baltic[75]

The 1974 Helsinki Convention for the Protection of the Marine Environment of the Baltic Sea Area was the first regional-seas treaty to cover control of marine pollution from all sources. It had an important influence on the formulation of the marine pollution provisions of the 1982 UNCLOS, and of UNEP's regional-seas treaties. By 1992 it was seen as outdated, and was replaced by a new and more comprehensive agreement whose objective is to promote restoration and preservation of the ecological balance of the Baltic Sea and coastal ecosystems 'influenced by the Baltic Sea'. Thus it not only deals with pollution but also applies to living resources and marine life and requires parties to conserve natural habitats, biological diversity and ecological processes, and ensure sustainable use of natural resources. The new treaty incorporates many of the pertinent Rio principles, including the precautionary principle and the polluter-pays principle. In principle at least, the 1992 Helsinki Convention is the first regional-seas agreement to be revised in accordance with Agenda 21 commitments. In 2003 a HELCOM Ministerial Declaration set priorities for action to conserve biodiversity, deal with eutrophication, and develop 'ecological quality objectives'.

(c) The Mediterranean and the Black Sea[76]

Adopted in 1976, the Barcelona Convention for the Protection of the Mediterranean Sea Against Pollution is the oldest UNEP regional-seas agreement, while the Convention on the Protection of the Black Sea Against Pollution is the newest. The Barcelona Convention regime is unusual in having to accommodate not only the interests of developed northern hemisphere industrialized economies but also the less-developed countries on its southern and eastern shores, and it is the only one to recognize the need for different standards according to the economic capacity of the parties and their

---

[73] See also 1998 Sintra Statement and Decision 98/2 on Disposal of Disused Offshore Installations.

[74] 1971 Copenhagen Agreement Concerning Cooperation in Taking Measures Against Pollution of the Sea by Oil; 1983 Bonn Agreement for Cooperation in Dealing with Pollution of the Sea by Oil and other Harmful Substances; 1990 Lisbon Agreement of Cooperation for the Protection of the North-east Atlantic Against Pollution; 1982 Paris Memorandum of Understanding on Port-state control (Paris MOU) on which see *infra*.

[75] See Ehlers, 8 *IJMCL* (1993) 191; Jenisch, 11 *IJMCL* (1996) 47; Platzoder and Verlaan, *The Baltic Sea: New Developments in National Policies and International Cooperation* (The Hague, 1997); Greene, in Victor et al, *The Implementation and Effectiveness of International Environmental Commitments*, 177; Fitzmaurice, 13 *IJMCL* (1998) 379; Ebbesson, 43 *GYIL* (2000) 38; Brusendorff and Ehlers, 17 *IJMCL* (2002) 351.

[76] Haas, *Saving the Mediterranean* (New York, 1991); Vallega, 19 *Marine Policy* (1995) 47; id, 31 *O&C Man* (1996) 199; id, 29 *O&C Man* (1996) 251; Scovazzi, 10 *IJMCL* (1995) 543; Raftopoulos, 7 *IJECL* (1992) 27; Chircop, 23 *ODIL* (1992) 17; Juste, in Miles and Treves (eds), *The Law of the Sea: New Worlds, New Discoveries* (Honolulu, 1992); Scovazzi (ed), *Mediterranean Specially Protected Areas: the General Aspects and the Mediterranean Regional System* (The Hague, 1999) Ch 7.

need for development.[77] In 1995 the Barcelona Convention also became the first to be comprehensively amended, expanded and re-named in line with Agenda 21.[78] Unlike earlier regional agreements in the Baltic and North Sea, the Barcelona Convention is a framework treaty, laying down only general rules that have subsequently been supplemented by more detailed protocols. This technique was followed by all subsequent UNEP regional-seas agreements; it has enabled new topics to be addressed without amending the basic treaty, and allows for differences in participation and the geographical scope of each protocol, while retaining common supervisory institutions. Current Mediterranean Sea protocols cover specially protected areas and biodiversity, emergency cooperation, dumping, land-based pollution, seabed pollution, and transboundary movement of hazardous waste.[79] A new Protocol on Integrated Coastal Zone Management was added in 2008.

Although adopted in 1992, the Black Sea Convention takes little explicit account of Agenda 21 concerns and differs from the original Barcelona Convention model only in acknowledging concern to protect fisheries and marine living resources from harmful effects. It is otherwise limited to general obligations to control all sources of pollution, although protocols adopted at the same time do establish further rules on land-based sources and prohibit dumping. However, in 1993 a ministerial Declaration on Protection of the Black Sea committed the parties to take appropriate measures to implement Agenda 21, Chapter 17 principles and objectives.[80] This declaration does at least illustrate how the parties are free to reinterpret and develop treaties whose texts were not drafted with Agenda 21 in mind. The same practice is potentially applicable to other unrevised pre-UNCED agreements, which do need to be read with this possibility in mind.

(d) Other UNEP regional-seas programmes[81]

UNEP's regional-seas programme, initiated in 1974, covers eleven areas where regional action plans are operative. Apart from the Mediterranean and the Black Sea, these regions include Kuwait (Persian Gulf), West and Central Africa, the wider Caribbean,

---

[77] 1996 Protocol on Pollution from Land-based Sources and Activities, Article 7. See *infra*, Ch 8.

[78] 1995 Convention for the Protection of the Marine Environment and the Coastal Region of the Mediterranean. Text in Scovazzi (ed), *Marine Specially Protected Areas*, 129. The revised convention entered into force in 2004.

[79] 1976 Protocol Concerning Cooperation in Cases of Emergency; 1994 Protocol on Pollution Resulting from Exploration and Exploitation of the Continental Shelf; 1995 Protocol Concerning Specially Protected Areas and Biological Diversity; 1996 Protocol on Prevention of Pollution by Transboundary Movements of Hazardous Wastes and their Disposal; 1996 Protocol on Pollution from Land-based Sources and Activities; 1996 Dumping Protocol; texts in Scovazzi (ed), *Marine Specially Protected Areas*, 141ff.

[80] For text see 9 *IJMCL* (1994) 72, and for the results see 1993 Black Sea Environment Programme and 2002 Strategic Action Plan.

[81] UNEP, *A Strategy for the Seas: the Regional Seas Programme, Past Present and* Future (Nairobi, 1983); id, *Achievements and Planned Development of UNEP's Regional Seas Programme* (Nairobi, 1982); id, *Assessment of UNEP's Achievement in Oceans Programme Element* (Nairobi, 1985); Sand, *Marine Environmental Law in the UNEP* (Dublin, 1988); Edwards, in Carroll (ed), *International Environmental Diplomacy* (Cambridge, 1988) 229; Vallega, 24 *O&C Man* (1994) 17; Verlaan and Khan, 31 *O&C Man* (1996) 83; Haas, 9 *Ocean Yb* (1991) 188; Akiwumi and Melvasalo, 22 *Marine Policy* (1998) 229.

the East Asian Seas, the South East Pacific, the North-west Pacific, the Red Sea and Gulf of Aden, the South Pacific, Eastern Africa, the South Asian Seas, and the North-east Pacific. Most of these action plans make provision for environmental assessment, management, legislation, and institutional and financial arrangements. They are of particular significance for developing states in facilitating cooperation and the provision of assistance in the management of marine pollution problems in regions where expertise and facilities may be lacking. Most of the regional programmes include arrangements for combating major incidents of marine pollution, and the regional treaties all have protocols on this subject.

Following the pattern established by the Barcelona Convention, most of the regional-seas programmes are now supported by framework conventions. These apply in the Persian Gulf, the Red Sea and Gulf of Aden, the East African side of the Indian Ocean, the South Pacific, the Latin American side of the South-east and North-east Pacific, the Caribbean, and the West African side of the South Atlantic.[82] Their geographical scope extends to the territorial sea and exclusive economic zones of participating states. All are comprehensive in their inclusion of sources of marine pollution, but the extent to which further protocols have been adopted varies widely. Most now give some form of protection to marine living resources and coastal ecosystems, usually by permitting the creation of specially protected areas.[83] In those areas designated under the Caribbean Protocol both the passage of ships and activities that could harm endangered species, their habitats or ecosystems are controlled. Other regional-seas protocols ban dumping in the South Pacific, the Black Sea, and the Mediterranean. Land-based pollution is regulated by protocols in the Caribbean, the Persian Gulf and the South-East Pacific, in addition to the Mediterranean and Black Sea.[84] A further development is the adoption of protocols on transboundary movement of hazardous wastes and pollution from continental shelf operations in the Mediterranean and the Persian Gulf.[85] Most of the UNEP regional agreements are thus capable in many respects of conforming to Agenda 21 requirements; only the Red Sea and the Western African Conventions have remained little more than bare framework regimes, limited to pollution, and with little evidence of further activity.

The regional seas programme has proved its utility as a model for facilitating the integration of marine environmental concerns into coastal development planning and coordinating training, technical and financial assistance and research. In general the more successful programmes appear to be those with a strong treaty basis and the political will to ensure the continued evolution of action plans, protocols and

---

[82] *Supra*, nn 54, 57, 58.

[83] 1985 Eastern African Protocol Concerning Specially Protected Areas and Wild Flora and Fauna (not in force 2000); 1986 Noumea Convention, Article 14; 1989 SE Pacific Protocol for the Conservation and Management of Protected Marine and Coastal Areas; 1990 Kingston Protocol Concerning Specially Protected Areas and Wildlife; for the Mediterranean and Black Sea, see previous section. See Scovazzi (ed), *Marine Specially Protected Areas*, Ch 2.

[84] 1983 SE Pacific Protocol; 1990 Kuwait Protocol; 1999 Caribbean Protocol.

[85] 1996 Mediterranean Protocol; 1998 Kuwait Protocol.

institutions. The least successful are those where the financing and infrastructure are weak. Overall, there has clearly been a shift from pollution control to sustainable management of the marine environment and its resources, in line with objectives outlined in Agenda 21. None of this is inconsistent with the 1982 UNCLOS; rather it builds on elements already found in the Convention, evidencing the shift from use-oriented to a resource-oriented approaches, which it has been said, is the essence of the new law of the sea.[86]

4 MARINE POLLUTION FROM SHIPS[87]

4(1) THE NATURE OF THE PROBLEM

Without the shipping industry much of the world's principal source of energy—oil—could not be moved from where it is extracted to where it is refined and marketed. Many other commodities are also moved in bulk by sea, including chemicals, wood pulp, and vegetable oil, to name only a few of the substances which have ended up on beaches after shipwrecks. Nor would international trade as currently understood be possible without container ships. The shipping industry is large, many of the ships are huge, and none are unsinkable. Over the past thirty years the industry has very substantially restructured. Most ships were once registered in and therefore regulated by a small number of advanced industrial economies with a long maritime tradition—principally the UK. Today, almost half the world's merchant fleet is still owned by Western European companies, the rest mostly by Japanese, Chinese, American, Russian, Korean, and Indian operators.[88] But many of these ships, and especially those involved in international trade, are now registered not where they are owned but in a growing list of 'flag of convenience' states. The advantage for the owners or operators of 'flagging-out' is that they pay less tax, they can employ cheaper crew, and regulation may be less stringent or less efficiently applied than it would be under more established flag states. Flag-of-convenience states have little or no connection with the shipping industry apart from offering the facility of an open register. Many of the newer ones are developing countries without a significant maritime tradition or infrastructure, such as St Kitts or Mongolia, but some such as Panama, Liberia, and Honduras have a long history as open registries. Other developing countries, including India and

---

[86] Haas, 9 *Ocean Yb* (1991) 211.

[87] See Tan, *Vessel-Source Marine Pollution* (Cambridge, 2006); Molenaar, *Coastal State Jurisdiction over Vessel-Source Pollution* (The Hague, 1998); Abecassis and Jarashow, *Oil Pollution from Ships* (2nd edn, London, 1985); Churchill and Lowe, *The Law of the Sea* (3rd edn, Manchester, 1999) 338ff; M'Gonigle and Zacher, *Pollution, Politics and International Law: Tankers at Sea* (London, 1979); Brown, *The International Law of the Sea* (Aldershot, 1994) I, Ch 15; Mitchell, *International Oil Pollution at Sea* (Cambridge, Mass, 1994); Kasoulides, *Port-state control and Jurisdiction: Evolution of the Port-state control Regime* (Dordrecht, 1993); Bodansky, 18 *ELQ* (1991) 719.

[88] See Tan, *Vessel-Source Marine Pollution*, 63–4 for details.

China, have also built up a substantial industry of their own, but this is unusual and Saudi Arabia, Singapore, Taiwan, and Malaysia are the only other developing states among the leading ship-owning nations.

These changes in the shipping industry are important for two reasons.[89] First, as we saw in Chapter 2, the main international regulatory body for shipping—IMO—is dominated by the largest flag states, and these are now mostly flag-of-convenience developing countries, some of which have only a limited interest in the quality and operating standards of the ships for which they are responsible in international law. Second, these same states will inevitably find it harder to regulate, inspect and enforce the law against ships which, while flying their flag, will rarely if ever enter any of their ports. In order to fulfil their regulatory responsibilities, the maritime administrations of these states therefore have to rely on the so-called 'classification societies' which historically have provided ship inspection and certification services for governments and insurance companies.[90] Some of these societies are very good, but some are sufficiently bad that governments have begun to prosecute or sue them for negligence when large and poorly maintained oil-tankers break up at sea.[91] Flag states and ship operators have considerable freedom in selecting where to go for these services, and there is little to prevent them choosing the most convenient rather than the best. In this environment, substandard ships that are older, or poorly maintained, or with inadequately trained crews, are an inevitable outcome. It is these ships which pose the biggest threat to the marine environment of coastal states. Flag-state enforcement will typically be poor or non-existent, even when infractions are reported by coastal states. Of course all ships have to call at ports and, as we will see, it is here that serious inspections, detentions and enforcement can be deployed to mitigate the risk. The most effective port-state controls are now in Europe, North America, and Japan, which import most of the world's trade in oil and other hazardous commodities. But not all ports are equally efficient at policing visiting ships, and in other regions of the world substandard ships are far less likely to be bothered.

Pollution from ships is generally of two kinds: operational and accidental. Operational pollution is a function of the manner in which ships operate. Oil tankers, for example, traditionally washed their oil tanks and disposed of oily residue at sea, causing significant volumes of pollution. Other ships also discharge oily wastes from engine rooms and cause significant pollution from sewage discharges and rubbish disposal at sea. Ballast water may contain cargo residues or alien species which when transported to other areas can cause serious ecosystem damage. The objective of international regulation in this context has been as far as possible to eliminate the need for such discharges, through technical solutions and the provision of shore facilities for the reception of waste and cargo residues. The second, more dramatic, form of marine pollution emanates from marine casualties. The sinking of large oil tankers such as the

---

[89] Ibid, 47–62.   [90] Ibid, 43–7.

[91] See IOPC Funds, *Annual Report* (2004) 77 (*Erika*) and 102 (*Prestige*). See also the *Annual Reports* of the Paris and Tokyo MOUs where the record of individual classification societies is analysed.

Torrey Canyon, Amoco Cadiz, Exxon Valdez, Nakhodka, Erika, or *Prestige* exemplifies the scale and potential severity of such accidents, whose seriousness derives mainly from the volume of oil or other pollutants released in one place. They harm coastal communities, fisheries, wildlife, and local ecology. In some areas, such as the Arctic or Antarctic, climatic conditions exacerbate both the long-term effects and the difficulty of dealing with this kind of pollution. The purpose of regulation here is to minimize the risk and give coastal states adequate means of protecting themselves and securing compensation.

Neither problem should be exaggerated; as we shall see in Chapter 8, the major sources of marine pollution are on land, not afloat. But, like nuclear installations, oil tankers and other vessels carrying hazardous and noxious cargoes represent a form of ultra-hazardous risk for all coastal states, which it is the object of international law to moderate and control. A dominant theme of the UNCLOS III conference was the failure of the traditional structure of jurisdiction over ships and maritime areas to protect the interests of those coastal states whose proximity to shipping routes made them particularly vulnerable. On the one hand the duty of the flag state to adopt and enforce appropriate regulations was too imperfectly defined and observed. On the other, the power of the coastal state to regulate shipping and activities off its coast was too limited. The 1973 MARPOL Convention and the 1982 UNCLOS address these problems by extending the enforcement powers of coastal and port states, at the expense of the flag state's exclusive authority, and by redefining and strengthening the latter's obligations towards the protection of the marine environment. The result is a relatively complex structure of authority over maritime activities, which tries to reconcile the effective enforcement of environmental regulations with the primary concern of maritime states in freedom of navigation.[92] How far this balancing act has been successful will be considered below: it has certainly led to improvements, but it has not eliminated vessel-source pollution.

4(2) REGULATION OF VESSEL POLLUTION

(a) Flag state jurisdiction and international standards

The primary basis for the regulation of ships is the jurisdiction enjoyed by the state in which the vessel is registered or whose flag it is entitled to flag ('the flag state'). Although Article 91 of the 1982 UNCLOS refers to the need for a genuine link between the state of nationality and the ship, this ambiguous provision was not intended to eliminate 'flags of convenience', where registration, rather than ownership, management, nationality of the crew, or the ship's operational base, is the only substantial connection. In the *MV Saiga Case* the ITLOS held that 'the purpose of the provisions of the Convention on the need for a genuine link between a ship and its flag State is to secure more effective implementation of the duties of the flag State, and not to

---

[92] Boyle, 79 *AJIL* (1985) 347; Bernhardt, 20 *VJIL* (1979) 265 and see generally Allott, 77 *AJIL* (1983) 1.

establish criteria by reference to which the validity of the registration of ships in a flag State may be challenged by other States'.[93] Thus, however tenuous the link, it is the flag state which is responsible for regulating safety at sea and the prevention of collisions, the manning of ships and the competence of their crews, and for setting standards of construction, design, equipment, and seaworthiness.[94] These responsibilities include taking the measures to prevent pollution referred to below.

Moreover, in customary law, only the flag state has jurisdiction to enforce regulations applicable to vessels on the high seas. In the *Lotus Case*,[95] the Permanent Court of International Justice referred to the principle that no state may exercise any kind of jurisdiction over foreign vessels on the high seas, but by this it meant only that foreign vessels could not be arrested or detained while on the high seas, not that regulations could not be enforced by other states once the ship had voluntarily entered port. As we shall see, this case forms the possible basis for port-state jurisdiction over high-seas pollution offences referred to in Article 218 of the 1982 UNCLOS. Even when the ship is within the territorial jurisdiction of other states, however, the flag state does not lose its jurisdiction; regardless of where it is operating, a ship must therefore comply with the laws of its own flag.

Customary international law thus gives the flag state ample power to regulate marine pollution from vessels, and other aspects of the operation of ships likely to pose a risk to the environment, such as seaworthiness standards. Moreover, as we have seen, it requires them to do so effectively, even if they may in practice have to act in cooperation with coastal and port states. Both the content of this duty, and the manner in which it is enforced, have been the subject of more specific international agreements negotiated mainly through IMO, which is usually the 'competent international organization' referred to in this context by the 1982 UNCLOS.

The purpose of these IMO agreements is to provide internationally recognized common standards for flag states and coastal states to follow in regulating the safety of shipping and the protection of the environment. They include the 1966 International Convention on Load Lines, the 1972 Convention on the International Regulations for Preventing Collisions at Sea (COLREGS), and the 1974 Safety of Life at Sea Convention (SOLAS), which are intended to minimize the risk of maritime accidents by regulating navigation, construction, and seaworthiness standards. A 1978 Protocol to the SOLAS Convention makes the use of certain additional safety features mandatory for oil tankers and other large vessels, both for safety of navigation and pollution prevention purposes. ILO Convention No 147 Concerning Minimum Standards in Merchant Ships and the 1978 IMO Convention on Standards of Training, Certification, and

---

[93] *MV Saiga (No 2) (Merits)* ITLOS No 2 (1999) paras 62–88, at para 84. However, whether a state has conferred the right to fly its flag is a question of fact: see *The 'Grand Prince' Case (Belize v France)* ITLOS No 8 (2001) paras 89–94.

[94] 1982 UNCLOS, Articles 94; 211(2); 1973/78 MARPOL Convention; 1974 Safety of Life at Sea Convention, and other IMO conventions. See generally Churchill and Lowe, *The Law of the Sea*, Ch 13; O'Connell. *The International Law of the Sea*, ii, Ch 20.

[95] PCIJ (1927) Ser A, No 10, 169.

Watchkeeping lay down additional standards for competency, hours of work, and manning of vessels.[96] The 2004 Ballast Water Convention attempts to control the global spread of invasive alien species in ship's ballast water.[97] It is the first IMO treaty to adopt a genuinely precautionary approach, insofar as there is uncertainty about which species will pose problems or where, but it is known that invasive species are an identifiable and often irreversible risk.

An important SOLAS amendment which came into force in 1998 makes compliance with IMO's Code on International Safety Management (ISM Code) mandatory, inter alia, for all oil and chemical tankers.[98] Ships can only be certified by the flag state if the operating company (this may be the owner, charterer, or manager) has in place safety and environmental policies, instructions and procedures in accordance with the Code. In effect an operator's licence, the certification required by the ISM Code, has been described as 'the most revolutionary change adopted by IMO in its 40 years of existence'. The underlying assumption is that operating companies are best able to ensure that ships meet adequate operational standards. Like airlines, shipping companies whose vessels do not do so will be unable to operate. Some 78 per cent of ships were thought to comply at the time of entry into force.[99]

Most of these agreements are very widely ratified and adopted by maritime states, and they can be readily amended and updated by IMO.[100] Although in most cases their primary purpose is to ensure better safety standards, they are also an essential means of reducing the threat to the marine environment posed by maritime accidents or the discharge of pollutants and invasive species. To that extent they constitute a form of international regulation of the environmental risks of transporting oil and other substances by sea, with IMO acting as the main regulatory and supervisory institution. The two agreements considered below deal specifically with operational pollution and the reduction of accidents: the 1954 London Convention for the Prevention of Pollution of the Sea by Oil, and its successor the 1973 International Convention for the Prevention of Pollution from Ships (MARPOL). The MARPOL Convention is important because it implements the relevant provisions of the 1982 UNCLOS (Articles 211 and 220) and provides a long-established and reasonably successful regulatory model whose real-world impact can be measured. The more recent Ballast Water Convention is modelled on MARPOL, uses the same regulatory techniques, and will be enforced by flag states and port states on the same basis. For that reason it will not be examined here.[101]

---

[96] See generally, Juda, 26 *ICLQ* (1977) 169; Blanco-Bazan, in Couper and Gold (eds), *The Marine Environment and Sustainable Development*, (Honolulu, 1993) 448; Valenzuela, in Soons (ed), *Implementation of the LOSC through International Institutions*, 187; Osieke, 30 *ICLQ* (1981) 497; Churchill and Lowe, *The Law of the Sea*, Ch 13; Molenaar, *Coastal State Jurisdiction over Vessel-Source Pollution*, 60ff.

[97] See Tsimplis, 19 *IJMCL* (2004) 411.

[98] See 1974 SOLAS Convention, Chapter IX, as amended 1994; IMO Res A 848 (20) 1997 and A 913(22) 1999; Valenzuela, in Vidas and Østreng (eds), *Order for the Oceans*, 502–4.

[99] 5% of ships inspected in the Paris MOU region in 1998 were detained for non-compliance with the code. The 2006 Paris MOU *Annual Report* notes a continuing rise in ISM Code deficiency rates, although the detention rate had diminished.

[100] *Supra*, Ch 2, section 4.

[101] For a detailed analysis see Tsimplis, 19 *IJMCL* (2004) 411. It is not yet in force.

(b) The 1954 London Convention

This Convention was the first to regulate oil pollution from tankers.[102] It was successively amended until its replacement in 1973 by the new MARPOL Convention. The 1954 Convention employed several techniques for minimizing operational discharges of oil. It controlled their location, by defining prohibited areas and excluding coastal zones; it controlled the quantity of pollution, by limiting the rate of discharge; it controlled the need for discharges, by setting construction and equipment standards intended to reduce the volume of waste oil, or to separate oil from ballast water, and by calling on governments to provide port discharge facilities. As the convention began to influence the construction of tankers, so it was possible to introduce progressively stricter standards, including the so-called 'load on top system' which enabled tankers to discharge oily residues to land-based reception facilities.

There was nothing inherently defective in this approach to the regulation of operational pollution, and the convention was clearly capable of responding to technical progress. It was not particularly successful, however, for two reasons. First, the enforcement record of flag states was not strong: many had insufficient interest in pursuing enforcement vigorously in areas beyond their territorial jurisdiction and they were in any case confronted with practical problems of collecting evidence and bringing proceedings against ships which rarely entered their ports. Second, not all flag states were parties to the convention, nor did the 1958 High Seas Convention, with its requirement only to 'take account' of existing treaty provisions, compel states to apply the London Convention. Some flags of convenience were thus able to avoid the more onerous regulations, which coastal states could do little to enforce. The Stockholm Conference in 1972 identified both failings in its recommendations on marine pollution, which called on states to accept and implement available instruments and to ensure compliance by their flag vessels.[103]

(c) The 1973/78 MARPOL Convention

This convention, first adopted in 1973, was substantially amended in 1978 to facilitate entry into force.[104] The convention's principal articles mainly deal with jurisdiction and powers of enforcement and inspection; the more detailed anti-pollution regulations are contained in annexes which can be adopted and amended by the Marine Environment Protection Committee of IMO, subject to acceptance by at least two-thirds of parties constituting not less than 50 per cent gross tonnage of the world merchant fleet. Annexes I and II, which regulate the carriage of oil and chemicals respectively, have been amended frequently in response to new technology and

---

[102] O'Connell, *The International Law of the Sea*, ii, 1000; Abecassis and Jarashow, *Oil Pollution from Ships*, Ch 3; M'Gonigle and Zacher, *Pollution, Politics and International Law*, 85ff.

[103] See generally Lowe, 12 *San Diego LR* (1975) 624; M'Gonigle and Zacher, *Pollution, Politics and International Law*, Ch 8; Birnie, in Cusine and Grant, *The Impact of Marine Pollution*, 95.

[104] See generally M'Gonigle and Zacher, *Pollution, Politics and International Law*, 107ff; Tan, *Vessel-Source Marine Pollution*, 107–75; O'Connell, *The International Law of the Sea*, ii, 1003; Abecassis and Jarashow, *Oil Pollution from Ships*, Ch 3; IMO, *Focus on IMO: MARPOL—25 Years* (London, 1998).

growing environmental awareness, and were further revised and simplified in 2004, partly in order to take account of the precautionary approach. However, as more ships flag out to developing country open registers, the 50 per cent tonnage requirement is becoming harder to achieve, and Annex VI on air pollution, adopted in 1997, did not enter into force until 2005.

All parties are bound by Annexes I and II. Other annexes are optional and participation varies but is still substantial. The parties to MARPOL in 2007 comprised over 98 per cent of merchant tonnage, which puts Annexes I and II in the category of 'generally accepted international rules and standards' prescribed by Article 211 of the 1982 UNCLOS as the minimum content of the flag state's duty to exercise diligent control of its vessels in the prevention of marine pollution. The same could be said for optional Annexes III–VI, whose tonnage participation rates in 2007 were 94%, 75%, 96%, and 74% respectively. As we have seen, there are also grounds for treating MARPOL regulations as a customary standard enforceable against vessels of all states, whether or not they have ratified the MARPOL convention.[105] At the same time, it must be remembered that, under Article 16 of this convention, states parties are not bound by amendments they have not accepted, so there may be different regulations in force simultaneously for different flag states. This undoubtedly complicates the question whether any particular regulation is 'generally accepted' when determining what rules a flag state must apply under Article 211.

The MARPOL Convention's approach to the regulation of oil pollution is broadly similar to the 1954 Convention in relying mainly on technical measures to limit the need for oil or chemical discharges at sea. Annexes I and II also specify construction standards in considerable detail. Later regulations do not normally apply to existing ships, because to do so might require substantial reconstruction, but they were nevertheless amended in 1992 to phase out older single-hull oil tankers and again in 2001 and 2003 to advance the deadline following the *Erika* and *Prestige* disasters.[106] These older vessels had become an unacceptable risk for coastal states and a liability for the industry, but IMO's action was precipitated by an imminent EU ban.[107] In general terms, MARPOL regulations take advantage of modern technology and operating methods to eliminate all but minimal levels of operational discharges, to ensure that these have the least impact on coastal states, and to emphasize port discharge for residues which cannot otherwise be disposed of. The most harmful Annex II residues will normally have to be off-loaded to a certified port discharge facility. The discharge at sea of oily waste and some chemical residues is still permitted in limited volumes, but only if it takes place en route, more than fifty miles from land and not in special areas where virtually all discharges are prohibited.[108] The special areas listed in the convention include the Mediterranean, the Black Sea, the Baltic, the Red Sea, and the Persian Gulf—all enclosed or semi-enclosed seas, where, as we saw earlier, more stringent

---

[105] *Supra*, section 2(2).

[106] Annex I, regulations 13F and G, or 20 and 21 in the revised Annex. The final phase-out date for all categories is 2010. See Tan, *Vessel-Source Marine Pollution*, 139–54.

[107] See *infra*, section 4(3).   [108] Annex 1, regulations 9 and 10; Annex II, regulations 3–6.

standards are necessary. The more open waters of the Gulf of Aden, the Gulf of Oman, the North Sea and North West European waters, the Caribbean, South African waters, and the Antarctic Ocean, have subsequently been added to this list.

In two respects the MARPOL Convention differs significantly from the earlier scheme. First, as we have seen, it is not confined to oil pollution, but also regulates other types of ship-based pollution, including the bulk carriage of noxious liquids, harmful substances, and garbage from ships.[109] It thus provides some evidence of internationally agreed standards of environmentally sound management for the transport of chemicals and hazardous wastes by sea, and will be relevant in determining the obligations of states under the 1989 Basel Convention, considered in Chapter 8.

Second, a more effective scheme of enforcement was adopted in response to pressure from coastal states dissatisfied with the observance of the 1954 treaty. This scheme involves the cooperation of coastal states, port states, and flag states in a system of certification, inspection, and reporting whose purposes are to make the operation of defective vessels difficult or impossible and to facilitate the performance by flag states of their primary jurisdiction to prosecute and enforce applicable laws. Better enforcement has made the MARPOL Convention a major advance on the 1954 treaty and provides evidence of the impact independent inspection can have in securing compliance with environmental protection treaties.

(d) Certification and inspection under the MARPOL Convention

The flag state has two main responsibilities in ensuring that its vessels comply with the technical standards set by MARPOL. It must inspect the vessel at periodic intervals, and it must issue an 'international oil pollution prevention certificate'.[110] This certificate provides prima facie evidence that the ship complies with the requirements of MARPOL: it 'shall be accepted by the other parties and regarded for all purposes covered by the present Convention as having the same validity as a certificate issued by them.[111] But the Convention does not leave the question of compliance to the flag state alone. A novel provision, subsequently adopted in other IMO Conventions, allows ships required to hold a certificate to be inspected by any party in whose ports they are present ('port states').[112]

This form of port-state control is not to be confused with the extended port-state jurisdiction provided for in Article 218 of the 1982 UNCLOS, since it involves no extraterritorial competence to legislate or enforce treaty-based or customary rules of law beyond the port state's own waters. MARPOL relies instead on the undoubted jurisdiction possessed by states to regulate conditions of entry to or passage through their internal waters, including ports.[113] In this sense the practice, while novel in its

---

[109] Annexes II, III and V. Annexes IV and VI deal with sewage and air pollution.

[110] Annex I, regulations 4, 5. A comparable requirement applies to chemical tankers and ballast water.

[111] Article 5(1).   [112] Article 5.

[113] Churchill and Lowe, *The International Law of the Sea*, Ch 3; Molenaar, 38 *ODIL* (2007) 225, but cf qualifications noted by Valenzuela, in Soons, *Implementation of the LOSC through International Institutions*,

application to pollution, is not a departure from existing principles of maritime jurisdiction referred to earlier.

Inspection under Article 5 of the MARPOL Convention may be carried out to confirm possession of a valid certificate, or to determine the condition of the ship where
there are 'clear grounds' for believing that it does not correspond 'substantially' with
the certificate. Since 1996 a new MARPOL regulation has also allowed port-state
inspection 'where there are clear grounds for believing that the master or crew are not
familiar with essential shipboard procedures relating to the prevention of pollution'.[114]
Where non-compliance with a MARPOL certificate is revealed, port states must not
allow such ships to sail unless they can do so without presenting an unreasonable
threat of harm to the marine environment. Their most effective sanction is therefore
to restrain the vessel in port until it can be repaired to a suitable standard or directed
to a repair yard. In less serious cases, the ship must be reported to the flag state for
appropriate action or prosecuted for any violation of the port state's own law which
arises from non-compliance with the convention.[115] The port state must not unduly
delay ships, however.[116]

Port-state inspection may also be used to supply evidence of a violation of the
Convention's discharge regulations. This facility may be crucial to the enforcement of
these regulations. The problem facing the flag state is that without cooperation from
port states in furnishing evidence it may be unable to mount successful prosecutions.
With this in mind, Article 6 of MARPOL therefore permits inspection by port states
for this purpose, and does not limit the power to situations where there are 'clear
grounds' for suspicion, as in Article 5. A report must be made to flag states when a discharge violation is indicated, and flag states must then bring proceedings if satisfied
that the evidence is sufficient. It is also open to any party, including a coastal state,
to request inspection by the port state if there is sufficient evidence that the ship has
discharged harmful substances 'in any place'. This would include high-seas violations
as well as violations in the maritime zones of other states. But, although port states
do prosecute pollution violations occurring in their own internal waters or territorial
sea, and Article 220(1) of the 1982 UNCLOS confirms their power to do so, MARPOL
confers on them no extraterritorial jurisdiction to prosecute violations which occur
elsewhere.[117]

An efficient scheme of port-state inspection and control is in many respects a more
practical means of deterring substandard vessels than flag-state enforcement of international rules and standards, since such vessels will more often come within the reach
of port states, where arrest or detention will provide a costly deterrent. It also reduces
the need for coastal states to interfere with passing traffic, while facilitating prosecution of those ships which offend within coastal zones. Moreover it has the merit that

---

200ff. On possible limits to port state jurisdiction see Molenaar, in Ringbom (ed), *Competing Norms in the Law of Marine Environmental Protection*, 201.

[114] Regulation 8A, Annexes I, II, III, V. See Valenzuela, in Vidas and Østreng (eds), *Order for the Oceans*, 500.

[115] Article 4, 5(3) and SOLAS.   [116] Article 7.   [117] But cf 1982 UNCLOS, Article 218, *infra*.

it can be applied to the vessels of non-parties to MARPOL or SOLAS as a condition of port entry. Article 5(4) of MARPOL supports this view by requiring port states to ensure that no more-favourable treatment is given to the ships of non-parties. State practice under port-state inspection schemes now in force in most of the major shipping regions indicates that non-parties have generally acquiesced in this application to their vessels of MARPOL and SOLAS standards.[118] Article 211(3) of the 1982 UNCLOS requires port states to give due publicity to port entry conditions, and to communicate them to IMO, but it too assumes their right to determine these conditions for themselves. The conclusion that non-party flag states are effectively bound by MARPOL and SOLAS in this manner further strengthens the earlier argument for treating these conventions as indicative of the flag state's obligations in customary law. It does mean that states have little to gain by staying outside either Convention.[119]

Since the impact of port-state inspection will tend to be reflected in traffic patterns, with substandard vessels favouring the more lenient ports, these inspection schemes will not work effectively unless they operate systematically and consistently. Where, as in Europe, ports in a variety of jurisdictions are potentially available, coordination is essential. Under the Paris Memorandum of Understanding on Port State Control the EU states, Canada, Norway, Iceland, and Russia cooperate in a programme of vessel inspection which aims to ensure that each participating administration inspects at least 25 per cent of foreign vessels calling at its ports annually.[120] The cumulative effect is that some 14,000 ships sailing to Europe are inspected annually, not only for compliance with MARPOL standards but also in respect of other IMO conventions and regulations including the 1974 SOLAS Convention. High-risk ships may be targeted and the ISM Code has become a particular focus of attention. The United States Coastguard achieves comparable levels of inspection, and there are similar schemes operating in Latin America, the Asia-Pacific Region, the Caribbean, the Mediterranean, the Indian Ocean, Western and Southern Africa, and the Black Sea, although most set lower inspection targets.[121] All of the regional schemes are modelled on the Paris MOU,[122] and provide good evidence of state practice on several points which are relevant to interpretation of Articles 211, 218, and 219 of UNCLOS. First, they are limited to ensuring compliance with treaties that are in force, and to which the state undertaking the inspection is a party, but it is not a requirement that the flag

---

[118] Molenaar, *Coastal State Jurisdiction*, 172–3. Handl, in Ringbom (ed), *Competing Norms*, 223, rejects the argument that port state application of IMO conventions to non-party vessels violates the *pacta tertiis* rule.

[119] See Valenzuela, in Soons, *Implementation of the LOSC through International Institutions*, 205ff.

[120] See Keselj, 30 *ODIL* (1999) 127; Schiferli, 11 *Ocean YB* (1994) 202; Kasoulides, *Port-state control*; Anderson, in Boyle and Freestone (eds), *Sustainable Development and International Law*, 325; Valenzuela, in Vidas and Østreng (eds), *Order for the Oceans*, 485; Kasoulides, *Port-state control and Jurisdiction* (Dordrecht, 1993) Ch 6.

[121] Usually 10–15%, but the Paris MOU requires 25% and the Tokyo MOU 50%. For a comparative survey see Hoppe, *IMO News* (1/2000) 9. See 1992 Viña del Mar Agreement on Port-state control in Latin America; 1993 Tokyo MOU on the Asia-Pacific Region; 1996 Caribbean MOU; 1997 Mediterranean MOU; 1998 Indian Ocean MOU, 2000 Black Sea MOU.

[122] For IMO guidelines see IMO Res A 787 (19) and A 882 (21).

state of the vessel should also be a party. Second, except where no valid certificate is produced (for example because the vessel is from a non-party to MARPOL or SOLAS), full inspection is allowed only if there are 'clear grounds' for believing that the vessel, or its equipment or crew, are substandard.[123] Third, there must be no discrimination between flags, but targeting priority inspections towards vessels from flags with a poor record is acceptable. In such cases 'clear grounds' for full inspection are deemed to exist. Finally, there is power in cases of serious deficiency to detain vessels or to ban them from ports in the region. As Kasoulides pointedly observes, however, unlike the Paris MOU, some of these schemes lack credible inspection and repair facilities, and produce little detailed inspection information.[124] Moreover, some are dominated by flag states which do not supervise their own ships adequately or are even blacklisted by the Paris MOU or the US Coastguard.[125]

(e) Jurisdiction under the MARPOL Convention

Negotiation of the MARPOL Convention coincided with increasing pressure from coastal states for extension of their pollution control jurisdiction beyond the narrow three-mile territorial sea which then prevailed for most states. It was clear that this controversial question would be an important topic for consideration in the UNCLOS III negotiations. For this reason MARPOL itself relies, like the 1954 Convention, primarily on regulation and prosecution by flag states, but it leaves open the possibility of extending the jurisdiction of coastal and port states by providing in Article 4(2) that 'Any violation of the requirements of the present Convention within the jurisdiction of any party to the Convention *shall* be prohibited and sanctions *shall* be established therefore under the law of that Party'. This can be read as a recognition of the customary rule that coastal states may regulate pollution within their own internal waters and territorial sea, although it arguably goes further by turning a power to regulate into a duty to do so. But Article 9(3) at the same time makes clear that the term 'jurisdiction' in the Convention 'shall be construed in the light of international law in force at the time of application or interpretation of the present Convention'. Thus it must now be read in the light of subsequent developments, including the emergence of coastal state pollution jurisdiction in the exclusive economic zone, considered below. The important point here is simply that MARPOL itself does not prevent the extension of jurisdiction beyond the territorial sea, but neither does it authorize or compel such action.

The convention does try to strengthen flag-state enforcement in a number of ways, however. Regardless of where they occur, violations must be prohibited, proceedings must be brought if there is sufficient evidence, and penalties must be adequate in severity. It is not open to the flag state to adopt a more lenient attitude simply because the offence is committed on the high seas or in the waters of some distant state: these

---

[123] On what constitute clear grounds see Paris MOU, Section 4.1.
[124] Ringbom (ed), *Competing Norms in the Law of Marine Environmental Protection*, 138. The Tokyo MOU is an exception, however: see its *Annual Reports*.
[125] Paris MOU, *Annual Report 2006*, 20.

are precisely the situations where its duty to act effectively requires emphasis. In order to facilitate flag-state prosecution of such offences, all parties are required to report incidents at sea involving harmful substances, and the flag state must then act appropriately when informed of suspected violations.[126] Moreover, as we saw earlier, evidential problems can be overcome if port-state inspections identify substandard vessels or discharge violations. Thus MARPOL does go some way towards promoting more effective enforcement by flag states, but it does not entirely remove the practical problems which in many cases have made port-state control the more realistic method of ensuring higher levels of compliance.

(f) Assessing the impact of MARPOL[127]

As we saw in Chapter 4, the implementation and effectiveness of most modern environmental treaties is monitored in some form by treaty supervisory institutions. States must report, non-compliance procedures exist to deal with complaints or difficulties, and funding and technical assistance may be available to help developing countries. The MARPOL Convention is unusual in lacking many of these features. Although flag states are required to report to IMO on action they have taken with regard to ships found to have violated MARPOL standards, and on a list of matters relevant to implementation of the Convention, their record of doing so is generally poor, and largely confined to developed states whose own tonnage is now a diminishing proportion of the whole.[128] Even if it does have information, IMO has no process for dealing effectively with non-compliance issues, such as the persistent failure of some states to provide the port discharge facilities required by Annexes I and II of MARPOL. In 1992 it did establish a Flag State Implementation Committee (FSIC) with responsibility for 'the identification of measures necessary to ensure effective and consistent global implementation of IMO instruments' by flag states.[129] The principle outcome has been the adoption of some useful recommendations and guidelines clarifying the responsibilities of flag states, but there is still no mechanism for dealing with non-performing parties, and the FSIC does not provide one. The problem of flag-state implementation is a broader one than compliance with MARPOL alone, but it is clear that while IMO has been an active regulatory body, with a good record in securing wide acceptance for safety and environmental standards, and in updating them, it has at best only a very weak supervisory role. In practice, implementation and compliance-control are left largely to the parties, and to port states. IMO itself may set standards for flag states, but it has little power or incentive to police them.

---

[126] Article 4.

[127] See Tan, *Vessel-Source Marine Pollution*, 230–85; Sasamura, in Couper and Gold (eds), *The Marine Environment and Sustainable Development* (Honolulu, 1993) 306; Mitchell, *Intentional Oil Pollution at Sea* (Cambridge, Mass, 1994); Peet, 7 *IJECL* (1992) 277.

[128] See Articles 4(3), 6(4), 11, and Mitchell, *Intentional Oil Pollution*, Ch 4.

[129] See Roach, in Nordquist and Moore (eds), *Current Maritime Issues and the IMO* (The Hague, 1999) 151; de La Fayette, 16 *IJMCL* (2001) 215–26.

While the evidence of port-state inspections undertaken in Western Europe and North America a decade ago showed high levels of compliance with various IMO conventions, including MARPOL,[130] it also indicated that the greatest percentage of deficiencies and detentions was represented by vessels from Eastern Europe, the southern and eastern Mediterranean, and certain flags of convenience, including Panama, St Vincent, Cyprus, Malta, Belize, and Honduras.[131] The average detention rate for substandard vessels in Paris MOU ports in 1996–8 was 15% of those inspected, but 30% to 62% for vessels from the worst flags: St Vincent, Thailand, Cambodia, Libya, Turkey, Romania, Morocco, Lebanon, Syria, Belize, and Honduras. The largest numbers of vessels detained (511) came from Cyprus, with a 19% detention rate. Eight years later a very significant improvement in the performance of Cyprus and Malta has been reported, with both these states now on the Paris MOU's 'white list'. Together with Bulgaria and Romania they have made sufficient progress to become members of the Paris MOU.[132] However, Cambodia, Belize, St Vincent, Morocco, Lebanon, Syria, and Honduras remained on the Paris MOU blacklist of substandard flags in 2006, along with North Korea, Albania, Brazil, Bolivia, Slovakia, Georgia, and St Kitts. Honduras, North Korea, Cambodia, Belize, and Georgia also featured on the Tokyo blacklist.

These results point to a continuing problem with the effectiveness of flag-state regulation which port-state control is only partly alleviating.[133] It cannot be assumed, however, that the problem is simply one of flags of convenience or developing state registers. A number of states in both categories, including Liberia and the Bahamas, have established good records. Strangely, while the worst performers in Latin American ports also include flag of convenience vessels from Cyprus and Malta, ships from Belize, Honduras, Panama, and St Vincent apparently perform much better there than in Europe or the United States.[134] Moreover, port-state control is not without problems of its own.[135] Deficiency rates have risen since 1997 under the Paris and Tokyo MOUs, but so have the number of inspections. Although detentions under the Paris MOU fell steadily until 2005, they have since risen again, but at 5.6 per cent of ships inspected are still well below the 1997 figure.[136] The detention rate under the Tokyo MOU rose every year until 2003, but was back to its 1997 level by 2006. While in part these figures might be explained by increased efficiency in targeting flags known to have high deficiency rates, this is not the outcome to be expected from an effective system of port-state control, since it suggests that substandard vessels are not yet deterred from returning to Paris or Tokyo MOU ports, and that shipping companies are not deterred

[130] The 2006 Paris MOU *Annual Report* notes that MARPOL 73/78 Annex operational deficiencies have increased by 38%, from 3,965 in 2005 to 5,453 in 2006. This may be caused by the concentrated inspection campaign on MARPOL 73/78, Annex 1, which took place in 2006.

[131] Paris MOU, *Annual Report* (1998).   [132] Paris MOU, *Annual Report* (2006) 20.

[133] See in particular Tan, *Vessel Source Marine-Pollution*, 239–85.

[134] Viña del Mar MOU, *Annual Report* (1998). Figures for the Tokyo MOU and the US Coastguard are closer to those for Europe; see Tan, *Vessel-Source Marine Pollution*, 250–1.

[135] See Kasoulides, *Port State Control and Jurisdiction*; Mitchell, *Intentional Oil Pollution*, 135ff; EC, *Common Policy on Safe Seas* (Brussels, 1993) 39ff, paras 61–8.

[136] 1174 in 2006, 944 in 2005, 1624 in 1997. But only 14 ships were banned in 2006 against 28 in 2005.

from flagging out to substandard registers. One problem is that, except where a sub-standard ship is detained or banned, there is no way of ensuring that any deficiency will be rectified. Banned ships simply move elsewhere. Another difficulty is the wide variation in inspection and detention rates for some countries in the Paris, Tokyo, and Viña del Mar schemes. Effective port-state control requires a commitment of expert-ise and technical resources which can no more be guaranteed when inspections are carried out by port states rather than by flag states. This suggests that extension of port-state control to other regions will not necessarily improve the performance of flag states. Even in Europe port-state control is far from perfect.

At the same time, MOU figures show that deficiency and detention rates for oil and chemical tankers are below the average for all ships.[137] By far the largest category of substandard vessels are the less potentially disastrous dry cargo and bulk carriers, although these are now one of the main source of operational discharges of oil at sea.[138] What does appear tenable is the conclusion that MARPOL and SOLAS, in con-junction with enhanced port-state control, have been substantially more effective than the 1954 London Convention in ensuring that oil and chemical tankers operating in the northern hemisphere conform to higher construction and equipment standards for pollution control and maritime safety.[139] It is of course this conclusion which is of most significance for protection of the marine and coastal environment, rather than the deficiency or detention rates for all ships. If MARPOL and SOLAS have undoubt-edly affected the way oil and chemical tankers are built and equipped, how has it affected the way they are operated? This is a more difficult question.

Illegal discharges can only be controlled if they are detected and if action is then taken. In practice this requires either port-state inspection relying on oil discharge records as evidence, or a level of surveillance and monitoring of vessels at sea which is only likely to be attainable by developed coastal states with appropriate resources in aircraft and naval or coastguard patrols. Moreover, the failure of many coastal states to adopt extended enforcement jurisdiction in their EEZ has meant that prosecutions for discharges in waters beyond the territorial sea remain largely the responsibility of flag states. Reports communicated to IMO concerning the application of MARPOL have given no reliable indication of the record of flag state prosecutions, nor of the Convention's success in reducing high-seas pollution, since only a minority of mainly developed states have submitted reports as required. These do show extensive referral of violations by port and coastal states, but subsequent flag-state action is reported in less than a quarter of such cases. One reason for this is that differing legal standards for exchange and admissibility of evidence continue to make successful prosecution

---

[137] 39% of oil tanker inspections in 2006 revealed some deficiencies, but less than 3% resulted in deten-tion. The average rate of detentions for all ships was 5.6% (Paris MOU). The 2006 oil tanker detention rate under the Tokyo MOU was 4.99% against an average for all ships of 5.71%.

[138] Paris MOU, *Annual Report* (2006); Tokyo MOU, *Annual Report* (2006).

[139] See Kasoulides, *Port State Control and Jurisdiction*; Mitchell, *Intentional Oil Pollution*, 135ff; EC, *Common Policy on Safe Seas* (Brussels, 1993) 39ff, paras 61–8.

of polluters difficult, and when fines are imposed, the average tends to be low.[140] These factors indicate that prosecution of ships is unlikely to be a significant factor in any reduction of oil in the sea.

GESAMP reports in the early 1990s consistently noted a decline in operational discharges and oil spillages at sea from tankers, and concluded that the entry into force of MARPOL 'had a substantial positive impact' in reducing operational pollution from all types of vessel.[141] This conclusion was shared by a report prepared for IMO by the US National Academy for Sciences in 1990, which found that a total of 568,800 tonnes of oil entered the sea from ships in 1989, compared to 1.47 million tonnes in 1981.[142] But of this total only some 114,000 tonnes resulted from accidents; most of the remainder was discharged by tankers during the course of ballasting and tank cleaning, or by other types of ship in the form of waste oil. The persistence of these operational discharges indicated a continuing inadequacy in the provision of port reception facilities, a long-standing problem despite the obligation to provide them placed on port states by the MARPOL Convention,[143] and the efforts of IMO through advice and assistance to ensure compliance. GESAMP's more recent assessment, covering the period 1988–97, shows some 457,000 tonnes of oil entering the sea annually from ships, a further decline on the 1989 figure, but still 70 per cent of the total from all human activities.[144] Of this total, 205,000 tonnes annually were estimated to come from operational sources (but only 4 per cent from tankers) and 164,000 tonnes from accidents at sea, mainly involving oil tankers. The decline in operational discharges from oil tankers may suggest improvements in port reception facilities over this period, but that merely shifts the problem of treatment and disposal of sometimes very hazardous wastes onto land. In one of the most serious incidents of its kind, hazardous MARPOL slops were denied offloading at Rotterdam, which could not handle them, but eventually discharged to a port reception facility in West Africa and then dumped in the surrounding city.[145] It can at least be said that the MARPOL prohibition on discharge at sea was effective in this case but that merely points up the absence of any comparable regulation of discharge on land. Provided the discharge is to a certified port reception facility, no law is broken.[146]

---

[140] Paris Memorandum, *Annual Report* (1990) 20; Kasoulides, in Soons (ed), *Implementation*, 432; Mitchell, *Intentional Oil Pollution*, Chs 5, 7; Peet, 7 *IJECL* (1992) 277.

[141] GESAMP, *The State of the Marine Environment* (Nairobi, 1990); id, *Reports and Studies No 50: Impact of Oil and Related Chemicals on the Marine Environment* (London, 1993).

[142] IMO, *Petroleum in the Marine Environment*, MEPC 30/INF 13 (London, 1990). See also Sasamura, in Couper and Gold (eds), *The Marine Environment and Sustainable Development*, 306.

[143] Annex I, Reg 12.

[144] GESAMP, *Reports and Studies No 75: Estimates of oil entering the marine environment from sea-based activities* (IMO, 2007). The remainder came from offshore installations (3%) coastal installations (17.8%) and small craft (8.2%).

[145] UNEP, Rept of 1st meeting of the Expanded Bureau of the 8th meeting of the Conference of the Parties to the Basel Convention (2007) UNEP/SBC/BUREAU/8/1/7, section III.

[146] MARPOL discharges are excluded from the Basel Convention on Transboundary Movement of Hazardous Wastes. See Article 1(4). The problems with port reception facilities are fully explored in Mitchell, *Intentional Oil Pollution*, Ch 6; Tan, *Vessel Source Marine Pollution*, 251–73.

Quantifying MARPOL's impact is thus not straightforward, and the data do not point to any clear conclusion, except that operational pollution from tankers does appear to have declined, while discharges from other types of vessel remain a problem. Major tanker disasters have continued to occur however, some of which indicate weaknesses in the proficiency of crews and the seaworthiness and construction standards of older vessels. The *Exxon Valdez, Aegean Sea, Haven, Braer, Sea Empress, Evoikos, Nakhodka, Erika,* and *Prestige* have all been the subject of large compensation claims.[147] With the exception of the *Exxon Valdez* all were registered in flag of convenience states: Greece, Liberia, Cyprus, Malta, and the Bahamas. These states account for only a small proportion of the hundred or more tanker incidents dealt with by the IOPC Fund, but their ships appear to have larger scale accidents than Japanese and Korean vessels, which account for more than half the total number of claims. Once single-hull tankers are all phased out the number of severe accidents may decline, but double hulls are not as easy to repair or inspect, and we will not know whether the policy has succeeded until these ships are twenty or thirty years old.[148]

(g) Flag state jurisdiction under the 1982 UNCLOS

The 1982 UNCLOS makes radical changes in the exclusive character of flag-state jurisdiction, but leaves intact the central principle of earlier law that the flag state has responsibility for the regulation and control of pollution from its ships. This duty is redefined, however, in terms requiring greater uniformity in the content of regulations. These must now 'at least have the same effect' as the MARPOL Convention, which as we saw earlier represents 'generally accepted international rules and standards' in this context. Since flag states retain a discretion under this wording to set more onerous standards, the effect of Article 211 of UNCLOS is to make MARPOL, and other relevant international standards referred to earlier, an obligatory minimum.

Article 217 reinforces this conclusion by requiring flag states to take measures necessary for the implementation and effective enforcement of international rules and standards. These measures must include the certification and inspection procedures instituted by MARPOL and SOLAS, and must be sufficient to ensure that vessels are prohibited from sailing until they can comply with the relevant regulations. The remaining provisions of Article 217 reiterate the obligation of flag states to investigate violations and bring appropriate proceedings, and to act on the request of other states where a violation is reported. In substance, therefore, a flag state bound by Article 217 is required to do all that the MARPOL Convention already demands. There is thus nothing novel in principle in the treatment of flag state regulation in the 1982 UNCLOS: it fully accords with existing customary and conventional law,[149] although as with other provisions of the convention these articles are part of a broader package deal and are not necessarily applicable in every respect to ships of non-parties.

---

[147] See *infra*, section 6(3).   [148] Frank, 20 *IJMCL* (2005) 1.
[149] Boyle, 79 *AJIL* (1985) 363ff; Popp, *CYIL* (1980) 3; Bernhardt, 20 *VJIL* (1979) 265.

4(3) COASTAL STATE JURISDICTION AND FREEDOM OF NAVIGATION

(a) In internal waters and the territorial sea

The coastal state's jurisdiction to regulate vessels depends on its sovereignty or sovereign rights over maritime zones contiguous to its coasts. Until the 1970s these zones were for the most part of limited extent. In internal waters, such as ports, the coastal state is free to apply national laws and determine conditions of entry for foreign vessels.[150] After the *Exxon Valdez* accident the United States became the first to ban all single-hull oil tankers from its ports without waiting for agreement in IMO.[151] The most obvious argument in favour of the lawfulness of this response is that it falls within the customary jurisdiction of a port state to regulate matters affecting the peace and good order of the port because of the risk of accidents and consequential pollution. No state is known to have objected to the US action; it represents a clear precedent for the subsequent introduction a similar ban by the EU following the sinking of the *Prestige*.[152] Legislation of this kind remains an unusual assertion of jurisdiction, however; for most states the interests of comity with other nations and freedom of navigation have until now dictated greater restraint in the unilateral regulation of foreign ships.[153]

In the territorial sea, the coastal state also enjoys sovereignty, and with it the power to apply national law.[154] The coastal state's right to regulate environmental protection in territorial waters has been assumed or asserted in national legislation and in treaties on such matters as dumping or pollution from ships. This right includes three important powers: the designation of environmentally protected or particularly sensitive sea areas,[155] the designation and control of navigation routes for safety and environmental purposes,[156] and the prohibition of pollution discharges.[157]

---

[150] *Nicaragua Case*, ICJ Reports (1986) paras 212–13; Churchill and Lowe, *The Law of the Sea*, 61; de La Fayette, 11 *IJMCL* (1996) 15–16.

[151] 1990 Oil Pollution Act. See critical analysis by Valenzuela, in Soons, *Implementation of the LOSC through International Institutions*, 212 ff.

[152] EC Regulation 417/2002, amended by Reg 1726/2003. See Boyle, 21 *IJMCL* (2006) 15; Frank, 20 *IJMCL* (2005) 1.

[153] See generally Churchill and Lowe, *The Law of the Sea*, Ch 3; O'Connell, *The International Law of the Sea*, Ch 22.

[154] 1982 UNCLOS, Article 2; Churchill and Lowe, *The Law of the Sea*, Ch 4; O'Connell, *The International Law of the Sea*, Chs 19, 24.

[155] See *infra*.

[156] 1982 UNCLOS, Article 22, which requires states to take into account IMO recommendations, but does not require IMO approval. Mandatory vessel traffic management (VTS) in the territorial sea and Mandatory Ship Reporting (MSR) are provided for under SOLAS 1974, Ch V; traffic separation schemes (TSS) under the 1972 Collision Regulations Convention. See IMO Resolutions A 857(20) Guidelines for vessel traffic services; A 851(20) General principles for ship reporting systems; A 572(14) General provisions on ships' routeing, as amended by MSC 165(78); and on routeing in PSSAs see IMO Res A 927(22). See generally Roberts, 20 *IJMCL* (2005) 135; Plant, in Ringbom (ed), *Competing Norms in the Law of Marine Environmental Protection*, 11; IJIstra, in Soons, *Implementation of the LOSC through International Institutions*, 216; Warren and Wallace, 9 *IJMCL* (1994) 523. On passage in straits, see 1982 UNCLOS, Article 41, and Oxman, 10 *IJMCL* (1995) 467.

[157] 1972 London Dumping Convention, Article 4(3); 1973 MARPOL Convention, Article 4(2); 1982 UNCLOS, Article 21(1)(f).

In each of these respects the coastal state enjoys a substantial measure of national discretion: it is, for example, free to set stricter pollution discharge standards than the international standards required by the MARPOL Convention. But unlike the earlier Territorial Sea Convention of 1958, or the 1973 MARPOL Convention, which are silent on the point, the 1982 UNCLOS excludes from the coastal state's jurisdiction the right to regulate construction, design, equipment, and manning standards for ships, unless giving effect to international rules and standards, which for this purpose means primarily the MARPOL Convention, and the 1974 Safety of Life at Sea Convention.[158] The reason for this exclusion is self-evident: if every state set its own standards on these matters ships could not freely navigate in the territorial sea of other states. This would contravene the most important limitation on the coastal state's jurisdiction with regard to any of the above matters: that it must not hamper the right of innocent passage through the territorial sea or suspend the right in straits used for international navigation.[159] This right is enjoyed by the vessels of all nations, and it is an essential safeguard for freedom of maritime navigation. Foreign vessels do not thereby acquire exemption from coastal state laws, but these laws must be in conformity with international law, and must not have the practical effect of denying passage.[160]

What then can a coastal state legitimately do when a foreign vessel is found violating international pollution regulations in the territorial sea, or when it poses a risk of accidental pollution or environmental harm? What the coastal state cannot do is to close its territorial waters to foreign ships in innocent passage, even where their cargo presents a significant environmental risk, as in the case of oil tankers.[161] Passage in these circumstances does not cease to be innocent, and must be afforded without discrimination. At most, the coastal state will be entitled to take certain precautionary measures to minimize the risk: it may, for example, require ships carrying nuclear materials or other inherently dangerous or noxious substances, such as oil or hazardous waste, to carry documentation, observe special precautionary measures approved by IMO or established by international agreements such as MARPOL, or confine their passage to specified sea lanes in the interests of safety, the efficiency of traffic, and the protection of the environment.[162] Following the *Braer* disaster off the Shetland Islands in 1993, IMO also amended the SOLAS Convention to allow coastal states to require

---

[158] 1982 UNCLOS, Article 21(2); Article 211(4). See especially the opposing views of Canada and Bulgaria on this question, 3rd UNCLOS, 6 *Official Records*, 109, 112.

[159] *Corfu Channel Case*, ICJ Reports (1949) 1; 1958 Territorial Sea Convention, Articles, 14–16; 1982 UNCLOS, Articles 17–19, 24–5; Churchill and Lowe, *The Law of the Sea*, 81ff, and see generally Ngantcha, *The Right of Innocent Passage and the Evolution of The International Law of the Sea* (London, 1990).

[160] Territorial Sea Convention, Article 17; 1982 UNCLOS, Article 21(4).

[161] 1982 UNCLOS, Article 24(1).

[162] 1982 UNCLOS, Articles 22(2), 23, and for IMO resolutions *supra*, n 156. On hazardous waste shipments see 1989 Basel Convention on the Control of Transboundary Movements of Hazardous Wastes, Article 4(12) and 1991 Bamako Convention, Article 4(4)(c) *infra*, Ch 8, section 4, but see *contra* Haiti, *Note Verbale* of 18 Feb 1988, in 11 *LOSB* (1988) 13 and Pineschi, in Francioni and Scovazzi (eds), *International Responsibility for Environmental Harm* (Dordrecht, 1991) 299.

ships to report their presence to coastal authorities when entering designated zones, including environmentally sensitive areas.[163]

The application of these principles can be observed in state practice concerning environmentally sensitive areas covered by special areas protocols,[164] or Particularly Sensitive Sea Areas (PSSAs) designated by IMO.[165] A PSSA is 'an area that needs special protection through action by IMO because of its significance for recognized ecological, socio-economic, or scientific attributes where such attributes may be vulnerable to damage by international shipping activities'.[166] They 'may be regarded as fulfilling general obligations in the LOS Convention and in a number of treaties designed to protect the marine environment and/or biodiversity'.[167] In such cases the passage of ships through the territorial sea may be regulated in order to minimize the risk of adverse environmental effects or serious pollution but, here too, the important point is that while ships may be required to avoid certain areas, the right of innocent passage is not lost.[168] Mandatory ship reporting is a common element of such schemes, but additional measures may also be taken with IMO approval. Thus in 1990, Australia obtained IMO designation of the Great Barrier Reef as a PSSA within an extended territorial sea and imposed compulsory pilotage requirements.[169] The United States also designated the Florida Keys as an 'area to be avoided' and prohibited the operation of tankers in these waters under the 1972 Marine Protection, Research, and Sanctuaries Act, again with the approval of IMO. However, as adopted by IMO in Resolution A 927(22), the PSSA concept does not expand the powers of coastal states in the territorial sea; it merely coordinates a range of available powers under the 1982 UNCLOS, 1974 SOLAS Convention, and 1972 COLREGS Convention, inter alia. PSSAs can extend into the exclusive economic zone—the North Sea/Western European PSSA is an example—but with more limited effects.[170]

Although the practical exercise of a right to arrest ships in passage poses serious dangers to navigation, and is rarely used as a means of enforcing anti-pollution regulations, both the 1972 London Dumping Convention and the 1973 MARPOL Convention require coastal states to apply and enforce their provisions against all vessels in the territorial sea. This right is recognized in the 1982 UNCLOS, subject to that Convention's provisions on innocent passage and the existence of clear grounds for suspecting a

---

[163] 1974 SOLAS, Chapter V, Regulation 8–1, and *supra*, n 156. See Plant, in Ringbom (ed), *Competing Norms*, 11.

[164] Mediterranean, Caribbean and East African protected areas protocols, *supra*, n 83.

[165] See IMO Res A 927(22) and materials collected in 9 *IJMCL* (1994). PSSAs designated by IMO include the Great Barrier Reef, the Florida Keys, the Wadden Sea, the Canary Islands, the Sabana-Camagüey Archipelago, the Torres Strait, and Western European waters.

[166] IMO Res A 982(24) annex, para 1.2.   [167] de La Fayette, 16 *IJMCL* (2001) 155, 186.

[168] 1982 Geneva Protocol Concerning Mediterranean Specially Protected Areas, Article 7(e); 1990 Kingston Protocol Concerning Specially Protected Areas, etc, of the Wider Caribbean, Article 5(2)(c); and see IMO, Working Group on Guidelines for Particularly Sensitive Sea Areas, MEPC 29 and 30 (1990). Cf, however, Canada's 1972 Arctic Waters Pollution Act, and 1982 UNCLOS, Article 234.

[169] MEPC 45/30 (1990) and MEPC 133/53 (2005) which extends the scheme to the Torres Strait. See Okkesen et al, 9 *IJMCL* (1994) 507.

[170] See *infra*, section 4(3)(b).

violation.[171] However, the mere violation of regulations will not necessarily deprive the vessel of its right of innocent passage. Innocent passage was defined by the 1958 Territorial Sea Convention as passage which is 'not prejudicial to the peace, good order or security' of the coastal state. This vague terminology appeared to allow coastal states ample room for subjective judgments of the question of innocence, and it is arguably not an accurate reflection of the treatment of innocent passage in the *Corfu Channel Case*. That decision implied a rather more objective test, now reflected in Article 19 of the 1982 UNCLOS. This provision was not intended to change the law but to clarify it in terms affording less scope for potentially abusive interference with shipping. The significant point is that only pollution which is 'wilful and serious' and contrary to the Convention will deprive a vessel in passage of its innocent character, which necessarily excludes accidental pollution from having this effect. Moreover, while operational pollution is invariably deliberate, it is less often serious, and may sometimes be justified by weather or distress. Under this formulation, therefore, it will rarely be the case that ships causing operational pollution will cease to be in innocent passage. Nor would it permit single-hull tankers to be banned from the territorial sea, since a mere violation of construction standards will not be enough to deprive a ship of its right to innocent passage. Only when they lose this right can their entry into territorial waters be denied, or their right of passage terminated by eviction or arrest. In most cases the preferable solution will be to rely on port states for enforcement purpose.

The 1982 UNCLOS does not alter these basic principles of customary law or extend the coastal state's rights in the territorial sea. In this context its purpose is simply to clarify and define the limits of those rights. The territorial-sea regime envisaged by the Convention is thus a compromise: it offers coastal states power to control navigation and pollution, while preserving rights of passage and international control of construction, design, equipment, and manning standards.[172] What the Convention does change is the breadth of the territorial sea, which it extends from three to twelve miles, a decision now overwhelmingly approved in state practice. By itself, however, this extension was not enough to satisfy the needs or claims of coastal states. The more important decision, therefore, was to go beyond the territorial sea by giving coastal states pollution control jurisdiction in a new exclusive economic zone created by the 1982 UNCLOS.

(b) Coastal state prescriptive jurisdiction in the EEZ

The major innovation of the 1982 UNCLOS provisions on the marine environment is the exclusive economic zone (EEZ), which extends to 200 nautical miles from the territorial-sea baseline and confers on coastal states sovereign rights over living and mineral resources, and jurisdiction with regard to the protection and preservation

---

[171] 1972 London Dumping Convention, Article 7; 1973 MARPOL Convention, Article 4(2); 1982 UNCLOS, Article 220(2).

[172] Boyle, 79 *AJIL* (1985) 347. See M'Gonigle and Zacher, *Pollution, Politics, and International Law*, 244–5 and Tan, *Vessel-Source Marine Pollution*, 176–229 for critical analysis of this part of the 1982 Convention.

of the marine environment.[173] This zone differs from the extended jurisdiction over fisheries recognized by the ICJ in the *Icelandic Fisheries Case* because it gives the coastal state rights to resources which are not merely preferential but potentially exclusive. Although in that sense the Convention's provisions make new law, the consensus behind the adoption of the EEZ was such that it has rapidly been translated into state practice by coastal state claims to exclusive fishing zones and full EEZs. In the *Libya-Malta Continental Shelf Case* the ICJ found that: 'the institution of the EEZ with its rule on entitlement by reason of distance is shown by the practice of states to have become part of customary law'.[174] Thus the principle of extended coastal-state rights beyond the territorial sea is now part of international law, although the precise claims made in this zone by individual states have varied, in some cases widely. It should be recalled moreover that the EEZ does not arise automatically: it has to be claimed, and, in the case of pollution jurisdiction, legislation will usually be necessary for the coastal state to acquire the necessary competence. Only a small number have legislation specifically incorporating coastal-state powers under Articles 211 and 220;[175] others, such as the United States, have asserted jurisdiction in their EEZ only for certain purposes, such as fisheries conservation or dumping, but have not legislated to control pollution from ships beyond the territorial sea. Some states have made no EEZ claims (e.g. in the Mediterranean), but a few of these, such as the United Kingdom, have nevertheless legislated on all or most of the matters covered by EEZ jurisdictional powers. A few others have EEZ pollution legislation which could be interpreted as exceeding what UNCLOS allows, notably on passage for ships carrying nuclear or hazardous waste, or which fails fully to reflect the carefully balanced qualifications and limitations laid down in the UNCLOS articles.[176]

Faced with the inadequacy of earlier attempts to control pollution from ships, a strong lobby at the UNCLOS III conference, led by Canada and Australia and supported by the majority of developing states, had sought a general extension of coastal state legislative and enforcement jurisdiction beyond the relatively limited changes wrought by MARPOL.[177] The adoption of the EEZ involved a compromise between the more extensive claims of these states and the concerns of maritime nations. Once coastal states had abandoned their support for a much broader margin of territorial sea, maritime states were prepared to accept the principle of extended jurisdiction for

---

[173] 1982 UNCLOS, Article 56. See Orrego-Vicuna, *The Exclusive Economic Zone: Regime and Legal Nature Under International Law* (Cambridge, 1989); Kwiatkowska, *The 200-Mile EEZ in the New Law of the Sea* (Dordrecht, 1989); Attard, *The Exclusive Economic Zone* (Oxford, 1987).

[174] ICJ Reports (1985) 13, para 34.

[175] Churchill and Lowe, *The Law of the Sea*, 352, list Russia, Bulgaria, Romania, Malaysia, Sweden, Antigua, St.Kitts, St.Lucia, and the Ukraine.

[176] See Churchill and Lowe, *The Law of the Sea*, 351–3; Molenaar, *Coastal State Jurisdiction over Vessel Source Pollution*, 363–82. For a full listing of national EEZ claims and legislation see Kwiatkowska, 9 *IJMCL* (1994) 199, 337; id, 10 *IJMCL* (1995) 53.

[177] *3rd UNCLOS, Official Records*, ii, 317–20; Nordquist and Park, *Reports of the US Delegation to the 3rd UNCLOS*, 47–51, 74, 89; M'Gonigle and Zacher, *Pollution, Politics and International Law*, Ch 6; Nordquist, *UNCLOS Commentary*, iv, 180ff.

specific purposes. The central feature of the new EEZ regime is that it preserves for all states high seas freedom of navigation within the zone, rather than the more restrictive territorial sea right of innocent passage, in contrast to earlier 200-mile claims made by a number of Latin American states.[178] Coastal states acquire responsibility for regulating pollution from seabed installations, dumping, and activities within the EEZ, but their regulatory jurisdiction over vessels is limited to the application of international rules for enforcement purposes only.[179]

The effect of this new regime is less radical than some coastal states had sought. That it does no more than permit them to apply MARPOL and other relevant instruments is evident from the wording of article 211(5) of the 1982 UNCLOS, which refers only to coastal state laws 'conforming to and giving effect to generally accepted international rules and standards' for the prevention, reduction, and control of vessel-source pollution.[180] In this context MARPOL regulations and other international standards adopted by IMO thus represent the normal limit of coastal state competence and act as a necessary restraint where there is evident potential for excessive interference with shipping. Thus, coastal states have acquired little real discretion about the kind of anti-pollution legislation they may apply in the EEZ. In particular, as in the territorial sea, they are denied the power to set their own construction, design, equipment, and manning standards for vessels or to refuse passage. Following the *Prestige* disaster, unilateral action by some European states to ban single-hull oil tankers from their EEZs encountered strong opposition and could not easily be reconciled with UNCLOS, or with the new PSSA subsequently adopted for Western Europe.[181] Mandatory reporting or routeing schemes require IMO approval if they extend to the EEZ and must be supported by scientific and technical evidence.[182] Nor does the designation of special areas or PSSAs by IMO confer any power on coastal states to act unilaterally in setting construction or equipment standards for ships entering the EEZ, although it does permit them to apply national standards relating to pollution discharges or to control navigation.[183]

The solitary exception to the Convention's preference for the application of international regulations in the EEZ is found in Article 234. This article was a concession to Canadian and Russian interests in the protection of the Arctic Ocean. It applies to ice-covered areas within the limits of the EEZ, and allows coastal states a broad discretion, free from IMO supervision, to adopt national standards for pollution control,

---

[178] 1982 UNCLOS, Articles 56(2), 58. On earlier Latin American claims to 200-mile jurisdiction, see Orrego Vicuna, *The EEZ: A Latin American Perspective* (Boulder, Colo, 1984) Ch 2.

[179] Articles 208, 210, 211(5)–(6).

[180] On the meaning of this phrase, see Molenaar, *Coastal State Jurisdiction over Vessel Source Pollution*, Ch 10.

[181] Frank, 20 *IJMCL* (2005) 9–10. See generally Laly-Chevalier, 50 *AFDI* (2004) 581.

[182] 1974 SOLAS, Regulation V/8 and V/8–1. See Plant, in Ringbom (ed), *Competing Norms in the Law of Marine Environmental Protection*, 11; Roberts, 20 *IJMCL* (2005) 135.

[183] For a fuller analysis of UNCLOS Article 211(6) and its relationship to PSSAs and MARPOL special areas, see Frank, 20 *IJMCL* (2005) 28–38; de La Fayette, 16 *IJMCL* (2001)155, 190–2. de La Fayette emphazises the importance of PSSAs in providing additional powers within the EEZ, with IMO approval.

provided only that these have due regard for navigation and are non-discriminatory. It remains uncertain whether this Article goes as far as Canada's 1970 Arctic Waters Pollution Act in authorizing limitations on navigation.[184]

In general, the 1982 UNCLOS can best be seen as serving the interests of maritime states within the EEZ although the extension of jurisdiction does give a wider area of control to coastal states if they choose to use it. In the exercise of jurisdiction within the EEZ, coastal states must have due regard for the rights and duties of other states, including the right of freedom of navigation. This freedom is largely protected by ensuring uniformity of applicable pollution standards, and by preserving the ability of maritime states to influence the formulation of those standards within IMO. Although the international regulations adopted through that body represent an expression of compromise and common interest among the various groups represented there, including environmental NGOs and industry associations, there is little doubt that maritime states have tended to predominate.[185] However, the continued growth of flags of convenience since 1982 makes the identification of 'maritime states' an increasingly difficult task. Thus, it should not be assumed that states with a low registered tonnage, such as the United States, do not have a substantial interest in maritime navigation, or that their influence in IMO can be disregarded. Nevertheless the essential point remains that the Convention's articles on the regulation of vessel pollution by coastal states are primarily important as a basis for enforcement of MARPOL and other international standards, and do not authorize 'creeping jurisdiction' over the high seas.

(c) Enforcement jurisdiction of coastal and port states under UNCLOS[186]

It was eventually accepted during the UNCLOS negotiations that the problem of non-compliance with international regulations could not be remedied by flag-state enforcement alone, and that the port-state control provisions of MARPOL were not in themselves a sufficient alternative. The main question was whether to allow coastal states full authority to arrest and prosecute vessels for pollution offences within the EEZ, a solution consistent with the extension of their prescriptive jurisdiction, or whether to concentrate instead on the increased use of port-state jurisdiction as the main complement to the flag state's authority. The advantage of the former was that it would give those states which suffered most from poor enforcement the opportunity to protect themselves directly, rather than by relying on flag states. The disadvantages were the threat to freedom of navigation, and as in the territorial sea, the practical

---

[184] McRae and Goundrey, 16 *UBCLR* (1982) 197; Pharand, 7 *Dalhousie LJ* (1983) 315; Johnson and Zacher, *Canadian Foreign Policy and the Law of the Sea* (Vancouver, 1977) Ch 3. Canada has subsequently redrawn its territorial sea baselines to extend its jurisdiction over the waters of its northern archipelago, and it has also claimed a 200-mile EEZ.

[185] See especially McGonigle and Zacher, *Pollution, Politics and International Law*, Chs 3, 7; Hayashi, 16 *IJMCL* (2001) 501; de La Fayette, 16 *IJMCL* (2001) 215–20; Gaskell, 18 *IJMCL* (2003) 172–4; Tan, *Vessel-Source Marine Pollution*, 29–74.

[186] Molenaar, *Coastal State Jurisdiction over Vessel Source Pollution*, 382–99; id, in Freestone, Barnes and Ong (eds), *The Law of the Sea*, Ch 11; Kasoulides, *Port-state control and Jurisdiction*.

dangers of interfering with ships at sea. Moreover, coastal-state enforcement afforded no remedy for high-seas pollution offences outside the EEZ. From this perspective, port-state jurisdiction to prosecute violations emerged as the more attractive alternative, since it presented no danger to navigation and afforded better facilities for investigation and the collection of evidence concerning offences, regardless of where they had taken place.[187]

The result, once more, is a compromise between the two extremes. Coastal states are not given full jurisdiction to enforce international regulations against ships in passage in the EEZ. They can do so if the vessel voluntarily enters port,[188] but otherwise their powers in the EEZ itself are graduated according to the likely harm. Only when there is 'clear objective evidence' of a violation of applicable international regulations resulting in a discharge of pollution which causes or threatens to cause 'major damage' to the coastal state are arrest and prosecution permitted, but where the violation has resulted only in a 'substantial discharge' causing or threatening 'significant pollution', the vessel may be inspected for 'matters relating to the violation'—that is, in effect, for evidence of the illegal discharge, provided this is justified by the circumstances, including information already given by the ship.[189] The ship may in this case only be detained if necessary to prevent an unreasonable threat of damage to the marine environment.[190] Where none of these conditions exist, the coastal state is confined to seeking information concerning the ship's identity and its next port of call.[191] The port state may then be asked to take appropriate action.

Although these graduated enforcement powers in the EEZ leave coastal states considerable latitude in determining what action is justified in individual cases, and may for that reason lead to uncertainty and inconsistency in their use, they do amount to rather less than the competence enjoyed by coastal states in the territorial sea, and in less serious cases they still leave enforcement to flag states, or as we shall see, to port states. In this form the jurisdiction of coastal states remains a limited one for protective purposes only, but this is consistent with the nature of their rights in the EEZ. In practice, few states have resorted to the exercise of these powers in full and it is doubtful whether in this respect Article 220 of the 1982 UNCLOS has had any significant effect, so far.[192]

In contrast to the limited jurisdiction of coastal states, the more radical development is that Article 218 gives port states express power to investigate and prosecute discharge violations wherever they have taken place. This power covers both high-seas offences, and violations within the coastal zones of another state, although in the latter

---

[187] Lowe, 12 *San Diego LR* (1975) 624; Bernhardt, 20 *Vand JTL* (1979) 265; Kasoulides, in Soons, *Implementation of the LOSC through International Institutions*; ILA, *Report of the 56th Conference* (1974) 400–8.

[188] Article 220(1). This power applies only to violations which have occurred 'within the territorial sea or the exclusive economic zone of *that* state'.

[189] Article 220(5)–(6).   [190] Article 226(1)(c).   [191] Article 220(3).

[192] For the drafting history of Article 220, see Nordquist (ed), *UNCLOS Commentary*, iv, 281ff. For national legislation, see Molenaar, *Coastal State Jurisdiction over Vessel Source Pollution*, 389–98.

case the port state may only act in response to a request from the state concerned. Apart from this limitation, the port state's jurisdiction under this article is independent, in the sense that no request from the flag state is necessary, but the flag state does enjoy a right of pre-emption, considered below.

The obvious advantage of Article 218 is that it may ensure prompt prosecution where the coastal state is unable or incompetent to act, or where the vessel is unlikely to come within the flag state's authority. In effect this article recognizes the inability or ineffectiveness of flag states when dealing with pollution incidents on the high seas, and gives the port state the power to act in the public interest, independently of any effects on its own waters or of any jurisdictional connection based on nationality, territory, or protection. In that sense, Article 218 creates a form of universal jurisdiction, concurrent with that of the flag state, and in some cases, with the coastal state.[193]

It is, however, a novel development in the law of the sea to confer jurisdiction on port states in this way. Although the *Lotus Case* did permit Turkey to prosecute a foreign vessel in a Turkish port for an offence which had occurred on the high seas, that decision owed much to the erroneous equation of ships with floating territory, and the court's specific conclusion regarding collisions has since been reversed by treaty.[194] Thus it cannot convincingly be asserted that the exercise of port state jurisdiction over high-seas pollution offences contemplated by Article 218(1) is based on pre-UNCLOS customary law. Only two states and the EU are known to have implemented Article 218 (1);[195] port-state practice otherwise appears to remain within the more limited regime provided by MARPOL and the regional schemes considered earlier. However, given the extensive and largely unopposed way in which port-state control and jurisdiction in general have developed since 1982, and the consensus surrounding UNCLOS provisions, it may be that no state would now deny that Article 218 has become customary law.[196]

One result of Article 218 is that flag states no longer enjoy exclusive jurisdiction over all high-seas offences, although this is not concurrent jurisdiction in the ordinary sense, where either party is entitled to prosecute. Except in cases of major damage to the coastal state, the flag state under the 1982 Convention has in all cases a right of pre-emption[197] which enables it to insist on taking control of any prosecution. It must continue the proceedings, and it loses the right if it repeatedly disregards its obligation

---

[193] See *supra*, Ch 5 for further discussion, and see generally Nordquist (ed), *UNCLOS Commentary*, iv, 258ff.

[194] PCIJ (1927) Ser A, No 10, 169 and cf 1952 Brussels Convention for the Unification of Certain Rules Relating to Penal Jurisdiction; 1958 High Seas Convention, Article II; 1982 UNCLOS, Article 97. For criticism of the *Lotus Case*, see II *YbILC* (1956) 281; Brownlie, *Principles of Public International Law* (6th edn, Oxford, 2005) 300–1.

[195] Belize, Maritime Areas Act 1992, s 24(4); United Kingdom, Merchant Shipping (Prevention of Oil Pollution) Regulations, 1996, regs 34–9, SI 1996 No 2154; EC Directive 95/21 (1995) Article 3(1)(e) on which see Ringbom, *The EU Maritime Safety Policy and International Law* (The Hague, 2008) Ch 5 .

[196] Cf the cautious views of Kwiatkowska, *The 200 Mile EEZ*, 184 and Churchill and Lowe, *Law of the Sea*, 352–3, with the more positive conclusion of Anderson, in Boyle and Freestone (eds), *International Law and Sustainable Development*, 343. See generally McDorman, 28 *JMLC* (1997) 305.

[197] Article 228. See Kwiatkowska, *The 200-Mile EEZ*, 184; Nordquist, *UNCLOS Commentary*, iv, 348ff.

of effective enforcement of international regulations. Nevertheless, in most cases it remains the flag state which will determine whether proceedings by coastal states or port states are to be allowed.

Finally, in exercising any of these enforcement powers, coastal or port states must observe certain safeguards whose purpose is to prevent excessive exercise of their authority.[198] In particular they must not act in a discriminatory fashion. Monetary penalties only may be imposed for violations, except in the case of wilful and serious pollution of the territorial sea. There are also special rules safeguarding passage in straits used for international navigation. Military or government-owned vessels in non-commercial service continue to enjoy immunity from the jurisdiction of port and coastal states in all circumstances, although states must ensure that these act in a manner consistent with the Convention's provisions on the environment 'so far as is reasonable and practicable',[199] and should presumably discipline officers responsible for pollution offences, including collisions.

5 POLLUTION INCIDENTS AND EMERGENCIES AT SEA

5(1) INTERNATIONAL COOPERATION AND ASSISTANCE[200]

International cooperation to deal with pollution incidents or emergencies at sea is primarily a matter of prudent self-interest, but international law does impose certain obligations on states confronted with such risks. Both customary law and Article 198 of the 1982 UNCLOS indicate that once they are aware of imminent or actual pollution of the marine environment, states must give immediate notification to others likely to be affected.[201] This requirement is also reiterated in most regional-seas agreements.[202] In addition, regional agreements, and the 1982 UNCLOS require states to cooperate, in accordance with their capabilities, in eliminating the effects of such pollution, in preventing or minimizing the damage, and in developing contingency plans.[203]

---

[198] Articles 223–33; Nordquist, *UNCLOS Commentary*, iv, 320ff.

[199] Article 235; 1926 Brussels Convention for the Unification of Rules Concerning the Immunity of State Owned Ships.

[200] See generally Kiss, 23 *GYIL* (1980) 231; Abecassis and Jarashow, *Oil Pollution from Ships*, Ch 7; IMO/ UNEP, *Meeting on Regional Arrangements for Cooperation in Combating Major Incidents of Marine Pollution* (London, 1985); de Rouw, in Couper and Gold, *The Marine Environment*.

[201] *Supra*, Ch 3, section 4.

[202] See e.g. 1976 Barcelona Convention, Article 9(2); 1983 Cartagena Convention, Article 11(2); 1978 Kuwait Convention, Article 9(b); 1983 Bonn Agreement for Cooperation in Dealing with Pollution of the North Sea by Oil and Other Harmful Substances, Article 5. See also 1990 International Convention on Oil Pollution Preparedness, Response and Cooperation, Article 5(1).

[203] 1982 UNCLOS, Article 199; 1983 Bonn Agreement; 1971 Copenhagen Agreement Concerning Cooperation in Measures to Deal with Pollution of the Sea by Oil; 1974 Helsinki Convention on the Protection

Article 7 of the 1990 Convention on Oil Pollution Preparedness, Response, and Cooperation (OPPRC), a global instrument adopted by IMO following the *Exxon Valdez* disaster in Alaska, further commits parties to respond to requests for assistance from states likely to be affected by oil pollution. IMO must be informed of major incidents,[204] and under Article 12, it is given responsibility for coordinating and facilitating cooperation on various matters, including the provision on request of technical assistance and advice for states faced with major oil pollution incidents. Parties may also seek IMO's assistance in arranging financial support for response costs.[205] A protocol adopted in 2000 extends the principles of the 1990 Convention to pollution incidents involving hazardous and noxious substances.[206]

IMO's role under the OPPRC Convention and the HNS Protocol is comparable to that played by IAEA under the Convention on Assistance in Cases of Nuclear Emergency.[207] Although not then in force, the 1990 Convention provided the basis for IMO coordination of technical support and financial assistance for governments dealing with serious marine pollution during the conflict in the Persian Gulf in January 1991.[208] Further coordination is provided regionally by centres established with the assistance of IMO and UNEP.[209] In the North Sea, the 1983 Bonn Agreement divides that area into zones for which states are individually or in some cases jointly responsible, but other parties remain obliged to use their best endeavours to provide assistance if requested. Although these agreements generally allocate the costs of cooperative action to the state requesting assistance, or to those which act on their own initiative, this is usually without prejudice to rights to recover these costs from third parties under national or international law.[210]

5(2) CONTROLLING POLLUTION EMERGENCIES AT SEA

(a) General obligations

Quite apart from their obligation to cooperate, states may also be required to respond to pollution emergencies individually, in cases where the incident falls within their

---

of the Marine Environment of the Baltic Sea Area, Annex VI; 1976 Barcelona Protocol Concerning Cases of Emergency; 1978 Kuwait Protocol Concerning Cases of Emergency; 1981 Abidjan Protocol Concerning Cases of Emergency; 1981 Lima Protocol on Regional Cooperation Cases of Emergency; 1982 Jeddah Protocol Concerning Cases of Emergency; 1983 Cartagena Protocol Concerning Cooperation in Combating Oil Spills; 1987 Noumea Protocol Concerning Emergencies; 1985 Nairobi Protocol Concerning Cases of Emergency, 1990 Lisbon Agreement of Cooperation for the Protection of the North-East Atlantic Against Pollution. See also bilateral arrangements between the UK and France, UK and Norway, Denmark and Germany, and Caribbean Island states, listed by IMO *supra*, n 200 at para 2.10. Other bilateral agreements apply between the United States and Canada and the United States and Mexico.

[204] Article 5(3).   [205] Article 7(2).

[206] Defined by reference to those listed in IMO Conventions and Codes.   [207] See *infra*, Ch 9.

[208] UNCED, Prepcom, UN Doc A/CONF 151/PC/72(1991).

[209] E.g. the Regional Marine Pollution Emergency Response Centre in Malta, the Marine Emergency Mutual Aid Centre in Bahrain, and the Regional Coordination Unit, in Jamaica. See IMO/UNEP, *Regional Meeting, supra*, n 200.

[210] 1983 Bonn Agreement, Article 9; 1990 Oil Pollution Preparedness, Response, and Cooperation Convention, Annex.

jurisdiction or control. Failure to do so may then amount to a breach of the state's obligations in customary law to control sources of pollution, even if the emergency itself is not attributable to state action or inaction.[211] This assumption is consistent with the 1982 UNCLOS, which requires states to ensure that pollution arising from 'incidents or activities' under their jurisdiction or control does not spread beyond areas where they exercise sovereign rights, or is not transferred to other areas.[212] Moreover, Article 194 specifically mandates measures to prevent accidents and deal with emergencies emanating from all sources of marine pollution. Such detailed requirements are not generally found in regional treaties, however.[213]

The 1990 OPPRC Convention and the HNS Protocol apply these basic principles to pollution incidents caused by ships, offshore installations, and port-handling facilities which threaten the marine environment or the coastline or related interests of individual states.[214] The parties must take all appropriate measures to prepare for and respond to such incidents. In particular, a national system capable of responding promptly and effectively must be established, including the designation of a competent national authority and a national contingency plan. Information concerning these arrangements must be provided to other states. Parties are also required to ensure that offshore oil operations within their jurisdiction, and port-handling facilities, are conducted in accordance with emergency procedures approved by the competent national authority. These provisions are somewhat stronger than those generally found in a number of regional or bilateral schemes.[215]

Although the primary responsibility for responding effectively will thus fall in most cases on the relevant coastal states, flag states also have a responsibility for ensuring that their vessels are adequately prepared to deal with emergencies. Article 3 of the 1990 Convention requires the parties to ensure that vessels flying their flag have on board an oil pollution emergency plan in accordance with the IMO provisions. For this purpose the Convention provides that vessels are subject to port-state inspection under existing international arrangements referred to earlier.

(b) Coastal-state powers of intervention[216]

It is unrealistic to expect flag states themselves to maintain the capacity to respond to accidents involving their vessels wherever they occur, and apart from the provisions of Article 3, the 1990 Convention does not attempt to make them do so. The right of coastal states to intervene beyond their territorial sea in cases of maritime casualties involving foreign vessels that are likely to cause pollution damage is, therefore, an important safeguard for these states in protecting themselves from the risks

[211] See e.g. *Corfu Channel Case*, ICJ Reports (1949) 3 and *supra*, Ch 3, section 4.

[212] Articles 194(2), 195.

[213] But see 1981 Lima Convention, Articles 3(5), 6; 1978 Kuwait Convention, Article 9(a); 1976 Barcelona Protocol, Article 9; 1990 Lisbon Agreement.

[214] De Rouw, in Couper and Gold (eds), *The Marine Environment* (Honolulu, 1991).

[215] 1978 Kuwait Convention, Article 9 and protocol; 1982 Jeddah Protocol; 1981 Abidjan Protocol; 1981 Lima Protocol; 1976 Barcelona Protocol; 1983 Cartagena Protocol.

[216] Abecassis and Jarashow, *Oil Pollution from Ships*, Ch 6.

posed by oil tankers and other ships carrying toxic or hazardous substances in passage near their shores. Although as we have seen, in principle, vessels exercising high-seas freedoms are subject only to the jurisdiction of the flag state, an exceptional right of coastal-state intervention in international law can be derived from the principle of necessity or, less convincingly, from the right of self-defence.[217] Following doubts raised about British intervention in the *Torrey Canyon* tanker disaster, however, the rights of coastal states were clarified by the 1969 Convention on Intervention on the High Seas in Cases of Oil Pollution Casualties.[218] This convention was extended to other forms of pollution by a 1973 protocol.

There can be little doubt today that a right of intervention beyond the territorial sea has become part of customary law. Apart from the widespread ratification and implementation of the 1969 Convention itself, Article 221 of the 1982 UNCLOS and Article 9 of the 1989 International Convention on Salvage respectively assume the right of coastal states to take measures under customary and conventional international law or under generally recognized principles of international law,[219] despite important differences in the wording of these provisions. The 1969 Convention permits parties to take:

Such measures on the high seas as may be necessary to prevent, mitigate or eliminate grave and imminent danger to their coastline or related interests from pollution or threat of pollution of the sea by oil, following upon a maritime casualty or acts related to such a casualty which may reasonably be expected to result in major harmful consequences.[220]

This article places significant limitations on the coastal state's right of intervention beyond the territorial sea. First, it applies only to cases of maritime casualties, defined as:

collision of ships, stranding or other incident of navigation, or other occurrence on board a ship or external to it resulting in material damage or imminent threat of material damage to a ship or cargo.[221]

This definition would not cover operational pollution, however serious, or dumping at sea, even if illegal. Moreover, no measures may be taken against warships or

---

[217] Brown, 21 *CLP* (1968) 113; Jagota, 16 *NYIL* (1985) 266–74; Abecassis and Jarashow, *Oil Pollution from Ships*, 116f.

[218] O'Connell, *The International Law of the Sea*, ii, 1006; Abecassis and Jarashow, *Oil Pollution from Ships*, 116, paras 6–14.

[219] Churchill and Lowe, *The Law of the Sea*, 355; de Rouw, in Couper and Gold (eds), *The Marine Environment*. A Soviet proposal to incorporate an explicit right of intervention in the 1982 UNCLOS was not accepted: see UN Doc A/CONF 62/C.3/L25, 3rd UNCLOS, 4 *Official Records* (1975) 212. The Soviet delegation interpreted the words 'pursuant to international law, both customary and conventional' in Article 221 as giving states not parties to the 1969 Convention the right to intervene 'within the limits defined by that Convention': 3rd UNCLOS, 9 *Official Records*, 162, para 52. See also Nordquist, *UNCLOS Commentary*, iv, 303ff.

[220] Article 1(1). A British proposal to apply the 1969 Intervention Convention to the territorial sea was rejected as unnecessary and undesirable by the Brussels Conference: see Abecassis and Jarashow, *Oil Pollution from Ships*, 121f. Churchill and Lowe, loc cit, argue that 'on the high seas' includes intervention in the EEZ.

[221] Article 2(1).

government ships under the convention, although in such cases a defence of necessity might nevertheless be relied upon.

Second, the references to 'grave and imminent' danger of pollution resulting in 'major harmful consequences' were intended to establish a high threshold of probability and of harm, so as to avoid the danger of precipitate action by coastal states causing undue interference with shipping beyond the territorial sea.[222] Following the *Amoco Cadiz* accident, however, some states, including France, argued strongly that the wording of 1969 Convention was too restrictive, and that intervention should be permitted at an earlier stage.[223] Although the 1969 Convention remains unchanged, the text of Article 221 of the 1982 UNCLOS was altered during negotiations to omit any reference to 'grave and imminent danger', and it now assumes a right of intervention when there is merely 'actual or threatened damage' which may 'reasonably be expected' to result in 'major harmful consequences' to the coastal state's interests.[224] Under the 1969 Convention these harmful consequences include direct effects on coastal activities such as fishing, tourist attractions, public health, and the wellbeing of the area concerned, 'including conservation of living marine resources and of wildlife'.[225] This is broad enough to justify action necessary to protect the coastal environment.

Third, the measures which coastal states are entitled to take are not specified by the 1969 Convention, but depend on what is necessary for their protection, and must be proportionate to the risk and nature of the likely damage.[226] In the *Torrey Canyon* disaster military aircraft were used to destroy the vessel and set fire to the oil; such extreme action will rarely now be regarded as necessary or useful and is unlikely in most cases to be justified given present experience in handling shipping casualties. The more appropriate response will usually involve the assistance of tugs and salvage services. The main significance of the right of intervention is thus that it allows coastal authorities to override the ship's master's discretion in seeking salvage assistance, and may enable them to direct damaged vessels away from their shores. This may not always be the right response: in some cases it would be better to allow damaged vessels to enter port or head for sheltered areas where their cargo can safely be offloaded. There is some evidence that in directing the *Prestige* away from their shores Spain and Portugal

---

[222] The non-application of the 1969 Convention to the territorial sea has left states free to set more liberal conditions for intervention there: see e.g, UK Merchant Shipping Act, 1995, 55, 137–141 which allow intervention if 'urgently needed' to deal with a shipping accident which will or may cause pollution 'on a large scale' in the UK or its waters, but with exceptions, adaptations or modifications for foreign ships outside United Kingdom waters.

[223] See Lucchini, 24 *AFDI* (1978) 721; Nordquist (ed), *UNCLOS Commentary*, iv, 313.

[224] Cf Article 222, ICNT, and see 3rd UNCLOS, 8 *Official Records*, 152; 10 ibid, 100. Note, however, the view of the Soviet delegation at UNCLOS that the proposed text of Article 221 'should not be held to give the coastal state more extensive rights of intervention in cases of maritime casualty than the rights of intervention it already enjoyed under the terms of the International Convention Relating to Intervention on the High Seas', quoted in Nordquist (ed), *UNCLOS Commentary*, iv, 313. Kwiatkowska, 22 *ODIL* (1991) 173 notes that a right of intervention based on the wording of Article 221 has been adopted by Bulgaria, Romania, Malaysia, New Zealand, and Russia.

[225] Article 2(4).   [226] Article 5.

made the eventual pollution disaster inevitable and worsened its effects. While coastal states may be within their rights to deny a safe refuge to such vessels even in distress, it needs to be recalled that Article 195 of UNCLOS specifically prohibits states from acting 'to transfer, directly or indirectly, damage or hazards from one area to another'. In such circumstances the appropriateness of any action a coastal state may take will depend on what is necessary to protect all those who may potentially be affected.[227] The 1969 Intervention Convention also seeks to limit excessive coastal-state action by requiring it to consult and notify the flag state and report measures to IMO.[228] The final right of decision remains with the coastal state, however. Damage caused by measures taken in excess of the convention must be compensated, and disputes are subject to compulsory conciliation and arbitration.[229]

(c) Notification by vessels and offshore installations

Coastal states can only intervene effectively if informed of impending disasters in a timely manner, whether by surveillance, by other states, or by the masters of vessels, including those in distress. A number of treaties, including the 1990 Convention on Oil Pollution Preparedness, Response, and Cooperation, provide for states to request or require masters of ships and aircraft to report casualties and pollution observed at sea;[230] as we saw earlier, there is also provision for states themselves to report known pollution hazards to other states. The 1990 Convention also applies to offshore installations.

A serious weakness of the 1969 Intervention Convention was its failure to deal with the crucial issue of notification by the master of the vessel involved in the maritime emergency. Subsequent treaties have not been wholly successful in remedying this omission. The MARPOL Convention requires masters of vessels involved in pollution incidents to report without delay, but does not say to whom.[231] The 1982 UNCLOS merely provides that international rules and standards should include those relating to prompt notification to coastal states, but seems to assume that no such rules yet exist.[232] A more satisfactory formulation is found in Article 4 of the Oil Pollution Response Convention, under which the flag state is responsible for requiring masters to report without delay to 'the nearest coastal state' any event on their ship involving the discharge or probable discharge of oil. The HNS Protocol applies the same rule to the wide variety of other toxic substances now likely to be involved in maritime accidents and emergencies.

---

[227] Frank, 20 *IJMCL* (2005) 1, 53–62. In 2003 IMO adopted Guidelines on Place of Refuge for Ships in Need of Assistance, IMO Res A 949(23).

[228] Article 3.   [229] Articles 6, 8.

[230] See also 1983 Bonn Agreement. Protocols in UNEP Regional Conventions invariably take the stronger form. See e.g. Barcelona Protocol, Article 8.

[231] Article 8 and Protocol 1. See also IMO Res A 851(20). The provisions of UNEP Regional Seas Protocols will also apply. In some cases these assume that reports will go to the flag state and be communicated from there: see e.g. Barcelona Protocol, Article 8.

[232] Article 211(7). Protocol 1 of the MARPOL Convention could constitute such 'international rules and standards'.

An alternative and possibly more effective approach would concentrate on the power of coastal states to regulate the provision of information by ships concerning pollution incidents in their EEZ or territorial sea. Coastal state interests are sufficiently strongly involved to justify such action to reinforce flag state control. Article 211(5) of the 1982 UNCLOS may provide the legal basis for coastal state regulation based on Protocol 1 of the MARPOL Convention, although none of the regional agreements appears to adopt this approach. Mandatory reporting by vessels may also be required under the 1974 SOLAS Convention.[233]

(d) Salvage

The basis on which most maritime salvage services have traditionally operated is the 'no cure no pay' principle. This provides salvors with no reward for work carried out benefiting the coastal state and reducing the liability of the vessel owner for pollution damage if the vessel itself is lost. Coastal-state intervention may exacerbate this problem if it renders salvage of the vessel more difficult. The 1969 Intervention Convention allows coastal states to override the master's discretion in calling for salvage assistance and empowers them, as we have seen, to take necessary measures to protect the coastal environment, but it provides no incentive for salvors themselves to assist in this task. Following measures already taken by Lloyds to revise salvage contracts, a new convention dealing, inter alia, with the environmental aspects of salvage was adopted by IMO in 1989.[234]

The 1989 International Convention on Salvage is mainly concerned with private-law matters, and the rights of coastal states to intervene remain unaffected, although Article 11 requires them to take account of the need to ensure the efficient and successful performance of salvage operations, and thus may affect decisions on matters such as access to ports. The convention applies to judicial or arbitral proceedings brought in a state party and which relate to salvage operations, but it also covers salvage operations conducted by or under the control of public authorities.[235] It does not cover warships or government non-commercial ships entitled to immunity, nor does it apply to offshore installations.[236]

There are two main features of the convention. Salvors are entitled to 'special compensation' for salvage operations, in respect of a vessel or its cargo, which have prevented or minimized damage to the environment, and they have a duty of care to carry out salvage operations in such a way as to prevent or minimize this damage.[237] Thus the convention does not apply to environmental protection unrelated to the salvage of a vessel or its cargo, but it has the important effects that protection of the environment

---

[233] Regulation V/8, adopted 1994, in force 1996.

[234] Redgwell, 14 *Marine Policy* (1990) 142; Gold, 20 *JMLC* (1989) 487; Kerr, ibid, 505.

[235] Articles 2, 5.   [236] Articles 3, 4.

[237] Articles 8, 14. 'Damage to the environment is defined in Article 1(d) to mean substantial physical damage to human health or to marine life or resources in coastal or inland waters or areas adjacent thereto caused by pollution, contamination, fire, explosion or similar major incidents.'

is regarded as a 'useful result' even if the vessel itself is lost, and also that expenses are recoverable in excess of the limit for salvage of the vessel or cargo alone.[238]

Salvors thus have a continued incentive and obligation to mitigate environmental damage even after the vessel is saved, or after it sinks. The salvor is correspondingly penalized by loss or reduction of his reward if through negligence or misconduct damage to the environment is not averted or minimized.[239] However, consistently with the traditional 'no cure no pay' principle the salvor will remain uncompensated for efforts, however great, which lead to no useful result, whether because the vessel is lost, or because damage to the environment cannot be reduced or averted. This convention came into force in 1986.

6 RESPONSIBILITY AND LIABILITY FOR MARINE POLLUTION DAMAGE

6(1) STATE RESPONSIBILITY

Article 235(1) of the 1982 UNCLOS affirms the orthodox proposition that 'states are responsible for the fulfilment of their international obligations concerning the protection and preservation of the marine environment' and goes on to add that 'They shall be liable in accordance with international law'. There is no reason to doubt that this responsibility extends to flag states in respect of their vessels, and to coastal states in respect of activities which they permit within their jurisdiction or control.[240] A number of authors have argued that in respect to ultra-hazardous activities at sea, such as the operation of large oil tankers, the liability of the flag state is strict, and the same view may be taken regarding offshore oil installations because of the serious risks these pose for other states.[241] As we saw in Chapter 4 the evidence in support of a standard of strict liability for states is not strong. Moreover it has not been applied by the 1982 UNCLOS to state responsibility for deep seabed operations. Instead, Article 139 of the convention provides only that in respect of damage resulting from deep seabed operations, states are liable only for a failure to carry out their responsibilities, and shall not be liable for damage caused by national operators 'if the state partly has taken all necessary and appropriate measures to secure effective compliance' with the requirements of the Convention. This clearly points to a due diligence standard of liability for states, although operators themselves would be subject to a

---

[238] Cf. Article 13 which limits the reward for salvage of the vessel or property to the salved value thereof.
[239] Articles 14(5) 18.
[240] Smith, *State Responsibility and the Marine Environment* (Oxford, 1988) Chs 10–12 and *supra*, Ch 4.
[241] See e.g, Smith, ibid, 114–18, 160–3, 210–13; and Handl, 74 *AJIL* (1980) 547, where the state practice and literature are reviewed.

strict liability standard in draft regulations proposed by the preparatory commission for the ISBA.[242]

A second reason for doubting academic views on the responsibility of states for damage to the marine environment is that there is almost no state practice from which to draw conclusions. In a few cases, flag states have paid compensation for pollution from oil tankers, and some writers treat this as supporting a principle of strict or absolute liability comparable to the position asserted by Canada in the Cosmos 954 claim.[243] These are exceptional examples, however; in general, pollution from ships has not been the subject of interstate claims, even in cases as serious as the *Amoco Cadiz* or the *Prestige*, but has instead been dealt with under national law or civil liability and compensation schemes considered below. The same is true of most oil spills from offshore installations. In one of the most serious of these, the IXTOC I blowout, Mexico refused to accept any responsibility for injury caused in the United States, and the matter was ultimately resolved in civil claims.[244] This is consistent with the approach adopted in UNEP's 'Study of Legal Aspects' of offshore mineral exploration and drilling,[245] and with bilateral and regional arrangements elsewhere,[246] all of which assume or require that operators will be made liable in civil law. Although in 1986 the parties to the London Dumping Convention called for the development of 'procedures for the assessment of liability in accordance with the principles of international law regarding state responsibility for damage to the environment of other states or to any other area of the environment resulting from dumping',[247] no progress has been made, and the question of state responsibility for dumping remains unresolved, under this convention and under all of the regional agreements.

Thus, although at a theoretical level, it is quite correct to conclude that 'the international legal order currently possesses a perfectly adequate foundation for an equitable and effective regime of state responsibility for marine environmental injury',[248] the failure of states to resort to this foundation is its most conspicuous feature. Alternative approaches based instead on the liability of the polluter have proved more appealing in practice, and for all of the reasons already observed in Chapter 5, these are probably also preferable in principle.

---

[242] Prepcom Doc LOS/PCN/SCN 3/WP 6/Add 5, Article 122.   [243] *Supra*, Ch 4, section 2.

[244] IXTOC 1 Agreement, 22 *ILM* (1983) 580; Smith, *State Responsibility and the Marine Environment*, 117.

[245] UNEP/GC 9/5/Add 5/App III (1981).

[246] 1977 International Convention on Civil Liability for Oil Pollution Damage from the Exploration for or Exploitation of Submarine Mineral Resources (No ratifications); 1983 Canada-Denmark Agreement for Cooperation Relating to the Marine Environment, Article 8, 23 *ILM* (1983) 269; 1974 Offshore Pollution Liability Agreement, 13 *ILM* (1974) 1409 (since updated); 1994 Madrid Protocol for the Protection of the Mediterranean Sea against Pollution from the Continental Shelf, Article 27. See also 1990 Kuwait Protocol on Pollution from land-based sources, Article 13, and generally Caron, 10 *ELQ* (1983) 641; de Mestral, 20 *Harv ILJ* (1979) 469.

[247] Resolution LDC 21(9) 1986; Kasoulides, 26 *San Diego LR* (1989) 497. See also 1996 Protocol, Article 15.

[248] Smith, *State Responsibility and the Marine Environment*, 255.

6(2) CIVIL LIABILITY FOR MARINE POLLUTION DAMAGE

(a) OECD and the polluter-pays principle

OECD's polluter-pays principle was examined in Chapter 5. As we saw there, the principle is primarily intended to ensure that the costs of dealing with pollution are not borne by public authorities but are directed to the polluter. OECD has recommended that this principle should be taken into account in calculating the costs of measures taken to prevent and control oil spills at sea, and that liability for the costs of 'reasonable remedial action' should be assigned to the polluter.[249] The effect of this policy is that liability would not be limited to compensation for direct injury, but would include some part of the capital outlay and running costs of maintaining a response capability and of restoring the environment to an acceptable state. These costs can be recovered in a variety of ways: through fines, charges, or civil actions for damages.[250] The preamble to the 1990 Oil Pollution Response Convention describes the polluter-pays principle as a 'general principle of international environmental law', and a number of regional seas treaties adopted or revised since the Rio Conference call on states to apply it more generally to the costs of marine pollution and environmental damage caused by ships, land-based activities and dumping.[251]

Despite this general endorsement of the polluter-pays principle, there is little evidence that it has influenced state practice or resulted in more comprehensive schemes of liability for damage to the marine environment at global or regional level. Parties to the revised London Dumping Convention continue to 'undertake to develop procedures regarding liability' for marine pollution damage, as do the parties to several regional seas agreements, but no progress has been made in this regard over many years.[252] The only significant extension of maritime liability which might be linked to the polluter pays principle is the 1992 revision of the Oil Pollution Liability and Fund Conventions and the adoption in 1996 of a new Convention on Liability and Compensation for the Carriage of Hazardous and Noxious Substances by Sea.[253]

These treaties illustrate two of the limitations of the polluter-pays concept. First, the question who is the polluter is not self-evident in a complex industry such as shipping. In one sense the operator of an oil or chemical tanker is the polluter and should be

---

[249] Recommendation C(81) 32 (Final).

[250] OECD, *Combating Oil Spills* (Paris, 1982) 24, gives examples of national legislation. See also OECD, *Economic Instruments for Environmental Protection* (Paris, 1989).

[251] 1992 Paris Convention, Article 2(2)(b); 1992 Helsinki Convention, Article 3(4); 1995 Barcelona Convention, Article 4(3)(b).

[252] This provision follows 1982 UNCLOS, Article 235(3). See 1996 Protocol on the Prevention of Marine Pollution by Dumping, Article 15; 1995 Barcelona Convention, Article 16; 1986 Noumea Convention, Article 20; 1983 Caribbean Convention, Article 14; 1982 Jeddah Convention, Article 13; 1981 Abidjan Convention, Article 15; 1978 Kuwait Convention, Article 13. Cf 1981 Lima Convention, Article 11, which instead reiterates UNCLOS Article 235(2). Attempts to conclude a liability protocol to the Barcelona Convention foundered in 1997: see UNEP (OCA)/MED WG 117/3 (1997). See generally Lefeber, in Vidas and Østreng (eds), *Order for the Oceans*, 507.

[253] See next section.

responsible if the ship sinks. But it can equally be said that the cargo causes the damage and the cargo owner is the real polluter. Alternatively, it might be argued that the ship-owner is most directly responsible for seaworthiness, and has the strongest interest in insuring his vessel, and should therefore be treated as the polluter. Then again, ships sink and cause pollution for various reasons. Sometimes a third party such a harbour pilot or a navigation authority is at fault. Who among all these possibilities should be made liable for the damage is a policy choice, not one capable of being answered by the polluter-pays concept. Sensibly, the present internationally agreed scheme of liability and compensation for pollution from ships treats both the ship's owner and the cargo owner as sharing responsibility, while excluding the liability of any other potential defendant in order to facilitate easy recovery by plaintiffs.

A second problem is that it is not necessarily realistic to expect the 'polluter' to pay in full for all the damage caused. This is especially so in the shipping industry, where insurance is the main source of a shipowner's liability funding. All of the maritime liability treaties limit this liability, as well as the compensation from industry funds, and also exclude certain kinds of loss. This has significant implications when it comes to making the polluter pay for environmental damage. When compensation is limited, there may not be enough to meet all claims for death, injury, property loss, economic loss, and environmental harm. Some of these losses may have to be prioritized, or paid pro rata, or excluded altogether. Again, this is a policy choice; as implemented in the present series of maritime liability and compensation treaties the main conclusion is that not all environmental loss is covered.

The most notable exclusion is environmental damage on the high seas beyond the exclusive economic zone. The point is exemplified by Article 3 of the 1992 Oil Pollution Fund Convention, which is expressly confined to pollution damage in the territory, territorial sea, EEZ, or within 200 miles of the state concerned, and to 'preventive measures, wherever taken, to prevent or minimize *such* damage'.[254] The 1989 Salvage Convention is similarly limited; although it provides 'special compensation' for salvage which prevents or minimizes 'damage to the environment', this phrase is defined to mean 'substantial physical damage to human health or to marine life or resources in coastal or inland waters or areas adjacent thereto'.[255] This does not include salvage on the high seas if no state is likely to benefit from the actions taken.

There is no inherent reason why liability and compensation schemes of this kind could not apply to damage to common spaces and resources. The point, however, is whether it makes sense to deal with the problem in this way. There is a strong case for doing so in regard to clean-up costs, if only because this may prevent damage affect-ing other states or the marine environment. There may also be a case for measures to restore the marine environment to its natural state. But suppose the spill cannot be cleaned up, and no harm to other states ensues, and restoration will take place naturally or is not possible? The role, if any, of damages in this context cannot be

---

[254] Emphasis added. See also 1992 Convention on Civil Liability for Oil Pollution Damage, Article 2.
[255] Articles 1(d), 8, 14.

compensatory, since there is no measurable loss to anyone, nor can it be restorative.[256] Rather, it becomes punitive. Punishment in these circumstances is better left to criminal prosecution for violation of MARPOL or SOLAS regulations, if any.[257]

(b) Civil liability for oil pollution from ships

The problems of jurisdiction, choice of law, standard of liability, and enforcement of judgments which typically affect transboundary claims for pollution damage[258] are amplified in the case of ships and can result in protracted and unsatisfactory litigation when maritime accidents cause serious pollution. The *Torrey Canyon* disaster of 1967 showed the need for international agreement on a regime of civil liability for such accidents and prompted IMO to call an international conference in 1969.[259] Resolving the difficulties confronting coastal states in securing adequate compensation was not simply a matter of removing jurisdictional obstacles, harmonizing liability, and ensuring the polluter would pay, however. Rather more important was the question how the loss should be distributed, given the long-standing tradition of permitting shipowners to limit their liability in maritime claims and the argument that in the case of oil, the cargo owners might reasonably be expected to share in the burden.

The 1969 Convention on Civil Liability for Oil Pollution Damage, in conjunction with the 1971 Convention on the Establishment of an International Fund for Compensation for Oil Pollution Damage, represent one approach to the establishment of a more satisfactory regime for oil pollution liability.[260] This scheme was partially based on the earlier nuclear liability conventions, which are considered in detail in Chapter 9 and to which reference should be made. The oil pollution conventions enable claims for 'pollution damage' to be brought in the courts of the state party where the damage occurs, regardless of where the ship[261] causing the damage is registered. Like port-state enforcement of the MARPOL Convention, the vessel does not have to be from a state party to the Liability Convention: the coastal state has jurisdiction because that is where the damage occurs. The 1969 and 1971 Conventions were amended by Protocols adopted in 1992, the principal effects of which are to raise liability and compensation limits, to include pollution damage in the EEZ as well as in the territory and territorial sea of a party to the Conventions, and to include the cost of

---

[256] See UNCC practice, *supra*, Ch 4, section 2(4).

[257] See Boyle, in Wetterstein (ed), *Harm to the Environment* (Oxford, 1997) 95ff, but cf Leigh, 14 *Australian YIL* (1993) 143–5.

[258] *Supra*, Ch 5, section 3.

[259] IMCO, *Official Records of the International Legal Conference on Marine Pollution Damage* (London, 1969) and see Keaton, 21 *CLP* (1968) 94; Brown, ibid, 113.

[260] See Abecassis and Jarashow, *Oil Pollution from Ships*, Chs 10, 11; de La Rue (ed), *Liability for Damage to the Marine Environment* (London, 1993); Gauci, *Oil Pollution at Sea: Civil Liability and Compensation for Damage* (Chichester, 1997); de La Rue and Anderson, *Shipping and the Environment* (London, 1998); Tan, *Vessel-Source Marine Pollution*, 286–342.

[261] 'Ship' means 'any seagoing vessel…constructed or adapted for the carriage of oil in bulk as cargo': 1992 Oil Pollution Convention, Article 1(1). Interpretation of Article 1(1) in IOPC Fund *Annual Report* (1999) para 9. Oil spills from non-tankers are thus excluded.

preventive measures for the first time.[262] In this section attention will focus primarily on the differences between the oil pollution and nuclear liability regimes.

The most important difference concerns the allocation of liability and the distribution of compensation costs. The 1992 Oil Pollution Liability Convention channels liability not to the ship's operator, nor to the cargo owner, but to the shipowner, who may be sued only in accordance with the Convention, and who is required to carry insurance for this purpose. Under Article 3 no claim for compensation may be made against the ship's manager, operator, charterer, crew, pilot, salvor, or their servants or agents, unless the damage resulted from their personal act or omission 'committed with intent to cause such damage, or recklessly and with knowledge that such damage would probably result'.[263] While this provision will preclude strict liability or negligence claims for pollution damage against any of these third parties, they may remain liable to recompense the owner in accordance with national law. The owner's liability under Article 3 is strict, rather than absolute, in the sense that although no fault or negligence need be shown, no liability arises where the owner can prove that the loss resulted from war, hostilities, insurrection, civil war, or natural phenomena, such as hurricanes, of an 'exceptional, inevitable and irresistible character', or was wholly caused intentionally by a third party or by the negligence of those responsible for navigation aids.[264]

The owner is entitled to limit liability[265] according to a formula related to the tonnage of the ship, and to an overall total, currently 14 million Special Drawing Rights (SDRs) under the 1969 Convention (c US$22 million). This limit allowed significantly greater sums to be recovered for oil pollution damage than for other forms of damage covered by maritime liability conventions in 1969, but by 1990 it was clearly insufficient. Even when additional compensation payable under the 1971 Fund Convention was added, the maximum available under the old scheme could no longer ensure full compensation for the largest accidents, particularly once environmental damage is included. The 1971 limit was far exceeded by claims arising out of the *Nakhodka* spill, when a total of US$220 million was paid out by the old fund and the 1992 Fund. One purpose of the 1992 Protocols and the amendments adopted in 2000 was therefore to raise these limits substantially. The owner's liability for damage rises to a maximum

---

[262] Liability limits have been raised again under additional protocols adopted in 2000. References are to articles in the 1969 and 1971 Conventions *as amended in 1992 and 2000* unless otherwise stated. The 1971 Fund Convention ceased to have effect in 2002. The 1969 and 1992 Liability Conventions will coexist until all parties denounce the earlier text.

[263] Compare the 1969 text of the Liability Convention, which did not bar claims against the operator of the *Amoco Cadiz* in US courts, rather than suing the owner in France under the CLC Convention. See Abecassis and Jarashow, *Oil Pollution from Ships*, 555, and Eskenazi, 24 *JMLC* (1993) 371. Under the 1992 version of Article 3, proceedings against a ship operator would no longer be possible, nor would claims against the ship's pilot found responsible for the *Sea Empress* disaster.

[264] Article 3(2). See also Article 3(3).

[265] Article 5. The 1969 Convention removes this right in case of 'actual fault' by the owner; the 1992 text does so only where the damage is caused intentionally or recklessly. On limitation of liability in maritime law see Popp, 24 *JMLC* (1993) 335.

of 89.7 million SDRs (c US$139 million) for the very largest tankers;[266] thereafter, the International Oil Pollution Compensation Fund (IOPC Fund) is liable to compensate for any damage in excess of the owner's liability,[267] up to a total of 203 million SDRs (c US$315 million, including whatever is obtained from the owner). The creation of a supplementary fund in 2003 will take the limit to 750 million SDRs or about US$1165 million.

Unlike the nuclear conventions, contributions to the IOPC Fund come not from states, but from the a levy on oil importers, mainly the oil companies whose cargoes the vessels are likely to be carrying.[268] The combined effect of the Oil Pollution Liability and Fund Conventions is thus that, in the more serious cases, the owners of the ship and the owners of the cargo are jointly treated as 'the polluter' and share equitably the cost of accidental pollution damage arising during transport. As with nuclear accidents, the capacity of the insurance market has been a factor in determining the limit of the owner's liability,[269] although unlimited liability in the United States has not prevented shipowners from securing insurance cover. In addition to raising the limit of this liability under the CLC, another important change made by the 1992 Protocols is to abolish the shipowner's right to have recourse to the Fund in order to relieve a portion of their liability. Under Article 5 of the 1971 Fund Convention this was permitted even where the total damage did not exceed the limit set by the 1969 Liability Convention. Shipowners will now have to bear the costs of any oil spill up to the full limit of their liability, and only for additional losses thereafter will the Fund's resources be called on. One calculation indicates that under the 1992 Protocols the shipowner's average share of the amount payable for pollution damage will rise from 47 to 68 per cent.[270] This should give insurers a stronger incentive to monitor the quality of the ships they insure.

But the Fund Convention also has an additional, wider, purpose of providing compensation even where no liability for damage arises under the Liability Convention, or where the shipowner's liability is not met by the compulsory insurance he is required to carry, leaving him financially incapable of meeting his obligations.[271] In these respects the Fund provides a form of security for claimants which governments provide under the nuclear liability conventions. However, the IOPC Fund is exonerated from liability where the pollution damage results from an act of war, hostilities, civil war or insurrection, or where the oil is discharged from a warship or government-owned ship entitled to immunity, or where the claimant cannot prove that the damage resulted from

---

[266] I.e. more than 140,000 tons: Liability Convention, Article 5(1). Smaller ships are liable on a graduated scale: a 50,000-ton tanker would be liable to a maximum of about US$42 million. The *Amoco Cadiz* was 230,000 dwt.

[267] Fund Convention, Article 4(1)(c). These figures apply to incidents after 1 November 2003. The Fund's early practice is reviewed by Brown, in Butler (ed), *International Shipping*, 275; for details of more recent awards and claims see *Annual Report of the IOPC Funds* (London, 2006).

[268] But under Article 14 governments may assume this responsibility.

[269] Abecassis and Jarashow, *Oil Pollution from Ships*, 215.   [270] Ibid, 241.

[271] Article 4(1)(a)–(b).

'an incident involving one or more ships'.[272] The importance of the last provision is that where the source of the oil is unidentified, no compensation is obtainable. Thus there remain certain situations in which the innocent victim will be without any effective recourse. It should also be observed that parties to the Liability Convention are not obliged to become parties to the Fund Convention, but virtually all have done so.

(c) Environmental damage

The 1969 Liability Convention covers 'pollution damage', defined by Article 2 as 'loss or damage caused outside the ship' and occurring on the territorial sea or territory of a contracting party, and it expressly includes the costs of preventive measures taken to minimize damage. It does not refer explicitly to environmental damage, however. The IOPC Fund has interpreted the phrase 'pollution damage' in the 1969 Convention to cover costs incurred in clean-up operations at sea and on the beach, preventive measures, additional costs, and a proportion of the fixed costs incurred by public authorities in maintaining a pollution response capability, as well as economic loss suffered by persons who depend directly on earnings from coastal or sea related activities, including fishermen and hoteliers, and damage to property.[273] But as Abecassis observes, 'The [1969] Convention's definition of pollution is so vague it is not really a definition at all'.[274] This has left interpretation in practice to national legal systems, which as in the cases of the *Antonio Gramsci*,[275] or the *Patmos*,[276] might allow claims for the notional costs of damage to the marine environment. A similar claim was initially allowed by a US court in the case of the *Zoe Colocotroni*,[277] where a value was put on the estimated loss of marine organisms and the cost of replanting a mangrove swamp, although this case was not governed by the 1969 Convention. Compensation was, however, reduced on appeal to 'reasonable' measures of restoration. A more precise definition was needed both to give uniformity to these interpretations, to ensure that some recovery of environmental costs would be available in the courts of all parties to the convention, but also to ensure that excessive environmental claims did not reduce the sums available to pay other claims.

Article 1(6) of the 1992 Liability Convention is thus an improvement on the 1969 Convention in making clear that compensation for impairment of the environment is recoverable, but the relatively narrow terms in which it does so should be noted.[278] Compensation is limited to 'the costs of reasonable measures of reinstatement actually undertaken or to be undertaken'. This would not be broad enough to cover the

---

[272] Article 4(2).

[273] See IOPC Fund, *Annual report* (1988) 58, and cf 1969 Liability Convention, Articles 1(6), 2.

[274] *Oil Pollution from Ships*, 209.

[275] Ibid, 209; Brown, in Butler, *International Shipping*, 282ff.

[276] See Bianchi, in Wetterstein (eds), *Harm to the Environment*, 113ff.

[277] *Commonwealth of Puerto Rico v SS Zoe Colocotroni*, 456 F Suppl 1327 (1978); 628 F 2d 652 (1980); see Abecassis and Jarashow *Oil Pollution from Ships*, 551; de la Rue and Anderson, *Shipping and the Environment*, 522ff.

[278] de La Fayette, 20 *IJMCL* (2005) 167; Abecassis and Jarashow, *Oil Pollution from Ships*, 237, 277; Jacobson and Trotz, 17 *JMLC* (1986) 467; Wetterstein, *LMCLQ* (1994) 230.

loss of marine organisms included in the *Zoe Colocotroni Case*, or the notional formula for water pollution damage used by the Soviet court in the *Antonio Gramsci
Case*, and accords with the view of the IOPC Fund Assembly that pollution damage
assessment 'is not to be made on the basis of an abstract quantification of damage
calculated in accordance with theoretical models'.[279] The new definition also allows
recovery for loss of profit arising out of impairment of the environment, for example
in the case of losses suffered by fishermen or hotel owners, but, as we have seen, such
claims had already been allowed by the IOPC Fund. It also includes pollution damage
in the coastal state's EEZ, or in an area up to 200 miles from its territorial sea baselines.
The Protocols' environmental perspective is clearly preferable to the very limited definition of damage found in the 1969 and 1971 Conventions, but it still stops short of
using liability to penalize those whose harm to the environment cannot be reinstated
or quantified in terms of property loss or loss of profits, or which the government concerned does not wish to reinstate, or which occurs on the high seas.[280] To this extent
the true environmental costs of oil transportation by sea continue to be borne by the
community as a whole, and not by the polluter.

(d) An assessment of the Oil Pollution Liability and Compensation Scheme

The Liability and Fund Conventions have generally worked well in the large majority
of over one hundred incidents resulting in claims to the IOPC Fund. Almost all of
these claims have been met promptly and in full without resort to litigation. Claims
allowed have included clean-up costs, preventive measures, and lost income for fishermen, fish processors, and the tourist industry. Some have also involved environmental
restoration costs, such as mangrove swamps. Over one hundred states have become
parties to the 1992 Protocols, representing some 92–95 per cent of relevant tonnage.
Some significant oil-importing states have declined to do so, however, including the
United States, mainly because the liability limits were still thought by Congress to be
too low. Prompted by the *Exxon Valdez* disaster in Alaska, the US Oil Pollution Act
of 1990 introduced limits on liability under US law greatly in excess even of the 1992
Protocols, and allowed unlimited liability in a wider range of situations, including
gross negligence, wilful misconduct, and violation of applicable Federal regulations.[281]
This must be seen against total clean-up costs for the *Exxon Valdez* incident estimated
at US$2,500 million, but it has the effect of precluding US ratification of the Fund and
Liability Conventions. The 1992 protocols would not guarantee full compensation for
such damage. Moreover even the smaller claims made in respect of the loss of the

---

[279] IOPC Fund Resolution No 3 on Pollution Damage (October, 1980). See also the claims made in respect
of the *Antonio Gramsci* (No 2) and the *Patmos*, reported in IOPC Fund, *Annual Report* (1990) 23, 27, and
the *Haven*, id, *Annual Report* (1999) para 10.2. In all three cases the Fund rejected claims for unquanti-
fied environmental damage. See Maffei, in Francioni and Scovazzi (eds), *International Responsibility for
Environmental Harm*, 381.

[280] Boyle, in Wetterstein (ed), *Harm to the Environment*, 83.

[281] The Act also leaves individual US states free to adopt their own higher liability standards. See Ruhl
and Jewell, 8 *OGTLR* (1990) 234; *eid*, 9 *OGTLR* (1990) 304; George and de La Rue, 11 *OGTLR* (1990) 363;
Noyes, 7 *IJECL* (1992) 43.

Erika and the *Prestige* exceeded the maximum then available from the 1992 Fund.[282] When this happens, payment of individual claims is not only reduced but delayed until contested claims are resolved, either by negotiation or in court, and governments may have to forego some of their clean-up and environmental-restoration claims.[283] The implications of this for the inclusion of environmental damage in a scheme intended principally to compensate individuals for property and economic loss are obvious, and have prompted the question: 'What is the use of comprehensive liability if it can be subject to considerable limitations?'[284] We can see immediately why the liability and compensation limits were further raised in 2000, and a Supplementary Fund established. It seems likely that this will sustain the Fund's capacity to meet the cost of future large-scale pollution disasters, and the ability to respond in this way is some indication of the importance attached to the scheme by the industries which benefit from it.

Like the nuclear liability and compensation conventions, the oil pollution scheme is a precedent for other forms of hazardous activity and an alternative to reliance on state responsibility for environmental damage.[285] As with other such schemes, limitation of liability and equitable sharing of the costs remain controversial, but it is of course precisely those features which make the Oil Pollution Liability and Fund Conventions broadly acceptable to the shipping industry and which ensure that the oil industry cannot offload all of the incidental cost of moving its products by sea. Nevertheless, when substandard vessels—such as the *Erika* and the *Prestige*—can cause such enormous losses, it is worth asking whether limits on the shipowner's liability can still be justified, and whether the cargo receivers should not also be required to contribute rather more for the privilege of transporting oil in defective ships. Proposals of this kind were considered at IMO but rejected after opposition from some flag states.[286] Another option pursued by Spain following the *Prestige* disaster was to sue the classification society for negligently failing to detect corrosion and other structural defects. In this instance the claim was dismissed on the ground that the Liability Convention bars such actions.[287] Finally, accidents involving defective ships may result in criminal prosecution of those involved. In the case of the *Erika*, France successfully prosecuted the owner, the management company, the classification society and the cargo owner. The court imposed fines on all the defendants totalling 900 million euros, and awarded damages of 192 million euros.[288] When payouts from the IOPC Fund are added, the *Prestige* accident becomes the second most expensive environmental disaster in maritime history after *Exxon Valdez*. Given the persistence of substandard

---

[282] IOPC Funds, *Annual Report* (2004) 45.

[283] See IOPC Funds, *Annual Report* (2004) for details of incidents involving the *Haven*, the *Braer*, the *Nakhodkha*, the *Aegean Sea*, the *Prestige*, and the *Erika*.

[284] Wetterstein, *LMCLQ* (1994) 230, 243. On the question how far general economic loss should be compensated see ibid, 14 *Ann Droit Mar & Oceanique* (1996) 37.

[285] *Supra*, Ch 4, section 2.   [286] See IOPC Funds *Annual Report* (2004) 34–5.

[287] See Article III(4)(b) and *Kingdom of Spain v American Bureau of Shipping*, US Dist Ct, SD New York (2008).

[288] Paris Tribunal de Grande Instance, judgment of 16 January 2008.

ships, extending the renewed focus on criminal sanctions in European law may be an inevitable response to the limitations of civil liability and the IOPC Fund.[289]

(e) Liability for other forms of pollution from ships[290]

The Liability and Fund Conventions cover only oil from oil tankers or ships carrying oil as cargo. They do not constitute a universal regime for all types of cargo, or for all types of ship. A 1971 Convention extends the liability of an operator of a nuclear instal-lation to the maritime carriage of nuclear material; in most situations a shipowner will not be liable.[291] A more significant development is the adoption by IMO in 1996 of a Convention on Liability and Compensation for the Carriage of Hazardous and Noxious Substances by Sea.[292] If it ever comes into force the key risks in international maritime transport will all have been covered. The legal regime created by this treaty is similar to the 1992 version of the Oil Pollution Liability and Fund Conventions in almost all respects. The strict liability of the shipowner is channelled and limited in the same way, and contributions to the HNS Fund come from the receivers of HNS cargoes, or from governments on their behalf. The HNS Convention applies to a range of noxious, dangerous, or hazardous liquids, gases, substances and bulk chemicals as defined in Annex II of the MARPOL Convention and in other international codes. It does not apply to oil pollution damage as defined in the Oil Pollution Liability Convention, but oils listed in Annex I of MARPOL are nevertheless included. Neither treaty covers bunker fuel.[293] A protocol to the 1989 Basel Convention provides a separ-ate and slightly different regime of liability and compensation for the transboundary movement of hazardous waste.[294] However, few states have shown any desire to ratify these liability agreements and to date they remain mere precedents.

Like the Oil Pollution Convention, the HNS Convention covers reinstatement of environmental damage occurring in the territory, territorial waters or exclusive eco-nomic zone of any party. An Australian proposal to include high seas environmental damage was not accepted, but the agreed text of Article 3 does apply to damage (includ-ing preventive measures) anywhere at sea, provided it is not 'damage by contamination of the environment'.[295] This text should enable fishermen to claim for economic losses if high-seas fish stocks are poisoned,[296] and it would also cover precautionary high-seas clean up intended to protect potentially affected states, but it would seem to rule out environmental reinstatement of the high seas, insofar as that might be possible, or any claim to notional damages for pure environmental loss, wherever suffered. Oil is

---

[289] Directive 2005/35/EC applies only to reckless discharges or intentional damage. At present it does not apply to accidents. See *Intertanko Case* (2007) ECJ C-308/06.

[290] See generally de La Fayette, 20 *IJMCL* (2005) 167.   [291] *Supra*, Ch 9, section 5.

[292] See Wetterstein, *LMCLQ* (1994) 230; de la Rue and Anderson, *Shipping and the Environment*, Ch 7. An attempt to adopt a convention at IMO in 1984 was not successful. See Resolution 1, IMO LEG/CONF 6/64/ Add 1, and Draft Convention, IMO LEG/CONF 6/3.

[293] A convention on liability for bunker oil was adopted in 2001, but it is not in force.

[294] See *infra*, Ch 8.   [295] Article 3(c).

[296] This was also an Australian proposal: see IMO LEG 65/3/4 (1991).

much less likely to harm high-seas fish stocks, so the exclusion of high-seas damage from the 1992 Oil Pollution Convention is probably of little practical significance.

7 CONCLUSIONS

This chapter has demonstrated the extent to which an international legal regime for the control of marine pollution from ships has developed since 1972, and the degree to which it has proved effective. Although in certain respects there remain significant problems in enforcing international pollution regulations at sea, and in controlling the risks of serious accidents, there is evidence that relevant international and regional conventions, most notably the 1973/8 MARPOL Convention, have led to improved protection of the marine environment. There is also some reason to conclude that international regulation of serious environmental risks has proved more successful with regard to ships than for other comparably hazardous undertakings. The regulatory system based on MARPOL and on other conventions such as the 1974 SOLAS has worked reasonably well under the supervision of IMO, which has shown the flexibility and responsiveness necessary to keep pace with new developments, and has successfully provided a forum in which competing interests can be balanced. Moreover, the system of enforcement employed against delinquent vessels has overcome some of the earlier problems of exclusive reliance on flag state control, although it is clear that further improvements remain necessary.

The 1982 UNCLOS has in many respects codified the existing rules of customary and conventional law and has proved largely uncontroversial in its approach to protection and preservation of the marine environment. An acceptable balance of interests between maritime states and coastal states appears to have been achieved. It has largely put an end to unilateral claims and 'creeping jurisdiction' over the high seas.[297] But it is more doubtful whether the Convention's carefully structured extension of coastal and port-state jurisdiction has, in reality, had much impact on the control and reduction of pollution from ships, although the EEZ regime does have significant implications for dumping at sea and the conservation of living resources. The Convention has also been less satisfactory in dealing with other sources of marine pollution, in particular land-based sources, as the following chapter makes clear. Perhaps the most positive element of part XII of the Convention is its elevation of international conventions such as MARPOL to the status of international standards within a global regime potentially applicable to all states. The Convention's impact in this respect will largely have been achieved irrespective of its entry into force, or of the continued non-participation of the United States.

Widespread ratification and entry into force of the 1982 UNCLOS is important, however. Its more novel provisions on matters such as port-state jurisdiction over

---

[297] Churchill, 48 *GYIL* (2005) 81; Franckx, 48 *GYIL* (2005) 117.

high-seas pollution offences and international management and regulation of deep seabed mining have come into effect. Most importantly, the dispute settlement machinery has operated to restrain unilateral or regional claims to jurisdiction over shipping or natural resources and to protect the 'package deal' on which the Convention is based.[298] It is true that UNCED has shown the Convention's articles on straddling and highly migratory fish stocks, on land-based sources of marine pollution, and on protection of the marine ecosystem and biodiversity to be insufficient. Yet it is also clear that the Convention has not prevented the law of the sea from continuing to evolve in a way that is responsive to these environmental concerns.[299] From that perspective the importance of UNCED for the marine environment can be seen in the substantial rewriting of regional fisheries law by the 1995 Straddling and Highly Migratory Fish Stocks Agreement; in the revision of the Baltic, Mediterranean, and North-East Atlantic regional seas treaties to take account of Agenda 21; in the prohibition of dumping under the 1996 Protocol to the Dumping Convention; in the revision and extension of maritime environmental liability and compensation schemes; and in the more modest developments relating to land-based sources of marine pollution. While it is still correct to observe that the 1982 UNCLOS has generally been more successful in addressing specific sources of pollution such as ships or dumping than in establishing a comprehensive and integrated 'system for sustainable development', it has shown its value as a foundation for the continued development of marine environmental law.

[298] *Supra*, Ch 4, section 4.
[299] See Boyle, 54 *ICLQ* (2005) 563; Birnie, 12 *IJMCL* (1997) 307, and see *infra*, Chs 8, 13.

8

INTERNATIONAL REGULATION
OF TOXIC SUBSTANCES

1 INTRODUCTION

1(1) THE PROBLEM

Toxic substances such as chemicals, industrial wastes, or agricultural pesticides create environmental risks which are international in several senses.[1] First, the release of persistent and potentially toxic substances into the environment may have long-term and cumulative effects on human and animal health over a wide area. Studies have shown how over many decades persistent organic pollutants have been transported to the Arctic, where marine life and animals show significantly higher levels of bio-accumulation than at lower latitudes. These pollutants originate in the industrial areas of Europe, Asia, and North America, but migrate northwards under the influence of winds and oceanic currents. While in some cases their release into the environment is caused by disposal as waste at sea or in rivers, or through airborne emissions, ultimately this problem can only be addressed by minimizing the use of these chemicals in industrial products and processes and for agricultural purposes. Second, international trade in hazardous wastes and chemicals poses a potential risk of accidental pollution of the marine environment and of transit states. Importing states are at also risk where trade takes place without their knowledge or consent, or where, as in the case of some developing states, they possess inadequate management and scientific facilities or limited understanding of the risks involved. Many developing countries thus continue to use pesticides and other chemicals long banned or restricted in more

---

[1] UNGAOR, 44th Session, *Rept of the Secretary General on Illegal Traffic in Toxic and Dangerous Products and Wastes*, UN Doc A/44/362 (1989); Pallemaerts, *Toxics and Transnational Law* (Oxford, 2002) Ch 1.

developed states. Trade in these circumstances may be a consequence of lower stand-ards of regulation or of a willingness to accept for use or disposal substances banned or regulated elsewhere. Taking advantage of these lower standards involves a transfer of environmental costs from manufacturers in developed industrialized economies to the peoples and environment of developing states who may be least able to bear them. It may also result in significant effects on the rights to life or health, or on other human rights of populations in areas where waste is disposed of or recycled.[2]

Trade in hazardous wastes will be advantageous, however, if it removes for reproc-essing or safe disposal substances which could not be dealt with in an environmentally sound manner in the country of origin, or which would otherwise be disposed of at sea. The bulk of this trade does not involve developing states, and a general policy of eliminating it among industrialized nations would be environmentally and econom-ically inefficient and hamper attempts to reduce marine pollution from dumping or land-based sources. Elimination of trade among developed countries would also put further pressure on developing states in Africa, Latin America, and the Caribbean who are already the main recipients of illegal traffic in toxic waste for disposal. The disappearance of landfill sites in industrialized countries, escalating disposal costs, and the difficulty of obtaining approval for incineration facilities have all contrib-uted to a growing demand for waste disposal in the developing world. It is mainly to counter this problem that international regulation of transboundary movements of hazardous waste has proved necessary.

1(2) INTERNATIONAL POLICY

As we will see, the London Dumping Convention, the Basel Convention on the Control of Transboundary Movements of Hazardous Wastes, the Convention on Persistent Organic Pollutants and, in somewhat weaker form, the regional agreements on land-based sources of marine pollution, share a common philosophy indicative of the trend of contemporary international policy.[3] In general, these agreements have endorsed a precautionary approach which, inter alia, favours reducing the generation of toxic and hazardous waste through cleaner production technology and processes, eliminating the most harmful chemicals from production and use, and controlling trade in other categories of hazardous wastes and substances. International policy can thus be sum-marized as an attempt to balance environmental protection and economic develop-ment. Agenda 21 of the 1992 Rio Conference set out three priorities. First, it endorsed environmentally sound management, giving priority to waste reduction.[4] Second,

---

[2] See UNHRC, *Rept of the Special Rapporteur on the adverse effects of the illicit dumping of toxic and dan-gerous products and wastes*, UN Doc A/HRC/7/21 (2008) and *infra*, section 4(7).

[3] See generally Pallemaerts, *Toxics and Transnational Law*; Wirth, in Bodansky, Brunnée, and Hey (eds), *Oxford Handbook of International Environmental Law* (Oxford, 2007) Ch 17.

[4] *Agenda 21*, Ch 20. See also UNEP, GC Decision SS 11/4 B (1990) 20 *EPL* (1990) 157 and OECD Council Recommendation C(90) 164 on integrated pollution prevention and control, 21 *EPL* (1991) 90.

it proposed international action on land-based sources of pollution.[5] Third, it called for better risk assessment of chemicals and the phasing out or banning of chemicals 'that pose an unreasonable and otherwise unmanageable risk to the environment or human health and those that are toxic, persistent and bio-accumulative and whose use cannot be adequately controlled'.[6] UNEP, GATT, FAO, and WHO were invited to consider the conclusion of legally binding instruments on prior informed consent for chemicals and pesticides in international trade. These decisions point towards an increasing integration of policy on international management and control of hazardous substances, but it remains true that '[t]here is at present no single, overarching international institutional framework for addressing environmental and public health risks from hazardous substances and activities'.[7] Nevertheless, UNEP, IMO, and FAO have become significant actors in this context, and it is largely through their agency that some progress has been made.

2 INTERNATIONAL REGULATION OF TOXIC CHEMICALS

2(1) INTRODUCTION

If pollution is principally a harmful change in the chemical composition of air, water, and soil, then it could be said that much of international environmental law involves the regulation of chemicals. That is certainly true of air pollution resulting in acid rain, or ozone depletion resulting from the migration of CFCs and other chemicals into the upper atmosphere. We considered all of these problems in Chapter 6. International regulation of land-based sources of marine pollution, dumping at sea, and international trade in hazardous waste also addresses emission and disposal of chemicals, together with heavy metals, radioactive substances and biological matter. These subjects are dealt with in later sections of this chapter. In this section we look at international regulation specifically aimed at toxic chemicals, in particular the Rotterdam Convention on Prior Informed Consent (PIC) and the Stockholm Convention on Persistent Organic Pollutants (POPS). There is plainly a need to coordinate measures adopted in each of these different but overlapping fields. Cooperation between the Basel Convention, the POPS Convention, and the PIC Convention is thus essential.[8]

---

[5] *Agenda 21*, Ch 17, on which see *supra*, Ch 7, section 1(2).
[6] *Agenda 21*, Ch 19.   [7] Wirth, in Bodansky, Brunnée, and Hey (eds), *Handbook of IEL*, 421.
[8] See UNEP, *Rept of Ad hoc Joint WG on Enhancing Cooperation and Coordination*, UNEP/FAO/CHW/ RC/POPS/WG 2/18 (2008). In 1995 FAO, ILO, OECD, UNEP, UNIDO, and WHO also created an Inter-organization Programme for the Sound Management of Chemicals: see 34 *ILM* (1995) 1311.

2(2) TRADE IN CHEMICALS: THE ROTTERDAM PIC CONVENTION

International trade in chemicals and pesticides is regulated in several ways. Transport of chemicals by sea is regulated by IMO and is covered by Annexes II and III of the 1973/8 MARPOL Convention.[9] Trade in waste containing toxic chemicals is subject to the prior informed consent and environmentally sound disposal requirements of the 1989 Basel Convention.[10] Together with guidelines on trade in chemicals and pesticides adopted by UNEP and FAO,[11] the latter convention provided a model for the Rotterdam Convention on the Prior Informed Consent Procedure for Certain Hazardous Chemicals and Pesticides in International Trade, adopted in 1998.[12] This convention applies only to international trade in 'banned or severely restricted chemicals' and 'severely hazardous pesticides' judged to pose a risk to human health or the environment.[13] It does not prohibit trade, but creates a procedure designed to ensure prior informed consent by the state of import. Essentially, each party must notify the Convention secretariat whether it wishes to ban, limit, or permit import of the chemicals and pesticides listed in Annex III. States that indicate their willingness to permit import are presumed to have consented on the terms specified. States that ban imports must also prohibit production for domestic consumption (Article 10(9)) in order to comply with WTO rules on non-discrimination.[14] The state of export must then take appropriate steps to ensure that exporters comply with the import requirements specified by other states (Article 11). Where the state of export itself bans or severely restricts use of a chemical it must give prior notification of any export to other states and provide the required information. It is for the state of import to determine its response in accordance with its rights under the Convention (Article 12). Chemicals listed in Annex III or banned by the state of export must also be suitably labelled with warnings and health information when exported to other states (Article 13). The International Register of Potentially Toxic Chemicals, a UNEP agency, acts as a repository of information and advice on hazardous chemicals and the implementation of policies for controlling potential hazards and evaluating effects on health and the environment.[15]

The key to the Rotterdam Convention is the listing in Annex III. At the time of writing twenty-four pesticides, four severely hazardous pesticides and eleven industrial chemicals were included. Others can be added or removed by amending Annex III, but proposals to add chemicals must first be made by states in at least two regions.[16]

---

[9] See *supra*, Ch 7, section 4.   [10] See *infra*, section 4.

[11] FAO, International Code of Conduct on the Distribution and Use of Pesticides (rev'd 2002); UNEP, London Guidelines for the Exchange of Information on Chemicals in International Trade (rev'd 1989). See Pallemaerts, *Toxics in Transnational Law*, 441–556; Victor, Raustiala and Skolnikoff (eds), *The Implementation and Effectiveness of International Environmental Commitments* (Cambridge, Mass, 1998) Ch 6.

[12] See Pallemaerts, *Toxics in Transnational Law*, 557–94.

[13] Article 3. For definitions of these terms see Article 2.

[14] On the WTO aspects of the negotiation see Pallemaerts, *Toxics in Transnational Law*, 584–94.

[15] UNEP/GC 15/28 (1989) *Rept of the Governing Council*, 153.

[16] Article 5(5). There are 7 regions: see *Rept of 1st COP*, decision RC-1/2 (2002).

Thus a chemical widely banned in Europe could not be considered for listing unless a state in another region supported the proposal. Additional pesticides can be proposed by any developing state or transitional economy 'that is experiencing problems caused by a severely hazardous pesticide formulation under conditions of use in its territory'.[17] All proposals are reviewed by an expert Chemical Review Committee. Recommendations made by this body are based on information provided by the proposing state and the secretariat. Criteria set out in Annexes II and IV require the Review Committee to make a scientific assessment of the proposing state's risk evaluation and the need for PIC controls to be applied.[18] Among other factors, they must take into account whether the risk exists 'only in a limited geographical area or in other limited circumstances'. Risk evaluations conducted for the Stockholm POPS Convention and the Montreal Ozone Protocol would be regarded as providing adequate support.[19] Although the Convention does not define the term, the negotiating committee understood 'risk evaluation' to mean 'evaluation of intrinsic toxicological and ecotoxicological properties and actual or expected relevant exposure, including actual incidents and scientific evidence of hazard'.[20] How this is interpreted and applied in practice will be crucial to the success of the Convention, but Pallemaerts notes that 'it is quite clear that the level of detail and the amount of scientific data and evidence required will make it almost impossible for any regulatory actions taken by developing countries to qualify for consideration'.[21] Moreover, the decision whether to amend the list is a political judgement taken by the Conference of the Parties.[22] Such decisions require consensus, which gives every state a veto, but once adopted they enter into force for all parties without the need for further ratification and with no right to opt out.[23] This is an unusual procedure, about which some states had expressed concern during negotiations, and it was not adopted in the Stockholm POPS Convention, which follows the more common majority vote/opt-out procedure also employed by the Ozone Protocol for adding additional ozone-depleting substances.

Listing of additional chemicals in Annex III is thus far from automatic and may not be easy. Although several additions were made at the 1st COP, at the 3rd COP in 2006 it was noted that some 160 chemicals banned by various states could not be reviewed or added to Annex III without the necessary support from at least one other region.[24] Moreover, a recommendation to list one chemical banned in several regions and supported by the Review Committee was not adopted despite meeting all the necessary criteria. While many states took the view that in such circumstances listing should normally follow, and some relied on the precautionary principle to the same effect, others questioned the scientific basis of the recommendation and the need to control

---

[17] Article 6(1).   [18] Articles 5(6), 6(5).

[19] *Rept. of 3rd COP*, UNEP/FAO/RC/COP 3/26 (2006) para 66.

[20] *Rept of the INC, 5th Session*, UNEP/FAO/PIC/INC 5/3 (1998) para 82. Compare *EC—Measures Concerning Meat and Meat Products*, WT/DS26/AB/R (1998) paras 182–7; *Japan—Measures Affecting the Import of Apples*, WT/DS245/AB/R (2003) para 202.

[21] Pallemaerts, *Toxics in Transnational Law*, 576.   [22] Article 7(2).

[23] Article 22(5).   [24] *Rept of 3rd COP*, para 28.

trade.[25] Since consensus could not be achieved after further diplomatic efforts, no decision to list was adopted. The ability of any state to block the listing of additional chemicals or pesticides, however harmful they are shown to be, is plainly open to abuse and seems an extraordinary provision to include in a convention whose only purpose is to facilitate respect for import restrictions in other states. It is also extraordinary that states whose unilateral import bans are lawful under WTO agreements when aimed at public-health protection and based on a precautionary risk assessment[26] cannot rely on the PIC procedure to protect them from illegal trade if listing is vetoed by a handful of states in the Rotterdam COP.

It is noteworthy that the Rotterdam Convention makes no reference to the precautionary principle. While this omission may in practice have made no difference to the unsuccessful attempts at listing, the Stockholm POPS Convention does not make the same mistake.[27] It is also notable that, unlike the Basel Convention, the Rotterdam Convention makes no provision for illegal traffic nor does it require the state of export to accept reimportation of illegally exported chemicals. This is a particularly unfortunate omission since the UNEP Governing Council had drawn attention to illegal traffic in the decision initiating the negotiations.[28] Although Article 17 requires a non-compliance procedure to be negotiated 'as soon as practicable', agreement could still not be reached at the 3rd COP. There is thus considerable room for further evolution in a dysfunctional convention whose already modest terms reflect the influence of a powerful international chemical industry and the resistance of a number of industrialized states. It is not surprising that the procedures of the older UNEP and FAO voluntary schemes are regarded as more environmentally friendly.[29] The only industrialized state not a party to the PIC Convention in 2007 was the United States.

2(3) PERSISTENT ORGANIC POLLUTANTS: THE STOCKHOLM POPS CONVENTION

A small group of chemicals have become the subject of specific international regulation because of their persistent, toxic, and bio-accumulative character. Known generically as persistent organic pollutants (POPS) these chemicals are now recognized as posing long-term hazards to human and animal health over a wide area, often far from where they originate. Some are produced for industrial or agricultural use, such as PCBs and DDT. Others, mainly dioxins and furans, are emitted incidentally by industrial processes. All can end up in the food chain. Like CFCs, the most appropriate policy for all of them is to phase out production and consumption, while allowing for essential uses and encouraging a switch to less harmful substitutes and processes. These are the principal objectives of the Stockholm Convention on Persistent Organic Pollutants, adopted in 2001. Following preparatory work undertaken by the Intergovernmental

---

[25] Ibid, paras 67–79.   [26] *Supra*, n 20 and see *infra*, Ch 14.   [27] See next section.
[28] UNEP GC, Decision 18/12 (1995). See also UNCED, *Agenda 21*, Ch 19, paras 19.66–8 and UNGA Res 44/226 (1989) both of which refer to 'illegal traffic in toxic and dangerous products and wastes'.
[29] Pallemaerts, *Toxics in Transnational Law*, 578.

Forum on Chemical Safety, described as 'an uncommon structure—one that combines experts and representatives from both the public and private sectors',[30] UNEP convened a negotiating conference. In addition to states, a wide range of other entities participated in the negotiations, including the chemical industry, public health, and environmental NGOs, indigenous peoples' organizations, WHO, FAO, and the GEF.[31] The outcome is a treaty with five distinct features.

First, it expressly proclaims a precautionary approach to the protection of human health and the environment (Article 1). On that basis, and following the model of the Ozone Protocol and the 1998 UNECE POPS Protocol,[32] states are required to prohibit or eliminate the production or use of nine chemicals listed in Annex A, and to restrict production and use of DDT as indicated in Annex B (Article 3). Specific exemptions allow continued import and use of some of these substances for a limited period, provided that each state making use of this facility is identified on a public register held by the secretariat (Article 4). This system of country-specific exceptions was designed to allow for special needs of particular countries to be identified, subject to periodic review by the parties. A state wishing to renew an exception must justify its request to the other parties. This appears to imply that the parties may reject the application if they are not satisfied by the reasons given. If that is correct then it gives the POPS Convention a control mechanism which effectively reverses the burden of proof and leaves no possibility of retaining an exemption by opting out of COP decisions. This resembles the prior-justification procedure once used to control dumping of waste at sea under the Oslo Dumping Convention. Once all exemptions have expired no further requests may be made and use of that chemical is then banned outright.[33]

Second, measures must be taken to deal with existing stocks of POPS and the processes which emit them. Stockpiles of substances listed in Annexes A and B are to be identified, managed, and disposed of in a 'safe, efficient and environmentally sound manner'. (Article 6). Ultimate disposal will entail destruction of their persistent organic content. Anthropogenic releases of POPS listed in Annex C must be minimized and eventually eliminated 'where feasible' through action plans, substitute materials and processes, and other practical measures that can 'expeditiously achieve a 'realistic and meaningful level of release reduction or source elimination'.[34] For this purpose parties must 'promote' the use of best available techniques (BAT) and best environmental practices (BEP) for existing sources and they must require new sources to use them within four years from entry into force. The Convention defines BAT and BEP (Article 5) and gives detailed guidance in Annex C. This aspect of the Convention represents a considered compromise between those who sought complete elimination and other states that regarded this as unrealistic in the short term.[35] Initial proposals to set targets and a timetable for reducing and eliminating emissions were not pursued, and Article 5 emerged as an obligation of conduct (to take the specified

---

[30] Lallas, 95 *AJIL* (2001) 692, 695.   [31] Id, 19 *UCLA J Env L&P* (2000/1) 83, 114–46.
[32] 1998 POPS Protocol to the 1979 Convention on Long-range Transboundary Air Pollution, *supra*, Ch 6.
[33] Article 4(9).   [34] Article 5(b).   [35] Lallas, 95 *AJIL* (2001) 702.

measures)—rather than one of result (reducing/eliminating emissions). It was the subject of litigation in the *Pulp Mills Case* where Uruguay argued that the technology it proposed to use met the BAT standard required.[36]

Third, again following the model of the Ozone Protocol, trade is restricted. Export and import of listed chemicals or wastes is banned unless intended for permitted use or for environmentally sound disposal (Article 3(2)). Export to non-parties is allowed only if they also comply with the principal requirements of the Convention.[37] None of these trade restrictions poses any problem of compatibility with GATT rules: they are non-discriminatory, have protection of human and animal health as their principal aim, and cannot be characterized as a 'disguised restriction on international trade'.[38]

Fourth, although the POPS Convention is not a framework convention in the normal sense, further annexes can be added and it is open to the parties to list additional chemicals in the annexes—at present only twelve are listed. Like the Rotterdam Convention, proposals to add other chemicals are assessed by chemical experts in a Review Committee whose processes are designed to allow transparency and informed recommendations based on a 'risk profile' which identifies the likelihood of 'significant adverse human health and/or environmental effects such that global action is warranted'.[39] Here too the precautionary principle reappears: 'Lack of full scientific certainty shall not prevent the proposal from proceeding'.[40] While recommendations of the Review Committee will reflect a scientific judgement, the final decision is a political one made by the Conference of the Parties 'in a precautionary manner', suggesting that, unlike the Rotterdam Convention, uncertainty will be resolved in favour of listing.[41] Such decisions can be made by a three-quarter majority vote if there is no consensus, but it remains open to any state to opt out within a year if it does not wish to be bound.[42] As in the Ozone Protocol, no state party can be forced to restrict or eliminate newly listed chemicals if it does not wish to do so. Unlike Rotterdam, no state can stop other parties from agreeing to do so.

Finally, while there is no express reference to 'common but differentiated responsibility' in the Convention, it shares the main elements of this concept with the Ozone Protocol. Most importantly there are commitments by developed states to make technology, technical assistance, and funding available to developing states parties.[43] It is recognized that 'the extent to which developing country Parties will effectively implement their commitments' will depend on the developed countries fulfilling their side of this bargain.[44] Moreover, while sustainable economic development and poverty eradication are acknowledged to be the 'first and overriding priorities' of developing states, Article 13 appears to envisage a balance between these considerations and 'the need for protection of human health and the environment'. The 'specific needs and

---

[36] ICJ Reports (2006) (Provisional Measures). See oral arguments and Uruguay's Counter-memorial.
[37] See Article 3(2)(b).   [38] 1994 GATT, Article XX. See *infra*, Ch 14.
[39] Article 8. See Annexes D, E, F for details of information required to make this judgement.
[40] Article 8(7)(a).   [41] Article 8(9).
[42] Article 22(3). See also Article 25(4) which allows a party to substitute an opt-in procedure at the time of ratification.
[43] Articles 12, 13.   [44] Article 13(4).

special situation' of the least developed states and small island states are also to be taken fully into account. Unlike the Ozone Protocol, however, there are no special timescales for developing state elimination of listed chemicals, but developing states are more likely to rely on the exemptions for continued use of certain POPS. All of these provisions suggest that developing country elimination of POPS will proceed more slowly than elsewhere unless other parties show adequate solidarity. It is particularly important therefore that a financial mechanism administered by the GEF is created for the purpose of assisting developing countries to implement the convention (Article 13(6)). The Conference of the Parties is empowered to give guidance to the GEF mechanism on policy and programme priorities and to review the effectiveness of the Convention and the financial mechanism at periodic intervals.[45] As we saw in Chapter 2 the GEF has a good record of facilitating implementation of MEAs, including the Ozone Protocol. Finally, there are requirements for all parties to report on national implementation (Article 15). A non-compliance procedure remains to be negotiated.[46] It is too early to assess the impact of the POPS Convention, but at the time of writing it was in force with 146 parties. Of the main industrialized states only Russia and the United States had still not ratified by 2007.[47]

3 PROTECTION OF THE MARINE ENVIRONMENT FROM TOXIC SUBSTANCES

3(1) INTRODUCTION

Although estimated to contribute over 80 per cent of all marine pollution, disposal of hazardous wastes at sea was subject to few restraints under international law until the first regional treaties of the 1970s. As we saw in Chapter 7, the High Seas Convention of 1958 only required states to regulate oil pollution, to take measures to prevent pollution from the dumping of radioactive waste, and to cooperate in preventing pollution from activities involving radioactive materials or other harmful agents.[48] Only with the adoption of the 1982 UNCLOS was there general recognition of an obligation to protect the marine environment and to control pollution originating from land-based sources.[49] Regional treaties amplify and implement the general provisions of Part XII of UNCLOS.[50]

---

[45] Articles 13(6), 13(7), 16.

[46] For draft see *Rept of 3rd COP*, UNEP/POPS/COP 3/30 (2007) decision SC-3/20.

[47] On the US position see Fuller and McGarrity, 28 *Wm & Mary Env L & Pol Rev* (2003) 1.

[48] Articles 24, 25. The ILC commentary indicates that the latter part of Article 25 was drafted with nuclear tests in mind. See II *YbILC* (1956) 286; 1st United Nations Conference on the Law of the Sea, *Official Records* (1958) iv, 84ff and Resolution II, adopted 23 Apr 1958; *Official Records*, ii, 143.

[49] 1982 UNCLOS, Articles 192, 194(2).

[50] 1978 Convention on Protection of the Marine Environment from Pollution ('Kuwait Convention') Articles 3, 6; 1981 Convention for the Protection and Development of the Marine and Coastal Environment

The 1982 Convention does no more than establish a general framework for the regulation of land-based sources of marine pollution. Article 207 requires states to take measures, including the adoption of laws and regulations, to prevent, reduce, and control pollution from land-based sources. Its definition of 'land-based sources' includes 'rivers, estuaries, pipelines and outfall structures', to which regional treaties usually add pollution from coastal establishments, and sometimes also from airborne sources.[51] The 1996 Mediterranean Protocol and the 1999 Caribbean Protocol cover 'activities' as well as sources, while the 1992 OSPAR and Helsinki Conventions take a novel approach which refers to pollution from 'point or diffuse inputs from all sources on land', whether these are waterborne, airborne, or come directly from the coast. It is clear that these definitions are meant to be fully comprehensive of all possible inputs to the sea. However, seabed installations are generally dealt with separately by all of the relevant treaties, including the 1982 UNCLOS, and for that reason are not considered here.[52]

Unlike the 1982 UNCLOS articles dealing with pollution from ships, dumping, or seabed installations, Article 207 does not require adherence to any minimum international standards established by international organizations. States must, however, take account of 'internationally agreed rules, standards and recommended practices

of the West and Central African Region ('Abidjan Convention') Articles 4, 7; 1982 Convention for the Conservation of the Red Sea and Gulf of Aden ('Jeddah Convention') Articles 1, 6; 1983 Convention for the Protection and Development of the Marine Environment of the Wider Caribbean ('Cartagena Convention') Articles 4, 7; 1985 Convention for the Marine and Coastal Environment of the East African Region ('Nairobi Convention') Articles 1, 7; 1986 Convention for the Protection of the Natural Resources and Environment of the South Pacific Region ('Noumea Convention') Articles 5, 7; 1992 Convention for the Protection of the Marine Environment of the NE Atlantic ('OSPAR Convention') Article 2; 1992 Convention for the Protection of the Marine Environment of the Baltic Sea Area ('1992 Helsinki Convention') Article 3; 1992 Convention on the Protection of the Black Sea Against Pollution ('Black Sea Convention') Articles 5, 7; 1995 Convention for the Protection of the Marine Environment and Coastal Region of the Mediterranean ('1995 Barcelona Convention') Articles 4, 8.

[51] See for example 1983 Quito Protocol, Article 2; 1981 Abidjan Convention, Article 7; 1983 Cartagena Convention, Article 7; 1985 Nairobi Convention, Article 7; 1986 Noumea Convention, Article 7; 1974 Nordic Convention for the Protection of the Environment, Article 1; 1990 Protocol for the Protection of the Marine Environment against Pollution from Land-based Sources ('Kuwait Protocol') Article 1; 1992 Protocol on Protection of the Black Sea Marine Environment against Pollution from Land-based Sources, Article 1; 1996 Protocol for the Protection of the Mediterranean Sea against Pollution from Land-based Sources and Activities ('Mediterranean Protocol') Article 1; 1999 Caribbean Protocol, Article 1.

[52] See 1982 UNCLOS, Article 208. All UNEP agreements acknowledge an obligation to control pollution from this source. See also 1994 Protocol for the Protection of the Mediterranean Sea against Pollution Resulting from Exploration and Exploitation of the Continental Shelf ('Madrid Protocol'); 1992 Helsinki Convention, Article 12 and Annex VI; 1992 OSPAR Convention, Article 5 and Annex III; 1990 Kuwait Protocol Concerning Marine Pollution Resulting from Exploration and Exploitation of the Continental Shelf; 1973/78 MARPOL Convention, Article 2(4) and Annex 1, Reg 21; 1981 UNEP Conclusions of a Study of Legal Aspects of the Environment Relating to Offshore Mineral Exploitation and Drilling, UNEP/GC 9/5/Add 5/Annex III, 7 EPL (1981) 50; de Mestral, 20 Harv ILJ (1979) 469; Rémond-Gouilloud, in Johnston, The Environmental Law of the Sea (Berlin, 1981) 245; Gavounelli, Pollution from Offshore Installations (Dordrecht, 1995); Vinogradov and Wagner, in Gao (ed), Environment Regulation of Oil and Gas (The Hague, 1998) Ch 3.

and procedures'.[53] National laws must also minimize 'to the fullest extent possible' the release of toxic, harmful, noxious, or persistent substances, but it is for each state to determine what measures to take and whether action should be global, regional, bilateral, or national. It is also for each state to determine which substances require regulation and control; the essential point is that it is not discharges of waste which are the object of this obligation, but only discharges which result in 'pollution' as defined by Article 1(4). As we saw in Chapter 3, this term provides only the most general guidance, and precludes useful generalization. Its effect is to give states a further discretion in their implementation of Article 207. This partly explains the significant variations in what different regional treaties prohibit or control, despite their almost identical definition of pollution,[54] and shows how contingent on the circumstances of each sea interpretation of this term proves to be in practice. Thus, one of the objects of regional treaties is to identify which substances will be treated as causing 'pollution' and in what circumstances.[55]

Articles 122 and 123 of the Convention, which deal with enclosed and semi-enclosed seas, merely reaffirm the general position that states must cooperate in measures of environmental protection. They do not alter the conclusion that, with regard to the control of land-based pollution, states have a wide discretion concerning the action they must take. At most, these articles may sustain a stronger obligation to cooperate in negotiating common pollution standards than is implied for oceanic areas by Article 207 alone.[56] Major regional agreements on land-based marine pollution are not limited to enclosed or semi-enclosed seas, nor do institutional arrangements treat enclosed and semi-enclosed seas differently from other oceanic areas.[57] The evidence does not go so far as to support the view that those enclosed or semi-enclosed seas are 'shared resources' subject to the principle of equitable utilization. Thus, although it provides the convention's only significant legal basis for protecting the marine environment from land-based pollution, Article 207 is drafted in terms which give no specific content to the underlying obligation of due diligence found in customary law. Like the comparable provision dealing with atmospheric pollution (Article 212)

[53] Articles 207(1), (5). See also 3rd UNCLOS, *Official Records*, ii (1974) 317, para 20 (Canada), 328 (China), and cf Kenyan draft articles A/CONF 62/C 3/42 (1974) and 10-power draft, A/CONF 62/C 3/L 6 (1974) ibid, iii, 245, 249. For the drafting history of Article 207, see Nordquist (ed), *United Nations Convention on the Law of the Sea: A Commentary*, iv (Dordrecht, 1991) 125–34.

[54] Based on Article 1(4) of UNCLOS. Some of the newer treaties refer to 'marine ecosystems' rather than 'marine life'. See 1992 OSPAR Convention, Article 1(d); 1992 Helsinki Convention, Article 2(1); 1995 Barcelona Convention, Article 2; 1999 Caribbean Protocol, Article 1(3); 1992 Black Sea Convention, Article 2(1); 1983 Quito Protocol, Article III; 1982 Jeddah Convention, Article 1(3); 1985 Nairobi Convention, Article 2(b); 1978 Kuwait Convention, Article 1(a); 1986 Noumea Convention, Article 2(f).

[55] Compare 1996 Mediterranean Protocol, Annex 1; 1992 Helsinki Convention, Annex 1; 1992 OSPAR Convention, Annex 1, and see *infra*.

[56] Vukas, in Vidas (ed), *Protecting the Polar Marine Environment* (Cambridge, 2000) Ch 2.

[57] See *infra*, and cf UNEP, Principles of Conduct in the Field of the Environment Concerning Natural Resources Shared by Two or More States, *supra*, Ch 3. The Executive Director of UNEP has referred to enclosed and semi-enclosed seas as examples of shared resources, UNEP Doc GC/44, (1975) para 86.

it lacks both the more precise content of the articles concerned with pollution from dumping or from ships, or any comparable means for its direct enforcement.[58]

The reasons for this are that states were generally unwilling to adopt a stronger text during the UNCLOS negotiations. They wished to preserve for themselves as much freedom of action as possible in balancing environmental protection measures against the needs of their own economies, where land-based activities generated much of the most harmful pollution. Concern for development priorities is also evident in the general provisions of the 1982 UNCLOS. Article 193 refers to the sovereign right of states to exploit their own natural resources pursuant to their environmental policies, and in accordance with their duty to protect the marine environment. Article 194(1) moderates the obligation to protect the environment by reference to the use of 'the best practicable means at their disposal and in accordance with their capabilities'. Moreover, although Article 207(4) refers to the establishment of 'global and regional rules, standards and recommended practices' for the control of land-based pollution, it allows account to be taken of 'characteristic regional features, the economic capacity of developing states and their need for economic development'.[59]

This phraseology leaves little doubt that states did not wish to commit themselves to the same level of international control as is imposed on other sources of marine pollution. The social and economic costs of such measures were seen as unacceptably high, and the preferred solution was thus a weaker level of international regulation, a greater latitude for giving preference to other national priorities, and resort to regional cooperation as the primary level at which international action should occur. The largely hortatory character of this policy is evident in the wording of Article 207(3)–(4) which provides that states shall 'endeavour' to harmonize their policies at the appropriate regional level and to establish global and regional rules. Article 123 is similarly elusive with regard to enclosed or semi-enclosed seas, requiring states only to 'endeavour' to coordinate the implementation of their rights and duties with respect to protection of the marine environment. These formulations are without significant normative content. They tend to demonstrate that, as it stands, Article 207 does not require states to take strong or effective measures.

At the time it was drafted, Article 207 did correspond to the practice of states, regionally and nationally. When compared to the most advanced regional regimes in operation thirty years later, it is less clear that it still does so. It does not necessarily follow that Article 207 can no longer be taken as a statement of general international law, because it was never intended as more than a minimum standard, but it is undoubtedly inadequate for the purpose of giving effect to the objectives of sustainable development and integrated coastal zone management outlined in UNCED Agenda 21.[60]

---

[58] Cf *supra*, Ch 7, and *infra*, section 3(6).

[59] See also 1996 Mediterranean Protocol, Article 7(2); 1983 Quito Protocol, Article 6, and 3rd UNCLOS, *Official Records*, *supra*, n 53.

[60] See Tanaka, 66 *ZAÖRV* (2006) 535; Franckx, 13 *IJMCL* (1998) 307; Mensah, in Boyle and Freestone (eds), *International Law and Sustainable Development* (Oxford, 1999) Ch 13; Pallemaerts, *Toxics and*

3(2) REGIONAL ADOPTION OF COMMON STANDARDS

As we have seen elsewhere, the main environmental benefit of common standards of pollution prevention is that they ensure a coordinated approach in areas of common interest such as enclosed or semi-enclosed seas. In the case of industrial pollution an important further benefit is the economic advantage derived from a reduction in unfair competition. The counter-arguments applied to land-based sources of pollution are also important however. Strict regulation of this form of pollution has substantial economic, social, and political implications for industrial economies and developing states alike. Those wishing to protect their freedom to decide for themselves how to develop sustainably may rely on assertions of national autonomy in the use of territory and permanent sovereignty over natural resources to limit the possibilities for international regulation, oversight, and enforcement. Moreover, geographical and ecological considerations point to substantial differences in the absorbtive capacity of different seas. Although land-based pollution affects most coastal areas, shallow, enclosed or semi-enclosed, seas such as the Baltic, North Sea, or Mediterranean are especially sensitive,[61] and need greater protection than open oceanic areas. All of these considerations may point to the doubtful utility of seeking detailed international regulation of land-based sources of pollution, and help explain the relatively weak framework approach adopted by the 1982 UNCLOS and the UNEP regional-seas programme. Not surprisingly, where they have been willing to cooperate, states have preferred regional or subregional arrangements, believing that they offer greater flexibility in accommodating the economic, geopolitical, and ecological needs of particular seas and their adjacent states and provide a better basis for common standards of regulation. But the main consequence of this regionalization of the problem has been the legitimation of weak standards and weak supervisory institutions. States have not always addressed the regional problems with the seriousness merited by scientific reports.

(a) UNEP's regional-seas programme

UNEP's regional-seas treaties all require states to endeavour to control land-based pollution. These general provisions are no more specific than Article 207 of the 1982 UNCLOS and merely repeat the duty to 'take measures', but they do offer a framework for the negotiation of regional controls, particularly in developing states. Despite its relative success in mobilizing cooperation on other matters and involving a large number of states, the potential of the regional-seas programme has only slowly been realized. In the Mediterranean, south-east Pacific, Persian Gulf, and Black Sea, protocols

---

Transnational Law, Ch 3; Nollkaemper, *The Legal Regime for Transboundary Water Pollution* (Dordrecht, 1993).

[61] On the specific problems of these seas see OSPAR, *Quality Status Report 2000 for the North-East Atlantic* (London, 2000); Helsinki Commission, *Fourth Periodic Assessment of the State of the Marine Environment of the Baltic Sea Area* (Helsinki, 2001); Plasman, 13 *IJMCL* (1998) 325.

on land-based sources of marine pollution have entered into force; not until 1999 was a protocol covering the Caribbean region adopted.

The 1983 Quito Protocol covering the SE Pacific illustrates weaknesses typical of most of the older generation of land-based pollution agreements, including in many respects the 1992 Black Sea Protocol.[62] The Quito Protocol requires the parties only to 'endeavour' to adopt measures to prevent, reduce and control marine pollution from specifically listed substances; those on the black list are generally distinguished by toxicity, persistence, or bioaccumulation and the aim is to eliminate discharges; those on the grey list must be controlled so that the amount and location of discharge are compatible with protection of the marine environment, but emissions need only be progressively reduced. However, discharge of blacklisted substances is not immediately prohibited; instead it is for the parties individually or jointly to decide on timetables, priorities, and measures, taking into account capacity to adapt existing facilities, the economic capacity of the parties and their development needs.

Similar language continues to be found in the revised 1996 Mediterranean Protocol,[63] and in the 1999 Caribbean Protocol.[64] It is a common feature of the UNEP LBS protocols to acknowledge the differentiated responsibility of developing state parties. In practice this allows a great deal of leeway for developing states to act in accordance with their own priorities and capabilities, and in that respect nothing has changed in agreements negotiated or revised since UNCED. Moreover, although there is greater emphasis on environmental impact assessment and monitoring in post-UNCED agreements,[65] and the black- and grey-listing of harmful substances has been abandoned in favour of a less rigid approach which encourages use of 'best available' or 'most appropriate' technology, references to the precautionary principle and the polluter-pays principle remain conspicuously absent from the texts of all except the revised Mediterranean LBS protocol. Although UNCED and Agenda 21 have had some influence, most notably on the strengthened Mediterranean Protocol, and also on the practice and policies of the parties, the newer UNEP agreements remain largely within the very loose framework provided by UNCLOS Article 207. Even this watered-down approach has proved too much for the United States, whose refusal to ratify the Caribbean protocol has prevented it from entering into force.

(b) European agreements on land-based sources of marine pollution

The oldest and most developed regional agreements regulating land-based sources of marine pollution are those applicable to the North-East Atlantic[66] and the Baltic.[67] Both have been renegotiated since UNCED, and the new Paris and Helsinki

---

[62] But on steps to modernize the Black Sea regime see Vinogradov, 22 *IJMCL* (2007) 585.

[63] See Article 7.   [64] See Article 3.   [65] See next section.

[66] 1992 Paris Convention, replacing 1974 Paris Convention. See Hey, IJIstra, Nollkaemper, 8 *IJMCL* (1993) 1; Juste, 97 *RGDIP* (1993) 365; Hilf, 55 *ZAÖRV* (1995) 580; Pallemaerts, 13 *IJMCL* (1998) 421; de La Fayette, 14 *IJMCL* (1999) 247.

[67] 1992 Helsinki Convention, replacing 1974 Convention. See Fitzmaurice, *International Legal Problems of the Environmental Protection of the Baltic Sea* (Dordrecht, 1992); Ehlers, 8 *IJMCL* (1993) 191; Jenisch, 11

Conventions entered into force in 1998 and 2000 respectively. These treaties do not follow the UNEP model and are not confined to land-based sources. They have many of the characteristic features of other regional regulatory regimes, and are comparable in many respects to the Rhine Protection Convention or the Great Lakes Water Quality Agreement reviewed in Chapter 10. The Paris and Helsinki Commissions function as regional supervisory institutions. An important feature, however, has been the interplay with other more overtly political bodies, notably the International North Sea Conference, the Organization for Security and Co-operation in Europe, and the European Community. These bodies have at various times helped set the political agenda for policy and regulatory action by the Paris and Helsinki Commissions.[68]

Although both agreements affirm the duty of parties to prevent and eliminate land-based marine pollution, like the UNEP Regional Seas Treaties they do not as such prescribe detailed standards for doing so. Only the Helsinki Convention actually bans the discharge of a small number of substances.[69] Otherwise, national authorities remain responsible for setting pollution control standards, as well as for the grant of permits and inspection. However, parties are required to follow priorities listed in annexes to both treaties and to use (or to take into account) 'best available technology' and 'best environmental practice'. What these terms mean is only partially answered by the treaties themselves, and requires further elaboration by the parties.[70] Coordination of treaty implementation thus depends partly on adherence to licensing criteria indicated in the treaties, and partly on the success of the regional supervisory bodies in negotiating common standards, guidelines and timetables.

Agreement on these matters has not always been easy to reach, and remains far from comprehensive.[71] A further problem common to all the European treaties on marine pollution is that standards once adopted only have the status of recommendations (as in the Helsinki Convention)[72] or if binding (as under the 1992 Paris Convention) do not apply to states which opt out by timely objection.[73] Enforcement of agreed standards remains the responsibility of national authorities alone; there is no provision for independent inspection, or for prior approval of permits by intergovernmental bodies, but parties must institute their own system for regular monitoring and inspection to ensure compliance with national authorizations and regulations.

IJMCL (1996) 47; Fitzmaurice et al, 13 IJMCL (1998) 379–420; Pallemaerts, ibid, 421; Ebbesson, 43 GYIL (2000) 38.

[68] See section (c) infra.   [69] Annex 1, Part 2: principally DDT and PCBs.

[70] See criteria in Annex II of the 1992 Helsinki Convention and for OSPAR practice see Pallemaerts, 13 IJMCL (1998) 440–6.

[71] See Pallemaerts, ibid, and infra, section (c).

[72] See Fitzmaurice, International Legal Problems of the Environmental Protection of the Baltic Sea, 72–82. On non-binding recommendations under OSPAR see Nollkaemper, 13 IJMCL (1998) 355, and generally in The Legal Regime for Transboundary Water Pollution: Between Discretion and Constraint (Dordrecht, 1993) Ch 5.

[73] 1992 Paris Convention, Article 13.

(c) The North Sea and the Mediterranean

Two examples, the North Sea and the Mediterranean, indicate the essential point common to all four schemes: that even these developed regimes are only as good as the parties allow them to be. The North Sea states are a relatively cohesive and homogeneous group with a strong political commitment to environmental protection, initially through the International North Sea Conference,[74] but currently through the OSPAR Commission and the European Community. The OSPAR Commission's area of responsibility includes the North Sea and it has adopted common standards for emission of various harmful substances.[75] EC directives have harmonized some standards for North Sea member states, but the Community has also been a significant obstacle to adoption of stricter standards.[76] After 1984, the International North Sea Conference's calls for stricter regulation and substantial reductions in pollution gradually quickened progress and led to the adoption of new measures aimed through better use of technology at reducing the need for polluting emissions.[77] Cooperation on standard-setting within the region has as a result become more extensive. But the main contribution of the North Sea Conference lies less in concrete action than in the policies it has endorsed: a precautionary approach to integrated protection of the ecosystem, substantial reduction in inputs of all substances that are toxic, persistent and bio-accumulative, and specific targets for reducing certain major pollutants. Implementing INSC objectives within the timescales set requires not only coordinated national action, but cooperation within the EC, the OSPAR Commission, and, for international watercourses, the Rhine, Meuse, Scheldt, and Elbe Commissions.[78]

Views differ on how successful the INSC and the OSPAR Convention have been in protecting the North Sea. The INSC has generated new targets for pollution reduction, and as we have seen this has had some effect on the Commission, but those targets have not always been met.[79] Pallemaerts argues that the INSC process has been attractive to governments 'precisely as a convenient, symbolical means of creating and maintaining the illusion of progress'.[80] Certainly, increased regulatory activity does not necessarily result in decreases in pollution. Nevertheless, decisions and recommendations adopted by the OSPAR Commission do 'represent a more comprehensive

---

[74] 1st INSC, Bremen Declaration, 1984, 14 *EPL* (1985) 32; 2nd INSC, London Declaration, 1987, 27 *ILM* (1988) 835; 3rd INSC, Hague Declaration, 1990, IMO Doc MEPC/29/INF 26; 4th INSC, Esbjerg Declaration (1995). See Ehlers, 5 *IJECL* (1990) 3; Hayward, ibid, 91; Pallemaerts, 7 *IJMCL* (1992) 126; id, 13 *IJMCL* (1998) 421. On the legal status of North Sea Conference Declarations see Nollkaemper, 13 *IJMCL* (1998) 355.

[75] Article 31 provides that decisions, recommendations and agreements adopted under the 1974 Paris Convention continue to be applicable under the new Convention unless incompatible with it or expressly terminated by the parties. For a list of measures so terminated see OSPAR Decision 98/1. For a review of PARCOM practice see Pallemaerts, 13 *IJMCL* (1998) 421.

[76] See Saetevik, *Environmental Cooperation Among North Sea States* (London, 1986); Prat, 5 *IJECL* (1990) 101; de La Fayette, 14 *IJMCL* (1999) 247; Pallemaerts, 13 *IJMCL* (1998) 452–6.

[77] Hayward, 5 *IJECL* (1990) 94–6; Wettestad and Andresen, *The Effectiveness of International Resource Cooperation* (Lysaker, 1991) 56–73; de La Fayette, 14 *IJMCL* (1999) 247; Pallemaerts, 13 *IJMCL* (1998) 421; Sadowski, in, Ringbom (ed), *Competing Norms in the Law of Marine Environmental Protection* (London, 1997) Ch 6; Skaerseth, *North Sea Cooperation* (Manchester, 2000).

[78] See *infra* Ch 10.   [79] 1995 Esbjerg Declaration, para 17ff.   [80] 13 *IJMCL* (1998) 468.

and integrated approach to the prevention of marine pollution from land-based activities than the earlier piecemeal approach',[81] and to this extent UNCED objectives have been taken into account. However, the revision of the Paris Convention in 1992 is less radical than it appears; it largely incorporates and consolidates principles and policies already adopted under the old convention, such as the precautionary principle. Pallemaerts concludes that it 'certainly does not indicate any clear intention to make radical changes in existing practices'. Thus he criticizes the new treaty as 'disappointingly general', for failing to set quantitative targets and deadlines, for not transforming INSC commitments into binding law, and for a 'loss of focus and normative force'.[82] On the other hand the 1992 Convention also makes new provision for a non-compliance process, for NGO access to Commission proceedings, for limited public access to information, and for protection of marine ecosystems and biodiversity.[83] Moreover, the replacement of black and grey lists with a single list of priority substances 'is undoubtedly an important change', as is the commitment in the 1996 Action Plan to use risk assessment as an instrument of priority setting.[84] Most importantly, as Redgwell notes, 'Both the 1992 OSPAR Convention and the 1996 Protocol [to the London Dumping Convention] signalled a fundamental shift in regulatory approach, from 'permitted unless prohibited' to 'prohibited unless permitted'.[85] In that sense the current North Sea regime is much more precautionary and evolutionary in approach than its predecessor.[86]

The Mediterranean region is larger, and shows greater economic, social, and political diversity than the North Sea. Land-based pollution in this area is regulated by the 1980 Athens Protocol to the Barcelona Convention; a revised protocol was adopted in 1996, but is not yet in force.[87] Explicit recognition of the needs of developing states on the southern and eastern shores of this region has made it more difficult to achieve agreement on common standards.[88] In the Genoa Declaration of 1985, however, the parties committed themselves to a programme intended to lead to substantial reduction in industrial pollution and waste disposal, the provision of sewage treatment plants, and reductions in air pollution affecting the marine environment. Common measures have subsequently been adopted which set quality standards for bathing and shellfish waters and control emissions from some Annex 1 substances.

In 1990 the Conference on Security and Co-operation in Europe recommended that policies for controlling pollution of the Mediterranean should be guided by the polluter-pays principle and the 'precautionary approach', and it urged parties to the

---

[81] Ibid, 446. [82] See also Hey, IJlstra, and Nollkaemper, 8 *IJMCL* (1993) 1.

[83] Articles 9, 11, 22, 23, and Annex V (1998) and *supra*, Ch 7. There is no provision for public participation: cf 1999 Caribbean Protocol, Article X, and 1998 Aarhus Convention, *supra*, Ch 5.

[84] Pallemaerts, 13 *IJMCL* (1998) 439, 450.

[85] In Freestone, Barnes and Ong (eds), *The Law of the Sea* (Oxford, 2006) 188.

[86] Hey, 17 *IJMCL* (2002) 325, 348.

[87] See Pallemaerts, *Toxics and Transnational Law*, Ch 6; Scovazzi (ed), *Marine Specially Protected Areas: the General Aspects of the Mediterranean Regional System* (The Hague, 1999) Ch 7; Raftopoulos, *The Barcelona Convention and its Protocols* (London, 1993).

[88] Article 7.

Barcelona Convention to strengthen all aspects of its implementation, in particular by encouraging non-polluting methods of production and the reduction of waste generation.[89] Its conclusions recognized the inadequacy of progress made until then in protecting the Mediterranean environment and implementing the Athens protocol. The revised protocol adopted in 1996 incorporates many of these elements, and was intended as a response to UNCED, the 1994 Tunis Declaration on Sustainable Development in the Mediterranean, and the Washington Declaration and Global Plan of Action agreed in 1995. Its geographical scope is broadened to cover the entire hydrologic basin of the Mediterranean Sea. The parties undertake generally to 'eliminate' pollution from land-based sources and are specifically required to give priority to phasing out inputs of substances that are toxic, persistent, and liable to bioaccumulate. In doing so they must take account of factors listed in the protocol or its annexes, including, inter alia, best available techniques and practices, and clean technology, 'where appropriate'.[90] They are also expected to formulate and adopt common guidelines and standards on such matters as effluent treatment, water quality, and discharge concentrations. However these must take into account not only local conditions and existing pollution, but also, as we have seen, the economic capacity of the parties, and their development needs.[91] The obligation to eliminate and phase out pollution must therefore be read with these substantial qualifications in mind. The preamble suggests that this obligation must also be read with the precautionary principle in mind, but the only article on this is found in the revised Convention, not in the Protocol. The Convention's general provisions on sustainable development, the polluter-pays principle, integrated coastal-zone management, protection of areas of ecological importance, and conservation of natural resources are also relevant.[92] A non-compliance procedure included in the Convention is applicable to the protocol.[93] Finally, there is provision for monitoring and reporting on the effectiveness of measures taken. The existing Mediterranean Action Plan was also revised, and further programmes have since been adopted.

The 1996 protocol has been described as a compromise between environmentalist NGOs and the chemical industry, allowing binding measures and timetables to be adopted, while postponing phase-out of emissions until agreement can be reached.[94] Potentially the Protocol is stronger than its predecessor. Whether in practice it proves to be so will depend entirely on what decisions the parties are able to take.

The regional nature of these treaty regimes, the scope for national discretion in the administration of permits, the recognition of a double standard for developing countries, and the absence in some cases of regional agreement on specific standards sharply differentiate control of land-based pollution from the international regulation of pollution from ships, or from dumping. Apart from the obligation to eliminate a

---

[89]   CSCE/RMP 6, *Rept of the Meeting on the Mediterranean* (1990).

[90]   Article 5. Criteria for the definition of BAT and BEP are listed in Annex IV and are taken from the 1992 Paris Convention.

[91]   Article 7.   [92]   Article 4.   [93]   1995 Barcelona Convention, Article 27.

[94]   Article 15 and Scovazzi, *Marine Specially Protected Areas*, Ch 7.

flexible category of more harmful substances, regional agreements provide insufficient evidence of uniformity of practice to constitute an international or global standard, and suggest that the customary obligation to prevent marine pollution from land-based sources has remained essentially general in character, with little objective content. Its implementation remains dependent primarily on national action, regional cooperation, and further agreement. The slow progress of such cooperation indicates the continuing importance of industrial and economic factors in this sphere and the desire of states to balance those considerations against the needs to environmental protection.

3(3) EIA AND RISK AVOIDANCE

Regulation is only part of the answer to the problem of protecting the marine environment from land-based sources of pollution. Two procedural obligations are widely recognized in this context: prior environmental impact assessment, and monitoring of the environmental effects of any discharges.[95] These obligations assume particular importance in those regional seas where no agreement on coordinated regulatory standards exists, since in these cases they afford the only mechanism for limiting unilateral decisions which disregard impacts on the quality of the marine environment.

As we saw in Chapter 3, prior environmental impact assessment facilitates informed decisions. By enabling the risk of pollution to be identified in advance, it may give the state an opportunity to require measures to be taken which will prevent or mitigate this risk.[96] The view that such assessments are required by customary law for impacts on the marine environment is reinforced by the 1982 UNCLOS and regional agreements. Article 206 of the 1982 Convention provides:

When states have reasonable grounds for believing that planned activities under their jurisdiction or control may cause substantial pollution of or significant and harmful changes to the marine environment, they shall as far as practicable assess the potential effects of such activities on the marine environment and shall communicate reports of the results of such assessments [to the competent international organizations].

Article 206 is silent on the question of what is required in an EIA, and in contrast to Articles 207–11 it makes no reference to internationally agreed rules and standards. The evidential standard for showing the 'reasonable grounds' required for the application of Article 206 is unlikely to be an onerous one.[97] Some of the regional treaties

---

[95] 1978 Kuwait Convention, Articles 10, 11; 1981 Abidjan Convention, Articles 13, 14; 1983 Cartagena Convention, Articles 12, 13; 1982 Jeddah Convention, Articles 10, 11; 1985 Nairobi Convention, Articles 13, 14; 1986 Noumea Convention, Articles 16, 17; 1981 Lima Convention, Articles 8, 9; 1983 Quito Protocol, Articles 8, 9; 1990 Kuwait LBS Protocol, Articles 7, 8; 1992 OSPAR Convention, Annex I, Article 2; 1992 Helsinki Convention, Articles 3(5) 7; 1995 Barcelona Convention, Articles 4(3) 12; 1996 Mediterranean LBS Protocol, Article 8; 1999 Caribbean LBS Protocol, Articles 6, 7. Note that the OSPAR Convention makes no provision for prior impact assessment, but see *infra*, n 98.

[96] UNEP Montreal Guidelines, Article 12; 1986 Noumea Convention, Article 16(2); 1983 Cartagena Convention, Article 12(2).

[97] *Supra*, Ch 3, section 4.

refer only to 'major projects',[98] so there is some latitude for judgement in determining when the obligation arises and when 'reasonable grounds' exist. Although the Paris Convention does not explicitly mention prior assessment, or include such assessments in licensing criteria, EC law, the 1991 Espoo Convention on EIA in a Transboundary Context, and the practice of the states concerned make such an express provision unnecessary.[99]

Neither the 1982 UNCLOS nor UNEP's framework treaties require notification and prior consultation with other states likely to be affected by land-based sources of marine pollution. But such an obligation is recognized by the Paris Convention,[100] the Quito Protocol,[101] and by a few treaties dealing with offshore operations.[102] Such treaties cannot be explained by reference to obligations attending the use of 'shared natural resources', since they are not confined to enclosed or semi-enclosed seas, but illustrate the broader customary principle examined in Chapter 3 which requires notification and prior consultation in cases of transboundary risk. Moreover, we saw in Chapter 7 that 'the duty to cooperate is a fundamental principle in the prevention of pollution of the marine environment under Part XII of the Convention and general international law'.[103]

The more difficult question is how to apply this principle of 'good neighbourliness' to cases where harm to the marine environment is foreseen. Without exception, all the treaties call for states to monitor pollution and make reports to other parties through regional institutions.[104] Consistent support for this obligation is reflected in Article 204 of the 1982 UNCLOS. But in contrast to situations where other states are at risk, and regional commissions may recommend solutions to parties in dispute,[105] no prior consultation or dispute settlement is required by any of the treaties where only the marine environment is affected; at most, the reporting procedure enables meetings of the parties to review the effectiveness of measures adopted and press for remedial action: it does not give them a right to be consulted in advance.[106]

---

[98] 1985 Nairobi Convention, Article 13; 1983 Cartagena Convention, Article 12; 1986 Noumea Convention, Article 16. Compare 1981 Abidjan Convention, Article 13; 1983 Kuwait Convention, Article 11; 1981 Lima Convention, Article 8; 1995 Barcelona Convention, Article 4; 1999 Caribbean LBS Protocol, Article 7, which apply to 'any planned activity'. Article 7 of the Helsinki Convention applies only where an EIA 'is required by international law or supra-national regulations'.

[99] Paris Commission, 9th meeting 1987. See *supra*, Ch 3.   [100] Article 21.

[101] Article 12.

[102] 1986 Canada–Denmark Agreement for Cooperation Relating to the Marine Environment, Article 4; 1989 Kuwait Protocol on Marine Pollution from Exploration and Exploitation of the Continental Shelf, Article IV; 1994 Protocol for the Protection of the Mediterranean Sea Against Pollution Resulting from the Exploration and Exploitation of the Continental Shelf and Sea-bed, Article 26; and see also UNEP GC 9/5/ Add 5/Article III, Aspects Concerning the Environment Related to Offshore Drilling and Mining Within the limits of National Jurisdiction, 1981, Part E.

[103] *MOX Plant Case (Provisional Measures)* ITLOS No 10, para 82; *Land Reclamation Case (Provisional Measures)* ITLOS No 12, para 92.

[104] See 1982 UNCLOS, Articles 204, 205, and *supra*, n 98.

[105] 1992 Paris Convention, Article 21; 1983 Quito Protocol, Article 12; 1996 Mediterranean LBS Protocol, Article 12, which allow solutions to be recommended to parties in dispute.

[106] Cf 1989 Kuwait Offshore Protocol, Article 4, which requires prior impact assessment before the grant of a licence for offshore operations and calls for consultation with all other contracting states through the

These provisions on prior assessment and monitoring reflect relevant provisions of the 1982 UNCLOS, but they do not compare favourably with the stronger regimes of prior consent or prior assessment and consultation through international organizations found in the London Dumping Convention, the Basel Convention, or the POPS Convention. They do not fully reflect more recent endorsement of the 'precautionary principle' but are much closer to the procedures adopted in international watercourse agreements. This tends to confirm the earlier conclusion that controls on all sources of land-based pollution remain relatively underdeveloped, but generally consistent with customary principles.

3(4) RELATIONSHIP WITH THE LAW OF INTERNATIONAL WATERCOURSES

As we will see in Chapter 10, international watercourses are not only a source of transboundary pollution, but a major contributor to marine pollution. The development of regional regimes to regulate watercourse environments has many similarities to those now controlling land-based sources of pollution.[107] Nevertheless there are differences between the two categories, and coordination gives rise to certain problems. First, it is doubtful whether the concept of equitable utilization has a role in regulating the marine environment, in contrast to the law of international watercourses.[108] Although the obligation to protect the marine environment is not absolute, and allows a significant balancing of interests at various levels, this is not the same as saying that states need only prevent pollution which is inequitable or unreasonable, nor does it imply that abuse of rights is the conceptual basis for pollution control. None of the treaties, including the 1982 UNCLOS and those dealing with enclosed or semi-enclosed seas, supports reliance on equitable utilization or abuse of rights in this way. Second, equitable utilization is mainly concerned with reconciling the interests of riparians, not those of coastal states or of the international community. A system which looks only at riparian interests in individual rivers will fail to offer a basis for common regional standards of environmental protection focused on the needs of particular regional seas. Moreover, equitable utilization is defective in giving too little weight to environmental considerations among a range of other relevant circumstances.[109] Even when implemented by institutional arrangements, as in the Rhine, these are likely to represent the wrong states with the wrong perspective: that of riparian rights.

regional organization. This is aimed at protecting the marine environment as such, not merely other states. On dumping, see *infra*, section 3.

[107] See Pallemaerts, *Toxics and Transnational Law*, Ch 7.

[108] Boyle, 14 *Marine Policy* (1990) 151. Cf the now discarded ILC draft Article 17(2) on 'International Watercourses', and commentary, *Rept of the ILC*, 43rd Session (1988) UN Doc A/43/10, 6972 and compare 1997 UN Watercourses Convention, Article 23. The latter makes no reference to equitable utilization: see *Rept of the* (1990) UN Doc A/45/10, 169, and *supra*, Ch 10.

[109] See *infra*, Ch 10, and Kuwabara, *Protection of the Mediterranean Sea Against Pollution from Land-based Sources*, 34.

For all these reasons, the regional treaties on prevention of marine pollution from land-based sources offer a more appropriate and efficient approach to the problem of protecting the marine environment. Their institutional structure more readily accommodates a balance of interests between the needs of the source states, and the capacity of the marine environment to absorb polluting inputs, since states with a direct interest in use of the sea will be involved. One method of integrating the protection of international watercourses into this system is to create institutional links between watercourse and regional seas commissions, including representation of landlocked riparians and non-riparian coastal states in the appropriate regional bodies. The role played by the International North Sea Conference in securing Swiss participation, and in persuading the Rhine Commission to adopt protection of the marine environment as an objective, offers an example of this approach.[110] However, such links by themselves are insufficient; what must be emphasized is that the obligations of all states with regard to land-based pollution of the marine environment should be fully applied to international watercourses. European and Mediterranean practice follows this principle explicitly or implicitly.[111] In these cases primary responsibility for agreed measures remains with the relevant international watercourse commission, but riparians assume a responsibility for protecting the marine environment and a duty in customary law towards coastal states and other users of the adjacent seas.[112]

3(5) A GLOBAL REGIME FOR LAND-BASED SOURCES?

The preference of states for regional agreements to control land-based sources of pollution has meant that no global treaty comparable to the London Dumping Convention exists. In advance of the 1992 Rio Conference, several proposals were made for a new global instrument intended to strengthen the existing law on land-based sources of marine pollution and provide better institutional arrangements for coordinating regional action.[113] Agenda 21, Chapter 17 called on states to consider updating, strengthening, and extending the earlier 1985 Montreal Guidelines on Land-Based

---

[110] Burchi, 3 *Ital YIL* (1977) 133; Kwiatkowska, 14 *ODIL* (1984) 324 ff; 9th Ministerial Conference of the International Commission for the Protection of the Rhine, 1988. See Nollkaemper, 5 *IJECL* (1990) 125. Switzerland is not a party to the Paris Convention, but it is a party to the 1999 Rhine Convention, on which see *infra*, Ch 10.

[111] 1980 Athens Protocol and 1996 Revised Protocol, Article 11(1); 1992 Helsinki Convention, Article 6(4); 1992 OSPAR Convention, Annex 1, Article 2. At its 3rd meeting, the OSPAR Commission resolved that 'there was no doubt that the scope of the Convention included "such discharges into watercourses as affect the maritime area" and the setting of limit values for those discharges', PARCOM III/10/1. On the Black Sea, see Vinogradov, 22 IJMCL (2007) 585.

[112] Nollkaemper, 5 *IJECL* (1990) 123; Rémond-Gouilloud, in Johnston, *The Environmental Law of the Sea*, 236; 1997 UN Watercourses Convention, Article 23; 1994 Danube Convention, Preamble and Article 2; 1999 Rhine Convention, Article 3(5) and commentary, *infra*, Ch 10; *contra* Burchi, 3 *Ital YIL* (1977) 115, but his conclusion relies too heavily on the erroneous view that conventions on land-based sources do not apply to international watercourses.

[113] See *Rept of 13th Consultative Meeting*, IMO/LDC 13/15 (1990) Annex 4; Resolution LDC 40/13 (1990) and *Rept of the Intergovernmental Meeting of Experts on Land-based Sources of Marine Pollution*, UN Doc /A/CONF 151/PC/71, 3; UNEP proposals for a global convention, a non-treaty instrument, or a global

Sources of Marine Pollution, and UNEP was invited to convene a conference. The outcome was the adoption in 1995 of the Washington Declaration on the Protection of the Marine Environment from Land-based Activities,[114] together with a Global Programme of Action (GPA). In the Declaration, participating states reaffirmed the importance of integrated coastal zone and catchment area management, and their common intention to take 'sustained and effective action' to deal with all land-based impacts on the marine environment. Commitments included periodic intergovernmental review of the Global Programme of Action; making available funding for implementation; promoting access to clean technology; and giving priority to wastewater treatment.[115] However, the only legally binding global commitment specifically envisaged was the negotiation of a treaty on persistent organic pollutants, which it was recognized could not be addressed adequately on a regional basis.[116]

Like the North Sea Declarations, the Washington Declaration and Programme of Action provide some evidence of a political commitment to stronger action and an indication of agreed priorities. As we saw earlier, all these declarations may have had some influence on the further development of regional treaties and regimes. Nevertheless, the Washington Declaration and GPA fall well short of the initial proposals for a binding global treaty which several governments and NGOs had supported. The reasons for this are easy to identify. Developing countries did not see the need for stronger action. There was a widespread belief that the problems were regional rather than global and that differences between regions made a common global approach difficult. Many countries continued to prefer action at national, sub-regional or regional level, and viewed stronger global regulation as an interference in internal matters. For all these reasons it has been argued that 'the objective of a global legal instrument has turned out to be both unrealistic and indeed unnecessary'.[117] It is also true that higher standards of pollution control would not flow from a global treaty that merely reflected existing priorities, and that intergovernmental supervision of stronger political commitments in the Global Programme of Action does not necessarily require a treaty basis. A more sceptical view is that once again economic and industrial priorities have prevailed, making harmonization more difficult, and delaying a more significant transformation of the applicable international law.[118] In these respects the contrast with the evolution of international law relating to dumping is striking. There is nothing in the Washington Declaration or its subsequent history

---

convention and action plan, ibid, 10, and UNEP decision SS 11/6 (1990) calling for strengthened institutions, legal and other measures at regional and global level.

[114] UNEP (OCA)/MED IG 6/5, in 6 *YbIEL* (1995) 883. See Mensah, in Boyle and Freestone (eds), *International Law and Sustainable Development* (Oxford, 1999) Ch 13. For *travaux préparatoires* see reports of the Intergovernmental Meetings of Experts held at Halifax, 1991; Nairobi, 1993; Rekjavik, 1995. On subsequent implementation of the GPA see UN, *Rept of the Secretary General on Law of the Sea* (New York, 1999) and subsequent years.

[115] On the role of the GEF see Freestone, Barnes and Ong (eds), *The Law of the Sea*, Ch 16.

[116] *Supra*, section 2.

[117] Mensah, in Boyle and Freestone (eds), *International Law and Sustainable Development*, 312.

[118] Nollkaemper, 27 *ODIL* (1996) 153.

to suggest that it has in any way changed international law relating to pollution of the sea from land-based activities.

3(6) DUMPING AT SEA[119]

With limited exceptions, the dumping of waste at sea is now illegal. In 1972, the Stockholm Conference called for an international regime to regulate dumping,[120] and the London Dumping Convention was duly concluded in the same year. It was later supplemented by regional treaties, considered below. These precedents formed the basis for Articles 210 and 216 of the 1982 UNCLOS which require states to regulate and control pollution of the marine environment caused by dumping at sea, but do not prohibit it. A review of long-term strategy for the London Convention was initiated by the 13th Consultative Meeting.[121] In 1993 extensive revisions were made,[122] and in 1996 the Convention was replaced entirely by a new Protocol which has since entered into force for most of the industrialised world except Russia and the United States.[123] The revisions and the new protocol effectively put an end to dumping of potentially hazardous waste at sea or the export of such waste for dumping by non-parties. The global dumping regime has thus become one of the strongest applications of a precautionary approach to environmental risk. In effect, the London Convention has become a non-dumping convention whose only real challenge is to ensure that compliance is more fully monitored and effectively controlled.[124]

The existence and widespread ratification of a convention applicable to all marine areas outside internal waters means that dumping is the subject of a global regime, not primarily a regional one. Regional agreements were mainly of significance in imposing higher standards in enclosed or semi-enclosed seas in advance of the more general prohibition agreed in 1996. As indicated by Article 210 of the 1982 UNCLOS, this global regime is based on attainment of international minimum standards by all states, which limits their national discretion and makes no allowance for double standards or economic development.[125] Given its widespread ratification, it is clear that the London Dumping Convention provides these minimum international standards, and that it is to this Convention and its annexes that Article 210 of the 1982 UNCLOS refers.[126] In this respect, the legal regime of dumping is closer to the regulation of

---

[119] Churchill and Lowe, *The Law of the Sea* (3rd edn, Manchester, 1999) 363ff; Letalik, in Johnston (ed), *The Environmental Law of the Sea*, 217ff; de La Fayette, 13 *IJMCL* (1998) 515; Redgwell, in Freestone, Barnes and Ong (eds), *The Law of the Sea* (Oxford, 2006) Ch 10.

[120] Recommendation 86(c) Action Plan for the Human Environment.

[121] *Rept of 13th Consultative Meeting*, IMO/LDC 13/15 (1990).

[122] Birnie, 12 *IJMCL* (1997) 488, 514–31; Res LC 49(16); Res LC 50(16) Res LC 51(16) (1993) amending Annex 1. See also 1997 Waste Assessment Guidelines, which modify the application of Annex III.

[123] For drafting history see *Rept of 18th Consultative Meeting* (1996) para 5.

[124] de La Fayette, 13 *IJMCL* (1998) 515.

[125] 1982 UNCLOS, Article 210(6). For an account of the drafting of Article 210, see Nordquist, *Commentary*, iv, 15568.

[126] de La Fayette, 13 *IJMCL* (1998) 516; Redgwell, in Freestone, Barnes and Ong (eds), *The Law of the Sea*, 184–6.

pollution from ships than to pollution from land-based sources. Only a limited range of largely harmless matter may now be dumped under permit.[127] This is a much more stringent application of the precautionary principle than is found in most regional controls on land-based pollution. Finally, dumping is subject to supervision by an international forum, the London Convention Consultative Meeting, in addition to regional bodies.[128]

(a) Why prohibit dumping?

The major argument against dumping at sea is that it allows a small number of industrialized states acting for their own benefit to impose pollution risks on many others, perhaps extending into future generations.[129] While prior assessment of the risks involved, and of the suitability of sites, will minimize the possibility of future harm, it cannot eliminate scientific uncertainty or risk entirely. Like nuclear power or the carriage of oil by sea, the main issue is thus not solely the availability of less-harmful alternatives; rather, the acceptability of dumping depends significantly on the degree of risk, if any, which the international community is willing to accept without any countervailing benefit for potentially affected states. Treaty commitments have moved away from the view implicit in the original text of the London Convention that dumping at sea is permissible unless proven harmful. Following endorsement of the precautionary approach by the parties in 1992, leading to revision of the Convention in 1993 and explicit incorporation in Article 3(1) of the 1996 Protocol, as well as in regional treaties, the position now is that dumping is permissible only if there are no alternatives and it can be proven harmless to the environment, a significant reversal of the burden of proof.[130] Thus, the proposition that dumping remains in principle a legitimate use of the oceans, notwithstanding the possibility of disposal on land, and the possible risk to other states, is now untenable in the light of recent state practice and treaty commitments. In this context it is not inappropriate to draw conclusions concerning the development of customary law from the practice of parties to the London Convention and the various regional agreements. Those parties include nearly all the industrialized nations and a comparable number of developing states. There is no evidence, unusually, of any non-party dumping significant wastes at sea, or asserting a

---

[127] E.g. dredged material, sewage sludge, organic material, ships, platforms and other structures: see 1972 Convention, Annexes I and II as revised 1993; 1996 Protocol, Annex 1; 1992 OSPAR Convention, Annex II, Article 3; 1995 Barcelona Protocol, Article 4 (but sewage may not be dumped). Under the 1992 Helsinki Convention only dredged material may be dumped: see Article II and Annex V. Following the *Brent Spar* controversy, OSPAR Decision 98/3 (1998) prohibits parties from dumping disused offshore installations in the NE Atlantic and North Sea: see Kirk, 46 *ICLQ* (1997) 957; id, 48 *ICLQ* (1999) 458; de La Fayette, 13 *IJMCL* (1998) 522–6. The Helsinki Convention does not permit dumping of such installations in the Baltic.

[128] See *infra.*

[129] Boehmer-Christiansen, 10 *Marine Policy* (1986) 131; Bewers and Garrett, 11 *Marine Policy* (1987) 121f.

[130] LDC Res 44 (14); 1972 Convention, Annex I as revised 1993; 1996 Protocol, Articles 3(1), 4(1)(2) and Annex 2; 1997 Waste Assessment Guidelines; 1992 OSPAR Convention, Article 4; 1992 Helsinki Convention, Article 3 (2). See Hey, *The Precautionary Approach and the LDC*, published as LDC 14/4 (1991); de La Fayette, 13 *IJMCL* (1998) 515; Kirk, 46 *ICLQ* (1997) 957, and *supra*, Ch 3.

freedom to do so beyond that implied by the 1982 UNCLOS and the various global and regional instruments.

(b) What is 'dumping'?

Dumping is defined by the 1972 London Convention and the 1982 UNCLOS as the 'deliberate disposal at sea of wastes or other matter'.[131] It includes disposal of redundant ships, aircraft, or oil and gas platforms, including abandonment or toppling of these and other man-made structures at sea.[132] Discharges occurring in the normal operation of ships or platforms do not constitute dumping, nor, a fortiori, do accidental spillages. Incineration at sea is explicitly covered by the 1993 revisions and the 1996 Protocol, as is disposal 'in the sea-bed or subsoil', but only if accessed by vessels or structures 'at sea'.[133] However, amendments adopted in 2006 permit permanent carbon sequestration under the seabed in accordance with guidelines adopted by the parties. This will facilitate a possible method for reducing atmospheric CO_2 emissions from power stations and other industrial sources.[134]

(c) Radioactive waste dumping[135]

The need to find a safe medium for disposal of radioactive waste material is one of the more intractable problems of nuclear power. Disposal in Antarctica is forbidden by treaty;[136] disposal or reprocessing on land carries risks for the health of present and future generations. One response, initially adopted by several nuclear states including the UK, United States, and Japan, was to dump radioactive waste at sea. The 1972 London Convention for that reason prohibited the dumping only of high-level radioactive matter defined by IAEA as unsuitable for this form of disposal, and it permitted the dumping of low-level waste to be conducted subject to IAEA guidelines.[137] Some states regarded the IAEA standards as being unacceptably low, however, and applied

---

[131] 1972 Convention, Article 3(1); 1982 UNCLOS, Article 1(5); 1992 Helsinki Convention, Article 2(4); 1976 and 1995 Barcelona Protocol, Article 3. Compare 1972 Oslo Convention, Article 19 and 1996 Protocol to the London Convention, Article 1(4)(1) which define dumping as deliberate disposal 'into the sea', and 1992 OSPAR Convention, Article 1(f) which defines it as disposal 'in the maritime area' (emphasis added).

[132] 1972 Convention, Article 1(1) as interpreted by the Parties in *Rept of the 13th Consultative Meeting*, LDC 13/15, para 7.4; 1996 Protocol, Article 1(4); 1992 OSPAR Convention, Article 1(f); 1992 Helsinki Convention, Article 2(4); 1992 Black Sea Convention, Article 2; 1995 Barcelona Protocol, Article 4(2)(d).

[133] Article 1(4)(1). This definition appears exclude tunnelling from shore. See also 1986 Noumea Protocol, Article 10.

[134] See Scott, 18 *Georgetown IELR* (2005) 57.

[135] Hey, 40 *NILR* (1993) 405; Welsch, 28 *GYIL* (1985)322; Curtis, 14 *ODIL* (1984) 383; Mani, 24 *Indian JIL* (1984) 235; Van Dyke, 12 *Marine Policy* (1988) 82; Boehmer-Christiansen, 10 *Marine Policy* (1986) 119; Bewers and Garrett, 11 *Marine Policy* (1987) 121, review the scientific studies.

[136] 1959 Antarctic Treaty, Article 5; Recommendation VIII-12, 8th Antarctic Treaty Consultative Meeting, 1975; 1991 Antarctic Protocol, Annex III, Article 2.

[137] Annex 1, para 6; Annex II, para (d). The IAEA's definition and recommendations appear in IAEA Doc INFCIRC/205/Add 1 (1975) and INFCIRC/205/Add 1/Rev 1 (1978); see now IAEA, Safety Series No 78, *Definition and Recommendations for the Convention on the Prevention of Marine Pollution, etc* (Vienna, 1986) adopted 1986 at the 10th Consultative Meeting of the LDC.

their own more stringent rules. Regional practice was overwhelmingly opposed to radioactive dumping, particularly in enclosed or semi-enclosed seas.[138] Growing opposition among a majority of London Dumping Convention parties and pressure from NGOs led to a moratorium on all radioactive dumping at sea, pending further study.[139] In 1993 Annex I was amended, and the moratorium became binding on all parties, save for Russia, which eventually withdrew its objections in 2005.[140] All radio-active waste dumping is now prohibited under the 1996 Protocol.

(d) Licensing and enforcement

The essence of the London Convention and of the regional agreements is that per-mitted matter may not be dumped at sea without a prior permit issued by the relevant national authorities.[141] Both the 1996 Protocol and the Waste Assessment Guidelines adopted in 1997 by the parties to the 1972 Convention emphasize that the use of waste prevention techniques, the 'practical availability of other means of disposal', 'environmentally friendly alternatives', and the need for a 'comparative risk assess-ment involving both dumping and the alternatives' must be taken into account.[142] The guidelines state categorically that a permit to dump 'shall be refused' if there are opportunities to re-use, recycle or teat the waste without 'undue risks to human health or the environment or disproportionate costs'. Uncertainties in assessing impacts on the marine environment must be considered and the precautionary approach applied. The final judgement on the grant of permits rests with the national licens-ing authority. Moreover, since the object of the London Convention is to set min-imum standards of acceptable national regulation, it is open to licensing authorities to adopt additional criteria, or more stringent regulations, or to prohibit dumping altogether.[143] Primary responsibility for issuing permits rests with the state where the waste is loaded, regardless of the nationality of the ship or aircraft, or where the dumping is to take place. Vessels of parties to the convention cannot escape this pro-vision by loading in non-party states; in this case the flag state is required to act as a

---

[138] 1992 Helsinki Convention, Article 11; 1986 Noumea Convention, Article 10, (Article 11 also pro-hibits storage of radioactive wastes or matter in the Convention area); 1989 Protocol for the Protection of the South-East Pacific Against Radioactive Pollution; 1992 Black Sea Protocol, Article 2 and Annex 1; 1992 OSPAR Convention, Annex II, Article 3(3); 1995 Barcelona Protocol for the Prevention of Pollution by Dumping, Annex 1.

[139] LDC Resolution 14(7) 1983 and Resolution LDC 21(9) 1985. See Bewers and Garrett, 11 *Marine Policy* (1987) and Forster, 16 *EPL* (1986) 7.

[140] Resolution LC 51 (16); 1996 Protocol, Annex I. See de La Fayette, 13 *IJMCL* (1998) 515; IMO, *Rept of 21st Consultative Meeting*, LC 21/13 (1999) para 6.

[141] 1996 Protocol, Article 4; 1992 OSPAR Convention, Annex II, Article 4; 1992 Helsinki Convention, Annex V; 1992 Black Sea Protocol on Dumping, Articles 3, 4; 1995 Barcelona Protocol on Dumping, Articles 5, 6; 1986 Noumea Protocol on Dumping, Articles 5, 6.

[142] 1996 Protocol, Article 4(1)(2) and Annex 2; 1997 Guidelines for the Assessment of Wastes or Other Matter that May be Considered for Dumping. The 1997 Guidelines are largely identical to Annex 2 of the 1996 Protocol and in effect amend Annex III of the 1972 Convention. See de La Fayette, 13 *IJMCL* (1998) 521.

[143] 1996 Protocol, Articles 3(4), 4(2); 1982 UNCLOS, Article 210(1) and (6) and Commentary in UN, *Pollution by Dumping: Legislative History* (New York, 1985) 21.

licensing authority.[144] Moreover, since flag states will retain concurrent jurisdiction over their vessels,[145] they will have a right independent of the London Convention to regulate dumping notwithstanding the grant of a permit elsewhere.

It is also clear that no dumping may take place within the internal waters or territorial sea of another state without its consent; since no claim to innocent passage will be involved where dumping is under way, the coastal state will necessarily enjoy full jurisdiction over ships engaged in this activity.[146] Article 210(5) of the 1982 UNCLOS extends this principle of prior consent to dumping in the exclusive economic zone and on the continental shelf, in respect of which coastal states enjoy sovereign rights.[147] Coastal states thus have jurisdiction to issue licences, and to regulate or prohibit all dumping within 200 miles of their coast, after due consideration of the matter with other states which may be affected. Thus the main significance of the 1982 Convention with regard to dumping is that it gives coastal states a regulatory jurisdiction that was not expressly provided for in the London Convention, and which, as in the case of flag-state regulation, may be invoked notwithstanding the grant of a permit elsewhere. This conclusion is further strengthened by the Basel Convention on the Control of Transboundary Movement of Hazardous Waste which requires prior consent to be obtained from importing states before dumping at sea within their jurisdiction.[148] Despite its global status, the London Convention is not a complete code for the regulation of dumping; it must be read in conjunction with the jurisdiction conferred on coastal and flag states under other treaties and customary international law.

Jurisdiction to enforce laws relating to dumping follows the same pattern. Each party must take measures with respect to vessels or aircraft registered in its territory or flying its flag, or loading matter which is to be dumped, or believed to be engaged in dumping 'under its jurisdiction'.[149] The latter phrase can now be taken as a reference to dumping inside territorial waters, the territorial sea, exclusive economic zone, or continental shelf, as provided for in Article 216 of the 1982 UNCLOS.[150] Both conventions are imperative in requiring states to enforce laws on dumping.[151]

---

[144] 1996 Protocol, Article 9(2); 1992 Helsinki Convention, Article 11; 1992 Black Sea Protocol, Annex V; 1995 Barcelona Protocol on Dumping, Article 10(2); 1986 Noumea Protocol on Dumping, Article 11(2). The OSPAR Convention refers only to 'the appropriate national authority' without definition.

[145] *The Lotus Case,* PCIJ Ser A, No 10 (1927); 1982 UNCLOS, Article 211(2); 1996 Protocol, Article 10(1).

[146] 1982 UNCLOS, Articles 18, 19(2)(h), 210(5), and *supra*, Ch 7. Note that the application of the 1996 Protocol to internal waters is restricted by Article 7.

[147] 1982 UNCLOS, Articles 55–7; *Libya–Malta Continental Shelf Case,* ICJ Reports (1985) 13; *North Sea Continental Shelf Case,* ICJ Reports (1969) 3.

[148] See *infra*, section 4.

[149] 1996 Protocol, Article 10(1); 1992 OSPAR Convention, Article 10(1); 1992 Black Sea Protocol, Article 8; 1995 Barcelona Protocol on Dumping, Article 11; 1986 Noumea Protocol on Dumping, Article 12. Cf 1992 Helsinki Convention, Article 11, which does not extend coastal state powers beyond the outer limit of the territorial sea.

[150] Article 216(1)(a); UN, *Pollution By Dumping,* 15–17, 29; 1972 London Convention, Article 13; Letalik, in Johnston, *The Environmental Law of the Sea*, 224. The Black Sea Protocol is the only one to refer expressly to the EEZ.

[151] cf Article 216(2) of the 1982 UNCLOS, however: 'No state shall be obliged by virtue of this article to institute proceedings when another state has already instituted proceedings in accordance with this article.'

There is little doubt that these provisions reflect customary law, including the evo-lution of the exclusive economic zone and extension of coastal state jurisdiction, con-current with that of the flag state. However, they leave open the question of high-seas enforcement. Since port-state enforcement jurisdiction is confined to cases of actual loading, it will not cover high-seas dumping.[152] Beyond the EEZ, or in cases where the coastal state does not claim jurisdiction, only the flag state will have jurisdiction to enforce dumping regulations and, as we saw in Chapter 7, this may often be an inef-fective remedy.

(e) Regional treaties

Both the London Dumping Convention and the 1982 UNCLOS accept the possibility of regional arrangements for the control of dumping.[153] Article 8 of the London Convention refers in particular to parties 'with common interests to protect in the marine environment in a given geographical area', and allows them to take account of characteristic regional features. Regional agreements may set higher standards, but must be consistent with the global requirements of the London Convention. Regional agreements or protocols apply in the North-East Atlantic and North Sea, the Baltic, the Mediterranean, the Black Sea, and the South Pacific, areas which are mostly enclosed or semi-enclosed seas and in which dumping may cause special problems.[154] As we have already seen, most of the applicable treaties and protocols are fully consistent with the revised London Convention and the 1996 Protocol. The African Convention on Transboundary Movement of Hazardous Waste also prohibits all dumping of haz-ardous waste at sea by the parties and within the parties' maritime zones.[155]

In all other respects the regional treaties are modelled closely on the London Convention, including their licensing, enforcement, and supervision arrangements. By adding an additional level of institutional supervision they provide a more immediate focus for ensuring compliance, but it seems clear that unlike the control of land-based pollution of the sea, one of the factors which has made the control of dumping effect-ive is the interplay of global and regional rules and institutions. This does suggest that however strong the case for regional arrangements to cater for special circumstances, these are best located within a clear global framework of minimum standards of suf-ficient stringency, reinforced by the wider community pressure which a body such as the Consultative Meeting of the parties to the London Convention can provide.

---

[152] 1982 UNCLOS, Article 216(1)(c); 1996 Protocol, Article 10(1). UNCLOS Article 218, which confers port-state jurisdiction over high seas pollution 'discharges' from ships, would not appear to apply to 'dump-ing'. See *supra*, Ch 7. However, 1996 Protocol, Article 10(3) and 1992 OSPAR Convention, Article 10(2) envisage cooperation and reporting procedures for high-seas dumping.

[153] London Convention, Article 8; 1996 Protocol, Article 12; 1982 UNCLOS, Article 210(4).

[154] 1995 Barcelona Protocol for the Prevention of Pollution of the Mediterranean Sea by Dumping from Ships and Aircraft; 1986 Noumea Protocol for the Prevention of Pollution by Dumping; 1992 OSPAR Convention; 1992 Black Sea Convention.

[155] Article 4(2). See also 1995 South Pacific Regional Convention on Hazardous Wastes, Article 4(3) although this merely reaffirms commitments under other treaties.

3(7) ASSESSING THE LONDON DUMPING CONVENTION

The London Dumping Convention is generally regarded as one of the more success-ful regulatory treaties of the 1970s. A report prepared by IMO in 1991[156] attributed reductions in dumping at sea to the efforts of contracting parties to find alternative disposal methods, to recycle wastes, and to use cleaner technology, and it concluded that the Convention had provided an effective instrument for the protection of the marine environment. Since then decisions taken by the parties with regard to incin-eration and radioactive and industrial waste have strengthened this trend towards elimination of dumping at sea as a method of waste disposal. Another measure of the Convention's relative success is the number of regional agreements which now supple-ment its global provisions.

In Chapter 2 we noted that one of the main reasons for the Convention's evolu-tion in this way has been the range and diversity of parties participating in regular consultative meetings. The Consultative meeting has been notably successful in gen-erating international consensus on the development of policy for dumping at sea. It has facilitated the adoption of increasingly stringent standards, and enabled a wider community of states not engaged in this activity to apply pressure on those who are involved to moderate or abandon practices which posed a risk to the marine environ-ment. It has also provided a forum for resolving disputed issues, such as sub-seabed disposal of radioactive waste. Only about forty parties regularly participate in con-sultative meetings, but among these there is an approximate balance of industrial-ized and developing states. It cannot be said that the Convention is of interest only to industrialized nations, and even some of these, such as the Scandinavian states, have long been opposed to dumping as a method of waste disposal. Although membership is thus far from universal, the Convention is plainly not controlled by pro-dumping states, nor is there evidence that significant dumping is practised by non-parties. Moreover, the involvement of NGOs has been an important feature of the Consultative Meetings, enabling environmental and industry groups to lobby members and pro-vide expert advice for the delegations of several states. Greenpeace and ACOPS have been particularly active and effective in pressing for development of the Convention and in bringing to the attention of parties evidence of violations, such as the alleged dumping of radioactive waste by the USSR disclosed at the 14th Consultative Meeting in 1991.[157] As this example shows, the consultative meetings were able to exercise some control over compliance under the 1972 Convention, despite the absence of a formal non-compliance procedure, but the 1996 Protocol now provides for one.[158] In practice, therefore, the Convention has largely achieved its objective of establishing a global framework for international action.

---

[156] UNCED Prepcom, UN Doc A/CONF 151/PC/31 (1991).

[157] On progress in eliminating further Russian dumping see *Rept of the 21st Consultative Meeting*, paras 6.15–6.22, and Stokke, in Victor et al (eds), *Implementation and Effectiveness of International Environmental Commitments* (Cambridge, Mass, 1998) Ch 11.

[158] Article 11. A compliance procedure was adopted in 2007. See *Rept of the 29th Consultative Meeting*, LC 29/17 (2007) para 5 and Annex 7.

4 INTERNATIONAL TRADE IN HAZARDOUS SUBSTANCES

4(1) THE PERMISSIBILITY OF TRADE IN HAZARDOUS WASTES AND SUBSTANCES

It is undoubtedly the transboundary impact of disposal of hazardous waste which underlies the regime of shared responsibility found in the 1988 Basel Convention and regional conventions dealing with this subject.[159] Unlike state practice in the case of nuclear installations, air pollution, or international watercourses, where the polluting state's freedom of action is limited only by its obligations of due diligence, notification and prior consultation, the Basel convention firmly asserts the sovereignty of the receiving state to determine what impacts on its territory it will accept. Above all, the principle of prior informed consent on which it is based points to an important difference in approach. It cannot now be assumed that waste disposal in other states is permissible unless shown to be harmful. Instead, a strong form of the precautionary approach obliges the export state to demonstrate that the wastes will be managed in an 'environmentally sound manner'.

Prior to the 1992 Rio Conference, international policy declarations disclosed differing views on the permissibility of trade in hazardous waste. Industrialized economies represented in OECD and the EC accepted that production of hazardous wastes should be minimized as far as possible, that disposal should take place within member states where consistent with environmentally sound management, and that trade in wastes should be reduced and should take place on a basis of prior notification and environmentally sound management. Nevertheless, developed states did not seek to eliminate transboundary disposal entirely.[160] Regional groupings of developing states, in contrast, condemned all trade involving export of waste from developed to developing countries for disposal in their territories.[161] Their belief was that regulation

---

[159] Handl and Lutz, 30 *Harv ILJ* (1989) 351; Kummer, *International Management of Hazardous Wastes: The Basel Convention and Related Legal Rules* (Oxford, 1995); Louka, *Overcoming Barriers to International Waste Trade* (Dordrecht, 1995); Bitar, *Les Mouvements Transfrontières de Déchets Dangereux Selon la Convention de Bâle* (Paris, 1997); Hackett, 5 *AUJILP* (1990) 291; Bothe, 33 *GYIL* (1990) 422; Desai, 37 *Indian JIL* (1997) 43.

[160] OECD, Recommendation C(76) 155; Decision/Recommendation C(83) 180; Resolution C(85) 100; Decision/Recommendation C(86)64; Decision C(88) 90; Resolution C(89) 112; Decisions C(90) 178; C(92)39; C(2001)107; EC, Regulation 259/93; 1986 Canada–US Agreement on the Transboundary Movement of Hazardous Waste; 1986 US–Mexico Agreement Regarding Transboundary Shipments of Hazardous Wastes and Substances. On OECD, EC and North American practice see Kummer, *International Management of Hazardous Wastes*, 113–71.

[161] ACP/EEC Joint Assembly, Madrid, 1988; ECOWAS, 11th Summit, Lomé, 1988; Final Document of the First Meeting of States of the Zone of Peace and Cooperation in the South Atlantic, Rio, 1988; Organization of African Unity, Resolution CM/Res 1153, 28 *ILM* (1989) 567. Developing states which have prohibited waste imports include Haiti, Constitution, Article 391; 258; Ivory Coast, Law on Toxic and Nuclear Waste, 1988, 28 *ILM* (1989) Gambia, Environmental Protection Act, 1988, 29 *ILM* (1990) 208; Nigeria, Decree No 42, 1988,

would merely legitimise an unacceptable practice. Among the strongest exponents of this view was the Organization of African Unity, which declared dumping of nuclear and industrial wastes a crime against the African people, and called on African states not to accept waste from industrialized countries. OAU policy is reflected in the 1991 African Convention on Transboundary Movements of Hazardous Wastes, which prohibits imports into Africa from non-parties and regulates trade in waste among African states.[162] Regional treaties covering the Mediterranean and the South Pacific also prohibit export of hazardous waste to developing state parties and small island state parties respectively, and ban imports by those states.[163] In addition, the fourth Lomé Convention, concluded in 1989, committed the EC to prohibit exports of radioactive or hazardous waste to any African, Caribbean, or Pacific Island states parties, and prohibited those states from importing such waste from the EC or from anywhere else.[164]

Like OECD, UNEP policy in promoting a global agreement initially preferred effective control of the waste trade rather than prohibition. Its Cairo Guidelines[165] acknowledged the need to respect international law applicable to protection of the environment, and sought to ensure environmentally sound management of wastes. They formed the basis for the main international regulatory regime, the Basel Convention on the Control of Transboundary Movements of Hazardous Wastes and their Disposal. Although unable to secure a trade ban, African states participated in the Basel negotiations, and their proposals on specific points were accepted.[166] The Basel Convention quickly attracted widespread support from over one hundred developed and developing countries, including many African states.

The Rio Conference did not support a ban on waste trade with developing countries. Nevertheless, Principle 14 called on all states to discourage or prevent transboundary transfer of substances hazardous to health or the environment. In 1994, developing countries, supported by Greenpeace, persuaded the 2nd Conference of the Parties to the Basel Convention to agree to ban the export from OECD countries of hazardous waste destined for disposal or recycling in non-OECD countries. This

---

Article 1; Togo, Environmental Code, 1988; Lebanon, Act No 64/88 (1988); see also Ghana, declaration on signature of Final Act of Basel Convention. UNEP/CHW 4/Inf 7 (1997) also lists Argentina, Brazil, Bahamas, Barbados, China, Colombia, Cyprus, Ecuador, Egypt, India, Iran, Jordan, Maldives, Oman, Panama, Peru, Philippines, Qatar, Singapore and Zambia.

[162] 21 *EPL* (1991) 66. See also the comparable 1992 Central American Agreement on the Transboundary Movement of Hazardous Wastes, Article 3(1). See Kummer, *International Management of Hazardous Wastes*, 99–103; Biggs, 5 *Colorado JIELP* (1994) 333.

[163] 1996 Mediterranean Protocol on Transboundary Movement of Hazardous Waste; 1995 Waigani Convention on Hazardous Wastes within the South Pacific Region. For a survey of regional agreements see UNEP/CHW 4/Inf 12 (1998).

[164] Article 39, and Annexes VIII–X, 29 *ILM* (1990) 783. See Kummer, *International Management of Hazardous Wastes*, 107–12.

[165] Cairo Guidelines and Principles of Environmentally Sound Management of Hazardous Wastes, 1985, UNEP/WG 122/3; 16 *EPL* (1986) 5, 31, approved by UNEP/GC 14/30 (1987).

[166] UNEP, *Proposals and Position of the African States During Negotiations on the Basel Convention* (1989); Dakar Ministerial Conference on Hazardous Wastes, 1989.

decision was formally incorporated in the Convention by amendment the following year, but in 2007 it had not yet entered into force.[167] If it does, OECD states parties to the amended Convention will thus have accepted that export to developing states of hazardous wastes covered by the ban will not normally constitute environmentally sound management. The ban will apply only to an agreed list of hazardous wastes,[168] but it makes no distinction between disposal of waste and recycling, nor does it distinguish between developing states which possess adequate waste disposal or recycling facilities and those which do not. The ban has been implemented by the EC, so transboundary export from Europe to any developing state party will be an offence.

It does not follow that all trade in waste involving developing countries will be prohibited. The wording of Article 4A would appear to ban export from OECD state parties to any non-OECD state,[169] whether or not the latter has accepted the amendment. However, under the Basel Convention, the African Convention, and the South Pacific Convention, trade in waste among developing states parties is not prohibited, nor is export from these states to developed states parties. It is important also to remember that those OECD states which have not accepted the ban amendment may continue to export waste to developing state parties, provided those states comply with the other requirements of the Basel Convention. Moreover, Article 11 of the Basel Convention permits parties to conclude regional agreements with other parties *or non-parties*, provided these agreements 'do not derogate from the environmentally sound management of hazardous wastes and other wastes as required by this Convention'. If they meet this standard,[170] and comply with the notice requirements of Article 11(2) developing state parties will be able under such agreements to continue to import waste from non-party developed states, although many of them will be debarred from doing so under regional agreements or the Lomé Convention.

In the absence of a wider consensus among exporting and importing states, it cannot be said that a policy of ending all trade in hazardous wastes has prevailed at a global level, nor that all waste exports to developing countries are illegal. What has been achieved is a compromise that places three important and far-reaching restrictions on this trade. First, as the 1991 African Convention indicates, it is clear that all states have the sovereign right to ban imports individually or regionally and that this right

---

[167] Decision II/12, *Rept of 2nd COP*, UNEP/CHW 2/30 (1994); Decision III/1, *Rept of 3rd COP*, UNEP/CHW 3/35 (1995) inserting new preambular paragraph 7bis, new Article 4A, and new Annex VII. Only Russia expressly refused to accept the ban, but the United States is also opposed, although not a Basel party. For background see Kitt, 7 *Georgetown IELR* (1995) 485.

[168] See Decision IV/9, adding new annexes VIII and IX, *Rept of 4th COP*, UNEP/CHW 4/35 (1998).

[169] I.e. to 'any state not listed in Annex VII'. The only parties so listed are OECD states, Liechtenstein and the EC. Some states have argued that other non-OECD parties might be added.

[170] It might be argued that a developing state which accepts the ban amendment thereby also accepts that it may not meet the standard of environmentally sound management with regard to waste from OECD states and, if so, that it will be in breach of its obligations under the Convention if it accepts such imports, even if trade takes place under an Article 11 agreement. See Crawford and Sands, *The Availability of Article 11 Agreements in the Context of the Basel Convention's Export Ban on Recyclables* (ICME, Ontario, 1997) 22. See also de La Fayette, 6 *YbIEL* (1995) 703 and Kummer, *International Management of Hazardous Wastes*, Ch 3.

is recognized in the Basel Convention and by OECD states.[171] The Basel Convention further strengthens this right to prohibit trade in waste by providing for import bans to be notified to other parties through the secretariat; no state may then permit transboundary movement of wastes to a party prohibiting their import nor, save by special agreement, is transport for disposal by non-parties permitted.[172]

Second, transboundary movement is permitted only in circumstances where the state of export does not have the capacity or facilities to dispose of the wastes in an environmentally sound manner itself, unless intended for recycling. To this end, the Basel Convention is based on a philosophy of minimizing the generation of hazardous waste and promoting disposal at source. The African, South Pacific, and Mediterranean Conventions place additional emphasis on the use of clean production methods 'which avoid or eliminate the generation of hazardous wastes'. They represent the strongest indication of the growing international emphasis on waste disposal at source and the adoption of a precautionary approach to pollution control.[173]

Lastly, the Basel and regional conventions demonstrate widespread agreement that trade which does take place requires the prior informed consent of transit and import states,[174] that illegal trade must be prevented, that illegally exported waste should be accepted for reimport by the state of origin,[175] and that conditions of management, transport, and ultimate disposal must be compatible with the protection of health, the environment, and the prevention of pollution.[176]

These principles probably already represent customary law, since they are supported in part by state practice, by the sovereign right of states to control activities in their own territory, and by the responsibility of exporting states for activities within their jurisdiction which harm other states or the global environment.[177] By also placing on importing states an obligation of environmentally sound management,[178] the Basel Convention recognizes that they too have a responsibility in international law for the

---

[171] Basel Convention, Preamble, and Declaration annexed to the Final Act of the Basel Conference, 1989. See also OECD Decision C(83) 180, Preamble; African Convention, Article 4(1). Some 107 states were reported to have banned waste imports by 1995.

[172] Articles 4(1), (2)(e), (5), 7, 11, 13. See also OECD Decision C(83) 180, Principle 8; Decision C(86) 64, para I, and African Convention, Article 4(3)(11).

[173] Basel Convention, Preamble and Articles 4(2)(a),(b),(d), 4(5), (9); Cairo Guidelines, Principle 2; African Convention, Preamble, and Articles 1(5) and 4(3); South Pacific Convention, Article 4(4); Mediterranean Protocol, Articles 5, 6; OECD Recommendation C(76) 155, Annex, Para 3; UNGA Res 43/212 (1988) 19 *EPL* (1989) 29; OECD Decision C(90) 178, and Recommendation C(90) 164.

[174] Basel Convention, Article 6; African Convention, Articles 4, 6, 7; South Pacific Convention, Article 6; Mediterranean Protocol, Article 6(3). See also OECD Decision C(86) 64, para I; Council Regulation COM (90) 415 Final; UNGA Res 43/212 (1988).

[175] Basel Convention, Article 9; African Convention, Article 9; South Pacific Convention, Articles 8, 9; Mediterranean Protocol, Articles 7, 9. See also OECD Decision C(83) 180, Principle 9; UNGA Res. 43/212 (1988).

[176] Basel Convention, Preamble and Articles 4(2)(c)–(e), (g), 7, 8; African Convention, Article 4. See also OECD Decision C(83) 180.

[177] Handl and Lutz, 30 *Harv ILJ* (1989) 359–60; Kummer, *International Management of Hazardous Wastes*, Ch 7; UNGA Res 43/212 (1988); 1985 Cairo Guidelines, Principle 2.

[178] Article 4.

protection of their own environment, peoples, and future generations, and it makes their management of imported waste a matter of legitimate international concern. Uniquely, the Basel Convention is thus based on a system of environmental responsibility shared among all states involved in each transaction.

4(2) THE SCOPE OF THE BASEL CONVENTION

The Basel Convention is concerned only with household and hazardous waste disposed of or intended for disposal.[179] 'Disposal' is defined in broad terms.[180] It includes landfill, release into watercourses, the sea, or seabed, incineration, permanent storage, or recycling. One consequence is that the Basel Convention will apply to waste exported for dumping in coastal state maritime zones where, as we have seen, Article 210(5) of the 1982 UNCLOS already requires coastal state consent.[181] Wastes are 'hazardous' only when listed in the Convention's annexes, or if defined as such by national law and notified to the Convention's Secretariat.[182] Radioactive wastes are excluded because they are covered by other arrangements.[183] So are wastes derived from the 'normal operations of a ship', thus enabling oil or chemical cargo residues to be discharged to a port reception facility if in accordance with the MARPOL Convention.[184] Unlike the London Dumping Convention, there are no categories of hazardous waste which may not be exported. OECD's definition follows the same pattern, but allows for bilateral or unilateral departure from the basic classification.[185] The Basel Convention acknowledges no such freedom but instead sets an obligatory minimum standard for states.[186]

Trade in hazardous substances not intended for disposal is not regulated by the Basel Convention, although the African Convention does apply where substances have been banned, refused registration, or voluntarily withdrawn in the country of manufacture for health and environmental reasons. With this exception the main legal constraints are those supplied by customary law, non-binding instruments such as UNEP's Guidelines for the Exchange of Information on Chemicals in International Trade or FAO's Code of Conduct on the Distribution and Use of Pesticides, and the 1998 Convention on the Prior Informed Consent Procedure for Certain Hazardous Chemicals and Pesticides in International Trade.[187] Like the earlier guidelines, the latter convention provides further evidence that international law recognizes the shared responsibility of importing and exporting states for the protection of health and the environment, and an obligation of good neighbourliness.

---

[179] Articles 1, 2(1), Annexes I, II.   [180] Article 2(4) and Annex IV.
[181] See *supra*, section 3.
[182] Article 3. Cf the African Convention, Article 2, which is broader than the Basel definition.
[183] See *supra*, Ch 9. The African and South Pacific Conventions do cover nuclear waste.
[184] Article 1(4). On MARPOL see *supra*, Ch 7.   [185] Decision C(88) 90, 28 *ILM* (1989) 257.
[186] Article 1(1).   [187] *Supra*, section 2(2).

4(3) THE REQUIREMENT OF PRIOR INFORMED CONSENT

Only rarely does international law require the prior consent of other states before environmentally harmful activities may be undertaken. As we saw in Chapter 3 the *Lac Lanoux Case* expressly rejects such a rule for the use of shared resources, nor does it normally apply to pollution of common spaces. In these cases, prior informed consultation at most is called for.[188] Unusually, the essence of the control system established by the Basel Convention is the need for prior, informed, written consent from transit states and the state of import.[189] Only in the case of transit states which are parties to the Convention can this requirement be waived in favour of tacit acquiescence.[190] Information must be supplied which is sufficient to enable the nature and effects on health and the environment of the proposed movement to be assessed.[191]

There are two ways in which the requirement of prior informed consent is enforced. The first is by making the state of export accept the return of illegal waste where practicable or, where the importer is at fault, imposing on the state of import a duty to ensure safe disposal of the waste.[192] There is some evidence that state practice already favours the return of illegally exported waste to the state of origin, as in the case of the *Karin B*, whose cargo Italy was obliged to accept back.[193] The second method employed by the Basel Convention is to ensure that states punish illegal traffic as a criminal offence.[194] It is possible that this provision might justify an extraterritorial protective jurisdiction over foreign nationals engaged in the illegal export of hazardous waste to a country which has prohibited its import.[195] This would provide an additional enforcement mechanism where the exporting state's procedures are lax or inadequate. One difficulty with these otherwise salutary enforcement rules is the possibility that they may result in illegal dumping at sea; the phasing out of dumping at sea will resolve this difficulty, however.[196] Another problem is the qualified nature of the duty to reimport: 'impracticability' is a vague and subjective notion which the exporting state itself is left to interpret. Once again the African Convention is stronger: Article 9 simply compels the exporting state to ensure that illegal waste is taken back within thirty days, without reference to practicality.

The requirement of prior consent, as we have seen, is simply an expression of the sovereignty of a state over the use of its territory and resources. It is this which differentiates transboundary disposal of wastes from the use of common spaces or shared resources. Where transit takes place through maritime areas, however, no such basis

---

[188] See *supra*, Ch 3, section 4(3) and *infra*, Ch 10.

[189] Articles 4(1)(c), 4(2)(f), 6(1)–(2), 6(10), 7.   [190] Article 6(4).

[191] Articles 4(2)(f), 6(1), and Annex V.

[192] Basel Convention, Article 9; African Convention, Article 9; Mediterranean Protocol, Article 7; South Pacific Treaty, Article 8.

[193] UK House of Lords, *2nd Rept of the Environment Committee on Toxic Waste*, i (1988–9) para 253; Handl and Lutz, 30 *Harv ILJ* (1989) 360; Weinstein, 9 *IJMCL* (1994) 135.

[194] Articles 4(3)–(4), 9(5). See also African Convention, Article 4(1); Mediterranean Protocol, Article 9(2); South Pacific Treaty, Article 9(2).

[195] *The Lotus Case*, PCIJ Ser A, No 10 (1927) 28.   [196] *Supra*, section 3.

in territorial sovereignty exists. In the exclusive economic zone, foreign vessels enjoy high-seas freedom of navigation.[197] In the territorial sea, although subject to coastal state sovereignty, they have a right of innocent passage.[198] Ships carrying dangerous or noxious substances in the territorial sea may be confined to the use of designated sea lanes and are required to carry documents and observe special precautionary measures established by international agreement, but they do not lose their rights of passage, and may not be discriminated against.[199] Article 4(12) of the Basel Convention appears to leave these navigational rights in the EEZ and territorial sea unaffected. In general, maritime states have interpreted this to mean that prior notice or consent for the passage of vessels carrying hazardous wastes or substances is not required, but not all coastal states accept this view.[200] As with oil tankers, the more convincing conclusion is that the passage of ships carrying dangerous cargoes may be regulated by coastal states according to international standards, but these vessels cannot unilaterally be excluded from exercising their rights of navigation, despite the risk they pose.[201] However, in appropriate circumstances the designation of Particularly Sensitive Sea Areas, areas to be avoided, traffic lanes and compulsory pilotage schemes, inter alia, will allow passage to be controlled.[202]

4(4) ENVIRONMENTALLY SOUND MANAGEMENT

The primary obligation imposed by the Basel Convention is to manage the transboundary movement of waste in an environmentally sound manner. This obligation applies to exporting, transit, and importing states alike,[203] and also to trade with non-parties, which may only be conducted under an agreement providing for management no less environmentally sound than is required by the Convention.[204] The crucial point is that states must not permit export or import of waste if they believe that it will not be handled in an environmentally sound manner.[205] Developing states do not escape this responsibility for sound management of imported waste; if they cannot meet it, they must either seek assistance, relying on the Convention's provisions for international

[197] 1982 UNCLOS, Article 58.

[198] 1958 Convention on the Territorial Sea and Contiguous Zone, Articles 1, 14–17; 1982 UNCLOS, Articles 2, 17–21; *Corfu Channel Case*, ICJ Reports (1949) 3.

[199] 1982 UNCLOS, Articles 22–5; 1958 Convention on the Territorial Sea and Contiguous Zone, Article 16(3). Documentation and special precautionary measures are required by the 1973/78 MARPOL Convention for oil, noxious liquids, and chemicals in bulk.

[200] See e.g. the British declaration on the Basel Convention, 39 *ICLQ* (190) 944, but *contra*, Haiti *Note Verbale* of 18 Feb 1988, 11 *LOSB* (1988) 13, and Article 6(4) of the 1996 Mediterranean Protocol. Article 4(4)(c) of the African Convention recognizes 'the exercise by ships and aircraft of all states of navigation rights and freedoms as provided for in international law and as reflected in relevant international instruments'. Article 2(5) of the 1995 South Pacific Treaty preserves rights and obligations under UNCLOS.

[201] 1982 UNCLOS, Articles 21(2), 211; but see Pineschi, in Francioni and Scovazzi (eds), *International Responsibility for Environmental Harm* (Dordrecht, 1991) 299.

[202] See *supra*, Ch 7, section 4(3).   [203] Article 4.

[204] Articles 4(5) and 7 as qualified by Article 11. Article 6 of the 1996 Protocol to the London Dumping Convention prohibits export of waste for dumping at sea by non-parties.

[205] Articles 4(2)(e), (g), and 4(8); African Convention, Article 4(3)(n).

co-operation, or prohibit the import.[206] Nor can the exporting state escape its obligations by transferring responsibility to the state of transit or import; wherever the waste
is sent the exporting state retains a responsibility for ensuring its proper management
at all stages until final disposal, and must permit reimport if necessary.[207]

What is meant by 'environmentally sound management' is defined in the Convention
only in general terms: 'taking all practicable steps to ensure that hazardous waste or
other wastes are managed in a manner which will protect human health and the environment against the adverse effects which may result from such wastes'.[208] More detailed
guidance is given in guidelines adopted by the parties.[209] These guidelines explain
what the parties mean by 'environmentally sound management', and are intended to
be a point of reference for the development of national waste-management strategies.
The principal aims of the Convention are reiterated, including waste prevention and
minimization, least transboundary movement, recycling, self-sufficiency and proximity of disposal. Criteria to be used in assessing the soundness of waste-management
standards include the following: whether the regulatory and enforcement infrastructure can ensure compliance, whether waste sites are authorized and of adequate standard to deal with the waste in question, whether operators of waste sites are adequately
trained, whether sites are monitored, and whether waste generation is minimized
through best practice and clean production methods. What is environmentally sound
in the country of import may also depend on the level of technology and pollution
control available in the exporting country: the implication is that it is unlikely to be
environmentally sound to import waste from states with higher standards of waste
disposal.[210] Additional guidance is provided for wastes identified as requiring priority
attention. Although these guidelines are not obligatory, their adoption by the parties
gives them persuasive force as a basic standard for states to meet in fulfilling their obligations under the Basel Convention. As such they have a legal significance comparable
to IAEA guidelines for the disposal of radioactive waste.

International standards for the carriage of dangerous goods also govern some
aspects of the transport of hazardous waste.[211] In some cases, such as annexes to the

---

[206] Articles 4(2)(g) and 10; Handl and Lutz, 30 *Harv ILJ* (1989) 363.

[207] Articles 4(10) and 8; African Convention, Articles 4(3)(o) and 8.

[208] Article 2(8); African Convention, Article 1(10).

[209] See in particular Basel Declaration on Environmentally Sound Management, Decision V/1, *Rept of* 5th
COP, UNEP/CHW 5/29 (1999) Annex II; Decision II/13 on Technical Guidelines for the Environmentally
Sound Management of Waste, *Rept of 2nd COP*, UNEP/CHW 2/30 (1994); Decision VI/20 on Technical
Guidelines for the Environmentally Sound Management of Biomedical and Health-care Wastes; Decision
VI/21 on Technical Guidelines for the Identification and Environmentally Sound Management of Plastic
Wastes; Decision VI/24 on Technical Guidelines for the Environmentally Sound Management of the Full
and Partial Dismantling of Ships, *Rept of 6th COP*, UNEP/CHW 6/40 (2003). See also UNEP's 1985 Cairo
Guidelines.

[210] 1994 Technical Guidelines, para 9(b). See also the amendments to the Convention adopted in
1995, *supra*.

[211] E.g. 1973/78 MARPOL Convention, Annexes II, III; IMO International Maritime Dangerous Goods
Code (IMDG); 1944 Convention on International Civil Aviation, Annex 18; 1957 European Agreement
Concerning the International Carriage of Dangerous Goods By Road; 1985 Convention and Regulation on
the International Carriage of Dangerous Goods by Rail.

MARPOL Convention and the IMDG Code, these are already legally binding, but the Basel Convention goes further by requiring that packaging, labelling, and transport should conform to generally accepted rules and standards and take account of internationally recognized practices, whether or not these are otherwise obligatory.[212] This is a strong indication that transport failing to comply with these standards cannot be regarded as meeting the obligation of environmentally sound management.

In substance, this obligation is no more than a reformulation of the standard of due diligence which has generally been employed to describe international obligations for the control of environmentally harmful activities or substances.[213] Like the 1982 UNCLOS, the Basel Convention identifies the detailed content of this standard by reference to other instruments, and allows for further development. In this sense its provisions on environmentally sound management are a framework only, not a complete code in themselves.

4(5) IMPLEMENTATION AND SUPERVISORY INSTITUTIONS

Further development of the convention regime is the responsibility of the conference of the parties established for this purpose. It has power to adopt decisions, amendments and protocols, and to undertake any additional action required to further the objectives of the Conventions.[214] The obligatory provision of information from parties regarding transboundary movements, their effects on health and the environment, and any accidents during transport or disposal,[215] gives the Conference a basis on which to review the effectiveness of the convention and the policies of states. In most respects the Basel Convention's provision for international supervision thus follows the typical pattern adopted in many environmental treaties.[216] Unusually, the COP has pioneered direct participation by industry as a means of securing agreement on how to handle end-of-life electronic equipment such as mobile phones and computers.

Although several additional functions are given to the secretariat, including assistance in identifying illegal traffic,[217] the role of this body in verifying alleged breaches of obligation under Article 19 of the Convention is confined to relaying 'all relevant information' to the parties. This allows it only a limited monitoring function which falls well short of some proposals made at the Basel Conference to give the secretariat stronger verification powers.[218] Neither the secretariat nor other parties are given any power of independent inspection, an omission which limits the potential effectiveness of the Convention's control and supervision regime. However, a procedure adopted in 2003 allows possible non-compliance to be referred by the party in difficulty, or by another party, or by the secretariat.[219] In common with most non-compliance procedures, a committee nominated by the parties has power to offer advice or make

---

[212] Article 4(7)(b); African Convention, Article 4(3)(m).   [213] *Supra*, Ch 3, section 4.
[214] Article 15.   [215] Article 13.   [216] *Supra*, Ch 2, section 5.   [217] Article 16.
[218] See Kummer, 41 *ICLQ* (1992) 530 and proposal by Nigeria, UNEP/WG 191/CRP 14. Cf Article 13 of the 1996 Mediterranean Protocol.
[219] Decision VI/12, *Rept of 6th COP*, UNEP/CHW 6/40 (2003).

recommendations to facilitate compliance. Cautions may only be issued by the conference of the parties. Although there is no express provision for suspension of trade rights, in an appropriately serious case such a response would be consistent both with the law of treaties and practice in other trade-related MEAs, such as the 1973 CITES Convention.[220] The alternative is to resort to dispute settlement machinery, but this requires the agreement of the parties concerned.[221]

4(6) STATE RESPONSIBILITY AND CIVIL LIABILITY

A major defect of the Basel Convention at the time of its adoption was the absence of any agreement on principles of liability and compensation for damage resulting from transboundary movements of waste. The Convention does require the parties to cooperate in adopting a protocol on this question, and it recognizes that states are liable in international law for the non-fulfilment of their environmental obligations.[222] Potential recourse to customary principles of state responsibility for environmental damage is a necessary element of any regime of environmental protection but, as in the case of nuclear damage, it must be combined with an effective scheme of transboundary civil liability if compensation is to be a realistic remedy in cases of illegal traffic where recourse is sought against the exporter. Negotiations began in 1990 to identify the elements of such a protocol, including an international fund from which compensation payments could be made to claimants bringing legal proceedings in national courts.[223]

The Protocol on Liability and Compensation,[224] adopted by the parties in 1999, shares many of the essential features of other liability treaties but differs in certain important respects. It applies only to damage resulting from the transboundary movement and disposal of waste. No single operator is liable at all stages, nor is the generator always liable. Instead, generators, exporters, importers, and disposers are all potentially liable at different stages of the waste's journey to its eventual destination. In general, during export and transit the person who notifies the states concerned of a proposed transboundary movement of waste will be liable (this will be either the generator or the exporter of the waste); then the ultimate disposer of the waste assumes liability once possession is transferred. In this case, the shipper and the importer will not be liable. Where the waste is classified as hazardous only in the state of import, then the importer will also be liable until the disposer takes possession. There are additional rules covering who is liable when no notification is given, or when waste has to be returned to the state of origin.

---

[220] *Supra*, Ch 4, section 3.   [221] Article 20, Annex VI.   [222] Article 12 and Preamble.

[223] *2nd Rept of the ad hoc Working Group of Legal and Technical Experts*, UNEP/CHW/WG 1/2/L1 (1991) and corr 1. See generally Kummer, *International Management of Hazardous Wastes*, Ch 6; Handl and Lutz, 30 *Harv ILJ* (1989) 359; Murphy, 88 *AJIL* (1994) 24. Muchlinski, *The Right to Development and the Industrialisation of Less Developed Countries: The Case of Compensation for Major Industrial Accidents* (Commonwealth Secretariat, London, 1989) offers a valuable critique of the issues from the point of view of less developed countries.

[224] See *Rept of 5th COP*, UNEP/CHW 5/29 (1999) Annex III; Soares and Vargas, 12 *YbIEL* (2001) 69.

Liability under the protocol is strict, subject to a limited range of defences. Additional fault-based liability is placed on any person whose failure to comply with laws implementing the Basel Convention or whose wrongful, intentional, reckless, or negligent acts or omissions have caused the damage. Where several parties are liable, which is clearly possible, liability is joint and several. There is a right of recourse against any other person liable under the Protocol, or under a contract, or under the law of the competent court. There are no limits on the amount recoverable for fault-based liability. Other liability limits are determined by national law, but the protocol sets a minimum level in accordance with a formula based on the amount of the waste (Annex B) and insurance or other financial guarantee is compulsory. Supplementary compensation covering environmental damage is provided on an interim basis from a fund established by the Conference of the Parties.[225] It is available only to developing state parties or economies in transition. This limitation is not a feature of other compensation schemes. Another difference is that the fund is financed by voluntary contributions from the parties to the Convention. There is no requirement for industry to contribute.

A number of states and NGOs voiced serious criticisms of the protocol.[226] African states criticized the failure to provide an adequate and permanent compensation fund. Australia, Canada, and NGOs were concerned that parties to Article 11 agreements could opt for alternative liability arrangements, thereby creating confusion and protracted litigation as to which liability regime is applicable. They also believed that channelling liability to the exporter/notifier, rather than to the person in operational control (i.e. the waste generator) did not properly reflect the polluter pays principle. Waste generators would be able to pass on the burden of liability to exporters, and would have less incentive to monitor disposal standards themselves. Leaving national law to determine maximum liability limits would also create further uncertainty and inconsistency, while the minimum limits based on waste tonnage would in some cases be too low, in others too high, depending on the nature of the waste. In their view, shared by others, these deficiencies were likely to delay ratification, and indeed the protocol had not yet entered into force by the end of 2007.

Regional agreements also make some provision for civil liability. In Europe, the 1993 Lugano Convention on Civil Liability would apply insofar as waste disposal or recycling involve production, handling, storage, use, or discharge of dangerous substances.[227] Article 4(3)(b) of the African Convention requires the parties to impose 'strict, unlimited liability as well as joint and several liability on hazardous waste generators'. Neither agreement is in force. The 1996 Mediterranean Protocol calls on the parties to develop liability rules, but ten years later they had still not been able to agree on a text. The 1986 US–Canada and US–Mexico Agreements allow for compulsory

---

[225] Decision V/32, *Rept of 5th COP*, UNEP/CHW 5/29 (1999) and Decision VI/14, *Rept of 6th COP*, UNEP/CHW 6/40 (2003). Compare the 1992 Convention on the Establishment of an International Fund for Compensation for Oil Pollution Damage, *supra*, Ch 7.

[226] *Rept of the 5th COP*, UNEP/CHW 5/29 (1999) paras 83–9; 30 *EPL* (2000) 43.

[227] *Supra*, Ch 5.

insurance as a condition of entry, and in the latter case also require the authorities where practicable to secure compensation through existing national law.[228]

4(7) AN ASSESSMENT OF THE BASEL CONVENTION

The most serious criticisms of the Basel Convention are that it legitimizes trade which cannot adequately be monitored or controlled, and leaves developing states vulnerable to unsafe disposal practices.[229] The adoption of the ban on waste exports from OECD to non-OECD countries goes some way towards addressing the second problem, even though it is not yet fully in force. Moreover, the Convention leaves open the possibility of import bans on a national or regional basis, and provides an effective mechanism for publicizing these or other restrictions. The 1991 African Convention indicates how regional measures to give stronger protection to third world countries remain a viable option under the Basel Convention. This is undoubtedly a more realistic means of safeguarding these countries than a complete international ban on all trade in hazardous waste.[230]

Developing countries remain particularly vulnerable to illegal waste trade, however. This is probably the biggest problem facing the Basel Convention. Indeed it is sufficiently serious to be characterized by the UN Human Rights Commission as a form of 'environmental racism' and a serious threat to the rights to life and health in Africa and developing nations elsewhere.[231] The Commission acknowledged that the 1995 amendment banning the export of hazardous wastes from OECD to non-OECD countries should lead to a major reduction in such trade, but it pointed to the difficulties faced by developing countries in implementing the Convention effectively within their territories, and the need for stronger action by developed states to prevent illegal traffic. Fraud, corruption, and the use of 'shell companies' all undermine efforts to control a trade which has significant connections with organized crime. So does uncertainty about the boundary between the MARPOL and Basel Conventions, a problem illuminated by the serious health effects of waste offloaded from an oil tanker in Abidjan.[232] In this case prosecutions and a large mass-damages action have resulted. The parties to the Basel Convention have called for stronger measures to deal with illegal traffic, including appropriate sanctions or penalties, and cooperation

---

[228] Articles 9 and 14 respectively. For US law see the 1980 Comprehensive Environmental Response, Compensation and Liability Act, which creates a 'superfund' for clean-up costs and imposes strict liability on anyone with a legal interest in the waste disposal site.

[229] See Handl, in Canadian Council on International Law, *Proceedings of the 18th Annual Conference* (1989) 367.

[230] Ibid, 371.

[231] Resolution 1997/9, UN Doc E/CN 4/RES/1997/9 (1997). The Commission appointed a special rapporteur to investigate the issue. See UN Commission on Human Rights, 57th session, *Rept on Adverse Effects of the Illicit Movement and Dumping of Toxic and Dangerous Products and Wastes on the Enjoyment of Human Rights*, UN Doc E/CN 4/2001/55 (2001).

[232] *Supra*, Ch 7, and UNEP, *Rept of 1st meeting of the Expanded Bureau of the 8th meeting of the Conference of the Parties to the Basel Convention* (2007) UNEP/SBC/BUREAU/8/1/7, section III.

through Interpol and the World Customs Organization.[233] However, apart from seeking to assist developing countries to enhance their capacity to control illegal trade, there is little the Convention organs can do about it: jurisdiction over criminal activity remains a matter for individual parties. When detected, illegal exports can be returned to the state of export. This does happen, but it is not always easy to identify the export state nor is it necessarily practical to secure return of the waste. Although it gives export states some incentive to control illegal traffic, the duty to reimport is not by itself sufficient to ensure effective suppression.

Other aspects of the Basel Convention also require consideration if it is to succeed in reducing the risks of unregulated waste disposal. Although progress has been made in defining in more detail what 'environmentally sound management' consists of, the Convention's implementation remains dependent on assumptions that importing states have the expertise and technology required to handle this trade, if they choose to do so, and that exporting states are realistically in a position to assess the capabilities of importers. A regime of shared responsibility may be desirable, but it is not clear that importing states will necessarily have the ability to protect themselves, nor that exporting states will in practice do this for them. The obvious risk is that both exporting and importing states may take an essentially subjective view of what constitutes 'environmentally sound management' and of the risks involved in transboundary waste movements. The argument that informed public scrutiny is likely to be the most effective way of policing transboundary waste movements is a cogent one,[234] but this implies a level of transparency and public access to decision-making which the Basel Convention does very little to require or promote.[235]

The Convention offers a model for regulating other problems of transboundary trade, whether in hazardous chemicals or technologies,[236] and it affords evidence of the development of customary principles which may govern these activities. As we have seen, some of its main principles are already applied by analogy to international trade in chemicals. The Bhopal chemical plant accident indicates some of the legal complexities affecting trade in hazardous technology, however, particularly in questions of liability and the obligations of importing states.[237] It remains doubtful whether states have recognized a shared responsibility in this context.[238] Yet it is difficult to resist the

---

[233] Decision IV/12, *Rept of 4th COP*, UNEP/CHW 4/35 (1998).

[234] Handl and Lutz, 30 *Harv ILJ* (1989) 373.

[235] Cf Article 10(4) and OECD's Decision and Recommendation C(88) 55 Concerning Provision of Information to the Public and Public Participation in Decision Making Processes Related to the Prevention of and Response to Accidents Involving Hazardous Substances, 28 *ILM* (1989) 277; EC Directive 90/313/EEC on Freedom of Access to Information on the Environment; 1998 Aarhus Convention on Public Participation, *supra*, Ch 5.

[236] See Handl and Lutz, *Transferring Hazardous Technologies and Substances: The International Legal Challenge* (The Hague, 1989) and compare the Rotterdam Chemicals Convention, *supra*, section 2.

[237] See generally Muchlinksi, 50 *MLR* (1987) 545; Anderson, in Butler (ed), *Control Over Compliance with International Law* (Dordrecht, 1991) 83; Francioni, in Francioni and Scovazzi, *International Responsibility for Environmental Harm*, 275.

[238] See Handl and Lutz, 30 *Harv ILJ* (1989) 357–61; Scovazzi, in Francioni and Scovazzi, *International Responsibility for Environmental Harm*, 395; Charney, *Duke LJ* (1983) 748.

conclusion that here too the principle of prior informed consent, and the assurance of environmentally sound management, would have an important potential role in any dispute.

5 CONCLUSIONS

The importance of adequate institutional machinery for supervising implementation of environmental protection treaties and ensuring their continued development is clearly illustrated in this chapter. The relative success of the London Dumping Convention and the Basel Convention in evolving to meet new priorities and needs, the slower progress of regional institutions dealing with land-based marine pollution, and the severe limitations of the Rotterdam Chemicals Convention, indicate both the strengths and weaknesses of international regulation. Continuing problems of illegal traffic in hazardous waste and chemicals also show that an international regime is only as strong as the capacity of national administrations to implement and enforce it. The lack of adequate compliance machinery is only part of the reason for the difficulty of enforcing the Basel Convention.

Nevertheless, the evidence of state practice and international conventions considered here support the propositions expressed by Articles 192 and 194 of the 1982 UNCLOS that states are obliged by international law to protect the marine environment by taking diligent measures to prevent, reduce, and control pollution of common areas. The trend towards phasing out most forms of dumping, both globally and regionally, suggests that the dumping of potentially toxic waste at sea is now unlawful. Moreover, the acceptance, both in state practice and in international conventions, of the principle of prior informed consent as a condition for the disposal of toxic wastes and substances in the territory or maritime zones of other states supports the view that this has become a requirement of international law. Growing support for a precautionary approach to protection of the environment is apparent in the development of clean technology requirements, in the prohibition of dumping and the stronger regulation of land-based disposal to the marine environment, and in the requirement of prior environmental impact assessment for waste-disposal activities affecting other states and the sea. The Stockholm POPS Convention also indicates the influence of the precautionary principle in international regulatory regimes, although the Rotterdam Chemicals Convention plainly does not. However, the evidence supports the view expressed in Chapter 3 that it is premature to treat the precautionary principle as a rule of customary international law, or to draw firm conclusions regarding its specific content.

It must also be concluded that the generality and weakness of the provisions of the 1982 UNCLOS and of regional conventions in dealing with land-based sources of pollution have both undermined their effectiveness and contributed to their failure to give more concrete content to customary law. While a global convention might lead to improved institutional supervision of measures to deal with this source of pollution, effective action requires a level of political commitment and international consensus, supported by necessary economic and technical assistance and cooperation, that has so far been absent. Renewed attempts to deal more successfully with these problems, and to integrate the prevention of land-based marine pollution into a much broader framework of sustainable development of coastal zones and ocean resources, have resulted from the 1992 UNCED Conference. What has emerged is a new approach to marine resource management which encompasses pollution control, living resource protection, the impact of climate change, the regulation of dumping, and the role of international institutions at global and regional level, and which no longer assumes that the oceans are an 'infinite sink or receptacle for wastes and an endless supply of free and open access resources'.[239] In particular, the post-UNCED agreements and other instruments stress the need to adopt a precautionary approach, and to harmonize management of coastal areas and exclusive economic zones. It still remains to be seen whether this appreciation of the limitations of earlier international law and institutional arrangements for the management of the relationship between land-based activities and their impact on the oceans will lead to more radical and effective measures of international and regional cooperation.

---

[239] See UNEP, *Rept of the Meeting of Government–Designated Experts*, UNEP (OCA)/WG 14/L1/Add 2 (1991); UNCED, *Rept of the Sec Gen of the Conference on Protection of Oceans, etc*, UN Doc A/CONF 151/PC/30 (1991); id, UN Doc A/CONF 151/PC/42 (1991); id, UN Doc A/CONF 151/PC/69 (1991).

9

NUCLEAR ENERGY AND
THE ENVIRONMENT

1 INTRODUCTION

As the Chernobyl reactor accident in 1986 showed, nuclear power creates unavoidable risks for all states, whether or not they choose to use this form of energy. Every state, and the environment, is potentially affected by the possibility of radioactive contamination, the spread of toxic substances derived from nuclear energy, and the long-term health hazards consequent on exposure to radiation.[1] In catastrophic cases the level of injury to individual states and the global environment may be severe. International law is capable of moderating these ultra-hazardous risks by assuring stronger regulation, more effective multilateral oversight, and enhanced provision for liability and compensation in cases of transboundary damage. Such a policy entails limitations on the freedom of states to conduct hazardous activities within their own territory which they have sometimes been reluctant to endorse, but it represents a price which may have to be paid if nuclear energy is to remain internationally acceptable. At the same time, nuclear power offers a carbon-free alternative to fossil fuels in the generation of electricity. Safe, efficient, and economically viable nuclear industries enable France and Japan to generate far less CO_2 per capita than other industrialized nations, but relatively free of the nuclear safety problems which have affected Eastern Europe, the United States, and the United Kingdom. As with oil tankers, the varying age and quality of the technology in use and the way it is managed may greatly affect the level of risk

---

[1] See IAEA, *Summary Report on the Post Accident Review Meeting on the Chernobyl Accident* (Vienna, 1986); UKAEA, *The Chernobyl Accident and its Consequences* (London, 1987); NEA/OECD, *The Radiological Impact of the Chernobyl Accident in OECD Countries* (Paris, 1988); *Report of the United Nations Scientific Committee on the Effects of Atomic Radiation*, GAOR 37th Session (New York, 1982) and 41st Session (New York, 1986); IAEA/INFCIRC 383 (1990); and INFCIRC 510 (1996). See also *Report of the President's Commission on the Accident at Three Mile Island* (Washington DC, 1979).

to human health and the environment. The nuclear industry and the oil tanker industry are vulnerable to their weakest performers, usually those with the oldest technology or the least well regulated and supervised by national authorities. Collectively both industries have a strong vested interest in the assurance of safety and the elimination of major accidents. In both cases the terms on which such ultra-hazardous technology will be tolerated have been determined multilaterally, through international organizations, rather than by the users alone. Nuclear power and maritime transport of oil are thus the leading examples of international regulation of a whole industry on safety and environmental grounds by an intergovernmental agency. International regulation and oversight are necessary but have not been wholly sufficient in either case; both have noticeably been strengthened and improved in response to disasters. Whether the nuclear power industry has now attained acceptable levels of risk to international society cannot be answered in the abstract or solely by reference to regulatory standards and technical capabilities, but must take into account public perceptions of risk, as well as the alternatives and the competing risks, such as climate change. For all governments these are inevitably difficult policy choices in which there are few electoral advantages.

1(1) INTERNATIONAL NUCLEAR POLICY

In the early days of nuclear energy it was widely believed that the benefits outweighed the risks and could be shared by all.[2] This optimistic view was reflected in international policy. The International Atomic Energy Agency was created in 1956 with the object of encouraging and facilitating the spread of nuclear power.[3] Nuclear energy, it was assumed, would contribute to 'peace, health and prosperity' throughout the world.[4] The prevalent belief then was that the health and environmental risks could be managed successfully by governments and the IAEA through cooperation on safety matters. Successive declarations of international bodies maintained this belief in the dissemination of nuclear energy. In 1977 the UN General Assembly reaffirmed the importance of nuclear energy for economic and social development and proclaimed the right of all states to use it and to have access to the technology.[5] The success of this early exercise in technology transfer can be measured today in over 450 nuclear power plants operating in thirty countries.

There were fewer illusions about nuclear weapons. Non-proliferation beyond the five permanent members of the UN Security Council quickly became an international

---

[2] Agreed Declaration on Atomic Energy, Washington, 1945, 1 *UNTS* 123 (United States, Canada, UK); UNGA Res 1(1) (1945); President Eisenhower's 'Atoms for Peace Address', GAOR 8th Session, 470th meeting, paras 79–126; Szasz, *The Law and Practices of the IAEA* (Vienna, 1970) Chs 1, 2; McKnight, *Atomic Safeguards* (New York, 1971) Ch 1.

[3] IAEA Statute, Articles III(1)–(4) amended (1961) 471 *UNTS* 334; (1970) 24 UST 1637.

[4] IAEA Statute, Article III.

[5] UNGA Res 32/50 (1977). See also UNGA Res 36/78 (1981) and GAOR, 41st Session, 1987, *Report of the Preparatory Committee for the UN Conference for the Promotion of Industrial Cooperation in the Peaceful Uses of Nuclear Energy.*

arms-control policy, although not accepted by all. Thus, a second role for the IAEA was to ensure that nuclear power was used for peaceful purposes only.[6] In 1968, the policy of non-proliferation and the powers of the IAEA were strengthened by the Nuclear Non-Proliferation Treaty.[7] Three nuclear powers and a large majority of UN members acknowledged 'the devastation that would be visited upon all mankind by a nuclear war', and agreed further measures intended to prevent the spread of nuclear weapons. Although the treaty reaffirmed the belief that nuclear technology, including weapons technology, had beneficial peaceful applications which should be available to all, the linkage between non-proliferation and the peaceful uses of nuclear power has remained controversial for some states, such as India, and hindered agreement on further nuclear cooperation.[8]

The 1968 treaty did nothing to reduce the arsenals of existing nuclear weapons powers. At first the testing of those arsenals proceeded freely, without objection, even in the South Pacific where it was mainly carried out. In the 1950s the main reservations about these tests concerned disruption of local populations and interference with high-seas freedoms.[9] The existence of a threat to health and the environment was recognized, however, by three nuclear powers, in the 1963 Partial Test Ban Treaty which banned nuclear weapons tests in the atmosphere, outer space, and under water.[10] But testing by France and China continued, prompting condemnation at the Stockholm Conference in 1972[11] and at the UN.[12]

Australia and New Zealand failed in their attempts to have the ICJ declare further French atmospheric and underground tests illegal.[13] Their experience, reinforced by mounting evidence of the long-term effects of earlier tests in Australia and elsewhere,[14]

---

[6] Statute, Articles II, III. See Lamm, *The Utilization of Nuclear Energy and International Law* (Budapest, 1984); Potter, *Nuclear Power and Non-Proliferation* (Cambridge, Mass, 1982); Willrich, *International Safeguards and Nuclear Industry* (Baltimore, Md, 1973). The 1957 Euratom Treaty provides for safeguards against diversion among European member states.

[7] See Goldblat, 256 *Recueil des Cours* (1995) 9–192; Müller, Fischer, Kötter (eds), *Nuclear Non-Proliferation and Global Order* (Oxford, 1994); Fischer, *The Non-Proliferation of Nuclear Weapons* (New York, 1971); Willrich, *Non-Proliferation Treaty* (Charlottesville, 1968).

[8] UN, *Rept of the Prepcom for the UN Conference for the Promotion of International Cooperation in the Peaceful Uses of Nuclear Energy*, GAOR, 37th Session, 1983 and 40th Session, 1986. In 2007 the only other nuclear-armed non-parties were Pakistan, North Korea and Israel. On the future of the NPT see Bosch and Reisman, in de Chazournes and Sands (eds), *International Law, the ICJ and Nuclear Weapons* (Cambridge, 1999) 375, 473.

[9] McDougal and Schlei, 64 *Yale LJ* (1995) 648; Margolis, ibid, 629.

[10] 1963 Treaty Banning Nuclear Weapons Tests in the Atmosphere, in Outer Space and Under Water.

[11] A/CONF 48/14/Rev. 1; Res 3(1) 4 June 1972.

[12] UNGA Res 3078 XXVIII (1973). Similar resolutions had been passed annually since 1955.

[13] *Nuclear Tests Cases (Australia v France)* ICJ Reports (1973) 99 (Interim measures); ICJ Reports (1974) 253 (Jurisdiction); *(New Zealand v France)* ICJ Reports (1973) 135 (Interim Measures); ICJ Reports (1974) 457 (Jurisdiction); Prott, 7 *Sydney LR* (1976) 433; Dugard, 16 *VJIL* (1976) 463; New Zealand Ministry of Foreign Affairs, *French Nuclear Testing in the Pacific* (Wellington, 1973); Dupuy, 20 *GYIL* (1977) 375; MacDonald and Hough, ibid, 337; Kos, 14 *VUWLR* (1984) 357. On the 1995 ICJ case see *supra*, Ch 3, section 4.

[14] See *Rept of the UN Scientific Committee on the Effects of Atomic Radiation* (1972) GAOR 27th Session, Suppl No 25 and (1982) GAOR, 37th Session, Suppl No 45.

prompted the creation in 1985 of a South Pacific Nuclear Free Zone.[15] The prohibition among the parties of nuclear tests or the dumping of radioactive waste at sea within this zone indicated the growing strength of regional and international opposition to such activities on environmental grounds. That opposition contributed to the adoption of a Comprehensive Test Ban Treaty in 1996. If it ever enters into force this agreement will prohibit all nuclear tests and institute a strong scheme of international verification, but it remains unratified by China, India, Israel, Iran, Pakistan, and the United States. All five permanent members of the Security Council have nevertheless ceased nuclear weapons testing.[16] At the same time the ICJ has held that the threat or use of nuclear weapons is not per se unlawful under customary international law, but in terms which place severe limits on their use.[17] In addition to other constraints, the Court reiterated both the obligation to protect the natural environment against the widespread, long-term and severe damage that nuclear weapons would cause, and the need to meet standards of necessity and proportionality in pursuing otherwise legitimate military objectives. Implicitly the ICJ also recognized the inter-generational implications of the use of nuclear weapons, but it stopped short of expressly acknowledging rights for future generations.

1(2) NUCLEAR POWER: THE EMERGENCE OF ENVIRONMENTAL CONCERN

It was the popularity of nuclear power as an answer to the oil crisis of the 1970s which ultimately brought long-term health and environmental consequences to the forefront of international concern. The Stockholm Conference in 1972 had called for a registry of emissions of radioactivity and international cooperation on radioactive waste disposal and reprocessing.[18] It recognized that the latter was a growing problem, caused by the increasing use of nuclear power, but offered no clear policy. Oceanic dumping of nuclear waste was partially banned in 1972, suspended entirely in 1983, and banned outright by the 1996 Protocol revising the London Dumping Convention, leaving disposal on land or reprocessing as the only viable options.[19] But nuclear reactor accidents at Three Mile Island in the United States and Chernobyl in the Soviet Union showed how serious were the risks for health, agriculture, and the environment posed

[15] 1985 South Pacific Nuclear Free Zone Treaty. See also 1995 South Pacific Regional Convention on Hazardous Wastes (Waigani Convention). Other nuclear weapons-free zones have been created in Latin America (1967 Tlateloco Treaty for the Prohibition of Nuclear Weapons in Latin America), Africa (1996 African Nuclear Free Zone Treaty, 35 *ILM* 698) and Asia (1996 ASEAN Nuclear Free Zone Treaty, 35 *ILM* 635) on which see Goldblat, 256 *Recueil des Cours* (1995) 108–38.

[16] *Infra*, section 3.

[17] *Advisory Opinion on the Threat or Use of Nuclear Weapons*, ICJ Reports (1996) 226. See de Chazournes and Sands (eds), *International Law, the ICJ and Nuclear Weapons*; Mahmoudi, 66 *Nordic JIL* (1997) 77, and *supra*, Ch 3, section 4.

[18] A/Conf 48/14/Rev 1, Rec 75, *Action Plan for the Human Environment*.

[19] *Supra*, Ch 8, section 3. Problems arising from the illegal transboundary movement and disposal of nuclear waste are also considered in Ch 8.

by nuclear power.[20] Spreading contamination over a wide area of Eastern and Western Europe, the accident at Chernobyl in 1986, like the sinking of the *Torrey Canyon* oil tanker in 1967, revealed the limitations of international policy for containing catastrophic risks, and some of the true costs of nuclear power.

Chernobyl cast doubt on the adequacy of national and international regulation of nuclear facilities. It showed how limited were the powers of IAEA,[21] and how little agreement existed on questions of liability and state responsibility. It gave new importance to the interest of neighbouring states in the siting of nuclear power plants, the opportunities for consultation on issues of safety, and the right to prompt notification of potentially harmful accidents. It demonstrated too, that the fundamentally benign view of nuclear power adopted in the 1950s now required modification, with new emphasis on stronger international control of safety matters.[22] For the first time, an international body, the Council of Europe, was prepared to describe nuclear energy as 'potentially dangerous', to recommend a moratorium on construction of new facilities, and the closure of those that did not meet international standards.[23] Some states, mainly in Western Europe, abandoned plans to build new reactors. Within IAEA, however, the predominant belief remains that, through stronger international cooperation and more modern technology, the risks of nuclear energy can be contained and made environmentally acceptable, thereby reducing reliance on fossil fuels, and helping to counter global warming.[24] Nevertheless, one of the beneficial effects of Chernobyl has been the development and strengthening of the international regulatory regime for the safe use of nuclear energy.[25]

2 THE INTERNATIONAL REGULATION
OF NUCLEAR ENERGY

Like oil tankers, nuclear installations are potentially hazardous undertakings whose risk to health, safety, and the environment is best met by regulation. Because the consequences of failure to regulate adequately may cause injury or pollution damage to other states and the global environment, international regulation—the setting of

---

[20] *Supra*, n 1.

[21] Barkenbus, 41 *International Organization* (1987) 483; Cameron et al (eds), *Nuclear Energy Law After Chernobyl* (London 1988); 159ff, 179ff; Handl, 92 *RGDIP* (1988) 5; Sands, *Chernobyl: Law and Communication* (Cambridge, 1988).

[22] See IAEA General Conference, Special Session, 1986, IAEA/GC (SPL 1)/4 and GC(SPL 1)/15/Rev 1, at 25 *ILM* (1986) 1387ff; OECD Nuclear Energy Agency, 15th Report, *NEA Activities in 1986*, 29ff; European Community, *20th General Report* (1986) paras 759–62; WCED, *Our Common Future* (Oxford, 1987) 181ff.

[23] Parliamentary Assembly Rec 1068 (1988).

[24] Blix, 18 *EPL* (1988) 142; 1996 Moscow Declaration on Nuclear Safety and Security, IAEA/INFCIRC/509 (1996) and see IAEA's statement on the environmental benefits of nuclear power at the Kyoto meeting of the parties to the UNFCCC, IAEA/PR97/40 (1997).

[25] For an overview see IAEA, *International Nuclear Law in the Post-Chernobyl Period* (Vienna, 2006).

common standards, supervised by international institutions—offers the best means of ensuring a generally accepted minimum level of environmental protection. The benefits of this approach accrue to the international community, which gains protection from unilaterally chosen levels of risk, but the burdens fall on national governments, which lose the freedom to determine for themselves the most appropriate balance of safety and development in their own territories.

For oil tankers, the choice of international regulation was made in the 1970s. The minimum duties of flag states in matters of environmental protection were laid down in detail in international conventions, and given additional legal force by the 1982 UN Convention on the Law of the Sea.[26] A relatively strong scheme of enforcement exists. For nuclear power it was not until the adoption of Conventions on Nuclear Safety and the Safety of Spent Fuel and Radioactive Waste Management in 1994 and 1997 that binding minimum standards of environmental protection from nuclear risks could be comparably assured. These treaties have codified much of the customary international law relating to nuclear activities and have given greater legal force to IAEA safety principles and standards. Both treaties represent an important stage in the evolution of international regulation and supervision of nuclear power and its waste products.

2(1) IAEA AND THE REGULATION OF NUCLEAR RISKS

The International Atomic Energy Agency was the product of compromise following failure to agree on US proposals for international management of all nuclear power by an international body.[27] Its main tasks were confined to encouraging and facilitating the development and dissemination of nuclear power,[28] and ensuring through non-proliferation safeguards that it was used for peaceful purposes only.[29] Setting standards for health and safety in collaboration with other international agencies was very much an incidental or secondary responsibility.[30]

The Chernobyl accident resulted in a significant alteration of the Agency's priorities. The IAEA provided the main forum for consideration of measures made necessary by the accident and member states endorsed the importance of the Agency's role in safety and radiological protection matters.[31] Among the recommendations of a review group were that the Agency should promote better exchanges of information among states on safety and accident experience, develop additional safety guidelines,

---

[26] 1982 UNCLOS Articles 211, 217–8, 220; *supra*, Ch 7.

[27] Szasz, *The Law and Practices of the IAEA*, Ch 1; Potter, *Nuclear Power and Non Proliferation* (Cambridge, Mass, 1982) Ch 2; McKnight, *Atomic Safeguards*, Ch 1.

[28] Statute, Article III(1)–(4). In practice the development of the international nuclear industry has relied more heavily on assistance from other states than on the IAEA. See Cavers, 12 *Vand LR* (1958) 68; Szasz, *The Law and Practices of the IAEA*, Ch 2; McKnight, *Atomic Safeguards*, Ch 2.

[29] Statute, Article III(5).

[30] Statute, Article III(6); Szasz, *The Law and Practices of the IAEA*, Ch 22.

[31] IAEA, 30th Conference, Special Session, GC/SPL 1/Res 1. See also statement of the Group of Seven on the implications of the Chernobyl Accident, 15 *ILM* (1986) 1005. See Handl, 92 *RGDIP* (1988) 50; Blix, 18 *EPL* (1988) 142.

and enhance its capacity to perform safety evaluations and inspections on request.[32] The Convention on Assistance in cases of Nuclear Emergency also gives it the new task of coordinating assistance and responding to requests for help, while the Nuclear Safety and Radioactive Waste Conventions adopted in 1994 and 1997 have enhanced its importance as the principal international regulatory body for civil nuclear power. Thus despite its very different objectives in 1956, the Agency has developed a significant nuclear safety role. Rather like the IMO after the *Torrey Canyon* disaster, it has acquired a new environmental perspective as perhaps the one positive result of Chernobyl.

(a) Powers over health and safety

Article III.A.6 of the IAEA Statute authorizes the Agency to adopt 'standards' of safety for the purposes of protecting health and minimizing danger to life and property from exposure to radiation, in collaboration with other UN agencies, such as WHO, FAO, ILO, or the OECD. The term 'standards' includes regulations, rules, requirements, codes of practice and guides. Those adopted by the IAEA have taken a variety of forms depending on their function, but three basic categories can be distinguished.[33] 'Safety fundamentals' provide a statement of basic objectives, concepts and principles for ensuring safety in general terms. 'Safety requirements' lay down detailed regulatory standards which must be satisfied in order to ensure the safety of specific types of installation or activity. 'Safety guides' are recommendations, based on international experience, and usually deal with ways and means to ensure the observance of safety requirements.

IAEA standards cover such subjects as radiation protection, transport and handling of radioactive materials, radioactive-waste disposal, and safety of nuclear installations. They are regularly updated in the light of current technical advice from the agency's own independent specialist advisory bodies and the International Commission for Radiological Protection, whose recommendations seek to limit the incidence of radiation-induced cancers and genetic disorders to an 'acceptable' level. The Board of Governors first approved radiation protection requirements in 1962 and has revised periodically thereafter.[34] Agency regulations on safe transport of nuclear material were adopted first in 1961, and a Code of Practice on the International Transboundary Movement of Radioactive Waste was added in 1990 in order to exclude such material from the Basel Convention on Transboundary Movements of Hazardous Waste.[35] In

---

[32] IAEA, *Summary Report on the Post Accident Review Meeting on the Chernobyl Accident* (Vienna, 1986).

[33] For a fuller account see IAEA, *Measures to Strengthen International Cooperation in Nuclear Radiation and Waste Safety*, IAEA/GC(41)/INF/8, Pt B, and IAEA/GC(43)/INF/8 (1999).

[34] See now International Basic Safety Standards for Protection Against Ionising Radiation (1996) IAEA Safety Series No 115. These are approved jointly by IAEA, FAO, ILO, WHO, OECD/NEA, and the Pan American Health Organization.

[35] See Regulations on Safe Transport for Radioactive Materials (2005) Safety Series TS-R-1; Code of Practice on the International Transboundary Movement of Radioactive Waste, IAEA/INFCIRC/386 (1990) and 1989 Basel Convention, Article 1(3) on which see *supra*, Ch 8.

1974 IAEA initiated the Nuclear Safety Standards Programme (NUSS), establishing basic international minimum safety standards and guiding principles regulating the design, construction, siting, and operation of nuclear power plants.[36] The important point is thus that the Agency has competence over a wide range of safety and health issues relating to all aspects of the use of nuclear energy: what it lacked until 1994 was the ability to give any of these standards obligatory force.

(b) The legal effect of IAEA health and safety standards

Nothing in the Statute confers any binding force on IAEA health and safety standards, or requires member states to comply with them.[37] While, under the statute, the same is true of non-proliferation safeguards, in practice IAEA enjoys much stronger power in that field as a result of the 1968 Non-Proliferation Treaty and regional agreements.[38] The effect of the NPT treaty is to make obligatory the acceptance of non-proliferation safeguards through bilateral agreements with the Agency, and to allow periodic compulsory Agency inspection for the purpose of verification.[39] Compliance with the overall scheme of non-proliferation safeguards is monitored by the UN General Assembly and Security Council.

No comparable attempt has been made to require universal adherence to health and safety standards.[40] Safeguards agreements and safeguards inspections relate only to non-proliferation; they give IAEA no power over health and safety.[41] Only where the Agency supplies materials, facilities, or services to states does the statute give it the power to ensure, through project agreements, that acceptable health, safety, and design standards are adopted.[42] In such cases, but only in such cases, it also has the right to examine the design of equipment and facilities to ensure compatibility with its standards, and the right to send inspectors to verify compliance.[43] If these are not met,

---

[36] IAEA GC(XXXII)/Res/489 first approved texts of five NUSS codes in 1988. According to the director general these establish 'the objectives and basic requirements that must be met to ensure adequate safety in the operation of nuclear power plants', 30 *IAEA Bulletin* (1988) 58. For the current list of standards see IAEA, *Status of the IAEA Safety Standards* (Vienna, 2007).

[37] Szasz, *The Law and Practices of the IAEA*, 679ff.

[38] *Supra*, nn 6, 7. For differences between statutory and NPT Safeguards, see Szasz, in Willrich, *International Safeguards and the Nuclear Industry*, Ch 4, and McKnight, *Atomic Safeguards*, Chs 7 and 9. Non-proliferation safeguards must also be accepted when IAEA provides assistance: Statute, Article XII.

[39] Article III, NPT Treaty.

[40] Barkenbus, 41 *International Organization* (1989); Szasz, *The Law and Practices of the IAEA*, Ch 22; Cameron et al, *Nuclear Energy Law after Chernobyl*, 4ff.

[41] IAEA/INFCIRC/153, paras 46, 71–3; Szasz, *The Law and Practices of the IAEA*, 662f. See e.g. Safeguards Agreement between the Agency, Israel, and the United States, 1975, TIAS 8051 and others listed, Ruster and Simma, *International Protection of the Environment* (hereafter 'Ruster and Simma') xiii, 6468ff. IAEA/INFCIRC/153, para 28 defines the objective of NPT safeguards as 'the timely detection of diversion of significant quantities of nuclear material from peaceful nuclear activities to the manufacture of nuclear weapons or of other explosive devices or for purposes unknown, and deterrence of such diversion by the risk of early detection'.

[42] Articles III(6) XI, XII. The Agency does not in fact receive or supply materials as envisaged in Article IX; it now arranges for others to do so.

[43] Statute, Article XII; Inspectors Doc/IAEA/GC(V)/INF 39, Annex, paras 9, 11.

further assistance may be terminated and membership of the Agency withdrawn.[44] Considerable latitude is normally allowed, however, provided national practices meet the minimum criterion of offering an 'adequate' means of controlling hazards and ensuring effective compliance.[45]

These powers over safety relate only to materials or facilities supplied by[46] or through[47] IAEA; states cannot be required to place their other facilities or materials under its standards merely because they seek its assistance, although they may do so voluntarily.[48] Where assistance is supplied under bilateral agreement without IAEA involvement, even these limited powers are lost, and the practice in such cases has been to provide only for safety consultations with the supplier state.[49]

It is clear therefore that as a general rule the IAEA Statute confers no binding force on any of the Safety Standards adopted by IAEA. Nevertheless, despite their non-binding character, IAEA health and safety standards have been a significant contribution to controlling the risks of nuclear energy. Governments are consulted during the formulation stage[50] and drafting is carried out in cooperation with specialist bodies, such as International Committee on Radiological Protection.[51] The Agency's standards thus reflect a large measure of expert and technical consensus, and it is for this reason, rather than their legal status, that they have been influential and serve as important guidelines for most states in regulating their nuclear facilities. They have resulted in an appreciable degree of harmonization.[52]

Given their undoubted influence on the regulation of nuclear risks at national level, can IAEA standards then be regarded as 'soft law', providing evidence of *opinio juris* in support of developing legal principles, or as a codification of existing customary law, or an amplification of general rules of custom or treaty? One problem with this view is that IAEA standards are not necessarily adopted by the Agency's General Conference, in which all member states are represented, but by the Board of Governors.[53] They may thus lack the evidence of international support which approval by the IMO Assembly confers on non-binding IMO resolutions under Article 16 of the IMO Convention. In such cases it is more difficult to describe IAEA standards as 'soft law', or to regard

---

[44] Statute, Article XII.   [45] INFCIRC/18/Rev 1, paras 2, 4.

[46] See e.g. agreements listed in Ruster and Simma xii, xxvii.

[47] See e.g. trilateral agreements between IAEA, the United States, and Argentina, 30 UST 1539; Indonesia, 32 UST 361; Malaysia, 32 UST 2610.

[48] Statute, Articles III(6), XII A; IAEA/INFCIRC/18/Rev 1, para 25.

[49] See e.g. US–Brazil Agreement, 1972, 23 UST 2478; US–Thailand Agreement, 1974, TIAS 7850; FRG–Brazil Agreement, 1975, Ruster and Simma, xiii, 6472ff, and others listed at 6415–29.

[50] Szasz, *The Law and Practices of the IAEA*, 672f; IAEA, *Experience and Trends in Nuclear Law* (Vienna, 1972).

[51] The ICRP is a private association of scientific experts, comparable to ICES or SCAR: see Smith, 30 *IAEA Bulletin* (1988) 42. For IAEA cooperation with other international bodies, see Szasz, *The Law and Practices of the IAEA*, Ch 12, IAEA, *Measures to Strengthen International Cooperation in Nuclear Radiation and Waste Safety*, GC(43)/INF/8/(1999).

[52] Dickstein, 23 *ICLQ* (1977) 437; Szasz, *The Law and Practices of the IAEA*, 673, 682ff; Cameron et al (eds), *Nuclear Energy Law after Chernobyl*, 4, 159ff.

[53] Szasz, *The Law and Practices of the IAEA*, 669ff.

them as representing a standard of due diligence for states to meet as a matter of customary law. But approval by the General Conference of some of the more important standards, including the NUSS Codes, may indicate an appreciation of this weakness and an intention to give them a politically more authoritative status which can be translated more easily into soft law.[54] A second problem is that IAEA standards are themselves divided between those written in mandatory form, using the word 'shall', and those using the more recommendatory 'should'. Use of the mandatory form, coupled with endorsement by the General Conference does suggest a higher level of commitment than mere recommendations.[55]

Whatever the correct view of the legal status of IAEA standards adopted under the IAEA Statute, there is no doubt that other treaties do give binding force to certain IAEA standards for parties to the relevant agreements. Immediately following the Chernobyl disaster IAEA's soft law guidelines for early notification of nuclear accidents were transformed into a now widely ratified treaty.[56] More recently, the Convention on Nuclear Safety and the Joint Convention on the Safety of Spent Fuel and Radioactive Waste Management[57] have incorporated as binding obligations the main elements of IAEA's fundamental safety standards for nuclear installations,[58] radioactive-waste management[59] and radiation protection,[60] and most of its Code of Practice on the Transboundary Movement of Radioactive Waste.[61] Moreover, those remaining IAEA standards which retain a soft law status[62] may still be relevant when determining how the basic obligations of states parties to these agreements are to be implemented. Under the Joint Convention there is also an obligation to take account, inter alia, of relevant IAEA standards in national law. As we shall see in the next section, these various agreements have significantly strengthened the legal force of IAEA standards and, in conjunction with non-binding common safety standards, have created a somewhat more convincing legal framework for the international regulation of nuclear risks.[63]

(c) IAEA as an international inspectorate and review body

IAEA has only a limited power to act as an international nuclear safety inspectorate under its Statute. Compulsory inspections are possible only where an assistance agreement with the Agency is in force, and in practice this power is rarely used.[64] However, the Agency can, if requested, also provide safety advice and a review of safety practices

---

[54] IAEA/GC (XXXII)/Res/489 (1988).

[55] See e.g. IAEA Safety Series No 111-S, *Establishing a National System for Radioactive Waste Management* (Vienna, 1995) and compare the more recommendatory wording of the 1990 Code of Practice on International Transboundary Movement of Radioactive Waste, *infra*.

[56] See *infra*, section 3(2).   [57] See *infra*, section 2(2).

[58] IAEA Safety Series No 110 *The Safety of Nuclear Installations* (Vienna, 1993).

[59] IAEA Safety series No 111-F *The Principles of Radioactive Waste Management* (Vienna, 1995).

[60] IAEA Safety Series No 120 *Radiation Protection and the Safety of Radiation Sources* (Vienna, 1996).

[61] IAEA GC (XXXIV)/939 (1990).   [62] E.g. the NUSS codes *supra*, n 36.

[63] IAEA, *Nuclear Safety Review 1997*, GC(41)/INF/8 (1997).

[64] Statute, Article 12; Szasz, *The Law and Practices of the IAEA*, 696.

for any nuclear installation or waste disposal site. An important recommendation acted on in response to the Chernobyl accident was that IAEA should enhance its capability for providing such services and that states should make more use of them.[65] Different aspects of nuclear safety are now covered by a range of IAEA review programmes. Of these the most prominent is the OSART programme for reviewing safety at nuclear reactors.[66] This facility has become quite widely used by states. For example, in 1997 and 1998 a total of ten OSART missions were conducted at reactors in China, France, Mexico, Bulgaria, Pakistan, Kazakhstan, and Slovakia, and there were six follow-up inspections elsewhere. Other IAEA missions reviewed safety at waste disposal sites in France, Serbia, Mururoa, and the USA, as well as regulatory practices in Bulgaria.

IAEA safety inspections are valuable to governments because of their independence and the reassurance they provide. Assessments of Soviet and Russian dumping in the Kara and Barents Seas and in the North Pacific concluded that the current radiological risks are small,[67] despite the international concern aroused by the discovery that this form of disposal had occurred. Nevertheless, if unsafe practices are found, the Agency can only recommend, not enforce changes. Thus, when it inspected Bulgaria's only reactor in 1991 and found it in very poor condition, with various safety-related deficiencies, the Agency urged the Bulgarian government to take immediate measures, but it could not compel closure. Similarly, an IAEA inspection of the Chernobyl plant in 1994 disclosed continuing serious deficiencies and a failure to meet international safety standards. Although the Agency cannot ensure compliance with international safety standards, making safety audits of this kind an accepted practice does provide a means for distinguishing good from bad safety performers, and brings international pressure to bear on the latter. In the case of Chernobyl it has also helped generate an international campaign to provide finance and assistance with upgrading.

While the Chernobyl accident showed the usefulness of IAEA in coordinating responses to serious accidents and in acting as a forum for considering further measures, it also exposed its weakness as a safety inspectorate.[68] Because they take place only in response to a request, the Agency's procedures by themselves cannot ensure systematic assessment of the safety of nuclear installations, nor are they reinforced by any safety reporting obligations under the Statute. IAEA member states thus had no basis on which to review and monitor each other's practices. Without such supervision, there was no means, prior to adoption of the Nuclear Safety Convention in 1994, of ensuring that agreed international safety standards were met. Now that binding minimum international standards for nuclear installations and radioactive waste have been laid down by treaty,[69] obligatory reporting has at last been introduced. How far

---

[65] IAEA, *Summary Report of the Post Accident Review Meeting on the Chernobyl Accident* (Vienna, 1986).

[66] OSART stands for Operational Safety Review Team. IAEA/GC(XXXII)/Res/459 invites member states to use OSART on a voluntary basis. Other types of safety review include ASSET, the Assessment of Safety Significant Events Team, and IRRT, the International Regulatory Review Team. For fuller details see IAEA, *Nuclear Safety Review 1997*, GC(41)/INF/8, Annex C-5.

[67] Ibid.   [68] Barkenbus, 41 *Int Org* (1987) 487ff; Handl, 92 *RGDIP* (1988) 18.

[69] See next section.

this may provide a basis for more systematic review by the parties of national safety standards is considered below. However, it remains the case that IAEA has no general power of compulsory inspection, and no power to close down a nuclear installation, however unsafe.[70]

2(2) INTERNATIONAL AGREEMENTS ON NUCLEAR SAFETY

At a special review conference held following the Chernobyl accident, IAEA member states affirmed their individual responsibility for ensuring nuclear and radiation safety, security, and environmental compatibility, while acknowledging the central role of IAEA in encouraging and facilitating cooperation on these matters.[71] At the same time they also considered the possibility of adopting mandatory international minimum safety standards for reactors as a means of strengthening international regulation of nuclear energy. No agreement could be reached for a variety of reasons. There were practical problems: reconciling different national standards, modifying existing installations, added financial and administrative burdens. There were also significant political and policy obstacles: establishing mandatory international standards would require some surrender of national sovereignty in this field, and assumes that uniform standards for all reactor types are possible and would indeed enhance overall safety. This assumption was not universally accepted, even after the Chernobyl accident.[72]

However, the realization that Chernobyl-type reactors would remain in widespread use in Eastern Europe, and that they could not easily be upgraded by the states in which they were located, prompted further discussions, including an international conference on the safety of nuclear power. Following this, in 1991, the General Conference of the IAEA, representing all member states, invited the Agency to prepare an outline of a nuclear safety convention, and to develop a common basis on which to judge whether the safety of existing reactors built to earlier standards is acceptable.[73] Two years later the General Conference also requested the Agency to prepare a convention on the safety of radioactive-waste management.[74] These decisions led to the adoption of a Convention on Nuclear Safety in 1994 and a Joint Convention on the Safety of Spent Fuel and Radioactive Waste Management in 1997. Neither convention was negotiated as a consensus 'package deal'; unlike almost every other global environmental agreement reservations are not prohibited. Although the Nuclear Safety Convention was in fact adopted by consensus, the Joint Convention was opposed by Pakistan and

---

[70] On the closure of unsafe installations see Nuclear Safety Convention, Article 6, considered *infra*.

[71] IAEA, 30th Conference, Special Session, 1986, 16 *EPL* (1986) 138. UNGA Res 41/36 (1986) called for the highest standards of safety in the design and operation of nuclear plants. See also 1996 Moscow Declaration on Nuclear Safety and Security, IAEA/INFCIRC/509.

[72] See Reyners and Lellouche, in Cameron et al (eds), *Nuclear Energy Law after Chernobyl*, 16f, 164f, 182f; Handl, 92 *RGDIP* (1988) 5, 7ff; and cf Kamminga, 44 *ICLQ* (1995) 872.

[73] IAEA, GC(XXXV)/RES/553 (1991).   [74] IAEA, GC(XXXVII)/RES/615 (1993).

New Zealand and several articles were also adopted by majority vote, in some cases against strong opposition.[75]

These two conventions are similar in their relatively conservative approach to the regulation of nuclear risks. By rejecting initial proposals for more elaborate framework conventions and making no provision for the adoption of further regulatory protocols,[76] or for the parties to adopt further regulatory measures or even to make recommendations for further measures,[77] responsibility for the future development of international nuclear safety remains in the hands of IAEA member states acting outside the framework of the two nuclear safety conventions. Of course, how the conventions develop in practice may be quite different from the initial conception. Moreover, referring disputes concerning interpretation or application of both conventions to the meeting of the parties for consultation may permit a more expansive interpretation of each convention, including the phrase 'appropriate steps'.[78] Their effect on international nuclear law, and on the power of IAEA, could thus be considerably more dynamic than appears at first sight. But at present, neither the Nuclear Safety Convention nor the Joint Convention establishes a 'regulatory regime' comparable to the Ozone Convention or the Convention on Long-Range Transboundary Air Pollution.

Both conventions rely on a process of reporting and peer review by the conference of the parties to ensure effectiveness, but in this respect they do nothing to enhance, or detract from, the existing limited powers of IAEA. Their most important feature, however, is that for the first time they give binding treaty status to some of IAEA's most fundamental standards of nuclear safety law affecting most aspects of civil nuclear reactors, radioactive-waste management, and spent fuel disposal and reprocessing. Turning soft law into hard law does not necessarily mean that the law itself has changed, for, though formally non-binding, some of these instruments reflected what were already rules of customary law such as the diligent regulation of transboundary risks or the requirement of prior informed consent for transboundary waste disposal. Nevertheless, incorporation of these basic principles in treaty form does reinforce their status, and more especially so in those Eastern European states where the problems of nuclear safety are most acute, such as Russia, Bulgaria, and Slovakia.

(a) The Nuclear Safety Convention

The Nuclear Safety Convention's objectives are to maintain a high level of nuclear safety in civil nuclear power plants and related facilities, to protect individuals, society

---

[75] Article 3(1) was adopted by 60–3, with 7 abstentions; Article 27 (1)(ii) by 57–5, with 2 abstentions. However a proposed New Zealand amendment to Article 27(1)(ii) had earlier been defeated by 28–25 with 19 abstentions, and a Turkish amendment by 29–13 with 30 abstentions.

[76] de La Fayette, 5 *JEL* (1993) 31.

[77] Nuclear Safety Convention, Article 20; Joint Convention, Article 30. It is of course open to the member states of IAEA to adopt further measures or make recommendations.

[78] Nuclear Safety Convention, Article 29; Joint Convention, Article 38.

and the environment from harmful radiation, and to prevent or mitigate accidents.[79] It seeks to pursue these objectives by enhancing national measures and international cooperation, rather than by fully internationalizing the regulation and supervision of the nuclear industry. Instead, it reaffirms that 'responsibility for nuclear safety rests with the state having jurisdiction over a nuclear installation', and requires each party to establish and maintain a national legislative and regulatory framework for the safety of nuclear installations, including a system of licensing, independent inspection, and enforcement of applicable regulations.[80] It entails, in the words of the preamble, 'a commitment to the application of fundamental safety principles for nuclear installations rather than of detailed safety standards'.

The principal obligations embodied in the Convention are based largely on IAEA's own safety fundamentals for nuclear installations.[81] They also represent, according to the director general of IAEA, 'an international consensus on the basic concepts underlying the regulation and management of safety and the operation of nuclear installations'.[82] Parties are thus required to take 'appropriate steps' to ensure that safety at nuclear installations is given 'due' priority, that levels of trained staff are adequate, that quality assurance programmes are established, that comprehensive and systematic safety assessments are carried out periodically, that radiation exposure is as low as reasonably achievable, and that emergency plans are prepared.[83] Further articles specify appropriate steps with regard to the siting, design, construction, and operation of civil nuclear installations.[84] What is 'appropriate' in all these different instances will have to be assessed in the circumstances of each case, and may change as safety standards evolve. While guidance may be derived from other standards concerning nuclear power adopted by IAEA or other international bodies, the cautious wording of the preamble, and the *travaux préparatoires*, suggest that there is no intention to make compliance with any of these other standards obligatory.[85]

Thus the Convention does take a significant step towards defining the obligations of states operating nuclear installations, but only in fairly general terms. Insofar as it gives effect to IAEA 'safety fundamentals' it can be seen as an elaboration of the general rule of customary international law regarding diligent regulation and control of potentially harmful activities in accordance with Principle 2 of the Rio Declaration and other precedents, rather in the same way that Articles 206–12 of the 1982 UNCLOS elaborate the same general rule in regard to protection of the marine environment.[86] Where the Nuclear Safety Convention differs from UNCLOS is that it

---

[79] Preamble and Article 1. For *travaux préparatoires* see IAEA, *Convention on Nuclear Safety* (IAEA Legal Series No 16, Vienna, 1994); see also Kamminga, *supra*, n 72; de La Fayette, *supra*, n 76.

[80] Articles 7–9.   [81] IAEA Safety Series No 110, *The Safety of Nuclear Installations* (1993).

[82] IAEA, *Convention on Nuclear Safety*, Legal Series No 16, at 65, para 16.   [83] Articles 10–16.

[84] Articles 17–19.

[85] Thus as well as emphasising that the Convention does not commit states to the application of *detailed safety standards*, it also refers to 'internationally formulated safety guidelines which are updated from time to time and so can provide *guidance* on contemporary means of achieving a high level of safety' (emphasis added).

[86] See *supra*, Ch 7.

does not directly incorporate all the more detailed safety standards for nuclear power adopted by IAEA in the way that UNCLOS incorporates and renders directly binding on parties the 'generally accepted rules and standards' of the MARPOL annexes and other internationally agreed instruments.[87]

Article 6 attempts to deal with the problem of unsafe existing nuclear reactors by requiring the party concerned to ensure that 'all reasonably practicable improvements' are made as a matter of urgency to upgrade safety. Where that is not possible the reactor must be shut down 'as soon as practically possible'. This does not necessarily mean immediately, however: account may be taken of the availability of alternative energy sources, as well as the 'social, environmental and economic impact'. The practical effect of this latitude is that Eastern European Chernobyl-style reactors will remain in operation until economic alternatives are found, but reports on progress in upgrading or closure will be subject to review by the meeting of the parties in accordance with Articles 5 and 20. Decisions on the future of such reactors are thus not left entirely to the discretion of the state concerned.[88] Given the importance of nuclear power to Eastern Europe, Article 6 represents an inevitable compromise, whose success will depend on the availability of appropriate technical assistance from other states and IAEA.

IAEA's own commentary on the Convention notes that 'It is not designed to ensure fulfilment of obligations by parties through control and sanction', but will function by a process of 'peer review'. Article 20 provides for the parties to meet periodically to review reports on measures they have taken to implement their international safety obligations. The first such review was held in 1999. Article 20(3) also specifies that each party 'shall have a reasonable opportunity to discuss the reports submitted by other Contracting Parties and to seek clarification…' The purpose of these review meetings is to allow experts 'to identify problems, concerns, uncertainties, or omissions in national reports, focusing on the most significant problems or concerns';[89] they are not meant to enable parties to review the safety of individual installations, but to learn from each other through 'a constructive exchange of views' after a 'thorough examination of national reports'. The expectation is that technical cooperation measures may then be identified with a view to resolving any safety problems. This is not explicitly a non-compliance procedure, nor does the Convention contemplate any machinery for independent verification or inspection of national reports, but the right to seek clarification and to comment on reports does provide an opportunity for scrutiny.[90] Such additional information as IAEA possesses could presumably also be called upon for assistance if necessary. Another omission is the failure to afford transparency to the process of review. Only intergovernmental organizations, but not NGOs, may be

---

[87] Ibid.

[88] See concerns expressed in *1st Review Meeting of the Parties* (1999) IAEA/GOV/INF/1999/11-GC(43)11, Annex II. But cf Kamminga, 44 *ICLQ* (1995) 872.

[89] Annex to the Final Act, para 3. See also *1st Review Meeting of the Parties* (1999) Annex II, para 4; IAEA, *Guidelines under the INSC Regarding the Review Process* (1998) IAEA/INFCIRC/571.

[90] Ibid.

invited to send observers to participate in meetings of the parties. Although a summary of discussions and conclusions must be made public, individual countries will not be named and the content of peer reviews must remain confidential.[91]

The Nuclear Safety Convention's control regime has much in common with early environmental treaties, but it compares unfavourably with most of the more recent global agreements: one critical commentator describes the Convention's review system as 'rudimentary', but he accepts that it may develop a momentum of its own, as other environmental agreements have done.[92] Another feature which may give it more bite is that the Convention is open to participation by 'all states', including non-nuclear states, who may have a stronger interest in ensuring effective oversight of non-complying parties than the nuclear powers who effectively dictated its terms. Moreover the Convention's potential impact in mitigating the risks of nuclear power should not be viewed in isolation from the safety-related work of IAEA as a whole. As we saw in the previous section, reporting by the parties to the NSC undoubtedly provides a more systematic basis for safety review than ad hoc IAEA inspections alone, and it provides a more informed basis for establishing which countries merit further voluntary inspection.

(b) The Joint Convention on the Safety of Spent Fuel and Radioactive Waste Management

This agreement, adopted by IAEA member states in 1997, follows the model of the Nuclear Safety Convention, and it has the same objectives of ensuring high safety standards and prevention of accidents.[93] Article 1 also recognizes the intergenerational implications of nuclear-waste disposal, and these are further addressed in the convention's specific obligations. In accordance with Article 3 the convention applies both to radioactive-waste disposal and spent-fuel management,[94] but with two notable exceptions which make it less than comprehensive. First, due to Indian and Pakistani opposition, reprocessing of spent fuel, and spent fuel held for reprocessing, are included only if the relevant contracting party so declares. However, the three main reprocessing states, France, Japan, and the United Kingdom all made voluntary declarations of inclusion during the negotiation of the Convention.[95] Second, spent fuel or waste from military installations are included only if transferred to permanent civilian control, or if the relevant party so declares. No declarations on this matter were made at the conference.

---

[91] See Articles 24–5, 27, and *Guidelines under the INSC Regarding the Review Process* (1998).

[92] See Kamminga, 44 *ICLQ* (1995) 872.

[93] For summary records of the Diplomatic Conference held in 1997 and other *travaux préparatoires* see IAEA GOV/INF/821-GC(41)/INF/12 (1997). See also de Kageneck and Pinel, 47 *ICLQ* (1998) 409.

[94] The Joint Convention will in some cases overlap with the Nuclear Safety Convention: the latter applies to radioactive waste or spent fuel held 'on the same site' and 'directly related to the operation of [a] nuclear power plant': Article 2(i). Once a nuclear plant ceases to be a 'nuclear installation' it moves out of the Nuclear Safety Convention and into the Joint Convention: NSC, Article 2(i).

[95] *Summary Record of the 4th Plenary Meeting*, RWSC/DC/SR 4, paras 93–5, in IAEA/GOV/INF/821-GC(41)/INF/12(1997).

The main provisions of the convention are similar to those found in the Nuclear Safety Convention. They set out general safety requirements for the management of spent fuel and radioactive waste, the design, siting, and operation of related facilities, and the establishment of a regulatory framework and independent regulatory body.[96] These obligations are based mainly on IAEA's 1995 Principles of Radioactive Waste Management,[97] which thus become the second of IAEA's fundamental safety standards to acquire a new binding treaty status. The Joint Convention also has exactly the same kind of control regime as the Nuclear Safety Convention, although the national reporting requirements are more detailed and potentially onerous.[98] Some elements of the Joint Convention go beyond what is required by the earlier convention, however.

In keeping with agreements relating to other types of hazardous waste,[99] and with Article 19(viii) of the Nuclear Safety Convention, generation of radioactive waste must be kept to a minimum, but parties must also must aim to avoid imposing 'undue burdens' on future generations, including burdens that are greater than permitted for present generations. Although still heavily qualified, this appears to be the strongest provision on intergenerational equity in any environmental treaty.[100] More specifically, consistently with Antarctica's status as a world park, storage or disposal of nuclear waste or spent fuel on the continent is wholly prohibited by Article 27(1). This reiteration of Article 5 of the 1959 Antarctic Treaty has the effect of making the latter provision applicable to third states who are parties to the Joint Convention.

Compared to the Nuclear Safety Convention, the Joint Convention gives somewhat greater effect to IAEA or OECD/NEA soft law in setting minimum standards for national regulation. Not only must national law provide 'effective' protection for individuals, society and the environment, it must also give 'due regard to internationally endorsed criteria and standards'.[101] This formulation does not make IAEA or OECD/NEA soft law binding on parties to the Joint Convention, but it strengthens the view that nuclear soft law is particularly relevant in deciding whether states have taken the 'appropriate steps' required by the principal provisions of the convention. Moreover, whereas the Nuclear Safety Convention provides only that radiation exposure shall not exceed prescribed *national* dose limits,[102] Article 24 of the Joint Convention requires national radiation limits to have 'due regard to internationally endorsed standards on radiation protection'. Article 24 also requires parties to the Joint Convention to implement 'appropriate corrective measures' to control or mitigate accidental releases of radioactivity; strangely there is no comparable obligation in the Nuclear Safety Convention, despite the greater risk of accidents.[103]

---

[96] Articles 4–26.

[97] IAEA Safety Series No 111-F (1995). See also IAEA Safety Series No 111-S, *Establishing a National System for Radioactive Waste Management* (1995).

[98] Articles 29–37.   [99] See *infra*, Ch 8.

[100] Articles 4(v)–(vi), 5(vi)–(vii). On intergenerational equity see *supra*, Ch 3.

[101] Articles 4(iv), 11(iv). These will include radiation protection standards, including those in IAEA Safety Series No 120 *Radiation Protection and the Safety of Radiation Sources* (Vienna, 1996).

[102] Article 15.   [103] See *infra*, section 3(3)(b).

Article 27 also gives binding force for the first time to the main provisions of IAEA's 1990 Code of Practice on the International Transboundary Movement of Radioactive Waste,[104] a soft-law instrument whose recommendations were based on the 1989 Basel Convention.[105] Waste or spent fuel may only be exported if the state of destination has the requisite capacity to handle such materials in a manner consistent with the convention and if it has given its prior informed consent. If these conditions are not met, reimport of the material must be allowed. However, disputes among the negotiating states about freedom of navigation at sea resulted in a provision on the rights of transit states which differs from the Code of Practice.[106] Instead of affording transit states the same right of prior informed consent as enjoyed by the state of intended disposal, and as provided for in the 1990 Code of Practice, Article 27(1) of the Joint Convention merely stipulates that 'transboundary movement through States of *transit* shall be subject to those international obligations which are relevant to the particular modes of transport utilised' (emphasis added), without making clear what those obligations are. What appears from the conference records is that, in the view of the bare majority of states who supported the text as finally adopted, international law does not require prior notice and consent for transit through the territorial waters or exclusive economic zone of another state.[107]

2(3) OTHER INTERNATIONAL REGULATORY BODIES

(a) Euratom

The Euratom Treaty was signed by EC member states in 1957 for the purpose of creating a nuclear common market.[108] It continues to provide the basis of EC competence in this field. The treaty's objectives include the application of uniform safety standards to protect the health of workers and the general public against radiation.[109] Other provisions are intended to ensure non-diversion of nuclear materials for military purposes.[110] Safety is thus only one aspect of EC nuclear responsibilities. Unlike the IAEA Statute, however, the Euratom Treaty requires member states to implement safety directives and to ensure that they are enforced.[111] But the safety measures it has adopted are limited in scope and some of those referred to below were only adopted belatedly in response to the Chernobyl accident, which revealed little coordination or agreement among member states.

---

[104] IAEA GC (XXXIV)/939 at (1990) 30 *ILM* (1991) 55. The 1990 Code is a good example of IAEA soft law at its weakest: most provisions are written in non-mandatory terms, using the word 'should'.

[105] See *infra*, Ch 8. The Basel Convention does not apply to nuclear waste specifically covered by other international instruments: see Article 1(3).

[106] See *Summary Records of the 4th Plenary Meeting*, RWSC/DC/SR 4 and SR.5, paras 119–139, and 1–40.

[107] For fuller discussion see *supra*, Ch 8.

[108] 1957 Euratom Treaty, Article 2 and Ch IX; IAEA, *Nuclear Law for a Developing World* (Vienna, 1969) 39ff; Grunwald, in Cameron et al (eds), *Nuclear Energy Law after Chernobyl*, 33.

[109] Articles 2(b), 30, 31. See *European Parliament v Council* [1991] ECR I-4529 ('*Chernobyl II*').

[110] Article 2(e) and Ch VII.   [111] Articles 33, 38.

Community directives lay down basic radiation standards for health protection.[112] The object of these is to ensure that Community citizens are protected to internationally agreed levels, and that all exposures are adequately regulated and kept as low as reasonably achievable. Radioactivity levels must be controlled by member states and are monitored by the European Commission through national reporting.[113] Following the Chernobyl accident the Commission temporarily restricted the import of affected foodstuffs, and it has since adopted regulations allowing it to specify permitted levels of radiation contamination in food.[114] At present these are the only aspects of nuclear health and safety covered by Community law. Due to opposition from some member states there are no EC rules setting standards for design, construction, and operation of nuclear installations, radioactive emissions into air or water, or management of radioactive waste. The 'Seveso' directives, which require that adequate measures be taken to prevent the risk of major accidents at chemical plants or industrial enterprises, do not apply to nuclear installations and reprocessing facilities.[115]

Faced with a reluctance on the part of some member states to allow the Community or the European Parliament to regulate nuclear power more comprehensively,[116] the main protection against nuclear risks which Community law and the Euratom Treaty offer other states is the right of the Community to be consulted or to inspect in certain circumstances. Article 34 of the treaty obliges states to consult the Commission when they propose to conduct particularly dangerous nuclear experiments in their territories, and to obtain its consent if these are liable to affect other member states. This is stronger than the consultation requirements of customary international law considered below because it gives the Commission a power of veto, and suggests that such experiments will otherwise be unlawful. Article 37 requires notification to be given to the Commission when radioactive substances may contaminate other states, for example by disposal at sea or into rivers.[117] Although the Commission may only comment on the proposal, the process nevertheless involves independent expert review, and the findings would provide some indication of likely problems, if any. The Article 37 procedure has been used, inter alia, to review nuclear fuel reprocessing facilities at Sellafield and the findings were relied on by the United Kingdom in the MOX Plant litigation. Other states have no right to participate in the review, however. Finally, Community law requires nuclear states to give urgent notice to their neigh-

---

[112] See e.g. Directives 96/29/EURATOM (1996) on Basic Safety Standards for Health Protection against Ionising Radiation; Directive 92/3/EURATOM (1992) on Shipments of Radioactive Waste and Regulation 1493/93 (1993) on Shipments of Radioactive Substances and Waste.

[113] Articles 35, 36 Euratom Treaty. In 1989, the Commission decided to exercise its power of inspection of environmental radioactivity monitoring facilities under Article 35 Euratom in order to ensure their proper functioning and efficiency.

[114] Council Regs 3954/87, 2218/89, 2219/89; Commission Reg (Euratom) 770/90.

[115] Directive 82/501/EEC ('Seveso I') replaced by 96/82/EC ('Seveso II'). See Cameron et al (eds), *Nuclear Energy Law after Chernobyl*, 40ff.

[116] Cameron, 19 *JEL* (2007) 71, 75–6.

[117] In ECJ Case 187/87 (1988) *Land Sarre v Minister for Industry, Posts and Telecommunications*, 1 *CMLR* (1989) 529, the ECJ determined that article 37 required notification to be given before *authorization* of any discharge.

bours of any accident which involves exposure of the population to radiation and to give information on how to minimize the consequences of the accident or of measures taken to deal with it.[118] The Euratom Treaty and Community law nevertheless fall well short of creating an obligation for member states to submit all their nuclear installations to independent environmental or safety assessment by the Commission. These remain national responsibilities. Despite its apparent advantages, therefore, the Euratom Treaty has neither supplanted nor extended the IAEA Statute as a basis for regulating nuclear environmental risks.

(b) OECD

Some 85 per cent of all civil nuclear installations are in OECD member states, and the OECD's Nuclear Energy Agency has become an important forum for cooperation at various levels, including the harmonization and development of national nuclear law on a consensus basis.[119] The aims of this organization are similar to those of IAEA, without its safeguards role. They include encouraging the adoption of common standards dealing with public health and the prevention of accidents.[120] Standards on such matters as radiation protection and waste management have been developed in collaboration with IAEA and other bodies, but once again there is no power to compel compliance. OECD has also been responsible for initiating and revising conventions on third-party liability.[121]

(c) ILO

ILO has sponsored a widely supported convention (ILO Convention No 115, 1960) on protecting workers against radiation and it issues various non-binding recommendations on the subject.

2(3) THE EFFECTIVENESS OF INTERNATIONAL REGULATION

There have undoubtedly been improvements in the international regulation of nuclear safety since the Chernobyl accident. Legally binding treaty commitments and improved opportunities for international supervision and inspection have reduced the freedom governments enjoy to determine their own balance of safety and economic interest. Although the Report of the 1st Review Meeting of the Parties to the Nuclear Safety Convention does little more than describe the system of review now in operation,[122] it does mark a new phase of collective oversight of nuclear safety which has some

---

[118] Council Decision 87/600/Euratom; Council Directive 89/618/Euratom; Council Directive 96/29/Euratom, Articles 50, 51(5). See generally, Cameron et al (eds), *Nuclear Energy Law after Chernobyl*, 40ff.

[119] See Strohl, in IAEA, *Licensing and Regulatory Control of Nuclear Installations* (Vienna, 1975) 135; Cameron et al (eds), *Nuclear Energy Law after Chernobyl*, 6ff; Reyners, 32 *European Yearbook* (1984) 1.

[120] ENEA Statute, Article 1.

[121] 1960 Convention on Third Party Liability in the Field of Nuclear Energy, with 2004 Protocol, *infra*, section 5.

[122] IAEA/GOV/INF/1999/11-GC(43)11.

resemblance to those in place for other forms of ultra-hazardous health, safety, and environmental risks. Subsequent review meetings have covered a wide range of topics, including security questions and the structure and functioning of national regulatory bodies. Some concern has been expressed about their independence from political control.[123]

In 1999 an intergovernmental conference concluded that considerable progress had been made in improving national regulation and the independence and competence of nuclear regulatory authorities in Eastern Europe, although it noted the continuing need to improve technical capabilities and ensure adequate resources for national regulators.[124] These developments lend some substance to the commitment made by governments in the 1996 Moscow Declaration on Nuclear Safety and Security to give 'absolute priority' to using nuclear power consistently with fundamental principles of nuclear safety. Whether, as claimed in the Declaration, nuclear power is consistent with and can contribute to sustainable development, or provide an environmentally safe alternative to fossil fuels, depends entirely on the public acceptability of the risk, however small, and however well controlled, which nuclear power installations continue to represent for both present and future generations.

3 CONTROL OF TRANSBOUNDARY NUCLEAR RISKS

3(1) INTERNATIONAL OBLIGATIONS

The 1994 Nuclear Safety Convention and the 1997 Joint Convention are the first global treaties to commit states to control the risks of nuclear energy for environmental objectives. Nevertheless, there is ample evidence that states had already recognized the existence of an obligation to minimize nuclear risks and to prevent injury to other states, or radioactive pollution of the global environment.[125] Nuclear powered merchant ships[126] and satellites[127] must comply with internationally agreed standards of safety and radiation protection, and the same principle is accepted for

---

[123] See *Report of the 3rd Review Meeting* (2005).

[124] International Conference on Strengthening Nuclear Safety in Eastern Europe, IAEA/GC(43)INF/6 (1999).

[125] IAEA/GC(SPL 1)Res/1 (1989); Okowa, *State Responsibility for Transboundary Air Pollution in International Law* (Oxford, 2000) Ch 4; Kirgis, 66 *AJIL* (1972) 290. In the dispute over nuclear testing in the Pacific, France accepted 'its duty to ensure that every condition was met and every precaution taken to prevent injury to the population and the fauna and flora of the world' (note to New Zealand of 19 Feb 1973, in *French Nuclear Testing in the Pacific*).

[126] 1974 Safety of Life at Sea Convention, Annex, Ch 8, and Attachment 3.

[127] UNGA Res 47/68 (1992); 1967 Treaty on Principles Governing the Activities of States in the Exploration and Use of Outer Space.

the transboundary transport of radioactive substances.[128] Only the military uses of nuclear power fall outside these rules, which show that in contrast to their practice concerning nuclear power plants, states have been more willing to accept obligatory standards of international regulation for nuclear risks when these occur in common spaces. Thus the problem of defining the content of an obligation of due diligence, posed by the uncertain legal status of IAEA standards, is confined mainly to the operation of nuclear power stations within national borders.

Moreover, the dumping of radioactive waste at sea, or its discharge into the marine environment through land-based or airborne sources is now largely prohibited. Insofar as it was formerly permitted on the high seas, dumping had to comply with international regulations and the requirements of relevant treaty regimes, and is now banned on precautionary grounds.[129] Further prohibitions on radioactive-waste disposal exist in the Antarctic,[130] in Asia and the Pacific,[131] and in Africa.[132] It was argued in Chapter 3 that what constitutes 'pollution' varies according to context, so these precedents are particularly important in showing that the emission of radioactive substances into the environment of common spaces is presumed to constitute prohibited pollution irrespective of any threshold of material injury or interference with amenities or resources.[133] The only possible exception is that below a certain level of radioactivity some proof of harm may be needed.[134]

With regard to nuclear explosions the same conclusion is indicated by the 1963 Nuclear Test Ban Treaty. This treaty prohibits weapons test explosions in the atmosphere, outer space, at sea, in Antarctica, or in any circumstances where radioactive debris spreads beyond the territory of the testing state. Its effect is that tests must be conducted underground and cause no escape of pollution. Not all nuclear powers are parties to this treaty, however,[135] and its status in customary law has been disputed. In the *Nuclear Tests Case*,[136] the ICJ declined to decide whether atmospheric tests carried out by France violated customary international law, but it did hold that France

---

[128] 1997 Joint Convention, *supra*, section 2; 1989 Basel Convention on the Control of Transboundary Movements of Hazardous Wastes, *supra*, Ch 8; 1990 Code of Practice on the International Transboundary Movement of Radioactive Waste, ibid.

[129] See *supra*, Ch 8.

[130] 1959 Antarctic Treaty, Article 5; Recommendation VIII-12, 8th Antarctic Treaty Consultative Meeting, 1975; 1997 Joint Convention, Article 27(1).

[131] 1986 Noumea Convention for the Protection of the Natural Resources and Environment of the South Pacific, Article II; 1989 Protocol for the Protection of the South East Pacific Against Radioactive Pollution; 1995 Waigani Convention on Hazardous Wastes in the South Pacific; 1996 ASEAN Treaty on the SE Asia Nuclear-Weapon Free Zone, Article 3.

[132] 1991 Bamako Convention, *supra*, Ch 8; 1996 African Nuclear Free Zone Treaty, Article 7.

[133] Kirgis, 66 *AJIL* 1972) and *supra*, Ch 3, section 4(6).

[134] E.g. in the case of land-based discharges of low-level radioactive waste.

[135] North Korea, France and China are the main nuclear states to remain outside the 1963 treaty. France is a party to the 1996 Comprehensive Test Ban Treaty (CTBT) however. China, India, Iran, Israel, Pakistan, North Korea, and the United States are not parties to the CTBT.

[136] Cf Judges Gros, ICJ Reports (1974) 279ff; Petren, 305ff; de Castro, 389ff; Barwick, 427ff. Note also Judge Barwick's point that 'there is a radical distinction to be made between claims that violation of territorial and decisional sovereignty by the intrusion and deposition of radioactive nuclides...is unlawful

had by its public statements unilaterally committed itself to conduct no more tests of this kind.[137] Since 1980 all Chinese tests have in practice also complied with the 1963 Treaty.[138] Regional agreements prohibit all nuclear weapons testing in the territory of Latin American, South Pacific, South-east Asian, and African states parties.[139]

Given the weight of international opposition expressed in these agreements to all forms of deliberate radioactive pollution of common spaces, and the tacit compliance of non-parties with the 1963 Treaty since 1980, the case for a prohibition of nuclear testing founded on customary law, but excluding underground tests, is now strong.[140] This conclusion does not extend beyond deliberate nuclear tests or peaceful explosions, however. It does not mean that accidental radioactive explosions, such as the Chernobyl reactor accident, per se represent a violation of international law without showing a failure of due diligence,[141] nor does it imply that the actual use of nuclear weapons is forbidden by international law. Although some writers argue that this is the case, their views are based on the indiscriminate character of nuclear weapons and other humanitarian considerations.[142] While recognizing the importance of these considerations in its *Advisory Opinion on Nuclear Weapons*, the International Court did not find the threat or use of nuclear weapons in all circumstances illegal, but it did recognize the customary status of explicit treaty limitations on methods of warfare which cause widespread, long-term, and severe damage to the natural environment.[143] However, the use of nuclear weapons is prohibited entirely in Latin America, Africa, South-east Asia, and the Pacific.[144] The 1977 Additional Protocol

according to international law, and the claim that the testing of nuclear weapons has become unlawful, according to customary law', at 248. See also Pleadings (1978) I, 500ff; II, 264ff.

[137] On the legal force of unilateral undertakings in international law, see *Nuclear Tests Cases,* ICJ Reports (1974) 253; *Paramilitary Activities in Nicaragua Case,* ICJ Reports (1986) 14.

[138] China announced in 1986 that it did not intend to conduct further atmospheric tests. Its last atmospheric test took place in 1980. See SIPRI, *Yearbook* (Oxford, 1987) 45–52. Subsequent North Korean, Indian, and Pakistani tests have all taken place underground.

[139] 1967 Tlateloco Treaty for the Prohibition of Nuclear Weapons in Latin America and the Caribbean, Article 1; 1985 South Pacific Nuclear Free Zone Treaty, Article 6; 1996 ASEAN Nuclear Weapon-Free Zone Treaty, Article 3; 1996 African Nuclear Weapon-Free Zone Treaty, Article 5. The Tlateloco Treaty permits nuclear explosions for peaceful purposes.

[140] Lammers, *Pollution of International Watercourses* (Dordrecht, 1984) 319–27; Kirgis, 66 *AJIL* (1972) 295f, but cf Margolis, 64 *Yale LJ* (1955) 648 and McDougal and Schlei, ibid, 629, who support only a standard of reasonableness but disagree about its implications for the permissibility of nuclear tests. Singh and McWhinney, *Nuclear Weapons and Contemporary International Law* (2nd edn, Dordrecht, 1989) 230–3, conclude that the number of adherents indicates that the 1963 Treaty is now accepted as customary law. Okowa, *State Responsibility for Transboundary Air Pollution in International Law,* 99–110, concludes that atmospheric testing is not unlawful.

[141] Boyle, 60 *BYIL* (1989) 272–4, 290–6; id, in Butler (ed), *Perestroika and International Law* (Dordrecht, 1990) 203. See *supra,* Ch 3.

[142] See Pogany (ed), *Nuclear Weapons and International Law* (Aldershot, 1987); de Chazournes and Sands (eds), *International Law, the ICJ and Nuclear Weapons,* 131–448.

[143] ICJ Reports (1996) 226; 1977 Additional Protocol 1 to the Geneva Red Cross Conventions, Articles 35, 55, and see de Chazournes and Sands (eds), *International Law, the ICJ and Nuclear Weapons.*

[144] 1985 South Pacific NFZ Treaty; 1967 Tlateloco Treaty; 1996 African and ASEAN Nuclear Weapon-Free Zone Treaties.

also prohibits attacks on nuclear power stations not used in support of military operations.[145]

As we saw in Chapter 3, the *Nuclear Tests Cases*[146] raised the question whether the deposit of radioactive particles on the territory of another state, or on the high seas, constitutes serious harm or an interference with high-seas freedoms. The peculiar difficulty which radioactive fallout poses is that injury may not be immediate or apparent, and the claimants in the *Nuclear Tests Cases* did not allege that they had suffered actual harm, but based the main part of their claim on a violation of their territorial sovereignty. The development of international standards of radiation exposure, based on evidence of long-term effects, provides an obvious method for establishing an agreed threshold of harm which takes account of the absence of immediate injury.[147] Inconsistent practices among those affected were revealed by the Chernobyl accident, and the work of the ICRP, IAEA, WHO, and FAO has in their respective fields subsequently concentrated on elaborating common guidelines. Thus it is now easier than it was in 1974 to determine when serious radiation injury or harm has occurred, and this should no longer constitute an obstacle to international claims.

With remarkable consistency, the precedents considered here point to the conclusion that Principle 2 of the Rio Declaration, and other authoritative statements of the obligation to control sources of environmental harm are applicable to nuclear risks.[148] States do have an international responsibility based in customary law for the safe conduct of their nuclear activities, notwithstanding that they may take place entirely within their own borders.

3(2) NUCLEAR INSTALLATIONS: NOTIFICATION AND CONSULTATION

The evidence of bilateral agreements among European states, as well as the Nuclear Safety Convention and the Joint Convention on Spent Fuel and Radioactive Waste, confirm that principles of notification and consultation intended to minimize transboundary risks have been applied to planned nuclear installations, although most of these treaties are limited to installations within 30km, 'or in the vicinity' of, an international border.[149] All require a full exchange of information on the proposed installation, so that other states may review the decision-making process and data and offer appropriate comments on safety and health protection. In most cases permanent commissions

---

[145] 1977 Additional Protocol I, ibid. Article 56. See also the condemnation of Israel's attack on an Iraqi nuclear reactor: UNSC Res 487 (1981); IAEA Board of Governors, Res S/14532 (1981) in 20 *ILM* (1981) 963, but note the US attack on Iraqi nuclear facilities during the 1991 Kuwait conflict.

[146] *Supra*, n 13. [147] Handl, 92 *RGDIP* (1988) 55; Sands, *Chernobyl*, 15.

[148] *Supra*, Ch 3, section 4, and Okowa, *State Responsibility for Transboundary Air Pollution in International Law*, 110–30.

[149] E.g. 1980 Agreement between Spain and Portugal on Cooperation in Matters Affecting the Safety of Nuclear Installations in the Vicinity of the Frontier, Ruster and Simma, xxvii, 420; 1977 Netherlands–FRG Memorandum on Exchange of Information and Consultation in Border Areas, ibid, 275; 1977 Denmark–FRG Agreement Regulating the Exchange of Information on the Construction of Nuclear Installations along the Border, 17 *ILM* (1978) 274; Nuclear Safety Convention, Article 17; Joint Convention, Articles 6, 13.

are established to consider matters of joint interest affecting public health,[150] but these bodies have no power to limit the parties' freedom of action. None of these treaties gives neighbouring states a veto, nor suggests that the siting of nuclear installations near borders is impermissible or subject to any equitable balance of interests.[151] However, Articles 6 and 13 of the 1997 Joint Convention do require the siting of waste or spent-fuel installations to conform to general safety principles set out in Article 4 of the Convention. This is at present the only acknowledgement that there may be some limits on the freedom of states to locate nuclear installations near a border, but there are some indications that it reflects state practice in this respect. Thus in 1996 Ireland made representations to a public inquiry in the United Kingdom, successfully opposing on safety grounds the licensing of a deep storage facility at Sellafield, bordering the Irish Sea. In 1997 a proposal to dispose of Taiwanese nuclear waste at border sites in North Korea was similarly shelved after South Korean protests over safety.

In contrast, port visits by nuclear-powered vessels have entailed the prior negotiation of bilateral agreements and are subject to the consent of the port state.[152] Where such vessels are merely in transit through the territorial sea of another state, however, the principle of innocent passage applies, as for all vessels, and no obligation of prior notice or consent appears to arise.[153] Such ships may be required to carry documents and observe special precautionary measures established by the SOLAS Convention, however.[154]

Lastly, both the use of nuclear power sources in outer space, and the conduct of nuclear explosions for peaceful purposes appear to require prior notification to the relevant international organization, and must be preceded by a safety assessment. Information on radioactive fallout must be communicated, and in case of unplanned satellite re-entry, sub-orbital states are to be consulted.[155]

These precedents all point first to the conclusion that states are not debarred by international law from acquiring and using nuclear technology simply because it poses a risk of injury to other states or to the environment, nor are they precluded from siting nuclear installations near borders.[156] Subject only to restraints implied by

---

[150] E.g. 1966 Belgium–France Convention on Radiological Protection with regard to the Installations of the Ardennes Nuclear Power Station, 988 *UNTS* 288; 1982 Switzerland–FRG Agreement on Mutual Information on Construction and Operation of Nuclear Installations in Border Areas, II *Bundesgesetzblatt* (1983) 734 and agreements listed *supra*, n 149 between Spain–Portugal and Netherlands–FRG.

[151] Cameron et al (eds), *Nuclear Energy Law After Chernobyl*, 73ff, but cf Handl, 7 *ELQ* (1978) 1, who argues that affected states are entitled to an equitable solution, i.e. more than consultation and negotiation, but less than a veto. See *supra*, Ch 3, section 4(5).

[152] Boulanger, in IAEA, *Experience and Trends in Nuclear Law*, 125; Haselgrove, ibid. In part the insistence on prior agreement reflects the failure of nuclear ship operators to ratify the 1962 Brussels Convention on the Liability of Operators of Nuclear Ships, *infra*, section 5.

[153] 1982 UNCLOS, Articles 17–19, 21–4. See *supra*, Ch 7. Article 5 of the 1985 South Pacific Nuclear Free Zone Treaty preserves the rights of innocent passage, archipelagic sea lanes passage, and transit passage for nuclear-armed ships in the South Pacific NFZ. See also 1996 African NWFZ Treaty, Article 2(2) and 1996 ASEAN NWFZ Treaty, Article 7.

[154] 1982 UNCLOS, Article 23.

[155] UNGA Res 47/68 (1992); Tlateloco Treaty, Article 18, but cf Article 34, Euratom Treaty, *supra*, section 2.

[156] Lenaerts, in Cameron et al (eds), *Nuclear Energy Law After Chernobyl*, 73ff; Reuter, 103 *Recueil des Cours* (1961) 592. But cf Handl, 7 *ELQ* (1978) 35, who argues that for activities carrying a risk of catastrophic

compliance with the required standards of diligent control and procedural obligations considered above, 'each state is free to act within the limits of its sovereignty',[157] and to act on its own assessment of the risk.

Second, leaving aside the exceptional rules applied to nuclear ships, the evidence of state practice examined here is consistent with the view that states must notify and consult their neighbours in cases of serious or appreciable transboundary risk, with a view to ensuring reasonable regard for the rights and legitimate interests of other states.[158] As we saw in Chapter 3, the application of this rule to transboundary risks such as nuclear installations represents a logical extension of the *Lac Lanoux Case*.[159] Although in its 2001 Articles on Prevention of Transboundary Harm the ILC requires the negotiation in these cases of an equitable balance of interests,[160] state practice continues to favour the more limited rule indicated here.

The narrowness of this obligation as it has been applied in state practice should be observed, however, particularly in its application to nuclear power. The Chernobyl reactor was not in a border area, and states have not consulted in such cases, save, as we shall see, in cases of emergency.[161] In contrast, it is significant that the ILC's 2001 articles extend the requirement of consultation to all activities creating significant transboundary risk wherever located.[162] Moreover, it is questionable whether for nuclear installations transboundary consultation is enough to ensure that neighbouring states and the environment are adequately protected from unilaterally determined nuclear risks. What is lacking in such cases is a rule comparable to that applied in certain cases of dumping at sea, requiring prior consultation and approval of the relevant international organization.[163] This solution seems preferable to one making nuclear activities dependent on the agreement of neighbouring states, but avoids the excessive unilateralism of the present law.

3(3) COOPERATION AND ASSISTANCE IN CASES OF NUCLEAR EMERGENCY

(a) Notification

The existence of a general obligation to notify other states and cooperate in cases where they are at risk from nuclear accidents or incidents is confirmed both by regional practice in Western Europe, and by international conventions. Most of the European

---

effects, 'barring a special relationship between risk exposed states such as reciprocity of risk creation, or a sharing of benefits to be derived from the proposed activity, such an activity should be considered impermissible, and Kirgis, 66 *AJIL* (1972) 294, who argues for a reasonableness test.

[157] ICJ Reports (1973) 131, per Judge Ignacio Pinto; ICJ Reports (1974) 253, 457. Note that the court's 1973 decisions ordered France by way of interim measures to 'avoid nuclear tests causing the deposit of radioactive fallout' on the plaintiffs' territory. Cf also New Zealand's reply to the French note regarding nuclear tests, cited, *supra*, n 125: 'an activity that is inherently harmful is not made acceptable even by the most stringent precautionary measures'.

[158] Lenaerts, in Cameron et al, *Nuclear Energy Law*, 73–8; cf Handl, 7 *ELQ* (1978) however.

[159] *Supra*, Ch 3, section 4(5).   [160] Articles 9(2),10, on which see *supra*, Ch 3, section 4(5).

[161] See *infra*, section 3(3).   [162] *Supra*, Ch 3, section 4(5).   [163] *Supra*, Ch 8, section 3.

treaties contain provisions for the timely supply of information in cases of emergency and require radioactivity monitoring systems to be established to alert governments of the danger.[164] A small number also require cooperation in response to such an emergency. Following the Chernobyl accident, the Soviet Union was criticized for failing to give adequate and timely information to other states likely to be affected by the disaster. Implicit in this criticism was a belief that such notification should reasonably be expected.[165] In addition to the practice of a growing number of states supporting such an obligation, IAEA had developed guidelines on reporting of incidents and information exchange in 1985,[166] but these were non-binding.

One result of Chernobyl was the opening for signature of the 1986 Convention on Early Notification of a Nuclear Accident.[167] This imposes on parties a duty to notify other states likely to be affected by transboundary releases of 'radiological safety significance'. Information on the occurrence and on means of minimizing its radiological consequences must be supplied, to enable other states to take all possible precautionary measures. The Convention specifies in detail what information is to be given, and requires states to respond promptly to requests for further relevant information. It is less clear, however, at what point a release acquires radiological safety significance; this provision deliberately avoids objective definition, and thus leaves substantial discretion to states where incidents occur. The effectiveness of the Convention is also dependent on states possessing a basic radiological monitoring and assessment capability. Unlike bilateral treaties in Europe, the Convention does not require states to acquire this capability; where it is lacking, it is difficult to see how they will be able to respond effectively.[168]

Due to superpower opposition, the Convention does not cover nuclear accidents involving military facilities, such as nuclear submarines, but the Soviet Union gave

---

[164] Agreement between Spain and Portugal, *supra*, n 148; Belgium–France Convention, *supra*, n 149; 1979 Agreement between France and Switzerland Concerning Exchange of Information in Case of Accidents, *Ruster and Simma*, xxvii, 382; 1983, UK–France Exchange of Notes Concerning Exchanges of Information, 60 *UKTS*, Cmnd 9041; 1978 Agreement between Switzerland and FRG Concerning Radiological Disaster Relief, *Ruster and Simma*, xxvii, 337; 1981 Agreement between France–FRG on Mutual Information in the event of Radiological Incidents, I *Bundesgesetzblatt*, 885; 1983 Agreement between France and Luxemburg on Exchange of Information in Case of Radiological Emergencies, 34 *NLB* (1984) 42. A further series of such agreements have been prompted by the Chernobyl accident; 1987 Agreement between Belgium and the Netherlands on Cooperation in Nuclear Safety, 41 *NLB* (1988) 42; 1987 Norway–Sweden Agreement on Exchange of Information and Early Notification Relating to Nuclear Facilities, 17 *EPL* (1987) 41; 1987 UK–Norway Agreement on Early Notification, Cmnd. 371; 1987 Finland–USSR Agreement on Early Notification of a Nuclear Accident, 39 *NLB* (1987) 4; 1987 FRG–GDR Radiation Protection Agreement, 40 *NLB* (1987) 44; 1987 Denmark–Poland Agreement on Exchange of Information, 41 *NLB* (1988) 49, and similar agreements with the FRG, USSR, UK, and Finland. These are all intended to give effect to the provisions of the 1986 IAEA Notification Convention.

[165] Group of Seven, Statement on the Implications of the Chernobyl Nuclear Accident, 25 *ILM* (1986) 1005; IAEA General Conference, Special Session, 1986, IAEA GC (SPL 1)/Res/1.

[166] IAEA/INFCIRC/321, Guidelines on Reportable Events, 1985.

[167] See generally Cameron et al (eds), *Nuclear Energy Law After Chernobyl*, 19ff; Adede, *The IAEA Notification and Assistance Conventions* (Dordrecht, 1987); Handl, 92 *RGDIP* (1988) 24ff.

[168] Rosen, *IAEA Bulletin* (1987) 34f.

notice when two such vessels ran into difficulty, and the United Kingdom has undertaken to do so.[169] Since the Convention applies only to 'transboundary releases', it would seem that accidents whose consequences do not extend beyond national borders, or which occur wholly on the high seas are also excluded.[170]

A number of states, including the Soviet Union and the United Kingdom, declared that they would observe the Convention pending ratification, and several agreements apply its provisions bilaterally.[171] Although the Convention is open to criticism for the apparent looseness of its terminology, and the range of excluded occurrences, it does now seem to justify the conclusion that the principle of timely notification of nuclear accidents likely to affect other states is a customary obligation. States also support the same principle in the case of accidents affecting nuclear-powered merchant ships or spacecraft.[172]

(b) Assistance

Assistance in cases of nuclear emergency is also the subject of an IAEA Convention, which allows states to call for international help to protect 'life, property and the environment' from the effects of radioactive releases.[173] IAEA is given a coordinating role, and an obligation to respond to a request by making available appropriate resources. No explicit obligation to render assistance is place on other states, however, even where an installation within their territory is the cause of harm, nor is there any provision for joint contingency planning comparable to that found in many maritime treaties.

Thus, in general, the Convention facilitates, but does not require a response to, nuclear accidents or emergencies. It main achievement is to give assisting states and their personnel immunity from legal proceedings brought by the requesting state, and an indemnity for proceedings brought by others. These provisions are open to reservation, however.[174]

Like the small number of bilateral treaties which provide in more general terms for emergency assistance,[175] the IAEA Convention leaves responsibility for making the request and taking or directing appropriate action in its territory with the state which needs help.[176] It creates no duty either to seek assistance, or to control the emergency.

---

[169] 25 *ILM* (1986) 1369. The UK declaration specifically includes voluntary notification of military accidents; others refer to 'all' or 'any' accidents.

[170] Cameron et al (eds), *Nuclear Energy Law After Chernobyl*, 24.   [171] *Supra*, n 164.

[172] 1974 SOLAS Convention, Regulation 12; UNGA Res 47/68 (1992) Principle 5.

[173] 1986 Convention on Assistance in the Case of a Nuclear Accident or Radiological Emergency; see also IAEA/INFCIRC/310, Guidelines for Mutual Emergency Assistance Arrangements. See generally Cameron et al (eds), *Nuclear Energy Law After Chernobyl*, 26ff; Adede, *The IAEA Notification and Assistance Conventions*.

[174] Articles 8, 10. Four states have excluded Article 8; two have excluded Article 10.

[175] E.g. 1963 Nordic Mutual Emergency Assistance Agreement in Connection with Radiation Accidents, 525 *UNTS* 76; 1966 Belgium–France Convention, *supra*, n 150; 1981 Belgium–France Agreement on Mutual Assistance in the Event of Catastrophic and Serious Accident, 34 *NLB* (1984) 42; 1977 France–FRG Agreement on Mutual Assistance in the Event of Catastrophic and Grave Disasters, II *Bundesgesetzblatt* (1980) 33; 1980 FRG–Belgium Agreement on Mutual Emergency Assistance, ibid. (1982) 1006.

[176] Article 3.

A failure to do so may of course incur state responsibility if it results in harm to others, under general principles discussed below. But unlike maritime casualties, where states also have a recognized right of intervention or self-help to protect their own coasts,[177] there is no generally accepted basis in international law for intervention by neighbouring states seeking to avert the consequences of a nuclear catastrophe, such as Chernobyl. Any attempt to take unilateral preventive action within another state, or to render unrequested assistance in these circumstances would in principle appear to be a violation of the source state's sovereignty.[178] At most, necessity might be pleaded in defence of any state undertaking such intervention in circumstances of grave and imminent peril.[179] By leaving the requesting state the decisive role, the IAEA Convention does nothing to disturb this position. Assistance, as provided for in the instruments referred to here is thus sharply different from intervention or self-protection. In short, it is not obligatory, it need not be sought, and it cannot be given without consent.

4 STATE RESPONSIBILITY FOR NUCLEAR DAMAGE

4(1) STRICT OR ABSOLUTE RESPONSIBILITY

The ultra-hazardous character of nuclear installations, in the sense that damage caused by accidents may be widespread, serious, and long-lasting, is for some writers the basis for asserting that state responsibility in such cases will be strict or absolute.[180] That position, and its application to nuclear energy, is the major focus of attention in this section, although it is questionable whether the ultra-hazardous category is wide enough to cover all nuclear activities, including those, such as discharge of radioactive waste into the sea, whose effects are cumulatively harmful rather than immediately catastrophic.[181]

---

[177] 1969 Convention on Intervention in Case of Maritime Casualties; 1982 UNCLOS, Article 221, *supra*, Ch 7.

[178] Cf the Security Council's condemnation of Israel's attack on an Iraqi Nuclear reactor: UNSC Res 487 (1981); see also IAEA Board of Governors Resolution S/14532, 20 *ILM* (1981) 963; *Corfu Channel Case*, ICJ Reports (1949) 32–6; *Case Concerning Diplomatic and Consular Staff in Tehran*, ICJ Reports (1980) 43, but see Bilder, 14 *Vand JTL* (1981).

[179] ILC, 2001 Articles on State Responsibility, Article 25, on which see *Gabčíkovo-Nagymaros Case*, ICJ Reports (1997) 7, paras 49–58.

[180] Jenks, 117 *Recueil des Cours* (1966) 105; Smith, *State Responsibility and the Marine Environment* (Oxford, 1987) 112–15; Handl, 16 *NYIL* (1985) 68ff; Hardy, 36 *BYIL* (1960) 237; Goldie, 16 *NYIL* (1985) 204ff; *contra*, Okowa, *State Responsibility for Transboundary Air Pollution in International Law*, 110–130, and see *supra*, Ch 4.

[181] Jenks, 117 *Recueil des Cours* (1966) 122, views *Trail Smelter* as a case of liability for ultra-hazardous operations. This is very much broader than most interpretations, however.

The main argument advanced by writers rests on inferences drawn from the use of strict or absolute liability as a general principle in national legal systems and civil liability treaties concerned with nuclear accidents.[182] The tendency of the treaties, however, is to avoid direct implication of the source state in responsibility for damage and to emphasize the liability in national law of the operator or company which caused the damage.[183] The possibility of state responsibility is not precluded, but the scheme of these civil-liability treaties involves states only as guarantors of the operators' strict liability, or in providing additional compensation funds. Moreover, the burden of this residual responsibility is either spread equitably across a group of nuclear states, or left in part to lie where it falls through limitation of liability. In neither case does the polluting state bear responsibility for the whole loss.[184] The extent of its liability is further limited by the narrow definition of nuclear damage used in the older treaties.[185]

These factors make the nuclear liability conventions weak precedents for any particular theory or standard of state responsibility for harm; they seem inconsistent with the view that states are absolutely or strictly responsible in international law for damage emanating from their territory even in cases of ultra-hazardous activities.[186] As with national laws employing standards of strict or absolute liability contingent on compulsory insurance and limitation of liability, it is difficult to treat complex schemes of loss distribution as indicating a standard of responsibility for states themselves in the less highly developed circumstances of international law.

A second argument concerning the standard of liability is based, as we saw in Chapter 4, on the concept of objective responsibility for breach of obligation. When applied to accidental injury emanating from nuclear installations, this concept focuses on the conduct of the state in failing to meet its obligation of diligent control, and is distinguishable from fault only in eliminating subjective elements of intention or recklessness. Responsibility in such cases is neither strict nor absolute since it cannot be established by proof of damage alone. But where nuclear damage is the result of some internationally prohibited activity, such as the dumping of radioactive waste at sea, or atmospheric nuclear tests, objective responsibility results not from a failure of due diligence, but simply from the harm caused in deliberate violation of international law. This is much closer to a standard of strict or absolute responsibility, and offers a sounder basis for such concepts than any inferences from national law or civil-liability conventions.[187] While the evidence of state practice reviewed below does not unequivocally support this analysis, some of the claims in question predate the present

---

[182] See esp Goldie, 14 *ICLQ* (1965) 1189, and *supra*, Ch 4, section 2.   [183] See *infra*, section 5.

[184] Ibid. Compare the 1972 Convention on International Liability for Damage Caused by Space Objects which places no limit on liability.

[185] But for revised formulations see *infra*, section 5(7).

[186] Miatello, in Spinedi and Simma (eds), *UN Codification of State Responsibility* (New York, 1987) 306ff; Handl, 92 *RGDIP* (1988) 35ff. *Contra*, Smith, *State Responsibility and the Marine Environment*, 114ff, and Kelson, 13 *Harv ILJ* (1972) 197. Poor ratification of all but the Paris Convention is another factor lessening the significance of these conventions: see *infra*, section 5(8).

[187] On objective responsibility see Ch 4, section 2. On the prohibition of deliberate pollution see *supra*, section 3.

consensus on prohibition of deliberate radioactive pollution, and cannot be taken as a wholly reliable guide to the present law.

4(2) STATE CLAIMS

State claims or settlements involving damage caused by nuclear activities provide little support for any one standard of responsibility. Rather, they demonstrate the lack of international consensus on this point. In 1955 the United States paid compensation to Japanese fishermen injured by one of its nuclear tests, but disclaimed any admission of legal responsibility.[188] Japan and New Zealand reserved the right in diplomatic protests to hold the United States and France responsible for any loss or damage inflicted by further tests in the Pacific,[189] but made no claims. Canada asserted in 1979 that the standard of absolute responsibility for space objects, including those using nuclear power and causing the deposit of radioactive material, had become a general principle of international law, and it relied on this in a successful claim for compensation from the Soviet Union following the crash of Cosmos 954. But this claim was supported by the 1972 Space Objects Liability Convention, to which both states were party;[190] the very different approach of the nuclear-liability conventions undermines the relevance of this precedent in other cases of accidental harm.

   Responses to the Chernobyl disaster provide the most telling evidence of state practice so far. This accident caused widespread harm to agricultural produce and livestock in Europe and affected wildlife, in some cases severely.[191] Clean-up costs were incurred and compensation was paid by several governments to their own citizens for produce which was destroyed as a precautionary measure, or which was rendered unusable. Evidence of long-term health risks has yet to emerge, but remains possible.[192]

   Despite this provable loss, no claims were made against the Soviet Union by any affected state, although the possibility was considered by some governments.[193] Uncertainty over the basis for such a claim, reluctance to establish a precedent with possible future implications for states which themselves operate nuclear power plants, and the absence of any appropriate treaty binding on the Soviet Union are the main reasons for this silence.[194] It is also unclear whether liability would extend to damage to the environment, or to the costs of precautionary measures taken by governments.

---

[188] Settlement of Japanese Claims for Personal and Property Damage Resulting from Nuclear Tests in Marshall Islands (1955) 1 *UST* 1, *TIAS* 3160, 4 Whiteman, *Digest* 553; Margolis, 64 *Yale LJ* (1955) 629; McDougal and Schlei, ibid, 648.

[189] Whiteman, *Digest* 585f; *Nuclear Tests Cases*, ICJ Pleadings (1978) II, 22–30; Australian notes on the subject made no reference to compensation, but did assert that the tests should be terminated: ibid, I, 2ff. In an exchange of notes dated 10 December 1993 Australia accepted an *ex gratia* payment of £20million from the United Kingdom in settlement of all claims relating to UK nuclear tests that took place on Australian territory in the 1950s and 60s.

[190] *Claim for Damage Caused by Cosmos 954*, 18 *ILM* (1979) 902; 1972 Convention on International Liability for Damage Caused by Space Objects. The USSR denied the applicability of the 1972 Convention to the damage which had occurred.

[191] *Supra*, n 1.   [192] IAEA, *One Decade After Chernobyl*, IAEA/INFCIRC/510(1996).

[193] West Germany, Sweden, and the UK reserved their position.   [194] Sands, *Chernobyl*, 27.

The Soviet Union made no voluntary offer of compensation, and questioned the necessity of precautionary measures taken by its neighbours, maintaining that they suffered little or no damage.[195] The failure to demand, or to offer compensation in this case shows the difficulty of reconciling doctrinal support for any standard of strict or absolute responsibility with the evidence of state practice, limited as it is. It points to the conclusion that responsibility for a failure of due diligence, that is for causing avoidable loss only, provides a more convincing interpretation of the actual practice of states and the present state of customary law in cases of accidental environmental damage.[196]

4(3) REFORMING THE LAW OF STATE RESPONSIBILITY FOR NUCLEAR INJURY

As we saw in chapter 4, the desirability of securing international agreement on appropriate principles of state responsibility for harm resulting from nuclear accidents was acknowledged as one of the lessons of Chernobyl.[197] In 1990 the IAEA established a Standing Committee on Liability for Nuclear Damage to undertake a comprehensive review of this problem, including revision of the existing Vienna Convention on Civil Liability for Nuclear Damage.[198] Initially the ILC's articles on 'International Liability' attracted some attention as a possible model for new provisions based on the strict liability of the state where the nuclear installation is located, and proposals were made by a number of states.[199] Opposition from the leading nuclear powers made this an untenable option, and the revised Vienna Convention does not address the question of the liability of states in international law, apart from acknowledging that the rights and obligations of the parties under general international law remain unaffected by the Convention. However, the parties did agree to adopt a new publicly funded compensation scheme, based on the earlier European scheme established in 1963, under which the state in which the installation is situated provides limited additional funding, and thereafter other states parties also contribute up to a ceiling.[200] Nuclear states cannot be compelled to participate in this scheme, however,

Despite the undoubted improvements made since 1990 to the global scheme for civil liability and compensation, recourse to state responsibility will remain necessary

---

[195] USSR Proposed Programme for Establishing an International Regime for the Safe Development of Nuclear Energy, 1986, repr Ibid, 227.

[196] See *supra*, Ch 4, section 2, and Okowa, *State Responsibility for Transboundary Air Pollution in International Law*, 110–30.

[197] USSR Proposed Programme, *supra*, n 195; Handl, 92 *RGDIP* (1988) 5; id, in NEA/OECD, *Nuclear Accidents: Liabilities and Guarantees: Proceedings of the NEA/OECD Symposium* (Paris, 1992).

[198] See IAEA, *Reports of the Standing Committee on Liability for Nuclear Damage,* 1st -17th sessions (1990–97).

[199] See IAEA/Gov/INF/509 and Politi, in Francioni and Scovazzi (eds), *International Responsibility for Environmental Harm* (Dordrecht, 1991) 473; Handl, 92 *RGDIP* (1988) 5. Poland's proposal for a supplementary scheme of state liability is in IAEA/SCNL/11/3 (1996).

[200] See 1997 Convention on Supplementary Compensation for Nuclear Damage, *infra*, next section.

if affected states are to be fully compensated in the event of a serious accident causing damage in excess of the limits for liability and compensation under the Vienna
Convention. Moreover, civil liability and compensation schemes do not apply to military installations. For these reasons, the two systems of public and private liability
remain complementary rather than alternative elements in the overall legal regime for
nuclear accidents. The more convincing proposals for reform which were not adopted
would have incorporated elements from both systems, possibly in a unified claims
process modelled in part on the precedent set by the UN Compensation Commission
for claims arising out of Iraq's invasion of Kuwait.[201]

Without further agreement on whether state responsibility for nuclear damage is
strict or requires a failure of diligence, on a forum in which claims can be brought,
and on how the burden of reparation should be allocated among public and private
actors, it is difficult to conclude that state responsibility at present affords a sufficiently
principled basis for the settlement of international claims arising out of accidental
nuclear damage. It is likely to remain an unpredictable option for any state seeking
redress, and there is no doubt that in most cases reliance on the revised civil liability
and compensation schemes provided by the 1997 Protocol to the Vienna Convention
and the 2004 Protocol to the Paris Convention will be preferable. This is especially the
case now that non-party claims are possible.[202]

5 CIVIL LIABILITY FOR NUCLEAR DAMAGE

Civil liability proceedings are the preferred method employed by the majority of
nuclear states for reallocating the costs of transboundary nuclear accidents. In a few
cases, bilateral arrangements simply apply the principle of equal access and non-discrimination to nuclear risks, and a number of national legal systems also facilitate
transboundary proceedings, including forum shopping.[203] The limited utility of equal
access has persuaded most nuclear states to adopt a more sophisticated model. This
is provided by four international conventions which create a special regime of civil
liability.[204] Nuclear incidents within Western Europe are covered by the OECD Paris
Convention of 1960,[205] to which all Western European nuclear states are party. The

---

[201] Handl, 92 *RGDIP* (1988) 5. On the UNCC see *supra*, Ch 4.   [202] *Infra*, section 5(6).

[203] 1974 Nordic Convention on the Protection of the Environment, Article 1; 1976 Nuclear Liability Rules
(US–Canada); 1986 Agreement on Third Party Liability in the Nuclear Field (Switzerland-FRG). On equal
access and forum shopping see *supra*, Ch 5.

[204] See generally, Lee, 12 *JEL* (2000) 317; Miatello, in Spinedi and Simma (eds), *United Nations Codification
of State Responsibility* (New York, 1987) 287; IAEA, *Nuclear Law for a Developing World*, 109–82; Hardy,
36 *BYIL* (1960) 223; Cigoj, 14 *ICLQ* (1965) 809; Reyners, in IAEA, *Licensing and Regulatory Control of
Nuclear Installations*, 243; IAEA, *Experience and Trends in Nuclear Law*, 69ff; Arrangio Ruiz, 107 *Recueil
des cours* (1962) 575ff; Fornassier, 10 *AFDI* (1964) 303; Cameron et al, *Nuclear Energy Law*.

[205] Amended by 1964 and 1982 Additional Protocols both in force, and 2004 Protocol, not yet in force.
See Berman and Hydeman, 55 *AJIL* (1961) 966; Arrangio-Ruiz, 107 *Recueil des Cours*, 582ff, and explanatory
memorandum, 8 *European Yearbook* (1960) 225.

Vienna Convention of 1963 offers a comparable scheme for global participation.[206] A Joint Protocol links the two conventions and allows claims to be made under either.[207] Revisions to the Vienna Convention in 1997, coupled with a new Convention on Supplementary Compensation for Nuclear Damage, have encouraged participation by all the Eastern European nuclear states, including Russia, whose Soviet-era reactors continue to pose a higher risk of serious accidents with transboundary effects.[208] Finally, two more treaties deal with nuclear ships[209] and maritime carriage of nuclear materials,[210] but neither is widely ratified.

All four treaties seek to harmonize important aspects of liability for nuclear accidents and incidents in national laws, without requiring complete uniformity in every respect. They create a common scheme for loss distribution among the victims, making the operator liable but reinforced by state-funded compensation schemes. These aspects distinguish the scheme from equal access to national remedies adopted by OECD, and make it more beneficial to litigants, who are given the assurance of compensation without proof of fault. At the same time, the scheme is also intended to give the nuclear industry protection from unlimited, unpredictable liability involving multiple actions against suppliers, builders, designers, carriers, operators, and states as potential defendants.[211] Although this kind of protection is now difficult to justify in the case of the highly developed nuclear industry in Western Europe, North America, or Japan, it remains an essential element of international efforts to provide help to the East European nuclear industry.[212]

The nuclear liability conventions thus reflect on the one hand an early recognition of the need for a stronger system of loss distribution, appropriate to the serious risks of nuclear accidents, and on the other a desire to encourage the infant nuclear industry. Both points again distinguish nuclear liability from transboundary air or water pollution, where equal access has generally remained the limit of state practice in civil liability matters.[213] While this special nuclear regime does not go so far as the

---

[206] See IAEA, *Civil Liability for Nuclear Damage, Official Records* (Vienna, 1964). On the 1997 Protocol to amend the Vienna Convention see IAEA, *Reports of the Standing Committee on Liability for Nuclear Damage,* 1st–17th sessions (1990–97). The final report of the committee is in IAEA/Gov/2924.

[207] 1988 Joint Protocol Relating to the Application of the Vienna Convention and the Paris Convention. See also Paris Convention, Article 2, as amended 2004.

[208] The 1963 Vienna Convention had 35 parties in 2007. Argentina, Brazil, Chile, Cuba, Mexico, Peru, and Uruguay were among the parties. Three of the world's main nuclear states, Canada, Japan, and the USA, were not parties.

[209] 1962 Brussels Convention on the Liability of Operators of Nuclear Ships; Hardy, 12 *ICLQ* (1963) 778; Konz, 57 *AJIL* (1963) 100; Szasz, 2 *JMLC* (1970) 541; Colliard, 8 *AFDI* (1962) 41; Cigoj, 14 *ICLQ* (1965) 809. The Convention is not in force. None of the states which license nuclear ships is a party.

[210] 1971 Brussels Convention Relating to Civil Liability in the Field of Maritime Carriage of Nuclear Material, IAEA, *International Conventions on Civil Liability for Nuclear Damage,* 55; Strohl, in IAEA, *Experience and Trends in Nuclear Law,* 89.

[211] Preamble to the Paris Convention, IAEA, *Conference on Civil Liability,* 66f; Berman and Hydeman, 55 *AJIL* (1961); Konz, 57 *AJIL* (1963) 105; Cameron et al (eds), *Nuclear Energy Law After Chernobyl,* 98f.

[212] See also the 2003 Framework Agreement on a Multilateral Nuclear Environmental Programme in the Russian Federation which indemnifies nuclear suppliers upgrading Russian nuclear reactors.

[213] *Supra,* Ch 5, section 4. But compare the 2004 Kiev Protocol on Civil Liability and Compensation for Damage Caused by the Transboundary Effects of Industrial Accidents on Transboundary Waters.

Convention on Liability for Damage Caused by Space Objects,[214] in that liability is not placed directly on the state, the influence of the nuclear example can be seen in later treaties dealing with liability for oil pollution from ships.[215]

5(1) THE SCHEME OF THE CONVENTIONS

Although there are variations, the overall scheme of the four conventions is based on the same five elements, as reflected in the protocols of 1997 (Vienna Convention) and 2004 (Paris Convention):[216]

(i) Liability is absolute and requires only proof that the damage was caused by a nuclear incident. No proof of fault or negligence is required as a condition of liability. Certain exceptions such as armed conflict, civil war, or negligence of the victim are allowed.[217] However, damage caused by terrorist acts are not an exception.

(ii) Liability is channelled exclusively to the operator of the nuclear installation or ship which causes the damage, and all other potential defendants are protected.[218] Operators are liable only in accordance with the relevant convention. In certain cases a carrier or handler of nuclear material may be treated as an operator, and several operators may be jointly liable.[219]

(iii) Limitations may be placed on the total amount and duration of liability but this is not obligatory except in the cases of ships.[220]

(iv) Payment up to the prescribed limit of liability is supported by compulsory insurance or security held by the operator, and guaranteed by the state of installation or registry.[221] For accidents covered by the Paris and Vienna Conventions, additional public funds are provided under supplementary conventions.[222]

(v) Rules determine which state or states have jurisdiction over claims and all other recourse to civil proceedings elsewhere is precluded.[223]

---

[214] *Supra*, Ch 4, section 2.

[215] 1969 International Convention on Civil Liability for Oil Pollution Damage with 1984 Protocol; *supra*, Ch 7.

[216] At the time of writing the former had 5 parties and was in force; the latter had no parties.

[217] Vienna Convention, Article IV; Paris Convention Articles 3, 9; Brussels Convention on Nuclear Ships, Articles II, VIII. The 1997 and 2004 Protocols delete the previous 'grave natural disaster' exception.

[218] Vienna Convention, Article II; Paris Convention, Articles 3, 6; Brussels Convention on Nuclear Ships, Article II. The Convention Relating to Maritime Carriage, Article I, channels liability to operators who would be liable under the Paris or Vienna Conventions, or under national laws which are at least as favourable to those suffering damage.

[219] Vienna Convention, Article II(2); Paris Convention, Article 4(d).

[220] Vienna Convention, Articles V, VI, as amended 1997; Paris Convention, Articles 7, 8, as amended 2004; Brussels Convention on Nuclear Ships, Articles III, V.

[221] Vienna Convention, Article VII, as amended 1997; Brussels Convention on Nuclear Ships, Article III; Paris Convention, Article 10, as amended 2004.

[222] 1963 Convention Supplementary to the Paris Convention with Additional Protocols of 1964, 1982, and 2004; 1997 Vienna Convention on Supplementary Compensation for Nuclear Damage.

[223] Vienna Convention, Article XI; Paris Convention, Article 13 as amended 2004; Brussels Convention on Nuclear Ships, Article X.

This scheme draws partly on the example of early national nuclear legislation, notably the United States Price-Anderson Act of 1957.[224] In most cases, the treaties leave states some discretion to modify their basic elements, however. National laws may thus adopt different limitation periods or insurance and liability ceilings.[225] Some states have used this power to set much higher liability ceilings; a few, such as the Federal Republic of Germany, have opted for unlimited liability in certain circumstances.

Although fewer variations are allowed under the Brussels Convention on Nuclear Ships, none of the treaties requires complete uniformity of implementation. Rather, as the IAEA commentary on the Vienna Convention explains, the principal objectives are to enumerate minimum international standards which will be flexible and adaptable to a variety of legal, social, and economic systems, while also designating which state will have exclusive legislative and jurisdictional competence.[226]

The Conventions cover most, but not all, potential sources of nuclear damage. The Paris and Vienna Conventions apply to 'nuclear installations', a term broadly defined to include reactors, reprocessing, manufacturing, and storage facilities, where nuclear fuel, nuclear material, and radioactive products or waste are used or produced.[227] They also apply to the transport of nuclear material or the handling of nuclear waste.[228] The revised Paris Convention has been extended to cover installations 'in the course of being decommissioned.'[229] The Brussels Convention covers nuclear-powered ships, their fuel and incidental waste, but not the carriage of nuclear material by sea.[230] This latter is subject to other conventional regimes.[231] Most uses and by-products of civil nuclear power will thus fall under one or other of these headings, and only nuclear tests, military installations, nuclear weapons, and peaceful nuclear explosions are excluded.[232]

5(2) WHY LIABILITY WITHOUT FAULT?

The combination of no-fault liability with a ceiling on damages, supported by insurance and state indemnity, made civil liability for nuclear risks unusual when the

---

[224] Atomic Energy Damages Act 1957, 42 USC 2011–284, as amended. See Cameron et al (eds), *Nuclear Energy Law After Chernobyl*, Chs 9, 10; and Tomain, *Nuclear Power Transformation* (Bloomington, 1987) Chs 1, 8. The Act imposes a liability ceiling, requires compulsory insurance, and provides for Federal indemnity payments; it does not make operators exclusively liable, however, and it leaves the standard of liability to be settled by each state.

[225] Vienna Convention, Article V, as amended 1997; Paris Convention, Articles 7, 8, as amended 2004. Germany and Austria had already reserved the right to make liability absolute.

[226] IAEA, *Conference on Civil Liability*, 67.

[227] Vienna Convention, Article I, as amended 1997; Paris Convention, Article 1, as amended 2004.

[228] Vienna Convention, Article II; Paris Convention, Article 4.   [229] Article 1, as amended 2004.

[230] Article XIII.

[231] i.e. the Paris or Vienna Conventions, or other conventions governing maritime cargoes, to the extent that these are not displaced in favour of the Paris and Vienna Conventions by the Convention on Maritime Carriage of Nuclear Material, 1972. See Strohl, in IAEA, *Experience and Trends in Nuclear Law* (Vienna, 1972) 89.

[232] Article 3 of the 1997 Protocol specifically excludes 'nuclear installations used for non-peaceful purposes'.

conventions were first adopted, although they have since become the pattern for later liability schemes.[233] An OECD study notes that these elements are found in national laws and are not new, but:

The originality of the system of nuclear liability lies rather in the fact that for the first time these various notions have been systematically applied to a whole industry and have been broadly accepted internationally.[234]

The choice of no-fault liability was justified on several grounds: it would relieve courts of the difficulty of setting appropriate standards of reasonable care, and plaintiffs of the difficulty of proving breach of those standards, in a relatively new, complex, and highly technical industrial process; the risk of very serious and widespread damage, despite its low probability, placed nuclear power in the ultra-hazardous category; it would be unjust and inappropriate to make plaintiffs shoulder a heavy burden of proof in respect of such an industry whose risks are only acceptable because of its social utility as a source of energy.[235] Thus the arguments are broadly comparable to those used in the case of state responsibility.

Whether liability is described as absolute, or merely strict, is a matter of degree.[236] The more exculpating factors are recognized the less appropriate it becomes to use the term absolute. Liability is then strict in the limited sense that fault or negligence are not required; in effect the burden of proof is moved to the defendant. On this spectrum, the nuclear liability conventions fall some way between liability for oil pollution damage, where liability is strict rather than absolute,[237] and liability for space objects, where the launch state is exonerated from absolute liability only when the damage on Earth results from the intention or gross negligence of a claimant state or persons it represents.[238]

The imposition of strict or absolute liability for nuclear incidents is supported by a substantial body of national legislation, including some states not parties to the conventions themselves.[239] Reference to national tort laws or civil codes may also

---

[233] *Supra*, Ch 5, section 4.

[234] OECD Environment Committee, *Compensation for Nuclear Damage*, 20 *NLB* (1977) 50.

[235] *Conference on Civil Liability*, 76; Cigoj, 14 *ICLQ* (1965) 831ff; OECD Environment Committee, *Compensation for Nuclear Damage*, 52. See generally, Goldie, 14 *ICLQ* (1965) 1189; Kelson, 13 *Harv ILJ* (1972) 151; Jenks, 117 *Recueil des Cours* (1966) 99.

[236] Goldie, 14 *ICLQ* (1965) 1215; and id, 16 *NYIL* (1985) 317. Some writers use these terms interchangeably, however, while others prefer to substitute the term 'responsibility for risk': see e.g. de Arechaga, 159 *Recueil des Cours* (1978) 271ff. These authors are, however, discussing primarily the responsibility of states in international law, not civil liability.

[237] See *supra*, Ch 7.

[238] 1972 Convention on International Liability for Damage Caused by Space Objects, Article VI; Cheng, *Studies in International Space Law* (Oxford, 1997) 326–7.

[239] See NEA, *Nuclear Legislation: Third Party Liability* (Paris, 1976). Non-parties with strict liability laws include Canada, Nuclear Liability Act, 1970; Japan, Acts Nos 147, 148 of 1961, Act No 53 of 1971; Brazil, Act No 6453, 1977, 21 *NLB* (1978) (Suppl) 3; Switzerland, Act on Third Party Liability, 1983, 32 *NLB* (1983) (Suppl) 3. US Federal Law, 42 USC 2210, does not specifically impose strict liability but allows for a waiver of defences and of questions of negligence, contributory negligence, and assumption of risk in indemnity cases. In *Duke Power Co v Environmental Study Group*, 438 US 59 (1978) this was held to establish the right to

supply evidence of a general principle of strict or absolute liability for dangerous or unusual activities, but such principles do not invariably cover nuclear installations.[240] One important benefit of the nuclear conventions is thus to clarify and harmonize the standard of liability in national law.

5(3) THE CHANNELLING OF LIABILITY

The channelling of all liability to the operator of nuclear installations or nuclear ships has the advantages of simplifying the plaintiff's choice of defendant and establishing a clear line of responsibility,[241] since one who is not an operator may not be held liable for incidents falling within the terms of the conventions.[242] The possibility of transferring liability to a carrier of nuclear material[243] or a handler of radioactive waste[244] does not materially diminish this concentration of liability, although it provides for an alternative and more extended definition of the term 'operator', and recognizes that there may be a need for special treatment in such cases.[245] Several operators may also be held jointly and severally liable for the same nuclear incident,[246] and the conventions provide rules for determining when liability for materials in transport passes from one operator to another, and when operators become or cease to be liable for material imported or exported.[247]

The choice of the operator as the focus of liability, rather than any other potential defendant, is based on the assumption that the operator of an installation or a ship is usually in the best position to exercise effective responsibility for it, and to secure adequate insurance.[248] This assumption is not universally shared; German, Greek, and

compensation without proof of fault. In cases not covered by Federal Law, strict liability is a matter for state law: see *Silkwood v Kerr McGee Corp*, 464 US 238 (1984); Stason, 12 *Vand LR* (1958) 93.

[240] Goldie, 14 *ICLQ* (1965) 1247; Kelson, 13 *Harv ILJ* (1972) 197; Hardy, 36 *BYIL* (1960) 223. It is doubtful whether in the UK publicly operated nuclear installations would at common law be subject to strict liability, either under *Rylands v Fletcher* (1868) LR 3 HL 330 (see *Dunne v NW Gas Board* [1964] 2 QB 806) or nuisance (see *Allen v Gulf Oil* [1981] 1 All ER 353) but liability for nuclear installations is now based on the Nuclear Installations Act 1965.

[241] *Conference on Civil Liability*, 72; Hardy, 36 *BYIL* (1960) 247ff; Cigoj, 14 *ICLQ* (1965) 822ff.

[242] Vienna Convention, Article II(5) but see also Articles II(2) and IV(5). Paris Convention Article 6(b); Brussels Convention on Nuclear Ships, Article II(2).

[243] Vienna Convention, Article II(2); Paris Convention Article 4(d).

[244] Vienna Convention, Article II(2); there is no comparable provision in the Paris Convention. See also Brussels Convention on Nuclear Ships, Article II(4).

[245] Vienna Convention, Article II(1); Paris Convention, Article 4; Hardy, 36 *BYIL* (1960) 247f; *Conference on Civil Liability*, 74.

[246] Vienna Convention, Article II(3) (4); Paris Convention, Article 5(d); Brussels Convention on Nuclear Ships, Article VII; *Conference on Civil Liability*, 75.

[247] Vienna Convention, Article II(1); Paris Convention, Articles 4(a) (b); *Conference on Civil Liability*, 73.

[248] Hardy, 36 *BYIL* (1960) 247; Cigoj, 14 *ICLQ* (1965) 823; Konz, 57 *AJIL* (1963) 105; Strohl, in IAEA, *Experience and Trends in Nuclear Law*, 89. But cf the 1969 Convention on Civil Liability for Oil Pollution Damage, *supra*, Ch 7, which places liability on the owner of the ship, rather than the operator. However, this Convention allows a right of recourse against operators or others who cause damage intentionally *or recklessly*.

Austrian reservations to the Paris Convention allow for persons other than the operator to be held additionally liable.[249] The main argument for this extension is that it
strengthens the incentive for all concerned, including manufacturers and suppliers, to
behave responsibly.

To some extent the nuclear conventions accept this point, by allowing a liable operator a right of recourse against those who cause nuclear damage intentionally.[250] This
is a narrow exception, however, which still leaves the operator solely responsible for
the negligence or carelessness of others,[251] unless broader indemnities can be voluntarily negotiated. For most European states, this arrangement has proved acceptable,
since operators will be adequately protected by insurance. The criticism that denying
wider recourse dilutes the incentive for others to behave responsibly[252] can be met in
two ways; states are free to employ criminal law or civil penalties,[253] and the efficient
control of construction and operational standards for nuclear installations is arguably
a sufficient safety policy.[254]

It is important to note that it makes no difference that the operator of a nuclear
installation or ship will in many cases be a state, or state entity. The civil liability conventions ensure that states or their organs are precluded from invoking jurisdictional
immunities, except in relation to the execution of judgments.[255] Thus, apart from this
exception, states sued under the Conventions in their own courts will be subject to the
same liability, and enjoy the same defences, as other categories of defendants.

5(4) ALLOCATION OF LOSS

The scale of potential damage a serious nuclear accident could cause is likely to be
well beyond the capacity of individual operators of nuclear installations to bear.[256]

---

[249] Legislation in Austria and Germany has, however, remained within the terms of the Paris Convention
on this point. For the position in the United States, see Cameron et al (eds), *Nuclear Energy Law After
Chernobyl*, Ch 9.

[250] Vienna Convention, Article X; Paris Convention Article 6(f); Brussels Convention on Nuclear Ships,
Article II(6).

[251] Cf the broader right of recourse allowed under that 1969 Convention on Civil Liability for Oil Pollution
Damage, *supra*, Ch 7, section 6(2).

[252] Pelzer, 12 *NLB* (1973) 46.

[253] *Conference on Civil Liability*, 83; this argument has been the focus of debate in the United States: see
Cameron et al (eds), *Nuclear Energy Law After Chernobyl*, 146f.

[254] OECD, Environment Committee, *Compensation for Nuclear Damage*, 20 *NLB* (1977) 76.

[255] Vienna Convention, Article XIV; Paris Convention, Article 13(e); Brussels Convention on Nuclear
Ships, Article X(3). The exclusion of jurisdictional immunities was opposed by Soviet bloc representatives
at the Vienna Conference, and the inclusion of this provision is one reason for their failure to sign the
Convention.

[256] The Three Mile Island accident is thought to have cost US $1 billion; $52 million was paid out by
insurers: Cameron et al (eds), *Nuclear Energy Law After Chernobyl*, 151ff. Estimates of the possible cost
of a core meltdown in the United States reach $15 billion: US GAO report, *Nuclear News*, Sept. 1986. The
Chernobyl accident may have caused damage in the USSR totalling $3 billion, including $1.2 billion in compensation payments: Shapar and Reyners, *The Nuclear Third Party Liability Regime in Western Europe: The
Test of Chernobyl* (OECD, Paris, 1987).

All the nuclear conventions allow each state party to limit the operator's liability. The option of doing so is intended primarily to make insurance easier to obtain. Without it, insurers might be reluctant to cover such potentially enormous risks, or to do so fully.[257] Compulsory insurance is what guarantees the operator's liability.[258] If insurance funds prove insufficient for this purpose, the state must step in and provide them. This is a unique feature of the nuclear conventions; it acknowledges the residual responsibility of states to compensate for damage caused by nuclear activities where the operator is unable to do so or is itself a state.[259] In return for this guarantee of compensation for plaintiffs, it also protects the industry itself from a burden of ruinous liability.[260] Since much will depend on the views of individual insurance markets, and their ability to pool risks internationally, the conventions set only minimum limits and allow states to fix higher ones, or to have no limit at all.[261]

Although all the nuclear conventions focus liability on the operator as the source of damage or pollution, two Supplementary Compensation Conventions acknowledge that this approach is insufficient, and involve states in meeting substantial losses in excess of the operator's capacity to cover them through insurance. It cannot be said that any of the nuclear liability conventions fully implements the polluter-pays principle, or recognizes the unlimited and unconditional liability of states within whose border nuclear accidents occur. What they do recognize, if imperfectly, is that the scale of possible damage has to be widely and equitably borne if nuclear power is to be internationally acceptable. This conclusion further weakens the already tenuous case for treating any of these agreements as evidence for the strict or absolute liability of the source state in international law for the full measure of any damage its nuclear activities may cause.

(a) The Paris Convention Scheme

The scheme adopted in the liability conventions is not intended to cover all loss in full, for by permitting limitation of the operator's liability it necessarily envisages wider distribution of uninsured loss. Partly because the Paris Convention operator liability

---

[257] *Conference on Civil Liability*, 78; Hardy, 36 *BYIL* (1960) 240ff; Cameron et al (eds), *Nuclear Energy Law After Chernobyl*, 109.

[258] Vienna Convention, Article VII, as amended 1997; Paris Convention, Article 10; Brussels Convention on Nuclear ships, Article III.

[259] Vienna Convention, Article VII; Brussels Supplementary Convention, Article 3(b)(i). See Miatello, in Spinedi and Simma, *United Nations Codification of State Responsibility*, 297–9, 302–5. There is no comparable arrangement under the 1969 Convention on Civil Liability for Oil Pollution Damage.

[260] *Conference on Civil Liability*, 78.

[261] Vienna Convention, Article V; Paris Convention, Article 7; *Conference on Civil Liability*, 78. Note that the Brussels Convention on Nuclear Ships, Article III, sets a single obligatory limit, following the practice of maritime liability conventions. The Federal German Atomic Energy Act, 1985, was the first to abolish liability ceilings in a Paris Convention state, although for internal claims only. See Pfaffelhuber and Kuchuk, 25 *NLB* (1980) 70. Switzerland and Japan, who are not parties, also have unlimited liability. See Shapar and Reyners, *Nuclear Third Party Liability*, for comparative tables of national liability limits, and Deprimoz, 32 *NLB* (1983) 33.

limit of around €20 million[262] has always been low compared to the probable cost of a serious accident, this Convention is supplemented by a long-established system of state-funded compensation at a level greatly above the minimum liability limits.[263] The European scheme thus spreads the burden of serious losses more broadly, first to the installation state and then across the community of Western European states as a whole. The important question is whether the overall scheme is adequate and strikes the right balance between state-funded compensation, industry protection, and victim protection. In practice, until revised in 2004, the Paris Convention and the Brussels Supplementary Convention placed the main burden of compensation on governments. The scale of this redistribution can be seen in the figures. Beyond the operator's basic liability a further 175 million SDRs would be drawn from the contracting party in whose territory the nuclear installation is situated and an additional 125 million from all other contracting parties.[264] Once the 2004 Protocols come into force, however, the operator's minimum liability will rise massively to a minimum of €700 million—roughly thirty-five times the present limit—and additional state-funded compensation will take the total available to €1500 million. Moreover, the formula whereby all states parties contribute compensation funds to the common pool has been altered so that 65% of the contribution is based on installed nuclear power and only 35% on GNP, rather than 50% as before. This will make the new scheme a little more attractive to non-nuclear states, although Ireland and Luxemburg remain non-parties at the time of writing. Thus the main burden of funding nuclear damage will shift significantly to nuclear operators (and their insurers) and the total available will offer greater potential for meeting the cost of a significant nuclear accident.

Despite these improvements, however, a really serious accident on the scale of Chernobyl could still result in uncompensated damage beyond the limits of the Paris/Brussels scheme. In this remote possibility, that part of the loss will then lie where it falls, although claims under the general international law of state responsibility remain possible in respect of the uncompensated loss.[265]

Compensation amounts under the revised Paris and Brussels Conventions (2004)

	Before revision	After revision
First tier Operator's liability insurance	SDR 15 million or national limit	€700 million minimum

---

[262] Article 7 establishes a normal minimum level of 15 million SDRs, equivalent to approximately 20 million Euros.

[263] 1963 Brussels Supplementary Convention on Third Party Liability in the Field of Nuclear Energy, 1041 *UNTS* 358, as amended by a Protocol of 1982. See Lagorce, in IAEA, *Nuclear Law for a Developing World* (Vienna, 1969) 143; Fornasier, 8 *AFDI* (1962) 762.

[264] 1982 Protocol. 100 million SDRs is worth approximately 140 million Euros.

[265] *Supra*, section 4.

Continued

	Before revision	After revision
Second tier Installation state public funds	Difference between the first tier and SDR 175 million	Difference between first tier and €1200 million
Third tier All parties contribute according to GNP and installed reactor power (Article 12)	SDR 125 million ----------------------	€300 million ----------------------
	TOTAL SDR 315 million = €440 million	*TOTAL €1500 million*

(b) The Vienna Convention scheme

The Paris Convention scheme for limited liability plus supplementary state-funded compensation provided the model on which revision of the Vienna Convention in 1997 is based.[266] Greatly increased sums are now available to victims of nuclear accidents under this revised scheme which came into force in 2003. First, in all but special cases,[267] the operator's liability under the Vienna Convention will rise to a minimum of 300 million SDRs[268] (approximately US$400 million at 1999 values). Under a new Convention on Supplementary Compensation, the installation state will provide a further 300 million SDRs, and thereafter all other parties also contribute according to a formula under which non-nuclear states contribute less, and the poorest nothing at all, in return for simplified access to compensation at levels that could now exceed US$1 billion.[269] Losses beyond that limit could only be recovered in international claims against the state concerned.

In order to make the benefits of the 1997 Supplementary Convention as widely available as possible, participation is not confined to parties to the Vienna Convention, but is also open to Paris Convention states and to states not party to either convention if their law conforms to the same basic principles of liability for nuclear accidents.[270] The United States was one of the first nuclear states to ratify the Supplementary Convention,

[266] See IAEA, *Reports of the Standing Committee on Liability for Nuclear Damage,* 1st–17th sessions (1990–97).

[267] Under Article 5 of the Vienna Convention, as amended 1997, the lowest possible liability which may be set by installation states 'having regard to the nature of the nuclear installation or the nuclear substances involved and to the likely consequences of an incident' is 5 million SDRs. This is not intended to be an appropriate limit for a nuclear reactor.

[268] Vienna Convention, Article V, as amended 1997. A 15-year transitional period is allowed.

[269] 1997 Supplementary Convention, Articles III(1), IV. The Convention was not force at the time of writing.

[270] 1997 Supplementary Convention, Articles XVIII, XIX. The requirements which must be met by non-parties to the Paris and Vienna Conventions are set out in an annex.

although it does not participate in the Liability Convention. For all these states the advantages of participation are twofold: they gain access to compensation in the event of a serious accident affecting them, as well as the assurance that their own liabilities will be shared across all participating states. Paris Convention states have perhaps most to gain from becoming parties to the 1997 Supplementary Convention because it assures them compensation in the event of another Chernobyl-type accident in one of the nuclear states in Eastern Europe, provided these states are themselves parties to the Supplementary Convention. Those with least to gain are the non-nuclear states such as Ireland who are not parties to the Paris or Vienna Conventions, because they would have to contribute to the general compensation pool, albeit at a much reduced level. However, to cater for such cases the convention does make provision for non-party claims.[271]

There is one important limitation on participation in the 1997 Supplementary Convention: it is only open to those states that are also parties to the 1994 Nuclear Safety Convention.[272] Few states would wish to commit themselves to contribute to a compensation fund if the accident risks in some participating states are much higher than in others. In effect, this requirement compels Eastern European states to meet IAEA fundamental safety requirements[273] if they wish to have access to the protection of the Supplementary Convention. For their neighbours it has the double benefit of reducing the risk while ensuring compensation. This will be a significant achievement if Eastern Europe participates as hoped.[274]

5(5) BRINGING CLAIMS UNDER THE CONVENTIONS

The nuclear conventions simplify the jurisdictional issues which would otherwise arise under national law in bringing transboundary civil actions. First, they determine which state has jurisdiction over claims against operators or their insurers. In the case of nuclear installations, the location of the nuclear incident causing the damage, or exceptionally, of the installation itself, is normally the deciding factor.[275] The object of this extended definition, and the reason jurisdiction does not simply follow the location of the installation, is to cater for incidents caused by material in transit. Cases of multiple jurisdiction are to be dealt with by agreement of the parties under the Vienna Convention[276] or by a tribunal under the Paris Convention.[277] This tribunal would decide which court was 'most closely related to the case in question'. However, acknowledging the concerns of coastal states over the risk of pollution damage arising from maritime transport of nuclear cargoes, the 2004 revision of the Paris Convention gives the courts of the coastal state exclusive jurisdiction over claims arising out of incidents in the exclusive economic zone.[278] This conforms to the jurisdictional provisions of the 1992 Convention on Civil Liability for Oil pollution Damage.[279] In the

---

[271] *Infra*, section 5(6).   [272] Articles XVIII, XIX.   [273] *Supra*, section 2.
[274] At the time of writing only Morocco and Romania were parties.
[275] Vienna Convention, Article XI, as amended, 1997; Paris Convention Article 13.
[276] Article XI(3).   [277] Article 13(c).   [278] Article 13(b).   [279] See *supra*, Ch 7.

case of nuclear ships, however, both the licensing state and the state or states where the damage occurs have jurisdiction.[280]

Second, judgments given by courts competent in accordance with the conventions must be recognized and enforced in other member states, with certain limited exceptions which do not allow reconsideration of the merits of the case.[281] This facility is now of limited practical importance within most of Western Europe, since judgments will normally be recognized under EC law,[282] but elsewhere it is an important further guarantee of access to compensation funds in transboundary cases.

Lastly, actions brought pursuant to all these conventions must commence within the appropriate limitation period, which in most cases is now thirty years from the date of the nuclear incident, unless national law or the conventions provide differently.[283]

Major international accidents at Chernobyl and Bhopal, as well as the damage done to Kuwait in 1991, have shown the need for a claims procedure capable of handling the large number of potential actions which may arise out of a serious accident. The 1997 revisions to the Vienna Convention do not create any special procedure for this purpose, but for the first time they do permit states to bring actions on behalf of their own nationals, domiciles or residents who suffer damage.[284]

5(6) NON-PARTY CLAIMS

The major argument against allowing non-party claims is that with limited funds to call on, adding more claimants will reduce the share available for those in contracting states, without reciprocal benefits. Extension to non-parties may be advantageous, however, if it permits operators to limit their liability to non-party claimants and it may facilitate transport of nuclear materials across non-party territories.[285] A provision on non-parties was deleted from the 1963 text of the Vienna Convention after opposition to the notion that they might benefit.[286] No consistent practice was followed by contracting parties to the 1960 Paris Convention, but several did allow non-party claims to be made.[287] With some qualifications, both the revised Vienna Convention and the Paris Convention now extend the benefit of their provisions

---

[280] Brussels Convention on Nuclear Ships, Article X.

[281] Vienna Convention, Article XII, as amended, 1977; Paris Convention, Article 13(d); Brussels Convention on Nuclear Ships, Article XI(4).

[282] 1968 and 1978 Conventions on Civil Jurisdiction and the Enforcement of Judgements, *supra*, Ch 5.

[283] Vienna Convention, Article VI, as amended 1997; Paris Convention, Article 8, as amended 2004. See FRG, Atomic Energy Act 1985, s 32; UK, Nuclear Installations Act, 1965; Switzerland, Act on Third Party Liability, 1983.

[284] Vienna Convention, as amended 1997, Article XIA. In the Bhopal accident, the Indian Government passed legislation permitting it to take over the claims brought by the injured victims: *supra*, Ch 5. See also the claims procedure adopted for the UN Compensation Commission, *supra*, Ch 4.

[285] *Conference on Civil Liability*, 184, para 55.

[286] Ibid, Committee of the Whole, 183f; Plenary, 121ff.

[287] Germany, Atomic Energy Act 1985, s 24(4); Denmark, Compensation for Nuclear Damage Act, 1974, s 5(1); Finland, Nuclear Liability Act 1972, s 4; Netherlands, Act on Liability for Damage Caused by Nuclear Incidents, s 26(1); Sweden, Nuclear Liability Act s 3; UK, Nuclear Installations Act, 1965, ss 7, 12.

on operator liability to claimants who suffer damage in the territory of a non-contracting state, or to incidents which arise there,[288] but non-party claimants are denied recourse to additional public funds provided under the two Supplementary Conventions unless the other parties agree.[289] Non-parties with nuclear installations on their territory who do not afford reciprocal benefits are also excluded from the liability conventions.[290] Both conventions provide jurisdictional rules for incidents occurring outside the territory of a party,[291] but these provisions are intended to resolve conflicts, not to extend the application of either instrument.

None of these changes are helpful in the case of accidents like Chernobyl, since the issue there involved the liability of a non-party operator rather than extension of benefits to non-party claimants. Non-party operators cannot be held liable under any of the conventions, and jurisdiction will in such cases be determined by ordinary rules of national law, with all the difficulties referred to earlier. Participation in the conventions by nuclear states—the source of potential defendants—is for this reason the best way of gauging international acceptance of the civil liability regime.

5(7) NUCLEAR DAMAGE AND THE ENVIRONMENT

A common feature of the nuclear conventions before 1997 had been their relatively narrow definition of 'damage'. Like the *Trail Smelter Case* their focus was on loss of life, personal injury, or loss or damage to property.[292] The Brussels and Vienna Conventions allowed parties to extend this definition, but the legislation of OECD states closely followed the provisions of the Paris Convention.[293] What was clearly missing was a broader environmental or ecological perspective.

Following the model for a new definition of damage in the 1992 Convention on Civil Liability for Oil Pollution Damage,[294] the revised Paris and Vienna Conventions have now been extended to include the costs of preventive measures and reinstatement of the environment, as well as loss of income.[295] This definition affords a more realistic approach to damage if the true costs of nuclear incidents are to be borne by the nuclear industry. Such additional environmental costs might also be recoverable against states in international law, following the outcome of the Canadian claim for clean-up costs arising out of the Cosmos 954 crash.[296]

---

[288] Paris Convention, Article 2, as amended 2004; Vienna Convention as amended 2004, Article 1A.

[289] Vienna Supplementary Convention, Article V(1); Brussels Supplementary Convention as amended, Article 2(a) but see also Article 15 which allows extension to non-parties by agreement. But non-parties to the liability conventions may also participate in the Supplementary Compensation Conventions.

[290] Paris Convention, Article 2, as amended 2004; Vienna Convention as amended 2004, Article 1A.

[291] Vienna Convention, Article XI(2); Paris Convention Article 13(b).

[292] Vienna Convention, Article 1(1)(K); Paris Convention, Article 3(a); Brussels Convention on Nuclear Ships, Article 1(7); Noltz, *NLB* (1987) 87, and *supra*, Ch 3, section 4(6).

[293] See OECD, *Nuclear Legislation: Third Party Liability* (Paris, 1976).   [294] *Supra*, Ch 7.

[295] Vienna Convention, Article 1(1)(K), as revised, 1997; Paris Convention, Article 1, as revised 2004.

[296] See *supra*, Ch 4, section 2.

6 CONCLUSIONS

Despite their longevity, no significant claim has ever been brought under either of the principal nuclear liability conventions, in itself something of a demonstration of the safety of nuclear reactors in the countries which are parties to the relevant conventions. The positive features of the nuclear conventions as models for other environmental liability regimes are self-evident: they facilitate individual access to legal remedies, they eliminate or minimize difficult issues of proof and liability, and they offer a scheme which ensures the availability of compensation funding regardless of the solvency of the defendant. They also provide a precedent for treating ultra-hazardous but socially acceptable activities as risks which require exceptional provision for wider loss distribution, based only in part on the absolute or strict liability of the polluter.

Given the pattern of participation by nuclear states, the Paris and Vienna Conventions' practical significance is mainly confined to Europe and Latin America. The most immediate consequence of the Chernobyl accident has been the growth in parties to the 1963 Vienna Convention, which now include all of Eastern Europe and most of Latin America. Not only has this made upgrading East European reactors less of a liability risk for contractors and those providing assistance, it has also ensured that Western and Eastern Europe are covered by comparable and linked liability regimes. This is important since Europe has the world's largest concentration of nuclear facilities and the highest likelihood of transboundary consequences arising from nuclear incidents. Of course, until the 1997 Supplementary Compensation Convention actually enters into force, the revised Vienna Convention alone cannot afford adequate redress in the event of a serious accident either in Eastern Europe or Latin America. Nor are the United States, Japan, or Canada parties to any nuclear liability regime. These remain weaknesses in the IAEA's attempts to improve both the regulatory and liability regimes for nuclear power.

Moreover, as we have seen, the difficulties of resorting to an international claim against a nuclear state have not been directly addressed, and render this alternative one of questionable value unless the respondent state has failed to exercise its regulatory responsibilities diligently. However, in providing evidence of an internationally agreed standard of due diligence, the Nuclear Safety Convention does make it easier to identify with more precision what those responsibilities are, and thus potentially provides the basis for a claim in general international law should legal proceedings ever prove necessary.

The evidence considered here does not show that nuclear activities involving significant transboundary risk are prohibited by international law, nor does it indicate that they may take place only on equitable terms agreed with states likely to be affected. Instead, the international community has generally accepted the lawfulness of nuclear power generation, provided it is regulated to a high standard, adequately monitored by independent national regulatory authorities, and subject to peer review by IAEA member states, with liability regimes in place that afford some assurance of redress for transboundary victims in the event of an accident. These are, in effect, the conditions under which the inherent risk imposed on international society by nuclear states is rendered lawful. This suggests that any state which cannot or will not adequately regulate its nuclear industry to international standards, or make satisfactory arrangements for compensating its non-nuclear neighbours in the event of serious accident, should not be permitted the freedom to pursue nuclear activities. The assertion that all states have the right of access to nuclear technology must be seen in this light.

10

INTERNATIONAL WATERCOURSES: ENVIRONMENTAL PROTECTION AND SUSTAINABLE USE

1 INTRODUCTION

A sustainable supply of fresh water is not merely fundamental to environmental protection, biodiversity, and so on, but to life itself. Over a billion people lack adequate access to potable water or basic sanitation. Access to clean water was a priority issue in the UN's Millennium Development goals and the 2002 World Summit on Sustainable Development. Reports for the Stockholm Water Conference in 2001 and the UN World Water Report in 2006 have shown that severe water shortages could affect one-third of the global population by 2025, and will extend well beyond existing arid and semi-arid countries. Water supply is already seriously inadequate in much of equatorial Africa and Central Asia; desertification is exacerbated by over-extraction of underground water supplies; pollution has reduced the supply of potable water; irrigation, which accounts for 80 per cent of water consumption in many developing countries, is wasteful, causes salinity and renders soil ultimately unusable for agriculture; the construction of massive dams for water-management and hydro-electric purposes in developing countries has resulted in large-scale population transfers and causes great hardship for the poor and for indigenous peoples whose interests are often disregarded; population growth and increased living standards are reflected in demand for water at rapidly increasing levels that cannot be met indefinitely; faced with large-scale diversion, extraction, or loss of natural water supplies, many rivers and lakes no longer support a natural ecosystem, leading to loss of wetlands, swamps, and other natural habitats for wildlife. Some major watercourses, such as the Aral Sea, are at risk of disappearing. Others, including the Yangtse, suffer periodic interruptions due to reduced rainfall. Added to these problems of poor management and inadequate governance are the effects of climate change on freshwater supply, with melting of mountain glaciers in all continents and changing rainfall patterns already posing a real threat to the continued flow of major rivers.

Historically, international water law has not been particularly concerned with these problems. Its principal focus, evident in the ILA's codification of 1966 (The Helsinki Rules), has mainly been the rules and principles for allocating water supply in international watercourses between upstream and downstream states, and only incidentally have environmental or sustainability concerns been served. As we shall see later in this chapter, serious efforts have been made to address these shortcomings and to give international water law a broader ecological perspective within a legal framework more attuned to sustainable use and water shortage than hitherto. Nevertheless, it remains true that international law has very little to say about freshwater resources as such, unless they are part of an international watercourse, or cause marine pollution, or unless supply problems become so severe that the human rights of users are affected.

1(1) THE SCOPE OF INTERNATIONAL WATERCOURSE LAW

The term 'international watercourse' is used in this chapter primarily as a convenient designation for rivers, lakes, or groundwater sources shared by two or more states. Such watercourses will normally either form or straddle an international boundary, or in the case of rivers, they may flow through a succession of states.[1] In dealing with shared or transboundary watercourses a second problem of geographical definition arises. How much of such a watercourse system is it proper to include? The possibilities range from simply that portion which crosses or defines a boundary, to the entire watershed or river basin, with its associated lakes, tributaries, groundwater systems, and connecting waterways wherever they are located. The latter interpretation may result in limitations on the use of a very substantial proportion of a state's internal river systems and their catchment areas,[2] and lead to the imposition of a responsibility on watercourse states to protect their own environment, as well as that of their neighbours. But if the narrower approach is preferred, the efficient environmental management of transboundary flows may be seriously impeded. For this reason the broadest possible geographical scope for the law of international watercourses is to be preferred. As the Commentary to the 1966 Helsinki Rules notes: 'The drainage basin is an indivisible hydrologic unit which requires comprehensive consideration in order to effect maximum utilization and development of any portion of its waters.'[3] International codification and state practice reflect differing views on this question,

---

[1] See McCaffrey, *The Law of International Watercourses* (2nd edn, Oxford, 2007) Ch 2.

[2] Sette-Camara, 186 *Recueil des Cours* (1984) 117, 130.

[3] ILA, Helsinki Rules on the Uses of the Waters of International Rivers ('Helsinki Rules') *Rept of 52nd Conf* (1966) 485; ILA, Berlin Rules on Water Resources ('Berlin Rules') *Rept of 71st Conf* (2004) 344; Teclaff, *The River Basin in History and Law* (The Hague, 1967).

however. Modern bilateral and regional treaties have tended to adopt the basin approach, because it is the most efficient means of achieving control of pollution and water utilization.[4] Examples of such arrangements are widespread in Africa,[5] but also include the Amazon, the Plate, and the Mekong.[6] In Europe the basin concept has been used in controlling pollution of the Rhine, Danube, Elbe, Meuse, and Scheldt rivers[7] and, in North America, of the Great Lakes.[8] It has been favoured by declarations on international conferences, including the Stockholm and Rio Conferences[9] and the UN Water Conference held at Mar Del Plata in 1977,[10] and it forms the basis of codification undertaken by the Institut de Droit International[11] and of the International Law Association's Helsinki and Berlin Rules. The ILA's definition of an international drainage basin is the most extensive: 'covering a geographical area extending over two or more states determined by the watershed limits of the system of waters, including surface and underground waters, flowing into a common terminus'.[12] Despite the obvious utility of a broadly comprehensive definition of a watercourse, and its clear endorsement in international policy, this remains a relatively recent approach only partially reflected in state practice.

Older treaties are more likely to follow the narrower definition found in the Final Act of Congress of Vienna, which focused on international rivers separating or traversing the territory of two or more states and declared them open for navigation

---

[4] Kearney, II *YbILC* (1976) Pt 1, 184ff.

[5] Examples include the 1999 Protocol on Lake Victoria; 1995 Protocol on Shared Watercourse Systems in the Southern African Development Community, Article 1, in, FAO, *Treaties Concerning the Non-Navigational Uses of International Watercourses: Africa* (Rome, 1997) 146; the 1972 Senegal River Basin Treaty, UN Doc ST/ESA/141, *Treaties Concerning the Utilization of International Watercourses*, 16; 1987 Zambezi River System Agreement, 27 *ILM* (1988) 1109; 1963 Act Regarding Navigation and Economic Co-operation between States of the Niger Basin, Ruster and Simma, *International Protection of the Environment* (New York, 1977) xi, 5629; 1964 Convention and Statute Relating to the Development of the Chad Basin, Ruster and Simma, xi, 5633. See McCaffrey, *3rd Rept on International Watercourses, etc,* UN Doc A/CN 4/406 (1987) 18; Godana, *Africa's Shared Water Resources: Legal and Institutional Aspects of the Nile, Niger and Senegal River Systems* (London, 1985).

[6] See 1978 Treaty on Amazonian Cooperation, 17 *ILM* (1978) 1045; 1969 Treaty on the River Plate Basin, 875 *UNTS* No 12550, and the 1995 Agreement for Sustainable Development of the Mekong River Basin, 34 *ILM* (1995) 865.

[7] 1976 Convention on the Protection of the Rhine against Chemical Pollution; 1999 Convention for the Protection of the Rhine; 1990 Convention for the Protection of the Elbe, Article 1, OJEC No C93/12 (1991); 1990 Agreement on Co-operation on Management of the Water Resources in the Danube Basin (Germany/Austria/ EC) OJEC No L90/20 (1990); 1994 Convention on Co-operation for Protection and Sustainable Use of the Danube River, Articles 1(b), 3; 1994 Agreement on the Protection of the Rivers Meuse and Scheldt, Articles 1, 3, 34 *ILM* (1995) 854.

[8] 1978 Great Lakes Water Quality Agreement, 30 UST 1383, TIAS 9257, amended 1983, TIAS 10798. See Utton and Teclaff, *Transboundary Resources Law* (Boulder, 1987) 27ff.

[9] 1972 UNCHE, Action Plan for the Human Environment, Rec 1, UN Doc A/Conf 48/14/Rev1; 1992 UNCED, Agenda 21, Ch 18.9, UN Doc A/Conf 151/26/Rev1.

[10] *Rept of the UN Water Conference*, Mar Del Plata, 14–25 Mar 1977. See generally II *YbILC* (1986) Pt 1, 325ff.

[11] 49 *Ann Inst DDI* (1961) Pt II, 381; 58 *Ann Inst DDI* (1979) Pt II, 197; Salmon, ibid, 193–263.

[12] ILA Helsinki Rules, Article II; ILA Berlin Rules, Article 3.

by all riparians.[13] Although inappropriately narrow for environmental purposes, this definition has remained influential.[14] The 1992 UNECE Convention on the Protection and Use of Transboundary Waters and Lakes[15] adopts essentially the same definition of 'transboundary waters'. These are 'surface or ground waters which mark, cross or are located on boundaries between two or more states'. It requires only these waters, rather than the river basin or watershed, to be managed and conserved in an ecologically sound and rational way and used reasonably and equitably; at the same time, parties are also required to control transboundary impacts, including pollution, to ensure conservation and restoration of ecosystems, and to cooperate in protecting the environment not just of transboundary waters but also of 'the environment influenced by such waters, including the marine environment'.[16] In practice this comes closer to a basin approach; certainly it involves more than the management of 'transboundary waters' alone. The 1992 UNECE Watercourses Convention is now the principle multilateral treaty governing environmental protection of European watercourses and the first regional framework convention dealing with international watercourses.[17] Treaties negotiated under it are less circumspect in their geographical scope: the 1994 Danube Convention applies to the Danube River basin and catchment area and it is not limited to control of transboundary impacts; the 1994 Agreements on the Meuse and Scheldt require the parties to take measures across the whole drainage area of these rivers, while the 1999 Rhine Convention applies to the Rhine, ground water and ecosystems interacting with the Rhine, and its catchment area, insofar as it contributes to pollution or flooding of the Rhine. Moreover, in 1997, parties to the 1992 UNECE Convention adopted the Helsinki Declaration,[18] in which they recognized the need for integrated management of all freshwater sources and committed themselves 'to apply, as appropriate, the principles of the Convention when drawing up, revising, implementing and enforcing' national laws and regulations on the management of internal as well as transboundary water resources.

Among some states, usually those enjoying an upstream position, there is resistance to the more extensive basin concept as a basis for environmental control.[19] For this

---

[13] See *ILC Report*, II *YbILC* (1979) Pt 1, 153f; Utton and Teclaff, *Transboundary Resources Law*, 2.

[14] See *Territorial Jurisdiction of the International Commission of the River Oder Case*, PCIJ Ser A No 23 (1929) 27–9; Lammers, *Pollution of International Watercourses* (Dordrecht, 1984) 110–13; 1909 US–Canada Boundary Waters Treaty, *repr* 146 *Recueil des Cours* (1975) 307. Cf 1960 Netherlands–FRG Frontier Treaty, Ruster and Simma, xi, 5588.

[15] For background material see: *Rept of the Working Party on Water Problems*, 5th Special Session, ENVWA/WP 3/CRP 9 (1991); draft convention, ENVWA/WP 3/R 19/Rev1 (1991); *Rept of the 1st Meeting of Parties*, ECE/MP WAT/2 (1997); Nollkaemper, *The Legal Regime for Transboundary Water Pollution: Between Discretion and Constraint* (Dordrecht, 1993).

[16] Articles 2, 3.

[17] See also 2000 Protocol on Shared Watercourse Systems in the Southern Africa Development Community, *infra*, section 3(3).

[18] *Rept of the 1st Meeting of Parties, supra*, n 15, annex. See also the Protocol on Water and Health adopted in 1999. Article 5(j) calls for integrated management of 'the whole of a catchment area', including natural ecosystems, groundwaters, and coastal waters.

[19] Schwebel, II *YbILC* (1979) Pt 1, 153ff; Evensen, ibid, (1984) Pt 1, 104f; McCaffrey, ibid, (1986) Pt 1, 101, para 16.

reason, the International Law Commission, in its work on the non-navigational uses of international watercourses, avoided reference to drainage basins. As special rapporteur Evensen reported in 1983:

For several reasons, the concept of 'international drainage basin' met with opposition in the discussions both of the Commission and of the Sixth Committee of the General Assembly. Concern was expressed that 'international drainage basin' might imply a certain doctrinal approach to all watercourses regardless of their special characteristics and regardless of the wide variety of issues of special circumstances of each case. It was likewise feared that the 'basin' concept put too much emphasis on the land areas within the watershed, indicating that the physical land area of a basin might be governed by the rules of international water resources law.[20]

Subsequent ILC draft articles and the 1997 UN Convention on International Watercourses, which seeks to codify much of the law on this subject,[21] have therefore referred only to 'international watercourses',[22] but have defined the term watercourse broadly, to mean 'a system of surface waters and groundwaters constituting by virtue of their physical relationship a unitary whole and normally flowing into a common terminus'.[23]

Despite support for the drainage basin concept in modern treaty practice and the work of international codification bodies, the evidence of disagreement in the ILC suggests that it is premature to attribute customary status to this concept as a definition of the geographical scope of international water-resources law.[24] With respect to pollution control, however, this conclusion may not greatly matter. As Lammers argues,[25] even where pollution obligations are placed only on a particular portion of an international watercourse, such as the boundary waters, it will still be necessary for states to control pollution of the wider drainage basin to the extent necessary to produce the desired result in boundary areas. In consequence, 'This means that for the question of legal (in)admissibility of transfrontier water pollution, it makes little sense to distinguish between such concepts as "international watercourse" or "waters of an international drainage basin"'.[26] Experience with the pollution of European and US–Canadian boundary waters[27] suggests that this conclusion may be optimistic, however.

---

[20] II *YbILC* (1983) Pt 1, 101, para 16.

[21] See *Gabčíkovo-Nagymaros Case*, ICJ Reports (1997) 7. Only France, China and Turkey opposed adoption of the Convention, on which see Wouters, 42 *GYIL* (1999) 293; McCaffrey and Sinjela, 92 *AJIL* (1998) 100; Bourne, 35 *CYIL* (1997) 222; McCaffrey, *The Law of International Watercourses*, Ch 9; Tanzi and Arcari, *The United Nations Convention on the Law of International Watercourses* (The Hague, 2001).

[22] 1984 Draft Articles, II *YbILC* (1984) Pt 1, 101; 1991 Draft Articles, *ILC Report* (1991) GAOR A/46/10, 161; 1997 UN Convention, Article 1. A watercourse is 'international' if parts are in two or more states: ibid, Article 2(b).

[23] 1997 UN Convention, Article 2. See also II *YbILC* (1986) Pt 2, 62, para 236, and *ILC Report* (1991) 154–60, where objections to the term 'watercourse system' are noted.

[24] Sette-Camara, 186 *Recueil des Cours* (1984) 128. Some writers disagree, however. See Lipper, in Garretson et al, *The Law of International Drainage Basins* (New York, 1967) 15ff.

[25] Lammers, *Pollution of International Watercourses*, 110–13.   [26] Ibid, 343.

[27] See *infra*, section 3, and Nollkaemper, *The Legal Regime for Transboundary Water Pollution*.

1(2) WATER RESOURCES: PRINCIPLES OF ALLOCATION

One approach to the admissibility of watercourse pollution is to treat it as an aspect of the allocation of water resources. Before considering specific issues relating to pollution and environmental protection it is therefore necessary to establish the basis on which water resources will be allocated among those states with a claim to their use. Four theories are commonly advanced:[28] territorial sovereignty, territorial integrity, equitable utilization, and common management.

(a) Territorial sovereignty

One view is that states enjoy absolute sovereignty over water within their territory and are free to do as they please with those waters, including extracting as much as necessary, or altering their quality, regardless of the effect this has on the use or supply of water in downstream or contiguous states. This theory is often known as the Harmon doctrine, after the United States Attorney General who asserted the absolute right of the United States to divert the Rio Grande.[29] Modern commentators mostly dismiss the doctrine. Apart from its bias in favour of upstream states, it has little support in state practice and does not seem to represent international law.[30] Even the United States quickly retreated from the full Harmon doctrine in treaties with Mexico[31] and Canada[32] which are more consistent with the principle of equitable utilization. There

---

[28] McCaffrey, *The Law of International Watercourses*, Ch 5; Colliard, in OECD, *Legal Aspects of Transfrontier Pollution* (Paris, 1977) 263; Teclaff and Utton (eds), *International Environmental Law* (New York, 1974) 155; Lipper, in Garretson et al, *The Law of International DrainageBasins*, 15ff; Dickstein, 12 *CJTL* (1973) 487; Bourne, 6 *UBCLR* (1971) 115; Cohen, 146 *Recueil des cours* (1975) 227; Caflisch, 219 *Recueil des Cours* (1989) 48ff.

[29] 'The fact that the Rio Grande lacks sufficient water to permit its use by the inhabitants of both countries does not entitle Mexico to impose restrictions on the United States which would hamper the development of the latter's territory or deprive its inhabitants of an advantage with which nature had endowed it and which is situated entirely within its territory. To admit such a principle would be completely contrary to the principle that the United States exercises full sovereignty over its national territory', 21 *Ops Atty Gen* (1895) 274, 283.

[30] McCaffrey, *The Law of International Watercourses*, Ch 4; Teclaff and Utton, *International Environmental Law*, 156; Lipper, in Garretson et al, *The Law of International Drainage Basins*, 23; Lester, 57 *AJIL* (1963) 828, 847; Dickstein, 12 *CJTL* (1973) 490ff; Bourne, 3 *CYIL* (1965) 187, 294ff; Lammers, *Pollution of International Watercourses*, 96.

[31] See 1906 Convention between the United States and Mexico concerning the Equitable Distribution of the Waters of the Rio Grande for Irrigation Purposes, 34 *Stat* 2953; 1944 Treaty between the United States and Mexico Relating to the Utilization of the Waters of the Colorado, Tijuana and Rio Grande Rivers, 3 *UNTS* 314; 1973 Agreement on the Permanent and Definitive Solution of the International Problem of the Salinity of the Colorado River, 12 *ILM* (1973) 1105. See Brownell and Eaton, 69 *AJIL* (1975) 255; Arechaga, 159 *Recueil des cours* (1978) 188ff. McCaffrey, II *YbILC* (1986) Pt 1, 105–9, concludes: 'viewed in the context of United States diplomatic and treaty practice, the "Harmon Doctrine" is not, and probably never has been actually followed by the state that formulated it'.

[32] 1909 Boundary Waters Treaty, *supra*, n 14; 1961 Treaty Relating to the Cooperative Development of the Water Resources of the Columbia River Basin, 542 *UNTS* 244. McCaffrey, II *YbILC* (1986) Pt1, 108, observes that 'the reservation by each party in Article II [of the 1909 Treaty] of 'exclusive jurisdiction and control' over successive rivers within its territory is far from being tantamount to an assertion of a right to use waters within its territory with no regard whatsoever for resulting damage to the other country'. See generally,

are echoes of the doctrine in a few other transboundary river disputes. India at one time asserted 'full freedom...to draw off such waters as it needed' from the Indus, but here again, the treaty which concluded this dispute is generally regarded as effecting an equitable apportionment of the waters.[33] The Harmon doctrine has never had much currency in Europe because of its fundamental inconsistency with the freedom of navigation which characterized major European rivers after 1815.[34]

(b) Territorial integrity

Equally questionable is the obverse of the Harmon doctrine, the principle of absolute territorial integrity or riparian rights. This theory would give the lower riparian the right to a full flow of water of natural quality. Interference with the natural flow by the upstream state would thus require the consent of the lower riparian. In this form the doctrine appears devoid of more than limited support in state practice, jurisprudence, or the writings of commentators.[35] It is sometimes confused with the idea that states may acquire servitudes in the use of rivers, and with the principle that states may not use or permit the use of their territory in such a manner as to cause harm to other states.[36] But these are separate principles: neither or them necessarily benefits only downstream or contiguous states, nor can it safely be assumed that they confer rights amounting to absolute territorial integrity.

(c) Equitable utilization

The most widely endorsed theory treats international watercourses as shared resources, subject to equitable utilization by riparian states.[37] This proposition requires some clarification, however. The view that international watercourses are 'shared resources' was initially adopted by the ILC, and enjoys some support,[38] but the concept itself has encountered significant opposition among states on account of its alleged novelty and uncertain legal implications. Specific reference to 'shared resources' was deleted from ILC draft articles in 1984,[39] in the belief that nothing of substance was thereby lost and that what mattered was the elaboration of obligations and rights attaching to

---

Zacklin and Caflisch, *The Legal Regime of International Rivers and Lakes* (The Hague, 1981) Ch 1; Cohen, 146 *Recueil des Cours* (1975); Ross, 12 *NRJ* (1972) 242; Arechaga, 159 *Recueil des Cours* (1978) 189ff.

[33] McCaffrey, II *YbILC* (1986) Pt 1, 109f. See 1960 Indus Waters Treaty, 419 *UNTS* 125.

[34] Cohen, 146 *Recueil des Cours* (1975) Ch 1, contrasts European and N American experience: transboundary navigation was less important in the latter case. Austria appears to have supported the doctrine, however: Bourne, 3 *CYIL* (1965) 205.

[35] Lipper, in Garretson et al, *The Law of International Drainage Basins*, 18; Bourne, 6 *UBCLR* (1971) 119.

[36] Colliard, in OECD, *Legal Aspects of Transfrontier Pollution*, 265, uses the phrase 'absolute territorial integrity' in this way.

[37] McCaffrey, *The Law of International Watercourses*, Ch 10; Lipper, in Garretson et al, *The Law of International Drainage Basins*, 41ff; Dickstein, 12 *CJTL* (1973) 492ff; Bourne, 6 *UBCLR* (1971) 120; Arechaga, 159 *Recueil des Cours* (1978) 192ff.

[38] *Rept of the Executive Director of UNEP*, UNEP/GC/44, para 86; *Lac Lanoux Arbitration*, 24 *ILR* (1957) 119, which refers to 'sharing of the use of international rivers'; Draft Articles on Int Watercourses, Article 5, II *YbILC* (1980) Pt 2, 120–36; Lammers, *Pollution of International Watercourses*, 335.

[39] Evensen, II *YbILC* (1984) Pt 1, 110, para 48.

watercourses which are in practice shared.[40] Among these obligations is the principle of equitable utilization.

Equitable utilization rests on a foundation of shared sovereignty, and is not to be confused with equal division.[41] Instead, it will generally entail a balance of interests which accommodates the needs, and uses of each state. This basic principle enjoys substantial support in judicial decisions, state practice, and international codifications. In the *River Oder Case*, the Permanent Court of International Justice had to consider the right of lower riparians to freedom of navigation in Polish waters upstream. Its main finding favoured a community of interest in navigation among all riparian states, based on equality of rights over the whole navigable course of the river.[42] Although confined to navigation, the principle on which this case is based supports a comparable community of interest in other uses of a watercourse.[43] It is implicitly followed in the *Lac Lanoux* arbitration, where the tribunal recognized that, in carrying out diversion works entirely within its own territory, France nevertheless had an obligation to consult Spain, the other riparian, and to safeguard her rights in the watercourse.[44] This does not mean that any use of an international watercourse affecting other states requires their consent, but it does indicate that the sovereignty of a state over rivers within its borders is qualified by a recognition of the equal and correlative rights of other states.

Settlements of river disputes in North America and the Indian subcontinent by states which had previously asserted a different position tend to confirm this conclusion.[45] These and other examples of state practice listed in the work of the International Law Commission have persuaded successive rapporteurs to endorse equitable utilization as an established principle of international law.[46] This view has generally been supported by states,[47] and by the ICJ.[48] Article 5(1) of the 1997 UN Watercourses Convention thus provides:

Watercourse states shall in their respective territories utilize an international watercourse in an equitable and reasonable manner...

---

[40] McCaffrey, ibid, (1986) Pt 1, 103, para 74: 'It therefore appears that, while the reformulation of article 6 has resulted in the loss of a new and developing concept [shared natural resources], it has produced greater legal certainty, and, when viewed in connection with other draft articles, has not resulted in the elimination of any fundamental principles from the draft as a whole.'

[41] Lipper, in Garretson et al, *The Law of International Drainage Basins*, 44f; Arechaga, 159 *Recueil des Cours* (1978) 192; McCaffrey, II *YbILC* (1986) Pt 1, 103f.

[42] *Territorial Jurisdiction of the International Commission of the River Oder Case*, PCIJ Ser A No 23 (1929). See also *Diversion of Water from the Meuse Case*, PCIJ Ser A/B No 70 (1937).

[43] Arechaga, 159 *Recueil des Cours* (1978) 193ff; Lipper, in Garretson et al, *The Law of International Drainage Basins*, 41ff; Lammers, *Pollution of International Watercourses*, 507; McCaffrey, II *YbILC* (1986) Pt 1, 114.

[44] 24 *ILR* (1957) 101; Lester, 57 *AJIL* (1963) 828. See *infra*, section 2.   [45] *Supra*, nn 31–3.

[46] McCaffrey, II *YbILC* (1986) Pt 1, 103–5, 110ff; Schwebel, ibid, (1982) Pt 1, 75ff.

[47] *ILC Report* (1987) GAOR A/42/10, 70; Evensen, II *YbILC* (1984) Pt 1, 110; Schwebel, ibid, (1982) Pt 1, 75. See also Recommendation 51 of the UN Conference on the Human Environment which calls on states to 'consider' when 'appropriate' the principle that 'the net benefits of hydrologic regions common to more than one national jurisdiction are to be shared equitably by the nations affected'.

[48] *Gabčíkovo-Nagymaros Case*, ICJ Reports (1997) 7, para 55.

The same principle has also been adopted in other codifications, such as the ILA's Berlin Rules,[49] and in the 1992 UNECE Convention on Transboundary Watercourses and Lakes.[50]

What constitutes 'reasonable and equitable' utilization is not capable of precise definition. As in other contexts, whether the delimitation of continental shelves according to equitable principles, or the allocation and regulation of shared fishing stocks, the issue turns on a balancing of relevant factors and must be responsive to the circumstances of individual cases.[51] Article 6 of the 1997 UN Watercourses Convention identifies factors relevant to determining what is equitable and reasonable utilization.[52] These include:

(a) geographic, hydrographic, hydrological, climatic, ecological, and other factors of a natural character

(b) the social and economic needs of the watercourse states concerned

(c) the population dependent on the watercourse in each state

(d) the effects of the use or uses of the watercourse in one watercourse state on other watercourse states

(e) existing and potential uses of the international watercourse

(f) conservation, protection, development, and economy of use of the water resources of the watercourse and the costs of measures taken to that effect

(g) the availability of alternatives, of corresponding value, to a particular planned or existing use.

This list is not meant to be exhaustive; consideration must be given to all the interests likely to be affected by the proposed use of the watercourse.[53] Both the benefits and the negative consequences of a particular use are to be taken into account.[54] Moreover, a listing of factors says nothing about the priority or weight given to each one, or how conflicts are to be reconciled. These remain matters calling for comparative judgement in individual cases,[55] and for this reason, uncertainty in application is the main

---

[49] ILA Berlin Rules, Article 12. See also ILA Helsinki Rules, Article IV and Institute of International Law, Salzburg Session, 1961, Resolution on the Utilization of Non-maritime International Waters, Article 3: 'If states are in disagreement over the scope of their rights of utilization, settlement will take place on the basis of equity, taking particular account of their respective needs, as well as of other pertinent circumstances.'

[50] Article 2(2) requires states to ensure that transboundary waters are used in a 'reasonable and equitable way'.

[51] *North Sea Continental Shelf Case*, ICJ Reports (1969) 50, para 93. See also *Tunisia–Libya Continental Shelf Case*, ICJ Reports (1982) 18; *Malta–Libya Continental Shelf Case*, ICJ Reports (1985) 13; *Gulf of Maine Case*, ICJ Reports (1984) 246; *Icelandic Fisheries Cases*, ICJ Reports (1974) 3; and 1982 UNCLOS, Articles 69, 70, 87, and *supra*, Ch 3.

[52] Compare ILA Berlin Rules (2004) Article 13; ILA Helsinki Rules (1966) Article V, and *Rept of the African-Asian legal Consultative Committee*, summarized in II *YbILC* (1982) Pt 1, 87, paras 94–8. For a comprehensive discussion see Fuentes, 67 *BYIL* (1996) 337.

[53] *Lac Lanoux Arbitration*, 138f, 'Account must be taken of all interests, of whatsoever nature, which are liable to be affected by the works undertaken, even if they do not correspond to a right'; see also ILA Helsinki Rules, Commentary, 488, and 1997 UN Watercourses Convention, Article 6(1), (3).

[54] UNGA, 51st Session, *Rept of the 6th Committee Working Group*, GAOR A/51/869 (1997) para 8.

[55] 1997 UN Watercourses Convention, Article 6(3); *ILC Report* (1994) 235; ILA, Helsinki Rules, Commentary, 489.

difficulty affecting the principle of reasonable and equitable use. Unlike the delimitation of continental shelves, third-party settlement has not been widely used in river disputes and comparable judicial elaboration is lacking.[56] The better solution given the greater complexity of the balancing process involved and the likelihood that the needs of states may change, is probably some form of common management designed to achieve equitable and optimum use of the watercourse system.[57] Thus the principle of equitable utilization leads naturally to the fourth theory on which the allocation of water resources has been based, that of common management.

(d) Common management

Common management is the logical combination of the idea that watercourse basins are most efficiently managed as an integrated whole, and the need to find effective institutional machinery to secure cooperation on environmental, social, and economic objectives.[58] It represents a community-of-interest approach which goes beyond the allocation of equitable rights, however, and opens up the possibility of integrating development and international regulation of the watercourse environment.[59] This important trend has already been referred to. As we have seen, modern state practice prefers the basin or hydrologic-system approach to watercourse management.[60] This is usually accompanied by the creation of international institutions in which all riparian states cooperate in formulating and implementing policies for the development and use of a watercourse. Examples of such arrangements are the Lake Chad Basin Commission,[61] the River Niger Commission,[62] the Permanent Joint Technical Commission for Nile Waters,[63] the Zambezi Intergovernmental Monitoring and Co-ordinating Committee,[64] the Intergovernmental Co-ordinating Committee of the River Plate Basin,[65] the Amazonian Cooperation Council,[66] and the Danube River

---

[56] But see *Gabčíkovo-Nagymaros Case, supra*, n 48.

[57] Schwebel, II *YbILC* (1982) Pt 1, 76, para 70; McCaffrey, ibid, (1986) Pt 1, 132, para 177.

[58] Schwebel, ibid, (1982) Pt 1, 76, para 70; Fitzmaurice, 14 *YbIEL* (2003) 3.

[59] McCaffrey, *The Law of International Watercourses*, 147–70; Benvenisti, *Sharing Transboundary Resources* (Cambridge, 2002); Toope and Brunnée, 91 *AJIL* (1997) 26; Benvenisti, 90 *AJIL* (1996) 384; Lipper, in Garretson et al, *The Law of International Drainage Basins*, 38. See also Scanlon and Iza, 14 *YbIEL* (2003) 81 who develop the concept of 'environmental flows' for this purpose.

[60] *Supra*, nn 4, 5.

[61] 1964 Convention and Statute Relating to the Development of the Chad Basin, *supra*, n 5.

[62] 1963 Act Regarding Navigation and Economic Co-operation between the States of the Niger Basin, *supra*, n 5.

[63] 1959 Agreement Between the UAR and the Republic of the Sudan for the Full Utilization of Nile Waters, and 1960 Protocol Establishing Permanent Joint Technical Committee, in UN, *Legislative Texts and Treaty Provisions Concerning the Utilization of International Rivers for Purposes Other than Navigation*, UN Doc ST/LEG/Ser B/12, 143ff.

[64] Agreement on the Action Plan for the Environmentally Sound Management of the Common Zambezi River System, *supra*, n 5. See *infra*, section 3.

[65] 1969 Treaty on the River Plate Basin, *supra*, n 6; 1973 Treaty on the River Plate and its Maritime Limits, 13 *ILM* (1973) 251.

[66] 1978 Treaty for Amazonian Cooperation, *supra*, n 6.

Protection Commission.[67] The US–Canadian International Joint Commission[68] is an example of common management applied to a more limited watercourse area. These institutions vary in their detailed form and the scope of their responsibilities. Some are not involved in environmental management;[69] in other cases, such as the International Commission from the Protection of the Rhine,[70] or the Moselle Commission,[71] this is their only purpose. As in the case of fisheries or wildlife conservation commissions their success is dependent on the degree of cooperation they can engender.[72]

Common management institutions have become the basis for environmental regulation and sustainable development of a number of international watercourses.[73] Progressive development of this approach has long been endorsed by international political institutions,[74] and adopted by codification bodies. Both the Stockholm Declaration on the Human Environment[75] and the UN Water Conference Mar Del Plata Action Plan[76] in 1977 called on states to establish such commissions where appropriate for coordinated development, including environmental protection. This policy is reflected in the draft articles produced by the Institute of International Law,[77] and the ILC.[78] Both the 1992 UNECE Watercourses Convention and the 1997 UN International Watercourses Convention include provision for common management institutions, but in notably different terms. The 1992 UNECE Convention is the stronger, requiring riparian states both to conclude bilateral or multilateral agreements or arrangements to prevent, reduce, and control transboundary pollution or other impacts, and to establish joint bodies, whose tasks are defined in some detail. States are entitled to participate in these arrangements 'on the basis of equality and reciprocity', although coastal states may join only at the invitation of riparians. Not only is this blueprint for future regional management of European watercourses obligatory for parties to the Convention, but existing arrangements must also be modified to ensure consistency with its 'basic principles'.[79]

---

[67] 1994 Convention on Cooperation for the Protection and Sustainable Use of the Danube River.

[68] 1909 Boundary Waters Treaty, *supra*, n 14.

[69] E.g. the Nile Commission.   [70] *Infra*, section 3.

[71] 1961 Protocol Concerning the Constitution of an International Commission for the Protection of the Moselle Against Pollution, Ruster and Simma, ii, 5618.

[72] See *supra*, Ch 2, section 5.   [73] See *infra*, section 3.

[74] See e.g. UN Committee on Natural Resources, UN Doc E/C 7/2 Add 6, 1–7; Economic Commission for Europe, Committee on Water Problems 1971, UN Doc E/ECE/Water/9, annex II; Council of Europe Rec 436 (1965). For a useful survey of lessons learned, see 1998 Berlin Recommendations on Transboundary Water management (UNECE).

[75] 1972 Stockholm Action Plan for the Human Environment, UN Doc A/Conf 48/14/Rev 1, Rec 51.

[76] *Rept of the UN Water Conference,* Mar del Plata, 1977. See also UN, *Experience in the Development and Management of International River and Lake Basins* (New York, 1981).

[77] 1961 Session, Resolution on Non-Maritime International Waters, Article 9; 1979 Session, Resolution on Pollution of Rivers and Lakes, Article 7(G).

[78] II *YbILC* (1984) Pt 1, 112–16.

[79] See generally Article 9. An earlier reference to participation on an 'equitable' basis was changed in the final text in favour of 'equality' of participation: see UNECE, *2nd Draft Convention,* ENVWA/WP.3/R.19/ Rev1 (1991) 5. Watercourse Agreements concluded in accordance with the 1992 Convention include the 1999 Convention for the Protection of the Rhine; the 1994 Convention on Co-operation for the Protection

In contrast, under the provisions of the 1997 UN International Watercourses Convention the parties need only 'consider' the creation of joint mechanisms or commissions as a means of giving effect to their duty of cooperation and consultation regarding optimal utilization and management of an international watercourse.[80] Moreover, unlike the 1992 UNECE Watercourses Convention or the 1995 UN Fish Stocks Agreement,[81] the 1997 Convention does not alter existing watercourse agreements, such as those governing the Nile or the Amazon, nor does it necessarily require that future watercourse agreements be consistent with its basic principles.[82] On the contrary, under Article 3, parties to later agreements may 'apply and adjust' the provisions of the Convention to the characteristics and uses of specific watercourses. The 1997 Convention is thus an optional framework code or 'guideline' whose provisions are not only subject to reservation, but may be departed from ad hoc by any of the parties.[83] While this may facilitate or even encourage common management of international water resources, the Convention does not require it. However, every watercourse state is entitled to participate in watercourse negotiations or agreements on terms set out in Article 4 of the Convention,[84] and also to participate 'in an equitable and reasonable manner' in the use, development and protection of the watercourse in accordance with Article 5(2). In the *Gabčíkovo-Nagymaros Case* the ICJ viewed the latter article as reflecting 'in an optimal way' the concept of common utilization of shared resources and noted that re-establishment of a joint management regime by the parties to the dispute would accord with its terms.[85] McCaffrey notes that while the idea behind Article 5(2) is well developed in many river basins, its codification by the ILC is novel.[86]

Although cooperation in joint management institutions is not obligatory as a matter of general international law, the foregoing treaties and declarations do recognize that it is a necessary and desirable principle, aptly described by the ILC's special rapporteur as a 'principle of progressive international law'.[87] Examples of state practice in the functioning of such institutions are considered further below.[88]

---

and Sustainable Use of the Danube River; and the 1994 Agreements on the Protection of the Rivers Meuse and Scheldt.

[80] See Articles 8, 24. McCaffrey, 92 *AJIL* (1998) 104, criticizes Article 24 as 'too modest'. Cf Vinogradov, 3 *Colorado JIELP* (1991) 238, and see Schwebel, 3rd *Rept*, II *YBILC*, Pt 1 (1982) 65; McCaffrey, 6th *Rept*, II *YBILC*, Pt 1 (1990) 42–52; *ILC Report*, II *YBILC*, Pt 2 (1991) 73–4.

[81] *Supra*, Ch 2, section 5.

[82] Article 3. Parties may 'consider' harmonizing existing agreements with the Convention's basic principles. See McCaffrey, 92 *AJIL* (1998) 98. Contrast Article 311(2), (3) of the 1982 UNCLOS. Ethiopia, France and Turkey voted against adoption of Article 3.

[83] See Article 3(3) and agreed statements of understanding in UNGA, 51st Session, *Rept of the 6th Committee Working Group*, GAOR A/51/869 (1997) para 8, in 36 *ILM* (1997) 719. Reservations are not prohibited. On the 1997 Convention see generally McCaffrey, *The Law of International Watercourses*, Ch 9.

[84] In this respect the 1997 Convention follows the strong precedent set by the 1995 UN Fish Stocks Agreement, *supra*, Ch 2, section 5. Note however that the entitlement is limited to negotiations or agreements that affect the *entire* watercourse. For negotiations affecting only part of the watercourse see Article 4(2) and McCaffrey, 92 *AJIL* (1998) 98–9.

[85] ICJ Reports (1997) 7, para 147.   [86] 92 *AJIL* (1998) 100.

[87] II *YbILC* (1984) Pt 1, 112, para 59.   [88] See *infra*, section 3.

2 PROTECTION OF WATERCOURSE ENVIRONMENTS

2(1) POLLUTION AND PERMISSIBLE USES OF WATERCOURSES

River pollution generally originates from industrial effluent, agricultural run-off, or domestic sewage discharge. Apart from specific treaty regimes, there is little contemporary support for the view that such polluting uses are per se impermissible.[89] The evidence of state practice is inconsistent, but few modern treaties endorse an absolute prohibition on detrimental alteration of water quality.[90] Instead, the modern trend is to require states to regulate and control river pollution, prohibiting only certain forms of pollutant discharge, and distinguishing between new and existing sources.[91]

Early European practice frequently prohibited industrial or agricultural pollution harmful to river fisheries or domestic use of water.[92] Only as the balance of demands on river utilization changed did this strict approach give way to a more varied pattern. For major industrial rivers, such as the Rhine, the later treaties show clearly a greater tolerance of polluting uses.[93]

---

[89] Salmon, 58 *Ann Inst DDI* (1979) 193–9; Sette Camara, 186 *Recueil des Cours* (1984) 117, 163; Fuentes, 69 *BYIL* (1998) 145–62.

[90] Colliard, in OECD, *Legal Aspects of Transfrontier Pollution*; Lammers, *Pollution of International Watercourses*, 122ff; McCaffrey, *4th Rept on International Watercourses* (1988) UN Doc A/CN 4/412/Add 1, 1–18. For a full list see Fuentes, 69 *BYIL* (1998) 146–50.

[91] See *infra*, section 2(3). Few watercourse treaties define the term pollution, however. Differing definitions are offered by the ILA's Helsinki Rules, Article 9, the IDI's 1979 Resolution on the Pollution of Rivers and Lakes, Article 1, and the 1997 UN International Watercourses Convention, Article 21(1). See also 1978 Great Lakes Water Quality Agreement Article 1(J); and the UNECE Guidelines on Responsibility and Liability Regarding Transboundary Water Pollution, Article 1(1)(b).

[92] 1869 Convention Between the Grand Duchy of Baden and Switzerland Concerning Fishing in the Rhine, Ruster and Simma, ix, 4695; 1887 Convention Establishing Uniform Provisions on Fishing in the Rhine and its Tributaries, Article 10, ibid, x, 4730; 1893 Convention Decreeing Uniform Regulations for Fishing in Lake Constance, Article 12, ibid, x, 4759; 1923 Agreement between Italy and Austria Concerning Economic Relations in Border Regions, Article 14, ibid, xi, 5504; 1922 Provisions relating to the Belgian–German Frontier, part III, Article 2, ibid, xi, 5495; 1882 Convention between Italy and Switzerland Concerning Fishing in Frontier Waters, ibid, 5413; 1906 Convention between Switzerland and Italy Establishing Uniform Regulations Concerning Fishing in Border Waterways, Article 12, ibid, xi, 5440; for more examples, see 1957 Agreement Concerning Fishing in Frontier Waters (Yugoslavia–Hungary) Article 5, ibid, ix, 4572; 1971 Frontier Rivers Agreement (Finland–Sweden) Ch 1, Articles 3, 4, Ch 6, Article 1, ibid, x, 5092. See generally Colliard, in OECD, *Legal Aspects of Transfrontier Pollution*.

[93] 1892 Convention between Luxemburg and Prussia Regulating Fisheries in Boundary Waters, para 11, Ruster and Simma, ix, 4753; 1922 Agreement Relating to Frontier Watercourses, Article 45 (Denmark–Germany) ibid, 5473; 1958 Convention Concerning Fishing in the Waters of the Danube, Article 7, UN, *Legislative Texts, supra*, n 15, 427; 1912 Agreement on the Exploitation of Border Rivers for Industrial Purposes (Spain–Portugal) Ruster and Simma, xi, 5449; 1956 Convention on the Regulation of the Upper Rhine (France–FRG) UN, *Legislative Texts*, 660.

North American practice followed a similar trend. A prohibition of pollution of boundary waters applied only when human health or property were injured.[94] Despite the explicit priority given to domestic and sanitary uses by the 1909 Boundary Waters Treaty, industrial and agricultural pollution of the Great Lakes became established, until a new regulatory regime was agreed in 1972.[95] Until 1973 the United States maintained that it was not required to deliver to Mexico water of any particular quality from the Colorado River, provided its polluting use of the river for irrigation was reasonable.[96] Nor do treaties elsewhere typically prohibit polluting uses. The 1960 Indus River Treaty limited industrial use and required measures to prevent undue pollution affecting other interests, but the implication that polluting uses are entitled to consideration consistent with equitable utilization is clear.[97]

State practice regarding land-based sources of pollution in general points to the prohibition of discharges of certain toxic substances, especially if these are persistent or highly radioactive.[98] But so long as no such substances are involved, the main conclusion must be that most polluting or environmentally harmful uses of international rivers are wrongful only if they infringe the rights of other states or the limits specifically prescribed by particular river treaties.[99] States do, however, have a number of claims on the quality of a watercourse. These include the right to equitable utilization, to protection from sources of serious harm, and to procedural rights of information exchange, consultation, and negotiation.[100]

Moreover, these rights must now be set in the context of the emergence of an obligation to regulate and control sources of river pollution and environmental damage, in particular where these contribute to pollution of the marine environment.[101] This approach to pollution control is important because it moves the issue away from exclusive concentration on the rights of riparians and acknowledges the broader international significance of watercourse environments; it places more emphasis on environmental protection, and illustrates in particular how equitable utilization, the most widely accepted principle of watercourse law, is perhaps the least useful for the development of environmental law.

---

[94] 1909 US–Canada Boundary Waters Treaty, Article IV. See Zacklin and Caflisch, *International Rivers and Lakes*, Ch 1; Bourne, 28 *NILR* (1981) 188; Fuentes, 69 *BYIL* (1998) 150–5.

[95] See *infra*, section 3.

[96] See 1944 Colorado River Treaty, UN, *Legislative Texts*, 236 and cf 1973 Agreement on Permanent and Definitive Solution of the International Problem of the Salinity of the Colorado River, 12 *ILM* (1973) 1105; Brownell and Eaton, 69 *AJIL* (1975) 255.

[97] Article 4.   [98] See *infra*, Ch 7.

[99] See generally, Salmon, 58 *Ann Inst DDI* (1979) 193–263; Lester, 57 *AJIL* (1963); Dickstein, 12 *CJTL* (1973); Bourne, 6 *UBCLR* (1971); Sette Camara, 186 *Recueil des Cours* (1984); Lammers, *Pollution of International Watercourses*; Zacklin and Caflisch, *The Legal Regime of International Rivers and Lakes*, 331; Fuentes, 69 *BYIL* (1998) 162–3.

[100] Other approaches, such as abuse of rights or good neighbourliness are sometimes referred to in the literature but there is no evidence that these reflect international practice or afford additional bases for resolving pollution disputes: Lester, 57 *AJIL* (1963) 833ff; Sette Camara, 186 *Recueil des Cours* (1984) 164 ff, and see generally, *supra*, Ch 3, section 6.

[101] See *infra*, Ch 7.

2(2) ENVIRONMENTAL HARM AND EQUITABLE UTILIZATION

The relationship between equitable utilization of an international watercourse on the one hand and the control of pollution and protection of the environment on the other has been among the more controversial problems affecting the codification of international law relating to freshwater resources. From the perspective of equitable utilization, water quality, and environmental protection are relevant factors to take into account when balancing the interests of the riparians involved, although they will not necessarily outweigh competing needs such as industrial use or irrigation.[102] In the *Gabčíkovo-Nagymaros Case*,[103] the ICJ held that Czechoslovakia, 'by unilaterally assuming control of a shared resource, and thereby depriving Hungary of its right to an equitable and reasonable share of the natural resources of the Danube—with continuing effects on the ecology of the riparian area of the Szigetköz—failed to respect the proportionality which is required by international law'. In this case, environmental effects had a significant impact on the overall equitable balance.

The strongest view is that pollution, or environmental damage, will be impermissible if, but only if, another state is thereby deprived of its claim to equitable utilization of the waters.[104] Advocates of this position argue that in determining the permissibility of pollution or other environmentally harmful uses, equitable utilization must take precedence over competing principles, including any obligation to prevent potential harm to other states. This approach, it is said, ensures that upstream states are not prevented from developing new uses for their watercourses in ways that might adversely affect established uses in downstream states. If this is correct, then 'an equitable use by one state could cause "appreciable" or "significant" harm to another state using the same watercourse, yet not entail a legal "injury" or be otherwise wrongful'.[105] If, alternatively, 'A watercourse state's right to utilize an international watercourse in an equitable and reasonable manner finds its limit in the duty of that state not to cause appreciable harm to other watercourse states',[106] then dams or irrigation projects that would reduce the flow of water could be constructed only with the consent of affected states. For this reason, upstream states were generally most in favour of equitable utilization as the controlling principle during negotiation of the UN International Watercourses Convention. Downstream states were naturally more concerned to secure a greater and more predictable level of protection than would flow from equitable balancing.[107] These competing views were reflected in the long-standing

---

[102] See ILA, Berlin Rules, Article 13; Helsinki Rules, Articles IV and X, *Rept of 52nd Conference* (1966) 484, 496–7; Montreal Rules on Pollution, Article 1, *Rept of 60th Conference* (1982) 531–5; Seoul Complementary Rules, Article 1, *Rept of 62nd Conference* (1986) 232.

[103] ICJ Reports (1997) 7, para 85.

[104] Bourne, 3 *CYIL* (1965) 187; Handl, 13 *CYIL* (1975) 156; id, 14 *RBDI* (1978) 40; Lipper, in Garretson et al, *The Law of International Drainage Basins*, 45ff; Lester, 57 *AJIL* (1963) 840; Dickstein, 12 *CJTL* (1973) 492ff.

[105] McCaffrey, II *YbILC* (1986) Pt 1, 133ff. See also Schwebel, ibid, (1982) Pt 1, 103, draft Article 8(1) and Handl, 13 *CYIL* (1975) 180.

[106] *ILC Report* (1988) GAOR A/43/10, 84.

[107] Crook and McCaffrey, 91 *AJIL* (1997) 374; Rahman, 19 *Fordham ILJ* (1995) 24.

debate within the ILC over the drafting and relative priority of Articles 5 and 7 of the Convention, dealing respectively with equitable utilization and the prevention of harm to other states.[108]

There are four problems with giving equitable utilization priority over obligations to prevent harm, including environmental harm. First, the apparent conflict between these principles is unreal and often based on a misunderstanding of the obligation to prevent harm in international law.[109] This is not an absolute obligation—international law simply does not prohibit all transboundary harm, even through the medium of a river. As we saw in Chapter 3, what it does require is that states take adequate steps to control and regulate sources of transboundary harm within their territory or subject to their jurisdiction. Thus formulated, the obligation is one of conduct, of due diligence, rather than an outright prohibition.[110] If this is correct—and the state practice, treaties and work of the ILC overwhelmingly suggest that it is[111]—then there is no real need to determine whether equitable utilization takes precedence or not. A state which fails to do its best to control avoidable harm to other states cannot easily maintain that it is acting equitably or reasonably, whichever principle prevails. Neither does an obligation to do its best to minimize unnecessary or avoidable harm to other states impede the reasonable and equitable development of a watercourse or the use of its waters in whatever way a state chooses.

Second, the evidence for applying equitable balancing to obligations of pollution control or environmental protection of international watercourses is weak. None of the treaties which regulate these matters does so.[112] The *Lac Lanoux Case* was not concerned with pollution, except as a possible violation of Spain's rights to share in the watercourse, and it held only that diversion of the waters which caused no such injury to Spain and which was accompanied by a full opportunity for consultation did not require her consent or violate any international obligation.[113] Handl's argument that the case confirms recourse to a balancing of interests as a means of determining responsibility for pollution injury rests on slender inference from Spanish interpretation of the relevant treaty.[114] Indeed, by accepting that 'only a limited amount of damage' might be caused to other states, Spain's argument rather points in the opposite direction.[115] Reliance on *Trail Smelter*[116] to support a balance of interests is similarly unconvincing, because this interpretation confuses responsibility for harm with the availability of injunctive relief under a *compromis*.[117] This factor also makes analogous

---

[108] See McCaffrey, 17 *Denver JILP* (1989) 505–10; Handl, 3 *Colorado JIELP* (1992) 123; Bourne, 35 *CYIL* (1997) 222. For the final ILC commentary on the issue see II *YbILC* (1994) Pt 2, 96–105. Only four states voted against Articles 5–7 as finally adopted: China, France, Turkey, and Tanzania.

[109] McCaffrey, 4th Rept, UN Doc A/CN 4/412/Add 2 (1988); Fuentes, 69 *BYIL* (1998) 135–45. But cf Handl, 3 *Colorado JIELP* (1992) 123.

[110] II *YbILC* (1994) Pt2, 103, 124, and see generally Ch 3 *supra*, section 4(2).   [111] Ibid.

[112] See *infra*, section 2(3).

[113] 24 *ILR* (1957) 101, 111–12, 123–4. See Lester, 57 *AJIL* (1963) 838ff.

[114] Handl, 13 *CYIL* (1975) 180f. See also Dickstein, 12 *CJTL* (1973) 494f. Cf Handl, 26 *NRJ* (1986) 405, 421f, however.

[115] At 124.   [116] 33 *AJIL* (1939) 184 and 35 *AJIL* (1941) 684.

[117] But cf Dickstein, 12 *Columbia JTL* (1973) 493ff.

decisions of federal courts questionable precedents on the role of equity in water pollution cases.[118] On the contrary, the US decisions relied on in *Trail Smelter*, and the *Trail Smelter Case* itself, insist that states have no right to cause serious injury by pollution, not that they have no right to cause inequitable or unreasonable injury.[119]

Third, Article 5 of the 1997 Convention itself indicates that the equitable and reasonable use of a watercourse must be consistent both with sustainable use and with the 'adequate protection of the watercourse'. The ILC commentary notes that this provision is meant to cover, inter alia, conservation, water flow, and control of pollution, drought and salinity, and that it 'may limit to some degree the uses that might be made of the waters'. Equitable use is thus not an unfettered right.[120]

Finally, the view that ecological factors can only constrain inequitable uses of an international watercourse allows insufficient weight to be given to the principle of sustainable development. As we saw in Chapter 3, sustainable development entails the integration of environmental protection and economic development. Integration is not simply a matter of equitable balancing between competing factors, however; it is a process which involves continuing obligations of environmental impact assessment, monitoring, and preventive action which cannot be disregarded merely because the proposed use is not inequitable. This much appears to have been recognized by the ICJ in the *Gabčíkovo-Nagymaros Case*.[121]

Among international codifications, only the 1966 Helsinki Rules explicitly require states to prevent pollution injury 'consistent with the principle of equitable utilization'.[122] This provision purports to rely mainly on *Trail Smelter* and other authorities considered here; not surprisingly it has been strongly criticized.[123] The 1997 UN Watercourses Convention and the ILA Berlin Articles adopt a different approach. First, Article 6 of the Watercourses Convention includes ecological factors and protection and conservation of the watercourse as relevant factors when determining whether a use is equitable. This is uncontroversial, as reflected in the ICJ's judgment in *Gabčíkovo*. Second, Article 7(1) codifies a general obligation to take all appropriate measures when utilizing an international watercourse to prevent significant harm to other watercourse states, but in terms which recognize this as an obligation of due diligence, not an absolute prohibition of all harm.[124] Third, Articles 20 and 21 explicitly

---

[118] Lammers, *Pollution of International Watercourses*, 486ff.   [119] Handl, 26 *NRJ* (1986) 421f.

[120] II *YbILC* (1994) Pt 2, 97. On sustainable use see *infra*, section 2(5).

[121] ICJ Reports (1997) para 140, and see *infra*, section 2(5).

[122] Article 10(1). The commentary notes, at 499: 'the international duty stated in this article regarding abatement or the taking of reasonable measures is not an absolute one. This duty, therefore, does not apply to a state whose use of the waters is consistent with the equitable utilization of the drainage basin.' See also 1982 ILA Montreal Rules on Transfrontier Pollution, Article 1, and the 1973 Draft Declaration of the Asian-African Legal Consultative Committee, II *YbILC* (1974) Pt 2, 338.

[123] Dickstein, 12 *Columbia JTL* (1973) 495ff; Handl, 26 *NRJ* (1986) 421ff.

[124] See McCaffrey and Sinjela, 92 *AJIL* (1998) 100; Bourne, 35 *CYIL* (1997) 223–5. An explicit requirement to 'exercise due diligence' in the ILC's 1994 draft of Article 7 was altered to read 'take all appropriate measures' in the 1997 Convention text, but no change in meaning results. The same phraseology is used in many other environmental treaties, including the 1992 UNECE Transboundary Watercourses Convention, Article 2(1). Other variants include 'all measures necessary': see Pt 12 of the 1982 UNCLOS, and *supra*, Ch 3,

require watercourse states to protect and preserve international watercourse ecosystems and to prevent, reduce and control pollution of a watercourse causing significant harm to other states, their environment, their use of the waters, or the living resources of the watercourse.[125]

The only plausible reading of Articles 7(1), 20, and 21 is that these obligations of due diligence are not themselves subject to equitable balancing, but must be complied with independently of any claim of equitable utilization. Bourne summarizes the point exactly:

> if a state is acting within its rights as defined in Articles 5 and 6, it is under a duty to prevent, eliminate, or mitigate harm to other watercourse states by all appropriate, presumably reasonable measures; in short it must act without malice and with due diligence—a proposition that is not disputed.[126]

However, where *despite taking all appropriate measures* significant harm nevertheless results, Article 7(2) then, but only then, requires the parties to negotiate an equitable solution. At this point, equity does take over in defining the rights of the parties. As McCaffrey points out, Article 7(2) acknowledges that harm may in some cases have to be tolerated; he concludes that 'The facts and circumstances of each case, rather than any *a priori* rule, will ultimately be the key determinants of the rights and obligations of the parties.'[127] This approach is largely consistent with the ILC's draft Articles on the Prevention of Transboundary Harm: it accepts that unavoidable harm is not per se wrongful or prohibited, but that a failure to mitigate or compensate for it may be inequitable.[128] Precisely what the rights of watercourse states are in this situation cannot be stated with precision, beyond saying that they must negotiate and that the factors listed in Article 6 of the 1997 UN Convention will be relevant. At the same time, the Convention as a whole suggests that the general requirement to exercise due diligence to prevent avoidable harm to the environment of other states applies to the use of international watercourses in the same way that it applies to other activities within a state's jurisdiction or control.

Equitable balancing is thus applicable to pollution and environmental protection of international watercourses in two situations only: where the harm is less than 'significant', or where it is significant but unavoidable by the exercise of due diligence. In carrying out this balancing process, two points are particularly relevant to pollution and environmental issues. Where potential uses conflict, such as industrial waste disposal and fishing, no priority can be assumed. While some treaties do establish a

---

section 4(2). Compare the ILC's 1991 draft Article 7, which read: 'Watercourse states shall utilize an international watercourse in such a way as not to cause appreciable harm to other watercourse states.'

[125] See next section.   [126] Bourne, 35 *CYIL* (1997) 225.

[127] McCaffrey and Sinjela, 92 *AJIL* (1998) 101–2. See also Bourne, 35 *CYIL* (1997) 223–5.

[128] *Supra*, Ch 3, section 4(1). Note also the agreed statement of understanding adopted with regard to Article 7(2): 'In the event such steps as are required by article 7(2) do not eliminate the harm, such steps as are required by article 7(2) shall then be taken to mitigate the harm': UNGA, 51st Session, *Rept of the 6th Committee Working Group*, GAOR A/51/869 (1997) para 8.

priority, there is no settled practice and each river must be considered individually.[129] Article 10 of the 1997 UN Watercourses Convention recognizes this point by providing that no category of use has inherent preference over any others.[130] Thus protection of the river environment and its living resources must compete with other equitable claims. Second, there is no automatic preference for established uses. An inflexible rule protecting such uses would in effect allow the creation of servitudes. These have not generally found favour with states.[131] Instead, commentators and the views of codification bodies suggest that an equitable balance of interests may in an appropriately strong case allow for the displacement or limitation of earlier established uses. At most these earlier uses enjoy a weighty claim to qualified preference.[132] European and North American practice referred to earlier seems consistent with this conclusion, which the *Lac Lanoux Case* implicitly supports.[133]

Equitable utilization is useful as a means of introducing environmental factors into the allocation of shared watercourse resources, but as a basis for comprehensive environmental protection of those watercourses it is a principle of only modest utility. Not only is it unpredictable in application, through its stress on the individuality of each river and the multiplicity of relevant factors,[134] but it tends to neglect the broader environmental context of rivers as part of a hydrologic cycle affecting the health and quality of the oceans.[135] Moreover, the common regional standards of water quality necessary in that context are less likely to find a place in equitable arrangements balancing only the needs of riparians.[136]

As we have seen, equitable utilization is generally workable on a multilateral basis only if supported by appropriate institutions and coordinated policies. Thus, only as part of the trend to common management and international regulation of transboundary watercourses does it have a more convincing role in resolving environmental disputes.[137]

---

[129] See e.g. 1909 Boundary Waters Treaty, Article VIII; 1960 Indus Waters Treaty, Articles 3, 4; 1976 Rhine Chemicals Convention, Article 1.

[130] 'Special regard' must be given to the requirements of 'vital human needs', however. See also ILA Helsinki Rules, Article VI and Berlin Rules, Article 14; Lipper, in Garretson et al, *The Law of International Drainage Basins*, 60ff and *infra*, section 2(5).

[131] See Lester, 57 *AJIL* (1963) 834ff: 'The concept of international servitudes is thus of negative value, since its characteristics illustrate the irrelevance of municipal law notions of property and permanence to the problem of international river pollution.'

[132] Lipper, in Garretson et al, *The Law of International Drainage Basins*, 50–8; ILA Helsinki Rules, *supra*, n 3, Articles V(d), VII, VIII, and commentary at 493.

[133] Bourne, 3 *CYIL* (1965) 187, 234–53

[134] Lipper, in Garretson et al, *The Law of International Drainage Basins*, 66; Handl, 13 *CYIL* (1975) 189f.

[135] See *infra*, Ch 7.

[136] Boyle, 14 *Marine Policy* (1990) 151; Handl, 13 *CYIL* (1975) 191f. Note also his observation that in a bilateral context, 'it is entirely conceivable that ecological factors, to the extent they are of actual or potential concern to other riparian states, might after all be insufficiently taken into account or altogether disregarded in a solution that primarily promotes the interests—and at that perhaps those of a socio-economic nature at the cost of ecological ones—of the directly involved states'.

[137] A point recognized by Article 5(2) of the 1997 UN Convention. See also Lester, 57 *AJIL* (1963) 84f; Dickstein, 12 *Columbia JTL* (1973) 498f; Bourne, 6 *UBCLR* (1971) 136; Teclaff and Utton, *International Environmental Law*.

2(3) PREVENTION OF POLLUTION AND TRANSBOUNDARY ENVIRONMENTAL HARM

As we have seen in the previous section, the proposition that states are under a customary obligation to take appropriate measures to prevent or minimize significant transboundary harm through their use of an international watercourse is not itself controversial. Article 7 of the 1997 UN Watercourses Convention states the general principle, which successive rapporteurs and the ILC have regarded as a codification of established customary law for all forms of damage to other states.[138] In defining the threshold at which this obligation operates, the ILC initially preferred the term 'appreciable harm', meaning more than perceptible, but less than 'serious' or 'substantial'.[139] What it envisaged was harm of some consequence, for example to health, industry, agriculture, or the environment. Subsequent adoption of 'significant' harm as the appropriate threshold in Articles 7 and 21(2) of the 1997 Convention is largely a cosmetic change.[140] The general principle clearly includes pollution or environmental damage, as Article 21(2) goes on to provide:

Watercourse states shall, individually, and where appropriate, jointly, prevent, reduce and control pollution of an international watercourse that may cause significant harm to other watercourse states or to their environment, including harm to human health or safety, to the use of the waters for any beneficial purpose or to the living resources of the watercourse...[141]

This provision is based on Article 194 of the 1982 UNCLOS and other precedents considered in Chapter 3 and is supported by international codifications, and by numerous writers;[142] the number of watercourse treaties which expressly or implicitly incorporate such an obligation has grown steadily.[143] The *Trail*

---

[138] Schwebel, II *YbILC* (1992) Pt 1, 91, para 111; Evensen, ibid, (1983) Pt 1, 172; McCaffrey, ibid, (1986) Pt 1, 133; *ILC Report*, GAOR A/43/10 (1988) 88ff. See generally McCaffrey, *The Law of International Watercourses*, Ch 11.

[139] II *YbILC* (1982) Pt 1, 98, paras 130–41; *ILC Report* (1988) GAOR A/43/10, 85–6.

[140] See *supra*, Ch 3, section 4.

[141] For commentary, see *ILC Report* (1990) GAOR A/45/10, 159. For earlier versions, see Evensen, *2nd Rept*, I *YbILC* (1984) Pt 1, 118–20, Articles 20–3; Schwebel, *3rd Rept*, II *YbILC* (1982) Pt 1, 144, Article 10, *ILC Report* (1988) GAOR A/43/10, 57, Article 16(2).

[142] Commentary, (1990) GAOR A/45/10, 159ff, and see ILA Helsinki Rules, Article X, and commentary, *1966 Rept*, 497f; Lammers, *Pollution of International Watercourses*, 123, 342; Zacklin and Caflisch, *The Legal Regime of International Rivers and Lakes*, 336; Salmon, 58 *Ann Inst DDI*, 209; Sette-Camara, 186 *Recueil des Cours* (1984) 165, and see the survey of opinions by Schwebel, *3rd Rept*, II *YbILC* (1982) 92ff.

[143] See e.g. 1909 Boundary Waters Treaty (US–Canada) Articles II, IV; 1960 Indus Waters Treaty (India–Pakistan) Article 4; 1922 Agreement Relating to Frontier Watercourses (Germany–Denmark); 1960 Convention on the Protection of Lake Constance Against Pollution; 1950 Treaty Concerning the Regime of the Soviet Hungarian Frontier, Article 17; 1960 Treaty Concerning the Course of the Common Frontier (Germany–Netherlands) Article 58; 1976 Convention on the Protection of the Rhine Against Chemical Pollution; 1990 Agreement Concerning Co-operation on Management of Water Resources of the Danube Basin (EC–Austria) OJ NO L/90/20; Article 3; 1992 UNECE Convention on the Protection and Use of Transboundary Waters and Lakes, Article 2; 1994 Agreements on Protection of the Rivers Meuse and Scheldt, Article 3, 34 ILM (1995) 854; 1994 Convention on Co-operation for the Protection and Sustainable

Smelter,[144] and *Lac Lanoux Arbitrations*,[145] decisions of some national courts,[146] and a number of international declarations[147] provide further confirmation of the Commission's view that Article 21(2)'s antecedents are well grounded in state practice.[148]

As we saw earlier, however, views differ on whether the obligation not to cause harm represents the limit of equitable utilization of a watercourse, or is itself subject to equitable balancing involving other factors.[149] Moreover, it encounters in this context the same difficulties of interpretation as elsewhere, notably whether the obligation is one of due diligence in preventing harm, or whether the state must meet a stricter standard.[150] International claims concerning watercourse damage, such as the *Gut Dam* arbitration, do not permit useful inferences on these questions.[151] The work of the ILC and the 1997 UN Watercourses Convention have provided useful clarification, however.

One ILC rapporteur, McCaffrey, dealt with the choice between a standard of due diligence and more stringent obligations of pollution prevention in international watercourses. Although the latter interpretation is implicit in the view of some members of the Commission who continued to favour a regime of strict liability for watercourse pollution, the rapporteur could find little or no evidence of state practice recognizing strict liability for damage which was non-accidental or did not result from a dangerous activity.[152] In his view, this indicated that the standard required of the state was generally one of due diligence, implicit in the *Trail Smelter* arbitration and supported by state practice. This standard afforded the appropriate flexibility and

---

Use of the Danube River, Articles 5–6; 1994 Agreement on the Protection and Utilization of Transboundary Waters (China–Mongolia) Articles 4, 6; 1995 Mekong River Agreement, Article 7; 1995 Israel–Jordan Peace Treaty, Article 6 and Annexes II, IV; 1995 Protocol on Shared Watercourse Systems in the Southern African Development Community, Article 2; 1999 Convention on the Protection of the Rhine, Article 5. See Fuentes, 69 *BYIL* (1998) 145ff; Nollkaemper, *The Legal Regime for Transboundary Water Pollution: Between Discretion and Constraint* (Dordrecht, 1993).

[144] See *supra*, Ch 3, section 4.   [145] Ibid.

[146] See *Trail Smelter Arbitration*, 35 *AJIL* (1941) 686, 714–17; *Missouri v Illinois*, 200 US 496 (1906); *New York v New Jersey*, 256 US 296 (1921); *North Dakota v Minnesota*, 263 US 365 (1923). See Lammers, *Pollution of International Watercourses*, 486. Many commentators are critical or cautious of the use of federal case law in this context: see Handl, 13 *CYIL* (1975) 182ff; Rubin, 50 *Oregon LR* (1971) 259, 266ff; Lester, 57 *AJIL* (1963) 844–7. The role of equity in these cases is another uncertain factor. In *Handelskwekerij Bier v Mines de Potasse d'Alsace* (1979) *Nederlandse Jurisprudentie*, No 113, 313–20, a Dutch Court, relying on *Trail Smelter*, applied the principle *sic utere tuo* as a principle of international law in determining the liability of a French undertaking for river pollution damage in the Netherlands, but this was overturned on appeal: see *supra*, Ch 5, section 3.

[147] 1971 Act of Asuncion on the Use of International Rivers, Resolution No 25, para 2; 1971 Act of Santiago Concerning Hydrologic Basins, para 4; African–Asian Legal Consultative Committee, Draft Declaration on the Law of International Rivers, 1973, paras IV, VIII.

[148] *ILC Report* (1988) GAOR A/43/10, 60, para 148 (draft Article 16(2)).

[149] See *supra*, section 2(2).   [150] See *supra* Ch 3, section 4.

[151] *Gut Dam Arbitration, Settlement of Claims* (US–Canada) excerpted in *Rept of the Agent of the United States*, 8 *ILM* (1968) 118; *Diversion of Water from the Meuse Case*, PCIJ Ser A/B No 70 (1937) 16. Both cases were concerned only with interpretation and application of bilateral treaties. See Lammers, *Pollution of International Watercourses*, 504. On the *Gabčíkovo-Nagymaros Case* see *supra*, Ch 3.

[152] *ILC Report* (1988) GAOR A/43/10, 64f.

allowed for adaptation to different situations, including the level of development of the state concerned.

McCaffrey's due diligence interpretation is explicit throughout Articles 7, 21(2), and 23 of the 1997 UN Watercourses Convention. Most of the more modern treaties support his view, although others which prohibit environmental harm, or pollution, or specified pollutants, may sustain a stricter interpretation.[153] Thus although the context and formulation of individual treaties is important and may lead to a different conclusion, the evidence does tend to favour the rapporteur's interpretation of a general duty of due diligence in the regulation and control of transboundary water pollution. Moreover, use of the formula 'prevent, reduce and control' in Article 21 is intended to allow for differentiation in measures taken with regard to new or existing sources of pollution, and to that extent also supports the conclusion that there is no absolute obligation of prevention. In this respect the ILC commentary notes that the practice of states 'indicates a general willingness to tolerate even significant pollution harm, provided that the watercourse state of origin is making its best efforts to reduce the pollution to a mutually acceptable level'.[154]

Cooperation between riparians in the elaboration and supervision of detailed standards of pollution control and prevention through international river commissions is, as in other contexts, an important means of giving concrete content to this general obligation of due diligence. Article 21(3) neatly summarizes the practices which are common in most of the modern watercourse treaties: it calls for mutually agreed measures such as establishing lists of prohibited and controlled substances, water quality objectives and criteria, and techniques and practices to deal with point and diffuse sources of pollution.[155] The 1992 UNECE Transboundary Watercourses Convention goes further than the 1997 UN Convention in certain respects, including specifying that pollution prevention measures shall if possible be taken at source, and be 'guided by' the precautionary principle, the polluter-pays principle, and the needs of future generations. Article 3 requires the development of limits on pollution discharges based on 'best available technology' or 'best environmental practices', emissions reduction through use of non-waste technology, and application of the 'ecosystems approach' to sustainable water resources management. There are additional requirements of environmental impact assessment and monitoring of transboundary impacts. This Convention has provided the framework for subsequent negotiation of

---

[153] See e.g. Articles 7 and 8 of the 1995 Mekong River Basin Agreement, which require parties to make every effort to 'avoid, minimise and mitigate' harmful effects to the environment, but also call for cessation of uses causing substantial damage, and compensation therefor. In effect this latter provision amounts to a prohibition of such harmful uses.

[154] II *YbILC* (1994) Pt 2, 122, para 4, and *ILC Report* (1990) GAOR A/45/10, 161. See also 1992 UNECE Watercourses Convention, Articles 2(2), 3, and *supra*, Ch 3. The same point is evident in Article 5(4)(b) of the 1999 Rhine Convention, which commits the parties only to a gradual reduction in discharges of hazardous substances, but compare 1995 Mekong Agreement, previous note.

[155] See generally, Nollkaemper, *Transboundary Water Pollution*. In this respect the Convention also reflects practice in regional treaties on land-based sources of marine pollution. See *supra*, Ch8.

environmental protection agreements for European rivers, including the 1999 Rhine Convention and the 1994 Danube Convention.[156]

As we saw in Chapter 3, it is difficult to make confident assertions concerning the general applicability of the precautionary principle or approach. From that perspective, the failure of the 1997 UN Convention to refer to precaution is unhelpful, but not necessarily significant. The ILC's view that the precautionary principle is implicit in Articles 20 and 21 of the 1997 Convention[157] derives some support from its inclusion in the 1992 UNECE Convention and subsequent European watercourse agreements, although only in its weakest form as guidance to the parties.[158] The principle is also found in newer agreements on land-based sources of marine pollution, such as the 1992 Paris Convention, which applies to most Western European rivers.[159]

It is now generally accepted that states have a duty to protect the marine environment, and in particular to control land-based sources of marine pollution. These sources include pollution from rivers. Article 23 of the 1997 UN Convention recognizes this point. Corresponding closely to Article 207 of the 1982 UNCLOS, which deals generally with land-based pollution, Article 23 sets no specific standard of conduct beyond an obligation to take all necessary measures to protect estuaries and the marine environment, 'taking into account generally accepted international rules and standards'.[160] The regional-seas treaties considered in Chapter 8 support the underlying implication of the ILC's codification that the basis of pollution control in international rivers is no longer to be found mainly in customary obligations concerning equitable utilization or harm prevention, but in regional regimes employing common standards of environmental protection for river pollution, and in the requirements of international cooperation. As we saw in Chapter 8, there remain problems of coordinating the operation of watercourse and regional seas commissions in a manner which achieves the ILC's objective.

2(4) PROTECTION OF WATERCOURSE ECOSYSTEMS

The environmental obligations of watercourse states are not limited to protecting other states or the marine environment from pollution. As we saw in the previous section, Articles 20 and 22 of the 1997 UN Convention also provide for the protection and preservation of the ecosystems of international watercourses. They are modelled respectively on Articles 192 and 196 of the 1982 UNCLOS. The International Law Commission's commentary treats Article 20 as a specific application of the more general rule in Article 5 concerning optimal and sustainable use of an international watercourse 'consistent with the adequate protection thereof,' and it concludes that

---

[156] See 1999 Rhine Convention, Articles 3–5; 1994 Danube Convention, Articles 5, 6 , 7, and Annex 1; 1994 Agreements on the Meuse and Scheldt, Article 3.

[157] II *YbILC* (1994) Pt 2, 120, paras 9 and 122, para 4.

[158] 1992 UNECE Convention, Article 2(5); 1999 Rhine Convention, Article 4; 1994 Agreements on the Meuse and Scheldt, Article 3; 1994 Danube Convention, Article 2(4).

[159] *Infra*, Ch 7.   [160] Ibid.

'[t]here is ample precedent for the obligation contained in Article 20 in the practice of States and the work of international organizations'.[161] The draft article was accepted without opposition in 1997. Article 22 deals with the introduction of new or alien species detrimental to the ecosystem, and according to the ILC it is necessary because 'pollution' does not include biological alterations. There are few precedents for it in other watercourse treaties.[162]

In both articles the obligation to 'protect' or 'preserve' the ecosystem from harm or the threat of harm once again requires the exercise of due diligence. 'Preservation' applies particularly to 'freshwater ecosystems that are in a pristine or unspoiled condition'; according to the ILC, these must be maintained 'as much as possible in their natural state'.[163] The Commission also suggests that Article 20 provides an 'essential basis for sustainable development' and gives priority to maintaining the viability of aquatic ecosystems as life support systems. However, this preservationist interpretation not only goes well beyond any concept of equitable balancing, it is inconsistent with the ICJ's more cautious approach to sustainable development in the context of the previously pristine Danube.[164] Where the ILC seeks preservation from development, the ICJ opts merely for integration.

Reflecting its earlier desire to avoid reference to shared natural resources or drainage basins, the Commission justifies its focus on the watercourse 'ecosystem', rather than the watercourse 'environment', by pointing to the latter's potential inclusion of surrounding land areas. Thus the 'watercourse ecosystem' is not intended to cover areas beyond the watercourse itself.[165] This narrow conception of ecosystem protection is not found elsewhere,[166] and it has been criticized as a missed opportunity to develop what in policy terms can be seen as a desirable basis for water management.[167] However, the ILC commentary goes on to define an ecosystem as 'an ecological unit consisting of living and non-living components that are interdependent and function as a community' and thus comes close to recognizing that interdependence cannot be confined to the watercourse alone; a major watercourse system or basin will cover a multiplicity of 'ecosystems' existing—or coexisting—at various levels of interdependence within and beyond the physical confines of the watercourse itself. Moreover, thus defined, an 'ecosystem' is indistinguishable from 'the environment' as used in Article 21, which according to the Commission includes 'flora and fauna dependent

---

[161] II *YbILC* (1994) Pt 2, 119. See also *ILC Report*, GAOR A/45/10 (1990) 147, 169; Toope and Brunnée, 91 *AJIL* (1997) 26; Bourne, 35 *CYIL* (1997) 215; Fuentes, 69 *BYIL* (1998) 119; McCaffrey, *The Law of International Watercourses*, Ch 12. See also ILA Berlin Rules, Ch V.

[162] For ILC Commentary see II *YbILC* (1994) Pt 2, 122. See also 1995 Protocol on Shared Watercourse Systems in the Southern African Development Community, Article 2(11).

[163] II *YbILC* (1994) Pt 2, 119.

[164] See *Gabčíkovo-Nagymaros Case*, ICJ Reports (1997) 7, *supra*, Ch 3, section 2. See also *Pulp Mills Case*, ICJ Reports (2006). For a different view of Article 20 see *infra*, and see also Bourne, 35 *CYIL* (1997) 215.

[165] II *YbILC* (1994) Pt 2, 118.

[166] Compare Article 2 of the 1999 Rhine Convention, which applies to 'aquatic *and terrestrial* ecosystems which interact or could again interact with the Rhine', and the *Gabčíkovo Case*, *supra*, text at n 104.

[167] Toope and Brunnée, 91 *AJIL* (1997) 26. But cf Fuentes, 69 *BYIL* (1998) 119.

on the watercourse'. It is doubtful if the Commission's careful choice of terminology really does confine the potential scope of this obligation in a meaningful way. Any attempt to protect a river 'ecosystem' cannot avoid affecting the surrounding land areas or their 'environment'.

A final problem which Article 20 throws up but fails to answer is the question of whose ecosystem it protects. Is the article aimed at protecting other states? Or is it also, or only, aimed at protecting a watercourse state's own ecosystem? Only if it does both is it consistent with a full ecosystem approach.[168] The subsequent articles of Part IV of the 1997 UN Convention are all concerned with harm to other states or the marine environment, and can be said to codify existing customary law on these matters. This may suggest that Article 20 is merely a chapeau to these articles and must accordingly be construed narrowly, thereby eliminating from its scope any ecosystem damage that remains purely internal in character. If this is correct, then the ecosystem approach endorsed by the Convention is further narrowed.[169] However, the ILC commentary clearly views watercourse ecosystem protection as a specific application of a more general obligation to protect ecosystems, regardless of any transboundary impact.[170] This view does make sense, since it recognizes the ecological unity of the watercourse and the artificiality of international boundaries when ecosystem management is imperative. Article 20 may thus imply that the legal obligations attaching to the use and management of an international watercourse are no longer determined solely by its transboundary aspects, but also apply to internal environmental protection.

It is thus apparent that the 1997 UN Convention is ambiguous, and possibly even confused, in the scope and depth of its commitment to watercourse ecosystem protection. Not surprisingly, Article 20 has been criticized both for going beyond customary law and for not being ambitious enough in developing the law on an ecosystem basis.[171] It is also true that whatever its merits, comprehensive ecosystem protection remains an underdeveloped concept in general international law, and that it is not yet possible to conclude that states have a general duty to protect and preserve ecosystems in all areas under their sovereignty.[172] Do regional treaties and practice lend stronger support to the narrower proposition that there is a developing obligation with regard to watercourse ecosystems?

It has been argued that the 1992 Transboundary Watercourses Convention makes a more significant commitment to watercourse ecosystem protection than the 1997 UN Convention.[173] Article 2(2) specifically requires parties to 'ensure conservation and, where necessary, restoration of ecosystems', and Article 3 calls for measures to

---

[168] Toope and Brunnée, loc cit, previous note.   [169] Ibid, 51.

[170] II *YbILC* (1994) Pt 2, 120. McCaffrey, *The Law of International Watercourses*, 458–60, takes the same view, and concludes that 'unlike Article 21, the obligation is not triggered by significant harm to another watercourse state or the threat thereof'.

[171] Compare Fuentes, 69 *BYIL* (1998) 119, and Toope and Brunnée, 91 *AJIL* (1997) 26. Bourne, 35 *CYIL* (1997) 215, appears to see the article as an expression of the principle of equitable use, and thus of existing customary law.

[172] See *infra*, Ch 11. But for a detailed treatment see Benvenisti, *Sharing Transboundary Resources*, Ch 5.

[173] Toope and Brunnée, 91 *AJIL* (1997) 26. On the 1992 Convention see *supra*, n 15.

promote sustainable water resource management and 'the application of the ecosystems approach'. Both provisions are placed within articles expressly aimed at preventing or controlling transboundary impact and all the subsequent monitoring and control provisions focus on transboundary rather than internal impacts. This may indicate no greater commitment to comprehensive ecosystem protection than the later UN Convention. However, the 1997 Helsinki Declaration[174] committed the parties to regulating internal waters in accordance with appropriate provisions of the Convention in order to ensure consistency with the management of transboundary waters. The parties also adopted a programme of integrated management of water and related ecosystems. Moreover, treaties governing the Rhine, the Danube, the Meuse, and the Scheldt, all of which were negotiated in accordance with the 1992 Convention, show a similarly broad commitment to ecosystem protection. They do not deal only with transboundary impacts, nor do they adopt a narrow definition of the relevant ecosystem.[175] Recent watercourse agreements between developing states follow a comparable pattern. The 1995 Mekong Agreement is the most comprehensive. It requires the parties to protect the environment, natural resources, aquatic life, and 'ecological balance' of the Mekong River basin, and to avoid or minimize harmful effects.[176]

These agreements do support the ILC's conclusion that ecosystem protection is a developing element in the law and practice of states relating to international watercourses, and they suggest that Article 20 of the 1997 UN Convention should not be interpreted too narrowly or limited to the control of transboundary harm. It is also noteworthy that in no case are obligations of ecosystem protection or preservation subject to equitable balancing; this does not mean, however, that they necessarily take precedence over watercourse development, or that ecosystems must be preserved from all development. The overriding objective of sustainable development is acknowledged, especially in developing country agreements.[177] In effect therefore, a balance is required, integrating economic and social development on the one hand and ecosystem and environmental protection on the other, and it is in this sense that the ILC's references to protection and preservation of ecosystems probably should be understood.

As we saw in Chapter 8, the now extensive system of regional treaties on land-based sources of pollution supplies some of the same ecosystem protection for

[174] 1st Meeting of the Parties, *supra*, n 15.

[175] 1994 Danube Convention, Article 2(3), (5); 1994 Agreements on the Protection of the Meuse and Scheldt, Article 3; 1999 Rhine Convention, Articles 2, 3, 5. See also 1990 Elbe Convention which requires parties to cooperate to achieve a healthy diversity of river species and as natural an ecosystem as possible.

[176] Articles 3, 7. See also 1994 China–Mongolia Treaty on Joint Watercourses, Article 4; 1994 Israel–Jordan Peace Treaty, Annex IV. Cf the 1995 Protocol on Shared Watercourse Systems in the Southern African Development Community, which recognizes the need for environmentally sustainable management and a proper balance between development and adequate protection of the watercourse, but refers explicitly to ecosystems only in Article 2(11) dealing with alien species.

[177] See e.g. 1995 Mekong River Treaty; 1995 Southern African Protocol; 1999 Rhine Convention; 1994 Agreements on the Rivers Meuse and Scheldt. And see 1992 Dublin Statement on Water and Sustainable Development; 1998 Declaration of the UN Conference on Water and Sustainable Development, UN Doc E/CN 17/1998/16, Annex 9/4 (1998).

otherwise non-international watercourses. The 1992 Convention on Biological Diversity and the 1971 Ramsar Convention on Wetlands of International Importance also place important ecological obligations on states affecting both international and non-international watercourses and these considerations are recognized in a few watecourse treaties.[178] Once watercourse ecosystem protection and sustainable use of water resources is embraced by international law, a sharp division between international and non-international watercourses becomes much more difficult to maintain.

2(5) SUSTAINABILITY AND CONSERVATION OF WATER RESOURCES

(a) Sustainable development and water resources law

As the *Gabčíkovo-Nagymaros* and *Pulp Mills Cases* show, international watercourse development is constrained in part by the limits of equitable use, in part by evolving environmental obligations, and in part by considerations of sustainable development.[179] In *Pulp Mills* the ICJ noted that 'the present case highlights the importance of the need to ensure environmental protection of shared natural resources while allowing for sustainable economic development'.[180] In Chapter 3 it was argued that sustainable development is best viewed as an objective or consideration to guide national or international policies or decisions on resource use, rather than as substantive standard appropriate for judicial review and determination. The implications of sustainable development are thus primarily procedural. What is required is a process which integrates both development objectives and environmental protection, and which takes account of future as well as present needs. The balance which emerges from this process is necessarily a value judgement in which neither the environment nor the needs of the future will necessarily prevail. However, it is a judgement which affects not only boundary or transboundary watercourses but all water resources within all states. Unlike equitable utilization, sustainable development is thus not a principle to be applied only in the context of transboundary impacts on other watercourse states, but a principle of general or universal application. A watercourse development may be equitable as between two riparians but it will not necessarily be consistent with the principle of sustainable development if it does not also integrate environmental, developmental, and intergenerational considerations in the manner envisaged by the Rio Declaration on Environment and Development. This is not to say that third states are entitled to challenge watercourse development not undertaken on such a basis of sustainability, but it is inevitable that the international community's collective commitment to the pursuit of sustainable development will also have implications for the cooperative management of transboundary water resources. In particular, institutions and policies established by watercourse treaties will have to reflect these new

---

[178] See 1990 Elbe Convention, Article 1(2); 1999 Rhine Convention, Article 3(1) and see *infra*, Chs 11–12.
[179] *Supra*, Ch 3, section 2(1).   [180] ICJ Reports (2006) para 80.

considerations, as they have done in other treaties, such as those concerned with climate change, fisheries management, or ozone depletion. Participating watercourse states will thus be entitled to insist on a management process which affords a proper place to sustainable development. This is recognized explicitly in Article 24 of the 1997 UN Watercourses Conventions and it one of the implicit lessons of the *Gabčíkovo-Nagymaros Case*.[181]

It is this changed perspective which is perhaps the most remarkable feature of watercourse treaties concluded since 1990, and which has begun to alter the existing law on water resources in quite subtle ways, as it has also done for fisheries law.[182] We can see that most of the new watercourse agreements now recognize in some form the importance of sustainable development, sustainable use, or sustainable management as an aim or objective.[183] Environmental protection obligations in these agreements are no longer confined to pollution control and transboundary damage, but require a more comprehensive integration of ecological considerations affecting a watercourse, including impacts on biological diversity, ecosystems, and the marine environment.[184] Water resources must be conserved and used sustainably. In many cases the precautionary principle is to be applied by governments and watercourse commissions when taking decisions or adopting policies concerning watercourse management.[185] Nor is this emphasis on sustainability confined to rivers in the developed world: it is equally evident in treaties such as the 1987 Agreement on the Action Plan for the Environmentally Sound Management of the Common Zambezi River System, the 1995 Protocol on Shared Watercourse Systems in the Southern African Development Community, or the 1995 Agreement on Cooperation for the Sustainable Development of the Mekong River Basin.

Moreover, although as we saw earlier the 1997 UN Watercourses Convention does not alter existing treaties,[186] the *Gabčíkovo-Nagymaros Case* illustrates that older watercourse treaties may nevertheless be affected by the objective of sustainable development and the need to integrate environmental and economic considerations in an inter-generational perspective. The International Court found in this

---

[181] At paras 140–2. See also *Pulp Mills Case*, ICJ Reports (2006).

[182] On fisheries law see Boyle and Freestone (eds), *International Law and Sustainable Development* (Oxford, 1999) especially Chs 6–8, and *infra*, Ch 13.

[183] 1988 Agreement on the Zambezi River, Preamble; 1992 UNECE Convention on Transboundary Watercourses, Preamble, Articles 2, 3; 1994 Danube Convention, Preamble, Article 2; 1994 Conventions on the Meuse and Scheldt, Article 3; 1995 Mekong River Basin Agreement, Article 1; 1995 SADC Protocol on Shared Watercourses, Preamble, Article 2, with 2000 Revised Protocol, Article 2; 1999 Rhine Convention, Preamble, Articles 3, 4; 1997 UN Watercourses Convention, Preamble, Articles 5, 6, 24; 1999 Rhine Convention, Preamble, Articles 3, 4; 1999 UNECE Protocol on Water and Health, Articles 1, 4. See also 1992 UNCED, *Agenda 21*, Ch 18; 1992 Dublin Statement on Water and Sustainable Development; 1998 Declaration of the UN Conference on Water and Sustainable Development, UN Doc E/CN 17/1998/16, Annex.

[184] See previous sections.

[185] 1992 UNECE Watercourses Convention, Article 2; 1994 Danube Convention, Article 2(4); 1994 Conventions on the Meuse and Scheldt, Article 2(3); 1999 Rhine Convention, Article 4; 1999 UNECE Protocol on Water and Health, Article 5(a).

[186] Article 3; see *supra*, section 1(2)(d).

case that although a bilateral treaty dating from 1977 continues to govern the parties' relationship with regard to the operation of the dam, it does so not in static isolation but in dynamic conjunction with other rules and principles of international
law relating to international watercourses, sustainable development, and environmental protection, as they evolve.[187] In effect the Court interpreted the 1977
treaty by reference to these evolving rules, while at the same time drawing heavily
on the principal obligations codified in the 1997 UN Watercourses Convention.
It was this view which enabled the Court to hold that, notwithstanding the 1977
Treaty's silence on the subject, the monitoring of environmental effects is a continuing obligation for the parties under general international law, and new norms
of international law, including those relevant to sustainable development, have to
be taken into account for continuing activities as well as for new developments.
This approach may have similar implications for the interpretation of other older
watercourse treaties, such as those governing the Nile or the Indus. In addition, it
suggests that watercourse agreements are neither self-contained regimes,[188] nor do
they freeze the applicable law at the date of the conclusion of the relevant treaty.
A watercourse treaty governs what it governs—if, for example, it makes no provision for environmental impact assessment or monitoring of future projects, there
is no evident reason why the general law on EIA and monitoring should not apply,
unless of course the treaty expressly or impliedly excludes it. Problems remain in
determining the precise relationship between such a treaty and general law, but the
Court's conclusion that the law governing a complex and ongoing project of this
kind cannot be viewed in static terms is surely correct.

(b) Sustainable utilization and the right to water

The obligation of states to utilize their natural resources sustainably was considered
in Chapter 3. As we saw there, it has become a prominent element in post-1992 treaties concerned with tropical timber and straddling and highly migratory fish stocks.
Article 5 of the 1997 UN Watercourses Convention also refers to attaining 'optimal
and sustainable utilization'[189] of international watercourses, while the 1992 UNECE
Transboundary Watercourses Convention requires parties to reduce transboundary
impacts by ensuring 'sustainable water-resources management'.[190] Similarly, the 1995
Mekong River Basin Agreement calls for cooperation in 'sustainable development,
utilization, management and conservation of water', and it goes on to lay down rules
to maintain minimum water flows during dry periods.[191] There is enough evidence

---

[187] At paras 112, 140. See also *Pulp Mills Case*, ICJ Reports (2006).

[188] On self-contained regimes see *Case Concerning Diplomatic and Consular Staff in Tehran*, ICJ Reports
(1980) 3, and Simma, 16 *NYIL* (1985) 111.

[189] On the principle of 'optimal utilization', see Hafner, 45 *Austrian JPIL* (1993) 45. Cf ILA Berlin Rules,
Article 7, which requires states to take 'all appropriate measures to manage waters sustainably'. This is not
limited to international waters.

[190] Article 3. See also 1994 Danube Convention, Article 2; 1999 Rhine Convention, Article 3(1) but this
agreement does not refer to sustainable use as such.

[191] Articles 1, 6.

here to show that sustainable utilization is at least an evolving element of international watercourses law, and an essential element if the objectives of sustainable development and international policy are to be fully realized.[192]

It is relatively easy to see what the concept of sustainable use means when applied to tropical timber or fish: use should be non-exhaustive, that is the resource should as far as possible be conserved so that it is available indefinitely.[193] Conservation in this sense is not a new element in international watercourses law. Fuentes points out that it was relevant to establishing an equitable regime for the Indus River in 1942 and 1960. She concludes that intentional or negligent wastefulness demonstrates the absence of any real need for the water.[194] Article 5 of the ILA's 1966 Helsinki Rules reflects this by listing 'the avoidance of unnecessary waste' as an equitable factor. Article 6 of the 1997 UN Watercourses Convention prefers 'conservation, protection, development and economy of use...and the costs of measures taken to that effect'. This formulation allows for lack of means as a justification. In some cases wasteful use is more than merely an element in an equitable balance. The 1992 UNECE Convention requires states to take all appropriate measures to ensure the conservation of transboundary waters,[195] while the Mekong Agreement calls for cooperation in this respect. Pollution is arguably one form of 'unnecessary' waste of water, and the development of stronger controls on harmful emissions will also contribute to conservation of water resources.

More often the problem affecting international watercourses is not wasteful or exhaustive use but priority between competing uses, and the question is not whether a use is sustainable, but sustainable for what purpose? As Article 10 of the 1997 UN Watercourses Convention indicates, '[i]n the absence of agreement or custom to the contrary, no use of an international watercourse enjoys inherent priority over other uses'. At the same time the article goes on to accord special regard in any equitable balance to 'vital human needs', suggesting at least an inchoate priority, though without specifying whether these needs are limited to drinking water and sanitation, or also include economic and agricultural needs.[196] Sustaining human life and health as a priority for water resource allocation in situations of scarcity can be supported by reference to international human-rights law, especially the right to life or the right freely to dispose of natural resources.[197] The UN Committee on Economic, Social and Cultural Rights has also concluded that states are required to ensure an adequate and accessible supply of water for drinking, sanitation, and nutrition, based on Articles 11 and

---

[192] See in particular 2002 World Summit on Sustainable Development, *Plan of Implementation*, UN Doc A/CONF 199/20, 6, paras 23–8 and Epiney, 63 *ZAÖRV* (2003) 377.

[193] See *supra*, Ch 3, section 2(2).   [194] 69 *BYIL* (1998) 179–85.

[195] Article 2. See also 1994 Danube Convention, Article 2.

[196] The 6th committee commentary indicates that 'In determining "vital human needs" special attention is to be paid to providing sufficient water to sustain human life, including both drinking water and water required for the production of food in order to prevent starvation.' *Rept of the 6th Committee Working Group*, GAOR A/51/869 (1997).

[197] *Supra*, Ch 5, section 2.

12 of the 1966 UN Covenant.[198] These at least would appear to be vital human needs, and a conflicting use is arguably neither sustainable nor equitable if it prevents them from being met.[199] There is little doubt that the UN Watercourses Convention and other watercourses treaties would be interpreted and applied taking these rights into account.[200] Moreover, whatever the legal status of sustainable use as a legal principle, it is clear from these various precedents that where human rights are sufficiently affected unsustainable use of water will violate applicable human-rights standards.[201]

2(6) TRANSBOUNDARY ENVIRONMENTAL COOPERATION[202]

(a) Notification, consultation, and negotiation in cases of environmental risk

The application to international watercourses of the rule that states are entitled to prior notice, consultation, and negotiation in cases where the proposed use of a shared resource may cause significant injury to their rights or interests is amply supported by UNGA Resolution 2995 (1972), by the 1997 UN Watercourses Convention,[203] by other international codifications,[204] declarations,[205] case law,[206] and commentators.[207] In this context procedural requirements are particularly important as a means of giving effect to the principle of equitable utilization and for avoiding disputes among riparians over the benefits and burdens of river development.[208]

The inclusion of articles on transboundary notification and consultation in the 1997 UN Watercourses Convention was opposed by only three states, all upstream: Ethiopia, Rwanda and Turkey. As McCaffrey observes, acceptance by most delegations of the basic obligation to provide prior notification is itself important: 'it provides

---

[198] UNCESCR, General Comment No 15: The Right to Water, UN Doc E/C 12/2002/11 (2003); WHO, *The Right to Water* (Geneva, 2003); McCaffrey, 5 *Georgetown IELR* (1992) 1; Benvenisti, 90 *AJIL* (1996) 406ff; Tully, 14 *YbIEL* (2003) 101; Fitzmaurice, 18 *Fordham ELR* (2007) 537.

[199] See 1999 UNECE Protocol (to the 1992 Convention) on Water and Health, which commits parties to ensuring provision of adequate supplies of wholesome drinking water, adequate sanitation, and other measures to protect human health. The Protocol takes priority over other less stringent agreements: Article 4 (9).

[200] *Supra*, Ch 1.   [201] See also World Bank practice, *supra*, Ch 2, section 4(7).

[202] *Supra*, Ch 3, section 4, and see generally McCaffrey, *The Law of International Watercourses*, Ch 13; Salman and de Chazournes (eds), *International Watercourses: Enhancing Cooperation and Managing Conflict* (World Bank, 1998).

[203] Articles 8–9, 11–19. For commentary see *YbILC* (1994) Pt 2, 105–8; *ILC Report* (1988) GAOR A/43/10, 114ff.

[204] ILA Berlin Rules, Chs VI, XI; ILA, Montreal Rules, Articles 5, 6; Institute of International Law, 1961 Resolution on the Utilization of Non-Maritime International Waters, Articles 5–8;

[205] E.g. 1933 Montevideo Declaration on the Industrial and Agricultural Use of International Rivers, 28 *AJIL Supp* (1934) 59–60; Stockholm Conference on the Human Environment, 1972, UN Doc, A/Conf 48/14, 'Action Plan', Recommendation 51; Council of Europe, Recommendation 436 on Fresh Water Pollution Control, 1965, and 1967 European Water Charter, II *YbILC* (1974) Pt 2, 341ff.

[206] *Lac Lanoux* Arbitration, 24 *ILR* (1957) 101; *Gabčíkovo-Nagymaros Case,* ICJ Reports (1997) 7; *Pulp Mills Case,* ICJ Reports (2006).

[207] Kirgis, *Prior Consultation in International Law* (Charlottesville, Va, 1983) Ch 2, reviews the state practice in detail. See also Bourne, 22 *UTLJ* (1972) 172; ibid, 10 *CYIL* (1972); Evensen, *1st Rept*, II *YbILC* (1983) Pt 1, 173ff; McCaffrey, *3rd Rept* (1987) UN Doc A/CN4/406, Add 2, 139ff.

[208] McCaffrey, *2nd Rept*, II *YbILC* (1986) Pt 1, 139. See generally *supra*, Ch3, section 4(5).

further evidence that the international community as whole emphatically rejects the notion that a state has unfettered discretion to do as it wishes with the portion of an international watercourse within its territory'.[209]

These procedural principles are generally regarded as applicable where the proposed use of a watercourse creates a risk of significant harm or adverse effects in another state.[210] Moreover, although many older treaties are concerned only with works which affect navigation or the flow or course of a river, the same procedural norms have been applied to the adverse effects of river pollution or the risk of serious environmental harm.[211] Treaties expressly requiring prior consultation in such cases include the Convention on the Protection of Lake Constance,[212] the 1994 Danube Convention,[213] and the 1974 Nordic Convention on the Protection of the Environment.[214] In other treaties, such as the 1973 Agreement between the United States and Mexico,[215] references to consultation in case of possible 'adverse effects' or 'transboundary impacts' will also cover pollution or environmental harm, unless as in the case of the 1960 Indus Waters Treaty, their terms are too specific to include consultation in such situations.[216] This conclusion is implicitly supported by the 1997 UN Convention, which does not distinguish consultation in cases of environmental harm from other possible adverse effects. Furthermore, the growing practice of information exchange and consultation, through international river commissions, on the establishment of pollution emission standards, toxic discharges, and measures threatening increased pollution points to an obligation covering these matters even where there is no treaty requirement to consult.[217] Treaties relating to land-based sources of pollution provide further evidence

---

[209] 92 *AJIL* (1998) 103.

[210] 1997 UN Watercourses Convention, Article 12; ILA Berlin Rules, Articles 57, 60; 1961 Salzburg Rules, Articles 4, 5; ILA Helsinki Rules, Article XXIX; Bourne 22 *UTLJ* (1972) 174–5, 233, n 143. See generally, 1978 UNEP Principles of Conduct Relating to Natural Resources Shared by Two or More States; Kirgis, *Prior Consultation in International Law*, 359.

[211] Kirgis, op cit, 40, 86.

[212] 1960 Convention on the Protection of Lake Constance Against Pollution, Article 1(3) UN *Legislative Texts*, UN Doc ST/LEG/SER B/12, 438 and see also 1966 Treaty Regulating the Withdrawal of Water from Lake Constance, 620 *UNTS* 198; Kirgis, *Prior Consultation*, 24 observes: 'These two treaties set up a comprehensive prior consultation system for Lake Constance, without requiring prior consent.'

[213] Articles 10(f), 11. See also 1990 Agreement Concerning Co-operation on Management of Water Resources in the Danube Basin.

[214] *Supra*, Ch 5, section 3. See also 1994 Israel–Jordan Peace Treaty, Annex II, Article 5, 34 *ILM* (1994) 46.

[215] 1973 US–Mexico Agreement on the Permanent and Definitive Solution to the International Problem of the Salinity of the Colorado River, *supra*, n 97, Article 6. Kirgis, *Prior Consultation*, 66 notes: 'Arguably the 1973 agreement represents United States acquiescence in repeated Mexican assertions that the Wellton-Mohawk project violated its rights. One result of that assertion-acquiescence process was the US promise to engage in consultation before embarking on any similar project in the future. Thus it is a particularly significant indication of current normative expectations regarding changes in the water quality of a successive river.' See also the 1960 Netherlands–FRG Frontier Treaty, Articles 60–2; Kiss and Lambrechts, 15 *AFDI* (1969) 726ff.

[216] This treaty requires consultation only in respect of engineering or hydro-electric works causing interference with waters: Kirgis, *Prior Consultation*, notes: 'the Treaty neither expressly nor by implication requires consultation before new potential pollutants are introduced into the waters', at 44–5.

[217] 1997 UN Watercourses Convention, Article 21(3). See also 1992 UNECE Transboundary Watercourses Convention, Articles 9–13; 1994 Danube Convention, Article 12; 1964 Statute Relating to Development of

of the importance of this form of institutional consultation machinery in relation to river pollution.[218]

As in other respects, regional patterns may be significant, and Europe and North America offer the most developed examples of cooperation in matters of notification and consultation. But although practice with regard to environmental risks for international watercourses elsewhere is less extensive, there is no evidence of any substantial departure from the general principles under discussion here.[219] Nor has any distinction been drawn in an environmental context between contiguous and successive rivers or lakes.[220] Only a few states, such as Brazil, have previously opposed explicit consultation obligations for successive watercourses, and the normative significance of such practice is questionable.[221] But while the general principle is beyond serious argument, its application may pose difficulties in particular cases. One of the most difficult questions remains that of deciding who determines when the circumstances require prior notification and consultation. The principle of good faith imports some limit of reasonableness in unilateral assessments by the proposing state, and in the *Lac Lanoux* arbitration, the tribunal observed:

A state wishing to do that which will affect an international watercourse cannot decide whether another state's interests will be affected; the other state is sole judge of that and has the right to information on the proposals.[222]

Thus the decision is not one for the proposing state alone to take once the possibility of adverse effects is foreseen.[223] The affected state is itself entitled to initiate the process of notification and consultation, if the proposing state does not act.[224]

There is scope for abuse in this formulation, however, which prompted the ILC to prefer a broader, additional, requirement of notification, consultation and negotiation

---

the Chad Basin, Article 5; 1962 Convention Concerning the Protection of the Waters of Lake Geneva Against Pollution, Ruster and Simma, x, 4872, on which see Kiss and Lambrechts, 15 *AFDI* (1969) 732–3; Kirgis, *Prior Consultation*, 25; the same point applies to the Rhine, Moselle, and Saar Commissions and to the 1909 US–Canada Boundary Waters Treaty (Under Article 9); see Kirgis, ibid, 28, who notes other examples.

[218] See *supra*, Ch 8.

[219] See e.g. 1964 Agreement Concerning the Niger River Commission, Article 12, 587 *UNTS* 19; 1964 Statute Relating to Development of the Chad Basin, Articles 5, 6, *supra*, n 5; 1968 African Convention on the Conservation of Nature and Natural Resources, Articles 5(2), 14(3), Ruster and Simma, v, 2037; 1971 Act of Santiago Concerning Hydrologic Basins, II *YbILC* (1974) Pt 2, 324; 1971 Buenos Aires Declaration on Water Resources, ibid, 324; 1971 Act of Buenos Aires on Hydrologic Basins, ibid, 325; 1995 Mekong River Basin Agreement, 34 *ILM* (1995) 865; 1995 Protocol on Shared Watercourse Systems in the Southern African Development Community, *supra*, n 5; Kirgis, *Prior Consultation*, 77; Bourne, 22 *UTLJ* (1972) 172.

[220] Kirgis, op cit, 26.

[221] Brazilian opposition to prior consultation requirements is summarized ibid, 72ff. The text of a bilateral agreement of 29 September 1972 between Argentina and Brazil that settled their dispute over consultations with respect to the Parana River was later adopted by the General Assembly as Resolution 2995 (1972). Brazil did not vote against part III of the 1997 UN Watercourses Convention.

[222] 24 *ILR* (1957) 101, 119.

[223] Kirgis, op cit, 41 argues: 'Any reasonable doubt must be resolved in favour of notification.'

[224] 1997 UN Convention, Article 18.

wherever there are 'possible effects' of whatever kind, including beneficial ones.[225]
This is complemented by a more general provision for cooperation in the exchange of
information relating to the state of the watercourse.[226] Although the 1933 Montevideo
Declaration and the 1992 UNECE Transboundary Watercourses Convention[227] are
among a few instruments supporting notification and consultation in situations
unqualified by reference to possible adverse effects, it is arguable whether such an
extensive obligation represents established law.[228] The most that can be said is that a
state must notify and consult wherever a possible conflict of interest exists.

The purpose of prior notification is of course to provide adequate information
on which consultation can if necessary take place. An obligation to notify is widely
accepted in watercourse treaties and international declarations.[229] It has been treated
as customary law by successive rapporteurs of the ILC.[230] Articles 12 and 13 of the
1997 UN Convention provide that notification must be timely, allow six months for
reply, and contain sufficient information for evaluation of the proposal, including the
results of any environmental impact assessment undertaken. The ILC's reports provide substantial evidence of the adoption of these principles in agreements among
riparian states, although in certain respects articles go beyond international practice,
for example in stipulating six months as a reasonable maximum period for reply.[231]

Where notification confirms the existence of a conflict of interests, or where
affected states request it, consultation and negotiation are required. The *Lac Lanoux
Arbitration* shows how the process of prior consultation and negotiation has been
interpreted by an international tribunal, not only as a treaty stipulation, specific to
relations between France and Spain,[232] but more generally as a principle of customary
law.[233] The tribunal found that: 'The conflicting interests aroused by the industrial use

---

[225] 1997 UN Convention, Article 11; cf Article 12, and see McCaffrey, 17 *Denver JILP* (1989) 505, 511f;
Handl, 3 *Colorado JIELP* (1992) 127–9, and for commentary, II *YbILC* (1994) Pt 2, 111.

[226] Article 10; see *infra*, section 2(6)(b).

[227] Articles 10, 13. See also 1999 Rhine Convention, Article 5; 1994 Danube Convention, Articles
10(f) 11, 12.

[228] See Bourne 22 *UTLJ* (1972) 173ff; Kirgis, *Prior Consultation*, 41, n 146, observes that the *Lac Lanoux*
arbitration leaves this question undecided.

[229] See *ILC Report* (1988) GAOR A/43/10, 117–24; McCaffrey, *3rd Rept,* II *YbILC* (1987) Pt 1, 28–35, and
e.g. 1923 Convention Relating to the Development of Hydraulic Power Affecting More Than One State,
36 *UNTS* 77; 1960 Convention on the Protection of Lake Constance; 1960 Indus Waters Treaty; 1975 Statute
of the River Uruguay, Articles 7–12; 1990 Danube Basin Agreement; 1995 Mekong River Basin Agreement.

[230] *ILC Report* (1988) 115–26; 1984 draft articles 11, 12; Evensen, *2nd Rept,* II *YbILC* (1984) Pt 1, 114 and
1st Rept, ibid, (1983) Pt 1, 174–6. See also ILA Helsinki Rules, Article XXIX, and IDI Salzburg Resolution,
1961, Article 5.

[231] *ILC Report* (1988) 125ff. Article 15 requires the notified state to respond as early as possible *within* the
six month period. Cf Evensen, *1st Rept*, 175, where six months is proposed only as a reasonable *minimum*
period for reply, and Article 3(1) of the 1990 Danube Basin Agreement, *supra*, n 146 which provides for consultations within 3 months of notification.

[232] 1866 Treaty of Bayonne and Additional Act, 56 *BFSP*, 212, 226.

[233] 24 *ILR* (1957) 101, 129f. See Bourne, 22 *UTLJ* (1972) 197: 'This decision of course was based on the
terms of the treaty. Nevertheless, it does intimate that there is a general principle of customary international
law requiring states to take the interests of co-basin states into consideration and thus necessarily leads to

of international rivers must be reconciled by mutual concessions embodied in comprehensive agreements'.[234] Consultation and negotiation in good faith are required, not as a mere formality, but as a genuine attempt to conclude an agreement. Each state is obliged to give a reasonable place to the interests of others in the solution finally adopted, even if negotiations for this purpose are unsuccessful, 'though owing to the intransigence of its partner'.[235] But subject to compliance with these procedural obligations, other states have no veto over the development of a river.[236]

In most respects the 1997 UN Watercourses Convention closely follows the principles laid down in the *Lac Lanoux* arbitration, the *Icelandic Fisheries Case*,[237] and the *North Sea Continental Shelf Case*[238] concerning the conduct of consultations and negotiations.[239] Where the implementation of planned measures would be inconsistent with Articles 5 or 7 of the Convention, because it entails inequitable utilization of the watercourse or would cause appreciable harm to other states, an 'equitable resolution' is called for on the basis of 'reasonable regard' for each party's rights and legitimate interests.[240] Although reliance on equitable solutions in cases of transboundary harm has been criticized earlier, the Commission's conclusion that international law requires states to notify and negotiate as a means of reconciling conflicting rights and interests is clearly consistent with the recognition of equitable utilization as the main basis for allocation of rights and interests in shared water resources.

The 1997 Convention also indicates some of the consequences of a failure to notify or negotiate with affected states. This will first be a breach of obligations and may render the state responsible for harm caused by the omission.[241] Another possible consequence is the loss of any claim to priority,[242] but this is rejected by Bourne as unsupported by authority.[243] As we have seen, the 1997 Convention allows the potentially affected state to request information and negotiation, if it has reasonable grounds for the request.[244] This approach is consistent with the view of the *Lac Lanoux* tribunal that 'if the neighbouring state has not taken the initiative, the other state cannot be denied the right to insist on notification of works or concessions which are the object of a Scheme',[245] and it accords with state practice in several disputed cases.[246]

---

the obligation to give notice, to consult and to negotiate.' Kirgis, *Prior Consultation*, 39, views the case as supporting a customary obligation to engage in 'meaningful preliminary negotiations'.

[234] 24 *ILR* (1957) 101, 119.   [235] Ibid, 141, and see 119, 128.

[236] Ibid, 128–38. Some treaties do, however, require prior *consent* of the affected riparians before works can be undertaken: this practice is reviewed by Kirgis, *Prior Consultation*, 40, who concludes that it is mainly European but does not apply to pollution or environmental harm.

[237] ICJ Reports (1974) 3, paras 71, 78.   [238] ICJ Reports (1969) 3, paras 85, 87.

[239] See *ILC Report* (1988) 131–3; Kirgis, *Prior Consultation*, 362ff.   [240] Articles 15, 17.

[241] Bourne, 22 *UTLJ* (1972).   [242] ILA Helsinki Rules, Article XXIX(4).

[243] 22 *UTLJ* (1972) 190.

[244] Article 18, and see *ILC Report* (1988) 134–6. See also Danube Basin Agreement, Article 3.

[245] 24 *ILR* (1957) 101, 138.

[246] See e.g. the Sudanese-Egyptian dispute regarding consultation over the Aswan High Dam and the US–Mexico dispute regarding salinity of the Colorado River, noted in *ILC Report* (1988) 131–3; Kirgis, *Prior Consultation*, 43, 66.

Failure to respond to notification, or to an offer of consultation, may indicate tacit consent to any proposed works.[247] On the other hand, the 1997 Convention provides that although the proposing state may then proceed with its plans, it remains subject to obligations of equitable utilization and the prevention of serious injury.[248] The implication here is that whatever tacit consent arises from a failure to reply or partici- pate in negotiations does not extend to a breach of the proposing state's obligations. This conclusion is more in keeping with the situation following an unsuccessful attempt to negotiate a settlement. But in cases where negotiations fail, the argument for tacit consent of any kind is clearly absent; where they never take place at all this is less apparent, and the Convention leaves unresolved what role tacit consent does then play.

The ILC has adopted the view that during the period for reply, consultation, and negotiation, good faith requires that implementation of any plans be postponed, but not indefinitely.[249] Prolonging negotiations unilaterally will itself be inconsistent with good faith, and to counter this possibility, the 1997 Convention adopts a six-month limit during which to resolve the dispute.[250] State practice undoubtedly favours post- ponement, but the evidence suggests that this is often much more protracted than the Commission envisages.[251]

(b) Information exchange

The regular exchange of data and information on the state of the watercourse, and on the impact of present and planned uses can also be regarded as part of a general obligation to cooperate. The ILA's 1966 Helsinki Rules recommend such an exchange, while the 2004 Berlin Rules and Article 9 of the 1997 UN Convention require it.[252] The ILC's rapporteur has pointed to the large number of agreements, declarations, and resolutions which provide for exchanges of information,[253] such as the 1944 US–Mexico Boundary Waters Agreement, the 1960 Indus Waters Treaty, the 1961 Columbia River Treaty, and the 1964 River Niger Treaty. Additionally, Article 5 of the ILA's 1982 Montreal Rules on Water Pollution in an International Drainage Basin

---

[247] Bourne, 22 *UTLJ* (1972) 181.   [248] Article 16. See *ILC Report* (1988) 129ff.

[249] 1997 Convention, Articles 14, 17(3); *ILC Report* (1988) 127ff, 130ff.

[250] Article 17(3). Cf Article 6 of the 1961 IDI Salzburg Resolution which allows for negotiations 'within a reasonable time' and see Bourne, 10 *CYIL* (1972) 231f.

[251] E.g. the *Lac Lanoux* negotiations, which began in 1917, and the proposal eventually considered by the tribunal was put forward in 1950. The case was referred to arbitration in 1956. Negotiations between Sudan and Egypt over the Aswan Dam took five years: see Garretson et al, *The Law of International Drainage Basins*, 274f. See *ILC Report* (1988) 131–3; Kirgis, *Prior Consultation*, 73 observes that Brazil's objections to prior consultation may be attributable to the likelihood of delays in its economic development. For examples of treaties which support postponement, see 1964 Chad Basin Statute, and 1960 Convention on the protec- tion of Lake Constance, Article 1.

[252] Helsinki Rules, Article XXIX(1); Berlin Rules, Article 56.

[253] *4th Rept* (1988) UN Doc A/CN 4/412, paras 15–27; *ILC Report* (1988) 106–14.

requires states to exchange information on pollution of basin waters.[254] The practice of river commissions dealing with pollution has facilitated and encouraged such
exchanges.[255]

Bourne, reviewing the state practice, concluded that a general obligation to exchange
information about watercourses had not yet crystallized into international law,[256] but
in view of the ILC's more recent evidence, this is too cautious. Moreover the importance of regular exchanges of information in fulfilling the obligations of equitable utilization of a shared resource and preventing harm to other states or the environment
can be emphasized in support of the UN Convention article.[257]

(c) Emergency cooperation

The general principle that states must notify each other and cooperate in cases of
emergency to avert harm to other states applies also to international watercourses.
Bourne views it as part of a state's duty of reasonable care in the supervision of its
territory;[258] McCaffrey treats it as part of the duty of equitable utilization.[259] Most of
the treaties are concerned more with natural disasters, such as floods,[260] but a few such
as the 1976 Rhine Chemicals Convention,[261] require notification to other states and
relevant international organizations in cases of accidental discharge of toxic or seriously polluting substances likely to affect other states. Switzerland was criticized by its
neighbours in 1986 for its failure to offer timely warning under Article 11 of this agreement when fire at the Sandoz Chemical plant caused toxic pollution of the Rhine.[262]
Resolutions of the IDI and ILA also support notification to other states where there
is a risk of sudden increase in transboundary pollution.[263] Article 28 of the 1997 UN
Convention takes the broader approach and requires expeditious notification of any
emergency posing an 'imminent threat' of serious harm to other states, whether from
natural causes or human conduct, 'such as industrial accidents'. However, both the
wording and the antecedents of this article strongly suggest an intention to cover pollution or environmental emergencies.[264]

---

[254] See also the 1987 ECE Principles on Cooperation in the Field of Transboundary Waters, UN Doc
E/ECE 42/L 19, and 1979 IDI Resolution on the Pollution of Rivers and Lakes, Article 7.

[255] See e.g. 1976 Rhine Chemicals Convention, Articles 2, 8, 12; 1978 Great Lakes Water Quality
Agreement, Article IX; 1992 UNECE Transboundary Watercourses Convention, Articles 6, 13; 1994 Danube
Convention, Article 12; 1999 Rhine Convention, Article 5(1).

[256] 22 UTLJ (1972) 206.

[257] McCaffrey, *3rd Rept* (1987) paras 29–38; *4th Rept* (1988) paras 12–14, 27.

[258] 22 UTLJ (1972) 186ff.   [259] *4th Rept* (1988) para 27.   [260] Bourne, 22 UTLJ (1972) 182.

[261] Article 11. See also the 1976 Convention on the Protection of the Rhine Against Pollution by Chlorides,
Articles 4, 11; 1978 US–Canadian Great Lakes Water Quality Agreement, Article X (2).

[262] Rest, 30 GYIL (1987) 160, 162, 165.

[263] IDI, 1979 Resolution on the Pollution of Rivers and Lakes, Article 7, *supra*, n 11; ILA, Montreal Rules
on Water Pollution in an International Drainage Basin, Article 5, *60th Conference* (1982) 540.

[264] Compare the ILC's 1991 draft Article 25(2) which applied explicitly to 'pollution or environmental
emergency'. See also *ILC Report* (1988) para 180; McCaffrey, *4th Rept*, (1988) para 27; Evensen, *1st Rept* (1983)
para 176.

The 1997 Convention extends the obligations of a riparian beyond mere notification in cases of emergency, and requires it to take action to prevent, mitigate, or neutralize the danger to other watercourse states.[265] This is in keeping with precedents in other fields, such as the Law of the Sea, and with the obligation of due diligence on which the decision in the *Corfu Channel Case*[266] is based, but it is as yet reflected in only a few watercourse treaties such as the 1961 Columbia River Basin Treaty.[267]

3 REGIONAL COOPERATION AND ENVIRONMENTAL REGULATION

The management of international watercourses through regional cooperation provides the most comprehensive basis for environmental protection and pollution control. First, the institutional framework of river commissions which usually accompanies such regional schemes offers a forum for notification, consultation, and negotiation to take place, for coordinating responses to emergency situations, for data and information on environmental matters and water quality to be collected and disseminated, and for the coordination of research These are important functions for such bodies.

Second, international river commissions facilitate adoption, implementation, and periodic review of common environmental standards.[268] Not all river commissions have this role, but the growing number which do is evidence of their significance in controlling watercourse pollution.[269] Moreover these river commissions are complemented by a series of multilateral treaties which establish institutions and standards for the regulation of marine pollution from land-based sources, including national and international rivers.[270] Thus in north-western Europe, the 1974 Paris Convention and its successor 1992 Convention have become the main basis for

---

[265] Articles 27–28.   [266] ICJ Reports (1949) 4; *supra*, Ch 3, section 4.

[267] Article 18(3). See also the 1990 ECE Code of Conduct on Accidental Pollution of Transboundary Inland Waters, E/ECE/1225, and *supra*, Ch 7.

[268] See especially 1992 UNECE Transboundary Watercourses Convention, Article 9.

[269] See 1964 Finland–USSR Agreement Concerning Frontier Watercourses, 537 *UNTS* 231: 1962 Convention Concerning the Protection of the Waters of Lake Geneva Against Pollution; 1961 Protocol Establishing an International Commission for the Protection of the Saar Against Pollution, Ruster and Simma, xi, 5613; 1961 Protocol Concerning the Constitution of an International Commission for the Protection of the Moselle Against Pollution, 1963 Agreement Concerning the International Commission for the Protection of the Rhine Against Pollution, Ruster and Simma, x, 4820; 1975 Statute of the River Uruguay, Article 56; 1976 Rhine Chlorides and Chemicals Conventions; 1971 Finland–Sweden Frontier Rivers Agreement, II *YbILC* (1974) Pt 2, 319; 1909 US–Canada Boundary Waters Treaty; 1978 US–Canada Great Lakes Water Quality Agreement; 1973 Argentina–Uruguay Treaty Concerning the River Plate; 1964 Statute Relating to the Development of the Chad Basin; 1987 Agreement on the Action Plan for the Environmentally Sound Management of the Common Zambezi River System; 1990 Magdeburg Convention on the International Commission for the Protection of the Elbe, OJ/EEC/No C93 (1991) 12; 1994 Danube Convention; 1999 Rhine Convention.

[270] See *supra*, Ch 8, section 3.

regional control of river pollution, together with measures adopted by the EC. From this perspective the relative weakness of earlier international commissions established to protect European rivers such as the Rhine, Moselle, and Saar from pollution is less significant than it might appear,[271] and the treatment of land-based sources of marine pollution in Chapter 7 should be read in conjunction with the comments made here.

Individual river commissions differ in their exact functions, in their powers, and in their success at persuading member governments to adopt and implement effective environmental measures. Nevertheless they share certain common characteristics.[272] The most important of these are their inherent flexibility and their dependence on agreement among their members. With some exceptions, they are aptly described as resembling intergovernmental conferences in many respects.[273] Thus, as we saw in Chapter 2, their effectiveness is primarily dependent on negotiated solutions to shared pollution problems. These points are well illustrated by consideration of some of the more significant commissions in Europe, North America, and Africa.

3(1) THE INTERNATIONAL COMMISSION FOR PROTECTION OF THE RHINE

This commission was established in 1950 and reorganized in 1963.[274] Its functions were initially to arrange for research into Rhine pollution, and to make proposals and prepare guidelines for protection of the river from pollution.[275] However, these required the unanimous agreement of the parties.[276] Beyond collaboration through the commission, no other obligations of pollution control were created. Despite serious problems of chemical and salt pollution in the river, Lammers, reviewing the work of the commission in its first twenty years concluded that 'the Rhine Commission has not been able to achieve any result of significance'.[277] Investigations had been carried out, but inability to reach agreement on specific measures had blocked progress.

Not until 1976 was it finally possible to negotiate, through the Commission, framework conventions on chemicals and chlorides pollution. Under the 1976 Rhine Chemicals Convention, the parties committed themselves to progressive elimination or strict regulation of specified groups of pollutants.[278] Emissions were controlled by a system of prior authorization by governments, and emission standards and timetables for eliminating the more serious pollutants are proposed by the Commission. Standards

---

[271] See generally Nollkaemper, *The Legal Regime for Transboundary Water Pollution* (Dordrecht, 1992); Pallemaerts, *Toxics in Transnational Law* (Oxford, 2002) Chs 4–7.

[272] See generally, Kiss and Lambrechts, 15 *AFDI* (1969) 718; Godana, *Africa's Shared Water Resources*, Ch 6.

[273] Kiss and Lambrechts, 15 *AFDI* (1969) 728. See generally, *supra*, Ch2, section 5.

[274] 1963 Agreement concerning the International Commission for the Protection of the Rhine. See Lammers, *Pollution of International Watercourses*, 168. The Rhine Protection Commission should not be confused with the General Commission for the Rhine established by the Congress of Vienna in 1815, on which see *supra*, Ch 2, section 5.

[275] Article 2.   [276] Article 6.   [277] *Pollution of International Watercourses*, 175.

[278] 1976 Convention on the Protection of the Rhine Against Chemical Pollution, Article 1, and Annexes I, II; Lammers, *Pollution of International Watercourses*, 187; Pallemaerts, *Toxics in Transnational Law*, 206–28.

for other pollutants would be determined nationally.[279] The Rhine Commission was also given responsibility for coordinating national programmes, receiving reports from governments, evaluating results, and proposing further measures. It thus performed monitoring, regulatory, and supervisory functions in respect of member states fulfilment of their obligations, but effective implementation continued to depend on further agreement on emission standards and the coordination of national measures.[280] The development of EC emission and water-quality standards for most of the Rhine's riparians has gone some way towards achieving this.[281]

Both the 1963 Rhine Commission Agreement and the 1976 Chemicals Convention were replaced by the 1999 Convention on the Protection of the Rhine.[282] Adopted in accordance with the 1992 UNECE Convention on Transboundary Watercourses, to which all the Rhine states are party, the new Rhine Convention for the first time provides a comprehensive approach to environmental protection which is no longer limited to the control of chemical pollution. Instead, its explicit objective is the sustainable development of the Rhine ecosystem.[283] The pre-existing approach to pollution control is largely maintained and strengthened,[284] but the parties are now also committed, inter alia, to the pursuit of environmentally sound and rational management of water; protecting species diversity; conserving, restoring, and improving natural habitats, flood plains, and riverbeds and banks; taking account of ecological factors when developing the waterway; and helping to restore the North Sea. In pursuing these aims, the parties are to be guided by the precautionary and preventive principles, the polluter-pays principle and sustainable development. They are to afford priority to 'rectification at source', apply 'best environmental practice', and avoid increasing or transferring damage. To some degree these provisions in Articles 3 and 4 of the 1999 Convention consolidate developments and decisions that had already taken place, notably under the Rhine Action Programme, adopted in 1987 following the Sandoz accident.[285] Decisions and recommendations adopted under the earlier treaties will remain in force under the new regime.

The 1999 Convention also gives the Rhine Commission stronger powers to take binding decisions and enhances the transparency of its work. In particular, decisions on measures adopted by unanimity must be implemented by all member states in a manner and to a timetable stipulated by the Commission.[286] Inability to implement must be reported; on that basis, or following further consultations among the parties, the Commission may decide on measures to assist implementation.[287] In effect, this provision creates a form of non-compliance procedure. Observers, including

[279] Cf Articles 3–5 (Annex 1 substances) and Article 6 (Annex II substances).

[280] Lammers, *Pollution of International Watercourses*, 189–90.

[281] See Nollkaemper, *The Legal Regime for Transboundary Water Pollution*, Ch 3. Switzerland is the only non-EC riparian. The EC is a party to the Rhine Chemicals Convention.

[282] In force for all the Rhine states and the EC in 2003. See Pallemaerts, op cit, 229–32.

[283] Article 3.   [284] See Articles 5(4), 8(1).

[285] 8th Ministerial Conference of the Rhine States, 1987. See Nollkaemper, *The Legal Regime for Transboundary Water Pollution*, Ch 3, esp 100, 127; Pallemaerts, *Toxics in Transnational Law*, 216–26.

[286] Articles 5(5), 10, 11.   [287] Article 11(3), (4).

relevant NGOs, may make reports or be consulted as specialists and can participate in Commission meetings if invited.[288] The Commission also has a duty to consult affected NGOs before decisions are taken, and to publicise reports on the state of the Rhine and the results of its work.[289]

The 1976 Rhine Chlorides Convention[290] is intended to reduce French chloride discharges into the river, and to prevent any increase in discharges by other parties. After a long delay, occasioned by France, the treaty entered into force in 1985. The Rhine Commission's functions under this treaty include receiving national reports, making proposals for further limitations, and monitoring compliance with chloride levels set by the Convention.[291] This treaty sets an unusual precedent in distributing across all riparians, including injured states downstream, the costs of measures taken by France to control chloride pollution.[292] In most watercourse treaties these costs fall on the polluting state. What the Chlorides Convention represents is an attempt to produce an equitable solution of the dispute between France and the Netherlands in which neither side pressed its legal rights to the full. However, one detailed study shows that while the Convention has been implemented, it has played little part in reducing chloride pollution or in mitigating environmental impact: these have instead come about mainly through industrial re-structuring.[293]

The three Rhine treaties provide for compulsory unilateral arbitration[294] as a remedy for breach of obligation by states parties, but no such claims have been made, even when, as in the Sandoz accident, there is evidence of a possible breach of obligation.[295] Instead, damage occurring in downstream states has been the subject of civil actions in national courts or before the European Court of Justice. These cases illustrate the value of European Community law in affording a choice of venue for claims brought directly against polluters in private law, and a preference for local remedies over international claims even for clean-up costs incurred by riparian governments.[296]

Historically, the original regime for protecting the environment of the Rhine could be criticized mainly for dealing inadequately with pollutants and for the slow pace of progress towards broader environmental protection. As Lammers points out, it has been easier to secure commitments to prevent new or increased pollution than to

---

[288] Article 14.   [289] Articles 14(3), 8(4).

[290] 1976 Convention on the Protection of the Rhine Against Pollution by Chlorides, as amended by Additional Protocol, 1991. See Lammers, *Pollution of International Watercourses*, 183ff; Bernauer, in Keohane (ed), *Institutions for Environmental Aid* (Cambridge, Mass, 1996).

[291] Articles 2, 3, 6, 9. For detailed regulations see 1991 Additional Protocol.

[292] Lammers, *Pollution of International Watercourses*, 176ff. France and Germany pay 30% each; the Netherlands, 34%; Switzerland, 6%; 1991 Additional Protocol, Article 4. See also *Rhine Chlorides Convention: Arbitral Award of 12 March 2004* (France/Netherlands) PCA.

[293] Bernauer, *supra*, n 290.

[294] 1999 Convention, Article 16; Chlorides Convention, Article 12(3); Chemicals Convention, Article 15.

[295] D'Oliviera, in Francioni and Scovazzi (eds), *International Responsibility for Environmental Harm* (Dordrecht, 1991) 429.

[296] *Handelskwekerij Bier v Mines de Potasse d'Alsace*, II ECR (1976) 1735, interpreting the proceedings in the place of injury or in the place of discharge. See *supra*, Ch 5, section 3. See also Rest, 5 *EPL* (1979) 85; id, 30 *GYIL* (1987) 160; Lammers, *Pollution of International Watercourses*, 196–206.

reduce existing pollution.[297] But the institutional structure now compares favourably with other such bodies and the 1999 Convention has the significant merit of applying to the Rhine Basin and ecosystem, not just to the Rhine itself.

Moreover, following inclusion in the Rhine Action programme of a commitment to protect water quality in the North Sea, it is likely that operation of the Rhine Commission will increasingly be coordinated with the OSPAR Commission and the International North Sea Conference.[298] Thus, the Rhine now offers an example of progress in the regional management of international watercourse pollution and environmental protection and the first to take account of the marine environment.

3(2) THE US–CANADIAN INTERNATIONAL JOINT COMMISSION

The International Joint Commission was established by the 1909 Boundary Waters Treaty with jurisdiction over all rivers and lakes along which the US–Canadian border passes.[299] This is not fully a 'basin treaty', since for most purposes 'boundary waters' excludes tributaries or rivers flowing across the boundary,[300] but it does cover the Great Lakes, and transboundary pollution.[301]

Uniquely, and unlike the Rhine Commission, the IJC does not resemble an intergovernmental conference. Rather, it is more like an administrative agency, composed not of representatives of the parties, but of independent experts who function quasi-judicially through public hearings and whose decisions are rendered by majority vote.[302] Its unity, its independence of both governments, and the binding character of its decisions are its most important and unusual characteristics.[303]

The importance of these features is that the Commission's approval is required before either state may permit the use, obstruction, or diversion of waters affecting the natural level or flow.[304] Although for these purposes each state enjoys 'equal and similar rights', the Commission's decisions apportion those rights according to criteria which protect existing uses and give preference to domestic and sanitary purposes, navigation, power, and irrigation in that order.[305] Thus its primary function is to make binding determinations regarding the equitable utilization of the flow of the waters.

But these powers apply only within a narrow field of uses; they do not address questions of water quality and are therefore of limited environmental relevance. The

---

[297] *Pollution of International Watercourses*, 192f. For other criticisms see Nollkaemper, *The Legal Regime for Transboundary Water Pollution*, Ch 3.

[298] On the OSPAR Commission and the INSC, see *supra*, Ch 7.

[299] Text in Cohen, 146 *Recueil des Cours* (1975) 221; see also Bourne, 28 *NILR* (1981) 188; Le Marquand, 33 *NRJ* (1993) 59; Schmandt, Clarkson, and Roderick (eds), *Acid Rain and Friendly Neighbors* (2nd edn, Durham, NC, 1988) Ch 8; Graham, in Zacklin and Caflisch, *International Rivers and Lakes*, 3; Bilder, 70 *Michigan LR* (1972) 469.

[300] Preliminary article.

[301] Article IV, dealing with pollution, applies to 'waters flowing across the boundary'.

[302] Boundary Waters Treaty, Articles 7, 8, 12; Cohen, 146 *Recueil des Cours*, 257ff. and 267ff.

[303] Cohen, 146 *Recueil des Cours*, 257; Bilder, 70 *Michigan LR* (1972) 518ff.

[304] Boundary Waters Treaty, Articles 3, 4.

[305] Boundary Waters Treaty, Article 8; Cohen, 146 *Recueil des Cours*, 254–6.

Boundary Waters Treaty prohibits pollution of boundary waters and waters flowing across the boundary,[306] but only if it causes injury to health or property, and the parties have in practice treated this provision as a basis for compromise and balancing of interests, not as an absolute prohibition.[307] Moreover, the Commission's role under the treaty in pollution disputes is essentially one of conciliation and inquiry: it makes findings of fact and recommendations on matters referred to it by either party.[308] These findings and recommendations are not binding, and the terms of reference are carefully controlled by the parties. Thus its independence in investigating pollution matters is strictly limited in scope, and may even hamper its usefulness as a bargaining forum.[309]

On a few occasions since 1945 environmental problems have been referred to the Commission, and this has enabled it to fulfil some of the monitoring and policy-formation functions of other more recently established bodies. Its most significant achievement has been a report on the Great Lakes, resulting in the negotiation of two agreements on Great Lakes Water Quality in 1972 and 1978.[310] As an ILC study notes: 'This report and full response by Governments dramatically illustrates the increasingly important role that the Commission is playing in dealing with environmental questions along the Canada–United States boundary.'[311] Generally the Commission has had a record of making politically acceptable recommendations and a good reputation for fact finding; its flexibility has been a major asset.[312] It has not found favour in its other role as an arbitral body however,[313] mainly because it lacks appropriate expertise. The *Trail Smelter* and *Gut Dam* arbitrations[314] were conducted by ad hoc tribunals; in all other cases direct negotiation has been the parties' preferred method of dispute settlement.[315]

The Great Lakes Water Quality Agreement of 1978 replaced the earlier agreement of 1972.[316] Its purpose is to restore and maintain the waters of the Great Lakes basin ecosystem and its geographical coverage is therefore broader than the 1909 treaty (Article II). The parties undertake to reduce or eliminate to the maximum extent practicable the discharge of pollutants, to prohibit toxic discharges, and to adopt water quality standards and regulatory measures consistent with minimum quality objectives set

---

[306] Article IV.   [307] Bilder, 70 *Michigan LR* (1972) 511–17.

[308] Article IX; Cooper, 24 *CYIL* (1986) 247, 285–90, who also notes the Commission's role as a mediator; Bilder, 70 *Michigan LR* (1972) 513ff. An unratified treaty drafted in 1920 would have given the Commission power to investigate violations of Article IV of its own motion and required parties to take proceedings against the persons responsible. Ruster and Simma, xi, 5704; Bilder, ibid, 490f.

[309] Bilder, 70 *Michigan LR* (1972) 520f.

[310] Ibid, 489ff. Schmandt, Clarkson, and Roderick, *Acid Rain*, 194–7.

[311] II *YbILC* (1974) Pt 2, 355.

[312] Schmandt, Clarkson, and Roderick, *Acid Rain and Friendly Neighbors*, 191–4; Bilder, 70 *Michigan LR* (1972) 520f.

[313] 1909 Boundary Waters Treaty, Article X.   [314] 8 *ILM* (1969) 118.

[315] Cooper, 24 *CYIL* (1986).

[316] On the 1972 Agreement, see Cohen 146 *Recueil des Cours*, 278ff; Kiss and Lambrechts, 20 *AFDI* (1974) 797. On the 1978 Agreement, see Rasmussen, *Boston CICLJ* (1979) 499; Toope and Brunnée, 91 *AJIL* (1997) 26, 52–8.

out in the treaty (Articles II–V). These objectives are kept under review by the parties and the IJC, which makes appropriate recommendations (Article IV(2)). Further measures involving the treatment of discharges from industrial, agricultural, municipal, and other sources are also specified (Article VI). The agreement is comprehensive in character, comparable to treaties on land-based sources of marine pollution.[317]

Under it, the IJC acquires additional powers and responsibilities in collecting data, conducting research and investigations, making recommendations, and reporting on the effectiveness of measures taken under the Agreement (Article VII). For these purposes it uses its own scientific and quality advisory boards. Unusually it also has authority to verify independently the data and information supplied by the parties. Thus it now performs most of the characteristic roles of other pollution commissions, save that of acting as a forum for intergovernmental negotiation. The parties are, however, required to consult and review the Commission's periodic reports and consider appropriate action (Article X), so it may act as a useful catalyst for negotiation.

Recognition of the need for an ecosystem approach combined with comprehensive environmental policies based on adequate research and monitoring are the most significant features of this agreement.[318] The IJC's role is important in providing the necessary independent review and enabling policy to evolve in an adaptable and informed way. In all of these respects the 1978 Agreement is one of the more advanced watercourse agreements; as already observed, it is perhaps closer in form to treaties aimed at protecting regional seas from land-based pollution. However, it is noteworthy that the parties have not extended this comprehensive approach to other elements of their transboundary watercourse system.[319] North American practice thus falls short of cooperation to protect the ecosystem of their shared watercourse system,[320] but, in respect at least of the Great Lakes, it offers a strong example of such cooperation.

As in Western Europe, equal access to national remedies is the preferred means of affording redress for damage caused by transboundary water pollution under the Boundary Waters Treaty. Article 2 is an early example of equal access for individual litigants in North American practice. US case law and some Canadian provincial statutes offer scope for applying this principle to transboundary water pollution, as well as to air pollution. Significant jurisdictional and procedural problems nevertheless remain.[321] In a recent dispute US courts held that US legislation applied to transboundary water pollution emanating from Canada and they allowed a claim against the Canadian defendants to proceed.[322]

---

[317] See *infra*, Ch 7.

[318] Schmandt, Clarkson, and Roderick, *Acid Rain and Friendly Neighbors*, 203; Toope and Brunnée, 91 *AJIL* (1997) 26.

[319] Cf 1961 Columbia River Basin Treaty.

[320] 1997 UN Watercourses Convention, Article 20, *supra*, section 2(4).

[321] *Michie v Great Lakes Steel Division*, 495 F 2d 213 (1974); Cooper, 24 *CYIL* (1986) 271–81; and see generally, *supra*, Ch 5, section 3.

[322] *Pakootas v Teck Cominco Metals Ltd* [2004] US Dist Lexis 23041 (ED Wash) [*Trail Smelter II*]. *Supra*, Ch 5, section 3(3).

3(3) SHARED WATERCOURSES IN SOUTHERN AFRICA

The 1987 Agreement on the Action Plan for the Environmentally Sound Management of the Common Zambezi River System,[323] and the Protocol on Shared Watercourse Systems in the Southern Africa Development Community (SADC Protocol),[324] represent the most ambitious approach to environmental protection of river basins in the developing world. They are untypical of earlier treaties in Africa, whose main concern was river development, but exemplify the potential of common management in addressing environmental problems.[325]

The 1987 Agreement provides a comprehensive environmental management programme for the Zambezi River drawn up with UNEP assistance and based on recommendations of the Stockholm Conference, the Mar Del Plata Action Plan, and the Cairo Programme for African Cooperation on the Environment. It forms part of UNEP's programme for environmentally sound management of inland waters[326] and seeks to deal with water resources and environmental protection in a coordinated manner intended to ameliorate existing problems and prevent future conflicts. States are required to take 'all appropriate measures' to implement the policies and objectives established by the plan. An Intergovernmental Monitoring and Coordinating Committee provides policy guidance, oversees implementation, and evaluates results. But this body has few real powers; it lacks a regulatory function and has no right to be consulted before states make adverse use of the resource. Like other commissions it cannot compel action, and its success will turn largely on its ability to negotiate detailed measures with individual governments, and in acting as an effective forum for information gathering and environmental assessment.

The SADC Protocol represents an attempt to address sustainable development of Southern Africa's watercourses on a regional basis. It is only the second such framework agreement to be adopted.[327] Full implementation will necessitate the creation of intergovernmental commissions, management boards, and monitoring units for each of the shared drainage basins in the region. The objectives of these institutions will include promoting equitable utilization and development of shared water resources. They are to be empowered, inter alia, to undertake harmonization of national water law and policy, and to promote measures aimed at flood control and drought mitigation, control of desertification, protection of the environment, environmental impact assessment, monitoring of environmental effects and of compliance with water law.[328] The 2002 Incomati River Basin Agreement is the first to be adopted within this framework.

---

[323] 1987 Zambezi River System Agreement.

[324] A revised protocol agreed in 2000 replaced an earlier protocol adopted in 1995. It is modelled closely on the 1997 UN Watercourses Convention. See 40 *ILM* (2001) 317. See also 1999 Protocol on Lake Victoria.

[325] Godana, *Africa's Shared Water Resources*.

[326] Rummel-Bulska, 54 *Ybk of the AAA* (1984) 75.

[327] See also 1992 UNECE Convention on Transboundary Watercourses and Lakes, and Article 6 of the 2000 Revised SADC Protocol.

[328] See Articles 3–5. But compare the new institutions envisaged by the 2000 Revised Protocol, Article 5.

Article 2 of the Protocol also codifies certain basic principles of international law which the parties agree to apply to the region's watercourses. It affirms the sovereign rights of each riparian and basin state over utilization of watercourses within its territory, but parties undertake to respect and apply existing general international law, 'and in particular…the principles of community of interests in the equitable utilization' of their shared watercourses. Factors listed as relevant to equitable utilization differ from Article 6 of the 1997 UN Convention in omitting all reference to ecological protection and water conservation, but Article 2 commits parties (a) to promote sustainable development by maintaining a 'proper balance' between resource development and conservation and enhancement of the environment and (b) to protect shared watercourses from pollution or environmental degradation. This approach suggests more clearly than the 1997 UN Convention that environmental protection is viewed as an obligation separate from equitable utilization. However, the Revised Protocol agreed in 2000 eliminates these differences and instead adopts the wording of the UN Convention on sustainable and equitable use, protection of ecosystems and prevention of pollution.[329] It thus becomes the first agreement to apply the provisions of that convention.

As in Europe, the value of a framework convention of this kind is twofold. First, it identifies basic principles on which the parties can agree regardless of the adoption of further agreements covering specific watercourses. Second, it provides a flexible basis for the development of institutions and the harmonization of law and policy for each regional watercourse. Its value in this context will depend entirely on the successful negotiation and implementation of more detailed agreements for individual watercourses. Once again it also illustrates the influence which the 1992 Rio Declaration and the commitment to sustainable development have had on international law relating to freshwater resources.

4 CONCLUSIONS

The law of international watercourses has for most of its history been concerned with the allocation and use of a natural resource of international significance, not with its conservation or environmental protection. The point was made in Chapter 3, however, that requirements of conservation and sustainable use are of increasing importance in regard to these resources, and the evidence of this chapter indicates how far such obligations now affect the management of international water resources.

While it can be asserted with some confidence that states are no longer free to pollute or otherwise destroy the ecology of a shared watercourse to the detriment of their neighbours or of the marine environment, definitive conclusions concerning the law

---

[329] 2000 Revised Protocol, Articles 2–4.

in this area are more difficult to draw. There is first the major problem of the diversity of watercourse systems and the regional and bilateral arrangements governing their use. From this body of treaty law and state practice only the most general of inferences can usefully be made. With regard to pollution control and environmental protection the difficulties of generalization are exacerbated by the relatively sparse and recent character of the precedents and practice which can be relied on.

Second, although the 1997 UN Convention on International Watercourses reflects existing international law, it remains in certain respects controversial. In particular, the relationship between equitable utilization, which is a right as well as a duty, and the obligation of harm prevention, is a continuing source of difficulty. This is of less significance for pollution control, where the general obligations of states to control this form of harm are fairly well accepted, than for other uses of a watercourse.

These difficulties, and other objections to the 1997 Convention expressed by some governments and writers, should not be exaggerated. It must be stressed that international watercourses are not the subject of a separate and wholly self-contained body of law, but are also governed by rules and principles, and in some cases also by international agreements, of more general significance. As we have seen, the law of the sea may be particularly relevant where pollution affects the marine environment. But it is not simply pollution which is the main problem, but a broader question of ecological protection. Many international and national watercourses are also important habitats for wildlife and migratory species, such as salmon, and these may be seriously affected by the building of dams, or the re-routeing of rivers and draining of wetlands. Thus conservation treaties and related rules of international law governing living resources, including fisheries, are of particular importance in this context, and reference should be made to later chapters where these matters are considered.

The importance of viewing an international watercourse not merely as a shared natural resource to be exploited, but as a complete ecosystem whose development has diverse effects of an international character also emphasizes the limited utility of the principle of equitable utilization. Although correctly seen as the main principle of international watercourse law, this principle cannot sustain more than a modest role mainly confined to allocating riparian rights. It affords an insufficient basis for measures of more comprehensive environmental protection. Nor does it ensure the integration of ecological, developmental and inter-generational considerations which is central to sustainable development as the overriding objective of contemporary water resources policy.

Such measures can only usefully be negotiated multilaterally, with their implementation subject at least to intergovernmental supervision and control, as we saw in Chapter 2. In this respect, the development of cooperative regimes for the common management of international watercourses has not yet been sufficiently comprehensive or effective. Environmental protection arrangements in Europe and North America are incomplete, apply only to certain rivers, and have only slowly been implemented. Many African watercourse treaties are sophisticated in content, but of little practical importance due to their limited implementation, and some rivers, most notably the Nile, are still managed on the basis of outdated regimes agreed many years ago. The record of states in the cooperative management of watercourse resources is thus an inadequate one, despite the general international endorsement of this approach in principle.[330]

[330] See 1998 Berlin Recommendations on Transboundary Water Management (UNECE).

11

CONSERVATION OF NATURE, ECOSYSTEMS, AND BIODIVERSITY

1 INTRODUCTION

Humanity's survival depends on the conservation of nature—of the natural resources of the planet in the form of soil, water, the atmosphere, and of the forests, plants, and life forms that these sustain. The massive growth in world population and changes in lifestyles brought about by economic growth and technology in the past century, whether in developed or developing states, have greatly increased demands on these resources, and led to accelerating degradation and loss of nature, natural resources, and biodiversity.

It is estimated that the number of known species is about 1.4 million but that far more are as yet uncatalogued; possibly the total is about 12 million, including the insects and smaller organisms.[1] Of the 43,850 species of vertebrates known to be extant only some 4,000 are mammals, 9,000 birds, 6,300 reptiles and 4,180 amphibians, whereas a minimum of 50,000 different species of molluscs have been identified. This diversity of species has emerged through mutation and expansion into hitherto vacant niches over the past 4.5 billion years. Only towards the end of this period, for reasons still unknown, did more complex organisms and further significant speciation occur. These unknown events appear to have generated the present range and dimensions of biodiversity, since when the rates of speciation and natural extinction have been in balance. It is thought to be unlikely that further speciation will occur.

---

[1] Swanson, *Global Action for Biodiversity* (London, 1997), 7–16. See generally Edmund Wilson's classic study, *The Diversity of Life* (London, 1992).

Thus the amount of biological diversity now extant is thought likely to be at its maximum. In this context diversity must be regarded as a non-renewable resource. Should it be threatened by large-scale degradation or destruction whether from natural or human activities this diversity is irreplaceable. If such a disaster occurs, modern technology cannot reproduce in laboratories the subtle differences between varieties that have evolved over millions of years, or their interactions with different ecosystems. As Swanson puts it: 'Biodiversity is valuable precisely because it is the output of this four billion-year-old evolutionary process, not for the sake of the variety itself'.[2] It is valuable, therefore, for the evolutionary range of variety and because it therefore has fine-tuned resilience to physical conditions, as well as powers to adapt to them and thus provides a buffer against future assaults on life supporting systems. Unlike such non-reusable resources as minerals biological diversity cannot be substituted for by human innovation; it is 'valuable for its naturalness'. What has happened rather is that as humans have depleted the natural range of natural resources, including species, they have replaced them by limited cultivation and domestication of a few selected species, thus reducing diversity and expanding their own niche by increasing the populations of their own and these chosen species, without much regard for ensuring that these developments are compatible with maintaining diversity and thus sustainable in the long term.

The extent of the threats to so many species, their habitats, ecosystems, and biodiversity and whether or not further development of modern technology can resolve these, is not easy to identify, requiring as it does extensive and often controversial scientific research and investment of economic, including technological, resources. The view that imminent disaster threatens the planet is not shared by all; some take the view that the market economy can best resolve the threats[3] or even question whether it would matter if neither humankind nor species survived.[4] A fierce debate continues between the many concerned scientists, naturalists, environmentalists, philosophers, and economists, which is outlined below, but whatever the reality of the situation it is clear that there is considerable cause for concern and a need to adopt a precautionary approach both to identification of serious threats to biodiversity and the measures now required to counter these, bearing in mind that in some sense we are responsible for the survival of nature, not just to present and future generations, but also to other existing and potential species. The significance of the 1992 Rio Convention on Biological Diversity is that it both provides a framework for such an approach and offers support to developing countries to enable them to bear the additional burdens involved.

In this chapter the principles of international law relating to protection of nature will be identified, including those relating to protection and conservation of living resources, biological diversity, biological resources, and ecosystems. To understand

---

[2] Swanson, *Global Action for Biodiversity* (London, 1997), 9.

[3] Lomborg, *The Skeptical Environmentalist* (Cambridge, 2001) and Rogers, 76 *Int Affairs* (2000), 315–23, esp 323.

[4] Rogers, 76 *Int Affairs* (2000), 323.

the complexities of conservation of biodiversity, some appreciation of the gradual development of new principles, policies, strategies, and obligations leading to the present framework of international law is necessary.

2 CONCEPTS OF NATURE CONSERVATION AND NATURAL RESOURCES

2(1) NATURE AND ECOSYSTEMS

'Nature', like 'environment', as pointed out in Chapter 1, is not a term of art and has never been clearly defined in international law. Forty years ago dictionaries did no more than to refer to a 'state of nature', being 'the condition of man before society was organized' and 'animals and plants were uncultivated or undomesticated'.[5] More recently such definitions have been refined to include 'the external world in its entirety; a creative and controlling force in the universe'.[6] Clearly it is not possible to conserve the whole of nature in this sense. This is beyond the scope of the concepts and rules of current international environmental law as outlined in Chapter 3, although in relation to some aspects of conservation the law has become both better established and wider in scope.[7]

Historically, concern was first generated by the destruction and even disappearance of wildlife and trees, though they have long been valued by humankind as exploitable natural resources, prized for their economic rather than their intrinsic value. Early conservatory regulation thus aimed at securing sustainable exploitation.[8] Ecologists, however, traditionally approached nature not as a collection of discrete exploitable resources but as a series of overlapping but integrated biological systems or ecosystems. In their view the natural world is intricately organized and vital to human existence; nature is a world of living things, constantly busy in discernible patterns producing goods and services essential for one another. An ecosystem is a subset of nature's global economy, a local or regional system of plants, micro-organisms, and animals working together to survive.[9] These are the living (biotic) components of an ecosystem and their functioning in this way provides the services upon which life on earth depends.[10] A less rigid view has since been adopted by some ecologists rejecting the idea of natural stability, balance, and order and emphasizing the profound changes that have already occurred in nature over the aeons.[11] This allows for a more

---

[5] E.g. *Concise Oxford Dictionary* (5th edn, Oxford, 1964) 303.
[6] *Penguin Pocket English Dictionary* (2nd edn, London, 1987).   [7] *Infra*, Chs 12, 13.
[8] See Worster, *The Wealth of Nature* (Oxford, 1993) 144–6; Nash, *The Rights of Nature*, (Madison, 1989).
[9] Worster, *The Wealth of Nature*, 52, 149.
[10] Glowka, et al, *A Guide to the Convention on Biological Diversity*, IUCN, Environmental Policy and Law Paper No 30 (Cambridge, 1994) 20, hereafter *Guide to the CBD*.
[11] Worster, *The Wealth of Nature*, 150–3.

permissive approach to human activity, within which some change, albeit at a slower rate, is acceptable; but it creates ambiguity concerning previous theory, ecologists having impressed upon us how ecosystems could collapse if exploitation reaches a critical level. Effective conservation of nature thus depends heavily on scientific advice relating to the working and interrelationships of the component species and of their ecosystems in order to devise formulae on which ecological sustainability can be built.

In all these circumstances it is not surprising that a more precautionary approach to conservation was called for in the Rio Declaration,[12] despite the somewhat restrictive and ambiguous language in which this approach was articulated in that instrument, and in numerous new or revised treaties and protocols concerning conservation of various aspects and components of nature. The applicability of a precautionary approach to the conservation of living resources and their habitats is discussed in Chapters 12 and 13. Its application is important also to protection of species habitats from pollution and other forms of degradation, discussed in Chapters 6–10. Problems have, however, arisen with the new approaches to ensuring sustainable use of nature and its living resources since it has proved much more difficult, in the light of the current state of scientific knowledge, to devise formulae for successful management of living resources than was originally envisaged,[13] particularly bearing in mind the obligation to conserve their biodiversity, for the reasons outlined in the following section.

2(2) NATURAL RESOURCES

The commonly used term 'natural resources' is unpopular with many environmentalists since it comprehends both living and non-living resources; the former are distinguished from the latter by the fact that they are renewable if conserved and destructible if not whereas the latter include non-renewable minerals such as oil, gas, coal, and metals mined commercially on land and at sea, sometimes to the point of virtual exhaustion, for human purposes. This activity is mostly subject to national regulation, with international overview generally limited to the tranboundary consequences of such actitivies.[14] The conservation of living resources requires inclusion of plants, animals, micro-organisms, and the non-living elements of the environment on which they depend.[15] Preservation of their habitat and of related species is thus an important part of their conservation. This chapter identifies the emerging principles of international law relating to the protection and conservation of nature, its ecosystems and biodiversity. Chapter 12 will then address, in this context, the measures developed to conserve land-based living resources, forests, and deserts, and Chapter 13 marine resources, though clearly some problems and methods of regulation are common to

---

[12] Principle 15; for discussion of this and its status in international law see Ch 3, section.

[13] Worster, *The Wealth of Nature* (Oxford, 1993) 52, 149.

[14] See generally Redgwell, in Roggenkamp, Redgwell, del Guayo, and Ronne (eds) *Energy Law in Europe: International, EU and National Law and Regulation* (Oxford, 2007), Ch 2, section G 'Energy and Environment'.

[15] De Klemm, 29 *NRJ* (1989), 932–78; ibid, 9 *EPL* (1982), 117.

both. This applies in particular to common threats to endangered species, such as trade, draining of wetlands, and capture during regular migrations, or to species of special global concern that are regarded as part of the world's natural heritage. In both chapters attention will be focused particularly on the problems and emergent principles of conservation and management of migratory and endangered species, as they are the ones whose preservation particularly requires international cooperation and development of international law.

There are, however, also important differences between terrestrial and marine living resources. The latter will more often constitute common property or shared resources, and, though subject to over-exploitation, are at least in principle regulated in international law by obligations of conservation and equitable utilization.[16] The former, apart from a few migratory species, will generally remain within the territory of the state or states where they are found, and their international regulation is accordingly more difficult, requiring as it does limitations on the permanent sovereignty of states over their own natural resources, and resort to concepts such as common interest, common concern, or common heritage to justify such interference, or to the language of animal rights which is discussed below. Moreover, although some species of animals and plants reproduce prolifically and can thus recover quickly from over-exploitation, as can some species of fish, mammals reproduce more slowly and are thus more susceptible to extinction resulting from over-exploitation, habitat destruction, and other adverse environmental factors, such as pollution. Animals and plants are also generally more easily accessible to plunder on land. On the other hand, terrestrial species are more often domesticated, while only a few marine species are tamed, mainly in zoos, dolphinaria or 'Sea Worlds'. Terrestrial species, especially 'charismatic mega-fauna', are also more likely to be valued for their own sake, for example elephants, eagles, and many other large mammals and birds, whereas in the seas such value is placed mainly on whales, dolphins, and pinnipeds, although recently smaller species such as turtles and corals have attracted attention.

The threats to wildlife arise from a wide variety of sources. Various species have been captured throughout the centuries not only for food, but for their skins, feathers, and other products used or traded by man; for display in zoos; for scientific research; as pets; and for medicinal, cultural, religious, and artistic purposes, amongst others. Such activities, if excessive, are now seen not only as threats to the existence of individual species or habitats but also to the biodiversity they represent, which provides, inter alia, a gene pool of immense present and future value to humankind, as now recognized in the Biodiversity Convention.

International law has, until recently, tended to adopt an ad hoc approach to wildlife protection, related to identification of 'endangered species', that is species, or discrete populations thereof, which are threatened with extinction, such as those endangered by trade, habitat loss, or excessive exploitation. In contrast, the law concerning conservation of fisheries has been dominated by their exploitation and has thus

---

[16] See *infra*, Ch 13.

concentrated on the need to maintain catches at sustainable levels whilst respecting the principle of equitable utilization through quota systems. Though public perspectives and the law in relation to their preservation are changing, they are doing so only slowly and problems remain, especially in relation to infusing the post-UNCED principles and perspectives, based on the need for conservation of biodiversity, ecosystems, and more precautionary approaches, into existing agreements concluded before UNCED.

2(3) THE CONCEPT OF BIOLOGICAL DIVERSITY

Biological diversity, or biodiversity, is the variability of life in all its forms, levels, and combinations. It is not, as is often wrongly assumed, the sum of all ecosystems, species, and genetic materials. Rather, as IUCN's guide to the 1992 Convention on Biological Diversity puts it, 'it represents the variability within and among them and is, therefore, an *attribute* of life, in contrast with 'biological resources' which are tangible biotic components of ecosystems'.[17]

The 1992 Convention on Biological Diversity thus defines 'biological diversity' as meaning 'the variability among living organisms from all sources, inter alia, terrestrial, marine and other aquatic ecosystems and the ecological complexes of which they are part' including diversity 'within species, between species and of ecosystems' (Article 2). According to IUCN, biodiversity is most conveniently, but not exclusively, defined in terms of three conceptual levels: ecosystem diversity, species diversity, and genetic diversity—the frequency and diversity of different genes and/or genomes. We shall return to these approaches in our discussion of the Convention.

2(4) MEANING OF CONSERVATION

(a) Conservation of living resources

Since this and the following chapters are primarily concerned with identifying principles and rules of international law relating to the protection and 'conservation' of living resources, a threshold question is how do we identify the meaning or meanings of 'conservation' and of 'living resources'.

Van Heijnsbergen traces the use of 'conservation' to Article III of the 1781 Convention between the King of France and the Prince Bishop of Basel and to various late nineteenth- and early twentieth-century treaties.[18] Few modern conventions specifically define the term, however; most approach it obliquely, defining, for example 'conservation status', as in the 1979 Convention on Conservation of Migratory Species of Wild Animals, or leaving its meaning to be implied from the nature of the measures presented to achieve the aims of conservation expressed in the preamble or

---

[17] Glowka et al, *Guide to the CBD*. The use of these and other terms are defined at 16–24.
[18] Van Heijnsbergen, *International Protection of Wild Flora and Fauna* (Amsterdam, 1997) 45.

substantive articles, as in the 1980 Convention on Conservation of Antarctic Marine Living Resources (CCAMLR).[19]

Conservation has in the past not become an issue until the level of threat to a species either endangers its survival or threatens seriously to deplete it or a particular stock.[20] The idea of conserving species for their own value and not simply as resources exploitable by man is of comparatively recent origin as we have seen and still controversial in some respects. Thus it is not surprising that the sole specific definition of the term in the substantive articles of a treaty, so far as can be ascertained, states that:

As employed in this Convention the expression 'conservation' of the living resources of the high seas means the aggregate of the measures rendering possible the optimum sustainable yield for these resources so as to secure a maximum supply of food and other marine products.[21]

It adds that 'conservation programmes should be formulated with a view to securing in the first place a supply of food for human consumption'. However, this definition is confined by its terms to the purposes of a convention which has never been widely ratified,[22] and it is notable that the 1982 United Nations Convention on the Law of the Sea (UNCLOS) does not offer any similar definition, despite providing in various articles for 'conservation of marine living resources'[23] although it does lay down in Article 61 certain conservation and management objectives discussed in Chapter 13.

The ordinary meaning of 'conservation' and 'conserve'—namely 'to keep in safety or from harm, decay or loss; to preserve in being; to keep alive' or now, more usually, 'to preserve in its existing state from destruction or change',[24] or from 'destructive influences, decay or waste' or 'in being and health'[25]—suggest that a higher standard of care is necessary to fulfil conservatory objectives than is actually required by existing conventions. These allow qualification of that objective by economic, social, and developmental requirements despite the fact that threats to both marine and terrestrial resources are of growing severity and are now much more widely perceived. Until the 1972 Stockholm Conference, over-exploitation was seen (except by a few ecologists) as the only problem. Ecologists' arguments that destruction of habitat by man, pollution, and introduction of alien species which prey on and may eventually replace existing species are equally serious threats, if not more so, are now widely accepted.

---

[19] See Munro and Lammers, *Environmental Protection and Sustainable Development* (Dordrecht, 1986) 25–33.

[20] Hey, *The Regime for the Exploitation of Transboundary Marine Fisheries Resources* (Dordrecht, 1989) 77.

[21] 1958 Geneva Convention on Fishing and the Conservation of the Living Resources of the High Seas, Article 2.

[22] By 1981 only forty-six states had become party to it including the UK, USSR, USA, Spain, and France but not Canada, Iceland, Japan, Korea, or China (PRC).

[23] E.g. in Preamble, para. 4; Articles 21(1)(d), 56(1)(a), 61, 78(i), 117, 118, 119(1), 123(a), 277(a).

[24] *Shorter Oxford English Dictionary* (3rd edn, Oxford, 1944), 404.   [25] Ibid, as revised, 1978, 404.

Thus, IUCN's World Conservation Strategy (WCS),[26] the purpose of which was to draw attention to the urgent need for the conservation of the world's land and marine ecosystems as an integral part of economic and social development, saw conservation as the maintenance of life support systems, preservation of genetic diversity, and sustainable utilization of species and ecosystems. It did not suggest that species should not be used but left it to be determined what form and level of use met these conservatory requirements. As we shall see, this strategy has evolved to take more account of the developmental implications of environmental measures within the context of sustainable development advocated in the UNCED Declaration, Agenda 21, and related instruments.

Van Heijnsbergen, after reviewing references to 'conservation' in various treaties, concludes that 'the present concept of "conservation" as developed at least by the IUCN and the WCS, includes both the "classic"' elements of protection and preservation, including restoration, and the safeguarding of ecological processes and genetic diversity besides management of natural resources in order to sustain their maintenance by sustainable utilization'.[27] But many conventions including that on biodiversity avoid references to 'preservation' and instead require 'conservation' and 'sustainable use'. Management concepts for achieving any of these aims have proved difficult to formulate and are still being refined.

(b) Maximum sustainable yield and other management concepts

To achieve these conservatory objectives the concept of maintaining 'maximum sustainable yield' of living resources is that most widely relied on, at least as a starting-point. It was defined for and refined at the 1955 Rome Technical Conference that preceded the first UN Conference on the Law of the Sea (UNCLOS I) held in Geneva in 1958, which adopted the Convention on Fishing and the Conservation of the Living Resources of the Sea.[28] But, as De Klemm has observed, it is paradoxical that the concept became quasi-institutionalized by international law (being found in most fisheries and related conventions in its original or modified form) at a time when scientists were increasingly questioning its applicability to a large number of practical situations.[29] The problem now, therefore, is to redefine the legal content of conservation and secure the necessary consequential changes in fisheries and other relevant living-resource conventions. In the MSY concept 'the maximum sustainable yield' is the greatest harvest that can be taken from a self-regenerating stock of animals year

---

[26] Prepared by IUCN, UNEP, and WWF, in 1980, in collaboration with FAO and UNESCO, and the revised programme *Caring for the Earth: A Strategy for Sustainable Living* (Gland, 1991), *supra*, Ch 2, section 2(3).

[27] International Legal Protection of Wild Fauna and Flora (Amsterdam, 1997), 51–2.

[28] UN International Technical Conference on the Conservation of the Living Resources of the Sea, *Technical Papers and Reports* (FAO, Rome, 1955). See also Johnston, *The International Law of Fisheries: A Framework for Policy-Oriented Enquiries* (New Haven, Conn, 1965) 50, 59, 76, 100, 337, 344–5, 411–15, 439.

[29] De Klemm, in Johnson, *The Environmental Law of the Sea* (Berlin, 1981) 118.

after year while still maintaining the average size of the stock'.[30] It aims at maintaining the productivity of the oceans by permitting taking of only that number of fish from a stock that is replaced by the annual rate of new recruits (young fish of harvestable size) entering the stock. Thus MSY is obtained when both fishing mortality and recruitment to the stock are maximized at the same time.

It is not, however, as easy as was thought in the 1950s for population dynamicists confidently and with accuracy to calculate MSY, although a qualified version of it is included in UNCLOS Article 56. Generally scientific advice consists of a range between a minimum and maximum figure, but this is not the only weakness of the approach. Even in 1958 some scientists challenged the assumption that MSY could be calculated solely on the basis of biological criteria, since these required too high a fishing intensity and would be uneconomic. They proposed the objective of 'eumetric fishing'—a state of optimum fishing—within which economic interests could be balanced, with regulation of the fishery being based equally on biological, economic, and social factors and the benefits to producers being accompanied by assured supplies of fish. This would require that an optimum yield (OY) be set, and that it be lower than MSY.[31] Thus, MSY as originally expressed is no longer acceptable as a conservation objective because it fails to take account not only of economic objectives but of the ecological relationships of species with each other and with their habitat and the quality status of that habitat, of the limits of the given area's biomass, and of factors disturbing the environment, such as pollution, habitat loss, disease, current and temperature changes, failures in the food chain of the oceans from disease, and other causes. Similar considerations arise in relation to conservation of forms of living resources other than the marine.

Suggested alternative conservation strategies have included maintaining an optimum population (OP), or optimum sustainable population (OSP), or optimum levels thereof (OL), or optimum (or maximum) economic yield (OEY/MEY), or the more complex optimum ecological resource management (OERM).[32] All share the concept of sustainability of use, as we have noted in Chapter 3. One of the most sophisticated formulae for ensuring an ultra precautionary and readily adjustable approach to sustainable use of a living resource is that used in the Revised Management Procedure (RMP) developed by the International Whaling Commission in the 1990s, though its operation is contingent on completion of a comprehensive Revised Management

---

[30] Holt and Talbot (eds), *The Conservation of Wild Living Resources*, Report of Workshops held at Airlie House, Va, February and April 1975 (unpublished) 30, on file with the authors.

[31] See Scarff, 6 ELQ (1977), 387–400; Johnston, *The International Law of Fisheries: A Framework for Policy Orientated Enquiries* (New Haven, Conn, 1965) 49–51.

[32] These theories were particularly discussed in relation to improving the conservation of whales. A useful summary is given in the Draft Report of a Consultation on Marine Mammals held at Bergen, Norway, in 1977; see the Food and Agriculture Organization Advisory Committee on Marine Resources Research Working Party on Marine Mammals, FAO ACMRR/WP/MM, ss 9–10; the report of the consultation was published as *Mammals in the Sea*, i–iv, FAO Fisheries Series No 5, 1978–80. See also Holt and Carlson, *Implementation of a Revised Management Procedure for Commercial Whaling*, International Fund for Animal Welfare (Crowborough, 1991).

Scheme (RMS), which is to include some form of international observation and inspection system. This and other new approaches incorporated in the 1995 UN Fish Stocks Agreement are further discussed in Chapter 13. Views differ on which method is to be preferred, although there is now general agreement, as evidenced in Principle 15 of the Rio Declaration, that a precautionary approach to environmental protection be applied, and that lack of full scientific certainty should not be used to postpone taking of measures when threats of serious damage exist.

One of the closest existing approaches to a broader environmental/ecosystem approach is found in the 1980 Convention on Conservation of Antarctic Marine Living Resources (CCAMLR),[33] the preamble to which recognizes the need to protect the integrity of the ecosystem of the seas surrounding Antarctica and to increase knowledge of its component parts. The substantive articles extend its scope to *all* marine living resources in the area within the *whole* Antarctic ecosystem (that is, that lying within the Antarctic convergence, a natural, not a man-made boundary) defined as 'the complex of relationships of Antarctic marine living resources with each other and with their physical environment';[34] they make it clear that birds are included within these resources. 'Rational use'[35] of species is allowed but harvesting must be based on ecological principles with the aim of avoiding reduction of a population to levels below those which ensure its stable recruitment; the stock level is to be maintained close to that which ensures the greatest net annual recruitment. This avoids reference to the criticized criteria of MSY, MEY, OP, etc. The problem of determining this level still remains, however, and progress on conservation under CCAMLR has been slow, even though the Commission and Scientific Committee established by it meets annually;[36] in practice national fishery interests take precedence over the ecosystem approach and fishing by third states has proved difficult to control, even today. Practice under the US Marine Mammal Protection Act 1972,[37] which pioneered this approach, has continued to evidence this difficulty. The linking of 'conservation' and 'rational use' in CCAMLR exacerbates the difficulties of following scientific advice, even when available. We discuss these problems further in Chapter 13.

The IUCN General Assembly had, as early as 1976, adopted 'Principles replacing maximum sustainable yield as a basis for management of wild life resources'.[38] These principles required that ecosystems should be maintained in such a state that both consumptive and non-consumptive values could be realized on a continuing basis, ensuring maintenance of both present and future options and minimizing the risk of irreversible change or long-term adverse effects; that management decisions should include a safety factor to allow for limitation of knowledge and imperfections of management;

[33] Bowman, Davies, and Redgwell, *Lyster's International Wildlife Law* (2nd edn, Cambridge, 2009), Ch 12 (hereafter *Lyster's International Wildlife Law*); Vignes, in Francioni and Scovazzi (eds), *International Law for Antarctica* (Milan, 1987), 341.

[34] Article 1.   [35] Article 2.

[36] Howard, 39 *ICLQ* (1989) 104–49; Redgwell, in Boyle and Freestone (eds), *International Law and Sustainable Development* (Oxford, 1999) Ch 9. See further, *infra*, Ch 13.

[37] US Pub L 92522, 4972, as amended.

[38] IUCN Resolution No 8, 12th General Assembly of IUCN, 1976.

that measures to conserve one resource should not be wasteful of another; that monitoring, analyses, and assessment should precede planned use and accompany actual use of a resource, and the results should be made available promptly for critical public review. It is very useful to bear these optimal objectives in mind when evaluating the regimes for conservation of wildlife that have been established in recent decades, especially the relevant provisions of the UNCLOS 1982 and their relationship to the Biodiversity Convention. Such approaches require multi-species management—a highly complex operation—but, as we shall see, many regimes relate to single species and despite the value of an ecosystem approach it is extremely difficult to model it. Moreover it is now even being put forward for purposes not envisaged by environmentalists when they first advocated it, namely to justify culling of whales and seals to maintain fish populations (see Chapters 12 and 13). Thus it has had many critics[39] and the law can do no more than require it in general terms. Furthermore, it is clear that any concept of conservation must now take account of such closely related issues as climate change, preservation of biological diversity, land-use management, and protection of the oceans from pollution.

It is not, in these circumstances, so surprising that most legal instruments, policy statements, and strategies avoid too rigid a definition of 'conservation' and the Legal Experts Group of WCED preferred a definition in general terms only. For its purposes, the term was used to mean:

the management of human use of a natural resource or the environment in such a manner that it may yield the greatest sustainable benefit to present generations while maintaining its potential to meet the needs and aspirations of future generations. It embraces the preservation, maintenance, sustainable utilization, restoration, and enhancement of a natural resource or the environment.[40]

The WCED gave no indication of the specific measures actually required to achieve this objective and the UNCED and WSSD Declarations provide no guidance, as we have noted in Chapter 2. For this purpose we have to turn to specific sectoral treaties, soft-law instruments, and policy declarations considered below and in the two subsequent chapters.

3 THE ROLE OF LAW IN THE
PROTECTION OF NATURE

3(1) EARLY APPROACHES

Law can and has served a number of functions in relation to living resources: it can be distributive, determining who is to have ownership or access to the resources;

---

[39] E.g. Gulland, 11 *Marine Policy* (1987), 259–72 considered that a comprehensive multi-species approach would make a complex situation even more complex.

[40] Legal Experts Group report in Munro and Lammers, *Environmental Protection and Sustainable Development* (Dordrecht, 1986) 9n.

conservatory, preserving the resources as such, or at least doing so at levels that can sustain exploitation; or proscriptive, prohibiting, for conservatory, ethical, or moral reasons, exploitation of the resource or particular forms and methods of exploitation.

Although there have been national laws protecting terrestrial and marine living resources since comparatively early times, the perception that species require conservation under an international legal regime is of comparatively recent origin. It was not until over-exploitation of living resources, especially those hunted by two or more states, began to lead to failures of stocks or herds of particular species so severe that they might be in danger of extinction that serious interest was taken in the need to develop legal obligations and principles for their protection and conservation on a sustainable basis. Birds, salmon, and whales were amongst the first species to excite such interest, originally at the national level. Whales, for example, were regulated ad hoc by one or two states from 1597 onwards; national control of the taking of such migratory species was recognized not to be sufficient to conserve them since it could not be enforced on foreign territory or on foreign vessels outside national jurisdiction.[41] The first relevant treaties were the 1882 North Sea Overfishing Convention, and the 1885 Convention for the Uniform Regulation of Fishing in the Rhine.[42] But by then the exploitation of such species had in many cases been taking place for hundreds of years, without any control and the theoretical basis of the first legal regimes to be developed necessarily had to take account of this fact.[43] Living species were not treated very differently from other resources, such as minerals, and indeed to this day are frequently included, as we have seen, within the general description of 'natural resources', though as sustainable living creatures they—especially those that migrate—are very different from static non-renewable minerals. As a result both living and non-living resources were long regarded as being as 'mineable' as minerals.[44] Even the Convention on Biological Diversity refers to 'biological resources', which it defines as including 'genetic resources, organisms or parts thereof, populations, or any other biotic components of ecosystems with actual or potential use or value for humanity',[45] under the heading of 'Sustainable Use of Biological Diversity', requiring its parties to 'integrate consideration of the conservation and sustainable use of biological resources into national decision-making'.[46] The implications of this definition and the limitations placed on this requirement are discussed below.

---

[41] Birnie, *International Regulation of Whaling* (Dobbs Ferry, NY, 1985), I, 102–4, gives examples of whaling regulations.

[42] Reprinted respectively in Marine Mammal Commission, *Compendium of Selected Treaties*, 2nd Update, 475, and *Ruster and Simma*, xxv, 200.

[43] Johnston, *The International Law of Fisheries: A Framework for Policy Orientated Enquiries* (New Haven, Conn, 1965), 157–252.

[44] Holt, 9 *Marine Policy* (1985), 192–213.   [45] Article 2.

[46] Article 10; on the legal status of natural resources see *supra*, Ch 3, section 5. With respect to the components of biodiversity, however, the 2004 Addis Abbaba Principles and Guidelines for the Sustainable Use of Biodiversity, adopted by COP Decision VII/12, call for the 'more efficient, ethical and humane use' of such components.

Since throughout history mankind has sought to exploit the wealth that such resources bring, the law has primarily been concerned with the problems of allocation of rights over them. The first approaches to this problem were simplistic; as territorial states had sovereignty over their territory, they were assumed to have exclusive rights to all the natural resources found therein and this was extended to the territorial sea and airspace, whether or not the resources were living and migratory. Thus once they were found in areas subject to sovereignty no other state could have access to them or play a role in their management without the express consent of the territorial sovereign. Natural resources found in areas beyond national jurisdiction, for example, on the high seas or the seabed below it or in the airspace above it, and indeed the air itself were regarded as common property and a doctrine of freedom of access for all states was applied.

It was only following increasing evidence of the serious adverse effects of over-exploitation of certain species, particularly at sea, that development of more sophisticated legal regimes began, mainly, but not exclusively, in the second half of the twentieth century. Until the late nineteenth-century, scientists had taken little interest in marine biology and it was not until 1902 when the International Council for the Exploration of the Sea (ICES)[47] was formed, following proposals first made at the International Geographic Congress of 1895, that international efforts were made to coordinate, on the basis of an informal 'Gentlemen's Agreement', scientific research on fisheries and to plan, collect, and evaluate data on an international basis.[48] Even today, it is often the research of scientists in a few countries that initiates conservatory legal developments. But as scientific knowledge has grown so too have the perceived dimensions of the legal problems of conservation.

Legal developments have also been influenced by the changing perceptions of philosophers and moralists in relation to living creatures. Early philosophers, such as Plato, made no attempt to distinguish individual animals or accord them rights. They viewed their special attributes as representative of the whole species; it was not considered that the taking of individuals from that species damaged the species as a whole.[49] This belief was reinforced by the view that, unlike humans, animals could not be subject to duties.[50] Even when science and philosophy combined in the Middle Ages in the doctrine of 'natural philosophy' each discipline continued to embrace the generalized concept of 'species' rather than concentrating on individual specimens.

These concepts were underpinned by the Roman law doctrine that animals *ferae naturae* did not belong to any person and could, therefore, be captured by anyone when found in international areas, such as the high seas and the airspace above them. Species

---

[47] Went, *Seventy Years Agrowing: A History of the International Council for the Exploration of the Sea 1920–1972* (Charlotteslund, 1972).

[48] Ibid.

[49] Clark, *The Moral Status of Animals* (Oxford, 1977), 64–5; he provides a bibliography of relevant works.

[50] Linzey, *Animal Rights* (London, 1976); ibid, 12 *Jnl of Legal Education* (1964–5), 185ff; Singer and Regan (eds), *Animal Rights and Legal Obligations* (New York, 1976); Tribe, 83 *Yale LJ* (1976), 1315ff.

which could not be corralled and domesticated, such as fish, marine mammals, and birds outside national territory, were thus regarded as common property resources.[51] These perceptions are now beginning to change, however.[52] Renewed attention is being paid to the concept of animal rights and the common property doctrine is being overlaid with new concepts of 'common heritage', 'common inheritance', 'common interest', and 'common concern'.

3(2) DEVELOPMENT OF NEW APPROACHES

(a) Animal rights

In national law, states at first simply regarded animals as either useful or vicious[53] and thus protected only the economic value of wildlife as a source of food and clothing, limiting the hunting of certain species to maintain their population levels for these purposes or encouraging the killing of animals thought harmful to humans and their activities. Later, wildlife law responded to protect the value placed on hunting and fishing as recreational activities. It is only fairly recently that public concern has developed for protection of animals and for their welfare, as species valuable for their own sake, with special emphasis on endangered species, habitats, and rational management.[54] Legal writers, following the first preoccupations of environmental activists in the Western Hemisphere, have been concerned initially with protection of a few species, for example whales, polar bears, porpoises, dolphins, sea otters, bald eagles, condors, and the snail darter, in isolation from land-use regulation.[55] A major problem of this topic, presented in this context, is that it is highly complex, involving a wide variety of subjects and issues as well as different jurisdictions and disciplines. It is thus difficult, at both national and international levels, to identify a discrete body of law protecting animals although recent publications will facilitate research on this[56] and increasing attention is being paid to the close relationship between legislation

---

[51] See Fulton, *The Sovereignty of the Seas* (Edinburgh, 1911), v–vii; Grotius, *The Freedom of the Sea or the Right Which Belongs to the Dutch to Take Part in the East India Trade*, trans Magoffin and Scott (New York, 1916); *infra*, Ch 13.

[52] Gillespie, *International Environmental Law, Politics and Ethics* (Oxford, 1997) *passim*, and the extensive bibliography provided at 179–210; Sarkar, *Biodiversity and Environmental Philosophy* (Cambridge, 2005); Light and Rolston (eds), *Environmental Ethics: An Anthology* (Oxford, 2003); Stone, in Bodansky, Brunnee, and Hey (eds), *The Oxford Handbook of International Environmental Law*, Ch 13; and *Lyster's International Wildlife Law*, Ch 3.

[53] Linder, 12 *Harv ELR* (1988) 157–200.

[54] Linder, loc cit, 157–8; see also Bean, *The Evolution of National Wildlife Law* (2nd edn, Washington DC, 1983), and works cited in Coggins and Smith, 6 *Environmental Law* (1976) 583; Coggins and Patti, 4 *Harv ELR* (1980) 164. On animal welfare provisions in national, including constitutional, law see Gillespie, 6 *JIWLP* (2003) 1.

[55] Coggins and Patti, 4 *Harv ELR* (1980) 181.

[56] E.g. Wilkins (ed), *Animal Welfare in Europe: European Legislation and Concerns* (The Hague, 1997) *passim*. The second edition of *Lyster's International Wildlife Law* (Cambridge, 2009), includes a new chapter on wildlife law and animal welfare (Ch 20). Austen and Richards (eds), *International Animal Welfare Law* (The Hague, 2000), collect the texts of relevant international, regional, and European instruments.

protecting animal welfare and its role in conserving animals and incidentally bio-diversity, as we shall see.[57]

It is important at this stage to distinguish the different perspectives of animal rights and welfare advocates,[58] who consider that all species should be protected for ethical and humanitarian reasons however adverse their effect on humans or on populations or individuals of other species,[59] and of environmentalists who urge that particular species should be protected for ecological reasons, that is, as part of an ecosystem, which includes the animals, plants, and micro-organisms together with the non-living components of their environment. This difference in views is reflected in the progress of both national and international law and the number and nature of the instruments adopted. It is not possible here, for reasons of space, to examine in detail the arguments of the animal-rights group based on the moral considerability of animals, although there is a growing literature on this aspect and drafts of an international Declaration of Animal Rights,[60] as well as of a convention,[61] have been under consideration for some years at the non-governmental level. This draft declaration is without legal status but has served to focus attention on gaps in the law by laying down in detail certain principles relating to animal protection. So far, however, the international commu-nity has not developed a specific legislative response to the question whether killing animals is wrong or whether all or only some animals are to be regarded as sharing sufficient human characteristics to have individual rights attributed to them and to be legally protected from so-called 'speciesism', as humans are protected from racism. It has, rather, followed the environmentalist view.

Gillespie's examination of international law, policy, and ethics concluded that the central basis of international environmental law remains anthropocentric, based on a mélange of self interest and economic advantage (especially in the case of developing states) as well as some religious, aesthetic, and cultural practices but finds, nonetheless,

[57] On this, see Bowman, 1 *JIWLP* (1998) 9–63.

[58] On the notion of 'rights' in this context see *supra*, Ch 5, section 1(1) and Stone, 45 *S Cal LR* (1972) 450, 488.

[59] See Linder, 12 *Harv ELR* (1988) 175ff; Regan, *The Case for Animal Rights* (New York, 1983); Singer, *Practical Ethics* (New York, 1979); ibid, *In Defence of Animals* (Washington DC, 1985); Bowman, in Bowman and Redgwell (eds), *International Law and the Conservation of Biological Diversity* (London, 1996) 5–32, Cheyne, 12 *JEL* (2000) 293–316; Harrop, ibid, 333–60; McIntyre (ed), *Mind in the Waters* (New York, 1974); Tribe, 83 *Yale LJ* (1974) 1315; Reed, 12 *Idaho LR* (1976) 153; Sagoff, 84 *Yale LJ* (1974) 33; Allen, 28 *NY Law School LR* (1983) 377–429; Stone, 45 *Scal LR* (1972), 450; Winters, 21 *SDLR* (1984), 911–40; Hersovice, *Second Nature: The Animal Rights Controversy* (Toronto, 1985) 42–55; Gillespie, *International Environmental Law, Politics and Ethics* (Oxford, 1997) *passim* and 141–4.

[60] Universal Declaration of the Rights of Animals, proclaimed on 15 Oct 1978 by the International League of Animal Rights. Its Preamble recognizes that 'all animals have rights'; Article 1 provides that 'All animals are born with an equal claim on life and the same rights to existence'; Article 2 that 'Man as an animal species shall not arrogate to himself the rights to exterminate or inhumanly exploit other animals'; Article 3 that 'All Animals shall have the right to the attention, care and protection of man'; texts in Allen, 28 *NY Law School LR* (1983) 414–5, n 259. Several members of the Council of Europe had relevant laws by the 1970s: see Taylor, 1 *Animal Reg Stud* (1977) 73; the USA has extensive legislation, Allen, op cit, 422–5.

[61] Progress on this is reported *passim* in the Newsletter of the International Committee for a Convention for the Protection of Animals.

that new non-anthropocentric developments reveal growing recognition of intrinsic values, ecological interdependence, and the need for a holistic approach. He accepts that international law still does not recognize animal rights, apart from in those treaties (considered in our Chapters 12 and 13) which aim to prevent extermination of certain species, and that the anthropocentric justification for nature protection fails to encapsulate its essential value. Alternative approaches, based on the moral considerability of animals and utilitarianism, are similarly flawed since they do not provide for inclusion of wider environmental considerations embracing entities and ecosystems which are neither sentient nor of intrinsic value. Even the so-called 'life approach', recognizing the moral worth of all living entities, fails to include ecosystems. Similarly, the 'land ethic' or 'deep ecology' perspectives, though they do emphasize ecological and ecosystemic holism, are regarded by Gillespie as too misanthropic, providing no social system for implementation of their goals.[62]

Cheyne, on the other hand, in examining the role of new ethical theories in the trade and environment debate arising out of US attempts to prevent incidental catch of dolphins in the purse-seine nets of Mexican fishermen, notes that the GATT panel did not consider the environmental or ethical issues.[63] They were, however, raised in the US Congressional debate on the subsequent amendment of the US Marine Mammal Protection Act which focused, inter alia, on the moral considerability of animals and the differences between biocentric (all life has intrinsic value) and ecocentric (all life has value as part of a complex ecosystem) approaches. She concluded that the debates revealed that the relationship between law and ethics remained complex and dynamic and that national lawmaking, international trade policy, and competing ethical theories could not easily be subsumed within the competition between trade and environment. She suggests that they even throw doubts on 'the rhetoric of sustainable development' and its goals, the incompatibility of which is revealed by further examination of the ethical dimension. The value placed on dolphins by Congress was 'anthropocentric in every respect' and exposed the risk of ignoring species with which humankind has little or no affinity.[64] Some speakers were prepared to sacrifice turtles were this necessary to save dolphins; other found a certain level of dolphin mortality acceptable. It was assumed by most speakers that there was a right to exploit the resources of the sea even if it resulted in killing dolphins and turtles.[65] The lack of clarity and openness in ethical thought and argument in the debates, as exposed by Cheyne, reflects the problems presented by such issues when they are presented to wider international society. Cheyne concludes that no *coherent* policy (or presumably legal) response will be possible unless the ethical approaches are made more explicit and their contradictions understood.[66] This is true not only in the case of trade and environment issues which are further discussed in Chapter 14 but also in relation to development of international environmental law generally in which these issues

---

[62] Gillespie, *International Environmental Law, Politics and Ethics* (Oxford, 1997) 176–8.

[63] Cheyne, 12 *JEL* (2000) 293. But see *infra*, Ch 14 and discussion there of the WTO Appellate Body's *Shrimp-Turtle* decision.

[64] Cheyne, loc cit, 314.   [65] Cheyne, loc cit, 310.   [66] Cheyne, loc cit, 315.

continue to arise, generating argument concerning measures necessary to protect biodiversity.

Harrop makes a similar point—the need for more coherence in environmental regimes—in the context of evaluating attempts to introduce international regulation of animal welfare and conservation issues by setting European Community standards for trapping wild animals.[67] He notes that regulation of wild animals' welfare is often entangled in treaty issues as, for example, in the case of CITES' regulation of animals in transit and detention or as in the Berne Convention in relation to indiscriminate methods of trading or killing. In response to calls for a ban on importing foreign furs the EC has now adopted a Leghold Trap Regulation,[68] entered into an Agreement on International Humane Trapping Standards with Canada and the Russian Federation,[69] and concluded an Agreed Minute with the USA on Humane Trapping Standards.[70] He fears, however, that these could retard development of international standards because their priorities remain trade-related.[71]

Supporting the view that the biodiversity concept must logically be based on recognition of the intrinsic value of individual organisms, Bowman suggests, however, that this approach does not involve acceptance of such controversial concepts as animal rights since there is not necessarily any incompatibility between accepting the importance of biological communities as unified systems and according value to individual creatures.[72] Bowman accepts that in support of these legal arguments much weight is placed on the preambles of relevant international legal instruments, both binding ones such as the ASEAN, Berne, CITES, and Western Hemisphere Conventions, and goal-setting ones, such as the World Charter for Nature and the World Conservation Strategy; but he regards this, correctly, as a legitimate means of establishing their underlying philosophy and object and purpose.[73] Bowman and others have also pointed out, in support of the moral considerability of animals, that CITES, for example, contains provisions aimed at securing the welfare of animals introduced into international trade.[74]

To date, it is only at the regional level, through the Council of Europe—which as early as 1961 declared that the humane treatment of animals is 'one of the hallmarks of Western civilization'—that a series of conventions has been concluded specifically protecting animals from suffering.[75] The European Community has also

---

[67] Harrop, 12 *JEL* (2000) 333.   [68] Regulation 3254/91 OJEC 1991, L/308/1.

[69] OJ L 042, 14.2.98, 43–57.   [70] OJ L 219, 13.7.98, 24–25.

[71] Harrop, 12 *JEL* (2000) 360; on such problems see also *infra*, Ch 14.

[72] Bowman, in Bowman and Redgwell (eds), *International Law and the Conservation of Biological Diversity*, 25–31; see also *Lyster's International Wildlife Law*, Ch 20.

[73] Ibid.

[74] E.g. Article 3(2)(c). See Bowman, 1 *JIWLP* (1998) 9–63; Harrop and Bowles, ibid, 64–94.

[75] These include the 1968 Convention for the Protection of Animals During International Transport, *ETS* No 65, (with 1979 Additional Protocol, *ETS* No 103, updated in 2003, *ETS* 193); the 1976 Convention for the Protection of Animals kept for Farming Purposes, *ETS* No. 87 (with 1992 Additional Protocol No 145); the 1979 Convention for the Protection of Animals used for Slaughter, *ETS* No 102; the 1986 Convention for the Protection of Vertebrate Animals used for Experimental and other Scientific Purposes, *ETS* No 123 (with Additional Protocol of 1998); and the 1987 Convention for the Protection of Pet Animals, *ETS* No 125.

adopted decisions which make these conventions binding in all EU member states.[76] Nonetheless, at the international level generally, controversy still surrounds the introduction of welfare protection into treaties concerning exploitation even of endangered species and is seen as peripheral to environmental concerns within the global goal of sustainable development. Thus in 1999 the parties to the Whaling Convention, under pressure from those few states still whaling, changed the name of its long-standing 'Working Group on Humane Killing' to 'Working Group on Killing Methods and Associated Welfare Issues'.[77] Animal welfare issues are thus not wholly irrelevant to the development of international and national law protecting biodiversity, but they are not yet a dominant concern.[78]

(b) Common property, common heritage, and common concern

The underlying concepts of common property and related concepts affecting the legal status of natural resources and common spaces have already been outlined in Chapter 3.[79] As we saw there, new concepts such as 'common heritage'[80] and 'common concern'[81] have, in the case of the former, been confined to certain mineral resources and not applied to shared natural resources and in case of the latter, while of growing importance, have as yet been included only in hortatory preambles of the Climate Change and Biological Diversity Conventions and some of the growing numbers of codes, declarations, and strategies for conservation. Thus common property remains a basic concept of international wildlife law, even though, when coupled with the principle of free access, it leads to over-exploitation and decline of species if exploitation expands unchecked. The doctrine of permanent sovereignty over natural resources has also encouraged over-exploitation in the absence of clearly established and implemented international conservatory obligations.[82] It is thus vital to conservation of living resources and biodiversity both to develop new legal principles and to conclude bilateral, regional or global regulatory agreements which define 'conservation' and prescribe appropriate measures, as there is no accepted international definition of this

---

See also Pavan, *A European Cultural Revolution: The Council of Europe's Charter on Invertebrates*, Council of Europe (Strasbourg, 1986).

[76] This ensures that there are explicit legal obligations within the EU to consider animal welfare. See also Camm and Bowles, 12 *JEL* (2000) 197–205.

[77] IWC, *Chairman's Report of the 51st Annual Meeting*, 24–8, May 1999, 6–10; the Working Group was established in 1982 and has had workshops on killing methods every 3–5 years since 1992, most recently in 2006. See, generally, Harrop 6 *JIWLP* (2003) 79 and *Lyster's International Wildlife Law*, Ch 20. Note also the failure of the International Standards Organization's Draft Humane Trapping Standards, 1998 ISO/DIS 10990–5, to attract consensus because of the difficulty of defining the term 'humane'.

[78] For discussion of whether welfare considerations are emerging as a general principle of international law, see *Lyster's International Wildlife Law*, Ch 20.

[79] *Supra*, Ch 3, section 5(1)–(4); see also Brunnee, in Bodansky, Brunnee, and Hey (eds), *The Oxford Handbook of International Environmental Law*, Ch 23.

[80] *Supra*, Ch 3, section 5(4).   [81] *Supra*, Ch 3, section 3(1)(a–c).

[82] For discussion of the interplay of permanent sovereignty over natural resources and sustainable development, see Schrijver, *Sovereignty over Natural Resources: Balancing Rights and Duties* (Cambridge, 1997), and *infra*, Ch 3.

term. Moreover, as Brunnee observes, since 'international law continues to struggle with "collective" or "community" aspirations', treaty regimes at least have 'the potential to turn pragmatic cooperation into genuine normative communities' and offer 'promising settings in which to mediate between "individual State interest" and "the global concerns of humanity as a whole"'.[83]

3(3) THE ROLE OF COOPERATION

It is now at least clear that the development of law taking account of all the international aspects of the problem of conservation of nature, including wildlife, must be based on recognition of certain important factors, inter alia: that many species and some of the threats to them migrate across national frontiers; that migratory and non-migratory species need to be protected from over-exploitation resulting from trade; and that it is necessary to protect the whole environment supporting the life-cycle of the species concerned.[84] It must also aim to conserve biodiversity, i.e. the frequency and variety of life in all its forms, levels, and combinations; including the differences within and between them, not just the components of biodiversity.[85]

Experience derived from the first attempts to conserve such species established three preconditions for ensuring the effectiveness of international conventions for this purpose: first, exploitation, when permitted, must be conducted on a rational basis, that is with conscious, reasonable objectives, taking account of scientific advice; second, the species concerned must be regulated as a biological unit, that is through its whole range; and third, all the relevant ecological factors that affect the conservation of a species and its habitat must be considered. To these has now been added the need, in order to conserve biological diversity, of both *in situ* and *ex situ* conservation of ecosystems and natural habitats and the maintenance and recovery of viable populations of species in their natural surroundings, which themselves must be protected from undue degradation.

Securing these aims requires that states cooperate on the widest possible basis in subjecting national sovereignty to the necessary coordinated international obligations. Thus the conventions and strategies outlined in this chapter and in Chapters 12 and 13 constitute, albeit on a somewhat ad hoc and incomplete basis, the emerging regime for conservation of nature and biodiversity. The evolution of the regime concerning marine living resources, in particular (see Chapter 13), indicates that merely to allocate migratory living species to national control, or to accord them common property or *res nullius* status in international areas, does not provide an effective solution; both international obligations and international institutions must be established.

The Biodiversity Convention specifically provides that it does not affect rights and responsibilities deriving from existing international agreements unless their exercise

---

[83] Brunnee, in Bodansky, Brunnee, and Hey (eds), *The Oxford Handbook of International Environmental Law*, 572, drawing on the language of the separate opinion of Judge Weeramantry in the *Case Concerning the Gabčikovo-Nagymaros Project (Hungary v Slovakia)* [1997] ICJ Reports 7.

[84] De Klemm, 29 *NRJ* (1989) 932, *passim*.   [85] *Supra*, section 2(3).

would cause harm to biological diversity.[86] However, this does not mean that the many other relevant agreements do not remain important to conservation of biological diversity, rather that cooperation and coordination between and among them in order to conserve biodiversity within their jurisdiction is required. Moreover, the fact that conservation of biodiversity has been declared the 'common concern of humankind' has, as explained in Chapter 3, given this objective a legal status involving some form of global accountability which is clearly different from previous agreements dealing with nature and living resources.[87]

3(4) INSTITUTIONAL REQUIREMENTS OF AN EFFECTIVE LIVING-RESOURCE REGIME

Assuming that conservation and management principles can be agreed, the basic legal requirements for the institution of an effective conservation and management regime which provides for conservation of biodiversity are as before:[88] establishment of the source of jurisdiction over the resource or resources concerned and their habitats; obligations to conduct scientific research and take account of scientific advice, subject now to the need, as appropriate, to adopt a 'precautionary approach'; prescription of regulations; establishment of permanent international institutions to provide a forum for discussion, evaluation, coordination, and adoption of required measures, inter alia; compliance and enforcement mechanisms; and dispute settlement arrangements. Chapters 12 and 13 address these issues and trace the emergence of the legal regimes for marine and other living resources. They also consider their role in providing the necessary coordination and integration to ensure conservation of biodiversity in the light of the terms set out in the 1992 Convention on Biological Diversity and the extent to which they have adapted their institutions and measures to achieve its aims.

4 CODIFICATION AND DEVELOPMENT OF INTERNATIONAL LAW ON NATURE PROTECTION

It cannot be said that prior to the 1972 Stockholm Conference on the Human Environment any principles specifically concerning conservation of wildlife or biodiversity had clearly emerged in international customary law. The Stockholm Declaration adopted by this Conference identified a number of relevant and important

---

[86] Article 22. For analysis see contributions by Boyle, Redgwell, and Frankx, in Freestone, Barnes and Ong (eds), *The Law of the Sea: Progress and Prospects* (Oxford, 2006); and *infra*, Ch 13.

[87] *Supra*, Ch 3, section 3(1)(c).

[88] De Klemm, in Johnston (ed), *The Environmental Law of the Sea* (Berlin, 1981), 85–90, and see generally, *supra*, Ch 3.

principles which have since been elaborated upon in other sets of principles, guidelines, and standards, and have formed the basis of treaties concluded between 1972 and 1992, but it cannot really be said to have codified or developed international law on nature protection. More significant attempts at codification and development of legal norms were made by UNEP and IUCN.

4(1) UNEP PRINCIPLES OF CONDUCT IN THE FIELD OF THE ENVIRONMENT FOR THE GUIDANCE OF STATES IN THE CONSERVATION AND HARMONIOUS UTILIZATION OF NATURAL RESOURCES SHARED BY TWO OR MORE STATES 1978[89]

Although, as we saw in Chapter 3,[90] these principles are relevant to mineral and water resources and pollution, they can also apply to protection of migratory species of animals and transboundary nature reserves and parks. They require cooperation in conservation and use, conclusion of agreements, creation of institutions, environmental impact assessment, joint research, exchange of information, and notification and consultation on the basis of good faith and good neighbourliness. They have to be applied in a way that enhances development, based on the concept of equitable utilization.

The legal status of these and similar sets of principles was discussed in Chapter 1; they exemplify the soft-law approach to lawmaking often favoured by UNEP. However, the analysis provided in Chapter 12 indicates that these UNEP principles are to a remarkable degree reflected in the provisions of the major wildlife conventions, and although some have not been acted upon, most have. As we saw in earlier chapters, in certain important respects they reflect existing customary law.

4(2) WORLD CHARTER FOR NATURE (WCN)[91]

In developing a more comprehensive legal regime for conservation of nature, wildlife, and biodiversity, account has also to be taken of the WCN which represented the acceptance, expressed in the form of a Resolution adopted by a majority of the General Assembly, that mankind is responsible for all species, and promulgated provisions for fulfilling this responsibility. It required, inter alia, that 'Nature shall be respected and

---

[89] UNEP/IG, 12/28 (1978). See also *supra*, Ch 3. The Experts Group on Environmental Law of the World Commission on Environment and Development preferred the term 'transboundary natural resources' to 'shared natural resources' because the latter has given rise to difficulties associated with claims to sovereignty: Munro and Lammers, *Environmental Protection and Sustainable Development* (London, 1987) 8, 37.

[90] *Supra*, Ch 3, section 5(2).

[91] See Consideration and Adoption of the Revised Draft World Charter for Nature: Report of the Secretary General, 37/UN GAOR (Agenda Item 21), UN Doc A/398 (1982); UNGA Res 37/7 (1982), reproduced in 23 *ILM* (1983) 455–60; 111 states voted for this resolution, one against (USA), and eighteen abstained (Algeria, Argentina, Bolivia, Brazil, Chile, Colombia, Dominican Republic, Ecuador, Ghana, Guyana, Lebanon, Mexico, Paraguay, Peru, Philippines, Surinam, Trinidad and Tobago, Venezuela). See also Burhenne and Irwin, *The World Charter for Nature: A Background Paper* (Berlin, 1983); International Council for Environmental Law, *Commentary on the World Charter for Nature*, IUCN Environmental Law Centre (Bonn, 1986).

its essential processes not impaired' (Article 1), that 'The genetic viability on the earth shall not be compromised; the population levels of all life forms, wild and domesticated, must be at least sufficient for their survival, and to this end necessary habitats shall be safeguarded' (Article 2).

So far as implementation was concerned, the WCN offered nothing more than general admonitions and though its general principles are expressed in mandatory terms ('shall' is used throughout rather than 'should'), they are expressed also in very general terms. A French commentator regretted 'son apparence pseudojuridique', adding that 'Il à est craindre que pour avoir vouler proposer du "droit doux" le législateur ne propose plus ici de droit de tout…pourquoi alors ce masque? Si cette pseudo-règle peut, on espère, servir la cause de la nature, elle ne peut que contribuer a descréditer celle du droit'.[92]

The legal status of this Charter must be assessed by the same tests as other UN resolutions (see Chapter 1). Despite the expression of contrary views,[93] it is difficult to argue that in relation to conservation of resources it had any binding legal status; indeed its drafters accepted that 'by its very nature, the Charter could not have any binding force, nor have any regime of sanctions attached to it'.[94] The use of 'shall' was purely declaratory.[95] Nonetheless, it has been suggested that it should 'be regarded as an instrument having a special character, a declaration of principles after the fashion of such General Assembly Resolutions as the Universal Declaration of Human Rights'[96] and it did have some moral and political force, as its restatement in subsequent strategies evidences. Its attempt to set the equilibrium between the use of nature and its conservation accords with current goals of sustainable development and its provisions have had more influence on subsequent international policymaking than was predicted at the time of its adoption, as Chapters 12 and 13 establish.

In addition to the principles referred to, the WCN prescribed certain 'functions'. Article 10 required 'wise use', namely, that states must not use resources beyond their natural capacity for regeneration, and Article 11 that activities which might impact on nature must be controlled, using 'best available technologies'. Unique areas must be specially protected, as must representative samples of ecosystems and habitats of rare or endangered species. Ecosystems and organisms used by man are to be managed to sustain optimum productivity without endangering coexisting ecosystems or species. Natural resources must not be wasted but can be used, as long as this does not come close to exceeding their regenerative capacity. Principle 21 of the Stockholm Declaration is reiterated[97] with the injunction that attention be paid to ensuring that

[92] Rémond-Gouilloud, 2 *Rev jurid de l'env* (1982), 120–4.   [93] Wood, 12 *ELQ* (1985) 981.

[94] *Report of the Ad Hoc Group Meeting on the Draft World Charter for Nature*, held at Nairobi, 24–7 August 1981, 36 UN GAOR, Annex (Agenda Item 23) 7, UN Doc A/539 (1981).

[95] Wood, 12 *ELQ* (1985), 982–4. See also views of Kiss and Singh on the significance of the word 'shall', 14 *EPL* (1985) 37–70; cf Caldwell, *International Environmental Policy* (2nd edn, Durham, 1900) 90–3, and 'Note on the Use of the World "Shall"', in Nordquist (ed), *United Nations Convention on the Law of the Sea: A Commentary* (London, 1991), iv, xli–xlii.

[96] Jackson, 12 *Ambio* (1983), 133.   [97] *Supra*, Ch 3, section 4(2).

activities within a state's jurisdiction or control do not cause damage to natural systems in other states or areas beyond national jurisdiction and that nature in the international area is safeguarded. Activities causing irreversible damage must be avoided and their likely risks to nature must be examined beforehand; environmental impact assessment must be undertaken; and agriculture, grazing, and forest practices must be adapted to the natural characteristics and constraints of given areas.

Article 22 formulated the obligations as those of states in providing that 'Taking fully into account the sovereignty of states over their natural resources, each state shall give effect to the provisions of the present Charter through its competent organs and in co-operation with other states', whilst Article 23 required that all *persons* must have the opportunity to participate in formulating decisions directly concerning their environment and be provided with access to means of redress if it is damaged, requirements subsequently endorsed by UNCED's Principle 10 and, to a limited extent, section 15.5 of Agenda 21's Chapter 15 on Conservation of Biodiversity. Article 24, however, affirms the personal obligation of each *person* to act in accordance with the provisions of the WCN and to 'strive to ensure' that its objectives are met.

The Charter was clearly intended by the UN majority to be a contribution to the creation of new binding international law on conservation and, if systematically applied and elaborated, its rules could be transformed into customary international law. They have been reflected in the UNCED instruments including the Convention on Biological Diversity. Article 14 requires that its principles be reflected both in the law and practice of each state and at the international level.

4(3) THE 1987 REPORT OF THE WORLD COMMISSION ON ENVIRONMENT AND DEVELOPMENT (WCED)[98]

The Brundtland Report, which the General Assembly transmitted to all governments and organs, organizations, and programmes of the UN system, inviting them to take account of its analysis and recommendations in determining their policies and programmes,[99] reinforced the UNEP and WCN proposals and principles and strongly promoted the aims of sustainable development, focusing on nature as a resource. It concluded that preservation of soil, water, and of the nurseries and breeding grounds of species cannot be divorced from conserving individual species within natural ecosystems, which contributes to the predominant goals of sustainable development. It identified the role in this process of various international organizations, such as FAO, UNEP, IUCN, and UNESCO, and the need for norms and procedures to be established.

The report laid special stress on the protection of biological diversity. It drew particular attention to UNESCO's establishment of biosphere reserves as 'biotic provinces' and called for a new species convention to be concluded to protect 'universal resources'. It postulated collective responsibility for species as a 'common heritage',

---

[98] *Our Common Future* (Oxford, 1987). See further, *supra*, Ch 2.   [99] UN Doc A/C 2/42/L 81.

which status, it suggested, required that other states provide financial help for their conservation within national boundaries through establishment of a trust fund to which the states benefiting most from resource exploitation would contribute the most, though an equitable share of the benefits of development of the resources would be attributed to the 'possessor' nations. An environmental role for the World Bank in undertaking environmental impact assessment of its development projects was conceived, with particular attention being accorded to habitat preservation and life support systems. This accords with the current practice of the World Bank as indicated in Chapter 2.

The WCED Report was accompanied by a Report of an Experts Group on Environmental Law. This Group's mandate was to report on legal principles for environmental protection and sustainable development and to make proposals for accelerating the development of relevant international law. The Group approved twenty-two articles stating legal principles which have been referred to throughout this work.[100] All are expressed in mandatory terms, that is, using the word 'shall'.[101] Relevant principles for our purpose include the 'General Principles, Rights and Responsibilities', referred to in Principles 1–7, such as the fundamental human right to an adequate environment; inter- and intra-generational equity; maintenance of ecosystems, biological diversity, and optimum sustainable yield of living resources; establishment of adequate environmental standards and monitoring thereof; prior environmental assessment; prior notification of activities with adverse effects; ensuring that conservation is an integral part of planning and implementation of development processes; and recognizing an obligation to cooperate in good faith in implementing all these rights and obligations. Of these Principle 3 is of particular relevance to formulation of the Convention on Biodiversity. It requires states to '(a) maintain ecosystems and related ecological processes essential for the functioning of the biosphere in all its diversity, in particular those important for food production, health and other aspects of human survival and sustainable development;' and '(b) maintain maximum biological diversity by ensuring the survival and promoting the conservation in their natural habitat of all species of flora and fauna, in particular those which are rare, endemic or endangered'.

Twelve others (Principles 9–20) are grouped as 'Principles, Rights and Obligations Concerning Transboundary Natural Resources and Environmental Interferences'. In order to obviate arguments about national sovereignty, these require states to use transboundary natural resources in a reasonable manner; prevent and abate harmful interferences; take precautionary measures to limit risk and to establish strict liability for harm done; apply, as a minimum, the same standards for environmental conduct and impacts concerning such resources as are applied domestically; cooperate in good faith to achieve optimal use and prevention or abatement of interference with such resources; provide prior notification and assessment of activities having

---

[100] *Supra*, Ch 3, n 9.
[101] For the significance of this usage, see Wood, 12 *ELQ* (1985) 977, and works cited *supra*, n 91

significant transboundary effects and engage in prior consultation with concerned states; cooperate in monitoring, scientific research and standard-setting; develop contingency plans for emerging situations; and provide equal access and treatment in administrative and judicial proceedings to all affected or likely to be so. The two remaining principles relate to state responsibility, requiring states to cease activities breaching international obligations regarding the environment and to provide compensation for harm, and the requirement that states settle environmental disputes by peaceful means.

Though the WCED legal principles are most often discussed and used, as in this work, in relation to transboundary pollution, they are equally applicable to interference with and harm to living resources and the natural environment. Moreover, as we saw in Chapter 3, many of them codify or have come to reflect customary international law.

4(4) THE 1992 UN CONFERENCE ON ENVIRONMENT AND DEVELOPMENT

(a) The Rio Declaration

As noted in Chapter 2, the Rio Declaration adopted by the UNCED did not include any provisions concerning natural resources as specific as those proposed in the instruments discussed above, since its prime concern was to recognize the need for, and to promote sustainable development.[102] Still less did it address animal rights. Its aims are anthropomorphic, the stated goal 'working towards international agreements, which respect the interests of all and protect the integrity of the global environmental and developmental system'.[103] Notably, these are not regarded as separate components but as an integral system. However, this does not mean, as we discuss more fully later, that sustainable development does not require restraint in the use of natural resources since 'sustainable utilization' or 'use' is a key element independent of 'sustainable development',[104] and it is required not only in the Convention on Biological Diversity but also in the Desertification[105] and Climate Change[106] Conventions and those terms are used in other important agreements concluded after Rio. They also underpin, though not precisely in the same language, the management concepts used in many pre- and post-UNCED agreements mentioned in Chapters 12 and 13. As we have noted, Principle 15 of the UNCED Declaration also contributes to sustainable resource utilization by applying the precautionary approach to accommodate uncertainty.[107] Principle 17 requiring conduct of environmental impact assessment, as well as other principles, are also relevant in this context, as we have pointed out.[108] Crucial to conservation of biodiversity in particular is the recognition of states' rights

---

[102] *Supra*, Ch 2, section 2(4), (5), and Ch 3, section 1(2).   [103] Preamble to UNCED Declaration.

[104] *Supra*, Ch 3, section 2(2); see also Schrijver, *Sovereignty over Natural Resources: Balancing Rights and Duties* (Cambridge, 1997), esp Pt III.

[105] Articles 2, 3; see *infra*, Ch 12 and comments of Bekhecki, 101 *RGDIP* (1997) 101.

[106] See *supra*, Ch 3, section 2(2).   [107] *Supra*, Ch 3, section 4(2).   [108] Ibid.

to exploit their own resources, albeit conditioned by the common but differentiated responsibilities of developed and developing states and the special needs of developing countries.[109]

(b) Agenda 21[110]

Agenda 21, consisting of 40 chapters, is a much more ambitious and lengthy framework than the UNCHE Action Plan. Its chapters include one (Chapter 13) on biological diversity. Though the Agenda is divided into four parts which cover the Social and Economic Dimensions (Part I), Strengthening the Role of Major Groups (Part III) and Means of Implementation (Part IV), it is only the second part consisting of fourteen chapters on 'Conservation and Management of Resources for Development' that need concern us here and for purposes of Chapters 12 and 13. This includes chapters on combating deforestation (Chapter 11); managing fragile ecosystems including desertification and drought (Chapter 12) and sustainable mountain development (Chapter 13); promoting sustainable agriculture and rural development (Chapter 14); conservation of biological diversity (Chapter 15); environmentally sound management of biotechnology (Chapter 16); and protection of oceans, all kinds of seas, including enclosed and semi-enclosed seas, and coastal areas and the protection, rational use and development of their living resources (Chapter 17). Chapters 18–22 are also relevant since they address the environmental problems concerning conservation of habitat of living resources (including freshwater resources) by control of discharge and transport of toxic chemicals, hazardous waste, solid waste and sewage-related issues, and radioactive waste all of which can contribute to the degradation of the habitats of terrestrial and marine living resources.

In Johnson's view the precise legal status of Agenda 21 is 'a matter of some speculation' since it is clearly not a legally binding text, governments have not subscribed to all its details, it does not require ratification and is not justiciable in any international court.[111] He regards it as a candidate for soft law status, since it has moral if not legal force and may play, and in the event in many cases has played, a role in underpinning both national actions and subsequent, possibly more stringent, international agreements. This it has indeed done, inter alia, in relation to straddling and highly migratory fish stocks (see Chapter 13). Practice in relation to it does give support to this view as we shall see. Ansari and Jamal reviewing Chapter 15 of Agenda 21, take a similar view concluding that though it is not a binding document 'the guidelines have persuasive value as soft law, thus they are being implemented by the states'.[112] We shall return to this issue after evaluating subsequent state practice in concluding binding agreements based on relevant chapters of this document not only in this chapter but in Chapters 12 and 13.

---

[109] Principles 2, 7, and 6 respectively; *supra*, Ch 3, section 3(3).   [110] *Supra*, Ch 2, section 2(4).

[111] Johnson, The Earth Summit: The United Nations Conference on Environment and Development (Dordrecht, 1993) 127.

[112] Ansari and Jamal, 88 *Indian JIL* (2000), 134, 151.

Although it is fair to say that the cumulative measures concluded by 1992 to protect wildlife represent an ad hoc and pragmatic response to the problems involved, nonetheless an examination of the most important texts does reveal that the problems of implementing the strategies adopted at the more comprehensive international level were and continue gradually to be addressed, as in the Convention on Biological Diversity, discussed below and those considered in Chapters 12 and 13.

4(5) DRAFT IUCN INTERNATIONAL COVENANT ON ENVIRONMENT AND DEVELOPMENT 2000

Following UNCED and the recommendations made in Agenda 21 for integration of environment and development issues at all levels, IUCN, in conjunction with other concerned bodies, has since prepared a Draft International Covenant on Environment.[113] It consists of seventy-two articles, setting out ten fundamental principles, and both general and specific obligations (Articles 11–15 and 16–22 respectively). These last include obligations relating to natural systems and resources (Article 20), biological diversity (Article 21), and cultural and natural heritage including Antarctica (Article 22). Provisions concerning processes and activities cover pollution, waste, and introduction of alien or modified organisms. Those relating to global issues address developmental, trade, and environment issues (Articles 27–33). Three dealing with transboundary issues include one on transboundary natural resources (Article 34). Others deal with aspects of implementation and cooperation (Articles 36–46), responsibility and liability (Articles 47–55), application and compliance (Articles 56–63), and Final Clauses (Articles 64–72). The draft is well founded on existing treaties, UN Resolutions, and other international documents, legislation, national constitutions and legislation, and European Union Regulations and Directives, as well as various leading cases and decisions and other relevant material. The draft was first launched in 1995; its updating takes account of new international agreements, including the UN Agreement on Straddling Fish Stocks, the Convention on Desertification and that on public participation in decision-making as well as of state practice evidencing integration of environment and development.[114] The articles are all expressed in very general terms. Those on natural systems, biological diversity, and natural heritage are so brief as to add little to existing conventions on these subjects. The aim is rather, as is made clear in the Preamble to 'recognize the unity of the biosphere, a unique and indivisible ecosystem, and the interdependence of all its components' (emphasis added).

It seems that though IUCN is convinced of the need for such an 'umbrella agreement' to effect the necessary integration of socio-economic development within maintenance of renewable natural resources,[115] states in general, as yet, are not. No

---

[113] *Supra*, Ch 2, n 188. A second edition was published in 2000.
[114] A Table of Authorities is provided at 169–94.
[115] Foreword to second edition, xi. IUCN's case for the Covenant is outlined at xii–xx.

doubt the scale and range of commitments is beyond the capability of many states at present, as are the formidable political difficulties both of securing a consensus on such a draft and enacting its requirements into national legislation. IUCN accepts that a broad consensus of states is required even to negotiate such an agreement and that while all states aim to promote sustainable development, the integration of *all* the legal requirements of sustainable development presents problems for many.[116] In the meantime, it reports that a consensus favouring such an agreement is growing and many states already have, or are contemplating, a framework law to integrate their own relevant sectoral laws or are using this Draft Covenant as an authoritative reference and checklist for national legislation fostering sustainable development.[117]

4(6) THE UN GENERAL ASSEMBLY AND NATURE PROTECTION

At the same time that it recommended the WCED Report to governments and UN bodies to take account of in their policies and programmes, the UNGA adopted the 'Environment Perspective to the Year 2000 and Beyond',[118] prepared by a UNEP intergovernmental group 'as a broad framework to guide national action and international co-operation on policies and programmes aimed at achieving environmentally sound development' and specifically as a guide to the preparation of system-wide medium-term programmes of the UN. The 'Perspective' addresses development issues and the need for environmentally sound development but includes the need to take note of cross-sectoral impacts and co-ordination, and responsibility for damage, and acknowledges that renewable resources can have sustainable yields only if system-wide effects of exploitation are taken into account. The Environment Perspective declares that safeguarding species is a *moral obligation* of humankind, and urges peaceful settlement of environmental disputes. More recently, at the end of 2006, the UN General Assembly declared 2010 'The International Year of Biodiversity',[119] motivated by a concern for the continued loss of biological diversity with an 'unprecedented effort' required to achieve by 2010 a significant reduction in such loss and 'deeply concerned by the social, economic, environmental and cultural implications' of such loss, including upon the Millenium Development Goals. While concrete measures are called for, none are contained in the resolution which merely calls on member states and the CBD Secretariat 'to take action'.

---

[116] Foreword, xiii.   [117] Ibid.

[118] UN Doc A/C 2/42/L 80, text in 18 *EPL* (1988) 37–8. See also the *World Conservation Strategy* (1980), prepared by IUCN, UNEP, and WWF, in collaboration with the FAO and UNESCO, and the same organization's revised programme *Caring for the Earth: A Strategy for Sustainable Living* (Gland, 1991), *supra*, n. 26 and Ch 2, section 2(3).

[119] See UNGA Res A/Res/61/203, 19 January 2007.

4(7) THE 2002 WORLD SUMMIT ON SUSTAINABLE DEVELOPMENT AND THE 2005 WORLD SUMMIT[120]

As indicated above in Chapter 2, the WSSD and 2005 World Summit added little by way of new policies and principles. Nonetheless, for present purposes their value lies in the further recognition of the contribution which conservation of biological diversity can make to the sustainable development process, and to poverty eradication in particular. Chapter IV of the Johannesburg Plan of Implementation is addressed to 'Protecting and managing the natural resource base of economic and social development' and seeks to strengthen participation in, and the implementation of, key instruments such as the CBD and the Desertification Convention. In particular, Paragraph 44 of the Plan reinforces the target of 2010 for achieving a 'significant reduction' in the rate of biodiversity loss agreed by CBD COP6 and the focus of the UN General Assembly's 2010 'International Year of Biodiversity' discussed above. Biodiversity has also been discussed by the Commission on Sustainable Development on several occasions and is one of the themes for discussion in the 2012/13 two-year cycle.

More important perhaps than reinforcement of existing policy is the useful opportunity provided to take stock of the achievements of a 'very substantial body of international legislation for the conservation of wildlife and the natural environment'.[121] UNEP's report[122] to the WSSD, and the Millenium Ecosystem Assessment in 2005,[123] provided stark reminders of the continuing rate of species extinction and ecosystem degradation, largely as a product of human activities, notwithstanding the extent of international regulation. The 'impression persists of a continuing escalation in the pressures upon wildlife which generated the need for the adoption of these instruments in the first place' and of inadequate mechanisms for implementation and enforcement of existing instruments.[124]

In sum, there is a considerable similarity and overlap between the policies and principles laid down in the strategies outlined in this section. Only the WCED Legal Experts formulate the principles precisely in specifically legal form, based on analysis of considerable supporting evidence in the form of existing practice and consultations. The repetition of the strategic principles has had significant effect in drawing attention to them but does not in itself confer legal status on them. This may only properly be assessed in the context of an examination of the extent to which the 'very substantial body of international legislation for the conservation of wildlife and the natural environment' referred to above rely upon these principles. Accordingly, the remainder of this chapter will consider the framework 1992 Convention on Biological Diversity,

---

[120] *Supra*, Ch 2, section 2(3).   [121] *Lyster's International Wildlife Law*, Ch 1, n 100.

[122] UNEP's report to the WSSD revealed that some 11,046 species of flora and fauna were known to be facing a high risk of extinction: UNEP, *Global Environmental Outlook-3 (Geo-3)* (2002).

[123] A global inventory of natural resources compiled by 1300 scientists from 95 countries, the Assessment concluded that about 60% of the planet's ecosystems are being degraded or used unsustainably: Millenium Ecosystem Assessment, *Ecosystems and Human Well-Being: Biodiversity Synthesis* (Washington, 2005).

[124] *Lyster's International Wildlife Law*, Ch 1.

and its 2000 Cartagena Protocol, before turning in Chapters 12 and 13 to assess other agreements for the protection of terrestrial and maritime biodiversity.

5 THE CONVENTION ON BIOLOGICAL DIVERSITY

5(1) INTRODUCTION

On the eve of UNCED, in a major breakthrough, a global Convention on Biological Diversity, under negotiation since 1988, was concluded. This has significantly enhanced the scope and potential effectiveness of the international legal regime for conserving the earth's biological diversity and ensuring the sustainable use of its components. It goes well beyond conservation of biological diversity per se and comprehends such diverse issues as sustainable use of biological resources, access to genetic resources, the sharing of benefits derived from the use of genetic material, and access to technology, including biotechnology.[125] This Convention, which was opened for signature at UNCED and entered into force on 29 December 1993, had 191 parties by mid-2008,[126] and has thus become one of the most widely ratified of all environmental conventions.

5(2) THE BACKGROUND TO ITS NEGOTIATION

As we noted earlier, previous strategies and conventions have been concerned with ensuring, on an ad hoc basis, the 'rational' or 'wise' use of common property or shared resources such as fish and marine mammals,[127] with the protection of migratory species and their habitats or with preventing over-exploitation of certain species of wild fauna and flora through control of international trade.[128] More recently treaties have addressed conservation of the ecosystems of particular areas such as Antarctica, certain regions in south-east Asia, the Caribbean and the western Indian Ocean, or outstanding natural heritage sites listed under the World Heritage Convention. These have all contributed considerably to protection of biodiversity, and continue to do so, but in a piecemeal fashion.[129] Another significant initiative was the adoption in 1983 by an FAO Conference of an Undertaking on Plant Genetic Resources which aimed to ensure that these should be explored, preserved, evaluated, and made available for plant breeding and scientific purposes which are considered further below.[130] This nascent

---

[125] Burhenne-Guilmin and Casey-Lefkowitz, 3 *YbIEL* (1992) 43.

[126] For the declarations made on adoption or signature see Sec VIII, *Handbook of the Convention on Biological Diversity* (3rd edn, Montreal, 2005), hereafter *CBD Handbook*.

[127] *Infra*, Ch 13.   [128] *Infra*, Ch 12.   [129] Ibid.

[130] Resolution 8/83 adopted by the 22nd FAO Conference on 23 November 1983 as amended by 'interpretations' adopted in 1989 and 1991. On this see Rose, in Bowman and Redgwell (eds), *International Law*

regime, however, did not represent a comprehensive global approach to protection of the earth's biodiversity and did little to protect resources found wholly within a state's national jurisdictional limits. The Convention on Biodiversity is therefore the first attempt to deal with the lacunae arising from the old system by establishing a more comprehensive and inclusive regime for conservation of biodiversity as such. While recognizing the intrinsic value of biodiversity to humankind and its future survival, at the same time it also allows for sustainable use of biological resources and incorporates many of the new conservatory principles and strategies that have developed in contemporary environmental law.

The WCED's Expert Group on Environmental Law was, however, the first to articulate specific legal principles requiring states to maintain ecosystems for the functioning of the biosphere 'in all its diversity', to maintain 'maximum biodiversity' by ensuring the survival and promoting the conservation of all species of flora and fauna in their natural habitat, based on observance of the optimum sustainable yield principle of exploitation.[131] This Group's proposals were followed by a report from UNEP's Executive Director on rationalization of existing international conventions on biodiversity which in turn, led UNEP's Governing Council in 1989 to initiate the drafting of a convention,[132] building on work already initiated by IUCN. However, although the need for such a convention was by then widely recognized, the difficulties encountered in negotiating the convention which was ultimately adopted have been described in detail by numerous informed commentators.[133]

Securing a consensus resulted in a text with many ambiguities and omissions, much bland language and qualified commitments. Major discrepancies in the views of developed and developing states emerged. Developing states envisaged the Convention as part of their agenda for restructuring world economic relations in order to gain access to resources, technology, and markets to enable sufficiently speedy and sustainable development to meet the needs of their populations.[134] They thus proposed establishment of (i) a special system of intellectual property rights; (ii) mechanisms

and Biodiversity (The Hague, 1996) 150. The 1991 modification still recognizes plant genetic resources as the 'heritage of mankind' but subject to the sovereignty of the state with property rights exercisable over them. In 2001 the Undertaking was replaced by a Treaty: see *infra*, section 5(7)(a) and discussion in Louka, *International Environmental Law: Fairness, Effectiveness, and World Order* (Cambridge, 2006), Ch 7.

[131] *Supra*, previous section.   [132] UNEP/GC/Res 15/34, 1989.

[133] E.g. Burhenne-Guilmin and Casey-Lefkowitz, 3 *YbIEL* (1992) 43; McConnell, *The Biodiversity Convention: A Negotiating History* (The Hague, 1996); Koester, 27 *EPL* (1997) 175; Svensson, in Sjøstedt et al (eds), *International Environmental Negotiations: Process, Issues and Context* (Stockholm, 1993) 164–91; Boyle, in Bowman and Redgwell (eds), *International Law and the Conservation of Biological Diversity* (The Hague, 1996) 33. On the Convention generally, see Hermitte, XXXVIII *AFDI* (1992) 844; Convention on Biological Diversity Handbook (CBD Secretariat, 2001) hereafter *CBD Handbook*; Klemm and Shine, *Biological Diversity Conservation and Law: Legal Mechanisms for Conserving Species and Ecosystems*, IUCN Environmental Policy & Law Paper Series No 29 (Gland, 1993); Redgwell, in Koufa (ed), *Protection of the Environment for the New Millenium, Thesaurus Acroasium*, Volume XXXI (Thessaloniki, 2002) 355–96; and 6:3 (1997) and 11:1 (2002) *RECIEL passim*.

[134] South Centre, *Environment and Development: Towards a Common Strategy of the South in the UNCED Negotiations and Beyond* (Geneva, 1991); Ansari and Jamal, 88 *Indian JIL* (2000) 134.

for compensating them for the use of biodiversity resources which their countries provided; (iii) mechanisms that would provide them with access to the biotechnology developed through use of the genetic resources provided by them; (iv) additional sources of funding to facilitate implementation of the Convention and access to technology. Most of these objectives were achieved.

Developed states also pursued economic objectives but from a different perspective. The USA contested the draft Convention's proposals concerning transfer of technology, financing, biotechnology, and access to resources and initially refused to sign it stating that the final text 'Threatened to retard biotechnology and undermine the protection of ideas'.[135] On signing the Final Act of the Conference[136] it drew attention to weaknesses in its provisions on intellectual property rights (IPR), finance (including the role of the GEF), environmental impact assessment, its relation to other conventions, and the scope of its obligations concerning the marine environment. It regretted that 'a number of issues of serious concern to the United States had not been adequately addressed' and that, therefore, in its view the text was seriously flawed 'whether because of the haste with which we have completed our work or the result of substantive disagreement'. It believed 'the hasty and disjointed approach' to the Convention's preparation had deprived delegations of the ability to consider it as a whole before adoption. Nonetheless, it confirmed that the United States 'strongly supports the conservation of biodiversity' and noted that it 'was an original proponent of a convention on this important subject', adding that 'we continue to view international cooperation in this area as extremely desirable'. In the event, President Clinton's administration signed the Convention but the USA has still not ratified it, and it seems unlikely at the time of writing that it will do so in the foreseeable future. Thus it joins only two other states—Somalia and Iraq—as non-parties to the Convention. Of the presently 191 Parties, thirty-two made individual or joint declarations concerning various aspects of the Convention either on its adoption or on signing or ratifying or both.[137]

The final text, in order to attract agreement, included many of the changes proposed by the developing states but omitted several substantive provisions on which no agreement could be reached. These included the precautionary principle, referred to only in the Preamble; responsibility for damage to biodiversity, whether in national or international areas—a provision rare, in any case, in international conventions; and a compilation of global lists of protected areas and species, as, inter alia, in the World Heritage Convention, and, for their particular purposes, the Bonn and Berne Conventions and CITES. These lists are left to the parties' national measures but could still be added in a subsequent Protocol or Protocols to the CBD. The process by which final agreement was reached on a text notably different from the fifth draft produced

---

[135] Statement by President Bush, USA, to the UNCED, 12 June 1992; see Coughlin, 31 *Col JTL* (1993) 337.

[136] The Convention was adopted by the Intergovernmental Negotiating Committee for a Convention on Biological Diversity, during its Fifth Session, held at Nairobi from 11–22 May 1992. It was opened for signature at Rio de Janeiro by all states and regional economic integration organizations.

[137] Excluding declarations made pursuant to Article 27 regarding dispute settlement: for text see Sec VIII, *CBD Handbook*.

by the INC,[138] and the trade-offs involved, have been described and illuminated by Koester amongst others.[139]

It is notable that none of the national experts involved at the start of this process recommended a new 'umbrella' convention though most did support elaboration of a new convention.[140] As Koester points out 'The Convention represents a North/South political compromise and hence the art of the possible and should be assessed bearing this in mind although judgments vary', as indeed they do. He notes, for example, the view of the US delegation's chief legal negotiator that for the reasons outlined earlier, the text would 'cause the utmost distress for international lawyers and policymakers'[141] and of Boyle's guarded support for the US view of its unsatisfactory nature,[142] but that, on the other hand, an IUCN lawyer, who was a main author of the IUCN's Draft Convention, considered that it could 'be hailed as a landmark from several points of view'[143] and that others support this view, though not without qualification.[144] Koester's own view is that as the Convention is process-oriented it can be considered, from that perspective, a success given the large number of parties, which include developed and developing states and those with economies in transition.[145] Other commentators taking a more positive view have noted that a treaty is only useful if it results in measures that would not otherwise have been taken[146] and that 'The most effective treaties are not necessarily those that are the most precisely drafted',[147] whilst an NGO representative from India considered that it is likely to become one of the world's most significant treaties.[148] In contrast a French legal expert has suggested that as the final text was one that included contradictory compromises, losing sight of its original objective, its ecological objectives might have been more effectively achieved by simply extending existing international instruments to cover biodiversity aspects.[149] We shall return to this wide range of views in our final conclusions.

---

[138] UNEP/Bio Div/N7-ING 5/2 (1992).

[139] Head of the Danish delegation at all the CBD negotiation meetings. He notes that the role of UNEP's then Executive Director, Dr MK Tolba, in facilitating the final agreement has been remarked upon by several writers. See Koester, 27 *EPL* (1997) 175, 181.

[140] Ad hoc Working Group of Experts on Biological Diversity convened by UNEP in 1988. UNEP acted as Secretariat for the negotiating process.

[141] 27 *EPL* (1997) 175, 187.

[142] 'There is much sense in the US objections to the weakness and unsatisfactory nature of the Treaty text', in Bowman and Redgwell (eds), *International Law and the Conservation of Biological Diversity*, 48.

[143] 27 *EPL* (1997) 175, 187.

[144] E.g. Burhenne-Guilmin and Casey-Lefkowitz, 3 *YbIEL* (1992) 43; Burhenne-Guilmin and Glowka, 4 *YbIEL* (1993) 245; Stoell, in Kiss and Burhenne-Guilmin (eds), *A Law for the Environment: Essays in Honour of Wolfgang E. Burhenne* (Bonn, 1994) 33–7.

[145] The UN Secretary General took a similar view in relation to reform of aspects of the UN System, in coining the phrase 'reform is not an event but a process', as cited by Asadi, 30 *EPL* (2000) 2–17, 17. The process could, of course, be never ending.

[146] Sjöstedt, et al, *International Environmental Negotiations: Process, Issues and Context* (Stockholm, 1993) 184.

[147] Palmer, 86 *AJIL* 259 (1992) 269.

[148] Mc Dougall, in Hall (ed), *Intellectual property rights and the Biodiversity Convention: The Impact of GATT* (Bedford, 1995) 11; Koester, 27 *EPL* (1997) 175, 188.

[149] Hermitte, 38 *AFDI* (1992) 844–70.

On this last aspect, namely the Convention's relation to existing international agreements concerning nature protection, its provisions afford only vague guidance, as we shall see in our discussion below. It is possible, however, that the concept of biodiversity, as defined in the Convention, could become the 'organizing' or at least the 'integrating' concept for relating relevant existing agreements, both to bring them into closer relation with each other, by embodying common concepts, and to the aims of the Biodiversity Convention. This is likely to require either full use of the opportunities for effective cooperation which are provided by the Convention's new institutions and mechanisms, such as the Biodiversity Liaison Group outlined later, or establishment of new institutions and further conventions as proposed in various articles of the Biodiversity Convention. We shall discuss this further in Chapters 12 and 13.

A unique feature of the Biodiversity Convention is that its provisions are mostly expressed as overall goals, rather than precisely defined obligations.[150] Hence, its status, along with the Ozone and Climate Change and similar conventions discussed in Chapter 6, not as an 'umbrella' but as a 'Framework' convention, *viz.* one that lays down various guiding principles at the international level which states parties are required to take into account in developing national law and policy to implement its objectives, but to which can also be added subsequent *ad hoc* protocols on related issues laying down more specific and detailed requirements and standards. The Biodiversity Convention specifically provides in Article 28 that parties must cooperate in formulating protocols and then adopting them at their Conferences of the Parties (COPs). To date only the 2000 Cartagena Protocol on Biosafety, trailed in Article 19(3) of the Convention, has been concluded and is discussed further below.

5(3) OBJECTIVES OF THE BIODIVERSITY CONVENTION[151]

In general, it can be said that the Convention aims to achieve an equitable balancing of the interests of developed and developing states. Article 1 sets out as the Convention's three main objectives: (a) the conservation of biodiversity, (b) the sustainable use of its components, and (c) the fair and equitable sharing of the benefits arising from the utilization of genetic resources, leaving the details of law and policy required to achieve these to be subsequently developed, to the extent that this is not already provided for in existing international and regional agreements and national laws. Articles 6–20 of the Convention translate these guiding objectives into binding commitments in substantive provisions, which include key provisions on, inter alia, measures for conservation and sustainable use of biological diversity[152] and, in more guarded language, of its components,[153] both *in situ*[154] and *ex situ*;[155] incentives for the conservation and sustainable use of biological diversity;[156] research and training;[157] public awareness and education;[158] assessing the impacts of projects upon biological diversity;[159] regulating

---

[150] De Klemm, 26 *EPL* (1996) 247, 252.   [151] See Chandler, 3 *Col JILP* (1993) 141.
[152] Article 6.   [153] Article 10.   [154] Article 8.   [155] Article 9.   [156] Article 11.
[157] Article 12.   [158] Article 13.   [159] Article 14.

access to genetic resources;[160] access to and transfer of technology;[161] and the provision of financial resources for national activities intended to achieve the Convention's objectives.[162]

The Convention clearly illustrates the extent to which biological diversity is an issue that cuts across all the issues covered in Chapters 12 and 13, inter alia. Both its Preambular assertions and substantive articles are relevant, for example, to combating deforestation and desertification, planning and management of land resources, managing fragile ecosystems on land and at sea, promoting sustainable utilization of all living resources and, as its parties have observed, it 'ushers in a new era' concerning access to genetic resources governed by the Convention.[163]

5(4) PROVISIONS OF THE CONVENTION RELEVANT TO ACHIEVEMENT OF ITS OBJECTIVES

As is inevitable in this style of framework treaty, with broad objectives of exceptionally wide scope, emerging from highly contentious negotiations among polarized groups, the Biodiversity Convention has many grey areas. Both its Preambular recitals and its substantive articles are expressed in broad terms, the requirements of which are often further weakened by such additional qualifications. These include such phrases as 'as appropriate', 'as far as possible', 'practicable in accordance with particular conditions and capabilities', 'taking into account special needs', 'likely to', 'grave and imminent', 'significant', and such limited requirements as to 'endeavour', 'encourage', 'promote', and 'minimize'.[164] Though these have been much criticized, without them the Convention would not have been concluded; states were clearly reluctant to accept more precise commitments and anxious to postpone to further negotiation or national decision-making clarification of the details of such commitments. We must look, therefore, to related agreements, protocols, and annexes to the Convention, as well as to state practice in implementing it at national, regional, and international levels before any meaningful evaluation can be made of its success. Particularly important to this will be the extent to which both developed and developing countries fulfil each other's respective expectations—concerning provision of financial aid and technological transfers on the former's part and access to genetic resources on fair and equitable terms on the latter's. We must, in other words, look more to the implementation process than textual analysis of the Convention's provision in order to measure its contribution to conservation of biodiversity. But this does not mean that the latter does not have value, particularly in highlighting terms and issues where difficulties of interpretation and performance are likely to arise. In this respect the Convention's preambular declarations are as relevant as the substantive articles.

---

[160] Article 15.   [161] Article 16.   [162] Article 20.

[163] *Statement from the Conference of the Parties to the Convention on Biological Diversity to the Commission on Sustainable Development at its third session*, Annex to Decision 1/8, paras. 9–10.

[164] For detailed analysis of the Preamble and each article see Glowka et al, *Guide to CBD* and *CBD Handbook*.

(a) Significance of the Convention's Preamble

Preambular recitals, however vaguely expressed, are nonetheless important as a guide to the parties' intentions in adopting particular measures. It has been observed by an eminent authority that 'the interpretational conclusions to be drawn from the Preamble are as binding upon the parties as those from any other part of the treaty'[165] Many of the contentious issues were avoided rather than resolved by relegating them in opaque language to the Preamble and the question of their value in interpreting its substantive provisions thus arises, as the following examples illustrate.

(b) Intrinsic and other values of biodiversity[166]

The Preamble's first recital begins by recognizing, without further explanation, 'the intrinsic value of biological diversity', as well as a range of other values—ecological, genetic, social economic, scientific, educational, cultural, recreational, and aesthetic. It does not mention the problem of attributing value to genetically modified organisms (GMOs).[167] The other Preambular recitals refer to biodiversity, however, solely as a 'resource'. The substantive articles define 'biological resources' as including 'genetic resources organisms or parts thereof, populations or any other biotic component of ecosystems with actual or potential use or value to humanity', a more anthropocentric approach. The Preamble reinforces this in noting that conservation and sustainable use of biodiversity is critical for meeting the food, health, and other needs of the growing world population.

(c) Needs of developing countries

The Preamble recognizes 'the special needs of developing countries' for 'new and additional financial resources' and for 'appropriate' access to relevant technologies. It is widely perceived that these must certainly be provided for if there is to be a substantial increase in the world's ability to address biodiversity loss. Several articles of the Convention address these concerns. The Preamble also notes in this regard the 'special conditions' of the least developed countries and of small island states (susceptible to inundation resulting from possible sea-level rise), both of which groups' special interests are otherwise unacknowledged in the Convention's substantive articles, although the overriding priority of economic and social development and eradication of poverty for developing countries is recognized. Several of the latter, however, do provide for financial aid and transfer of technology, including biotechnology, but not to the

---

[165] Fitzmaurice, 33 *BYIL* (1957) 200, 229; Brownlie, *Principles of Public International Law* (5th edn, Oxford, 1998) 632, also notes that the Court's jurisprudence supports the view that the best guide to the parties common intention is the intention *as expressed in the text*; Aust, *Modern Treaty Law and Practice* (Cambridge, 1999) 185, is less convinced.

[166] Tinker, 28 *Vand JTL* (1995) 778, 800, notes the difficulties of valuing biodiversity as the value of genes, species, and ecosystems is little understood; there are both direct and indirect values, mere existence values, as yet unknown uses and store house values; i.e. preserving stocks of genes and micro-organisms that might permit organisms and ecosystems to recover. See also *Lyster's International Wildlife Law*, Ch 3.

[167] On this see, Tew, Kate, and Laird, 76 *Int Affairs* (2000) 241–65, who underline the different perceptions that value can have on access and benefit sharing arrangements.

extent that developing countries had hoped for, as we shall see. In general, however, since the Preamble does not create obligations, it is notably more ecocentric than the substantive articles, which reflect more anthropocentric concerns.

(d) The legal status of biodiversity: implications of common concern

This highly contentious issue has been resolved by 'affirming' in the Preamble only that 'the conservation of biodiversity is a common concern of humankind'. Although this is also the solution adopted in the Framework Convention on Climate Change,[168] the precise scope of this formulation of value remains obscure, as was no doubt the intention. As we saw in Chapter 3, at the very least it does provide some general basis for international action, giving all states an interest in, and the right to conserve, biodiversity and for the parties to the Convention, and even non-parties, to observe and comment upon the progress of others in fulfilling their respective obligations and responsibilities for this purpose, both within their own national jurisdiction and beyond it, as discussed below. The meetings of the Conference of the Parties (COP), at which non-party states and various international organizations (as well as governmental and non-governmental bodies qualified in relevant fields) can have observer status,[169] provides a forum in which criticism can be voiced and common problems and solutions discussed, now that the Convention is operational. Much depends on effective use of these processes if the Convention is to achieve its aims. Adoption of this approach also makes it clear that biological resources are neither shared resources nor common property available for appropriation and use by all, as are migratory species of animals or fish which cross national boundaries or are found in the high seas, the conservatory problems concerning which are discussed in Chapters 12 and 13.

(e) The precautionary approach and inter-generational equity

The Preamble and Article 2 on 'Use of Terms' are the repository of the only references in the Convention to these important conservatory principles, whose legal significance is considered in other chapters of this work.[170] However, the Preamble does not refer to these two principles in the terms used in the Rio Declaration. Whereas the latter states that 'the right to *development* must be fulfilled so as to equitably meet the developmental *and* environmental needs of present and future generations',[171] the Convention's Preamble merely expresses, and only in its last recital, the parties 'determination' 'to conserve and sustainably use biological diversity for the *benefit* of present and future generations', omitting the reference to development and thus giving it a more environmental perspective. This rather weakly expressed inter-generational perspective is only partially reinforced by the definition of 'sustainable use' laid down in Article 2, requiring use of biological diversity in a way that maintains its potential 'to meet *the needs and aspirations* of present and future generations'.[172]

---

[168] *Supra*, Ch 10.   [169] Article 23(5).   [170] See esp Ch 3.   [171] Emphasis added.
[172] Emphasis added.

Second, whilst the Rio Declaration calls for a 'precautionary approach', expressly stating that 'when there are threats of serious or irreversible damage, lack of full scientific certainty shall not be used as a reason for postponing cost effective measures to prevent environmental degradation',[173] the Convention's Preamble merely notes that 'where there is a threat of significant reduction or loss of biodiversity, lack of full scientific certainty should not be used as a reason for postponing measures to avoid or minimize such threat'. In both cases the formulation is significantly weaker than in the Rio instrument and, incidentally, the more robust approaches in recent environmental conventions which are discussed in other chapters of this work—though the failure to cite the precautionary principle explicitly is to some extent offset by the Convention's provisions on environmental impact assessment. Moreover, the substantive articles of the Convention are also ambiguous, as we shall see. The Preamble thus provides little encouragement for application of the Rio principles to biodiversity conservation, though it is possible for any related agreements to apply these Rio principles more effectively, as is illustrated in Chapters 12 and 13, so as to further the aims of sustainable use of biological resources.

5(5) JURISDICTIONAL SCOPE

As observed earlier, the Convention applies to biodiversity from all sources, viz terrestrial, marine, and other aquatic sources. It also distinguishes, in Article 4, between its application to the components of biodiversity found within the territory of a state party, which they must protect, and processes and activities carried out under their jurisdiction or control regardless of where their effects occur, which they must at least identify and monitor, both within their territories and beyond the limits of national jurisdiction. So far as rights within their own territories are concerned Article 3 reiterates Principle 21 of the 1972 Stockholm Declaration but omits the developmental aspects introduced by the Rio Principle 2 formulation of this right.[174] Thus it merely recognizes the sovereign right of states to exploit their own resources, i.e. within their own territory, pursuant to their own environmental policies, subject to ensuring that activities within their jurisdiction or control do not cause harm to other states or areas beyond their national jurisdictional limits. The legal implications of this 'responsibility' are unclear since no guidelines are provided, again reflecting the disagreements during the negotiations between developed and developing states.[175]

The view of the developed states who did not want a generalized declaration of principles is evidenced by the interpretive declaration made by the UK stating that this 'Principle' was intended to apply only to the Biodiversity Convention.[176] This has resulted in a somewhat perfunctory treatment of the transboundary issue since

---

[173] Principle 15, on which see *supra*, Ch 3, section 4.   [174] See *supra*, Ch 3, section 4(2).

[175] *Supra*, Ch 3, section 4.

[176] The UK made a Declaration to the effect that Article 3 sets out a guiding principle to be taken into account in the implementation of the Convention, i.e. that it does not create a general principle of international law.

customary international law, as well as several international agreements, at least require notification and consultation between states. Moreover, in the view of some authorities, permanent sovereignty now includes, as a minimum, a duty to cooperate for the good of the international community.[177] Article 5 does require states to cooperate, directly or through international organizations concerning areas beyond national jurisdiction and other matters of mutual interest for conservation and sustainable use of biological diversity, but this is too general a provision to clarify issues concerning liability for transboundary harm in the absence of any relevant guidance from other provisions or direct invocation of the precautionary principle. These lacunae do not mean that states can disregard the possible consequences of their actions since Article 14 requires parties, albeit only 'as far as possible and appropriate', to 'introduce appropriate procedures' requiring environmental impact assessment of proposed projects 'likely to have significant adverse impacts on biological diversity with a view to avoiding or minimizing such effects', and 'to introduce appropriate arrangements to ensure that the environmental consequences of its programmes and policies that are likely to have significant adverse impacts on biological diversity are duly taken into account'.[178] Though this provision is weakened by use of vague terms such as 'likely to', it does apply to assessments within national boundaries, not solely, as does the 1991 EIA Convention,[179] to transboundary effects. However, Article 14 does not create so precise an obligation as regards the kinds of activities to be assessed or the documentation required. By leaving much detail to the individual judgement of states parties, as well as requiring them to act only 'as far as possible and appropriate' to assess whether or not particular projects and programmes are 'likely to have a significant adverse impact', the parties may well escape any form of EIA, particularly when the possible risks may be long-term and difficult to predict.

5(6) OBLIGATIONS CONSTRAINING THE EXERCISE OF NATIONAL SOVEREIGNTY

As the Convention applies, within the jurisdictional scope outlined in the previous section, to all processes and activities significantly impacting on conservation and sustainable use, some limitations on national sovereignty inevitably follow. These especially affect the conservatory obligations set out in Articles 5–10 and in particular in Articles 8–10 which relate to *in situ* and *ex situ* conservation and sustainable use of the components of biodiversity respectively and will be considered in these contexts.

(a) Sustainable use[180]

This, it will be recalled, means using the components of biodiversity 'in a way and at a rate that does not lead to the long-term decline of biological diversity' and in so

---

[177] Handl, 1 *YbIEL* (1990) 32.   [178] Article 14(1)(b).   [179] *Supra*, Ch 3, section 4(3).

[180] On the background of the concept and the ambiguities inherent in the term, see Johnston, in Bowman and Redgwell (eds), *International Law and the Conservation of Biological Diversity*, 51–69, and see further, *supra*, Ch 3, section 2(2)(c).

doing 'meet the needs and aspirations of present and future generations'. Some of the basic features of sustainable use include: monitoring of use; management on a flexible basis attuned to the goals of observing biological unity, adopting a holistic ecosystem approach; restoring areas of depleted biodiversity; adoption of both an integrated and a precautionary approach; ensuring inter-generational equity; and basing measures on scientific research. Certainly the various strategies outlined earlier in this chapter have identified these requirements but at present it is not clear to what extent state practice on these aspects has developed the concept of sustainable use beyond its formulation as a guiding principle into a legally binding obligation and if so what its content is. The main purpose of using this term in the Convention was indeed to allow a variety of flexible approaches so long as their goal is achieved. Nonetheless, this said, Article 6 of the Convention does require parties, to this end, to develop national strategies, plans, or programmes for conservation and rational use, or adapt existing ones to reflect the Convention's requirements and integrate conservation and sustainable use into relevant sectoral or cross-sectoral plans, programmes, and policies (though only to the extent of their capabilities), whilst Article 7 specifically requires identification of components of biodiversity 'important' for conservation and use, which are indicated, in very general categories, on the list provided in Annex I.[181] These must also be monitored, with particular regard to those requiring 'urgent' conservation measures and those offering the 'greatest potential for sustainable use'. Finally, parties are required to identify processes and categories of activities which have, or are likely to have 'significant adverse impacts' on conservation and sustainable use of biodiversity, monitor their effects and 'maintain and organize' by 'any mechanism', the data derived therefrom. These provisions of the Convention have been amplified by the Addis Ababa Principles and Guidelines for the Sustainable Use of Biodiversity were adopted at the 7th Conference of the Parties to the CBD in 2004.[182]

(b) Conservation of biological diversity and biological resources

This is the prime objective of the Convention. The requirements are broad. Parties must adopt national strategies, plans or programmes for their conservation and sustainable use and integrate these and sustainable use into their national sectoral or cross-sectoral plans, programmes, and policies, monitor identified components of biodiversity, and identify processes and categories of activities impacting adversely upon it. But the most significant obligations placed on parties concern *in situ*, and to a lesser extent, *ex situ* conservation which are dealt with under Articles 8 and 9.

'*Ex situ* conservation' means, according to Article 2, 'conservation of components of biological diversity outside their natural habitats' (i.e. removing specimens or parts thereof from the wild and keeping them in a viable conditions elsewhere; generally in zoos, aquaria, and wildlife parks). '*In situ* conservation' means 'the conservation of

---

[181] These relate to specified ecosystems and habitats; species and communities; described genomes and genes which are either important or threatened.
[182] See Decision VI/45.

ecosystems and natural habitats and the maintenance and recovery of viable populations of species in their natural surroundings, and in the case of domesticated or cultivated species in the surroundings where they have developed their distinctive properties'. '*In situ* conditions' refers to the situation 'where genetic resources exist within ecosystems and natural habitats, and, in the case of domesticated or cultivated species, in the surroundings where they have developed their distinctive properties'. The interpretation and application of these definitions thus rests largely on scientific advice concerning the viability of species and habitats. Article 9(a) makes it clear that *ex situ* conservation is predominantly to be used for the purpose of complementing *in situ* measures.

Article 8 lists the wide range of measures required to protect the diffuse elements which collectively constitute the essential elements of *in situ* biodiversity. They include (a) protected areas; (b) regulation and management of biological resources both inside and outside protected areas; (c) protection of ecosystems and natural habitats and populations of species; (d) environmentally sound and sustainable development in areas adjacent to protected areas; (e) rehabilitation of degraded areas and recovery of species; (f) control of use and release of modified living organisms when they are likely to have adverse environmental impacts; (g) protection of threatened species and populations; (h) regulation or management of processes and activities which threaten biodiversity.

After an exhaustive analysis of existing approaches to *ex situ* conservation practices in various parts of the world, Warren concluded that though *ex situ* conservation in the past has been regarded as a cul de sac and thus most conservation effort has concentrated on habitat protection as the main device for maintaining species, the view that *ex* and *in situ* measures are complementary is now widely accepted but their relative importance is irrelevant; rather what matters is that the optimum blend of measures to deal with individual management problems should be sought. Moreover, in the case of endangered species, prohibitions on taking all wild specimens can be unhelpful, when there is a need to remove specimens from the wild for captive breeding in order to preserve and restore them. Warren's survey of existing relevant laws, international conventions, and European Union measures establishes that exceptions are usually made for these purposes, as in some international agreements.[183]

In both the cases of *in situ* and *ex situ* conservation, parties are required (under Articles 8(m) and 9(e) respectively) to cooperate in providing financial and other support for the conservation measures listed, especially to developing countries. In the case of the latter, they must also cooperate in establishing and maintaining *ex situ* conservation facilities in developing countries.

---

[183] See Warren, in Bowman and Redgwell (eds), *International Law and the Conservation of Biological Diversity*, esp 135–42.

(c) Alien species

Various problems are posed by the introduction of so-called 'alien,' 'exotic', or 'non-indigenous species' into the environment.[184] Despite recognition of the ecological damage caused by such introductions, the pursuant loss of biological diversity and the potential for severe economic and developmental losses, such introductions seem to be increasing. As Rayfuse notes, international trade has enhanced the pathways for introduction of invasive alien species, including through ballast water—since 2004 the subject of an IMO Convention—raw wood products and packaging materials, and intentional imports for the pet and ornaments trade.[185] There are also dangers in manipulating nature by transplanting specimens bred in captivity into *in situ* locations or introducing some species from the wild, into such locations, whether accidentally or deliberately. Examples of disastrous results abound. Views also differ concerning whether the main aim of *ex situ* conservation should be to provide a store of species and genetic material for further return to nature, despite the difficulties involved in current lack of knowledge concerning the effects. Particular concern is engendered by growth of artificial breeding and gene manipulation, since not all agree that the scientific basis is yet adequate for evaluation of environmental risk to be made with confidence.

International concern relating to introductions of alien species has been evidenced for some years by inclusion of reference to the problem in a growing number of instruments at international and regional levels and concerns expressed in several international organizations.[186] Several sets of recommendations, guidelines, codes of conduct, and the like have now been promulgated by, inter alia, FAO and IMO, as well as the Council of Europe.[187] But there is an inconsistency in treatment of the problems involved, particularly in relation to the specifics of implementation and key issues such as control or elimination after release, or the questions of responsibility for damage resulting from such introductions, remain unaddressed.[188] However, international regulation of invasive alien species has been piecemeal and inconsistent, lacking common definitions and approaches. For example, alien invasive species are included in

---

[184] Ibid; Glowka and De Klemm, 26 *EPL* (1996) 247–54; Perrault and Muffett, 11 *RECIEL* (2001) 211; Rayfuse, in Bodansky, Brunnee, and Hey (eds) *The Oxford Handbook of International Environmental Law*, 385–7.

[185] Rayfuse, ibid, 386. Thus, for example, CBD COP7 called on Parties to consider risks of invasive species introduction when reviewing international, bilateral and regional arrangements, such as trade arrangements, and called on the CBD Executive Secretary to collaborate with the WTO Secretariat: see Decision VII/13, paragraph 5(d)–(e).

[186] Glowka and De Klemm, 26 *EPL* (1996) 247; Perrault and Muffett, 11 *RECIEL* (2001) 211. See also the range of instruments and institutions identified in the CBD SBSTTA's in-depth review of ongoing work on alien species that threaten ecosystems, habitats or species

[187] Ibid; see also Rayfuse, in Bodansky, Brunnee, and Hey (eds) *The Oxford Handbook of International Environmental Law*, 385–7.

[188] In their survey of existing instruments, Glowka and De Klemm note that similar differences in coverage arise in relation to national laws on the subject: Glowka and De Klemm, ibid, 249–50.

instruments regulating pests[189] and have been addressed in instruments addressed to particular pathways through which invasive alien species may be introduced. For example, Chapter 17 of Agenda 21 acknowledged the need to develop rules on ballast water discharges, and in 2004 an IMO Convention for the Control and Management of Ships' Ballast Water and Sediments was concluded which calls on States to prevent, minimize, and ultimately eliminate the transfer of harmful aquatic organisms and pathogens through such ballast and sediments.[190]

Article 8(h) of the Biological Diversity Convention calls on parties to 'prevent the introduction of, control or eradicate those alien species which threaten ecosystems, habitats or species', without offering guidance on the criteria for determining the occurrence of a 'threat'. Invasive alien species are a cross-cutting issue under the Convention, with other articles also relevant, notably Article 7 requiring parties, particularly for purposes of Articles 8–10, to identify and monitor the components of biodiversity and to identify processes and categories of activities which have or are likely to have significant adverse impacts on conservation and use of biological diversity and monitor their effects through sampling and other techniques.

Although there have been calls for the conclusion of a Protocol on invasive species,[191] thus far the response of the COP has been to develop, through the Convention's Subsidiary Body on Scientific, Technical and Technological Advice (SBSTTA), guiding principles for the prevention, introduction, and mitigation of impacts of alien species and to establish, again through SBSTTA, an Ad Hoc Technical Expert Group on Gaps and Inconsistencies in the International Regulatory Framework in Relation to Invasive Species. COP6 adopted 'Guiding Principles', annexed to its decision on alien species,[192] to be applied 'as appropriate' in the context of activities aimed at implementing Article 8(h). These principles call for measures of prevention and mitigation, including control and eradication, and require that such measures 'should, as appropriate' be based on precautionary and ecosystem approaches.[193] The COP has also requested the Global Invasive Species Programme, in developing a programme to deal with such species, to ensure consistency with the Article 8(h) provisions and relevant provisions of other articles, including Article 15 on access to genetic resources.[194] Convention parties have been encouraged to develop, inter alia, country-driven

---

[189] See the 1951 FAO International Plant Protection Convention, as revised, and the 1959 Agreement Concerning Cooperation in the Quarantine of Plants and Their Protection against Pests and Diseases.

[190] See *supra*, Ch 13.

[191] Glowka and De Klemm, 26 *EPL* (1996) 247 after reviewing global and regional treaties referencing introduction of non-indigenous species and relevant national legislation, propose that, because it is a global problem, the COP should address this issue as part of its medium-term programme with a view to adopting a Protocol or Annex. COP Decision V/8, paragraph 16, calls for consideration of the possibility of developing an international instrument.

[192] Decision VI/23 (2000). The Guidelines had been adopted on an interim basis from COP5, Decision V/8.

[193] Australia objected to the wording of the precautionary approach contained in Guiding Principles 1 and 10, and entered a formal objection to the wording and to the consensus adoption of the text in the light of such objection: see UNEP/CBD/COP/6/20, paras 294–324.

[194] See Decision V/8.

projects at all levels (national, regional, subregional, and international) to address this issue and have requested the financial mechanism established pursuant to the Convention to provide adequate support for these.[195] Gaps in the international regulatory framework were considered by the ad hoc technical experts group established in 2004 with recent COP decisions[196] stressing the need for cooperation with and participation in other treaty instruments addressed to invasive alien species such as the International Plant Protection Convention and the Ballast Water Convention noted above. Rather than seek to plug the gap itself, in 2008 the COP called on other bodies, including the WTO, the the World Organization for Animal Health, and the FAO, to 'note' the lack of international standards pertaining to non-pest invasive alien species.[197] The various pathways for introduction are recognized in the request to the CBD's Executive Secretary to collaborate with IMO, ICAO, and the CITES secretariat, to address regulatory gaps but also to reduce duplication of effort. The 2004 Guidelines will thus continue to provide the framework for national implementation of Article 8(h) under the Convention for the foreseeable future, with parties encouraged to submit 'case studies, lessons learned and best practice' in their implementation of the Guidelines with respect to risk assessment, monitoring and surveillance, management of pathways, and on restoration and rehabilitation, with SBSTTA playing a further technical role in the identification and dissemination of best practice.[198]

(d) Role of indigenous peoples rights in relation to biodiversity[199]

Increasing recognition of the interrelationship between the natural environment, sustainable development, and the well-being of indigenous peoples is evident in general international law and in the Biological Diversity Convention. ILO Convention 169 Concerning Indigenous and Tribal Peoples in Independent Countries gives indigenous peoples the right to be consulted and to participate in national and regional development plans and strategies, for their cultures and relationship to the environment to be respected, their rights to natural resources in their lands safeguarded, and to participate also in use, management, and conservation of these resources.[200] While significant as the only treaty in force that specifically addresses indigenous peoples' rights and interests, it has not been widely ratified by countries with indigenous populations.[201] Until the Rio Conference, developed states had also been reluctant to accept the value, now recognized in Agenda 21, of 'holistic, traditional scientific knowledge of their lands, natural resources and environment'.[202] Further recognition of rights and standards in this field came in 2007, after nearly twenty-five years of contentious negotiations,

---

[195] See, for example, Decision III/9 and Decision IV/1.6.
[196] See Decisions VIII/27 (2006) and IX/4 (2008).   [197] Decision IX/4 (2008).   [198] Ibid.
[199] See Shelton, 5 *YbIEL* (1994) 77; Woodliffe, in Bowman and Redgwell (eds), *International Law and the Conservation of Biological Diversity*, Ch 13.
[200] Sutherland, 27 *EPL* (1997) 13–30, 16; see also Triggs, in Zillman, Lucas, and Pring (eds), *Human Rights in Natural Resource Development* (Oxford, 2002).
[201] For two Latin American studies see Aguilar Fabra and Fernandes, in Boyle and Anderson (eds), *Human Rights Approaches to Environmental Protection* (Oxford, 1996), Chs 13–14.
[202] Agenda 21, Ch 26.1.

with the adoption[203] by the United Nations General Assembly of a Declaration on the Rights of Indigenous Peoples,[204] including those relevant to environment and development. The preamble recognizes 'that respect for indigenous knowledge, cultures and traditional practices contributes to sustainable and equitable development and proper management of the environment' while Article 25 confirms the right of indigenous peoples 'to maintain and strengthen their distinctive spiritual with their traditionally owned or otherwise occupied and used lands, territories, waters and coastal seas and other resources and to uphold their responsibilities to future generations in this regard'. Article 29 acknowledges that indigenous peoples 'have the right to the conservation and protection of the environment and the productive capacity of their lands or territories and resources' and links this to a state obligation to provide assistance programmes for such conservation and protection.[205] While no doubt influential in terms of its reflection of the aspirations of indigenous peoples, the Declaration is not binding, with four developed states with indigenous populations voting against the resolution (Australia, Canada, New Zealand, and the United States), and a number of other states expressing reservations owing to the Declaration's provisions on, inter alia, land and resources.[206]

While recognizing 'the close and traditional dependence of many indigenous local communities embodying traditional lifestyles on biological resources', the Preamble and Article 8(j) of the Biological Diversity Convention notably avoid the use of either the terms 'rights' or 'peoples'. Moreover, the Convention does not define 'indigenous communities', there is no cross-referencing to any definitions provided in ILO or other conventions,[207] and the most recent COP (2008) merely 'took note' of the 2007 Declaration.[208] The ambiguous language of the Preamble and Article 8(j) arises from the fact that international law on indigenous peoples and protection of the environment of indigenous peoples remains controversial.[209]

The Convention Preamble recognizes only 'the desirability' of 'sharing equitably' the benefits arising from use of traditional knowledge. Article 8(j) goes little further. It provides that each party shall 'as far as possible and appropriate' and subject to its national legislation, 'respect, preserve and maintain knowledge, innovations and practices of indigenous and local communities embodying traditional lifestyles relevant for the conservation and sustainable use of biological diversity and promote their

---

[203] UNGA Res 61/295, adopted on 13 September 2007, by 143 votes in favour, 4 against (Australia, Canada, New Zealand, and the United States) and 11 abstentions (Azerbaijan, Bangladesh, Bhutan, Burundi, Colombia, Georgia, Kenya, Nigeria, Russian Federation, Samoa, and Ukraine). For explanation of the voting see A/61/PV 107.

[204] The Declaration was drafted by the Working Group on Indigenous Populations of the UN Sub-Commission on the Prevention of Discrimination and Protection of Minorities, within the context of the UN's 1994–2004 Decade of the World's Indigenous Peoples.

[205] See also Article 29(2) which prohibits the storage or disposal of hazardous materials on lands or territories of indigenous peoples without their 'free, prior and informed consent'.

[206] See n 203 above.   [207] The most important of these is ILO Convention No 169 (1989).

[208] Decision IX/13 (2008).

[209] For an overview of progress in this field see Sutherland, 27 EPL (1997) 13–30.

wider application with the approval and involvement of the holders of such knowledge, innovations and practices and encourage the equitable sharing of the benefits arising from the utilization of such knowledge, innovations and practices'.[210] The Convention says nothing about the important role played by indigenous communities and local people in the *in situ* management of wildlife and habitats.[211]

The CBD's COP has established an Ad Hoc Working Group to address implementation of Article 8(j) which could eventually lead to clarification of some issues.[212] Thus far, voluntary guidelines have been adopted for the conduct of cultural, environmental, and social impact assessment of development planned for, or likely to impact on, sacred sites and lands and waters traditionally occupied or used by indigenous and local communities.[213] Parties involved in the Working Group are merely 'encouraged' to include in their delegations representatives of concerned indigenous and local communities with lifestyles relevant to conservation and sustainable use of biological diversity. It seems unlikely that the COP will provide the vehicle for further clarification of indigenous and local communities rights; rather it is endeavouring to ensure that, to the extent permitted by the parties, it will provide the forum[214] within which such communities can participate and thus influence the parties when developing policies, guidelines or protocols impinging upon their interests, including their lands and resources, contributing their own unique perspective and knowledge.

(e) Living modified organisms (LMOs) and biosafety[215]

Article 8(g) requires parties to establish or maintain means to regulate risks arising from biotechnology, taking into account those associated with use and release of LMOs, which are likely to have adverse environmental impacts that could affect conservation and sustainable use of biotechnology, taking into account also the risks to human health. This obligation is not geographically limited under the Convention, so it applies not only to components of biological diversity within the limits of national jurisdiction, but also to processes and activities, regardless of where they occur, which are carried out under its jurisdiction and control. This article is closely related to

---

[210] Nor has significant progress been made through the Article 8(j) Ad Hoc Working Group, which is collaborating with the Ad Hoc Open-ended Working Group on Access and Benefit Sharing to negotiate an international regime on access and benefit sharing which is relevant to traditional knowledge, innovations and practices associated with genetic resources, and in developing fair and equitable sharing of benefits arising from their utilization.

[211] See Harland, *Killing Game* (Westport, 1994).

[212] Article 8(j) is a cross-cutting issue under the Convention. Thus decisions pertinent to indigenous and local communities have also been taken pursuant to Articles 10(c), 15, 16, 17(2), 18(4), and 19, as well as under thematic work programmes relating to marine and coastal, agricultural, inland water and forest biodiversity, and biodiversity of dry and sub-humid lands.

[213] Adopted at COP7; Decision VII/16 F COP9 (2008) also took note of further revised draft elements of a code of ethical conduct to ensure respect for the cultural and intellectual heritage of indigenous and local communities relevant for the conservation and sustainable use of biological diversity, on which comments are sought for possible adoption at COP10. For text see the Annex to ibid.

[214] There is also close cooperation between the CBD and the United Nations Permanent Forum on Indigenous Issues.

[215] On trade-related aspects see *infra*, Ch 14, section 9.

Article 19 concerning the handling of biotechnology and its benefits. The responsibility for taking measures falls on the parties. The Convention does not define 'LMOs' but it was understood that it includes 'genetically modified organisms' (GMOs), provided these are alive.[216] There are two distinct kinds of LMOs. The first category includes organisms whose genetic material has been modified by traditional or conventional techniques such as plant breeding or artificial insemination; the second includes organisms whose genetic material has been modified more directly, e.g. through recombitant DNA technology; these are the ones generally referred to as GMOs.[217] The extent to which LMOs developed from modern biotechnological techniques to present environmental and health risks is controversial. Determining the likelihood of risk requires scientific input and a precautionary approach based on assessment, consequent regulation, and either management or control of the risks. A major factor in US reluctance to ratify the Convention was its fear that this provision might inhibit the application and commercialization of biotechnologies, fail to protect intellectual-property rights, and reduce royalty payments, especially to pharmaceutical companies which need biological resources as raw materials for development of drugs.

Although the Convention offers no guidance, there exists a considerable number of policy guidelines developed through FAO, OECD, UNIDO, and the WHO which could form a basis for developing future regulation. Implementing effective programmes involves not only issues of law and economics, but of biological science. Thus many developing countries are likely to need help on all these aspects as well as financial and technical assistance. It also involves fulfilment of obligations under Article 19(4) to provide information on available use, safety, and environmental impact information when a specific LMO is exported to another party. Article 19 relates to handling of biotechnology generally and distribution of its benefits. Article 19(3) requires parties to consider the need for a protocol setting out procedures on safe transfer, handling, and use of LMOs that may have an adverse effect on conservation and sustainable use of biodiversity, including in particular provision for advanced informed agreement.[218]

The first COP of the CBD parties in 1994 initiated consideration of a protocol.[219] Negotiations focused on such issues as objectives, definitions, scope, application of the Advanced Informed Agreement Notification procedures, relation to agreements other than the protocol, aspects of risk, relevant national authorities, capacity building, illegal traffic, liability and redress, and the financial mechanisms and resources. Disagreement on most of these and other issues was such that concern was expressed that if an insufficiently precautionary approach was adopted to the little understood impacts of LMOs on biodiversity-rich countries, the resultant instrument would be no more than a mechanism for information exchange. Safety, not trade, should be its main objective on this view, based on the precautionary principle—otherwise the

---

[216] See 22 *EPL* (1992) 205, 206.   [217] Glowka, et al, *A Guide to the CBD*, 45–6.

[218] McGraw, 11 *RECIEL* (2002) 19, refers to criticisms of this choice as reflecting an absence of 'sound science'—why not a Protocol on traditional knowledge or on alien species, for example?

[219] 28 *EPL* (1998) 268–73.

importing countries would bear an unfair burden.[220] The inability to reach agreement reflected the clash between the trade interests of the USA (which, though not a party to the CBD, participated in the negotiation of the Protocol) and other GMO crop exporters and the environmental concerns of others, as well as the treatment of commodities and domestic regimes in contrast to international regulatory regimes; the USA insisting that WTO rules must prevail over any biosafety agreement.[221] Such significant disagreements prevented adoption at Cartagena in 1999 but a resumed session in Montreal in 2000 achieved consensus, with the Protocol duly adopted on 29 January 2000 and opened for signature on 15 May 2000.[222] It entered into force on 11 September 2003 and presently has 147 parties. Its provisions are considered in more detail below, while potential conflicts between the Protocol and WTO law are discussed in Chapter 14.

5(7) INCENTIVES TO PARTICIPATION AND COMPLIANCE

A remarkable feature of the Convention is the incentives it offers to developed and developing states to participate, to implement it, and to cooperate in balancing their different interests. Inclusion of provisions safeguarding access to genetic resources was an essential element so far as developed states were concerned. Sharing the financial burden and other burdens of conserving resources by enhancing access to funding, technology, information, training, education and scientific research, enabling them to conserve and sustainably exploit their biological resources, were key objectives of the developing states, as we have seen.[223] Compromises were arrived at on all these goals in the interests of consensus.

(a) Fair and equitable sharing of benefits

Fair and equitable sharing of resources is the second of the Convention's main objectives and its implementation will be a key to its success. Whilst again confirming, in Article 15(1), states' sovereign rights to natural resources and their authority to determine access to genetic resources, parties are required by Article 15(7) to take measures aimed at sharing in a fair and equitable way, not only the results of research and development, but the benefits arising from commercial and other uses of these resources with the party providing them, upon mutually agreed terms. It thus leaves the balancing to further negotiation. Provider parties are also required to create conditions facilitating access by other parties for environmentally sound uses (as no criteria are provided for 'soundness' the provider party is left to apply its own) and must also

---

[220] Ibid, 273.

[221] Some of these issues are addressed in the *EC—Biotech Case* in the WTO, and considered in Chapter 14 below. On the background to the Protocol see 29 *EPL* (1999) 84–5, and Draft Text Submitted by the Chair, ibid, 138.

[222] See Stoll, 10 *YbIEL* (1999) 82; Quereshi, 49 *ICLQ* (2000) 535 and *infra*, Ch 14.

[223] Ansari and Jamal, 88 *Indian JIL* (2000) 134; Nayar and Ong, in Bowman and Redgwell (eds), *International Law and the Conservation of Biological Diversity*, Ch 12.

minimize restrictions on access which would defeat the Convention's aims. Other paragraphs address the benefits deriving from actual use of the genetic resources, which might include participation in scientific research based on these (Article 15(b)) as well as those referred to in Article 5(7). More specific benefits are referred to in other articles, including Articles 16(3), 19(1), and 19(2), concerning various uses of relevant technology. It remains to be seen whether the provider parties will fulfil their part of the bargain in allowing access and whether parties seeking access will offer sufficient quid pro quo in terms of inducements such as technology transfer, participation in the scientific research involved, and other forms of genuine benefit sharing.

Meanwhile, the COP has confirmed that human genetic resources are not included within the Convention's scope[224] and concentrated on collecting and sharing information on all national and regional approaches to regulatory access to genetic resources and disseminating this. It has thus asked parties to supply the relevant information on their national legal, policy, and administrative measures in order to produce a survey, and appointed a regionally balanced expert panel to work on development of a common understanding of basic concepts and options for access and benefit-sharing on mutually agreed terms, including guiding principles, guidelines and codes of best practice for access and benefit sharing. These might address requirements for prior informed consent in provider countries; a clearly established mechanism for giving consent; mutually agreed terms on benefit sharing, intellectual-property rights, and technology transfer; reference to country of origin in patent applications; efficient permitting and regulatory procedures; and incentive measures to encourage the conclusion of contractual partnerships. It is possible, by analogy with UNEP's and IMO's practice, that some form of 'soft law' guidelines or codes may emerge from these initiatives in the long-term. Indeed, in 2002 the Bonn Guidelines were adopted as an attempt to streamline access and benefit-sharing procedures, but have served only further to burden the parties with a daunting checklist of procedures and requirements.[225]

In this context it is worth noting that cross-reference is frequently made to the FAO International Undertaking on Plant Genetic Resources for Food and Agriculture and its revision.[226] As Rose observes, the Biodiversity Convention's approach emerged from a conservation ethic and is concerned with all biological resources with emphasis on control of future foreign access to each state's biodiversity, whereas the finance and technology benefits derived by the Plant Genetic Resource (PGR) source states under the Biodiversity Convention can be used for any purpose, including such economic enterprises as logging or land clearance.[227] Under the PGR Undertaking the regime is based on uncontrolled access, modified by rewards for access in the form

---

[224] *CBD Handbook*, Sec IV, Decision II/11, para 2, ref Article 2, use of terms.

[225] For assessment see Etty, 2006 YBIEL 506 (2007).

[226] See Rose, in Bowman and Redgwell (eds), *International Law and the Conservation of Biological Diversity*, 150–156; Glowka et al, *A Guide to the CBD*, 78–9. In 2001 a Treaty on Plant Genetic Resources for Food and Agriculture was concluded, which entered in force on 29 June 2004 and at mid-2008 had 118 parties.

[227] Rose, op cit, 169.

of historic 'Farmer's Rights', backed by a fund, directed to conservation of PGRs.[228] The evident link between access to these resources and their conservation may not be realized in practice. It is possible that similar conclusions may be arrived at in relation to Article 15 of the Biodiversity Convention. It has to be recalled, however, that though Article 15 does recognize state sovereignty over these resources, their use and terms of access thereto remain a common concern of humankind; and that contracting parties must represent this interest at the COPs and within other institutions of the Convention which are outlined later. Article 15 is a key provision in achieving equitable sharing of the benefits of utilization: sovereignty is tempered by the requirements governing access which must observe the need for this. It is a core element of the incentives provided for participation and implementation of the Convention. Thus the policies pursued by the COP and codes produced by it could be an important means for achieving rights over and access to genetic resources and sharing the required equitable balancing of the interests involved in qualifying sovereign benefits of their use.

(b) Financial incentives

It was accepted at the start of negotiations that developing countries would require substantial assistance to enable them to implement the Convention and that the financial burden would have to be shared among all parties.[229] Agenda 21 estimated that in the period 1993–2000 about US$3.5 billion would be needed annually to fund required conservatory activities; others put this at US$17 billion. Article 20 places different responsibilities on all parties and on developed-state parties. Thus all parties must, but only 'in accordance with (their) capabilities', 'undertake' to provide 'financial support' and 'incentives' for implementation of the Convention,[230] subject to Article 11's qualifications concerning adoption of 'economically and socially sound measures'[231]—a phrasing described as 'subtle and deceptive',[232] since it allows for wide choice. What is really required are more specific and direct incentives and disincentives, with avoidance of so-called 'perverse' incentives which can have undesirable effects.

For the first time in any global environmental treaty, Article 20(2) lays down a clear obligation on the parties, not just an 'undertaking', to provide 'new and additional financial resources to enable developing state parties to meet the agreed full incremental costs to them of the implementing measures which fulfil the obligations of this Convention'. This provision, vital to the Convention's success, thus includes several ambiguities. The qualification that the source of funds be new and additional

---

[228] Rose, op cit. On related aspects such as of safeguarding intellectual property rights see *infra*, Ch 14; Walden, in Bowman and Redgwell (eds), *International Law and the Conservation of Biological Diversity*, 181, and Gollin, in World Resources Institute, *Biodiversity Prospecting* (Washington DC, 1993).

[229] See, Johnston, in Bowman and Redgwell (eds), *International Law and the Conservation of Biological Diversity*, 271–88.

[230] Article 20(1).

[231] On the wide variety of tools available see Glowka et al, *A Guide to the CBD*, 63–4.

[232] On its limitations see ibid, 63.

necessitates establishment of new funding mechanisms which are not part of exist-ing development assistance and do not undermine existing sources. Both the costs of conservation measures adopted by developing states and of measures to build up their administrations and develop necessary technology can be recovered by them, but this is not an unfettered right; such costs have to be 'agreed' upon between the developing country concerned and the financial mechanisms established under Article 21; more-over the measures taken must aim to achieve the Convention's obligations. In effect these new finances represent the inducement required to persuade developing coun-tries to conserve their genetic resources. This is underlined by the condition included in Article 20(4) which determines that 'the extent to which developing country par-ties will effectively implement their commitments under this Convention will depend on the effective implementation by developed country parties of their commitments under this Convention related to financial resources and transfer of technology'. The close linkage of performance to 'conservation obligations with provision of funding' is apparent but developing states use of any funds provided is, under Article 21(2), subject to monitoring and evaluation on a regular basis; both the COP and the fund-ing mechanism (GEF) play a role in this[233] since the latter has to ensure that measures for which funding is sought conform to policies, strategies, and priorities determined by the former.[234] In effect this modifies Article 3, since developing states are thus only free to decide their own environmental polices if they do not apply for fund-ing.[235] In 1997 the COP and the GEF adopted a Memorandum of Understanding between them to give effect to Article 21(1) of the Convention and paragraph 26 of the GEF Instrument, which provides that the COP assesses the amount of replenish-ment funds, on the basis of guidance given by the COP itself. It also covers cooper-ation between the Convention and the GEF.[236] It has been suggested that whether or not developing states observe this system, which means that their own policies become integrated into general international policy on utilization and conservation, will depend on whether the benefits of international funding exceed the benefits of utilization of the relevant resources or areas deriving from policies formulated solely at the national level.[237] Thus the Convention could become the source of funding pro-vided the activities in issue at least do provide for management or protection of bio-logical diversity. In this way this incentive is aimed at compensating the developing

---

[233] On the role of the restructured GEF see *supra*, Ch 2, section 4(4). The GEF has established *Operational Criteria for Enabling Activities: Biodiversity* (Washington, 2000), which have been revised on several occa-sions to take account of guidance from the COP.

[234] As required under Article 21(2), comprehensive guidance was issued at COP1 and at each subsequent COP this guidance has been refined and augmented: see, for example, Decision IX/31 (COP9, 2008). In add-ition there is regular review of the effectiveness of the financial mechanism, with a 3-year review cycle.

[235] Wolfrum (ed), *Enforcing Environmental Standards: Economic Mechanisms as Viable Means* (Berlin, 1996) 39–93.

[236] For the text, see *CBD Handbook*.

[237] Wolfrum (ed), *Enforcing Environmental Standards: Economic Mechanisms as Viable Means* (Berlin, 1996).

states concerned for losses deriving from reorientation of their current economic uses of such biological resources as rain forests.

(c) Access to and transfer of technology

Articles 16–19 deal with transfer of technology in several different senses. First, the parties undertake in Article 16(1) to provide or facilitate access and transfer to other parties of technologies 'that are relevant to the conservation and sustainable use of biological diversity or make use of genetic resources and do not cause significant damage to the environment'. Second, parties must take measures 'with the aim that' parties which provide genetic resources have access to and transfer of technology which makes use of those resources.[238] Third, parties must take measures to provide for the 'effective' participation in biotechnology research of those providing genetic resources, and to 'promote and advance priority access on a fair and equitable basis' to the results and benefits of biotechnologies based on the provision of genetic resources.[239] Transfer of technology provisions in earlier treaties, such as the 1982 UNCLOS, have usually been controversial, on several grounds. There is first the reluctance of governments to compel companies and private parties to transfer technologies that may not be commercially available; second there have been objections to the terms on which any transfer will take place, particularly if this is not at market prices; and, third, there is the question of intellectual property rights which may be lost if transfer is required. The Biodiversity Convention attempts to deal with some of these issues.

Transfers under Article 16(1) must be on 'fair and most favourable terms', and in other cases on 'mutually agreed' terms. Governments are specifically required by Article 16(4) to ensure that the private sector facilitates access to, and joint development and transfer of, technology. These provisions are likely to be easiest to implement in the case of countries providing access to genetic resources since they will again be in a position to bargain for the benefits they will receive, but for some governments, such as the USA, the suggestion of compulsion placed on industry is undoubtedly objectionable and has, inter alia, inhibited its ratification of the Convention. Intellectual property issues are important because the transfer of patented technology is specifically envisaged.[240]

Article 16(2) provides that access and transfer 'shall be provided on terms which recognize and are consistent with the adequate and effective protection of intellectual-property rights', while Article 16(5) calls for the parties to cooperate to ensure that intellectual-property rights 'are supportive of and do not run counter to' the objectives of the Convention. This appears to be an attempt to satisfy both sides; intellectual

---

[238] Article 16(3).

[239] Article 19(1), (2). See Coughlin, 31 *Col JTL* (1993), 337, for examples of access agreements which provide for technology transfer.

[240] There is a large literature on the problems arising; see Walden, in Bowman and Redgwell (eds), *International Law and the Conservation of Biological Diversity*, 171–89; Footer, 10 *YbIEL* (1999) 48; Asebey and Kempenaar, 28 *Vand JTL* (1995) 703; Kushan, ibid, 755 and Winter, 2 *JEL* (1992) 167. See also *infra*, Ch 14.

property rights are to be respected but only insofar as they assist rather than hinder implementation of the Convention.

However, behind these references there remain unresolved questions about the scope of intellectual property rights and whether they benefit the providers of genetic resources or only those who make use of them. Natural genetic resources, or genetically altered organisms which result from experimentation, are not necessarily always patentable or a source of legally protectable rights. Discovery of a new species of fish, for example, could not be patented; like most natural resources it is simply a commodity which can be bought and sold by anyone. Patentable rights may arise either in respect of a new process for isolating and developing substances, or for new uses for existing substances or possibly in respect of a substance which had no previous known existence. The extent to which these principles enable the products of biotechnology to be protected will vary, and remains controversial in national patent systems. It is, for example, still uncertain whether genetically altered organisms can be patented as such, or how far patent law will always protect new uses for existing substances. How far this part of the Convention will be important thus depends in part on how far intellectual property itself is prepared to go in protecting the products of biotechnology and the original natural genetic resource. For the USA it is clear that the risk of losing protection for genetic engineering is thought to be too high to support the Convention; this is not a problem which has deterred other developed states, such as the EC countries, however, from ratifying the Convention. The COP has taken some decisions aimed at resolving some of these problems, including encouraging cooperation with WIPO and the WTO.[241]

5(8) INSTITUTIONAL SUPERVISORY BODIES AND COMPLIANCE PROCEDURES[242]

(a) Compliance procedures

As Bothe has pointed out, trends concerning means and techniques to induce compliance reveal a complicated picture, with tension between unilateral or bilateral approaches and multilateral areas; old methods of unilaterally imposed sanctions are declining and national means of verification of other states' performance are increasingly problematic as is even the traditional approach to international responsibility. As we saw in Chapter 4, traditional methods of dispute settlement, even if included in modern treaties are often unused. However, what Bothe calls 'true multi-lateral implementation procedures' are developing in the form of reporting systems, systematic implementation review based on national reporting and other information, new non-compliance procedures and financial instruments, and in particular systems of remuneration of compliance. But these methods are not without difficulties. An

---

[241] E.g. Decisions III/7 and Annex. See also *infra*, Ch 14.

[242] See generally *supra*, Ch 4 and Bothe, in Wolfrum (ed), *Enforcing Environmental Standards: Economic Mechanisms as Viable Means* (Berlin, 1996) 13–38, esp conclusions at 38.

enhanced role for NGOs providing more non-governmental expertise and pressure, as a form of international public conscience, is still required, with less reliance on inter-governmental pressure and the politesse of diplomacy. The Convention on Biological Diversity offers a prime opportunity for this role, which, as we have seen, is encouraged in its substantive articles and the practice of its institutions.[243]

The Convention makes no provision for enforcement in the sense of establishing an international inspection or observer system; indeed that would be an impossibility for a Convention of this kind which provides a broad framework of 'soft' obligations and requires much enactment of national legislation of its efficacy. As already remarked, however, it is unusual, indeed unique, in the extent to which its provisions provide inducements for participation and compliance.

The Convention's Preamble notes that the fundamental requirement for conservation of biological diversity is *in situ* conservation of ecosystems and natural habitats and maintenance and recovery of viable populations and species in their natural surroundings. As the majority of the areas and species concerned are found within national jurisdiction, enforcement *strictu sensu* is, therefore, a matter for national authorities. But, as the conservation of biodiversity is categorized as 'a common concern of humankind', the efficiency with which its contracting parties, and even non-parties, fulfil this obligation is potentially subject to international overview and complaints. The effectiveness of this criticism depends largely on the institutional structures available for voicing it both inside the Convention's structure and in the wider international community.

At the international level, as already observed, the Convention establishes numerous incentives aimed at inducing compliance. At the national level it adopts a similar approach. Article 11 requires that each contracting party shall 'as far as possible and appropriate', 'adopt economically and socially sound measures that act as incentives for the conservation and sustainable use of components of biological diversity'. It does not provide guidance concerning what these incentives might or should be. The COP, however, having affirmed that implementation of incentive measures, in a broad social, cultural, and economic context, is of central importance to the realization of the three objectives of the Convention, resolved that such measures would be included ('as appropriate') on the COP's agenda and integrated into the sectoral and thematic items under its medium-term work programme. It also encouraged parties to review their existing legislation and economic policies, identify and promote incentives for conservation and sustainable use, stressing the importance of taking appropriate action on incentives that threaten biological diversity. It encouraged parties to incorporate market and non-market values of biological diversity into policies,

---

[243] See Article 23(5) which accords observer status to the UN, its specialized agencies, the IAEA and non-party states and allows any other body, or agencies, whether governmental or non-governmental qualified in fields relating to conservation and sustainable use of biological diversity, to be represented as an observer, though only as long as at least one- third of the parties do not object. As evidenced by the practice in other bodies, this provides ample opportunity for lobbying.

programmes, national accounting systems, and investment strategy (such plans, etc, being required in Article 6).[244]

Otherwise, the COP relied on promotion of other methods advocated in the Convention such as development of training and capacity-building programmes (Article 12); public education and awareness (Article 13); impact assessment—it encourages parties to incorporate biological diversity considerations into this— (Article 14); exchange of information (Article 17); and cooperation, which is referred to in several articles and on which we elaborate below. It invited parties to 'share their experiences on these incentive measures with and make available case studies to the Secretariat' with a view to the Secretariat providing guidance to the parties on designing and implementing incentive measures.

Reporting procedures for complaints with overview and comment from treaty bodies is a feature of some of the other environmental conventions referred to in this work, but not yet under the Biodiversity Convention (but see the Cartagena Protocol, below). However, it does require each party to present to the COP reports on measures taken by it to implement the Convention and their effectiveness in meeting the objectives of the Convention.[245] This provides an opportunity for the COP, and any committees it might duly establish to overview these reports, to comment on any weaknesses or failures of parties in this respect. The Convention's institutional structure is thus an important part of the supervisory structures and could extend its role, as has been done under the Montreal Protocol and Ramsar Convention for example, if parties agree to this.[246]

Responsibility for overviewing compliance with the Convention's requirements in areas beyond national jurisdiction will generally fall within the competence, if any, of appropriate international and regional bodies; Article 5 requires parties to cooperate 'as far as possible and appropriate' with other parties, directly or through competent international organizations, in respect of these areas on matters of mutual interest, and we must assume that compliance is such a matter. Whilst Article 22 asserts that the Convention does not affect parties' rights (and obligations) deriving from other international agreements to which they are party, unless their exercise would damage or threaten biodiversity, it also requires that parties implement the Convention, so far as it relates to the marine environment, 'consistently' with states' rights and obligations under the law of the sea. This raises interesting possibilities concerning application of the Law of the Sea Convention's provisions on enforcement, compliance, and dispute settlement to biodiversity issues.

---

[244] For assessment of National Biodiversity Strategies and Action Plans, see Herkenrath 11 *RECIEL* (2002) 29.

[245] Article 26.

[246] A subsidiary implementation review body could be established by the COP in accordance with the powers conferred by Article 23(4)(g) of the Convention for example.

(b) Institutional structure[247]

The Convention's governing body is the Conference of the Parties (COP) established under Article 22. Its key function is to keep the Convention's implementation under review.[248] This and other functions are set out in Article 23. As well as reviewing scientific and other sources of advice,[249] it can adopt protocols[250] and amendments to the Convention and its annexes[251] and consider further annexes.[252] It can also establish such subsidiary bodies as are deemed necessary to implement the Convention,[253] and contact (through the Secretariat) executive bodies of conventions dealing with CBD matters in order to establish 'appropriate forms' of cooperation with them.[254] It is not, however, given any explicit independent role of monitoring or inspection but, as already mentioned, has in practice 'encouraged' initiatives relating to this. The Secretariat, established under Article 24, can inter alia perform any function assigned to it by any protocol,[255] report to the COP,[256] coordinate with other relevant international[257] bodies, enter into relevant contractual arrangements,[258] as well as performing any other functions assigned to it by the COP.[259] UNEP was designated to fulfil the Secretariat function. Unfortunately despite the parties now numbering over 180, only a small number attend the COPs; but COP itself has initiated several lines of communication with all of them. In addition to these bodies, the Convention established a Subsidiary Body on Scientific, Technical and Technological Advice,[260] and also envisaged a Clearing House Mechanism (CHM),[261] established as a pilot phase and since reviewed to promote and facilitate technical and scientific cooperation. The COP has also established other subsidiary organs, including an Open Ended Working Group on Biosafety, an Expert Panel on Access and Benefit Sharing, and an Open Ended Ad Hoc Working Group on Article 8(j)[262] to provide advice.

What remains to be seen is whether, and if so when, the COP will tackle the problem of resolving at least some of the ambiguities latent in the Convention, given that it is unlikely that formal dispute settlement procedures will be invoked (see below). Here, however, its practice in negotiating the Protocol on Biosafety offers some encouragement. Given the numerous proposals now made by various commentators for further protocols or annexes, there seems to be no reason why this procedure should not be invoked ad hoc if the political support and necessary budget and infrastructure are forthcoming. What the subject matter of this might be is referred to in our conclusions. Although the Madrid Protocol to the Antarctic Treaty on Environmental Protection provides a better model both for openness, publicity of information, and effective supervision, it is perhaps unfair to compare treaties which have so many disparities, not least in the very different number of parties, most of which are developing

---

[247] On the limitations of these arrangements see the *CBD Handbook*, xvi–xx and *passim*.
[248] Decision IV/10 A, para 5(b).   [249] Article 23(4)(b).   [250] Article 23(4)(c).
[251] Article 23(4)(e).   [252] Article 23(4)(f).   [253] Article 23(g).   [254] Article 23(4)(h).
[255] Article 24(a).   [256] Article 24(i)(b).   [257] Article 24(c).   [258] Article 24(d).
[259] Article 24(e).   [260] Article 25.   [261] Article 18(3).
[262] Decisions II/5, IV/8, and IV/9 respectively.

states without resources, and one of which has global scope whereas the other relates only to a remote and mostly frozen wilderness.

Meanwhile, the COP has adopted an ecosystem approach as the framework for the analysis and implementation of the objectives of the Convention.[263] Although not referred to in the CBD Preamble, the term is defined in Article 2 as meaning 'a dynamic complex of plant, animal and micro-organism communities and their non-living environment interacting as a functional unit', which seems surprising given that 'biodiversity' as defined in that article has wider implications, including both variability among living organisms and 'diversity within species, between species and of ecosystems'.

(c) Dispute settlement

There are several issues raised by the Convention's wording which are likely to require resort to effective dispute settlement machinery. Article 27 does provide for disputes concerning 'interpretation and application' of the Convention and its protocols—including the Cartagena Protocol, below[264]—and Annex II sets out arbitration procedures, but the only compulsory method of settlement is negotiation. All else, including resort to arbitration or the ICJ, is optional, although states may declare acceptance of one or both of these methods as compulsory. This is the typical clause found in most environmental treaties; it offers little or no assurance that unresolved matters of interpretation, or alleged excess of power by the Conference of the Parties or the financial mechanism can be settled by any third-party process.[265]

(d) Liability and responsibility

The perfunctory treatment of transboundary issues in the CBD has already been noted above, with Article 14(1) doing little more than restate the customary law obligation to notify of transboundary harm.[266] There is little remaining in the final text of the CBD relating to responsibility[267] and liability issues, a contentious issue during negotiations, with Article 14(2) merely calling on the parties to 'examine... the issue of liability and redress, including restoration and compensation, for damage to biodiversity except where such liability is purely an internal matter'. Although a working group of legal and technical experts was established to consider the issue, little headway has been made.[268]

---

[263] Decisions II/8; SBSTTA Recommendation V/10. See also the 'Jakarta Mandate' on Marine and Coastal Biological Diversity adopted by the COP in 1997, *infra*, Ch 13, section 6.

[264] Article 27 extends to the Cartagena Protocol with the crucial distinction that the Protocol contemplates in Article 34 thereof, and indeed has established, a compliance mechanism which is 'without prejudice' to the operation of Article 27. See section 5(9)(e) below and, generally, Fitzmaurice and Redgwell, XXXI *NYIL* (2000) 35.

[265] Cf the *ICAO Council Case, ICJ Rep* (1972) 6, 56–60, and see generally *supra*, Ch 4.

[266] See Ch 4, *supra* and, more generally, Okowa 71 *BYbIL* (1996) 275.

[267] The responsibility clause of draft 5 was dropped from the final text of the CBD.

[268] See for example Decision VI/11.

5(9) THE CARTAGENA PROTOCOL[269]

(a) Regulation of biosafety under the Protocol: Advanced Informed Agreement

As we noted above, the CBD expressly recognized the need to develop further international regulation of the transfer and use of LMOs which may have adverse effect on the conservation and sustainable use of biodiversity, and the Cartagena Protocol was duly concluded in 2000. It defines 'living modified organism' as 'any living organism that possesses a novel combination of genetic material obtained through the use of modern biotechnology' (Article 3(f)). In fact the Protocol addresses two general categories of LMO: (i) those intended for release into the environment (e.g. seeds for cultivation or animal breeding stock); and (ii) those intended for use in food or feed, or for processing (e.g. corn, cotton, and soy). The latter are of particular concern to the United States as the chief exporter of genetically modified crops. In the event the Protocol distinguishes between these categories, subjecting organisms intended for direct use as food or feed, or for processing, to a less onerous regime (Article 11) than that applicable to LMOs intended for direct release into the environment (Articles 7–10).

A marked feature of the Protocol is its overtly precautionary approach, with Article 1 making express reference to the precautionary approach contained in Principle 15 of the 1992 Rio Declaration; implicit reference is found in the conditional language of '*may* have an adverse effect' on biodiversity and/or human health. The chief regulatory technique employed is the 'advanced informed agreement' (AIA) procedure, trailed in the CBD but set out in more detail here in Article 7, which is designed to ensure that Contracting Parties are provided with the information necessary to make informed decisions before agreeing to the import of LMOs into their territory. AIA marks the Protocol out from the 'prior informed consent' procedures of the 1989 Basel and 1998 Rotterdam Conventions,[270] which are based on prior multilateral agreement on the hazardous substances to be regulated and which are set out in annexes. Prior informed consent has been applied where substances have already been adjudged hazardous; the primary purpose of the Cartagena Protocol is to facilitate early assessment by each Contracting Party of the potential risks in accordance with the Protocol. As Stoll observes, the Cartagena Protocol's 'unique combination between import State control and risk assessment results from the fact that it does not contain an agreed definition of materials that the importing State may refuse without condition or even

---

[269] For coverage of the final negotiating session see (2000) 9:137 *Earth Negotiations Bulletin*, 1–11; see also CBD, *The Cartagena Protocol on Biosafety: A Record of the Negotiations* (Montreal, 2003), hereafter 'Record of the Negotiations'. On the Protocol generally, see Hagan and Weiner, 12 *Georgetown Environmental Law Review* (2002) 697; Burgiel, 11 *RECIEL* (2002) 53; McKenzie et al, *An Explanatory Guide to the Cartagena Protocol on Biosafety*, IUCN Environmental Policy and Law Paper No 46 (Gland, 2003), hereafter 'Explanatory Guide to the Protocol'. On biotechnology more widely see Mackenzie, 13 YbIEL (2002) 97–163; Redgwell, 60 *CLP* (2007); Francioni and Scovazzi (eds), *Biotechnology and International Law* (Oxford, 2006).

[270] The 1998 Rotterdam Convention on Prior Informed Consent expressly excludes LMOs from its scope to eliminate the possibility of conflict arising between it and the Cartagena Protocol.

an agreement that the substances that it regulates are "undesirable".[271] Indeed, the flexibility of the rules under the Protocol has led to suggestions that it represents a form of 'treaty-based environmental unilateralism' and that it is a 'prototype of minimum harmonisation legislation'.[272] It establishes principles and procedures to guide national decision-making based on risk assessment and risk management, without mandating a particular outcome.

The AIA procedures must be read with the risk-management provisions for the safe use, handling, and transboundary movement of LMOs;[273] emergency measures in the event of unintentional release of LMOs;[274] and provisions on handling, transport, packaging, and indentification.[275] Illegal transboundary movements are regulated by Article 25, which includes a 'take-back' provision: the country of origin may be requested to dispose of the LMO at its own expense. Similar provisions are found in the PIC and Basel Conventions, for example. To facilitate information exchange each contracting party must designate a national focal point for liaison with the Secretariat and a competent national authority to perform the administrative tasks required in implementing an AIA procedure.[276] Monitoring and reporting, so common in international environmental agreements, is also required under the Protocol (Article 33). It 'piggy-backs' on the institutions established under the CBD[277] discussed above—including dispute settlement—but does establish its own Biosafety Clearing-House mechanism to facilitate the exchange of scientific, technical, environmental and legal information.[278] This mechanism, combined with its capacity-building provisions,[279] is designed to facilitate developing states' participation. As Kameri-Mbote observes, scientific capacity-building at the national or regional level will 'go a long way in shaping the potential of the GMO revolution used to address local needs and the requirements for sustainable development'.[280] As yet, however, the biosafety CHM contains only

---

[271] Stoll, 10 *YbIEL* (1999) 91.

[272] Pavoni, X *Italian Yearbook of International Law* (2000) 113, 115–6. But note that Article 14 expressly provides for bilateral, regional and multilateral agreements and arrangements regarding intentional movement of LMOs so long as such arrangements do not provide a lower level of protection than that provided for by the Protocol—either equal protection or in fact a form of bilateral and/or multilateral upward derogation, and certainly precluding 'contracting out' of the Protocol's level of protection. Article 24 also envisages such agreements being concluded between Contracting Parties and non-parties to the Protocol.

[273] Article 16.   [274] Article 17.   [275] Article 18.   [276] Article 19.

[277] The Protocol relies on the institutions established under the CBD, including the Secretariat (Article 31), the COP which serves as the Meeting of the Parties to the Protocol (Article 29), and any subsidiary bodies under the Convention which the MOP determines may also serve the Protocol (Article 30). It also shares the financial mechanism of the CBD (Article 28).

[278] Article 20. This builds on the clearing house mechanism already established under the CBD, as well as establishing a gateway to other biosafety information exchange sites such as UNIDO's Biosafety Information Network and Advisory Service (BINAS) and UNEP's Information Resource for the Release of Organisms (IRRO), as provided for in Article 20(2) of the Protocol.

[279] Which in turn are closely linked with Articles 16 (access to and transfer of technology) and 18 (technical and scientific cooperation) of the CBD. Under the Protocol, capacity building is viewed as of particular importance for developing countries without domestic biosafety systems, and is closely linked with Article 28 of the Protocol (financial mechanism and resources).

[280] Kameri-Mbote, 11 *RECIEL* (2002) 62, 73.

seven entries containing data regarding decisions taken under AIA but 1756 records with respect to risk assessments and 536 entries under Article 11, which is the stream-lined decision-making procedure in respect of LMOs for food feed and processing.

(b) Public awareness and participation in biosafety decision-making

The AIA approach of the Biosafety Protocol is dependent on the ability of receiving states to conduct some form of risk assessment; for non-contained LMOs this may be part of a broader environmental impact assessment (EIA) exercise in which public par-ticipation is central. In the biosafety field, consultation will likely embrace a wide range of stakeholders—civil society, research institutes, and the biotechnology industry, for example. The Protocol requires states to ensure that the public is actively consulted on LMOs and biosafety to promote transparency and informed decision-making—but only 'in accordance with their respective laws and regulations' (Article 23). Significant differences in institutional and technical capacity exist between states, differences that are only partly addressed through the Protocol's provisions on capacity building and information sharing through, inter alia, the clearing house mechanism already briefly touched upon. A question arises whether international rules on public participation specifically tailored to biosafety decision-making are necessary.

This question has been faced squarely in the discussion of the role of civil soci-ety in biosafety decision-making under the 1998 Economic Commission for Europe's Aarhus Convention on access to information, public participation in decision-making, and access to justice in environmental matters.[281] When Article 6 was originally concluded, decisions on GMOs (the terminology of the Aarhus Convention) were expressly excluded from its binding requirements on public participation, with the parties required to apply its terms to decisions on whether to permit the deliberate release of GMOs into the environment only 'to the extent feasible and appropriate'. This weak provision resulted from a lack of agreement on the issue between the parties during the negotiation of the Convention, and was clearly going to be revisited once the Convention entered into force.

In May 2005 agreement was reached on an amendment to the Convention which, once it enters into force,[282] will require parties to inform and consult the public in decision-making regarding the deliberate release and placing on the market of GMOs. The public would have the right to submit comments and public authorities would be expected to take these into account in the decision-making process. Once made, the decision taken should be publicly available together with the reasons and consider-ations upon which it is based. Information associated with GMO decisions would be made available to the public, subject to the usual protection for commercially confi-dential information. However, confidentiality may not be extended to information on the intended uses of the release or regarding assessment of environmental risk. This

[281] Concluded 25 June 1998 and in force 30 October 2001, available at 38 *ILM* (1999) 517. The Convention presently has 36 parties.

[282] In the meantime, non-binding Guidelines adopted at MOP-1 in 2002 will apply, providing particular inspiration for states without domestic biosafety legislation. See Etty, 2006 *YBIEL* 506 (2007).

is clearly intended to prevent abuse of the confidentiality exception, and to ensure full transparency in respect of the use and environmental impact of GMOs and mirrors the language of Article 21(6) of the Cartagena Protocol. Upward derogation—that is, the flexibility for parties to adopt more expansive measures for public participation and access to information in GMO decision-making[283]—is also provided for. Overall, this compromise embeds national and regional flexibility whilst establishing international minimum standards for public participation in GMO decision-making, and seeks further to fill the biosafety regulatory gap which persists in some Central and East European and newly independent states. For states party to both the Aarhus Convention and the Cartagena Protocol (and that have also accepted the amendment and when it has entered into force), these provisions on the pubic right to participate in GMO decision-making will serve as a modest strengthening of the public awareness and participation provisions of Article 23 of the Protocol.

(c) Risk assessment

The AIA procedure set forth in Article 7 of the Cartagena Protocol is buttressed by provisions addressing notification[284] and decision procedures (Articles 8–10) in which, as was discussed above, there may be a role for public participation. The import of LMOs may be approved by the designated national authority with or without conditions, prohibited, or additional information may be requested. Silence in response to an initial notification from the party of export does not imply consent to transboundary movement (Article 9(4)). There is also provision for review of decisions in the light of new scientific information regarding the potential adverse effects of the LMO (Article 12). The Protocol stresses that lack of scientific certainty due to insufficient information available about the potential negative effects of LMOs on biodiversity, including taking into account risks to human health, will *not* prevent the importing/receiving state from taking decisions in respect of LMOs in order to avoid or minimize potential adverse effects (Article 10(6)). However, such decisions must be taken in accordance with the risk-assessment procedure stipulated in Article 15 and Annex III of the Protocol. And, whilst states are expressly permitted to take action more protective of biodiversity than provided for in the Protocol, such action must be consistent both with the Protocol *and* with that party's other obligations under international law (e.g. trade obligations). The socio-economic impact of LMOs on biodiversity, especially its value to indigenous and local communities, may also be taken into account by contracting parties, but again to the extent consistent with their other international

---

[283] Access to justice, the third pillar of the Aarhus Convention, is not addressed in the amendment regarding GMOs, though clearly could be embraced in the exercise of such upward derogation.

[284] The question whether transit states should have the same right to AIA as importing states was discussed at COP/MOP 4. With regard to the information submitted with the notification, confidentiality may be preserved in accordance with Article 21. This includes a list of what is not considered confidential, including '[a] summary of the risk assessment of the effects on the conservation and sustainable use of biological diversity, taking into account risks to human health' (para 6) and information relating to '[a]ny methods and plans for emergency response' (para 7).

obligations (Article 26).[285] Thus in both instances—a more stringent approach to LMO regulation, and taking into account in risk assessment non-scientific factors such as the socio-economic impact of LMOs on biodiversity—individual response is conditioned by compliance with wider international obligations, including trade obligations.[286]

During the negotiation of the Protocol there was some divergence between developed and developing states regarding the purpose of risk assessment. One of the most contentious issues was whether to include in the decision-making process the precautionary principle and socio-economic considerations just mentioned. For developed states, in particular those members of the 'Miami Group' keen to facilitate LMO trade,[287] the key point was to ensure that assessments were based on the most up-to-date scientific data (the 'sound science' approach). The inclusion of 'extraneous' matters such as socio-economic impact was viewed as encouraging disguised restrictions on trade.[288] The trade group also favours a minimalist (and less costly) approach to the documentation and labelling requirements of the Protocol.[289] Developing states considered scientific data alone to be insufficient to assess the full range of possible impacts on conservation and sustainable use of biological diversity, socio-economic factors, and risks to agriculture and to human health. This broader approach necessitates a multidisciplinary approach to risk assessment,[290] the implementation of which requires a case-by-case approach. Arguably the flexibility to maintain a multidisciplinary case-by-case approach is provided by the Cartagena Protocol, whilst also ensuring that possible impacts on human health and on the conservation and sustainable use of biological diversity are an integral part of the risk-assessment process, the 'backbone of the decision-making process' under the Protocol.[291] Precaution is an integral part of the AIA decision-making procedure, and socio-economic concerns are catered for to an extent in the provisions permitting taking account of the concerns of indigenous and local communities. But it is clear that decision-making regarding LMOs must be grounded in 'sound science' and that non-scientific factors alone—for example, a

---

[285] This concern with non-scientific factors is reflected in the ecosystem approach of the parent Biodiversity Convention which 'establishes the importance of including the socio-economic dimensions of nature management when implementing the CBD': see 'The Convention on Biological Diversity and the World Summit on Sustainable Development' at <http://www.biodiv.org/events/wssd.asp>.

[286] This may be compared with, for example, the 2003 GM Food and Feed Regulation in the EU (Regulation 1829/2003, OJ [2003] L268/1). There the legitimate objectives that may be pursued by a system of prior approval embrace not only internal market objectives and concerns for the protection of human life and health and of the environment, but also animal health and welfare and consumer interests in relation to genetically modified foodstuffs in particular. On the other hand, the 2001 Deliberate Release Directive (Directive 2001/18/EC, OJ [2001] L106/1) is addressed only to protection of human health and the environment. See further Scott, 2006 *CLP* 444.

[287] Comprising Argentina, Australia, Canada, Chile, Uruguay, and the United States, i.e. the major actual or likely exporters of LMOs. Three of the Miami Group—Argentina, Canada, and the United States—launched proceedings under the WTO's dispute settlement procedure challenging the EU's biosafety regime: WT/DS292, WT/DS292, and WT/DS293, *EC—Measures Affecting the Approval and Marketing of Biotech Products*, discussed *infra*, Ch 14 section 9.

[288] Burgiel, 11 *RECIEL* (2002) 53, 55.   [289] Etty, 2006 *YBIEL* 499 (2007).

[290] CBD/UNEP, *Record of the Negotiations*, 51.   [291] Kameri-Mbote, 11 *RECIEL* (2002) 62, 63.

generalized consumer concern regarding genetically modified foodstuffs—will not provide unchallengeable grounds for refusal to import LMOs under the Protocol.

The requirement that risk assessments 'shall be carried out in a scientifically sound manner' entails taking account not only of the provisions of the Protocol but also of 'recognized risk assessment techniques'—i.e. those recognized at the national, regional and international levels.[292] There is no definition of 'scientifically sound manner' in the Protocol though similar language may be found in other agreements.[293] 'Sound science' should entail independence, transparency, scepticism, peer review and accountability.[294] While in general terms these are not matters prescribed at the international level but left for domestic or regional implementation, Annex III of the Biosafety Protocol does set forth certain general principles of risk assessment which include the requirement that it 'should be carried out in a scientifically sound and transparent manner' (Article 3). As Mackenzie et al observe, this absence of an agreed definition of 'scientifically sound manner' may give rise to disagreements between states both as to the meaning of the phrase and as to the validity of inevitably diverging scientific views 'about the manner in which an inserted gene is likely to modify characteristics of the organism other than the intended changes, about the interpretation of data, and about the ecological and environmental effects of LMOs'.[295] Part of the difficulty in establishing international minimum harmonized standards for risk assessment, as observed by Australia in the negotiation of the Protocol,[296] is the diverse range of national regulatory measures already in place for undertaking risk assessment.[297] As we saw above, this problem has also beset efforts to draft binding international rules on public participation in GMO decision-making.

There are clearly both benefits and drawbacks to the Cartagena Protocol's approach to maintaining the diversity of national and regional approaches to living modified organisms. The benefit lies in preserving divergence, albeit consistent with other international obligations, with the principal focus the impact of LMOs on biological diversity which necessarily varies from state to state. Yet the tether for diversity is the application of the precautionary principle, which requires a degree of objectivity in

---

[292] Mackenzie et al, *Explanatory Guide to the Protocol*, 110. On the international level these might include UNEP's *International Technical Guidelines on for Safety in Biotechnology*, which a number of delegations in the Protocol negotiations viewed as a valuable source of guidance. See UNEP/CBD/BSWG/1/4/ paras 57–63, and CBD/UNEP, *Record of the Negotiations*, 50.

[293] See also the SPS Agreement—'scientific principles' (Article 2(2)); 'scientific justification' (Article 3(3)); and 'scientific evidence' (Articles 2(2) and 5(2)), discussed further *infra*, Ch 14. The provisions on the application of the precautionary approach in the 1995 Straddling Stocks Agreement refer to the 'best scientific information available' (Article 6): see Ch 13.

[294] Stirling, *On Science and Precaution in the Management of Technological Risk*, vol 1, EC Institute for Prospective Technological Studies, EUR 19056 EN Spain (1998), cited in Macrory, 54 *CLP* (2001) 640.

[295] Mackenzie et al, *Explanatory Guide to the Protocol*, 108.

[296] See CBD/UNEP, *Record of the Negotiations*.

[297] COP/MOP 3 established an Ad Hoc Technical Expert Group on Risk Assessment in 2005. The need for a common approach to risk assessment and risk management is widely appreciated, but no consensus exists on how to achieve it, e.g. whether a permanent scientific subsidiary body should be established for this purpose.

its application. Subjective concerns about the impact of LMOs are left outwith this process, save to the extent that socio-economic impact may be taken into account where impacting on indigenous and local peoples. International regulation of LMOs thus reflects a rationalist faith in the objective application of scientific principles; what Holder has referred to as a 'technocratic approach to environmental problems'.[298] This is well-illustrated by the role of science in the application of the precautionary concept under the Cartagena Protocol.[299]

This approach may be out of step with recent scientific developments, in particular 'sustainability science'. This is multidisciplinary, combining scientific, economic, legal, and other disciplinary understandings and knowledge. It recognizes the limitations of traditional scientific inquiry in dealing with the complex reality of social institutions interacting with natural phenomena. It is also a recent phenomenon— since 2001 or so—and seeks a rapprochement between science and sustainable development.[300] This multidisciplinary approach is reflected in the IUCN's 2004 report on GMOs and biosafety which identifies the single most important factor in resolving conflict over GMO regulation as the development of 'reliable information and analysis' in a multidisciplinary range of fields—biology, ecology, law, economics, ecosystem management, and social policy.[301] This is also recognized in the CBD's 2004 Addis Ababa Principles, principle 6 of which stresses the importance of interdisciplinary research for the successful implementation of the CBD.[302] However, it remains to be seen whether, in implementing the Protocol, these more dynamic scientific approaches emerge, or whether the Protocol's approach to 'sound science' risks being yet another example of the law entrenching established (and perhaps old-fashioned) ways of understanding and doing.

(d) Trade implications

Several of the Protocol's provisions have a clear potential for conflict with other international obligations, most notably trade-related obligations. These are discussed in more detail in Chapter 14. For present purposes, it should be noted that the precautionary approach, such a key feature of the Protocol as we have noted,[303] allows importing countries to ban imports because of lack of scientific certainty. Unlike under the Agreement on the Application of Sanitary and Phytosanitary Measures (SPS Agreement), there is no obligation to seek further information to enable a more

---

[298] Holder, 53 *CLP* (2000) 152.

[299] For an EU perspective, see Hervey, 10 *RECIEL* (2001) 321.

[300] Clark and Dickson, 100 *Proceedings of the National Academy of Sciences of the United States of America* (2003) 8061: Kates et al, 292 *Science* (2001) 641–2.

[301] IUCN–The World Conservation Union, *Genetically Modified Organisms and Biosafety: A background paper for decision-makers and others to assist in consideration of GMO issues* (Gland, 2004), 5. It identifies three, often disconnected, strands in GMO discourse, namely: (i) science; (ii) economics; and (iii) socio-cultural issues.

[302] The Addis Ababa Principles and Guidelines for the Sustainable Use of Biodiversity were adopted at the 7th Conference of the Parties to the CBD in 2004.

[303] In addition to the preambular provisions and Article 1 cited above, see Articles 10(6), 11(8).

objective, informed assessment of the risk and to review the SPS measure within a reasonable time. Thus a trade-restrictive measure under the Cartagena Protocol may be of unlimited duration, or at least until the importing country decides that scientific certainty exists regarding the effects of products on biodiversity and human health.[304] The Protocol does address its relationship with trade agreements—a contentious issue during negotiations—in the preamble,[305] which repeats nearly verbatim the preambular language of the 1998 Rotterdam Convention on Prior Informed Consent. The Preamble to the Cartagena Protocol recognizes that trade and environment agreements should be mutually supportive with a view to achieving sustainable development. It then emphasizes that 'this Protocol shall not be interpreted as implying a change in rights and obligations of a Party under any existing international agreements' whilst immediately asserting, potentially paradoxically, that this recital 'is not intended to subordinate this Protocol to other international agreements'. There is an obvious contradiction between asserting on the one hand no change in rights and obligations yet on the other rejecting any hierarchy between agreements in the event of conflict. The answers are far from clear and have been the subject of much discussion, though such conflict will only materialize in fact when a decision taken thereunder is challenged as trade restrictive. In the *EC—Biotech Case*, discussed further in Chapter 14, the EC relied on the precautionary principle as articulated in, inter alia, the Cartagena Protocol, to which it is a party, but the WTO Dispute Settlement Panel did not apply it.[306]

(e) Subsequent developments under the protocol: liability and non-compliance

Owing to the subject matter of the Protocol, it is unsurprising to find that, unlike its parent Convention, provisions were included providing for the subsequent elaboration of rules and procedures on liability and redress (Article 27) and the conclusion of a compliance mechanism (Article 34). A facilitative compliance mechanism has been established, though in common with the mechanisms established under other treaty instruments, the Compliance Committee has spent its first meetings elaborating rules of procedures, aided by an assessment of the practice of other environmental agreements' compliance procedures. This process was necessitated by the political compromises embedded in this weak compliance mechanism adopted in 2004, with further elaboration necessary. At the time of writing it had yet to consider specific instances of non-compliance in the absence of submissions to it, although it has reviewed compliance—in general terms—based on the national reports submitted by the parties after four years' operation of the Protocol.[307] This absence of 'business' is a

---

[304] See Zarilli, in Francioni (ed), *Environment, Human Rights & International Trade* (Oxford, 2001) Ch 3, esp 57–64; Hagan and Weiner, 12 *Georgetown Environmental Law Review* (2002) 697; Gaston and Abate, 12 *Pace Int'l L Rev* (2000) 107; and *infra*, Ch 14, section 9.

[305] For thorough analysis see Stoll, 10 *YbIEL* (1999) 91, and Gaston and Abate, ibid.

[306] See *infra*, Ch 14, section 9, and Ch 1 above.

[307] See, for example, the Report of the Compliance Committee submitted to COP-MOP 4 (2008) at UNEP/CBD/BS/COP-MOP/4/2; for pertinent decisions of the COP/MOP, see Decisions BS-I/7, BS-II/1, BS-III/1 and BS-IV/1.

reflection upon the slow rate of implementation of the Protocol, hinging in part on dis-agreement over key aspects such as risk assessment, discussed above, and lack of pro-gress on liability and redress.[308] With respect to the latter, at COP-MOP 4 (2008) the parties agreed to draft legally binding rules and procedures for liability and redress for potential damage caused from the transboundary movement of LMOs for consider-ation at the next COP-MOP in 2010. This will provide a clearer legal framework for the liability and redress where transboundary movement of LMOs causes transboundary harm.

6 CONCLUSIONS

Much of the success of the Biodiversity Convention in ensuring responsible exercise of state sovereignty when identifying and using biological resource depends on the willingness of parties to fulfil their various duties under it to cooperate, especially on providing the finance, technology, and other forms of support required for suc-cessful operation. This requires cooperation not only within the Convention's own institutions, but through existing relevant agreements to which they are and should now become party. Duties of cooperation are laid down in several articles of the Convention, including those on providing financial and other support, particularly for developing countries for *in situ* conservation (Article 8(a)) and *ex situ* conserva-tion, including establishment and maintenance of relevant conservation facilities in such countries (Article 9(e)); research and training especially concerning use of scien-tific advances in biological diversity research in developing methods for conservation and sustainable use of biological resources (Article 12(c)); and public education and awareness concerning conservation and sustainable use (Article 13). There are signs of the COP, the Secretariat, and the CBD's other institutions initiating a considerable amount of activity.

Article 5 of the Convention specifically requires parties in general to cooperate with each other, as do several other articles which address specific issues, referred to earlier. Article 5, however, only requires them to do so 'as far as possible and appropriate', either directly or through competent international organizations, on areas beyond national jurisdiction and on other concerns of mutual interest for conservation and sustainable use of biodiversity. Although the Convention does not define the former terms it does define the latter, in terms of using its components 'in a way and at a rate that does not lead to long-term decline, thereby maintaining its potential to meet the needs and aspirations of present and future generations', on the ambiguities of which we have already remarked.

---

[308] An Ad Hoc Working Group on Liability and Redress was established pursuant to Decision BS-I/8 and met five times between 2005 and 2008. For background on the key liability and redress issues, see the *Report of the Technical Group of Experts on Liability and Redress in the Context of the Cartagena Protocol on Biosafety* UNEP/CBD/BS/TEG-L&R/1/3, 9 November 2004.

It is too early to say whether the Convention will succeed in achieving its wide-ranging and challenging objectives but the criticisms and predictions of failure made at the time of its conclusion seem premature and somewhat misplaced in the light of its activities; these are necessarily embryonic at present. There is still much to be done, as its parties and institutions are aware. Despite the valued criticisms that can be made of both the Convention's and the Cartagena Protocol's weaknesses and ambiguities, there seems to be ongoing a serious attempt to make progress. In doing so, further challenges must be tackled especially in clarifying the ambiguities. The likely failure to achieve a slowing of the rate of biodiversity loss by 2010 suggests both unrealistic targets and a lack of political will to give effect to the Convention. Under both the Convention and the Protocol, 'agreed' text embedded many ambiguities and compromises which resurface to inhibit or prevent effective implementation and even, according to more severe critics, imperilling the viability of the instrument.[309]

National regimes, vital to effective *in situ* conservation, need to be developed. Other relevant agreements need to be integrated,[310] as do the relevant Rio Principles and proposals of Agenda 21. More state practice under the Convention is required to define its vague terms. The inducements offered to fulfil its aims—finance, technology transfer, other forms of support for developing country parties—must be made good. The supporting infrastructure at national and international levels requires development, perhaps on the lines of CITES.[311] As wide as possible, continual external overview is required not only by the bodies appointed under the Convention but, as has occurred to some extent already, by the UN itself through its Special Sessions of the General Assembly and by the Commission on Sustainable Development.

---

[309] Etty 2006 *YBIEL* (2007) 498, with reference particularly to the Cartagena Protocol.
[310] See *infra*, Chs 12, 13.   [311] See *infra*, Ch 12.

12

CONSERVATION OF MIGRATORY AND LAND-BASED SPECIES AND BIODIVERSITY

1 INTRODUCTION

As we have noted in Chapter 11, 'biological diversity' is a comprehensive term encompassing the entire variety of nature—all species of plants, trees, animals, and micro-organisms as well as the ecosystems of which they are part and which provide their habitat. The Biodiversity Convention defines biodiversity in terms of this variability of living organisms 'from all sources', including 'terrestrial, marine, and other aquatic complexes of which they are part', not just in terms of preserving particular species of animals or protecting particular areas or regions although hitherto protection had been based on these approaches.

Effective conservation of living resources, not only for their value to biodiversity, but for other values, requires that the protection of species in general and of endangered ones in particular be ensured on a sustainable basis. This necessitates regulation on a flexible basis to make sure, inter alia, that species can be added to conventions, as they become threatened; habitats and ecosystems are preserved; introduction of exotic species is controlled; reserved areas are set aside; and that trade in endangered species and their products is limited.

The global and regional conservation conventions discussed in this chapter impinge on various issues of biological diversity but do so sectorally, addressing specific problems; they do not deal with biological diversity as such. For this, a more comprehensive approach is required, establishing general obligations to conserve biological diversity as such within one framework since it would be impossible to renegotiate or amalgamate all these conventions. As we saw in the previous chapter, this is now provided by the

Biological Diversity Convention. It is the purpose of this chapter to consider some of the most important existing conventions relevant to conserving various components of biodiversity, to evaluate their appropriateness for fulfilling the Convention's objectives, and indicate any other agreements that might still be required for this purpose. Means of coordinating these agreements and integrating them into the Convention's system for conserving terrestrial biodiversity will be considered and progress on this identified.

As pointed out in the introduction to Chapter 11, there are differences between land-based and marine species that merit addressing the problems of their conservation in separate chapters, despite several common problems. Insofar as these problems are common they have mainly been addressed in comprehensive conservation treaties. Though applying largely to land-based species, these often list some threatened marine species in their annexes, and require comparable forms of protection, whether against harmful effects of trade, or because their habitat is threatened or because of their unique value. We pointed out in the previous chapter that unlike marine species, terrestrially based species fall wholly under the sovereignty of the state within whose land frontiers or airspace they are found, even if migratory, and that their regulation, for purposes of conservation and sustainable use, necessitates that states cooperate and accept limitations on unfettered claims of sovereignty or sovereign rights over their natural resources in order to protect biological diversity. We also emphasized that there are far more terrestrially based mammals, and that they are, with some exceptions, more accessible and vulnerable to capture, over-exploitation, habitat destruction, and the effects of industrialization than those inhabiting the oceans. These threats are increasing as human population expands, the need for animals and their products as food or sources of income accelerates, the means of capturing them become ever more technologically sophisticated both on land and in the sea, and their habitats are destroyed, degraded, or otherwise threatened.

Resolution of the problems affecting wildlife conservation has mainly been achieved through the conclusion of international conventions at the global, regional, and subregional level depending on the extent of the areas which threatened species inhabit or through which they migrate. The new environmental principles and strategies outlined in Chapters 2 and 11 have had a considerable influence on the development of treaty law in this field even before conclusion of the Biodiversity Convention.

2 IMPLEMENTATION OF PRINCIPLES AND STRATEGIES THROUGH CONSERVATION TREATIES

A wide variety of treaties implementing the principles and strategies referred to in Chapter 11 now exists at the global, regional, and bilateral levels, but no convention

protects *all* wildlife globally.[1] The Biological Diversity Convention is limited to protection of biodiversity, not species as such. Some treaties protect a single species, such
as polar bears or vicuña,[2] or a group of species, such as whales or migratory birds,
from excessive exploitation.[3] Others adopt a regional approach to conservation, for
example, in the Western Hemisphere (North and South America), Africa, Europe,
South-east Asia, the South Pacific, and Antarctica.[4] Many of the newer treaties no
longer confine themselves to regulating hunting, as did the earlier ones, but provide
also for habitat protection. There are also many bilateral treaties, especially for protection of birds and seals,[5] which reflect these trends. The importance of protecting
natural ecosystems as such had begun to be more widely perceived well before 1992.
Since UNCED, further conventions and principles have been adopted for protecting
such wide ranging habitats as deserts,[6] forests,[7] and mountain areas.[8]

In addition to the species-specific treaties, there are a number of treaties introducing protective techniques and approaches. Four, referred to by Lyster as the 'Big
Four', remain of particular significance and importance to the regime for protection
of wildlife, both marine and terrestrial, namely the 1971 Convention on Wetlands
of International Importance (Ramsar Convention);[9] the 1972 Convention for the
Protection of the World Cultural and Natural Heritage (World Heritage Convention);[10]
the 1973 Convention on International Trade in Endangered Species of Wild Fauna and
Flora (CITES);[11] and the 1979 Convention on the Conservation of Migratory Species
of Wild Animals (Bonn Convention).[12] To these must now be added the Biodiversity
Convention itself. These remain of particular significance as being the main global
conventions for fulfilling the aims of that Convention insofar as wildlife protection is
concerned. These Conventions will be considered later in this chapter.[13]

---

[1] For a comprehensive overview of the contribution of existing strategies and agreements, see Bowman
and Redgwell (eds), *International Law and the Conservation of Biodiversity* (London, 1996) esp Ch 4. See also
Bowman, Davies and Redgwell, *Lyster's International Wildlife Law* (2nd edn, Cambridge, 2009) (hereinafter
Lyster's International Wildlife Law); De Klemm, 29 *NRJ* (1989) 932–78; ibid, 9 *EPL* (1982) 117–28.

[2] 1973 Agreement on the Conservation of Polar Bears; 1979 Andean Convention for the Conservation
and Management of Vicuña.

[3] 1946 International Convention for the Regulation of Whaling; 1995 Agreement on Conservation of
African–Eurasian Migratory Water Birds.

[4] See the 1940 Convention on Nature Protection and Wildlife Preservation in the Western Hemisphere;
1968 African Convention on the Conservation of Nature and Natural Resources, to be replaced by the 2003
revision when it enters into force; 1979 Convention on the Conservation of European Wildlife and Natural
Habitats (Berne Convention); 1985 ASEAN Agreement on the Conservation of Nature and Natural Resources
(not in force); 1976 Apia Convention on Conservation of Nature in the South Pacific; 1980 Convention on the
Conservation of Antarctic Marine Living Resources.

[5] E.g. 1916 US–UK Convention for the Protection of Migratory Birds, 12 *TIAS* 375; 1936 US–Mexico
Convention for the Protection of Migratory Birds and Game Mammals, 178 *LNTS* 309, supplemented by
Agreement of 1972, 837 *UNTS* 125.

[6] *Infra*, section 4(1).   [7] *Infra*, section 4(2).   [8] *Infra*, section 4(3).

[9] *Lyster's International Wildlife* Law, 183–207; Navid, 29 *NRJ* (1989) 1001.

[10] Administered by UNESCO in cooperation with IUCN; Lyster, *International Wildlife Law* (Cambridge,
1985), 208–38.

[11] *Lyster's International Wildlife Law*, 239–77.   [12] Ibid, 278–304.

[13] *Infra*, section 3.

Also worthy of special mention are the 1980 Convention for Conservation of Antarctic Marine Living Resources (CCAMLR),[14] referred to in Chapters 11 and 13, since its definition of marine living resources includes birds and it adopts a holistic ecological approach to conservation whereby the effects of exploitation of one species on all other species and on the ecosystem as a whole must be taken into account in taking measures. The Madrid Protocol added to the Antarctic Treaty in 1991 also provides a vehicle for application of the Biodiversity Convention's holistic ecological approach as it aims to provide comprehensive environmental protection to the whole Antarctic area and its living resources.

A number of the above Conventions apply, in various ways and to various degrees, the principles examined in Chapter 11, though the 'Big Four' cover only internationally important sites, specific ecosystems, or a particular group of species. An overview of these instruments indicates that they are not necessarily preservationist in their approach to wildlife conservation. In order for them to attract a wide range of ratifications, fair and rational use and exploitation had to be allowed. The Biological Diversity Convention additionally requires such use to be sustainable, but it does not alter the basic approach. To achieve these aims states parties must provide on a cooperative basis for equitable utilization of so-called 'shared' or 'transboundary' species as outlined in Chapter 11 and as articulated in the Stockholm Declaration, the relevant UNEP Principles, and those evidenced in the Rio Declaration and the Biodiversity Convention. They must also, to the extent appropriate, take account of the relevant chapters of Agenda 21. There is growing evidence that many wildlife and related conventions are adapting to this situation though not necessarily as fast and as comprehensively as environmentalists would like. The one exception is the Madrid Protocol, which is wholly aimed at preservation of the Antarctic environment, and even regulates tourism.

There are now certain key issues for which successful wildlife and related conventions must provide: sustainability of use, particularly if species are threatened; flexibility in their regulatory systems for listing species that become threatened; maintenance of habitats and ecosystems; control of introduction of exotic (so-called 'alien') species; creation of protected areas or reserves; and limitations or prohibition, as appropriate, of trade in endangered species of animals and plants. More controversial is the question of whether certain 'charismatic mega-fauna', such as elephants, tigers, eagles, and whales, should ever be exploited, so vulnerable are they to capture and over-exploitation.

2(1) SPECIES PROTECTED BY CONVENTIONS

The main international and regional conventions relevant to conservation of biodiversity have been surveyed elsewhere.[15] The number of parties varies greatly as

---

[14] Lyster's International Wildlife Law 156–82, and see infra, text at n 36.

[15] For a succinct résumé of twelve leading conventions, see Churchill, in Bowman and Redgwell, *International Law and the Conservation of Biodiversity* (London, 1996) 73, 77; Van Heijnsbergen, *International Legal Protection of Wild Fauna and Flora* (Oxford, 1997) 9–36.

does their level of activity. Much of their effect varies depending on how well they are implemented and how well they are adapted to changes both in international law and perceptions concerning the best techniques for, inter alia, protecting the components of biodiversity.

(a) Global conventions

There are a number of conventions that aim to protect a particular species or group of species on a global basis. They include the 1946 International Convention for Regulation of Whaling (ICRW),[16] which covers the taking of the whales in 'all waters where whaling takes place', and the 1979 Bonn Convention on Conservation of Migratory Species of Wild Animals, which includes in that term 'the entire population or any geographically separate part of the populations of any species or lower taxon of wild animals, a significant proportion of whose members cyclically and predictably cross one or more national jurisdictional boundaries'.[17] The particular species protected at any given time are listed, in the case of ICRW, on the amendable schedule, and in the case of the Bonn Convention on an amendable appendix. Treaties and other instruments relating exclusively to birds, seals, and small cetaceans are all regional or bilateral.

(b) Regional conventions[18]

Most regional conventions cover a variety of species. The Preamble to the 1940 Western Hemisphere Convention expresses the intention of the American Republics to protect 'representatives of all species and genera of their native flora and fauna, including migratory birds, in sufficient numbers and over areas extensive enough to assure them from becoming extinct through any agency within man's control'. These species are then listed in an amendable Annex. Unfortunately, however, its nineteen parties have not been active in these respects at the international level, hence Lyster's eponymous reference to it as a 'sleeping treaty'.[19] The 1968 African Convention ensures in Article VII, the 'conservation, wise use and development of faunal resources' which it lists in an annex. It requires parties to maintain a variety of existing conservation areas and consider the need for others to protect ecosystems important to conservation of species. These obligations are repeated, and elaborated upon in Articles X–XII of the 2003 African Convention, a revision of the 1968 Convention which is not yet in force.[20] It replaces 'faunal resources' with 'natural resources', which is defined to include flora and fauna, and also refers to 'threatened species' of flora and fauna. Such species are not listed in the annexes, which do contain further elaboration of the definition and management objectives of conservation areas, definition of critically endangered, endangered, and vulnerable species, and lists the prohibited means

---

[16] See *infra*, Ch 13.   [17] Article 1(1)(a)

[18] See *Lyster's International Wildlife Law*, Pt III, Chs 8–12.

[19] Lyster, *International Wildlife Law* (1st edn, Cambridge, 1985). The second edition notes, however, that the Convention has likely had a catalytic effect on national legislative efforts, especially in the establishment of protected areas: ibid, Ch 8.

[20] See further Mekouar, 34/1 *EPL*, 43, and *Lyster's International Wildlife Law*, Ch 9.

of taking. The 1979 Berne Convention on the Conservation of European Wildlife aims, in Article 1, to conserve those wild fauna in Europe which are listed in amendable appendices. The Convention is not limited to members of the Council of Europe but is also open to non-members that participated in its elaboration, the European Community, and any other states invited to sign. The 1980 CCAMLR extends to all Antarctic marine living resources, including birds (Article 1). The parties to the 1985 ASEAN Agreement aim at 'ensuring the survival and promoting the conservation of all species under their jurisdiction and control' (Article 3) but only endangered species are listed in an appendix. As early as 1950 an International Convention for Protection of Birds[21] stated that 'all birds should in principle be protected', and that endangered and migratory species require special protection. The 1995 Agreement on the Conservation of African–Eurasian Migratory Water Birds covers a much larger area, encompassing not only the whole of Europe and Africa, but also Arabia and part of the Arctic. It requires parties to conserve all such birds, defined as those that are 'ecologically dependent on wetlands for at least part of their annual cycle', and it gives 'special attention' to endangered species.[22] As already indicated, there are also international conventions protecting single species in specific regions, for example, the 1973 Agreement on the Conservation of Polar Bears and the 1974 Convention for the Conservation and Management of the Vicuña. More recently, the parties to the 1993 North American Agreement on Environmental Cooperation concluded, under the auspices of the Commission on Environmental Cooperation, a Monarch Butterfly Sister Protected Area Network and a Northern American Monarch Conservation Plan, to protect the habitat of this migratory, though not yet endangered, species.

2(2) DEFINITION OF 'CONSERVATION'

The Biodiversity Convention does not define this term in its general definitions, except in relation to *in situ* conservation. It is left to related agreements and other instruments to do so for their purposes. It has been remarked that three concepts are used in relation to fauna and flora, often interchangeably, viz 'protection', 'preservation', and 'conservation'.[23] However, the Biodiversity Convention states its aim in Article I as 'conservation' of biological diversity. The interpretive problem arises both in relation to marine and terrestrial species.

The lack of any clear definition of 'conservation' was observed in Chapter 11; although the purpose of all the conventions referred to in the section above is 'conservation' none, except the Biodiversity Convention, defines the term. The discrepancies between the 'ecosystem' definition given by IUCN in the World Charter for Nature, 'the sustainable use' and 'development' meaning attributed to the term by the WCED

---

[21] Open only to European States; now, superseded by the EC Birds Directive 1979; see Birnie, in Bowman and Redgwell (eds), *International Law and the Conservation of Biodiversity* (London, 1996) 221–5.

[22] This Agreement is concluded under Article IV of the 1979 Bonn Convention.

[23] Van Heijnsbergen, *International Legal Protection of Wild Fauna and Flora* (Oxford, 1997), Ch 3, 43–52.

Legal Experts Group, and that provided in the 1958 High Seas Convention,[24] explains why the Conventions evade this problem and resort to specification of measures to be taken, expressing their conservatory aims only in general terms.

The 1979 Bonn Convention, however, requires parties to conserve migratory species and take action to this end, paying special attention to 'species the *conservation status* of which is unfavourable'.[25] It then defines not 'conservation' but 'conservation status', which it postulates as 'the sum of the influences acting on the migratory species that may affect its long-term distribution and abundance' and lists the factors to take into account in determining this. The interpretations of the 'wise use' prescribed in the 1971 Ramsar Convention outlined later in this chapter are also relevant. The WCED's Group of Legal Experts, as noted in Chapter 11, favoured a definition based on 'optimum sustainable yield' (OSY) in order to achieve and maintain sustainable utilization, since 'sustainable yield' does not allow for error, lack of data, or other uncertainties, or interdependence of exploited species and other species or ecosystems. If both predator and prey are taken, MSY cannot be upheld. To be successful as a conservation model, MSY must be based on reliable scientific advice and the data on which this is to be based must also be reliable. But not only are data often non-existent or insufficient but scientific theories used to interpret them often themselves prove inadequate and the advice given is either imprecise or offers wide ranges of allowable catch. Moreover, the applicable data and factors relevant to terrestrial species are very different from those used by marine biologists for marine species. Advice may also be compromised by the economic, social, and political needs of those exploiting a species or its habitat.[26] Unfortunately, as knowledge advances the management theories become more complex and uncertain.

Nonetheless, though MSY is increasingly discredited as application of the precautionary principle increases,[27] it remains an important, if not the predominant, conservation concept. Because of these difficulties, some environmental NGOs have begun to use 'preservation' or 'protection' as the favoured goal, rather than 'conservation'. The tension between 'conservation' and sustainable economic development is expressed in the African Convention which noted, as early as in its unrevised 1968 text, that 'the interrelationship between conservation and socio-economic development implies both that conservation is necessary to ensure sustainability of development, and that socio-economic development is necessary for the achievement of conservation on a lasting basis'. One of the expressly stated purposes of the 2003 revision of the 1968 African Convention is to expand elements related to sustainable development. 'Conservation and sustainable use' is the language of the revised 2003 African Convention, the objectives of which include enhancing environmental protection and fostering the conservation and sustainable use of natural resources, 'with a view to achieving ecologically rational, economically sound and socially acceptable

---

[24] *Supra*, Ch 11.   [25] Article I(1)(b)–(c), emphasis added.

[26] Andresen and Ostreng (eds), *International Resource Management: The Role of Science and Politics* (Oslo, 1990) 17–23; Andresen, 13 *Marine Policy* (1989) 99–118.

[27] See *infra*, Ch 13.

development polices and programmes' (Article II). While 'conservation' is not defined, the 2003 Convention does include definition of 'conservation area' by the purpose served by such conservation, eg 'ecosystem protection and recreation' for National Parks designation and 'conservation through management interventions' for Habitat/ Species Management Areas, with further elaboration of conservation area management objectives (Annex 2) and according to resource type (Articles VI–X).

2(3) THE NATURE AND LEGAL STATUS OF THE INTERNATIONAL COMMUNITY'S INTEREST IN NATURAL LIVING RESOURCES

The Biodiversity Convention, as we have seen, merely 'affirms', and then only in its Preamble, that conservation of biodiversity is a 'common concern of mankind'. We have already considered the implications of this in Chapters 3 and 11. The issue here is whether living resources per se have any international legal status, and, if so, what it is. Here we focus on the confusing variety of terms used in agreements protecting various aspects of nature. There is no doubt that the international community has an interest in protection of certain species, but the extent and nature of this community interest is difficult to determine at present. Whilst it cannot be said that the substantive provisions of the conventions treat living resources as 'common heritage' or give full effect to inter-generational rights as conceived by Brown Weiss[28] and included in the environmental strategies considered in Chapter 11, some conventions do recognize in their preambles the moral force of this concept and treat conservation of living resources as, at the least, a matter of community interest. But there is a lack of coherent conceptual thinking on this, though, unlike later fisheries conventions even in 1946 the Preamble to the Whaling Convention recognized 'the *interest* of the nations of the world in safeguarding for future generations the great natural resources represented by the whale stocks' and was the first to do so.[29] Similarly the unrevised African Convention (1968), still in force, regards soil, water, and faunal resources as constituting 'a capital of vital importance for mankind', while the 1985 ASEAN Agreement's preamble recognizes 'the importance of natural resources for present and future generations'; the 1971 Ramsar Convention, more weakly, merely acknowledges 'the interdependence of man and his environment'. More positively, the 1972 World Heritage Convention declares that 'parts [sic] of the natural heritage are of outstanding interest and therefore need to be preserved as part of the world heritage of mankind as a whole'. The Preamble to the 1973 CITES refers, however, to wild fauna and flora as 'an irreplaceable part of the natural systems of the earth which must be protected for *this and future generations to come*'.[30] The revised African Convention of 2003, refers to 'the interest of present and future generations' as part of the 'fundamental objective' of implementing all measures necessary to achieve the objectives of the Convention (Article IV) and to in the Preamble refers to 'the natural environment of Africa and the natural resources with which Africa is endowed' as 'an irreplaceable part of the African heritage' which

---

[28] See *supra*, Ch 3.   [29] Emphasis added.   [30] Emphasis added.

'constitutes a capital of vital importance to the continent and humankind as a whole'; the Preamble also states that 'the conservation of the global environment is a common concern of human kind as a whole'.

The concept of 'common heritage' as the basis of a new international regime for the exploitation of the deep seabed is considered in Chapter 3; it has undoubtedly influenced discussion in other forums, but in a negative sense: the form it took in the 1982 UNCLOS is not reflected in living resources conventions. States, in relation to living resources within their territory, are not willing to establish supranational institutions. The 1972 World Heritage Convention comes closest to that concept, without establishing any comparable international institutions with responsibility for its manifestation. The Preamble declares that 'deterioration or disappearance of any item of the cultural or natural heritage constitutes a harmful impoverishment of the *heritage of all nations of the world*';[31] that UNESCO's constitution requires it to spread knowledge by assessing conservation of the world's heritage and recommending the necessary international conventions for achieving this; and that existing conventions, etc, show the importance of 'safeguarding this unique and irreplaceable *property to whatever people it may belong*',[32] parts of which of outstanding interest need to be preserved 'as part of the *world heritage of mankind as a whole*'.[33] The UNESCO General Conference expressed the view, evidenced in the Preamble, that new conventional provisions were necessary to establish an effective system of *collective* protection. The protective responsibility is placed initially on states but Article 6, whilst respecting state sovereignty, also recognizes that the cultural and natural heritage constitutes 'a *world* heritage' for whose protection '*it is the duty of the international community as a whole to cooperate*'.[34] An inter-governmental World Heritage Committee (WHC) is established by Article 8 to maintain a World Heritage List of properties submitted for inclusion by states and to lay down the criteria for this (Article 11). It is assisted by a secretariat provided by UNESCO but no independent authority is established to regulate activities in relation to this heritage, in contrast to the International Seabed Authority created by the 1982 UNCLOS; this is left to national legislation.

Though the Preamble to the 1973 CITES Convention acknowledges that wild flora and fauna must be protected for '*future generations to come*',[35] it adds that 'people and states are and should be the best protectors of their own wild fauna and flora'. Whilst noting that in addition 'international cooperation is essential for protection against over-exploitation through international trade', it too does not establish any international management body. Rather, a Management and a Scientific Authority

---

[31] Emphasis added. For analysis of the preamble, see Francioni, in Francioni and Lenzerini (eds), *The 1972 World Heritage Convention: A Commentary* (Oxford, 2007).

[32] Emphasis added.

[33] Emphasis added. On protecting natural heritage and transmission to future generations see Redgwell, in Yusuf (ed), *Standard-setting in UNESCO Vol 1: Normative Action in Education, Science and Culture* (Paris, 2007) 267.

[34] Emphasis added.   [35] Emphasis added.

are to be established in each state party, backed by an international secretariat and a biennial Conference of the Parties.

The 1979 Bonn Convention's Preamble is the most positive in stating international community and inter generational rights. It recognizes that 'wild animals are an irreplaceable part of the earth's natural system, which must be conserved for the good of mankind' and that 'each generation of man *holds* the resources of the earth for future generations and has an *obligation* to ensure that this legacy is conserved and, when utilized, is used wisely'.[36] This is the clearest articulation yet in a wildlife convention in force of intergenerational rights and obligations and is more ecocentric than Rio Principle 3's reformulation of the principle, viz that 'the right to development must be fulfilled so as to equitably meet developmental and environmental needs of present and future generations'. Its parties have recently become more active in implementing it and have now concluded several subsidiary agreements.[37] It stresses that *states* are the protectors of the species within national boundaries, although recognizing that conservation and effective management of migratory species require the concerted action of all states within whose boundaries they spend part of their lifecycle. No international authority is established; only a small Secretariat, a Scientific Council, and a triennial Conference of the Parties. Finally, in the context of community interest, it should be noted that a Ramsar Convention Conference in 1987, as part of its definition of 'wise use' as employed in that Convention, defined 'sustainable use' as 'human use of a wetland so that it may yield the greatest continuous benefit to present generations whilst maintaining its potential to meet the needs and aspirations of future generations'. The most recent definition of 'wise use' adopted at COP 9 in Kampala (2005), which is discussed further below in section 3(1), refers expressly to 'the context of sustainable development'.

The preambular articulation of international community interest or inter-generational interest in protection of living resources is generally coupled not with the institution of international management bodies with independent powers but with expression of the duty of states parties to cooperate and establish machinery through which they can do so.[38] This is evidenced in all the conventions cited so far, the Biodiversity Convention being no exception, confining recognition of 'the common concern of mankind' to its Preamble and merely expressing therein also 'determination' to 'conserve and use' biodiversity for 'the benefit of present and future generations', without concession to their 'interest'. Of particular relevance in this respect also are the regional conventions, even those not identifying 'common interest' or 'concern' as such. The Preamble to the 1979 Berne Convention merely expresses the need for greater 'unity' and cooperation among members. No international authority is established; action is left to each contracting party, though the Convention does institute a Standing Committee of the Parties and secretariat functions are fulfilled by the Council of Europe itself.

---

[36] Emphasis added.   [37] See *infra*, section 3(3).
[38] *Report of United Nations Conference on the Human Environment*, 1972, 12.

Another regional convention, the 1980 CCAMLR, which adopts an ecosystem approach to conservation of Antarctic marine life, refers in its Preamble to the need for international cooperation and to the 'prime responsibilities of the Antarctic Treaty Consultative Parties for Antarctic environmental protection'. It recognizes the need to establish machinery for coordinating measures and studies, institutes a small Secretariat (Article XVII), and a Commission of the Parties which is accorded international personality (Article VII) and which, inter alia, formulates conservation measures (Article IX) advised by a Scientific Committee of Commission Members. In practice, however, the parties have not been able to adopt many cooperative measures, due to the consensus required by Article XII and the objection procedures provided by Article IX.[39] Those that it has adopted have been undermined by illegal, unreported fishing, addressed through CCAMLR Conservation Measures.[40] Of course this is a problem not just for the Southern Ocean; global and other regional conservatory developments are referred to in Chapter 13. Here it suffices to note that although the 1991 Antarctic Protocol adopts an ecosystem approach, the Antarctic Treaty consultative parties considered that 'the requirements for coordination [with the Convention on Biological Diversity] were specific to each of the agreements and that primary responsibility for ensuring such coordination lay with the parties to the Antarctic Treaty that were parties also to the other agreements'.[41] In other words, states parties, not the Antarctic Treaty System as such, are responsible for giving effect to any 'common concern' that may arise out of biodiversity degradation in Antarctica. It is possible that the obligations of states party to both conventions could clash, but this seems unlikely in the light of the Antarctic Protocol's ecosystem approach and emphasis. With the establishment of the Antarctic Treaty Secretariat in 2004 there are perhaps greater prospects for institutional cooperation and coordination.[42]

---

[39] Howard, 38 ICLQ (1989) 135; Lyster's International Wildlife Law, Ch 11; Wettestad and Andresen, The Effectiveness of International Resource Cooperation: Some Preliminary Findings (Lysaker, 1991) 28; Redgwell, in Bowman and Redgwell (eds), International Law and the Conservation of Biodiversity, 109–28, and ibid in Boyle and Freestone (eds), International Law and Sustainable Development (Oxford, 1999) Ch 9. See also French, 2 JIWLP (1999) 291, who argues that the lesson has been learned in Antarctica that preserving ecosystems is a pre-condition to sustainable development and that this necessarily limits states' sovereignty and activities there as a requirement of international law, not just of relevant treaties, and Rothwell, 29 EPL (1999) 17–24, who draws attention to UNEP's potential role in Antarctica.

[40] See for example CCAMLR Conservation Measures 118/XVI, 119/XVI.

[41] See Chilean Working Paper and Draft Final Report of XVIIIth ATCM, ATCM/WP 37, 22 April 1994, para 55, cited by Redgwell, in Bowman and Redgwell (eds), International Law and the Conservation of Biodiversity, 127.

[42] However, the unresolved question of territorial sovereignty over the Antarctic may prove an obstacle to such cooperation. Gardner, a member of the US delegation to Ramsar COP 9, recounts how a Swiss resolution to encourage cooperation between the Ramsar and Antarctic Treaty Secretariats to prepare a list of areas in the Antarctic such as glacial lakes for inscription under Ramsar was withdrawn at the COP 9 meeting in Kampala '[i]n part out of a concern that such a process could encourage countries to take action with respect to territorial claims on Antarctica': Gardner, Ninth Meeting of the Conference of the Contracting Parties to the Convention on Wetlands, available at <http://www.ramsarcommittee.us>, citing 17:23 Earth Negotiations Bulletin (2005).

The 1968 African Convention also failed to provide any new international machinery for cooperation in disbursement of what it refers to as 'mankind's capital' of living resources—not even a regular meeting of the conference of the parties. This failing will be remedied when the revised 2003 version of the Convention enters into force, since it provides for a secretariat and for regular meetings of the COP and empowers the COP to establish further subsidiary bodies of a scientific and technical nature in particular (Article XXVI). But this falls far short of institutional management of the 'natural resources' regulated by the Convention. The 1985 ASEAN Agreement expresses the desire to take both individual and joint conservatory actions, recognizes that international cooperation is essential to attain many of these goals and that the Agreement is essential to achieving these purposes, but again no *supra* national authority is established. The Agreement has never entered into force, though this has not prevented a degree of environmental cooperation within ASEAN including a non-binding 2003 Declaration on Heritage Parks which notes the *in situ* conservation requirements of the Biodiversity Convention and an Agreement for Regulation of Wildlife Trade to bring it into line with CITES.

There exists also a large number of bilateral cooperative agreements on conservation of nature,[43] a few of which recognize, in terms similar to the multilateral conventions, the international value of the resources concerned. A good example is the 1987 US–Canadian Agreement on the Conservation of the Porcupine Caribou Herd, which recognized that it is 'a unique and irreplaceable natural resource of great value which each generation should maintain and make use of so as to conserve them for future generations'.[44] It also recognizes the traditional harvesting rights of indigenous peoples and acknowledges the need to establish cooperative bilateral mechanisms to coordinate the parties' conservatory activities but adds that it should be implemented by existing rather than new management structures.

It is clear from this résumé of the relevant provisions of the leading conservation agreements at international, regional, subregional, and bilateral level, that international conservation law as yet neither recognizes that living resources in general or migratory species in particular are a 'common heritage' in the UNCLOS sense nor the subject of inter generational rights as such. There are no provisions corresponding to the establishment by US law of wildlife as a public trust,[45] nor has any wildlife body

---

[43] The number of such bilateral arrangements is too extensive to list in full here. An interesting example of the interplay between bilateral, trilateral, and multilateral endeavours is the regulation of the polar bear. The previous edition of this volume noted that the Memorandum on Implementation of the Agreement between the USA and the USSR on Cooperation in the Field of Environmental Protection, which includes conservation of rare and endangered species of animals and plants, general wildlife conservation, and management, facilitated conclusion of the multilateral 1973 Polar Bears Agreement. This multilateral agreement has in turn been enhanced by the conclusion in 2000 between the USA and the Russian Federation, after eight years of negotiations, of the Agreement on the Conservation and Management of the Alaska–Chukotka Polar Bear Population: see 97 *AJIL* (2003) 192–3.

[44] UST, *TIAS* 11259.

[45] Nanda, 4 *Millennium* (1975) 101–11, esp 107–9; Redgwell, *Intergenerational Trusts and Environmental Protection* (Manchester, 1999) Ch 3.

corresponding to the International Seabed Authority established by the UNCLOS 1982 been instituted. Terrestrial wildlife remains the property of the state within whose boundaries it resides, albeit temporarily; in international areas it is regarded as a common property resource akin to fisheries. But increasingly it is recognized that cooperation between states in conservation regimes is vital to the survival of migratory species. The treaties and agreements evidence such a degree of specific acceptance of the need for such cooperation that both conservation (though undefined) and cooperation can, it is submitted, now be regarded as duties established as part of customary law by state practice.[46] The increasing reference to conservation of species and habitat as community concerns, whatever form of expression is used, enhances the emergence of these duties even in relation to living resources located within areas of national jurisdiction. There is some, but less extensive, evidence on the basis of the growing number of bilateral and regional agreements, that the principle of good neighbourliness is also recognized and that it requires cooperation, notification, and consultation on matters affecting conservation. This conclusion is supported also by the variety of political and administrative bodies established for developing cooperative regulatory measures at national and international levels, such as regular Conferences of the Parties, Scientific Committees and/or Councils, Management Authorities, Standing Committees, Commissions, and Secretariats.[47] Every agreement has either established such a body, or required designation of the appropriate national agencies, or use of existing international organizations, such as the AU, OAS, UNESCO, the Council of Europe, IUCN, FAO, UNEP, or a combination of these. The Biodiversity Convention has built on these developments, as we have seen, stressing in Article 22 that its provisions do not affect parties' rights and obligations deriving from *any* existing agreement unless their exercise would cause a serious damage or threat to biological diversity. Several Memoranda of Cooperation with the institutions of other relevant conventions have been concluded.[48]

2(4) COOPERATIVE AND CONSERVATORY TECHNIQUES

It is important also, therefore, in the light of Article 22 of the Biodiversity Convention, to consider the variety of techniques available under the other conventions for development of cooperative measures. Many of these techniques can only work on the basis of cooperation, reciprocity, and mutual trust; for example permit systems, establishment of protected areas; listings of endangered species, joint inspection or enforcement schemes, exchange of scientific data, and other information.

(a) Listing, permit systems, and other techniques

The main technique used in the conventions is to list species, sites, etc requiring regulation in annexes, appendices, or simply 'lists'. Generally this is combined with a system of

[46] On transboundary cooperation generally see *supra*, Ch 3, section 4.   [47] *Supra*, Ch 1.
[48] *Supra*, Ch 11.

permits, each state party being required to enact the necessary legislation. In conjunction with the provision of a regular forum within which the parties can meet, discuss, exchange information and otherwise inform, and negotiate—whether it be an ad hoc commission established by the Convention, regular conferences of the parties, or use of an existing international organization—this institutes the flexible system necessary to fine-tune the requisite conservatory measures to both internationally agreed scientific advice and political support, taking account of the economic and social as well as the environmental effects of the measures and of their impact on development. These procedures and institutions can now be used to conserve biodiversity among the species regulated. As an ultimate safeguard of national interests most species conventions, though allowing regulations to be adopted by various forms of majority vote, also include an objections procedure,[49] whereby if states formally object to a new measure within a specified period, they are not bound by it; this undermines the effectiveness of some measures but ensures wider participation in the Convention.[50] Alternatively, some conventions provide that if states do not notify any objection they are bound (sometimes referred to as the 'tacit amendment' procedure), which makes introduction of changes somewhat easier than the formal objection procedure.

Listing is a popular conservatory measure, despite its omission from the Biodiversity Convention's toolbox. It remains a basic technique of fisheries and marine mammal conventions.[51] The 1968 African Convention[52]—but not its 2003 revision—lists natural resources according to the degree of protection required: those threatened with extinction are banned from hunting unless this is required in the national interest or for scientific purposes; the others can be listed only under special authority. These provisions can be applied to unlisted species to preserve particular national fauna. Measures taken must be scientifically based and reconciled with customary rights.

The Bonn Convention also provides for listing of threatened species in appendices according to the degree of threat.[53] The need for conservatory measures depends on whether a species has a favourable or unfavourable 'conservation status', namely, the sum of the influences acting on it that may affect its long-term distribution and abundance (Article 1(1)(c)). Species are listed, on the basis of reliable scientific evidence, in one of two appendices according to their degree of endangerment. Parties that are 'Range States' of that species, that is states exercising jurisdiction over any part of the range of a migratory species that is listed as having an unfavourable conservation status, or whose flag vessels take it beyond national jurisdictional limits, must conclude international agreements to conserve them (Article 2).[54]

The Berne Convention also lists endangered species on two appendices according to the degree of threat (Article 7) and requires parties to take such measures as closed seasons, prohibition of taking (as required), and prohibition of indiscriminate means

---

[49] As in the 1946 Whaling Convention, on which see *infra*, Ch 13.

[50] *Supra*, Ch 2.   [51] *Infra*, Ch 13.

[52] See *Lyster's International Wildlife Law* 278–304; ibid, 29 *NRJ* (1989) 979–1000; De Klemm, 29 *NRJ* (1989) 935–78.

[53] See *Lyster's International Wildlife Law*, 129–55.   [54] See *infra*, section 3(3).

of capture, though exceptions can be permitted. Parties are also required to take appropriate measures to conserve the habitat of species listed on the appendices and there are special provisions for migratory species. Its Standing Committee of member states of the Council of Europe can make recommendations on all these matters and has done so. The listing system is also used to protect wetlands (as defined therein) in the Ramsar Convention,[55] which now has over 150 parties. Each party must designate suitable wetlands in its territory for inclusion in a List of Wetlands of International Importance (Article 2), maintained by a Bureau established under the Convention. The choice is made on the basis of their international significance in terms of ecology, botany, zoology, limnology, or hydrology. The wetlands remain subject to national sovereignty but parties must promote their conservation in conformity with the international obligations laid down in the Convention. Conferences meet regularly: they can give advice on, amongst other things, conservation, wise use, and management. The parties have been increasingly active on all these issues, as illustrated later in this chapter, even though their obligations are expressed in general terms only. In 1987 many improvements were introduced to make the Convention more relevant to developing countries. There is less emphasis on wetlands and waterfowl protection as such, more on their value to people and on wise use; further developments have occurred following adoption of UNCED instruments including the Rio Declaration, Agenda 21, and the Biodiversity Convention and these are outlined below.

Under the 1972 World Heritage Convention,[56] areas that are listed constitute a world heritage for whose protection it is the duty of the international community as a whole to cooperate (Articles 6 and 11), but remain under the sovereignty of the state in which it is located (Article 2). The WHC maintains a list of those areas considered to be of outstanding universal value in terms of criteria established by it.[57] Thus it is not all natural heritage which is to be protected, conserved, and transmitted to future generations and which will be eligible for inscription on the World Heritage List.

Finally, mention must be made of the system underlying the 1973 CITES,[58] which now has 173 parties and more than 30,000 animal and plant species under its remit, and which is one of the most effective and important wildlife conventions. It deals with the threat to survival of many commercially attractive animals species posed by trading in them or their products. It thus requires that international trade between parties be sustainable in terms of the survival of the species, subspecies, and populations concerned. This and other synergies between the CITES and other related conventions, including the Biodiversity Convention, have been pointed out by some commentators.[59] CITES parties need to identify the species so threatened and monitor trade imports, on the

---

[55] See *Lyster's International Wildlife Law*, 183–207.   [56] See ibid, 208–38.

[57] See *infra*, section 3(2).

[58] See *Lyster's International Wildlife Law*, Ch 15; Favre, *Convention on Trade in Endangered Species* (Dordrecht, 1990) *passim*; for recent development see Ong, 10 *JEL* (1998) 291–314; Hepworth, 1 *JIWLP* (1998) 412; Wijnstekers, *The Evolution of CITES* (8th edn, CITES Secretariat, Geneva, 2005); on its trade, conservation, and animal welfare dimensions, see Bowman, 1 *JIWLP* (1998) 9–63.

[59] De Fontaubert, Downes, Agardy, *Biodiversity in the Seas* (CIEL, Washington DC, 1995).

basis of the precautionary approach now approved by both Conventions though not spelt out in the substantive articles of either. New science-based listing criteria thus have to be devised: the Memoranda of Cooperation concluded between the CITES and CBD Secretariats is conducive to this, as also are relevant Decisions of the COP of the CBD[60] which spell out the subject matter of coordination and cooperation, not only with CITES, but also with some other relevant conventions of importance outlined in this chapter. Under CITES, species whose survival is threatened by international trade therein or in specimens thereof or which may become so unless trade is regulated, are listed on appendices, which can be amended at the biennial conferences of its parties. Export and import of those threatened with extinction (listed on Appendix 1) requires prior issue and presentation of an export and import permit; these are issued only if certain conditions are met (Article III). Re-export similarly requires a prior permit. The advice of both the national Scientific and Management Authorities, established under the Convention, must be sought on questions such as whether export will be detrimental to the species' survival, whether or not the specimen was obtained in breach of state laws, and whether the method of shipment minimizes risk of injury, damage to health, or cruel treatment, etc, of animals concerned. The export-import permit system is the crux of this Convention but exemptions are permitted, for example, if the specimen was acquired before the Convention applied, or the specimens are household effects (subject to various exceptions). An incentive for participation and compliance is that trade with states not party to the Convention is permitted only if 'comparable documentation' to that required by CITES is issued by the state concerned. As CITES membership expands there are fewer non-parties with which other non-parties can trade. There is much for the small Secretariat established under it to do since, inter alia, it can invite the parties' attention to any matter 'pertaining to the aims of the convention' (Article XII (2)(e)) and can communicate to the parties concerned relevant information about species and specimens in transit and the status of relevant permits. Whether or not the CITES system is the best approach to conserving wildlife and biodiversity is, however, now being called into question, as indicated in section 5 below.

(b) Protection of habitat

The strategies outlined in earlier sections of this chapter stress the need to conserve species' habitats as an integral part of their effective conservation. Fishery conventions generally ignore this aspect, although, even in 1957, the Bering Fur Seals Convention required research on the relationship between fur seals and other marine resources and on whether fur seals had adverse effects on other resources exploited by its parties, and the more recent North-east and North-west Atlantic Fisheries Conventions require scientific advice on ecological and environmental factors to be obtained as indicated in Chapter 13. Several of the major wildlife conventions, many of which

---

[60] *Handbook of the CBD*, Sec VIII, esp Decision III/21; this built on Decisions II/13 and 14 adopted by the 2nd COP.

list some marine mammals, now specifically provide for habitat protection. Amongst these is the 1968 African Convention which provides for the creation of 'special reserves' set aside for conservation of wildlife and protection of its habitat (Article III), within which killing and human settlement is controlled, and also for 'partial reserves' or 'sanctuaries' set aside to protect particularly threatened animal or plant species (especially those listed) and the biotypes necessary for their survival. It also requires maintenance and extension of existing conservation areas and possible creation of new ones to protect representative ecosystems and those peculiar to a territory and that parties establish protective zones round these areas for control of detrimental activities (Article X, 1968). The 2003 revision provides similarly for 'conservation areas' to conserve representative ecosystems or areas with a high degree of biological diversity, and ensure conservation of species, including those threatened or of special scientific or aesthetic value (Article XII). Buffer zones are also to be established where activites outside a conservation are detrimental to the purposes for conservation within the conservation area (Article XII(4)). The definition and management objectives for different categories of conservation area—strict nature reserve, wilderness area, national park, natural monument, habitat/species management area, protected landscape/ seascape, and managed resource protection area—are set forth in Annex 2. These categories clearly reflect the influence of other instruments, including the Biodiversity Convention and the World Heritage Convention.

The 1971 Ramsar Convention is concerned with protecting 'the fundamental ecological functions of wetlands as regulators of water regimes and as habitats supporting a characteristic flora and fauna, especially waterfowl'. The 1972 World Heritage Convention defines 'natural heritage' to include 'areas which constitute the habitat of threatened species of animals of outstanding universal value from the point of view of science or conservation' (Article 2). The 2005 Operational Guidelines state that nominated natural heritage properties must contain, inter alia, 'the most important and significant natural habitats for *in-situ* conservation of biological diversity, including those containing threatened species of outstanding universal value from the point of view of science or conservation'.[61] The 1979 Bonn Convention defines habitat as 'any area in the range of a migratory species which contains suitable living conditions for that species'. Range states of the Appendix I species must try to conserve and restore habitats important to removing these species from danger of extinction (Article III(4)(a)) and agreements concluded by range states must provide for conservation and restoration of habitats important in maintaining a favourable conservation status (Article V(5) (e)). The 1979 Berne Convention's stated titular and preambular aims include conservation of natural habitats, as also do its general provisions. This is a major purpose of the Convention. Several articles lay down obligations on parties to promote policies, enact legislation, and take other measures for this purpose (Articles 3, 4, and 12). The

---

[61] *Operational Guidelines for the Implementation of the World Heritage Convention* WHC 05/2, 2 February 2005, para 77. For fuller disussion see Redgwell, in Francioni and Lenzerini (eds), *The 1972 World Heritage Convention: A Commentary* (Oxford, 2008), Ch 2.

1940 Western Hemisphere Convention's aim is also to protect representatives of species in their natural habitat.

Despite these provisions in major conventions, however, the record of states parties in implementing habitat protection measures is generally considered to be less good than that in implementation of permit systems. States often limit habitat protection to national parks or nature reserves (see below) or do not extend it to certain species. State practice and response to pressure from NGOs in this respect varies as the different fates of certain loggerhead turtle nesting sites in Greece and Turkey earlier revealed: in the former case, tourist development threatening such sites was stopped; in the latter it was not, though both states concerned are parties to the Berne Convention;[62] these examples are often repeated. It remains to be seen whether the influence of the UNCED instruments, including the Biodiversity Convention's holistic approach to nature conservation will overcome the sectoralism of the existing system in this context, but as we shall see both the CBD COP and its other institutions, as well as those of the major relevant conventions, do appear to be responding to these new demands and incentives to some extent.

(c) Creation of nature reserves, marine parks, and protected areas

National parks and nature reserves are a means of giving special protection to endangered wildlife and ecologically important areas. Antarctica is the largest and most important nature reserve specifically so designated and protected by treaty. In addition to a ban on all mineral extraction, the 1991 Antarctic Environment Protocol provides, inter alia, for measures to conserve flora and fauna.[63] Both the 1940 Western Hemisphere Convention and the 1968 African Convention, with its 2003 revision, also encourage the creation of national parks, nature reserves, nature monuments, and strict wilderness reserves, all of which are defined and for which various protective measures are laid down.[64]

UNEP has added protocols on Specially Protected Areas to its Mediterranean and Caribbean Regional Seas Conventions which are discussed further in Chapters 7 and 13.[65] Although these aim to protect marine resources, the consequent coordination and implementation problems provide lessons for similar terrestrial situations. The Protocol to the Barcelona Convention requires, in Article 3, that such areas be

---

[62] Lyster, 'Protection of Wildlife from the Point of View of the North', Paper given at Dartmouth College Colloquium on International Governance, Hanover, USA, 17–19 June 1991; unpublished; on file with the authors.

[63] Article II and Annex 2.

[64] 1968 African Convention on Conservation of Nature, Articles 3, 10; 1940 Convention on Nature Protection and Wildlife Preservation, Article II. See *Lyster's International Wildlife Law*, Chs 8 (Western Hemisphere), 9 (African Convention). As indicated above, Annex 2 of the 2003 revision to the African Convention defines and sets forth management objectives for 7 categories of conservation area: strict nature reserve; wilderness area; national park; natural monument; habitat/species management area; protected landscape/seascape; and managed resource protection area.

[65] 1995 Barcelona Protocol Concerning Mediterranean Specially Protected Areas; 1990 Kingston Protocol Concerning Specially Protected Areas and Wildlife.

established to safeguard in particular (a) sites of biological and ecological value; the genetic diversity, as well as satisfactory population levels, of species, and their breed-ing grounds and habitats; representative types of ecosystems as well as ecological processes; and (b) sites of particular importance because of their scientific, aesthetic, historical, archaeological, cultural, or educational interest. It is thus the most ambi-tious of all instruments in this respect. The parties are required to develop standards for selecting, establishing, managing, and notifying information on such protected areas. The aim is to have a series of interlinked areas throughout the Mediterranean but the obligations are expressed subjectively in 'soft terms': parties are required only 'to the extent possible' to establish such areas and to 'endeavour to undertake the action necessary' in order to protect and, as appropriate, restore them 'as rapidly as possible'. The possible scope of the subject matter of the measures is, however, spelt out in Article 7 and is quite broad.

A potentially controversial issue is the regulation of passage, stopping, and anchor-ing of ships within these areas; conflicts could develop if the rules concerning inno-cent passage and rights established under IMO and other relevant conventions are not observed. However, both these Protocols and the 1986 Noumea Convention for the Protection of the Natural Resources and Environment of the South Pacific Region do, for the first time, bring together in one instrument, outside the 1982 UNCLOS itself, the regulation of all sources of pollution and the conservation of living resources. This is now seen to be the approach required for effective conservation on an ecologi-cal basis and is commended as such in the various strategies laid down internation-ally for this purpose. Implementation problems can arise where treaties overlap and not all parties to the regional-seas agreement are party to the global treaty or treaties upon which it builds.[66] Many of the UNEP Conventions overlap with the global IMO and other conventions; but there are many compatible provisions, as well as unique elements: the CBD's *in situ* requirements go beyond the SPAW Protocol, for exam-ple. The tendency is to enact broad, umbrella-type legislation and leave overlaps to be resolved by production of subsequent management plans; the Protocols do, however, require the adoption of a precautionary approach requiring that states 'shall manage species of flora and fauna with the objective of preventing species becoming threat-ened or endangered'.[67] The SPAW/CBD Memorandum of Understanding, initiated by the SPAW Secretariat in 1994 to promote cooperation and coordination, noted that SPAW was a fundamental instrument toward securing implementation of the CBD in the Caribbean Region, though the Memorandum has serious weaknesses.[68]

The ASEAN Convention, in Article 13, requires its parties to establish 'terrestrial, freshwater, coastal or marine protection areas' to safeguard essential ecological proc-esses, representative samples of ecosystems, natural habitat (especially of rare or

---

[66] For problems developing national implementing leglislation under the SPAW Protocol, see Anderson, 28 *EPL* (1998) 237ff.

[67] Freestone, in Bowman and Redgwell (eds), *International Law and the Conservation of Biodiversity* (London, 1996) 91–107.

[68] Anderson, 28 *EPL* (1998) 241.

endangered species), gene pools, and reference sources for research, inter alia, thus being one of the first conventions to provide for preservation of biological diversity. Several states parties have enacted national legislation establishing near-shore marine parks,[69] with consequent problems arising from the interface of coast and sea, but whether or not they have done so in pursuit of the conventions or strategies is difficult to determine. Undoubtedly these are having some effect.

(d) Provision of financial assistance

Both the taking of necessary conservation measures and the non-exploitation of wildlife can have adverse economic consequences, especially serious for developing states. To achieve sustainable development on a global basis, and especially to preserve biological diversity, it was suggested that compensation should be available in such circumstances long before conclusion of the Biodiversity Convention which made specific provision for this in Article 20.

Only one convention originally established a fund to help achieve its purposes, namely, the World Heritage Convention, Articles 15–18 of which establish the World Heritage Fund for the Protection of the World Cultural and Natural Heritage of Outstanding Universal Value, as a trust fund in accordance with UNESCO's financial regulations. The moneys are drawn from five sources: compulsory and voluntary contribution of states parties; contributions, gifts, or bequests made by other states, UNESCO, and other UN bodies and intergovernmental organizations, public or private bodies, and individuals; interest accruing on the Fund; benefit events for the Fund; and other authorized sources drawn up by the World Heritage Committee (WHC). The World Heritage Convention requires states to contribute to the trust fund on a basis related to their contributions to UNESCO; thus the richer states are expected to pay most. There is, of course, nothing to stop parties and non-parties voluntarily contributing more than these amounts or assisting in other forms of fund-raising. The funds can be used only for purposes defined by the WHC in Articles 19–26. Operational guidelines have been promulgated which categorize assistance as preparatory, emergency, or training and technical cooperation, and which lay down priorities. Formal agreements are concluded between the WHC and the party concerned.

In the 1980s a Wetlands Conservation Fund was established under the Ramsar Convention to facilitate participation by developing states, whose involvement was seen to be increasingly crucial to that convention's success.[70] Contributions derive mainly from the industrialized states parties and are used to promote wetland conservation in developing states. A Protocol was also added to the 1985 Ozone Convention (see Chapter 6) establishing funds to assist poor states to reduce chlorofluorocarbon emissions. This has the incidental effect of helping to protect species and habitats from the

---

[69] De Saussay, *Principles, Criteria and Guidelines for the Establishment of Mediterranean Marine and Coastal Protected Areas*, IUCN (Gland, 1981); Salm and Clark, *Marine and Coastal Protected Areas: A Guide for Planners and Managers*, IUCN (1983); see, for legislative and institutional support, 35–52, esp 44–8 on international aspects.

[70] *Proc of the 4th Conf of the Contracting Parties* (Ramsar Bureau, 1990) 141.

adverse effects of ozone depletion. Finally, the World Bank's Global Environmental Facility (GEF), outlined in Chapter 2, has been established specifically to aid developing countries to relieve pressures on global ecosystems, including preserving biological diversity and natural habitats. Recently the Biodiversity Liaison Group, representing the five treaty secretariats (CBD, which takes the lead, and the World Heritage Convention, CITES, CMS, and the Bonn Convention), has called for the GEF to finance all five biodiversity-related instruments given their overlapping mandates.[71]

In the wildlife field in general, however, provision of financial assistance is a neglected area of international environmental law. Clearly more states would be prepared to join in conservation conventions and enact the necessary controls if they could be compensated for the economic costs of taking the required restrictive measures. Many other writers have canvassed proposals for taxes and other sources of revenue to provide funds for compensation of the costs of environmental protection.[72] The argument was succinctly put by a president of Tanzania as follows: 'That Tanzania has a rich wildlife resource is an accident of geography. It belongs to all mankind. The international community should therefore contribute to its survival.'[73] The CBD's acknowledgement that conservation of biodiversity is a 'common concern of human kind' endorses this approach, but without vesting property or concomitant rights of unfettered access in the international community. Bargains therefore remain to be struck and negotiated.

Glennon has argued that certain resources *should* be regarded as global environmental resources (for example tropical rain forests and the elephant); all states would then have a right to expect the state of their location to protect them; correspondingly, the other states would have a duty to share the burden of preserving these resources.[74] He categorizes these as *custodial* (the state of location's duty to preserve the resource) and *support* obligations (the duty of other states to contribute to the preservatory conduct of the custodial state), which could involve both compensation for resulting loss of export income or paying the enforcement costs of stopping poaching of elephants, etc, or both. This financial support could either be organized multilaterally through establishment of international funds or unilaterally through the so-called 'debt swap' or 'debt for nature' agreements, whereby lenders to developing countries forego some or all of the debt repayment in return for the taking by the borrower state of environmentally protective measures, as has already been arranged in some cases.[75] In some cases NGOs have taken over the debt in return for similar commitments which, though laudable, has had slight impact on conservation given the small scale of such activities.[76]

---

[71] 3rd Report of the Biodiversity Liaison Group, Gland, Switzerland, 10 May 2005, BLG-3/REP, 8 June 2005, para 9.

[72] See works cited by Glennon, 84 *AJIL* (1990) 28, n 233.   [73] Ibid, 28 and n 232.

[74] Ibid, 28.

[75] For examples, see ibid, 36; see also letter from Mrs Thatcher (then UK Prime Minister) to Dr Holdgate, Director-General, IUCN, responding positively to such proposals, 20 *IUCN Bull* 46 (1989) 24.

[76] Glennon, 84 *AJIL* (1990) 36; Wee, 6 *JEL* (1994) 1.

The enthusiasm for public-private partnerships evident in some domestic juris-dictions has its reflection in international treaties, with both the Ramsar and World Heritage Convention participating in such arrangements. For example, in 2004 the International Corporate Wetlands Restoration Partnership was established as a joint initiative of the UN Foundation with the Nature Conservancy and the Gillette Company, designed to leverage private financial contributions to match existing inter-national mechanisms under these Conventions. The first large project is Sian Ka'an in Mexico, a Ramsar and World Heritage site as well as a biosphere reserve. In 2001, the Great Apes Survival Project (GRASP) was launched as a public/private partnership led by UNESCO and UNEP. It now involves twenty-three range states, several donor nations, thirty NGOs, and four conventions: CITES, the World Heritage Convention, the CMS, and the CBD.[77]

3 SIGNIFICANCE AND EFFECTIVENESS OF THE MAJOR GLOBAL WILDLIFE CONVENTIONS

It is virtually impossible to assess the effectiveness of the wildlife conservation regime from a cross-sectoral perspective, for example, to evaluate the effect on conservation of one species of all the measures that have been—or might be—applied to it under the full range of conventions, and particularly in the context of the broad requirements of the Biodiversity Convention. It is somewhat easier to evaluate the relative effectiveness of the techniques provided under particular conventions, although even here it is not possible to give an overview of all state practice in implementation of a convention; some global conventions are less well ratified than others, as in the case of the Bonn Convention, and this per se reduces their effectiveness. Glennon, in his article assess-ing the effectiveness of international law for conserving the elephant, concentrated entirely on criticizing the provisions and operation of CITES, which he found defect-ive, and made little attempt to identify the relevance and potential of conventions such as the Bonn Convention or World Heritage Convention, to which he made only curs-ory reference,[78] but the requirements of the Biodiversity Convention now necessitate a broader approach to coordination and cooperation among all the relevant sectoral conventions at all levels, as recognized in the practice of its institutions to date noted in this chapter.

It has always to be borne in mind that a whole range of concepts, principles, and measures, specific and non-specific, can be invoked to protect living resources. Some are undoubtedly more effective than others. It is now over thirty-five years since the adoption of the UNCHE Declaration, Recommendations, and Action Plan, which

---

[77] See further Redgwell, in Francioni and Lenzerini (eds), *The 1972 World Heritage Convention: A Commentary* (Oxford, 2008) 388–90.

[78] Ibid, *passim*; and see *infra*.

greatly accelerated the conclusion of wildlife conventions in pursuance of their principles, which themselves have been kept in the forefront of international action to preserve endangered species by the numerous strategies adopted since. It is over fifteen
years since adoption of UNCED's Declaration, Agenda 21 and related conventions and
principles which augment these and place them within the framework of achievement
of sustainable development. There is thus now considerable state practice under the
major conventions. This has accrued in the form of resolutions, amendments to the
relevant appendices, and states' acceptance or rejection of these, making it possible
at least to review this aspect. Reviewing all the developments within these conventions, and even more so the relevant national laws implementing these, is too vast a
task for a work of the present kind. Fuller treatment is found in Lyster's seminal work
International Wildlife Law, the first edition of which outlined progress up to 1984
under twenty-seven treaties and refers to many others, with a second edition due in
early 2009 which adds to this tally. In this section, we shall again confine our review
mainly to Lyster's 'big four' treaties which remain the centrepiece of wildlife law and
were listed at the outset of this chapter—the Ramsar, World Heritage, CITES, and
Bonn Conventions. By virtue of their relevance to the objectives of conservation strategies outlined in this chapter, especially those now set by the Biodiversity Convention,
these treaties continue to have the most influential effect on the development of the
international law of conservation of living resources. Together with the Biodiversity
Convention discussed in detail above, these comprise a 'web' of biodiversity-related
treaties with increasing linkages between them, whilst each maintains a legally separate and dynamically evolving structure.

3(1) THE RAMSAR CONVENTION ON WETLANDS OF INTERNATIONAL IMPORTANCE 1971[79]

At every one of its meetings, the Biodiversity Convention's COP has reaffirmed the
importance it attaches to cooperation and coordination between it and other relevant
conventions, institutions, and processes.[80] Thus a Memorandum of Cooperation has
been concluded between the CBD Secretariat and that of the Ramsar Convention
in 1996, replaced and updated in 2005. The CBD COP's decisions, inter alia, regularly invite it to cooperate as a lead partner in implementing its decisions concerning inland water biodiversity[81] and it has approved a joint work plan between them

---

[79] *Lyster's International Wildlife Law*, Ch 13; Ramsar, *The Quarterly Newsletter of the Convention on Wetlands of International Importance Especially as Wildfowl Habitat*, Nos 1 (1987) onwards; Ramsar Convention Secretariat, *The Ramsar Convention Manual: A Guide to the Convention on Wetlands* (4th edn, Gland, 2006); Navid, 29 *NRJ* (1989) 1001–16; 20 *IUCN Bull* 4–6 (1989); Special Report: Wetlands; Bowman, 42 *Neths ILR* (1995) 1–52; Bowman, 66 *ICLQ* (1995) 540–559; ibid, 11 *JEL* (1999) 87, 281; Owen, 13 *JEL* (2001) 21ff.; Matthews, *The Ramsar Convention on Wetlands: Its History and Development* (Ramsar Convention Bureau, 1993); Shine and de Klemm, *Wetlands, Water and the Law* (IUCN Environmental Policy and Law Paper No 38, Gland, 1999); Farrier and Tucker, 12 *JEL* (2000) 21–42, provide illuminating insight into its implementation in general and in Australia in particular.

[80] See *CBD Handbook*, Sec IV, Decisions 1/5, 11/13, 111/21, IV/15, and Guide to Article 26.

[81] Decision III/21, para 7.

covering twenty-five areas of collaborate activity.[82] The Ramsar parties in turn have noted that it will be natural for it to play a leading role in the conservation of wetland biodiversity.[83] The Ramsar Convention is essentially sectoral and its approach is accordingly limited, not well tuned to the holistic, broadly ecological approach required to effectively implement the Biodiversity Convention, but its practice now presents an interesting case study of an ability to adapt and progress, without the benefit of formal amendment procedures, towards integration and sustainable developmental goals. It was both the first wildlife convention, the ICRW apart, to aim at global participation and the first to be concerned, at that level, solely with protection of habitat. Its most important requirements in relation to conservation of biodiversity relate to the obligations to record internationally significant wetlands on its List of Wetlands of International Importance and 'promote' their conservation, and to 'promote', as far as possible, the 'wise use' of all wetlands within the territory of the parties.[84]

The general nature of its provisions has given rise to problems of interpretation and weakness of obligations. It was not clear, for example, whether parties had an obligation to promote conservation of listed sites in all states parties or only of their own sites. There are, unusually in relation to the other three 'lead' conventions, no amendment procedures. Its parties have had to resort to interpretative recommendations in lieu of these. Although, for its purposes, the Biodiversity Convention allows 'sustainable use' of biodiversity, the Ramsar Convention permits undefined 'wise use' of sites recorded on a list maintained by its Bureau and neither forbids nor regulates the taking of species for any purpose, though such use must not affect the ecological characteristics of wetland. The Bureau, originally provided by IUCN on an interim basis, has, since 1988, been established as an independent office headed by a secretary general,[85] which has greatly strengthened its role.

Despite the fact that originally it had a relatively small number of predominantly European parties, that it is underfunded, and has only a small Bureau compared to the other major conventions, the parties have been able gradually but relatively effectively to use its provisions and machinery to promote the Convention's objectives, although it has proved more attractive to list wetlands than to provide effectively for their 'wise use' in the broad sense, now essential for ecological conservation. On the eve of the adoption of the CBD, 549 wetlands in sixty-five countries had been placed on its list; sixteen years later, its 158 parties have designated 1,757 sites covering a surface of 161,000,000 hectares, many of which are in developing states.[86] Many parties have

---

[82] Decision IV/13, para 2.   [83] Resolution 5.1, 5th COP, Kashiro, Japan, 1993.

[84] Article 3(1).

[85] Ramsar Convention, *Report of the Third Meeting of the Conference of the Contracting Parties*, Regina, Canada 1987, 27 May–5 June, Resolution on Secretariat Matters, 1–2. Secretariat established by amendments adopted at an extraordinary conference of the contracting parties, held at Regina, Saskatchewan, Canada, 28 May–3 June 1987; see Report of this Conference and texts, 3. The Convention will maintain its own independent offices both at IUCN, Gland, Switzerland and at the International Waterfowl Research Bureau, UK.

[86] *Directory of Wetlands of International Importance*, prepared by IUCN. The current ambitious target of expanding the Ramsar list to at least 2500 sites covering 250,000,000 hectares by 2010 (see Resolution IX.1, Annex B) is unlikely to be met.

exceeded its minimum legal requirement of one site designation, though both distribution and size of areas covered requires further continual enlargement for conservation purposes, particularly in view of the scope of the Biodiversity Convention
requirements. It is not enough, however, for purposes of ensuring conservation of biodiversity within that Convention's framework, merely to list sites; its requirements for
in situ conservation (Article 8) need to be observed.

At the first Ramsar Convention meeting, in Cagliari in 1980, detailed criteria for
listing of sites were adopted and recommended to the parties. Notably, though the
Convention's requirement of 'wise use' of wetlands was not defined, this conference recommended that the term be interpreted as involving 'maintenance of their ecological
character, as a basis not only for conservation, but for sustainable development',[87]
though later thought to be too technical a definition for a broad audience. Though this
goal might differ between states it was considered that there was no fundamental difference between them in the ways through which it could be achieved. Thus the Regina
Conference in 1987 redefined 'wise use' of wetlands as 'their sustainable utilization for
the benefit of human kind in a way compatible with the maintenance of the natural
properties of the ecosystem'.[88] This conference also established a Working Group on
Criteria and Wise Use and defined 'sustainable utilization' as 'human use of a wetland so that it may yield the greatest continuous benefit to present generations whilst
maintaining its potential to meet the needs and aspirations of future generations' for
purposes of fulfilling the Article 3 requirement of the Ramsar Convention that parties
supply the Bureau with information on 'wise use'. Finally, it defined 'natural properties of the ecosystem' as 'those physical, biological or chemical components, such as
soil, water, plants, animals and nutrients and the interactions between them'.

Writing in 2000, Farrier and Tucker pointed out that the Biodiversity Convention's
emphasis on interaction between 'conservation' and 'sustainable use', and relega-
tion of other values to its Preamble contrasts with the Ramsar Convention's separate
requirements of promotion of conservation of listed wetlands and wise use of the rest,
which envisages more prudent management of the former.[89] This contrast is no longer
as sharp, however, with the further refinement of the 'wise use' definition which took
place at the Kampala Conference in 2005 with the adoption of a revised 'Conceptual
Framework for the Wise Use of Wetlands and the Maintenance of their Ecological
Character'. It defines 'wise use of wetlands' as 'the maintenance of their ecological
character, achieved through the implementation of ecosystem approaches, within the
context of sustainable development'.[90] This 'slightly delphic allusion to "ecosystem

---

[87] Cagliari Conference, Recommendation 104; see also Recommendation 3.3 of the Regina Conference
1987 which upgraded these criteria.

[88] *Rept of 3rd Mtng of the Conf of the Contracting Parties*, Rec C 3.3 (Rev).

[89] Farrier and Tucker, 12 *JEL* (2000) 21; on the parameters of 'wise use', see also 30–1.

[90] Resolution IX.1, Annex A (2005). Further guidance is found in guidelines on the practical application
of 'wise use', first elaborated at the Regina Conference in 1987. There are now 14 *Handbooks for the Wise
Use of Wetlands* (3rd edn, Ramsar Convention Secretariat, 2007) which include guidelines adopted at the
7th (1999), 8th (2002) and 9th (2005) Meetings of the Conference of the Parties.

approaches" is intended to reflect the practice of the Biodiversity Convention', with recent Ramsar resolutions appearing to treat 'conservation' and 'wise use' as 'a sort of composite concept' without clear distinction between them.[91] This is not to suggest that development is an objective for every wetland, since 'wise use' of wetlands clearly demands 'the maintenance of their ecological character'.[92]

Some sites have been protected under national law before listing; but listing them, as in the case of World Heritage sites, becomes a means of raising their profile and securing national action when they are threatened;[93] other states list sites not yet protected. State practice varies in interpreting the Convention, which is unspecific on this point. Many sites at the time of listing are already within nature reserves; some become so after listing but only a few states take measures restricting activities *outside* these areas to protect them from harm. However, although Article 4(1) of the Convention only requires parties to 'promote' the conservation of the sites and establish nature reserves and wardens, parties must inform the Bureau of changes in the sites' ecology, thus enabling evaluation of their performance by the Conference of the Parties and some evaluation of its correspondence to the requirements of the Biodiversity Convention's articles. Though not all parties provide this information, many have reported instances of substantial enhancement of conservation measures taken to avoid disturbance of listed sites.[94] Action has also been taken on the requirement that parties encourage research and exchange of data and relevant publications and promote training of personnel, which should encourage participation and enhance compliance of developing states, but the absence originally of any fund established by the Convention to provide financial assistance limited participation by developing states. Parties were recommended to provide such assistance[95] and, as indicated in section 4(b)(d) above, have now done so. There was a notable difference in the number of states party to the Ramsar Convention compared to the World Heritage Convention when the latter but not former had a fund. However, the establishment of a fund coupled with the offer by an NGO to provide funding for the operation of the new Monitoring Procedures, if contracting parties matched this contribution,[96] once in place led to a dramatic increase in the number of Ramsar parties. Entry into force of the Biodiversity Convention, and nearly universal participation in it, has added to the pressure to assist developing countries to meet Ramsar's aims.

---

[91] *Lyster's International Wildlife Law*, Ch 13, n 80, citing Resolution VIII.14, para 11, as a particularly good example.

[92] Ibid.

[93] For example, public protest at UK government proposals to blow up an oil tanker off a listed site in Suffolk, resulted in its being towed twenty miles out to sea for this purpose; *Lyster's International Wildlife Law*, Ch 13, n 46.

[94] Ibid, 192–3.

[95] A Recommendation to the Multilateral and Bilateral Development Assistance Agencies concerning Wetlands urging them to use their influence to promote 'wise use' of wetlands was adopted at the Regina Conference in 1987; Rec C.3.4. (Rev).

[96] Ibid, 17.

Several parties, though not required so to do, have enacted legislation requiring environmental impact assessment of development projects that might affect the listed sites[97] and the Second Conference of the Parties held at Groningen in 1984, recommended for priority consideration seven of the Thirty Action Points set out in a Framework Document for Implementation of the Convention,[98] and consequently further measures have been introduced.

The lack of amendment procedures is a serious defect in a wildlife conservation convention since it inhibits its flexibility in adapting it to changed perceptions and needs, including the need to conserve biodiversity, now considered vital to successful conservation in general. Protocols have been adopted to bring about substantial changes but costly extraordinary conferences have to be convened for this purpose and not all parties to the main convention necessarily become parties to the protocols.[99] Similar problems beset other conventions. However, the Third Meeting of the Parties established a Standing Committee to carry out various duties between and during conferences. This Committee has approved a Monitoring Procedure, giving the Bureau an active role when it receives reports of changes in the ecological character of wetlands,[100] and Bowman has shown how far, despite the lack of specific amendment procedures, the treaty has been brought into line with recent developments and concepts of international environmental law,[101] within the existing rules and processes of international treaty law.

Despite the growing activity under this Convention, national reports submitted by contracting parties reveal many persistent problems.[102] However, the strengthening through successive Conferences of the Parties, of its administrative procedures, the establishment of a permanent Secretariat, a Standing Committee, a financial regime of contributions based on the UN scale, the increase in authority accorded to the Conference and its productive use of Resolutions have all enhanced the effectiveness of this innovative Convention, and encouraged increasing cooperation between its Bureau and those of other conventions, especially those of the Bonn and Biological Diversity Conventions.[103] It also, in 1999, concluded a cooperative Memorandum with the World Heritage Secretariat which encouraged active contribution to achieving the CBD goals, instructing its scientific and technical bodies to exchange information, cooperate and coordinate activities. There are now over 30 sites jointly designated under the Ramsar and World Heritage Conventions. The need to take not only

---

[97] See *Lyster's International Wildlife Law*, Ch 13 and EC Council Directive 85/337/EEC, as amended, discussed in Davies, *European Union Environmental Law* (Aldershot, 2004) Ch 5.

[98] May 1984. For more recent points of action, see *Lyster's International Wildlife Law*, Ch 13.

[99] See, e.g. 1982 Protocol, 22 *ILM* (1983) 698–702.   [100] *Rept of 3rd Mtng*, 1987.

[101] Bowman, 66 *ICLQ* (1995) 560.

[102] See most recently the *Report of the Secretary General on the Implementation of the Convention at the Global Level*, Ramsar COP9 DOC 5 (2005). This has been referred to as a 'reality check' with the San Jose Conference of 1999 representing the high water mark in terms of setting quantitative targets which subseqently proved over-optimistic: see *Lyster's International Wildlife Law*, Ch 13(6)(a)(i).

[103] Navid, 29 *NRJ* (1989), 1001, *passim*; for specific examples of cooperation, see 1014–15.

the CBD but other relevant conventions' goals into account in applying the Wise Use Working Group's guidance has also been emphasized.

Nonetheless, problems remain in applying the definition of 'wise use', given that the original 'naturalness' of wetlands' ecosystems has been so long modified by humankind that applying the concept and returning them to some natural state is virtually impossible.[104] Moreover, knowledge of the working of wetland ecosystems is such that decisions have to be made on the basis of great scientific uncertainty in many states parties, despite the adoption by the Ramsar COP of a Resolution on Ecological Character.[105] Adoption of a precautionary approach, despite its omission from the substantive articles of both the Biodiversity and the Ramsar Conventions remains a necessity although socio-economic considerations of use may override it in practice. This view is reinforced by the outcome of a three-year study overseen by the Wise Use Working Group, of existing management practices, that when the activities affecting wetlands should be governed by the precautionary principle and when comprehensive understanding of the ecological constraints upon them was lacking, they should be prohibited. This view, however, is not reflected in current guidance adopted by the Ramsar parties. Nonetheless it should be since, as Australian experience illustrates, the problems are even more acute when proposals relate to use of new wetlands.[106]

Whilst the Ramsar Convention parties, through its institutions, have clearly developed the 'wise use' concept, but the pragmatic listing concept is not conducive to the holistic approach upon which the Biodiversity Convention goals are premised, and it is restricted by its focus on 'wetlands' divorced from their wider catchment areas, a perspective challenged by scientists and not adopted in the CBD since 'wise use' requires regulation of and management of biological resources important to its aims whether inside or outside protected areas.[107] The Convention may have 'come of age', as Bowman concluded, but it still needs to mature.

3(2) WORLD HERITAGE CONVENTION 1971[108]

Articles 2 and 16 of this Convention impose an obligation on parties to conserve and protect the natural heritage, including habitats of 'threatened species of animals and plants of outstanding universal value' from the scientific and conservation viewpoint.

---

[104] Resolution RES C 5.6 (Annex), 5th COP, Kashiro, Japan, 26.

[105] REC C 4.8, on Change in Ecological Character of Ramsar Sites, 4th COP, Montreux, Switzerland, 1990.

[106] CBD Article 8(c)–(d); see Introduction to Wise Use Group's Additional Guidance for the Implementation of the Wise Use Concept, and Farrier and Tucker, who outline and critique Australia's National Strategy for Ecologically Sustainable Development based in pursuit of this.

[107] Convention on Biodiversity Article 8(c)–(d).

[108] Lyster, *International Wildlife Law*, 208–38; Atherton and Atherton, 69 *ALJ* (1995) 631ff; Churchill, in Bowman and Redgwell (eds), *International Law and the Conservation of Biodiversity* (London, 1996) 83; Francioni and Lenzerini (eds), *The 1972 World Heritage Convention: A Commentary* (Oxford, 2008).

As at November 2007, it had 185 parties, including many developing states. It has one important characteristic in common with the Ramsar Convention, with which it has concluded a Memorandum of Understanding: it works on the basis of maintaining a list of protected sites. To date, there are 878 sites of 'outstanding universal value' listed in 145 states of which 174 are outstanding areas of natural heritage and a further twenty-five of which are mixed sites, combining elements of natural and cultural heritage. The IUCN conducts the original review of natural sites, though the sites are nominated by the state party in whose territory they are located; and it retains a role under the Operational Guidelines in evaluating the natural heritage nominations, which are submitted to it by the Secretariat. A precise procedure has been laid down; a small Bureau of members of the World Heritage Committee, consisting of twenty-one states, overviews proposals on the basis of 'Operational Guidelines' and distributes its recommendations to all states parties; listing thus takes time.[109] The World Heritage Fund provides an incentive for developing states to list sites, and today the World Heritage Convention enjoys participation by virtually all states whose participation is vital to global conservation of outstanding natural sites.

The guidelines laid down for listing natural sites, referred to earlier, narrow the choice to physical areas of outstanding universal value, though these can include marine as well as terrestrial sites. The Convention is thus useful to conservation of wildlife only in protecting certain habitats (mostly in national parks[110]); a species itself, however extraordinary, cannot be listed, in contrast to the Bonn Convention or CITES. One of these guidelines enables a site to be listed if it provides an important habitat for a threatened species of universal value even if the area has no other outstanding features; namely, if it contains the most important and significant natural habitats where threatened species of animals and plants of outstanding universal value from the point of view of science or conservation still survive.[111] The site has to fulfil 'conditions of integrity' which ensure that it is large enough to comprehend the essential components of the support system it represents and that it is sustainable. Outstanding universal value and conditions of integrity are linked with protection and management of properties with the requirement for adequate long-term legislative, regulatory, institutional, and/or traditional protection and management to ensure their safeguarding.[112] Individual nominations must now be drawn from the state's 'tentative list'—essentially an inventory of natural and cultural heritage suitably for inclusion on the List—to be reviewed and resubmitted every decade or so.[113] This

---

[109] Hales, 4 *Parks* (1980) 1–3; see also Francioni and Lenzerini, ibid.

[110] The most common legal management tool for World Heritage natural sites is national park or other protected area designation under national law: *Implementation of the Convention in the light of twenty-five years' practice*, WHC-96/CONF 201/15, Paris, 29 October 1996, 8, para 3.1.

[111] Guideline (x).

[112] Operational Guidelines 2005, para 97. The purpose of management is 'to ensure the effective protection of the nominated site for present and future generations': para 109.

[113] Operational Guidelines 2005, paras. 62, 65.

forms a benchmark against which to measure the inclusiveness of the List. However, the 2007 report by IUCN to the Convention highlights a continuing cultural bias in the tentative lists and their poor technical quality, thus diminishing their value as a planning and evaluation tool.[114] IUCN also prepared independent lists, with regional and biome studies to enhance knowledge of natural heritge of outstanding universal value, and in 1996 launched a Natural Heritage Programme to support development of a global strategy for natural heritage sites. The 1997 review of wetland and marine protected areas concludes that the World Heritage Convention protects sites with a broader range of biome values than under the Ramsar Convention because of the role of the World Heritage Committee.[115]

Listing is subject to the decision of the World Heritage Committee. Thus, though sites must be selected on their own merits, considerations of balance with cultural sites and cost of and availability of funds for protection are likely to have some influence and political difficulties can intervene if title to the territory concerned is disputed. However, the increasing number of sites of outstanding natural heritage now listed, including marine sites, does represent an important contribution to the network of conventions relevant to biodiversity conservation, and the Secretariat of the Biodiversity Convention has participated in a project to harmonize the reporting requirements of this Convention, as well as those of the CITES, Ramsar, and CMS Conventions and has developed joint work programmes.[116] Today an estimated 50 per cent of global natural heritage of oustanding universal value is on the List, a significant achievement. But the cultural 'bias' of the List persists. Recently the Convention has sought to encourage parties to nominate natural as well as cultural sites to address concerns regarding the representivity of the World Heritage List, with indifferent success.[117] The 2007 additions to the List contained sixteen new cultural properties and only two natural properties.

On the other hand, that same year fourteen of the thirty properties on the World Heritage in Danger List were threatened natural heritage. Under this list, sites must be threatened by 'serious and specific danger' (Article 11(4)); the guidelines require that this be 'proven and specific'; for example, that there is a threat of a serious decline in the population of an endangered species or the site is under 'major threats which could have deleterious effects on its inherent characteristics', such as a development plan. Threats must be of a kind that are removable by human action.

The obligations concerning conservation are spelt out in Articles 4 and 5 of the Convention. Parties must do all they can to ensure identification, protection, and

[114] See WHC-07/31 Com/9, 23 May 2007.

[115] Thorsell, Levy and Sigaty, *A Global Overview of Wetland and Marine Protected Areas on the World Heritage List* (Gland, 1997) 1.

[116] *Handbook of the CBD*, Sec. IV, Guide to Decisions, cooperation with other biodiversity-related conventions processes and organizations, Notes on COP's consideration of cooperation with these, Dec. IV/15, para. 2.

[117] See further discussion in Redgwell, in Francioni and Lenzerini, *The 1972 World Heritage Convention: A Commentary* (Oxford, 2008) 81–2.

transmission of the natural heritage, which surely now includes its biodiversity, to future generations, using to the utmost their own resources and, when appropriate and obtainable, international financial, scientific, and technical aid and cooperation. They must adopt protective policies, set up management services for conservation, carry out relevant research to remove threats, take other appropriate measures, and institute training. The High Court of Australia held in the case of *Commonwealth of Australia v The State of Tasmania*[118] in 1983 (with the Chief Justice dissenting) that these provisions imposed a legal duty on Australia, a party to the World Heritage Convention, to protect its listed wilderness parks in Tasmania, despite the generality of the expressions used in these articles and the degree of discretion left to states concerning the precise measure to be taken; Australia must act in good faith to do all it could to achieve the objectives of these articles. As no other such cases have arisen, so far as the authors are aware, it is impossible to say whether other states' courts would hold likewise. These obligations, under the Convention, extend also to non-listed sites that are 'natural heritage' within the Convention's definitions and situated in the territory of the state party concerned. In certain circumstances, properties that have so deteriorated as to lose the characteristics qualifying them for inclusion in the list of threatened sites may be removed from the list. This happened for the first time in 2007 with the removal of the Oman Arabian Oryx Sanctuary from the List after numbers of this endangered species tumbled to a mere four viable breeding pairs and the sancutary was reduced 90 per cent in size, a downgrading the World Heritage Committee considered to be incompatible with the values for which the natural heritage site was inscribed in 1994.

Finally, in another provision which accords with the Biodiversity Convention's requirements and should encourage them to respect them and their ecological as well as aesthetic values, states parties must educate their populations to appreciate and enjoy the sites and submit, through the Committee, biennial reports to the General Conference of UNESCO on the relevant legislative and administrative measures taken by them. Protection of sites thus becomes a matter of national pride; there is considerable evidence that this is so, but this can also attract additional visits and cause environmental degradation, requiring further protective measures.

The World Heritage Convention both overlaps and goes beyond Ramsar's scope in relation to conserving habitats in that it lays more stringent and specific obligations on its parties to take conservation measures and its provisions for financial assistance have provided the model for Ramsar and other conventions which have subsequently followed its example. For sites listed, it provides real protection but the limitations on listing, and the problem of securing ongoing protection and integrity of inscribed sites with the ultimate 'sanction' being removal from the List, prevent it from being the major instrument of habitat protection.

---

[118] 46 *ALR* (1983) 625.

3(3) THE 1979 CONVENTION ON THE CONSERVATION OF MIGRATORY SPECIES OF WILD ANIMALS (BONN CONVENTION)[119]

This Convention, which as of mid-2008 has 109 parties, originally encountered many problems. It conserves habitat, inter alia, as well as aiming to protect species as such during their migrations, in fulfilment of Recommendation 32 of the UNCHE Action Plan. However, little progress was made at the first meetings of its parties held after its entry into force in 1983.[120] Its small Secretariat, provided initially by UNEP, is located in Bonn but its underfunding, because of failure of many parties to pay their contributions and expenses (only a third are developed states though they include the EC), has long limited its staffing, convening of meetings of its Standing Committee, and scope for action.

Conservation of those migratory species which during their lifecycle range across national boundaries requires concerted action by all states that exercise jurisdiction over any part of the range of a particular species. The Bonn Convention provides a framework within which these states can cooperate in undertaking scientific research, restoring habitats, and removing impediments to the migration of species listed in Appendix I (which covers migratory species that are endangered, i.e. in danger of extinction throughout all or a significant portion of their range). It also provides for the conclusion of formal conservation 'AGREEMENTS', (rendered thus to distinguish them from the other type of agreement referred to in the Convention) which are explained below. The success of this Convention depends on conclusion of such AGREEMENTS. They are to be concluded among range states of particular migratory species listed on the Convention's Appendix II as having 'unfavourable conservation status' and requiring an international agreement for their conservation and management, or as having a conservation status that would significantly benefit from international cooperation achieved by international agreement. There is thus a considerable difference in the method of protecting species adopted under these two appendices: mandatory obligations are laid down in the CMS for Appendix I species, whereas AGREEMENTS are required for Appendix II species. The taking of Appendix I species must be prohibited by range-state parties, though exceptions, governed by criteria laid down in the Convention, can be made.

Species, including marine species, may, however, be listed on both Appendix I and Appendix II, even if they are already within the scope of other relevant treaties, including fishery or marine mammal treaties. For example, the blue, humpback, right, and bowhead whales and the Mediterranean monk seal are listed on Appendix I, along with various terrestrial mammals, and Appendix II now includes white whales and certain populations of common, grey, and monk seals and the sea cow (dugong). The

---

[119] *Lyster's International Wildlife Law*, Ch 16; Lyster, 29 *NRJ* (1989) 979–1000; Osterwoldt, ibid, 1017–49; Johnson, in Soons (ed), *Implementation of the Law of the Sea Convention Through International Institutions* (Honolulu, 1990) 363; Glowka, 3 *JIWLP* (2000) 205–52; Anastassiadis, 30 *EPL* (2000) 49ff.

[120] See *Proc of the 1st COP*, Bonn, 1985, vols I–II; *Proc of the 2nd COP*, Geneva, 1988.

Second Conference of the Parties added harbour porpoises, bottlenose, common, risso's, white-beaked, and white-sided dolphins, and the long-finned pilot whale. AGREEMENTS have since been concluded dealing, inter alia, with seals, small cetaceans, and various bird species.[121]

As indicated earlier two kinds of agreement are provided for—referred to as AGREEMENTS and agreements—both of which should cover the whole range and be open to all range states whether or not parties to the Convention. The form of AGREEMENT for Appendix II species to which reference has already been made, must provide for conservation, restoration of habitats important to favourable conservation status (as necessary and feasible), and protection from disturbance of that habitat, including, inter alia, introduction or control of exotic species detrimental to it. If required, the AGREEMENT should institute appropriate machinery to execute its aims, monitor its effectiveness, and prepare the necessary reports to the Conference of the Parties. Cognizance is taken of the Bonn Convention's overlap with the 1946 International Convention for the Regulation of Whaling; thus AGREEMENTS relating to cetaceans should, at the least, focus on prohibiting any taking that is not allowed under other agreements and should provide for accession by non-range states. Article XX(2) of the Bonn Convention provides also that its provisions will not affect the rights and obligations of any party under any existing treaty; even by 1990 there were at least thirteen treaties that impinge or could impinge on rights concerning marine species alone[122] and there are now undoubtedly more. If parties to these conventions are simultaneously parties to the Bonn Convention and plan to conclude AGREEMENTS thereunder, it will thus be necessary for them to establish whether any of these other conventions provides for the adoption of stricter regional measures and to take these fully into account.

The second kind of agreement arises under Article IV(4) of the Convention. This article encourages parties to conclude an agreement for any population or any geographically separate part of the population of any species of the lower taxon of wild animals, members of which periodically cross one or more jurisdictional boundaries. These broad terms allow inclusion of species not listed in Appendix II or even falling within the definition of 'migratory' given in the Convention. The aim is to promote agreements protecting species that would benefit from international cooperation but whose circumstances either do not fulfil the criteria listed on Appendix II or have not yet led to such listing.

---

[121] 1990 Bonn Agreement on the Conservation of Seals in the Wadden Sea; 1992 New York Agreement on Conservation of Small Cetaceans of the Baltic and North Seas (ASCOBANS); 1996 Agreement on Conservation of Cetaceans of the Black Sea, Mediterranean Sea and Contiguous Atlantic Areas (ACCOBAMS); on all of which see *infra*, Ch 13, n 237; 1996 Convention on the Conservation of African-Eurasian Migratory Waterbirds; 1999 Agreement on Conservation of Bats in Europe; 1996 Agreement on Conservation of African-Eurasian Migratory Waterbirds, and Memoranda of Understanding on Conservation of Siberian Crane, and on Slender Billed Curlews and Bustards, on which see 10 *YbIEL* (1999) 315–18.

[122] They are listed by Johnson, in Soons (ed), *Implementation of the Law of the Sea Through International Institutions* (Honolulu, 1990) 363.

Definitions of 'range' and 'range states' are laid down in the Convention and a list of range states is maintained by the Secretariat; parties inform it concerning which of the migratory species listed in the appendices they consider themselves to be in the relation of range state; this includes submitting information on vessels registered under their flag engaged in taking these species (which could include birds) outside national jurisdictional limits and plans for such activities concerning relevant species. However, many of the Convention's terms are ambiguous, including the definition of 'migratory species' in Article 1 to mean, inter alia species that 'cyclically and predictably' cross boundaries. The Second Conference of the Parties adopted guidelines for application of the term 'migratory species', indicating that 'cyclically' relates to a cycle of any nature, such as astronomical (circadian, annual, etc), life, or climatic cycles, and of any frequency, and that 'predictably' implies that a phenomenon can be expected to recur in a given set of circumstances, though not necessarily regularly in time. This removed some of the ambiguity inherent in the original definition. Progress on these definitional problems has encouraged wider participation in the Convention; practical application by conclusion of AGREEMENTS is the best clarifier of its inadequacies.

It appeared at an earlier stage that some states parties were inhibited from concluding AGREEMENTS because they considered them a form of treaty, requiring parliamentary or other official approval for adoption—a complex problem in federal states— which might have to be sought annually as AGREEMENTS proliferate.[123] The Second Conference of the Parties agreed that a less formal agreement, such as a Memorandum of Understanding, could appropriately be concluded between governmental administrations, as a preliminary to a more formal agreement[124] and more AGREEMENTS have now, as we have seen, been concluded, though still too few effectively to achieve the Convention's aims. Another impediment to the conclusion of AGREEMENTS has been that other international organizations or treaty bodies have interests in the protection of the species discussed. There is both considerable overlap and considerable diffusion of responsibility among relevant conventions, concerning particular aspects or techniques of conservation, for example between the Ramsar and Berne Conventions and ad hoc conventions on particular species such as whales, seals, birds and turtles, polar bears, and vicuña. There is clearly a need to improve coordination and cooperation between these conventions on the grounds of both efficiency and the need for a more holistic approach. We shall return to this point in our conclusions.

The Bonn Convention's broadly drafted terms nonetheless open up many advantageous new approaches to conservation of *all* migratory species, including finfish and

---

[123] As an example of the early internal domestic legislative and other problems inhibiting conclusion of Agreements, see Osterwoldt, 29 *NRJ* (1989) 1035–48, on the difficulties facing Germany, Denmark, and the Netherlands, whose different perceptions concerning the 'taking' of seals under the Bonn Convention, inhibited conclusion of an agreement for conservation of the harbour seals in the Wadden Sea.

[124] Lyster, 29 *NRJ* (1989) 992–3; see Aust, 35 *ICLQ* (1986) 787–812, on the theory and practice of such informal agreements; for outstanding examples of use of this technique in protecting the marine environmental/ habitat from vessel source pollution—see the now numerous Memoranda of Understanding on Port State Control, considered *supra*, Ch 7.

shellfish.[125] Its definition of such species allows geographically separate populations to be considered independently. Several such groups have been listed on Appendix I. States with unendangered, well-managed populations can thus still allow some exploitation of species endangered in other states; vice versa, the latter states can protect populations of species not endangered elsewhere. Even a relatively sedentary species can be listed if a significant proportion of its number migrate. Its Scientific Council has been able to offer advice to member states on these matters, but they are not bound to accept this since Article VIII states that the role of that Council is merely to 'provide advice on scientific matters'. It is the Conference of the Parties that determines the Scientific Council's functions, which may only include 'making *recommendations*'[126] on species to be included in the appendices, together with an indication of their range and on the specific measures to be included in the AGREEMENTS.

Despite the potential of the Bonn Convention for provision of comprehensive protection of endangered migratory species, this potential is currently far from fully realized; neither of the techniques it provides has yet been fully or effectively used. Though the recent increase in the number of parties and AGREEMENTS is encouraging, the success of the Bonn Convention depends not only on the existence and use of these techniques but on participation in the Convention by all states that are range states of threatened species, which in practice means that near universal membership is required, especially now that the Biological Diversity Convention is in force. Neither the USA nor Canada are party to the Convention, arguing that existing conservation measures or those planned in their countries would not be benefited by the Bonn Convention.[127] Many species are already covered by bilateral agreements listed earlier in this chapter. This, coupled with the fact that not all threatened migratory species have been listed, adds to its limitations. Moreover, non-ratification of the Convention by any of the range states of some of the species listed on Appendix I means that the Convention's provisions for their protection are nugatory. There are nine Appendix I species for which none of the range states are parties to the CMS;[128] and, of the major non-participants, China, Russia, the two Koreas, Japan, Brazil, and the United States are all range states for over twenty-five Appendix I species, thus imperilling their full protection. Such weaknesses have rendered the Bonn Agreement less effective than it might be. However, though it long remained a 'sleeping treaty',[129] outcomes since the 6th Meeting of the Parties have indicated significant improvements.[130] Synergies with other conventions such as the Ramsar, CITES, and Biodiversity Conventions, were highlighted and further cooperation encouraged, along with new AGREEMENTS.

---

[125] Lyster, 29 *NRJ* (1989) 979–1000. See also Osterwoldt, ibid, 1017.

[126] Article VII(5), emphasis added.

[127] Osterwoldt, 29 *NRJ* (1989) 1028. Threatened species in these countries are mainly migratory birds covered by the 1916 Convention between the USA and Great Britain for the Protection of Migratory Birds.

[128] See the 2005 analysis by the Secretariat—Analysis and Synthesis of National Reports, UNEP/CMS/ Conf 8.5/Add 1, para 9.

[129] *Lyster's International Wildlife Law*, 301.   [130] Anastassiadis, 30 *EPL* (2000) 49–51.

With respect to the former, the current Strategic Plan for the CMS[131] confirms its primary goal is to ensure the favourable conservation status of migratory species, thereby contributing to global sustainability; it has harmonised its work with that of the CBD and the 2010 target of signficantly reducing the rate of biodiversity loss. With respect to the latter, there has been significant development especially with the conclusion of instruments for the conservation of Appendix II species 'largely due to imaginative exploitation of the flexibility offered by Article IV(4)' to conclude MoUs.[132] Thus the CMS seems at last to be advancing in the right direction.[133]

3(4) THE CONVENTION ON TRADE IN ENDANGERED SPECIES 1973 (CITES)[134]

CITES is, in many respects, one of the most effective regulatory structures since it provides sanctions for non-compliance. Moreover, unlike the Bonn Convention, it has a large number of parties—173 as at mid-2008—but it is also one of the most controversial conventions. Though unique and remarkable in many ways, and thus meriting extensive analysis, CITES is not designed directly to conserve migratory or other species in their habitats or protect them from threats to their existence such as pollution, over-exploitation, or by-catches, so its role in furthering the Biodiversity Convention's goals is limited, though not inconsequential. Its sole aim is to control or prevent international commercial trade in endangered species or their products, but as it covers not only species of animals but also of plants, it does play a role in preserving component parts of the habitat of some species and is not without value in the array of treaties through which the Biodiversity Convention's aims can be prosecuted.

Many species are declining not only because of loss of habitat but also because of increased exploitation. A major contributory factor to this is trade, an especially serious threat since the growth of modern transport facilities by sea, air, and land have facilitated the shipping of live animals and plants and their products all over the world. This trade is very lucrative; millions of live animals and birds are transported to meet the demands of the pet trade, ornamental plants are in great demand, and furskins, shells, leather, timber, and artefacts made from these products are all traded in on a large scale, as also was ivory until recently. The technique of controlling import and export of such species and

---

[131] Strategic Plan 2006–2011, Annex to Resolution 8.2, para 29.

[132] See *Lyster's International Wildlife Law*, Ch 13(8). Thus, for example, China and Russia participate in the conservation arrangements for the Siberian Crane, pursuant to an MOU, though neither is a party to the CMS; and NGOs may participate in these non-treaty arrangements, such a the International Council for Game and Wildlife Conservation with respect to the MoU concerning the slender-billed curlew.

[133] Ibid, esp 51; see also Glowka, 3 *JIWLP* (2000) 205–52.

[134] There is now a large literature on this; see, inter alia, Hutton and Dickson (eds), *Endangered Species, Threatened Convention: The Past, Present and Future of CITES* (London, 2000); Sand, 8 *EJIL* (1997) 29, esp 52–3; Baker, 2 *JIWLP* (1999) 1; Bowman, 2 *JIWLP* (1999) 9–63; Hepworth, 1 *JIWLP* (1998) 412; Ong, 10 *JEL* (1998) 291–316; Ruiz Muller, *IUCN Newsletter* (1997) 1; Wijinstekers, *The Evolution of CITES* (8th edn, Cambridge, 2005); Harland, *Killing Game* (Westport, 1994); *Lyster's, International Wildlife Law*, Ch 15; Lyster, 29 *NRJ* (1989), 979; De Klemm, ibid, 953.

products is, as remarked earlier in this chapter, also found in some regional and other conventions. The innovatory aspect of CITES is that it has established this technique on a global scale. It consists of regulating by means of a permit system international trade in species that are listed on its three appendices. Trade, with some exceptions, is forbidden for species listed on Appendix I, that is those threatened with extinction.[135] Trade is permitted, subject to control, in species listed on Appendix II, that is those not yet threatened with extinction but which may become so if trade is not controlled and monitored. So that threatened species are not traded under the pretext that they are species of similar appearance, some non-threatened species are included in this Appendix.[136] International trade is permitted only if there is proper documentation issued by the exporting state. Parties that have stricter legislation, that is restricting export of species *not* already listed in Appendices I or II, can add these species to Appendix II, whereupon other parties also must regulate trade in them. Appendix III includes all species the parties identify as being subject to regulation in their jurisdiction for purposes of preventing or restricting exploitation and needing other parties' cooperation to control trade.

The basis of the Convention, and, in the view of its supporters, the main reason for its relative effectiveness, compared to other treaties, is that it has an elaborate but workable operational system in which a national export/import permit system is combined with a national institutional system. In the light of subsequent events in international law and policy, particularly in the context of the goal of achieving sustainable development, critics have, however, emerged, some of whom go so far as to press for its discontinuance. In order to evaluate these different views, it is necessary first to understand the basic tools available under the CITES system and its operations to date.

CITES requires that each party has to establish at least one Management Authority and Scientific Authority, which is responsible for checking that the required conditions for issue of permits (laid down respectively in Articles III, IV, and V for each Appendix) have been fulfilled and for granting the permit only if they have been complied with. It lays down conditions for export, re-export, and import permits, as required. Article III prohibits the export of specimens of Appendix I species without the prior grant and submission of an export permit. An export permit is issued only if the Management Authority is satisfied not only that the species has been legally obtained but that, if they are to be exported alive, conditions for their transportation conform to the standards laid down in the Convention and only if the Scientific Authority is satisfied that export will not be detrimental to the species' survival. Each transhipment

---

[135] Included in this list, inter alia, are all apes, lemurs, the giant panda, many South American monkeys, great whales, cheetahs, leopards, tigers, Asian and African elephants, all rhinoceroses, many birds of prey, cranes, pheasants, all sea turtles, some crocodiles and lizards, giant salamanders and some mussels, orchids (8 species), and cacti. There were 450 species on the Appendix I list when the Convention entered into force; today there are over 800 species with a greater variety of wildlife, and around 300 species of endangered plants represented.

[136] This list is much larger than Appendix I, with over 30,000 species. Included in this list are primates, cats, otters, whales, dolphins and porpoises, seahorses, birds of prey, all species of flamingo, tortoises, crocodiles and orchids (around 30,000 species), mahogany, fur seals, the black stork, birds of paradise, the coelacanth, some snails, birdwing butterflies, and black corals.

requires an individual permit. Re-export of Appendix I species is banned unless a re-export certificate is issued for which similar prerequisites apply. An export permit cannot be issued for Appendix I species unless an import permit has already been issued; this latter is not a prerequisite for export of Appendix II species, however. It is the requirement of an import permit, which supporters of CITES endorse, that represents the most effective enforcement technique and, in the case of live specimens, that the intended recipient has the necessary equipment to accommodate and care for it. The further requirement that the relevant Management Authority must also be satisfied that the specimen will be used primarily for non-commercial purposes effectively limits trade among parties to specimens used only for scientific and educational purposes or, in certain circumstances, for hunting trophies, subject to modifications introduced at the Gaborone Conference in favour of small, exceptional quotas of specimens of species otherwise prohibited from import.[137] Import permits *are not* required for Appendix II species. A large trade in many of these, therefore, takes place, which has been a matter of concern over the years to the Conference of the Parties. It accordingly has made recommendations to ensure that such trade conforms to the CITES requirement that export will not be in such quantities as to be detrimental to the species survival.[138] Each state party is then responsible through exercise of its customs controls, inter alia, for ensuring that listed species and specimens imported and exported are covered by the appropriate permits. The CITES Secretariat in Switzerland is responsible for monitoring the operation of the treaty and encouraging and facilitating the exchange of information and liaison between member states, other authorities, and organizations. The parties themselves, at their biennial meetings, review the working of the CITES and discuss possible changes to the appendices including removal of particular species from the list or from Appendix I to Appendix II—so-called 'downlisting'.

The role of NGOs is crucial to the success of CITES and they have been particularly active in it, even for a time securing the listing of all elephants on Appendix I, a ban subsequently modified at the 10th COP in Harare in 1997. This amendment to Appendix I was driven by concerns regarding the economic and environmental problems to which the ban gave rise in a few African developing states with elephant populations said to be thriving and effectively managed, and where ivory trade would be used to finance conservation efforts; accordingly, elephant populations in Botswana, Namibia, and Zimbabwe were moved to Appendix II and tightly monitored trade in ivory permitted.[139] Data for purposes of monitoring trade are collected by the NGO Wildlife Trade Monitoring Unit (WTMU) located in the UK. It receives governmental information and also information from the IUCN/WWF TRAFFIC[140] offices in

---

[137] *Lyster's International Wildlife Law*, Ch 15.   [138] Ibid.

[139] On this see, Mofson, in Hatton and Dickson (eds), *Threatened Convention: The Past, Present and Future of CITES* (London, 2000) 107–22; and *Lyster's International Wildlife Law*, Ch 16. Three sales of ivory have taken place, the last in January 2007 of all stocks owned by each of the governments, with no further sales envisaged for the following nine years.

[140] Trade Records Analysis of Flora and Fauna in Commerce.

various states. This, backed by information supplied by other NGOs, depending on its accuracy, quantity, and speed of flow, enables the CITES Secretariat to identify problems and take countermeasures, if controls are, or are about to be evaded. Annual reports from member states back up this process. As information accrues, the assumption is that the effectiveness of CITES is correspondingly enhanced. Nonetheless, smuggling is widespread, particularly through Taiwan, which because of the ambivalence surrounding its territorial status is not a party to CITES.

Interpretative problems also remain, inter alia, as do those of identifying plants and animals in the customs posts, especially as Article II(2)(b) allows so-called 'look alike' species to be added to Appendix II, even if not threatened, to enable effective enforcement; these are 'specimens' of species, defined in Article I(b)(i) as an animal or plant, whether alive or dead, including (for Appendix I and II species) 'any readily recognizable part or derivative thereof'. Such parts include ivory, horns, and skins but, as the term 'readily recognizable' is not defined in CITES, it is left to each state to compile its own list or deal with this problem ad hoc since it is essential to effective enforcement that customs officials should be enabled to identify such items. Thus CITES presents another example of a treaty in relation to which many developing states, to the extent that they now support the system, need training and advice if they are effectively to comply with its demands.

The Conferences of the Parties have, however, dealt over the years with many of the interpretational and operational problems arising. For example, the first meeting at Berne (1976) laid down criteria for the listing and de-listing of species on the appendices[141] which, under Article XV(1)(b), requires a two-thirds majority of the parties present and voting; proposed controversial listing of species have been dealt with ad hoc at subsequent meetings which meetings have also dealt with a wide variety of other questions. The 1978 San José Second Conference recommended detailed restriction on import of hunting trophies,[142] the 1982 New Delhi Third Conference recommended that parties follow a standard, conference-approved model permit and use special security paper or serially numbered adhesive security stamps.[143] The 1983 Gaborone Fourth Conference recommended identification of species subject to 'significant' international trade in relation to which there was insufficient scientific information on their ability to survive such an amount of trade.[144] The 1985 Buenos Aires Fifth Conference agreed that 'primarily commercial purposes' covered 'all uses whose non-commercial aspects do not clearly predominate' (it being for the importer to establish this) and that 'commercial' included any such transaction even if not wholly commercial.[145] The 1986 Ottawa Sixth Conference recommended various measures concerning shipment of live animals in order to ensure their safe handling and welfare in transit and on arrival.[146]

[141] *Proc 1st COP*, Conf 1.2, 33.   [142] *Proc 2nd COP*, Conf 2.11, 48.
[143] *Proc 3rd COP*, Confs 3.6, 3.7, 46–52.   [144] *Proc 4th COP*, Conf 4.7, 49–50.
[145] *Proc 5th COP*, Doc 5.10.   [146] *Proc 6th COP*, Doc 6.19; Resolution 6.2.4.

However, major changes occurred after the Seventh Conference in Berne in 1987 agreed to place the African elephant on Appendix I,[147] since poaching and sale of ivory had caused severe decline, with adverse economic and to some extent, environmental effects on a few developing countries. This prohibited all trade in elephant ivory, after which trade declined dramatically. There was subsequently pressure from states such as Namibia, Tanzania, Uganda, and Zambia (whose elephant herds, under good management were reputed gradually to have recovered from the effects of over-exploitation) to be allowed to carry out limited culls and sell the resulting products in order to generate income for further conservation measures. This was at first resisted at the Eighth Conference of the Parties held in Kyoto in 1992, since it is impossible to distinguish ivory so obtained from ivory taken from illegally poached specimens. Some scientists were, however, critical of this decision, arguing that it neither encouraged nor rewarded wise conservation and local respect for the law, which necessarily, in their view, included culling as herds recover. They considered that trade is not per se bad for conservation. In the event, and as related above, proposals made by Zimbabwe, Botswana, and Namibia to downlist some of the African elephant populations, allowing resumption of trade only on specific conditions, were accepted. Mofson concludes that this establishes that CITES membership has made a difference to Zimbabwe, influencing it to adhere to the ban on trade whilst working to overturn it (a reversal of its previous conceptualization of its national interest) and that it has been able to use and change the regime to its advantage.[148] She cites the view expressed by one Zimbabwe official that it was 'better to work on CITES from within. It doesn't end with elephants; once you are an outsider you have no input or involvement. We realize we will benefit from staying in ... and ... we are hosting the next COP'.[149]

Opinions are, however divided concerning the effectiveness of CITES in protecting wildlife.[150] Some, like Lyster, consider that real progress has been made under it and especially commend its administrative system that enables the Secretariat to receive and circulate information vital to detection of movement of illegal specimens, and applaud its wide ratification. Others, however, consider that it has limited practical success and may even have promoted over-exploitative trade.[151] Critics point to over-zealous listing of specimens not seriously endangered, to CITES' weakness in allowing major exemptions, which provide loopholes for illegal trade, and to the practical difficulties of enforcement, which enable large numbers of species listed on all appendices to escape detection since enforcement is left to individual states parties, whose domestic wildlife laws, scrutiny, and controls vary greatly in scope and

---

[147] See Rolfes, in Hatton and Dickson, (eds), *Threatened Convention: The Past, Present and Future of CITES* (London, 2000) 74–8, 86; Barbier, et al, *Elephants, Economics and Ivory* (London, 1990).

[148] Mofson, in Hatton and Dickson (eds), *Threatened Convention: The Past, Present and Future of CITES* (London, 2000) 107–22.

[149] Ibid, 114.

[150] Contrast for example *Lyster's, International Wildlife Law*, Ch 16 and Favre, *Convention on Trade in Endangered Species* (Dordrecht, 1990). Baker sees much room for improvement on compliance: see Baker, 2 *JIWLP* (1999) 1.

[151] Shonfield, 15 *CWILJ* (1985) 111, 127–58.

stringency of enforcement. The Secretariat thus arranges enforcement seminars for customs officers and Interpol, facilitates cooperation between them, offers training to Management Authorities, and maintains a collection of slides depicting forged documents. Some parties provide funds for technical assistance. The permission of trade with non-parties has also presented problems. TRAFFIC, however, is an effective part of a network cooperating with the IUCN in monitoring international trade in wildlife and plants. It reports on the data gathered and provides analyses of wild-life trade statistics. Publicizing this trade in itself provides one of the most effective controls on it.[152]

The Convention has been shown to have other weaknesses. The non-binding nature of Conference resolutions and the fundamental weakness of the reservations system, which, since it exempts parties formally entering objections to a listing from being bound by it, in effect puts such parties in a position equivalent to non-parties with whom trade is permitted, and undermines the aims of the Treaty regime. Reservations can be lodged, on adhering to the Convention, to listings on Appendices I and II or within ninety days of their adoption by the Conference, and subsequently at any time in written form, without specification of reasons,[153] a procedure that gives rise to many uncertainties concerning the status and interpretation of the resultant obligations.[154] Exhortations by successive conferences that parties should refrain from use of these procedures has had little effect. Compilation by the Secretariat of lists of non-parties whose scientific assessment of whether proposed trade 'substantially conforms' to CITES requirements are found by it not to meet the required standards for issue of permits has been more effective, according to these commentators.

These weaknesses are not insurmountable; parties have the power to resolve the textual ambiguities and to use enforcement powers effectively, if so minded and have done so. Amendment procedures are also available, both for the CITES substantive articles and its appendices. Even early critics conceded that CITES provides 'a highly practical mechanism incorporating a structure designed to deal with a complex inter-national situation'[155] which attempts to balance legitimate trade interests in renewable resources with the need to protect endangered species.[156] There is considerable scope for revision,[157] for example, it has been suggested that a limit could be placed on the number of reservations a party may enter; their duration could be limited and all reservations should be periodically reviewed.[158] Reservation or objection procedures, as we have established in this chapter and Chapter 13, are not unusual. For reasons of political expediency, to maximize participation and protect national interests, most

---

[152] The information is published in the Traffic Newsletter.

[153] Steward, 14 *Cornell ILJ* (1981) 424–55.

[154] Steward gives practical examples of these problems, ibid, 434–55.

[155] Shonfield, 15 *CWILJ* (1985) 127.

[156] Steward, 14 *Cornell ILJ* (1981) 429; Blanco-Castillo, 'An Analysis of the 1973 Convention on International Trade in Endangered Species of Wild Flora and Fauna', M Phil thesis (Univ of Nottingham, 1988) 302–7.

[157] See Shonfield, 15 *CWILJ* (1985), and Steward, 14 *Cornell ILJ* (1981) *passim*.

[158] Steward, 14 *Cornell ILJ* (1981) *passim*.

wildlife conventions permit reservations, just as some national legislation permits exceptions to be made for the taking of species otherwise protected.[159]

Despite the support offered by the 1994 Lusaka Agreement on Cooperative Enforcement Operations Directed at Illegal Trade in Wild Fauna and Flora and Bowman's analysis of CITES' contribution to animal welfare,[160] a real challenge to CITES now comes from the changed framework of perceptions concerning use of wildlife following the adoption of the UNCED instruments and their goal of 'sustainable development', including the Rio Declaration's requirement that future international law be developed 'in the field of sustainable development'. Presenting a broad review of the operation of CITES, twenty-five years after its entry into force, Hatton and Dickson expose the heated arguments that have thus arisen at CITES meetings over its basic assumptions. It is now questioned whether its failures are attributable to weaknesses in its enforcement or to its basic approach to conservation, in particular whether other approaches would now be more successful and how the Convention might now evolve, since, in the view of some, recent experience suggests that trade is not as serious a threat to wildlife as was perceived in 1973. The threat posed by habitat destruction has prompted proposals that permissible human use of wildlife, and commercial trade in particular, should encourage conservation, as long as it is sustainable. Some ad hoc recognition of this has now been conceded, as illustrated by the outcome of the African elephant case. Through this and other debates, developing countries, to some extent prompted by developed states with an interest in specific trades in issue, have pressed these arguments more forcefully against the developed states who largely initiated the original treaty. Development issues have prompted more input in the debate by social scientists, as the complexity of the relationship of wildlife and human social needs has been grasped. Finally, along with the other treaties in this chapter, the conclusion of the Biological Diversity Convention with its broader approaches to conservation has added to the emerging challenges.

However, as the wide range of opinions ventilated in Hatton and Dickson's study illustrates, views on CITES' future and possible alternatives differ widely, ranging from increasing international regulation to reallocation of management to the local community level. Ong concludes that despite the recent apparent relaxation of controls over trade in endangered species at both the international and EC level, an argument can still be made that controls at these levels are better focused and are more likely to achieve the goal of sustainable development. Thus much now depends on their effective implementation in order to achieve the balance between progressive socio-economic development and the conservation of wildlife for future generations.[161] He observes that the democratization of the decision-making powers represented by the enhanced position of range states now accommodates many different perspectives

---

[159] E.g. the US Endangered Species Act (ESA) 1973, PL 93–205, 28 Dec 1973, 87 Stat 884, which has been subjected to criticism on this account, though otherwise regarded as a pioneering model in this field; see Campbell, 24 *Environment* 5 (June, 1982) 6–42. There are both similarities and differences, however, between the ESA and CITES.

[160] Bowman, 1 *JIWLP* (1998) 9–63.   [161] Ong, 10 *JEL* (1998) 291–314.

within institutions where the rival claims can be scrutinized and no one claim taken for granted, as is appropriate within the sustainable development framework.

4 POST-UNCED INSTRUMENTS FOR CONSERVATION OF NATURE AND BIODIVERSITY

It was hoped that the Rio process would bring about not only a convention conserving biodiversity but conventions on desertification and forests. From 1975 onwards, the UN, UNEP, and various conferences of concerned international organizations and bodies had drawn attention to the increasingly serious economic consequences of the expansion of arid lands[162] and destruction of forests, especially tropical forests. Various recommendations emerged from these and were promoted, inter alia, by UNEP, UNESCO, and FAO, but action lagged until the spread and severity of desertification and rate of destruction of forests led to intensified demands for action. This was inhibited, however, by the insistence of the states concerned that the issues involved fell wholly within their national sovereignty. Thus, although some progress was made on definitional aspects, the goal of concluding conventions on these topics was not attained at UNCED, though Agenda 21 did define and draw attention to desertification, and a non-binding statement of principles relating to forests was adopted.

4(1) THE CONVENTION TO COMBAT DESERTIFICATION

Following a recommendation made in Agenda 21, the UNGA initiated negotiation of a convention focusing particularly on states experiencing serious drought in Africa.[163] States were, however, anxious to avoid conflict and overlap with existing conventions, such as those on climate change and biodiversity. Problems also arose concerning the conclusion and status of specific regional instruments which it was agreed should be an integral part of the convention. A Convention to Combat Desertification (UNCCD) was eventually concluded in 1994, with four annexes covering Africa, Latin America and the Caribbean, Asia, and the Northern Mediterranean.[164] It entered into force on 26 December 1996 and, as of mid-2008, had 193 parties. It thus enjoys

---

[162] UNGA Res 3511 (XXX) 1975, instructing UNEP and UNDP to convene a UN Conference on desertification which took place in Nairobi in 1977, informally coordinated with the UN Water Conference held in Mar del Plata, Argentina earlier that year; on this see Tolba, *The United Nations Conference on Desertification: A Review*, 6 Mazingara, 1982, 14–23; Biswas, 5 *Envl Consvn* (1978) 69–70, 267–72; 6 *Envl Consvn* (1979) 80–1.

[163] UNGA Res 47/188 (1992); text in 23 *EPL* (1993) 43–6.

[164] For reports on the difficulties experienced in negotiation, see 23 *EPL* (1993) 202–3; 24 *EPL* (1994) 36; on the COPs, 26 *EPL* (1996) 462; 27 *EPL* (1997) 80, 169; 28 *EPL* (1998) 46; 30 *EPL* (2000) 32–3. See generally Bekhechi, 101 *RGDIP* (1997) 101.

the most widespread participation of any of the instruments considered here, but as we will see below this high level of participation has not yet translated into effective implementation of the UNCCD, not least because the Convention is weak on specific commitments.

This Convention, as in the case of the Biodiversity Convention, confines many problematic issues giving rise to disagreement to its Preamble: human beings are recognized as being at the centre of concerns to combat desertification and mitigate drought. The 'urgent concern of the international community' about the adverse impacts of these problems is 'reflected' in the text, though as the problems are stated to be of 'global dimensions in that they affect all regions of the world', it is 'acknowledged' that joint action of that community is needed to combat them. Stress is laid on the need to resolve the economic and social problems of the areas concerned, the prevalence of developing states in the areas, and the need for sustainable economic growth. The parties reaffirm Rio Declaration Principle 2 concerning the right to pursue their own developmental as well as environmental policies and assert that national governments play a crucial role in combating the problems involved, but they also draw attention to the accompanying need for 'new and additional funding' and access to technology, without which they state it will be difficult for them to comply. They do however, recognize the relationship between desertification and other global environmental problems and 'bear in mind' the contribution that combating desertification will have to achieving their objectives under the Climate Change and Biological Diversity Conventions.[165] They also note that it will be necessary to base strategies on rigorous scientific knowledge if they are to be effective, and stress the urgent need to improve 'the effectiveness and coordination of international cooperation'. The need to take 'appropriate action' against desertification and drought for the benefit of present and future generations is acknowledged but the precautionary approach is not affirmed. 'Desertification' is defined in Article 1 as meaning 'land degradation in arid, semi-arid and dry humid areas resulting from various factors', including climatic variations and human activities; 'combating' it includes activities aimed at (i) prevention or reduction of land degradation, (ii) rehabilitation of partly degraded land, and (iii) reclamation of desertified land. Nevertheless, the substantive articles are weak on positive commitment. As in the case of the Biodiversity Convention, reference is made in the Preamble to the Rio Declaration's goal-setting principles, such as sustainable development and accounting for the interests of future generations, but much development of the implementing measures required will depend on the degree of transfer of technology and financial support, invoked in other articles, so far as the many developing countries in the desertified areas are concerned.

One of the key instruments for the implementation of the Convention is the development of national, subregional and regional action programmes which are being developed by country parties affected by desertification in Africa, Asia, Latin America,

---

[165] The CBD's SBSTTA has recommended improving synergies between the CBD and UNCCD rgarding dry and sub-humid lands biodiversity: CBD COP8 (2006).

the Caribbean, and the Northern Mediterranean. Developed country parties have the obligation to support affected countries through the provision of additional financial resources and by facilitating access to technology, knowledge, and know-how (Articles 6 and 20). Current efforts are focused on enhancing the implementation of the Convention, which is at an early stage. There is a Committee for Review of Implementation of the Convention (CRIC) which, within the framework of a ten-year strategic plan (2008–18) to enhance implementation of the Convention, is to consider progress in implementation of strategic objectives 1, 2, and 3—with the second of particular note: 'to improve the condition of affected ecosystems'—based on the work of the Convention's Committee on Science and Technology. However, though the Convention has now been in force for over a decade, political support remains weak notwithstanding the large number of parties. Despite the great need to combat the problems of desertification and aridity, it is too early to say whether the Convention will engender the urgent and positive action required, although its progress will also periodically be subject to review, as in the case of the other conventions, by the UN, the CSD, and UNEP.

4(2) THE FOREST PRINCIPLES AND RELATED INSTRUMENTS[166]

Forests have value as an exploitable reservoir of timber and fuel, as a source of food, as a habitat rich in wildlife, and as a major reservoir of biodiversity. In addition they act as sinks for absorption of carbon. Despite the high profile given to deforestation, little has been done to control this problem internationally. The instruments adopted to date are weak. A new International Tropical Timber Agreement was concluded in 2006, replacing an earlier 1983 agreement revised in 1994 and subsequently renewed. The 2006 Agreement, though paying greater attention to sustainable development, is still effectively little more than a commodity-market adjustment among consumer and producer states, with a commitment to increase international trade in tropical timber from sustainably managed and legally harvested forests. Some forests are also to some extent protected by the World Heritage Convention.[167] A number of regional treaties contain general provisions on rational or sustainable use of tropical forests;[168]

---

[166] On these see Schally, 4 YbIEL (1993) 30–50; Szekeley, in Campiglio et al (ed), *The Environment after Rio* (The Hague, 1994) 65–9; Tarasofsky, *The International Forest Regime: Legal and Policy Issues* (Bonn, 1995); König, in Wolfrum (ed), *Enforcing International Environmental Standards* (Heidleberg, 1996) 337–71; Canadian Council on International Law, *Global Forests and International Environmental Law* (The Hague, 1996); Yamin, 9 YbIEL (1998) 316–19; Saint-Laurent, in Dodds (ed), *The Way Forward* (London, 1999) 65; Sand, 1 *Int Envtl Agmts: Politics, Law and Economics* (2001) 33, 41.

[167] *Supra*, section 3(2) and *Commonwealth of Australia v State of Tasmania*, 46 ALR (1983) 625; see also IUCN, *A Global Overview of Forest Protected Areas on the World Heritage List* (Gland, 1997).

[168] See the 1993 Central American Convention on Management and Conservation of Natural Forest Ecosystems and Forest Plantation Development and the 1978 Treaty for Amazonian Cooperation, 17 *ILM* (1978) 1045. Article 4 of the latter affirms the exclusive sovereignty of each state over its own forests, but does promote cooperation. The 1989 Declaration of San Francisco adopted by the parties, inter alia, recognizes the importance of the Amazonian ecosystem for biodiversity, the need for joint preservation policies and the rational use of forest resources.

of these only the 1985 ASEAN Convention requires a serious commitment to forest protection in a broader environmental context, and it is not in force.[169]

As Peter Sand has pointed out, responsibility for forest conservation is divided, and even contested among several institutions, including FAO's Committee on Forestry (COFO); UNCTAD's International Tropical Timber Organization, and the open ended Inter-Governmental Forum on Forests (IFF), whose work is overseen by the Commission on Sustainable Development. None are located in the same country so that coordination is difficult. Attempts to negotiate at Rio an International Convention on Conservation and Development of Forests, as proposed by the UN in 1990, were blocked by the irreconcilable concerns of developed and developing states, led especially by Brazil and Malaysia. Instead, the curiously entitled 'Non-legally Binding Authoritative Statement of Forest Principles' was adopted which, as Szekely pithily concludes, falls 100 per cent short of providing even the most elementary basis for the protection of the world's forests. The failure of the negotiations at UNCED was partly attributable to the fact that developed states did not propose to submit their own boreal forests to criteria for sustainable utilization and the European Community attempted to trade developed states' agreement to a desertification convention as a quid pro quo for developing states' acceptance of a forest treaty.[170] The resulting polarization and sensitivity over sovereignty issues still inhibits conclusion of a comprehensive global convention despite the accelerating destruction of tropical forests. Thus, in contrast with the successful completion of a new ITTA noted above, the UN Forum on Forests has since 2000 sought to strengthen the International Agreement on Forests, but without success. As Forner relates, the only agreement seems to be on goals rather than upon how to achieve them, namely reversal of loss of forest cover worldwide; enhancement of 'forest-based benefits'; a significant increase in the area of protected forest; and a reversal in the decline in official development assistance for sustainable forestry management.[171] Forests have also been the subject of negotiation in the Conference of the Parties to the Kyoto Protocol on Climate Change,[172] and they could potentially be addressed by a protocol to the Biological Diversity Convention—where forest biodiversity is one of its five thematic areas—though the parties to the CBD have no present intentions to do so.[173]

4(3) PROTECTION OF LANDSCAPE: EUROPEAN LANDSCAPE CONVENTION[174]

In addition to the 1991 Alpine Convention, which is now in force,[175] the Council of Europe (CE) concluded, in 2000, a European Landscape Convention, which is (so far

---

[169] The Treaty was drafted by IUCN. See Article 6.

[170] Since then, however, the EU has promulgated a coordinated forest strategy to secure recognition of European forests' diversity, 29 EPL (1999) 48–69.

[171] Forner, 16 *YBIEL* (2007) 488.   [172] See *supra*, Ch 10.

[173] The ASEAN Convention provides a possible model.

[174] European Landscape Convention and Explanatory Report, Council of Europe, Strasbourg, 2000.

[175] 25 *EPL* (1995) 105; 27 *EPL* (1997) 407; 29 *EPL* (1999) 31.

as the authors are aware) the first of its kind and which came into force on 1 March 2004. Its Preamble invokes, in an unusual context, many of the UNCLOS and UNCED principles, records the CE's aim of 'safeguarding and realising the ideals and principles which are their common heritage', and notes the 'important public interest role of landscape' which is a 'basic component of the European natural cultural heritage'. It notes the accelerating transformation of landscapes resulting from a number of impacts of modern developments, many economically based. It aims to preserve the high quality landscapes as 'key elements of individual and social well-being', using measures that 'entail rights and responsibilities for everyone'. 'Landscape' for its purposes amorphously means 'an area, as perceived by people, whose character is the result of the action and interaction of natural and/or human factors'. It will surely be difficult to select areas for protection from the vast number of potential sites which are likely to fall within such a broad definition. In 2008 the parties adopted Guidelines for the Implementation of the Convention to assist the development of national landscape policy.[176]

5 THE REGIONAL APPROACH

The major regional conventions—the 1968 African Convention for Conservation of Nature and its 2003 revision; the 1940 Western Hemisphere Convention; the 1985 ASEAN Convention; and the 1979 Berne Convention on Conservation of European Wildlife and Natural Habitats—have already been referred to in this chapter; space does not permit further elaboration and they have recently been comprehensively reviewed by others.[177] It suffices to say here that the first three initially fell within Lyster's category of 'sleeping treaties', though they introduced some innovatory conservation techniques at the regional level and attempts are now being made to reactivate them. Clearly, regional bodies, though important, cannot protect highly migratory species that migrate globally or traverse the waters or territories of several regions or frontiers that border two or more regions. There is a need for overarching global conventions to protect such species and for coordination between the institutions and measures established to administer and operate the regional conventions. A regional approach, though valuable within the region, is not sufficient to solve the problems addressed by the global conventions discussed above, although insofar as species reside in particular regional areas for part of their lifecycle, they can be effectively protected by local

---

[176] Recommendation CM/Rec (2008) 3 of the Committee of Ministers to member states on the guidelines for the implementation of the European Landscape Convention, adopted by the Committee of Ministers on 6 February 2008.

[177] See esp Churchill, in Bowman and Redgwell (eds), *International Law and the Conservation of Biodiversity*, 71–90, esp 73–7, 80–5; Bowman, in Anke, Tegner, and Basse (eds), *Effectiveness of International Nature Conservation Agreements* (Copenhagen, 1997) 105–54; Gehring, 1 *YbIEL* (1990) 35ff; *Lyster's International Wildlife Law* Part III 'Regional Wildlife Regulation'.

measures as long as they are at least as effective as those required under the global conventions.

6 COORDINATION OF CONVENTIONS AND ORGANS

Coordination has become the most urgent and overarching need of terrestrial wildlife and habitats if related environments and their biodiversity, as defined and required in the Biodiversity Convention, are to be conserved. The strategies and principles outlined earlier in this chapter and in Chapter 11 point to the urgent and indispensable need given the rapid growth in conventions and other instruments for better coordination and cooperation between all bodies concerned in conservation and harmonization of measures both in pursuit of 'holism', to the extent that this is feasible, and of sustainable development. This need has been intensified by conclusion of the Biodiversity Convention, as we have illustrated. A major purpose of UNCED was to review the UN system with these goals in mind. When a particular species is protected under more than one convention, especially if the conventions address only one aspect of the needs of conservation, for example, hunting, habitat, or trade, it is essential that coordination of the measures and organs of the relevant treaties be established. The Biodiversity Convention reinforces this in requiring that, in Article 5, that parties *must* cooperate, a requirement reinforced in many other articles. The general problems of coordination of activities of international bodies concerned in the same issues have been discussed in Chapter 2 and those concerning living resources and biodiversity in Chapters 11 and 13 as well as herein. The institutions established under the Biodiversity Convention, its COP, Secretariat, SBSTTA, Open Ended Ad Hoc Working Groups, Clearing House Mechanism (CHM), and work programmes show that it is making serious efforts to promote cooperation and coordination. How successful these efforts will be remains to be seen.[178]

On a wider basis, initiatives have been taken by both IUCN and UNEP to further coordinate and reduce overlap by convening meetings of concerned secretariats. IUCN early convened a meeting, instigated by the Ecosystem Conservation Group (consisting of FAO, UNEP, and UNESCO), to which the secretariats of the Bonn, Berne, CITES, Ramsar, and World Heritage and Whaling Conventions were invited, to consider the possibilities of cooperation and it was suggested that the secretariats of the various conventions might be able to relocate their secretariats within the new IUCN headquarters in Switzerland, though in the event this has not occurred owing to a variety

---

[178] The *Handbook of the Convention on Biodiversity* lists over 20 initiatives on cooperation but many more appear under headings on specific subjects, including Global Plans of Action and interrelationship with particular related international bodies and conventions, including those within its Jakarta Mandate on Marine and Coastal Biodiversity highlighted in Ch 13.

of political and financial factors.[179] In the context of preparations for UNCED and in particular for conclusion of the Convention on Biological Diversity, which required a wide range of coordinated actions, UNEP convened meetings of representatives of governments, international organizations, and relevant convention secretariats, inter alia, to rationalize actions under all these conventions and to maximize individual and collective potential and effectiveness in this field. These meetings acted as a catalyst for organizing further participation in each other's meetings on the part of all the concerned bodies; exchange of observers was frequent and well-established long before adoption of the UNCED strategies and instruments but has of necessity been intensified since 1993 when the Biodiversity Convention entered into force. In particular, the lead role of the CBD in the Biodiversity Liaison Group, with joint meetings of representatives of the secretariats of the CBD, CMS, CITES, World Heriatge and Bonn Conventions, has facilitated both more formal—e.g. MoUs with joint work programmes—and less formal—e.g. information sharing—arrangements amongst them, described above. Although UNEP underwent radical reorganization to enable it to exercise a more effective coordinating role in relation to its many conventions, it has not developed a lead role in this regard.

7 CONCLUSIONS

It was argued by Glennon, writing before conclusion of the UNCED and post-UNCED Conventions, Declarations, and other instruments, that 'It is now possible to conclude that customary international law requires states to take appropriate steps to protect endangered species'.[180] This conclusion was said to be based on (i) state practice, which in his view evidenced that 'like highly codified humanitarian law norms that have come to bind even states that are not parties to the instruments promulgating them, wildlife norms also have become binding on non-parties as customary law';[181] (ii) customary norms created by conventions when such agreements are intended for adherence by states generally and are in fact widely accepted;[182] (iii) norms created by 'general principles of law recognized by civilized nations'.[183] He suggested, for example, that because CITES is widely implemented in domestic law, the general principles embodied in states' domestic laws on endangered species may be relied upon as another source of customary law.[184] He found further support for this view in the relevant resolutions of the General Assembly and international conferences.

The survey of strategies, principles, the conventions implementing them, and state practice in putting them into effect conducted in this and other relevant chapters, indicates that more cautious conclusions should still be drawn than those indicated by Glennon. As we saw in Chapter 1, customary law can emerge from conventions

---

[179] By Holdgate, then director general, IUCN, 3 *Ramsar Journal* (April 1989) 1.
[180] Glennon, 84 *AJIL* (1990) 30.   [181] Ibid.   [182] Ibid.   [183] Ibid, 31.   [184] Ibid.

and bind states that have not ratified them only if the provisions in issue are of a fundamentally norm-creating character, both generalizable and applied in state practice with the sense of obligation necessary to establish custom.[185] Even enactment of legislation, let alone mere adoption of treaties, is not conclusive evidence of this obligation; it is necessary to ascertain whether the norm or treaty embodying it is applied and enforced and whether or not the state against whom it is applied persistently objects. It is extremely difficult to establish practice on these aspects and it has been possible only to review a few known examples in this chapter.

As we have observed, it is not easy to identify the meaning of 'sustainable development', which is a key premise of almost all the conventions surveyed in this chapter. As we saw in Chapter 3, after analysing the decision of the ICJ in the *Case Concerning the Gabcíkovo-Nagymoros Dam*, Lowe concludes that 'the process of developing a precise and coherent concept' of sustainable development has some way to go 'before it is well suited to application by tribunals as a component of judicial reasoning'.[186] Though some strands are common to most of its formulations they are—in Lowe's view, which we share—'more of a procedural than a substantive nature'. He suggests that at least the concept, when at issue before them, requires that tribunals should allow disputing parties to address the developmental/environmental issues within a broader 'holistic' context and on the basis of an equitable approach, despite the ambiguities inherent in establishing what is required under such an approach. It is clear, he concludes, that it does not allow property owners to contend that such ownership confers unrestricted rights to use it as they determine, disregarding the interests of others. 'Property' in the context of the issues discussed in this chapter, can surely be interpreted as the territory and resources over which most states jealously assert sovereign rights.

The implications of this approach could, in the long run be far reaching, if unsustainable developmental practices result in serious environmental damage or harm. The numerous cases of evasion of CITES and other wildlife conventions reported by TRAFFIC show that enforcement of wildlife conventions, even by states parties, is often poor. Chapter 13 shows how prevalent illegal, unregulated fishing still is and how many states still do not participate in regulatory international and regional fisheries organizations. The limited implementation of many conventions, especially the regional ones, and the fact that many states still exploit most species, does not suggest that protection of endangered species is a requirement of customary law, however desirable it is that it should be. Even the cessation of whale-catching was achieved only through adoption of regulations by states party to the ICRW setting quotas at zero on an interim basis for a limited period. That ban is currently being reviewed and there is strong pressure to resume whaling on the basis of sustainable development.

These views seem more in accord with emerging state practice in this field than Glennon's. The adoption of the series of conservation strategies; declarations of principles; the conventions concluded at global, regional, multilateral, and bilateral levels;

---

[185] *North Sea Continental Shelf Cases*, ICJ Rep (1969) 41–2, para 41; and *supra*, Ch 1.
[186] Lowe, in Boyle and Freestone (eds), *Sustainable Development and International Law*, Ch 2.

and practice in relation to these, is creating a framework in which conservatory, economic, and social goals can be balanced and achieved within the widely accepted but generalized policy of sustainable development. The relevant strategies should not be examined for legal content—except insofar as they do incorporate existing rules or norms of customary international law—but set goals, many of which have been achieved through legal processes. These goals include those laid down in the WCN, such as control of adverse impacts, avoidance of damage, protection of unique areas and habitats; in the WCS, such as maintenance of ecological processes, preserving, maintaining, using, restoring, and enhancing resources, minimizing threats to trade, conditioning access, helping poorer countries to sustain development; and in the WCED report, such as preserving biodiversity, coordinating activities of organizations, establishing trust funds, controlling access to enable sustainable levels of exploitation, helping poorer countries to sustain development, and improving enforcement. Many of these goals overlap and there is thus much repetition, which serves to draw attention to the issues concerning effective conservation. But adoption of these goals, except the last, does not take place on a global basis, or wholly through legal developments; progress is made partly through legal measures and partly through public acknowledgement of the moral values of many 'principles' that are evidenced in their reiteration. It is important in this context to separate goal-setting provisions from legal-norm-creating ones, and to recall that enunciating provisions of any kind does not per se make them legally binding as *lex lata*; rather it elevates them to soft law or law-in-the-making *lex ferenda* status.

There is nonetheless now much evidence of adoption of relevant controls ad hoc through conventions at various levels, for example on hunting and taking of particular species; for establishment of parks and reserved areas; maintaining optimum sustainable yields; and improving enforcement systems by instituting permit systems backed by penalties, monitoring and data collection, much of which is enacted into national laws. There is widespread evidence that most states do accept that it is their duty: to cooperate in protection of living resources but not that they are under a legal obligation to participate in existing conventions for this purpose as the slow rate of ratification of some conventions evidences; to act in good faith; to arrange some form of equitable use of shared living resources; and to act as good neighbours at the regional level, as required by the UNEP Principles on Shared Natural Resources and subsequent and numerous Declarations referred to in this chapter.

It is, however, difficult to go further than that; if it can be said that there is a recognition of a duty to conserve resources its content is unclear—definitions of conservation are broadly based and differ widely, as we saw in Chapter 11. Similarly, some form of common international interest in certain endangered species is evident but the different terminology used to express this and lack of institutional support make it clear that no internationalization of such living resources has yet occurred. Though the Biodiversity Convention's recognition that its conservation is a common concern of humankind is significant it has yet to be established what this involves in practice. While 'rights of future generations' are acknowledged in a moral sense, they remain inchoate and to some extent incoherent (see Chapter 3). What is increasingly recognized is the need for regulation, on a scientific basis, founded on treaties to protect wildlife and for widespread participation, implementation, enforcement and coordination of these. Such treaties do enable specific measures of conservation to be identified and prescribed in a variety of contexts, as we have seen. Yet it should be recalled that one of the most widely ratified, CITES, deals only with threats represented by trade, not with habitat disturbance, over-exploitation, or the problems of migration, and that wildlife conventions in general are not only poorly related to or coordinated with each other but also those dealing with the activities and sources of pollution and other forms of disturbance most threatening to wildlife. The legal regime established by the existing network of global and regional conventions, though it has greatly expanded under the impetus of the UNCHE and UNCED outcomes, is still far from comprehensive, universal, or effective in scope or operation. Applicable equitable principles do not yet provide a clear guide for resolving the problems of sustainable utilization of living resources, as we shall see in Chapter 13, where further conventions at the international level have been required in an effort to establish a more precautionary approach to sustainable use of fisheries. In most cases this has singularly failed to conserve stocks at a level permitting sustainable use.

13

CONSERVATION OF MARINE LIVING RESOURCES AND BIODIVERSITY

1 INTRODUCTION

The oceans which cover 70 per cent of the Earth's surface represent its most extensive but least understood ecosystem.[1] It has become increasingly apparent that conservation of marine living resources presents much more complex problems of regulation and management than hitherto envisaged during the centuries over which they have been exploited by humans. The need to conserve commercial fisheries and the great whales has long attracted attention but conservation of other marine species that are not commercially attractive or particularly charismatic has garnered little support. Conservation of marine habitats and spawning grounds, including the very rich biodiversity found in coral reefs, seamounts and some near-coastal areas, has been similarly neglected. Coastal development, together with sea-level rise, higher ocean temperatures, and acidification caused by climate change are progressively degrading marine ecosystems such as mangrove swamps, wetlands, and estuaries, threatening the loss or destruction of many marine species, including a third of all coral species.[2] Pollution from land-based sources adds to the destructive impact on the coastal environment. Nor is the harm limited to coastal areas. High-seas species such as sharks, rays, turtles, and various species of tuna are among the many that have suffered disastrous declines, and in some cases may face extinction. Not all of these species are

---

[1] See de Klemm, in Hey (ed), *Developments in International Fisheries Law* (The Hague, 1999) 423; Joyner, 28 *Vand JTL* (1995) 635.

[2] See *Report of UNCED*, Agenda 21, Ch 17; IUCN, Press Release 10.7.08 at <http://www.cms.iucn.org>, and see *supra*, Chs 7–8.

directly exploited. Some, such as the albatross, are merely incidental victims of need-lessly wasteful fishing methods. Many newly targeted deep-sea stocks are so poorly understood that fishing has resulted in particularly rapid declines because the fish mature and reproduce slowly. In effect they are being mined rather than managed. Fisheries science cannot realistically provide enough data about an environment that is still less well known than outer space. Uncertainty abounds, and the once-common belief that fish stocks recover rapidly has been discredited by the evidence. But, if rational management requires good science, it also requires decision-makers to follow scientific advice, which in this field they often do not do, for short-term reasons, with inevitable consequences.

The rise in fish catches has been phenomenal and now represents a major threat to marine biological diversity and the sustainable use of marine resources.[3] In 1938 the world catch was 15 million tonnes (mt); by 1958 it had risen to 28 mt, by 1978 to 64 mt, and by 1992 to 90 mt, although by 2000 it had begun to decline. The reasons for this prolonged increase include rising demand and the growth in fishing by developing states but, above all, the enormous advances in technology for catching and process-ing fish. From use of rod and line and small boats operating close inshore with sisal nets and taking fish mainly for human consumption locally, developed sections of the industry have progressed to the use of sonar and satellites for locating fish shoals, and factory/freezer vessels which can store and process fish on board and stay at sea for months at a time, operating in large fleets. The increased capital cost of modern fisheries leads in turn to more intensive catching efforts, while older boats are simply sold on to other users. Fishing methods are often highly destructive. Bottom trawling damages coral reefs and seamounts; nylon driftnets float like a curtain and when lost at sea can trap a variety of species, including seals, turtles and dolphins. Longline fish-ing attracts and snares seabirds in large numbers. Paradoxically the viability of some stocks is threatened by certain conservation restrictions. Targeting only larger fish alters the genetic diversity of the stock and results eventually in smaller fish. 'Discards', fish thrown away because quotas have been exceeded, add a growing element of point-less waste to the overfishing of many traditionally rich fishing grounds, including the north-west Atlantic and north-east Pacific. In so-called 'industrial fishing' fish are not taken for human consumption but are processed into meal for use as cattle or poultry feed or as fertilizer; it matters little what species are taken or of what size. Such fishing has lead to reductions in seabird colonies unable to feed their young.

The effect of all these developments on certain species has been devastating; not only are they taken in much larger amounts but frequently the species on which the larger fish, seabirds, and some marine mammals predate are also removed, which aggravates the decline since the biomass of a given area can only support so much fish life. The exploitation of marine living resources is thus an environmental problem

---

[3] See FAO, *World Fisheries Ten Years After the Adoption of the 1982 United Nations Convention on the Law of the Sea*, FAO Doc COFI/93/4 (Rome, 1992); FAO, *The State of World Fisheries and Agriculture* (Rome, 2006) 5.

pre-eminently because it has been and is increasingly pursued unsustainably with, as we can see, broader ecological effects than simply the loss of communities and livelihood for fishermen that have resulted from the collapse of major fisheries.

Although in Chapter 11 we noted important differences between terrestrial and marine-based living resources, the management factors, principles, and strategies outlined there are equally applicable to fisheries and to the various species of marine mammals. Regimes for conservation of marine living resources thus have to address not only sustainable use of targeted stocks, but also incidental catch of other species, depletion of biological diversity, and degradation of marine ecosystems. Some fish are highly migratory, such as salmon and tuna, while marine mammals, being larger and warm blooded, reproduce slowly and give birth to live progeny which require nursing. They are thus more vulnerable to capture and over-exploitation and need special protection of various kinds. Because of their special characteristics, many marine mammal species are included in some of the conservation conventions discussed in Chapter 12. As we saw there, these treaties cover only such species as are listed in the appendices. Fish are more rarely listed under conservation treaties than other marine species, but replenishment of some badly affected stocks may take many years, and certain species are increasingly endangered.[4]

International law on the management of marine living resources has developed on an ad hoc basis with little, if any, of the coordination and integration required for effective conservation or the assurance that it will be based on scientific advice. If ecosystem protection and conservation of marine biodiversity have been overlooked in the past, addressing them now has raised urgent questions of law reform, not only in the law of the sea but also in international trade law.[5] The paradox with which lawyers have to grapple in this context is that biologically the oceans are an ecosystem, or a series of interlocking ecosystems, but legally we have divided them into arbitrary jurisdictional zones whose only merit is that they are easier to plot on maps. As a result fisheries conservation is probably the least successful part of the 1982 UN Convention on the Law of the Sea: a triumph, at best, of hope over experience.

Marine living resources are subject to the exclusive rights of a state only when they are within its internal waters, territorial seas, or 200-mile exclusive economic zone (EEZ) or exclusive fishery (EFZ) zone. They frequently migrate through or straddle a variety of jurisdictional zones, including the high seas, where historically they have been regarded as common property. As we saw in Chapter 3, the salient characteristics of common-property resources, as applied to the high seas, are that they do not fall within the sovereignty or sovereign rights of any state, and are free for use and exploitation by vessels of all nations. The history of whaling, pelagic sealing, and now high-seas fisheries is such that it would be entirely reasonable to argue that sustainable development of common property in this context is an oxymoron. High-seas fishing

---

[4] On the possible application of the CITES Convention to marine fisheries see Franckx, in Freestone, Barnes, and Ong (eds), *The Law of the Sea: Progress and Prospects* (Oxford, 2006) Ch 12.

[5] On the trade law implications see *infra*, Ch 14 and McDorman, in Hey (ed), *Developments in International Fisheries Law*, 501–31.

is only partially regulated by regional agreements, while flag-of-convenience trawl-ers operate freely outside many of the applicable treaties. Fisheries enforcement on the high seas is weak and illegal or unreported fishing is thought to account for some 30 per cent of catches. Garrett Hardin's description of the 'tragedy of the commons' remains the most compelling analysis of the problem of sustainability of common property: free access to a free resource which no one controls and everyone can exploit leads inexorably to over-consumption, unrestrained competition, and ultimate ruin for all.[6] Marine living resources present no better proof of the accuracy of this conclu-sion. The task of international law since the earliest conservation agreements has been to try to ameliorate this powerful tendency.

The EEZ regime agreed during the UNCLOS III negotiations sought to address the problems of sustainable exploitation of common property by largely removing living resources from that status. Coastal states were given the exclusive right to con-trol access, exploitation, and conservation—the very opposite of high-seas freedom.[7] This approach relied on national self-interest, not international cooperation, to ensure rational and sustainable use. Some 90 per cent of all fish are caught within 200 miles of the coast, and most states now have such a zone, or at least an exclusive fisheries zone. However, as we explain below, exclusive jurisdiction has not put an end to the overfishing which seriously affects not only the sustainability of many fish species but also the survival of entire coastal ecosystems. Much depends on whether coastal states make effective use of this opportunity to conserve fisheries on a sustainable basis. It is not always easy to do so, especially for developing states with extensive EEZs. The cost of collecting the necessary data, maintaining surveillance over the zone, and actively enforcing conservatory laws is greater the larger the area. Very few states have scientific research vessels. The possibility of arresting violators at sea, or of making use of the right of 'hot pursuit' of offending vessels,[8] requires availability of naval vessels, aircraft, satellites, and highly trained personnel. This problem can be ameliorated by flag states of distant water vessels applying stricter sanctions, by regional cooperation, by pooling resources, and by provision of technical assistance and advice by international organizations, such as FAO, regional commissions, and by other states or groupings thereof, including for example, the European Community. A remarkably successful initiative was taken by the sixteen states of the South Pacific Forum Fisheries Agency (FFA) in relation to enforcement of the FFA's conservatory regulations for highly migratory tuna in its region, where large-scale illegal fish-ing had taken place. The 1992 Niue Treaty on Cooperation in Fisheries Surveillance and Enforcement in the South Pacific Region instituted a regional register of vessels licensed to fish, and set minimum terms and conditions, backed by strong aerial and surface surveillance and enforcement capacity, as well as a data and communication network and training.[9] Its success depends heavily on a high level of material support from Australia and New Zealand for surveillance patrols, all its other parties being small-island developing states.

---

[6] *Science,* 162 (1968) 1243–8. See also Wijkman, 36 *Int Org* (1982) 511.   [7] See *infra,* section 4(2).
[8] Codified in UNCLOS, Article 111.   [9] See Lodge, 2 *RECIEL* (1993) 277–83.

Nevertheless, there is cogent evidence that even developed states are not always successful in managing and conserving fisheries in their EEZs or EFZs.[10] This well illustrates that few fisheries are immune to improvident policies motivated by short-term social and political concerns. But the fundamental point is the simplest and most obvious: 'Reducing the killing power/overcapacity of the world's fishing fleets is an essential first step towards ecosystem-based fisheries management'.[11] Fishing as presently practiced by many states represents unsustainable development at its worst. Growing international concern is evident in UN General Assembly resolutions,[12] and in reports produced by the Secretary General, FAO, the OECD, the EU, and various NGOs. Not surprisingly, the Conference of the Parties to the Convention on Biological Diversity selected marine and coastal biodiversity as one of the topics for early consideration under that Convention.[13] The 2002 Johannesburg World Summit on Sustainable Development reiterated these concerns.

2 JURISDICTION OVER FISHERIES AND MARINE MAMMALS

2(1) EVOLUTION OF HIGH-SEAS FREEDOM OF FISHING

Modern fisheries problems originate in concepts and doctrines of the law of the sea attuned to the interests of earlier centuries. Grotius sought to establish the *inclusive* interest of the whole community in the 'free seas'/'common property' approach to high-seas resources, based on the impossibility, as then perceived, of either occupying those areas or of exhausting their fish resources, though he accepted that if a great many people hunt on land or fish in a river the species are easily exhausted and control becomes expedient.[14] Others, however, sought to extend *exclusive* rights over the seas and its resources, as did King James I and VI in 1609 over the British and Irish Seas.[15] Following a change of policy in Britain later in the seventeenth century,[16] the common interest in fisheries predominated for the next three hundred years, with major maritime states seeking to maximize the area of the high seas and minimize the breadth of the territorial sea, widely accepted until the 1960s to be three nautical miles. Given the

---

[10] See Ulfstein, Andersen, and Churchill, *The Regulation of Fisheries: Legal, Economic and Social Aspects* (Council of Europe, 1986); Johnston, 22 *ODIL* (1991) 199; Beckman and Coleman, 14 *IJMCL* (1999) 491; Saunders, *Policy Options for the Management and Conservation of Straddling Stocks*, Research Paper—Royal Commission on Renewing and Strengthening our Place in Canada (St John's, 2003); EC, *Fishing Opportunities for 2009: Policy Statement from the European Commission*, COM(2008) 331 final.

[11] Parsons, 20 *IJMCL* (2005) 421.   [12] See e.g. UNGA Res 59/25 (2005)

[13] COP, 2nd meeting, 1994; see *Handbook of Biological Diversity* (London, 2001) and *infra*, section 6.

[14] Grotius, *The Freedom of the Sea or the Right Which Belongs to the Dutch to Take Part in the East India Trade*, trans Magoffin and Scott (New York, 1916) 1, 28, 43, 57.

[15] Selden, *Mare Clausum* (1635) cited in Fulton, *The Sovereignty of the Sea* (Edinburgh, 1911) 366–72.

[16] Fulton, op cit, 352ff.

prevailing doctrine, those few states which claimed a wider territorial sea, or sought to reserve to themselves fishing or sealing in a particular coastal area, generally encountered strong protests. Objections by Britain to Russia's attempt to extend its jurisdiction over foreign vessels sealing within one hundred miles of Alaska led indirectly to the seminal *Behring Sea Fur Seals Arbitration*.[17]

Faced with continued decline in fur seals because of over-exploitation on the high seas, despite enactment of laws to conserve them and protect their breeding grounds, which lay within US territorial jurisdiction, the United States arrested British (Canadian) vessels taking the seals on the high seas, arguing that it had a right of protection and property in the fur seals frequenting the Pribilof Islands even when found outside the US three-mile limit. The United States contended that this right was based upon the established practice in common and civil law, the practice of nations, upon the laws of natural history, and upon the common interests of mankind, in view of the fact that the fur seals were bred within its territory, were protected there by the United States, and were a valuable resource and source of income for its people. The United States regarded itself as the trustee of the herd for the benefit of mankind. Britain (for Canada) argued that it had the right to hunt seals on the high seas; they were either *res communis* or *res nullius* in status, not the exclusive property of the United States. The United States countered that the high seas were 'free only for innocent and inoffensive use, not injurious to the just interests of any nation which borders upon it', and also that the seals had an *animus revertendi*, returning cyclically to US territory, and were thus to be equated to domesticated animals which could be the subject of property rights.[18] The arbitral tribunal found against the US arguments. It held that as Britain had protested against the Russian decree, Russia had neither held nor exercised exclusive rights in the Behring Sea beyond areas of national jurisdiction. Thus the United States had not acquired such rights from Russia, had no property rights in the seals, and no right to protect them beyond the three-mile limit. Freedom of the high seas was held to be the prevailing doctrine.

The importance of this decision to the development of the law concerning conservation of marine living resources cannot be overstressed. It laid the twin foundations for subsequent developments over the next century. First, it confirmed that the law was based on high-seas freedom of fishing and that no distinction was to be made in this respect between fisheries and marine mammals despite the very different characteristics of the latter. Second, it recognized the need for conservation to prevent over-exploitation and decline of a hunted species, but because of the former finding, it made this dependent on the express acceptance of regulation by participants in the fishery.

The two parties in this case had asked the tribunal, if it found against the United States, to recommend the required conservation regulations. Its nine-point plan for conservation provides a model for fishery commissions to this day: a prohibited zone; a closed season in a defined area of the high seas, with specific exceptions in favours of indigenous peoples as long as they hunted for traditional purposes, using traditional

---

[17] Moore, *Int Arb Awards*, I (1898) 811. Reproduced in 1 *IELR* (2000) 43.   [18] Ibid, 812, 839, 883–4.

methods; a limitation on the type of vessels used; a licensing system to be operated by the governments concerned; use of a special flag while sealing; the keeping of catch records; exchange of data; governmental responsibility for selection of suitable crews; and the provisions to continue for five years or until abandoned by agreement. Moreover the tribunal went on to recommend that these regulations be enacted into uniform national laws in *both* states and that national measures be adopted to ensure their enforcement. Thus the choice of national measures of enforcement, rather than international means, was also established. Finally, a three-year ban on all sealing was recommended, the foundation of the moratorium approach to conservation of marine mammals.

The measures recommended were not conservatory in the modern sense of being based on scientific findings, theories of sustainable yield or population, or catch quotas, but were influenced by the adoption in 1882 of the pioneering Convention on North Sea Overfishing, the first of its kind. This had introduced several progressive measures to establish order among states fishing in that area by harmonizing the registration and numbering of vessels, prescribing the use of certain kinds of gear, the salvage of derelict gear, and the supervision of these matters by national fisheries protection vessels. Attempts to follow this up by convening a conference to discuss the scientific aspects of fisheries problems eventually led to the establishment of ICES (International Council for the Exploration of the Sea), a cooperative group of scientists drawn from North Atlantic states.[19]

Thus, although it perpetuated the high-seas freedom of fishing and hence made conservation more difficult, especially in relation to enforcement, the *Behring Sea* arbitral tribunal strongly supported the need for restraint in exploitation, clearly indicated the requisite measures, and recognized that freedom was not absolute but had to be regulated to take reasonable account of the interests of other states. Its decision, however, failed in the short term to have the desired conservatory effect because it could be addressed to only two of the four states engaged in hunting the Behring Sea fur seals; Russia and Japan were not involved in the case. US and Canadian vessel owners re-registered under Japanese and other flags to evade the US and Canadian regulations. Naturally, the decline in seal stocks continued until it was eventually realized by all participants that only an international regulatory treaty among all the states involved in sealing could save them.[20] This cycle of events has been repeated in almost all exploited fisheries as the following sections illustrate.

[19] *Supra,* Ch 2.

[20] 1911 Convention on Behring Sea Fur Seals, 104 *BFSP* (1911) 175, based on the arbitral award. Replaced in 1957 by Interim Convention on North Pacific Fur Seals, since terminated. See Lyster, *International Wildlife Law* (1st edn, Cambridge, 1985) Ch 3. The 1957 convention was innovative in several respects, including its ban on pelagic (high seas) sealing, its provision for high seas enforcement by any party, and a sharing of the income among all four parties to compensate Canada and Japan for loss of pelagic catches. Compare 1972 Convention for the Conservation of Antarctic Seals, on which see Lyster, op cit.

2(2) 1958 GENEVA CONVENTIONS AND JURISDICTION OVER MARINE LIVING RESOURCES

The 1958 Geneva Convention on Fisheries Conservation and Management was the first multilateral treaty to attempt to codify and develop international fisheries law. It recognized only the 'special interest' of the coastal state in conservation of high-seas fisheries adjacent to its territorial sea.[21] Zones beyond that limit in which coastal states could assert exclusive or preferential rights to fisheries were not generally recognized, whether for conservatory or exploitative purposes. Instead, Article 2 of the 1958 High Seas Convention reiterated the customary freedom to fish on the high seas, without specific reference to conservation, but exercisable only 'with reasonable regard to the interests of other states'.

The 1958 Geneva Fisheries Convention was not a success. Supported mainly by distant water fishing states, it failed to establish a balance of interests widely acceptable to coastal fishing states. Those Latin American states that had from 1947 onwards declared 200-nautical-mile maritime zones in which, inter alia, they asserted 'sovereignty' over living resources did not renounce their claims. Following the failure of the UNCLOS I and II to deal with these problems, new claims to extended fisheries jurisdiction were made by other states for a variety of reasons, including the failure of many international fishing commissions to preserve or restore stocks to MSY and thus maintain catch levels.

Iceland was one of the states which opposed the establishment of the six-plus-six-nautical-mile formula for extension of coastal state control over fisheries proposed unsuccessfully at UNCLOS I and II. For this reason it did not participate in the 1964 European Fisheries Convention. Its declaration of a twelve-mile territorial sea provoked the first dispute with the UK, but this was settled by negotiation. The further extension of its exclusive fishery zone to fifty nautical miles in 1972, however, provoked disputes with the UK and Germany which were submitted to the International Court of Justice.[22] The Court was asked to decide the legality of Iceland's extension of its fisheries jurisdiction and the continuing rights of the UK and the Federal Republic of Germany to fish in the area, and to pronounce on any requirements for cooperation in adopting conservation measures. In the *Icelandic Fisheries Cases* the Court found, after surveying existing fisheries conventions and state practice, that claims to a 12-mile exclusive zone were not unlawful, that the UK and Germany had not acquiesced in or accepted Iceland's claim to an exclusive zone beyond that limit, but that Iceland did have preferential rights in the allocation of quotas (although it did not fix any spatial limit for these). The UK and Germany retained rights to fish beyond Iceland's 12-mile zone, based on long-standing historic exercise of high-seas freedoms. The Court held, however, that the parties' respective rights were not absolute; both had

---

[21] Article 6. For a short account of the 1958 Convention see Nelson, in Boyle and Freestone (eds), *International Law and Sustainable Development* (Oxford, 1999) 113–8.

[22] *Icelandic Fisheries Cases (UK v Iceland)* (Merits) ICJ Reports (1974) 3 and (*FRG v Iceland*) (Merits) 175. See Churchill, 24 *ICLQ* (1975) 82–105.

to take account of and accommodate not only each other's rights but also the needs of fisheries conservation:

Both states have an obligation to take full account of each other's rights and of any fishery conservation measures the necessity of which is shown to exist in those waters. It is one of the advances of maritime international law, resulting from the intensification of fishing, that the former *laissez-faire* treatment of the living resources of the high seas has been replaced by a recognition of a duty to have due regard to the rights of other states and the *needs of conservation* for the benefit of all. Consequently, both Parties have the obligation to keep under review the fishery resources in the disputed waters and *to examine together,* in the light of scientific and other available information *the measures required for conservation* and development of *equitable* exploitation of these resources.[23]

The parties were held to be under an obligation to negotiate and cooperate in good faith, to accommodate equitably their respective rights and interests under Article 2 of the High Seas Convention, to regulate catches and to take full account of fishery conservation needs.[24]

Subsequently, in the *Gulf of Maine*[25] and *Jan Mayen Cases,*[26] the ICJ delimited maritime boundaries between the overlapping continental shelves and exclusive fisheries/ economic zones of the respective parties. The boundaries drawn by the court cut across fishing grounds. Rejecting American arguments in the *Gulf of Maine Case* based on the unity of the marine ecosystem, the court considered that any adverse effects on fisheries from this bisection would not be sufficiently serious to affect the proposed boundary and that any difficulties could be resolved by cooperation, which had become 'all the more necessary' as a result of its decisions.[27]

These cases indicate that cooperation remains necessary when natural resources are shared across maritime boundaries or in international areas.[28] States must, for this purpose, have due regard to other states' rights; provide for management of the resource for the benefit of all interested states; examine jointly the measures necessary for conservation and development of the fishery; and arrange for equitable exploitation. Only then will true 'optimum utilization' be achieved, which, in Hey's view, means use in the best interests of all participants. She submits that this qualification of sovereignty and sovereign rights has changed the role of these concepts and shifted the burden of proof; states do not have an unfettered right to exploit shared resources that fall only partly within their territory or jurisdiction, but may only claim an equitable share of

---

[23] *Icelandic Fisheries (UK v Iceland)* 31, para 72; *(FRG v Iceland)* 200, para 64, emphasis added.

[24] *Icelandic Fisheries (UK v Iceland)* 31–3, paras 73–5 and *(FRG v Iceland)* 200–1, paras 64–7.

[25] *Gulf of Maine Case,* ICJ Reports (1984) 246.

[26] ICJ Reports (1993) 38; Churchill, 9 *IJMCL* (1994) 1.

[27] On the limited effect of fisheries on maritime boundary delimitation see Churchill, 17 *Marine Policy* (1993) 44, but compare the *Yemen–Eritrea Maritime Boundary Arbitration* (2000) which reserved a right of continued access to traditional fishing grounds for fishermen from the other party. See Antunes, 50 *ICLQ* (2001) 299, 301–16.

[28] Hey, *The Regime for the Exploitation of Transboundary Marine Fishery Resources,* 34–5; she considers that the ICJ would have been more forthright in the *North Sea* and *Gulf of Maine Cases* if the issue had not been secondary to the primary purpose of establishing the principles of boundary delimitation.

the benefits derivable from these resources.[29] She thus disagrees with the conclusion of Judge Schewbel, when special rapporteur for the ILC on international watercourses, that the duty to cooperate in such cases is an exception to the concepts of permanent sovereignty over natural resources embodied in General Assembly resolutions.[30] Hers is certainly a more attractive view to take from the conservatory standpoint. It remains to be seen below to what extent it is supported in the 1982 UNCLOS.

3 THE DEVELOPMENT OF INTERNATIONAL FISHERIES REGIMES

3(1) CONSERVATORY CONVENTIONS AND COMMISSIONS

It is essential to an understanding of the development of the law for conservation of marine living resources to examine the problems faced in achieving the necessary regulation. These problems have never been satisfactorily resolved and remain acute, exacerbated by the use of modern technology for both ships and gear, and the solutions adopted have frequently been called into question. The establishment of regional fisheries commissions, and the gradual enlargement of their powers, was a seminal development.[31] As we saw in Chapter 7 they are an important contribution to implementing UNCLOS and giving effect to the goals of Chapter 17 of Agenda 21 and the 2002 Johannesburg Declaration and Plan of Implementation.

There is a symbiotic relationship between the development of the law of conservation and the development of scientific knowledge. Though the former necessarily lags behind the latter for political, economic, and social reasons, it cannot progress without an appropriate scientific basis; it must respond both to new scientific data and new scientific theories and take account also of economic, social, and political factors. Regional fisheries commissions provide the forum in which the necessary discussions and decisions can take place. They face many problems, however, in reducing catch to levels that can sustain exploitation on a continuing basis.

Fisheries commissions usually have to meet annually to set new quotas and revise or adopt other measures. Conventions typically differentiate between amendment to the substantive articles of the convention, which generally requires ratification by states parties, and decisions of the parties required annually to amend regulations concerning catch, gear used, etc. The latter are usually not included in the main

---

[29] *Supra*, Ch 3, section 5.   [30] *Supra*, Ch 10.

[31] See Koers, *The International Regulation of Marine Fisheries* (London, 1973); Knight (ed), *The Future of International Fisheries Management* (St Paul, 1975); Hey, *The Regime for the Exploitation of Transboundary Marine Fishery Resources* (Dordrecht, 1989) 133–274; Stokke (ed), *Governing High Seas Fisheries* (Oxford, 2001); Kaye, *International Fisheries Management* (The Hague, 2001); Henriksen, Hønneland, Sydnes, *Law and Politics in Ocean Governance: The UN Fish Stocks Agreement and Regional Fisheries Management Regimes* (Leiden, 2006).

convention but placed in an Appendix or Annex, which forms an integral part of the convention but is amendable by a two-thirds or three-quarters majority without the need for ratification. This system provides a flexible means of adapting the convent-ions to changing scientific advice and other values, but its fundamental weakness is that any state is free to opt out of regulations adopted in this manner.[32] Not infre-quently the use of this objections procedure has destroyed the ability of such bodies to take effective measures.[33]

Fisheries treaties in the period before UNCLOS III were more concerned with estab-lishing national quotas for fish stocks than with conservation of the marine environ-ment as such; in so far as they had a conservatory effect it derived incidentally from the regulation of access. They offered a variety of approaches—some were species spe-cific (halibut, salmon, tuna); others regional (Behring Sea, North-east or North-west Atlantic, Indian Ocean); some were both. Some had closed membership, others were open to all interested states. A few provided techniques for persuading non-members to join, such as prohibiting trade in fish with non-parties. Though regulatory powers of fisheries commissions were wide in scope—setting a total allowable catch (TAC), allocating national quotas, regulating fishing gear and net mesh sizes, establishing closed areas or seasons, etc—none limited entry or effort. Enforcement was mainly left to national means, that is to coastal states in the territorial sea/EEZ and to the flag state on the high seas; only the 1957 North Pacific Fur Seals Convention provided for international enforcement (including arrest and prosecution) though other agree-ments subsequently instituted limited international surveillance based on mutual inspection. Under this system, vessels of one party would inspect suspected offending vessels of the other(s) on the high seas but could only report offences to the flag state; they could not arrest them. No independent observers or inspectors were carried on board vessels. Finally, though the promotion of scientific research was stipulated by most conventions, some left its execution to national means; some allowed for the appointment of in-house scientists; others used ICES, establishing a special liaison committee for this purpose, with ICES and government scientists on their country's delegations to these commissions meeting together. Some treaties provided for spe-cialized committees for scientific and technical matters, which could be established by the commissions or by other organs so empowered.

Despite these protective treaty provisions, many fisheries continued to decline partly because of the inadequacies of scientific knowledge and management theory; partly because such advice as scientists gave was not followed; partly because there was no attempt to limit effort and little attempt to limit the number of vessels having access; and partly because of the lack of fully international inspection and enforce-ment. Most of these weaknesses derived from the underlying common property/free

---

[32] *Supra*, Ch 4, section 3.

[33] See generally Koers, *The International Regulation of Marine Fisheries*. The Canada–Spain dispute over turbot caused by the inability of the North-west Atlantic Fisheries Commission to control Spanish overfish-ing provides a good example of this problem. See Davies and Redgwell, 67 *BYIL* (1996) 199–217; Joyner and von Gustedt, 11 *IJMCL* (1996) 425.

access doctrine and the limited powers of fishery commissions.[34] Beyond requiring states to cooperate in the conservation and management of fish stocks,[35] UNCLOS did little to rectify the shortcomings of regional fisheries cooperation; nor, until the adoption of the 1995 UN Agreement on Straddling and Highly Migratory Fish Stocks ('UN Fish Stocks Agreement'), did FAO.

3(2) THE ROLE OF FAO IN FISHERIES MANAGEMENT AND LAW

Although suggestions have been made from time to time for the establishment of a World Fisheries Organization nothing has come of them.[36] However, the creation of the Food and Agriculture Organization (FAO) in 1945 provided the UN with a means of promoting the establishment of regional fisheries bodies and of monitoring and coordinating their activities. As we saw in Chapter 2, Article XIV of the FAO treaty allows the FAO Conference to approve agreements relating, inter alia, to fisheries. Not all agreements on marine living resources come under its jurisdiction however. It is notable that the International Whaling Commission, which the United States had at the outset thought should be incorporated into FAO, voted against such a move when the opportunity arose. More recently regional fisheries agreements involving 'fishing entities' (i.e. Taiwan) have been concluded outside FAO in deference to Chinese wishes.[37]

FAO's main responsibilities with respect to fisheries rest on Article I(2) of the FAO Constitution, which requires it 'to promote and where appropriate to recommend national and international action with respect to the conservation of natural resources and the adoption of improved methods of agricultural production', and Article IV, which empowers FAO, by a two-thirds majority, to submit conventions on these subjects to its members. Under Article XVI 'agriculture' includes fisheries and marine products. FAO issues reports on fisheries problems and on national legislation and provides technical assistance and advice, including legal advice, to the developing countries which make up the majority of its membership. Faced with the disparate national interests of its members—which include developed and developing states, coastal, artisanal, and distant water-fishing states—it has eschewed any attempt at a global or regional managerial role, confining itself instead to promoting effective management of world fishery resources. Where no fisheries commissions exist, it has established regional advisory bodies with responsibility for data collection, scientific research, training, and development (including aquaculture). A Committee on

---

[34] *Supra*, Ch 4. For case studies of this failure in the period up to UNCLOS III see Koers, *The International Regulation of Marine Fisheries*; Kaye, *International Fisheries Management*, 43–88.

[35] Articles 61(2), 63–5, 66(4), 118.

[36] E.g. Koers, *The International Regulation of Marine Fisheries*, 307–24 and Appendix I, 331–9 (draft text of Convention for the Establishment of a World Marine Fisheries Organization). Nor were high-seas fisheries included in the common heritage regime administered by the International Seabed Authority established by Part XI of the 1982 UNCLOS.

[37] See Edeson, 22 *IJMCL* (2007) 485.

Fisheries (COFI) and various committees of independent fisheries experts advise the Director General. Their reports have helped underline the frailty of estimates of maximum sustainable yield (MSY), the closeness of most of the world's fishing resources to maximum catch limits, and the manifestation of signs of biological degradation and economic waste.[38]

These considerations resulted in a reassessment of international fisheries policy and law during and after the 1992 Rio Conference. Placing international fisheries policy in a broader environmental context, Agenda 21 gave new vigour to the importance of sustainable use and conservation of marine living resources, and recognized once more the need for more effective regional cooperation. FAO has since played a leading role in the negotiation of new agreements on straddling and highly migratory fish stocks, sustainable fishing, and compliance with regional fisheries agreements. Intended to supplement the existing provisions of the 1982 UNCLOS, these agreements underline FAO's importance in the process of law-reform relating to international fisheries.[39] In particular, the 1995 UN Fish Stocks Agreement has for the first time provided a framework for regional agreements, revising those already in existence and requiring the negotiation of new ones. We return to this important development in section 5 below.

4 THE 1982 UN CONVENTION ON THE LAW OF THE SEA

4(1) GENERAL APPROACH

The 1982 UN Convention on the Law of the Sea is the foundation for the modern law relating to international fisheries.[40] As we saw in Chapter 1, the 1982 UNCLOS was negotiated and adopted as a 'package deal'. States had to reach compromises on some issues to secure agreement on others of particular concern to them. Fisheries articles

---

[38] See *Contribution of the Committee on Fisheries to Global Fisheries, Governance 1977–1997*, FAO Fisheries Circular No 938, FIPL/C938; *Summary Information on the Role of International Fishery and Other Bodies with Regard to the Conservation and Management of Living Resources of the High Seas*, Fisheries Circular No 908, FILP/C908; *Marine Fisheries and the Law of the Sea: A Decade of Change*, FAO Fisheries Circular No 853, FID/C853, and other reports cited *supra*, n 3.

[39] See in particular Edeson, in Boyle and Freestone (eds), *International Law and Sustainable Development*, Ch 8; Moore, in Hey (ed), *Developments in International Fisheries Law*, 55ff; Reyfuse, ibid, 107ff; and *infra*, section 5.

[40] See Churchill and Lowe, *The Law of the Sea* (3rd edn, Manchester, 1999). With regard to fisheries, they stress the extent of the consensus arrived at on the relevant provisions and their status as customary law. See generally Burke, *The New International Law of Fisheries* (Oxford, 1994); Hey (ed), *Developments in International Fisheries Law* (The Hague, 1999); Stokke (ed), *Governing High Seas Fisheries* (Oxford, 2001); Lucchini and Voeckel, *Le Droit de la Mer* (Paris, 1996); de Yturriaga, *The International Regime of Fisheries: From UNCLOS to the Presencial Sea* (Dordrecht, 1997); Bowman, Davies and Redgwell, *Lyster's International Wildlife Law* (2nd edn, Cambridge, 2009), Ch 5.

could not be voted on separately from those relating to the territorial sea, high seas, continental shelf, or settlement of disputes. The necessary compromises were often achieved by the use of ambiguous language or by leaving difficult issues, such as precise formulae for allocation of fish catches or calculation of MSY, to be determined by subsequent agreement or left to the discretion of coastal states or the decisions of international tribunals.

The 1982 Convention incorporates the conclusions of the *Icelandic Fisheries Case* only in part. While nominally retaining freedom of fishing on the high seas, it responds to pressure from coastal states by allowing them to adopt a 200-nautical-mile exclusive economic zone for fisheries, thus removing them from a high-seas common-property regime. It also adopts special rules for certain species of fish and marine mammals. Despite the coordinated ecosystem strategies referred to earlier, the 1982 UNCLOS does not provide any mechanism for coordinating existing fisheries commissions or the relationship between fisheries conservation and other conservatory conventions in general. Nor does it deal effectively or in detail with the crucial problem of common stocks, namely stocks that migrate between or among zones, though it does address it in general terms. It does not clearly endorse an ecosystem- or habitat-preservation approach, though its main article on conservation (Article 61) goes some way towards this and Article 194(5) is relevant to certain endangered species' habitats. Finally, it provides no mechanism for considering or clearly identifying the close interrelationship of the fisheries conservation (Parts V and VII) and pollution prevention articles (Part XII), although as the Convention was negotiated as a 'package deal' the relationship is inherent and the title of Part XII—'Protection and Preservation of the Marine Environment' (rather than 'prevention of pollution') is aimed at emphasizing this.[41]

Despite these limitations, it must be recalled that not only is the 1982 UNCLOS in force for a substantial number of states, but the consensus on most of its provisions during and after the UNCLOS III conference, combined with subsequent state practice, are strong evidence of the extent to which many of its provisions represent customary international law. This is especially so with regard to jurisdictional questions.[42]

4(2) COMPETENCE OVER CONSERVATION OF MARINE LIVING RESOURCES UNDER UNCLOS

On one aspect of fisheries problems—the attribution of jurisdiction over conservation and use of marine living resources—the 1982 UNCLOS is an important step forward.

---

[41] Nordquist (ed), *UN Convention on the Law of the Sea: A Commentary* (Dordrecht, 1991) iv, 9–12; the commentator suggests that 'preserve' means to conserve the natural resources and retain the quality of the marine environment over the long term (at 11–12). See also Van Heijnsbergen, *International Legal Protection of Wild Flora and Fauna* (Amsterdam, 1997) who examines the concepts of 'protection', 'preservation' and 'conservation' and their use in different instruments, 43ff, and concludes that they are often used interchangeably.

[42] In the *Malta–Libya Continental Shelf Case*, ICJ Reports (1985) 13, paras 26–34, the ICJ held that the 200-mile exclusive economic zone had become customary law on the basis of widespread state practice since first agreed at UNCLOS III in 1976–7.

Moreover, both the obligation to conserve and manage and, to some extent, its specific content can be identified. The relevant provisions for fisheries are as follows.

(a) Territorial sea (TS)

Article 3 of the 1982 UNCLOS establishes a twelve-mile limit for the territorial sea, over which the coastal state has sovereignty, subject to any requirements of the UNCLOS and other rules of international law, including any conservatory conventions to which that state is party and which by their terms apply within that area. Foreign fishing vessels must refrain from fishing activities in the territorial sea.[43] The coastal state can adopt laws and regulations, consistent UNCLOS and other international rules, to prevent infringement of its fishery laws.[44]

(b) Archipelagic waters

Archipelagic states, as defined in the UNCLOS, can draw straight baselines joining the outermost points of their outer islands and reefs.[45] Within the area enclosed the waters fall within the sovereignty of the archipelagic state, with a status akin to that of the territorial sea, but subject to UNCLOS provisions on jurisdiction and on the right of innocent passage. As the baselines enclosing the archipelago now also form the baselines for the territorial sea, the continental shelf and the exclusive economic zone, archipelagic states control fishing in vast areas of sea. Article 51, however, requires them to respect existing agreements with other states, including those on fisheries, and to recognize in certain areas the traditional fishing rights of immediately adjacent neighbouring states, which can be regulated by bilateral agreement. Though no specific reference is made to conservation this could be required under the relevant agreements. An archipelagic state has the same powers to prohibit fishing and scientific research by vessels in passage through any archipelagic sea lanes it may designate as have coastal states over transit passage through international straits.[46] The conservation of fisheries in the EEZ of archipelagic states is, of course, subject to the requirements of Article 61 of the UNCLOS.[47]

(c) Exclusive economic zone (EEZ)

In establishing the EEZ, subject to coastal-state jurisdiction, in an area not exceeding 200-nautical-mile from the low-water baseline of the territorial sea,[48] the UNCLOS negotiators sought to provide a more effective basis for conservation and sustainable management of marine living resources. The EEZ is not an area in which the coastal state has territorial sovereignty but a more limited functional zone,[49] in which the

---

[43] Articles 19(2)(i); 42(1)(c).   [44] Article 21(1)(e).   [45] Articles 46–53.   [46] Article 54.
[47] *Infra.*

[48] Articles 55–7. Generally the baseline will be the low-water line along the coast, but there are exceptions: see UNCLOS, Articles 5–14. Where an EEZ would otherwise overlap with the maritime zones of an adjacent or opposite state, an equitable boundary is delimited. This will often, but not always, be the median line: see *Gulf of Maine Case*, ICJ Reports (1984) 246 and *Jan Mayen Case*, ICJ Reports (1993) 38.

[49] See Barnes, in Freestone, Barnes and Ong (eds), *The Law of the Sea*, Ch 13; Christie, in Hey (ed), *Developments in International Fisheries Law*, 395–419; Burke, *The New International Law of Fisheries*, Ch 2;

coastal state is accorded 'sovereign rights for the purpose of exploring, exploiting, *conserving and managing* the natural resources, whether living or non-living, of the water superjacent to the seabed and its subsoil'.[50] It also exercises jurisdiction, as provided for in the Convention, with regard to marine scientific research and protection and preservation of the marine environment.[51] Coastal states must have 'due regard' to the rights and duties of other states and their actions must be compatible with UNCLOS. In the EEZ there is neither freedom of fishing for all states, nor unfettered freedom of scientific research.[52] To that extent fish within the zone thus cease to be high-seas common property. Although other states may in certain circumstances have a claim to share in EEZ fishing,[53] the coastal state determines the total allowable catch (TAC) for harvesting the living resources and allocates fishing rights.[54]

Conservatory obligations laid down in the 1982 UNCLOS qualify the sovereign right to exploit the EEZ's living resources. They are expressed in general terms in Article 61 but create complex obligations. In determining the TAC the coastal state, taking account of the best scientific advice available to it (no criteria are provided for evaluating this) must ensure 'through proper conservation and management measures' that the living resources of the EEZ are maintained and not threatened by over-exploitation.[55] It must cooperate with 'competent' international organizations, whether subregional, regional, or global. This conservatory aim, however, is offset by the need to promote 'optimum utilization' and to select measures which will maintain or restore populations—of harvested species only—at levels which can produce MSY (now, as indicated in Chapter 11, a somewhat discredited concept) but only as qualified by 'relevant environmental *and* economic factors'.[56]

Optimum utilization, however, does not require full utilization; the coastal state is not tied to any specific level and could hold back on full exploitation in the interests of conservation. Whether it has a right *not* to exploit otherwise abundant fisheries is doubtful, except as regards marine mammals, specifically allowed for in Article 65 or under other agreements. Other states cannot insist on access to a surplus in such circumstances; the declaration of a TAC is excluded from the UNCLOS compulsory dispute settlement procedures by Article 297(3)(a)–(b), although the coastal state's 'manifest failure' to ensure, by proper conservation and management, that the zone's living resources are not endangered must be submitted to conciliation procedures established under the UNCLOS. A non-exhaustive list of the factors to be taken into account includes the economic needs of coastal fishing communities, special needs of developing states, fishing patterns, the interdependence of stocks, and any 'generally recommended international minimum standards whether subregional, regional or global.'[57] In formulating measures the coastal state must 'take into consideration' such ecological factors as 'effects on species associated with or dependent upon harvested

Attard, *The Exclusive Economic Zone in International Law*, 146–91; Kwiatkowska, *The 200 Mile EEZ in the Law of the Sea*, 45–103.

[50] Article 56(1)(a), emphasis added.   [51] Ibid, (b)–(c) and see *supra*, Ch 7.
[52] Articles 58, 87.   [53] Articles 62(2), 69–70.   [54] Article 61(1).   [55] Article 61(2).
[56] Article 61(3), emphasis added.   [57] Ibid.

species' with a view to maintaining or restoring these populations 'above levels at which their reproduction may become seriously threatened'.[58] The coastal state and all states participating in the fishery must regularly contribute and exchange a wide range of scientific information and data relevant to conservation through 'competent international organizations' at all levels.

Clearly, the above provisions of the 1982 UNCLOS afford a better approach to conservation than did the 1958 Fisheries Conservation Convention, but the short-term national interests of some states have still tempted them to give more weight to the economic than the environmental considerations. One study concludes that the failings of the EEZ regime 'render the conservation obligations of States largely illusory'.[59] No mechanism is provided to hold states accountable for the management and conservation of fish stocks within their own territorial sea or EEZ, since compliance with the relevant articles is excluded from compulsory dispute settlement by Article 297, while FAO has no power to exercise any kind of oversight.[60] In any event the factors to take into consideration are complex and difficult to assess with certainty, and collection of the necessary data requires a good deal of expensive scientific research. Despite the fact that fish migrate to areas beyond one EEZ, states may tend to regard the resources of the EEZ as their 'national property' and resist cooperation with neighbouring states or the application of international regulation. This is evidenced by the regulatory structure of the North-East Atlantic Fisheries Commission (NEAFC) and North-West Atlantic Fisheries Organization (NAFO) reconstituted following the adoption of EFZs and EEZs by their states parties.[61] These conventions now divide their areas of application into 'Regulatory' and 'Non-Regulatory' sub-areas, the latter being within the EEZs of one or more states parties. Binding regulations adopted by the Commissions apply only in the high-seas area; only non-binding recommendations apply to the coastal states' EEZ stocks and only on the latter's initiatives. The two treaty bodies are thus left largely with a coordinating and harmonizing role in relation to measures adopted for Regulatory and Non-Regulatory areas; they have no management powers in relation to straddling stocks.[62]

The role of fisheries commissions has thus been much reduced by the advent of EEZs and EFZs. This makes cooperative management of shared EEZ stocks all the more difficult, and has contributed to the evidence of catastrophic stock collapse in the North-west Atlantic and North Sea. In all these areas national EEZs abut each other,

---

[58] Article 61(4).   [59] Barnes, in Freestone, Barnes and Ong (eds), *The Law of the Sea*, 234.

[60] See Barnes, loc cit, 257–60; Churchill, 22 *IJMCL* (2007) 383 and on Article 297 *supra* Ch 4, section 4(3).

[61] See 1978 Convention on Future Multilateral Cooperation in the North-West Atlantic and 1980 Convention on Future Multilateral Cooperation in the North-East Atlantic; on these see Applebaum and Donohue, in Hey (ed), *Developments in International Fisheries Law*, 217–69. For an overview of regional fisheries organizations and their mandate, see Marashi, *Summary Information on the Role of International Fishery and Other Bodies with Regard to the Conservation and Management of the Living Resources of the High Seas*, FAO Fisheries Circular No 908 (Rome, 1996) 60–80 and Swan, *Summary Information on the Role of International Fishery Organizations or Arrangements and other Bodies concerned with the Conservation and Management of Living Aquatic Resources*, FAO Fisheries Circular No 985 (Rome, 2003) 31–3, 36–8.

[62] On straddling stocks see *infra*, section 5.

and stocks naturally straddle several zones, including the high seas. In effect they are no longer an exclusive resource, but a shared one. In such circumstances, effective cooperation remains necessary for sustainable management, but this is just as difficult to achieve under an EEZ regime as it had been before UNCLOS under a high-seas regime. All that UNCLOS provides in this respect is that states shall agree on necessary measures so as to ensure coordination and conservation of these stocks.[63]

In the North Sea, comprehensively covered by EEZs or EFZs, problems of overfishing have been exacerbated by the European Union's Common Fisheries Policy (CFP).[64] This gives all EU member states equality of access to fishing throughout the North Sea. The EU Fisheries Council sets and allocates the TAC and promulgates the relevant conservatory measures. The European Commission also represents its member states in the NEAF Commission, North-West Atlantic Fisheries Organization, etc, voting on behalf of all EU member states. The EU regime does not appear to have been any more effective than regulation by traditional fisheries commissions—indeed EU fisheries are among the most overfished, over-resourced and unsustainably managed in the world.[65] Even the European Commission believes that less fishing would eventually result in higher catches. TACs have been set too high for political reasons; conservation measures have been inadequate and poorly enforced and too many fish, especially juvenile fish, have been discarded at sea under an enforcement regime attempting to discourage catching of undersized fish. That even the EU, with far more regulatory authority and resources at its disposal than any intergovernmental fishery commission, cannot succeed in ensuring sustainable fishing within its own marine area is a telling commentary on the assumption that national management of ocean resources is necessarily more effective than international management.

(d) Continental shelf

The continental shelf is a relatively shallow area of seabed over which a great deal of marine life is found. Adjacent coastal states have sovereign rights over the seabed mineral resources of the shelf.[66] The 1982 UNCLOS makes no reference to the precise status of these waters (it simply states that the shelf rights do not affect their status).[67] As the waters above the continental shelf are not included in the areas to which Part VII (high seas) is specifically applied,[68] marine living resources found over the continental shelf will either have the status of EEZ resources, or of high-seas resources. However, 'living organisms belonging to sedentary species' are within the definition of the 'natural resources' of the continental shelf over which the coastal state exercises sovereign rights.[69] As the coastal state now has wide powers to take conservatory

---

[63] Article 63(1).

[64] See Churchill, *EEC Fisheries Law* (Dordrecht, 1987); id, in Hey (ed), *Developments in International Fisheries Law*, 534–73.

[65] EC, *Fishing Opportunities for 2009: Policy Statement from the European Commission*, COM(2008) 331 final.

[66] Article 77.   [67] Article 78(1).   [68] Article 86.

[69] CSC, Articles 1, 2(1)–(2), (4); UNCLOS, Article 77.

measures (taking account of the interdependence of species, etc) and to control pollution and scientific research in the EEZ (see below) this should improve conservation of sedentary species,[70] most of which are found well within the 200-mile limit.

(e) The high seas[71]

Many fish migrate between EEZs and the high seas and many species of marine mammals spend a considerable part of their lives there during migrations. Though Part VII of UNCLOS recognizes that all states have the right for their nationals to engage in fishing on the high seas, this is subject to existing treaty obligations and to the rights, duties, and interests of coastal states in conserving stocks that migrate between EEZs (or EFZs) and the high seas, as set out in Articles 63–7.[72] Article 117 lays down the duty of states to take, or to cooperate with other states in taking, the measures for their nationals that may be necessary to conserve high-seas living resources. This includes marine mammals.[73]

About 400 species are found outside 200-mile zones—including cephalopods, sharks, marine mammals, but also many species of fish, such as tuna, swordfish, halibut, and turbot. The increased scale of high-seas fishing beyond 200 miles and within EEZs has put pressure on some of these stocks and shown that some form of integrated management is essential.[74] No harmonized standards for conservation of such stocks on the high seas are laid down in the UNCLOS, nor are they obligatory in EEZs. Article 63(2) obliges coastal states and states fishing stocks beyond EEZs to seek 'to agree on the measures necessary to coordinate and ensure the conservation and development of such stocks', but allows them to do this either 'directly' *or* through appropriate regional or subregional organizations; in other words, they are not *required* to use the latter process. Article 118 also spells out a duty to cooperate in the management of high-seas fisheries and requires that states exploiting the same resources or resources in the same area 'enter into negotiations with a view to taking the measures necessary for the conservation'. This somewhat imprecise formulation reflects the terminology used in the 1958 Fisheries Conservation Convention.[75] States are also required to cooperate in establishing regional and subregional fisheries organizations for this purpose but only 'as appropriate', and coverage of the high seas by regional fisheries bodies remains fragmentary.[76] However, Article 119 does specify the factors that states must take into consideration in determining the TAC and other conservation measures for the high seas, in terms somewhat similar to Article 61 (though

---

[70] Though Article 56(3) subjects EEZ rights relating to the seabed and subsoil to the provisions of Part VI concerning the continental shelf, which make no reference to any obligation to conserve sedentary species.

[71] See Stokke (ed), *Governing High Seas Fisheries*; Burke, *The New International Law of Fisheries*, Ch 3; Nelson, in Boyle and Freestone (eds), *International Law and Sustainable Development*, 113–34.

[72] Articles 87, 116. Article 119(3) also requires that conservation measures do not discriminate in form or in fact against fishermen of any state on the high seas.

[73] Article 120.

[74] Saunders, *Policy Options For the Management and Conservation of Straddling Fisheries Resources* (St John's, 2003).

[75] Article 4.   [76] Article 118. See Molenaar, 20 *IJMCL* (2005) 533–70.

unlike that article, it does not clearly require states to establish a TAC). These articles do not expressly require, as does Article 61, that states 'ensure through proper conservation and management measures that the maintenance of living resources is not endangered by over-exploitation'. The concept of management based on MSY qualified by both economic and environmental factors is, however, retained along with reference to interdependence of stocks, effects on associated species, and any 'generally recommended international minimum standards'.

These provisions of the 1982 UNCLOS neither clarify the rights of coastal states if agreement on high-seas conservation measures is not possible, nor do they address the broader objectives of ecosystem protection and conservation of biological diversity which cannot be achieved without coordinating law and policy for the EEZ and the adjacent high-seas area. The 1995 UN Fish Stocks Agreement is intended to remedy these defects of the UNCLOS text, whose articles must now be interpreted from the perspective of that treaty, which is considered in detail below.[77]

(f) Deep seabed

Questions have arisen concerning the legal status of living resources found at great depths in the vicinity of hydrothermal vents on the deep seabed.[78] Over 200 species of micro-organisms, crustaceans, molluscs, and other species have been identified in these vent areas. Because of their genetic material they are of great interest for biotechnological purposes, with potential pharmaceutical applications. Neither the UNCLOS nor the Biodiversity Convention specifically covers their use for pure scientific research or commercial purposes. Nor is research or exploitation of these species constrained by the UNCLOS provisions governing the deep seabed in areas beyond national jurisdiction. Those provisions apply only in respect of mineral resource activities 'in' the deep seabed.[79] Deep-seabed species are thus not common heritage resources and do not fall directly within the management responsibilities of the International Seabed Authority;[80] rather they appear to be EEZ or high-seas resources depending on where they reside. As such, relevant provisions of the 1982 Convention and customary law concerning equitable utilization and conservation of marine living resources will apply.[81] However, the International Seabed Authority's jurisdiction to carry out research, regulate pollution or prevent interference with the ecological balance of the marine environment would apply to living organisms found around deep-sea vents if affected by seabed mineral resource activities.[82]

It is clear that the Biodiversity Convention also applies in principle to these resources.[83] Deep-seabed species have a potentially high value as 'genetic resources' and 'genetic material' within the objectives of the Convention. As such they are

---

[77] See *infra*, section 6.

[78] See Glowka, 12 *Ocean Yb* (1996) 156; Hayes, in Nordquist et al (eds), *Law, Science and Ocean Management* (Leiden, 2007) 683–700; Lodge, 19 *IJMCL* (2004) 299.

[79] Articles 133–4.   [80] Articles 136–7, and on common heritage see *supra*, Ch 3, section 5.

[81] Articles 61, 117–9. See *infra*.   [82] Articles 143, 145.

[83] CBD Articles 1, 2, 3, 4(b), 5, and 22 are potentially applicable.

subject to relevant obligations such as sustainable use, maintenance of variability among living organisms, 'appropriate access', fair and equitable sharing of benefits arising from their use, and, to the extent applicable, the 'appropriate' transfer of technologies.[84] However, unless exploitation of deep-seabed vent resources would seriously damage or threaten marine biodiversity, the CBD in effect defers to the UNCLOS.[85] Scovazzi, having pointed out the complexities of the legal situation, arrives at no clear-cut conclusions, while others take the view that a new protocol dealing specifically with deep-seabed living resources is needed, or that regulation already falls within the mandate of the International Seabed Authority.[86] We must agree that the issue remains open since neither UNCLOS nor the CBD took clear cognizance of it.

4(3) THE SPECIES APPROACH

It was agreed at UNCLOS III that special regimes should be laid down for certain species that migrate in various ways. The origins of this approach lie more in allocation of access and jurisdictional rights than in conservation, but the provisions, of course, also allocate control for this purpose. The 1982 Convention specifically addresses the following five categories.

(a) Highly migratory species (HMS)[87]

These are listed in Annex I and include various species of tuna, marlin, sailfish, sword-fish, dolphin, shark, and cetacea . The Annex is, however, neither comprehensive (it does not include squid or krill, for example) nor easily amendable.[88] In addition to the other EEZ requirements, Article 64 requires coastal and other states fishing in a region for HMS to cooperate directly or through 'appropriate' international organizations 'with a view' to ensuring and promoting optimum utilization, within *and* beyond the EEZ—thus giving this aim priority over conservation. Unlike marine mammals (Article 65) HMS are not removed from the requirement of optimum use. If no relevant organization exists, the states involved must cooperate to establish one and participate in it; the alternative of direct cooperation means that some HMS may

---

[84] *Supra*, Ch 11.

[85] CBD, Article 22, on which see *infra*, section 6. The CBD's 2nd COP commissioned a joint study under the Executive Director in consultation with the UN Office of Ocean Affairs and Law of the Sea of the relationship between the two conventions and sustainable use of these deep seabed resources: see UNEP, *Handbook of the Biodiversity Convention*.

[86] See Scovazzi, 3 *RECIEL* (1992) 481; de La Fayette, 24 *IJMCL* (2009); and the variety of views canvassed by states and NGOs in UNGA, Report of the Ad Hoc Open-ended Informal Working Group on Conservation and Sustainable Use of Marine Biological Diversity Beyond Areas of National Jurisdiction, UN Doc A/61/65 (2006).

[87] See Burke, *The New International Law of Fisheries*, Ch 5.

[88] Although Article 65 protects marine mammals, cetaceans were left on Annex I because small cetaceans are caught incidentally in the monofilament nylon nets used by the tuna industry and it falls within the ambit of ICCAT and the ITTC to deal with this problem.

not be conserved throughout their entire range.[89] Conservation objectives may thus be compromised if no agreement is concluded for high-seas areas (as is required under Article 63(2) for stocks within the EEZ) and if the wide discretion accorded to coastal states within their EEZ undermines the aims of Article 64. The problem of by-catches of dolphins, etc is not directly addressed; the use of driftnets has, however, become such a serious problem that it has been the subject of UNGA resolutions and a regional convention.[90]

The weaknesses of Article 64 stem from the United States wish to remove HMS as far as possible from coastal state control in the EEZ and subject their management to international regulation. The coastal state thus cannot exercise its right to make decisions until it has discharged its duty to cooperate with other states in promoting conservation and use. Developing coastal states, however, wanted to protect their sovereign rights to tuna, etc as EEZ resources and had been seeking in the tuna commissions higher quotas for 'resource adjacent nations'. Article 64 tries to accommodate both views. Following the establishment in 1987 of the South Pacific Forum Fisheries Agency (SPFFA)[91] under the auspices of FAO, it introduced a licensing system for the catching, inter alia, of tuna in the Convention area, which comprises the 200-mile zones of participating states and entities, the high-seas areas enclosed by these, and certain other specified areas in the Pacific Ocean. The United States initially objected but eventually paid a considerable sum to the Commission in return for access to a fixed quota of tuna.

The 1995 Agreement on Straddling and Highly Migratory Fish Stocks makes important changes to the law and Article 64 must now be read in the light of that agreement.[92] As Schram and Tahindro conclude, 'The Agreement put flesh on the bones of the obligation to conserve' and it is clear that it will represent a major step towards more adequate management of these stocks.[93]

(b) Marine mammals

These include the twelve species of so-called great whales, many of which were previously hunted to near extinction, as well as small cetaceans, dolphins, porpoises, seals, dugongs, and marine otters. Some of these species are listed in the 1982 UNCLOS as

[89] See Burke, 14 *ODIL* (1984) 283–93. Relevant organizations cover Atlantic tuna (ICCAT), Inter-American tropical tuna (ITTC), southern bluefin tuna (CCSBT); Indian Ocean tuna (IOTC); South Pacific tuna (SPFFA).

[90] 1989 Wellington Convention for the Prohibition of Fishing with Long Driftnets in the South Pacific; UNGA Res 44/225 (1989); 45/197 (1990); 46/215 (1991); 59/25 (2004). See FAO, *The Regulation of Driftnet Fishing on the High Seas: Legal Issues* (Rome, 1991); Kaye, *International Fisheries Management*, 188–94; Carr and Gianni, in Van Dyke, Zaelke, Hewison (eds), *Freedom of the Seas in the 21st Century: Ocean Governance and Environmental Harmony* (Washington DC, 1993) 272; Burke, Freeburg, and Miles, 25 *ODIL* (1994) 127.

[91] See Swan, in Soons (ed), *Implementation of the Law of the Sea Convention Through International Institutions* (Honolulu, 1990) 318–43, for details of the practice of the SPFFA; see also Tsamenyi, 10 *Marine Policy* (1986) 29–41, who points out the need to retain ambiguity concerning sovereignty over HMS in order to secure an agreement (31–6, 41).

[92] *Infra*, section 6.

[93] Schram and Tahindro, in Hey (ed), *Developments in International Fisheries Law* 251, 285–6.

highly migratory and are thus covered by Article 64. However, it is Article 65 which gives more general protection to all marine mammals. It is *not* limited to the EEZ.[94] These species are thus, for the first time, fully protected in a UN Convention. Article 65 provides that:

Nothing in this Convention restricts the right of a coastal state or international organization, as appropriate, to prohibit, limit or regulate the exploitation of marine mammals more strictly than provided for in this Part. States shall co-operate with a view to the conservation of marine mammals and in the case of cetaceans shall in particular work through the appropriate international organization for their conservation, management and study.

This removes all marine mammals from the full application of Part V in that optimum utilization is not required. States can thus prohibit all taking unilaterally or through international organizations. At the same time, Article 65 does not itself prohibit the taking of marine mammals or whaling, nor does the only regional agreement currently existing, which established the North Atlantic Marine Mammal Conservation Organization (NAMMCO).[95]

Article 65 does not in terms require states to join any particular international body—merely to cooperate and, for cetaceans, to 'work through' the 'appropriate body'. In the view of many, the International Whaling Commission (IWC) is that body. However, some states argue that as Article 65 refers to 'organizations' in the plural, it does not exclusively envisage the IWC and that the state concerned can determine which organization is appropriate.[96] Moreover, the Canadian view on withdrawing from the IWC in the 1980s was that the obligation to 'work through' is fulfilled if the organization is merely consulted or its scientific advice sought. For small cetaceans within the Canadian EEZ it would thus be for Canada to manage them; consultation could be with NAFO, would be voluntary and on Canada's initiative.

The IWC was established by the 1946 International Convention for the Regulation of Whaling, the principal treaty under which states cooperate in the management of the marine mammals pursuant to Article 65.[97] Adopted for the purpose of restoring depleted whale stocks to a level that would permit hunting, the Whaling Convention

---

[94] Article 120 specifically extends this article to the high seas. Whether it applies to the territorial sea is disputed. For a detailed account of the negotiating history of Articles 65 and 120, and current disputes relating thereto, see Birnie, in Freestone, Barnes and Ong (eds), *The Law of the Sea*, Ch 14.

[95] The 1992 Agreement on Research, Conservation and Management of Marine Mammals in the North Atlantic, II *MMC* 1618. NAMMCO's purpose is 'the rational management, conservation and optimum utilisation of the living resources of the sea'. Its Convention is carefully drafted to avoid conflict with the ICRW. It reports on hunting methods, by-catch, scientific studies and improving public appreciation of marine mammal products. It has no power to set quotas. See NAMMCO, *Annual Report 2006* (Tromso, 2007); Birnie in Hey (ed), *Developments in International Fisheries Law*, 381–3. Caron, 89 *AJIL* (1995) 154–174, argues that NAMMCO poses only a limited challenge to the IWC at present.

[96] E.g. in the North Atlantic NAFO or NAMMCO.

[97] See generally Birnie, *International Regulation of Whaling*, 2 vols (Dobbs Ferry, 1985); id, in Hey (ed), *Developments in International Fisheries Law*, Ch 13; id, 12 *IJMCL* (1997) 307, 488; Burke, *The New International Law of Fisheries*, Ch 6; D'Amato and Chopra, 85 *AJIL* (1991) 21; Maffei, 12 *IJMCL* (1997) 287; Churchill, in Boyle and Freestone (eds), *International Law and Sustainable Development*, Ch 10.

provides a unique example of the use of conservation techniques borrowed from fishery commissions in order to achieve a strongly preservationist objective. It empowered the IWC to regulate whaling. As one commentator has remarked, although its full procedures have been unaltered for fifty years, '*de facto* the IWC has become a new organization',[98] and had it not been for the conflicts in it 'we would have known far less than we do today about the status of the various stocks of whales'.[99] The IWC has continued to focus on the twelve large whale species that were originally the targets of the whaling industry and it has not regulated (with minor exceptions) the small cetaceans.[100] The votes necessary to amend the shedule for this purpose have never been obtainable. Attempts have instead been made to protect at least some of these species by listing them on the appendices of the Bonn, Berne, and CITES Conventions.[101]

The Whaling Convention includes a schedule of regulations which can be added to or amended annually by a three-quarter majority vote in the IWC. Objecting states may opt out of IWC regulations under Article 3,[102] but this option is used much less than in the past because of conservationist pressure from NGOs and non-whaling states. Catches can be limited by quotas and stocks are assessed in relation to maximum sustainable yield, with due allowance being made for environmental factors affecting this calculation. As quotas can be set at zero, all taking of exploited species can be totally prohibited by issuing no permits. Since 1985 an IWC moratorium on commercial whaling has been in force, reviewed at each meeting of the Commission. In effect a treaty originally intended to regulate whaling has through this simple device become a treaty to protect whales, albeit with strenuous objections from Japan, Iceland, and Norway. Some former whaling states have instead turned to promoting whale watching as an acceptable non-consumptive alternative. In 1994 the Southern Ocean was declared a whale sanctuary in which all whaling would be banned as a precautionary measure, although Japan continues to permit the taking of whales there for scientific research purposes under Article VIII of the ICRW.[103] Proposals for a South Pacific sanctuary have not yet been approved. A proposal for the establishment of a whale sanctuary in the South Atlantic also failed to achieve the required three-quarter majority votes during the 59th Annual Meeting in 2007.

Although regulations must be based on 'scientific findings' (Article V), the IWC's Scientific Committee has developed a much more precautionary policy on methods of setting quotas, based on the view that the available scientific information and population theory is so uncertain that catch quotas could not safely be set for any species, though states such as Iceland, Japan, and Norway do not agree and contend that certain stocks

---

[98] Andresen, in Andresen, Skodvin, Underdahl, and Wettestad (eds), *Science and Politics in International Environmental Regimes* (Manchester, 2000) 65. For the current activities of the International Whaling Commission see IWC, *Chairman's Report of the 59th Annual Meeting* (2007).

[99] Ibid, 66.

[100] Birnie, 29 *NRJ* (1989) 903–34; id, 10 *Georgetown IELR* (1997) 1. Two regional agreements on small cetaceans have been adopted under the 1979 International Convention on the Conservation of Migratory Species: see Churchill, in Boyle and Freestone (eds), *International Law and Sustainable Development*, Ch 10.

[101] See *supra*, Ch 12.   [102] *Supra*, Ch 2, section 5.   [103] Gillespie, 15 *IJMCL* (2000) 293.

and species could still be taken without risk.[104] IWC policy thus provides an example of the application in a wildlife context of a rather stronger version of the precautionary approach than that applied to fish by the UN Fish Stocks Agreement.[105] The sophisticated policy finally adopted, the Revised Management Procedure, is thought to be the most conservatory of any system currently existing for setting quotas. Any state wishing to resume commercial whaling will have to satisfy the Commission that the relevant stock can be exploited sustainably. It is agreed that a Revised Management Scheme will also have to be agreed before any commercial whaling can recommence, and that it should include (i) an effective observation and inspection system, (ii) arrangements to ensure that total catches over time are within prescribed limits, and (iii) incorporation into the Schedule of the requirements of the Revised Management Procedure and all other elements of the Revised Management Scheme.[106] However, at the IWC meeting in 2008 member states remained deadlocked on proposals to lift the moratorium in return for an end to unregulated scientific whaling.

In the course of time and in the light of changing opinions about whaling, the IWC has also passed several non-binding resolutions (which require only a simple majority for their adoption). Inter alia, these ban transfer of vessels, equipment, and knowhow to non-member states; prohibit trading in whales and whale products (the EC has implemented this by adopting a regulation banning their import into member states);[107] call for humane killing, and require collection of data on small cetaceans.[108] Following the model of the 1911 Fur Seals Convention, the Schedule itself was also used to permit, exceptionally, aboriginal subsistence whaling in Siberia and Alaska, but only if using traditional, simple means of killing the whales. More controversially the Makah tribe of native Americans was permitted to take a gray whale, after a gap of over seventy years.

Conservatory techniques applied to other marine mammals include those laid down in the now terminated 1957 North Pacific (Behring Sea) Fur Seals Convention (as amended), which introduced the 'abstention principle'. It prohibited pelagic sealing (also with exceptions for native peoples) and established a commission to recommend conservatory measures for the taking of the seals on land, on the basis of coordinated scientific research. Only the USSR and United States were permitted to continue sealing on land and in return undertook to deliver 15 per cent of the sealskins to Canada and Japan. This separation of the right to exploit a resource from the right to share in the proceeds is arguably the most advanced application of the UNEP principles of equitable utilization to be found in any wildlife or fisheries convention, and for

---

[104] Iceland withdrew from the IWC shortly after the establishment of the moratorium, to which it did not enter a reservation. It rejoined at the 53rd Meeting in 2001, but with a reservation concerning the whaling moratorium. Some states questioned its validity.

[105] See *infra*, section 5, and on the precautionary approach see *supra* Ch 3, section 4.

[106] IWC, *Chairman's Report of the 51st Annual Meeting* (1999) 24.

[107] Council Regulation No 348/81, Article 1; OJ EEC No L 39 (12 Feb 1981) 1 as corrected on OJ No L 132 (19 May 1981) 30. CITES has continued to list whales barred from taking by the IWC on Appendix I, which prevents trade in these species.

[108] For texts of these and related resolutions, see Birnie, *International Regulation of Whaling*, ii, 775–97.

many years it provided an effective control on over-exploitation.[109] It has, however, remained a unique model, contrasting sharply with the precautionary approach taken by the IWC and also with the 1972 Convention on Conservation of Antarctic Seals. The latter agreement follows the more orthodox approach of establishing catch quotas, designating areas, gear, etc, to be implemented through a permit system enacted by each state party, but in practice no quotas have ever been set and no sealing takes place in Antarctica.[110]

(c) Anadromous species[111]

Anadromous species (such as salmon) spawn in freshwater rivers, but spend the major part of their lives at sea, passing through territorial sea and EEZ to the high seas before returning to die in the rivers in which they originated. Conservatory measures adopted by the state of origin are rendered useless if the species are over-exploited in the EEZ or on the high seas. Article 66 of the 1982 UNCLOS provides that the state in whose rivers the stocks originate has the *primary* interest in and responsibility for these stocks[112] but, in return, it must ensure their conservation by establishing appropriate regulatory measures for this purpose and for determining access to these stocks landward of the outer boundary of its own EEZ.[113] Anadramous species can only be taken on the high seas in exceptional circumstances,[114] but fishing in other states' EEZs or in the rivers of downstream states is not banned. Where the stock migrates through the EEZ of another coastal state, the parties must cooperate on conservation and management.[115] It is not clear whether other coastal states can exercise jurisdiction over stocks not originating in their territory and which they have never fished.[116] TACs *can* be set by the state of origin in consultation with other interested states,[117] but it is not obliged either to do so or to determine its own harvesting capacity. It retains the discretion to adopt other measures that ensure conservation.

If banning fishing on the high seas causes economic dislocation in other states,[118] the state of origin must consult them 'with a view to achieving agreement on terms and conditions of such fishing', including determining the necessary conservation measures. Enforcement (which must respect high-seas freedoms) must be agreed among the state of origin and the others concerned. The state of origin must also cooperate in minimizing economic dislocation to all other states where fishing has taken place.[119] Special arrangements for harvesting the stock must be made with states which have invested in stock renewal in cooperation with the state of origin.[120]

---

[109] Lyster, *International Wildlife Law*, 40–9.   [110] Ibid, 112–28.

[111] See Burke, *The New International Law of Fisheries*, Ch 4; Birnie, in Hey (ed), *Developments in International Fisheries Law*, Ch 13; Orrego Vicuña, 22 *ODIL* (1991) 133–51.

[112] UNCLOS, Article 66(1); Article 116(b) also subjects freedom of fishing on the high seas to the rights and interests of coastal states 'as provided in the Convention', i.e. including Article 66.

[113] Article 66(2).   [114] Article 66(3)(a).   [115] Article 66(4).

[116] Hey, *The Regime for the Exploitation of Transboundary Marine Fishery Resources*, 64.

[117] Article 66(2).   [118] Article 66(3)(a).

[119] Article 66(3)(b). E.g. in the EEZ of another coastal state.

[120] Article 66(3)(c). E.g. a downstream state that has to maintain salmon weirs.

Article 66 thus establishes a special discrete conservatory regime, apart from others in Part V; conservation is the main aim here, with the secondary interests of other states balanced by cooperation through consultation. Most fisheries conventions do not apply to salmon and we have to look for evidence of state practice in the conclusion of specific conventions, in particular the innovatory 1982 Reykjavik Convention for the Conservation of Salmon in the North Atlantic Ocean (NASCO)[121] and the 1992 Convention for the Conservation of Anadromous Stocks in the North Pacific.[122] With limited exceptions, both agreements ban all high-seas fishing for salmon.

Problems arise, however, concerning intermingling of wild salmon with farmed salmon which have escaped. Not only does this put the wild salmon at risk from disease but it may lead to irreversible genetic change and ecological interactions.[123] This could threaten maintenance of biodiversity. Meanwhile, NASCO has developed principles for ensuring that a precautionary approach is taken into account in decisions that may have adverse impacts for salmon habitats. The International Baltic Sea Fishery Commission has also recommended urgent action to control numerous pollution threats which are depleting salmon stocks.[124] These changes evidence the impact of post-UNCED developments and principles, including the UN Fish Stocks Agreement. They also reveal how important not only effective enforcement has become but also how problems of habitat protection and conservation of biodiversity must be addressed in order to ensure successful maintenance and continuing sustainable use of anadromous species. Adoption of the precautionary approach becomes indispensable in the situations now faced in such commissions and necessitates cooperation and coordination with related institutions for protection of the marine environment.

(d) Catadromous species

Catadromous species are the opposite of the above; they are spawned at sea and spend the major part of their lives in rivers and lakes. The species of main commercial interest are eels on which coastal industries are based in several states. Article 67 provides that coastal states in whose waters these species spend the major part of their lifecycle are responsible for their conservation and management;[125] they have the primary interest. Exploitation is permitted only to landward of the outer limit of the EEZ. Exploitation in the EEZ is subject to the provisions of Article 67 and those relating to

---

[121] The original parties were Canada, EEC, Denmark (for Faroe Islands and Greenland), Finland, Iceland, Norway, Sweden, United States. See Churchill, *EEC Fisheries Law*, 189.

[122] The parties are Japan, United States, Canada, Russia. See Birnie, in Hey (ed), *Developments in International Fisheries Law*, Ch 13. See also 1985 Treaty Concerning Pacific Salmon between Canada and the United States. Yanagida, 81 *AJIL* (1987) 577–91, draws attention to the practical difficulties of operating the complex devolved solutions this treaty provides.

[123] See NASCO, *Ten Year Review of the Atlantic Salmon Conservation Organization* (Edinburgh, 1995); id, *Report of the 17th Annual Meeting of the Council* (Edinburgh, 2000) 271, 285–7; Hansen and Windsor, *Interactions between Aquaculture and Wild Stocks of Atlantic Salmon and other Diadromous Fish Species: Science and Management, Challenges and Solutions* (Trondheim, 2006).

[124] IBFSC, *Report of the IBSFC: Extraordinary Session on IBSFC Salmon Action Plan 1997–2010* (1997) 98–9.

[125] UNCLOS, Article 67(1).

the EEZ.[126] When migrating through another state's EEZ, they are to be regulated both by the state in whose waters they spend the major part of their life-cycle and the state through whose waters they migrate, which must conclude agreements providing for rational management, taking account of the special interest of the former state. As exploitation beyond the EEZ is banned, no agreements will be needed for high-seas stocks. As no particular manner of cooperation is prescribed states can act bilaterally or through international organizations.

4(4) NATIONAL IMPLEMENTATION OF UNCLOS FISHERY PROVISIONS

It is clearly important for conservation of high seas and EEZ fisheries that states implement in good faith a conservatory and management regime based on the principles and considerations set out in Articles 61 and 119 of UNCLOS. It is apparent from the compendia of national fisheries legislation produced by the FAO and the UN and various individual analyses of state practice,[127] that states are not doing so in any uniform fashion. That is not to say that in their administrative practice they do not heed these conservatory requirements, but that they do not obligate themselves to do so in their relevant national legislation partly because of the difficulties encountered in interpreting these provisions.

Over one hundred states have now asserted sovereign rights over fisheries up to 200 miles from their coastline. Since the 1970s many of these have sought advice from FAO, either on the drafting of their new legislation, or the management and development of their fisheries or both.[128] Whilst FAO cannot take any particular view on the interpretation of ambiguous provisions in the UNCLOS, it can advise on the choices facing its member states concerning interpretation and the complex problems of enactment and implementation of these provisions. This it has done, encouraging multidisciplinary studies, introduction of legal and administrative measures, reviewing existing agreements, evaluating the enforcement problems, and providing reports and draft laws.

Most developing states inherited their legislation from the former colonial powers, based on the pre-1982 UNCLOS regime and inappropriate to extended coastal-state management powers. Modern fisheries legislation, especially if drafted under FAO auspices, now typically provides for a Fisheries Management and Development Plan related to a specific management area and to exploited fisheries only. The United States Marine Mammal Protection Act 1972[129] and the Fishery Conservation and

---

[126] Article 67(2).

[127] E.g. Juda, 18 *ODIL* (1987) 305; Smith, *Exclusive Economic Zone Claims*; Wolfrum, 18 *NYIL* (1987) 121; Hey, *The Regime for the Exploitation of Transboundary Marine Fishery Resources*; Kwiatkowska, *The 200 Mile EEZ in the Law of the Sea*, 45–93, esp 45–6, 91–3; Attard, *The Exclusive Economic Zone in International Law*, 146–91, and esp 152–6.

[128] Information supplied by Dr W Edeson, FAO.

[129] 16 USC, ss 1361–2, 137–84, 1401–7 (revised several times since 1972).

Management Act 1976[130] provided models for this, although more recent examples in developing country practice are simpler.[131] There has thus been a move away from the old-style conservation statute, as exemplified in UK fisheries laws, based on highly specific prohibitions of the various fishing techniques, etc, outlined earlier in this chapter, towards a more general enunciation of objectives and the means of achieving them, an approach hitherto more familiar in civil than common-law systems. This leaves details to be worked out in the light of subsequent experience but results in a diversity of solutions which makes evaluation of state practice difficult. It is important, given the multiplicity of factors affecting fishery conservation, that flexibility be maintained in national legislation and that it be constantly revised.

5 POST-UNCLOS DEVELOPMENTS

5(1) UNCED AND THE CONSERVATION OF HIGH SEAS LIVING RESOURCES

As we saw in Chapter 7, the Rio Conference treated the 1982 UN Convention on the Law of the Sea as a codification of the existing law relating to the marine environment, but Agenda 21 nevertheless placed new emphasis, inter alia, on ecosystem and biodiversity protection, application of the precautionary approach, and sustainable use of marine living resources. It was noted in particular that the management of high-seas fisheries had been inadequate. Problems identified included a failure to adopt, monitor and enforce effective fisheries conservation measures, unreliable data regarding high-seas stocks and catches, evasion of controls by re-flagging of vessels, excessive fishing-fleet size, and a lack of sufficient cooperation between states. While acknowledging that the relevant provisions of the 1982 UNCLOS represented the rights and obligations of states with respect to conservation and sustainable use of high seas living resources, Agenda 21 called for the convening of a UN conference on straddling and highly migratory fish stocks, and for more effective cooperation through regional fisheries organizations and agreements.[132] The Rio Conference thus initiated some important developments in the law relating to marine living resources, including not only the conclusion in 1995 of the UN Agreement on Straddling and Highly Migratory Fish Stocks ('UN Fish Stocks Agreement') but also the adoption by FAO of the 1993 Agreement to Promote Compliance with International Conservation and Management Measures by Fishing Vessels on the High Seas,[133] the 1995 Code of

---

[130] 16 USC, ss 1801 *et seq.*

[131] See examples in FAO, *Legislative Series No 21* (Rome, 1990) 120.

[132] *Rept of UNCED*, UN Doc A/CONF 151/26/Rev 1, Vol I (1992), Ch 17, paras 44–63.

[133] Edeson, in Boyle and Freestone (eds), *International Law and Sustainable Development*, 165. Adopted by FAO to reinforce flag state obligations in respect of high-seas fishing, this agreement might be regarded as another UNCLOS 'implementing agreement.'

Conduct for Responsible Fisheries,[134] and the International Plan of Action on Illegal, Unregulated and Unreported Fishing.[135] In the assessment of one writer,

There can be little doubt that the sum total of the changes introduced has substantially strengthened the regime of the 1982 UN Convention... [T]hese instruments have ensured that the importance of the long-term sustainable use of marine living resources has been placed in the forefront of any serious analysis of the legal regime...[136]

One consequence is that the traditional concept of high-seas freedom of fishing has been substantially altered since the 1995 Fish Stocks Agreement entered into force in 2001, if indeed it can be said to had survived at all.[137] Another is that international fisheries law has acquired a stronger environmental dimension, integrating it more closely with Part XII of the 1982 UN Convention and the 1992 Convention on Biological Diversity.[138] As Freestone concludes, freedom of fishing is no longer the dominant community interest; instead the protection of the marine environment has become a fundamental element in international fisheries law.[139] However, other studies point to the ineffectiveness of regional fisheries organizations and the inability of too many flag states to ensure that their vessels fish legally and comply with applicable conservation measures. As we shall see below it remains unclear that any of these changes in the law will significantly affect the uncertain future of marine living resources.[140]

5(2) ALTERNATIVE APPROACHES TO MANAGEMENT OF HIGH SEAS FISHERIES

Notwithstanding the very widespread adoption of the 200-mile EEZ, the over-exploitation of fish stocks in the North Pacific, the Behring Sea, the Antarctic, the North Atlantic and the North Sea shows that the UNCLOS strategy for sustainable fishing has not worked as intended.[141] As we saw earlier, one reason for this failure is that some coastal states have failed to ensure sustainable fishing within their own EEZs. Another closely connected problem is that some important fish stocks are not confined to the EEZ but can also be taken on the high seas. Highly migratory species such as tuna clearly fall into this category, but other less-mobile stocks are also found straddling the remaining high-seas areas and adjacent EEZs. Fishing effort on the high seas has not been eliminated by the extension of coastal-state jurisdiction, but

---

[134] See Edeson, 11 *IJMCL* (1996) 97.   [135] See Edeson, 16 *IJMCL* (2001) 603.

[136] Edeson, loc cit, *supra*, n 133.

[137] See Orrego Vicuña, in Stokke (ed), *Governing High Seas Fisheries*, 23; Örebech et al, 13 *IJMCL* (1998) 140–1.

[138] Freestone and Makuch, 7 *YbIEL* (1996) 3.

[139] In Boyle and Freestone (eds), *International Law and Sustainable Development*, 164.

[140] See Gjerde, in Freestone, Barnes, and Ong (eds), *The Law of the Sea*, Ch 15. For comprehensive studies of high-seas fisheries law and governance see articles collected in 19 *IJMCL* (2004) 209–363 and 20 *IJMCL* (2005) 323–629.

[141] See Ulfstein, Andersen, and Churchill, *The Regulation of Fisheries: Legal, Economic and Social Aspects* (Council of Europe, 1986); Meltzer, 25 *ODIL* (1994) 255; Burke, *The New International Law of Fisheries*.

transferred beyond 200 miles, and competition for stocks made more intense. This has seriously affected the viability of some adjacent EEZ fisheries. Redrawing the boundary between coastal-state jurisdiction and the high seas has not done away with the unavoidable facts of geography: in a divided ocean, most fish are inevitably at least a shared EEZ resource and will in some cases also be a high seas common property resource.

One possible response—the further extension of coastal state jurisdiction—adopted so far only by Chile and briefly by Canada, would destroy the consensus arrived at in the UNCLOS Convention, and once again generate serious conflict with distant-water fishing states.[142] Another solution would entail the abolition or suspension of high-seas exploitation rights, based on a 'precautionary approach' to environmental risks.[143] At its strongest, the precautionary approach may result in a 'preservationist' model of sustainability if, for example, a workable scheme of sustainable exploitation proved impossible to devise. The moratorium on whaling in force since 1983 arguably reflects this form of precaution; so for somewhat similar reasons does the prohibition of sealing or the taking of salmon on the high seas under an increasing number of regional agreements.[144] Limited versions of the same approach are evident in the revival of the high seas abstention doctrine to contain Japanese, Korean, and Taiwanese fishing in the North Pacific,[145] and in the attempt to outlaw mainly Japanese drift-netting in the South Pacific.[146] All of these possibilities were rejected during negotiation of the 1995 Fish Stocks Agreement in favour of a more moderate version of the precautionary approach, considered below.[147]

One serious weakness of the UNCLOS negotiations was that they did not address problems of institutional cooperation on fisheries conservation: as a recent study by Lodge and Nandan shows, the analysis of their failure given by Koers remains just as pertinent to contemporary analysis of NAFO, CCAMLR, and other post-UNCLOS fisheries commissions.[148] The lesson to be learnt from this experience is self-evident: if a resource allocated on the principle of common property cannot be exploited sustainably without the support of effective institutional arrangements to ensure rational cooperation, then the fundamental problems of regime participation,

---

[142] See Orrego Vicuña, 55 ZAÖRV (1995) 520; Davies and Redgwell, 67 BYIL (1996) 199; Saunders, Policy Options for the Management and Conservation of Straddling Stocks (St John's, 2003).

[143] FAO, The Precautionary Approach with Reference to Straddling Fish Stocks and HM Fish Stocks, UN Doc A/Conf 164/INF/8 (1994) and see for an example the 1993 amendments to the 1972 London Dumping Convention which phase out industrial dumping at sea, supra, Ch 8.

[144] 1982 UNCLOS, Article 66; 1982 North Atlantic Salmon Convention; 1991 Convention for the Conservation of Anadramous Stocks in the North Pacific; Burke, The New International Law of Fisheries, Ch 4.

[145] Joint Resolution of the 5th Conference on the Conservation and Management of the Living Marine Resources of the Central Bering Sea, August 14, 1992; see Meltzer, 25 ODIL (1994) 283–90.

[146] 1989 Convention for the Prohibition of Fishing with Long Drift Nets in the South Pacific.

[147] For an account of the negotiations on this issue see Boyle and Freestone (eds), International Law and Sustainable Development, 154; Hewison, 11 IJMCL (1996) 301.

[148] Lodge and Nandan, 20 IJMCL (2005) 345, especially annexes, and cf Koers, International Regulation of Marine Fisheries (London, 1973).

effective regulation based on adequate scientific information, adequate dispute settlement arrangements, and high-seas enforcement need to be addressed once more. Recognition of this elementary lesson is apparent in the UN General Assembly resolution convening the conference on conservation and management of straddling and highly migratory fish stocks.[149] Reviewing the work of the second session of the conference, the chairman observed that governments must be flexible and 'not insist on old rules of the game which are no longer appropriate, whether they apply to areas under national jurisdiction or to the resources of the high seas'.[150]

The most radical alternative to 'the old rules of the game' would involve extending the common heritage concept to high-seas fisheries. As this would entail surrendering management and regulatory authority to an international body, comparable to the International Seabed Authority,[151] or to similar regional bodies, it was not a solution proposed either at UNCED or during negotiation of the 1995 Fish Stocks Agreement. This is politically understandable, but only at the cost of ignoring the economic logic of separating the right to fish from the right to own or profit from the catch.[152] Without such a separation it will always be in the economic interest of distant-water fishing nations to tolerate unrestrained fishing on the high seas, whatever international law may provide. It is against this economic logic that the 1995 Agreement must be assessed.

5(3) 1995 AGREEMENT ON STRADDLING AND HIGHLY MIGRATORY FISH STOCKS (UNFSA)

The 1995 UN Fish Stocks Agreement represents an attempt to deal with the serious problems of sustainable fishing by building on the existing provisions of the 1982 UNCLOS.[153] Nevertheless, the Agreement is in many respects radical in its reform of international fisheries law; it introduces new obligations of sustainable use; requires a precautionary approach to be applied to the conservation and management of stocks and broadens this obligation to include associated ecosystems; seeks to ensure compatibility between EEZ and high-seas conservation measures, and places on parties a more extensive obligation of cooperation through regional fisheries bodies, without which they risk losing the right to fish on the high seas. Although the 1995 Agreement is to be interpreted and applied 'in the context of and in a manner consistent with the [1982] Convention' and is without prejudice to the rights, jurisdiction and obligations

---

[149] UNGA Res 47/192 (1992).   [150] 24 *EPL* (1994) 144.

[151] *Supra*, Ch 2, section 5(3). Malta's proposal for a treaty establishing an international agency for this purpose limited it to assuming jurisdiction over the seabed 'as a trustee for all countries': Draft Ocean Space Treaty: Working Paper submitted by Malta, UN Doc AC 138/53, 5 (1973).

[152] Compare the 1957 North Pacific Fur Seals Convention, *supra*, section 4(4).

[153] See Anderson, 45 *ICLQ* (1996) 463; Balton, 27 *ODIL* (1996) 125; Freestone and Makuch, 7 *YbIEL* (1996) 3; Davies and Redgwell, 67 *BYIL* (19996) 199; Hayashi, 29 *O&C Man* (1995) 51; Hayashi, in Vidas and Østreng (eds), *Order for the Oceans at the Turn of the Century* (The Hague, 1999) 37; Örebech, Sigurjonsson, and McDorman, 13 *IJMCL* (1998) 119–42. For drafting history see FAO Fisheries Circ 898, *Structure and Process of the UN Conference on Straddling Fish stocks and Highly Migratory Fish Stocks* (Rome, 1995).

of parties to the 1982 UNCLOS,[154] in effect it not only amplifies that convention, but amends other regional fisheries treaties covering straddling and highly migratory stocks. Moreover, in accordance with the general rules on interpretation of treaties, the 1995 Fish Stocks Agreement can provide guidance on, or confirmation of, the inherently evolutionary meaning of Articles 63 and 116–19 of the 1982 UNCLOS.[155] The fact that it was negotiated and adopted by consensus, including all the major distant water and coastal fishing states, reinforces this conclusion.

(a) Application of the 1995 Fish Stocks Agreement

The Fish Stocks Agreement as a whole applies only to straddling and highly migratory fish stocks in areas beyond national jurisdiction—i.e. on the high seas.[156] Neither the terms 'straddling' nor 'highly migratory' are defined, although highly migratory species are listed in Annex I of the 1982 Convention. Not all high-seas stocks necessarily fall into one or other of these categories, so the Agreement is not a comprehensive framework for regulating all high seas fisheries. Moreover, it does not cover stocks which are exclusive to one EEZ or which only straddle other EEZs. However, there are, exceptionally, certain articles which also apply to straddling and highly migratory stocks within the EEZ and which thus place some obligations on coastal states with regard to their conservation and management. The essential point is that, within the EEZ, coastal states are required to apply the general principles concerning sustainable use in Article 5, the precautionary approach in Article 6, and to a more limited extent the compatibility provisions of Article 7. These are of course precisely the matters which are most likely to affect fish stocks and other marine species in adjacent EEZs and on the high seas, and to that extent the unity of marine ecosystems is implicitly acknowledged, regardless of boundaries.

In addition to states parties, under Article 1(3) the Agreement also applies *mutatis mutandis* to 'other fishing entities whose vessels fish on the high seas'. This novel provision is intended to allow for Taiwanese acceptance of the Agreement, without having to address that country's uncertain international status.[157] It thus addresses for the first time the application of international wildlife conservation agreements to a country whose inability to participate in other treaties such as CITES has provided a significant loophole for unregulated trade and fishing.

---

[154] Article 4. However, a state can be a party to the 1995 Agreement without being party to UNCLOS: in that limited sense it is a 'stand alone' treaty.

[155] See 1969 Vienna Convention on the Law of Treaties, Article 31(3); Freestone, in Boyle and Freestone (eds), *International Law and Sustainable Development*, 160.

[156] Article 3. It is noteworthy that, at the time of writing, FAO has been developing International Guidelines for the Management of Deep-Sea Fisheries in the High Seas, which are not encompassed by the Fish Stocks Agreement. See *FAO Technical Consultation on International Guidelines for the Management of Deep-Sea Fisheries* (Rome, 2008).

[157] See Edeson, 22 *IJMCL* (2007) 485. Note however that there is no provision for a 'fishing entity' to become a party to the agreement. Since no treaty can bind a non-party without its consent (Vienna Convention on the Law of Treaties, Articles 35–7) it must be assumed that 'application' of the agreement to a fishing entity can only create rights and obligations with the consent of the entity concerned. Taiwan has not yet given its consent.

(b) Conservation, sustainable use and ecosystem protection

As we saw in Chapter 11, the concept of 'maximum sustainable yield' has proved difficult to determine with accuracy, and largely inadequate to the task of conserving fish stocks and minimising the broader ecological effects of fisheries. Although reiterated in Article 119 of UNCLOS in terms which allow for environmental factors and effects on associated or dependent species to be taken into account, conservation measures under that article are still supposed to maximize the allowable catch, having regard, inter alia, to economic considerations and the special needs of developing states. It is far from clear that Article 119 obliges states to fish at sustainable levels.[158] In determining total allowable catches this formulation has proved notoriously open to over-optimistic assessments by the members of high-seas fisheries commissions. Not infrequently, scientific advice has been disregarded or uncertainty and inadequate data relied on to justify higher-than-prudent levels of fishing. Many fisheries commissions have not established conservation measures until the scientific evidence is sufficiently compelling to demonstrate that a stock is under real threat.[159]

The 1995 Fish Stocks Agreement retains the wording of Article 119, but places maximum sustainable yield within the context of a proactive, precautionary, and more environmentally focused approach to conservation and sustainable use.[160] In giving effect to their duty to conserve marine living resources, states are now required by Article 5 to adopt measures designed to ensure 'long-term sustainability... and optimum utilisation' of straddling and highly migratory fish stocks. These include preventing overfishing and removing excess capacity, as well as improving collection and dissemination of fisheries data and using more selective, environmentally safe and cost effective fishing gear. There is an obligation to assess the impact of fishing, other human activities, and environmental factors, on the target fish stock and its ecosystem. Conservation measures must protect not only the fish, but also their associated ecosystems, and marine biodiversity. Measures must also be taken to minimize pollution, waste, and catches of other non-target stocks or species. As the chairman of the 1995 conference pointed out: 'the collective interest of the international community must [also] be taken into account if sustainable use of high seas resources was to be secured'.[161]

FAO uses a mixture of hard- and soft-law instruments to promote implementation of the fisheries conservation provisions of the 1982 UNCLOS and the 1995 Agreement. The 1993 Agreement to Promote Compliance with Conservation Measures on the High Seas regulates reflagging of fishing vessels and other activities that undermine the effectiveness of conservation agreements.[162] Though a binding treaty, it forms an

---

[158] Freestone, in Boyle and Freestone (eds), *International Law and Sustainable Development*, 146–7.

[159] See e.g. Redgwell's account of the practice of the Commission for the Conservation of Antarctic Marine Living Resources in Boyle and Freestone, op cit, 216.

[160] Articles 5, 6.

[161] Ambassador Satya Nandan, quoted in FAO Fisheries Circular 898, *Structure and Process of the UN Conference etc*, para 4.5.

[162] See *infra*, section (e).

integral part of the non-binding 1995 Code of Conduct on Responsible Fishing,[163] which is itself further implemented by other soft-law measures including the 2001 Plan of Action on Illegal, Unreported and Unregulated Fishing,[164] and the 2003 FAO Guidelines on the Ecosystem Approach to Fisheries.[165] The choice of soft-law instruments to promote an ecosystem approach can partly be explained by the opposition of some states to binding agreements. Another reason, however, is that they are aimed at regional fisheries organizations and the fishing industry as well as states, and contain some elements which are unlikely to find their way into treaty form. They are also easier to amend or replace than treaties, requiring simply the adoption of another instrument. Negotiated in the same manner as treaties, and adopted by consensus in FAO,[166] these non-binding 'voluntary instruments' also complement the 1995 UN Fish Stocks Agreement and seek to promote implementation of elements of that agreement by non-parties.

Thus, it is not only exploited fish stocks which benefit from the approach outlined in the 1995 Agreement and Code of Conduct. Recognizing the overriding need for an ecosystem approach, the ultimate objectives of Articles 5 and 6 are to protect marine living resources and biological diversity, including non-target stocks and associated and dependent species, and preserve the marine ecosystem in general. There is now an obligation, as there was not under the 1982 UNCLOS,[167] to assess and monitor the impact of fishing on ecosystems, other species and their habitats, and to take and keep under review measures to conserve and protect them. This is very much in keeping with Article 194(5) of the 1982 UNCLOS, and with the general obligation to protect the marine environment codified in Part XII,[168] but it is the first time it has been spelt out explicitly in a major fisheries agreement. It has been suggested that, as a result, the 1995 Fish Stocks Agreement is more important for the protection of marine biological diversity than the Convention on Biological Diversity itself, and that 'sustainability in the Agreement is to be read in ecosystem and biodiversity terms, rather than, as before, in terms of constant food supply.'[169]

Nevertheless, considerable work remains to be done to 'operationalize' the ecosystem approach to fisheries, which in the view of one FAO official 'is still largely political

---

[163] See Edeson, 11 *IJMCL* (1996) 97.

[164] See Edeson, 16 *IJMCL* (2001) 603. See also the International Plans of Action on Longline Fisheries; Conservation and Management of Sharks; and Management of Fishing Capacity, adopted by FAO in 1999.

[165] FAO, *Fisheries Management: The Ecosystem Approach to Fisheries*, FAO Technical Guidelines for Responsible Fisheries No 4, Suppl 2 (Rome, 2003).

[166] However some states expressed significant reservations when adopting the Plan of Action on IUU Fishing: see FAO, *Rept of the Committee on Fisheries*, 24th Session (2001).

[167] Compare 1982 UNCLOS, Article 119(1)(b) which merely requires effects on associated and dependent species to be 'taken into account' when setting a total allowable catch and establishing other conservation measures.

[168] Freestone, in Boyle and Freestone, *International Law and Sustainable Development*, 148–9, and see *supra*, Ch 7.

[169] Freestone and Makuch, 7 *YbIEL* (1996) 50.

and conceptual'.[170] FAO's technical guidelines encourage states to 'apply an integrated approach to fisheries within ecologically meaningful boundaries', taking into account 'the knowledge and uncertainties about biotic, abiotic and human components of eco-systems and their interactions'.[171] This has been described as 'somewhat fuzzy', and the same writer cautions against seeing the concept as a panacea.[172] Over-exploitation and depletion of stocks 'usually result from failure to apply the scientific advice being given on single species approaches'.[173] He advocates incremental development of exist-ing regimes, building in particular on the experience of CCAMLR and advice given by ICES, and above all, reducing fishing capacity.

(c) Application of the precautionary approach

Another indication of the 1995 Agreement's environmental perspective is the require-ment to apply a precautionary approach to fishing and to the protection of associ-ated ecosystems and species. A precautionary approach may already be implicit in the 1982 UNCLOS,[174] but what this entails is set out explicitly and in some detail by the 1995 Agreement. The moderate version of the precautionary approach incorporated in Article 6 reflects the realization that 'with an imperfect knowledge of fish popula-tion and dynamics and an incomplete understanding of socio-economic dynamics', the continued use of maximum sustainable yield as a management target is 'neither efficient nor safe'.[175] In combination with the other measures or agreements referred to above, it seeks sustainability through improving data collection and techniques for dealing with risk and scientific uncertainty. These include setting 'precautionary ref-erence points' for specific fish stocks, enhanced monitoring, and broadening the range of factors to be taken into account.

Reference points identify the safe biological limit for harvesting, and other relevant constraints.[176] They are to be determined in advance of using the best scientific infor-mation available, but uncertainties are also to be taken into account and the absence of adequate information 'shall not be used as a reason for postponing or failing to take conservation and management measures'. In the case of a new fishery, 'cautious con-servation and management measures' are to be adopted until there is enough data to permit assessment of the impact on long-term sustainability.[177] Thus the importance of

---

[170] Garcia, in Nordquist et al (eds), *Law, Science and Ocean Management*, 171–216, 173. The oldest and most advanced application of an ecosystem approach is the CCAMLR, on which see Miller, Sabourenkov and Ramm, 19 *IJMCL* (2004) 317.

[171] FAO, *Fisheries Management: The Ecosystem Approach to Fisheries*, 6.

[172] Parsons, 20 *IJMCL* (2005) 381, 419.   [173] Ibid, 420–1.

[174] Freestone, in Boyle and Freestone, *International Law and Sustainable Development*, 141, and see *Southern Bluefin Tuna Cases*, ITLOS Nos 3 and 4 (2000); *supra*, Ch 3, section 4(3).

[175] 24 *EPL* (1994) 142; a lesson already learned in the International Whaling Commission in reformulat-ing its management procedures, see *supra*, section 4(3). See Kimball, *Treaty Implementation: Scientific and Technical Advice Enters a New Stage* (Washington DC, 1996).

[176] See Annex II of the 1995 Agreement, and FAO Fisheries Circular 864, *Reference Points for Fisheries Management: Their Potential Application to Straddling and Highly Migratory Resources* (Rome, 1993).

[177] Article 6(6).

the precautionary approach is that states are no longer free to ignore conservation until a stock is shown to be under stress. As Freestone points out, 'This represents a major change in the traditional approach of fisheries management which until recently has tended to be reactive to management problems only after they arrived at crisis levels.'[178] Timely action must therefore be taken to ensure that precautionary reference points are not exceeded; if stocks are under threat, conservation and management measures must be reviewed. However, in such cases nothing in the Agreement expressly requires a halt to fishing or a moratorium; as we saw above, the parties rejected the automatic application of such outcomes. This does not mean that fishing of depleted stocks can lawfully continue, merely that what response is appropriate will depend on the circumstances and will be determined by the relevant regional fisheries body.[179]

As we saw in Chapter 3, requiring states to apply a precautionary approach does not of itself determine what measures must be adopted: it merely helps determine when action is necessary. The approach taken in the International Whaling Commission and in the UN's drift- net resolutions has already been noted. There the onus of proving by scientific evidence that resumption of hunting or fishing will not be environmentally harmful is shifted to the proponents, although in the IWC the burden of formulating an appropriate procedure is delegated to the Scientific Committee. The 1994 Bering Sea Pollock Convention expressly prohibits fishing unless the parties determine that the total biomass of pollock exceeds a stipulated level; only if a stock is above that level can a total allowable catch be set.[180] In effect this agreement specifies a precautionary reference limit in the treaty, and compels a fishing moratorium when that limit is exceeded, whereas the 1995 Fish Stocks Agreement leaves parties to negotiate such limits, and the consequences of exceeding them.[181] More recently, the states participating in the negotiations to create the South Pacific Regional Fisheries Management Organisation have adopted interim measures based on the precautionary approach, limiting bottom trawling in the region until the Convention establishing the organization enters into force.[182] It is interesting to note that this body will have a mandate to deal with discrete high-seas stocks in addition to straddling stocks, as provided for by the 1995 Agreement. Since the 1995 Agreement is essentially a framework for the negotiation of regional agreements covering very diverse fisheries, its less robust approach to precautionary measures is inevitable. Nevertheless, it does create a presumption in favour of conservation and long-term sustainability,[183] and the parties must apply it accordingly.

[178] Boyle and Freestone (eds), *International Law and Sustainable Development*, 160.

[179] Freestone and Makuch, 7 *YbIEL* (1996) 3, 28; Nelson, in Boyle and Freestone (eds), *International Law and Sustainable Development*, 129.

[180] Convention on Conservation and Management of Pollock Resources in the Central Bering Sea, 34 *ILM* (1994) 67. See Balton, in Stokke (ed), *Governing High Seas Fisheries*, 143; Dunlop, 10 *IJMCL* (1995) 114ff.

[181] Starting in 1991, precautionary limits for toothfish and krill have been agreed by the Commission for Antarctic Marine Living Resources, but Redgwell, in Boyle and Freestone (eds), *International Law and Sustainable Development*, 217, points out the serious difficulty in doing so when there is little data on stocks or their interaction with other species. See also Herr, in Stokke (ed), *Governing High Seas Fisheries*, 304.

[182] SPRFMO, *Interim Measures* (2007).

[183] Boyle and Freestone (eds), *International Law and Sustainable Development*, 158.

(d) Cooperation through regional fisheries bodies

Underlying the 1995 Fish Stocks Agreement is a recognition that its objectives can only be achieved through improved regional cooperation between coastal and distant-water fishing states. Like UNCLOS, Article 8 spells out the duty of all states fishing on the high seas to cooperate in order to 'ensure effective conservation and management of such stocks'. They can do so directly, or through regional fisheries management organizations (RFMOs), which must if necessary be created.

Unlike the 1982 UNCLOS, the Fish Stocks Agreement lays down detailed provisions on the functions of these bodies.[184] Inter alia, Article 10 rather bluntly requires RFMO members to:

- *agree on and comply with* conservation and management measures to ensure the long-term sustainability of straddling fish stocks and highly migratory fish stocks

- *adopt and apply* any generally recommended international minimum standards for the responsible conduct of fishing operations

- *obtain and evaluate* scientific advice, review the status of the stocks and assess the impact of fishing on non-target and associated or dependent species

- *establish* appropriate cooperative mechanisms for effective monitoring, control, surveillance, and enforcement

- *agree on* decision-making procedures which facilitate the adoption of conservation and management measures in a timely and effective manner.

These provisions represent a fairly bold attempt to put some serious content into fishery conservation agreements and to compel member states to adopt and comply with the necessary measures. Compliance is obligatory: arguably, even a state party which opts out of RFMO conservation measures in such a way as to defeat their purpose will not be compliant with Article 10, and the continued use of such opt-outs may itself fail to meet the required standard of timely and effective decision-making.[185] Moreover, it seems possible within the terms of this article for 'generally recommended international minimum standards' to be adopted by intergovernmental organizations, including FAO, the CBD, and the UN General Assembly,[186] opening up the possibility of these bodies in effect legislating for RFMO member states in the same way that IMO resolutions or IAEA Codes may become binding under Part XII of UNCLOS or the Nuclear Safety Convention.[187] This is particularly relevant to FAO's Code of Conduct

---

[184] UNFSA, Articles 8–12. See generally *supra*, Ch 2, section 5(2), and Lodge and Nandan, 20 *IJMCL* (2005) 345; Molenaar, ibid, 533; Henriksen, Hönneland and Sydnes (eds), *Law and Politics in Ocean Governance: The UN Fish Stocks Agreement and Regional Fisheries Management Regimes* (Leiden, 2006).

[185] For a comprehensive analysis of alternative approaches to decision-making under Article 10 see McDorman, 20 *IJMCL* (2005) 423.

[186] Lodge and Nandan, 20 *IJMCL* (2005) 365–72.

[187] *Supra*, Ch 1. Contrast UNCLOS Article 119(1)(a) under which generally recommended international minimum standards need only be taken 'into account'.

on Responsible Fishing and UNGA resolutions on driftnets and bottom trawling.[188] It also provides a possible basis on which FAO or the CBD could recommend the creation of high-seas protected areas where fishing is banned or severely restricted, or impose a moratorium on certain kinds of fishing, in cases where RFMOs themselves have failed to take the necessary action.

Article 12 adds the important rider that 'States shall provide for transparency' in the decision-making processes and activities of regional fisheries bodies. It goes on to give NGOs and intergovernmental organizations 'concerned with' straddling or migratory fish stocks a right to participate in meetings and to have timely access to reports and records—an attempt to move fisheries agreements beyond the closed-door world in which some have operated.[189] With a view to updating and amendment, Article 13 requires states to cooperate to strengthen existing subregional and regional fisheries management organizations and arrangements in order to improve their effectiveness.

Where there is an appropriate regional body, states fishing for high-seas stocks and relevant coastal states 'shall give effect to their duty to cooperate by becoming members of such organization', or by agreeing to apply its rules.[190] Failure to do so will entail loss of the right to engage in the high-seas fishery.[191] States with a 'real interest' in the fishery have a right to membership on non-discriminatory terms,[192] and new participants can expect to be treated in accordance with factors set out in Article 11, but this does not guarantee them a quota. One problem with these attempts to control or deny access is that it may simply lead to an increase in IUU fishing. In theory non-parties to the UN Fish Stocks Agreement are bound by none of these provisions, although states parties have committed themselves to taking measures to deter non-party vessels from undermining the effective implementation of the Agreement.[193] This is mainly likely to involve denial of port access, or of access to EEZ fishing. However, the more important risk that non-parties face is that eventually, even in the face of their persistent objection, the Fish Stocks Agreement will come to be regarded as establishing new rules of access to high-seas fishing that are no longer based on high-seas freedoms.[194] Once that occurs they will lose altogether the right to fish except in accordance with regional agreements and their vessels might be apprehended if they attempt to do so. At that point a new conception of common property on the high seas will finally have emerged.[195]

At present, however, the coverage of and participation in high-seas RFMOs is not yet comprehensive nor do all such bodies conform to the terms of the Fish Stocks Agreement. Most tuna stocks, together with salmon and certain other high seas fish,[196] are subject to species-specific regional agreements. Negotiations are still in progress to adopt comprehensive agreements covering the Southern Pacific and the Southern

---

[188] FAO Plans of Action and the 2001 Reykjavik Declaration on Responsible Fisheries are also relevant.
[189] On transparency see *supra*, Ch 2, section 5(2).   [190] Article 8(3).   [191] Article 8(4).
[192] Article 8(3). See Molenaar, 15 *IJMCL* (2000) 475; id, 18 *IJMCL* (2003) 457.   [193] Article 33.
[194] See Charney, 61 *BYIL* (1985) 1.   [195] See Örebech et al, 13 *IJMCL* (1998) 119.
[196] Eg Pacific halibut, central Bering Sea Pollock. See Meltzer, 20 *IJMCL* (2005) 571–604.

Indian Ocean. Further agreements will be needed for much of the South-west and Central Atlantic, and for certain species, including swordfish stocks in the South-eastern Pacific, where Chile and the European Union are in dispute over an access and conservation regime. Existing agreements, including NAFO and NEAFC, will have to be amended, given broader mandates or operated in accordance with new policies, but some participants are not yet bound by the Fish Stocks Agreement, so progress has been slow.[197] Moreover, many flag-of-convenience fishing states also remain outside applicable regional agreements. Their vessels will continue to fish unregulated until either access to ports or a market for their fish can be denied, or until lawmaking efforts by FAO and the UN General Assembly succeed in changing the applicable customary law to allow arrest at sea, or UNCLOS itself can be reinterpreted in accordance with the Fish Stocks Agreement. In this respect it is worth recalling that high-seas fishery disputes (and the UN Fish Stocks Agreement) are subject to compulsory settlement in accordance with Part XV of UNCLOS. Since many flag-of-convenience states are UNCLOS parties, they can thus be held to account for overfishing or ecosystem destruction on that basis, in a way that coastal states cannot.[198] Arguably, since conservation of biodiversity is the 'common concern of humanity', any UNCLOS party should be entitled to initiate such proceedings, whether or not they have a real interest in the fishery.[199] However, the Fish Stocks Agreement makes no provision for any form of non-confrontational non-compliance procedure comparable to other MEAs, nor is there any mechanism for reviewing the performance of RFMOs, although the Agreement itself has been reviewed in a UN conference. While it undoubtedly promotes changes to the architecture of regional agreements, there remains considerable room for improving accountability mechanisms,[200] since states are understandably reluctant to address the mismanagement of high-seas living resources by RFMOs in adversarial judicial processes.

(e) Compatibility of EEZ and high seas conservation measures

Article 63(2) of the 1982 UNCLOS merely provides that coastal states and those whose vessels fish straddling stocks in adjacent high-seas areas shall seek agreement on conservation measures for those areas.[201] Article 64 similarly requires cooperation on the conservation of highly migratory stocks in the EEZ and on the high seas. One of the principal purposes of the Fish Stocks Agreement is to 'ensure that the measures taken for conservation and management in the EEZs and in the adjacent high seas areas

---

[197] Molenaar, 20 *IJMCL* (2005) 533, 546–7. A number of RFMOs have adopted recommendations on precautionary and ecosystem approaches to fishing.

[198] UNCLOS Article 297(3), *supra* Ch 4, section 4.

[199] On common concern see *supra*, Ch 3, section 3, and on *erga omnes partes* obligations see *supra*, Ch 4, section 2.

[200] Gjerde, in Freestone, Barnes and Ong (eds), *The Law of the Sea*, 298–301; Lodge and Nandan, 20 *IJMCL* (2005) 357–9.

[201] But not in the EEZ. The coastal state alone determines these, and its determination cannot be challenged, except in non-binding conciliation: see 1982 UNCLOS, Article 297(3); 1995 UN Fish Stocks Agreement, Article 32.

are compatible and coherent, in order to take into account the biological unity of the stocks and the supporting ecosystem'.[202] Article 7 thus amplifies Articles 63 and 64 of UNCLOS by requiring these states to cooperate to ensure compatibility between the measures adopted for high-seas areas and those for areas under national jurisdiction. The article lists various matters to be taken into account in determining compatibility, including the measures adopted by coastal states within their EEZ, the biological unity of the stocks, and the impact on other marine living resources. States whose vessels fish the adjacent high seas are required to ensure that measures they take do not undermine the effectiveness of coastal-state conservation and management measures within the EEZ.[203] Pointedly, Article 7 does *not* say that measures applied in the EEZ and on the high seas should be the same.

The objective of this article is obvious, but it is less clear what happens if the parties cannot agree on compatible measures for the high seas. The Fish Stocks Agreement itself says only that any of the states concerned may invoke dispute settlement procedures, which include seeking provisional measures and special arbitration by fisheries experts.[204] However, while this may allow an independent tribunal to determine the question and indicate compatible measures if asked to do so,[205] it should be appreciated that not all disputes relating to straddling or highly migratory stocks will necessarily be subject to compulsory jurisdiction.[206] Failing agreement or a third-party determination, can the coastal state unilaterally insist on the non-discriminatory application of its own conservation measures to straddling or highly migratory stocks in adjacent high seas areas? Coastal states did have such a power under Article 7 of the 1958 Geneva Convention on Fisheries Conservation, but there is no comparable article in the 1982 UNCLOS or the 1995 Fish Stocks Agreement, although some authors have argued that Article 116 (b) of UNCLOS gives such a priority to the special interests of coastal states.[207] Even if this is correct, coastal states have no power to enforce their own conservation laws by arresting and prosecuting foreign fishing vessels on the high seas, but a number of coastal states have sought to do so indirectly by denying such vessels access to ports. For distant-water fishing vessels this can cause serious supply problems, and it is no idle threat. Arguably, unilateral action of this kind is a violation of the GATT Agreement, provided that the distant-water states have shown their willingness to negotiate in good faith,[208] but this does not solve the problem if the parties

---

[202] FAO Fisheries Circular 898, para 4.4, at 15.   [203] Article 7(2)(a).

[204] Article 7(4)–(5). On settlement of disputes see Articles 27–32, and *supra*, Ch 4, section 4.

[205] Provisional measures were sought successfully in the *Southern Bluefin Tuna Cases* (1999) ITLOS Nos 3 and 4. See various authors in 10 *YbIEL* (1999) and Kwiatkowska, 15 *IJMCL* (2000) 1.

[206] See *Southern Bluefin Tuna Arbitration*, ICSID (2000); Boyle, 14 *IJMCL* (1999) 1; Churchill, 22 *IJMCL* (2007) 383.

[207] Miles and Burke, 20 *ODIL* (1989) 343, 352. See also Orrego Vicuna, 55 *ZAÖRV* (1995) 520.

[208] On freedom of transit through ports see 1947 GATT, Article V. On unilateral action see WTO Appellate Body, *US Import Prohibition of Shrimp and Certain Shrimp Products* ['Shrimp-Turtle Case'] 37 *ILM* (1998) 832, *infra*, Ch 14. In 2000 the European Community and Chile initiated parallel proceedings before the WTO and ITLOS after failing to agree on measures to protect straddling swordfish stocks. The cases were provisionally settled shortly thereafter.

still cannot agree and no dispute settlement forum has jurisdiction. This omission remains one of the major uncertainties left over from the 1995 negotiations.

(f) Compliance and enforcement

One of the most important objectives of post-UNCED fisheries law reform has been to improve law enforcement and compliance by fishing vessels on the high seas. UNCLOS left fisheries enforcement on the high seas in the hands of flag states, exclusively. Relying solely on flag-state enforcement, or mutual observer schemes,[209] has not been effective at controlling illegal fishing. Moreover, fishing vessels have found it easy to evade flag-state control by the simple expedient of re-flagging when necessary, usually to states not party to the relevant regional fisheries treaty.[210] Some states have made use of their EEZ powers to arrest foreign vessels transhipping fish illegally caught on the high seas,[211] but although there are various grounds on which foreign vessels can also be boarded or arrested on the high seas, illegal fishing is not one of them.[212] Much of the high seas, especially in the southern hemisphere, is effectively unpoliced. In these circumstances, cooperation is essential to law enforcement.

The UN Fish Stocks Agreement is one of several global and regional treaties which have created a new enforcement and compliance regime for high seas fishing.[213] The new regime has three elements.

First, flag-state regulatory and enforcement responsibility is reiterated in much more specific terms in both the UN Fish Stocks Agreement[214] and the FAO Compliance Agreement.[215] Inter alia, vessels must be licensed and their catches monitored; high-seas fishing must be regulated and violations investigated, prosecuted, and effective sanctions imposed. It remains primarily the duty of the flag state to ensure that vessels flying its flag comply with conservation and management measures adopted by regional fisheries organizations. It should not authorize vessels to fish if it cannot do so effectively. These provisions are designed not only to strengthen flag-state control but also to deter evasive re-flagging of vessels.

Second, port states may take non-discriminatory measures to promote the effectiveness of international conservation and management measures.[216] In the Fish Stocks Agreement this includes a power to inspect vessels in port and to prohibit landing or

---

[209] See e.g. 1980 Convention on the Conservation of Antarctic Marine Living Resources, Article 24.

[210] See Birnie, 2 *RECIEL* (1993) 270.   [211] UNCLOS, Article 73.

[212] See Articles 105, 108–111.

[213] For innovative provisions in recent regional treaties, see 1992 Convention for the Conservation of Anadramous Stocks in the North Pacific, Article 5; 1994 Convention on the Conservation and Management of Pollock Resources of the Bering Sea, Article 11; 1992 Niue Treaty on Cooperation on Fisheries Surveillance and Law Enforcement in the South Pacific, Articles 4–6. See generally, Moore, 24 *ODIL* (1993) 197; Edeson, in Boyle and Freestone (eds), *International Law and Sustainable Development*, Ch 8; Joyner, in Hey (ed), *Developments in International Fisheries Law*, Ch 12; Rayfuse, 20 *IJMCL* (2005) 509.

[214] Articles 18–19.

[215] Articles III-IV. See Birnie, 2 *RECIEL* (1993) 245; Edeson, in, Boyle and Freestone (eds), *International Law and Sustainable Development*, Ch 8.

[216] UNFSA, Article 23; Compliance Agreement, Article V. See Anderson, in Boyle and Freestone (eds), *International Law and Sustainable Development*, Ch 14; Molenaar, 38 *ODIL* (2007) 225.

transhipment of illegally caught stock. If the port state does not prosecute the vessel, it can report its findings to the flag state, which then has a duty to investigate and take action.[217] These powers do not in reality depend on the Fish Stocks Agreement, which merely codifies them. They exist as a matter of customary law by virtue of the port state's sovereignty over its ports and are exercisable by any port state.[218]

Third, in high-seas areas covered by a regional or subregional fisheries organization, inspectors from any member state may board and inspect where there are 'clear grounds' for believing that a fishing vessel has engaged in illegal fishing.[219] The findings are then reported to the flag state. If the flag state does not respond and the violation is serious, for example where the vessel is unlicensed or operating under a false identity, has no catch records, is caught fishing in a closed area, taking prohibited stocks, or using prohibited gear, it may be arrested and brought into port for further enquiry, and prosecution by or with the agreement of the flag state.[220]

The power to board and detain is hedged about with extensive safeguards, both to prevent abuse or the use of excessive force, and to protect the position of the flag state.[221] The flag state may at any point require the vessel to be released into its custody and take further proceedings itself.[222] There are also prompt release procedures and limitations on the penalties for arrests within the EEZ,[223] but these do not apply to high-seas arrests.[224] Concerns about high-seas arrests may have deterred some fishing states from ratifying the Fish Stocks Agreement. Nevertheless, the Agreement expands significantly the enforcement powers available to members of regional fisheries bodies, and facilitates greater cooperation in this respect between flag, coastal, and port states. For the first time, fishing vessels are no longer immune from non-flag-state inspection and arrest on the high seas, and their access to ports provides a further instrument of control and supervision of illegal fishing.

6 CONSERVATION OF MARINE BIODIVERSITY[225]

6(1) EVOLUTION OF THE LAW ON MARINE BIODIVERSITY

The relationship between the 1982 UNCLOS and the 1992 Convention on Biological Diversity (CBD) shows how successive treaties on rather different topics can

---

[217] UNFSA, Article 19.   [218] *Supra*, Ch 7.

[219] UNFSA, Article 21. See Hayashi, 9 *Georgetown IELR* (1996) 1.   [220] UNFSA, Article 21(8)–(11).

[221] UNFSA, Article 22.   [222] UNFSA, Article 21(12)–(13).

[223] UNCLOS Articles 73(2)–(3), 292. See also *MV Saiga* (1998/9) ITLOS Nos 1 and 2; Mensah, 22 *IJMCL* (2007) 425; Rothwell, 53 *ICLQ* (2004) 171.

[224] Churchill, 22 *IJMCL* (2007) 402–5.

[225] See generally, Angel, in Petersen (ed), *Diversity of Oceanic Life: An Evaluation Review* (Washington, 1992) 23–59; Joyner, 28 *Vand JTL* (1995) 635–87; de Klemm, in Hey (ed), *Developments in International Fisheries Law*, 423–99; Pullen and Warren, 1 *Int Jnl of Biosciences and the Law* (1997) 249.

nevertheless contribute to the development of an integrated legal regime. The 1982 Convention makes no reference to biological diversity, although Article 194(5) does require parties to take measures necessary 'to protect and preserve rare or fragile eco-systems as well as the habitat of depleted, threatened or endangered species and other forms of marine life'. It is also clear from the totality of Articles 192–6 that Part XII was never intended to be simply about pollution, and that it encompasses protection of ecosystems, conservation of depleted or endangered species of marine life, and control of alien species.[226] A decade later the 1992 Rio Conference on Environment and Development adopted the CBD, whose provisions apply both to terrestrial and marine biodiversity. Clearly, each agreement is relevant for the purpose of interpreting the other. Equally clearly, the increasingly devastating effect of unsustainable fishing practices on marine biodiversity and ecosystems is a matter that directly affects the CBD. There is thus a possibility that implementing the later treaty could affect rights and obligations under UNCLOS. Moreover, Agenda 21 of the Rio Conference, the Convention on Biological Diversity and the UN Fish Stocks Agreement all give a broad reading to the responsibilities of states with regard to protection of the marine environment. In this context conservation and sustainable use of marine living resources, ecosystems, and biological diversity are important elements, and the 1982 UNCLOS must be interpreted and applied accordingly.[227]

(a) Agenda 21

A more ecological approach to 'Protection of the Oceans and all Kinds of Seas', including their living resources, was first addressed in Chapter 17 of UNCED Agenda 21,[228] the opening paragraph of which asserts that 'the marine environment—including the oceans and all seas and adjacent coastal areas—forms an integrated whole that is an essential part of the global life-support system', which it also recognizes as 'a positive asset that presents opportunities for sustainable development'. Whilst asserting that international law as reflected in UNCLOS provides the basis for pursuing protection and sustainable development of the marine and costal environment, it stresses that this requires *new approaches to marine and costal management and development at the national, subregional and global levels, approaches that are integrated in content and are precautionary and anticipatory in* ambit'.[229]

Agenda 21 identifies seven programme areas covering the actions required to achieve these objectives in all sea areas. Those most pertinent to biodiversity conservation generally include: integrated management, marine environment protection, addressing critical uncertainties for the management of the marine environment and climate change, and strengthening international, including regional, cooperation.[230]

---

[226] *Supra,* Ch 7.
[227] See generally Molenaar, 22 *IJMCL* (2007) 89; Gjerde, 'Ecosystems and Biodiversity in Deep Waters and High Seas', *UNEP Regional Seas Reports and Studies* No 178 (2006).
[228] *Rept of the UNCED,* UN Doc A/CONF 151/26/REV 1, Vol I (1992).
[229] Para 17.1, emphasis added.
[230] Ch 17 makes no reference to Ch 15 on conservation of biodiversity, presumably because the Biodiversity Convention was not concluded until the eve of UNCED and Ch 15 is itself drafted in very general terms.

These remain the key considerations for effective implementation of the Biodiversity Convention, as also does the accompanying warning that implementation by developing countries of the activities set out in Chapter 17 'shall be commensurate with their individual technological and juridical capacities' as well as their developmental priorities, and 'ultimately depends on the technology transfer and technological resources required and made available to them'.[231] The Biological Diversity Convention addresses these requirements,[232] but UNCLOS does so only in general and somewhat ambiguous terms,[233] requiring 'promotion' of development and transfer of marine technology; international cooperation—including among international organizations—and establishment of national and regional marine scientific and technological centres, all of which is left to subsequent negotiation. The emphasis of these weakly drafted UNCLOS provisions, however, focuses on the anthropomorphic goal of accelerating economic and social development.

Chapter 17 of Agenda 21, however, spells out the relevant requirements for protection of marine living resources and the marine environment much more clearly. It specifies establishment of coordinating mechanisms to further integrated management; consultation with interested groups; prior environmental impact assessment; conservation and restoration of critical habitats in all marine areas; a precautionary and anticipatory approach to protection from degradation; use of resources; and development of aquaculture and mariculture. Although its tenor also is anthropomorphic, it does specifically encourage states to identify marine ecosystems exhibiting high levels of biodiversity and productivity and other critical habitat areas and to establish necessary limitations on use of such areas through, inter alia, designation of protected areas (in particular coral reef systems) estuaries, temperate and tropical wetlands, including mangroves, seagrass areas, and other spawning and nursery areas all of which are generally rich providers of biodiversity.

(b) The Convention on Biological Diversity

The COP to the Biological Diversity Convention identified marine and coastal biodiversity as an early priority for action and at its first meeting requested the Subsidiary Body on Scientific, Technical and Technological Advice (SBSTTA) for advice. It is worth examining the content and development of the proposals it made in some detail as they represent the main initiative under this Convention. COP 2 adopted an important decision, based on the SBSTTA's advice, relating to development of a work programme and cooperation with the related conventions and relevant international and regional organizations discussed earlier in this chapter. It also issued a ministerial statement, known as the Jakarta Mandate on Marine and Coastal Biological Diversity,[234] acknowledging a new global consensus on the importance of this topic,

---

[231] Ch 17, para 17.2.   [232] In Articles 16, 18, 20, 21, on which see *supra*, Ch 11.
[233] In Part XIV, Development and Transfer of Marine Technology, Articles 266–78. See e.g. Article 266(3): states 'shall endeavour to foster economic and legal conditions for the benefit of all parties concerned on an equitable basis'.
[234] See COP Decision II/10.

reaffirming the critical need for the COP to address conservation and sustainable use of marine and coastal biodiversity and urging parties to initiate immediate action to implement these COP decisions. Based on expert recommendations, the SBSTTA produced a three-year work programme,[235] which was adopted by COP 4.[236] It specifically addressed, in addition to the general mandate, the issues of coral bleaching and related biodiversity loss and the special needs of small island states in implementing the programme. Its basic principles include, inter alia, ecosystem and precautionary approaches; the importance of science; use of local and indigenous community knowledge; the need for primary action at local and national levels (as well as at the global and regional); and strong coordination between the Biodiversity Convention and other relevant bodies. Its five main thematic areas relate to: integrated marine and coastal management; sustainable use of the resources concerned; marine and coastal protected areas; mariculture; and alien species.[237] Operational objectives are set for all these thematic areas.[238] COP V urged the SBSTTA and Secretariat to complete this programme. It is noteworthy that COP VII expressed concern about threats to conservation of biodiversity in marine areas beyond national jurisdiction, particularly to vulnerable marine ecosystems.[239]

Progress is, and will doubtless remain, inevitably slow, given the number of the CBD's parties, the complexity of the issues, the lack of scientific data, and so on. But a start has been made in bringing together and applying in a more integrated way all the strategies, principles and existing international frameworks outlined in this chapter and Chapters 11 and 12 in order to focus on the need for marine biodiversity protection. The Jakarta Mandate goes some way to meet the disappointment expressed by the United States in its declaration on adoption of the Convention concerning the limited scope of its obligations respecting the marine environment.[240] Many of the actions required are already within the scope of existing conventions concerned with wildlife conservation, insofar as they list marine species or marine protected areas in their annexes.[241] As the Ramsar Convention includes wetlands with some marine water (depending on depth) its listings include shallow coastal waters. The World Heritage List now also includes some coastal and marine reef areas; all cetaceans and some seals and other marine mammals have been listed on CITES Appendix I and are thus banned from trade. Some species of whales and seals, the dugong, and porpoises are

---

[235] SBSTTA Recommendation III/2, as amended by COP III.   [236] Decision IV/5 and Annex.

[237] See COP Decision VII/5, Annex I.

[238] For further details see *CBD Handbook*, Sec IV, Guide to Decisions of the Conference of the Parties: Thematic Work Programmes.

[239] COP Decision VII/5.   [240] *Supra*, Ch 11.

[241] Notably the 1971 Convention on Wetlands of International Importance for Wildfowl Habitat; 1972 Convention for the Protection of the World Cultural and National Heritage Convention; 1973 Convention on International Trade in Endangered Species; 1979 Convention on Migratory Species of Wild Animals (Bonn Convention); 1979 Convention on Conservation of European Wildlife and National Habitats (Berne Convention); and the 1980 Convention on Conservation of Antarctic Marine Living Resources (CCAMLR). See *supra*, Ch 12, section 2; Churchill, in Bowman and Redgwell (eds), *International Law and the Conservation of Biological Diversity*, 71–89.

listed in the Bonn Convention, under which several relevant Agreements have now been concluded.[242] There are also ad hoc treaties providing for conservation of specific marine species such as the antarctic seals,[243] polar bears,[244] and sea turtles.[245]

Most regional-seas agreements were originally limited to preventing pollution, but as awareness of the importance of the marine environment as the habitat of marine species has grown, not only have many of original conventions been revised to adapt them to a broader role in protecting ecosystems and marine biodiversity.[246] Protocols to protect various species of marine wildlife and establish specially protected areas have been added.[247] Awareness has developed within the institutions of some of the older regional-seas commissions and organizations concerning the importance of maintaining the quality of waters forming the habitat of marine species and organisms. The OSPAR Commission adopted the Sintra Statement phasing out certain polluting discharges by 2002, applying all the new principles for sustainable development and preservation of the marine environment, and adding a new annex and appendix on the Protection and Conservation of Ecosystems and Biological Diversity of the Maritime Area.[248] Similarly, progress has been made in transforming the London Dumping Convention by a protocol which eliminates all dumping at sea.[249] Further examples include actions within the Helsinki Commission[250] aimed at restoring habitats important to fish and sustainable aquaculture. Thus the 1982 UNCLOS and treaties on land-based marine pollution have begun to protect marine ecosystems.

Other developments supporting restoration of marine habitats include the series of measures adopted through the International Maritime Organization, pursuant to Part XII of UNCLOS, Chapter 17 of Agenda 21, the Commission on Sustainable

---

[242] 1990 Bonn Agreement on the Conservation of Seals in the Wadden Sea; 1992 New York Agreement on Conservation of Small Cetaceans of the Baltic and North Seas (ASCOBANS); 1996 Agreement on Conservation of Cetaceans of the Black Sea, Mediterranean Sea and Contiguous Atlantic Areas (ACCOBAMS); 1996 Convention on the Conservation of African-Eurasian Migratory Waterbirds; 2001 Agreement on Conservation of Albatrosses and Petrels (ACAP). On ASCOBANS and ACCOBAMS see Churchill, in Boyle and Freestone, *International Law and Sustainable Development*, Ch 10; Nijkamp and Nollkaemper, 9 *Georgetown IELR* (1997) 281.

[243] 1972 Convention on the Conservation of Antarctic Seals. See Lyster, *International Wildlife Law* (Cambridge, 1985) Ch 3.

[244] 1973 Agreement on the Conservation of Polar Bears; 2000 Agreement on the Conservation and Management of the Alaska-Chukota Polar Bear Population. See Lyster 2nd edn, op cit, Ch 11.

[245] 1996 Inter-American Agreement on the Conservation of Sea Turtles, 1 *JIWLP* (1998) 179; MOU Concerning Conservation Measures for Marine Turtles of the West Coast of Africa, 39 *ILM* (2000) 1.

[246] See *supra*, Ch 7.

[247] See *e.g.* 1995 Protocol Concerning Specially Protected Areas and Biological Diversity in the Mediterranean Sea; 1985 Protocol on Protected Areas and on Wild Fauna and Flora in the East African Region; 1990 Protocol on Specially Protected Areas and Wildlife in the Wide Caribbean Region (SPAW Protocol); 1989 Paipa Protocol for the Conservation and Management of Protected Marine and Coastal Areas in the South East Pacific. The Black Sea Convention concluded a protocol in 2001. See de Klemm, in Hey (ed), *Developments in International Fisheries Law*, 441–7.

[248] *Supra*, Ch 8.   [249] Ibid.

[250] Ibid. The Helsinki Commission launched an Agenda 21 for the Baltic region in 1996, focusing, inter alia, on fisheries and strengthened relations with the Baltic Sea Fishery Commission.

Development's decision on 'Oceans and Seas',[251] and the 2002 World Summit on Sustainable Development (WSSD) Plan of Implementation.[252] Despite past reluctance to invade the role of other UN specialized agencies and bodies it is now cooperating with many of these.[253] The Biological Diversity Convention has influenced IMO's agenda in various ways. IMO was addressing all five of the major threats to marine biodiversity even before receiving the CSD's request that it should do so, viz: alteration and loss of habitat, chemical pollution and eutrophication, climate change, invasion of alien species, and over-exploitation of marine and coastal resources. It has adopted a variety of instruments on these issues.[254] The 2001 Convention on Control of Harmful Anti-Fouling Systems on Ships restricts the use chemicals that have been particularly harmful to certain marine species.[255] A Convention for the Control and Management of Ships' Ballast Water and Sediments was adopted in 2004 in order to reduce the increasingly serious problem of alien species transported worldwide in ships' ballast water.[256]

Clearly, in the light of so many marine initiatives and instruments, there is an urgent need not only for oversight of implementation, but also for coordination and integration of the activities of the many concerned bodies. The existing governance system is undeniably ad hoc and fragmented,[257] confined within artificial boundaries either of a jurisdictional nature or by species or pollutant, whereas the marine biological diversity conservation problem is essentially ecosystemic. Moreover, both enforcement and promulgation of relevant detailed regulations depend largely on action by national authorities. As noted in a UNEP/FAO Report,[258] the practical implications of regional fishery bodies (RFBs) and regional seas conventions (RSCs) adopting an ecosystem approach have only begun to attract international attention.[259] At the international level implementation of this approach would prompt changes to institutional, monitoring,

---

[251] CSD Decision 7/1.   [252] WSSD Plan of Implementation, UN Doc A/Conf 199/20.

[253] With FAO, ILO, IAEA, UNEO, the Secretariats of the Basel Convention, UNFCCC, OSPARCOM and the UN Division of Ocean Affairs and the Law of the Sea (DOALOS); see de La Fayette, 16 *IJMCL* (2001) 155; also Birnie, in Nordquist and Norton Moore (eds), *Current Maritime Issues in the IMO* (The Hague, 1999) 301, 376ff.

[254] *E.g.* Guidelines to Minimize the Transfer of Harmful Aquatic Organisms and Pathogens Through Ballast Water and Regulations requiring ships to carry approved ballast water management plans and conduct surveys, though it is working towards a convention on this; Annex VI to the MARPOL Convention on Air Pollution From Ships and a Protocol to the OPPRR Convention on Pollution Incidents by Hazardous and Noxious Substances. See de La Fayette, loc cit, previous note and *supra*, Ch 7.

[255] The Annex currently lists only tributyl.   [256] Vallega, 19 *IJMCL* (2004) 411–82.

[257] See Molenaar, 22 *IJMCL* (2007) 89 and articles collected in 19 *IJMCL* (2004) 209–363.

[258] *Report on Ecosystem-Based Management of Fisheries: Opportunities and Challenges for Coordination Between Marine Regional Fishery Bodies and Regional Seas Conventions*, 2nd Meeting of FAO and Non-FAO Regional Fishery Bodies or Arrangements, Rome, 20–21 February 2001, RFB/II/2001/7; see also Keckes, *Review of International Programmes Relevant to the Work of the Independent World Commission on the Oceans*, January 1997.

[259] Notably, at a symposium on 'Ecosystem Effects of Fishing,' convened by ICES in March 1999, and the 2001 Reykjavik Conference on Responsible Fisheries in the Ecosystem, which makes various proposals for structural adjustments and changes in the UN systems at VI4 and VI5. See the 2001 Reykjavik Declaration on Sustainable Fisheries and FAO, *Fisheries Management: The Ecosystem Approach to Fisheries*, FAO Technical Guidelines for Responsible Fisheries No 4 Suppl 2 (Rome, 2003).

evaluation, governance and regulatory requirements. Actions proposed for RFBs included defining ecosystem objectives parallel to current conservation objectives of fisheries management. It was suggested that these should address biodiversity, habitat productivity, and marine-environmental quality. Once these considerations are factored into fisheries management, enhanced cooperation on ecosystem-based fishery management will be required, building on existing experience of cooperation between RFBs and RSCs, adapted accordingly.[260]

6(2) THE RELATIONSHIP BETWEEN UNCLOS AND THE CBD

The Convention on Biological Diversity does not give blanket priority to UNCLOS.[261] On marine environmental matters Article 22 specifically requires parties to implement the CBD 'consistently with the rights and obligations of States under the law of the sea'. This suggests that they could not, for example, ignore the rights of ships to freedom of navigation in the EEZ and high seas, whether under UNCLOS or under customary law. To that extent Article 22 of the CBD reinforces the terms of Article 311(3) of UNCLOS. Within these limits UNCLOS will prevail in any conflict. On the other hand, as Article 237 of UNCLOS makes clear, agreements relating to the marine environment do not have to conform to Part XII of the Convention, but need only be carried out in a manner consistent with its 'general principles and objectives'. This should allow CBD parties much greater latitude to depart from the terms of Part XII than from other parts of the Convention since, as a *lex specialis,* Article 237 overrides Article 311(3).[262] Save in an extreme case, the CBD regime will therefore prevail over Part XII of UNCLOS.

More importantly, however, while Article 22 also provides that existing treaty rights and obligations are not affected by the CBD, this exclusion does not apply where 'the exercise of those rights and obligations would cause serious damage or threat to biological diversity'. While in general terms the effect of Article 22 is to ensure that UNCLOS will normally prevail, states parties to the CBD cannot rely on UNCLOS to justify—or to tolerate—fishing which causes or threatens serious damage to biodiversity. To that extent the CBD may have modified the fisheries provisions of UNCLOS. Moreover, since conservation of marine living resources and protection and preservation of 'rare or fragile ecosystems' and the habitat of 'depleted, threatened or endangered species and other forms of marine life' are already envisaged by UNCLOS,[263] the Convention's objects and purposes can readily be interpreted to include measures aimed at protection of marine biodiversity. Thus, for example, the adoption under the CBD of protected zones intended to reduce serious damage to biodiversity from high-seas fishing would not be incompatible with UNCLOS, and would be consistent with Article 22 of the CBD. However, such zones would not be opposable to non-parties to

---

[260] Reykjavik Conference, *Executive Summary*, 2–3.
[261] See generally Wolfrum and Matz, 4 *Max Planck YbUNL* (2000) 445.
[262] Nordquist (ed), *UNCLOS Commentary*, IV, 423–6.   [263] Articles 61, 64–7, 117–20, 194(5).

the CBD, whose UNCLOS rights Article 311 expressly protects.[264] Any meaningful attempt to regulate marine biodiversity thus in practice depends principally on the parties to UNCLOS, not on the parties to the CBD. Thus the most important agreement on marine biodiversity—the UN Fish Stocks Agreement—is formally an agreement implementing UNCLOS, not an agreement implementing the CBD. We can see from this example how a major lawmaking treaty such as UNCLOS has an ongoing impact on the structuring of later lawmaking agreements. The range of matters covered by the 1995 Agreement simply could not have been addressed with the same freedom or priority as an addendum to the CBD.

A final point is that we can see from the relationship between UNCLOS and the CBD that international law on conservation of marine living resources and ecosystems is not the exclusive preserve of either treaty. A coherent and comprehensive understanding of the present law requires consideration of both treaties.

7 CONCLUSIONS

As we have seen, developing a legal regime that provides for sustainable use and conservation of ocean-living resources and biological diversity within the framework of the general law of the sea has presented virtually insuperable problems for the international community since the late nineteenth century. The ad hoc and sectoral approach to conservatory regulation of marine species, though initially regarded as a major advance, has in practice adversely influenced subsequent attempts to establish a more comprehensive and rational regime. Despite four international conferences on the Law of the Sea between 1930 and 1982 which attempted to establish jurisdictional limits within which states' responsibilities for development of a conservatory regime would be exercised, both overfishing and increasing degradation of the habitat of marine species has largely continued unabated, with disregard not only for the socio-economic implications but also for the wider threat to marine biodiversity highlighted in the negotiations preceding the 1992 Convention on Biological Diversity.

UNCLOS III sought to deal with the problems of ocean space as a 'closely interrelated...whole' and establish a legal order which, inter alia, would at one and the same time promote 'the conservation of their living resources and protection of the marine environment'.[265] It was and remains undoubtedly an advance on the previous regime and its provisions concerning fisheries have led to creation of many more fisheries organizations at international, regional, and subregional levels both under the auspices of the FAO and outside it, with the result that fewer marine areas within which fisheries are conducted now remain outside the scope of a regulatory regime.

---

[264] But a recommendation from the CBD that fishing be discontinued in certain high seas areas or using methods harmful to biodiversity would appear to be binding on RFMOs pursuant to Article 10 of the UN Fish Stocks Agreement, *supra*, section 5(3).

[265] *Supra*, Ch 7.

Despite this success, fisheries within the new jurisdictional zones, whether on the high seas or under national jurisdiction, have continued to decline and are almost everywhere in trouble.[266] A pessimistic report on EU fish stocks concluded that: 'Despite substantial efforts, there are no significant signs of stock recovery nor of reductions in overfishing since 2003. Fisheries management in the European Union is not working as it should and the objective of achieving long-term sustainability is not being reached.'[267] The state of more than half the EU stocks is unknown, and only 32% of the rest are sustainably managed. Globally, over 25% of all stocks are overfished and 50% are fished to capacity.

The causes, as outlined in this chapter, are multi-fold: subsidizing of uneconomic fisheries, a huge increase in vessel numbers, and the advanced technology used by them. These fundamentals have not changed despite changes in the law. Moreover, setting sustainable TACs based on reliable scientific formulae has become increasingly difficult as awareness of the complexity of the problem has grown, exacerbated by the Biodiversity Convention's requirements for conservation of marine biodiversity. The extent to which the collapse or decline of specific fisheries now poses a threat of serious damage to biodiversity is gradually becoming clearer and is a matter to be considered by the parties to fishery conventions and the COP of the Biodiversity Convention, in pursuance of its Jakarta Mandate and role in reviewing related policies and reports submitted by the parties. Much also depends on the effective implementation of the UN Fish Stocks Agreement in bringing about changes in fisheries governance and introducing new principles.[268] It remains premature to determine whether or not this agreement and the Biodiversity Convention will succeed in implementing their shared goals of sustainable use and conservation of marine living resources and biodiversity for the benefit of present and future generations. Greater cooperation is clearly called for by all the instruments, declarations, strategies, and conventions considered in this chapter.[269] But effective use must also be made of the proliferating international institutions established under the increasing number of related multilateral fisheries and environmental agreements.[270]

---

[266] OECD, *Towards Sustainable Fisheries: Economic Aspects of the Management of Living Marine Resources* (Paris, 1999).

[267] *Fishing Opportunities for 2009: Policy Statement from the European Commission*, COM (2008) 331 final, 5.

[268] For a comprehensive review see Lodge and Nandan, 20 *IJMCL* (2005) 345.

[269] On the difficulties and uncertain legal content of the obligation of cooperation see Stoll, in Wolfrum (ed), *Enforcing Environmental Standards: Economic Mechanisms as Viable Means* (Berlin, 1996) 39–93.

[270] See Churchill and Ulfstein, 94 *AJIL* (2000) 623, esp 658–9; Molenaar, 22 *IJMCL* (2007) 89; and *supra*, Ch 4, section 3.

14

INTERNATIONAL TRADE AND ENVIRONMENTAL PROTECTION

1   INTRODUCTION

Promotion and liberalization of free trade in goods and services has been the objective of international trade law since the General Agreement on Tariffs and Trade (GATT) was first adopted in 1947.[1] Many states have subsequently become parties to what is now a complex system of international trade agreements based on GATT. Since the Marrakesh Agreement of 1994 entered into force these agreements have been administered by the World Trade Organization (WTO). The WTO now provides the principal forum for negotiations on multilateral trading relations among

---

[1] For texts of the 1947 GATT as amended in 1994, the 1994 Marrakesh Agreement Establishing the World Trade Organization, and related agreements, understandings, and decisions, see WTO, *The Legal Texts: The Results of the Uruguay Round of Multilateral Trade Negotiations* (Cambridge, 1999). On WTO law and policy see: Trebilcock and Howse, *The Regulation of International Trade*, (2nd edn, London, 1999); Jackson, *The World Trading System*, (2nd edn, Cambridge, Mass, 1997); Kreuger (ed), *The WTO as an International Organization* (Chicago, 1998); Jackson, *The World Trade Organization: Constitution and Jurisprudence* (London, 1998); Jackson, Davey, and Sykes, *Legal Problems of International Economic Relations* (5th edn, St Paul, Minn, 2008); Matsushita, Schoenbaum and Mavroidis, *The World Trade Organization: Law, Practice and Policy* (2nd edn, Oxford, 2006); Van den Bossche, *The Law and Policy of the World Trade Organization: Text, Cases and Materials* (2nd edn, Cambridge, 2008)

member states, and for the binding settlement of disputes arising under WTO agreements. These institutional and dispute settlement features of the WTO, contrasted
with the decentralized and consensual dispute settlement features of international
environmental agreements, have further fuelled the 'trade and environment debate'
with the propsect that trade and environment disputes would inevitably fall for resolution before a trade body perceived to be inimical to environmental concerns.[2] In
practice, however, this 'centrifugal pull' of the WTO has not resulted in a multitude
of cases before the WTO dispute- settlement body arising from trade and environment conflicts. Nonetheless, as we discuss further below, though few in number the
impact of the WTO's trade and environment cases has been significant, and reveals a
more nuanced approach to environmental issues than that displayed by the pre-WTO
GATT panel in *Tuna-Dolphin*.[3]

A policy of free trade will inevitably involve some conflict with international environmental agreements or environmental-protection requirements in national law that
have the effect of restricting trade in certain goods. Although some commentators
condemn free trade as generally bad for the environment,[4] most focus their critique
on specific issues, arguing (i) that the rules of the multilateral trading system may pose
difficulties for the implementation of multilateral environmental agreements that use
trade restrictions to protect the environment, such as the 1973 Convention on Trade in
Endangered Species, the 1987 Protocol for the Protection of the Ozone Layer, the 1989
Basel Convention on the Control of Transboundary Movement of Hazardous Wastes
and the 2001 Rotterdam Convention on the Prior Informed Consent Procedure for
Certain Hazardous Chemicals and Pesticides in International Trade (PIC Convention);
(ii) that the rules of the multilateral trading system frustrate attempts to protect
resources and the environment in areas beyond national jurisdiction (e.g. the oceans),
as in the US–Mexico dispute concerning dolphin-friendly tuna-fishing regulations, or
the similar attempt to protect sea turtles from shrimp fisheries; (iii) that the rules of the
multilateral trading system prevent nations from adopting measures to protect their
domestic environment, such as setting high environmental standards for products
and services, labelling, packaging, recycling, and conservation of natural resources;
and (iv) that the rules of the multilateral trading system obstruct efforts to compel
other countries to adopt high environmental standards, although these may be necessary to prevent or correct transboundary pollution, to remove competitive advantages
in attracting investment and in selling products and services, or to conserve natural
resources. This chapter focuses on these issues.[5]

[2] For the flavour of this debate following the GATT Panel decisions in *Tuna-Dolphin*, see the contributions by Weiss and by Schoenbaum, 86 *AJIL* (1992) 700.

[3] *US—Restrictions on Imports of Tuna*, Report of the Panel, 30 *ILM* (1991), 1598, para 5.28 (not adopted
by the GATT Council) (hereafter, '*Tuna-Dolphin I*'); see *infra*, section 4.

[4] Daly, 15 *Loyola ICLJ* (1992) 36. Compare OECD, *The Environmental Effects of Trade* (Paris, 1994), and
GATT, *Trade and Environment* (Geneva, 1991).

[5] On trade and environment generally see: Esty, *Greening the GATT: Trade, Environment, and the Future*
(Washington DC, 1994); Cameron, Demaret, Gerardin (eds), *Trade and Environment: The Search for Balance*
(London, 1994); Petersmann, *International and European Trade and Environmental Law after the Uruguay*

International policy does not seek to give free trade priority over environmental protection, but neither does it endorse any general exception for environmental purposes. Recognizing the potential for conflict, what is sought is balance between the two objectives. Thus the preamble to the 1994 Marrakesh Agreement Establishing the World Trade Organization acknowledges that expansion of production and trade must allow for:

the optimal use of the world's resources in accordance with the objective of sustainable development, seeking both to protect and preserve the environment and to enhance the means for doing so in a manner consistent with their respective needs and concerns at different levels of economic development.

As we will see below, this preambular reference to 'the objective of sustainable development' has influenced the interpretation of the WTO-covered agreements, including the GATT in the *Shrimp-Turtle Case*.[6]

At the same time, Principle 12 of the Rio Declaration calls for states to cooperate to promote an 'open international economic system that would lead to growth and sustainable development in all countries'. It provides that 'Trade policy measures for environmental purposes should not constitute a means of arbitrary or unjustifiable discrimination or a disguised restriction on international trade'. Unilateral measures aimed at extraterritorial environmental problems are to be avoided, and 'environmental measures addressing transboundary or global environmental problems should, as far as possible, be based on an international consensus'. Since 1994 a number of important decisions of the WTO Appellate Body have helped clarify how this balance between free-trade agreements and environmental protection is to be achieved, but the WTO itself has been less successful in its search for better ways to integrate both concerns. Multilateral environmental agreements concluded since 1994 addressing transboundary or global environmental problems have likewise sought accommodation between trade and environmental concerns, though often merely repeating in preambular terms the exhortation to balance trade and environmental concerns. The Cartagena Protocol on Biosafety and the PIC Convention are recent examples.[7] This may be explained by the fact that, in environmental treaty negotiations, there is a risk attached to the consideration of the compatibility of trade-related environmental

---

Round (The Hague, 1995); Wolfrum (ed), *Enforcing Environmental Standards: Economic Mechanisms as Viable Means* (Berlin, 1996); Van Calster, *International and EU Trade Law: The Environmental Challenge* (London, 2000); Steinberg, *The Greening of Trade Law* (New York, 2002); Sampson, *The WTO and Sustainable Development* (Tokyo, 2005); Goyal, *The WTO and International Environmental Law* (Oxford, 2006); Bernasconi-Osterwalder, *Environment and Trade: A Guide to WTO Jurisprudence* (London, 2006); Ward, 45 *ICLQ* (1996) 592; Schoenbaum, 91 *AJIL* (1997) 268; McRae, 9 *Otago LR* (1998) 221; Esty and Gerardin, 32 *JWT* (1998) 5; Trebilcock and Howse, *The Regulation of International Trade* (2nd edn, London, 1999) Ch 15; Scott, in Weiler (ed), *The EU, the WTO, and the NAFTA: Towards a Common Law of International Trade* (Oxford, 2000), Ch 5.

[6] WTO Appellate Body Report, *US—Import Prohibition of Certain Shrimp and Shrimp Products*, WT/DS58/AB/R, adopted 6 November 1998, paras 152–3.

[7] For further discussion of the 'savings clauses' adopted in the PIC Convention and substantially duplicated in the Cartagena Protocol, see Safrin, 96 *AJIL* (2002) 606.

mechanisms (TREMS) with WTO rules at the design stage of MEAs since 'the potential for conflict with WTO rules is near deal-breaking in new MEA negotiations, as demonstrated by the difficulty in drafting the Biosafety Protocol, the Kyoto Protocol and the Rotterdam (PIC) Convention'.[8]

2 THE MULITLATERAL TRADING SYSTEM

2(1) THE WORLD TRADE ORGANIZATION

The World Trade Organization (WTO) came into existence on 1 January 1995[9] as the successor to the General Agreement on Tariffs and Trade (GATT), which had operated 'provisionally' since 1947. The WTO has legal personality and enjoys privileges and immunities 'similar to' those of a specialized agency of the United Nations.[10] With over 150 members, including China, the European Community, Japan, and the USA, together with many developing states, it provides a common institutional framework for the conduct of trade relations among its members.[11] The WTO oversees the implementation, administration, and operation of the 'Multilateral Trade Agreements' which are legally binding upon its members. In addition to the General Agreement on Trade in Goods (GATT), these Agreements include the General Agreement on Trade in Services (GATS), the Agreement on Trade-Related Aspects of Intellectual Property Rights (TRIPS), the Agreement on Trade-Related Investment Measures (TRIMS), the Agreement on Technical Barriers to Trade (TBT Agreement), the Agreement on the Application of Sanitary and Phytosanitary Measures (SPS Agreement), the Agreement on Agriculture, and the Agreement on Subsidies and Countervailing Measures (SCM Agreement). As is discussed further below, trade-related environmental measures can fall for consideration under one or more of these agreements; in addition, most of them contain specific environmental exceptions, largely a product of the Uruguay round of negotiations from which the WTO emerged.[12]

---

[8] *Environment and Trade: A Handbook* (2000, New York, UNEP/IISD) 62. During negotiation of the 1992 Climate Change Convention, early drafts included a conflict clause which called for the decisions of the COP and other measures taken to combat climate change to be consistent with the GATT/WTO, but this did not find a place in the final text. For more recent analysis, including of the Kyoto mechanisms, see Green, 8 *JIEL* (2005) 143.

[9] 1994 Marrakesh Agreement Establishing the World Trade Organization (hereafter 'WTO Agreement'). For text see *supra*, n 1.

[10] Article VIII.   [11] Article II.

[12] For example, like GATT, GATS contains an exception for measures 'necessary to protect human, animal or plant life, or health' (Article XIV (b)); similar wording is found in TRIPS Art 27.2 where a patent may be refused where preventing the domestic commercial exploitation of an invention is necessary to protect human, animal, or plant life or health or to avoid serious prejudice to the environment. Risk-assessment criteria under Article 5.2 of the SPS Agreement include 'ecological and environmental conditions' while Article 6.2 refers to 'ecosystems' as one factor members should consider in determining pest or disease free areas. Protection of the environment is also a recognized legitimite objective under the TBT Agreement (Article 2.2). The Agreement on Agriculture provides certain exceptions from its subsidy

The main organs of the WTO are a Ministerial Conference, a General Council, which also functions as the WTO's Dispute Settlement Body and Trade Policy Review Body, and Councils for Trade in Goods and Services, and Trade-Related Aspects of Intellectual Property Rights.[13] Each member has one vote,[14] and decisions are usually taken by consensus, but when that is not possible, a simple majority of votes cast is normally sufficient.[15] Certain decisions, such as interpretation of the multilateral trade agreements, waivers, and amendments and accessions, can be taken only by a specified majority vote.[16] The GATT, newly promulgated as 'GATT 1994', is the fundamental trade agreement administered by the WTO, and it is to this agreement and its impact on TREMs that we now turn.

2(2) PRINCIPAL WTO/GATT NORMS RELEVANT TO THE ENVIRONMENT

(a) The most-favoured-nation principle and the national treatment principle

At the core of the WTO/GATT system are two non-discrimination principles: the most-favoured-nation principle (MFN) and the national treatment principle. These non-discrimination mandates are essential for the full implementation of the Schedules of Concessions—lowered tariffs—which are binding obligations under GATT Article II.

The most-favoured-nation principle of Article I is designed to ensure equality of treatment of 'like product[s] originating or destined for the territories of all other contracting parties'. This equal treatment must be accorded 'unconditionally' and extends to (i) 'customs charges and duties', (ii) 'all rules and formalities connected with importation or exportation', and (iii) internal taxes, charges, and domestic regulation of a product's distribution, sale, and use. The MFN principle was considered in the *Belgian Family Allowances Case*,[17] which involved a law that levied a charge on foreign goods purchased by public authorities when the countries in which the goods originated did not administer a system of family allowances similar to that required under Belgian law. A GATT dispute-settlement panel concluded that the charge was illegal under GATT Article I and that even internal charges cannot discriminate between like products on the basis of distinctions between the production conditions in different countries.

The national treatment provision (GATT Article III) applies broadly to all 'internal' requirements applied to imported products, including taxes, charges, and all manner of regulations. The equality of treatment between domestic and imported

---

reduction obligations for environmental measures (Article 6.1 and Annex II, paras 2(a), 8(a),12); but the SCM Agreement's five-year exception for governmental assistance to industry to adapt to new environmental requirements has not been renewed, with the possibility that such subsidies are now actionable (Article 8.2(c))

[13] Article IV.   [14] Article IX(1).   [15] Article IX(1).   [16] Articles XI, X, XII.

[17] *Belgian Family Allowances (Allocations Familiales)*, GATT BISD (1st Supp), 59 (1953).

products required by this provision is delicately worded. For regulations, two standards must be met, one positive and one negative: they must be applied to imported products to accord 'treatment no less favourable than that accorded to like products of national origin',[18] and they must not be applied 'to afford protection to domestic production'.[19] For internal taxes and charges, two negative criteria apply: they must not be 'in excess of those applied, directly or indirectly, to like domestic charges',[20] or 'applied to imported or domestic products so as to afford protection to domestic production'.[21] In the two leading cases concerning these provisions, *Japan Shochu* and *Asbestos*, the WTO Appellate Body noted that 'there can be no one precise and absolute definition of what is like ', but that the general principle of Article III 'seeks to prevent members from affecting the competitive relationship, in the marketplace, *between the domestic and imported products involved*, so as to afford protection to domestic production'.[22]

Important questions arise in connection with this scheme. One is whether the phrase 'laws, regulations, and requirements' in Article III is limited to the conditions of purchase or sale of products in the domestic market. The *Italian Agricultural Machinery Case* rejected this view, holding that 'the Article was intended to cover...not only the laws and regulations which directly governed the conditions of sale or purchase, but also any laws or regulations which might adversely modify the *conditions of competition* between the domestic and imported products on the internal market'.[23] Subsequent GATT panels have extended this interpretation to hold that the test of the words 'treatment no less favourable' in Article III(4) is whether imported products are given an equal chance to compete with domestic products: 'treatment no less favourable...call[s] for effective equality of opportunities in respect of the application of laws, regulations, and requirements affecting the internal sale, offering for sale, purchase, transportation, distribution, or use of products'.[24]

Just as Articles I and III are paired *in pari materia* in this respect, so, too, is the GATT's quota provision, Article XI, in relation to both articles. Article XI states:

No prohibitions or restrictions other than duties, taxes or other charges, whether made effective through quotas, import or export licenses or other measures, shall be instituted or maintained by any contracting party on the importation of any product of the territory of any other contracting party or on the exportation or sale for export of any product destined for the territory of any other contracting party.

---

[18] 1994 General Agreement on Tariffs and Trade (hereafter 'GATT 1994'), Article III(4).

[19] Article III(1).   [20] Article III(2).   [21] Article III(1).

[22] *Japan—Taxes on Alcoholic Beverages*, Appellate Body Report, WTO Doc AB-1996-2 (1996) 17–25 ['*Japan Shochu Case*']; *EC—Measures Affecting Asbestos and Asbestos-Containing Products*, WT/DS135/AB/R (2001) paras 87–100 ['*Asbestos Case*'].

[23] *Italian Discrimination against Imported Machinery*, GATT BISD (7th Supp) 60, para 12 (1959).

[24] *US—Section 337 of the Tariff Act of 1930*, 7 Nov 1989, GATT BISD (36th Supp), 345, para 5.1.1 (1990). This ruling means that the actual economic impact of a discriminatory measure or tax is irrelevant: see *US—Taxes on Petroleum and Certain Imported Substances*, GATT BISD (34th Supp), 136, para 5.19 (1988) (hereafter '*US Superfund*').

Article XI concerns more than just quotas. It also extends to 'other measures... instituted or maintained on the importation... or exportation... of any product'. The word 'measures' in this formulation was interpreted in the *Japan Semi-Conductor Case* to refer not only to laws and regulations, but also, more broadly, even to non-mandatory government involvement.[25] Thus, Article XI is comprehensive in scope; it deals with everything other than fiscal matters.

As for the relationship between Articles III and XI, in the *Canada Foreign Investment Review Act Case*,[26] the GATT dispute-resolution panel interpreted Article XI as regulating only measures affecting the importation (or exportation) of a product, not internal requirements affecting imported products, which are left to Article III. This mutual exclusivity of Articles III and XI often presents difficulty and can be understood only in the context of the correct methodology for applying the tests of the two articles. The measure in question should *first* be analysed as to whether it is protected by Article III. If it fails the tests of Article III, then Article XI is automatically applicable and, unless it falls under one of the narrow exemptions in that article, the measure will violate the GATT. One such exception is import restrictions on agricultural or fisheries products that are necessary for the enforcement of certain governmental measures.[27]

(b) GATT environmental exceptions

The 'General Exceptions' provision of the GATT, Article XX,[28] constitutes conditional exceptions to GATT obligations, including those in Articles I, III, and XI. Although the word 'environment' is not used,[29] Article XX may be applied to justify certain environmentally inspired rules that affect free trade. The pertinent wording of Article XX is as follows:

Subject to the requirement that such measures are not applied in a manner which would constitute a means of arbitrary or unjustifiable discrimination between countries where the same conditions prevail, or a disguised restriction on international trade, nothing in this

---

[25] *Japan—Trade in Semi-Conductors*, GATT BISD (35th Supp) 115, paras 106–9 (1989). The panel set out a two-part test for determining whether non-mandatory government requests could be regarded as 'measures' within Article XI: (i) whether there were sufficient incentives for the requests to take effect; and (ii) whether the operation of the measures was dependent on government action. Non-binding 'administrative guidance' by the Japanese government was ruled in the *Semi-Conductor Case* to be within Article XI.

[26] *Canada—Administration of the Foreign Investment Review Act*, GATT BISD (30th Supp) 140, para 5.14 (1984).

[27] Article XI(2) excepts three types of measures from the prohibition of Article XI(1), the other two being export restrictions to relieve critical shortages of foodstuffs and other products 'essential' to the exporting contracting party, and import or export restrictions necessary to the application of standards for grading or classifying commodities.

[28] As indicated above, a virtually identical 'General Exception' appears in Article XIV GATS.

[29] The word 'environment', meaning nature and the natural world, came into current use only in the 1960s. The GATT, drafted in 1947, uses the older term, 'natural resources': GATT 1994, Article XX(g). For detailed discussion of the drafting history of the environmental exceptions in Article XX, see Charnovitz, 25 *JWT* (1991) 37.

Agreement shall be construed to prevent the adoption or enforcement by any contracting party of measures:

...

   (b) necessary to protect human, animal or plant life or health;...

   (g) relating to the conservation of exhaustible natural resources if such measures are made effective in conjunction with restrictions on domestic production or consumption.

The burden of showing that an Article XX exception applies is placed upon the party asserting it as a defence.[30] This burden has not often been discharged, largely because of the strictness with which its provisions are interpreted. An understanding of Article XX requires careful interpretation.

(i) The chapeau   The entire catalogue of exceptions under Article XX is qualified by an introductory clause commonly termed the *chapeau*. Even if a measure otherwise falls within one of the exceptions in Article XX, it would be illegal under the *chapeau* if it constitutes (i) arbitrary or unjustifiable discrimination between countries where the same conditions prevail, or (ii) a disguised restriction on international trade. In 1996, the significance of the *chapeau* was emphasized by the WTO Appellate Body in the *US Gasoline Standards* decision.[31] This case involved the reformulated and conventional gasoline programmes established under the Clean Air Act Amendments of 1990. Both programmes required changes in the composition of gasoline sold to consumers, using 1990 as a baseline year. The baseline establishment rules of the Environmental Protection Agency (EPA), however, distinguished between foreign and domestic producers and refiners: domestic refiners were permitted to establish individual 1990 baselines, but foreign refiners generally were not allowed to do so and were required instead to use a statutory baseline established by the EPA. The WTO Appellate Body found that the measure could be justified under Article XX(g) but that it nonetheless constituted 'unjustifiable discrimination' and a 'disguised restriction on international trade' contrary to the *chapeau*. It noted that the USA could have avoided the discrimination involved in the baseline rules in two ways: either by imposing statutory baselines on both domestic producers and importers, or by making individual baselines available to all. The Appellate Body rejected the reasons the USA set forth for not following one of these options: administrative difficulties and problems of verification and enforcement. Thus, the Appellate Body interpreted the *chapeau* as invalidating a measure that otherwise meets the requirements of Article XX if it involves unjustified or arbitrary discrimination; and such discrimination tends to show that a measure is a 'disguised' trade restriction as well.

(ii) Article XX(b)   Interpreting Article XX(b) commonly requires a three-step analysis. First, does the measure in question protect human, animal, or plant life or health?

---

[30] *Canada—Administration of the Foreign Investment Review Act, supra*, n 26, para 5.20.

[31] *US—Standards for Reformulated and Conventional Gasoline*, Report of the Appellate Body, WT/DS2/AB/R (1996); 35 *ILM* (1996) 274 ['*US Gasoline Standards Case*'].

Second, is the measure for which the exception is being invoked *necessary* for this purpose? Third, is the measure applied consistently with the *chapeau*, avoiding arbitrary or unjustifiable discrimination and/or a disguised restriction on international trade?[32] The Appellate Body has held that a measure is 'necessary' under Article XX(b) if no GATT-consistent alternative is reasonably available and provided it entails the least degree of inconsistency with other GATT provisions.[33]

(iii) Article XX(g) Article XX(g) is an important GATT exception designed to allow WTO members to take action to conserve exhaustible natural resources. It contains four separate requirements: (i) that the measures for which the provision is invoked concern 'exhaustible natural resources' ; (ii) that these measures are related to the 'conservation' of those resources; (iii) that the measures are made effective in conjunction with restrictions on domestic production or consumption; and (iv) that the measures are applied in conformity with the requirements of the *chapeau* of Article XX.[34]

What is obvious from this brief preliminary discussion is that the GATT Agreement does not provide a simple or straightforward framework for resolving conflicts between free trade and environmental protection. Both the interpretation of Article XX and its application to multilateral environmental agreements have proved difficult in practice. These problems and the central dilemma of how to reconcile competing social and economic values have been addressed through two WTO institutions: the Committee on Trade and Environment, and the Dispute Settlement Body. It is also intended to be addressed in the current Doha round of trade negotiations, still ongoing as of mid-2008, with paragraph 31(i) of the Doha Ministerial Declaration, adopted in 2001, committing WTO members to negotiate on the relationship between WTO rules and 'specific trade obligations' set forth in MEAs.[35]

2(3) THE COMMITTEE ON TRADE AND ENVIRONMENT

At the meeting held to sign the Final Act Embodying the Results of the Uruguay Round of Multilateral Trade Negotiations in Marrakesh on 14 April 1994, the GATT contracting parties adopted a Ministerial Decision that formally established a new

---

[32] See the *Asbestos Case, supra*, n 22, paras 155–75, and *infra*, section 4(3).   [33] Ibid, paras 164–75.

[34] E.g., *US Gasoline Standards Case, supra*, n 31, where the Appellate Body held that clean air is an exhaustible natural resource. See section 4, *infra*.

[35] Para 31(i) instructs WTO Members to negotiate on 'the relationship between existing WTO rules and specific trade obligations set out in multilateral environmental agreements (MEAs). The negotiations shall be limited in scope to the applicability of such existing WTO rules as among parties to the MEA in question. The negotiation shall not prejudice the WTO rights of any Member that is not a party to the MEA in questions.' Paragraph 31(ii) is addressed to 'procedures for regular information exchange between MEA Secretariats and the relevant WTO committees, and the criteria for the granting of observer status' while the final paragraph addresses 'the reduction or, as appropriate, elimination of tariff and non-tariff barriers to environmental goods and services'. These negotiations take place in special sessions of the CTE, with proposals submitted by WTO members available at <http://www.wto.org>.

Committee on Trade and Environment (CTE)[36] under the auspices of the World Trade Organization. The CTE was charged with making appropriate recommendations on 'the need for rules to enhance the positive interaction between trade and environment measures for the promotion of sustainable development'. It was asked to address the following matters:

(1) the relationship between the provisions of the multilateral trading system and trade measures for environmental purposes, including those pursuant to multilateral environmental agreements

(2) the relationship between environmental policies relevant to trade and environmental measures with significant trade effects and the provisions of the multilateral trading system

(3) the relationship between the provisions of the multilateral trading system and:

    (a) charges and taxes for environmental purposes

    (b) requirements for environmental purposes relating to products, including standards and technical regulations, packaging, labelling and recycling

(4) the provisions of the multilateral trading system with respect to the transparency of trade measures used for environmental purposes and environmental measures and requirements which have significant trade effects

(5) the relationship between the dispute settlement mechanisms in the multilateral trading system and those found in multilateral environmental agreements

(6) the effect of environmental measures on market access, especially in relation to developing countries, in particular to the least developed among them, and environmental benefits of removing trade restrictions and distortions

(7) the issue of exports of domestically prohibited goods

(8) the relevant provisions of the Agreement on Trade-Related Aspects of Intellectual Property Rights

(9) the work programme envisaged in Decision on Trade in Services and the Environment

(10) input to the relevant bodies in respect of appropriate arrangements for relations with intergovernmental and non-governmental organizations.[37]

There has been little progress in the CTE on these issues. Directed by the Marrakesh decision to report to the first WTO Ministerial Conference in Singapore in 1996, this first report of the Committee[38] is primarily a compilation of the debates within the CTE and the views of its members. There is very little analysis and evaluation and

---

[36] *Trade and Environment*, GATT Ministerial Decision of 14 April 1994, 33 *ILM* (1994) 1267. See Charnovitz, 8 *YbIEL* (1997) 98, 106ff and Shaffer, in Steinberg (ed), *The Greening of Trade Law* (Rowman and Littlefield Publishers, 2002) 81–114.

[37] GATT Ministerial Decision, 1994, 1267–9.

[38] WTO Doc WT/CTE/1 (1996) (hereafter 'CTE Report').

virtually no recommendations for specific actions.[39] Seen in its best light, the report provided a foundation for future progress, confirming the need for transparency, cooperation and the determination to accommodate environmental values. This is reflected in the final declaration of the Singapore Ministerial Conference giving the CTE a mandate to continue its work.[40]

Since 1996, the CTE has not taken any concrete decisions on how to reconcile trade and environmental concerns. Its output has been meager, with annual reports notable principally for their brevity.[41] Its significance lies rather in the 'institutionalization of environmental issues into WTO processes' which it symbolizes, and the opportunity its meetings afford for 'socialization' between trade officials and representatives of selected MEAs.[42] Substantive progress in the CTE remains blocked, however, principally because there remain deep divisions between the most economically developed members, such as the EC and the USA, which support introducing environmental values more explicitly into trade agreements, and the majority of developing member states, who see this as a cover for discrimination against their products.[43] There are also growing differences between the EC and the USA over such matters as the precautionary principle, most recently reflected in the *EC—Biotech* dispute over GMOs. The cumbersome WTO decision-making process, relying on consensus, virtually assures continuing deadlock in meetings of the parties. Thus it is principally in the WTO Appellate Body that some progress has been made in meeting environmental concerns, most notably in the *Shrimp-Turtle* and *Asbestos* decisions considered below.[44]

2(4) WTO DISPUTE SETTLEMENT[45]

One of the great strengths of the WTO is the system of compulsory binding dispute settlement created by the Understanding on Rules and Procedures Governing the

---

[39] The report summarizes the result of two years of deliberations as follows: 'Work in the WTO on contributing to build a constructive policy relationship between trade, environment and sustainable development needs to continue': Ibid, 47.

[40] Singapore Ministerial Declaration, para 16, WTO Doc WT/MIN(96)/DEC/W (1996), 36 *ILM* (1997) 218, 224.

[41] See Charnovitz, 10 *JIEL* (2007) 685, 687 On the other hand, the WTO Secretariat's Trade and Environment Division has published background papers (e.g. WTO Special Studies, *Trade and Environment* (Geneva, 1999)) and a widely cited 1999 Report on Trade and Environment, *Report of the Committee on Trade and Environment*, WT/CTE/4 (1999).

[42] Ibid.

[43] See *Report of the Committee on Trade and Environment*, WT/CTE/4 (1999) and WTO Special Studies, *Trade and Environment* (Geneva, 1999).

[44] *US—Import Prohibition of Certain Shrimp and Shrimp Products*, WT/DS58/AB/R (1998); *European Communities—Measures Affecting Asbestos and Asbestos-Containing Products*, WT/DS135/AB/R (2001). See *infra*, sections 3, 4.

[45] See Petersmann, *The GATT/WTO Dispute Settlement System* (The Hague, 1997); Palmeter and Mavroidis, *Dispute Settlement in the World Trade Organization: Practice and Procedure* (The Hague, 1999); Trebilcock and Howse, *The Regulation of International Trade* (2nd edn, London, 1999) Ch 4; Matsushita, Schoenbaum and Mavroidis, *The World Trade Organization: Law, Practice and Policy* (2nd edn Oxford, 2006) Ch 2.

Settlement of Disputes adopted in 1994.[46] The WTO dispute-settlement system is administered by the Dispute Settlement Body (DSB). Disputes between members arising under the Multilateral Trade Agreements ('covered agreements') are first remitted to consultations,[47] but if these are not successful, may be adjudicated by panels and appealed to an Appellate Body.[48] Decisions must be implemented by the parties within a reasonable period of time, normally not more than fifteen months from the date of adoption of a panel or Appellate Body Report.[49] In the event of non-compliance, a member can be subjected to sanctions in the form of compensation and suspension of concessions.[50]

This system of dispute settlement is neither self-contained nor static, although the jurisdiction of the DSB extends only to matters arising under the 'covered agreements'.[51] In interpreting WTO agreements the Appellate Body has followed the general rule codified in Article 31(3) of the 1969 Vienna Convention on the Law of Treaties that account may be taken of 'any relevant rules of international law applicable in the relations between the parties'.[52] Since these rules necessarily develop over time, the interpretation given to provisions of WTO agreements is not static but evolutionary. Thus, in the *Shrimp-Turtle* decision, the Appellate Body referred, inter alia, to the 1992 Rio Declaration on Environment and Development, the 1982 UNCLOS, the 1973 CITES Convention, the 1979 Convention on Conservation of Migratory Species, and the 1992 Convention on Biological Diversity. Rather than interpreting GATT Article XX(g) ('exhaustible natural resources') in accordance with whatever might have been the intention of the drafters in 1947, the Appellate Body took account of these much later and directly relevant agreements. In this respect it was following the approach adopted by the International Court of Justice in the *Gabčíkovo-Nagymaros Case* when that Court read the 1977 treaty between Hungary and Czechoslovakia in conjunction with subsequent developments in international environmental law. However, in the more recent *EC—Biotech* decision, the Panel interpreted 'rules of

---

[46] Hereafter the 'DSU'. See also 1947 GATT, Articles XXII–XXIII and 1994 Agreement Establishing the World Trade Organization, Annex 2, in WTO, *Legal Texts, supra*, n 1.

[47] DSU, Article 4. Alternative dispute settlement procedures such as conciliation, good offices, mediation, and arbitration also may be employed: see Articles 5, 25.

[48] DSU, Articles 6, 17.

[49] DSU, Article 21. Reports of the panels and Appellate Body must be adopted unless there is a consensus against.

[50] DSU, Article 22. For an assessment of the effectiveness of WTO remedies, see Mavroidis, 11 *EJIL* (2000), 763.

[51] DSU, Articles 2–3. See, generally, Pauwelyn, *Conflict of Norms in Public International Law, How WTO Law Relates to other Rules of International Law* (Cambridge, 2003).

[52] See Sands, in Boyle and Freestone (eds), *International Law and Sustainable Development* (Oxford, 1999) Ch 3; Howse, in Weiler (ed), *The EU, the WTO and the NAFTA* (Oxford, 2000) 55–9; Boyle, in Bodansky, Brunnee and Hey (eds), *The Oxford Handbook of International Environmental Law* (Oxford, 2007) 136–8. On Article 31(3)(c) see McLachlan, 54 *ICLQ* (2005) 279; on the use of environmental agreements thereunder see French, 55 *ICLQ* (2006) 281; and see *supra*, Ch 3.

international law applicable' to mean those treaties applicable between all parties, and thus declined to use the Biodiversity Convention and Cartagena Protocol.[53]

Most importantly, Article 3(2) of the WTO Dispute Settlement Understanding expressly provides that the existing provisions of the 'covered agreements' are to be clarified 'in accordance with customary rules of interpretation of public international law'.[54] In a major break with pre-1994 GATT jurisprudence, the Appellate Body has made it clear that this means interpreting WTO agreements in accordance with international law on interpretation of treaties, as codified in Articles 31–3 of the Vienna Convention, and not in accordance with specific GATT canons of interpretation. The importance of this change in helping resolve trade-environment conflicts cannot be understated. As one author observes:

the very decision to follow these general public international law interpretative norms enhances the legitimacy of the dispute settlement organs in adjudicating competing values—because these norms are common to international law generally, including regimes that give priority to very different values, and are not specific to a regime that has traditionally privileged a single value, that of free trade.[55]

The Appellate Body's more consistent and internationally principled approach to interpretation, and the reference to sustainable development in the preamble to the 1994 GATT, have helped it move away from the more rigidly free trade focus of earlier GATT panel awards, such as the *Tuna-Dolphin Cases*. It has thus been able to begin the task of developing a new and more environmentally nuanced jurisprudence, in a manner which appears to justify the decision taken at Marrakesh in 1994 to create a more formally judicial dispute-settlement machinery. It should be noted that it has done so without the requirement for specific environmental expertise within the Appellate Body.[56] There is no provision in the Understanding on Rules and Procedures Governing the Settlement of Disputes (DSU) for panels adjudicating environmental cases to have specific environmental expertise, in contrast with, for example, the requirement that panels adjudicating 'prudential issues and other financial matters' under GATS have the necessary financial services expertise.

---

[53] Panel Report, *European Communities—Measures Affecting the Approval and Marketing of Biotech Products*, WT/DS291/R, WT/DS292/R, WT/DS293/R, adopted 21 November 2006, paras 7.70–7.95, hereafter *EC—Biotech*. For analysis on this point see Young, 56 *ICLQ* (2007) 907.

[54] These are codified in Articles 31–3 of the Vienna Convention. On treaty interpretation under the Vienna Convention see Sinclair, *The Vienna Convention on the Law of Treaties* (Manchester, 1984) 114–58 and Aust, *Modern Treaty Law and Practice* (Cambridge, 2000) Ch 13.

[55] Howse, in Weiler (ed), *The EU, the WTO and the NAFTA* (Oxford, 2000) 54. See also Palmeter and Mavroidis, *Dispute Settlement in the World Trade Organization: Practice and Procedure* (The Hague, 1999) 84–5; Nichols, 36 *VJIL* (1996) 379, 434–5.

[56] However, it has been noted that the presiding Judge in the Appellate Body which reversed WTO panel holdings which 'threatened to render the environmental exceptions unusable' in *US Gasoline Standards, Shrimp-Turtle* and *EC-Asbestos Cases* was Florentino Feliciano: see Charnovitz, 10 *JIEL* (2007) n 53; see also Jackson, in Charnovitz, Steger and van den Bossche (eds), *Law in the Service of Human Dignity. Essays in Honour of Florentino Feliciano* (Cambridge, 2005).

An issue considered by the CTE, but not yet by the Appellate Body, is what is the most appropriate forum for the settlement of a dispute over trade that arises in connection with a multilateral environmental agreement? The CTE's view is that, in the first instance, such disputes should be resolved through the mechanisms established by the multilateral environmental agreement, rather than through WTO procedures. In practice, however, this solution is largely illusory because, as we saw in Chapter 4, dispute settlement under multilateral environmental instruments is rarely compulsory or binding, and generally requires the agreement of the parties. Disputes involving trade and environment agreements have thus arisen, so far, only in compulsory proceedings before the WTO Dispute Settlement Body[57] and, as we discuss below, exclusively in the context of unilateral action by states.

3 MULTILATERAL ENVIRONMENTAL AGREEMENTS AND TRADE RESTRICTIONS

Nonetheless there remains a question of paramount importance: how will the WTO/GATT system accommodate multilateral environmental agreements (MEAs) that employ trade restrictions?[58] Leading examples of such MEAs include the Montreal Protocol on Substances that Deplete the Ozone Layer,[59] which adopts trade controls that are more restrictive as to non-parties than parties; the Convention on International Trade in Endangered Species (CITES),[60] which regulates imports and exports in certain species of animals and plants and allows punitive trade restrictions to be imposed on non-complying parties; and the Basel Convention on the Control of Transboundary Movements of Hazardous Wastes,[61] which prohibits exports and imports of hazardous and other wastes by parties to the Convention to and from non-party states.

---

[57] To date only three environmental disputes have been fully completed under the WTO's dispute settlement process: *US Gasoline Standards* (1996), *Shrimp-Turtle* (1998) and *EC-Asbestos* (2001). But see the parallel ITLOS/WTO proceedings in Chile–EC: *Case Concerning the Conservation and Sustainable Exploitation of Swordfish Stocks in the South-Eastern Pacific Ocean*, ITLOS No 7, Order No 2000/3 (2000), and EC–Chile: *Measures Affecting the Transit and Importation of Swordfish* (WTO, 2000) (WT/DS193). The 1982 LOSC remains the only agreement with environmental provisions whose interrelationship with WTO law has been explored by an international tribunal.

[58] See Cameron and Robinson, 2 *YbIEL* (1991) 3; Tarasofsky, 7 *YbIEL* (1996) 52; Brack, 9 *YbIEL* (1998) 13; and references in n 3 above. The WTO Secretariat has identified a least 14 MEAs which contain trade-related measures: Note by the Secretariat, *Matrix on Trade Measures Pursuant to Multilateral Trade Agreements*, WT/CTE/W/160/Rev 3 TN/TE/S/5/Rev 1, 16 February 2005.

[59] See *supra*, Ch 10. The question has also been raised whether the Multilateral Fund established under the Protocol amounts to an actionable subsidy contrary to the SCM Agreement: Benitah, *Subsidies, Services and Sustainable Development* (Geneva, 2004) 23 (in the context of GATS); Goyal, *The WTO and International Environmental Law; Towards Conciliation* (New Delhi, 2006) Ch 5.

[60] See *supra*, Ch 12.   [61] See *supra*, Ch 8.

No WTO/GATT dispute-resolution panel yet has directly addressed the conformity of any MEA trade restrictions with GATT rules. However, the validity of some MEA trade restrictions is at least doubtful, in particular those involving process and production methods, discrimination between parties and non-parties, and extra-territorial application.[62] The question of conformity between MEAs and the GATT was heightened by the promulgation of GATT 1994 and the creation of the WTO. These events reset the GATT from 1947 to 1994, theoretically allowing the GATT to trump any inconsistent provisions of an earlier MEA, even between parties that are parties to both treaty regimes.[63] Different solutions may be suggested according to whether the incompatibility arises between, say, a measure under the 1997 Kyoto Protocol and the GATT 1994, than for the 1973 CITES and GATT 1994. Further complexities arise due to the flexible nature of many environmental treaties, with subsequent amendment and use of additional trade-restrictive mechanisms (e.g. non-compliance procedures) rendering a 'one stop shop' approach to treaty interpretation insufficient to address the trade and environmental conflicts which may arise. As the Montreal Protocol[64] experience reveals, even where the trade/environment interface is addressed at the treaty design stage, the dynamic and evolutive character of contemporary MEAs requires some degree of ongoing monitoring of the potential for conflict. The provisions of the 1987 Montreal Protocol were submitted to the GATT Secretariat for an opinion (not binding either on the Parties to the GATT nor to the Montreal Protocol). Not addressed at that time was the design of the non-compliance procedure under the Protocol, which only came into operation in 1992 following further adjustments to the Protocol. Included within the list of indicative measures in response to non-compliance with the Protocol is the suspension of trading privileges under Article 4. In practice the decisions on non-compliance have generally relied on facilitative measures to assist in a return to compliance, but with the suspension of trading privileges held out as a possible further measure. This was threatened against Russia, which evidently gave consideration to remitting the non-compliance measures taken against it to the GATT/WTO for an assessment of their compatibility.[65]

Were such a challenge to be mounted, as a general matter it should be reinforced that both the WTO Committee on Trade and Environment and the Appellate Body are not 'anti-MEA'. The CTE has endorsed 'multilateral solutions based on international cooperation and consensus as the best and most effective way for governments to tackle environmental problems of a transboundary or global nature'.[66] The GATT panel in the *Tuna-Dolphin I Case* stated that dolphins could be protected through 'international cooperative arrangements'.[67] The WTO dispute-settlement panel and the Appellate Body in the *Shrimp-Turtle Case* expressed strong favour for MEAs as well, with the latter encouraging the USA to seek international agreement on turtle conservation

---

[62] See Wold, 16 *Envtl L* (1996) 841. [63] For further discussion see *supra*, Ch 1.
[64] See *supra*, Ch 10. [65] Werksman, 56 *ZAÖRV* (1996) 750.
[66] CTE Report, *supra*, n 38, para 171.
[67] *US—Restrictions on Imports of Tuna*, Report of the Panel, 30 *ILM* (1991) 1598, para 5.28 (not adopted by the GATT Council) (hereafter, '*Tuna-Dolphin I*').

and tolerant of the time-scale required to achieve such agreement.[68] Nonetheless, it is difficult to predict how a WTO panel would rule on particular MEAs. Thus, there is the need to clarify their legal status.

There are four basic ways in which the WTO could address the relationship between GATT and multilateral environmental agreements. First, each MEA could be examined on a case-by-case basis using Article IX(3) of the Agreement Establishing the World Trade Organization. This provision allows waiver of any obligation under 'exceptional circumstances' by vote of a three-fourths majority of the member states. For several reasons this solution seems unsatisfactory. The WTO would abdicate from setting criteria to influence MEAs and thus states would have no prior guidance when framing them. Moreover, the test of 'exceptional circumstances' is unduly vague. Approval under the waiver provision would be a political decision rather than one on the substance of the case. Furthermore, the status of MEAs would be doubtful until they had received the *ex post* blessing of a waiver.

A second possible solution is to follow the approach of the North American Free Trade Agreement (NAFTA), which provides that certain MEAs (such as the Montreal Protocol, CITES, and the Basel Convention) take precedence over NAFTA obligations.[69] This clarifies the status of certain existing MEAs, but does not provide a process for the addition of future MEAs so remains dependent on the agreement of all three NAFTA parties (Canada, USA, and Mexico) Furthermore, an ad hoc approach such as this may be workable for an organization of three states, but may not be for the WTO.

Two additional alternatives are either to amend Article XX by adding a provision on MEAs, or to adopt a collective interpretation[70] of Article XX, that would validate existing MEAs and provide for notification of future MEAs as well as setting out criteria, a 'safe harbour', they would have to fulfil to receive approval.[71] A model for MEAs might be GATT Article XX(h), which creates an exception for trade measures imposed pursuant to obligations in international commodity agreements that are otherwise illegal under the GATT. Article XX(h) sets out two methods of approval: first, commodity agreements that conform to specified criteria are valid automatically; second, other commodity agreements can be validated on an ad hoc basis if they are submitted to the GATT contracting parties and not disapproved. Hudec advocates a similar GATT

---

[68] *US—Import Prohibition of Certain Shrimp and Shrimp Products*, Report of the Panel, WT/DS58/R (1998), para 50; Report of the Appellate Body, WT/DS58/AB/R (1998) 68–9 ['*Shrimp-Turtle Case*']. On the failure to achieve a negotiated solution, see *US—Shrimp, Recourse to Art 21.5 of the DSU by Malaysia*, Report of the Appellate Body, WT/DS58/AB/RW (2001).

[69] 1992 North American Free Trade Agreement, Article 104(1), 32 *ILM* (1993) 296, 605. See Abbott, in Weiler (ed), *The EU, the WTO and the NAFTA: Towards a Common Law of International Trade* (Oxford, 2000) Ch 6.

[70] An interpretation can be adopted by a three-quarters majority vote of the WTO Ministerial Conference: WTO Agreement, Article IX (2) *supra*, n 1.

[71] These ideas are discussed in Rege, 28 *JWT* (1994) 95, 124–9; and in Hudec and Bhagwati (eds), *Fair Trade and Harmonization* (Cambridge, Mass, 1996) ii, 120–42. See also Charnovitz, 26 *EPL* (1996) 163.

amendment for MEAs.[72] Such an amendment[73] might provide (i) that negotiation of the MEA shall be under the auspices of the United Nations Environment Programme (UNEP) or a similar organization, and accession shall be open to all states that have a legitimate interest in the environmental problem addressed; (ii) that the problem dealt with must relate to serious environmental harm; (iii) that there be a reasonable relationship between the trade restrictions adopted and the object and purposes of the MEA; and (iv) that the MEA must be formally notified to the WTO. This would effectively immunize current and future MEAs from attack under WTO/GATT rules.

The likelihood of any of these changes being adopted is minimal, however, because of the deadlock in the CTE. Thus, it seems most probable that the task of reconciling MEAs with the GATT will primarily be a matter for the WTO dispute-settlement panels and the Appellate Body to resolve. In the *Shrimp-Turtle* decision the Appellate Body clearly upheld the right of WTO members to legislate for the protection of natural resources beyond national boundaries, provided they do so pursuant to an MEA. In coming to this conclusion, it adopted an interpretation of GATT Article XX which would permit MEAs in appropriate circumstances to derogate from GATT obligations.[74] This important decision, and its more controversial predecessors, are considered in the following section.

4 TRADE RESTRICTIONS TO PROTECT RESOURCES BEYOND NATIONAL JURISDICTION

4(1) UNILATERAL TRADE SANCTIONS UNDER 1947 GATT

Whether there is scope under GATT for unilateral state action to protect resources or the environment in areas beyond national jurisdiction was first addressed by the celebrated *Tuna-Dolphin I Case*[75] decided by a GATT panel in 1991. Acting under the Marine Mammal Protection Act (MMPA), the USA had banned imports of yellow fin tuna caught using methods that also kill dolphins, a protected species under the MMPA. Upon Mexico's complaint to the GATT, a dispute-settlement panel found that the US tuna embargo violated GATT Article XI(1), which forbids measures prohibiting or restricting imports or exports. The USA sought to justify the embargo under GATT Article III(1) and (4) since US fishermen were subject to the same MMPA rules. The GATT panel rejected the US argument on the grounds that Article III(1) and (4) permit only regulations relating to products as such. Since the MMPA regulations concerned

---

[72] Ibid, 125–45.

[73] A similar proposal has been put forward by the European Union. *See* CTE Report, *supra*, n 38, 5–6.

[74] *Shrimp-Turtle Case*, Appellate Body Report, paras 171–2, and see *infra*.

[75] *Tuna-Dolphin I, supra*, n 67. For an excellent commentary, see Kingsbury, 5 *YbIEL* (1994) 1.

harvesting techniques which could not possibly affect tuna as a *product*, the ban on tuna could not be justified. This reasoning was reiterated by a second GATT panel in the *Tuna-Dolphin II* decision,[76] which involved the legality of a secondary embargo of tuna products from countries that processed tuna caught by the offending countries. This GATT panel condemned the unilateral boycott in even stronger terms.[77]

Both *Tuna-Dolphin* panels also concluded that neither GATT Articles XX(b) nor XX(g) could justify the US tuna import ban. As to Article XX(b), both panels held that the ban failed the 'necessary' test. They rejected the US argument that 'necessary' means 'needed', stating that 'necessary' means that no other reasonable alternative exists and that 'a contracting party is bound to use, among the measures available to it, that which entails the least degree of inconsistency' with the GATT.[78] A trade measure taken to force other countries to change their environmental policies, and that would be effective only if such changes occurred, could not be considered 'necessary' within the meaning of Article XX(b).[79] Both panels similarly concluded that Article XX(g) was not applicable; they found that the terms 'relating to' and 'in conjunction with' in Article XX(g) meant 'primarily aimed at', and held that unilateral measures to force other countries to change conservation policies cannot satisfy the 'primarily aimed at' standard.[80]

The *Tuna-Dolphin* decisions must now be read in the light of later jurisprudence formulated by the WTO Appellate Body, considered below.

4(2) THE EXTRATERRITORIAL SCOPE OF ARTICLE XX (B) AND (G) UNDER 1947 GATT

The GATT panels in the two *Tuna-Dolphin Cases* came to different conclusions regarding the territorial application of Article XX(b) and (g). The *Tuna-Dolphin I* panel concluded that the natural resources and living things protected under these provisions were only those within the territorial jurisdiction of the country concerned.[81] This view, which was based on the belief that the drafters of Article XX had focused on each contracting party's domestic concerns, has been widely criticized.[82] The *Tuna-Dolphin II* panel, in contrast, 'could see no valid reason supporting the conclusion that the provisions of Article XX(g) apply only to ... the conservation of exhaustible natural resources located within the territory of the contracting party invoking

---

[76] *US—Restrictions on Imports of Tuna*, 33 ILM (1994) 839, para 5.29 (hereafter '*Tuna-Dolphin II*'). This decision was not adopted by the GATT Council.

[77] Ibid, paras 5.38–5.39.

[78] *Tuna-Dolphin I, supra*, n 67, para 5.27; *Tuna-Dolphin II, supra*, n 76, para 5.35.

[79] *Tuna-Dolphin I, supra*, n 67, para 5.27; *Tuna-Dolphin II, supra*, n 76, paras 5.36–5.38.

[80] *Tuna-Dolphin I, supra*, n 67, para 5.33; *Tuna-Dolphin II, supra*, n 76, para 5.26.

[81] *Tuna-Dolphin I, supra*, n 67, paras 5.26, 5.31.

[82] See, e.g. Snape and Lefkovitz, 27 *Cornell ILJ* (1994) 777, 782–90; Ferrante, 5 *J Transnatl L & Pol* (1996) 279, 297.

the provision'.[83] Nevertheless, the panel ruled that governments can enforce an Article XX(g) restriction extraterritorially only against their own nationals and vessels.[84]

To justify its ruling, the *Tuna-Dolphin II* panel distinguished between extraterritorial and extra-jurisdictional application of Article XX. This is a salutary distinction that makes eminent sense. The extraterritorial application of Article XX(b) and (g) is supported by analysis based on the norms of treaty interpretation under the Vienna Convention on Treaties, Article 31(1) of which requires that treaties be interpreted 'in good faith in accordance with the ordinary meaning [of] the terms of the Treaty in their context'. Together with the 'context', the parties should take into account 'any relevant rules of international law applicable in the relations between the parties'. It is well established as a matter of international law that states have an obligation to prevent damage to both the environment of other states and areas beyond the limits of national jurisdiction.[85] Thus, it should be beyond doubt that paragraphs (b) and (g) of Article XX permit national measures designed to protect extraterritorial resources.

The *Tuna-Dolphin II* panel's position on extraterritorial jurisdiction is based on the concept of nationality, under which a state may control the activities of its own citizens. Other theories of extraterritorial jurisdiction include passive personality jurisdiction over crimes against nationals; objective territorial jurisdiction, where the effect of an extraterritorial act is felt within a state; protective jurisdiction to deal with national security risks; and universal jurisdiction in cases of piracy and certain other crimes.[86] These other international law jurisdictional doctrines seemingly have little relevance to Article XX. Thus, the *Tuna-Dolphin II* panel's conclusion is essentially correct: Article XX may have *extraterritorial*, but not *extra-jurisdictional* effect.

4(3) THE NEW WTO APPROACH UNDER 1994 GATT

The two *Tuna-Dolphin* GATT panel decisions represented the first tentative steps of the multilateral trading system to come to terms with protection of the environment. Neither decision was binding under the GATT because they were not adopted by the contracting parties. Even if they had been, they would have little force as precedents because their reasoning was partially inconsistent and the decisions of prior GATT or WTO panels are not binding on future panels.[87] Moreover, these decisions pre-dated the entry into force of the WTO Agreement and the establishment of the new dispute settlement body. The WTO Appellate Body has been fashioning its own approach to interpretation of Article XX that makes significantly greater allowance for legitimate measures of environmental protection.

---

[83] *Tuna-Dolphin II*, para 5.20.   [84] Ibid.

[85] See, e.g. Rio Declaration on Environment and Development, Principle 2; 1982 UNCLOS, Articles 192–5, and *supra*, Ch 3.

[86] See Higgins, *Problems and Process: International Law and How We Use It* (Oxford, 1994) 56–77.

[87] *Japan Shochu Case*, *supra*, n 22, at 14.

(a) GATT Article XX(g)

A consistent theory of interpretation of Article XX(g) has been advanced by the Appellate Body in two important cases, the *US Gasoline Standards Case*[88] and the *Shrimp-Turtle Case*[89]. The latter is particularly relevant because it involved a trade measure similar to that employed in the *Tuna-Dolphin Cases*, a ban on imported shrimp from countries that do not require their fishermen to harvest shrimp with methods that do not pose a threat to sea turtles. As such it marks the contrast in approach by the WTO Appellate Body to environmental disputes compared with earlier GATT panels. The first issue that must be addressed under Article XX(g) is whether the particular trade measure[90] concerns the conservation of exhaustible natural resources.[91] The Appellate Body has taken a generous view of this matter, adopting an evolutive approach to the interpretation of the term 'natural resources' which does not have static content and 'must be read by a treaty interpreter in the light of contemporary concerns of the community of nations about the protection and conservation of the environment'.[92] A 'resource' may be living or non-living, and it need not be rare or endangered to be potentially 'exhaustible'. Thus, dolphins, clean air, gasoline, and sea turtles all qualify. Under this expansive interpretation, virtually any living or non-living resource, particularly those addressed by multilateral environmental agreements, would qualify.

The second 'relating to' element of Article XX(g) has proved more difficult to apply. Although a trade measure does not have to be 'necessary' (as in Article XX(b)) to natural resource conservation, the WTO/GATT panels have interpreted 'relating to' to mean that it must be 'primarily aimed at' conservation.[93] Thus phrased, this requirement has proved a difficult obstacle. The question arises whether the 'primarily aimed at' interpretation of 'relating to' is correct. Certainly, these phrases are *not* synonymous. The 'primarily aimed at' requirement seems to be an unwarranted amendment of Article XX. As the Appellate Body in *US Gasoline Standards* pointed out, 'the phrase "primarily aimed at" is not, itself, treaty language and was not designed as a simple litmus test' for Article XX.[94] In *Shrimp-Turtle* the Appellate Body took a more nuanced approach to the 'relating to' element, examining the relationship between the structure of the measure in question and the conservation objectives sought to be achieved and concluded that the US import ban on shrimp was 'reasonably related' to the turtle conservation measures sought to be achieved.[95]

A third requirement of Article XX(g) is that the measure in question must be 'made effective in conjunction with restrictions on domestic production or consumption'.

---

[88] *US—Standards for Reformulated and Conventional Gasoline, supra,* n 31.

[89] *Shrimp-Turtle* Appellate Body Report, *supra,* n 68. For discussion of the case see Mann, 9 *YbIEL* (1998) 28; Schoenbaum, ibid, 36; Wirth, ibid, 40.

[90] By 'measure' is meant the law or rule challenged as inconsistent with WTO/GATT norms: *US Gasoline Standards* App, *supra,* n 31, at 13–14.

[91] *Shrimp-Turtle* Appellate Body Report, *supra,* n 68, para 127.   [92] Ibid, paras 129–30.

[93] See *US Gasoline Standards* App, *supra,* n 31, at 16.

[94] *US Gasoline Standards* App, *supra,* n 31, at 19.

[95] *Shrimp-Turtle* Appellate Body Report, *supra,* n 68, para 141.

The definitive interpretation of this phrase was given by the Appellate Body in the *US Gasoline Standards Case*:

[T]he basic international law rule of treaty interpretation...that the terms of a treaty are to be given their ordinary meaning, in context, so as to effectuate its object and purpose, is applicable here...[T]he ordinary or natural meaning of 'made effective' when used in connection with a measure—a governmental act or regulation—may be seen to refer to such measure being 'operative', as 'in force', or as having 'come into effect'. Similarly, the phrase 'in conjunction with' may be read quite plainly as 'together with' or 'jointly with'. Taken together, the second clause of Article XX(g) appears to us to refer to governmental measures like the baseline establishment rules being promulgated or brought into effect together with restrictions on domestic production or consumption of natural resources...[W]e believe that the clause 'if such measures are made effective in conjunction with restrictions on domestic product[ion] or consumption' is appropriately read as a requirement that the measures concerned impose restrictions, not just in respect of imported gasoline but also with respect to domestic gasoline.[96]

As the Appellate Body further pointed out, however, the 'in conjunction with' element requires a certain amount of even-handedness, but not identity of treatment, and restrictions on either domestic production or consumption will be satisfactory.[97]

A similar approach was used in the *Shrimp-Turtle Case*.[98] As indicated above, the Appellate Body found that the import ban on shrimp was reasonably related to the purpose of protecting sea turtles (just as the Appellate Body in the *US Gasoline Standards Case* found that there was a reasonable relationship between the baseline establishment rules and clean air). In addition, the 'in conjunction with' requirement was satisfied because the USA required all shrimp trawlers to use turtle excluder devices in areas and at times when there is a likelihood of intercepting sea turtles. Thus, there are comparable restrictions on the domestic harvesting of shrimp.[99]

The approach to Article XX(g) now mandated by the Appellate Body is substantially different from the restrictive and somewhat illogical interpretations of GATT panels, particularly the *Tuna-Dolphin* decisions. In fact, the US restrictions on the harvesting of tuna would now pass Article XX(g) with flying colours. Dolphins clearly are an exhaustible natural resource; the import ban on tuna harvested by methods that kill dolphins clearly is related to the purpose of cutting dolphin mortality; and the requirements protecting dolphins also apply to US vessels and fishermen. Also important, the Appellate Body in the *Shrimp-Turtle Case* gave clear *extraterritorial* scope to Article XX(g): it applies without distinction to exhaustible resources beyond areas of national jurisdiction as well as to domestic resources.[100]

(b) Article XX(b)

As we saw earlier, in the *Asbestos Case*,[101] the Appellate Body has followed the interpretation given to the phrase 'necessary to protect human, animal or plant life or

---

[96] Ibid, 20.   [97] Ibid, 21.
[98] *Shrimp-Turtle* Appellate Body Report, *supra*, n 68, paras 138–42.   [99] Ibid, paras 143–5.
[100] Ibid, paras 132–3.   [101] *Supra*, n 22.

health' by panel decisions in *Tuna-Dolphin* and other cases. It has been said that this interpretation constitutes too great an infringement on the sovereign powers of states to take decisions by democratic means to solve problems and to satisfy their constituents, and that it underestimates the political difficulties and constraints, both domestic and foreign, with which a nation must deal.[102] Thus, in deciding what is 'necessary', WTO panels should employ a deferential standard of review that allows some freedom of action to member states. In the *Asbestos Case*, the Appellate Body appears to have been sensitive to these criticisms.

Upholding a French ban on imports of asbestos under Article XX(b), the Appellate Body held that where there is a scientifically proven risk to health, 'WTO members have the right to determine the level of protection of health that they consider appropriate ', based *either* on the quality of the risk (i.e. is it regarded as socially acceptable) or on the quantity of the risk (i.e. how likely is it). The more vital the common interests or values pursued, the easier it would be to accept as 'necessary' measures designed to achieve those ends. In this case it found that there was no alternative means of eliminating the risk. The Appellate Body's approach to the application of Article XX(b) thus brings it closer to the proportionality[103] or balancing analysis applied by the European Community and the USA[104] when testing the necessity of restrictions on trade for environmental purposes. In the *US-Gambling Case*[105] the Appellate Body stressed that the test whether a contested measure is 'necessary' is an objective one, with the burden of proof falling on the defending government to present the evidence to be weighed in the balance. Factors to be weighted could include: '(i) the relative importance of the common interests or value pursued by the measure, (ii) the contribution made by the measure to the realization of the ends pursued by it, and (iii) the restrictive impact of the measure on international commerce'.[106] In discharging the burden of proof in the face of scientific uncertainty, the Appellate Body in the *Asbestos Case* acknowledged that, in justifying the trade-restrictive measure, the defending government may 'rely in good faith, on scientific sources which, at that time, may represent a divergent, but qualified and respected, opinion'.[107]

(c) The chapeau of Article XX

As already noted, all the Article XX exceptions are qualified by the *chapeau*, which sets out the tests for the *manner* in which a trade measure is applied. Three standards are stated in the *chapeau*: (i) arbitrary discrimination, (ii) unjustifiable discrimination,

---

[102] See Croley and Jackson, 90 *AJIL* (1996) 193, 211–12.

[103] Others have argued that the language in *EC-Asbestos* amounts to a rejection of the proportionality test, leaving States free to set their own level of protection: see, for example, House and Türk, in Bermann and Mavroidis (eds), *Trade and Human Health and Safety* (Cambridge, 2006) 77, 113.

[104] *Infra*, nn 133–4.

[105] WTO Appellate Body Report, *US—Measures Affecting the Cross-Border Supply of Gambling and Betting Services*, WT/DS285/AB/R, adopted 20 April 2005, paras 304, 309–10. This case arose under GATS but (i) it mirrors the GATT Article XX exceptions and (ii) the Appellate Body expressly indicated that its analysis was based on the GATT Article XX jurisprudence.

[106] Charnovitz, 10 *JIEL*(2007) 685, 691; *US—Gambling*, ibid, para 306.   [107] *EC-Asbestos*, para 178.

and (iii) a disguised restriction on international trade. In the *Shrimp-Turtle Case*, the Appellate Body stated that the *chapeau* is (i) a balancing principle to mediate between the right of a member to invoke an Article XX derogation and its obligation to respect the rights of other members; (ii) a qualification making the Article XX exemptions 'limited and conditional';[108] (iii) an expression of the principle of good faith in international law; and (iv) a safeguard against *abus de droit*, the doctrine that requires the assertion of a right under a treaty to be 'exercised bona fide, that is to say reasonably'.[109] According to the Appellate Body, the *chapeau* protects 'both substantive and procedural requirements'.[110]

In the *Shrimp-Turtle Case*, the unilateral measures applied by the USA to protect sea turtles were found to violate the *chapeau*'s criteria against arbitrary and unjustifiable discrimination. The Appellate Body's reasoning focused on the manner of application of the US regulations. First, it found that there was 'arbitrary discrimination' because US law required a 'rigid and unbending...comprehensive regulatory programme that is essentially the same as the US programme, without inquiring into the appropriateness of that program for the conditions prevailing in the exporting countries'.[111] Arbitrary discrimination was found to exist separately because the US authorities, in their certification process for shrimp imports, did not comply with basic standards of fairness and due process with regard to notice, the gathering of evidence, and the opportunity to be heard. The Appellate Body found that the GATT requires 'rigorous compliance with the fundamental requirements of due process' with respect to exceptions to treaty obligations.[112]

Second, the US regulations were 'unjustifiable'[113] because they required (i) a duplication of the US programme without considering conditions in other countries and (ii) applied differing phase-in periods for countries similarly situated and impacted by the import ban. Most importantly, the Appellate Body held that it was unjustifiable discrimination for the USA not to have negotiated seriously with some of the affected countries: the subject matter—protection of sea turtles—demanded international cooperation, the US statute recognized the importance of seeking international agreements, and the USA had, subsequent to imposing its own restrictions, entered into the 1996 Inter-American Convention for the Protection and Conservation of Sea Turtles. The Appellate Body concluded: 'The Inter-American Convention thus provides convincing demonstration that an alternative course of action was reasonably open to the USA'.[114]

The *Shrimp-Turtle Case* is a well-reasoned decision of great importance for the trade/environment controversy. The Appellate Body, unlike earlier GATT panels, went out of its way to emphasize concern for protection of the environment and respect for both general international environmental law and international environmental agreements. Two striking conclusions emerge from its opinion.

---

[108] *Shrimp-Turtle* Appellate Body Report, *supra*, n 68, para 157.   [109] Ibid, para 158.
[110] Ibid, para 160.   [111] Ibid, para 177.   [112] Ibid, para 182.   [113] Ibid, para 182.
[114] Ibid, para 171.

First, the Appellate Body did not totally condemn unilateral action or declare it illegal per se as the GATT panels had done. The Appellate Body stated only that '[T]he unilateral character…heightens the disruptive and discriminatory influence of the import prohibition and underscores its unjustifiability'.[115] This leaves some room, albeit small, for unilateral measures to protect the environment beyond national jurisdiction. If, for example, the US measures in the *Shrimp-Turtle Case* had been tailored carefully to meet due process concerns and were suited to conditions in other countries, and especially if the countries concerned had spurned offers of negotiation or refused to negotiate in good faith, it is conceivable that unilateral measures to protect turtles would not be arbitrary or unjustifiable and would have been upheld. Of particular interest is the Appellate Body's emphasis on good faith as a principle of international law. If, in a given case, a state were to spurn environmental controls and refuse to enter into negotiations over the depletion of resources beyond national jurisdiction, it would be deemed to be in breach of the principle of good faith, and unilateral measures might be justified.

Second, the *Shrimp-Turtle* opinion provides a principled basis for upholding multilateral and bilateral environmental agreements under Article XX(b) and (g). By interpreting the requirements of (g) (and impliedly (b)) in a pro-environmental manner, it is virtually certain that MEAs, as well as bilateral environmental agreements, would be upheld. They would meet the requirements of the *chapeau* unless they contained substantial flaws or were disguised protectionist measures. Thus, the *Shrimp-Turtle Case* provides an important new basis for upholding trade-restrictive international environmental agreements.[116] Here the Appellate Body used international environmental agreements not binding on the parties as an aid to the interpretation of existing WTO provisions, not as the applicable law between the parties. This point was emphasized in the *EC—Biotech Case* where the panel considered whether, and how, agreements external to the WTO covered agreements could be taken into account.[117]

4(4) 'CREATIVE' UNILATERALISM

WTO and GATT jurisprudence have tended to frown on unilateral action.[118] However, there are at least two theoretical justifications for 'creative' unilateral action. First, a unilateral act can be *de lege ferenda*, new state practice that may mature into 'opposable' custom under accepted norms of international law.[119] The doctrine of

---

[115] Ibid, para 172.   [116] See Scott, 15 *EJIL* (2004) 311.

[117] Panel Report, *European Communities—Measures Affecting the Approval and Marketing of Biotech Products*, WT/DS291/R, WT/DS292/R, WT/DS293/R, adopted 21 November 2006, paras 7.70–7.95; see Young, 56 *ICLQ* (2007) 907.

[118] See in particular *Tuna-Dolphin I and II* and *Shrimp-Turtle*.

[119] An example of this is President Truman's unilateral proclamation of US 'jurisdiction and control' over the resources of the continental shelves of the USA in 1945. This act matured into the doctrine formulated in the 1958 Geneva Convention on the Continental Shelf. Thus, unilateral measures that are 'illegal' at first may come to be 'opposable' against some states and develop into international law. See also *Norwegian Fisheries Case*, ICJ Reports (1951) 116 (baselines claimed by Norway).

opposability—first employed by the International Court of Justice in the *Norwegian Fisheries Case*[120]—has two aspects: it allows a state to assert an important interest in ways that are not, strictly speaking, consistent with international law; and it serves to promote the adoption of new international-law norms where necessary to clarify 'grey areas' of international practice.[121] Opposability is thus a creative agent of change and an important part of the international 'legislative' process.

The second justification is that a unilateral act may be a countermeasure under international law. Countermeasures can be taken only under certain conditions.[122] A countermeasure must be in response to a prior act contrary to international law; there must be a prior request for redress; and the measure taken by the aggrieved state must not be out of proportion to the gravity of the original wrongful act.[123] Force, as well as extreme political and economic measures that represent a threat to a state's territorial integrity or political independence, must be avoided. Human rights and peremptory norms of international law must be observed, and legal obligations toward third states must be respected. Three examples make the point. First, the *Tuna-Dolphin* dispute might be viewed as an attempt by the USA to put forward a new principle of customary international law, the need to protect marine mammal species regardless of whether they are in danger of extinction. The US action might also be viewed as a countermeasure in retaliation for Mexico's disregard of the duty of all states, recognized under customary international law, as well as the 1982 UNCLOS, to protect marine living resources. However, this theory would not justify the US embargo of tuna imports from 'intermediary' nations (those that buy tuna from the country subject to the direct import ban) because countermeasures against third parties are generally prohibited.

A hypothetical instance of transboundary pollution serves as a second example. Although the duty of every state under customary law to prevent serious harm to its neighbours or to the global environment from activities in its territories is unquestioned, there is usually no forum with compulsory jurisdiction to adjudicate such questions.[124] Under those circumstances, unilateral action imposing an environmental trade restriction as a countermeasure may be permissible.[125]

---

[120] See also the *Icelandic Fisheries Cases*, ICJ Reports (1974) 3, 175.

[121] The ICJ cases suggest that to be opposable, a unilateral measure must: (i) be within the effective power of the asserting state; (ii) conform to a sense of equity and the general interest of the international community (not merely the special interest of a particular state); (iii) be asserted in good faith; and (iv) not be opposed by consistent objection.

[122] See ILC, 2001 Articles on State Responsibility, Articles 50–5, and generally, Schachter, *International Law in Theory and Practice* (The Hague, 1992) 184–200; Matsui, 37 *Japanese Ann IL* (1994) 1; Elagab, *The Legality of Non-forcible Countermeasures in International Law* (Oxford, 1988); Koskenniemi, 72 *BYIL* (2001) 337.

[123] See ILC 2001 Articles 50, 52, 53; *The Naulilaa (Germany v Portugal)*, 2 RIAA (1928), 1011; *Case Concerning the Air Services Agreement of March 27, 1946* (US–France), 18 RIAA (1978) 417.

[124] *Supra*, Chs 3, 4.

[125] Fox, 84 *Geo LJ* (1996) 249; Okowa, *State Responsibility for Transboundary Air Pollution in International Law* (Oxford, 2000) 248–54, who notes that the scope for other types of countermeasure in response to breaches of environmental obligations is limited because of the likelihood that third state rights will thereby be affected.

A third example is the controversy between Spain and Canada during 1995, when Spanish fishing vessels intensively fished the Grand Banks in the North Atlantic just beyond the Canadian 200-mile exclusive economic zone, thereby disrupting Canadian efforts to rebuild fish stocks.[126] The Spanish vessels' actions violated several provisions of the Northwest Atlantic Fisheries Organization Agreement.[127] If Canada had adopted environmental trade restrictions against Spain,[128] this would have been a permissible countermeasure.

Is unilateral action successful? The outcome of unilateral measures will vary according to the circumstances of the case. Consider the tuna-dolphin controversy. After the US ban on tuna caught in purse-seine nets was ruled inconsistent with the GATT, Mexico, the chief prevailing party, did not press for adoption of the GATT panel report by the GATT Council. In response to the panel decision, the USA passed the International Dolphin Conservation Act[129] and sought to negotiate an understanding with Mexico and Venezuela to create an international moratorium on the practice of fishing for tuna with purse-seine nets. Shortly thereafter, in 1992, the International Agreement for the Reduction of Dolphin Mortality was signed by twelve states, including the USA and Mexico, under the auspices of the Inter-American Tropical Tuna Commission. Within two years, this Agreement reduced incidental mortality of dolphins in the eastern tropical Pacific to below 4,000 animals, prompting the US Marine Mammal Commission to conclude that the incidental take of dolphins 'was no longer significant from a biological perspective'.[130] As a result, the USA revoked the tuna embargo.

Thus, the tuna-dolphin problem was resolved by preserving both free trade and dolphins. Would it have occurred without US unilateral action? Many commentators have pointed out that the USA tried unsuccessfully for twenty years to obtain an agreement reducing dolphin mortality.[131] Only after the tuna ban and the subsequent uproar over the *Tuna-Dolphin* decisions was it possible to negotiate an agreement.

5 TRADE RESTRICTIONS TO PROTECT THE DOMESTIC ENVIRONMENT

The protection of a nation's domestic environment may demand three different kinds of trade restrictions: (i) import restraints against products or services that do not

---

[126] See McLarty, 15 *Va Envtl LJ* (1996) 469 and Davies, 44 *ICLQ* (1995) 927.

[127] 1978 Convention on Future Multilateral Cooperation in Northwest Atlantic Fisheries. See *supra*, Ch 13 for a fuller discussion.

[128] For example, Canada could have adopted a ban on imports of fish products from Spain but did not do so because it chose to retaliate by pursuing and arresting the offending vessels.

[129] Pub L 102–583, 106 Stat 3425 (1992), codified at 16 USC §§1411–18 (1994).

[130] See Marine Mammal Commission, *Annual Report to Congress* (1994) 121.

[131] See, e.g. Dunoff, 49 *Wash & Lee LR* (1992) 1407, 1415–33.

comply with domestic environmental norms; (ii) requirements that imported as well as domestic products comply with regulations involving such matters as labelling, packaging, and recycling; and (iii) export restrictions to conserve natural resources.

5(1) IMPORT RESTRAINTS

Import restrictions on products must, of course, comply with Articles I, II, III, and XI of GATT 1994, or must find an applicable exemption under Article XX. In addition, product import restrictions are subject to the disciplines of two Uruguay Round codes: the Agreement on Technical Barriers to Trade (TBT)[132] and the Agreement on the Application of Sanitary and Phytosanitary Measures (SPS).[133] The TBT and SPS Agreements are mutually exclusive: the SPS Agreement deals with additives, contaminants, toxins, and disease-carrying organisms in food, beverages, and feedstuffs, while the TBT applies to all other product standards. Both Agreements seek to balance state autonomy with the concern that complete freedom to set standards would undermine the WTO/GATT aims. The Agreements successfully combat non-tariff barriers but allow states reasonable freedom to set environmental standards.

Article XX(b) of the GATT and the identically worded Article XIV(b) of the GATS are applicable to justify import restraints on environmentally harmful products or services. This provision can be invoked broadly to protect the domestic environment (although the wording 'human, animal, or plant life' would restrict protection to *living* things). The trade restriction must be 'necessary', and the wording of the *chapeau* of Article XX would appear to mean that like products or services produced domestically must be similarly restricted and discrimination among countries similarly situated would be prohibited. The country asserting this exception would bear the burden of proof and persuasion on these matters.

GATT Article XX(b) or GATS Article XIV(b) would apply to ordinary products and services. However, most trade restrictions would also implicate the TBT or SPS Agreements. The SPS is the more restrictive of the two agreements. WTO member states have the right to take sanitary and phytosanitary measures that are 'necessary' for the protection of human and animal health.[134] Six specific requirements must be fulfilled.

First, SPS measures must 'not be more trade-restrictive than required to achieve their appropriate level of...protection'.[135] This provision presumes the right of each state to choose *its own level* of protection unilaterally.[136] A footnote specifies that a measure is not more trade restrictive than required unless there is another

---

[132] *Legal Texts, supra*, n 1, at 163 (1994) (hereafter 'TBT Agreement').

[133] Ibid, 69 (hereafter 'SPS Agreement'). See Pauwelyn, 2 *JIEL* (1999) 641 and Scott, *The WTO Agreement on Sanitary and Phytosanitary Measures: A Commentary* (Oxford, 2007).

[134] SPS Agreement, Article 2(1)–(2). This repeats the language in GATT Article XX(b).

[135] Article 5(6).

[136] 'Appropriate' is the level of protection deemed appropriate by the member state. See Annex A, para 5.

measure *reasonably* available (meaning feasible) that would do the job.[137] This elaboration effectively gives the word 'necessary' a flexible interpretation.

Second, any SPS measure shall be applied 'only to the extent necessary' to protect human, animal, or plant life and health.[138] This seems to duplicate partially the first requirement; arguably, it places the emphasis on the obligation not to *apply* a measure so as to cause more trade restriction than necessary for the appropriate level of protection desired. Under this interpretation, the first two requirements are complementary: a state can neither *adopt* nor *apply* a measure that goes beyond its chosen level of protection.

Third, a measure must be based upon 'scientific principles' and 'sufficient scientific evidence'.[139] Even without sufficient scientific evidence, the SPS Agreement includes 'precautionary language' that permits standards to be adopted provisionally 'on the basis of available pertinent information'.[140] This does not relieve the state concerned from the continuing obligation 'to obtain the additional information necessary for a more objective assessment of risk' and to review the measure within a reasonable period of time.[141] Nor does it permit a measure to be justified on the basis of the precautionary principle—whatever the international legal status of that principle—if otherwise contrary to the explicit requirements of the SPS Agreement.[142] As we noted in Chapter 11 above, this is a point of potential conflict between the SPS Agreement and the Cartagena Protocol. Even with the Protocol subject to the international discipline of the SPS Agreement and capable of harmonization with it, there is inconsistency in the application of the precautionary principle. The Protocol explicitly adopts the precautionary principle for the regulation of food, feed, and processed LMOs, allowing import regulation even in the face of 'lack of scientific certainty due to insufficient scientific information'.[143] This may result in future conflict with the SPS Agreement, which allows the precautionary principle to be applied only to measures taken on a provisional basis where there is insufficient scientific evidence.[144] Direct conflict has thus far been avoided in so far as the Panel in the *EC—Biotech Case* did not apply the Biodiversity Convention and Protocol to its analysis of precaution under the SPS Agreement, thus at the same time raising high the hurdle for interpretation of WTO agreements in the light of other instruments.[145]

---

[137] SPS Agreement, Article 5(6), n 3.   [138] Article 2(2).

[139] Ibid. For a cogent critique of the use of scientific evidence by WTO panels see Christoforou, 8 *NYUEnvLJ* (2000) 622 and Green and Epps, 10 *JIEL* (2007) 285.

[140] Safrin, 96 *AJIL* (2002) 606, 610.

[141] SPS Agreement, Art 5.7. This was one of the points on which EC member State safeguard measures failed in the *EC—Biotech Case, supra*, n.0.

[142] *Beef Hormones* (AB), paras 124–5; see Peel, 5 *Melb JIL* (2004) 483, 493. Although relied upon by the EC in the *EC—Biotech Case*, as we noted above, the Panel did not consider the precautionary principle as reflected in e.g. the Cartagena Protocol.

[143] Article 11(8).   [144] See *supra*, text at n 139.

[145] See n.53 above; and criticism by Young, 56 *ICLQ*(2007) 907.

Fourth, measures must be based upon a risk-assessment process 'taking into account' available scientific evidence and economic factors, including the objective of minimizing negative trade effects.[146]

Fifth, Article 2(3) of the SPS Agreement repeats the requirements of the *chapeau* of Article XX, that the measure must not 'arbitrarily or unjustifiably discriminate between members' and must not be a 'disguised restriction on international trade'. Moreover, 'with the objective of achieving consistency', Article 5(5) also prohibits 'arbitrary or unjustifiable distinctions' in the levels of sanitary or phytosanitary protection considered appropriate. In practice and in the case law this provision is the real bite of the agreement.[147]

Sixth, there is an obligation at least to consider adopting international SPS standards in the interests of achieving harmonization.[148] Yet, the Agreement explicitly permits maintenance of higher standards if they are justified scientifically or required by the member state's own unilaterally determined higher level of protection.[149]

Under the TBT Agreement, member states pledge that technical regulations will not be allowed to create 'unnecessary obstacles to international trade. For this purpose, technical regulations shall not be more restrictive than necessary to fulfil a legitimate objective'.[150] Here again, the *level* of protection is up to the individual member state, and a high level of environmental protection can be chosen. Furthermore, member states are free to accept or reject international standards. International standards need not be applied when they would be 'ineffective or inappropriate' for the fulfilment of a legitimate objective. Thus, if a state chooses a strict level of environmental protection, it can employ stricter standards than international technical requirements.

Controversy has arisen, particularly under the SPS Agreement, over the issues of standard-setting and the application of a precautionary approach by some states. In the *Beef Hormones Case*,[151] which involved an EC import ban of meat and meat products derived from cattle to which natural or synthetic hormones had been administered for growth purposes, the Appellate Body clarified the criteria and the process

---

[146] Article 5.   [147] See *infra*, and see also Pauwelyn, 2 *JIEL* (1999) 641.

[148] Such standards are deemed under the SPS Agreement to include those emanating from three international standards-setting organizations—Codex Alimentarius for food safety, the International Office of Epizootics for animal health, and the Secretariat of the Plant Protection Convention for plant health. In addition, Annex A of the SPS Agreement includes 'appropriate standards' from other international organizations open to membership by all WTO members as identified by the SPS Committee. Interpretation of Annex A was a significant feature of the *EC—Biotech Case*; see discussion by Young, 56 *ICLQ* (2007) 907.

[149] Article 3.

[150] TBT Agreement, Article 2(2). 'Legitimate objective' is broadly defined as including 'national security requirements, prevention of deceptive practices, protection of human health or safety, animal, plant life, or health, or the environment'.

[151] *EC—Measures Concerning Meat and Meat Products* ['Beef Hormones Case'], Rept of the Appellate Body, WT/DS26/AB/R (1997). Two further cases have similarly struck down national food safety measures because of a lack of scientific evidence and the failure to carry out a risk assessment. See *Australia—Measures Affecting the Import of Salmon*, Rept of Appellate Body, WT/DS18/AB/R (1998), and *Japan—Measures Affecting Agricultural Products*, Rept of the Panel, WT/DS76/R (1998).

by which a WTO member can adapt and apply high-level sanitary and phytosanitary standards.

First, a member may either choose an international SPS standard, or may base its standard on the international standard without conforming to all its requirements, or may set a level of protection wholly its own.[152] When an international standard is used, there is a rebuttable presumption that it is consistent with the SPS Agreement and GATT 1994. If the national measure is based merely upon the international standard, but not in conformity with it, there is no presumption in its favour, but a complaining member must make a prima facie case in favour of inconsistency. If a member adopts its own level of protection under Article 3(3) of the SPS Agreement, it must be based on a 'risk assessment' (Article 5(1)) and 'sufficient scientific evidence' (Article 2(2)).[153]

Second, what is a sufficient risk assessment is not defined in the SPS Agreement either substantively or procedurally. A member, therefore, is free to consider both 'available scientific evidence' (Article 5(2)) and 'relevant economic factors' (Article 5(3)). But there must be a 'rational relationship between the trade measure and the risk assessment',[154] and the scientific reports relied upon must rationally support the import restriction. Since the risk assessment in the *Beef Hormones Case* failed these tests, the EC's import restriction was held to violate Article 5(1).

Third, Article 5(5) of the SPS Agreement requires the avoidance of arbitrary or unjustifiable discrimination and disguised restrictions on international trade. The Appellate Body, interpreting these elements in the context of SPS Article 2(3) (which is similarly worded), read this to require a showing of three elements: (i) that a member has adopted its own appropriate levels of SPS protection in several situations; (ii) that those levels of protection exhibit arbitrary or unjustifiable differences; and (iii) that these differences are discriminatory or a disguised restriction on international trade.[155] These three elements are cumulative: arbitrary or unjustifiable differences alone will not violate Article 5(5) unless they also result in discrimination or a disguised restriction on international trade.[156]

Several conclusions may be drawn from this brief analysis of the SPS and TBT Agreements. First, a WTO member may choose the level of protection it wants to adopt

---

[152] Paras 165–73. This interpretation is based upon Article 3(1)–(3) of the SPS Agreement. See also WT/DS231/AB/R *EC—Trade Descriptions of Sardines*, Report of the Appellate Body, para 245 (for domestic regulation based on international standards there must be a 'very strong and close relationship').

[153] Paras 176–80. Article 2(2) is to be read as informing the risk assessment obligation of Article 5(1). This interpretation of the SPS Agreement is curious since the relevant provision, Article 3(3), appears to state two ways of justifying a 'higher level' of protection: '[I]f there is a scientific justification or as a consequence of the level of…protection a Member determines to be appropriate in accordance with…Article 5.' Because of a footnote to this sentence requiring 'scientific information in conformity with the relevant provisions of this Agreement', the Appellate Body interpreted 'or' to mean 'and'. The reasoning of the Appellate Body in the *Beef Hormone Case* was followed by a WTO panel in *Australia—Measures Affecting Importation of Salmon*, Report of the Panel, WT/DS18/R (1998).

[154] *Beef Hormone Case*, para 193.   [155] Ibid, para 214.

[156] Ibid, para 2.44–2.46. The Appellate Body held that the EC's measures in the *Beef Hormone Case* were arbitrary in part but did not result in discrimination or a disguised restriction on international trade. See also *Australia—Measures Affecting Importation of Salmon*, Report of the Appellate Body, WT/DS18/AB/R (1998).

regarding its *own* natural resources, environmental quality, and health and safety. However, it must be prepared to justify such trade-restricting measures once a prima facie case of violation is made out by a complaining member. Second, the precautionary principle, whatever its status as a general rule or principle of international law,[157] cannot override the specific provisions of the SPS Agreement.[158] Third, harmonization and the adoption of international standards is encouraged, but not required. Fourth, only the *means* chosen to implement these domestic policies will be subject to WTO review when they impact international trade, and the tests employed attempt to balance the accommodation of national interests, on the one hand, and the need to police disguised trade restrictions on the other.[159]

It is informative to compare the WTO/GATT regime of regulation of disguised trade barriers to those adopted by the European Union and NAFTA.[160] The EU operates a tighter system of controls to ensure the free movement of goods under the European Community Treaty and other EU legislation. Articles 30 and 34 of the EC Treaty are interpreted to require, in principle, freedom of movement of goods among member states. Derogations are allowed under Article 36 for certain reasons, including environmental reasons; but national restrictions are subjected to a balancing test by the European Court of Justice. To survive, they must be 'necessary' and meet the test of 'proportionality'.[161] The NAFTA system to regulate SPS standards and technical barriers to trade is somewhat looser than the WTO/GATT system. Under NAFTA Article 904(4), no party may maintain a standard that is an 'unnecessary obstacle to trade', but such an obstacle shall not be deemed to be created if the purpose of a standard is to achieve a 'legitimate objective'. Article 905(3) of NAFTA also specifically validates national standards that result in a higher level of protection than would the relevant international standard. A similar savings clause applies to SPS standards under Article 713(3).

5(2) RECYCLING AND PACKAGING

Several countries have taken bold steps to introduce mandatory recycling of products and packaging to reduce the generation of waste and the resulting pollution and need for landfills. Germany has led the way, passing the *Verpackungsverordnung (Packaging*

---

[157] See *supra*, Ch 3, section 4(3)   [158] *Beef Hormone Case*, paras 123–5.

[159] This is the conclusion of most experts. See, e.g. Nichols, in Stewart (ed), *The World Trade Organization* (Washington DC, 1996) 191.

[160] For a comparative study, see Weiler (ed), *The EU, the WTO and the NAFTA: Towards a Common Law of International Trade* (Oxford, 2000). A fourth system for assuring free movement of goods and eliminating 'unnecessary' obstacles to trade is the US Commerce Clause: see *City of Philadelphia v New Jersey*, 437 US 617 (1978) (discrimination in interstate commerce is prohibited); *Hunt v Washington State Apple Advertising*, 432 US 333 (1977) (facially neutral legislation with a discriminatory effect must be justified); and *Pike v Bruce Church, Inc*, 397 US 137 (1970) (applying a balancing test for incidental burdens on commerce).

[161] *Rewe-Zentral AG v Bundesmonopolverwaltung für Branntwein* ['*Cassis de Dijon*' *Case*], Case 120/78, [1979] ECR 649; *Commission v Denmark* [1988] ECR 4607 ['*Danish Bottles Case*']. In addition, the EU institutions have wide powers to compel the harmonization and mutual recognition of standards.

Ordinance)[162] in 1991, which regulates the packaging of products and sets mandatory recycling requirements for packaging waste. The *Packaging Ordinance* requires the manufacturers of products to take back packaging wastes and to arrange for their recycling. They fulfil this duty by participating in a private waste collection system, which, for a fee, will handle this obligation by collecting waste from consumers. Participating manufacturers may mark their products with a green dot. The *Packaging Ordinance* applies to all products distributed within Germany.[163]

Largely because of this German initiative and in order to harmonize member-state legal regimes, the European Union adopted a Packaging Directive in December 1994.[164] The European Union directive sets target ranges for packaging waste recovery and recycling, standardizes methods of analysing product lifecycles and measuring toxicity of packaging components and waste, and sets maximum concentration levels for heavy metals in packaging. The directive applies to the packaging of all products sold in the European Union, including imports.[165]

These laws are part of an increasing trend in many industrialized countries to consider the environmental impact of products throughout their lifecycles to the point of their ultimate disposal. The purpose of these laws is to weaken this impact by (i) minimizing packaging waste, (ii) prohibiting the use of toxic and hazardous materials in packaging, and (iii) creating incentives or requirements for recycling, reuse, or proper disposal of both the packaging and the products themselves. Such laws have the potential to disrupt international trade. Manufacturing groups are alarmed that the spread of such lifecycle or 'producer responsibility laws' will have a protectionist effect, isolating national markets. Developing countries are especially concerned that their exporters will be unable to comply with these laws.

Nevertheless, life-cycle laws serve important purposes and the international trading system should be adjusted to accommodate them. Two separate sets of issues arise. The most serious problems come from the proliferation of such laws rather than their substantive requirements. If every country adopts its own national (or sub-national) system, trade will be disrupted simply by the burden of satisfying many different national bureaucracies. Moreover, though well intentioned, some packaging or product regulations may be environmentally harmful. The problems stemming from proliferation could be alleviated through international harmonization of product life-cycle regulation. This should be encouraged by the WTO's Committee on Trade and Environment, but is probably best left to private groups like the International Standards Organization that can work with national governments and industry and environmental interest groups. Harmonization efforts should emphasize environmental protection,

---

[162] 20 August 1991 BGBl I S 1234 *translated in* 21 *ILM* (1992), 1135. For commentary, see Goldfine, 7 *Georgetown IELR* (1994), 309.

[163] Bundesministerium für Umwelt, Naturschutz, and Reaktorsicherheit, *The Packaging Ordinance and International Trade* §1(1), 23 June 1993.

[164] Council Directive 94/62 EC, 1994 OJ (L 365) 10. See generally, Haner, 18 *Fordham ILJ* (1995), 2187; Comer, 7 *Fordham ELJ* (1995)163.

[165] Council Directive 94/62, para 2(1).

but should screen carefully the current array of laws for effectiveness and eliminate those that are not working. The second problem with such laws is that they may be more restrictive than necessary or may discriminate intentionally or unintentionally against foreign producers. To ensure that this does not happen, they should be held to scrutiny under international trade-law norms that recognize the necessity of environmental protection for national governments to have some flexibility in the remedies they adopt.

In principle, product lifecycle and producer responsibility laws are permitted under GATT Article III as long as they apply equally to domestic and foreign producers.[166] These laws should be subject to the discipline of the TBT Agreement,[167] which imposes the additional requirements that they must not create 'unnecessary obstacles to international trade' and not be 'more restrictive than necessary to fulfil a legitimate objective', including, of course, protection of the environment. These tests assure that a proper balancing process will be applied so that restrictive measures are not out of proportion to their benefits.[168]

5(3) ECO-LABELS

Another method of raising environmental standards is through eco-labelling. The theory behind eco-labels is that if consumers are informed, the market and consumer choice can be relied upon to stimulate the production and consumption of environmentally friendly products.[169] A great variety of eco-labelling schemes exist, sponsored by governments, private groups, or a combination of the two. They take several forms: mandatory 'negative content' labelling, mandatory 'content neutral' labelling, and voluntary 'multi-criteria' labelling.[170] Eco-labels can show product characteristics and/or process and production methods (PPMs). They can operate as a 'seal of approval' or objectively impart information. Well-known examples of eco-labelling plans include Germany's 'Blue Angel' programme and the 'White Swan' mark launched by the Scandinavian countries.[171] In the USA a private organization operates a 'Green Seal' programme. Increasingly, governments are adopting such programmes.[172] In 1992 the European Union established an eco-label scheme to 'promote the design, production, marketing, and use of products which have a reduced environmental impact during

---

[166] See *supra*, section 2(2).   [167] *See* text *supra*, n 150.

[168] A useful balancing test that might be employed is the concept of proportionality; see *Danish Bottles Case, supra*, n 161. The ECJ upheld a ban on non-returnable beverage containers, but held that a limitation on the sale of non-approved containers was discriminatory against foreign producers and out of proportion to the benefits served.

[169] See Ward, 6 *RECIEL* (1997) 139; Subedi, 2 *Brooklyn JIL* (1999) 373. For a sceptical view, see Menell, 4 *RECIEL* (1995) 304.

[170] US Environmental Protection Agency, *Status Report on the Use of Environmental Labels Worldwide* (1993).

[171] *See* Staffin, 21 *Col JEL* (1996) 205, 225.   [172] Ibid, 230–2.

their entire lifecycle, and provide consumers with better information on the environmental impact of products'.[173]

Eco-labelling must comply with WTO/GATT requirements. Even mandatory
eco-label requirements on products would be permissible if they are applied on a
non-discriminatory basis, adhering to the GATT 1994 MFN and national treatment
requirements. For example, under the US Energy Policy and Conservation Act,[174] corporate average fuel economy standards for automobiles must be calculated for domestic manufacturers and importers, and new automobiles sold in the USA must bear
a label stating the estimated miles-per-gallon rate for city and highway use.[175] This
programme was the subject of a GATT panel report in the *US Taxes on Automobiles
Case*,[176] which upheld the standards except for the separate foreign fleet accounting
aspects, which discriminated unfairly against foreign manufacturers.

Even eco-label schemes that pertain to PPMs may be upheld if they adhere to MFN
and national treatment norms. In the *Tuna-Dolphin I Case*, the panel accepted the
voluntary 'dolphin safe' labelling scheme for tuna products sold in the USA:

[T]he labelling provisions of the [US law] do not restrict the sale of tuna products; tuna
products can be freely sold both with and without the 'Dolphin Safe' label. Nor do these provisions establish requirements that have to be met in order to obtain an advantage from the
government. Any advantage which might possibly result from access to this label depends
on the free choice by consumers to give preference to tuna carrying the 'Dolphin Safe' label.
The labelling provisions therefore did not make the right to sell tuna or tuna products, nor
the access to a government-conferred advantage affecting the sale of tuna or tuna products,
conditional upon the use of tuna harvesting methods.[177]

In contrast, a discriminatory PPM labelling scheme would not be upheld. One that
singled out wood products made from tropical forests would fail if like products from
temperate forests were not included.[178]

Eco-labelling schemes must also comply with the TBT Agreement, which applies to
any technical regulation that deals with a product characteristic, including 'terminology, symbols, packaging, marking or labelling requirements as they apply to a product, process or production method'.[179] The Agreement requires that eco-labels 'fulfil a
legitimate objective', not be 'more trade-restrictive than necessary', and comply with
notice and transparency requirements, including the TBT Code of Good Practice.[180]

Additional steps should be taken as well by the WTO Committee on Trade and
Environment to ensure that eco-labelling does not become a barrier to trade. First,
eco-label schemes might be required to be registered with the WTO so that transparency

---

[173] Commission Regulation 880/92, Article I, 1992 OJ (L 99) 1.   [174] 17 USC §4001 (1994).

[175] 40 CFR Pt 600 (1996).

[176] *US—Taxes on Automobiles*, DS31/R, 11 Oct 1994 (Report not adopted by GATT Council) ['*Taxes on
Automobiles Case*'].

[177] *Tuna-Dolphin I*, supra, n 67, para 5.42. For a dissenting view that PPM labels would pass GATT mus-
ter, *see* Bartenhagen, 17 *Va Env LJ* (1997) 1.

[178] *See* Chase, 17 *Hastings ICLR* 349 (1994).   [179] TBT Agreement, *supra*, n 113, Annex I, para 1.

[180] Ibid, Annex III.

is guaranteed. National eco-label systems also should be open to all producers on a non-discriminatory basis, not contain requirements that favour domestic producers or be too costly or difficult to meet.

5(4) NATURAL RESOURCES

The issue arises whether a country may ban or restrict exports of natural resource products on the grounds that it is necessary for conservation purposes. Natural resources export bans would have to qualify either under GATT Article XI(2)(a), which permits an export prohibition or restriction to relieve temporary domestic 'critical shortages', or under Article XX(g), as a measure related to conservation of exhaustible natural resources. The limits of these sections can best be illustrated by examining a specific case: the US export ban on unprocessed logs from federal and state lands.[181] Section 488 of the US Forest Resources Conservation and Shortage Relief Act of 1990 states that timber is essential to the USA; that forests, forest resources, and the forest environment are exhaustible natural resources that require efficient and effective conservation efforts; that there is evidence of a shortfall in the supply of unprocessed timber in the USA; that any existing shortfall may worsen unless action is taken; and that conservation action is necessary with respect to exports of unprocessed timber. Among the stated purposes of the Act are to take action necessary under the GATT Article XI(2)(a) to ensure sufficient supplies of certain forest resources or products that are essential to the USA and to effect measures aimed at meeting these objectives in conformity with US obligations under the GATT.[182]

It is doubtful, however, whether this Act would survive the scrutiny of a WTO dispute resolution panel. Neither possible justification under the GATT seems to apply. Article XI(2)(a) would not be applicable since there is no evidence that timber or timber products are in 'critical' short supply in the USA. Article XI(g) would not apply because the export restrictions must be 'in conjunction with restrictions on domestic production or consumption'. There are no such domestic restrictions on timber in the USA. In fact, there is ample evidence that timber production is subsidized by low government prices for standing timber on federal and state lands. The real purpose of the ban, then, is more likely to create jobs in the domestic wood products industry by giving domestic mills the right to perform value-added processing.

In contrast, a ban on timber exports for true conservation purposes would be consistent with Article XX(g). For example, if a US ban on unprocessed logs over a certain diameter were accompanied by the elimination of domestic subsidies for timber cutting and restrictions on the cutting of 'old growth' forests,[183] it almost certainly would be upheld by the WTO.

---

[181] For discussion of these provisions in the context of exhaustible petroleum resources, see 10 *JERL* (1996) *passim*.

[182] 16 USC § 620 (1994).

[183] 'Old growth' or 'ancient' forests are terms given to forest habitat where trees vary considerably in age and size and there is a multilevel canopy that supports a rich ecosystem.

6 POLLUTION HAVENS: TRADE RESTRICTIONS TO IMPROVE THE ENVIRONMENT OF OTHER COUNTRIES

The trade/environment controversy may arise in the context of concern over low or non-existent environmental norms in other countries. This can be rooted in a sincere concern for pollution, environmental degradation, and exploitation of resources in other countries; concern over competitive disadvantages because lax environmental standards allow other countries to attract investment and sell their products more cheaply; or concern over transboundary pollution. It is obvious that the principle of the sovereign equality of states and limitations on the exercise of jurisdiction under international legal norms limit what a country can do directly to deal with environmental laxity in other countries. The question arises whether the problem can be addressed indirectly through trade sanctions or restrictions to punish countries that refuse to improve environmental standards. However, such measures engage the WTO/GATT rules.

6(1) PROCESS AND PRODUCTION METHODS

In addition to placing environmental trade measures on products, states also may concern themselves with how a product is produced, manufactured, or obtained— commonly referred to as process and production methods (PPMs). Some PPMs are directly related to the characteristics of the products concerned. For example, pesticides used on food crops produce residues on food products; cattle raised on growth hormones produce meat with hormone residues; and unsanitary conditions in slaughterhouses result in meat that may be contaminated with disease-causing organisms. PPMs such as these are covered by the SPS and TBT Agreements.[184] Thus, states may regulate such PPMs as long as they adhere to the disciplines in those Agreements. However, other PPMs that generally do not affect the product produced fall outside the existing trade agreements. A good example of a PPM of this type is the practice of catching tuna by setting fishing nets on schools of dolphins without requiring precautions to spare the dolphins. When the USA banned import of tuna caught by such methods, two GATT dispute-settlement panels declared this action inconsistent with GATT norms on the ground that it discriminated between 'like' products.[185] Thus, a state cannot adopt different treatment for two products with the same physical characteristics based upon how the products have been produced or harvested.[186]

---

[184] See TBT Agreement, Article 2(2) and Annex I, para 1; SPS Agreement, Annex A, para 1.

[185] *Supra*, nn 67 and 76. For extensive discussion see Choi, *'Like Products' in International Trade Law: Towards a Consistent GATT/WTO Jurisprudence* (Oxford, 2003).

[186] Another example of a PPM controversy is the EU proposal to prohibit the import of pelts and manufactured goods of certain animal species caught or killed by methods using leg-hold traps. See Council Regulation 3254/91, 1991 OJ (L 308) 1. Concerns regarding invalidity under WTO rules led to postponement

These controversial rulings have been opposed by two different groups. Environmentalists regard them as a setback to the goal of protecting ecosystems all over the world as well as the global commons. Others fear unfair competition from pollution havens, countries that maintain different conditions of production, particularly with respect to environmental, health, and safety laws and workers' rights and pay. This group wants the ability to 'level the playing field' by prohibiting imports from any country that refuses to adopt laws and regulations mirroring those of the importing country.

Scholars sympathetic to one or both of these views have called upon the WTO to overturn the *Tuna-Dolphin* rulings by (i) redefining 'like product' in GATT Article III so that products could be considered 'unlike' on the basis of how they are made, produced, or harvested;[187] (ii) adopting countervailing or 'eco-dumping' duties on products from countries that some believe constitute 'pollution havens' where products are made without adequate environmental controls;[188] or (iii) employing a new method of balancing trade and environmental interests by analysing the intent or effect of the measure, the legitimacy of the environmental policy, and the justification for the disruption to trade.[189] The first and second of these proposals could only be implemented by amendments to the GATT.[190] There are powerful arguments—both political and legal—against these ideas. Although the term 'like product' is defined flexibly on a case-by-case basis,[191] it would be a radical shift to differentiate products based on how they are produced, manufactured, or harvested.

The enforcement of PPMs in other countries could also be encouraged by replacing the current legal tests with a more lenient test that would allow WTO dispute-settlement panels to balance the legitimacy of the protected environmental value with the disruption to trading interests.[192] However, this proposal, which is derived from the way the US Supreme Court decides Commerce Clause cases,[193] may be unsuited to international tribunals like WTO panels whose ad hoc judges would, thereby, be delegated extraordinary discretion. Under this scheme, many PPM regulations undoubtedly would be upheld, but in the international context this would encourage nations

---

of the import ban and, in the event, agreement with Canada and the Russian Federation in the form of the 1997 Agreement on Humane Trapping Standards: see OJEC L 042, 14 February 1998, approved by EC Council Decision 98/142/EC. Nonetheless the Netherlands applied the import ban unilaterally: see Bowman, Davies and Redgwell, *Lyster's International Wildlife Law* (Cambridge, 2009), Ch 20, and Nollkaemper, 8 *JEL* (1996) 237.

[187] See especially, Snape and Lefkowitz, 27 *Cornell ILJ* (1994) 788–92.

[188] See the discussion in Esty, *Greening the GATT: Trade, Environment, and the Future* (Washington DC, 1994) 163–8.

[189] Ibid, 114–16. On the effect of the *Shrimp-Turtle Case*, see *supra*.

[190] Eco-dumping and countervailing duties are not authorized under the GATT Subsidies and Countervailing Duty Codes or current US law. For analysis, see Hudec, 5 *Minn J Global Trade* (1995) 1, 14–21.

[191] See *Japan Shochu Case*.

[192] See Esty, *Greening the GATT: Trade, Environment, and the Future* (Washington DC, 1994) 114–18.

[193] See, e.g., *Huron Cement Co v Detroit*, 362 US 440 (1960); see also Farber and Hudec, 1 *Fair Trade and Harmonization* (1996) 59, 64–8.

to violate fundamental principles of public international law, which, for the sake of harmony among nations, restrict the exercise of jurisdiction to accepted normative concepts.[194]

Instead of allowing unilateral regulation of PPMs to deal with environmental protection/pollution haven problems, other approaches might be considered, such as international environmental agreements, environmental management systems, and investment standards.

6(2) INTERNATIONAL ENVIRONMENTAL AGREEMENTS

The PPM/pollution-haven problem can be dealt with directly by encouraging countries to negotiate environmental agreements. If PPMs are causing transboundary pollution, the states concerned, relying on well-established principles of state responsibility under international law, may enter into an agreement to abate the pollution and compensate for its damage.[195] Where the problem is serious, as in the border region between the USA and Mexico, new institutions may be required both to deal with the pollution and to upgrade the environmental enforcement of the lax country concerned. Thus, the USA and Mexico have created a US–Mexican International Boundary Water Commission,[196] a Border Plan, and a Border Environmental Cooperation Agreement.[197] Mexico, Canada, and the USA have created a trilateral Commission for Environmental Cooperation to promote enforcement of environmental laws in the three countries.

Second, a specific problem may be addressed either through a bilateral or multilateral agreement designed to deal with it. An example is the tuna-dolphin dispute itself, which was addressed by the 1992 Agreement for the Reduction of Dolphin Mortality in the Eastern Pacific Ocean.[198] The Agreement has been implemented so successfully that scientists say that the eastern Pacific is now the 'world's safest tuna fishery for dolphins'.[199]

Third, regional pollution control agreements could be adopted following the model of the UNEP Regional Seas Programme[200] where 'framework' conventions have been concluded to preserve marine ecosystems in a number of regional-seas areas. These agreements are comprehensive in their regulation of all sources of marine pollution; they are models for facilitating cooperation and technical assistance, and new protocols can be added as needed to focus on particular pollution problems. A similar

---

[194] See generally, Brownlie, *Principles of Public International Law* (5th edn, Oxford, 1998) Ch 15.

[195] See, e.g. *Trail Smelter Arbitration*, 33 *AJIL* (1939) 182; 35 *AJIL* (1941), 684; 1991 Canada–US Agreement on Air Quality, 30 *ILM* (1991) 676; *supra*, Ch 6.

[196] 22 USC §§277–78b (1994). *See* Mumme, 33 *NRJ* (1993) 93.

[197] See Housman, *Reconciling Free Trade and the Environment: Lessons From the North American Free Trade Agreement* (UNEP, 1994).

[198] 33 *ILM* (1994) 936.

[199] *Int'l Herald Trib*, 26 June 1996, 6 (hereafter 'Dolphin Slaughter Ended').

[200] See Hulm, *A Strategy for the Seas: The Regional Seas Programme, Past and Future* (UNEP, 1983), and *supra*, Ch 7.

system of regional treaties could foster higher environmental PPMs, as well as control pollution on an appropriate regional basis.[201]

Fourth, appropriate international organizations can encourage the transfer of environmentally friendly technology[202] through development assistance or foreign direct investment. Thus, countries would upgrade PPMs in return for assistance in acquiring environmentally enhancing technology. In this way, as countries develop particular industrial sectors, they would acquire the means to control the environmental consequences. The transfer of technology also would promote voluntary standardization of PPMs. To some extent, this already is happening under international treaty regimes for the control of ozone-depleting substances and climate change.[203]

6(3) ENVIRONMENTAL MANAGEMENT SYSTEMS

Many environmentalists saw the *Tuna-Dolphin* decisions as an obstacle to the maintenance of high environmental standards because they invalidated efforts to require environmentally protective PPMs in other countries. How should the WTO respond to these concerns? Should international minimum PPM standards be required?

The term 'environmental standards' has various meanings. It can refer to the characteristics of products, PPMs, the cleanliness of the ambient environment, or procedural requirements. There are three general approaches to the international treatment of product standards: (i) national treatment, where each country determines its own standards and applies them to imported products; (ii) mutual recognition, where countries agree to recognize each other's standards; and (iii) harmonization, where, through negotiation, countries agree to adopt identical or similar standards, which become, therefore, international.

The WTO/GATT system, through the TBT and SPS Agreements, relies primarily on approaches (i) and (iii), encouraging harmonization and the adoption of international standards, but permitting national treatment. Empirical studies evaluating WTO/GATT harmonization of product standards find that, other than 'interface' harmonization (e.g., weights and measures), it has had very limited success, because the costs and benefits of harmonization are incommensurable, so that most countries perceive it as a 'lose-lose' exchange.[204] If harmonization of product standards on a worldwide basis has proved difficult, harmonizing PPMs would be impossible. There also are valid economic and environmental reasons why process standards should not be identical on a worldwide basis.[205] In addition, the putative international 'race to

---

[201] Compare, e.g. the 1979 Convention on Long-Range Transboundary Air Pollution, *supra*, Ch 6.

[202] This idea, advanced by Rege, 28 *JWT* (1994) 95, 113–16, is already occurring to some extent through environmental agreements and the Global Environmental Facility. See Doherty, 4 *RECIEL* (1995) 33.

[203] See *supra*, Ch 6.

[204] See Leebron, in Bhagwati and Hudec (eds), *Fair Trade and Harmonization* (Cambridge, Mass, 1996) I, 41.

[205] See Stewart, 102 *Yale LJ* (1993) 2039, 2051–7.

the bottom' has been much exaggerated. Actually, there is much evidence that trade between nations improves environmental standards of all kinds.[206]

If requiring worldwide PPM harmonization is not the answer, what can be done to ameliorate the PPM/pollution haven problem? PPMs can be upgraded through private efforts to protect the environment by means of corporate responsibility programmes and widespread adoption of environmental management systems such as the ISO 14000 Series.[207] ISO 14001 was developed by the International Standards Organization to identify the core elements of a voluntary environmental management system that would call on organizations to conduct their environmental affairs within a structured system integrated with ordinary management activity. The elements of such a corporate system are (i) adoption of a senior-management-level environmental policy; (ii) identification of the key environmental aspects of a company's operations; (iii) identification and implementation of legal requirements; (iv) identification of quantifiable environmental targets and objectives; (v) establishment of an environmental management system that allocates responsibility for environmental improvement; (vi) training of employees; (vii) establishment of monitoring, auditing, and corrective action; and (viii) establishment of management review and responsibility. The ISO 14001 EMS is not limited to compliance, but focuses on pollution prevention as well.

ISO 14001 is becoming established as the internationally accepted voluntary standard system of environmental management. Many companies are moving to adopt this system, and there is every indication that adherence to it will become a prerequisite for access to international markets. ISO 14001 does not establish specific PPMs or standards for pollution control. Rather, it requires companies to commit themselves to continual improvement of their environmental management systems' compliance with applicable laws and pollution prevention, but it leaves each company free to implement individual solutions to pollution and negative externality problems. Although adoption of ISO 14001 is voluntary, governments can provide incentives for its use through relief from 'command and control' regulation, enforcement policies that impose reduced penalties, and environmental privilege guarantees for companies that implement it.

6(4) INVESTMENT

An important aspect of the pollution-haven problem is the charge that countries with lax pollution standards attract industry and jobs away from countries with high standards. Empirical studies, however, fail to show much evidence of this loss of jobs.[208] The USA and other OECD countries enforce similar environmental standards and

---

[206] See Casella, in Bhagwati and Hudec (eds), *Fair Trade and Harmonization* (Cambridge, Mass., 1996) I, 119; Wilson, ibid, I, 393.

[207] See Roht-Arriaza, 22 *ELQ* (1995) 479; ibid, 6 *YbIEL* (1995) 107; Rodgers, 5 *NYU Env LJ* (1996) 181; and Morrison and Roht-Arriaza, in Bodansky, Brunnee, and Hey (eds) *The Oxford Handbook of International Environmental Law* (Oxford, 2007) Ch 21.

[208] See Carbaugh and Wassink, 16 *World Competition* (1992) 81.

spend about the same to control pollution, about 2 per cent of gross domestic product.[209] Even though certain developing countries have lower pollution standards and there is anecdotal evidence of job losses, empirical evidence again suggests cost differences in environmental standards play little role in company location decisions.[210] Environmental compliance costs in most industries are only a small percentage of production costs. Thus, cost differences in raw materials and wages probably are more significant.[211]

Nevertheless, it may be wise for the WTO to counter this concern by adopting an amendment to the Agreement on Trade Related Investment Measures[212] or a broader Multilateral Agreement on Investment, if one is negotiated.[213] A model might be the NAFTA provision on Environmental Measures:

The Parties recognize that it is inappropriate to encourage investment by relaxing domestic health, safety or environmental measures. Accordingly, a Party should not waive or otherwise derogate from, or offer to waive or otherwise derogate from, such measures as an encouragement for the establishment, acquisition, expansion or retention in its territory of an investment of an investor. If a Party considers that another Party has offered such an encouragement, it may request consultations with the other Party and the two Parties shall consult with a view to avoiding any such encouragement.[214]

Such a provision would not require any specific level of pollution control in the country where the investment is located, but it would set up a channel of complaint if environmental laxity is used to attract investment.

7 THE EXPORT OF HAZARDOUS SUBSTANCES AND WASTES

7(1) DOMESTICALLY PROHIBITED GOODS

Domestically prohibited goods are products whose sale and use are restricted in a nation's domestic market on the grounds that they present a danger to human, animal, or plant life, health, or the environment. They include unregistered pesticides, expired pharmaceuticals, alcohol, tobacco, dangerous chemicals, and adulterated food

---

[209] Ibid, 87–8.

[210] Leonard, *Pollution and the Struggle for World Product* (Washington DC, 1988); Pearson, *Down to Business: Multinational Corporations, the Environment, and Development* (New York, 1985).

[211] Carbaugh and Wassink, 16 *World Competition* (1992) 81, 88–90.

[212] The Agreement on Trade Related Investment Measures (TRIMs), *Legal Texts, supra*, n 1, was one of the key agreements of the GATT Uruguay Round.

[213] A proposed OECD Multilateral Agreement on Investment was abandoned in 1998: see McDonald, 22 *Melbourne ULR* (1998) 617–56; and Kodoma, 32 *JWT* (1998) 21–40. However, trade and investment is on the tentative agenda for a future WTO negotiating round.

[214] NAFTA, Article 1114(2).

products. For example, in the USA, the export of unregistered pesticides is permitted only under a system of notice that requires prior informal consent.[215]

Clearly a state may bar *imports* of a product that is banned for domestic sale or consumption. Can exports of such products also be restricted? This issue was addressed by a GATT working group in 1991,[216] but there was no consensus on its report; the issue was transferred to the agenda of the Committee on Trade and Environment (CTE). This was followed in 1998 by the negotiation of the Rotterdam Convention on the Prior Informed Consent Procedure for Certain Hazardous Chemicals and Pesticides in International Trade[217] establishing a prior informed consent (PIC) regime for banned or restricted chemical products and hazardous pesticide formulations that may cause health or environmental problems. The international shipment of these products would be barred without the prior notice and explicit consent of a designated national authority in the destination country. Do these export control and PIC regimes for dangerous products conform with WTO rules? The relationship of the PIC Convention with the WTO agreements was a controversial issue during negotiations, with a lack of consensus on the wording of a provision establishing an order of priority between them. As Kummer observes, '[c]ontroversy on this point appears to be inherent in multilateral environmental negotiations addressing transboundary transfer of potentially hazardous substances, since they deal with the interface of environment and trade considerations'.[218] In the event the preamble recognizes 'that trade and environmental policies should be mutually supportive with a view to achieving sustainable development'. Both the 2000 Cartagena Protocol and the 2001 Stockholm POP Convention employ this preambular language. The PIC Convention further emphasizes 'that nothing in this Convention shall be interpreted as implying in any way a change in the rights and obligations of a Party under any existing international agreement applying to chemicals in international trade or to environmental protection' whilst at the same time immediately recording the parties' '[u]nderstanding that the above recital is not intended to create a hierarchy between this Convention and other international agreements'. The Cartagena Protocol (but not the 2001 Stockholm POP Convention) repeats these preambular provisions virtually verbatim, though replaces 'hierarchy' with 'subordinate'. Neither approach is particularly helpful, not least because no specific guidance is given on how 'trade and environment' conflicts

---

[215] 7 USC §1360 (West Supp 1994).

[216] See *Report by the Chairman of the GATT Working Group in Export of Domestically Prohibited Goods and Other Hazardous Substances*, GATT Doc L/6872 (1991). This group recommended a code that would allow individual member states to decide whether their domestic restrictions should be carried over to exports.

[217] The Convention rests on three cornerstones: prior informed consent, exchange of information, and national decision-making processes, also found in the Basel Convention and the Cartagena Protocol: see Chs 8, 11. In contrast, the 2001 Stockholm Convention on Persistent Organic Pollutants provides for an outright ban on the export/import of the regulated substances. See further Redgwell, in Kiss, Shelton, and Ishibashi (eds), *Economic Globalization and Compliance with International Environmental Agreements* (The Hague, 2003) Ch 6. For analysis of the trade implications of a range of prior informed consent regimes, see Micklitz, 23 *Journal of Consumer Policy* (2000) 3, 12.

[218] 8 *RECIEL* (1999) 322, 325.

are to be resolved should they arise. The dispute settlement provisions of the PIC Convention adopt the familiar, non-compulsory, dispute settlement formula found in so many international environmental treaties.

Would it be permissible for a state to go beyond PIC and adopt a total ban on the export of certain categories of domestically prohibited goods? A PIC restriction or a total ban[219] may be carried out within current established legal limits. GATT Article XX(b) allows trade measures (affecting either imports or exports) that are 'necessary to protect human, animal, plant life or health'. Moreover, according to the *Tuna-Dolphin II* and *Shrimp-Turtle Cases*, nothing in Article XX prevents a state from imposing a trade measure to protect the health or safety of persons or the environment located *outside* the territory of that state. Under this interpretation, then, a PIC export regime or a total export ban would be justified.

However, further clarification by the CTE would remove any remaining uncertainty by reaffirming the requirements of current law and stating explicitly that they apply to domestically prohibited goods. The CTE could also adopt transparency requirements which would compel trade-restricting states to notify the WTO and publish in full all laws, regulations, and decisions relating to the products concerned. The WTO would thus provide a clearinghouse for the notification and publication of domestically prohibited goods restrictions, and they would be fully subject to the WTO dispute resolution regime.

7(2) WASTE

Export of hazardous wastes has received great attention from the international community. The Basel Convention on the Control of Transboundary Movements of Hazardous Wastes and Their Disposal[220] requires prior notification and informed consent of the receiving country as a precondition for authorizing international waste shipments. Furthermore, the Convention provides that parties must prohibit the export of the waste whenever there is reason to believe that it will not be managed in an environmentally sound manner.

Two aspects of the Basel Convention raise problems with respect to WTO rules. First, as we saw in Chapter 8, the Conference of the Parties adopted an amendment to ban the export of hazardous wastes from industrialized countries (the OECD, the European Union, and Liechtenstein) to developing countries. The ban applies both to hazardous waste intended for disposal and, since the end of 1997, to hazardous waste intended for reuse or recycling.[221] Second, Article 4(5) of the Convention prohibits exports and imports of hazardous and other wastes between parties and non-party states. These trade restrictions on wastes are based upon past experiences and future fears concerning the exploitation of developing countries. They also reflect certain principles adopted at the 1992 UN Conference on Environment and Development, notably Principle 14 of the Rio Declaration, which provides that states should cooperate

---

[219] For example, under the POPS Convention.   [220] See Ch 8.   [221] Ibid.

to prevent the movement of materials harmful to the environment and humans, and Principle 19, which requires prior notice to potentially affected states with regard to potentially harmful activities.

The international regime for the transboundary movement of hazardous waste is in marked contrast to that in effect domestically in the USA, where the Supreme Court has struck down state-imposed limitations on the import of hazardous waste as violating constitutional norms under the Commerce Clause.[222] On the other hand, the European Court of Justice in the *Belgian Waste Case*[223] stated that waste can be a threat to the environment because of the limited capacity of each region or locality to receive it. Accordingly, the Court ruled that it is permissible under the Articles 30 and 36 of the EC Treaty for a locality to adopt an import ban unless this is inconsistent with EC legislation.[224] The Court based its decision on the 'proximity principle'—that wastes should be treated at their source—and the importance of self-sufficiency regarding waste. The Court's ruling would seem to allow export as well as import restrictions on waste.

An export ban on *hazardous* wastes may be justified under GATT Article XX(b) on the same basis as export restrictions on domestically prohibited goods. Hazardous wastes have the potential to endanger human health and the environment; thus Article XX(b) may be interpreted to allow export bans to protect areas outside the territory of the trade restricting country. Even a discriminatory export ban may be upheld under Article XX(b) if the discrimination is not 'arbitrary or unjustifiable ... between countries where the same conditions prevail'. A ban that distinguishes between OECD and developing countries, arguably at least, could pass this test because of the very different conditions in developing countries. Thus, emerging international hazardous waste regimes seem reconcilable under the WTO/GATT system.

8   ENVIRONMENTAL TAXES

Many commentators have called on governments and public authorities to use market-based economic incentives[225] rather than command-and-control regulation to improve environmental quality. As a result, taxes may be used more frequently in the future, both to raise revenue and to achieve environmental goals. Environmental taxes are based on the principle that many resources are under-priced and, therefore, overused. Environmental taxes, in effect, raise the price of the use of these

---

[222]   E.g. *City of Philadelphia v New Jersey*, 437 US 617 (1978).

[223]   Case C-2/90, *Commission v Belgium* (1993) 1 *CMLR* 365 ['*Belgian Waste Case*'].

[224]   The Court upheld the ban as regards the importation of non-hazardous waste not covered by a Council directive. However, the Court ruled that to the extent that the ban related also to hazardous waste, Belgium had failed to fulfil its obligation to comply with Council Directive 84/631. Ibid, paras 38–9.

[225]   There are four basic types of economic incentives: (i) taxes on charges, (ii) transferable pollution permits, (iii) deposit-and-return systems, and (iv) information strategies. See Stewart, 102 *Yale LJ* (1993) 2039, 2093–4; Galizzi, 6 *Eur Env LR* (1997) 155.

resources. They have three purposes: (i) to discourage the consumption of goods and services that create environmental costs; (ii) to encourage producers to develop alternative production methods and products that are less harmful to the environment; and (iii) to implement the polluter-pays principle (PPP), which holds that the polluter should bear the expenses imposed upon society of ensuring that the environment is in an acceptable state.[226] In the *US Superfund Case*, a GATT panel stated: 'The General Agreement's rules on tax adjustment...give the contracting party the possibility to follow the polluter-pays principle, but they do not oblige it to do so'.[227]

Despite their attractiveness, environmental taxes are not yet widespread for several reasons. First, many people are opposed in principle to raising taxes. Second, analysis shows that some environmental taxes would be regressive, falling most heavily on the poor. Third, there is concern that countries employing them would no longer be competitive in the global marketplace, as their industries would suffer in comparison to industries in countries without such taxes. There are, in general, two solutions to this problem. Countries can cooperate and enter into an international agreement that requires all to levy environmental taxes on their producers; or countries that tax their own producers can levy a similar charge on 'like' imported products. Moreover, even if environmental taxes are imposed by international agreement, import taxes may be needed to even out unequal taxation. Charges on imports raise the issue of their consistency with the WTO system and GATT 1994.

There are three different categories of environmental taxes that governments may use. First, taxes can be imposed directly on the sale of a product that has potentially adverse environmental consequences. This category includes deposit-and-return systems, where 'tax' is rebated, and un-rebated taxes on environmentally unfriendly products such as cigarettes, certain types of energy, and certain chemicals. Second, the tax can be levied on the use of an environmental resource itself. Examples include charges for the emission of pollutants into the air, discharges into rivers or sewer systems, the 'congestion' of highways, and the use of landfills or hazardous waste disposal facilities. Third, environmental taxes may be imposed on *inputs* into products. Here, two kinds of measures may be distinguished: taxes on inputs that are physically incorporated into the final product (such as chemical feedstock incorporated into a plastic or petroleum product), and taxes on inputs that are completely consumed during production (such as fuel or energy used in making a manufactured product).

GATT distinguishes two principal categories of taxes and charges and submits them to different controls.[228] Article II(1), which applies to customs duties and import charges, prohibits WTO members from imposing higher charges than those specified

---

[226] On the polluter-pays principle see *supra*, Ch 3, and OECD, Recommendations C(72)128 on Guiding Principles Concerning International Economic Aspects of Environmental Policies, 11 *ILM* (1972) 1172; C(74)223 on the Implementation of the 'Polluter Pays' Principle, 14 *ILM* (1974) 234.

[227] *US—Taxes on Petroleum and Certain Imported Substances*, GATT BISD (34th Supp) (1988), 136, para 5.2.5.

[228] See generally Fauchald, *Environmental Taxes and Trade Discrimination* (The Hague, 1998); O'Riordan (ed), *Environmental Taxation* (London, 1995).

in their agreed schedules of concessions. Article III, which applies to internal taxes and charges, requires national treatment. To distinguish between the two, Article II(2)(a) provides:

Nothing in this Article shall prevent any contracting party from imposing *at any time* on the importation of any product:

> (a) a charge equivalent to an internal tax imposed consistently with the provisions of paragraph 2 of Article III in respect of an article *from which* the imported product has been manufactured or produced *in whole or in part*. [Emphasis added]

To further clarify the distinction, an interpretive Note Ad Article III states that '[a]ny internal tax . . . which applies to an imported product and to the like domestic product and is collected or enforced in the case of the imported product at the time of importation, is nevertheless to be regarded as an internal tax'.

This pattern of GATT regulation makes clear that the distinction between customs charges (Article II) and internal taxes (Article III) is not based on when or where the taxes are levied. Internal taxes can be adjusted at the border or anywhere else in the distribution process. The difference is that internal taxes on imports are 'equalizing' taxes for the purpose of subjecting imports to the equivalent tax regime for domestic like products. Environmental taxes are internal taxes subject to the discipline of Article III, not Article II. Thus, environmental taxes theoretically can be imposed on imports and be adjusted at the border.[229] Which kinds of environmental taxes can be applied to imports depends on the GATT's border tax adjustment rules.

Border tax adjustment (BTA) is the mechanism invented to harmonize the international taxation of products in accordance with the destination principle, which holds that goods should be taxed where they are used or consumed. BTA, which can be traced to the eighteenth century,[230] allows each nation to implement its own regime of domestic taxation while assuring that goods that move in international trade are neither exempt from taxation nor subject to double taxation. BTA allows (i) an internal tax to be imposed on imported products and (ii) the remission of internal taxes on domestic products destined for export.

What kinds of domestic taxes are eligible for BTA? From its origin in 1947, the GATT has maintained a fundamental distinction between taxes imposed on *products* (termed 'indirect' taxes) and taxes on various forms of income and the ownership of property (termed 'direct' taxes).[231] Only taxes imposed on *products*, indirect taxes, are eligible for BTA. For example, as to taxes remitted on export, Article VI(4) provides:

No product of the territory of any contracting party imported into the territory of any other contracting party shall be subject to an anti-dumping or countervailing duty by reason of the exemption of such product from duties or taxes borne by the like product when destined

---

[229] Of course, the requirements of Article III(2) must be met, which means that imports cannot be charged more than domestic products. However, in the *Japan Shochu Case*, the WTO Appellate Body held that Article III(2) embodies two standards.

[230] See Demaret and Stewardson, 28 *JWT* (1994) 5, 6–7.

[231] For the history of this distinction, see ibid, 9–12.

for consumption in the country of origin or exportation, or by reason of the refund of such duties or taxes.

The Note Ad Article XVI also makes this point: 'The exemption of an exported product from duties or taxes borne by the like product when destined for domestic consumption, or the remission of such duties or taxes in amounts not in excess of those which have accrued, shall not be deemed to be a subsidy'. In 1970, the GATT Working Party on Border Tax Adjustments made the distinction explicit, agreeing that 'taxes directly levied on products were eligible for tax adjustment', and that 'certain taxes that were not directly levied on products were not eligible for adjustment, [such as] social security charges...and payroll taxes'.[232]

The economic distinction between direct and indirect taxes originally was based on the idea that indirect taxes generally were passed on to the ultimate consumer, while direct taxes were not. It is now recognized that this distinction is too simplistic; many indirect taxes are absorbed by producers and direct taxes also can be passed on in the price of a product.[233] Thus, today the distinction rests on tradition and practicality. It is fundamentally a political compromise that allows equalization of some, but not all, of the differences in internal tax regimes; it is based on administrative practicality in that BTA would be much more difficult to apply to direct taxes; and also is based on the fact that taxes on products can be abused more easily for protectionist purposes.

(i) Taxes on products   Environmental taxes levied on products are eligible for BTA as long as they are consistent with the national treatment standards of GATT Article III. In the *US Superfund Case*, the panel made the point that the GATT 'does not distinguish between taxes with different policy purposes'.[234] The GATT requires only that 'like' imported and domestic products be taxed the same. Moreover, there is some flexibility in this national treatment standard. As stated above, when products are 'like' only in the sense of being 'substitutable or competitive' with each other, a higher tax on imports is allowable.[235] In addition, in the *US Automobile Taxes Case*,[236] the GATT panel upheld the validity of US taxes that fell more heavily on imported cars. This ruling seems to justify de facto (but not *de jure*) discrimination against imports as long as a tax has a valid environmental purpose. This decision is thrown into doubt, however, by the WTO Appellate Body's ruling in the *Japan Shochu Case* that the *purpose* of a tax is not a legitimate inquiry under GATT Article III.[237]

A deposit-and-return system of taxes on products is also permissible under GATT rules. In the *Canada Beer Cases*,[238] panels upheld the Canadian deposit/return system on beer containers as applied to imports; to meet the national treatment standard, however, the system had to be applied equally without different systems of delivery

---

[232]   *Border Tax Adjustments*, 2 Dec 1970, GATT BISD (18th Supp) 97, 100–01, para 14 (1972).

[233]   Hufbauer and Erb, *Subsidies in International Trade* (Washington DC, 1984) 23.

[234]   *US Superfund Case, supra*, n 19, para 5.2.8.   [235]   *Japan Shochu Case, supra*, n 22.

[236]   *Taxes on Automobiles Case, supra*, n 150.   [237]   *Japan Shochu Case, supra*, n 22.

[238]   *Canada—Import, Distribution, and Sale of Alcoholic Drinks by Canadian Provincial Marketing Agencies*, 22 March 1988, GATT BISD (35th Supp) 37 (1989) (hereafter 'Canada Beer I'); *Canada—Import, Distribution, and Sale of Alcoholic Drinks by Canadian Provincial Marketing Agencies*, 18 February 1992, GATT BISD (39th Supp) 27 (1993) (hereafter 'Canada Beer II').

to points of sale for imported and domestic beer.[239] Thus, GATT norms freely permit BTA with respect to environmental taxes on products.

(ii) Taxes on resource use   Environmental taxes and charges on resource use, such as effluent and emission charges, are not subject to BTA under GATT rules. Such taxes are not on products as such, even though they are incurred in connection with the manufacture of products. The GATT would classify these charges as direct taxes paid out of gross revenues not eligible for BTA.

(iii) Taxes on inputs   The leading case on environmental taxation of physically incorporated inputs is *US Superfund*, which ruled that taxes on articles used for the manufacture of domestic products may be taken into account in BTA of imported like products. In coming to this conclusion, the panel relied on an example provided by the 1947 drafting committee to explain the word 'equivalent' in Article II(2)(a): 'If a charge is imposed on perfume because it contains alcohol, the charge to be imposed must take into consideration the value of the alcohol and not the value of the perfume, that is to say the value of the content and not the value of the "whole"'.[240] The panel concluded that the tax met the requirements of Article III(2) because the chemical feed stocks taxed were 'used as materials in the manufacture or production' of the final product. '[T]he tax is imposed on the imported substances because they are produced from chemicals subject to an excise tax in the USA and the tax rate is determined in principle in relation to the amount of these chemicals used and not in relation to the imported substance'.[241] The *US Superfund* panel also upheld the method US authorities used in assessing the tax, which was to charge 5 per cent of the appraised value of the final product unless the importer furnished the information necessary to determine the exact amount to impose. This method was permissible[242] because the importer, by furnishing proper information, could avoid the penalty tax.

Thus, environmental taxes on inputs that are physically present in some form in the final imported product are properly subject to BTA. This means that BTA can be made, for example, for a tax on chlorofluorocarbons (CFCs) and other ozone-depleting substances with respect to the export/import of refrigerators in which they are incorporated.

The status of inputs consumed in the production process is more problematic, as is shown by the example of the UN Framework Convention on Climate Change.[243] Although the Convention merely requires parties to work toward the modest goal of reducing greenhouse gas emissions to 1990 levels by the year 2000,[244] the 1997 Kyoto Protocol[245] obliges most developed state parties to make binding reductions of the main greenhouse gases by the year 2012. The parties' implementation of greenhouse gas reductions could include taxes on carbon emissions or energy.[246] Although proposals to

---

[239] *Canada Beer II*, ibid, para 5.33.
[240] GATT Doc EPCT/TAC/PV/26, at 21 (1947), quoted in *US Superfund Case, supra*, n 19, para 5.2.7.
[241] *US Superfund Case, supra*, n 227, para 5.2.8.   [242] Ibid, para 5.3.9.   [243] *Supra*, Ch 6.
[244] Article 4.   [245] *Supra*, Ch 6.
[246] See generally, OECD/IEA, *Taxing Energy: Why and How* (Paris, 1993).

tax energy in both the USA[247] and the European Community[248] have proved politically unacceptable—and likely to remain so for the near future given the current high cost of energy—their allure to policymakers is undeniable: such taxes produce more governmental revenues while improving environmental quality. If energy taxes are to become politically palatable, many concerns must be addressed, such as their impact on poorer members of society, how the revenue produced will be used (for reduction of other forms of taxation, deficit reduction, or new programmes), and their impact on international competitiveness. To deal with the latter problem, BTA is essential.[249]

But the GATT is ambiguous about BTA for taxes on inputs consumed during the production process. Article III does not deal with this issue, but Article II(2)(a) appears to preclude BTA, since it allows a tax with respect to Article III only on inputs 'from which', *not* 'with the help of which', the imported and the like domestic product were produced. Hence, energy taxes apparently cannot be imposed on imported products because energy is consumed and is not physically incorporated into the product during its production. The 1970 GATT Working Party on Border Tax Adjustments noted a divergence of views on *taxes occultes*, that is, taxes on energy, advertising, machinery, and transport.[250] Thus, this point needs clarification.[251]

9 THE TRIPS AGREEMENT AND THE BIODIVERSITY CONVENTION

The WTO Agreement on Trade-Related Aspects of Intellectual Property Rights (TRIPs)[252] guarantees recognition and enforcement of intellectual property rights

---

[247] In 1993, President Clinton proposed a broad-based energy tax that would have applied to all fuels at a basic rate in proportion to their energy content as measured in British Thermal Units (BTUs). The Senate substituted a 4.3-cent per gallon increase in the tax on motor fuels, which became law. See HR Rep No 103–111, 103d Cong, 1st Sess (1993).

[248] In 1992, the European Commission proposed a hybrid carbon/energy tax to limit carbon dioxide emissions and to improve energy efficiency. See *Commission Proposal for a Council Directive Introducing a Tax on Carbon Dioxide Emissions and Energy*, 1992 OJ (L 196) 1; Christian, 10 *UCLA J Envtl L & Pol* (1992) 332, 342. This and modified versions of an energy tax have not been enacted, although a few member states have adopted their own energy taxes, including the UK and Denmark. However, energy products and electricity are taxed when used as motor or heating fuel, with lower minimum levels of taxation applicable to more environmentally friendly unleaded petrol: see Council Directive 2003/96/EC of 27 October 2003 restructuring the Community framework for the taxation of energy products and electricity For discussion of national, regional and international approaches, see Deketelaere, Milne, Kreiser, and Ashiabor (eds), *Critical Issues in Environmental Taxation* (Oxford, 2006).

[249] Another environmental tax of this kind is §4681 of the US Internal Revenue Code, which provides for a tax on 'any product (other than an ozone-depleting chemical) entered into the USA for consumption, use, or warehousing if any ozone-depleting chemical was used as material in the manufacture or production of such product'. This would cover such products even if the ozone-depleting chemicals were completely consumed in the production process.

[250] On border tax adjustments, see *supra*, section 8.

[251] This is one of the topics of discussion within the CTE: see *supra*, section 2(3).

[252] The text of TRIPS is reprinted in WTO, *The Legal Texts*, *supra*, n 1.

backed by the authority of the WTO's dispute settlement mechanism. As indicated above, the relationship between TRIPS and the environment is one of three areas of focus for the CTE identified in the 2001 Doha Declaration, with two features subsequently dominating CTE discussions: (i) transfer of environmentally friendly technology; and (ii) the general relationship between TRIPS and the Convention on Biological Diversity.[253] As we noted above in Chapter 11, the Biodiversity Convention provides that the genetic resources of plants and animals are under the sovereignty of the state in which they are located,[254] and developing countries have a right to benefit from the development of these resources as well as from the transfer of technology relevant to the development and use of genetic resources. The Biodiversity Convention also requires the recognition 'as far as possible and as appropriate' of the rights of 'indigenous and local communities' in 'innovations and practices' relevant to the conservation and use of biological diversity.[255] These two agreements contain the seeds of potential conflicts with vast implications not only for the environment, but also for the biotechnology, pharmaceutical, and agricultural industries.

The TRIPS Agreement and the Biodiversity Convention were developed, albeit at the same time, by different delegations, in different forums, with different objectives, and with almost no consultation or even communication between the two negotiations. The same is not true for the Cartagena Protocol, however, as we have noted, and subsequent developments under the Biodiversity Convention have seen increased cooperation between, for example, the Biodiversity secretariat and the WTO and WIPO secretariats.[256] Since the Biodiversity Convention is in force and accepted by nearly 190 States and the WTO/GATT by over 150, conflicts are most likely to arise between nations that have accepted both treaty regimes. In such a case, Article 22 of the Biological Diversity Convention adopts the following rule of priority:

1. The provisions of this Convention shall not affect the rights and obligations of any Contracting Party deriving from any existing international agreement, except where the exercise of those rights and obligations would cause a serious damage or threat to biological diversity.

2. Contracting Parties shall implement this Convention with respect to the marine environment consistently with the rights and obligations of States under the law of the sea.

As we noted above in Chapter 11, this 'serious damage or threat' standard is obviously vague and difficult to apply because it can be interpreted in different ways, and highlights the importance of dispute settlement when concrete issues arise. However, the Biodiversity Convention provides a flexible dispute settlement

---

[253] TRIPS Article 64, with a delayed implementation periods for developing countries which have now expired.

[254] For the particular problem of genetic resources on the deep seabed, see *supra*, Ch 13 and Scovazzi, in Francioni and Scovazzi (eds), *Biotechnology and International Law* (Oxford, 2006) Ch 4.

[255] Articles 3, 8, 10, 15, 16, 19.

[256] See Ch 11 above. While the TRIPS is a covered agreement under the WTO and is concerned with the trade-related aspects of intellectual property rights, the other international conventions referred to in it—on trademarks, copyright, and industrial property for example—are administered by WIPO.

mechanism in Article 27: parties are required to negotiate and they may refer the dispute by agreement to mediation, but arbitration or resort to the ICJ are compulsory only if both parties have made a declaration accepting jurisdiction. Since few states have accepted this option, most disputes under the Convention will be resolved by compulsory conciliation, which requires only that the states involved submit their dispute to a conciliation commission and consider the solution proposed by the commission 'in good faith'. This provision also applies to disputes under the Cartagena Protocol. It may be contrasted with the dispute resolution mechanism of TRIPS, where disputes are subject to resolution under GATT Articles XXII and XXIII and the WTO's Dispute Settlement Understanding detailed earlier in this chapter and featuring compulsory jurisdiction, a strict timetable, judicialized procedures, and mandatory compliance or punishment in the form of compensation or suspension of concessions.

Given these two separate regimes, disputes arising under both the Biodiversity Convention/Cartagena Protocol and TRIPS probably will be addressed by the WTO dispute settlement regime. This is because the WTO process is mandatory if either party brings a complaint; the other party will not be able to resist. Thus, conciliation under the Biodiversity Convention will take place only if both parties involved agree to forego resort to the WTO. In some cases disputes may arise between states that have accepted binding arbitration or adjudication by the International Court of Justice as well as the WTO regime. In such a case a true conflict may arise as to which dispute settlement body has primary jurisdiction.[257]

9(1) ACCESS TO GENETIC RESOURCES

Major industries, such as those relating to biotechnology, pharmaceuticals, and agriculture, are dependent on worldwide access to genetic resources. These and other industries use wild plants and animals in three basic ways. First, a species can be used directly as a source of natural chemicals or compounds for the production of drugs or other products. An example is the use of the Pacific yew tree to produce an anti-cancer drug. Second, a species' natural chemicals can provide information and ideas that can lead to the production of useful synthetic chemicals, drugs, and products. An example is aspirin, a drug developed as a synthetic modification of salicylic acid, which is found in plants. Third, a natural species can be a source of a gene or genetic sequence that can be used to develop new varieties through breeding or a genetically modified organism through implantation. The former process is essential to modern agriculture. Because crops and animals are susceptible to disease and adverse climatic conditions, it is critical to have access to natural gene pools (germ plasm) to develop more productive and

---

[257] A precedent for reconciliation of the jurisdiction of different international tribunals is Article 2005 of the North American Free Trade Agreement (NAFTA), which contains a complex regime for deciding when the parties to a trade dispute should go to the World Trade Organization and when the NAFTA dispute settlement provisions should be employed. See Abbott, in Weiler (ed), *The EU, the WTO and the NAFTA: Towards and Common Law of International Trade* (Oxford, 2000) 182–4.

disease resistant plants and animals. The latter process is critical to the biotech industry which develops new products through genetic modification and incorporation of genetic materials.

Article 15 of the Biodiversity Convention authorizes states to limit or place conditions on access to genetic resources.[258] The vague language of Article 15 provides a potential basis for a range of actions, from an export ban to market pricing. However, members of the WTO are required to observe GATT 1994 norms in its implementation. Most notably, export bans or conditions would have to comply with GATT Article XX(g), which requires that export restrictions must relate to the conservation of the resource and must be applied in conjunction with restrictions on domestic production or consumption. In addition, an Article 15 export measure must not employ 'arbitrary or unjustifiable discrimination between countries' or be a 'disguised restriction on international trade'. Thus, the vagaries of Article 15 are subject to the discipline of the GATT.

A striking exercise of Article 15 rights is the control regime adopted by Costa Rica, which, in 1992, passed amendments to its Wildlife Conservation Law declaring wildlife to be in the 'public interest' and requiring advance governmental approval for the export of genetic materials and for bio-genetic research.[259] This law is designed to give the Costa Rican government broad discretion in negotiating contracts with foreign firms that wish to employ genetic resources for research. A precursor of this contractual regime was the 1989 contract[260] signed by Merck & Company, the largest US pharmaceutical company, and the Instituto de Biodiversidad Nacional (INBIO), a non-profit institution created by the Costa Rican government. Under this arrangement Merck advanced $1 million to INBIO for the right to develop drugs from Costa Rican plants, insects, or microbes supplied by INBIO, and INBIO and the Costa Rican government will share an amount, reportedly between 1 and 3 per cent, of the revenues from any products developed from INBIO-supplied genetic resources.

GATT 1994 would not bar this arrangement or any other that requires compensation in the form of payment or royalties in return for resource use.[261] The GATT does not regulate pricing so that any payment arrangement would be permissible; however, if a state trading enterprise is involved, GATT Article XVII requires that purchases and sales must be in accordance with commercial consideration and must be made on a non-discriminatory basis.[262] Thus, the GATT and Article 15 of the Biological Diversity Convention are prima facie compatible.

---

[258] The provisions on access and benefit sharing in the CBD have been elaborated by the SBSTTA: see *supra*, Ch 11 section 5.

[259] See Aseby and Kempenaar, 28 *Vand JTL* (1998), 703.

[260] See Reid et al (eds), *Biodiversity Prospecting: Using Genetic Resources for Sustainable Development* (Washington DC, 1993); Powers, 12 *Wis ILJ* (1993) 103, 117–20.

[261] For a comprehensive review and analysis of contractual arrangements, see Aseby and Kempenaar, 28 *Vand JTL* (1995) 703.

[262] GATT Article XVII(1)–(2).

Perhaps the most important and troublesome question likely to arise in legislation and contracts implementing Article 15 is whether countries can discriminate against foreign companies, charging them for resource use while exempting domestic firms. The answer to this question depends on whether the charge is levied as a customs charge or an internal tax or charge. A true customs charge must comply only with the most-favoured-nation requirement of GATT Article I, while an internal charge must comply not only with Article I but also with GATT Article III, which requires national treatment. In the latter case it would be GATT-illegal to exempt domestic firms. Thus, foreign firms that establish and carry on research activities in the country of origin of the biological materials cannot be subjected to a discriminatory pricing arrangement.

While Article 15 is, in principle, compatible with the GATT, it may be difficult for substantial revenues to be derived from Article 15 by developing countries unless they illegally control exports and discriminate against foreign firms. First, only rarely will the biological materials concerned be limited to one country, and availability from multiple sources will reduce the price. For example, Eli Lilly Company produced two anti-cancer drugs, vinblastine and vincristine, from periwinkle leaves first obtained in Madagascar. However, the plant grows wild in many areas of the world including in Texas, where it is grown commercially. Although Eli Lilly has been criticized[263] for not providing compensation to Madagascar, it is not difficult to see why it did not do so. Second, few new drugs or products are made from unmodified biological resources; more often they will be derivatives or produced purely synthetically.[264] Thus, Article 15 seems to be deficient as a mechanism for achieving the goal of sustainable development.

9(2) PATENTABILITY

Patentability is important for the development of both beneficial biotechnologies and marketable environmental technologies that generate less waste and pollution. The TRIPS Agreement, by strengthening global intellectual property protection, will have a positive effect on both categories by providing incentives for research and development. Under TRIPS Article 27(1) patents must be available for products and processes in all fields of technology. TRIPS Article 8(1) permits 'measures necessary to protect public health and nutrition and to promote the public interest in sectors of vital importance to ... socio-economic and technological development', but this is qualified by the requirement that such measures must be 'consistent with ... this Agreement'. It would thus appear that Article 8(1) does not qualify the patentability requirement of Article 27. However, Article 27(2) allows members to exclude from patentability inventions that endanger human, animal or plant life or health, or the environment,

---

[263] See Stone, 256 *Science* (1992) 1624.
[264] Office of Technology Assessment, US Cong, *Biotechnology in a Global Economy*, 75–6 (Washington DC, 1991).

but the exclusion must be 'necessary', not 'merely because the exploitation is prohibited by their law'. Article 27(3) also allows plants, animals, and biological processes to be excluded from patentability, but micro-organisms, non-biological and microbiological processes must be patentable.

This formulation ensures that most biotechnological, pharmaceutical, and agricultural biotechnical inventions must be protected by patent law. Naturally occurring plants and animals are not patentable, but genetically modified micro-organisms, animal genes, human DNA sequences, human proteins, and human genes have all been patented in the USA and Europe.[265] Although TRIPS does not require parties to allow the patenting of genetically engineered animals, such as the 'Harvard mouse', an experimental animal developed for the study of breast cancer, the transgenic process by which such animals are developed would be patentable under TRIPS, either as a microbiological or a non-biological process.[266]

TRIPS also for the first time requires plant breeders rights (PBR) to be given world-wide protection. Although naturally occurring plants cannot be patented, TRIPS Article 27(3)(b) provides that 'Members shall provide for the protection of plant varieties either by patents or by an effective *sui generis* system or by any combination thereof'. The *sui generis* system refers to the International Union for the Protection of New Varieties of Plants (UPOV), established by the UPOV Convention in Paris in 1961 and periodically revised.[267] States adhering to UPOV undertake to create a system of granting PBRs under their domestic laws. TRIPS supplements UPOV by requiring all WTO member states to grant protection to PBRs, either through UPOV or by admitting their patentability.[268]

The Biodiversity Convention, in general, is consistent with the patentability provisions of TRIPS and places no limits on protection of genetic resources. However, the Convention calls for respect and preservation of the knowledge, innovations, and

---

[265] See generally Walden, in Bowman and Redgwell (eds), *International Law and the Conservation of Biological Diversity*, 171; Hedge, 38 *Ind JIL* (1998) 28. In *Diamond v Chakrabarty*, 447 US 303 (1980) the US Supreme Court held that a genetically altered micro organism was patentable under US law either as a 'manufacture' or a 'composition of matter'.

[266] Genetically altered animals are patentable under US law: see *Ex parte Allen*, 2 USPQ 1425 (1987). The US Patent and Trademark Office issued a patent in 1988 to the inventors of the 'Harvard mouse' (also known as the 'ONCO mouse'). In contrast, a similar patent granted by the European Patent Office in 1991 has been subject to opposition proceedings under Article 53 of the 1973 European Patent Convention, which provides that a patent should not be granted (a) for an invention the exploitation of which would be contrary to *ordre public* or public morality, and (b) for plant or animal varieties, or essentially biological processes for the production of plants or animals. Article 6 of the 1998 EC Directive 98/44/EC on Protection of Biotechnological Inventions retains similar but not identical morality provisions, although its general thrust is to provide for the patentability of biological material in EC member states.

[267] In 1972, 1978, and 1991. 'UPOV' stands for 'Union Internationale pour la Protection des Obtentions Végétales' and its members include the EC and the USA. On international regimes for plant genetic resources see Rose, in Bowman and Redgwell (eds), *International Law and the Conservation of Biological Diversity*, 145; Duffield, *Intellectual Property Rights, Trade and Biodiversity* (London, 1999); and *supra*, Ch 11, section 5.

[268] See Tilford, 30 *Case WRJIL* (1998) 373.

practices of indigenous and local communities.[269] It is not clear what impact, if any, these provisions were intended to have on intellectual property rights. Presumably, domestic legislation could provide for PBR for traditional societies and certain kinds of knowledge could be protected as trade secrets.[270] Thus, these provisions of the Biodiversity Convention may be accommodated under existing categories of intellectual property rights.

Another problem may be posed by the exception clause of TRIPS Article 27(2). On first reading, this exception seems very broad, freely allowing national exceptions to patentability. However, the two qualifying phrases, 'necessary' and 'not made merely because the exploitation is prohibited by their law' could, if interpreted strictly, mean that only when there is a substantial international consensus in favour of non-patentability and only where no other means is available to protect the environment, will this exception be triggered. As yet the meaning and scope of this Article 27(2) exception has not been clarified.[271]

9(3) ACCESS TO AND TRANSFER OF TECHNOLOGY

The Convention on Biodiversity and the TRIPS Agreement may come into conflict depending on how Article 16 of the Convention is interpreted concerning access to and transfer of technology. TRIPS mandates a private, free-market system for the acquisition and transfer of rights to intellectual property. Article 28 confers on the patent owner the right to prevent the selling or importing of patented products; patent owners also have the exclusive right to assign, transfer or license their patents. The Biodiversity Convention, in contrast, requires that the contracting parties provide for (i) priority or concessional access for developing countries; (ii) preferential terms for such countries; and (iii) joint research and development efforts by the firms that develop the IPRs and the country supplying the genetic resources.[272]

All of these requirements potentially conflict with the TRIPS regime, which would leave matters to the private sector to decide without governmental interference. For this reason, as we noted above in Chapter 11, the USA initially refused to sign the Biodiversity Convention,[273] and the Clinton administration essentially repudiated all three requirements in its statement supporting the Convention's ratification. President Clinton's Message to the Congress stated that sharing of results of research and benefits 'must take fully into account exclusive rights that a party may possess and that transfers of proprietary technology will take place only at the discretion of

---

[269] Articles 8(j), 10(c). See Shelton, 5 *YbIEL* (1994) 77, and *supra*, Ch 11, section 5. See also the UNESCO Convention on intangible property rights.

[270] See generally Starr and Hardy, 12 *Stan ELJ* (1993) 85.

[271] See Harper, 2 *Wm & Mary Envtl L & Pol Rev* (1997) 381.

[272] See Articles 15(7), 16(2)–(3), 19(1)–(2). See *supra*, Ch 11.

[273] See also Chandler, 4 *Col JILP* (1993) 141, 173–5.

the owner of the technology'.[274] Article 16 should be interpreted, the president stated, so 'that in the case of technology subject to patents and other intellectual property rights, such access and transfer shall be provided on terms that are consistent with the adequate and effective protection of intellectual property rights'.[275] The message further holds that:

technology transfer by the US private sector to other countries requires an economic infra-structure in the recipient country that encourages the voluntary transfer of technology and provides sufficient safeguards for investment…To be considered adequate and effective, a country's intellectual property system must make protection available for all fields of tech-nology and provide effective procedures for enforcing rights.[276]

These comments appear to disregard the primary requirements of Articles 15, 16, and 19 of the Biodiversity Convention and would amount to a reservation, should the USA move to ratification on this basis. However, no reservations are permitted.[277]

There is, perhaps, one way to reconcile the provisions of the Biodiversity Convention with the TRIPS Agreement and the protection of intellectual property rights. Articles 20 and 21 of the Convention provide for a 'financial mechanism' and the provision of financial resources to facilitate transfer of technology to developing countries on favourable terms. Nothing in the TRIPS Agreement would prohibit the use of an inter-national financial mechanism to assure access and the transfer of technology. Articles 15, 16, and 19 can be interpreted to mean that transfer of technology should be left to negotiations between private parties, but should be supplemented where needed by the financial mechanism established by the Convention's contracting parties under Articles 20 and 21.[278]

9(4) COMPULSORY LICENSING

An important question that may arise under the Biodiversity Convention and the TRIPS Agreement is whether a developing country that believes its rights under the Convention are being denied can resort to compulsory licensing. The Biodiversity Convention contains no specific authorization of compulsory licensing, but it does authorize 'legislative, administrative or policy measures, as appropriate' to gain the rights granted by the access to and transfer of technology and biotechnology pro-visions.[279] Compulsory licensing by WTO members would be controlled by TRIPS Agreement, which has specific provisions dealing with this issue. Article 30 of TRIPS permits 'limited exceptions to the exclusive rights conferred by a patent, provided [the

---

[274] Convention on Biodiversity: Message from the President of the US, 103 Cong Treaty Doc 103–20, Nov 1993, X1.

[275] Ibid, xi.   [276] Ibid.   [277] Article 37.

[278] Another possibility might be an Agreement on Implementation analogous to that adopted in 1994 with respect to the 1982 Law of the Sea Convention, which subjects the technology transfer provisions of Part XI on the deep sea bed to GATT disciplines: see Evans, in Evans (ed), *International Law* (2nd edn, Oxford, 2006) Ch 21.

[279] Articles 15(4), 16(3), 19(1).

exceptions] do not unreasonably conflict with the normal exploitation of the patent and do not unreasonably prejudice the legitimate interest of the patent owner…'. These conditions make Article 30 of TRIPS a poor vehicle to claim the transfer of technology benefits accorded by the Biological Diversity Convention. Article 30 envisages only ad hoc exceptions primarily for experimental purposes.

Article 31 of TRIPS authorizes compulsory licensing subject to highly restrictive conditions that would seem to make the use of compulsory licensing impractical to achieve the purposes of the Biodiversity Convention, except in extreme cases. Under TRIPS, the compulsory licensee must be remunerated based upon 'economic value', and it must be preceded by efforts to obtain authorization on 'reasonable commercial terms'. Thus, a developing country could not obtain the 'concessional and preferential terms' provided for by the Biodiversity Convention through compulsory licensing.[280] However, in 2005 an amendment to Article 31 was adopted to give effect to a waiver granted to make it easier for countries in need to import cheaper generic medicines made under compulsory licensing if unable to manufacture it for themselves.[281] This is the first amendment adopted to one of the 'core' WTO agreements and indicates a potential way forward where the political will to act—in this case to facilitate access to generic drugs for the treatment of HIV/AIDS.

10 CONCLUSIONS

The WTO's Committee on Trade and Environment has only taken the first steps in clarifying and reconciling the conflicts between protection of the environment and the rules of the multilateral trading system by ventilating the issues, marshalling different views, and calling for transparency and increased cooperation among WTO members, the public, and non-governmental organizations. Though the stage is now set for concrete decisions to deal with the issues enumerated in the committee's terms of reference, progress has been slow.

There is a need for the WTO to give specific recognition to environmental values. Article XX(b) of the GATT 1994 might be amended to provide a general exception for trade measures that are reasonably necessary for the protection of the domestic environment. This amendment would remove the overly strict 'least trade restrictive' criterion for such measures. In addition, Article XX might be amended to provide a 'safe harbour' for multilateral environmental agreements that employ trade measures

---

[280] Article 16(2).

[281] A waiver was granted on 30 August 2003 by decision of the General Council (WT/L/540), accompanied by an interpretative statement by the Chair, to give effect to paragraph 6 of the Doha Declaration on TRIPS and public health. At the Hong Kong Ministerial Meeting in December 2005 an amendment inserted a new Article 31 *bis* and Annex to TRIPs, rendering in binding legal form the 2003 Decision and accompanying Chair's statement upon receipt of instruments of ratification by 2/3 of WTO members: see WT/L/641, 6 December 2005.

which are reasonably necessary and reasonably related to the subject matter of the agreement, following the NAFTA example. There is also a need for the WTO to adopt a clear policy on the international use of environmental taxes, especially energy taxes, and food safety.

As for the controversy that became the cause célèbre, the *Tuna-Dolphin* dispute, there is a consensus that the decisions were correct insofar as they interpret the GATT to prohibit trade measures imposed by powerful states to enforce unilateral environmental policies. The goal of raising international environmental standards should be pursued, but there are more effective ways than licensing unlimited unilateral action. Nevertheless, it is no contradiction to say that the US ban on tuna imports was correct and ultimately successful in creating new rules of international law to stop the slaughter of dolphins. This highlights an important point: there is a place, even in the WTO system, for 'creative unilateralism' that operates within the accepted norms of public international law.

We should realize, however, that there will be no grand synthesis of the trade and environment conflict. Rather, the process of accommodation will be ongoing, demanding continual attention and work. Environmental considerations should become a continual concern at the WTO as work proceeds on the Doha Declaration negotiation priorities in the current round of trade negotiations. New trade and environment conflicts are on the horizon, especially in the areas of food safety, intellectual property, trade in services, and subsidies. Other important tasks facing the WTO are the careful monitoring of the impact of new environmental initiatives and protection of developing countries' access to global markets. Finally, the WTO should adopt thoroughgoing procedural reforms to improve the transparency of its decision-making process to both the public and non-governmental organizations. The relatively more transparent and participatory international environmental-treaty framework has had some impact on WTO processes which has recently seen the admission of amicus briefs, observer status for the hybrid state/NGO organization IUCN, and in increased cooperation between the WTO and MEA secretariats.[282]

[282] See Charnovitz, 10 *JIEL* (2007) 685.

BIBLIOGRAPHY

Only the principal periodical articles cited in the footnotes are listed here. A full reference for each book and monograph is given when first cited in each chapter.

ADEDE, AO, 'United Nations Efforts Toward the Development of an Environmental Code of Conduct for States Concerning Harmonious Utilization of Shared Natural Resources', 43 *Albany LR* 487 (1978–9)

—— 'Utilization of Shared Natural Resources: Towards a Code of Conduct', 5 *EPL* 66 (1979)

AGO, R, 'Nouvelles réflexions sur la codification du droit international', 92 *RGDIP* 532 (1988)

AKEHURST, M, 'Custom as a Source of International Law', 47 *BYIL* 1 (1974–5)

—— 'International Liability for Injurious Consequences Arising out of Acts Not Prohibited by International Law', 16 *NYIL* 8 (1985) 8

ALDRICH, GH, 'Progressive Development of the Laws of War: A Reply to Criticism of the 1977 Geneva Protocol 1', 26 *VJIL* 693 (1986)

—— 'Prospects for United States Ratification of Additional Protocol 1 to the 1949 Geneva Conventions', 85 *AJIL* 1 (1991)

—— 'Regional Arrangements in the Oceans', 71 *AJIL* 84 (1977)

—— 'Regionalism and the Law of the Sea: The Case of Semi-Enclosed Seas', 2 *ODIL* 151 (1974)

ALLEN, DW, 'The Rights of Non-Human Animals and World Public Order: A Global Assessment', 28 *NY Law School LR* 377 (1983)

ALLOT, P, 'State Responsibility and the Unmaking of International Law', 29 *Harv ILJ* 1 (1988)

—— 'Power Sharing in the Law of the Sea', 77 *AJIL* 1 (1983)

ALSTON, P, 'Conjuring up New Human Rights: A Proposal for Quality Control', 78 *AJIL* 607 (1984)

—— 'A Third Generation of Solidarity Rights: Progressive Development or Obfuscation of International Human Rights Law?' 29 *NILR* 307 (1982)

—— 'Making Space for New Human Rights: The Case of the Right to Development', 1 *Harv HRYb* 21 (1988)

AMERASINGHE, CF, 'Issues of Compensation for the Taking of Alien Property in the Light of Recent Cases and Practice' 41 *ICLQ* 22 (1992)

ANDRESON, S, 'Science and Politics in the International Management of Whales', 13 *Marine Policy* 99 (1989)

ANNACKER, C, 'Part Two of the ILCs Draft Articles on State Responsibility', 37 *GYIL* 206 (1994)

ANSARI, AH and JAMAL, P, 'The Convention on Biological Diversity: A Critical Appraisal with Special Reference to Malaysia', 88 *Ind JIL* 134 (2000)

ANTRIM, L, 'The UNCED Negotiating Process', 18 *O&CM* 79 (1992)

DE ARECHAGA, J, 'International Law in the Past Third of a Century', 159 *Recueil des Cours* 272 (1978)

ARNOLD, RP, 'The Common Heritage of Mankind as a Legal Concept', 9 *International Lawyer* 153 (1975)

ARRANGIO-RUIZ, G, 'Some International Legal Problems of the Civil Uses of Nuclear Energy', 107 *Recueil des Cours* 497 (1962)

ASEBY, EJ and Kempenaar, JD, 'Biodiversity Prospecting: Fulfilling the Mandate of the Biodiversity Convention', 28 *Vand JTL* 703 (1995)

AUST, A, 'The Theory and Practice of Informal International Instruments', 35 *ICLQ* 787 (1986)

AYLING, J, 'Serving Many Voices: Progressing Calls for an International Environmental Organisation', 9 *JEL* 243 (1997)

BAETTIG, MB, et al, 'Measuring Countries' Cooperation Within the International Climate Change Regime', 30 *Environmental Science and Policy* (2008)...

BAKER, J, 'A Substantive Theory of the Relative Efficiency of Environmental Treaty Compliance: The Case of CITES', 2 *JIWLP* 1 (1999)

BAKER, JE, 'A Substantive Theory of the Relative Efficiency of Environmental Treaty Compliance Strategies: The Case of CITES', 2 *JIWLP* 1 (1999)

BARKENBUS, J, 'Nuclear Power Safety and the Role of International Organisation', 41 *Int Org* 482 (1987)

BARTENHAGEN, E, 'The Intersection of Trade and the Environment: An Examination of the Impact of the TBT Agreement on Ecolabelling Programs', 17 *Va Envtl LJ* 1 (1997)

BARTELS, L, 'Article XX of GATT and the Problem of Extraterritorial Jurisdiction', 36 *JWT* 353 (2002)

BAUGHEN, S, 'Expropriation and Environmental regulation: The Lessons of NAFTA Ch11', 18 *JEL* 207 (2006)

BAXTER, RR, 'International Law in Her Infinite Variety', 29 *ICLQ* 549 (1980)

BEDERMAN, D and KESKAR, SP, 'Antarctic Environmental Liability: The Stockholm Annex and Beyond', 19 *Emory Int LR* (2005) 1383

BEEBY, C, 'The South Pacific Nuclear Free Zone Treaty', 17 VUWLR 33 (1987)

BEKHECHI, M, 'Une nouvelle étape dans le développement du droit international de l'environnement: la Convention sur la Désertification', 101 *RGDIP* 101 (1997)

BELLO, E, 'The African Charter on Human and Peoples Rights: A Legal Analysis', 194 *Recueil des Cours* 1 (1985)

BERMAN, WH and HYDEMAN, LM, 'A Convention on Third Party Liability For Damage From Nuclear Incidents', 55 *AJIL* 966 (1961)

BERNHARDT, R, 'A Schematic Analysis of Vessel-Source Pollution: Prescriptive and Enforcement Regimes in the Law of the Sea Conference', 20 *VJIL* 265 (1980)

BERNASCONI, C, 'Civil Liability resulting from transfrontier Environmental Damage: A case for the Hague Conference?' *Hague YIL* 35 (1999)

BEWERS, JM and GARRETT, C, 'Analysis of the Issues Related to Sea Dumping of Radioactive Waste', 11 *Marine Policy* 121 (1987)

BEYERLIN, U, 'New Developments in the Protection of the Marine Environment: Potential Effects of the Rio Process', 55 *ZAÖRV* 544 (1995)

—— 'State Community Interests and Institution-Building in International Environmental Law', 56 *ZAÖRV* 602 (1996)

—— and REICHARD, M, 'The Johannesburg Summit: Outcome and Overall Assessment', 63 *ZAÖRV* 213 (2003)

BIANCHI, A, 'The Harmonisation of Laws on Liability for Environmental Damage in Europe: an Italian Perspective', 6 *JEL* 21 (1994)

—— 'Controlling Great Lakes Pollution: A Study in United States/Canada Environmental Co-operation', 70 *Mich LR* 469 (1972)

—— 'The Role of Unilateral State Action in Preventing International Environmental Injury', 14 *Vand JIL* 51 (1981)

—— 'The Settlement of Disputes in the Field of the International Law of the Environment', 144 *Recueil des Cours* 139 (1975)

BIRNIE, PW, 'The Role of Developing Countries in Nudging the International Whaling Commission From Regulating Whaling to Encouraging Non-consumptive Uses of Whales', 12 *ELQ* 675 (1985)

—— 'International Legal Issues in the Management and Protection of the Whale: A Review of Four Decades of Experience', 29 *NRJ* 903 (1989)

—— 'Environmental Protection and Development', 20 *MelbULR* (1995) 66

BLIX, H, 'The Role and Development of Nuclear Power', 18 *EPL* 142 (1988)

BÖCKENFÖRDE, M, 'The Operationalization of the Precautionary Approach in International Environmental Law Treaties', 63 *ZAÖRV* 313 (2003)

BOCZEK, BA, 'Global and Regional Approaches to the Protection and Preservation of the Marine Environment', 16 *CWRJIL* 39 (1984)

BODANSKY, D, 'Scientific Uncertainty and the Precautionary Principle', 33 *Environment* 5 (1991)

—— 'Protecting the Marine Environment from Vessel-source Pollution: UNCLOS III and Beyond', 18 *ELQ* 719 (1991)

—— 'Managing Climate Change', 3 *YbIEL* 60 (1992)

—— 'The UN Framework Convention on Climate Change', 18 *Yale JIL* 451 (1993)

—— 'Customary (And Not So Customary) International Environmental Law', 3 *Indiana Journal of Global Legal Studies* 105 (1995)

—— 'The Emerging Climate Change Regime', 20 *Ann Rev Energy & Env* 425 (1995)

—— 'Rules vs Standards in International Environmental Law', 98 *Proc ASIL* 275 (2004)

—— 'The Legitimacy of International Governance', 93 *AJIL* 596 (1999)

Boehmer-Christiansen, S, 'Environmental Quality Objectives versus Uniform Emission Standards', 5 *IJECL* 139 (1990)

BONINE, J, 'Environmental Impact Assessment—Principles Developed', 17 *EPL* 5 (1987)

BOTHE, M, 'The Protection of the Environment in Times of Armed Conflict: Legal Rules Uncertainty, Deficiencies and Possible Developments', 34 *GYIL* 54 (1992)

—— 'International Regulation of Transboundary Movement of Hazardous Waste', 33 *GYIL* 422 (1990)

BOURNE, CB, 'International Law and Pollution of International Rivers and Lakes', 6 *UBCLR* 115 (1971)

—— 'Procedure in the Development of International Drainage Basins: The Duty to Consult and to Negotiate', 10 *CYIL* 212 (1972)

—— 'The Right to Utilize the Waters of International Rivers', 3 *CYIL* 187 (1965)

—— 'Procedure in the Development of International Drainage Basins', 22 *UTLJ* 172 (1972)

—— 'The Primacy of the Principle of Equitable utilisation in the 1997 Watercourses Convention', 35 *CYIL* 215 (1997)

BOWETT, DW, 'Reservations to Non-Restricted Multi-lateral Treaties', 48 *BYIL* 67 (1977)

BOWMAN, M, 'Conflict or Compatibility? The Trade, Conservation and Animal Welfare Dimension of CITES', 1 *JIWLP* 9 (1998)

—— 'International Treaties and the Global Protection of Birds', 11 *JEL* 87, 281 (1999)

—— 'The Ramsar Convention Comes of Age', 42 *Neths ILR* 1 (1995)

Bowman, M, 'The Multilateral Treaty Amendment Process, A Case Study', 66 *ICLQ* 560 (1995)

—— 'CITES: Trade Conservation and Animal Welfare', 2 *JIWLP* 9 (1999)

Boyle, AE, 'Marine Pollution Under the Law of the Sea Convention', 79 *AJIL* 347 (1985)

—— 'Nuclear Energy and International Law: An Environmental Perspective', 60 *BYIL* 257 (1989)

—— 'State Responsibility and International Liability for Injurious Consequences of Acts Not Prohibited by International Law: A Necessary Distinction', 39 *ICLQ* 1 (1990)

—— 'Dispute Settlement and the Law of the Sea Convention: Problems of Fragmentation and Jurisdiction', 46 *ICLQ* 37 (1997)

—— 'Globalising Environmental Liability: the Interplay of National and International Law', 17 *JEL* 3 (2005)

—— 'Further Development of the 1982 Law of the Sea Convention: Mechanisms for Change', 54 *ICLQ* 563 (2005)

Brack, D, 'The *Shrimp-Turtle* Case: Implications for the Multilateral Environmental Agreement—World Trade Organisation Debate', 9 *YIEL* 13 (1998)

Bradlow, D and Schlemmer-Schulte, S, 'The World Banks New Inspection Panel', 54 *ZAÖRV* 392 (1994)

Brölmann, C, 'Law-making Treaties: Form and Function in International Law', 74 *Nordic JIL* 383 (2005)

Brown, ED, 'Lessons of the Torrey Canyon', 21 *CLP* 113 (1968)

—— Dispute Settlement and the Law of the Sea: the UN Convention Regime, *21 Marine Policy* 17(1997)

Brown Weiss, E, 'The Planetary Trust: Conservation and Intergenerational Equity', 11 *ELQ* 495 (1984)

—— 'Our Rights and Obligations to Future Generations for the Environment', 84 *AJIL* 198 (1990)

Brownell, H and Eaton, SD, 'The Colorado River Salinity Problem with Mexico', 69 *AJIL* 255 (1975)

Brownlie, I, A Survey of International Customary Rules of Environmental Protection, 13 *NRJ* 179 (1973)

—— 'Legal Status of Natural Resources in International Law', 162 *Recueil des Cours* 245 (1979)

Brunnée, J, 'Common Interest—Echoes from an Empty Shell? Some Thoughts on Common Interests and International Environmental Law', 49 *ZAÖRV* 791 (1989)

—— and Toope, S, 'Environmental Security and Freshwater Resources: Ecosystem Regime Building', 91 *AJIL* 26 (1997)

—— and Toope, S, 'Environmental Security and Freshwater Resources: A Case for International Ecosystem Law', 5 *YbIEL* 41 (1994)

—— 'Of Sense and Sensibility: Reflections on International Liability Regimes as Tools for Environmental Protection', 53 *ICLQ* 351(2004)

—— and Toope, S, 'International Law and Constructivism: Elements of an Interactional Theory of International Law', 39 *Columbia JTL* 19 (2000)

—— 'COPing with Consent: Law-making Under MEAs', 15 *Leiden JIL* 1 (2002)

—— 'International Legal Accountability Through the Lens of State Responsibility', 36 *NYIL* 21 (2005)

—— 'International Environmental Law and the United States: Living with the Elephant', 15 *EJIL* 617 (2004)

Brusendorff, A and Ehlers, P, 'The HELCOM Copenhagen Declaration: A Regional Environmental Approach for Safer Shipping', 17 *IJMCL* 351 (2002)

BURCHI, S, 'International Legal Aspects of Pollution of the Sea from Rivers', 3 *Ital YIL* 115 (1977)

BURGIEL, SW, 'The Cartagena Protocol on Biosafety: Taking the Steps from Negotiation to Implementation', 11 *RECIEL* 53 (2002)

BURHENNE-GUILMIN, F and CASEY-LEFKOWITZ, S, 'The Convention on Biological Diversity: A Hard Won Global Achievement', 3 *YbIEL* 43 (1992)

BURKE, W.T, Highly Migratory Species in the New Law of the Sea, 14 *ODIL* 273 (1984)

—— 'Anadramous Species and the New International Law of the Sea', 22 ODIL 95 (1991)

—— FREEBERG, M and MILES, E, 'UN Resolutions on Driftnet Fishing: An Unsustainable Precedent', 25 *ODIL* 127 (1994)

BUZAN, B, 'Negotiating by Consensus: Developments in Techniques at the United Nations Conference on the Law of the Sea', 75 *AJIL* 324 (1981)

CAFLISCH, L, 'Règles générales du droit des cours d'eau internationaux', 219 *Recueil des Cours* 13 (1989)

CAMERON, P, 'The Revival of Nuclear Power: An Analysis of the Legal Implications', 19 *JEL* 71 (2007)

CAMERON, J and ROBINSON, J, 'The Use of Trade Provisions in International Environmental Agreements and their Compatibility with GATT', 2 *YbIEL* 3 (1991)

CAMM, T and BOWLES, D, 'Animal Welfare and the Treaty of Rome: A Legal Analysis of the Protocol on Animal Welfare and Welfare Standards in the European Union', 12 *JEL* 197 (2000)

CARON, D, 'Liability for Transnational Pollution Arising from Offshore Oil Development: A Methodological Approach', 10 *ELQ* 641 (1983)

—— 'The Nature of the Iran-US Claims Tribunal and the Evolving Structure of International Dispute Resolution', 84 *AJIL* 104 (1990)

—— 'The International Whaling Commission and the North Atlantic Marine Mammal Commission: The Institutional Loss of Coercion in Consensual Structures', 89 *AJIL* 154 (1995)

CARROZ, JE, 'International Aspects of Fishery Management Under the New Regime of the Oceans', 21 *San Diego LR* 516 (1984)

CAVERS, DF, 'International Cooperation in the Peaceful Uses of Atomic Energy', 12 *Vand LR* 17 (1958)

CHAMBERS, B, 'Emerging International Rules on the Commercialisation of Genetic Resources', 6 *J World Intellectual Property* 311 (2003)

CHANDLER, M, 'The Biodiversity Convention: Selected Issues of Interest to the International Lawyer', 3 *Colorado JILP* 141 (1993)

CHARNEY, J, 'Third State Remedies in International Law', 10 *Mich JIL* 57 (1989)

—— 'Transnational Corporations and Developing Public International Law', *Duke LJ* 748 (1983)

—— 'The Persistent Objector Rule and the Development of Customary International Law', 56 *BYIL* 1 (1985)

—— 'Entry Into Force of the 1982 UNCLOS', 35 *VaJIL* 381 (1995)

—— 'The Implications of the International Dispute Settlement System of the 1982 Convention on the Law of the Sea on International Law', 90 *AJIL* 69 (1996)

—— 'The Marine Environment and the 1982 UNCLOS', 28 *Int Lawyer* 879 (1994)

—— 'Progress in International Criminal Law?' 93 *AJIL* 452 (1999)

CHARNOVITZ, S, 'Exploring the Environmental Exceptions in GATT Article XX', 25 *JWT* 37 (1991)

—— 'Multilateral Environmental Agreements and Trade Rules', 26 *EPL* 163 (1996)

CHARNOVITZ, S, 'The World Trade Organization and the Environment', 8 *YbIEL* 98 (1998)

—— 'Non-Governmental Organizations and International Law', 100 *AJIL* 348 (2006)

—— 'The WTO's Environmental Progress', 10 *JIEL* 685 (2007)

CHATTERJEE, SK, 'The Charter of Economic Rights and Duties of States: An Evaluation of 15 Years', 40 *ICLQ* 669 (1991)

CHENG, B, 'The Moon Treaty: Agreement Governing the Activities of States on the Moon and other Celestial Bodies within the Solar System other than Earth', 33 *CLP* 213 (1980)

CHENG, B, 'United Nations Resolutions on Outer Space: "Instant" Customary Law?' 5 *Indian JIL* 23 (1965)

CHEYNE, I, 'Gateways to the Precautionary Principle in WTO Law', 19 *JEL* 155 (2007)

CHINKIN, CM, 'The Challenge of Soft Law: Development and Change in International Law', 38 *ICLQ* 850 (1989)

CHRISTIAN, AC, 'Designing a Carbon Tax: The Introduction of the Carbon Burned Tax (CBT)', 10 *UCLA J Envtl L & Poly* 332 (1992)

CHURCHILL, RR, KUTTING, G and WARREN, L, 'The 1994 UN ECE Sulphur Protocol', 7 *JEL* 169 (1995)

—— and ULFSTEIN, G, 'Autonomous Institutional Arrangements in Multilateral Environmental Agreements', 94 *AJIL* 623 (2000)

—— 'Civil Liability Litigation for Environmental Damage by Means of Treaties: Progress, Problems and Prospects', 12 *YbIEL* 3 (2001)

—— and SCOTT, J, 'The MOX Plant Litigation: The First Half-Life', 53 *ICLQ* 643 (2004)

—— '10 Years of the UNCLOS—Towards a Global Ocean Regime? A General Appraisal', 48 *GYIL* 81 (2005)

—— 'The Jurisprudence of the International Tribunal for the Law of the Sea Relating to Fisheries: Is there Much in the Net?' 22 *IJMCL* 383 (2007)

CICIN-SAIN, B and KNECHT, R, 'Implications of the Earth Summit for Ocean and Coastal Governance', 24 *ODIL* 323 (1993)

CIGOJ, S, 'International Regulation of Civil Liability For Nuclear Risk', 14 *ICLQ* 809 (1965)

CLARK, WC and DICKSON, NM, 'Sustainability Science: The emerging research program', 100:14 *Proceedings of the National Academy of Sciences of the United States of America* 806 (2003)

COASE, R, 'The Problem of Social Cost', 3 *Journal of Law and Economics* 1 (1960)

Cohen, M, 'The Regime of Boundary Waters: The Canadian–United States Experience', 146 *Recueil des cours* 219 (1975)

COLLIARD, C, 'La Convention de Bruxelles relative à la responsabilité des exploitants de navires nucléaires', 8 *AFDI* 41 (1962)

COMBACAU, J and ALLAND, D, '"Primary" and "Secondary" Rules in the Law of State Responsibility: Categorizing International Obligations', 16 *NYIL* 108 (1985)

CONTINI, P and SAND, PH, 'Methods to Expedite Environmental Protection: International Ecostandards', 66 *AJIL* 37 (1972)

COOMANS, F, 'The Ogoni Case before the African Commission on Human and Peoples Rights', 52 *ICLQ* 749 (2003)

COOPER, C, 'The Management of International Environmental Disputes in the Context of Canada–United States Relations: A Survey and Evaluation of Techniques and Mechanisms', 24 *CYIL* 247 (1986)

COUGHLIN, MD, 'Using the Merck-In Bio Agreement to clarify the Convention on Biological Diversity', 31 *Columbia JTL* 337 (1993)

CROLEY, SP and JACKSON, J, 'WTO Dispute Procedures, Standard of Review, and Deference to National Governments', 90 *AJIL* 193 (1996)

CROOK, JR, 'The UN Claims Commission' (1993) 87 *AJIL* 144

—— and McCAFFREY, SC, 'The United Nations Starts Work on a Watercourses Convention', 91 *AJIL* 374 (1997)

CULLET, P, 'Differential Treatment in International Law: Towards a new Paradigm of Inter-State Relations', 10 *EJIL* 549 (1999)

D'AMATO, A, 'Do We Owe a Duty to Future Generations to Preserve the Global Environment?', 84 *AJIL* 190 (1990)

—— and CHOPRA, SK, 'Whales: Their Emerging Right to Life', 85 *AJIL* 21 (1991)

DAM, S and TEWARY, V, 'Polluting Environment, Polluting Constitution', 17 *JEL* 383 (2005)

DE LA FAYETTE, LA, 'International Environmental Law and the Problem of Nuclear Safety', 5 *JEL* 31 (1993)

—— 'The ILC and International Liability: a Commentary', 6 *RECIEL* 321 (1997)

—— 'The OSPAR Convention Comes into Force: Continuity and Progress', 14 *IJMCL* 247 (1999)

—— 'The MEPC: The Conjunction of the Law of the Sea and International Environmental Law', 16 *IJMCL* 155 (2001)

—— 'New Approaches to Addressing Damage to the Marine Environment', 20 *IJMCL* 167 (2005)

—— 'A New Regime for the Conservation and Sustainable Use of Marine Biodiversity and Genetic Resources Beyond the Limits of National Jurisdiction', 24 *IJMCL* (2009)

DE KAGENECK, A and PINEL, C, 'The Joint Convention on the Safety of Spent Fuel Management and the Safety of Radioactive Waste Management', 47 *ICLQ* 409 (1998)

DE MESTRAL, A, 'The Prevention of Pollution of the Marine Environment Arising from Offshore Mining and Drilling', 20 *Harv ILJ* 469 (1979)

DE KLEMM, C, 'Migratory Species in International Law', 29 *NRJ* 932 (1989)

—— 'Conservation of Species: The Need for a New Approach', 9 *EPL* 117 (1982)

DAMRO, C and MENDEZ, PL, 'Emissions Trading at Kyoto', 12 *Environmental Politics* 2 (2003)

DAVIES, P, 'EC–Canada Fisheries Dispute', 44 *ICLQ* 927 (1995)

DEMARET, P and STEWARDSON, R, 'Border Tax Adjustment Under GATT and EC Law and General Implications for Environmental Taxes', 28 *J World Trade* 5 (1994)

DENNIS MJ and STEWART, DP, 'Justiciability of Economic, Social and Cultural Rights', 98 *AJIL* (2004) 462.

DESAI, B, 'Revitalising International Environmental Institutions: The UN Task Force Report and Beyond', 40 *Ind JIL* 455 (2000)

—— 'Regulating Transboundary Movement of Hazardous Wastes', 37 *Ind JIL* 43 (1997)

DIAZ, A, 'Permanent Sovereignty over Natural Resources', 24 *EPL* 157 (1994)

—— 'Private Rights Under the Environment and Labor Agreements', 2 *US-Mex LJ* 11 (1994)

DICKSTEIN, HL, 'International Lake and River Pollution Control: Questions of Method', 12 *CJTL* 487 (1973)

DOECKER, G and GEHRING, T, 'Private or International Liability for Transnational Environmental Damage: The Precedent of Conventional Liability Regimes', 2 *JEL* 1 (1990)

DOUMA, WTH, 'Fleshing out the Precautionary principle by the Court of First Instance', 15 *JEL* (2003) 394

DUNLOP, W, 'The Bering Sea: The Donut Hole Agreement', 10 *IJMCL* 114 (1995)

DUNOFF, G, 'Reconciling International Trade with Preservation of the Global Commons: Can We Prosper and Protect?' 49 *Wash & Lee L Rev* 1407 (1992)

DUPUY, P-M, 'L'affaire des essais nucléaires français et le contentieux de la responsabilité internationale publique', 20 *GYIL* 375 (1977)

—— 'Soft Law and the International Law of the Environment', 12 *Michigan JIL* 420 (1991)

—— 'Où en est le droit international de l'environnement à la fin du XXeme siècle?' 101 *RGDIP* 873 (1997)

—— 'Reviewing the Difficulties of Codification: on Ago's Classification of Obligations of Means and Obligations of Result in Relation to State Responsibility', 10 *EJIL* 371 (1999)

EBBESSON, J, 'Innovative Elements and Expected Effectiveness of the 1991 EIA Convention', 19 *EIA Rev* 47 (1999)

—— 'The Notion of Public Participation in International Environmental Law', 8 *YbIEL* 98 (1997)

—— 'A Critical assessment of the 1992 Baltic Sea Convention', 43 *GYIL* 38 (2000)

Edeson, W, 'The Code of Conduct for Responsible Fisheries: An Introduction', 11 *IJMCL* 97 (1996)

—— 'The International Plan of Action on Illegal, Unreported and Unregulated Fishing: The Legal Context of a Non-Legally Binding Instrument', 16 *IJMCL* 603 (2001)

—— 'An International Legal Extravaganza in the Indian Ocean: Placing the Indian Ocean Tuna Commission outside the Framework of FAO', 22 *IJMCL* 485 (2007)

EHLERS, P, 'The History of International North Sea Conferences', 5 *IJECL* 3 (1990)

ELDER, PS, 'Legal Rights for Nature: The Wrong Answer to the Right(s) Question', 22 *OsHLJ* 285 (1984)

ELKIND, JB, 'Footnote to the Nuclear Test Cases: Abuse of Right—A Blind Alley for Environmentalists', 9 *Vand JTL* 57 (1976)

ELIAS, O and LIM, C, 'General Principles of Law, Soft Law and the Identification of International Law', 28 *Neths YIL* 3 (1997)

EMOND, P, 'Cooperation in Nature: A New Foundation for Environmental Law', 22 *OsHLJ* 323 (1984)

EPINEY, A, 'Sustainable Use of Freshwater Resources', 63 *ZAÖRV* 377 (2003)

ERCMANN, S, 'The Contribution of the Council of Europe to the Protection of the Environment through Penal Law', 65 *Rev Int de Droit Pénal* 1199 (1994)

ESTY, D, 'NGOs and the WTO', 1 *JIEL* 123 (1998)

FARRIER, D and TUCKER, L, 'Wise Use of Wetlands Under the Ramsar Convention', 12 *JEL* 21 (2000)

FAUCHALD, OK, 'International Investment Law and Environmental Protection', 17 *YbIEL* 3 (2006)

FAWCETT, JJ, 'The Impact of Article 6(1) of the ECHR on Private International Law', 56 *ICLQ* 1 (2007)

FITCH, DA, 'Unilateral Action versus Universal Evaluation of Safety and Environmental Protection Standards in Maritime Shipping of Hazardous Cargoes', 20 *Harv ILR* 127 (1979)

FITZMAURICE, G, 'The Law and Procedure of the International Court of Justice: Treaty Interpretation and Other Points', 33 BYIL 200 (1957)

FITZMAURICE, M, 'International Law as a Special Field', 25 *NYIL* 181 (1994)

—— 'The Gabčíkovo-Nagymaros Case: the Law of Treaties', 11 *Leiden JIL* 321 (1998)

—— and REDGWELL, C, 'Environmental Non-Compliance Procedures and International Law', 31 *NYIL* 35 (2000)

—— 'Public Participation in the NAAEC', 52 *ICLQ* 334 (2003)

—— 'General Principles Governing the Co-operation between States in Relation to the Non-navigational Uses of International Watercourses', 14 *YbIEL* 3 (2003)

—— 'The Human Right to Water', 18 *Fordham ELR* 537 (2007)

FOOTER, M, 'Intellectual Property and Agro-biodiversity: Towards Private Ownership of Genetic Commons', 10 *YbIEL* 48 (1999)

FORNASIER, R, 'La Convention complémentaire à la convention de Paris de 29 Juillet 1960 sur la responsabilité civile dans la domaine de l'energie nucléaire', 8 *AFDI* 762 (1962)

FOSTER, WF, 'The Convention on International Liability for Damage Caused by Space Objects', 10 *CYIL* 136 (1972)

FOX, ST, 'Responding to Climate Change: The Case for Unilateral Measures to Protect the Global Atmosphere', 84 *Geo LJ* 249 (1996)

FRAENKEL, A, 'The Convention on Long-range Transboundary Air Pollution: Meeting the Challenge of International Cooperation', 30 *Harv ILJ* 447 (1989)

FRANCKX, E, 'Regional Marine Environment Protection Regimes in the Context of UNCLOS', 13 *IJMCL* 307 (1998)

—— 'The 200-Mile Limit: Between Creeping Jurisdiction and Creeping Common Heritage?' 48 *GYIL* 117 (2005)

FRANK, V, 'Consequences of the Prestige Sinking for European and Internatioanl Law', 20 *IJMCL* 1 (2005)

FREESTONE, D, 'Specially Protected Areas and Wildlife in the Caribbean: The 1990 Kingston Protocol to the Cartagena Convention', 5 *IJECL* 362 (1990)

—— 'The Road from Rio: International Environmental Law After the Earth Summit', 6 *JEL* 193 (1994)

—— and MAKUCH, Z, 'The New International Environmental Law of Fisheries : The 1995 UN Straddling Stocks Convention', 7 *YbIEL* 3 (1996)

FRENCH, D, 'Developing States and International Environmental Law: the Importance of Differentiated Responsibilities', 49 *ICLQ* 35 (2000)

—— 'Treaty Interpretation and the Incorporation of Extraneous Legal Rules', 55 *ICLQ* 281 (2006)

FRIEDMAN, W, 'The Uses of General Principles in the Development of International Law', 57 *AJIL* 279 (1963)

FUENTES, X, 'The Criteria for the Equitable Utilization of International Rivers', 67 *BYIL* 337 (1996)

—— 'Sustainable Development and the Equitable Utilisation of International Watercourses', 69 *BYIL* 119 (1998)

FULLER, L, 'The Forms and Limits of Adjudication', 92 *Harv LR* 353 (1978)

GALIZZI, P, 'Economic Instruments as Tools for the Protection of the International Environment', 6 *Eur Env LR* 155 (1997)

—— 'From Stockholm to New York Via Rio and Johannesburg: Has International Environmental law Lost Its Way on the Global Agenda?' 29 *Fordham ILJ* 952 (2006)

GASKELL, N, 'Decision Making and the Legal Committee of the IMO', 18 *IJMCL* 155 (2003)

GASTON, GL and RS ABATE, 'The Biosafety Protocol and the World Trade Organisation: Can the Two Co-Exist?', 12 *Pace Int'l L Rev* 107 (2000)

GAVOUNELI, M, 'Access to Environmental Information', 13 *Tulane Env LJ* 303 (2000)

GEHRING, T, 'International Environmental Regimes: Dynamic Sectoral Legal Systems', 1 *YbIEL* 35 (1990)

GIAGNOCAVO, C, and GOLDSTEIN, H, 'Law Reform or World Reform: The Problem of Environmental Rights', 35 *McGill LJ* 345 (1990)

GLENNON, MJ, 'Has International Law Failed the Elephant?' 84 *AJIL* 1 (1990)

GILLESPIE, A, 'The Search for a New Compliance Mechanism within the IWC', 34 *ODIL* 349 (2003)

GLOWKA, L and DE KLEMM, C, 'International Instruments and Processes and Non-Indigenous Species: Is a Protocol Necessary?' 26 *EPL* 247 (1996)

GLOWKA, L, Complementarities between the CMS and CITES, 3 *JIWLP* 205 (2000)

GOLD, E, 'Vessel Traffic Regulation: The Interface of Maritime Safety and Operational Freedom', 14 *JMLC* 136 (1983)

—— 'Marine Salvage: Towards a New Regime', 20 *JMLC* 487 (1987)

GOLDBLAT, J, 'The Nuclear Non-proliferation Regime: Assessment and Prospects', 256 *Recueil des Cours* 9 (1995)

GOLDIE, L, 'Concepts of Strict and Absolute Liability and the Ranking of Liability in Terms of Relative Exposure to Risk', 16 *NYIL* 175 (1985)

—— Liability for Damage and the Progressive Development of International Law, 14 *ICLQ* 1189 (1965)

GRAEFRATH, B, 'Universal Criminal Jurisdiction and an International Court', 1 *EJIL* 67 (1990)

GREEN, A, 'Climate Change, Regulatory Policy and the WTO: How Constraining Are Trade Rules?', 8 *JIEL* 143 (2005)

—— and EPPS, T, 'The WTO, Science and the Environment', 10 *JIEL* 285 (2007)

GRIFFITH, A, 'The South and UNCED: the Dawn of a Probable Turning Point in International Relations Between States', 18 *O&CM* 55 (1992)

GRUCHALLA-WESIERSKI, T, 'A Framework for Understanding Soft Law', 30 *McGill LJ* 37 (1984)

GUILLAUME, G, 'The Future of International Judicial Institutions', 44 *ICLQ* 848 (1995)

GUNDLING, L, 'The Status in International Law of the Principle of Precautionary Action', 5 *IJECL* 29 (1990)

—— 'Our Responsibility to Future Generations', 84 *AJIL* 207 (1990)

—— 'International Law and Protection of the Atmosphere', *Proc ASIL* 72 (1989)

GUPTA, J, 'The Role of Non-State Actors in International Environmental Affairs', 63 *ZAÖRV* 459 (2003)

HAAS, PM, 'Do Regimes Matter? Epistemic communities and Mediterranean Pollution Control', 43 *Int Org* 377 (1989)

—— LEVY, MA, and PARSON, EA, 'How Should We Judge UNCED's Success?' 34 *Environment* 6 (1992)

HACKETT, DP, 'An Assessment of the Basel Convention on the Control of Transboundary Movements of Hazardous Wastes and their Disposal', 5 *AUJILP* 291 (1990)

HAFNER, G, 'The Optimum Utilization Principle and the Non-Navigational Uses of Drainage Basins', 45 *Austrian JPIL* 113 (1993)

HAGAN, PE and WEINER, JB, 'The Cartagena Protocol on Biosafety: New Rules for International Trade in Living Modified Organisms', 12 *Georgetown Environmental Law Review* 697 (2000)

HANDL, G, 'The Principle of Equitable Use as Applied to Internationally Shared Natural Resources: Its Role in Resolving Potential International Disputes over Transfrontier Pollution', 14 *RBDI* 40 (1978)

—— 'National Uses of Transboundary Air Resources: The International Entitlement Issues Reconsidered', 26 *NRJ* 405 (1986)

—— 'An International Legal Perspective on the Conduct of Abnormally Dangerous Activities in Frontier Areas: The Case of Nuclear Power Plant Siting', 7 *ELQ* 1 (1978)

—— 'Après Tchernobyl: Quelques réflexions sur le programme législatif multilatéral à l'ordre du jour', 92 *RGDIP* 50 (1988)

—— and LUTZ, R, 'An International Policy Perspective in the Trade of Hazardous Materials and Technologies', 30 *Harv ILJ* 351 (1989)

—— 'Environmental Security and Global Change: The Challenge to International Law', 1 *YBIEL* 3 (1990)

—— 'International Liability for the Pollution of International Watercourses: Balancing Interests', 13 *CYIL* 156 (1975)

—— 'Liability as an Obligation Established by a Primary Rule of International Law', 16 *NYIL* 49 (1985)

—— 'State Liability for Accidental Transnational Environmental Damage by Private Persons', 74 *AJIL* 525 (1980)

—— 'Territorial Sovereignty and the Problem of Transnational Pollution', 69 *AJIL* 50 (1975)

—— 'Controlling Implementation of and Compliance with International Environmental Commitments: The Rocky Road From Rio', 5 *Colorado JIELP* 327 (1994)

—— 'The International Law Commission's Draft Articles on the Law of International Watercourses: Progressive or Retrogressive Development of International Law', 3 *Colorado JIELP* 123 (1992)

HARDY, M, 'Nuclear Liability: The General Principles of Law and Further Proposals', 36 *BYIL* 223 (1960)

—— 'The Liability of Operators of Nuclear Ships', 12 *ICLQ* 778 (1963)

HARROP, SR, 'From Cartel to Conservation and on to Compassion: Animal Welfare and the International Whaling Commission', 6 *JIWLP* 79 (2003)

HART, D and WHEELER, M, 'Night Flights and Strasbourg's Retreat from Environmental Human Rights', 16 *JEL* 132 (2004)

HASSAN, P, 'Toward an International Covenant on Environment and Development', *Proc ASIL* 513 (1993)

HAYASHI, M, 'Toward Elimination of Substandard Shipping: The Report of the International Commission on Shipping', 16 *IJMCL* 501 (2001)

HEDGE, VG, 'Intellectual Property Rights: National and International Legal Aspects Relating to Patenting of Life Forms', 38 *Ind JIL* 28 (1998)

HEIJNSBERGEN, P VAN, 'The Pollution Concept in International Law', 5 *EPL* 11 (1979)

HEPWORTH, R, 'The Independent Review of CITES', 1 *JIWLP* 412 (1998)

HERKENRATH, P, 'The Implementation of the Convention on Biological Diversity: A Non-Government Perspective Ten Years On', 11 *RECIEL* 29 (2002)

HERMITTE, MA, 'La Convention sur la biodiversité biologique', 37 *AFDI* 844 (1991) Hervey,).

HERVEY, T, 'Regulation of Genetically Modified Products in a Multi-Level System of Governance: Science or Citizens?', 10 *RECIEL* 321 (2001)

HEWISON, G, 'The Precautionary Approach to Fisheries Management: An Environmental Perspective', 11 *IJMCL* 301 (1996)

HEY, E, 'The International Regime for the Protection of the North Sea', 17 *IJMCL* 325 (2002)

—— 'Sustainable Development, Normative Development and the Legitimacy of Decision-making', 34 *NYIL* 3 (2003)

HIGGINS, R, 'The Development of International Law by the Political Organs of the United Nations', *Proc ASIL* 116 (1965)

HIGGINS, R, 'A Babel of Judicial Voices?' 55 *ICLQ* 791 (2006)

HILBORN, R, WALTERS, CJ and LUDWIG, D, 'Sustainable Exploitation of Renewable Resources', 26 *Ann Rev Ecol Syst* 45 (1995)

HILLGENBERG, H, 'A Fresh Look at Soft Law', 10 *EJIL* 499 (1999)

HOFFMAN, H, 'Germany's New Environmental Liability Act: Strict Liability for Facilities Causing Pollution', 38 *NILR* 27 (1991)

HOLDER, J, 'New Age: Rediscovering Natural Law', 53 *CLP* 152 (2000)

HOLT, S, 'Whale Mining, Whale Saving', 9 *Marine Policy* 192 (1985)

HOWARD, M, 'The Convention on the Conservation of Antarctic Marine Living Resources: A Five Year Review', 38 *ICLQ* 104 (1985)

HUDEC, RE, 'Differences in National Environmental Standards: The Level-Playing Field Dimension', 5 *Minn. J. Global Trade* 1 (1995)

HUTCHINSON, DH, 'Solidarity and Breaches of Multilateral Treaties', 59 *BYIL* 151 (1988)

IANNI, RW, 'International and Private Actions in Transboundary Pollution', 11 *CYIL* 258 (1973)

IJLSTRA, T, 'Regional Cooperation in the North Sea: An Inquiry', 3 *IJECL* 181 (1988)

JAGOTA, SP, 'State Responsibility: Circumstances Precluding Wrongfulness', 16 *NYIL* 249 (1985)

JENKINS, V, 'Placing Sustainable Development at the Heart of Government in the UK', 22 *Legal Studies* 578 (2002)

JENKS, W, 'Liability for Ultra-Hazardous Activities in International Law', 117 *Recueil des Cours* 99 (1966)

JENNINGS, RY, 'What is International Law and How Do We Tell it When We See It', 37 *Ann Suisse DDI* 59 (1981)

—— 'The ICJ After 50 Years' 89 *AJIL* 493 (1995)

—— 'The Judiciary, National and International, and International Law', 45 *ICLQ* 1 (1996)

JOYNER, C, 'UN General Assembly Resolutions and International Law: Rethinking the Contemporary Dynamics of Norm Creation', 11 *CWILJ* 446 (1981)

—— 'Biodiversity in the Marine Environment: Resource Implications for the Law of the Sea', 28 *Vand JTL* 635–687 (1995)

JUDA, L, 'IMCO and the Regulation of Ocean Pollution from Ships', 26 *ICLQ* 558 (1977)

—— 'Considerations in Developing a Functional Approach to the Governance of Large Marine Ecosystems', 30 *ODIL* 89 (1999)

KAMERI-MBOTE, P, 'The Development of Biosafety Regulation in Africa in the Context of the Cartagena Protocol: Legal and Administrative Issues', 11 *RECIEL* 62 (2002)

KAMMINGA, M, 'The IAEA Convention on Nuclear Safety', 44 *ICLQ* 872 (1995)

KASOULIDES, G, 'State Responsibility and Assessment of Liability for Damage Resulting from Ocean Dumping Operations', 26 *San Diego LR* 497 (1989)

KATES, RW et al, 'Sustainability Science', 292:5517 *Science* 641 (2001)

KELSON, J, 'State Responsibility and the Abnormally Dangerous Activity', 13 *Harv ILR* 197 (1972)

KERR, D, 'The 1989 Salvage Convention: Expediency or Equity?', 20 *JMLC* 505 (1989)

KEYUAN, Z, 'The Common Heritage of Mankind and the Antarctic Treaty System', 58 *NILR* 173 (1991)

KIMBALL, LA, 'International Law and Institutions: The Oceans and Beyond', 21 *ODIL* 147 (1990)

—— 'Towards Global Environmental Management: The Institutional Setting', 3 *YbIEL* 18 (1992)

KINDT, JW, 'The Effect of Claims by Developing Countries on Law of the Sea International Marine Pollution Negotiations', 20 *VJIL* 313 (1979)

KINGSBURY, B, 'The Tuna-Dolphin Controversy, The World Trade Organization and the Liberal Project to Reconceptualize International Law', 5 *YbIEL* 1 (1994)

—— 'The Concept of Compliance as a Function of Competing Conceptions of International Law', 19 *Mich JIL* 345 (1998)

—— KRISCH, N, and STEWART, R, 'The Emergence of Global Administrative Law', 68 *Law&Cont Problems* 15 (2005)

KIRGIS, FL, 'Standing to Challenge Human Endeavors that Could Change the Climate', 84 *AJIL* 525 (1990)

KISS, AC, 'International Cooperation for the Control of Accidental Marine Pollution', 23 *GYIL* 231 (1980)

—— 'Nouvelles tendances en droit international de l'environnement', 32 *GYIL* 241 (1989)

—— 'Dix ans après Stockholm: une decennie de droit international de l'environnement', *AFDI* (1982) 784

—— 'La Notion de patrimonie commun de l'humanité', 175 *Recueil des Cours* 99 (1985)

—— 'Compliance with International and European Environmental Obligations', *Hague YIL* 45 (1996)

KITT, JR, 'Waste Exports to the Developing World: A Global Response', 7 *Geo IELR* 485 (1995)

KLABBERS, J, 'The Substance of Form: The Case Concerning the Gabčíkovo-Nagymaros Project', 8 *YbIEL* 32 (1997)

—— 'The Undesirability of Soft Law', 67 *Nordic JIL* 381 (1998)

KLEIN-CHESIVOIR, C, 'Avoiding Environmental Injury: The Case for Widespread Use of Environmental Impact Assessment in International Development Projects', 30 *VJIL* 517 (1989–1990)

KNECHT, R, 'A Commentary on the Institutional and Political Aspects of Regional Ocean Governance', 24 *O&C Man* 39 (1994)

KNOX, J, 'Myth and Reality of Transboundary Environmental Impact Assessment', 96 *AJIL* 291 (2002)

KOESTER, V, 'The Biodiversity Convention Negotiating Process and Some Comments on the Outcome', 27 *EPL* 175 (1997)

—— 'Review of Compliance Under the Aarhus Convention', 2 *J Eur Env & Plng L* 31 (2005)

KONZ, P, 'The 1962 Brussels Convention on the Liability of Operators of Nuclear Ships', 57 *AJIL* 100 (1963)

KOSKENNIEMI, M, 'Breach of Treaty or Non-Compliance? Reflections on the Enforcement of the Montreal Protocol', 3 *YbIEL* 123 (1992)

—— 'Solidarity Measures: State Responsibility as a New International Order', 72 *BYIL* 337 (2001)

KRAVCHENKO, S, 'The Aarhus Convention and Innovations in Compliance with MEAs', 18 *Colorado JIELP* 1 (2007)

KUMMER, K, 'The International Regulation of Transboundary Traffic in Hazardous Wastes: The 1989 Basel Convention', 41 *ICLQ* 530 (1992)

—— 'Prior Informed Consent for Chemicals in International Trade: The 1998 Rotterdam Convention', 8 *RECIEL* 322 (1999)

KWIATKOWSKA, B, 'Creeping Jurisdictions Beyond 200 Miles in the Light of the 1982 Law of the Sea Convention and State Practice', 22 *ODIL* 153 (1991)

KWIATKOWSKA, B, 'Marine Pollution from Land Based Sources: Current Problems and Perspectives', 14 *ODIL* 315 (1984)

LALY-CHEVALIER, C, 'Les Catastrophes maritimes et la protection des côtes Françaises', 50 *AFDI* 581 (2004)

LANG, W, 'Compliance Control in International Environmental Law', 56 *ZAÖRV* 685(1996)

LAWRENCE, P, 'International Legal Regulation for Protection of the Ozone Layer: Some Problems of Implementation', 2 *JEL* 17 (1990)

LEONARD, L, 'Recent Negotiations Toward the International Regulation of Whaling', 35 *AJIL* 90 (1941)

LE MARQUAND, D, 'The International Joint Commission and Changing Canada-United States Boundary Relations', 33 *NRJ* 59 (1993)

LEE, M and ABBOTT, C, 'Usual Suspects? Public Participation Under the Aarhus Convention', 66 *MLR* 80 (2003)

LESTER, S, 'The Convention on the Conservation of Migratory Species of Wild Animals (the Bonn Convention)', 29 *NRJ* 979 (1989)

LESTER, A, 'River Pollution in International Law', 57 *AJIL* 828 (1963)

LEVY, R, HAAS, P and KEOHANE, M, 'Institutions for the Earth', 34 *Environment* 12 (1992)

LINDER, D, 'Are All Species Created Equal? And Other Questions Shaping Wildlife Law', 12 *Harv ELR* 157 (1988)

LODGE, M, Improving International Governance in the Deep Sea, 19 *IJMCL* (2004) 299

—— and NANDAN, S, 'Some Suggestions Towards Better Implementation of the United Nations Agreement on Straddling Fish Stocks etc', 20 *IJMCL* 345 (2005)

LOUCAIDES, L, 'Environmental Protection through the Jurisprudence of the ECHR', 75 *BYIL* 249 (2004)

LOWE, AV, 'The Enforcement of Marine Pollution Regulations', 12 *SDLR* 624 (1975)

McCAFFREY, S, 'The OECD Principles Concerning Transfrontier Pollution: A Commentary', 1 *EPL* 1 (1975)

——'Transboundary Pollution Injuries: Jurisdictional Considerations in Private Litigation Between Canada and the United States', 3 *CWJIL* 191 (1973)

—— and SINJELA, M, 'The 1997 UN Convention on International Watercourses', 92 *AJIL* 97 (1998)

McCONNELL, M and GOLD, E, 'The Modern Law of the Sea: Framework for the Protection and Preservation of the Marine Environment', 23 *CWRJIL* 83 (1991)

McDORMAN, TL, 'Implementing Existing Tools: Decision-making Processes of Regional Fisheries Management Organisations', 20 *IJMCL* 423 (2005)

McDOUGAL, M and SCHLEI, N, 'The Hydrogen Bomb Tests in Perspective: Lawful Measures for Security', 64 *Yale LJ* 648 (1955)

McGOLDRICK, D, 'Sustainable Development and Human Rights as an Integrated Conception', 45 *ICLQ* 796 (1996)

McGRAW, DM, 'The CBD: Key Characteristics and Implications for Implementation', 11 *RECIEL* 17 (2002)

McINTYRE, O, and MOSEDALE, T, 'The Precautionary Principle as a Norm of Customary International Law', 9 *JEL* 221 (1997)

McLACHLAN, C, 'The Principle of Systemic Integration in Treaty Interpretation and Article 31(3)(c) of the Vienna Convention', 54 *ICLQ* 279 (2005)

McRAE, DM, 'Trade and Environment: The Development of WTO Law', 9 *Otago LR* 221 (1998)

McRAE, DM and GOUNDREY, DJ, 'Environmental Jurisdiction in Arctic Waters: The Extent of Article 234', 16 *UBCLR* 197 (1982)

MACKENZIE, R, 'The International Regulation of Modern Biotechnology', 13 *YEL* 97 (2002)

MACRORY, R, 'Regulating in a Risky Environment', 54 *CLP* 640 (2001)

MAGRAW, DB, 'Transboundary Harm: The International Law Commission's Study of International Liability', 80 *AJIL* 305 (1986)

MAHMOUDI, S, 'The International Court of Justice and Nuclear Weapons', 66 *Nordic JIL* 77 (1997)

MANN, H, 'Of Revolution and Results: Trade and Environmental law in the Afterglow of the Shrimp Turtle Case', 9 *YbIEL* 28 (1998)

MANSELL, W and SCOTT, J, 'Why Bother about a Right to Development?' 21 *JLS* 171 (1994)

MARGOLIS, E, 'The Hydrogen Bomb Experiments and International Law', 64 *Yale LJ* 629 (1955)

MARTIN-BIDOU, P, 'Le Principe de précaution en droit international de l'environnement', 103 *RGDIP* 631 (1999)

MATSUI, Y, 'Countermeasures in the International Legal Order', 37 *Japanese Ann Intl L* 1 (1994)

MEKOUAR, MA, 'La Convention africaine: petite histoire d'une grande renovation', 34 *EPL* 43 (2004)

MEIJERS, H, 'How is International Law Made? The Stages of Growth of International Law and the Uses of its Customary Rules', 9 *NYIL* 3 (1978)

MERRILLS, JG, 'The Mosaic of International Dispute Settlement Procedures: Complementary or Contradictory', 54 *NILR* 361 (2007)

MENSAH, T, 'The Tribunal and the Prompt Release of Vessels', 22 *IJMCL* 425 (2007)

MICKLITZ, H, 'International Regulation on Health, Safety and the Environment: Trends and Challenges', 21 *Journal of Consumer Policy* 3 (2000)

MILLER, GM, SABOURENKOV, EN and RAMM, DC, 'Managing Antarctic Marine Living Resources: The CCAMLR Approach', 19 *IJMCL* 317 (2004)

MOLENAAR, E, 'The Concept of 'Real Interest' and Other Aspects of Co-operation Through Regional Fisheries Management Mechanisms', 15 *IJMCL* 475 (2000)

—— 'Participation, Allocation and Unregulated Fishing: The Practice of Regional Fisheries Management Organisations', 18 *IJMCL* 457 (2003)

—— Addressing Regulatory Gaps in High Seas Fisheries, 20 *IJMCL* 533 (2005)

—— 'Port State Jurisdiction: Toward Comprehensive Mandatory and Global Coverage', 38 *ODIL* 225 (2007)

—— 'Managing Biodiversity in Areas Beyond National Jurisdiction', 22 *IJMCL* 89 (2007)

MORGERA, E, 'Significant Trends in Corporate Environmental Accountability: The New Performance Standards of the International Finance Corporation', 18 *Colorado JIELP* 151 (2007)

MUCHLINSKI, P, 'The Bhopal Case: Controlling Ultra-hazardous Industrial Activities Undertaken by Foreign Investors', 50 *MLR* 545 (1987)

—— 'Corporations in International Litigation: Problems of Jurisdiction and the United Kingdom Asbestos Case', 50 *ICLQ* 1 (2001)

—— '"Caveat Investor"? The Relevance of the Conduct of the Investor under the Fair and Equitable Treatment Standard', 55 *ICLQ* 527 (2006)

MULDOON, P, 'The International Law of Ecodevelopment: Emerging Norms for Development Assistance Agencies', 22 *Texas ILJ* 1 (1987)

MURASE, S, 'Perspectives from International Economic Law on Transnational Environmental Issues', 253 *Recueil des Cours* 283 (1995)

MUSHAL, RM, 'Reflections Upon American Environmental Enforcement Experience', 19 *JEL* 201 (2007)

NAVID, D, 'The International Law of Migratory Species: The Ramsar Convention', 29 *NRJ* 1001 (1989)

NOLLKAEMPER, A, 'The Rhine Action Programme: A Turning Point in the Protection of the North Sea', 5 *IJECL* 123 (1990)

—— 'Norms in the Law of Marine Environmental Protection', 8 *IJMCL* 1 (1993)

—— 'Agenda 21 and Prevention of Sea-based Marine Pollution', *Marine Policy* 537 (1993)

—— 'Balancing Protection of Marine Ecosystems and the Economic Benefits from Land-based Activities: The Quest for International Legal Barriers', 27 *ODIL* 153 (1996)

—— 'The Legality of Moral Crusades Disguised as Trade Laws', 8 *JEL* 237 (1996)

—— 'The Distinction Between Non-legal and Legal Norms in International Affairs—with Reference to Protection of the North Sea from Hazardous Substances', 13 *IJMCL* 355 (1998)

NOYES, J, 'The International Tribunal for the Law of the Sea', 32 *Cornell ILJ* 109 (1998)

NURMUKHAMETOVA, E, 'Problems in Connection with the Efficiency of the World Bank Inspection Panel', 10 *Max Planck YbUNL* 397 (2006)

ODA, S, 'The ICJ Viewed from the Bench', 244 *Recueil des Cours* 127 (1993)

ODA, S, 'Dispute Settlement Prospects in the Law of the Sea', 44 *ICLQ* 863 (1995)

OKIDI, IO, 'Towards Regional Arrangements for Regulation of Marine Pollution: An Appraisal of Options', 4 *ODIL* 1 (1971)

OKOWA, P, 'Procedural Obligations in International Environmental Agreements', 71 *BYbIL* 275 (1996)

ONG, D, 'CITES: Implications of Recent Developments', 10 *JEL* 291 (1998)

—— 'The Impact of Environmental Law on Corporate Governance', 12 *EJIL* 685 (2001)

OPPENHEIMER M and PETSONK, A, 'Article 2 of the UNFCCC: Historical Origins, Recent Interpretations', 73 *Climatic Change* 195 (2005)

ORAKHELASHVILI, A, 'The World Bank Inspection Panel in Context: Institutional Aspects of the Accountability of International Organizations', 2 *Int Orgs LR* 57 (2005)

ÖREBECH, P, SIGURJONSSON, K and McDORMAN, TL, 'The 1995 United Nations Straddling and Highly Migratory Fish Stocks Agreement: Management, Enforcement and Dispute Settlement', 13 *IJMCL* 119 (1998)

ORREGO VICUÑA, F, 'International Cooperation in Salmon Fisheries and a Comparative Law Perspective on the Salmon and Ocean Ranching Industry', 22 *ODIL* 133 (1991)

OSIEKE, E, 'The International Labour Organization and the Control of Substandard Merchant Vessels', 30 *ICLQ* 497 (1981)

OSTERWOLDT, R, Implementation and Enforcement Issues in the Protection of Migratory Species, 29 *NRJ* 1017 (1989)

OWEN, D, 'The Application of the Wild Birds Directive beyond the Territorial Sea of EC Member States', 13 *JEL* 39 (2001)

PANJABI, R, 'From Stockholm to Rio: A Comparison of Declaratory Principles of International Environmental Law', 21 *Den JILP* 215 (1993)

PALLEMAERTS, M, 'International Legal Aspects of Long Range Transboundary Air Pollution', *Hague YIL* 189 (1988)

PALMER, G, 'New Ways to Make International Environmental Law', 86 *AJIL* 259 (1992)

PARSONS, S, 'Ecosystem Considerations in Fisheries Management: Theory and Practice', 20 *IJMCL* 381 (2005)

PAUWELYN, J, 'A Typology of Multilateral Treaty Obligations: Are WTO Obligations Bilateral or Collective in Nature?' 14 *EJIL* 907 (2003)

—— 'The Role of Public International Law in the WTO: How Far Can We Go?' 95 *AJIL* 535 (2001)

PAVONI, R, 'Assessing and Managing Biotechnology Risk under the Cartagena Protocol on Biosafety', X *Italian Yearbook of International Law* 113 (2000)

PEARCE, D, 'An Intellectual History of Environmental Economics', 27 *Annual Review of Energy and Environment* 57 (2002)

PEEL, J, 'Precaution: A Matter of Principle, Approach or Process', 5 *Melb JIL* 483 (2004)

PERRAULT, AM and MUFFETT, WC, 'Turning off the Tap: A Strategy to Address International Aspects of Invasive Alien Species', 11 *RECIEL* 211 (2001)

PETSONK, CA, 'The Role of UNEP in the Development of International Environmental Law, 5 *Am.UJILP* 351 (1990)

PHARAND, D, Canada's Arctic Jurisdiction in International Law', 7 *Dal LJ* 315 (1983)

PINTO, CW, 'Reflections on International Liability for Injurious Consequences arising Out of Acts Not Prohibited by International Law', 16 *NYIL* 17 (1985)

PISILLO-MAZESCHI, R, 'The Due Diligence Rule and the Nature of the International Responsibility of States', 35 *GYIL* 9 (1992)

PLANT, G, 'International Legal Aspects of Vessel Traffic Services', 14 *Marine Policy* 71 (1990)

PONTECORVO, G, 'The Enclosure of the Marine Commons: Adjustment and Redistribution in World Fisheries', 12 *Marine Policy* 361 (1988)

POPOVIC, NAF, 'In Pursuit of Human Rights: Commentary on the Draft Declaration of Principles on Human Rights and the Environment', 27 *Columbia HRLR* 487 (1996)

POSTIGLIONE, A, 'An International Court for the Environment?' 23 *EPL* 73 (1993)

PULLEN and WARREN, L, 'The Biodiversity Convention and its Implementation with Respect to Marine Biodiversity', 1 *Int Jnl of Biosciences and the Law* 269 (1997)

RAHMAN, R, 'The Law of the Non-navigational Uses of International Watercourses: Dilemma for Lower Riparians', 19 *Fordham ILJ* 9 (1995)

RAUSTIALA, K and VICTOR, D, 'The Regime Complex for Plant Genetic Resources', 58 *Int Org* 277 (2004)

RAYFUSE, R, 'From Promoting to Achieving Compliance in High Seas Fisheries', 20 *IJMCL* 509 (2005)

READ, J, 'The Trail Smelter Dispute', 1 *CYIL* 213 (1963)

REDGWELL, C, 'The Greening of Salvage Law', 14 *Marine Policy* 142 (1990)

—— 'Environmental Protection in Antarctica: the 1991 Protocol', 43 *ICLQ* 599 (1994)

—— 'Universality or Integrity? Some Reflections on Reservations to General Multilateral Treaties', 64 *BYIL* 245 (1993)

—— 'Biotechnology, Biodiversity and International Law', 58 *CLP* 543 (2005)

REID, E, 'Liability for Dangerous Activities: A Comparative Analysis', 48 *ICLQ* 731 (1999)

REST, F, 'The Sandoz Conflagration and Rhine Pollution Liability Issues', 30 *GYIL* 160 (1987)

RICHARDS, RW and HAHN, KR, 'The Internationalization of Environmental Regulation', 30 *Harv ILJ* 421 (1989)

RICUPERO, R, 'Chronicle of a Negotiation: The Financial Chapter of Agenda 21', 4 *Col JIELP* 81 (1993)

RIPHAGEN, W, 'From Soft Law to Jus Cogens and Back', 17 *VUWLR* 81 (1987)

ROBERTS, J, 'Protecting Sensitive Marine Environments: The Role and Application of Ships' Routeing Measures', 20 *IJMCL* 135 (2005)

ROBERTS, A, 'Traditional and Modern Approaches to Customary International Law: A Reconciliation', 95 *AJIL* 757 (2001)

ROBINSON, NA, 'Colloquium: The Rio Environmental Law Treaties: IUCN's Proposed Covenant on Environment and Development', 13 *Pace Env LR* 133 (1995)

RODGERS, KE, 'The ISO Environmental Standards Initiative', 5 *NYU Env LJ* 181 (1996)

ROGERS, B, 'The Nature of Value and the Value of Nature: a Philosophical Overview', 76 *Int Aff* 315 (2000)

ROHT-ARRIAZA, N, Shifting the Point of Regulation: The International Organization for Standardization and Global Lawmaking on Trade and the Environment, 22 *ELQ* 479 (1995)

—— 'Private Voluntary Standard Setting: The International Organization for Standardization and International Environmental Lawmaking', 6 *YbIEL* 107 (1995)

ROSAS, A, 'Issues of State Liability for Transboundary Environmental Damage', 60 *Nordic JIL* 29 (1991)

ROSENCRANTZ, A, 'The ECE Convention of 1979 on Long Range Transboundary Air Pollution', 75 *AJIL* 975 (1981)

ROSENCRANTZ, A, 'The Uniform Transboundary Pollution Reciprocal Access Act', 15 *EPL* 105 (1985)

ROSENNE, S, 'The Nuclear Weapons Advisory opinions of 8 July 1996', 27 *Israel YbHR* 263 (1998)

ROTHWELL, D, 'Illegal Southern Ocean Fishing and Prompt Release', 53 *ICLQ* 171 (2004)

RUBIN, A, 'Pollution by Analogy: The Trail Smelter Arbitration', 50 *Oregon LR* (1971) 259

RUHL, JB and JEWELL, MJ, 'The Oil Pollution Act of 1990: Opening a New Era in Federal and State Regulation of Oil Spill Prevention, Containment and Clean-up, and Liability', 8 *OGTLR* 234 (1990)

SACHARIEW, K, 'Promoting Compliance with International Environmental Legal Standards: Reflections on Monitoring and Reporting Mechanisms', 2 *YbIEL* 31 (1991)

SACHS, N, 'Beyond the Liability Wall: Strengthening Tort Remedies in International Environmental Law', 55 *UCLALR* 837 (2008)

SAFRIN, S, 'Treaties in Collision? The Biosafety Protocol and the World Trade Organization Agreements', 96 *AJIL* 606 (2002)

SALMON, J, 'La pollution des fleuves et des lacs et le droit international', 58 *Ann Inst DDI* 193 (1979)

SAND, PH, 'International Environmental Law After Rio', 3 *YbIEL* 3 (1992)

—— 'Institution-building to Assist Compliance with International Environmental law: Perspectives', 56 *ZAÖRV* 774 (1996)

—— 'Whither CITES? The Evolution of a Treaty Regime on the Borderland of Trade and Environment', 8 *EJIL* 29 (1997)

—— 'Compensation for Environmental Damage from the 1991 Gulf War', 35 *EPL* 244 (2005)

—— 'Information Disclosure as an Instrument of Environmental Governance', 63 *ZAÖRV* 487 (2002)

SANDS, P, 'The Environment, Community and International Law', 30 *Harv ILJ* 393 (1989)

—— 'International Law in the Field of Sustainable Development', 65 *BYIL* 303 (1994)

—— 'The New Architecture of International Environmental Law', 30 *RBDI* 512 (1997)

SCANLON, J and IZA, A, 'International Legal Foundations for Environmental Flows', 14 *YbIEL* 81 (2003)

SCARFF, J, 'The International Management of Whales, Dolphins and Porpoises: An Interdisciplinary Assessment', 6 *ELQ* 387 (1977)

SCHACHTER, O and SERWER, P, 'Marine Pollution Problems and Remedies', 65 *AJIL* 84 (1971)

SCHALLY, H, 'Forests: Toward an International Legal Regime?' 4 *YbIEL* 30 (1993)

SCHEIBER, H, 'From Science to Law in Politics: A Historical View of the Ecosystem Idea and its Effects on Resources Management', 24 *ELQ* 631 (1999)

SCHNEIDER, J, 'Codification and Progressive Development of International Environmental Law at the Third UNCLOS: The Environment Aspects of Treaty Review', 20 *Columbia JTL* 243 (1981)

SCHLEMMER-SCHULTE, S, 'The World Bank's Experience with Its Inspection Panel', 58 *ZAÖRV* 353 (1998)

SCHOENBAUM, T, 'International Trade and the Environment: the Continuing Search for Reconciliation', 91 *AJIL* 268 (1997)

—— 'The Decision in the *Shrimp-Turtle* Case', 9 *YbIEL* 36 (1998)

SCHWARTZ, B, and BERLIN, M, 'After the Fall: An Analysis of Canadian Legal Claims for Damage Caused by Cosmo 954', 27 *McGill LJ* 676 (1982)

SCHWELB, E, 'The Actio Popularis and International Law', 2 *Israel YbHR* 46 (1972)

SCOTT, J, 'European Regulation of GMOs: Thinking About Judicial Review in the WTO', 58 *CLP* 444 (2005)

—— 'International Trade and Environmental Governance: Relating Rules (and Standards) in the EU and the WTO', 15 *EJIL* 307 (2004)

SCOTT, KN, 'Ocean CO_2 Sequestration and the Future of Climate Change', 18 *Geo IELR* 57 (2005)

SCOVAZZI, T, 'Some Considerations on the Role of the International Seabed Authority', 19 *IJMCL* 383 (2004)

—— 'State Responsibility for Environmental Harm', 12 *YbIEL* 43 (2001)

SETTE-CAMARA, J, 'Pollution of International Rivers', 186 *Recueil des Cours* 117 (1984)

SHELTON, D, 'Human Rights, Environmental Rights, and the Right to the Environment', 28 *Stanford JIL* 103 (1991)

—— 'What Happened in Rio to Human Rights?' 3 *YbIEL* 91 (1992)

—— 'The Participation of NGOs in International Judicial Proceedings', 88 *AJIL* 611 (1994)

—— 'Fair Play, Fair Pay: Preserving Traditional Knowledge and Biological Resources', 5 *YbIEL* 77 (1994)

—— 'Decision Regarding case 155/96', 96 *AJIL* 937 (2002)

SIMMA, B, 'The work of the ILC at its 50th session', 67 *Nordic JIL* 444 (1998)

—— 'From Bilateralism to Community Interest in International Law', 250 *Recueil des Cours* 293 (1994)

—— 'Self Contained Regimes', 16 *NYIL* 111 (1985)

SKUBISZEWSKI, K, 'Enactment of Law By International Organizations', 41 *BYIL* 198 (1965)

SLAUGHTER BURLEY, AM, 'International Law and International Relations Theory', 87 *AJIL* 205 (1993)

SMETS, H, 'Le principe de non-discrimination en matière de protection de l'environnement', *Rev Eur Droit de l'Environnement* 3 (2000)

SMETS, H, 'Le principe pollueur payeur: un principe économique érigé en principe de droit de l'environnement?' 97 *RGDIP* 339 (1993)

SNAPE, W and LEFKOVITZ, N, 'Searching for GATTs Environmental *Miranda*: Are Process Standards Getting Due Process?' 27 *Cornell ILJ* 777 (1994)

SOARES, G and VARGAS, V, 'The Basel Liability Protocol', 12 *YbIEL* 69 (2001)

SOHN, L, 'The New International Law: Protection of the Rights of Individuals Rather than States', 32 *AULR* 1 (1982)

—— 'The Stockholm Declaration on the Human Environment', 14 *Harv ILJ* 423 (1973)

—— 'Settlement of Disputes Relating to the Interpretation and Application of Treaties', 150 *Recueil des Cours* 195 (1976)

—— 'Settlement of Law of the Sea Disputes', 10 *IJMCL* 205 (1995)

SPRINGER, AL, 'Towards a Meaningful Concept of Pollution in International Law', 26 *ICLQ* 531 (1977)

STAFFIN, E, 'Trade Barrier or Trade Boon? A Critical Evaluation of Environmental Labelling and Its Role in the Greening of World Trade', 21 *Columbia JEL* 205 (1996)

STARR, J and HARDY, K, 'Not by Seeds Alone: The Biodiversity Treaty and the Role for Native Agriculture', 12 *Stan ELJ* 85 (1993)

STEWART, RB, 'Environmental Regulation and International Competitiveness', 102 *Yale LJ* 2039 (1993)

—— and MARTINEZ, MA, 'International Aspects of Biotechnology', 1 *JEL* 157 (1989)

STONE, C, 'Should Trees Have Standing?—Towards Legal Rights for Natural Objects', 45 *Southern Cal LR* 450 (1972)

—— 'The Biodiversity Treaty: Pandora's Box or Fair Deal?', 256 *Science* 1624 (1992)

STRECK, C and SCHOLZ, SM, 'The Role of Forests in Global Climate Change: Whence We Come and Whence We Go', 82 *International Affairs* 861 (2006)

—— and GEHRING, M, 'Emissions Trading: Lessons From SOx and NOx Emissions Allowance and Credit Systems', 4 *Environmental Law Reporter* 10219 (2005)

SUBEDI, S, 'Balancing International Trade with Environmental Protection: International Legal Aspects of Eco-labels', 2 *Brooklyn JIL* 373 (1999)

SUNSTEIN, C, 'Montreal vs. Kyoto: A Tale of Two Protocols', 31 *Harv ELR* 1 (2007)

SZASZ, P, 'The Convention on the Liability of Operators of Nuclear Ships', 2 *JMLC* 541 (1970)

TANAKA, Y, 'Zonal and Integrated Management Approaches to Ocean Governance', 19 *IJMCL* 483 (2004)

—— 'Regulation of Land-based Marine Pollution in International Law: A Comparative Analysis Between Global and Regional Legal Frameworks', 66 *ZAÖRV* (2006) 535

TARASOFSKY, R, 'Ensuring Compatibility Between Multilateral Environmental Agreements and GATT/WTO', 7 *YbIEL* 52 (1996)

—— 'Legal Protection of the Environment During International Armed Conflict', 24 *NYIL* 17 (1993)

THORNTON, J and TROMANS, S, 'Human Rights and Environmental Wrongs', 11 *JEL* 35 (1999)

TILFORD, D, 'Saving the Blueprints: The International Legal Regime for Plant Resources', 30 *Case WRJIL* 373 (1998)

TINKER, C, 'Environmental Security in the United Nations: Not a Matter for the Security Council', 59 *Tennessee LR* 787 (1992)

TOMCZAK, M, 'Defining Marine Pollution: A Comparison of Definitions Used by International Conventions', 8 *Marine Policy* 311 (1984)

TRIBE, L, 'Ways Not to Think About Plastic Trees: New Foundations for Environmental Law', 83 *Yale LJ* 1315 (1974)

TRINDADE, AC, 'Coexistence and Coordination of Mechanisms of International Protection of Human Rights', 202 *Recueil des Cours* 9 (1987)

TRÜEB, HR, 'Natural Resource Damages: A Swiss Perspective', 27 *EPL* 58 (1997)

TSAMENYI, M, 'The South Pacific States, The USA and Sovereignty over Highly Migratory Species', 10 *Marine Policy* 29 (1986)

TSIMPLIS, M, 'Alien Species Stay at Home: The International Convention for the Control and Management of Ships Ballast Water', 19 *IJMCL* 411 (2004)

TULLY, SR, 'The Contribution of Human Rights to Freshwater Resource Management', 14 *YbIEL* 99 (2003)

USUKI, T, 'Measures to Ensure Compliance with the Montreal Ozone Protocol', 43 *Jap Ann IL* 19 (2000)

UTTON, AE, 'International Environmental Law and Consultation Mechanisms', 12 *Col JTL* 56 (1973)

VALLEGA, A, 'The Regional Scale of Ocean Management and Marine Regional Building', 24 *O&C Man* 17 (1994)

—— 'Management of Ships' Ballast Water and Sediments 2004', 19 *IJMCL* 411 (2004)

VAN DER MENSBRUGGHE, Y, 'Legal Status of International North Sea Conference Declarations', 5 *IJECL* 15 (1990)

VAN REENEN, W, 'Rules of Reference in the New Convention on the Law of the Sea', 12 *NYIL* 3 (1981)

VIGNES, D, 'La valeur juridique de certaines règles, normes ou pratiques mentionnées au TNCO comme généralement acceptées', *AFDI* 712 (1979)

VINOGRADOV, S, 'Observations on the ILC Draft Rules on Non-Navigational Uses of International Watercourses: Management and Domestic Remedies', 3 *Colorado JIELP* 235 (1992)

—— 'Marine Pollution Via Transboundary Watercourses: Regimes in the Wider Black Sea Region', 22 *IJMCL* 585 (2007)

VON BAR, C, 'Environmental Damage in Private International Law', 268 *Recueil des Cours* 303 (1997)

WAELDE T, and KOLO, A, 'Environmental Regulation, Investment Protection and Regulatory Taking in International Law', 50 *ICLQ* 811(2001)

WANG, CP, 'A Review of the Enforcement Regime for Vessel Source Oil Pollution Control', 16 *ODIL* 305 (1986)

WARD, H, 'Common but Differentiated Debates: Environment, Labour and The World Trade Organisation', 45 *ICLQ* 592 (1996)

—— 'Some Lessons From the Thor Chemical and Cape PLC Cases', 12 *YbIEL* 105 (2001)

WATTS, AD, 'The Convention on the Regulation of Antarctic Mineral Resource Activities 1988', 39 *ICLQ* 169 (1990)

WEE, L, 'Debt-for-Nature Swaps, A Reassessment of their significance in International Environmental Law', 6 *JEL* 1 (1994)

WEIL, P, 'Towards Relative Normativity in International Law?' 77 *AJIL* 413 (1983)

WELD, CM, 'Critical Evaluation of Existing Mechanisms for Managing Highly Migratory Pelagic Species in the Atlantic Ocean', 20 *ODIL* 285 (1989)

WERKSMAN, J, 'Compliance and Transition: Russia's Non-Compliance Tests the Ozone Regime' 36 *ZAÖRV* 750 (1996)

—— 'Consolidationg Governance of the Global Commons: Insights from the GEF', 6 *YbIEL* 27 (1995)

WERKSMAN, J, 'Compliance and the Kyoto Protocol: Building a Backbone into a Flexible Regime', 9 *YbIEL* 47 (1998)

WETTESTAD, J, 'Science, Politics and Institutional Design: Some Initial Notes on the Long Range Transboundary Air Pollution Regime', 4 *J Env & Devmnt* 165 (1995)

WIJKMAN, PM, 'Managing the Global Commons', 36 *Int Org* 511 (1982)

WILLHEIM, E, 'Private Remedies for Transfrontier Environmental Damage: A Critique of Equal Right of Access', 7 *AYIL* 174 (1976)

WILLIS, FM, 'Economic Development, Environmental Protection and the Right to Health', 9 *Georgetown IELR* 195(1996–7)

WINTER, G, 'Patent Law Policy in Biotechnology', 2 *JEL* 167 (1992)

WINTERS, MA, Cetacean Rights Under Human Laws, 21 *San Diego LR* 911 (1985)

WIRTH, D, The Rio Declaration on Environment and Development: Two Steps Forward and One Step Back, or Vice Versa, 29 *Georgetown LR* 599 (1995)

WIRTH, D, 'Some Reflections on Turtles, Tuna, Dolphin and Shrimp', 9 *YbIEL* 40 (1998)

WOLFRUM, R, 'Means of Ensuring Compliance with and Enforcement of International Environmental Law', 272 *Recueil des Cours* 110 (1998)

WOLFRUM, R and MATZ, NM, 'The Interplay of the UNCLOS and the Convention on Biological Diversity', 4 *Max Planck YbUNL* 445 (2000)

WOOD, H, 'The United Nations World Charter for Nature: The Developing Nations Initiative to Establish Protections for the Environment', 12 *ELQ* 977 (1985)

WRIGHT, A and DOULMAN, D, 'Drift Net Fishing in the South Pacific: From Controversy to Management', 15 *Marine Policy* 303 (1991)

YANAGIDA, J, 'The Pacific Salmon Treaty', 81 *AJIL* 577 (1987)

YOSHIDA, O, 'Soft Enforcement of Treaties: The Montreal Non-Compliance Procedure and the Functions of the Internal International Institutions', 10 *Colorado JIELP* 95 (1999)

YOUNG, MA, 'The WTO's Use of Relevant Rules of International Law: An Analysis of the Biotech Case', 56 *ICLQ* 907 (2007)

YTURRIAGA, J, 'Regional Conventions on the Protection of the Marine Environment', 162 *Recueil des Cours* 319 (1979)

INDEX